Modern Maritime Law

and Risk Management

Second Edition

Extensively revised and updated to include recent case law and legislation, this textbook lucidly examines the legal principles of both the jurisdictional and substantive aspects of maritime law, drawing attention to risk management issues.

It provides students, lawyers, shipping companies, P&I clubs, and others with a comprehensive analysis of principles and precedents in maritime law, as derived from important decisions, statutes, international conventions, as well as government consultation papers, EU directives and regulations, recent proposals of the European Commission and the IMO on marine safety and policy. It approaches the subject from a modern perspective.

This edition has been rearranged and covers all key areas of maritime law, including summaries of important case law. It is restructured into four parts:

- Part I (7 chapters) considers admiralty jurisdiction, with an extensive revision of the chapters concerning the Brussels Regulation, including the effect of recent European Court of Justice rulings upon English jurisdiction, particularly with regard to *lis pendens, forum non-conveniens* and anti-suit injunctions.

- Part II (9 chapters) deals with the substantive law, namely: the regulatory regimes and obligations of ship owners and managers in the context of international safety regulations and the legal implications of the International Safety Management Code have been reviewed; issues of seaworthiness under contracts of carriage of goods by sea and contracts of marine insurance as well as issues of limitation of liability and criminal liability, including the Corporate Manslaughter Act 2007, are contextually discussed. The other chapters relating to the law of ship mortgages, ship sale, ship building, collisions, salvage, towage contracts and ports have also been substantially reviewed. A new chapter on general average has been added.

- Part III (3 chapters) focuses on international conventions concerning limitation of liability for maritime claims, namely: the London Convention, as enriched by new case law, the Athens Convention and the Protocol 2002 (new chapter), and the conventions relating to Marine Pollution law (contributed to this edition by Elizabeth Blackburn QC).

- Part IV (2 chapters) comprises a comprehensively revised chapter on European legislation as compared with developments at the IMO, and the epilogue in which the book offers a 'bird eye' view on risk management issues.

This unique textbook is the first to discuss the importance of risk management in shipping and to offer guidance in relevant cases on how to minimise losses, making it essential reading for postgraduates, legal practitioners, shipowners and managers, insurers, brokers, bankers and other professionals in the shipping industry.

Professor Aleka Mandaraka-Sheppard, LLB, LLM, PhD, attorney-at-law (Athens Bar Ass) and solicitor, is the founder and director of the London Shipping Law Centre, a Risk Management Advisor, and visiting professor of maritime law, University College London (UCL), formerly, the Head of the Shipping Law Unit (1993–2006). She has 28 years' experience in the maritime industry, in both commercial and legal practice. As well as teaching and consulting in risk management, she is now practising as a Maritime Arbitrator.

Modern Maritime Law

and Risk Management

Second Edition

Aleka Mandaraka-Sheppard

informa

LONDON

2009

First published 2007
by Routledge-Cavendish
2 Park Square, Milton Park, Abingdon, Oxon OX14 4RN

Simultaneously published in the USA and Canada
by Routledge-Cavendish
270 Madison Ave, New York, NY 10016

© 2001, 2007 Dr Aleka Mandaraka-Sheppard
© Chapter 19 Elizabeth Blackburn, QC
Previous edition published by Cavendish Publishing Limited

First edition 2001, 2008

ISBN 978–1–84568–076–3 (hbk)
ISBN 978–1–85941–895–6 (pbk)
ISBN 978–0–203–94464–6 (ebk)

Reissued 2009 by

Informa Law
Mortimer House
37–41 Mortimer Street
London W1T 3JH
law.enquiries@informa.com

An Informa business

British Library Cataloguing-in-Publication Data
A catalogue record for this book is available
from the British Library

ISBN 978 1 84311 823 7

Whilst every effort has been made to ensure that the information contained in this
publication is correct, neither the authors nor Informa Law can accept any
responsibility for any errors or omissions
or for any consequences arising therefrom.

Typeset in Palatino by
RefineCatch Limited, Bungay, Suffolk
Printed and bound in Great Britain by
MPG Books Ltd, Bodmin, Cornwall
Printed on paper from sustainable sources

*Knowing the law is the beginning of a battle; knowing how to apply it is winning the battle;
and knowing how to practise risk management is winning the war.*

*To the young generation of shipping law and practice
And to my son Emmanuel-John*

FOREWORD TO THE FIRST EDITION

Anyone with knowledge of the boundless enthusiasm and apparently inexhaustible energy displayed by Dr Aleka Mandaraka-Sheppard in the conception and evolution of the London Shipping Law Centre is unlikely to be surprised at her successful achievement of another daunting goal, namely to publish a new and comprehensive work on shipping law.

There is of course nothing radical in itself about the idea of a modern work in this field. As the author rightly acknowledges, several valuable works on individual aspects of the general topic have been published in recent years, but there has long been the need for a comprehensive work from which both the student (at various levels) and the practitioner can gain a general perspective as well as concrete and detailed information. Perhaps the late Professor Cadwallader, to whom the author pays tribute, could if spared have tackled the task, but his former student has produced a volume of which he would have been proud, the more so given the striking expansion in volume of the law relating to ships and the sea which has occurred since his day. Even a glance at the table of contents will show the extent of the author's grasp of contemporary legal issues, and the thoroughness with which they have been explored.

In addition to the general merits of this book there is one particular theme which calls for particular mention. That is, the emphasis laid on risk management. In recent years this has become a commonplace of business law and practice in many areas, but with a few notable exceptions it has been an absentee from study and practice in the maritime world. Fortunately this is now changing, and Dr Mandaraka-Sheppard's focus on the subject will, it may be hoped, stimulate interest and promote a wider appreciation of its cardinal importance.

Shelves now groan under the weight of legal textbooks, and inches of shelf-room are at a discount, but place must be made for *Modern Maritime Law*, whose dimensions belie its approachability whilst evidencing its scope. This is a book for the library, the study and the office. I welcome it, and am sure that readers will do the same.

MJ Mustill
June 2001

FOREWORD TO THE SECOND EDITION

This is by any standards a magnum opus. Seven years have passed since Michael Mustill wrote the foreword to the first edition of 'Modern Maritime Law'. He paid tribute to the boundless enthusiasm and apparently inexhaustible energy displayed by Dr Aleka Mandaraka-Sheppard in the preparation of the first edition.

Both the enthusiasm and the energy are evident again in the preparation of the second edition. I cannot pretend that I have read every word of its 1000 pages. It would have been impossible to do so in the time available. However, those parts which I have been able to absorb have persuaded me, and am sure will persuade students and practitioners in maritime law in the future that this is a vital work for everyone interested in shipping law to have on their shelves. It has a breathtaking range. Try as I might, I have not been able to think of anything like it. Having spent some five years as the Admiralty judge and having before that practised for many years at the Admiralty and Commercial Bar, I am delighted that Aleka has had the time and energy to produce a second edition of her great work.

Like Michael Mustill, I am particularly struck by her focus on risk management, especially in the context of the management of ships and the ISM Code. The importance of risk management was brought home to me when I had the privilege of conducting the Thames Safety Inquiry and then the Formal Investigation into the collision between the MARCHIONESS and the BOWBELLE with its consequent loss of life. I hope that this book will help to underline this aspect of the legal responsibilities of shipowners, managers and charterers alike.

Finally, I especially appreciate the section on Admiralty Jurisdiction and Procedure because it brings back many happy days in front of the then Admiralty judge, Mr Justice Brandon, in the 1970s when the likes of the present Admiralty judge, Mr Justice David Steel, and I were kept on our metal by the intellectual rigour of the judge.

Future practitioners will have the great benefit of Dr Mandaraka-Sheppard's book with which to educate future Admiralty judges.

Sir Anthony Clarke
August 2007

ADDENDUM

SUMMARY OF THE ECJ CASE *THE FRONT COMOR*

In this reprinted edition, the opportunity has been taken to refer briefly to the recent decision of the ECJ in *The Front Comor*, which completes the relevant discussion in Chapter 7.

Case C-185/07: *(1) Allianz SpA (2) Generali Assicurazioni Generali SpA v West Tankers Inc*

West Tankers owned the vessel *Front Comor* which, in August 2000, was chartered to Erg Petroli SpA (Erg) when it collided with a jetty in Syracuse, Italy, also owned by Erg. Erg claimed compensation for the damage to the jetty from its insurers, Allianz and Generali, up to the limit of its insurance cover, claiming the excess from West Tankers in London arbitration, in accordance with an arbitration clause contained in the charterparty.

In July 2003, Allianz and Generali started proceedings against West Tankers in the Italian courts (based on their rights of subrogation) to recover the sums they had paid to Erg. West Tankers, in response, disputed the jurisdiction of the Italian courts on the basis of the existence of the arbitration agreement and in September 2004 brought proceedings in the English High Court, seeking a declaration that the dispute between itself and Allianz and Generali was to be settled in London arbitration, pursuant to the arbitration agreement. They also sought an anti-suit injunction to discontinue the Italian court proceedings, which was granted.

By leapfrogging the Court of Appeal, Allianz and Generali appealed to the House of Lords, which took the view that the judgments of *Gasser* and *Turner* would not apply in this particular case since this was a matter relating to arbitration, which is excluded from the operation of the EC Regulation by Article 1(2)(d). The House of Lords, nevertheless, referred the case to the ECJ, requesting a ruling as to whether it is incompatible with the EC Regulation for a court of a member state to make an order restraining a person from commencing or continuing proceedings before the courts of another member state on the ground that such proceedings would be contrary to an arbitration agreement, notwithstanding that arbitration is itself excluded from the EC Regulation.

The ECJ ruled that it would be incompatible to make such an order and gave the following reasons:

- If the subject matter of the dispute (e.g. a claim for damages under a contract) fell within the scope of the EC Regulation, a preliminary issue concerning the applicability of an arbitration agreement would also come within the scope of the EC Regulation.

- The general principle arising from the case law on the EC Regulation is that every court seised determines, under the applicable rules of the EC Regulation, whether it has jurisdiction to resolve the dispute. The EC Regulation does not authorise the jurisdiction of one court in a member state to be reviewed by a court in another member state.

- It follows that the objection of lack of jurisdiction raised by West Tankers on the basis of the existence of an arbitration agreement, including issues regarding the validity of such an agreement, falls within the scope of the EC Regulation. Accordingly, it is for the Italian courts to rule on its own jurisdiction.

Professor Aleka Mandaraka-Sheppard
March 2009

PREFACE TO THE SECOND EDITION

Since the first edition, 2001, there have been major developments in most areas of Admiralty and Maritime law, both at international and European levels as well as in English law.

There has been extensive revision of the first edition and, taking note of the advice of Professor Rhidian Thomas, three further chapters have been added, namely, The Athens Convention 1974 and the Protocol 2002, Pollution damage legislation, and General Average law. Considering the extended breadth of this edition, the previous title of the book, 'Modern Admiralty law', is changed to 'Modern Maritime Law', better to reflect the dimensions and scope of the book.

The book provides a comprehensive analysis of principles and precedents in maritime law and related aspects of law. The sources include important decisions, statutes, international conventions, as well as government consultation papers, EU directives and regulations, recent proposals of the European Commission and the IMO on marine safety and policy. The book approaches the subject from a modern perspective, focusing the mind on the importance of risk management in maritime operations and the law, and is the first of this kind. Its extent and depth ranges from basic principles of the law of contract and tort, including statutory controls, causation and remoteness of damages, to specialised maritime contracts, incorporating some cases and principles relating to carriage of goods by sea, insurance, agency, criminal law, as well as regulations pertaining to safety at sea and the protection of the environment. The book also encompasses international conventions regulating liabilities for maritime claims, complex jurisdictional issues in relation to multiple proceedings, forum shopping, arbitration, including injunctions, obtaining security for claims, and conflict of laws. Befitting to a modern era of the practice of maritime law and policy, it expands beyond what was, in the past, the remit of Admiralty law as taught by the late Professor Cadwallader who inspired many international students of maritime law.

The 2nd edition is re-structured into four Parts.

Part I covers Admiralty jurisdiction in depth (7 chapters) including an overview of wrongful arrest and the possibility of a further arrest of a ship for a maritime claim. Most importantly, there is discussion on the effect upon English jurisdiction and previous decisions of the English courts of the recent decisions of the European Court of Justice in *Gasser v Misat, Turner v Grovit* and *Owusu v Jackson* relating to lis pendens, forbiddance of anti-suit injunctions and the inapplicability of *forum non-conveniens*, when the Brussels Regulation 2001 applies. *The Front Comor*, concerning the question of anti-suit injunctions in the context of arbitration agreements, is also considered but, at the time of writing, a reference has just been made to the European Court of Justice on this issue by the House of Lords (chapters 6 and 7).

Part II deals with the substantive maritime law comprising 9 chapters. The book has been regarded as the first legal text to deal with risk management generally and, in particular, with safety regulations and the legal implications of the International Safety Management Code (ISMC) upon liabilities of ship owners and ship managers. In chapter 8, titled: ownership and management of ships, the regulatory regimes and the 'Quality Shipping Campaign' are examined; issues of seaworthiness under contracts of carriage of goods by sea and contracts of marine insurance as well as issues of limitation of liability and criminal liability, including the proposed Bill on Corporate Manslaughter 2006, are considered in the context of the additional obligations of owners and managers under the ISMC. The rules of attribution of liability are examined generally.

This Part reviews shipbuilding contracts in chapter 10 and includes recent decisions, such as: *Covington Marine v Xiamen Shipbuilding* (has there been a contract?); *Balmoral v Borealis* (validity of exclusion clauses in relation to fitness for purpose); *Haugland Tankers v RMK Marine Gemi Yapim Sanayii ve Deniz, and Ravennavi v New Century Shipbuilding* (option agreements); *Gold Coast v Naval Gijo* (premature cancellation of a contract); *Cenargo v Izar Construcciones Navale* (trifling breaches and penalty clauses). Chapter 11 examines the law of sale and purchase of ships: see the significance of *The Kriti Palm* in relation to what could amount to a false representation in negotiations or could just be mere fallibility. In *Fourie v Le Roux* it is confirmed that an accrued cause of action is needed before an application for a freezing order against the seller can be made, and as regards the risk of dissipation of assets the principles are reviewed in *Harrison Partners v Jevena* and *Laemthong International v ARTIS*. There are no major developments in ship mortgages (chapter 9) but confirmation is noted that the duty of a mortgagee to third parties lies in equity not in tort: *The Tropical Reefer*. The tort of wrongful interference with third parties' contracts is also discussed in the light of recent developments.

Furthermore, Part II examines collisions at sea in chapter 12. This chapter reviews criminal liability arising from breach of statutory duties; civil liability due to negligence of owners' servants, including a review of employer's liability for wrongful, deliberate acts of employees: *Attorney General of the British Virgin Islands v. Hartwell* (PC), *The Ocean Frost(HL)*, *Mattis v. Pollock (CA)*; expert evidence: *Bow Spring and Manzanillo II*; causation and remoteness of damages: *Lagden v O'Connor (HL)*, which overruled its previous decision in *The Edison*; pure economic loss: *The Sea Empress (CA)*, *The Braer*. There are some developments in the law of salvage, chapter 13, (e.g. *The Star Maria*, where the harbour master was awarded a salvage award; *The Great Peace* concerning what constitutes an operative mistake in sub-contracting a tug; *The Key Singapore* relating to negligence of salvors; *The Sea Angel* reviewing the foreseeability issue in frustration of contracts and in context of the SCOPIC). Places of refuge are considered and a new initiative for environmental salvage is briefly mentioned. Towage contracts are examined in chapter 14 in which there are some interesting recent decisions (*e.g. The Key Singapore, The Borvigilant and Romina*). The obligations of port authorities in a risk management era, particularly after *The Sea Empress*, are also reviewed in chapter 16 and a brief account of the Wreck Removal Convention 2007 is given. A new chapter 15 laying out the basic principles of General Average is added.

In Part III, this edition deals with International Conventions on maritime liabilities, limitation and compensation. Chapter 17 explores the law concerning limitation of liability for maritime claims under the London Convention 1976, as amended by the 1996 Protocol. There have been some interesting recent decisions, such as *The Tasman Pioneer, The CMA Djakarta, The Darfur, Thompson v. Masterton, The Robert Whitmore, The MSC Rosa M, Saint Jacques II and Gudermes, The Leerort, The Western Regent, ICL Vikraman*. This Part includes two new chapters: Liability to passengers of ships and compensation under the Athens Convention 1974, as amended by the

2002 Protocol, in chapter 18; liability and compensation for marine pollution damage, including hazardous/ noxious substances and nuclear damage, in chapter 19, which is contributed to this edition by Elizabeth Blackburn QC.

Part IV concerns, mainly, developments with regard to safety at sea that have taken place since the first edition, in chapter 20, which reviews European legislation and proposals for new directives and regulations, as compared with the parallel steps taken by the IMO. Technological developments in the running of ships, public concern for protection of the environment and criminalisation, international regulations for safety at sea, the campaign for quality shipping, insurance concerns and policy issues have all influenced the development of maritime law in recent years. The Epilogue in this Part gives an overview on the approach to risk management and highlights its significance by bringing the parts of this book together. Knowledge of how things did go wrong in previous cases and accidents will, hopefully, increase awareness of how to avoid the same or similar incidents.

Although the book was, originally, intended, primarily, for post-graduate students of shipping law and academics, it has found a useful purpose amongst practitioners of shipping law (world-wide), trainees, in-house lawyers, ship owners, ship managers, mortgagees, salvors, P & I Clubs, insurers, shipbrokers, traders, consultants, average adjusters, shipbuilders, classification societies, port authorities, and regulators.

It is a great reward for me to witness that the first edition did stimulate interest in the subject of risk management in the maritime world and promoted a wider appreciation of its importance, as Lord Mustill had expressed that hope in the foreword to the first edition.

Students of maritime law, practitioners and others studied the first edition with immense appreciation for being able to find the principles and important decisions of all aspects of Admiralty law in one volume and, in particular, for becoming aware of the importance of risk management in 21st century shipping. I am indebted to my LLM students of University of London for their comments which helped me to review the first edition.

I wish to express my gratitude, particularly, to my research assistant, Darren Wall, barrister, currently re-training as a solicitor with Mays Brown Solicitors, for his cheerful encouragement, help with research, footnote referencing, and ground work in the Athens Convention and General Average chapters. I am most grateful to Elizabeth Blackburn QC for her valuable contribution to the 2nd edition by writing the chapter on marine pollution law.

In addition, I would like to acknowledge my thanks to: Andrew Mitchell, formerly manager of marine management systems, Lloyd's Register, for his valuable comments on technical matters relating to the ISM Code, risk assessment issues and classification societies; John MacDonald, an experienced average adjuster, for his useful observations and suggestions on the GA chapter; Herry Lawford, formerly director of Thomas Miller, managers of the UK P & I Club, for his valuable observations on the Epilogue of this edition. Last, but not least, I owe my gratitude to my husband, Colin Sheppard, and our son Emmanuel, to many friends, and to Gerard Matthews, manager of the London Shipping Law Centre, for their support and patience while I was immersed in writing this edition.

I am particularly grateful to The Rt. Hon Sir Anthony Clarke, Master of the Rolls, for his generosity in writing the foreword to this edition.

Only important decisions published during the first part of 2007 are included in this edition.

Dr Aleka Mandaraka-Sheppard, solicitor,
Visiting Professor, University College London,
Founding Director, London Shipping Law Centre,
Risk Management Advisor
June 2007

ABBREVIATIONS

AA 1975/1996	Arbitration Act 1975/1996
AIS	Automatic Identification System
BIMCO	Baltic and International Maritime Council
C(RTP)A 1999	Contracts (Rights of Third Parties) Act 1999
CJJA 1982	Civil Jurisdiction and Judgments Act 1982
CLC 1969/1992	International Convention for Civil Liability arising from Pollution Damage 1969/1992
CMCIS	Community monitoring, control and information system
CMI	Comité Maritime International
Colregs	International Regulations for Preventing Collisions at Sea
COSS	Committee on Safe Seas and the Prevention of Pollution from Ships
CPR 1998	Civil Procedure Rules 1998
CRISTAL	Contract Regarding an Interim Supplement to Tanker Liability for Oil Pollution
DOC	Document of Compliance
DPA	Designated Person Ashore
DVA 1985	Dangerous Vessels Act 1985
dwt	dead weight
ECJ	European Court of Justice
EEZ	Exclusive Economic Zone
EL(DE)A 1969	Employers' Liability (Defective Equipment) Act 1969
EMSA	European Maritime Safety Agency
EU	European Union
FAAs	Fatal Accident Acts
H&M	Hull and Machinery
HA 1964	Harbours Act 1964
HDPCA 1847	Harbours, Docks and Piers Clauses Act 1847
HNS	Hazardous and Noxious Substances
HVR	Hague-Visby Rules
IACS	International Association of Classification Societies
IAEA	International Atomic Energy Authority
IMF	International Monetary Fund
IMO	International Maritime Organisation
ISM Code/ISMC	International Safety Management Code
ISPS Code	International Ship and Port Security Code
ISSC	International Ship Security Certificate
LLMC Convention	Limitation of Liability Convention for Maritime Claims
LOU	Letter of Understanding
LR(CN)A 1945	Law Reform (Contributory Negligence) Act 1945
MAIB	Marine Accidents Investigation Branch
MARPOL	International Convention for the Prevention of Pollution from Ships 1973/1978
MS(Reg)A 1993	Merchant Shipping (Regulation etc) Act 1993

MCA	Maritime Coastguard Agency
MCA 1911	Maritime Conventions Act 1911
MEHRA	Marine Environment High Risk Areas
MEPC	Marine Environment Protection Committee
MIA 1906	Marine Insurance Act 1906
MOA	Memorandum of Agreement
MOU	Memorandum of Understanding
MS(LSO)A 1958	Merchant Shipping (Liability of Shipowners and Others) Act 1958
MSA 1894/1958/1979/1995	Merchant Shipping Act 1894/1958/1979/1995
MSC	Maritime Safety Committee
MSMSA 1997	Merchant Shipping and Maritime Security Act 1997
MS(SP)A 1994	Merchant Shipping (Salvage and Pollution) Act 1994
NUCLEAR 71	1971 Convention relating to Civil Liability in the Field of Maritime Carriage of Nuclear Material
OCIMF	Oil Companies International Marine Forum
OECD	Organisation for Economic Co-operation and Development
OPPRC Convention	Oil Pollution, Preparedness, Response and Co-operation Convention 1990
P&I	Protection and Indemnity
PA 1987	Pilotage Act 1987
PSC	Port State Control
PTR 1992	Package Travel Regulations 1992
SCA 1981	Supreme Court Act 1981
SCJ(Con)A 1925	Supreme Court of Judicature (Consolidation) Act 1925
SCOPIC	Special Compensation of Protection and Indemnity Clause
SDR	Special Drawing Rights
SGSA 1982	Supply of Goods and Services Act 1982
SHIPMAN	Ship management form
SMM	Safety Management Manual
SMS	Safety Management System
SOLAS	International Convention for Safety of Life at Sea
SOSREP	Secretary of State's Representative for Maritime Salvage and Intervention
STCW Convention	Standard of Training Certification and Watch-keeping 1978 as amened
STOPIA	Small Tanker Oil Pollution Indemnification Agreement
TDA 1968	Trade Descriptions Act 1968
TMSA	Tanker Management Self Assessment
TOPIA	Tanker Oil Pollution Indemnification Agreement 2006
TOVALOP	Tanker Owners' Voluntary Agreement concerning Liability for Oil Pollution
UCTA 1977	Unfair Contract Terms Act 1977

UKSTC	United Kingdom Standard Towage Conditions of 1986
UNCLOS	United Nations Convention on the Law of the Sea 1982
VDR	Voyage Data Recorder
YAR	York Antwerp Rules

CONTENTS

PART I ADMIRALTY JURISDICTION
AND PROCEDURE

Contents

Contents

Contents

TABLE OF CASES

TABLE OF STATUTORY INSTRUMENTS

TABLE OF EUROPEAN LEGISLATION

TABLE OF EUROPEAN DIRECTIVES

TABLE OF INTERNATIONAL LEGISLATION

PART I

ADMIRALTY JURISDICTION AND PROCEDURE

INTRODUCTION

This Part deals with the nature of the admiralty jurisdiction, its extent, the types of maritime claims that can be enforced in the Admiralty Court, arrest of ships, and the aftermath, including the priorities of claims to be paid out of the fund from the sale of the ship by the Admiralty Marshal. The function of statutory rights *in rem* and maritime liens are also considered. How the jurisdiction of the court is affected by international conventions and other doctrines, such as *forum non-conveniens*, is a paramount consideration. While the jurisdiction of the court is quite wide, modern European and international jurisdictional developments and influences have impacted on the ambit of the court's jurisdiction, and indeed eroded the traditional jurisdictional chauvinism. This has occurred in recent years, for example, with the evolution of principles pronounced by the European Court of Justice in interpreting the Brussels Convention 1968 (now replaced by Council Regulation (EC) 44/2001) in relation to European civil jurisdiction, recognition and enforcement of judgments, which limit, to a certain extent, the jurisdiction of the English courts. There has also been a gradual judicial acceptance that the courts of other countries are competent to adjudicate on a matter, provided it is shown that a court of another country is the natural or an appropriate forum to which the parties are amenable and justice can be done for the interests of all parties.

Chapter 1 contains introductory elements. Chapter 2 examines the nature of the admiralty jurisdiction. Chapter 3 deals with the mode of exercise of jurisdiction in admiralty cases, with particular emphasis on the nature of the action *in rem*. Chapter 4 briefly outlines an overview of procedure, arrest of ships and the aftermath of sale of the ship by the court, priorities of claims and conflict of laws. Chapter 5 sets out rules and doctrines pertaining to restrictions of the jurisdiction to adjudicate on the merits of a case, and, in particular, if a stay of proceedings is warranted on grounds of *forum non-conveniens* or jurisdiction agreements, which are not within the scope of the Council Regulation on civil jurisdiction and judgments. Chapter 6 examines jurisdiction bases provided by international conventions separately, and deals in particular with the jurisdiction of Member States of the European Union in civil and commercial matters. This chapter has been substantially reviewed to take into account the impact of the decisions of the ECJ. Since the last edition of this book, significant changes have occurred in relation to anti-suit injunctions, by reason of the ECJ decision in *Turner v Grovit*, and are incorporated in Chapter 7.

CHAPTER 1

INTRODUCTORY ELEMENTS

1 THE JURISDICTION OF THE ADMIRALTY COURT – HISTORICAL OVERVIEW

Whether or not the admiralty jurisdiction in England originated from Saxon times, or from the times of Henry I, the authority of the Crown to administer justice in respect of piracy or spoil and other offences committed upon the sea was undisputed by the reign of Edward III.[1] The High Court of Admiralty was an instrument of the Lord High Admiral and had jurisdiction to hear all offences and disputes within the Admiral's jurisdiction. The judge of the court was a deputy of the Lord High Admiral. This jurisdiction was separate from that of the common law courts. However, apart from possessing criminal jurisdiction, the Admiral began, gradually, to hear disputes also in all civil matters connected with the sea. This resulted in usurping the jurisdiction of the common law courts in matters arising in inland tidal waters.[2] The encroachment of the Admiral's jurisdiction upon the common law courts' jurisdiction caused indignation and became intolerable to common law lawyers in the 13th and 14th centuries. The authority of the Admiral to determine disputes involving seizure at sea was denied by the Common Pleas in 1296.[3] Later a statutory restriction of the Admiral's jurisdiction was obtained by the Admiralty Jurisdiction Act 1389,[4] in the reign of Richard II. In addition, by the subsequent statute, the Admiralty Jurisdiction Act 1391, matters of contracts, pleas and quarrels, which arose within the body of a county, whether on land or water, were removed from the jurisdiction of the Lord Admiral and were only triable in common law courts.[5]

In the years that followed, common law lawyers still employed devices to enable them to adjudicate maritime matters, which were actually within the jurisdiction of the Admiralty Court. Attempts by the Lord High Admiral to proceed in the Admiralty Court, either by arresting the person of the defendant or seizing his goods within the jurisdiction (known as the 'maritime attachment') in order to compel the defendant to appear, had been thwarted by common law writs of prohibition.[6] The last known instance of admiralty jurisdiction by the arrest of the person was in 1780.[7]

---

1   *Halsbury's Laws*, Vol 1(1), 1989, para 301.
2   Ibid.
3   Marsden, *Select Pleas*, Vol 1.
4   This Act was finally repealed in 1879.
5   See details of this background in Wiswall, FL (Jr), *Development of Admiralty Jurisdiction Since 1800*, 1970, CUP; also see Roscoe's *Admiralty Jurisdiction and Practice*, 5th edn for a general overview in the introduction.
6   Op cit, Wiswall, fn 5, p 5.
7   See *The Clara* (1855) Swa 1 (arrest of a person for civil liability was considered out of order; perhaps the prohibition of such arrest marked the beginning of protection of human rights and liberties).

The long conflict between the Admirals and the superior common law courts led to the decline of the Admiralty Court. Eventually, at the end of the reign of William IV in the 1830s, the jurisdiction of the Admiralty Court was retained in matters such as droits of admiralty (wrecks at sea which were the Admiral's property rights) collisions, salvage, possession of ships, bottomry and seamen's wages.[8] During this time, Dr Lushington, who was also a Member of Parliament, succeeded Sir John Nicholas as judge of the High Court of Admiralty in 1838. He promulgated the passing of the Admiralty Court Act (ACA) 1840. This Act effectively abolished the restrictions of Admiralty Court imposed by the Acts of Richard II and extended the court's general jurisdiction, but it did not restore it to jurisdiction enjoyed in the ancient times in questions of contract, freight and charterparties. The new jurisdiction conferred by the Act included cognisance of mortgages on ships, questions of legal title and the division of proceeds of sale on suits of possession, and any claims in the nature of salvage services, provision of necessaries to a ship, as well as claims for towage. It was made clear, however, that none of this jurisdiction was exclusive, but concurrent with that of the courts of law and equity.[9]

The jurisdiction was extended, in certain cases specified in s 6 of the ACA 1840 (3 & 4 Vict c 65), so as to enable the court to adjudicate upon claims where the ship was within a body of a county, but there was no remedy *in personam* until 1854, by s 13 of the ACA 1854 (17 & 18 Vict c 78). The 1854 Act revived the obsolete proceedings *in personam*, and the Admiralty Court had power to proceed by way of monition. But the effect of these two Acts was only to enable the jurisdiction to be exercised in the body of a county and did not give any greater jurisdiction than the court had before.

By s 7 of the subsequent ACA 1861 (24 Vict c 10) jurisdiction was given over any claim for damage done by any ship. The effect of s 35 of this Act, which gave the Admiralty Court jurisdiction either by proceedings *in rem* or *in personam*, was only to enable proceedings *in personam* to be taken where the case was an admiralty suit, so that proceedings *in rem* would have lain against the ship or against the owners or persons identified to have an interest in the ship.

Dr Lushington was inclined to give the full literal meaning to the Acts of Parliament and thought that anything done at sea, or anything done anywhere by a ship, was to be considered as within the admiralty jurisdiction. Sir Robert Phillimore was more imbued with the idea that the Admiralty Court had the entire jurisdiction which it ever had, which was extended over every tort committed on the high seas.[10]

By 1868, the admiralty jurisdiction was considered to be of a double character. There was the original jurisdiction, which existed in the ancient Court of Admiralty (the jurisdiction of the Lord High Admiral), and there was the enlarged jurisdiction given by the aforesaid statutes. These statutes professed to enlarge and did enlarge

8   *Halsbury's Laws*, Vol 1, para 301.
9   Op cit, Wiswall, fn 5, pp 40–41. The author also explains, p 42, how Dr Lushington lost his seat in Parliament, which was the price he had to pay for the passing of the 1840 Act. An opponent of Dr Lushington insisted that a clause was inserted in the Act disqualifying the admiralty judge from sitting in Parliament.
10 Per Esher LJ in *The Zeta* [1892] P 285, pp 297–299.

the jurisdiction of the Admiralty Court. For the first time, the statutes gave admiralty jurisdiction within the body of a county as, for example, when a collision occurred between an object on the high seas and a ship. There was an undoubted jurisdiction of the Lord High Admiral over everything that happened upon the high seas and there was no prohibition about it to be found in the books.[11]

Thus, the admiralty jurisdiction as expanded by the Acts of 1840 and 1861 enjoyed exclusively the advantage of the proceeding *in rem*. Maritime law developed in a separate court, but it derived from law expounded in other courts. At the time of Sir Robert Phillimore's judgeship, the Royal Commission, which inquired into the structure of the court, reported in 1869 that the root cause of the need to extend the admiralty jurisdiction was the imperfection of the procedures of the common law system. The recommendations of the Royal Commission were enacted by Parliament by the first Supreme Court of Judicature Act 1873, which consolidated all courts, including the High Court of Admiralty, into the Supreme Court of Judicature.

This Court was divided into Her Majesty's High Court of Justice and Her Majesty's Court of Appeal to exercise appellate jurisdiction. The High Court was subdivided into five divisions: Queen's Bench, Common Pleas, Exchequer, Chancery, and Probate, Divorce and Admiralty (PDA or Admiralty Division).[12] By 1875, any imperfections of the Act were corrected and the long struggle between the Lord Admiral's jurisdiction and the common law courts ended. It was mainly done to foster the development of common concepts between these divisions of courts. The development of admiralty law has continued to be influenced by changes in concepts of common law and vice versa. The reform of the judicature system transformed the attitude of common law lawyers. The admiralty jurisdiction was as readily extended, as it was in the early days when it was in the hands of the civilian admiralty judges. There were frequently transfers of actions, which were not triable at common law, from the Queen's Bench Division to the Admiralty Court.[13]

Subsequent enactments modified the Judicature Acts and this led to the consolidation of all statutes by the Supreme Court of Judicature (Consolidation) Act 1925. In addition to the basic jurisdiction of the Admiralty Court, claims for necessaries supplied to any foreign ship anywhere and questions of title arising in suits of necessaries, claims for damage done by any ship (inclusive of personal injury and death), claims for salvage services (including life salvage) rendered anywhere and claims in the nature of towage were added.[14]

The admiralty jurisdiction was later affected by two subsequent Acts: the Crown Proceedings Act 1947 (concerned with limitation of liability and immunity from suit *in rem* of Crown vessels and aircraft) and the Civil Aviation Act 1949 (concerned with claims for salvage of or by an aircraft).

An opportunity for further judicial expansion of the admiralty jurisdiction was given by the Administration of Justice Act 1956. This Act confirmed the jurisdiction

---

11 Ibid, per Fry LJ, at pp 300–301 (see extracts in 1st edition of this book).
12 Op cit, Wiswall, fn 5, pp 100–02.
13 Op cit, Wiswall, fn 5, p 128.
14 Supreme Court of Judicature (Consolidation) Act 1925, ss 18 and 22.

the court already possessed and incorporated some provisions of the International Convention for the Arrest of Sea-going Ships 1952 (ratified in this country in 1959, but not all its provisions were introduced into English law).

2 ADMIRALTY JURISDICTION AT THE PRESENT TIME

The sources of admiralty jurisdiction can be found in statutes,[15] Conventions, rules of court and judicial doctrines. The present statute is the Supreme Court Act (SCA) 1981. The provisions of this Act will be examined in detail later. Conventions,[16] as enacted by various Acts of Parliament, play a major part in the expansion or restriction of admiralty jurisdiction. The rules of court for admiralty procedures can be found in Part 61 of the Civil Procedure Rules (CPR) 1998,[17] as amended, and new Practice Directions. These are the result of the Woolf Reform of Civil Justice[18] and relate only to procedure. The philosophy behind these rules is to encourage parties to a dispute to settle as early as possible and, should they have to litigate, an obligation is imposed upon them and their lawyers to prosecute and defend their proceedings efficiently and without unnecessary delays. The overriding objective is to make the procedures simple and easily understood by laymen and lawyers. There are some changes also in terminology; for example, latin terms are eliminated. So, apart from the words *'in rem'* and *'in personam'*, for which no replacement could be found, the word 'writ' has been replaced with 'claim form', and 'action' is now 'claim'. The old 'summons' or 'motion' is now 'application'. 'Plaintiff' has changed to 'claimant', 'pleading' has become 'statement of case', 'discovery of documents' has become 'disclosure', 'Mareva injunction' is now called 'freezing injunction' and 'Anton Piller order' is a 'search order'. 'Leave of the court' is substituted with 'permission'. 'Third party action', 'contribution proceedings' and a 'counterclaim against a new party' are now known as 'Part 20 claims'. 'Summary judgment under Order 14' is now found under Part 24. Since the application of the new rules, there has, gradually, been a cultural change, too, in that speed is required in the management of cases, and the judges take a very active role in the process of

---

15 The first statute was the ACA 1840 which gave statutory rights of arrest (*in rem* jurisdiction); this *in rem* jurisdiction was expanded by the Supreme Court of Judicature Acts 1873 and 1875, as consolidated in the Supreme Court of Judicature Act 1925. The Administration of Justice Act 1956 was passed mainly to give effect to two International Conventions: the Convention for the Arrest of Sea-going Ships 1952 and the Convention for the Prevention of Collisions at Sea 1952. The 1956 Act was amended and superseded by the present statute, the SCA 1981.

16 These include: the Arrest Convention 1952, the Convention for the Prevention of Collisions 1952, the International Salvage Convention 1989 (the Salvage Convention), Foreign Immunity 1978, the European Civil Jurisdiction and Judgments Conventions 1968 and 1988, the Athens Convention on Carriage of Passengers and their Luggage by Sea 1974, the Limitation of Liability Convention 1976 (International Convention relating to the Limitation of Liability of Owners and Others of Sea-going Ships), the Convention and Protocol for the Prevention of Pollution Damage 1992.

17 Prior to 1999 these Rules were embodied in the so-called 'White Book' for the practice in the High Court and in the 'Green Book' for the county courts' practice.

18 As regards a prediction of the effect of the Woolf reform upon the Admiralty and Commercial Court after the initial stages of its implementation, refer to the speeches by Clarke LJ and Rix J (as he then was) delivered at the second lecture in memory of Professor Cadwallader, the London Shipping Law Centre, 1999.

disposing litigation more efficiently. The intention is to curtail an unnecessary increase in legal costs. The role of expert witnesses has also changed in an attempt to prevent them from taking a partisan role. The court may direct that expert evidence, on particular issues, be given by a 'single joint expert'.[19]

The old terms are used here in the discussion of cases decided before the CPR 1998 were implemented.

3 FOREIGN ASPECTS AND EXTENT OF ADMIRALTY JURISDICTION

Admiralty law has developed from sources common to many maritime nations. Thus, through the ratification of International Conventions, the internal municipal laws of different countries show greater similarity to one another. The jurisdiction extends to all ships, hovercrafts[20] or aircraft,[21] British or foreign, wherever the residence or domicile of the owners[22] may be,[23] but it is limited by Crown and foreign sovereign immunity rules.[24] It applies to all maritime claims whenever arising.[25] Its extent is also subject to rules governing the mode of exercise of such jurisdiction and, in the case of collisions, the jurisdiction is restricted where the action is *in personam*.[26] In certain circumstances, the court may have to stay or decline its jurisdiction upon application of other rules and doctrines,[27] such as the European Convention on Civil Jurisdiction and Judgments[28] and the doctrine of *forum non-conveniens*. On the other hand, the expertise that exists in England in maritime matters encourages parties to choose English jurisdiction in their contracts or submit to English jurisdiction.

---

19 See a short summary of the CPR in [1999] LMCLQ 321.

20 Hovercraft Act 1968, s 2(1).

21 Where legislation provides; see *Glider Standard Austria* [1965] 2 Lloyd's Rep 189.

22 Provided the jurisdiction does not conflict with the provisions of the Civil Jurisdiction and Judgments Acts 1982, 1991, or the owners of the relevant property are not the Crown or a foreign State using the ship or cargo for public purposes.

23 SCA 1981, s 20(7)(a).

24 As apply by the Crown Proceedings Act 1947 and the State Immunity Act 1978.

25 SCA 1981, s 20(7)(b).

26 SCA 1981, ss 21 and 22.

27 See Chapter 5, below.

28 The Brussels Convention 1968, as amended, and the Lugano Convention 1988, enacted by the Civil Jurisdiction and Judgments Acts 1982 and 1991 respectively (the European Civil Jurisdiction Conventions). On 1 March 2002, amending Council Regulation (EC) 44/2001 (the Brussels Regulation) came into force which replaced the Brussels Convention 1968. The Convention still applies, however, to proceedings in Denmark, which has not adopted the Regulation. Case-law applying the 1968 Brussels Convention, as amended, will continue to be good law where the corresponding wording of the Regulation is the same or similar; see Chapter 6, in which reference is made to the Brussels Convention where the case in question was decided before the Regulation had effect.

4 THE CIVIL LAW AND COMMON LAW APPROACHES

In civil law systems, there are three distinct rules provided in civil procedure codes, namely: (a) rules for a provisional pre-trial remedy, such as conservatory measures to obtain security for a claim, called, in French, *saisie conservatoire*; (b) rules relating to establishing jurisdiction on the merits, which may be based on a substantive link between the claim and the particular jurisdiction; and (c) rules relating to the status of some claims as preferred claims over unsecured creditors.

By contrast, in the common law jurisdictions, the commencement of the *in rem* claim coupled with the arrest of the ship merges the three distinct functions set out above. Namely, it has the consequence of (a) obtaining security for the claim; (b) establishing jurisdiction on the merits[29] (even if there is no substantive link between the claim and the jurisdiction other than the presence of the arrested ship in the jurisdiction); and (c) securing the position of statutory maritime claimants as preferred creditors over unsecured ones by the issue of the proceedings *in rem*. Art 7 of the Arrest Convention 1952 adopted a middle position between common law and civil law, in that, where the arrest was made, that court should have jurisdiction on the merits, if its own domestic law permitted it, but allows the parties to agree another jurisdiction.

The SCA 1981 provides the means of enforcing those maritime claims specifically mentioned in s 20(2). They are statutory rights *in rem*. The prerequisite is, however, that there must exist a substantive cause of action.

5 UNIQUE ASPECTS OF THE ADMIRALTY JURISDICTION

The distinction between the action *in rem* and the action *in personam* (renamed '*in rem* claim' and '*in personam* claim' respectively by the CPR) is unique and is not familiar to other European jurisdictions.

The '*in rem* claim' was originally founded on the notion of maritime liens. Enforcement of judgment was allowed against the property arrested, on the theory that a maritime lien attached to the property from the moment of the creation of such a claim. That is why it became known as an '*action in rem*'.[30] The right to enforce a maritime lien by such an action was confined to the ship by which the damage was caused, or in relation to which the maritime lien arose, even if it was in the hands of an innocent purchaser.[31] Later, this jurisdiction was extended to other maritime claims provided by the statutes regardless of whether or not the claims gave rise to maritime liens.

It should be noted that, historically, a claimant had to secure an entry in the

---

29 Whether the court will exercise its jurisdiction will depend on there being no other court claiming to have exclusive jurisdiction based on either Convention rules, or a prior agreement between the parties to a dispute. See Chapter 6, below.

30 *Halsbury's Laws*, Vol 1, para 305.

31 *The Ripon City* [1892] P 226, pp 241–42.

action book kept in the Admiralty Registry stating his name and giving a description of the ship to be sued and the amount of the claim. Shortly thereafter, he had to execute an affidavit to lead a warrant of arrest of the ship. This particular procedure developed since 1801. All the *in rem* claims from the issue of the *in rem* claim form are registered in the Admiralty Registry. The procedural step of issuing the claim has the effect of crystallising the *in rem* claim on the ship as a statutory lien *in rem*, which is very important as a form of security in case the ship is, in the meantime, sold even to a bona fide purchaser. The recording of the issue in the Admiralty Registry has the effect of notice for those who wish to check the record of claims against the ship.

As mentioned earlier in the historical overview, apart from proceedings against the ship, there was also the availability of proceedings against the person interested in the property, by arresting the person or his property (known as the maritime attachment). The common law courts vehemently disapproved of the proceeding to arrest the person and caused it to become obsolete. The power of arrest was only retained in relation to property if it was the subject matter of the dispute.[32] Wiswall explains[33] that the procedure of maritime attachment was similar in outline to that of the action *in rem* and, because it involved seizure of a vessel, it was often referred to as a proceeding *quasi in rem*. The author further explains that such maritime attachment or *quasi in rem* proceeding should not be confused with the action *in rem* per se because it was a device designed to compel the appearance of the defendant in an action *in personam* and it was by no means an action *in rem*. It is important that this type of maritime attachment or *quasi in rem* claim should not be confused with the present position under the SCA 1981, which distinguishes claims *in rem* based on proprietary rights on the ship from those which do not have proprietary rights on the ship arrested, as will be seen later.

The procedure *in personam* was founded by the Merchant Shipping Act 1854 and was paralleled to a suit *in rem*, in which the defendant appeared collaterally to defend the *res*. The High Court of Admiralty was empowered to entertain proceedings commenced by personal service upon the owners of the property, which was the subject matter of the dispute. It was particularly useful when the property had been lost. Subsequently, s 35 of the ACA 1861 confirmed the Admiralty Court's jurisdiction by proceedings either *in rem* or *in personam*.

The distinguishing feature of the claim *in rem* has always been the ability of the maritime claimant to proceed against the ship directly, which was regarded as the defendant because the ship was personified as the actual defendant. This notion gave rise to the personification theory for the purpose of explaining the nature of the *in rem* action, because the ship was regarded to be the defendant and even more so if her owner, or the person interested in the ship, did not appear to defend the case but let the ship be sold by the court. If the person interested in the ship and in defending the claim appeared in the proceeding, or acknowledged service of the writ *in rem*, the action would become, also, an action against the person. This step in the action was significant to the advancement of the procedural theory, which

---

32 Op cit, Wiswall, fn 5, pp 12–17.
33 Ibid, p 165.

regards the *in rem* action merely as the necessary procedural step, the function of which is to bring the person liable for the claim in the proceedings. It will be seen later, in Chapter 3, how this theory evolved. In fact, since the House of Lords' decision in *The Indian Grace*, the procedural theory has been accepted as the correct theory in interpreting the *nature* of the action *in rem*.

The *in rem* claim can be brought into effect by service on, or arrest of, the relevant ship when she comes within the jurisdiction of the English court. When a claim attracts a maritime lien, the property to be arrested includes the cargo on board the particular ship and the freight due, in relation to the cargo and voyage of the ship arrested.

The *in rem* proceedings can even be brought simply to obtain security for claims referred to arbitration, or for claims for which a court, other than the Admiralty Court, has jurisdiction on the merits.[34] In the realm of the European Civil Jurisdiction Conventions, the action *in rem* has caused some debate but, recently, both the European Court of Justice and the House of Lords resolved the matter.[35] The result of the House of Lords' decision in *The Indian Grace*,[36] which will be discussed later,[37] seems to have been a complete overhaul of the *in rem* (action) claim.

English procedural rules do not require any connection between the claim and the jurisdiction. With regard to actions *in personam*,[38] jurisdiction is established by the service of the proceedings or claim form upon the person within the jurisdiction. However, in maritime or commercial claims, when, in most cases, the defendants are a company registered abroad, other rules have developed to serve them out of the jurisdiction, provided the claim comes within certain defined categories.[39]

6 THE ADMIRALTY COURT

The Administration of Justice Act 1970 (s 2(1)) abolished the PDA division of the High Court and provided for the constitution of the Admiralty Court of the Queen's Bench Division of the High Court. Section 6 of the SCA 1981 replaced this and further provided, by sub-s(2), that the judges are puisne judges of the High Court, nominated by the Lord Chancellor.[40] The Admiralty Marshal performs the arrest, appraisement and sale of a ship or property – being the subject of the *in rem* claim. The Admiralty Registrar carries out the functions of the Queen's Bench Master. The nautical assessors, known as Elder Brethren of Trinity House, who express their opinion in nautical matters, may assist the judge in technical cases. Their expert evidence is admissible in all courts on all issues of fact about seamanship.[41]

---

34 *The Bazias* [1993] 1 Lloyd's Rep 101.
35 See Chapter 6, para 1.6, below.
36 *Republic of India v India Steamship Co Ltd (No 2)* [1994] 3 WLR 818 (HL).
37 See Chapter 3, below.
38 For the advantages of the action *in rem* over the action *in personam*, see Chapter 3, below.
39 See Chapter 5, below.
40 SCA 1981, s 6(1)(b), (2).
41 *The Clan Lamont* (1946) LlL Rep 522.

The nautical assessor is not to be confused with the expert witness; he is not subjected to cross-examination, but the judge has discretion to choose between the opinion of differing nautical assessors.[42]

The SCA 1981 governs the jurisdiction of the Admiralty Court, ss 20–24. The *in rem* jurisdiction of the county courts was abolished in 1999.

The old Ord 75 of the Rules of the Supreme Court (RSC), relating to procedure in admiralty cases, has been replaced with CPR Pt 61 and Practice Direction 61 (PD 61), which were brought into force pursuant to Civil Procedure (Amendment No 5) Rules 2001 (SI 2001/4015). *In personam* claims are now governed by CPR Pt 58 and Practice Direction 58 (PD 58).

7 LIMITS OF EXERCISE OF ADMIRALTY JURISDICTION

An *in rem* claim is not allowed to be brought against ships of the Crown nor against those owned by foreign States. Section 38 of the Crown Immunity Act 1947 states that 'His Majesty's ships' means ships of which the beneficial interest vested in His Majesty, or ships which are registered as Government ships, or which are, for the time being, demised or sub-demised to or in the exclusive possession of the Crown; except that, the said expression does not include any ship in which His Majesty is interested, otherwise, than in right of His Government. By s 29 of the same Act, no proceedings *in rem* shall be brought for any claim against the property of the Crown whether a ship, cargo or aircraft. Section 24(2) of the SCA 1981 preserves that position. The jurisdiction may be exercised *in personam* against the Crown in accordance with the provisions of the Crown Immunity Act 1947.

Similarly, under s 10(1)–(3) of the State Immunity Act 1978, a foreign sovereign is immune[43] from either action *in rem* against a ship or a sister ship belonging to that State, or *in personam* for enforcing a claim in connection with such a ship unless, when the cause of action arose, the ship was (or, in a case of a sister ship, both ships were) in use, or intended for use, for commercial purposes. As regards claims *in rem* against cargo belonging to a foreign State, the immunity will apply if both ship and cargo carried on board were not used, or intended for use, for commercial purposes (s 10(4)(a)). An action *in personam* will be allowed for claims against the cargo belonging to the State, if the ship carrying it was used, or intended for use, for commercial purposes (s 10(4)(b)).

8 WHAT IS A SHIP?

One might possibly take the position of the gentleman who dealt with the elephant by saying that he could not define an elephant but he knew what it was when he saw

---

42 *The Australia* (1926) LlL Rep 142.

43 Congresso del Partido [1978] 2 QB 500, pp 537–38; and Kuwait Airways Corp v Iraq Airways Co [1995] 2 Lloyd's Rep 317 (HL).

one, and it may be that this is the foundation of the learned judge's decision, that he cannot define 'ship or vessel' but he knows that this thing is not a ship or vessel.[44]

8.1 Why is it important to define it?

Defining a ship is important in many areas of shipping law (including marine insurance) in order to determine whether the provisions of various statutes, which are intended to apply to ships, are applicable to structures other than those which are obviously a ship. A decision whether a particular structure is a ship or not will determine the basis of liability. For example, if a collision occurs between a floating beacon[45] and a ship, the provisions of the Merchant Shipping Act (MSA) 1995 in relation to apportionment of liability (the admiralty law rule) will not apply, because they only apply if there is a collision between two or more ships. Instead, common law principles will apply. Unlike the admiralty law rule of division of loss in accordance with the degree of blame, the common law did not allow for apportionment of blame between two wrongdoers, prior to the Law Reform (Contributory Negligence) Act 1945. It was, therefore, very important to determine whether a collision between a skiff with oars and a rowing boat involved a collision between two ships.[46]

Whether a subject matter will be referred to the jurisdiction of the Admiralty Court, will, again, depend on whether a ship was involved in the incident which gave rise to the cause of action. Limitation of liability will also depend on whether the 'thing' that gave rise to liability was a ship within the meaning of the MSA 1995. For the purpose of salvage, the Salvage Convention 1989 has extended the subject matter which can be subject to salvage.[47]

8.2 Old definition

The definition of a ship had baffled the courts for more than a century. The problem arose from the circular definition in s 742 of the MSA 1894, which stated:

> ... 'vessel' includes any ship or boat, or any other description of vessel used in navigation; 'ship' includes every description of vessel used in navigation not propelled by oars.

The origin of the word 'vessel' comes from Latin *vascellum* meaning a 'vas', and connotes something hollow, a kind of container. The definition of 'vessel' or 'ship' in s 742 required three elements: first, physical appearance; second, not to be propelled by oars;[48] third, a determined purpose, namely, used in navigation.

---

44 Merchant Marine Insurance Co Ltd v North of England P&I Assoc (1926) 26 LIL Rep 201 (CA), p 203, per Scrutton LJ.

45 It has been held that this is not a ship: *The Gas Float Whitton* [1897] AC 337 (HL).

46 See *Edwards v Quikenden and Forester* [1939] P 261.

47 See Chapter 13, below.

48 Such a requirement has now been eliminated from all relevant statutes which define a 'ship'.

An interesting explanation of the definition of a ship was given by Blackburn J in *Ex p Ferguson*[49] which is worth quoting, for it would be useful even today (save for the reference to oars, which has been eliminated from the present definition, see later).

It involved a collision between a steamer and a fishing coble, which had oars, but, when fully loaded with fish and wet nets, it did not use the oars at that time. In deciding whether or not the fishing coble was a ship (under s 2 of the MSA 1854), the judge said:

> The chief argument against that proposition [that it was a ship] is by referring to the interpretation clause ... [meaning s 2] which says: ' "ship" shall include every description of vessel used in navigation nor propelled by oars'. And the argument against the proposition is one which I have heard very frequently, viz. Where an Act says certain words shall include a certain thing, that the words must apply exclusively to that which they are to include. That is not so; the definition given of a 'ship' is in order that 'ship' may have a more extensive meaning. Whether a ship is propelled by oars or not, it is still a ship, unless the words 'not propelled by oars' exclude all vessels which are ever propelled by oars. Most small vessels rig out something to propel them, and it would be monstrous to say that they are not ships. What, then, is the meaning of the word 'ship' in this Act? It is this, that every vessel that substantially goes to sea is a 'ship'. I do not mean to say that a little boat going out for a mile or two to sea would be a ship; but where it is its business really and substantially to go to sea, if it is not propelled by oars, it shall be considered a ship for the purpose of the Act. Whenever the vessel does go to sea, whether it be decked or not decked, or whether it goes to sea for the purpose of fishing or anything else, it would be a ship.

The fishing coble was, therefore, a ship.

Many old cases dealt with the method of propulsion (which is no longer relevant), the purpose or use of the structure, or even the area where she was used (which are still relevant criteria today under the present statutes). In *The Gas Float Whitton (No 2)*, a boat-shaped gas float, moored in tidal waters to give light, was held not to be a ship for the purpose of salvage.[50] Lord Herschell said:[51]

> It was not constructed for the purpose of being navigated or of conveying cargo or passengers. It was, in truth, a lighted buoy or beacon. The suggestion that the gas stored in the float can be regarded as cargo carried by it is more ingenious than sound.

8.3 Modern definitions

The Concise Oxford English Dictionary defines vessel as: 'a hollow receptacle, especially for liquid, a ship or boat', while Collins English Dictionary gives a

---

49 (1871) LR 6 QB 280, p 291.

50 Under Art 1 of the Salvage Convention 1989, a gas float like this will be subject to salvage coming within the wide definition of vessel or property and being in any waters whatsoever (see Chapter 13 and, particularly, Brice, G, *Maritime Law of Salvage*, 4th edn, 2003, Sweet & Maxwell, pp 223–24).

51 [1897] AC 337, p 343.

broader definition: 'any object used as a container, especially for a liquid, or passengers or freight-carrying ship, boat, etc.' Both refer to its Latin origin. The Oxford English Dictionary gives a conventional broad definition of 'vessel' as 'a craft or ship of any kind now usually one larger than a rowing boat and often restricted to sea-going craft or those plying on the larger rivers or lakes'; it defines a 'ship' as 'a large sea-going vessel (opposed to boat)'.

When the conventional appearance and use of an object lead the mind to perceive that the object is a ship, there is no need for a definition, as Scrutton LJ put it so lucidly.[52]

Section 313(1) of the MSA 1995 defines a ship to include every description of vessel used in navigation.[53] The same definition is given by s 24(1) of the SCA 1981, which also includes a hovercraft in the definition. The purpose of being 'used in navigation' is important and these words have been carried forward from the old definition. Thus, only two elements are now considered in the definition of an object as a ship: its physical appearance and its use in navigation.

8.3.1 Physical appearance

It is relevant to quote what Sheen J said, in *Steedman v Scofield*,[54] concerning a jet ski[55] which was involved in a collision with a speed boat:

> To my mind the word 'boat' conveys the concept of a structure, whether it be made of wood, steel or fibreglass, which by reason of its concave shape provides buoyancy for the carriage of persons or goods. Thus, a lifeboat differs from a liferaft in that the boat derives its buoyancy from its shape, whereas a raft obtains its buoyancy from some method of utilizing air receptacles.

> The jet ski cannot be boarded until it has reached a speed – at which it is stable enough for a rider to pull himself aboard out of the water.

> A person cannot sit in a jet ski, which is stopped in the water, as he can in a boat. The manufacturers do not describe it as a boat, but as 'personal watercraft'. Giving the word 'boat' its ordinary and natural meaning, I do not think it encompasses a jet ski.

He referred to *Dependable Marine Co Ltd v Customs and Excise Commissioners*,[56] in which Roskill J had to decide whether a ski craft was exempt from purchase tax, being 'a boat or other vessel large enough to carry human beings':

> Whether this craft was a boat or vessel depended on first impressions. The clear primary purpose was to tow skiers and to enable them to have the benefit of a craft to move them without having to use a conventional motorboat together with some person to drive it. It was true that it was physically capable of carrying a human being, who could control the engine. But it had no navigation aids – no rudder, and

---

52 In *Merchant Marine Insurance Co Ltd v North of England P&I Assoc* (1926) 26 LlL Rep 201 (CA).

53 The requirement in the old statutes of 'not being propelled by oars' was excluded by the Merchant Shipping (Registration) Act 1993, which was consolidated by the present MSA 1995.

54 [1992] 2 Lloyd's Rep 163, pp 165, 166.

55 See further confirmation in *R v Goodwin* [2006] 1 Lloyd's Rep 432.

56 [1965] 1 Lloyd's Rep 550, p 553.

the only method of changing direction was for the skier or passenger to shift his weight. The phrase 'boats and other vessels' conveyed an element of carriage ability – ability to carry either passengers or goods. Those words conveyed something different from the mere physical ability of a craft to support a passenger. It is doubtful whether the average person would have said that this was a boat or vessel capable of carrying passengers in the normal sense of that phrase. Further, it was doubtful if the craft could be said to be a boat or vessel since it was designed to tow skiers and the ability to carry passengers was merely incidental to that primary function. Accordingly, this craft was not a boat or vessel . . .

As to 'vessel', Sheen J said that it is usually a hollow receptacle for carrying goods or people. In common parlance, 'vessel' is a word used to refer to craft larger than rowing boats and it includes every description of watercraft used or capable of being used as a means of transportation on water.

However, in a more recent case, the Court of Appeal held that the function of conveying persons and cargo from place to place was not an essential characteristic, so long as 'navigation' was a significant part of the function of the structure in question; the mere fact that 'navigation' was incidental to some more specialised function such as dredging or the provision of accommodation did not take it outside the definition. For example, oil rigs were capable of and used for navigation.[57]

8.3.2 Used in navigation

The phrase 'used in navigation' requires that the navigation occurs in navigable waters. If navigation occurs within an enclosed sheet of water, it will not normally be held to be navigable waters. A small artificial lake was held not to be navigable in *Southport Corp v Morris*,[58] while a non-enclosed canal which communicated via locks to the sea with vessels passing up and down was held to be navigable waters in *Weeks v Ross*.[59] The question whether a reservoir was 'navigable waters' and could be used by dinghies for navigation depended on whether vessels were proceeding from an originating place A to a terminus B for the purpose of discharging people or cargo at the destination point, in which case there was navigation. Henry J applied the previous two cases in *Curtis v Wild*.[60] This is consistent with some old cases, which dealt with the area and the object of the work.[61]

In *Steedman v Scofield*,[62] Sheen J said it might be possible to navigate a jet ski but it was not a vessel used in navigation.[63]

---

57 *Perks v Clark* [2001] 2 Lloyd's Rep 431 (CA).

58 [1893] 1 QB 359.

59 [1913] 2 KB 229.

60 See *Curtis v Wild* [1991] 4 All ER 172, in which it was held that sailing dinghies used in a reservoir were not used in navigation and, in particular, that 'navigable waters' meant waters used by vessels going from point A to point B, not simply for pleasure purposes, even though this involved steering.

61 *The Mac* (1882) 7 PD 126; *The Mudlark* [1911] P 116.

62 [1992] 2 Lloyd's Rep 163.

63 Cf the Court of Appeal in Florida has recently held that a jet ski is a pleasure craft that meets the definition of 'vessel' under the Limitation Act, 55 F Supp 2d 1367 (SD Fla) 1999.

... what is meant by 'used in navigation'? Navigation is the nautical art or science of conducting a ship from one place to another. The navigator must be able (1) to determine the ship's position and (2) to determine the future course or courses to be steered to reach the intended destination. The word 'navigation' is also used to describe the action of navigating or ordered movement of ships on water. Hence 'navigable waters' means waters on which ships can be navigated. To my mind the phrase 'used in navigation' conveys the concept of transporting persons or property by water to an intended destination. A fishing vessel may go to sea and return to the harbour from which she sailed, but that vessel will nevertheless be navigated to her fishing grounds and back again.

'Navigation' is not synonymous with movement on water. Navigation is planned or ordered movement from one place to another. A jet ski is capable of movement on water at very high speed under its own power, but its purpose is not to go from one place to another.

The phrase 'used in navigation' connotes that, irrespective of the actual current use, the ship is actually or potentially capable of being used for navigation. A ship remains 'used in navigation' although rendered incapable of navigation, provided there is a reasonable expectation that it would regain its capacity to navigate. By contrast, the phrase 'used for navigation' implies that the actual current use of the ship is for navigation. This was confirmed in *The Winnie Rigg*,[64] in which the judge applied principles derived from old decisions. The case concerned a moored yacht used for recreational purposes and as a holiday home, which was taken for repairs after having been moored in a harbour for 15 years. The port authority levied distrain on the ship claiming outstanding mooring charges and relied on powers based on harbour statutes. One of the issues was whether the yacht was, in those circumstances, a ship so as to be the subject of distrain under the statute for such a claim. It was held that she was a ship, but the port authority had no right to distrain on her because the mooring charges did not constitute ship dues, as provided by the statute.

Recently, the Court of Appeal confirmed in *R v Goodwin*[65] that a vessel used in navigation was confined to a vessel which was used to make ordered progression over the water from one place to another, although it was not a necessary requirement that it should be used in transporting persons or property by water to an intended destination. Craft that were simply used for having fun on the water without the object of going anywhere, such as jet skis, were not 'used in navigation' and were accordingly excluded from the definition of 'ship or vessel'.

It can be concluded that, when an object has the shape of a vessel and is used in navigation in navigable waters, in the sense discussed, it will be a ship for the purpose of the MSA 1995 and for the purpose of jurisdiction of the Admiralty Court.

Old cases which do not fit within this interpretation are not good law any longer, but if a pontoon is used to transport goods from one place to another, thus,

---

64 [1998] 2 Lloyd's Rep 675.
65 *R v Goodwin* [2006] 1 Lloyd's Rep 432.

being like a dumb barge,[66] it may be a ship, provided it is not just a floating crane.[67]

Whether a drilling unit could be embraced under this meaning is more difficult to answer. The relevant words in the definition of 'ship' and 'vessel' in the MSA 1995, 'used in navigation', relate to actual use and not the purpose, or main purpose, of the builders, as some authorities seemed to suggest.[68] Drilling units have to cross the waters and, thus, be navigable, and are intended to do their work on the seas, even though at one place at a time. While a definite answer depends on the facts of a particular case, it would seem quite possible that the definition of a ship would apply to drilling vessels, meaning those not attached to the seabed.[69]

In a recent Scottish case, **Global Marine Drilling & Co v Triton Holdings Ltd (The Sovereign Explorer)**,[70] a mobile offshore drilling unit was arrested for the purpose of obtaining security in relation to a dispute under a sub-charter party, which was referred to arbitration. An application by the defendant to set aside the arrest on the ground that *The Sovereign Explorer* was not a ship was refused by Lord Marnoch on 12 November 1999. There was an appeal to the Scottish Court of Session regarding the adequacy of the security offered for her release from arrest and this issue was not questioned.

In **Perks v Clark**,[71] Longmore LJ pointed out that watertight definitions do not exist even for ships and, although it is true that some of the authorities regard the function and purpose of the structure as important, the critical question is whether the structure is used in navigation. Drilling ships and drilling barges must be ships. Semi-submersible oil rigs in which drilling operations are carried out while the rig is in a floating condition, submersible oil rigs in which drilling is carried out when the rig is resting on the sea bed, and jack-up drilling rigs, are all different forms of structure. It could be said that, since the jack-up rigs cannot perform their main function without their legs being on the sea bed, they should be singled out and should not be regarded as ships. It would, however, be unsatisfactory if some forms of oil rigs were ships and others were not.

---

66 Dumb barges have been held to be ships: *The Mudlark* [1911] P 116; *The Harlow* [1922] P 175; barges with small sails intended to be towed from port to port with captain and crew, steering gear and anchors, are held to be ships: *St John Pilot Commissioners v Cumberland Rly & Coal Co* [1910] AC 208; even a 'blower boat' shaped like a ship, but having a flat bottom and flat ends, with the purpose of having barges to lay alongside and only being towed from time to time, was a ship: *Cook v Dredging and Construction Co Ltd* [1958] 1 Lloyd's Rep 334.

67 *Marine Craft Constructions Ltd v Erland Blomquist (Engineers) Ltd* [1953] 1 Lloyd's Rep 514.

68 *Merchant Marine Insurance Co Ltd v North of England P&I Assoc* (1926) 25 LlL Rep 446 (where it was said that the floating pontoon was designed and adapted to float and to lift and not to navigate, so it was not a ship); similar words were used in *The Gas Float Whitton* [1897] AC 337 (HL).

69 See Chapter 13, para 5.3, below.

70 [2001] 1 Lloyd's Rep 60.

71 [2001] 2 Lloyd's Rep 431, p. 441.

CHAPTER 2

NATURE OF THE ADMIRALTY JURISDICTION

1 INTRODUCTION

At the time of writing the first edition of this book, a new Arrest Convention 1999 was approved by a Diplomatic Conference, which – if enacted by the UK – would have the effect of enlarging the list of claims and maritime liens that could be enforced in the Admiralty Court.[1] Six years on, and the Arrest Convention has not been enacted.

At present, a list of the heads of maritime claims which are within the admiralty jurisdiction of the English Admiralty Court are found in s 20 of the Supreme Court Act (SCA) 1981.

It is essential to remember that the Act provides the means for the enforcement of maritime claims against the relevant ship and not the cause of action which must have arisen. Section 20 outlines the extent of the court's jurisdiction to entertain such claims on their merits. Section 21 specifies the mode of bringing a maritime claim in the Admiralty Court by commencing a claim either *in personam* (s 21(1)) or *in rem* (s 21(2)–(8)). These provisions are supplemented by the procedural rules as provided in Part 61 of the Civil Procedure Rules (CPR) 1998.

There are four jurisdictional heads under s 20(1), namely:

- jurisdiction to hear and determine any of the questions and claims mentioned in sub-s (2);

- jurisdiction in relation to any of the proceedings mentioned in sub-s (3), which comprises applications under the Merchant Shipping Act (MSA) 1995 and any action to enforce a claim for damages, loss of life or personal injury arising out of a collision between ships, or non-compliance with collision regulations;

- any other admiralty jurisdiction which it had immediately before the commencement of the Act; and

- any jurisdiction connected with ships or aircraft which is vested in the High Court apart from this section and is, for the time being, by rules of court made or coming into force after the commencement of this Act, assigned to the Queen's Bench Division and directed by the rules to be exercised by the Admiralty Court.

Section 20(2)–(6) elaborates on these heads. The individual heads of jurisdiction provided under s 20(2) are examined under para 3 below, with analysis of decided cases following the lettered sub-paragraphs of the sub-section. Most of these are

---

1   See Gaskell, N (Prof), 'Explanatory note of the new Convention' (1999) 6(4) *International Maritime Law*, May; and Gaskell, N and Shaw, R, 'The Arrest Convention 1999' [1999] LMCLQ 470, pp 470–90.

rudimentary, but essential in the understanding of the nature of jurisdiction and the construction of the words used in the statute by the courts.

Before the individual heads of claims are set out, it is important to refer briefly to the nature of maritime liens because it is relevant to the discussion of cases that follow under para 3, below.

2 MARITIME LIENS[2] CONTRASTED WITH OTHER STATUTORY RIGHTS *IN REM*

Statutory rights *in rem* embrace all claims that can be enforced in the Admiralty Court by virtue of the SCA 1981 and its predecessors. Some of the statutory rights *in rem* which are listed in the Act are maritime liens. But maritime liens are not just statutory rights. The substantive right of a maritime lien arises upon the incident of the mischief done by a ship. It exists irrespective of an action *in rem* but it needs to be enforced by the proceeding *in rem*, otherwise it may die by lack of endorsement.

By contrast, the other statutory rights *in rem*, which are not maritime liens, crystallise on the ship upon commencement of the proceeding *in rem*,[3] and are otherwise known as statutory liens.

A maritime lien is a privileged charge on maritime property and arises by operation of law. It does not depend on possession of the property or on agreement. It accrues from the moment of the event which gives rise to a cause of action, and travels with the property. A maritime lien is invisible because it is not subject to any scheme of registration. It survives into the hands of a bona fide purchaser for value without notice, and is enforceable by an *in rem* claim.

This concept was first defined by Sir John Jervis in **The Bold Buccleugh**[4] in which it was said that:

> ... a maritime lien is well defined ... to mean a claim or privilege upon a thing to be carried into effect by legal process ... that process to be a proceeding *in rem* ... This claim or privilege travels with the thing into whosoever possession it may come. It is inchoate from the moment the claim or privilege attaches, and, when carried into effect by legal process by a proceeding *in rem*, relates back to the period when it first attached.

A maritime lien has an advantage over other statutory rights *in rem* (known as statutory liens), in that the latter depend on the issue of the *in rem* claim form to crystallise on the property, while a maritime lien does not depend on the legal process for its attachment, although the legal process will bring it into effect. This was illustrated in **The Tolten**:[5]

> The essence of the privilege was, and still is, whether, in continental or English law, that it comes into existence automatically, without any antecedent formality, and

---

2   For details, read Thomas, R, 'Maritime liens', in *British Shipping Laws*, 1980, Stevens, Vol 14.
3   See *The Monica S* [1967] 2 Lloyd's Rep 113.
4   [1851] 7 Moo PC 267, p 284.
5   [1946] 2 All ER 372, p 379.

simultaneously with the cause of action, and confers a true charge on the ship and freight of a proprietary kind in favour of the privileged creditor. The charge goes with the ship everywhere, even in the hands of a purchaser for value without notice, and has a certain ranking with other maritime liens, all of which take precedence over mortgages.

Although a maritime lien is similar to a mortgage, in that both are charges on the ship and can be enforced against the owner and any subsequent purchaser, it is quite distinct from it for the following reasons: first, unlike a maritime lien, a mortgage is created by an agreement in a form prescribed by statute; second, a mortgage needs registration which functions as a notice to third parties and the date of registration determines its priority over subsequent registered mortgages; third, while a mortgage has priority over other statutory rights *in rem*, a maritime lien has priority over all other maritime claims; fourth, a maritime lien travels with the ship from the moment of its creation, even when the ship is transferred to a bona fide purchaser without notice.

A maritime lien is further distinguishable from the common law possessory lien, which is a right to retain possession of a chattel pending payment of an outstanding obligation for services rendered. Once possession is released, the right to lien is lost. This right is available to ship-repairers and, if possession is retained, it can take priority over later created liens or mortgages.[6]

Another type of lien is called an 'equitable lien' which is created by implication of law and does not depend on possession of the thing. It can, however, be lost by a sale of the thing to a bona fide purchaser for value without notice.

Under English law, the claims recognised as giving rise to maritime liens are:

- damage done by a ship;
- salvage;
- seamen's wages;
- master's wages and disbursements;
- bottomry bond[7] (which is no longer in use).

It suffices at this point to quote what Scott LJ said in *The Tolten*[8] about the nature and security element of maritime liens:

> The maritime lien is one of the first principles of the law of the sea, and very far-reaching in its effects. In the *Bold Buccleugh*, Sir John Jervis delivering the judgment of the Privy Council, said this: 'Having its origin in this rule of the civil law, a maritime lien is well defined by Lord Tenterden, to mean a claim or privilege upon a thing to be carried into effect by legal process; and Mr. Justice Story . . . explains that process to be a proceeding *in rem*, and adds, that wherever a lien or claim is given upon the thing, then the Admiralty enforces it by a proceeding *in rem*, and indeed is the only court competent to enforce it. A maritime lien is the foundation of the proceeding *in rem*, a process to make perfect a right inchoate from the moment the lien attaches . . .

---

6 See Chapters 4 and 9 below; see further about liens and priorities in Chapters 17–23, Jackson, DC, *Enforcement of Maritime Claims*, 4th edn, 2005, LLP.

7 See para 3.18, below.

8 [1946] P 135 (CA), pp 144–46.

In *The Sara*, Lord Macnaghten said:

> 'A "maritime lien", as was observed in the *Two Ellens* ... must be something which adheres to the ship from the time that the facts happened which gave the maritime lien, and then continues binding on the ship until it is discharge' ... It commences and there it continues binding on the ship until it comes to an end.'

In the *Ripon City*, Gorell Barnes J reviewed the history of the maritime lien in our law in a long judgment from which, so far as I know, there has been no subsequent dissent. The following extracts describe the essential characteristics. He said:

> 'The definition of a maritime lien as recognized by the law maritime given by Lord Tenterden has thus been adopted. It is a privileged claim upon a thing in respect of service done to it or injury caused by it, to be carried effect by legal process.'

Later on, Scott LJ continued:

> The result of my examination of these principles and authorities is as follows: the law now recognizes maritime liens in certain classes of claims, the principal being bottomry, salvage, wages, masters' wages, disbursements and liabilities, and damage. According to the definition above given, such a lien is a privileged claim upon a vessel in respect of service done to it, or injury caused by it, to be carried into effect by legal process. It is a right acquired by one over a thing belonging to another – a *jus in re aliena*. It is, so to speak, a subtraction from the absolute property of the owner in the thing ...

> In my opinion, it is right in principle and only reasonable, in order to secure prudent navigation, that third persons whose property is damaged by negligence in the navigation of a vessel by those in charge of her should not be deprived of the security of the vessel ...

> In most actions *in rem* for damage, the ship is released on bail, but cases may occur where the liens or rights *in rem* against the ship are so heavy as to exceed the ship's value to her owners, who, in such case, will probably not enter an appearance and obtain the ship's release on bail. The lien consists in the substantive right of putting into operation the Admiralty Court's executive function of arresting and selling the ship, so as to give a clear title to the purchaser and, thereby, enforcing distribution of the proceeds amongst the lien creditors in accordance with their several priorities, and subject thereto rateably. I call that function of the court 'executive' because, once the lien is admitted, or is established by evidence of the right to compensation for damage suffered through the defendant ship's negligence, there is then no further judicial function for the court to perform, save that in the registry where priorities, quantum and distribution are dealt with.

Maritime liens can be enforced, as all other maritime claims, by an *in rem* claim brought in accordance with the provisions of the SCA 1981, which is dealt with in Chapter 3. Priorities of maritime claims and conflict of laws issues, in the enforcement of maritime claims when a maritime lien is created under foreign law, follow later.[9]

---

9   In this respect, see Chapter 4, and Chapter 9 (on mortgages).

3 MARITIME CLAIMS UNDER s 20(2) OF THE SCA 1981

3.1 Any claim to the possession or ownership of a ship or to the ownership of a share therein (s 20(2)(a)) [10]

The power of the court to determine questions of title in the ship, ownership or possession is inherent and was conferred to the Admiralty Court for the first time by statute in the Admiralty Court Act (ACA) 1840, s 4. The same provision was carried forward in the subsequent Acts, but it was slightly restricted by the Administration of Justice Act (AJA) 1956 and this was followed in s 20(2)(a) of the SCA 1981. Any omissions are dealt with by the sweeping up provision, s 20(1)(c), which refers to the inherent jurisdiction of the court existing prior to statute. The extent of this power was exemplified in *The Bineta*,[11] in which the court had jurisdiction to make a declaration as to which party was entitled to be registered as the legal owner of a ship.

The registered owner of *The Bineta* sold her to G, who was then registered as owner, but the seller retained possession pending payment of the purchase price. Following the failure of G to pay the purchase price to the seller, the latter exercised his statutory lien of retention and resold *The Bineta* to X. A declaration by the court was necessary to allow X, as claimant, to obtain registration in place of the first purchaser, G, which was granted.

Questions of possession or ownership, both legal and equitable, regardless of the nationality or domicile or residence of the person who claims to be the owner of the ship – of which the ownership or possession is disputed – are within the admiralty jurisdiction of the court, unless the claim involves impleading a foreign sovereign State.

In *The Jupiter (No 2)*,[12] The Court of Appeal held that there was no established rule that the Admiralty Court would not entertain possession suits in respect of foreign vessels, except at the request of the parties or with the consent of the accredited representative of the country to which the vessel belongs. The matter is one for the discretion of the court.

The vessel was originally owned by a Russian company but the Soviet Government asserted ownership by a decree of nationalisation. The Russian company, having moved its business to France, sought possession of the vessel by an action *in rem* when the vessel was purported to be sold by an English company – representing the Soviet Government, pursuant to a contract made in London – to an Italian company.

Atkin LJ said,[13] in particular, that:

---

10 *The Glider Standard Austria* [1965] P 463: no application to aircraft.

11 [1966] 3 All ER 1007, [1966] 1 WLR 121; see also *The Cape Don* [2000] 1 Lloyd's Rep 388, in which the Australian Federal Court construed the equivalent provision of the Australian Admiralty Act 1988 as including a dispute concerning whether or not a sale contract about a ship had been concluded.

12 [1925] P 69.

13 *The Jupiter (No 2)* [1925] P 69, p 77.

The first question is as to the jurisdiction of the court to entertain this claim for possession by one foreigner against another foreigner in respect of a ship that is within the territorial jurisdiction. It appears to me now reasonably plain that there is jurisdiction in the court to entertain such a claim. I think there was jurisdiction before the Admiralty Act of 1840, and in my opinion there is statutory jurisdiction given by that Act.

The only question that is left is whether or not there is a discretion in the court to decline to exercise jurisdiction in such cases, and, if so, whether that jurisdiction ought to be so exercised in this case. As to that the law seems to me still to obtain that the court in such a case has a discretion as to whether it will exercise its jurisdiction or not, and in cases where the parties both belonging to a foreign State have merely taken the occasion of the ship being temporarily here to get a question of title, which depends on the municipal laws of another country, determined by the courts of this country, the court may in the exercise of its discretion decline to do so. But, in the facts of this case, there seems to me to be no reason why the court should not exercise its discretion and entertain the suit. The vessel has been in this country for a period of years and the question arises in respect of her disposition by a contract entered into in this country by a limited company of this country, the Arcos Shipping Company, Ltd, and although questions may arise as to the right of title of the vendors to the defendants, yet it appears to me to be a case which can properly be tried in this country, and I see no reason for interfering with the discretion of the learned President in that respect.

The foreign sovereign was not impleaded in this case, since the Soviet Government had sold the vessel.[14]

The English courts, in some cases, may regard another forum as being more appropriate for the particular dispute, as it did in *The Lakhta*,[15] in which the case was in every way connected with Russia (see Chapter 5).

The court has always had power under s 30 of the MSA 1894, now para 6 of Sched 1 to the MSA 1995, to order an injunction prohibiting the dealings with a ship on the application of an interested party made under s 20(2)(a), when there is a dispute. Schedule 1, para 6(1) provides:

> The High Court or in Scotland the Court of Session may, if they think fit (without prejudice to the exercise of any other power), on the application of any interested person, make an order prohibiting for a specified time any dealing with a registered ship or share in a registered ship.

This is a substantive right not a procedural right, which can be enforced in the Admiralty Court. An 'interested person' extends only to a person with a proprietary interest in the ship, or at least to a person having a claim against the ship leading to a proprietary right.[16] It does not include personal, non-secured, creditors.

---

14 In the earlier decision of the Court of Appeal concerning a writ *in rem* against the same ship by a French company claiming possession rights, *The Jupiter (No 1)* [1924] P 236, it had been held that the Soviet Government was impleaded by the action *in rem* and the court decided not to exercise its jurisdiction. At that time, the Soviet Government had claimed an interest in the ship and applied to set aside the writ on the ground of foreign immunity.

15 [1992] 2 Lloyd's Rep 269.

16 *The Siben* [1994] 2 Lloyd's Rep 420.

This was made clear in *The Mikado*,[17] in which a financial institution, having lent money for the construction of a yacht without obtaining a mortgage, was not considered to be an interested person under this provision for the purposes of preventing further dealings with the ship.

3.2 Any question arising between the co-owners of a ship as to possession, employment or earnings of that ship (s 20(2)(b))

The purpose of this provision is to curb the obstinacy of some part-owners from damaging the rights and interests of their co-owners. It derived from s 8 of the ACA 1861 which provided:

> The High Court of Admiralty shall have jurisdiction to decide all questions arising between the co-owners, or any of them, touching the ownership ... of any ship registered at any port in England or Wales, or any share thereof and ... may direct the said ship or any share thereof to be sold, and may make such order in the premises that it shall seem fit.

It includes the power of the court to settle any accounts outstanding between the parties in relation to the ship and to direct that the ship, or any share therein, be sold, or to make any order the court thinks fit (s 20(4)).

In practice today, the relations between part owners will normally be regulated by an agreement. In the event that there is no particular or clear provision about the employment of the ship, or there is a breach of any provision having been made in this connection, there is a remedy to be enforced under this sub-paragraph. If, for instance, the majority shareholders wish to employ the ship in a particular way which the minority object to, the latter may seek to restrain the majority by arresting the ship until security to the full value of the minority's interest in the ship is provided (see Chapter 8).

In *The Vanessa Ann*,[18] the minority shareholders were granted an equitable mortgage in return for the release of the ship from arrest. Once security is provided, the ship is released to perform the voyage at the risk, expense and profit of the majority owners.

In the reverse situation, where the minority are in possession and wish to send the ship to sea against the wishes of the majority, the latter may enforce their rights by bringing an action for possession.

The court also has power to exercise its discretion and order the sale of the ship when there is a co-ownership dispute. In *The Nelly Schneider*,[19] the minority applied to the court for sale of the ship, to recover damages from the majority and settle outstanding accounts, which was opposed by the majority owners.

Sir Robert Phillimore held:

> The court has full power to decree a sale of the ship, but it will be very reluctant to do so at the instance of part owners not possessing a majority of the shares. The

---

17 [1992] 1 Lloyd's Rep 163.
18 [1985] 1 Lloyd's Rep 549.
19 (1878) 3 PD 152.

defendants have the option allowed to them of purchasing such shares at the amount fixed at valuation. If the defendants do not exercise the option within a fortnight, the ship must be appraised and sold by the Marshal. The court had to consider whether the sale would be in the interests of all parties.

However, caution is exercised by the court in making an order of sale against the wishes of the majority. It may do so in exceptional circumstances. In *The Hereward*,[20] Bruce J said:

> ... that power may be exercised on the application of a minority of part owners; and it seems to me that, when part owners of the ship are unable to agree as to what is to be done with their common property, and there appears to be no way of preventing the sacrifice of the property except by a sale, the court ought to direct a sale.[21]

3.3 Any claim in respect of a mortgage of or a charge on a ship or any share therein (s 20(2)(c))

This provision covers all mortgages and charges, notwithstanding whether they are registered or not, legal or equitable, including those created by foreign law (s 20(2)(c) and (7)(c) of the SCA 1981).

The concept of a mortgage is examined in Chapter 9. Briefly, under English law, a mortgage is a statutory charge on a registered British ship for the security of a debt and must be in a statutory form. The rights and obligations of the lender (mortgagee) are regulated by the MSA 1995 and regulations issued pursuant to the Act. When a mortgage is not in the required statutory form, or not registered, it is an equitable mortgage, which does not enjoy the protection of the statute, but it is, nevertheless, protected by equitable principles.

Most ships, nowadays, are registered abroad under the laws of a particular State carrying the flag of that State. Other than the Commonwealth States and former British colonies, foreign systems of law do not recognise the concept of equitable mortgages. So, if the mortgage is unregistered under the system of the law in the State in which the ship is registered, such a mortgage cannot be enforced by an *in rem* claim against the ship, although the mortgagee will be able to sue the borrower (mortgagor) *in personam* and enforce his claim against any insurance proceeds of the ship, provided he has obtained an effective assignment of the insurance proceeds or policy of the ship. A very good example of this situation occurred in the following case.

The Angel Bell[22]

This concerned a Panamanian ship and mortgage. The substantive law governing the mortgage was the law of the flag of the ship, Panamanian. The mortgagee omitted to register his mortgage within six months after the provisional registration

---

20 [1895] P 284.
21 Ibid, p 285.
22 [1979] 2 Lloyd's Rep 491.

as was required by statute. The result of this was to deprive the mortgagee from his rights *in rem* against the ship. He never became a legal mortgagee under the statute. (Unlike English law, Panamanian law does not recognise equitable mortgages.) However, it had been agreed that the mortgagee would obtain assignments of the hull and machinery insurance policies and each policy would contain a 'loss payable' clause. The ship sank. The owners of the cargo on board the ship began proceedings against the defendants (shipowners) claiming damages for the loss of their cargo. They applied and were granted a Mareva injunction restraining the defendants from dealing with their assets within the jurisdiction, which were the insurance proceeds of the vessel. The mortgagee intervened in the action claiming that his claim as a lender was secured on the proceeds of the insurance policies. The issue was whether the mortgagee was a secured creditor by way of proper assignment of the insurance policies, so as to entitle him to obtain judgment and execute it upon the insurance proceeds.

Donaldson J examined the matter from various angles. It suffices to mention the two substantive reasons of his decision which lay down a general principle on the issue of assignment: (a) what was the effect of the 'loss payable' clause? It was accepted that such a clause would not have an effect unless it also constituted or evidenced an assignment of the assured's rights under the policy. Regardless of the fate of the Panamanian mortgage at the time of the renewal of the insurance policies, the mortgagee was under English law – by virtue of the oral agreement to obtain a mortgage on the ship governed by English law – an equitable mortgagee. Therefore, the wording of the loss payable clause in the renewed policies referring to him as 'interested in this insurance as mortgagees' (instead of as assignees) did not defeat the effect of the clause; and (b) what was the effect of assignments under notices of assignment endorsed on the policies? Although the notices had not been signed, there was evidence that undated notices are acceptable in the market. So, the mortgagee was an assignee of the policy in the customary manner.

In conclusion, the mortgagee was a secured creditor on the proceeds of the hull and machinery policies.

A charge in the context of this section means a charge in the nature of a mortgage. It does not cover a charge in its wider sense nor a lien for wages.[23] The word did not exist in the old statutes, but it was added in the AJA 1956. It was, perhaps, included for two reasons: (a) to ensure that those who have security on the ship by way of hypothecation,[24] under foreign law, which is a charge in the nature of a mortgage, can enforce their claim under this head; and (b) to ensure that equitable mortgages are within this provision.

In this connection, it is relevant to mention that matters of procedure, remedy and priorities are governed by the *lex fori*[25] (the law of the place where the matter has been submitted for adjudication), while questions of validity of a mortgage or charge are determined by the *lex loci contractus* (the law of the place in which the contract was made).

---

23 *The Acrux* [1965] 1 Lloyd's Rep 565.
24 Reference to it is made in the Arrest Convention 1952.
25 See, further, conflict of laws and priorities of maritime claims in Chapters 4 and 9.

3.4 Any claim for damage received by a ship (s 20(2)(d))

This head includes damage done to a ship by something other than a ship, such as a pier head, or a claim against the manufacturer whose defective equipment caused damage to the ship. There is no guilty ship to arrest. This ground of claim is omitted from s 21 of the SCA 1981, which defines the mode of enforcement of maritime claims against ships. Thus, it prevents enforceability of this claim by an *in rem* claim simply because the ship that receives the damage will be the claimant, as was explained by Lord Diplock in *The Eschersheim*.[26]

The plaintiffs could not invoke the admiralty jurisdiction by an action *in rem* against their own ship. The action must be in connection with a ship. That ship must be the ship specified in the Arrest Convention as the particular ship in respect of which the maritime claim arose – and, therefore, the inclusion of this head of claim could not lead to an action *in rem*.

3.5 Any claim for damage done by a ship (s 20(2)(e))

3.5.1 The ambit of sub-paragraph (e)

The cause of action for such claims to be enforced in the Admiralty Court under sub-paragraph (e) is based on tort. Originally and independently of statute the court of Admiralty exercised jurisdiction over all torts on the high seas and in harbours within the ebb and flow of the tide.[27] The first Admiralty Court Act (ACA) in 1840 did not distinguish between damage done and damage received by a ship. But the ACA 1861, by s 7, specifically enacted that the court shall have jurisdiction over any claim for damage done by any ship and, by s 35, that the jurisdiction of the court may be exercised either by proceedings *in rem* or *in personam* (see Ch 1, para 5).

Taking the words of the statute by themselves, they would appear to confer jurisdiction upon the Admiralty Court to entertain all claims in respect of damage done by a ship, whatever may be the nature of the damage, whether to person or to property; there is nothing in the context of the section to suggest that the word 'damage' should be limited. Thus, a wide construction was placed on the words 'damage done by a ship' as was decided in several old decisions.[28] However, the House of Lords in *The Vera Cruz* did not give as wide a construction as to cover

---

26 [1976] 2 Lloyd's Rep 1, p 9.

27 See *The Volent* (1842) 1 Wm Rob 383; *The Hercules* (1819) 2 Dod 353; *The Ruckers* (1801) 4 C Rob 73; *The Lagan & Mimax* (1838) 3 Hagg Adm 418.

28 See reference to them in *The Vera Cruz* (1884) 10 App Cas 59 (HL); the HL in *The Vera Cruz* was in agreement with the dissenting view of the Court of Appeal in *The Franconia* (1877) 2 PD 163. It should be noted that in both *The Sylph* (1867) LR 2 A & E 24, and *The Beta* (1869) LR 2 PC 447, in which the admiralty jurisdiction of the court was upheld, the claim was for personal injury, while in *Smith v Brown* (1871) LR 6 QB 729, in which the jurisdiction *in rem* was refused, the claim was for pecuniary loss by the relatives of the deceased seamen who were drowned after a collision between two ships. The Court of Appeal was of the opinion that the word 'damage' in s 7 of the ACA 1861 implied damage to property not to a person. This decision is not to be relied upon in view of subsequent statutory provisions which included loss of life and personal injury into the word 'damage': MCA 1911, s 5.

damage causing loss of life. It therefore refused the enforcement *in rem* of a claim by the relatives of a deceased who had a cause of action by virtue of the old Lord Campbell's Act (Fatal Accidents Act 1846) for pecuniary loss. It was thought that Lord Campbell's Act granted such a cause of action to be brought before the common law courts against the liable person, not against the ship *in rem* before the Admiralty Court.[29] Claims for personal injury, however, that did not cause death were viewed as being included within the word 'damage', although it was not decided in this case.

Subsequent to this decision, and in view of the doubt as to whether or not a wide interpretation should be given to the word 'damage', the Maritime Conventions Act (MCA) 1911, by s 5, expressly extended the ambit of 'damage' to include personal injury and loss of life. Thus, on this issue, it reversed the effect of *The Vera Cruz* decision.

Claims arising from personal injury or death can today be enforced *in rem* under the SCA 1981, s 20(2)(f), which is discussed later.

How the damage done by a ship must have occurred was explained by Lord Diplock in **The Eschersheim**:[30]

> The figurative phrase 'damage done by a ship' is a term of art in maritime law whose meaning is well established by authority: *The Vera Cruz* (1884) 9 PD 96 [(1884) 10 App Cas 59 (HL)]; *The Currie v M'Knight* [1897] AC 97. To fall within 'damage done by a ship' not only must the damage be the direct result or natural consequence of something done by those engaged in the *navigation of the ship*, but the ship itself must be *the actual instrument* by which the damage was done. But physical contact between the ship and whatever object sustains the damage is not essential, a ship may *negligently* cause a wash by which some other vessel or . . . property on shore is damaged. (emphasis added)

In this case, a collision took place off the coast of Spain between a Sudanese ship, *The Erkowit*, and a German ship, *The Dortmund*, as a result of which the engine room of *The Erkowit* was holed and became flooded. The tug, *Rotesand*, went to her aid and a salvage agreement on the Lloyd's Open Form (LOF) was signed. By the salvors' negligence in beaching *The Erkowit*, she was delivered in a sinking condition and became total loss. Most of her cargo and the crew's personal effects were lost or damaged. As some of her cargo was insecticide in drums, they were washed away causing pollution along the Spanish coast with consequential interference with fishing in that area. Various actions commenced; first, the owners of *The Erkowit*, her crew and the owners of the cargo on board commenced proceedings against the German ship. However, the respective lawyers of the above claimants had the foresight to protect the time limit for commencing an action against the salvors in the event they could not establish a cause of action for the damages suffered against the other ship. The claimants arrested two sister ships of the tug *Rotesand*, *The Jade* and *The Eschersheim*. Indeed, the proceedings against the German

---

29 *The Vera Cruz*, ibid, but such personal claims were and are admissible against the limitation fund established in the limitation of liability action pursuant to the Merchant Shipping Acts.

30 [1976] 1 WLR 430 (HL), p 438.

ship failed because the chain of causation of the damage suffered was broken by the subsequent negligence of the salvors.

Various issues arose which will be examined later under each sub-paragraph of the statute in which they fell.[31] The issue under this head was whether the claims against the salvors came within the admiralty jurisdiction, or should be referred to arbitration by virtue of the terms of the salvage agreement. The House of Lords decided that:

> The act of casting off *The Erkowit* in such a way as to beach her upon an exposed shore was something done by those engaged in the navigation of *The Rotesand*, as a result of which *The Erkowit* and her cargo were left exposed to the risk of being damaged by wind and wave if the weather worsened before she could be removed to a more sheltered position.[32]

Both shipowners' and cargo-owners' claims fell under this sub-paragraph (e) as well, although they were regarded to be a borderline case, being more appropriate for the one under (h) to be discussed later.

With regard to the claimants who sued for the pollution damage in this case, it was also held that a claim for pollution damage caused through escaping oil following the negligent beaching of the ship whilst being salved can be enforced under sub-para (e).

This provision (damage done by a ship) is now extended by virtue of s 20(5)(a) and (b) to cover any claim in respect of liability incurred under the MSA 1995, Sched 4 for pollution damage. The International Convention for Civil Liability arising from Pollution Damage 1969 (CLC) has been superseded by the CLC 1992, the 1992 Protocol. It came into force on 30 May 1996, although, so far as English law is concerned, it had already been enacted into English law, a year previously, by ss 152–70 of the MSA 1995. Pollution liability is discussed in Chapter 19, below.

3.5.2 The act must be an act of navigation

The damage may be done by a ship, regardless of direct physical contact, such as a collision; it can also be done by transmitted physical force, such as a wash of waves, but there must be an act of navigation.

This principle for enforcement of claims under this sub-paragraph was laid down by the House of Lords in ***Currie v M'Knight***.[33]

A heavy gale was raging when the vessel D and the vessel E were lying alongside one another in the port. In an attempt to put D out to sea, her crew cut off the ropes of E, so that the latter drifted ashore and was damaged. The question in the action was whether the wrongful act of D's crew was sufficient to create a maritime lien for the damage to E.

Lord Halsbury stated:

---

31 At the time of these actions, the claims were enforced in the Admiralty Court under the previous statute (the AJA 1956), therefore, the claim for damage done by a ship was numbered under the letter (d).

32 [1976] 2 Lloyd's Rep 1, p 8.

33 [1897] AC 97.

... the phrase that 'it must be the fault of the ship itself' is not a mere figurative expression, but it imports, in my opinion, that the ship against which a maritime lien for damages is claimed is the instrument of mischief, and that, in order to establish the liability of the ship itself to the maritime lien claimed, some act of navigation of the ship itself should either mediately or immediately be the cause of the damage.[34]

It was held that the act was a wrongful act of self-preservation, but was not an act of navigation, even though other ships were damaged. The section requires the act not just to be an act of the crew, but one in the course of their navigation. This act was done for the purpose of removing an obstacle, which prevented D from starting her voyage. The doctrine of maritime liens could not be extended to cover such a case.

The act of navigation can involve an act which deprives the victim from using a particular area for fishing when a wrongdoer ship drives it out from the area. A question arose in *The Dagmara and The Ama Antixine*[35] whether a claim for economic loss can be enforced under sub-para (e). The defendants' vessel A was being dangerously navigated around vessel D belonging to the claimants, in a deliberate attempt to drive the D away from the fishing grounds. For fear of their safety, the master and crew of ship D left the fishing grounds. The owners of D claimed in tort for damages in respect of damage suffered in the form of financial loss. It was held by Sheen J that they had a valid cause of action in tort to be enforced under this head. It should be noted, however, that such a claim was not for pure economic loss because the financial loss suffered was consequential to their boat being driven away from the fishing area by the wrongful act of the defendant, as if physical damage had been inflicted on the fishing boat. (For pure economic loss, see Ch 12, para 3.12.3.4.)

A claim for damage done by a ship gives rise to a maritime lien[36] and it can be enforced as such under s 21(3) of the SCA 1981.

3.6 Any claim for loss of life, personal injury ... (s 20(2)(f))

... sustained in consequence of any defect in a ship, her apparel or equipment, or in consequence of the wrongful act, neglect or default of:

(i) owners, charterers or persons in possession or control of a ship; or

(ii) the master[37] or crew of a ship, or any other persons whose wrongful acts, neglects or defaults the owners, charterers or persons in possession or control of a ship are responsible,

being an act or default in the navigation or management of a ship in the loading, carriage or discharge of goods on, in or from the ship, or in the embarkation of persons on, in or from the ship.

---

34 Ibid, p 101.
35 [1988] 1 Lloyd's Rep 431.
36 The nature of maritime liens, para 2, above.
37 Under SCA 1981, s 24(1), master includes every person, except the pilot, having command of the ship.

3.6.1 Origins of this provision

This sub-paragraph is very wide. The Administration of Justice Act 1956 borrowed the same provision from the Arrest Convention 1952. *In personam* jurisdiction for such claims existed even before the ACA 1861. Section 7 of the 1861 Act provided that there should be jurisdiction 'over any claim for damage done by any ship' and this included, as discussed earlier, at least originally, claims for personal injury and later since 1911 claims for loss of life. Under the present Act, SCA 1981, the provision has been separated from 'damage done by a ship' and has been expanded in order to include jurisdiction for incidents other than just those occurring by negligent navigation. Consistently with all other maritime claims, such jurisdiction is statutory for the purpose of enforcement of those claims.

3.6.2 Wrongful act, neglect or default in the navigation or management of a ship

The reason why this sub-paragraph is separate from the provision of 'damage done by a ship' under para (e) is that it includes negligence, not only in the navigation, but also in the management of the ship and any defect in the ship, her apparel or equipment, which may cause loss of life or personal injury, whether on board the ship or outside. It was the 1981 statute that extended it to defects of a ship and defaults of certain persons. The Arrest Convention 1952 covers such claims only if caused by any ship or by her operation, which is much narrower than the SCA 1981; but neither the Convention nor the Act precludes loss occurring outside the ship.

3.6.3 Sub-paragraph (f) covers incidents that occurred on board another ship

The Radiant and *The Maid of Kent* are good examples of how the courts have approached such situations. They involve defect in equipment of a guilty ship, other than the one on which the injured person was carried.

The Radiant [38]

This case concerned personal injury sustained by the skipper of a motor fishing vessel, *The Radiant*, owned by the employer of the skipper. The skipper's feet were amputated by a tow rope, which had wrapped around the skipper's legs when the tow rope was thrown out by a sister ship, *The Margaret Hamilton*, which was towing *The Radiant* after it had grounded due to the negligence of the sister ship. It was found that the cause of the accident was the grounding and the inadequacy of ropes in *The Margaret Hamilton*. It was held that defective equipment of one vessel could give rise to a cause of action at the suit of a person on board another vessel. There was no proof of contributory negligence on the part of the skipper.

---

38 [1958] 2 Lloyd's Rep 596, p 608.

The Maid of Kent [39]

A North Sea pilot was about to climb a ladder from the pilot launch to board the port side of the ship 'DS'. At the time, The Maid of Kent passed the DS too near and too fast, causing a wash, which struck the launch and caused her to roll violently against the DS. The pilot was crushed between the port side of the DS and the launch as a result. He fell into the sea and died. The administrator of his estate claimed under the FAAs that the owners of The Maid of Kent were liable for damages. Although the claim was dismissed at first instance, the Court of Appeal held that those in charge of The Maid of Kent were negligent, in that they failed to see the effect which the wash from their ship might have had on a small craft. The accident was foreseeable. The claim could be enforced under this statutory provision (s 20(2)(f) of the SCA 1981), as the words 'wrongful act or neglect or default' are very broad to cover such claims arising in connection with a ship.

3.6.4 Defect in a ship, her apparel or equipment under sub-para (f)

A claimant must first be able to rely on an actionable substantive cause of action, which he may then seek to enforce in the admiralty court through the provisions of the SCA. As explained earlier, the SCA provides a link between that cause of action and the in rem jurisdiction of the court. For example, in a case of a collision, or in the cases mentioned above, the cause of action is easily identifiable as a breach of the common law duty of care. Apart from cases of breach of contract, there are occasions where the cause of action may lie in statutes. Such statutes are, for present purposes, the Employers' Liability (Defective Equipment) Act (EL(DE)A) 1969 or the FAAs (currently 1976), or the Occupiers' Liability Act 1957, or the MSA 1995. Whether or not a ship is 'equipment' for the purpose of the application of the EL(DE)A 1969 was decided in **The Derbyshire**. [40]

The Derbyshire sank during a voyage from Canada to Japan with loss of all the lives on board. The action was brought by the personal representatives of the deceased (third engineer) to recover damages on behalf of his estate and for the benefit of his widow and daughter who were dependent on him. The cause of action was based on the EL(DE)A 1969. It was argued that his death was caused by a defect in equipment provided by the employer in the course of his business. Such equipment was the vessel, regardless that the defect was attributable to a third party, the shipbuilder. The issue was whether the vessel constituted 'equipment' within the meaning to be given to that word in the EL(DE)A 1969. The House of Lords answered the question in the affirmative (reversing the decision of the Court of Appeal). Lord Oliver explained[41] the origins of this provision:

> My Lords, it is common ground that the 1969 Act was introduced with a view to rectifying what was felt to be the possible hardship to an employee resulting from the decision of this House in Davie v New Merton Board Mills Ltd ([1959] 2 Lloyd's Rep 587; [1959] AC 604). In that case, an employee was injured by a defective drift supplied to him by his employers for the purpose of his work. The defect resulted from a

---

39 [1974] 1 Lloyd's Rep 434.
40 [1988] 1 Lloyd's Rep 109.
41 [1988] 1 Lloyd's Rep 109, pp 111–15.

fault in manufacture but the article had been purchased by the employers without knowledge of the defect from a reputable supplier and without any negligence on their part. It was held that the employers' duty was only to take reasonable care to provide a reasonably safe tool and that that duty had been discharged by purchasing from a reputable source an article whose latent defect they had no means of discovering. Thus, the action against them failed, although judgment was recovered against the manufacturer. Clearly, this opened the door to the possibility that an employee required to work with, on or in equipment furnished by his employer and injured as a result of some negligent failure in design or manufacture might find himself without remedy in a case where the manufacture and the employer were, to use the words of Viscount Simonds, 'divided in time and space by decades and continents' so that the person actually responsible was no longer traceable or, perhaps, was insolvent or had ceased to carry on business. Parliament, accordingly, met this by imposing on employers a vicarious liability and providing, in a case where injury was due to a defect caused by the fault of the third party, that the employer should, regardless of his own conduct, be liable to his employee as if he had been responsible for the defect, leaving it to him to pursue against the third party such remedies as he might have whether original or by way of contribution.

The purpose of the Act, as set out in the long title, is:

> ... to make further provision with respect to the liability of an employer for injury to his employee which is attributable to any defect in equipment provided by the employer for the purposes of the employer's business; and for purposes connected with the matter aforesaid.

The relevant provisions of the Act, for present purposes, are contained in sub-ss (1) and (3) of s 1 and are as follows:

> (1) Where after the commencement of this Act – (a) an employee suffers personal injury in the course of his employment in consequence of a defect in equipment provided by his employer for the purposes of the employer's business; and (b) the defect is attributable wholly or partly to the fault of a third party (whether identified or not), the injury shall be deemed to be also attributable to negligence on the part of the employer (whether or not he is liable in respect of the injury apart from this sub-section), but without prejudice to the law relating to contributory negligence and to any remedy by way of contribution or in contract or otherwise which is available to the employer in respect of the injury ...

> (3) In this section – 'business' includes the activities carried on by any public body; 'employee' means a person who is employed by another person under a contract of service or apprenticeship and is so employed for the purposes of a business carried on by that other person, and 'employer' shall be construed accordingly; 'equipment' includes any plant and machinery, vehicle, aircraft and clothing; 'fault' means negligence, breach of statutory duty or other act or omission which gives rise to liability in tort in England and Wales or which is wrongful and gives rise to liability in damages in Scotland; and 'personal injury' includes loss of life, any impairment of a person's physical or mental condition and any disease.

My Lords, if sub-s (1) stood alone without such assistance as provided by sub-s (3), I would not, for my part, have encountered any difficulty in concluding that, in the context of this Act, a ship was part of the 'equipment' of the business of a shipowner. In the Court of Appeal, O'Connor LJ, expressed the view that the word in its natural meaning denoted something ancillary to something else and an echo of this is to be found in the judgment of Glidewell LJ. Thus, both Lords Justices would, I think, regard machinery attached to a ship as 'equipment', because it would be ancillary to the main object, the vessel, but both regarded the word as inappropriate to describe the vessel itself. I do not doubt that the word is frequently and quite properly used to describe the appurtenances of some larger entity, but I can see no reason either in logic or as a matter of language why its use should be so confined. Indeed, there is nothing in the entry in the *Oxford English Dictionary* quoted by O'Connor LJ which necessarily imports that 'equipment' is restricted to parts of a larger whole. The meaning is given as:

> . . . anything used in equipping; furniture; outfit; warlike apparatus; necessaries for an expedition or voyage.

Moreover, your Lordships are concerned not with the meaning of 'equipment' simpliciter but of the composite phrase, 'equipment provided by his employer for the purposes of the employer's business'. Speaking for myself, I can think of no more essential equipment for the setting up and carrying on of the business of a shipowner than the ship or ships with which the business is carried on. This involves, in my judgment, no misuse of language . . .

In my judgment, a shipowner's fleet of ships is properly described as the equipment of his business. They are, in truth, the tools of his trade and I can see no ground for treating the word 'equipment' in sub-s (1)(a) – leaving aside for the moment the more difficult questions posed by sub-s (3) – as excluding this particular type of chattel as opposed to other articles, of whatever size or construction, employed by a trader in carrying on his trade.

With regard to sub-s (3), Lord Oliver had some difficulty in its construction, but he came to the same conclusion as the dissenting Lloyd LJ of the court below, that the wording of the sub-section intended to be clarifying rather than limiting the application of the section only to any plant and aircraft, but not ships.

Lord Goff added:[42]

> The real difficulty in the case, as it seems to me, arises from the fact that the word 'equipment' is defined in s 1(3) of the Act, and that the definition expressly includes any vehicle and aircraft, but makes no mention of ships or vessels . . . it seems to me that, in the case of ships, the distinction between the equipment on the ship and the structure of the ship is not only very difficult to draw in practice, but is artificial in the extreme. In any event, the duty of care imposed under the Occupiers' Liability Act 1957 may apply not only in respect of vessels, but also in respect of vehicles and aircraft. I have therefore come to the conclusion in agreement with my noble and learned friend, and with Lloyd LJ in the Court of Appeal, that the definition of equipment in s 1(3) of the Act of 1969 must have been included in the Act for the purpose of clarification only, and that the mere fact that ships and vessels were not expressly included in the definition cannot have been intended to have the effect of cutting down the ordinary meaning of the word 'equipment' by excluding ships or vessels from that word.

3.6.5 Claims in the Admiralty Court by foreigners against a foreign ship for a tort committed on the high seas

When a collision occurs between foreign ships in international waters resulting in damage to property, loss of life or personal injury, the tort of negligence is

---

42 [1988] 1 Lloyd's Rep 109, p 115.

committed outside the territorial waters of the United Kingdom. Claimants would be restricted from suing the defendant *in personam* in the English High Court, unless the conditions of s 22(2) of the SCA 1981 were satisfied. These conditions are:

- the defendant has his habitual residence or a place of business within England or Wales; or

- the cause of action arose within inland waters of England or Wales; or

- an action arising out of the same incident, or series of incidents, is proceeding in the court or has been heard and determined in the court.

If neither of these conditions applied, the claimants would be advised, in any event, to proceed *in rem* by issuing a claim form *in rem* and wait until the ship came within the English jurisdiction to arrest her by a warrant of arrest. Unlike the *in personam* claim, there would be no need for a substantive link between the jurisdiction and the claim other than the presence of the ship within the jurisdiction.

The cause of action of claimants in respect of property damage or personal injury would be based on the tort of negligence, while the cause of action of dependants of a deceased person would be based on the Fatal Accidents Acts (FAAs). The basis of the claim to which the Acts give statutory authority is negligence causing death. Although the death is an essential constituent of the right of action, the measure of damages is not the same as in an action by an injured person.

There have been numerous cases where the collision damage occurred on the high seas and the parties involved were foreigners. So, when the relevant ship was arrested in this jurisdiction, the courts had to consider whether the ambit of the English admiralty jurisdiction was extra-territorial in such cases. There was no problem in answering this question because such jurisdiction had been extended to adjudicate cases concerning any matters which occurred on the high seas, provided the relevant ship, which provides the link, was arrested in this jurisdiction. But when foreign dependants of a foreign deceased (who died due to a collision between foreign ships on the high seas) arrested a ship in this jurisdiction, the issue confronting the courts was whether the FAA applied to foreigners.

Although there had been several decisions decided on points of jurisdiction, the first case – in which this precise issue of tort on the high seas causing death involving foreign parties of which the claimants pursued the *in rem* claim under the FAAs was to be decided – was *The Esso Malaysia*.[43]

A collision occurred on the high seas between a trawler, registered in Latvia, and *The Esso Honduras*, registered in Panama and owned by the defendants, a Panamanian company. Twenty-four Russian seamen lost their lives. The administrator of the estates of the Russian seamen brought an action against *The Esso Malaysia*, a sister ship of *The Esso Honduras*, under the FAAs 1846 to 1959, for the benefit of the dependants of the deceased seamen. It was argued by the defendants that, on a true construction of the FAAs, a right of action was not conferred on a foreigner against a foreigner in respect of death occurring on the high seas and there was a presumption that the statute did not have extra-territorial effect.

After careful consideration of the issues, it was held by Brandon J that the

---

43 [1975] QB 198, pp 205–06.

plaintiff, as personal representative of the deceased seamen, had a good cause of action against the owners of the Panamanian ship for damages under the FAAs 1846 to 1959. He agreed with the comments made by the Divisional Court in *Davidson v Hill*[44] in which Kennedy J held:

> It seems to me that the Fatal Accidents Acts which are under our consideration in the present case embody legislation which is of a very different character. The basis of the claim to which they give statutory authority is negligence causing injury, and that is a wrong which I believe the law of every civilized country treats as an actionable wrong. They create, no doubt, a new cause of action . . . for previously the relatives of the deceased could not in England sue the wrong-doer. The measure of damages is not the same as in an action by the injured man, as the death is an essential constituent of the right of action. None the less, as I venture to think, is it true to say that in substance the purpose and effect of the legislation is to extend the area of reparation for a wrong which civilized nations treat as an actionable wrong . . . It appears to me, under all the circumstances and looking at the subject-matter, more reasonable to hold that Parliament did intend to confer the benefit of this legislation upon foreigners as well as upon subjects . . .

Although the point was obiter in this case, the decision had not been disturbed by higher authority for 75 years, and Brandon J in *The Esso Malaysia* agreed with the opinion of Kennedy J. It seems that, since the issue has not been challenged in subsequent decisions, it can be concluded that it has been settled.

The enforcement of such a claim or right against the ship can be in the Admiralty Court by virtue of sub-para (f) or, if any of the conditions of s 22(2) of the SCA 1981 is satisfied, by a claim *in personam*. It should be noted in this context that the master of the ship on which a seaman has been injured, or died, due to breach of duty by the master, can be sued *in personam*, if he is within the jurisdiction, by the injured seaman in tort, and by the executrix of the estate of a deceased seaman under the Fatal Accidents Act 1976.[45]

3.6.6 Do claims for personal injury or loss of life attract a maritime lien?

This issue is contested.

Claims which result from damage done by a ship are amongst the list of maritime liens.[46] A question has arisen whether claims for personal injury or loss of life attract a maritime lien,[47] or are just statutory rights *in rem*.

As regards personal injury claims, there has been no direct decision on whether or not these claims attract a maritime lien, although there had been conflicting decisions with regard to whether or not the claims come within 'damage done by a ship' (see para 3.5.1 above). As is seen earlier (under para 3.5.2), claims falling

---

44 [1901] 2 KB 606, pp 613–615 (here, the collision was between a Norwegian and a British ship; the Divisional Court decided in favour of personal representatives and expressed the view obiter that the result would have been the same even if all the ships were foreign).

45 See *Booth v Phillips and others (The Maysora)* [2004] 2 Lloyd's Rep 457, in which interesting issues of jurisdiction and *forum non-conveniens* arose.

46 *The Bold Buccleugh* (1851) 7 Moo PC 267.

47 Jackson, op cit, fn 6, pp 39–40.

within 'damage done by a ship', which is interpreted to be the result of an act in the course of negligent navigation (*Currie v M'Knight*), attract a maritime lien. Once such claims are within the category 'damage done by a ship', they should attract a maritime lien.

In *The Beta*,[48] the Privy Council Committee had affirmed that a personal injury claim was within 'damage done by a ship' and Lord Romilly expounded without doubt that:

> The words of the 7th section of the Admiralty Court Act 1861 . . . clearly include every possible kind of damage. Personal injuries are undoubtedly within the words 'damage done by any Ship'. The case of *The Sylph*,[49] which has been referred to, and in which it was so held, had not been appealed from. There was every reason for the Legislature enacting that which the judgment of the court below holds to have been enacted.

Later, the Maritime Convention Act 1911 followed by the Supreme Court of Judicature (Consolidation) Act 1925, see below, affirmed that 'damage' includes both personal injury and loss of life.

It should follow that, at least, as long as the personal injury is the result of negligent navigation, being undoubtedly damage done by a ship, it should attract a maritime lien.

So far as loss of life cases are concerned, the issue whether or not these attract a maritime lien is more complex. The dependants of a deceased sue the owner of the wrongdoing ship for pecuniary loss suffered by reason of being deprived of financial assistance which they would have received had it not been for the death of the person who supported them. The damage is caused to them indirectly by the negligent navigation of the ship which caused the death. The Fatal Accident Acts give statutory authority to their claim, the incident of which is the negligence causing the death.

Jackson, in his book, *The Enforcement of Maritime Claims*, proposes that, if claims for loss of life or personal injury are regarded as an extension of the 'damage lien', it may be argued that the maritime lien attracted to 'damage done by a ship' is extended by analogy to the statutory extension of jurisdiction with respect to these claims. But, if the jurisdiction is seen as a novel jurisdiction, or that a new action is created, such claims will suffer the fate of other novel claims created by statute and will be relegated to a statutory lien.

Thomas[50] has no doubt that there is a maritime lien for personal injury claimants, but not with regard to claimants who claim under the Fatal Accidents Act (FAA) 1976[51] in respect of loss of life of a relative, as the jurisdiction is solely statutory. In other words, a new action has been created by statute.[52]

However, such an interpretation provides a rigid construction of 'damage done

---

48 (1869) LR 2 PC 447, p 449; and *The Mary Ann* (1865) L.R. 1 A&E 8.
49 (1867) LR 2 A&E 24, pp 26–27.
50 On maritime liens; see op cit, Thomas, fn 2.
51 The successor to FAA 1846, as amended by the AJA 1982.
52 See an explanation of its origin given by Brandon J in *The Esso Malaysia* [1975] QB 198.

by a ship' (as was widely defined by the Maritime Conventions Act (MCA) 1911) and ignores that the basis of such claims attracts a maritime lien.

The MCA 1911 clarified what should be understood as being included in the word 'damage' referred to in any statute, which conferred jurisdiction to the court for such 'damage' claims. Section 5 provided that:

> Any enactment which confers on any court admiralty jurisdiction in respect of damage shall have effect as though references to such damage included references to damages for loss of life or personal injury, and accordingly proceedings in respect of such damages may be brought *in rem* or *in personam*.

The Supreme Court of Judicature (Consolidation) Act (SCJ(Con)A) 1925 repealed and replaced s 5 of the MCA with s 22. Thus, jurisdiction for loss of life and personal injury was always included in the provision of 'damage done by a ship'.

The occasion of claims by the dependants of a deceased is the death caused by negligent navigation. Although it is said that the cause of action of such claims was created by the FAAs, nevertheless, the Acts gave statutory authority to an existing right of action for negligence causing injury (see *Davidson v Hill*). The FAAs assisted relatives of the deceased to sue the wrongdoer in England. It is more plausible to accept the first proposition of Jackson (than the proposition of Thomas), that: claims for loss of life should be regarded as an extension of the 'damage lien', and thus the maritime lien attracted to 'damage done by a ship' is extended by analogy to the statutory extension of jurisdiction with respect to these claims.

A peripheral problem which might have confused matters further is the separation of these claims from the general category 'damage done by a ship' in the SCA 1981, which (like all previous statutes) is concerned with the enforcement of such claims by an action *in rem* and not with the cause of action. The separation was done for the purpose of clarification of the incidents that can give rise to such claims, so that a wider class of claims can be enforced in the Admiralty Court under sub-paragraph (f). The incidents referred to in sub-para (f) are obviously still within the broad category 'damage done by a ship', whether that damage was due to negligent navigation or due to defects in the ship.

It is submitted that personal injury and loss of life claims ought to be treated as an extension of the damage lien. There is no reason in terms of principle why these claims, if they arise from the same incident, damage done by a ship, should not be placed in the same position. If it were otherwise, this would mean that a property damage claimant would enjoy the priority of a maritime lien while personal claims would rank in priority lower than the property claims. At least, a maritime lien should attach on these claims when the cause of their occurrence is negligent navigation, as this would clearly be consistent with the treatment of other claims, which fall within 'damage done by a ship' (*Currie v M'Knight*). There may, however, be a policy reason to exclude claims of dependants from maritime liens to prevent giving priority to large claims over other claimants.

It should be noted that the International Convention for Maritime Liens and Mortgages 1993 classifies both types of claims for loss of life and personal injury amongst maritime liens, but the Convention is not yet in force.

3.7 Any claim for loss of or damage to goods carried on a ship (s 20(2)(g))

Sub-paragraph (g) permits the arrest only of the ship in which the goods (lost or damaged) were carried, or her sister ship, or any other ship beneficially owned by the person (the carrier) who would be liable for the claim *in personam*.[53] If the cargo-owner chooses to arrest the non-carrying ship, which might have caused the damage, he must rely on another sub-paragraph of s 20(2). So it was decided in *The Eschersheim* (see para 3.5.1, above) in which the cargo-owners arrested the sister ship of the tug claiming loss of their cargo carried on board the ship being salved, which was lost by the negligence of the salvors. The claim against the carrying ship will be subject to exclusion or limitation of liability under the contract of carriage, where the carriage by sea Conventions apply.[54] With regard to damage resulting from collision due to negligent navigation, cargo-owners may enforce their claim against the non-carrying ship under sub-para (e): damage done by a ship. The liability of the colliding ships is apportioned on the basis of their respective faults and includes liability incurred to third parties. The limitation of liability provisions applicable by the International Convention 1976 will affect the amount recoverable.[55]

3.8 Any claim arising out of an agreement relating to the carriage of goods[56] on a ship or to the use or hire of a ship (s 20(2)(h))

3.8.1 Interpretation and extent

Sub-paragraph (h) is wide enough to encompass claims in contract and tort arising out of any agreement relating to the carriage of goods in a vessel. It covers claims arising from fraud or the tort of deceit generally and, in particular, claims relating to ante-dated bills of lading.

The St Elefterio[57]

The plaintiffs were holders of a bill of lading for a cargo of cattle cake on board the defendants' steamship. They had bought the cargo from the shippers, who were also the charterers of the vessel, and had later resold the cargo to other purchasers. The bill of lading was endorsed in blank by the shippers and presented to the plaintiffs. On presentation of the bill to the subsequent purchasers of the cargo, the latter claimed a right to reject the goods on the ground that the bill was wrongly dated. It appeared that the goods had not been shipped on the day it was stated on

---

53 See conditions of arrest, in Chapter 3, below.
54 Hague Rules, Hague-Visby Rules or Hamburg Rules.
55 See Chapter 17, below.
56 A cif (cost, insurance, freight) contract for the sale of goods was not a contract relating to the carriage of goods on a ship: *The Maersk Nimrod* [1991] 1 Lloyd's Rep 269.
57 [1957] PD 179.

the bill. The plaintiffs sought to enforce their claim against the ship under sub-para (h) of the then Act, AJA 1956, for the loss they would sustain if the purchasers were held entitled to reject the goods under the sale contract. The defendants contended that the court had no jurisdiction to entertain the action and, in particular, under this paragraph. Willmer J held that the words used in the Act are wide enough to cover claims whether in contract or in tort arising out of any agreement relating to the carriage of goods.

In *The Sennar*,[58] in which the plaintiffs had purchased groundnut expellers from a Swiss company, the contract had provided that the cargo was to be shipped not later than August 1973. Although the shipping documents were presented to the plaintiffs showing the cargo as having been shipped, in truth, it had not been shipped until September. However, the master wrongly dated the bill of lading with an August date. After arbitration proceedings in London, the plaintiffs were ordered to make payment to the purchasers in the chain but were unable to get their money back from the Swiss company which had gone bankrupt. The plaintiffs, therefore, issued a writ *in rem* against *The Sennar* and other ships belonging to the defendants for a claim of indemnity or damages for fraud, breach of duty or negligence, in connection with the shipment of the cargo. The vessel was arrested. It was held that, in the ordinary meaning of the words in sub-para (h), the claim here did arise out of an agreement relating to the carriage of goods in a ship.

It is not necessary for the claim in question to be directly connected with the agreement of the kind referred to in this sub-section, or that it be the agreement made between the two parties to the action themselves. The phrase 'arising out of' does not mean 'arising under' an agreement and it has been given a broad meaning which can be equivalent to the phrase 'connected with' it.

A very wide interpretation of this sub-section was given by both the Court of Appeal and the House of Lords in the following case.

The Antonios P Lemos [59] (APL)

Containertank, the disponent owners of APL, chartered the ship to Sammisa (head charterers) for one year who, in turn, let the ship to the plaintiffs, Samick Lines (sub-charterers), for one time chartered trip. The vessel loaded corn at Houston for carriage to Alexandria. On arrival, the vessel was unable to berth because her draught exceeded 32 feet and some of the cargo had to be discharged into lighters. The operation caused delay and involved the plaintiffs in additional expense in respect of which they claimed damages from the disponent owners of the vessel, the defendants. The plaintiffs contended that the master of the ship was negligent in allowing the loading to exceed the vessel's draught on arrival. As there was no contract between the plaintiffs and the defendants, the claim was based in the tort of negligence and the ship was arrested. The issue was whether the claim was a claim arising out of an agreement relating to the use or hire of the ship under s 20(2)(h) of the SCA 1981.

---

58 [1983] 1 Lloyd's Rep 295.
59 [1985] AC 711 (HL).

The defendants sought to set aside the writ and warrant of arrest on the ground that the High Court had no admiralty jurisdiction in respect of the plaintiff's claim, since it did not fall within s 20(2) of the SCA 1981. The main issue was whether, for the claim to fall under sub-para (h), the 'agreement' in question should be between the plaintiffs and the defendants, or any agreement in relation to the carriage of goods in a ship or the use or hire of a ship, which could be within the chain of chartering. The learned trial judge held that the claim did not fall within s 20(2)(h), but Parker LJ in the Court of Appeal held:

> Section 20(2)(h) contains no words of limitation restricting the agreements mentioned to agreements between the plaintiff and the defendant. It would have been simple so to limit them if any such limitation had been intended. The Convention contains no words of limitation either. I am unable to find any sufficient reason for importing such words, and would only do so if compelled by authority. In the absence of such authority, I would accordingly hold that, if the plaintiff can establish that his claim arises out of an agreement of the relevant kind, that is, an agreement relating to the carriage of goods in a ship or to the use or hire of a ship, then even if such agreement is not one between himself and the defendant, that claim falls within para (h).
>
> It is sufficient for the purposes of this appeal to say that on the ordinary meaning of the words the plaintiffs' claim is, in my view, a claim arising out of the relevant agreement notwithstanding that such agreement is not between the plaintiffs and the defendants, and on that simple ground I would allow this appeal.[60]

The defendants appealed. Lord Brandon in the House of Lords, agreeing with the construction given by the Court of Appeal, said further:

> I would readily accept that in certain contexts the expression 'arising out of' may, on the ordinary and natural meaning of the words used, be equivalent of the expression 'arising under' and not that of the wider expression 'connected with'. In my view, however, the expression 'arising out of' is, on the ordinary and natural meaning of the words used, capable, in other contexts, of being the equivalent of the wider expression 'connected with'. Whether the expression 'arising out of' has the narrower or the wider meaning in any particular case must depend on the context in which it is used.[61]

Thus, it was sufficient, for the claim to be enforced under this paragraph, that the claim arose out of an agreement which, although it was not between the parties to the litigation, was nevertheless connected with it.

Sub-paragraph (h) also covers claims arising out of agreements relating to the use of boats for the mooring of vessels as well as the use of tugs for the assistance of vessels in distress.

The Queen of the South[62]

The Queen of the South, belonging to the defendants, was employed as a passenger vessel for day trips from London to Glasgow. The plaintiffs were watermen

---

60   [1985] AC 711, pp 717, 719, quoting Parker LJ.
61   Ibid, p 727.
62   [1968] P 449.

carrying on the business of ship mooring and contracted with the defendants to moor and unmoor the ship at her berth in London and convey her crew between the ship and the shore. They rendered the services but the sum due to them under the contract remained unpaid. To recover the cost of services they arrested the ship. In default of appearance by the defendants, the court ordered judicial sale. The Port of London Authority having a claim for unpaid port dues intervened and purported to seize the ship under their statutory powers. One of the questions was whether the plaintiffs' claim entitled them to bring an action *in rem* against the ship. The plaintiffs contended that their claim arose out of 'an agreement relating to the use or hire of a ship'. They argued that their services were rendered by the use of their motor boats suitably manned for the work to be done; therefore, their claim came under this sub-para (h). Counsel for the interveners in the action sought to draw a distinction between an agreement relating to the rendering of services, in the course of which a ship was used, and an agreement relating to the use of a ship. This claim, he argued, came within the first category and hence it was not within sub-para (h). But this fine distinction did not convince the judge, Brandon J:[63]

> I did not think that his argument based on this distinction was convincing. I can see that there might be an agreement for services, in the course of which there was only some incidental and minor use of a ship, which it might be inappropriate to describe as an agreement relating to the use of a ship. In the present case, however, it seems to me clear, on the written and oral evidence before me, that the whole of the services rendered by the plaintiffs were based on the use of motor boats owned and operated by them. It is true that in some cases the men engaged in mooring and unmooring did their work on a quay or on a buoy. But they were landed on the quay or on the buoy from a motor boat and taken off again by the same means.

It is clear from this case and *The Eschersheim* (see below) that use or hire of a ship under sub-para (h) can include any ship used or hired, and it can be a ship other than the ship against which the claim is enforced.

The Eschersheim[64]

The question was whether the claims of both the owners of the vessel salved and the owners of the cargo on board for damages caused due to salvor's negligence could be enforced under sub-para (h). It was held that, in deciding whether it was an agreement relating to the use of a ship, the courts should look at the substance of the matter. There was an agreement by which *The Rotesand* (tug) was to tow *The Erkowit* to a place of safety. This was considered to be an agreement for the use of a ship (that is, the tug) in the ordinary and natural meaning; thus, the claim was within this sub-paragraph.

Lord Diplock said:[65]

> The salvage agreement was entered into by the master of *The Erkowit* on behalf of the cargo-owners as well as the shipowners. The primary contractual obligation of the salvor under the agreement in Lloyd's Open Form is to use his best endeavours to

---

63   Ibid, pp 456–57.
64   [1976] 2 Lloyd's Rep 1.
65   Ibid, p 7.

bring the vessel and her cargo to a place of safety, providing at his own risk, in the time honoured phrase, 'all proper steam and other assistance and labour'. The only possible way in which the salvors could perform their contract was by taking *The Erkowit* in tow and using the tug that had been sent to the scene of the casualty for that very purpose – *The Rotesand*.

While, in this case, it was accepted that the agreement was for the use of the tug, the judge's interpretation of 'use or hire of a ship' in the following case does not accord with the width of the interpretation given by the House of Lords.

The Tesaba [66]

The vessel sailed with a cargo of steel coils and general cargo en route to Mediterranean ports. She ran aground shortly after setting sail and her owners entered into an agreement with the plaintiffs, well-known salvors, to salve the vessel and her cargo. The agreement was on the standard terms of Lloyd's form of salvage agreement, containing a clause which provided that the owners of the vessel shall use their best endeavours to ensure that security is provided by the cargo interests before the discharge of the cargo from the ship. The salvors were successful in refloating the vessel. At the end of the services, they made demands for security from the owners of the ship and the cargo. The owners provided security for the amount due for salvage of the ship, but they failed to ensure that the cargo owners provided security also before their cargo was discharged at Istanbul. The salvors issued proceedings in the Admiralty Court claiming damages from the defendants (shipowners) on the ground of breach of their obligation under the salvage agreement. The defendants moved to set aside the writ on arguing that the claim did not fall within any of the paragraphs under this sub-section of the 1956 Act and they succeeded.

Sheen J held that there was no reason for not giving the words in sub-para (h) their ordinary wide meaning. However, the plaintiffs' claims arose out of a breach by the defendants of the terms of the salvage agreement which was an agreement to salve *The Tesaba* and her cargo. The agreement was not in relation to the carriage of goods in *The Tesaba* nor was it an agreement for the use or hire of *The Tesaba*, but for the use or hire of the tugs.

This decision seems to contradict the decision of Brandon J in *The Queen of the South*, in which the claim of watermen for the costs of the services against the ship which was moored and unmoored with the assistance of the watermen's boats was held to be within 'an agreement for the use or hire' of the boats. In both cases, a ship was used to provide the services under an agreement. In both cases there was a breach of contract. The only difference between the two was that the claim of the watermen was for a debt in relation to the services provided by their boats, while the claim of the salvors in *The Tesaba* was in damages for breach of the agreement in relation to the use of their tug.

It also contradicts the decision in *The Eschersheim* and it is difficult to find a valid point of distinction between the two cases. In both, *The Eschersheim* and *The Tesaba*,

---

66   [1982] 1 Lloyd's Rep 397.

there was use or hire of a tug for the purpose of salvage. The respective claims in both cases were based on a breach of obligations under the salvage agreement. The only difference was that, in the former, the claim was by the owner of the salved ship against the salvor, while, in the latter, it was the other way round. Such a fine distinction is contrary to the general wide approach adopted by higher courts in the interpretation of this paragraph. In any event, such claims are covered under sub-para (j) (see later)

It should be noted that such claims have been included in the Arrest Convention 1999.

By contrast to the interpretation given by Sheen J in *The Tesaba*, Brandon J, in the following case relating to an agreement for towage, preferred a wide interpretation of sub-para (h).

The Conoco Britannia [67]

Under a towage contract containing the usual indemnity clause in favour of the supplier of a tug, the plaintiff supplied the defendant with a tug owned by a third party. The tug sank due to a collision with the defendant's ship, causing loss and damage. The plaintiff proceeded *in rem* against the defendant claiming indemnity as provided by the towage contract for liability incurred by him to the tugowners, or for payment direct to the tugowners, or damages for failure to indemnify. The claim was brought under s 1(1)(h) of the old statute, the 1956 Act, being equivalent to the present sub-para (h).

Brandon J held that the words relating to the use or hire of a ship were wide enough to cover hire of the tug under a towage contract. It could be given a wide interpretation because the spirit of the Act and history of jurisdiction was to widen jurisdiction and incorporate claims under the Arrest Convention 1952.

Even a claim involving loss arising out of the exercise of the right to lien on the cargo carried on the ship, which is a contractual entitlement of the carrier for unpaid freight or hire, is a claim which can be enforced under this paragraph, if it is alleged that the lien or detention of goods is wrongful.

The Gina [68]

The plaintiffs in this case instructed their forwarding agents to arrange shipment of three containers of aerosols. The agents arranged for shipment in the defendants' vessel. Eventually, only two containers were presented to the receivers at the port of discharge and the latter refused to obtain delivery – withholding payment of the freight. The defendants exercised lien upon the goods for freight. The plaintiffs issued a writ *in rem* against *The Gina* for wrongful detention of their goods, contending that it was the defendants' fault that only two containers reached destination. It was held that the vessel was properly arrested under sub-para (h) and the plaintiffs were entitled to use the procedures of an admiralty action *in rem* in order to obtain security for their claim.

---

67 [1972] QB 543, [1972] 1 Lloyd's Rep 342.
68 [1980] 1 Lloyd's Rep 398.

3.8.2 Claims excluded from sub-para (h)

Claims for insurance premiums

While the words of sub-para (h), 'relating to the use or hire of a ship', were given a wide interpretation, the House of Lords chose a narrow construction of the words 'an agreement relating to the carriage of goods in a ship', in the context of claims relating to non-payment of insurance premiums or brokerage in *The Sandrina*. Although it should be noted that, on the facts of this case, the insurance premium was in connection with the cargo carried on board and not with the ship, the decision seems to have wider application to the exclusion of any insurance premium claims from the *in rem* jurisdiction of the English court.

Gatoil International Inc v Arkwright-Boston Manufacturers Mutual Insurance Co (The Sandrina) [69]

The case concerned unpaid insurance premiums claimed by six insurance companies and an insurance broker against the owners of the ship for the insurance of cargo of oil carried on the ship. To obtain security for their claim, the ship *Sandrina* was arrested in Shetland Islands, Scotland.

The issue was whether the claim came within s 47(2)(e) of the AJA 1956, which applied in Scotland and had equivalent provisions to the English AJA 1956. Paragraph (e) provided:

> ... any agreement relating to the carriage of goods in any ship whether by charter-party or otherwise ...

This provision was similar in effect to s 20(2)(h) of the SCA 1981. The issue for interpretation was whether or not the words in the statute covered an agreement to pay premiums on a policy of insurance under a war risk open cover on cargo. If so, the arrest of the ship would be valid; if not, the arrest should be lifted. The matter reached the House of Lords.

After reviewing the relevant authorities, the House of Lords held that, for an agreement to come within that provision, it must have a reasonably direct connection with the carriage of goods in a ship and not merely a remote connection. A contract of insurance was not connected with the carriage of goods in a sufficiently direct sense to be capable of falling within that paragraph. The 1956 Act was passed in order to enable the UK to ratify and comply with the provisions of the 1952 Arrest Convention. In particular, Lord Wilberforce referred to the proceedings of the conference which led to the 1952 Convention. In that conference, the Netherlands had proposed the addition of insurance premiums due to underwriters as part of the claims justifying the arrest of a ship. The conference had expressly refused to include claims for insurance premiums among the maritime claims justifying arrest. The legislative intention behind the Convention must be treated as being the same as under the 1956 Act adopting its provisions.

During consideration of the issue, however, Lord Wilberforce admitted that the

---

69   [1985] AC 255 (HL), or [1985] 1 Lloyd's Rep 181.

words were ambiguous and raised the following questions: 'must the agreement be directly "for" carriage of goods in a ship, or is it enough that it involves directly or indirectly, or that the parties contemplated that there would be, such carriage as a consequence of the agreement? How close, in such a case, must the relationship be between the agreement and the carriage? Is any connection of a factual character between the agreement and some carriage in a ship sufficient? If not, what is the test of relevant connection?' It was clear from the deliberations of the conference, referred to above, that the matter was decided against including insurance premium amongst the maritime claims justifying arrest of a ship for reasons of policy.

Lord Keith referred to the only previous decision on this issue, *The Aifanourios* 1980 SC 346, which had been decided in Scotland, in which Lord Wylie had held that a claim arising out of an insurance contract did not come within the provision and, in particular, the insurance of a vessel was a matter directed to the convenience or protection of the owner; it was not essential for the operation of the vessel as such. Therefore, a more restricted construction of the provision was called for.

Lord Keith then continued:

> It is necessary to attribute due significance to the circumstance that the words of the relevant paragraphs speak of an agreement 'in relation to' not 'for' the carriage of goods in a ship and the use or hire of a ship. The meaning must be wider than would be conveyed by the particle 'for'. It would, on the other hand, be unreasonable to infer from the expression actually used, 'in relation to', that it is intended to be sufficient that the agreement in issue should be in some way connected, however remotely, with the carriage of goods in a ship or with the use or hire of a ship, and I think there is much force in the view expressed by Lord Wylie, in *The Aifanourios* . . . as to the inference to be drawn from the presence of certain other paragraphs in s 47(2). There must, in my opinion, be some reasonably direct connection with such activities. An agreement for the cancellation of a contract for the carriage of goods in a ship or for the use or hire of a ship would, I think, show a sufficiently direct connection. It is unnecessary to speculate what other cases might be covered. Each case would require to be decided on its own facts. As regards the contract of insurance founded on in the instant appeal, I am of opinion that it is not connected with the carriage of goods in a ship in a sufficiently direct sense to be capable of coming within para (e).

It should be noted that the Arrest Convention 1999 has incorporated insurance premiums and brokerage, including claims by a P&I club for unpaid calls, in the list of maritime claims. Such claims will qualify for an arrest of a ship to be made once the Convention comes into force in, or is enacted by, the UK.

Claims for container hire or damage to containers

This has been the subject of interesting decisions. Unless containers in relation to which a claim arises were supplied to a particular ship, the claim cannot be enforced by *in rem* proceedings under the SCA 1981. In practice, however, containers are supplied to shipowners under a long lease agreement. The container supplier is usually not aware of which particular ship will carry his containers, unless a specific mention is made in the agreement. When a dispute arises under the lease agreement, either for outstanding payment of hire, or for damage to containers, the container supplier may sue the shipowner *in personam*, but he will not be able to arrest a ship. This is so because such claims cannot be considered as 'arising out of any agreement relating to the carriage of goods in a ship'. So was held by Clarke J, in *The Lloyd Pacifico*[70] in which he followed Lord Keith's reasoning in *The Sandrina* that 'in relation to' does not mean 'for the carriage of goods in a ship' under sub-para (h). The containers must be provided to a particular ship as they were in *The Hamburg Star*,[71] in which containers with goods were shipped on this ship and some were lost. Whether or not such claims can be enforced under sub-para (m) is examined later.

In the Arrest Convention 1999, a claim arising from the provision of containers for use in a ship is included in the list of maritime claims, provided they are supplied to a particular ship.

Enforcement of an arbitration award obtained in relation to a charter party dispute

On the proper construction of sub-para (h), an action on an award was held in *The Bumbesti*[72] not to be within the wording of this paragraph, namely 'an agreement in relation to the use or hire of a ship' and the court had no jurisdiction to consider the *in rem* claim.[73]

The claimant detained two ships of the defendant in Constantza by order of the court for the enforcement of two awards obtained with regard to a repudiation of a charterparty. Later, the claimant arrested in England *The Bumbesti*, belonging to the defendant, for the enforcement of the awards in case the value of the other two ships was not sufficient. The *in rem* proceeding was based on s 20(2)(h) of the SCA 1981, and the issue was whether or not the claim came within the wording of this paragraph. It was held that:

> The claim in this case was the action on the awards and clearly arose out of the agreement to refer to arbitration the disputes that had arisen under the bareboat charter; but that agreement to refer disputes was not, itself, an agreement in relation to the use or hire of a ship since the arbitration agreement to refer was a contract that was distinct from the principal contract, that is, the bareboat charter.

The agreement to refer to arbitration disputes that had arisen under a charterparty was an agreement which was indirectly 'in relation to the use or hire of a ship' and it was not an agreement in sufficiently direct relation to the 'use or hire of a ship'; the arbitration agreement was, at least, one step removed from the 'use or hire' of a ship; the breach of contract relied on to found the present claim had nothing to do with the use or hire of a ship. It concerned an implied term to fulfil any award made pursuant to the agreement to refer disputes to arbitration, and the breach of contract relied on when suing on the award did not have a reasonably direct connection with the use or hire of the ship that was necessary to found jurisdiction.

---

70 [1995] 1 Lloyd's Rep 54.
71 [1994] 1 Lloyd's Rep 399, p 406.
72 [1999] 2 Lloyd's Rep 481.
73 The judge applied *The Beldis* (1936) 53 LlL Rep 255.

Security for enforcement of an arbitration award can be obtained under s 26 of CJJA 1982 and s 11 of the Arbitration Act (AA) 1996 (see Chapter 4).

3.9 Any claim for salvage services (s 20(2)(j))

Any claim (i) under the Salvage Convention 1989,[74] or (ii) under any contract for or in relation to salvage services;[75] or (iii) in the nature of salvage not falling within (i) or (ii) above, or any corresponding claim in connection with an aircraft.[76]

The predecessor to this paragraph referred only to 'claims in the nature of salvage', so it did not cover a claim against salvors for negligence, which was covered under sub-para (h) above (see *The Eschersheim*). It did not cover a claim for breach by a shipowner of his undertaking under salvage agreements to use his best endeavours to ensure that security is provided by the cargo interests in favour of the salvor prior to the discharge of the cargo from the ship. Now, apart from the considerable extension of this paragraph, there are explanatory provisions in s 20(6) of the Act which specifically refer to the inclusion of any claims whether or not arising during the provision of salvage services.

The Arrest Convention 1999 has also widened the scope of salvage claims that will be enforced by an action *in rem* by including any claims arising from a salvage agreement and claims for special compensation arising under Art 14 of the Salvage Convention 1989. Damage to the environment is also included as a ground for arrest, as are claims for wreck and cargo recoveries.

Claims for salvage give rise to a maritime lien.

3.10 Any claim in the nature of towage in respect of a ship or aircraft (s 20(2)(k))

Only when the aircraft is waterborne does its towage come within this provision.

Unlike salvage, towage does not give rise to a maritime lien.[77]

3.11 Any claim in the nature of pilotage in respect of a ship or an aircraft (s 20(2)(l))

Pilotage charges or dues are claims for which an arrest of a ship can be made, but such claims do not give rise to a maritime lien.

---

74 See Chapter 13 on salvage for its definition and elements.

75 The reference to salvage services includes services rendered in saving life from a ship and the reference to any claim under any contract for or in relation to salvage services includes any claim arising out of such a contract whether or not arising during the provision of the services: s 20(6)(b) of the SCA 1981, as amended.

76 The reference to a corresponding claim in connection with an aircraft is a reference to any claim mentioned in sub-para (i) or (ii) of para (j) which is available under Civil Aviation Act 1982, s 87: SCA 1981, s 20(6)(c).

77 See details of towage in Chapter 14, below.

Again, an aircraft must be waterborne when pilotage service is rendered for such a claim to be within this provision.

3.12 Any claim in respect of goods or materials supplied to a ship for her operations or maintenance (s 20(2)(m))

Containers have been regarded as 'goods' and are within the meaning of sub-para (m). The word 'supplied' in this paragraph includes supply by way of hire as well as sale, but containers are not supplied for the maintenance of the ship within the meaning of this paragraph. The only question for decision by the House of Lords in *The River Rima*[78] was whether or not the containers supplied to a ship were for the operation of the ship within the meaning of sub-para (m) in order for the action *in rem* to be entertained in respect of the claims made by the container supplier. To answer this question, it was necessary to determine whether the containers were supplied to the ship in question.

The case involved a vessel owned by the Nigerian National Shipping Line (NNSL). NNSL had a number of contracts whereby they leased containers from their owners including the plaintiffs at a daily rate. The plaintiffs claimed conversion of certain containers and breach of an obligation by NNSL under the contract to maintain the containers in good condition and repair. They issued a writ *in rem* and arrested *The Riva Rima* belonging to NNSL. The issue before the court was whether the action could be maintained as an action *in rem*.

It was decided that, unless the containers were supplied to a particular ship, any claim arising from a lease agreement with respect to containers would not be enforceable by *in rem* proceedings.

The House of Lords made a distinction between the kind of contract which expressly provides that goods are required for the use of a particular ship, identified, or to be identified, when the contract comes to be performed, and the kind of contract which makes no reference to a particular ship, leaving the shipowner to make his choice later. Claims arising under the first category of contract are enforceable under this paragraph. The crucial words are 'supplied to a ship', which require identification of the ship on which the containers will be placed. The reason for this decision was that, upon a historical analysis, the jurisdiction of the court regarding this provision derived from the court's jurisdiction in relation to necessaries supplied to a ship (s 1(1) of the AJA 1956), for which the identity of a ship was an essential ingredient.

As discussed earlier under sub-para (h), one would expect that such claims could be considered as 'arising out of any agreement relating to the carriage of goods in a ship' under s 20(2)(h). However, Clarke J (as he then was) rejected such a submission in *The Lloyd Pacifico*, mainly because the containers must be provided to a particular ship.

It should be noted that the Arrest Convention 1999 has included such claims

---

78 [1988] 2 Lloyd's Rep 193.

arising in relation to the supply of containers in the list of claims for which *in rem* proceedings can be issued, but the provision also states that the containers must be supplied to a particular ship.

Finally, sub-para (m) includes claims by ship's agents arising in relation to providing supplies to a ship for its operation or maintenance.

The Kommunar (No 1)[79]

The sub-agents of entities in South America had supplied goods and materials under two agreements to a number of named vessels belonging to the defendants. Their invoices were presented to the plaintiffs who paid for them. The plaintiffs sought to recover the amount paid and the interest due from the defendants under the agreement with them. They brought an action *in rem* under s 20(2)(m) and (p) of the SCA 1981. The defendants alleged that the court had no jurisdiction because under the agreement the plaintiffs' duty was the provision of finance to the ship-owners. Therefore, they were merely financiers and thus not entitled to bring their claim under s 20(2) of that Act. The defendants also alleged that the case did not fall within s 21(4) of that Act. The sub-agents were appointed for the purpose of supplying the goods and services to the defendants and it was the plaintiffs' responsibility to pay for the invoices tendered and later charge them to the defendants' account. It was held that, the fact that the claim was on a general account, did not, by itself, lead to the conclusion that the claim was not a claim in respect of goods or materials supplied to a ship. Clarke J held, thus:

> . . . in my judgment, they were not simply acting as bankers, they were not advancing moneys to the shipowner for the shipowner to purchase supplies. By the terms of the contract, it was their responsibility to pay for necessaries supplied by the supplier of the necessaries. I can see no reason why it should not be held that the claim to recover those moneys is in respect of the goods and materials supplied to the ship for her operation or maintenance.[80]

This paragraph also covers advances made by a ship's chandler for payment of crews' wages, the supply of bunkers[81] and the provision of officers and crew.[82]

The Arrest Convention 1999 clarifies the position of agents of a ship.

No maritime lien attaches under this head.

3.13 Any claim in respect of the construction, repair or equipment of a ship or dock charges or dues (s 20(2)(n))

Claims by shipbuilders and ship-repairers, port dues and charges are within this paragraph. No maritime lien attaches to these claims but the ship-repairer will have a right to detain the ship in his yard until payment of his charges is made. This is a

---

79   [1997] 1 Lloyd's Rep 1.

80   Ibid, p 7.

81   *The Fairport (No 4)* [1967] 1 Lloyd's Rep 602.

82   *The Nore Challenger and Nore Commander* [2001] 2 All ER (Comm) 667.

common law right, known as 'possessory lien', which is different from the nature of the maritime lien. It depends on possession of the ship.

Fuel is not within the term 'equipment', but it is covered under the previous sub-para (m).

The D'Vora [83]

An order had been made for the appraisement and sale of *The D'Vora*. The ship was sold and the proceeds were under arrest. The plaintiffs issued their writ and started proceedings claiming a sum for oil supplied to the vessel at Haifa. They claimed that the supply of fuel oil to an oil-burning ship was covered by 'equipment' and the claim could, thus, be brought under this paragraph. They contended that equipping meant 'making the ship ready to sail'. Willmer J rejected this contention and stated:

> In my judgment, there is an important difference between 'equip' and 'supply', 'supply' being a word which is appropriate for use in connection with consumable stores, such as fuel oil, whereas 'equip', to my mind, connotes something of a more permanent nature than consumable stores. I can well understand that anchors, cables, hawsers, sails, ropes and such things may be said to be part of a ship's equipment, and that, nonetheless, although they may have to be renewed from time to time; but such things as fuel, coal, boiler water and food-consumable stores – seem to me to be quite a different category. [84]

3.14 Any claim by master or crew of a ship for wages (s 20(2)(o))

Various questions about seamen's wages have been brought before the courts. It is important to know what is included in wages because they attract a maritime lien and this will affect the priority of payment out of the proceeds of sale of a ship when there are many claimants (see Chapter 4). The seamen's and master's lien for wages arises independently of contract for services rendered to a ship provided the seaman acted as a member of the crew. That was so, whether or not the owner of the ship had authorised his service unless the seaman was guilty of fraud or knew that he was not authorised to act as master or seaman (*The Ever Success*). [85]

3.14.1 What is included in seamen's wages

This question was thoroughly and comprehensively analysed by Brandon J in the following case.

The Halcyon Skies [86]

It concerned a claim by a seaman for employees' and employers' contribution to a pension fund. The first issue was whether the right to such payments was part of

---

83   [1952] 2 Lloyd's Rep 404.
84   Ibid, p 405.
85   [1999] 1 Lloyd's Rep 824.
86   [1976] 1 Lloyd's Rep 461.

wages since it arose from a special contract (that is, to be paid contributions to a special fund) and not from the general seaman's contract for wages. The second issue was whether the claims were in debt or in damages and, if it was the latter, could they still be part of wages so as to come within the admiralty jurisdiction. The third issue, which depended on the answer to the second, was whether the claims attracted a maritime lien.

A British Merchant Navy officer was employed by Court Line on board this ship. His contract provided that Court Line would pay employers' contributions to the Merchant Navy pension fund. Such contributions had not been paid when a petition to the Companies' Court was made for the winding up of Court Line and a liquidator was appointed. By an action *in rem*, brought by the second mortgagee of the ship, the ship was appraised and sold by the order of the Admiralty Marshal. The officer brought an action – with the leave of the Companies' Court – against the proceeds of sale, claiming priority over the mortgagee on the basis of a maritime lien attached on the ship in respect of the outstanding contributions.

Brandon J distinguished employees' from employers' contributions and considered first the issue of employees' contributions:[87]

> So far as a cause of action is concerned, the plaintiff has, in my opinion, a good claim in debt. He had under his contract of employment given Court Line authority to deduct such contributions from his pay and pay them to the fund. Court Line had acted on the first part of that authority but not on the second. In these circumstances the plaintiff was entitled to revoke the second part of the authority, namely for payment of the sums deducted to the Fund, and to require Court Line to pay such sums to him instead. This he did by issuing his writ in the present action. So far as the nature of the claim is concerned there can, I think, be no doubt that the sums concerned, having been deducted from the plaintiff's pay in the first place, were part of his wages for the purpose of s 1(1)(o) of the 1956 Act. I also think . . . that he had a maritime lien in respect of the claim.

As regards the disputed item of employers' contributions he examined the history of the court's jurisdiction and previous authorities about seamen's wages. He explained that, even before and indeed after the 1861 Act, the court had jurisdiction for unpaid wages as claims in debt and as claims in damages for wrongful dismissal:

> There were other extensions of the wages concept. The claims covered by it were held to include emoluments other than wages in the strict sense, which were payable direct to the seaman, such as victualling allowances and bonuses: *The Tergeste* [1903] P 26; *The Elmville (No 2)* [1904] P 422. This approach was in accordance with s 742 of the MSA 1894, which defined 'wages' as including 'emoluments'.

> It was further held in one case that the jurisdiction in wages extended to claims for damages for breach of a seaman's contract of employment during its subsistence. *The Justitia* (1887) 12 PD 145. That was a strange case, in which seamen recovered, in an admiralty action *in personam* for wages, general damages for hardship suffered and risks run when they were obliged to remain on board a ship while she was being used, contrary to the articles on which they had been engaged, as an armed cruiser in support of insurgents.

---

87   Ibid, p 463.

It is to be observed that, when the admiralty jurisdiction over claims for wages was redefined by Parliament in 1956, the requirement that wages should have been 'earned on board ship' was removed. This was in accordance with the description of the corresponding 'maritime claim' in para (1)(m) of Art 1 of the 1952 Brussels Ship Arrest Convention, which refers simply to claims arising out of 'wages of Masters, Officers, or crew'.

In *The Arosa Star* [1959] 2 Lloyd's Rep 396, the Supreme Court of Bermuda (Chief Justice Worley) held that a foreign seaman could recover, in an admiralty action *in rem* for wages and with the priority accorded by a maritime lien, full pay during sick leave and employer's contributions for social insurance, as being emoluments in the nature of wages to which he was entitled under his contract of employment.

In *The Arosa Kulm (No 2)* [1960] 1 Lloyd's Rep 97, Hewson J held that a foreign master and crew could recover, in an admiralty action *in rem* for wages, social benefit contributions said to be similar to National Insurance contributions, which were payable by the shipowners under their contracts of employment.

In *The Fairport* [1965] 2 Lloyd's Rep 183, Hewson J held that a foreign master could recover, in an admiralty action *in rem* for disbursements, notional deductions from unpaid seamen's wages in respect of insurance and pension contributions payable under their contracts of employment. He further expressed the opinion that the seamen themselves, who had already recovered their wages net of such contributions in an earlier action, would have been entitled to include the amounts of such contributions in their own wages claim.

In *The Fairport (No 3)* [1966] 2 Lloyd's Rep 253, the question arose whether the master's maritime lien for disbursements extended to the amounts recovered by him in respect of insurance and pension contributions under the judgment in the preceding case. Karminski J held that his lien did so extend, on the ground that such contributions formed part of the seamen's wages.

In *The Westport (No 4)* [1968] 2 Lloyd's Rep 559, Karminski J held that a foreign master could recover, in an admiralty action *in rem* for disbursements, firstly, sums which he was bound to pay in respect of deductions from seamen's wages for insurance, pension, provident and union contributions; and, secondly, sums which he was bound to pay jointly with the owners in respect of owners' own insurance and other contributions. The ground of the decision seems to have been that all the contributions concerned were emoluments of the seamen under their contracts of employment or according to their national law.[88]

Then, Brandon J examined whether the claim in this case was in debt or in damages, and continued:

It was argued for the first defendants that the plaintiff's only cause of action was in damages for breach of contract. It was argued for the plaintiff, on the other hand, that he had a cause of action in debt, on the basis that it was an implied term of his contract of employment that, if Court Line did not pay the employer's contributions to the fund, they would pay them to him instead. In my opinion it is not necessary to imply the term contended for in order to give business efficacy to the contract and it would not therefore be right to do so. The true view, I think, is that the failure of Court Line to pay the employer's contributions was a breach of contract for which the plaintiff is entitled to recover damages at law. It follows that his cause of action in

---

88   Ibid, pp 464, 465, 467.

respect of such contributions is in damages and not in debt. It seems that, if damages were not an adequate remedy, the plaintiff could seek the alternative equitable remedy of specific performance: *Beswick v Beswick* [1968] AC 58.

Does it make any difference that the plaintiff's claim is not, if I am right in my answer ... above, a claim in debt for the contributions themselves, but a claim in damages for breach of contract in failing to pay them? In my judgment, it does not, because the admiralty jurisdiction in wages has long extended, as I explained earlier, to claims founded in damages as well as debt. Further, that extended jurisdiction has not only been exercised regularly in respect of claims for damages after termination of the contract of employment by wrongful dismissal, but also at least once prior to 1951 in respect of a claim for damages for breach of such contract during its subsistence. Indeed, it may well be that the reason why the judges, who decided the group of further cases from 1951 to 1968 referred to above, did not pause to analyse the precise cause of action on which the claims in respect of employer's contributions succeeded was that they did not think it mattered, so far as the seaman's right to recover was concerned, whether such cause of action was in debt or in damages.

With regard to the third issue, whether these claims attracted a maritime lien, his answer was affirmative.

3.14.2 *The treatment of severance payments (redundancy pay) and pensions*

The Tacoma City [89]

The shipowners announced that they were ceasing trade at the end of May 1985. The first mortgagees (the bank) issued a writ *in rem*, arrested the vessel and it was sold by order of the court. There was a second mortgagee ranking immediately behind the bank. The plaintiffs were 20 officers, who had served aboard the ship. They claimed maritime liens for severance payments and wages in lieu of notice against the proceeds of sale of the ship, in priority to the claim of the second mortgagee. The question was whether severance payment agreements could fairly be regarded as the development of new terms in special contracts, which are as much 'additions to wages' as, for example, damages for wrongful dismissal or wages payable during sick leave.

Sheen J gave a number of reasons in support of his conclusion that this type of claim is not within wages, which included: (i) a severance payment is not payable 'for service to the ship', because it may be payable to one officer, who is declared surplus, and not to another who is not; (ii) a severance payment is 'compensation' for losing employment and is not part of the emoluments of employment; (iii) it is not paid for services rendered but because services are no longer required; and (iv) the essence of a severance payment is a reward for long service payable as compensation for having had the service cut short.

However, in the Court of Appeal, Gibson LJ explained that the reasons given by the judge cannot be regarded as forming any rule or principle:[90]

I do not think it is possible to formulate a principle based upon any of those reasons

---

89 [1991] 1 Lloyd's Rep 330.
90 [1991] 1 Lloyd's Rep 330, pp 344–45.

and to demonstrate that it is supported by any particular authority. The cases show a development of the concept of 'wages' based upon a liberal approach and a determination to do what is fair and just in order to secure to the seaman what he has earned by service to and in the ship.

The reasons for his conclusion given by Sheen J represent, I think, a description of aspects of these severance payments which together exclude them from the concept of wages rather than the formulation of any rule or principle. Thus, there is, in my view, no conclusive force in the fact that a severance payment may be payable to one officer who is declared surplus and not to another who is not. . . .

Further, I do not find anything conclusive in the fact that a severance payment is 'compensation for losing employment' or that it is paid 'because services are no longer required'. Damages for wrongful dismissal are paid because employment has been lost and wages during sick leave are paid because services cannot be rendered.

Sheen J viewed with concern the fact that, if the plaintiffs' claims to maritime liens were held to be good, the security provided by a mortgage on the ship would be greatly diminished, because those serving in the ship would have contingent rights to large sums of money by way of severance payments which would become due if the officers became surplus to the requirements of the owners at the end of service in the ship. Miss Bucknall has submitted that that is an irrelevant consideration. I accept that it is of no real weight. Those who lend money on ships are, no doubt, aware of the priority of a maritime lien for wages and can either require information as to the maximum risk for wages and for the payments and limit their lending accordingly or require the provision of sufficient security, by insurance or otherwise, against the risk.

I am, however, quite unable to accept the full extent of Miss Bucknall's argument, namely that any sum is 'wages' and gives rise to a maritime lien, if it is promised to be paid in consideration of service in a ship. If, for example, the payment of a pension upon retirement age was promised by a shipowner by terms incorporated in a crew agreement, to be taken as a lump sum or by future periodical payments, I do not accept that that lump sum, or the value of the pension, or even the sums which have fallen due at the time of the termination of employment in the ship, would fall within the concept of 'wages', for which the law would give a lien. Such claims would not, in my judgment, be 'wages', even though the immediate consideration for the promised pay was service by the seaman in the ship coupled with prior service to the shipping company or to other companies.

All the additions to wages, payable under special contracts, 'which the mariner can be fairly said to have earned by his services' (per Worley CJ in *The Arosa Star*, p 403) which have been accepted as giving rise to liens, have been claims which can be regarded as items in the quantification of the value of the current service in the ship by the seafarer. Pension, as contrasted with contributions towards a pension fund, is not part of the agreed value of the current service but, in substance, is the reward for past service.

Leggatt LJ stated:[91]

Since wages include 'emoluments', they are not confined to periodic payments. In its natural meaning of severance payment it does not constitute remuneration, because it is not paid for services rendered or for services that would have been rendered . . .

---

91 [1991] 1 Lloyd's Rep 330, p 346.

It is paid when a seaman who has been continuously employed for at least two years is dismissed by his employer. In other words, it is a payment made not for services to a ship, but to compensate the seaman for the termination of his employment after a reasonably long period of service to the same employer. It is not paid for past service, even though the amount of the payment is calculated by reference to the length of it. In my judgment severance pay does not constitute wages.

And Dillon LJ added:[92]

... the severance pay is to be calculated by reference to the whole of his service with the company or group in question. It is not paid as extra remuneration, or deferred remuneration on a contingency, for his services merely during the voyage in his last ship when he becomes surplus to requirements. Indeed, it is not paid as remuneration for his services at all; it is paid as compensation for the loss of the expectation he would otherwise have had that because of his long service he would have been offered further employment by the company or group after the end of what was in the event his final voyage in his last ship for the company or group.

It was held, therefore, that the appellants' claim for severance pay was not the subject of a maritime lien. The distinction made between damages for wrongful dismissal, on the one hand, and compensation to the seaman for being made redundant, on the other hand, was that the former is for services rendered or to be rendered under the seaman's contract, while the latter is for loss of expectation of further work, because he had already served the minimum of two years' employment. In other words, a loss of certainty of employment qualifies for a maritime lien while a loss of an expectation does not. Similarly, as Gibson LJ explained, a lump sum of pension or future periodic payments upon retirement for old age does not fall within the concept of wages.

Payment of wages to a ship agent on account of the crew under a contract of employment, which had been agreed to be paid to the agent with the consent of the crew as wages for their services, was not for the account of the agent. Thus, the payment attracted a maritime lien.[93]

3.15 Any claim by a master, shipper, charterer or agent in respect of disbursements on account of a ship (s 20(2)(p))

The Sea Friends[94]

The plaintiffs were Lloyd's brokers who incurred a liability to Lloyd's underwriters in respect of premiums for hull insurance on the vessel. A writ *in rem* was issued and they intended to arrest the ship as soon as it arrived within the jurisdiction. The question was whether their claim could come under s 20(2)(p), entitling them to arrest the vessel on its arrival. Therefore, it was necessary to consider whether the plaintiffs' insurance brokers could be regarded as 'agents' for the purpose of this

---

92 Ibid, p 348.
93 *The Turidu* [1998] 2 Lloyd's Rep 278; see voluntary payments of wages by third parties, and assignment of the wages claim in Chapter 4, para 7.2.
94 [1991] 2 Lloyd's Rep 322.

sub-section. Both the Admiralty Registrar and the trial judge held that the plaintiffs were not entitled to arrest the vessel under s 20(2)(p). On appeal to the Court of Appeal, it was reminded that the House of Lords in *The Sandrina*[95] had clearly shown that the legislative intention behind both the 1956 and the 1981 Acts was to exclude claims for insurance premiums from the list of maritime claims. They could, therefore, not be subtly included under sub-para (p). According to Lloyd LJ:

> Put in simple and non-technical language, bunkers are, to take just one example, a disbursement within (p) because bunkers are needed to keep the ship going. But insurance is not needed to keep the ship going. Insurance is needed to reimburse the shipowners in case a ship is lost or damages. The ship could very well sail uninsured, although, of course, it never, in fact, does. The disbursement in this case is, in my view, no more a disbursement on account of the ship than it would have been if the premium were in respect of insurance on freight.[96]

It was held that the disbursement must be something, which would ordinarily be regarded as a master's disbursement, whether that disbursement be incurred by the master himself or by the shippers or the charterers or the agents. Insurance premiums are not ordinarily included within the description of master's disbursements.

At common law, no maritime lien was attached to master's disbursements incurred on account of the ship (*The Castlegate*).[97] A statutory maritime lien was, however, given by statute (MSA 1970, s 18) which is now found in s 41 of the MSA 1995 and states:

> ... the master of the ship shall have the same lien for his remuneration and all disbursements or liabilities properly incurred by him on account of the ship, as a seaman has for his wages.

Such a maritime lien does not extend to others who incur expenses on account of the ship (shippers, charterers, ships' agents). They, as all maritime claimants, can enhance their position by issuing *in rem* proceedings pursuant to their statutory rights *in rem* under the SCA 1981, whereupon they become secured creditors irrespective of the subsequent winding up of the defendant company by petition to the Companies' Court. The following case illustrates the position.

The Zafiro[98]

The plaintiffs made necessary disbursements on account of the vessels *Oro* and *The Zafiro*, both of which were owned by the defendant. Subsequently, the defendant proposed a resolution for voluntary winding up of the company. The plaintiffs issued a writ *in rem* against *The Zafiro* claiming disbursements on account of the ship and arrested that vessel. The creditors of the company passed a resolution that the company should be wound up and appointed a liquidator. *The Zafiro* was sold and the proceeds were paid into court. In the first motion, the plaintiffs moved for a

---

95 [1985] AC 255.
96 [1991] 2 Lloyd's Rep 322, p 324.
97 [1893] AC 38 (HL).
98 [1960] P 1.

judgment in default of defence against the defendants and/or the proceeds of sale claiming payment of the sum due to them. In the second motion, the defendants moved for an order that the action be stayed on the ground that, since the issue of the writ, the resolution for the voluntary winding up of the defendant's company had been passed and that, before the issue of the writ, the plaintiffs had been given notice of the meeting at which such resolution was to be proposed. The defendant further sought an order that the proceeds of sale of *The Zafiro* be paid out to him after the satisfaction of the claim of the owners of another vessel, who had previously obtained judgment against *The Zafiro* in a collision action.

It was held that:

- the arrest of a vessel was not an 'execution' within the meaning of s 326 of the Companies Act 1948 and, accordingly, the plaintiffs were entitled to the benefit of the arrest of *The Zafiro* as against the liquidator in spite of the prior notice of the meeting at which a resolution for the winding up of the defendant company was to be proposed;

- by arresting *The Zafiro*, the plaintiffs had become secured creditors; and

- the general practice of the court was to stay all actions against the company after the commencement of the voluntary winding up of the company, save in special circumstances. This was an action for necessary disbursements, in which the writ had been issued prior to the commencement of the winding up.[99]

3.16 Any claim arising out of an act which is claimed to be a general average act (s 20(2)(q))

The elements of a general average act derive from s 66(2) of the Marine Insurance Act 1906 and the York-Antwerp Rules 1974, as amended in 1994. Briefly, for general average to qualify as such, there must be some intentional or voluntary sacrifice or expenditure reasonably made with regard to the ship or cargo in time of peril or danger for the common safety of the adventure (see Chapter 15). There is no maritime lien for general average claims. The shipowner has a possessory lien over the cargo for its proportionate contribution to general average, enforceable against the consignee of the cargo, notwithstanding that – at the time of the general average act – he may not be the owner of the cargo.[100]

3.17 Any claim arising out of bottomry (s 20(2)(r))

Bottomry bonds were contracts in the nature of a mortgage of a ship where the owner borrowed money while the ship was at sea to enable him to fit her as needed. He had to pledge the keel or the bottom of the ship as security for repayment. Such

---

99 For the provisions of the Insolvency Act 1986 and their effect upon statutory rights *in rem* and secured maritime creditors, see Meeson, N, *Admiralty Jurisdiction and Practice*, 3rd edn, 2003, LLP, pp 93–106 (There is now the Insolvency Act 2000.)

100 *Castle Insurance v Hong Kong Island Shipping* [1984] AC 226 (HL).

bonds are no longer in use today, but they gave rise to a maritime lien when used.[101] The Arrest Convention (1999) has deleted bottomry bonds from the list of maritime claims.

3.18 Any claim for the forfeiture or condemnation of a ship or for the restoration of a ship or goods after seizure or for droits of admiralty (s 20(2)(s))

The old MSA 1894 and the current 1995 Act have provided for occasions of forfeiture of a ship in case of contravention of the Acts by her owner or master. Some grounds of forfeiture are mentioned as examples below, where:

- a false declaration is made as to qualification to ownership of a British vessel, under s 3(1) of the MSA 1995, except where the false declaration is made for the purpose of escaping capture by an enemy of war (MSA 1995, s 3(2));

- the British character of the ship is concealed (MSA 1995, s 3(4) and (5));

- dangerous goods are shipped without marks or without notification (MSA 1995, s 87(1)); or

- there is contravention of Customs and Excise requirements.[102] A ship will be liable to forfeiture for contravening the Customs and Excise Management Act 1979. Examples of contravention include: exporting stores contrary to a prohibition or restriction (s 68); shipping coastwise contrary to regulations (s 74); concealing goods (s 88); jettison or destruction of cargo to prevent seizure (s 89); and inability of the master of a ship to account for missing cargo (s 90).

Droits of admiralty are abandoned property at sea which can be claimed by the Crown. Historically, this right of the Crown existed in the old MSA 1894 and now in the 1995 Act. Such property includes: jetsam, flotsam, lagan and derelict found at sea, which are not claimed by their owner 'in due time' (within a year and a day). It also includes goods and ships taken from pirates (but, apparently not property in the possession of pirates and belonging to others).

Presently, ss 241–44 of the MSA 1995 provide that Her Majesty is entitled to all unclaimed wrecks found in territorial waters in any part of Her Majesty's dominion. A good example of the territorial requirement of these provisions is found in *The Lusitania*.[103]

4 FURTHER JURISDICTION OF THE ADMIRALTY COURT IS GIVEN BY s 20(1)(b) AND (3)

This section includes:

- any application to the High Court under the MSA 1995;

---

101 The last reported case was *The Conet* [1965] 1 Lloyd's Rep 195.
102 *The Skylark* [1965] 3 All ER 380.
103 [1986] QB 384.

- any proceedings to enforce a claim for damage, loss of life or personal injury arising out of: (i) a collision between ships; or (ii) the carrying out of or omission to carry out a manoeuvre in the case of one or more ships; or (iii) non-compliance on the part of one or more ships with the collision regulations; or

- any action by shipowners or other persons for limitation of their liability under the MSA 1995.

Also, s 20(1)(c) has preserved any other admiralty jurisdiction which the court had immediately before the commencement of this Act, otherwise known as the 'sweeping up' provision, encompassing the court's inherent jurisdiction and such jurisdiction as the court had under the old ACAs 1840 and 1861. Examples of the court's inherent jurisdiction include jurisdiction over acts done on the high seas and power to award interest, which is now also statutory by virtue of s 35A of the SCA 1981.

Under s 20(1)(d), any other jurisdiction connected with a ship or aircraft which is vested in the High Court after the commencement of the SCA 1981 will be within the jurisdiction of this court.

5 POWER OF THE COURT TO GRANT INJUNCTIONS

Such power of the court existed since the Judicature Act 1873, s 25(8), which was re-enacted by s 45 of the SCJ(Con)A 1925. An injunction would be granted when the court thought it was just or convenient. The court's power to grant injunctions can be found in s 37(1) of the SCA 1981 which has replaced s 45 of the 1925 Act.

However, the general rule until 1975 was that a plaintiff, as a mere putative judgment creditor, could not obtain an injunctive order to prevent a defendant dealing with his own assets before judgment was obtained[104] (unless the assets belonged to the plaintiff – whereupon he would have a tracing or proprietary claim). Lord Denning MR, in 1975, sitting in the Court of Appeal, innovated an injunction – relying on s 45 of the SCJ(Con)A 1925 – upon an ex parte application by a shipowner to restrain a charterer from disposing or removing his assets from the jurisdiction before a judgment for unpaid hire was obtained.[105] Again, in the same year, Lord Denning MR (sitting in the Court of Appeal) granted the same injunction to shipowners in *Mareva Compania Naviera v International Bulkcarriers*,[106] hence the name of this injunction became known as a 'Mareva' injunction. Under the new Civil Procedure Rules, it is now named 'freezing' injunction or order.

The principal object of a freezing order made under s 37(1) is to ensure that the defendant's assets are not dissipated and that there is a fund to meet a judgment, or arbitration award, obtained by a claimant in the English courts, or arbitration (s 44 of the Arbitration Act 1996). Generally, the freezing order would be made in respect of assets beneficially owned by the defendant to the action. It is not a statutory

---

104 *Lister v Stubbs* (1890) 45 Ch D 1.
105 *Nippon Yusen Kaisha v G&J Karageorgis* [1975] 2 Lloyd's Rep 137 (CA).
106 [1975] 2 Lloyd's Rep 509.

remedy.[107] It is an interim and ancillary remedy covering any type of injunction sought to restrain a party from removing his assets located within the jurisdiction, or to restrain a party from dealing with any assets, whether located within the jurisdiction or not.[108]

The applicant (claimant), however, is not in the same position as a secured creditor and he has no proprietary claim to the assets which are subject to the injunction. Thus, his position differs significantly from the security provided by the arrest of a ship. The purpose of the injunction is to preserve assets of the defendant for execution of a judgment or the enforcement of an award obtained subsequently.[109] In principle, there can be no objection to a defendant being allowed by the court to employ such assets for the purpose of his business or, where appropriate, to pay living expenses or legal fees, or to seek in good faith to repay loans in the ordinary course of business.[110]

The claimant must show that he has a good arguable case, that is, a better than 50 per cent chance of success[111] of an accrued – not a future – cause of action,[112] that the defendant has assets within the jurisdiction, and there is a real risk[113] that such assets will be dissipated before a judgment can be enforced. The question of risk of disposal of assets is a question of fact judged from the surrounding circumstances, such as evidence of dishonesty or attempts by the defendant to remove or dissipate assets.[114] The applicant must make a full and frank disclosure in his statement of truth of all facts and circumstances[115] and give an undertaking in damages to the court, the effect of which is that the defendant can ask the court to enforce it, should he suffer any loss by the issue of the order. He should also give an undertaking to indemnify third parties who might be affected by the injunction and incur expenses.

A similar power has been given to the court by the old provision, s 30 of the MSA 1894, now para 6 of Sched 1 to the MSA 1995. However, unlike the freezing injunction, which is an ancillary relief, an application made under s 30 has been held to be a substantive right of relief, not being ancillary to any other cause of action.[116]

Originally, the Mareva injunction was limited to English proceedings in which the claimant was claiming a substantive relief against a foreign-based defendant

---

107 *Mercedes-Benz AG v Leiduck* [1995] WLR 718 (PC), p 728, per Lord Mustill.

108 CPR, r 25(1)(f).

109 The defendant may, upon application to the court, obtain a variation of the order if he can show that he needs to cover ordinary living expenses, or, if the defendant is a company, allowance may be made to use some of the assets for business expenses: *The Angel Bell* [1981] QB 65; Devonshire (1999) 62(4) MLR 539, pp 539–63.

110 *The Angel Bell* [1980] 1 Lloyd's Rep 632; *Derby v Weldon (Nos 3 and 4)* [1990] Ch 65 (CA); *The Coral Rose* [1991] 1 Lloyd's Rep 563 (CA).

111 *Ninemia Maritime Corp v Trave Schiffahrtsgesellschaft* [1983] 1 WLR 1412 (affirmed by the Court of Appeal [1983] 2 Lloyd's Rep 660).

112 *Veracruz Transportation Inc v VC Shipping Co Inc* [1992] 1 Lloyd's Rep 353 (CA).

113 *Third Chandris Shipping Corp v Unimarine SA* [1979] QB 645, p 669.

114 *Aiglon Ltd v Gau Shan Co Ltd* [1993] 1 Lloyd's Rep 164.

115 *The Giovana* [1999] 1 Lloyd's Rep 867 (concerning a non-sufficient disclosure).

116 See *The Mikado* [1992] 1 Lloyd's Rep 163 and *The Siben* [1994] 2 Lloyd's Rep 420.

and the injunction was sought to ensure that the defendant did not remove assets out of the English jurisdiction before judgment. It was also available in aid to arbitration proceedings by s 12(6)(f) and (h) of the AA 1950;[117] this has now been replaced by s 44 of the AA 1996, which gives power to the court to grant an injunction in aid to arbitration proceedings.

However, an injunction could not be granted when the only factor connecting the case with England was the presence of assets within the jurisdiction because it was ancillary to a pre-existing cause of action triable in England ('the Siskina barrier').[118] Thus, a claimant who was seeking to serve a defendant out of the jurisdiction would need to show that his cause of action fell within the provisions of court rules for service out of the jurisdiction (Ord 11, r 1) in order for the injunction to be granted;[119] in other words, the substantive cause of action should be triable in the English court.

Since the judicial innovation of the old Mareva order in the late 1970s,[120] the freezing injunction has been expanded by case law, practice directions and legislation.

In recent years, the freezing injunction has been subject to dramatic changes. It has gradually gained much wider scope applying to domestic or foreign proceedings, English or foreign defendants, English or foreign assets and even assets sheltered in offshore companies or trusts.[121] The combination of changes brought by case law,[122] statute[123] and statutory instrument[124] have allowed a free-standing

---

117 *The Rena K* [1979] QB 377.

118 *The Siskina* [1979] AC 210 (HL).

119 The Privy Council left the matter open as to whether there could be a free-standing injunction in *Mercedes-Benz v Leiduck* [1996] AC 284, while Lord Nicholls' dissenting advice was that 'justice and convenience suggests that the answer to the question is yes'.

120 *Mareva Compania Naviera v International Bulkcarriers* [1975] 2 Lloyd's Rep 509.

121 Such developments can be found in the most authoritative book of Gee, S, *Commercial Injunctions* (formerly *Mareva Injunctions and Anton Piller Relief*), Sweet & Maxwell, 5th edn (2004) with supplement 2007.

122 *Channel Tunnel Group Ltd v Balfour Beatty Constructions Ltd* [1993] AC 334 (HL), in which it was accepted that there was jurisdiction to grant an interlocutory injunction, although the English proceedings were stayed in favour of foreign arbitration.

123 Civil Jurisdiction and Judgments Act 1982, s 25 and AA 1996, s 44 adopted the wording of Art 24 of the Brussels Convention, which is now replaced by Art 31 of the Brussels Regulation. A straightforward interpretation of the meaning of provisional or protective measures under the old Art 24 of the Brussels Convention was given by the European Court of Justice in *Mario Reichert and Others v Dresdner Bank AG* (Case C–261/90) (1992): 'In matters within the scope of the Convention, provisional measures are intended to preserve a factual or legal situation so as to safeguard rights, the recognition of which is sought elsewhere, from the court having jurisdiction as to the substance of the matter.' Article 31 of the Regulation expressly provides that a court has jurisdiction under its national law to grant an application for provisional or protective measures, even if it does not have jurisdiction as to the substance of the matter. An order for interim payment of contractual consideration delivered by a court not having jurisdiction under the Brussels Regulation as to the substance of the matter is not a provisional measure capable of being granted under Art 31: *Hans-Hermann Mietz v Intership Yachting Sneek BV* (Case C–99/96) [1999] ECR I–2277 (referring to the old Art 24 of the Brussels Convention).

124 The CJJA 1982 (Interim Relief) Order 1997 (SI 1997/302).

freezing injunction and the 'Siskina barrier' to the service of originating process out of the jurisdiction seeking a free-standing interim relief has been removed.[125]

Further recent changes have also enabled claimants to obtain a worldwide freezing injunction. The first step towards this direction was made in 1987 when the question whether the court had jurisdiction to grant an order requiring the disclosure of foreign assets in support of a domestic Mareva injunction was negatively answered.[126] In 1990, however, three Court of Appeal decisions recognised a jurisdiction to grant injunctions against assets outside the jurisdiction, thus, permitting it to have extra-territorial effect.[127] The extra-territorial freezing injunction is a holding relief pending an order of the court having jurisdiction at the place where the account is held. In *Credit Suisse Fides Trust SA v Cuoghi*,[128] the Court of Appeal held that worldwide relief could be granted in proceedings, whether or not these were domestic or foreign, under s 25 of the Civil Jurisdiction and Judgments Act (CJJA) 1982, or in aid to foreign arbitration.

In addition, once there is a cause of action against a defendant, the court has power to order an injunction, or interim relief, against a non-party to the proceedings. The injunction or interim relief against that party is ancillary for the purpose of obtaining satisfaction on that cause of action or enforcement of judgment.[129]

More recently, the Court of Appeal set the following guidelines with regard to worldwide freezing injunctions in *Dadourian Group International Inc v Simms and others*:[130]

> The making of a worldwide freezing order in respect of foreign assets is a serious step which ordinarily requires an undertaking by the claimant not to enforce it without the permission of the English court. The court has a discretion to grant permission if it considers it just and convenient for the purpose of ensuring the effectiveness of the order and it is not oppressive to the parties to the English proceedings or to third parties who may be joined to the foreign proceedings. All the relevant circumstances and options need to be considered. In particular, consideration should be given to granting relief on terms, to the proportionality of the steps proposed to be taken abroad, and to the form of any order. The interests of the applicant should be balanced against the interests of the other parties to the proceedings and any new party likely to be joined to the foreign proceedings. Permission should not normally be given in terms which would enable the applicant to obtain relief in the foreign proceedings which is superior to the relief given by the worldwide freezing order. The evidence in support of the application for permission

---

125 RSC Ord 11 (now Section III of CPR Part 6) has been amended.

126 *Ashtiani v Kashi* [1987] 1 QB 888.

127 *Babanaft International Co SA v Bassatne* [1990] 1 Ch 13; *Republic of Haiti v Duvalier* [1990] 1 QB 202; and *Derby v Weldon* [1990] 1 Ch 48.

128 [1997] 1 WLR 871.

129 *C Inc v L* [2001] 2 Lloyd's Rep 459; an interesting recent series of decisions showing the extent of the court's power can be found in *Kensington International Ltd v Republic of Congo* [2006] EWHC 1848, from which the previous decisions on injunctive orders and interim relief can be traced. The cases involved fraudulent transactions and, apart from an injunction, a tracing order and interim relief from the English courts, there were also a foreign attachment as well as an undertaking and cross-undertaking for damages. In this particular case, an order was made against a non-party for cross-examination.

130 [2006] 1 WLR 2499.

should contain all the information (so far as it can reasonably be obtained in the time available) necessary to enable the judge to reach an informed decision, including evidence as to the applicable law and practice in the foreign court, the nature of the proposed proceedings to be commenced, the assets believed to be located in the jurisdiction of the foreign court, and the names of the parties by whom such assets are held. The applicant must show that there is a real prospect that such assets are located within the jurisdiction of the foreign court and that there is a risk of their dissipation. Normally the application should be made on notice to the respondent but, in cases of urgency, where it is just to do so, permission may be given without notice to the party against whom relief will be sought in the foreign proceedings, but that party should have the earliest practicable opportunity of having the matter reconsidered by the court at a hearing of which he is given notice.

Freezing orders are looked at again, in Chapter 11 below, in relation to the circumstances in which a buyer of a ship can obtain such an order.

CHAPTER 3

MODE OF EXERCISE OF JURISDICTION

1 INTRODUCTION

Thus far, we have seen that the admiralty jurisdiction is statutory, with specific heads of subject matter. It entertains both claims *in rem* and claims *in personam*. The *in rem* claim which, until recently, was known as the action *in rem*, has had a long history. It has been mentioned, in the introduction of Chapter 1, that the conflict between the common law courts and the Admiralty Court was settled first, by permitting the Lord Admiral to determine disputes in matters that concerned exclusively what happened at sea, such as collisions and salvage, as well as matters that involved mortgages on ships, and questions of possession of or title in a ship. The Lord Admiral was allowed to proceed with a suit only *in rem* against the ship. This perhaps marked the genesis of the 'truly *in rem*' causes, which involved claims concerned with proprietary rights on the ship and maritime liens and, in which, the defendant was the ship. The concept that the ship was the defendant in maritime claims was used to extend the jurisdiction of the court. The Admiralty Court Acts (ACA) 1840 and 1861 extended the admiralty jurisdiction to other maritime claims, referred to in this book as the 'non-truly *in rem*' because they are not concerned with proprietary rights in a ship, or maritime liens. The phrase 'quasi *in rem*' is avoided because that phrase was used with regard to the old 'maritime attachment', which was, as explained in the introduction of this book, related to the arrest of property or the person of the defendant in actions *in personam* (see Ch 1 para 5).

The merger of procedure for these additional claims with the procedure for the truly *in rem* claims, coupled with the merger of all courts by the Judicature Acts (JA) 1873–75, brought a fusion of actions so that both actions *in rem* and *in personam* could be tried in the same courts. The distinction, however, between truly and non-truly *in rem* claims and *in rem* or *in personam* proceedings has always been maintained in the mode of exercise of jurisdiction and can be found in the present statute, as will be seen later. Briefly, the truly *in rem* claims can be brought against the relevant ship without considerations of who would be liable *in personam* for the claim, or who is the beneficial owner of the ship to be arrested. The maritime lien is attached to the ship (see Ch 2 para 2), the mortgage is a legal or equitable right in a ship, claims of ownership or possession of a ship are rights in a ship. By contrast, considerations of ownership, or liability *in personam*, are taken into account when a non-truly *in rem* claim is brought against the relevant ship. Before examining these considerations in detail, it is important to understand, first, the nature and the functions of *in personam* and *in rem* claims, respectively. An examination of the effect of *The Indian Grace* on the nature of the *in rem* claim follows, after an analysis of how non-truly *in rem* claims can crystallise on the ship by institution of suit.

2 CLAIMS *IN PERSONAM* – s 21(1) OF THE SUPREME COURT ACT 1981

As the latin tag indicates, these are claims against the person or the owning company, or the demise charterer of the ship. By s 22(1) of the SCA 1981, a claim *in personam* may be brought in the High Court in all cases within the admiralty jurisdiction of that court. The proceedings may be brought, either by a claim form *in personam*, or through an *in rem* claim. Since shipping companies are normally incorporated abroad, personal service of the *in personam* claim form cannot be effected, unless the claim falls within certain categories of claims for which permission of the court can be obtained in accordance with the Rules of Court.[1] An *in personam* claim form may also be served out of the jurisdiction, where the defendant has agreed to submit to this jurisdiction, or the claim is about salvage for services rendered within the jurisdiction.[2]

There are, however, certain restrictions on jurisdiction imposed by other statutes or Conventions, such as the Brussels Regulation and the Lugano Convention, in the event of multiple proceedings, which will be examined in Chapter 6. There is also a limitation to commencing *in personam* proceedings in collision cases,[3] unless the defendant submits to this jurisdiction. Section 22(2) provides that the High Court shall not entertain such actions unless:

(a) the defendant has his habitual residence or place of business within England or Wales; or

(b) the cause of action arose within the inland waters of England or Wales or within the limits of a port of England or Wales; or

(c) an action arising out of the same incident or series of incidents is proceeding in the court, or has been heard and determined in the court.

There are two major weaknesses of the *in personam* proceedings: first, it may be difficult sometimes to obtain permission to serve the defendant out of the jurisdiction; second, unlike the *in rem* claim, the *in personam* does not provide security for the claim, so that a judgment, if obtained, will be an empty shell unless a quasi-security is obtained for satisfaction of the judgment, by means of a freezing injunction. However, as was explained in the previous chapter, a freezing injunction does not definitely secure the claimant. It does not provide security for the claim in the way the arrest of the ship does because, first, the asset made subject to the injunction may not be sufficient to satisfy the claim and, second, the defendant can obtain a variation of the injunction by which the asset may be used for his business expenses.

---

1 See, eg, *The Manchester Carriage* [1973] 1 Lloyd's Rep 386; *The Craiova* [1976] 1 Lloyd's Rep 356; Ord 11, now in CPR, Pt 6, Section III (rr 6.17–6.31) and PD 6B.

2 PD 58.

3 *The World Harmony* [1969] 1 Lloyd's Rep 350; contrast *The Fagerness* (1927) 28 LlL Rep 261; PD 58.

3 THE *IN REM* CLAIM (OR THE OLD ACTION *IN REM*)

3.1 The origins of non-truly *in rem* claims

Statutory rights by way of an action *in rem* were first created by the ACA 1840. It is illustrative to use the words of Brandon J in *The Monica S*:[4]

> Such rights were given by s 6 in respect, firstly, of claims for towage, and, secondly, of claims for necessaries supplied to foreign ships, whether within the body of a country or on the high seas. Further rights of the same kind were created by the ACA 1861. Such rights were given by s 4, in respect of claims for building, equipping or repairing a ship, if at the date of institution of the cause the ship or its proceeds were under arrest of the court; by s 5, in respect of claims for necessaries supplied to any ship elsewhere than in the port to which she belonged, unless at the time of institution of the cause any owner or part-owner was domiciled in England or Wales; by s 6, in respect of claims by holders of bills of lading of any goods carried into any port in England or Wales for damage to such goods, subject to the same proviso as to domicile of any owner or part-owner; and by s 10 in respect of masters' claims for disbursements. Section 35 further provided that the jurisdiction of the Admiralty Court could be exercised either *in rem* or *in personam*.

Later, the Judicature (Consolidation) Act 1925 expanded the list of claims which could be enforced by an action *in rem*, and further extension was achieved by the Administration of Justice Act (AJA) 1956, and the present statute, the Supreme Court Act (SCA) 1981 (as has already been seen).

3.2 Functions of the *in rem* proceedings

At its commencement, the *in rem* claim is against the property, such as the relevant ship or cargo or freight, as the case may be (see para 5, below). It requires the relevant ship or property to be within the jurisdiction for it to be arrested, unless the defendant submits to jurisdiction and provides security in lieu of arrest. The uniqueness of an *in rem* claim under English procedural law lies on its triple function, namely: it assists the claimant (a) to obtain security for the claim; (b) to invoke the jurisdiction of the English court on the merits of the claim; and (c) regarding 'non-truly *in rem*' claims, to have the right *in rem* crystallised on the property from the time of issue of the *in rem* claim form.[5] Functions (a) and (b) are discussed in Chapter 4. The origins of function (c) are examined next.

3.2.1 The crystallisation of non-truly in rem claims on the property

The crystallisation of the non-truly *in rem* claim on the ship (against which proceedings *in rem* have been issued) was established in 1967 by the decision of Brandon J, in *The Monica S*. This decision has had far-reaching effect upon purchasers of ships who may buy the ship after the issue of the *in rem* proceeding. It has remained

---

4   [1967] 2 Lloyd's Rep 113, pp 118–19, per Brandon J.
5   *The Monica S* [1967] 2 Lloyd's Rep 113.

unchallenged. It will later be examined whether or not the effect of this decision has been undermined by the decision of the House of Lords in *The Indian Grace*.[6]

The Monica S[7]

The cargo-owners of the cargo on board this ship claimed damages to their cargo and issued a writ *in rem*. At the time of the issue, the ship was named *Monica Smith* and was owned by S. Before the writ was served, *Monica Smith* was transferred to T and was renamed *Monica S*. The writ was subsequently amended, accordingly, to describe the name and the defendants as 'the owners of the ship formerly called *Monica Smith* and now known as *Monica S*' and was served on the ship. The new owner T entered conditional appearance and applied by motion to set aside the writ or the service. After the service, T sold the ship to someone else. T claimed, inter alia, a declaration that no lien or charge arose against *Monica S* by reason of issue of the writ or service on grounds that (1) T was not the owner of the vessel at the date of issue, or when the cause of action arose; (2) T would not be liable *in personam*; (3) the claim gave no rise to a maritime lien or charge on the ship. He claimed that the plaintiff had only a statutory right of action *in rem* under the AJA 1956, which was enforceable against the *res* if (i) the *res* was arrested while still owned by the person liable *in personam*, or (ii) the writ had been served before change of ownership.

Brandon J had to decide the issue whether a change of ownership of the ship, occurring after institution of proceedings but before service of process or arrest, defeated the statutory right of action *in rem*. He reviewed all previous authorities being relevant to the question and held:

> T was the owner of the vessel at the time of service of writ and had an interest in defending it. As a matter of principle, if creation of a substantive right could occur on arrest then it could occur at date of action brought. There was a preponderance of authority to show that the defendants' contention (that under the pre–1956 law a change of ownership after issue of writ, but before service or arrest, defeated a statutory right of action *in rem*) was wrong. There was no reason why, once the plaintiff had properly invoked jurisdiction under the 1956 Act by bringing an action *in rem*, he should not, despite a subsequent change of ownership of the *res*, be able to prosecute it through all its stages, up to judgment against the *res* and payment out of the proceeds.

The motion of the defendant, T, was dismissed. Brandon J referred to the following decisions, some of which, he thought, supported his view, although he accepted that none of them was exactly on the point, while others were conflicting. In *The Pacific*,[8] in which there was competition between a claim by a mortgagee and a claim for necessaries supplied to the ship, Dr Lushington had stated:

> The material(s) man . . . by the mere fact of his supplying necessaries, in no case obtains the ship as a security until he *institutes his suit* in this court . . . [he] has not a maritime lien; for a maritime lien accrues from the instant of the circumstances creating it, and not from the date of the intervention of the court. (emphasis added)

---

6   [1998] 1 Lloyd's Rep 1.
7   [1967] 2 Lloyd's Rep 113.
8   (1864) 1 Brown 7 Lush 243, p 246.

In *The Princess Charlotte*,[9] in which the sale of the ship took place the day after the institution of the cause and on the same day as the arrest, Dr Lushington again expounded that:

> I am of the opinion that the mere transfer of a foreign ship to a British owner does not bar the remedy ... and, moreover, in this case, the title (of the new owner) did not commence till *after the suit was instituted*.[10] (emphasis added)

In the subsequent case, *The Troubadour*,[11] Dr Lushington repeated his view expressed in his previous decision, *The Pacific*, that the necessary man did not acquire a lien on the ship until institution of suit, so the necessary man, again, came in priority after a mortgagee whose mortgage had been registered before institution of suit. In *The Two Ellens*,[12] the Privy Council – construing s 5 of the ACA 1861 – approved the decision in *The Pacific* and confirmed that the *res* did not become chargeable with the debt for necessaries until the suit was actually instituted. It was *the institution of suit*, Brandon J explained in *The Monica S*, commenting on another decision of Privy Council (*The Pieve Superiore*),[13] that gave a claimant the right to arrest and the arrest provided him with security. This case, however, did not absolutely support the judge's point of view, but he gave it a liberal interpretation.

Next he examined *The Aneroid*,[14] in which, however, Sir Robert Phillimore had said that a necessary man would have no cause of action if the sale of the ship preceded *the arrest* of the ship. Brandon J thought that, even if the judge in that case had put his mind to this point, it must have been *obiter*, as it was not relevant to the case, because, on the facts, the sale had occurred before the institution of the proceedings *in rem*.

What persuaded Brandon J most in his judgment was the statement of Lord Watson in *The Heinrich Bjorn*,[15] who had said:

> The position of a creditor who has a proper maritime lien differs from that of a creditor in an unsecured claim in this respect – that the former, unless he has forfeited the right by his own laches, can proceed against the ship, notwithstanding any change in her ownership, whereas the latter cannot have an action *in rem* unless, at the time of *its institution*, the *res* is the property of his debtor. (emphasis added)

In an earlier passage, however, Lord Watson had said that:

> The attachment of the ship by process of the court had the effect of giving the creditor a legal nexus over the proprietary interest of his debtor, as from the date of *the attachment*.[16] (emphasis added)

The plaintiffs in *The Monica S* argued that this passage was directed to the time from

---

9   (1864) LJ Adm 188.

10 But, at that time, it had been thought that a claim for necessaries conferred a maritime lien, which view was overruled by the House of Lords in *The Heinrich Bjorn* (1886) 11 App Cas 270 (HL) (see below).

11 (1866) LR A&E 302.

12 (1872) LR 4 PC 161.

13 (1874) LR 3 PC 482.

14 (1877) 2 PD 189.

15 (1886) 11 App Cas 270, p 276.

16 Ibid, p 276.

which the security, when obtained, took effect, and not to the time when the right to obtain it accrued. This interpretation was not accepted by Brandon J, because Lord Watson in the next case referred to by Brandon J, *The Sara*,[17] had approved what Dr Lushington had said about the effect of institution of suit in *The Pacific*.

In *The Cella*[18] case, at first instance, the judge referred to the correctness of *The Pacific*, but the Court of Appeal (Esher and Fry LJJ), having approved the first instance decision, used the word 'arrest' of the ship as being the critical time offering the greatest security for obtaining substantial justice. Esher LJ also referred to the alternative time of the service of the writ. Lopes LJ, however, said that, from the time of arrest, the ship is held by the court to abide the result of the action and the rights of the parties must be determined by the institution of the action and cannot be altered by anything which takes place subsequently. Brandon J preferred the words used by Lopes LJ, in that, *it is from the institution of suit that the rights of the parties are determined*. *The Cella* concerned the right *in rem* of a ship-repairer, who had issued a caveat against release of the ship (which had previously been arrested by its master) as against the liquidator of the shipowning company. Brandon thought that, because of the caveat, neither Esher LJ, nor Fry LJ, put their mind to the effect of the issue of the writ. In a much later decision, *The Zafiro*,[19] (to which Brandon J referred), the court upheld the claim of a necessary man secured on the ship by arrest against the liquidator of the company.[20] Two further decisions, *The James W Elwell*[21] and *The Colorado*,[22] seem to stress the incident of arrest of the ship as having the effect of creating security on the ship for a non-maritime lien claimant. Brandon J commented about these decisions that the point of distinction between issue of writ and arrest of the ship was not in issue.

Finally, Brandon J asserted that Sir Boyd Merriman, in *The Beldis*,[23] supported his view. Sir Boyd was, in fact, commenting on the contrast being made by the House of Lords' decision, in *The Heinrich Bjorn*, between the security aspect of maritime liens, which does not depend on bringing a suit, and other maritime claims which need the institution of suit in order to be attached on the ship.

Brandon J concluded that seven of these decisions supported or tended to support his view, six were against and one was neutral. On closer examination,

---

17 (1889) 14 App Cas 209: this case is now wrong on the point that the master does not have a maritime lien for disbursements on account of the ship.

18 (1888) 13 PD 82.

19 [1960] P 1.

20 However, when maritime creditors are in competition with the creditors of the company, there must have been an arrest of the ship belonging to the company prior to the commencement of the winding-up proceedings for maritime claims, other than maritime liens and mortgages, to be given priority over the company's unsecured creditors. Otherwise the arrest will be void for being equivalent to 'sequestration' under s 128(1) of the Insolvency Act 1986. The discretion of the judge in the company court is very important in this context. Issue of a caveat against release of the ship which has been arrested by another maritime claimant, will have the same effect, provided it is issued before the commencement of the winding-up proceedings: *Re Aro Co Ltd* [1980] Ch 196 (CA); for the extent of the discretion of the court, which will depend on the circumstances of each case, see *The Bolivia* [1995] BCC 666.

21 [1921] P 351.

22 [1923] P 102 (CA).

23 [1936] P 51.

however, bearing in mind that some of these decisions were strained in their inter-pretation by Brandon J, only six[24] of them seemed to support his view that the institution of suit causes a statutory right *in rem* to accrue on the ship. Three[25] decisions were not clear, or were not deciding the point and seemed to equate arrest with institution of suit. Five[26] referred directly to the incident of arrest and one[27] was neutral. One can hardly argue that there was a preponderance of opinion in favour of the judge's view.

It is important, however, to note that the procedure of the court between 1859 until 1874 (at which time the decisions that supported Brandon J's view were decided) required that a cause was instituted by having the cause written in the book. If the cause was *in rem*, a warrant for the arrest of the res was taken out, served and executed. In practice, arrest followed very soon, usually within one or two days of institution and there was not then any separation between service of process and arrest, both being carried out simultaneously.[28] There should be no surprise, therefore, that, in some of the decisions referred to by Brandon J, the issue of the writ and the arrest seemed to be equated by the judges. However, these authorities had been decided before the AJA 1956 and Brandon J was more con-cerned with the construction of the 1956 Act than previous authorities.

The judge thought that the passing of the Act made his argument stronger by reason of the statute's express requirements. In particular, s 3(4) provided:

> In the case of any such claim as is mentioned in para (d) to (r) of s 1(1), being a claim arising in connection with a ship, where the person who would be liable on the claim in an action *in personam* was, when the cause of action arose, the owner or charterer of, or in possession or in control of, the ship, the admiralty jurisdiction of the High Court ... may be invoked by an action *in rem* against (a) that ship, if at the time *the action is brought*, it is beneficially owned as respects all the shares therein by that person ... (emphasis added)

Thus, the critical time under the Act was when the 'action was brought' against the relevant ship, which caused the statutory right of action *in rem*[29] to accrue upon it irrevocably and, hence, be enforced against that ship, even if it had, in the mean-time, been transferred to a bona fide purchaser, who bought the ship for value and without knowledge of the issue of the writ at the time.[30] In essence, the gist of

---

24 *The Pacific* (1864) 1 Brown 7 Lush 243; *The Princess Charlotte* (1864) LJ Adm 188; *The Troubadour* (1866) LR A&E 302; *The Two Ellens* (1872) LR 4 PC 161; *The Sara* (1889) 14 App Cas 209; *The Cella* (1888) 13 PD 82: but, in the Court of Appeal the arrest or service was mentioned.

25 *The Pieve Superiore* (1874) LR 3 PC 482; *The Heinrich Bjorn* (1886) 11 App Cas 270 (CA) and (HL); *The Beldis* [1936] P 51 (CA).

26 *The Cella* (1888) 13 PD 82 (CA); *The Aneroid* (1877) 2 PD 189; *The James W Elwell* [1921] P 351; *The Colorado* [1923] P 102 (CA); *The Zafiro* [1960] P 1.

27 *The Igor* [1956] 2 Lloyd's Rep 271.

28 Summary given by Brandon J in *The Monica S* [1967] 2 Lloyd's Rep 113, p 119 (see above).

29 The judge also preferred the expression 'statutory right of action *in rem*' to the expression 'statutory lien', for it seemed to him to be a more accurate description of the right in question. But, he also thought that 'statutory lien' was a convenient expression if it was used to mean no more than an irrevocably accrued statutory right of action *in rem*.

30 It has been the practice of solicitors involved in the sale and purchase of ships to conduct a search in the Admiralty Registry, as part of the due diligence exercise, to see whether there are any outstanding claims *in rem* issued against the ship to be bought. PD 61, para 3.12 provides that any *in rem* form may be searched, whether it has been served or not.

Brandon J's decision is that, with the institution of suit *in rem*, a contingent right of security is created upon the ship which will be brought into effect by the arrest of the ship, regardless of change of ownership between the issue and the arrest. That was, he thought, the intention of the statute as derived from the words 'action is brought', and he disregarded persuasive arguments by the defendants' counsel about the meaning of previous authorities and the need to protect innocent purchasers. On balance, Brandon J preferred to protect maritime claimants, because a purchaser would be able to rely on the contractual indemnity obtained from the seller, if he did not become insolvent by the time it was discovered that the ship bought was encumbered by maritime liens[31] or other maritime claims giving cause for arrest of the ship. As far as statutory rights *in rem* are concerned, a purchaser can carry out a search in the Admiralty Registry.[32]

3.2.2 What does 'action brought' mean?

The foundation of *The Monica S* would crumble if the words 'action brought'[33] in the statute meant the service of the *in rem* proceedings on the ship, or the arrest of the relevant ship. Brandon J said on this point that:

> It seems to me that it would be strange if a statutory right of action *in rem* only became effective, as against a subsequent change of ownership of the res, upon arrest of the *res*, and yet, by the same statute, as conferred the right of action, arrest was in many cases prohibited.[34]

This is a very powerful judicial statement of a very experienced admiralty judge with an insight into the realities of shipping commercial practices. He rightly anticipated that shipowners, who would wish to avoid their liabilities, would only be too quick to sell their ship (against which a writ *in rem* had been issued) to avoid the consequences, if the effect of the issue of the writ was not to crystallise the claim on the ship from the time of issue. It seems that policy considerations were very important in his decision, which has remained unchallenged since 1967.[35]

---

31 Maritime liens cannot be registered, so there is no means of finding out about them from a public record, unless the purchaser inspects the log books of the ship, in case there are incidents recorded which might have given rise to maritime liens (see further Ch 11).

32 See fn 30.

33 The construction of these words under the Warsaw Convention for the Unification of Certain Rules relating to International Carriage by Air was given a broader meaning by the Court of Appeal in *Milor Srl and Others v BA plc* [1996] QB 702, in which Phillips LJ said: 'I accept that, in the appropriate context, the expression "to bring an action" can naturally mean "to commence an action". To find such a context, one need look no further than the next article of the Convention. Article 29 provides: "The right to damages shall be extinguished if an action is not brought within two years, reckoned from the date of arrival at the destination, or from the date on which the aircraft ought to have arrived, or from the date on which the carriage stopped." Plainly in Art 29 "brought" means "instituted or commenced". The natural meaning of "brought" will, however, depend upon its context. If a litigant says, "I brought a successful action", the natural meaning of "brought" embraces both the initiation and the pursuit of the action. In my judgment, the context of Art 28 is one in which "brought" naturally has the latter meaning, rather than meaning no more than "instituted".'

34 *The Monica S* [1967] 2 Lloyd's Rep 113, p 131.

35 The decision was approved by the Court of Appeal in *Re Aro Co Ltd* [1980] 1 Ch 196, where it was held that a plaintiff by commencing an action *in rem* against a ship, even if the writ has not been served or the ship has not been arrested, puts himself in the position of a secured creditor.

It remains to be seen whether his decision will remain unchallenged in the future.

It should be noted that, shortly after the decision of Brandon J, the phrase 'the jurisdiction may be invoked' of s 3(4) of the 1956 Act (which preceded the words 'when the action is brought') was construed by the Court of Appeal in *The Banco*.[36] Megaw LJ thought that the jurisdiction was invoked when the writ was served on the one ship chosen, and not at its issue (when more than one ship can be named in the writ). Lord Denning MR, in the same case, said that it was when the writ was served and a warrant of arrest was executed, because it was an action against the very thing itself. Cairns LJ was in the minority and agreed with what Brandon J said in *The Monica S*. Brandon J, in his subsequent decision, *The Berny*,[37] observed that, in the context of s 3 of the AJA 1956, the expressions used 'when the action is brought' and 'when the jurisdiction is invoked' were not intended to be the same thing. To support this, he drew a prima facie inference from the statute, which used both phrases in different parts of the sub-sections. Relying on older authorities,[38] he said that the jurisdiction of the court was invoked by the service and not by the issue of the writ.

It should be observed that the draftsman of s 21 of the SCA 1981, which replaced s 3 of the 1956 Act, has used the words 'action may be brought'[39] in all sub-sections. To avoid confusion, the words 'jurisdiction may be invoked' have been eliminated.

It is interesting to note that, in the context of the Brussels Regulation, Art 30, the court's jurisdiction, whether *in personam* or *in rem*, can only be invoked or seised by the issue of proceedings.

Before any conclusion can be drawn about the 'status' of *The Monica S* at the present time, it is essential to examine who has been regarded as the defendant in the *in rem* proceedings.

3.3 Who is the defendant in the *in rem* proceedings?

Historically, there have been two schools of thought. One school has viewed the *in rem* action (claim) as a means of compelling the defendant liable for the claim to appear in court and defend the claim personally (known as 'the procedural theory'). In other words, an *in rem* claim really aims at the person who is interested in the ship, who will – after appearance – be personally liable, beyond the value of the ship, if the claim exceeds its value.[40]

The other school has viewed the action as being against the *res* and has developed from the concept of maritime liens, which attach on the ship from the moment of the incident that gave rise to the claim (see Ch 2 para 2). In other words,

---

36 [1971] P 137.
37 [1977] 2 Lloyd's Rep 533.
38 *Société Générale de Paris v Dreyfus Brothers* (1885) 29 Ch D 239 and *The Hagen* [1908] P 189.
39 In PD 61, para 5.3(2)(c), the word 'issued' instead of 'brought' is used.
40 *The Dictator* [1892] PD 304, per Jeune J.

the *res* has been considered to be the 'personified' defendant, hence, the name attributed to this theory is known as the 'personification theory'.[41]

The procedural theory gradually gained preponderance amongst English judges over the personification theory, particularly since 1892, when Sir Francis Jeune decided *The Dictator*,[42] which, in fact, concerned the enforcement of a maritime lien claim for salvage, that is, a truly *in rem* claim. The owners of the ship had put up bail, but the sum awarded exceeded the bail. The question was, whether the owners were personally liable for the balance of the judgment, which exceeded the bail amount, and it was held that they were.

The decision was severely criticised by Wiswall,[43] who claimed with audacity that Sir Francis Jeune did not cite any authority for his proposition, which was in complete contradiction to what was thought at the time by other eminent judges. In particular, it has been argued by Wiswall that Jeune J confused the action *in rem* with the maritime attachment,[44] which was a procedural device designed to compel the appearance of a defendant in an action *in personam* (a jurisdiction *in personam*), if he was absent, by seizing his property. This was by no means a proceeding *in rem*. 'It is this crucial distinction,' the author says, 'which was so deftly grasped by Sir John Jervis in *Bold Buccleugh*[45] and so unfortunately ignored by Sir Francis Jeune'.[46] However, the procedural theory prevailed and, but for two decisions,[47] which concern truly *in rem* claims and seem to be against it, there have been no other authorities that are inconsistent with *The Dictator*.[48]

The effect of the procedural theory, as was pronounced by the House of Lords in *The Indian Grace* (below), is that the real defendant in the *in rem* proceedings is the person interested in the ship who appears in the action to defend the asset and the claim.

Before examining how the House of Lords in *The Indian Grace* treated *The Dictator*, it is important, first, to outline the features of the *in rem* proceedings as had prevailed up to this latter decision. Later, it will be seen to what extent *The Indian Grace* has affected the features of the *in rem* action or claim.

---

41 This derived from *The Bold Buccleugh* (1850) 7 Moo 267, p 282, in which the Privy Council (Sir John Jervis) had held that the action *in rem* was not a procedural device for obtaining personal jurisdiction over shipowners, but a unique proceeding directly against the ship.

42 [1892] PD 304.

43 See Wiswall, FL (Jr), *Development of Admiralty Jurisdiction Since 1800*, 1970, CUP.

44 See Chapter 1, para 1, above.

45 (1850) 7 Moo 267.

46 See Wiswall, op cit, fn 43, Chapter 6, 'The evolution of the action *in rem*', p 165.

47 *The Longford* (1889) 14 PD 34, which was not cited in argument, nor was it considered by the Court of Appeal in *The Gemma* [1899] P 285, which approved *The Dictator* [1892] PD 304. In *The Burns* [1907] P 137, Moulton LJ repudiated the procedural theory and in effect overruled Jeune J's decision on the point.

48 Wiswall, op cit, fn 43, p 198.

3.4 Nature and features of the *in rem* claim prior to *The Indian Grace (No 2)*[49]

(a) The *in rem* proceeding (whether the claim is truly *in rem* or not) is primarily a vehicle of obtaining security for the claim.

(b) It is also a vehicle of founding jurisdiction on the merits of the claim by the arrest of the ship within this jurisdiction (subject to certain limitations and restrictions, which will be examined later).

(c) With regard to a maritime lien, the *in rem* proceeding gives effect to an already accrued right on the ship, which dates back to the date of its creation. The maritime lien is enforceable against the relevant ship, notwithstanding the change of ownership, either prior to, or after the issue of the proceeding, or liability *in personam*.

(d) With regard to non-truly *in rem* claims, the *in rem* proceeding causes a statutory right *in rem* to crystallize on the ship from the time of issue of the *in rem* proceeding. From that time, the *in rem* claim, or statutory lien, is enforceable against the ship, regardless of a subsequent transfer of ownership to a bona fide purchaser without notice.

(e) In both truly and non-truly *in rem* claims, the value of the ship had always been the limit for the satisfaction of maritime claims, unless the defendant acknowledged service of the *in rem* proceeding, or otherwise submitted to the jurisdiction unconditionally, whereupon the action became also *in personam*.[50]

(f) In the absence of acknowledgment of service or submission to jurisdiction, the *in rem* proceeding, as far as domestic law was concerned, remained solely *in rem* and no personal jurisdiction over the owner, or the person liable *in personam*, would be created by service.

(g) A court sale by the Admiralty Marshal, consequent to judgment in the action *in rem*, extinguishes all encumbrances on the ship and gives a clean title to the purchaser.

3.5 The nature of the *in rem* claim after *The Indian Grace (No 2)*[51]

3.5.1 The decision

The House of Lords, in *The Indian Grace*, has brought some changes which may have drastically affected some features of the action *in rem*, or *in rem* claim, if the decision is given a wide interpretation.

It was held that the action *in rem* is against the owners of the ship from the

---

49 [1998] 1 Lloyd's Rep 1.
50 *The Nordglimt* [1988] QB 183; *The Maciej Rataj (sub nom The Tatry)* [1992] 2 Lloyd's Rep 552 (CA): after acknowledgment the action continued as a hybrid action, being both *in personam* and *in rem*, but without losing its previous *in rem* character; in *The Anna H* [1995] 1 Lloyd's Rep 11 (CA) the same principle was followed.
51 *The Indian Grace (No 1)* [1993] AC 410, [1993] 1 Lloyd's Rep 387.

moment of service of the writ (now claim form) (see 3.5.1.2 below). The reasoning of this decision is first examined and, then, an attempt is made to explore its consequences and effect on the features of the *in rem* claim, as seen above.

3.5.1.1 Factual background

A cargo of munitions was carried on board the vessel from Sweden to Cochin, India. During the voyage, fire broke out in No 3 hold, necessitating her to divert to the nearest port for inspection. Some shells and charges had to be jettisoned. The remaining cargo was repacked and re-stowed. Some of the boxes of the cargo showed damage but the vessel resumed her voyage and, finally, discharged the cargo at destination on 4 September 1987. The Ministry of Defence, on behalf of the Indian Government, wrote to the defendants claiming a total loss of £2.6 million. Eventually, on 1 September 1988, a claim *in personam* was brought in the Indian court by the Indian Government seeking damages from the owners of the ship only for the undelivered (that is, jettisoned) cargo for £7,000, on the ground of negligence and carelessness of the defendants while the cargo was in transit.

On 25 August 1989 (before judgment in the Indian action), the claimants brought an action *in rem* in England. On 16 December 1989, judgment was delivered in India. On 4 May 1990, *The Indian Endurance*, a sister ship of *The Indian Grace*, was arrested. The owners submitted to the English jurisdiction, provided security for the claim and the ship was allowed to sail. The claimants amended their claim, claiming damages for £2.6 million (in respect of the damaged cargo in hold No 3) on the ground of breach of contract by the owners of the ship in failing to make the ship seaworthy and failure to take reasonable care in the stowage and carriage. The owners pleaded, originally, issue estoppel as a defence, and were later allowed to amend their defence to rely on s 34 (*res judicata*) of the Civil Jurisdiction and Judgments Act (CJJA) 1982. Only s 34 is relevant here.

The judge struck out the English action because the cause of action was the same as that on which the claimants relied when they obtained a judgment in India. Section 34 was an absolute bar to it. The Court of Appeal dismissed an appeal by the claimants. At the House of Lords, it was raised for the first time that the judgment of the Indian Court was not a judgment between the same parties, as the parties in the *in rem* action. Thus, the case was remitted to the judge to determine this issue. Clarke J held that the *in rem* action was against the ship, while the Indian action was *in personam*. Therefore, s 34 did not apply to bar the English *in rem* action. The Court of Appeal reversed this decision on the ground that the owners of the vessel served with the action *in rem* were the same person as the defendants in the Indian action. The owners appealed.

One of the questions for the House of Lords, this time round, was whether a judgment obtained against the owners of the ship in India for shortage of cargo was a bar to the *in rem* claim brought by the claimants in England, by virtue of s 34, which provides that:

> . . . no proceedings may be brought by a person in England and Wales . . . on a cause of action in respect of which a judgment has been given in his favour in proceedings between the same parties, or their privies . . . in a court of an overseas country, unless that judgment is not enforceable or entitled to recognition in England and Wales.

Thus, the issue was whether the action *in personam* in India was between the same parties as the action *in rem* in England for the purpose of s 34.[52]

3.5.1.2 *Ratio decidendi*

It was held that, for the purpose of s 34, an action *in rem* was an action against the owners from the moment the Admiralty Court was seised with jurisdiction. The court was seised, or its jurisdiction was invoked, by the service of the writ, or where the writ was deemed to be served, as a result of acknowledgment of the issue of the writ by the defendant before service. From that moment, the owners were parties to the proceedings *in rem* and s 34 was a bar to the action *in rem*.[53]

3.5.1.3 *The reasons*

Lord Steyn, who delivered judgment, sought support for this conclusion from previous authorities, starting from a historical perspective[54] of the action *in rem*, as follows.

The historical background

During the struggle for power between the common law courts and the High Court of Admiralty, the common law courts effectively blocked the assumption by the High Court of Admiralty of *in personam* jurisdiction. This was done by writs of prohibition, which did not, however, extend to the admiralty jurisdiction over the ship. Admiralty practitioners and judges used the concept that the ship was a defendant in an action *in rem*, as a means of defending and extending the jurisdiction of the High Court of Admiralty. An enlarged view was taken of what constituted a maritime lien. The personification theory flourished. But, this struggle for power was ended by the Judicature Acts (JAs) in 1873–75. Although the ship was still regarded as both the source and limit of liability, the personification theory fell into decline after these Acts. Four reasons contributed to this decline (he said): first, the action *in rem* was permitted in new categories of claims not just maritime liens; second, there was a new procedure introduced in 1883 by which the owners of the vessel were named as defendants. It was easier to regard an action *in rem* as an action against the owners of the vessel. Thus, he said:

> ... the procedural theory stripped away the form and revealed that, in substance, the owners were parties to the action *in rem*.[55]

Third, until the JAs, it was not possible to combine actions *in rem* and *in personam*. Fourth, judges of the Admiralty Court, with its non-common law roots, were more

---

52 *The Indian Grace (No 2)* [1998] 1 Lloyd's Rep 1 (HL). See, also, Chapter 6, para 2.6.2 below.

53 Clarke J, at first instance – who followed Moulton LJ in *The Burns* [1907] P 137 (above): that 'the action *in rem* is against the ship itself' and Hobhouse J, in *The Nordglimt* [1988] QB 183 (above): that 'the action *in rem* is against the ship until the defendant acknowledges service of the proceeding' – held that s 34 was inapplicable because the parties in the two sets of proceedings were different at the inception of the proceedings and before acknowledgment of service.

54 For a more extensive historical perspective, see, also, Chapter 1, above.

55 *The Indian Grace (No 2)* [1998] 1 Lloyd's Rep 1, pp 6, 7.

sympathetic to the personification theory than those trained in the common law. But the breakthrough, Lord Steyn said, came with *The Dictator*[56] and quoted the well-known passage of Sir Francis Jeune, in that:

> ... the action *in rem* ... not only determines the amount of the liability, and in default of payment enforces it on the *res*, but is also a means of *enforcing against the appearing owners, if they could have been made personally liable* in the Admiralty Court, the complete claim of the plaintiff, so far as the owners are liable to meet it. (emphasis added)

Lord Steyn was convinced of the change in the character of the action *in rem* and said:

> ... since *The Dictator*, the law has been that once the owners enter an appearance (or in modern phraseology when they acknowledge issue of the writ) there are two parallel actions: the action *in personam* and the action *in rem*. From that moment the owners are defendants in the action *in personam*.[57]

To complete the historical perspective, he referred to all other cases supporting *The Dictator*. For example, he referred to Scrutton LJ in *The Tervaete*[58] who had affirmed the procedural view, thus:

> ... the action *in rem* was not based upon the wrongdoing of the ship personified as an offender, but was a means of bringing the owner of the ship to meet this personal liability by seizing his property.[59]

Further, he stressed that the Court of Appeal in *The Gemma*[60] endorsed *The Dictator*, which prevailed, despite the support of the personification theory by Moulton LJ in another Court of Appeal case, *The Burns*.[61] In addition, he said the House of Lords, in *The Cristina*,[62] unambiguously rejected the personification theory and adopted the view that, in an action *in rem*, the owners were the defendants.[63]

The sovereign immunity cases

Lord Steyn next relied on the sovereign immunity cases, such as *The Parlement Belge*,[64] *The Cristina*[65] and *The Arantzazu Mendi*,[66] which, he said, established that the sovereign is directly impleaded by the service of the action *in rem* on its vessel. Therefore, the sovereign immunity principle then applied.

---

56 [1892] P 304, p 320.

57 *The Indian Grace (No 2)* [1998] 1 Lloyd's Rep 1, p 7.

58 (1922) 12 LlL Rep 252, p 254.

59 This passage harks back to the maritime attachment which was possible through an action *in personam* mentioned by Wiswall, *op cit*, fn 43.

60 [1899] P 285, p 291.

61 [1907] P 137, p 149.

62 (1938) 60 LlL Rep 147.

63 Lord Steyn qualified the position with regard to maritime liens, to which the procedural theory would not be appropriate; but, since *The Indian Grace* was not concerned with a maritime lien, he put this issue to one side.

64 (1880) 5 PD 197.

65 [1938] AC 485 (HL).

66 (1939) 63 LlL Rep 89.

Recent decisions

Referring to more recent cases, he quoted Lord Brandon, in *The August 8*:[67]

> ... once a defendant in an admiralty action *in rem* has *entered an appearance* in such an action, he has submitted himself personally to the jurisdiction of the court, and *the result of that is that, from then on, the action continues against him not only as an action in rem but also as an action in personam* ... (emphasis added)

Furthermore, in the context of the European Civil Jurisdiction Conventions,[68] he drew support from *The Deichland*,[69] in which the Court of Appeal held that the owner of the vessel who is served with the proceedings *in rem* is 'sued' for the purpose of Art 2 of the Brussels Convention (which is now the Brussels Regulation). In this context, the European Court of Justice (ECJ) had previously ruled in *The Maciej Rataj (sub nom The Tatry)*[70] that an action *in rem* and an action *in personam* involved the same cause of action and the same parties for the purpose of Art 21 of the Brussels Convention 1968.[71]

Against this background, Lord Steyn concluded that, since Art 21 and s 34 had similar wording, it would be curious if one were to give a different meaning in interpreting the words 'between the same parties', which appear in both provisions. He said that, given the decision of the ECJ in *The Tatry*, *The Nordglimt*, on which Clarke J relied, in *The Indian Grace*, at first instance, was no longer good law.

3.5.2 Criticisms of the decision in The Indian Grace (No 2)

While the *ratio decidendi* of this decision does not seem to give rise to any objections, insofar as s 34 is concerned, the reasoning of Lord Steyn's judgment appears to have stripped the action *in rem* from its unique characteristic of being against the ship before the defendant acknowledges service. This involves certain implications with regard to the security aspects of the action *in rem*, as will be seen shortly. It would be sufficient for the purpose of s 34, which was the issue in this case, if Lord Steyn had relied only on judgments that dealt with the application of Art 21 of the Brussels Convention, which has a similar wording to s 34 of CJJA 1982. There was no need to overhaul the action *in rem*, as has been known in domestic English procedural law.[72] However, in practice there have not yet been any problems.

3.5.2.1 The misapplication of the procedural theory decisions

There is no doubt that, despite the origin of the action *in rem*, which was distinct from the old procedure of the maritime attachment (by which the defendant was compelled to appear in court in an action *in personam*), the procedural theory of an

---

67 [1983] 1 Lloyd's Rep 351, p 355.

68 This topic is discussed in Chapter 6 with the relevant cases.

69 [1989] 2 Lloyd's Rep 113.

70 [1995] 1 Lloyd's Rep 302 (ECJ).

71 This is now Art 27 of the Brussels Regulation.

72 See, also, in this respect a critique of *The Indian Grace* by Teare, N (QC), 'The admiralty action *in rem* and the House of Lords', 1998 LMCLQ 33, p 39.

action *in rem*, as developed since the decision of Jeune J in *The Dictator*, prevailed. But the problem arising from *The Indian Grace* does not stem from whether or not the procedural theory applies to *in rem* claims. It stems from the misapplication of the cases that advocated this theory.

All the cases upon which the House of Lords relied in *The Indian Grace* consistently referred to the 'appearance' of the defendant in the action *in rem* as being the trigger of creating a personal jurisdiction against the defendant. It should be noted that the procedure of 'appearance' used in old times has, in modern times, been equated to the procedure of 'acknowledgment' of service, or to acknowledgment of the issue of the proceedings (which would have been a 'deemed' service).

The House of Lords, in *The Indian Grace*, instead of applying the *ratio decidendi* and the *dicta* quoted from those authorities which expressly referred to the 'appearance' of the defendant, replaced the word 'appearance' with 'service' of the writ, or equated the word 'appearance' only with 'acknowledgment of issue of the writ' and not also with acknowledgment of service. While the service of the proceedings may compel the defendant to appear, he has not yet, at that time, taken a step in the proceedings, unless he had already chosen to acknowledge the issue of the proceedings.

The fact that there was a consistent reference in the old decisions to the 'appearance' of the defendant, which was regarded as the incident creating personal jurisdiction over him, is clearly shown from the following extracts of the relevant judgments.

In particular, Smith LJ had pointed out in *The Gemma*[73] that:

> . . . if the defendants had not appeared, and the proceedings had throughout been solely *in rem*, the judgment . . . according to the practice of Admiralty Court, would have been not . . . condemning the defendants . . . but would have condemned the ship alone.

And in *The Beldis*,[74] Sir Boyd Merriman said that:

> It is true that, unless the defendant appears to an action *in rem*, satisfaction of the judgment is limited to the value of the *res*, but if the defendant appears, the action proceeds *in personam*, as well as *in rem*. In such a case, as where the action is brought *in personam* in the first instance, execution can issue against any property of the defendant, including any surplus value of the *res* over and above the amount for which bail has been given.

Moulton LJ, in The Burns,[75] commented on *The Dictator* and *The Gemma* as follows:

> . . . both of them treat the appearance as introducing the characteristics of an action *in personam*. In other words, it is not the institution of suit that makes it a proceeding *in personam*, but the appearance of the defendant.

In the same vein of thinking, Hobhouse J, in *The Nordglimt*,[76] pointed out the time at which the action *in rem* would be enforceable also *in personam*, and said:

---

73 [1899] P 285, p 291.
74 [1936] P 51, pp 75–76.
75 [1907] P 137, p 148.
76 [1987] 2 Lloyd's Rep 470.

Unless and until anyone appears to defend an action *in rem*, the action proceeds solely as an action *in rem* and any judgment given is solely a judgment given against the *res*. It is determinative and conclusive as against all the world in respect of the rights in the *res*, but does not create any rights that are enforceable *in personam*. An action *in rem* may be defended by anyone who has a legitimate interest in resisting the plaintiff's claim on the *res*. Such a person may be the owner of the *res* but, equally, it may be someone who has a different interest in the *res* which does not amount to ownership, or, again, it may be simply someone who also has a claim *in rem* against the *res* and is competing with the plaintiff for a right to the security of a *res* of an inadequate value to satisfy all the claims that are being made upon it . . . Unless and until a person liable *in personam* chooses to defend an action *in rem*, the action *in rem* will not give rise to any determination as against such person or any personal liability on his part, nor will it give rise to any judgment which is enforceable *in personam* against any such person.[77]

Apparently, this was consistent with the authorities on which Lord Steyn relied in *The Indian Grace*, but, nevertheless, Lord Steyn declared that *The Nordglimt* was no longer good law.

There is further force in favour of the argument that the procedural theory was misapplied which derives from the Court of Appeal's decision in *The Aro*,[78] in which Brightman LJ firmly stated:

The service of the writ adds nothing to the status of the claimant vis-à-vis the vessel sued. This is established by the issue of the writ. As between the plaintiff and the defendant, service merely causes time to commence running within which the defendant must enter appearance in order to avoid being a respondent to a motion for judgment by default.[79]

3.5.2.2 *The sovereign immunity cases* [80] *– an inappropriate parallel*

These decisions apply provisions of sovereignty immunity statutes, which aim to protect a foreign sovereign from being compelled to come to this court. Briefly, the statutes provide that neither *in personam* nor *in rem* proceedings are permitted to be issued against a foreign sovereign, if its ships do not trade for commercial purposes. Scrutton LJ had explained, in *The Jupiter*,[81] the position of a foreign sovereign by referring to the old practice of the Admiralty Court:

The appearance of a person interested in property used to be enforced, either by seizing him to make him appear, or by seizing his ship, or by seizing his property other than his ship; but, the object of all the processes of seizing was to make the man appear, so that he might be a personal defendant to the action. *If he did appear, he at once became personally liable to the judgment of the court.* If he did not appear, the court, having given him the opportunity of appearing, might take away his property . . . The foreign government, which does claim a right or interest in the ship, must do one

---

77 [1987] 2 Lloyd's Rep 470, p 482.

78 [1980] 2 WLR 453, p 465, which was not referred to at the hearing of *The Indian Grace*.

79 Ibid, see further Chapter 4, para 3, below.

80 *The Parlement Belge* (1880) 5 PD 197; *The Cristina* (1938) 60 LlL Rep 147; *The Arantzazu Mendi* (1939) 63 LlL Rep 89.

81 [1924] P 236, p 243.

of three things. First, it may appear to defend, but it cannot be compelled to appear; secondly, if it were not to appear and let the action go on, the court might feel able to forfeit the property of a foreign sovereign; thirdly, it can come to the court and say: 'I am not going to discuss what my title is; I say I am a foreign sovereign; I claim a right in this property, and you cannot compel me to come to your court to show you that I have good cause for saying that it is my property.' (emphasis added)

Whether it is the issue of proceedings, or the service upon the foreign sovereign, or the arrest of a ship of a foreign sovereign that impleads it, the foreign immunity cases are not concerned with when the foreign State becomes a party to the *in rem* proceedings. They are concerned with the fact that 'the writ commands an appearance to be entered' and that alone would constitute impleading of the foreign sovereign.[82] In any event, in most cases referred to by Lord Steyn, the 'appearance' of the foreign sovereign, rather than the service of process upon it, was more relevant to the issue of impleading. There is ample evidence of this in this group of decisions, as well as, for example, in the above citation and in the speeches of both Lord Atkin and Lord Wright in *The Cristina*[83] (in which the ship had been arrested). In particular, Lord Atkin said:

> In any case, when they do appear as defendants, and as such I conceive that they are impleaded. And when they cannot be heard to protect their interest unless they appear as defendants, I incline to hold that . . . they are by the very terms of the writ impleaded.

3.5.2.3 Comparing Art 21 of Brussels Convention (now Art 27 of Brussels Regulation)[84] with s 34 of the CJJA 1982

It should be noted that under both the Brussels Convention (before its replacement by the Brussels Regulation) and under English domestic common law, *The Duke Yare*[85] (which is now not good law after Art 30 of the Brussels Regulation), the court was seised in a matter, or invoked, from the moment of service of the proceedings. The fact that the House of Lords held in *The Indian Grace* that the defendant owner, or the person interested in the ship, becomes a party to the *in rem* proceedings from the date of its service seems to have followed this principle. That was also the position previously, as had been held by the Court of Appeal in *The Deichland*.

---

82   *The Cristina* [1938] AC 485 (HL), *per* Lord Wright.

83   [1938] 60 LlL Rep 147, pp 157 and 163.

84   Article 27 of the Brussels Regulation, previously Art 21 of the Brussels Convention, regulates the jurisdiction of the court in cases of *lis pendens* in a court of another Contracting State (see Chapter 6). The proceedings in the court of one State may be *in personam* and in another court the proceeding may be *in rem*, but they must involve the same cause of action and be between the same parties for Art 27 to apply. To determine which of the courts has to decline or stay its proceedings in accordance with Art 27, it has to be ascertained which court was seised first of the matter. Article 30 of the Brussels Regulation provides that a court shall be seised of proceedings when the document instituting such proceedings is lodged with the court. So the time of issue of the proceeding is important. The court seised second of the matter is obliged to stay its proceedings until the jurisdiction of the court first seised is determined. With this change, the issue of when the court is seised in the matter under the Brussels Regulation is at variance with the issue of when the defendant becomes a party to the proceedings under *The Indian Grace*, but these issues may, or may not, be capable of distinction (see para 3.2.2, above).

85   *The Duke Yare* [1991] 2 Lloyd's Rep 557 (CA) and *The Freccia del Nord* [1989] 1 Lloyd's Rep 388.

In *The Deichland*,[86] in which one of the issues was whether the rules of the Brussels Convention applied to actions *in rem* when the court had to determine *lis pendens* under Art 21 of the Brussels Convention, it was explained by Sir Denys Buckley that, before unconditional appearance in the *in rem* proceedings, the defendant did not become liable *in personam*.[87] Neill LJ also said that 'it is Deich who is interested in contesting liability and against whom the plaintiff would wish to proceed *in personam* if an *appearance is entered*' (emphasis added).[88] Only for the purpose of the Convention, was it held that it was impossible to conclude that Deich was not being sued, even though, at that time, the proceedings were solely *in rem*. So, the action *in rem* and the action *in personam* were regarded, for the purpose of Art 21, as being between the same parties from the time of service. However, it was recognised that the action *in rem* had special characteristics, but that its characteristics could not affect the application of the rules of the Brussels Convention. Neill LJ said in this context:

> By English law an admiralty action *in rem* has special characteristics ... I do not consider, however, that the rules relating to such actions and governing the rights of a plaintiff to levy execution can affect the substance of the matter when the court is faced with an international convention designed to regulate the international jurisdiction of national courts.[89]

However, the incident of service, which then caused the jurisdiction of the court to be seised under the Convention, was distinct from the defendant's unconditional submission to jurisdiction, and the service was important to the extent of providing uniform rules under the European Civil Jurisdiction Conventions. Now, under Art 30 of the Brussels Regulation it is the issue of the proceedings that causes the court to be seised of the matter.

Since *The Indian Grace* concerned the application of s 34 of the CJJA 1982, which has similar wording to Art 21 of the Brussels Convention, or to Art 27 of the Brussels Regulation, the principle drawn from this case ought to be limited to what was in issue. Namely, whether an *in rem* action in England or Wales was barred by s 34 after judgment was given *in personam* in favour of the claimant in the foreign court on the ground that, if the respective actions concerned the same cause of action and persons, *res judicata* would apply. In other words, no new trial on the merits would be permitted afresh by an *in rem* action, but *in rem* proceedings for the purpose of obtaining security for the judgment should not be barred. Logically, therefore, the remaining *dicta* in the decision relating to the nature of the *in rem* action, which were not strictly relevant to determining this issue, ought to be disregarded. If this conclusion is not correct, the potential consequences of the decision are analysed below.

3.5.3 *Consequences of* The Indian Grace [90]

It has been trite procedural law that, until *The Indian Grace*, it was the acknowledgment of service of the *in rem* proceedings (or, as was previously known, the

---

86 [1990] 1 QB 361, the Court of Appeal held that the owner of the vessel, which is served with the proceedings *in rem*, is 'sued' for the purpose of s 2 of the CJJA 1982.

87 Ibid, p 389.

88 Ibid, p 373.

89 [1990] 1 QB 361, pp 373–74.

90 Op cit, Teare, fn 72.

'appearance' by the defendant) that rendered the defendant personally involved in the proceedings, so that payment of any unsatisfied balance of the claim over and above the value of the ship could be enforced against him (if he was found liable) by a writ of execution.[91] Seizure of another ship in his fleet (owned by the same company) by the sheriff would be possible only as a means of execution of judgment (CPR, Sched 1, Order 46) which is different from an arrest of the ship by a warrant of arrest. However, becoming personally a defendant in the proceedings was controlled by the defendant if he wished to take a step in the *in rem* action by acknowledging service. Normally, provision of sufficient security with the acknowledgment of service would obviate the exposure of other assets of the defendant to the claimants. The defendant, on the other hand, could choose not to acknowledge service and thus let the *in rem* action proceed in default of his appearance, whereupon it would remain solely an *in rem* action.

If the effect of *The Indian Grace* is that the service of the *in rem* proceedings – regardless of lack of acknowledgment of service or submission to jurisdiction by the defendant – goes beyond the scope of s 34, the following consequences might result, at least in theory.

3.5.3.1 *Has* The Indian Grace *undermined the principle of* The Monica S? *The position of a bona fide purchaser*

It is important to note that *The Monica S* decision was not referred to at the hearing in the House of Lords, although it was at first instance. The long-standing principle of *The Monica S* has been that, by the issue of the *in rem* proceeding, a statutory right *in rem* irrevocably accrues on the ship[92] and the ship can be arrested, even if she has subsequently been transferred to a bona fide purchaser without notice.[93] Since it was held in *The Indian Grace* that the *in rem* action is against the owner of the ship from the time of service, what would happen in the following scenario? A claimant has issued *in rem* proceedings in England but has not obtained security and the ship is not in the jurisdiction to be arrested; he has also issued *in personam* proceedings abroad which progress to obtaining a judgment *in personam* against the defendant. As has been seen, the *in personam* judgment is not of much use to the claimant without security to execute judgment against it. Considering the ruling of *The Indian Grace*, would the claimant (judgment creditor) be allowed to arrest the relevant ship, if it came within the jurisdiction, to execute the foreign judgment obtained against the defendant?

Assuming that the ship is still the property of the defendant, it is submitted that

---

91 See, eg, *The Gemma* [1899] P 285.

92 In a question before the court whether a maritime claimant becomes a secured creditor against the ship from the issue or the service of the writ, vis-à-vis the creditors of the shipowning company, which is faced with winding-up, the Court of Appeal held, unanimously, in *Re Aro Co Ltd* [1979] 2 WLR 150, that, regardless of whether the plaintiffs had invoked the jurisdiction of the Admiralty Court prior to the winding-up, they should be considered as having the status of secured creditors because, after the issue of the writ, they could have served it and could have arrested *The Aro* with the result that the vessel would effectively be encumbered with their claim (see p 85 above) per Brightman LJ in *The Aro* and Chapter 4, para 3, below).

93 This decision was not cited to the court, so the Lords did not put their mind to it.

the answer should be in the affirmative because the claimant, as a judgment creditor, would be seeking to execute judgment against the asset of the defendant. This should not be prevented by *The Indian Grace* ruling because, on the facts of *The Indian Grace*, the claimant arrested the ship after the Indian judgment had been obtained for the purpose of retrying the same issues.

Could the claimant arrest the ship, if – in the meantime – the ship had been transferred to a bona fide purchaser? The answer to this would appear to be more difficult after *The Indian Grace*, since it has been decided that from the time of service of the proceedings the *in rem* action is not against the ship, as a defendant, and the personification theory has been discarded. In this respect, *The Indian Grace* may have undermined the ruling of *The Monica S*. However, since this issue was not before the court in *The Indian Grace*, it would be more logical to conclude, until another decision determines this issue, that the ruling of *The Indian Grace* should be limited to the issue of *res judicata* in cases with the same facts as in *The Indian Grace*.

The Monica S dealt with the accrual of a security interest in the ship from the issue of the *in rem* proceedings, while *The Indian Grace* dealt with personal jurisdiction over the relevant defendant created from the time of service of the *in rem* proceedings for the purpose of *res judicata*. The effect of *The Indian Grace* is to make the previous owner, who would be interested in defending the claim, bound by the proceedings personally[94] from the time of the service.

A risk of arrest of the ship which is bought by an innocent purchaser has always been in existence. Upon service of the proceedings *in rem* on the ship, or upon its arrest, the new owner of the ship does not become personally liable. In practice, he acknowledges service conditionally to contest personal jurisdiction over him on the ground that he was not the person liable *in personam* for the relevant claim under s 21(4) SCA 1981.[95] He could do this, also, before *The Indian Grace*. The claimant, in reality, is after the person liable *in personam* hoping that, if he still exists, some pressure exercised upon him by the buyer will compel him to put up security for the claim through his P&I insurer.

If the seller (person liable for the claim) exists, then the buyer, who will incur expenses by reasons of the arrest, will be able to enforce his remedy for an indemnity or damages under the sale contract (see Chapter 11). If the seller does not exist, the value of the ship should still be the limit of liability for the claims against the ship. In the latter case, the risk for the buyer will be, as always has been, that he will have lost his asset and will be unable to obtain indemnity from the non-existing seller. Well-advised buyers do consider obtaining insurance against such a risk, or a bank guarantee from the seller in the event the ship is encumbered with liens and debts.[96] Obtaining some form of insurance or security for such a risk is very

---

94 In *The Dictator* [1892] PD 304, it was stressed that the action *in rem* was against 'the *appearing owner if he could be made personally liable*' (emphasis added).

95 This conclusion may be inferred from the actual judgment of Lord Steyn in *The Indian Grace (No 2)* [1998] 1 Lloyd's Rep 1 (HL), p 9.

96 See Chapter 11.

important, particularly if the ship is burdened with maritime liens. It could be possible to ascertain whether such debts giving rise to maritime liens exist if a proper investigation of the history of the owners and the trading of the ship was made before the ship is bought. Thus, as a policy issue, it was considered in *The Monica S* that buyers can have means of protection, while maritime claimants may not have; so they should be able to proceed against the ship.

3.5.3.2 *The effect of* **The Indian Grace** *on other assets of the defendant who would be liable* **in personam**

Prior to *The Indian Grace*, if the relevant person, who would be liable *in personam* for the claim, did not acknowledge service of the *in rem* proceeding, or did not submit to jurisdiction unconditionally, judgment obtained in the action would be executed only against the ship arrested and up to the value of that ship.

If the decision in *The Indian Grace* was intended to have a wider application than the issue of *res judicata*, it would certainly affect the extent of liability of owners and demise charterers of the ship in connection with which the claim arose because the *in rem* claim would not just be against the relevant ship but against them *in personam* from the time of service. Other ships in the fleet of the beneficial owner or demise charterer, even if they do not acknowledge service of the *in rem* claim form, may, in theory, be exposed to a risk of execution of judgment. Such a risk always existed before *The Indian Grace*, but only after acknowledgment of service of the *in rem* proceedings, not from the earlier time of the service of such proceedings. In practice, however, the liability is limited by the formation of one-ship companies.

3.5.3.3 *Risk management issues*

In rem proceedings can be served only on the ship and not on the defendant company. If the relevant ship, or a sister ship, was not due to come within the jurisdiction, so as to be served with the *in rem* claim form, it could perhaps be considered by solicitors acting for shipowners or demise charterers not to accept service of the *in rem* claim form. But this could be useful only in limited circumstances in practice.

In most cases, security is provided to a claimant who threatens to serve the *in rem* proceeding when the ship is about to come to the jurisdiction. In the event that the person interested in the ship provides or procures the provision of an undertaking for security of the claim – in consideration of no arrest or re-arrest of the relevant ship or any other ship in the same or associated ownership or management – it may be prudent to include, and in most cases it is included, that any judgment or award obtained will not be enforceable against the person liable for more than the amount given in the undertaking on his behalf, which may be limited to the amount of limitation provided for by the relevant international conventions.

Furthermore, in practice, *The Indian Grace* may not make any difference to personal liability, if the person who would be liable *in personam* did not have any other assets than the ship of the one-ship company.

The decision's possible effect on personal liability is also ameliorated when the person liable constitutes a limitation fund in accordance with the provisions of the

Limitation Convention 1976. Since the fund will be the limit of liability, payment for a claim which has been admitted in the fund will be made pro rata, taking into account other claims. The Convention does not permit other assets of the defendant to be arrested after the establishment of the fund.[97]

3.6 Extent to which the features of the *in rem* action are affected by *The Indian Grace*

Most of the features of the *in rem* action (mentioned under para 3.4, above) should still remain the same. Namely, (i) the *in rem* proceeding is a means of obtaining security for the claim, or judgment, or arbitral award, by arresting the ship; (ii) it gives effect to the inchoate right of a maritime lien, which can be enforced irrespective of who is liable *in personam*; (iii) it creates a security right on the ship from the moment of its issue, particularly in relation to non-truly *in rem* claims, on the assumption that *The Monica S* is not affected by *The Indian Grace*, as discussed earlier; (iv) it establishes jurisdiction on the merits of a case; and (v) sale of the ship by the Admiralty Marshal wipes out all encumbrances or claims on the ship. The decision may, however, have some unintended consequences which are capable of being resolved. In particular:

(a) In theory, the value of the ship will no longer be the limit of liability for the satisfaction of maritime claims, which arose in connection with the ship because, once the *in rem* claim form is served, the action becomes also an action *in personam* from that moment, whether or not the defendant chooses to acknowledge service.

Except in the case of a bona fide buyer of the ship, as explained earlier, personal liability of the owner or demise charterer (that is, the person liable *in personam*) will arise if the value of the ship is not sufficient to satisfy all the claims. However, in practice security is provided for the claim up to a maximum sum (see earlier) and in most cases ships are owned by a single-ship company; that ship may be the only asset of the defendant company.

(b) Although the House of Lords, in *The Indian Grace*, stated that the case before it did not concern maritime liens, nevertheless, it proceeded to support its reasoning by relying on authorities concerned with truly *in rem* claims. The question therefore, is this: could the enforceability of a maritime lien, which by its very nature is enforceable against the *res*, regardless of liability *in personam*, be barred by s 34 when a foreign judgment on liability has been obtained and remains unsatisfied? Although the House of Lords did not have to decide this, it is submitted that the answer would be in the negative for the following reasons:

(i) The old rule of no merger between a judgment *in personam* and proceedings

---

97 Limitation Convention 1976, Art 13(2); see Chapter 17.

in rem was necessary to protect maritime lien claimants,[98] who were concerned to realise their security by arresting the ship if security had not been obtained. For example, in old cases, when a claimant could not recover the fruits of his judgment at common law because the judgment remained unsatisfied, he was permitted to proceed *in rem*. In Dr Lushington's decisions, *The Bengal*[99] (master's wages) and *The John and Mary*[100] (collision case), the issue was one of realising the security attached on the ship, the maritime lien, and not an issue of jurisdiction on the merits, or jurisdiction *in personam*. Thus, it is submitted that the decision has not affected the enforceability of a maritime lien.[101]

(ii) The clear effect of *The Indian Grace*, whether the case is concerned with a claim which attracts a maritime lien or not, is that the person who has obtained a foreign judgment in his favour will be barred from re-litigating the same cause of action afresh through *in rem* proceedings, unless the judgment is not enforceable or entitled to be recognised in England and Wales or, as the case may be, in Northern Ireland. It would follow that, if the claimant has lost in the foreign proceedings, the section will have no application, although the principle of estoppel should operate to prevent a second action.

It is submitted that s 34 should not be a bar to *in rem* proceedings used only for the purpose of obtaining security or executing judgment as opposed to seeking the retrial of the same cause of action. This should be applicable to both truly *in rem* claims and to non-truly *in rem* claims.[102] Such an analysis is strengthened by the fact that, since s 26 of the CJJA 1982 has been in force, assistance is provided to all maritime claimants to arrest a ship to obtain security for the purpose of enforcing a foreign judgment or an arbitration award against that security. In any event, execution of an unsatisfied judgment *in personam*, after its recognition, can be effected by seizure of the defendant's assets by the sheriff.

In conclusion, *The Indian Grace* dealt with the issue of *res judicata* under s 34 of

---

98 The issue whether s 34 of CJJA 1982 has abolished the old rule, namely: 'That an unsatisfied foreign judgment obtained *in personam* is no bar to an action *in rem*, which had been established in cases of maritime liens', was not decided by the House of Lords in *The Indian Grace*. The rule was thought to be ancient and strange and Lord Steyn did not wish to extend it beyond the limits laid down by authority. There was discussion at the hearing that the rule of no merger would be irrelevant in cases of non-maritime liens when the ship has been transferred to a new owner after judgment because, in any event, it would not be possible to establish personal liability for the claim under the SCA 1981, s 21(4). Nigel Meeson, in *Admiralty Jurisdiction and Practice*, 3rd edn, 2003, LLP, discusses (pp 80–82) how *The Indian Grace* has not affected truly *in rem* claims, so a judgment in a claim truly *in rem* is not a bar to a subsequent claim *in personam* and vice versa.

99 (1859) Swab 468.

100 (1859) Swab 471.

101 Briggs, A and Rees, P (eds), in the recent edn of *Civil Jurisdiction and Judgments*, 4th edn, 2005, LLP at p 599 admit that the implications of the analysis of Lord Steyn in *Indian Grace* upon actions *in rem* are difficult to predict. In their previous edn (2002) the authors stated at p 492 that s 34 operates to give a defence to the defendant, unless he can be estopped from relying on this statutory defence.

102 Clarke J, who discussed these issues in *The Indian Grace* [1994] 2 Lloyd's Rep 331, p 351, was of the view that, although the old rule of no merger was developed in maritime lien cases, he could not see any reason why the general principle of permitting a maritime claimant to realise his security by *in rem* proceedings could not apply to non-maritime lien cases.

the CJJA 1982 and was not concerned with the enforcement of maritime liens, or an accrued statutory right *in rem*, or the right of a maritime claimant to obtain security by arresting a ship against which a foreign judgment can be enforced (see further Chapter 4, para 2.5.2).

3.7 Conclusion

It is submitted that the judgment in *The Indian Grace* has a limited application. This can be derived from the conclusion of the judgment, in which Lord Steyn stated:

> ... it is now possible to say that, for the purpose of s 34, an action *in rem* is an action against the owners from the moment the Admiralty Court is seised with jurisdiction.[103]

It is further submitted that, in the context of the issues involved in this case, no broad principle can be drawn from it.

In summary, it is suggested that the following proposals may iron out the difficulties created by this decision.

(a) The service of the *in rem* claim form creates a personal jurisdiction against the person who is interested to defend the claim on the merits, such as the owner or the demise charterer of the relevant ship, but it does not affect the security aspects of the *in rem* proceeding.

(b) As regards a bona fide purchaser of a ship, service of the *in rem* claim form does not create a personal jurisdiction over him because he is not the person liable for the claim. With regard to the enforcement of the security attached on the ship from the moment of the issue of the *in rem* proceeding and prior to the purchase of the ship by him, it is submitted that the claim should remain solely *in rem*, for this purpose, if another form of security has not been obtained.

(c) The point of service of *in rem* proceedings is only relevant to the res judicata issue. Thus, the defence of s 34 should not be a bar to *in rem* proceedings (whether they are concerned with truly or non-truly *in rem* claims), if they are brought only for the purpose of obtaining security, or realising the security attached on the ship (that is, maritime liens and crystallised rights *in rem*), unless sufficient security has already been obtained (see Chapter 4). It should be remembered that the claimants in *The Indian Grace* commenced the *in rem* proceedings in the Admiralty Court to re-litigate the same issues after their determination by the foreign court. On the very same issues, the claimants were, in fact, claiming higher damages than they had been awarded by the Indian judgment.

---

103 *The Indian Grace (No 2)* [1998] 1 Lloyd's Rep 1 (HL), p 10.

4 THE RELEVANT CONDITIONS OF BRINGING *IN REM* CLAIMS

Maritime claims, or rights of claim *in rem*, have been divided into two categories in s 21 of the Supreme Court Act 1981, which is the instrument entitling claimants to enforce their claims; different rules apply to each category for the purpose of arresting a ship in connection with which a claim arose:

(a) The first category includes claims which, in themselves, are regarded as having proprietary characteristics, 'the truly *in rem*' claims. These are: maritime liens (eg the damage lien, the salvage lien, the seamen's wages lien); those which are relevant to rights of owners or mortgagees of a ship; and those concerned with forfeiture of a ship and droits of admiralty (s 20(2)(a), (b), (c), (s));

(b) The second category encompasses all other maritime claims, or statutory rights *in rem*, which are labelled for the purpose of this book as 'non-truly *in rem*' claims.

4.1 No conditions are required to enforce truly *in rem* claims

By ss 21(2) and (3) of the SCA 1981, an action *in rem* can be brought against the ship without considering who is the owner of the ship at the time the claim form is issued, or who would be liable *in personam* when the cause of action arose. So, it is said that these claims are truly *in rem* because they arise and are enforced irrespective of ownership or personal liability criteria. They are proprietary rights attached on the relevant ship from the moment of their creation.

It will be seen that maritime liens (eg the damage lien, the salvage lien, the seamen's wages lien) are also enforceable under s 21(4), as they are statutory rights *in rem* like all maritime claims, and this usually causes confusion among students because they are included in the list of the non-truly *in rem* claims for the enforcement of which certain conditions are required.

4.2 Conditions for enforcement of non-truly *in rem* claims

In contrast with the truly *in rem* claims, for a claimant to enforce a non-truly *in rem* claim there has to be a personal liability link (s. 21(4)(b)), as well as an ownership link between the person liable and the relevant ship (s 21(4)(b) (i)(ii)).

4.2.1 In personam *link between the claim and the defendant when the cause of action arose*

An *in rem* claim form regarding claims which are listed in paras (e)–(r) of s 20(2) may be brought under s 21(4) of the SCA 1981 where:

(a) the claim arises in connection with a ship; and

(b) the person who would be liable on an action *in personam* (the relevant person) was, when the cause of action arose, the owner or charterer or person in possession or in control of, the ship.

It should be observed that the statutory rights under s 20(2) paras (e), (j) and (o) are also maritime liens enforceable under s 21(3), but for the purpose of s 21(4) they are treated as statutory rights *in rem*.

Section 21(4)(b) requires that, for claims arising from paras (e)–(r) of s 20(2), the claimant must identify first who would be liable *in personam*, if he were sued *in personam*. That person may have been either the owner, or charterer, or the person in possession or control of the ship *when the cause of action arose*.

'Owner' means the registered owner. Lord Donaldson decided, in *The Evpo Agnic*,[104] that, on a true construction, the word in s 21(4)(b), which refers simply to 'owners', is to be contrasted with 'beneficial owner' in sub-paras (i) and (ii) (see para 4.2.2 below). The Arrest Convention 1952 looks to ownership and registered ownership as one and the same. Registered owners appear in the registers of shipping, they are nominal owners, but in real commercial life, registered owners can be both legal and beneficial owners of all the shares in the ship:

> . . . in real commercial life . . . registered owners, even in one-ship companies, are not bare legal owners. They are both legal and beneficial owners of all the shares in the ship and any division between legal and equitable interests occurs in relation to the registered owner itself, which is almost always a juridical person. The legal property in its shares may well be held by A and the equitable property by B, but this does not affect the ownership of the ship, or of the shares in that ship. They are the legal and equitable property of the company.[105]

'Charterer' was then thought by Lord Donaldson, in the same case, to refer only to the demise charterer. However, later decisions contradicted him, and the prevailing judicial view is that 'charterer' can include either a charterer by demise, or time, or even a voyage charterer. This is derived from a true construction of the statute, in that, if the intention was to be restricted to the demise charterer only, the statute would have spelled that out.

The Permina [106]

By a time charterparty, *The Ibnu* was chartered by the appellants (charterers) and the charter hire was to be paid monthly. The respondents (owners) contended that the appellants had failed to pay hire due and, therefore, arrested the charterers' vessel *The Permina*. The charterers applied to set aside the writ and the warrant of arrest on the ground that the claim asserted in relation to the charter of *The Ibnu* had no connection with *The Permina* and that the word 'charterer' meant charterer by demise. At first instance, in Singapore, their motion was dismissed and the

---

104 [1988] 2 Lloyd's Rep 411 (CA).

105 Ibid, p 415; see, also, *Haji-Ioannou v Frangos* [1999] 2 Lloyd's Rep 337, that ownership of a ship for the purpose of the admiralty jurisdiction means legal ownership, except in those provisions where the word is qualified by the adjective 'beneficial'; *The Tian Sheng* [2000] 2 Lloyd's Rep 430 (HK Court of Final Appeal), in which it was explained that, in the general run of things, registration would be virtually conclusive, unless there was a fraudulent procurement of registration.

106 [1978] 1 Lloyd's Rep 311 (Singapore CA).

charterers appealed. They lost on appeal in which it was held that the ordinary meaning of the word 'charterer' did not mean only 'by demise'. If the legislature had intended to limit the operation of the sub-section to charterers by demise only, it would have expressly added those words.

This was affirmed by the English Court of Appeal in the following case.

The Span Terza [107]

The owners of the ship N issued a writ *in rem* and applied for a warrant of arrest against the vessel S, belonging to the time charterers. The application was made in respect of their claim to damages pursuant to a breach of the time charter of the ship N by the charterers. The application was turned down by the High Court, but on appeal to the Court of Appeal, the arrest was allowed. In the reasoning of the Court of Appeal, 'charterer' in that provision must include 'time charterer'. If it was meant to be construed only as a 'demise charterer', then the word 'demise' would have been inserted. Alternatively, the word 'charterer' could have been omitted and 'a person in possession or control of the ship' would have automatically included a demise charterer. Therefore, 'charterer' must be taken to mean both demise and time charterers and the time charterers' ship could be arrested for the claim against both.

It is now clear that 'charterer' includes even a voyage charterer, as has recently been decided in **The Tychy**,[108] with regard to a slot charterer, in which Clarke LJ said:

> ... the purpose of the 1981 Act was to ensure that, before a person's ship could be arrested in respect of a maritime claim, that person had some relationship with the ship in connection with which the maritime claim arose; there was no reason, in principle, why a time or a voyage charterer of the ship should not have been regarded as having a sufficient relationship and no reason to narrow the scope of that relationship by giving the words of s 21(4) other than their ordinary and natural meaning; and, in the case of a sister ship, the ship being arrested must be wholly beneficially owned by the person liable *in personam*; the expression 'the charterer' in s 21(4) was not confined to a demise charterer. If a charterer included a time charterer, it must include a voyage charterer; and it included a voyage charterer of part of a ship.'

'Person in possession or control' refers to a person in the position of a demise charterer. Such a person could be a manager and operator of the ship (see Ch 8), or a salvor (see Ch 13), or a mortgagee who has taken over the possession and manage-ment of the ship from the owner in the event of default of the loan conditions (see Ch 9).

The liability must have arisen when the owner or charterer or the person in possession or in control of the ship had that status at that particular time. Rix J said in *The Fajal*[109] that the words of the statute require looking at the status of the relevant person at the relevant time, namely when the cause of action arose.

---

107 [1982] 1 Lloyd's Rep 225 (CA).
108 [1999] 2 Lloyd's Rep 11 (CA).
109 [2000] 1 Lloyd's Rep 473.

4.2.2 Ownership criteria when the action is brought

After the identification of the relevant person as per s 21(4)(b), the section further provides that the action may be brought against:

(i)   *that* ship, if at the time when the action is brought the relevant person is either the beneficial owner of that ship as respects all the shares in it or the charterer of it under a charter by demise; or

(ii) *any other ship* of which, at the time when the action is brought, the relevant person is the beneficial owner as respects all the shares in it.

The expression *'or the charterer of it under a charter by demise'*, under (i) above, was not in s 3(4) of the AJA 1956, but it was added to s 21(4) of the 1981 Act.

4.2.2.1 Beneficial ownership and arrest of the relevant ship or a sister ship

Arrest of the relevant ship:

To recapitulate, for the purpose of arresting the ship in connection with which the claim arose, s 21(4) of the SCA 1981 requires that the arresting claimant must identify first the relevant person who would be liable *in personam when the cause of action arose*. That person can be either the owner, or the charterer, or the person in possession or control of the ship in connection with which the claim arose as discussed earlier. The same section also requires that, at the time *of issuing the claim form in rem* for the arrest of *that* ship, the relevant person must still be either the beneficial owner in respect of all shares in the ship,[110] or the demise charterer of the ship. For example, the person liable may have been the demise charterer, who is still the demise charterer of that ship, or may have been another charterer, who, by this time, has become the demise charterer.

Arrest of any other ship:

If the ship to be arrested is other than the ship in connection with which the claim arose, the relevant person must be the beneficial owner of *that other ship* (which may be either a 'sister ship' – meaning a ship owned by the same company which owns the ship in connection with which the claim arose – or a ship beneficially owned by the demise charterer of the relevant ship, or a ship beneficially owned by any of the other persons who would be liable in personam, as per s 21(4)(b), at the time of issuing the proceedings. For example, if the person who would be liable when the cause of action arose is not the owner of the relevant ship but the demise charterer, or another charterer, or a salvor, and it is not possible to arrest the ship in connection with which the claim arose (if, for example, she was lost after a collision incident), any ship beneficially owned by the demise charterer or another charterer, or the salvor, would be a target for arrest under s 21(4)(ii).

It is important to remember that when a ship other than the one in connection with which the claim arose is to be arrested, that other ship must be, at the time of issuing the writ, beneficially owned in all shares by the relevant person who was

---

110 In *The Afala* [1995] 2 Lloyd's Rep 286, the arrest of the ship, which had by agreement been sold to a third party although physical delivery had not yet taken place, was inept.

identified as the person who would be liable *in personam*. Since s 21(4) covers claims within paras (e)–(r), maritime liens can also be enforced this way. So, a sister ship can be arrested, but the maritime lien will obviously be lost because it only attaches on the ship in connection with which it arose. By contrast, there can be no sister ship arrest for claims in relation to ownership rights, or mortgages, or forfeiture (s 20(2)(a), (b), (c) and (r)), which are enforced only as provided by s 21(2).

Ownership under English law includes rights of exclusive enjoyment, destruction and alienation.[111] While 'owner' refers to the registered owner of the ship, and charterer includes also time and voyage charterers, beneficial ownership, which is not a term included in the Arrest Convention 1952, was originally thought to include the person in possession or control of the ship. This had been decided in the following case, which, however, is not now followed, but it is worth mentioning to illustrate the point.

The Andrea Ursula[112]

This case concerned the meaning of the expression 'beneficially owned', as used in s 3(4) of the AJA 1956 which stated 'beneficially owned as respects all the shares therein'. The issue was whether the phrase 'beneficial owner' was wide enough to include a demise charterer. Repairs had been carried out on the vessel under the instructions of the demise charterers and prospective owners of the vessel. Upon repudiation of the contract for repairs by the demise charterers, the repairs remained uncompleted and the plaintiffs, the shiprepairers, accepted the repudiation. Exercising their right of a possessory lien for unpaid costs, they detained the vessel and started *in rem* proceedings. At the time of issue of the writ, the defendants were still the demise charterers of the vessel, but had not yet bought the ship. The question for the court was whether the requirements of s 3(4) of the Act had been satisfied. This Act did not include 'demise charterer', as the present Act does under s 21(4)(i) in the requirements for arrest. In deciding whether the court had jurisdiction to entertain the action *in rem* for this claim, Brandon J held:

> There is no definition in the Act of the expression 'beneficially owned' as used in s 3(4). It could mean owned by someone who, whether he is the legal owner or not, is in any case the equitable owner. That would cover both the case of a ship, the legal and equitable title to which are in one person, A, and also the case of a ship, the legal title to which is in one person, A, but the equitable title to which is in another person, B. In the first case, the ship would be beneficially owned by A, and in the second case by B. Trusts of ships, express or implied, are, however, rare and the words seem to me to be capable also of a different and more practical meaning related not to title, legal or equitable, but to lawful possession and control with the use and benefit which are derived from them. If that meaning were right, a ship would be beneficially owned by a person who, whether he was the legal or equitable owner or not, lawfully had full possession and control of her, and, by virtue of such possession and control, had all the benefit and use of her which a legal owner would ordinarily have.[113]

---

111 *Halsbury's Laws*, 4th edn, Vol 35, para 1227.
112 [1973] QB 265, [1971] 1 Lloyd's Rep 145.
113 [1973] QB 265, p 269, [1971] 1 Lloyd's Rep 145, p 147.

It was held that 'beneficially owned' could, thus, include a demise charter, but a different view was held by Goff J, in the following case, the definition of which has been widely accepted. The issue was whether the operator or manager of a ship was a beneficial owner.

Congresso del Partido[114]

Goff J said:

> In my judgment, the natural and ordinary meaning of these words is that they refer only to such ownership as is vested in a person who, whether or not he is the legal owner of the vessel, is in any case the equitable owner ... Furthermore, on the natural and ordinary meaning of the words, I do not consider them apt to apply to the case of a demise charterer or indeed any other person who has only possession of the ship, however full and complete such possession may be, and however much control over the ship he may have ... such words are only appropriate when describing ownership in the ordinary sense of the word, and not possession which is concerned with a physical relationship with the vessel founded on control and has nothing to do with shares in the vessel. A demise charterer had, within limits defined by contract, the beneficial use of the ship, he does not however have the beneficial ownership as respects all the shares in the ship.

In *The Father Thames*,[115] the above definition was adopted.

The vessel was under a demise charter for a period of two years to B Ltd, and the owners had completely divested themselves of all control and possession of the vessel. During the demise charter, the ship collided with another. After the collision, the benefit and liabilities of the demise charter were assigned to P Ltd. A writ *in rem* was issued and *The Father Thames* was arrested. The owners claimed that there was no jurisdiction to proceed against their vessel because, at the time the cause of action arose (the collision), they were not liable for the negligent navigation and damage done. Under a demise charter, the crew were employees of the demise charterer. The problem was that the 1956 Act did not provide, as the present Act does, for the alternative requirement that the person who would be liable *in personam* could be the demise charterer when the writ was issued. The owners urged the court to follow the decision of Justice Brandon, in *The Andrea Ursula*, in that a beneficial owner included a demise charterer. On the facts of *The Father Thames*, however, the demise charterer was no longer the demise charterer when the writ was issued. It was held that 'beneficially owned' did not apply to a demise charterer; the decision in *Congresso del Partido* was followed. Nevertheless, although the person who would be liable *in personam* was not the beneficial owner of the ship, the writ *in rem* was not set aside because a maritime lien (having arisen due to the collision damage) had attached on the ship from the time of the incident.

As was seen earlier, for the arrest of the ship concerning claims under s 20(2)(a)–(c) and (s), and those attracting maritime liens, there is no need to identify the person who would be personally liable, nor to consider ownership criteria at any time (s 21(2) and (3)). The same applied under s 3(2) and (3) of the 1956 Act. The

---

114 [1978] 1 All ER 1169, pp 1201–02.
115 [1979] 2 Lloyd's Rep 364.

change brought by the 1981 Act is under s 21(4), in which the term 'charterer by demise' has been added, and this is relevant only to those *in rem* claims which are not maritime liens. The demise charterer must still be in that capacity when the action is brought.

A question may sometimes arise as to whether the demise charter had already been terminated at the time of issue of the proceedings. This was an issue in a decision of the New Zealand High Court of Admiralty in **Rangiora, Ranginui and Takitimu.**[116] These three ships were owned by Deil shipowners and were chartered by demise to South Pacific Shipping (SPS) in 1995. Due to outstanding areas of hire, the owners decided to terminate the charter arrangements and formal notices to that effect were given by Deil to SPS on approximately 16.00 hours, on 18 February 1998. The next day, a shareholders' resolution for voluntary winding up of SPS was passed. On 20 February, a stevedoring company commenced proceedings *in rem* against the vessel *Ranginui* for monies owed to it by SPS with regard to services rendered during the time of the demise charter. On the same day, Mobil Oil New Zealand commenced *in rem* proceedings against the *Rangiora*. The owners of the ships applied to set aside the proceedings, on the ground that the person who would be liable *in personam*, SPS, were no longer the demise charterers at the time the proceedings were issued. The claimants argued that the notices of termination of the charter did not have an immediate effect, but were notices of future intention, and that, in accordance with the construction of the charterparties, the charters were still in existence. So, SPS were still the demise charterers at the date of the issue of the writ. The court decided that the contractual status remained on foot until the owners took steps to proclaim recovery of possession of the ships from the charterers. Under German law, which applied to the contracts, a demise charter is brought to an end upon physical delivery. The owners' application was dismissed.

An interesting example of a company structure by which the arrest of the ship was successfully evaded, by the creation of various company structures to distance the beneficial owner or demise charterer from the claim, can be observed in a decision of the highest appellate Court of Hong Kong in **The Tian Sheng (No 8).**[117]

The owners (TSI) had chartered this ship by demise to T&R, who, in turn, chartered her on a time charter to Tiansheng Ocean, who were the carriers of the cargo and, on their behalf, the bill of lading was signed. The ship deviated and the cargo was sold by court order. The ship was sold to a company IRI before the issue of the writ by the cargo-owners who claimed damages for loss of their cargo carried on board. The ship, whose name was changed to *Resourse I*, was arrested and her new owners contested jurisdiction having obtained her release by putting up bail. Both the judge and the Court of Appeal (HK), suspecting that the documents were fabricated to disguise the real ownership of the person liable *in personam*, Ocean, held that the arrest was valid. The highest appeal Court of Hong Kong reversed the decision because neither the owner nor the demise charterer was the person liable

---

116 [2000] 1 Lloyd's Rep 36.
117 [2000] 2 Lloyd's Rep 430.

when the cause of action arose. So, when the writ was issued in Hong Kong, the person who would be liable was neither the beneficial owner, nor the charterer by demise of the ship for it to be arrested.

The facts of this case, as indeed of other cases involving a series of charterparties and the creation of companies, in order to distance the owner and the demise charterer from direct contractual arrangements with cargo-owners, may give cause for one to 'raise eyebrows'. However, since the company structure, in the eyes of the law, shields the person who would really be liable *in personam*, the decision is within the bounds of the law. Whether or not the court may order the lifting of the corporate veil for evidence to be adduced, or even order piercing of the corporate veil, will be seen later.

As discussed earlier, 'beneficially owned' refers to equitable ownership, whether or not accompanied by legal ownership. 'Equitable ownership' is meant to cover an owner for whose benefit the legal owner holds the shares in the ship under the English law concept of trust. Thus, the adjective 'beneficial' before owner ensures that, if the ship is operated under the cloak of trust, she can still be arrested for maritime claims. The commercial reality is that registered owners of ships are not just legal owners of bearer shares. They are both legal and beneficial owners of all shares in the ship. Any division between the legal and equitable interest in the ship occurs in relation to the registered ownership itself. For example, the legal property in the shares may be held by A and the equitable by B.

It is interesting to note from a recent decision of the court in Hong Kong, *Liberty Container and Mandarin Container*,[118] that, where a ship-owning company was liquidated, there was no change of equitable ownership so as to deprive the Admiralty Court of jurisdiction over the claim *in rem*.

4.2.2.2 *Minority shareholding in a ship not sufficient for the purpose of arrest*

For the purpose of arrest, it is not enough that the beneficial owner owns a fraction of 64 shares in the ship and not all of them. This was confirmed by the Federal Court of Canada in the following case.

The Looiersgracht[119]

This ship was arrested in respect of maritime claims, which arose in connection with her and five other vessels, which were believed to be her sister ships. The defendants claimed that security to be posted should not include security for alleged damage to cargo carried on the other five vessels, as they did not beneficially own all the shares therein. From the Lloyd's Register of Shipping, it was clear that the defendants were managing agents for many vessels and had minority ownership of some of them. Most of the vessels were owned by either one or more limited partnerships. The plaintiffs alleged that there was a common ownership based on the management of the fleet by the defendants, and, also on the part-ownership of the defendants in the shares of the ships. The defendants admitted

---

118 [2006] 2 Lloyd's Rep 556.
119 [1995] 2 Lloyd's Rep 411.

minority ownership interest in some of them, but maintained that each vessel-owning limited partnership was made up of a different group of participants. Canada is not a signatory to the 1952 Arrest Convention. It has, however, enacted parallel legislation, the Federal Court Act 1992, which is similar to the English statute, save for no reference to all shares in the ship with regard to beneficial ownership. The trial judge of the Canadian Federal Court, Hargrave J, stated:

> Under our legislation, it is not sufficient to show merely some beneficial interest. Our legislation requires that the sistership be 'beneficially owned by the person who is the owner of the ship that is subject of the action'. To come within the Canadian sister ship provisions, there must be common complete ownership of both vessels by the same owner or owners, for that is the plain and ordinary meaning of our legislation. It is not enough to be an owner, but rather it must be the owner, that is a similar complete ownership of both vessels.[120]

The judge also held that this was an instance in which a series of one-ship companies were not a sham to defeat legislation, but had been established for legitimate reasons.

4.2.2.3 Corporate veil and the beneficial owner

Under an old English authority, *Salomon v A Salomon & Co Ltd*,[121] the concept of legal personality given to a corporation means that, no matter who the shareholders are, the company is a separate person owning its own assets. Thus, creditors of the company cannot go behind the corporate veil to pursue the shareholders and persons controlling the company, or its subsidiaries, for liabilities of the company, unless there are special circumstances which indicate a mere façade concealing the true facts.[122]

The Court of Appeal, in *Adams v Cape Industries* (see below), delineated the circumstances that would constitute a façade. It gave guidelines that the court could make an order to pierce the corporate veil when a defendant had attempted by the device of a corporate structure to evade: (i) limitations imposed on his conduct by law; and (ii) such rights of relief against him as third parties already possess, but not rights that may be acquired in the future. But the veil would not be pierced, even if it was necessary to achieve justice.[123] This principle has prevailed ever since the *Salomon* case and there has been recognition of the separate legal identity of companies within a group.

Adams v Cape Industries[124]

Cape was the parent company in the case. It owned four subsidiary companies, Capaso, NAAC, E and Casap, for its mining and marketing activities for the USA and worldwide. One of its subsidiaries owned the asbestos mines from which came the asbestos dust used by its customers. One such customer was PCC, which purchased the asbestos and used it in its factory for 10 years, until the factory closed.

---

120 Ibid, p 415.
121 [1897] AC 22 (HL).
122 *Woolfson v Strathclyde RC* 1978 SLT 159 (HL).
123 *In re Company* [1985] 1 BCC 99.
124 [1991] 1 All ER 929.

People later became aware of the long-term damage caused by the use of asbestos and personal injury claims began to mount in court, from 1974 to 1979, by both factory workers and those who lived in the neighbourhood of the factory. Cape and her subsidiaries were defendants in the action, as it was alleged that they had been responsible for the supply of the asbestos used in the factory. The allegation against them was that, notwithstanding their knowledge about the dangers of asbestos, they failed to give adequate warning. It was alleged that this amounted to negligent acts and omissions and breaches of implied and express warranties. Judgment in default was entered in the action against Cape and her subsidiary Capaso in September 1983, in Texas. Capaso was the subsidiary which organised the sale of asbestos worldwide, to those who used it for industrial purposes. Both Cape and Capaso had been incorporated in the UK and some of the plaintiffs sought to enforce the judgments, entered against these defendants, in this country. At the trial for enforcement, the question was whether the foreign court, in Texas, had jurisdiction to give a judgment which was sought to be enforced in the UK. After the first set of proceedings had been heard in the US, the subsidiary NAAC was wound up and another subsidiary, AMC, was formed to continue trade in the USA. Another company, CPC, was to act as agent for AMC. The plaintiffs claimed that, although the defendants were incorporated in the UK, they were residents in the USA, at the time of the commencement of the proceedings. The presence of any of Cape's subsidiaries incorporated in the USA was sufficient to give the US court jurisdiction. The trial judge rejected this submission and the plaintiffs appealed. The plaintiffs claimed that Cape/Capaso and NAAC constituted one single commercial unit. Therefore, in relation to AMC and her agent CPC, the corporate veil should be pierced, so that their presence in the USA could also be treated as the presence of Cape and Capaso. The Court of Appeal re-emphasised the doctrine that every company is a separate legal person that cannot be identified with its members. Slade LJ stated:

> Our law, for better or worse, recognises the creation of subsidiary companies, which, though in one sense are the creatures of their parent companies, will nevertheless under the general law fall to be treated as separate legal entities with all the rights and liabilities which would normally attach to separate legal entities. In deciding whether a company is present in a foreign country by a subsidiary, which is itself present in that country, the court is entitled, indeed bound, to investigate that relationship between the parent and the subsidiary. In particular, that relationship may be relevant in determining whether the subsidiary was acting as the parent's agent and, if so, on what terms . . . However, there is no presumption of any such agency. There is no presumption that the subsidiary is the parent company's alter ego . . . If a company chooses to arrange the affairs of its group in such a way that the business carried on in a particular foreign country is the business of its subsidiary and not its own, it is, in our judgment, entitled to do so. Neither in this class of case, nor in any other class of case, is it open to this court to disregard the principle of *Salomon v A Salomon & Co Ltd*, merely because it considers it just so to do.[125]

This is of great significance to shipping companies. As has been seen earlier, the registered owner of a ship is a company which is the legal owner of the asset, the

---

125 [1991] 1 All ER 929, pp 1019–20.

ship, regardless of who is the real owner, the person or persons controlling the company. That company may own more than one ship, but this is not common.

The veil of one-ship companies

It is legitimate in shipping to arrange ownership of ships in the fleet by a series of one-ship companies, which may be sister companies, or a parent company with various subsidiaries, to protect the assets from various claimants. Following the principle of *Salomon v Salomon*, it is not permitted to seek an order from the court to lift or pierce the corporate veil of the company in order to find the real (beneficial) owner of the assets.

The courts have held that it is not permissible to pierce the corporate veil unless there is evidence of a sham transfer of the legal ownership of the ship. For this purpose, the court may order evidence to be produced, in certain circumstances, to investigate the beneficial ownership by lifting the veil in order to determine whether there has been a sham transfer.[126] If there is proof of a sham transfer, the court will order the piercing of the veil. However, it is legitimate for shipowners to arrange their affairs by running a series of one-ship companies as a group and cause them to use their individual assets to their mutual advantage. There is no reason why they should not do so without any risk of the arrangement being held to be a sham.[127]

The Evpo Agnic [128]

The plaintiffs were the cargo-owners of cargo laden on board the vessel *The Skipper*, which sank. They issued a writ *in rem* against 'the owners of that ship, or the ship *The Evpo Agnic*', for breach of duty in loading and handling of their cargo. *The Evpo Agnic* was owned by a separate company from that which owned *The Skipper*, but both companies were owned and controlled by the same shareholder and president, Mr Pothitos. According to the plaintiffs, the owners of the vessel *The Evpo Agnic* were, at all times, the owners of the vessel *The Skipper*. The defendants moved to set aside the writ *in rem* and the warrant for the arrest of *The Evpo Agnic*. Sheen J, in the lower court, ordered the defendants to disclose all documents relating to the ownership of both vessels. The defendants appealed against this order on the basis that the two vessels were owned by two separate 'one-ship' companies. It was held that there was no evidence that the holding company of the two sister companies was the beneficial owner of all the shares in *The Evpo Agnic* or her demise charter. Lord Donaldson MR refused to pierce the corporate veil and defined owner to mean the registered owner with no rights on the assets of a sister company. He said:

> I would be most reluctant to interfere with the exercise of judicial discretion in an admiralty action by a judge of the experience of Sheen J and there can be no doubt that discovery can be ordered, if there is any real indication that this may uncover a situation which will confirm, or for that matter negative, the court's jurisdiction. But,

---

126 See *The Aventicum* [1978] 1 Lloyd's Rep 184.
127 Lord Donaldson in *The Evpo Agnic* [1988] 2 Lloyd's Rep 411.
128 Ibid.

there has to be some real indication that further facts may exist which will affect the issue.[129]

Unlike flexible jurisdictions on arrest of ships, such as South Africa and probably France, under English law and in those jurisdictions which follow it (for example, Hong Kong) the controlling shareholders of two sister companies, each owning one ship, will not be sufficient evidence to pierce the corporate veil of a legitimate one-ship company for the purpose of arresting the asset belonging to the other sister company, unless there is fraud. Mr Pothitos' companies were legitimate, said Lord Donaldson, and he was not regarded the beneficial owner of the ships owned by the separate corporate structures.

It should be noted that in shipping it is not uncommon, before a claim has arisen, or a claim form has been issued, for a ship owned by one company to be transferred bona fide to another company (both of which are controlled by the same person). In such a case, the requirements of s 21(4) of the SCA 1981 will not be satisfied for an arrest of that ship to be effectively made. If, however, such a transfer is made to avoid the arrest of the ship when claims are anticipated or have arisen, the court may order evidence to be adduced to examine whether or not the corporate veil should be pierced.

Lifting the corporate veil

The courts are, sometimes, prepared to look behind the corporate veil (which is known as 'lifting the veil' to peep behind it), in order to determine whether there is a genuine link between corporate structures. The investigation may reveal that the corporate veil ought to be pierced in order to treat the liabilities of the relevant company as the liabilities of its shareholders or directors.[130]

Staughton LJ said in *The Coral Rose*[131] that, like all metaphors, the corporate veil can sometimes obscure reasoning rather than elucidate it. He explained, relying on the *Adams* case, that there were two senses in which the phrase is used and which needed to be distinguished:

> To pierce the corporate veil is an expression that I would reserve for treating the rights or liabilities or activities of a company as the rights or liabilities or activities of its shareholders. To lift the corporate veil or look behind it, on the other hand, should mean to have regard to the shareholding in a company for some legal purpose.

Thus the court may order evidence to be adduced for this purpose as is shown in the following cases.

The Kommunar (No 2)[132]

The plaintiffs applied for the appraisement and sale of the vessel K, which they had earlier arrested for reimbursement of sums owed to them with regard to services for

---

129 Ibid, p 415.
130 It seems that the distinction between 'lifting' and 'piercing' the corporate veil was made by Slade LJ in *Adams v Cape Industries* [1991] 1 All ER 929.
131 [1991] 1 Lloyd's Rep 563, p 571 (concerning a Mareva injunction).
132 [1997] 1 Lloyd's Rep 8.

the supply of goods and materials to the ship.[133] The services were provided to various Russian fishing vessels, which at the time were managed by an entity called POL. This entity was a State enterprise under the control of the Russian Ministry of Fisheries through the medium of another State enterprise, S. S had arranged for the plaintiffs to provide agency services to these vessels in Central and South America. POL was privatised in 1993 and became a public joint stock company limited by shares. It was no longer an emanation of the Ministry and it was renamed AOL. The plaintiffs, thus, alleged that AOL had taken over the debts of POL, including the debt owed to the plaintiffs. AOL applied for the arrest to be set aside on the grounds that, at the time the cause of action arose, they were not the owners, or charterers, nor in possession or control of the ship. They also submitted that, although they owned the vessel K, they were not the same legal person as POL. It was held that once there was discontinuity of legal personality, no amount of statutory transfer of assets or liabilities by means of legal succession could satisfy the provisions of s 21(4) of the SCA 1981. Colman J held that the wording of the legislation dealing with privatisation was significantly more consistent with discontinuity of legal personality than with continuity. Also, the kind of legal entity created in AOL differed fundamentally from the kind that existed up to that time. The creation of a joint stock company out of an unincorporated State enterprise was more than a mere change of name. The defendant's motion succeeded because the conditions of s 21(4) were not strictly satisfied.[134]

The Aventicum [135]

Three separate companies were part owners and controlling shareholders of another company, which, in turn, owned two subsidiaries, one of which owned the ship The Aventicum (A).

The plaintiffs, consignees of cargo, claimed damages for breach of contract and/or duty in the loading/handling of the cargo carried on board the vessel A in 1976. They issued a writ on 5 May 1977 and arrested the vessel in respect of their claim on 11 August 1977. The defendant owners of the vessel applied to have the writ, service of writ and all subsequent proceedings set aside, on the ground that the court had no jurisdiction over the vessel or her owners. The issue for decision was who owned the ship when the cause of action arose and whether that person was also the beneficial owner of all the shares in the ship when the writ was issued. At the time the cause of action arose, the vessel belonged to a company, Armadora, which was a subsidiary of company Scalotas. Scalotas was owned by three separate parent companies. After the cause of action had arisen, the ship was transferred to a sister company of Armadora, Longan. This company, with the ship, was later bought by Anglo Norse and a new subsidiary company was set up, Loquat, to which the ship was transferred again. The plaintiffs argued that the company Longan, which owned the ship by August 1976, belonged to Anglo Norse. At the time

---

133 See also *Kommunar (No 1)* [1997] 1 Lloyd's Rep 1. Chapter 2, para 3.12, with regard to s 20(2)(m) of the SCA 1981.

134 See, also, para 4.2.2.4, below.

135 [1978] 1 Lloyd's Rep 184.

the writ was issued, the vessel was owned by Loquat, which also belonged to Anglo Norse. In this manner, it could be said that Anglo Norse was, therefore, beneficial owner of both companies and still the beneficial owner of the shares in the ship. Although there had been changes in the registered ownership of this vessel, it was argued that the real owners had, throughout, remained the same and, if one looked at all the connecting links between these companies, the beneficial owners were the same person. The defendants urged the court not to lift the corporate veil, but to take matters at face value. Slynn J disagreed and ordered evidence to be adduced:

> I think that it is wrong and that where damages are claimed by cargo-owners and there is dispute as to the beneficial ownership of the ship, the court in all cases can and in some cases should look behind the registered owner to determine the true beneficial ownership . . . I have no doubt that on a motion of this kind it is right to investigate the true beneficial ownership. I reject any suggestion that it is impossible 'to pierce the corporate veil' . . . it is plain that s 3(4) of the Act intends that the court shall not be limited to a consideration of who is the registered owner, or who is the person having legal ownership of the shares in the ship; the directions are to look at the beneficial ownership.[136]

It was permitted, therefore, to look behind the corporate veil. However, on the evidence, the plaintiffs could not prove that the beneficial owner of the ship arrested was the same person with the person liable *in personam*. That was a smart way of avoiding claims already accrued, although the successive transfers of the ship from one company to another commenced after the claim had arisen. Perhaps, if the evidence had been more carefully scrutinised, a trace back to the person liable *in personam* could have been made. By contrast to this complex corporate structure, the following case concerned a simple structure of a parent and a subsidiary company.

The Maritime Trader[137]

The plaintiffs, owners of the vessel *Antaios*, time chartered her to MTO and claimed outstanding payment of hire. MTO was a parent company of MTS, which owned the vessel *The Maritime Trader*. The plaintiffs, believing that MTO had financial difficulties, issued a writ against *The Maritime Trader* and arrested her. The question was whether, at the time the action was brought, *The Maritime Trader* was beneficially owned in respect of all shares therein by MTO, the person who would be liable on the claim *in personam*.

It was held that it could not be said that *The Maritime Trader* was beneficially owned by MTO, unless the corporate veil was to be lifted. Without evidence of fraud, the court would not pierce the veil. There was no evidence of sham as the vessel had been owned by MTS ever since she was built, which was over four years before the charterparty contract was entered into between the plaintiffs and MTO.

In *The Glastnos*,[138] where there was a genuine transfer of the ship within a group of distinct legal entities for legitimate reasons, Steyn J (as he then was) said:

---

136 Ibid, p 187.
137 [1981] 2 Lloyd's Rep 153.
138 [1991] 1 Lloyd's Rep 482, pp 490, 491.

My conclusion is that all the companies in the Tolteca Group were distinct legal entities: to describe any as sham is simply not correct. I accept that Mr Farias resorted to the device of incorporation to attain the benefits of limited liability. That is, of course, why the shipping trade is structured on the basis of one-ship companies, but by itself it affords no basis for piercing the corporate veil, and the evidence before me certainly does not justify an inference that the companies were vehicles for the commission of fraud . . .

The companies in question were Tolteca SA, Tolteca Inc and, possibly, Marbank. One can readily accept that ultimate control rested with Mr Farias. A great many shipping groups, structured in one-ship companies, are ultimately controlled by one individual or family. By itself that proves nothing. What matters is how business and affairs are carried on.

Piercing the corporate veil

An order to pierce the veil will be made when it is found that there was a sham transfer of the ship to another company in an attempt to avoid liability to claimants.

The definition of a 'sham' transfer was given by Diplock LJ in *Snook v London and West Riding Investments Ltd*[139] concerning hire purchase:

> . . . it means acts done or documents executed by the parties to the 'sham' which are intended by them to give to third parties or to the court the appearance of creating between the parties legal rights and obligations different from the actual legal rights and obligations (if any) which the parties intend to create. But, one thing, I think, is clear in legal principle, morality and the authorities (see *Yorkshire Rly Wagon Co v Maclure* and *Stoneleigh Finance Ltd v Phillips*), that for acts or documents to be a 'sham,' with whatever legal consequences follow from this, all the parties thereto must have a common intention that the acts or documents are not to create the legal rights and obligations which they give the appearance of creating. No unexpressed intentions of a 'shammer' affect the rights of a party whom he deceived.

In shipping, the facts of the following cases illustrate what would not be regarded as a genuine single-ship company in the eyes of the law but only used to conceal the true ownership of a ship to evade liability to creditors.

The Saudi Prince[140]

In 1976, a cargo of ceramic tiles was carried on the ship A. At the time, the vessel was owned by Mr Orri, a Saudi businessman, who traded the ship under the company SEL. The cargo suffered damage before delivery and the cargo-owners claimed such damages from the carriers. When *The Saudi Prince*, also belonging to SEL, being a sister ship of A, came into the jurisdiction in August 1979, a writ *in rem* against her was issued and she was arrested. Mr Orri sought to have the writ set aside on the ground that, before the writ was issued, the legal ownership of the SP had been transferred to another company (SSST) in which he owned 80% of the shares, while his two daughters owned 20%. Even if it was permissible to regard the shareholders of the company as the beneficial owners of the SP, Mr Orri argued, he

---

139 [1967] 2 QB 786, p 802.
140 [1982] 2 Lloyd's Rep 255.

was not the beneficial owner of all shares therein. On the evidence, however, it was not shown that the vessel had been transferred to this company for value. There was no convincing evidence that his children paid money for the shares. The shares were just put in their name as nominees of Mr Orri to divest himself of shares, in name only. In any event, the company had not properly been incorporated in accordance with Saudi Arabian law. Therefore, it was held that an investigation of the true beneficial ownership of SP showed that Mr Orri was, at the time of the issue of the writ, the true beneficial owner of the vessel.

The Tjaskemolen [141]

The defendants, Bayland Navigation Inc (B), were a company being part of a group of companies which were formed for the purpose of owning this ship, T. B entered into a charterparty with the plaintiffs (charterers) for the carriage of steel from Rotterdam to Korea under which B warranted that the ship's certificates of class and seaworthiness were in order. The charterers in turn had contracted with D to sell and transport cargo of steel to Korea. When the notice of readiness for loading of the cargo was tendered by the charterers, the classification certificate was not on board. As a result, the charterers were unable to load and cancelled the charter-party. Consequently, the buyer of the steel, D, cancelled the sale contract. The charterers arrested the ship, seeking security in respect of their claim in damages, which had been submitted to arbitration. The defendants B applied for the release of the ship from arrest on the grounds that, at the time of the issue of the writ, she was not owned by them, nor was she chartered by demise to the person who would be liable for the claim *in personam*. They submitted that they had transferred legal and beneficial ownership to another company in the group, G, before the issue of the writ. The plaintiffs alleged that the agreement was a sham and that neither legal nor beneficial ownership could have passed until the vessel was deleted from the Register of Ships in Panama. This event did not occur until after the issue of the writ. On evidence, it was shown that, at the time the memorandum of agreement for the sale of the ship was signed, G did not exist and was not incorporated until afterwards. In addition, there was never any intention that G should pay a full price for the ship. It was held that the whole arrangement was a sham made only for the purpose of ensuring that the vessel was not made subject to security for any arbitration award.

The Ocean Enterprise [142]

The sale of a ship by a director of the owning company, who had no authority from the board of directors and the sale was in breach of his fiduciary duty, was declared invalid and fraudulent on the company. The beneficial ownership in the ship remained with the company. The buyer was not a bona fide purchaser for value and without notice of the defect in the title. On the facts, the director of the purchasing company was involved in a covering up for the seller in a series of sham sales and

---

141 [1997] 2 Lloyd's Rep 465.
142 [1997] 1 Lloyd's Rep 449.

registration of the ship. He was ordered by the court to pay damages to the plaintiff (the defrauded company) for conversion of its property.

By contrast to the above cases, Toulson J, in *The Rialto (No 2)*,[143] a case concerning a Mareva injunction, refused to pierce the corporate veil. Mr Yamvrias as a chartering broker had signed a charterparty on behalf of the contracting party, the charterers, who eventually repudiated it and the owners of the chartered ship claimed damages. On evidence, it was shown that Mr Yamvrias had control of the chartering company and, on the day of the repudiation of the charterparty, he had caused the transfer of money from the account of the charterers to other companies controlled by him, in order to protect the money from the owners' claim in damages. The judge distinguished the *Tjaskemolen* case from this one on the basis that, at the time of the transfer, liability had not yet arisen following the principle laid down in the *Adams* case seen earlier. This case shows that the technicality of the law can sometimes overrule common sense. It could not have been a more obvious deliberate evasion of liability by the charterers than the transfer of the money from the company's account on the day of the repudiation; but, technically, liability arose a few hours later on the same day.

4.2.2.4 *Beneficial ownership and privatisation of State-owned corporations*

The question whether a given corporate entity can be said to be the same legal personality as some previous legal entity[144] is, perhaps, best answered by investigating the different legal characteristics of the two to see whether continuity of the original entity has been broken or maintained.[145]

The Nazym Khikmet [146] (NK)

The plaintiffs were owners or parties interested in a cargo of tobacco, damaged on a voyage on board this ship, *NK*. Blasko, a State enterprise, was a managing company of a fleet for the Ukraine Government and, by reason of being in possession and control of the ship when the cause of action arose, Blasko was the person who would be liable *in personam*. The plaintiffs arrested Z, a sister ship of *NK*, and claimed that Blasko was the beneficial owner of Z, at the time the action was brought. Both Blasko and the Republic of Ukraine contended that, at the time of the issue of the writ, Z was not beneficially owned by Blasko, but by the Republic. Upon conclusive evidence, Clarke J held that, although Blasko had some rights of ownership, it did not have full rights to dispose of or mortgage the ship without the consent of the Government. The Court of Appeal affirmed his decision, and Sir Thomas Bingham MR stated:

> The evidence makes plain that the process of liberalisation, which took place in the Ukraine once it became independent, has involved a devolution of commercial authority to trading enterprises; this process has led to a loosening of the bonds of State control, but not to a severance of them. The State has retained its ownership of

---

143 [1998] 1 Lloyd's Rep 322.

144 For a summary of State reconstruction in Russia and its effect on arrest of ships bought by the new entity, see Thomas, R, 'State reconstruction and ship arrest' [1998] IJSL 236.

145 *The Kommunar (No 2)* [1997] 1 Lloyd's Rep 8, p 16, per Colman J.

146 [1996] 2 Lloyd's Rep 362.

the income earning assets of enterprises such as Blasko, and had retained the right and power of ultimate decision over the use and exploitation of those assets.[147]

At a later stage, however, as is shown in the following case, Blasko was thought to have taken over ownership rights by having power to mortgage the ship, which was arrested in respect of a claim of bunker suppliers. The Court of Appeal held in *Guiseppe di Vittorio* (below) that Blasko had the status of a demise charterer and, for that reason, the arrest of the ship could be maintained.

Guiseppe di Vittorio [148]

The plaintiffs supplied bunkers, on two occasions, to the ship G, which was operated by Blasko.[149] Remaining unpaid, the plaintiffs issued a writ *in rem*, arrested her and applied for an order that the vessel be sold *pendente lite*. The Republic of Ukraine intervened, claiming that it was the beneficial owner of the ship and not Blasko. Therefore, it contended that since it was a successor state of the USSR, the ship was not subject to arrest under the SCA 1981. The State Immunity (Merchant Shipping) (USSR) Order 1978 applied to a ship owned by it and it was immune from liability. The plaintiffs submitted that at the time the cause of action arose, Blasko was the beneficial owner, or demise charterer, of the vessel and there had been a transfer of property in the vessel to Blasko before the issue of the writ. They relied on a mortgage agreement by which it appeared that Blasko had power to mortgage the ship. The plaintiffs argued that this was an act consistent with Blasko being the legal and beneficial owner of the vessel. Although, at first instance, the judge held that it was, the Court of Appeal held that, on the evidence, there was no suggestion of a transfer either by Blasko's representatives, or by the Ministry of Transport. On the issue whether Blasko could be described as a demise charterer of the ship, the court held that there need not be a document which records a consensual agreement between the owner and the charterer, before the statutory definition of 'demise charterer' can be satisfied. The terms on which Blasko held the vessel were set out in a document described as a 'charter' and had the effect that Blasko could sell or mortgage its vessels, provided necessary government or State consent was obtained. Evans LJ held that Blasko's position vis a vis the Republic could be interpreted as a demise charterer and, as such, the provision of s 21(4) for the arrest of the ship was satisfied.

In situations of privatisation of State enterprises, a transfer of the whole undertaking of a fleet of ships from one corporation to another will be done effectively if continuity is broken, so that it can be said that the new corporation is a new entity. The Russian State had successfully broken that continuity, as was shown earlier in *The Kommunar (No 2)*.[150]

In this case, briefly, Russian fishing vessels, which were managed by a State enterprise and controlled by the Ministry of Fisheries, were transferred by privatisation of the managing company. It involved a conversion into a public joint stock,

---

147 Ibid, p 374.
148 [1998] 1 Lloyd's Rep 136.
149 See *The Nazym Khikmet* [1996] 2 Lloyd's Rep 362.
150 [1997] 1 Lloyd's Rep 8.

a company limited by shares, and change of its name. The conversion occurred after claims arose, but before the arrest of the ship in connection with which the claim arose. The beneficial owner, therefore, at the time of the issue of the writ was not the person who would be liable *in personam* when the cause of action arose. The ship was released from arrest.

4.2.2.5 Beneficial ownership and risk management

These cases illustrate that there are various ways of structuring the owning companies of ships, some of which are legitimate in the eyes of the law but others are illegitimate, if the intention is to avoid liabilities already accrued.[151] For purpose of risk management, a shipowner can legitimately arrange his affairs in such a way so that the exposure of his assets is limited.

Forming one-ship companies provides one legitimate method of limiting liability;[152] a parent company, and a series of subsidiary companies, is another. A genuine transfer of a ship from one sister company to another, before a suspected claim has arisen, may provide a shield to reaching the beneficial owner when the *in rem* claim form is issued.

Similarly, the ship can be chartered down the line, and the carrier of cargo, for example, can be a subsidiary company of the owning companies, which acts as a time charterer, signing bills of lading as carrier, but which does not own ships. So, although the contractual carrier would be liable personally for a cargo claim, the ship in connection with which a claim might arise might not be arrested because he would neither be the beneficial owner of that ship nor the charterer by demise at the time of issuing the *in rem* proceeding. If the carrier/charterer does not beneficially own ships itself, no other ship can be arrested under s 21(4) of the SCA 1981. In some cases, however, the claimant may be able to base his claim in tort against the owner of the ship, the performing carrier, in which case the ship could be arrested.

If an arrest of the ship or any 'other' ship is difficult, the claimant may be able to locate where the freight or hire is to be paid and apply for a freezing injunction, but that is often difficult and does not provide the security which is guaranteed by the arrest of the ship.

It has already been mentioned that, unlike the arrest of a ship, which is available as of right, an application to the court for an injunctive relief depends on judicial discretion. 'The eye of equity' can look behind the corporate veil in order to do justice.[153] Thus, the court may peep through the corporate status of a company as a legal entity and may consider who are the shareholders, or the people who direct

---

151 *Yukong Lines Ltd P of Korea v Rendsburg Investment Corp (The Rialto (No 2))* [1998] 1 Lloyd's Rep 322.

152 *Bakri Bunker Trading Co Ltd v The Owners of Neptune* [1986] HK LR 345. Single-ship companies and legal consequences have been examined by Christodoulou, D, *The Single-Ship Company*, 2000, Sakkoulas, which provides an interesting comparative study of the subject matter, particularly in relation to the position of creditors. The author examines the circumstances in which the courts in England, USA and Greece pay regard or disregard to the corporate personality, as well as the conditions of ship arrest under the more flexible legal systems, such as in France and South Africa. The viability of financial security for creditors is also examined and the reasons why the single-ship companies are justified.

153 *The Coral Rose* [1991] 1 Lloyd's Rep 563, p 569, per Neill LJ.

and control the activities of a company, where the character of a company, or the nature of persons controlling it, is a relevant feature.[154]

Furthermore, the English court has broken new ground in the piercing of the corporate veil on an issue arising under s 51 of the SCA 1981, relating to funding litigation under which the court has discretion to order any party to pay the costs of English proceedings, if that party financially supports the litigation.[155] In *The Ikarian Reefer*,[156] it was held that the director of a company, a non-party to previous proceedings brought by the assured (the company) against the hull underwriters of the ship for a total loss, was liable to pay the outstanding legal costs of those proceedings in which the assured had lost at the Court of Appeal on the ground of wilful misconduct.

Whether or not the Court of Appeal decision against the company was correct, the result of this case are alarming to shareholders or directors of one-ship companies who support litigation financially. Even if they are domiciled in a European Union State, they may be sued in the court seised of the original proceedings under Art 6(2) of the Brussels Regulation,[157] which provides for an alternative to the domicile rule, that being a special jurisdiction provided against a third party in any third party proceedings.

5 PROPERTY AGAINST WHICH AN *IN REM* CLAIM MAY BE BROUGHT

The ship with all appurtenances, including bunkers, the cargo on board, or every freight, are property being the subject of arrest.

The ship – in connection with which the maritime claim arose – and/or her sister ship are the primary property against which an *in rem* claim can be brought, provided the conditions laid down in s 21(4) of the SCA 1981 are satisfied. A sister ship is a ship owned by the same company, which owns the ship in connection with which the claim arose. For claims enforceable under s 21(2) and (3), however, there is no provision for a sister ship arrest. But, since the claims attracting maritime liens are also included in s 21(4), a sister ship arrest is allowed under this paragraph. The

---

154 *Merchandise Transport Ltd v British Transport Commission* [1962] 2 QB 173, p 206.

155 The material objectives of public policy which the court applies before it orders litigation funders to pay the costs of a successful defendant were recently summarised by Colman J in *Arkin v Borchard Lines and Others (No 2)* [2004] 1 Lloyd's Rep 88; the public policy objectives are: (i) the purpose of discouraging ill-founded claims or defences and of compensating those who had been obliged successfully to protect their rights in the course of litigation underlay the rule that in general a successful party was entitled to recover his costs; (ii) the purpose of facilitating access to justice for impecunious claimants needed to be supported but costs orders would act as deterrent to funders of weak claims; and (iii) the purpose of protecting the due administration of justice required the court to discourage interference by funders. In the exercise of the court's discretion, these public policy objectives may yield to the objective of making access to the courts available to impecunious claimants with claims of substance. In this case, MPC, the funders, were not ordered to pay the costs of the defendants.

156 *National Justice Compania Naviera SA v Prudential Assurance Co Ltd (The Ikarian Reefer (No 2))* [2000] 1 Lloyd's Rep 129 (CA).

157 See Chapter 6.

consequence of arresting a sister ship for a claim which attracts a maritime lien will, however, be the loss of the privilege of maritime lien because the sister ship is not the property on which the lien has attached.[158] If the ship is under a time charter, the bunkers on board the ship belong to the charterer.[159] So, if a mortgagee arrests the ship, the charterer can intervene in the action[160] and the proceeds of sale of the bunkers, if the ship is sold by a court order, will be paid to the charterer.[161]

The cargo on board the ship, or freight earned, may be subject to arrest only if there is a maritime lien attached, for example, when there have been salvage services rendered to save ship and cargo. The same would apply to the bunkers on board, which do not belong to the shipowner. An aircraft can only be the subject of arrest if it is waterborne and there has been salvage, or towage, or pilotage of the aircraft as per ss 21(3), (4) and 24(1).

---

158 *The Leoborg (No 2)* [1964] 1 Lloyd's Rep 380.
159 *The Span Terza (No 2)* [1984] 1 Lloyd's Rep 119 (HL).
160 *The Saint Anna* [1980] 1 Lloyd's Rep 180.
161 *The Eurostar* [1993] 1 Lloyd's Rep 106; *The Pan Oak* [1992] 2 Lloyd's Rep 36.

CHAPTER 4

PROCEDURE (OVERVIEW)

1 ISSUE OF THE *IN REM* CLAIM FORM, SERVICE AND ARREST

1.1 Issue

Pursuant to Civil Procedure Rules 1998 (CPR), 61.3(2), a claim *in rem* is started by the issue of an *in rem* claim form, as set out in the practice direction (PD 61).

An *in rem* claim form can be issued naming more than one ship, or separate *in rem* claim forms may be issued against different ships belonging to the same owner for the same claim, but only one ship can be arrested.[1] The claimant must elect which ship to arrest.[2] In practice, the claimant waits until one of the ships named comes within the jurisdiction, whereupon he amends the claim form and serves it on that ship.

The Berny[3]

This case involved claims in relation to cargo of sugar that was carried from Dunkirk to Dar-es-Salaam on the defendant's ship, *The Berny*. The plaintiffs/cargo-owners brought a number of actions for shortage of bags of cargo delivered. One was *in rem* against a number of sister ships of *The Berny*, another was against *The Berny* and a third was *in personam* against the defendants. As neither *The Berny* nor any of her sister ships visited a port within the jurisdiction and the time of the validity of the writs was about to expire, the plaintiffs applied for their renewal, which they obtained. A sister ship entered the jurisdiction and the shipowners/defendants, at the request of the plaintiffs, provided a letter of undertaking to nominate solicitors to accept service. Later, the writ in the action against *The Berny* was served upon her and the shipowners entered a conditional appearance, but they contended that the action should be stayed on the ground that, when it was begun, the cargo-owners had already invoked the jurisdiction of the court in respect of a sister ship. Therefore, the court had no jurisdiction to entertain the action against *The Berny*. The shipowner's contention was rejected.

It was held that the cargo-owners were entitled to institute proceedings *in rem* against more than one ship, provided they served proceedings on, or arrested, only one of such ships. The Administration of Justice Act 1956 (which was then applicable) gave the cargo-owners the option to invoke the admiralty jurisdiction of the court *in rem*, against either *The Berny* or any other sister ship. The right course of

---

1   *The Banco* [1971] 1 Lloyd's Rep 49; also s 21(8) of the SCA 1981.
2   *The Berny* [1977] 2 Lloyd's Rep 533.
3   Ibid.

action for the court was to compel them to elect against which of such ships they wished to continue. If they elected to continue against *The Berny*, the writ against the sister ship was to be set aside. It would not be right to compel them to continue against one of the sister ships rather than against *The Berny*, simply on the ground that the writ against a sister ship was issued first and the one against *The Berny* second.

1.2 Effect of issue

Unless the principle established by *The Monica S* has been undermined by *The Indian Grace* (as discussed in Chapter 3), the effect of the issue of the claim form is the crystallisation of the claimant's statutory right *in rem* against the relevant ship. The consequence of this is that, in the event of ownership transfer even to a bona fide purchaser of the ship before service of the claim form, the claim will still be enforceable against the ship by service and arrest. Therefore, prompt issue of the *in rem* claim form is essential.

1.3 Service of the *in rem* claim form

The service can be effected[4] either upon the property, by affixing the claim form (or a copy) on the outside of the property in a position where it may reasonably be expected to be seen; or upon the defendant's solicitor who has authority to accept service. The service does not constitute arrest without a warrant of arrest, which must be issued upon a separate application and executed by the Admiralty Marshal or his substitute. The effect of service or arrest is that the jurisdiction of the court is invoked[5] and, in addition, following *The Indian Grace*, the person named in the claim form, as the person who would be liable *in personam*, becomes a party to the proceedings.[6]

The *in rem* claim form cannot be served out of the jurisdiction (the ship must come within the jurisdiction) nor can an order for substituted service be made.[7] In most cases, in practice, however, when an undertaking is given by way of security for the claim to the claimant in an acceptable form prior to the service of proceedings and in lieu of arrest, there is a condition of that undertaking that solicitors will be appointed by the defendant to accept service unconditionally. The solicitors then accept service by endorsing on the claim form such acceptance, which amounts to submission to the jurisdiction of the court by the defendant. Alternatively, the defendant may choose to acknowledge the issue[8] of the claim form, which will amount to submission to jurisdiction. If he wishes to contest the jurisdiction of

---

4   See PD 61, para 3.6.

5   *The Freccia del Nord* [1989] 1 Lloyd's Rep 388.

6   But the claim should also continue to be a claim *in rem*. See conclusion on *The Indian Grace* in Chapter 3.

7   *The Good Herald* [1987] 1 Lloyd's Rep 236.

8   CPR, r 61.3(6).

the court, he may acknowledge service conditionally,[9] since unconditional acknowledgment will amount to submission.

The particulars of claim, subject to CPR, r 61.4 relating to collision claims, must be contained in or served with the claim form, or be served on the defendant by the claimant with 75 days after service of the claim form (CPR, r 61.3(3)).

1.4 Arrest by issue and execution of a warrant

The service of the *in rem* claim form on the ship does not constitute arrest. A separate application must be made for the issue of a warrant of arrest. Only the Admiralty Marshal or his substitute may effect the arrest of property.[10] An application to arrest (containing an undertaking to pay the Marshal's fees) may be made by filing an application notice in the Admiralty and Commercial Registry. Before the application is made, the applicant must carry out a search in the caveat book in order to ascertain whether there is a caveat against arrest. Then he must file a declaration in the prescribed form (ADM 5) containing the particulars of the claim, the property, the amount of the security and show that the requirements of s 21(4) of the Supreme Court Act (SCA) 1981 are met. The declaration must be verified by a statement of truth,[11] containing statements of information and belief about the particulars and sources thereof stated. The Admiralty Court may issue a warrant of arrest even if the declaration does not contain all the particulars.[12] The claimant no longer needs to make full and frank disclosure of all material facts, provided the requirements of CPR, rr 61.5(1) and PD 61, para 5 are complied with. He must, however, correct any inaccuracies promptly. Issue of an arrest warrant is as of right, that is, the court no longer has discretion, as it used to prior to the decision in *The Varna*.[13] One exception is provided by CPR, r 61.5(4), namely: a warrant of arrest may not be issued as of right in the case of property in respect of which the beneficial ownership has changed since the claim form was issued, as a result of a sale or disposal by any court in any jurisdiction exercising admiralty jurisdiction *in rem*.

The Admiralty Marshal, or his substitute, will serve the warrant on the ship or property to be arrested.[14] To prevent arrest, a caveat against arrest may be filed in the Admiralty and Commercial Registry accompanied by an undertaking to file an acknowledgment of service and to give sufficient security to satisfy the claim with interest and costs. The entry of a caveat against arrest shall not be treated as a submission to the jurisdiction of the English court and property may be arrested, notwithstanding a caveat against arrest. Where a defendant constitutes a limitation fund, in accordance with Art 11 of the Limitation of Liability Convention 1976, and

---

9   By acknowledging service, the right to dispute the court's jurisdiction is not lost (PD 61, para 3.11).

10 CPR, r 61.5(8).

11 PD 61, para 5.3.

12 CPR, rr 61.5(1); PD 61, para 5. An application for arrest must be in Form ADM4 containing an undertaking and a declaration in form ADM5.

13 [1993] 2 Lloyd's Rep 253.

14 For a useful outline of the procedure of arrest by the Admiralty Marshal, see *The Johnny Two* [1992] 2 Lloyd's Rep 257, per Sheen J.

desires to prevent the arrest of his property, he may file a caution against arrest.[15] If the property is already under arrest, any other person claiming to have a right *in rem* against the property under arrest may file a caution against its release.[16]

2 THE AFTERMATH OF ARREST

2.1 Rights of third parties

Once the ship or property is arrested, it is under the custody not the possession of the Admiralty Marshal. A pre-arrest right or remedy of a third party based on possession is not affected, such as a statutory right of detention of a port authority. The Marshal can apply to court for directions. In *The Queen of the South*,[17] the port authority's right to detain the ship, which was under the custody of the Marshal, was preserved. The port authority was allowed to receive payment for its outstanding dues from the proceeds of sale of the ship by the Marshal before other maritime claimants. Third parties whose rights are adversely affected by the arrest can intervene but any other interference with the arrest is a contempt of court being subject to committal.[18] If the port operations are affected the court has inherent jurisdiction to give directions to the Marshal as it thinks it may be appropriate.

The Mardina Merchant[19]

In this case, there was an application by the port authority to the Admiralty Marshal for direction to move a ship from her place of arrest to another place. The vessel had been arrested by various claimants and remained under arrest for a while, causing interference to the working of the port, thus, causing financial loss to the port and the owners of the berth. Under the rules of court, a third party could intervene only if it could show that it had an interest in the property arrested. Unless the court could exercise its inherent jurisdiction, the port authority, of course, could not show an interest. Brandon J held:

> I am of the opinion that there must be an inherent jurisdiction in the court to allow a party to intervene if the effect of an arrest is to cause that party serious hardship or difficulty or danger ... In all such cases it seems to me that the court must have power to allow the party who is affected by the work of the system of law used in admiralty actions *in rem* to apply to the court for some mitigation of the hardship or the difficulty or danger. If it were not so, then there would be no remedy available for such persons at all.[20]

Any other person interested in the property under arrest, or its proceeds of sale, whose interests are affected by any order sought or made, may be made a party to

---

15 CPR, r 61.7(1) and (2)(b). Prior to the CPR, the caution was known as 'caveat'.
16 CPR, r 61.8(2), (3).
17 [1968] P 449.
18 CPR, Sched 1, RSC Ord 52.
19 [1975] 1 WLR 147.
20 Ibid, p 149.

any claim *in rem* against the property or proceeds of sale where the court considers it would be just and convenient, and on terms the court may think fit.[21] If the ship is under arrest, but cargo on board her is not, and those interested in the cargo wish to secure its discharge, they may request the Marshal to take the appropriate steps, provided the applicant gives a written undertaking satisfactory to the Marshal to pay on demand the Marshal's fees and expenses to be incurred by him in taking the desired steps. The Marshal will apply to court for the appropriate order. Alternatively, they may intervene in the action. The same rules apply when the cargo is under arrest but the ship is not.[22]

2.2 Provision of security for the claim and release from arrest

When a ship is arrested, the defendant or the person interested in the ship may either acknowledge service and contest the arrest without submitting to the jurisdiction, or submit to the jurisdiction by acknowledging service and provide security in lieu of the release of the ship from arrest, or do nothing. In the latter case, the Admiralty Marshal will put the ship for appraisal and sale (see later). When security is offered, it may be placed either as a bail in court, or by way of an undertaking on behalf of the person interested in the ship. There are standard letters of undertaking provided either by the insurer for third party liability, the protection and indemnity insurer – known as P&I club (mutual insurance) – of the shipowner or demise charterer, or by their bank. The undertaking includes an undertaking that solicitors will be instructed to accept service on the owner's behalf and the owners will submit to jurisdiction. There is no requirement, as yet, for an undertaking in damages to be given by the arresting party to the shipowner in case of wrongful or unjustified arrest.[23] The amount of security for release of a ship must be reasonable and its assessment approximate. The form of guarantee provided is at the discretion of the court.[24]

The Moschanthy [25]

A consignment of second hand machinery was shipped on the defendants' motor vessel, *A*, at London for carriage to Tripoli, to be delivered to the plaintiffs' order. When the discharge was completed at Tripoli, the machinery was placed with the defendants' agents, who claimed a lien for unpaid freight. An application to the Lebanese court for an order of delivery of the goods against a bank guarantee was rejected. Later, the plaintiff issued a writ *in rem* in the English Court against the *M*, a sister ship of *A*, claiming damages or the value of the goods plus damages, and *M* was arrested in Liverpool. A high amount of security was requested for the release of the ship from arrest on the ground that the plaintiff expected to make a 100%

---

21   CPR, r 61.8(7).
22   CPR, rr 61.8–61.10.
23   See later under para 2.4. When the Arrest Convention 1999 is enacted by the UK, there will be such a provision therein.
24   *The Sovereign Explorer* [2001] 1 Lloyd's Rep 60.
25   [1971] 1 Lloyd's Rep 37.

profit from the sale of the goods. The defendants, who in the meantime had commenced an action in Lebanon claiming freight due, applied to stay the proceedings in the English Court on the ground, inter alia, that the security given was excessive and should be reduced. It was held that having regard to the value of the goods, and also the amount of interest and costs, which would ultimately be payable if the plaintiffs succeeded, any assessment of a reasonable figure for security could only be approximate. The amount requested fixed was not excessive.

Contrast the criteria applied in the following case.

The Tribels [26]

While the plaintiffs' vessel was entering into the harbour, she took to the ground due to a strong northeasterly wind. The master employed the defendants' harbour tugs on the standard Lloyd's form of Salvage Agreement. The salvors, pursuant to the contract, demanded security in the sum of £3,323,000. The plaintiffs asked for an injunction to prevent the salvors from demanding security, exceeding £1 million. The salved value was probably about £16,150,000. It was an implied term of the salvage agreement that the contractor would not ask for unreasonably high security. It was held that security in the sum of £1 million gave a very ample margin of protection in respect of whatever sum the arbitrator would award after the salvage. Taking the case at its most favourable to the salvor, the sum provided an ample margin of protection.

2.3 Release in particular circumstances

(a) Where a shipowner constitutes a limitation fund in accordance with the Merchant Shipping Act (MSA) 1995 and the Rules of Court,[27] he will be entitled to the release of the ship as of right, if the prerequisites of Art 13(2), (3) of the Limitation of Liability Convention 1976 are satisfied.[28]

(b) When a claim is subject to an arbitration agreement and in rem proceedings have commenced, the court will stay the proceedings upon the application of the defendant, and may order the release from arrest, provided sufficient security for the claim is given (s 26 of the Civil Jurisdiction and Judgments Act (CJJA) 1982). Prior to s 26, a vessel could be arrested for the purpose of provision of security to satisfy a judgment and not an arbitration award. If the proceedings were stayed in favour of arbitration pursuant to s 1 of the previous Arbitration Act (AA) 1975, the court had a wide discretion whether or not to maintain the arrest. If the court took the view that the proceedings would result in a judgment, the arrest could be maintained as security for that judgment.[29] Such a wide discretion is no longer needed. Section 26 of the CJJA 1982, coupled with s

---

26 [1985] 1 Lloyd's Rep 128.

27 CPR, r 61.11 and PD 61, para 10.

28 If a limitation decree is granted, any proceedings arising out of the occurrence may be stayed: CPR, r 61.11(3)(a)(i); see further, Ch 17, below.

29 *The Tuyuti* [1984] 2 All ER 545.

11 of the AA 1996, give the court power either to maintain the arrest as security for the arbitration award, or to order the release from arrest upon provision of security for the satisfaction of any such award. The following case confirmed that position, even before the AA 1996 was enacted.

The Bazias [30]

The plaintiffs were the bareboat charterers of two vessels, B1 and B2, which were owned by the defendants. They chartered the vessels under time charters to Sally Line Ltd (the time charterers) who employed the ships for cross-channel ferry services. The defendants withdrew their vessels from the services to plaintiffs on grounds of failure by the plaintiffs to pay hire and for other breaches of the bareboat charters. Sally Line gave notice to the plaintiffs ending the time charters, as they could no longer perform under the contract. The defendants in this action commenced arbitration proceedings against the plaintiffs, claiming unpaid hire and damages. The plaintiffs counterclaimed for loss of profits with respect to the remaining period of the bareboat charters and, in order to obtain security for their counterclaim, they issued proceedings *in rem* against the vessels; due warning had been given that they intended to arrest. Meanwhile, the defendants had already entered into bareboat charters with Sally Line Ltd, so that the cross-channel ferry service continued. *The Bazias* was arrested by the plaintiffs. The defendants applied for a stay, under s 1 of the AA 1975, on the ground that the dispute was referred to arbitration, and sought to set aside the warrant of arrest. All parties agreed that the defendants were entitled to a mandatory stay under the above section. The question in issue was whether the court still had a discretion to release the vessel according to pre-existing practice without requiring equivalent security, especially in the light of s 26 of the CJJA 1982. Counsel for the defendants argued that s 26 preserved the pre-existing wide discretion of the court in arbitration cases and the manner in which it was exercised. It was held that the reason for the wider discretion exercised by the court previously had gone with the advent of the CJJA 1982. This Act was drafted to cover all classes of cases. The usual practice was that the vessel would only be released on the provision of sufficient security to cover the amount of the claim plus interest and costs. Therefore, a stay was granted and it was ordered that the vessel remained under arrest until a further order of the Admiralty Court.

2.4 Wrongful arrest

The Arrest Convention 1952 has left the matter of remedies in case of wrongful arrest to the State parties. Under English law, the shipowner or demise charterer has to show that the arresting party was guilty of *mala fides* or *grossa negligentia* when they arrested the ship which ought not to have been arrested.[31]

The leading authority in this area is **The Evangelismos**, in which the Privy Council dealt with the conduct required to be proved by the shipowner in order to

---

30 [1993] 1 Lloyd's Rep 101; see, also, *The Jalamatsya* [1987] 2 Lloyd's Rep 164, and Ch 5 paras 3.5.2 & 3.5.3.

31 *The Evangelismos* (1858) 12 Moo PC 352; *Walter D Wallett* [1893] P 202.

succeed in his claim for damages in case of wrongful arrest. In the process of investigation the court has to ask the following question: is there or is there not reason to say that the action was so unwarrantably brought, or brought with so little colour, or so little foundation, that it rather implies malice on the part of the plaintiff, or gross negligence which is equivalent to it?[32]

Since the circumstances of this case afforded grounds for believing that there had been a genuine but understandable mistake by the arresting party of the identity of the ship arrested, it was held that there was no *mala fides* and the action for damages was dismissed.

There have been a few old decisions in which the court awarded damages for wrongful arrest,[33] and in some others the court awarded costs to the shipowner. It is beyond the scope of this chapter to analyse them, but readers are referred to another work[34] which criticises the narrow rule of *The Evangelismos* case and rightly suggests that the test for wrongful arrest should be reviewed by the English courts, as foreign courts (such as in Singapore and Hong Kong) have applied a more liberal approach to this issue in recent years.

In recent years, the decision of Colman J in **The Kommunar (No 3)**[35] shows how difficult it is for the owner to succeed in his claim for damages. Although the plaintiffs in this case knew that the beneficial owners and the party in possession of the ship were, when the cause of action arose, a different entity from the owners of the Kommunar at the time of the arrest (due to privatisation of the company which would be liable *in personam*), the owners did not succeed in their claim for damages. Contesting the arrest, the defendants argued that the plaintiffs' conduct amounted to *crassa negligentia* and on that basis they claimed damages. Colman J, referring to the dicta in *The Evangelismos* cited above, stated:

> Two types of cases are thus envisaged. Firstly, there are cases of mala fides, which must be taken to mean those cases where on the primary evidence the arresting party has no honest belief in his entitlement to arrest the vessel. Secondly, there are those cases in which objectively there is so little basis for the arrest that it may be inferred that the arresting party did not believe in his entitlement to arrest the vessel or acted without any serious regard to whether there were adequate grounds for the arrest of the vessel. It is, as I understand the judgment, in the latter sense that such phrases as 'crassa negligentia' and 'gross negligence' are used and are described as implying malice or being equivalent to it.

On the evidence, however, he held that there was no proof of mala fides conduct; whether or not the conduct amounted to crassa negligentia, he found it quite impossible to say that it should have been obvious to the plaintiffs or their legal advisors that the claim in England was bound to fail, given the relatively complicated privatisation process and the complex analysis of the Russian legislation.

---

32 Ibid, at 359.

33 Eg *The Cheshire Witch* (1864) Br & L 362 (substantive claim *in rem* dismissed); *The Cathcart* (1867) LR 1 A & E 333 (wrongful arrest by a mortgagee); *The Margaret Jane* (1869) LR 2 A & E 345 (salvors knew of the appraisal of the wreck but malice was not proved).

34 Nossal, S: 'Damages for the wrongful arrest of a vessel' [1996] LMCLQ 368.

35 [1997] 1 Lloyd's Rep 22.

The difficulty in granting damages, even for wasted costs or other expenses incurred during an unjustified arrest, which does not amount to wrongful in the sense of mala fides or crassa negligentia, is inherent in the principle of arrest under English law, and this was expressed by Colman J in *The Kommunar*:

> The *in rem* jurisdiction of the Admiralty Court required no undertaking in damages from a plaintiff who obtained the benefit of security for his claim by arresting a vessel; even if the plaintiff's claim failed or he was found to have wrongly invoked the jurisdiction he would not have to compensate the shipowners for the expenses and losses arising out of the arrest unless mala fides or crassa negligentia was proved; the potential injustice attributable to this feature of the Admiralty jurisdiction *in rem* was relevant to the exercise of the Court's discretion to direct that the defendants' recoverable costs should be discounted to take account of a benefit derived from bunkers provided and paid for by the plaintiffs in the course of arrest; unless the Court were satisfied that there would be no injustice by reducing recoverable costs, having regard to the possibility of the shipowners having suffered irrecoverable losses in addition to legal costs, attributable to an unjustifiable arrest of the vessel, it would be quite inappropriate for any such direction to be made.

By contrast, there was clear evidence of wrongful detention of both the ship and her crew in Nigeria and the arrest for the ship for an unsustainable claim in *Gulf Azov v Idisi*,[36] in which the arresting party acted without serious regard to whether there were adequate grounds for continuing the arrest in the extortionate amount claimed. But such cases of clear evidence showing either malice or *crassa negligentia* are rare, and make interesting reading. The problem of discharging the burden of proof of wrongful arrest lies with the run-of-the-mill cases.

It has been argued by some commentators that English law should be changed, and an undertaking for damages should be ordered by the court as a condition of arrest in case of wrongful arrest, as is the case of applications for freezing orders.[37] It should be noted, however, that in the latter cases the court has a wide discretion whether or not to grant the application for a freezing order, while the arrest of a ship is as of right and the court no longer has wide discretion since the decision in *The Varna*.[38] Others argue that, if the law changes, it may make it less attractive for litigants to effect an arrest in this country. It is submitted that such an argument is feeble and without foundation. The test of wrongful arrest can be changed by a practice direction to allow the court discretion to award damages not just when there is proof of malice or *crassa negligentia* but also in cases of an unjustified arrest, depending on the circumstances of a case. Support for this can be derived from *The Margaret Jane*.[39] To protect recovery of damages by the shipowner should there be a finding of an unjustified arrest, security must be allowed to be ordered by way of an undertaking provided for by the insurer of the claimant, not as a condition of arrest, since this may delay the exercise of the right of arrest, but immediately thereafter upon a separate application, if a case warrants such an application.

---

36 [2001] 1 Lloyd's Rep 727.
37 See further Eder, B (QC), 'Wrongful Arrest of Ships: Revisit' paper delivered at a seminar held by the London Shipping Law Centre in 1998 and at ICMA XV.
38 [1993] 2 Lloyd's Rep 253.
39 (1869) LR 2 A & E 345.

The 1999 Arrest Convention, by Art 6, permits the court to require the claimant, as a condition of arrest, to put up security in the event of wrongful or unjustified arrest, or when excessive security has been demanded and provided.[40] Perhaps a time will come when English law will be changed if the UK adopts this Convention but, as the law stands at present, a defendant will have great difficulty in proving even crassa negligentia, no matter how much injustice it suffers.

In the meantime, lawyers may invent other means of ensuring that their client shipowner is granted, at least, the cost or expense incurred during the period of an unjustified arrest. Could they make a case for breach of the Human Rights Act?[41] This is a difficult question to answer and the author does not see an easy way of enabling defendants to bypass the harshness of the present law. It is suggested that the English courts should review the justification of the present harsh test of wrongful arrest.

2.5 Can there be a re-arrest?

As is derived from old authorities, there can be no re-arrest when a judgment on the merits has been given and security had previously been obtained for the same cause of action for which judgment has been obtained.

In *The Kalamazoo*,[42] in which the bail given for a collision claim was found to be insufficient after judgment, Dr Lushington set aside a warrant of arrest by which the claimant sought to obtain further security. It was held that the bail represented the ship and it would be absurd to contend that you could arrest a ship, take bail to any amount, and afterwards arrest her again for the same cause of action.

He repeated the same principle in *The Wild Ranger*,[43] when he emphasised that: '... bail given for a ship in any action is a substitute for the ship; and whenever bail is given, the ship is wholly released from the cause of action and cannot be arrested again for that cause of action.' This principle, based on the notion that the cause of action had become merged in the judgment, therefore *res judicata*, was accepted to be correct in later decisions, *The Point Breeze*[44] and *The Alletta*.[45]

Bateson J expressed a pragmatic view in *The Point Breeze*,[46] in which bail had been given for a collision liability and the ship was re-arrested after judgment (that is, *res judicata*), the amount of which exceeded the bail. Disallowing the re-arrest, he said:

> If the plaintiffs are right in their contention that they are entitled to arrest this ship, it

---

40 See comments by Gaskell, N and Shaw, R, 'The Arrest Convention 1999' [1999] LMCLQ 470, pp 470–90.

41 See Eder B, op cit, fn 37.

42 (1851) 15 Jur 885, p 886.

43 (1863) Lush 553; (1862) 1 New Rep 132.

44 (1928) 30 LlL Rep 229.

45 [1974] 1 Lloyd's Rep 40.

46 (1928) 30 LlL Rep 229, p 231.

seems to me that it will open the door to the re-arrest of vessels, or arrest after getting bail, whenever a party thinks that his claim may be more than he originally thought it was. No immunity from arrest will be obtained by giving bail, and the result of that, on the question of maritime liens, might be very serious.

All the authorities were reviewed by Mocatta J in the *The Alletta*.

A claim arose out of a collision incident, security was provided in lieu of arrest of *The Alletta* and her owners submitted to the jurisdiction. A judgment for damages was obtained against the defendants, who were not able to limit their liability. It appeared later that the amount of the security was not enough to satisfy the full claim amount. Seven years later, the ship was sold and she was renamed, *The Tarmac I*. In the hands of her new owner, she was threatened to be arrested by the plaintiffs. The buyers knew nothing about the claim prior to delivery; subsequently, they claimed an indemnity from the previous owner (the first defendant in this action) and joined the action seeking an order for warrant of arrest to be set aside. It was argued that the plaintiffs' right to arrest, either by way of enforcing a maritime lien or a statutory right *in rem*, had been lost (i) by laches, or (ii) by the fact that the plaintiffs had obtained judgment against the first defendants. The laches point was not accepted, but on the second point, Mocatta J applied the previous authorities and stated a broad principle:

> If a ship may be arrested after judgment on liability has been obtained against her and she is by the date of the arrest the property of a third party, which had bought her without knowledge of the maritime lien, grave injustice may be done. The third party may have no right of indemnity or, which is less unlikely supposition, his indemnity may be worthless. His vendor may, through lack of adequate funds, incompetent legal advice or other reason, not properly and fully have contested the issue of liability . . . The position would be quite different from that obtaining when an arrest is effected after transfer of the res to such a third party, but before there had been judgment on liability. The third party can then intervene.[47]

It was held that the plaintiff's right of arrest was lost because it had become merged in the judgment.

It should be noted that, under CPR, r 61. 5(1), a judgment creditor can arrest a ship. That rule seems to presuppose that no security had been obtained before judgment, rather than suggesting that this rule has undermined *The Alletta*. It is interesting to note that the Singaporean court in *The Daien Maru*[48] criticised and did not follow *The Alletta*. However, from the facts of *The Daien Maru*, it will be seen that it can be distinguished from *The Alletta* because security had not been obtained before judgment.

The Singaporean court held that the plaintiff, who had instituted an action *in rem* against the ship to enforce a maritime lien for services provided to the ship, but had not obtained security, was entitled to arrest the ship for the same cause of action, even after he had obtained judgment. The facts were unusual. The ship was originally arrested by her owners for a claim of possession they had against the charterers. The crew, who had a claim for unpaid wages against the owners, issued

---

47 [1974] 1 Lloyd's Rep 40, pp 50–51, *The Point Breeze* [1928] P 135 was applied.
48 [1986] 1 Lloyd's Rep 387.

a caveat against release of the ship and proceeded to judgment. Thereafter, the owners persuaded the court to release the ship from arrest they had effected themselves. Then the crew arrested the ship to obtain security and execute judgment against it. The judge said that, although once a judgment has been obtained in an action the claim was merged in the judgment, it did not follow and there was no authority supporting the view that the right to security in the ship was lost or extinguished by such merger. The plaintiff who has instituted an action to enforce a maritime lien must be entitled to arrest the ship in the same action, even after he has obtained judgment, provided always that, in such a case, no bail has been previously put up for the ship in that action.

On the facts of this case, it would be unfair if the arrest of the ship was not permitted after judgment to enforce the judgment against the ship representing the security for the maritime lien.[49]

By contrast, *The Alletta*, in which security had been provided and the enforcement of the maritime lien against the ship by arresting it in the hands of an innocent purchaser took an unusually long time after judgment, is clearly distinguishable.[50]

When a domestic judgment *in rem* has been obtained after bail has been given, which represents the ship and has the effect of submission to jurisdiction by the defendant,[51] but the bail is not sufficient to satisfy the total amount of judgment, the judgment can be executed *in personam* against the defendant, whereupon seizure and sale of assets belonging to the defendant will be executed by the Sheriff by serving a writ of *fieri facias*.[52] These are *in personam* proceedings which involve a seizure of assets by the Sheriff.

In conclusion, a re-arrest, after a judgment has been given, will not be permitted unless the re-arrest is for the purpose of enforcement of a maritime lien, when security had not previously been obtained. This may occur in very few cases such as *The Daien Maru*.

2.5.1 There can be re-arrest with the leave of the court before judgment on liability is given

It follows that, before judgment on liability has been given, the court has power to direct measures to be taken to do full justice to the claimant and re-arrest may be allowed, if the bail given is not sufficient, as Dr Lushington decided in *The Hero*[53] in

---

49 See, also, Chapter 3.

50 That the claimant cannot re-arrest the vessel after judgment, having previously obtained bail up to her full value, was also held in: *The Freedom* (1871) LR 3 A&E 495; *The Gemma* [1899] P 285; *The Ioannis Vatis* [1922] P 213: '. . . having received bail in the full value of the defendants' vessel, the plaintiffs could not arrest her *in rem*, but could proceed *in personam* and were entitled to a declaration that the amounts due in respect of interest and costs were enforceable by seizure and sale of the vessel by a sheriff under a writ of *fi fa*.' The rule that the bail represents the ship and the court will not normally permit a second arrest is not without exception: *The Arctic Star* (CA *The Times*, Feb 5, 1985).

51 When bail is provided, it is linked with an undertaking given by the defendant to submit to jurisdiction: *The Prinsengracht* [1993] 1 Lloyd's Rep 41. Bail could be given under protest if there are grounds for the defendant to contest the jurisdiction of the court: *The Anna H* [1994] 1 Lloyd's Rep 287 (CA), per Hobhouse LJ.

52 CPR, Sched 1, Ords 46 and 47.

53 Dr Lushington in *The Hero* (1865) B&L 447.

which judgment had not been given at the time of re-arrest. In this case, in which a clerical error had been made about the amount of security, Dr Lushington distinguished his previous decisions, namely *The Kalamazoo* and *The Wild Ranger*, by saying[54] that: if the expressions in those cases were literally interpreted, it would indicate that the court would not have power to grant a re-arrest for the same cause of action after property had been released on bail. But what was said in those earlier cases must be read subject to the facts that formed the ground of the decisions. In each of those cases, the cause of action had passed into *res judicata* because judgment on liability had been given.

Another occasion of permitting re-arrest was, in the old days, when the bail had become insolvent, or the guarantee was inoperative.[55]

This is confirmed by the English court in recent cases, such as **The Ruta**,[56] in which Steel J held that the discretion of the court to allow re-arrest is a broad one and the courts adopt a pragmatic approach. The court will not normally permit a second arrest, and the justification for this rule is to avoid oppression and unfairness. CPR Part 61.6(2)(b) makes express provision for permitting an arrest or re-arrest so as to obtain further security. The judge explained that permission will only be granted in circumstances of oppression or unfairness and, in this case, the security was insufficient to cover the very substantial cost element brought about by the procedural complications of the default claim.

Also the New Zealand Court of Appeal in **The Clarabelle**[57] ordered the re-arrest of a ship applied for by the classification society for the purpose of obtaining adequate security. It was held that release and re-arrest did not involve the exercise of a broad and unfettered discretion but it was based on the claimant's best arguable case. This case fell within the exception to the rule against re-arrest on account of the inadequate security provided, and there was nothing oppressive or unfair on the part of the claimant. On the facts, it was shown that there was a genuine dispute as to the merits of the underlying debt for survey fees.

By contrast, if there is adequate security provided, a re-arrest will be an abuse of process of the court.[58]

2.5.2 A foreign in rem judgment can be executed by re-arrest in this jurisdiction

When a foreign *in rem* judgment has been obtained and is not satisfied, the duty of the English court, founded on international comity and on interest of justice with respect to execution of a foreign judgment based upon a maritime lien, had been

---

54 (1865) B&L 447, p 448.

55 The City of Mecca (1879) 5 PD 28; *The Christiansborg* (1885) 10 PD 141; see, also, *Westminster Bank Ltd v West of England Association* (1933) 46 LlL Rep 101, in which it was said that, when there has been a mistake about the amount of bail, or there is a question of solvency of the surety, the bail question may be re-opened. Also, when the security given is by way of a personal guarantee which may prove to be inoperative, further arrest may be allowed.

56 [2000] 1 Lloyd's Rep 359.

57 [2002] 2 Lloyd's Rep 479.

58 *The Bumbesti* [1999] 2 Lloyd's Rep 481.

established since 1608.[59] Sir Robert Phillimore in *The City of Mecca*[60] allowed a judgment obtained *in rem* in Lisbon in respect of a collision damage to be enforced by an action *in rem* in England.[61] It should be noted that the case concerned a foreign judgment for which security had not been provided.

In a 20th century case, Sheen J confirmed this principle in *The Despina GK*,[62] which concerned a cargo claim. The plaintiffs arrested the ship at a Swedish port and commenced an action in the Admiralty Court in Stockholm, which gave judgment and awarded a maritime lien on the vessel for the sum adjudged. Sheen J said:[63]

> There is, of course, a distinction between those claims which give rise to a maritime lien and which may, therefore, be enforced against the ship, notwithstanding a change of ownership, and those claims which may only be enforced by an action *in rem* if the person who would be liable *in personam* is still the owner of the ship at the time when the writ is issued.

> Likewise, there is the further distinction between an action *in rem*, which may be brought in the High Court against the ship, and execution of a judgment obtained in such an action . . .

> A judgment creditor who has obtained a final judgment against a shipowner by proceeding *in rem* in a foreign Admiralty Court can bring an action *in rem* in this court against that ship to enforce the decree of the foreign court *if that is necessary to complete the execution* of that judgment, provided that the ship is the property of the judgment debtor at the time when she is arrested.[64] (emphasis added)

2.5.3 *Prohibition of re-arrest by statute or conventions*

Subject to the foregoing, re-arrest of the ship or a sister ship is, generally, not allowed by s 21(8) of the SCA 1981 for claims mentioned in s 20(2)(e)–(r) with regard to proceedings in this country. Section 21(8) provides:

> Where as regards any such claim as is mentioned in section 20(2)(e) to (r) a ship has been served with a writ or arrest in an action *in rem* brought to enforce that claim, no other ship may be served with a writ or arrested in that or any other action *in rem* brought to enforce that claim.

It emphasises that, in this jurisdiction, only one ship can be arrested.[65] The prohibition, however, should be read in the light of the decisions discussed above, namely when the security provided is insufficient and there is no oppression or unfairness,

---

59   Sir Robert Phillimore explained in *The City of Mecca* (1879) 5 PD 28.

60   Ibid.

61   The judgment was reversed by the Court of Appeal (1881) 6 PD 106, as it appeared from a further affidavit that the facts upon which the decision was based were different from the facts proved. But the principle laid down by Sir Phillimore regarding enforcement of a judgment *in rem* by way of execution was not undermined (see Sheen J's comments in *The Despina GK* [1982] 2 Lloyd's Rep 555).

62   [1982] 2 Lloyd's Rep 555.

63   Ibid, pp 558–59.

64   The action must be for the purpose of execution (as the judge stressed) and not for the trial of the matter.

65   *The Kommunar (No 2)* [1997] 1 Lloyd's Rep 8; *The Banco* [1971] 1 Lloyd's Rep 49.

or when the security given is inoperative, or when there has b¢
the amount of security requested.

Article 3(3) of the 1952 Arrest Convention provides specifically oi
which re-arrest or multiple arrest is permitted in Contracting Statι
the bail or other security, that was provided originally for the releas
has been released. That is a very rare occasion.

> A ship shall not be arrested, nor shall bail or other security be given more than ι
> in any one or more of the jurisdictions of any of the Contracting States in respect o.
> the same maritime claim by the same claimant: and, if a ship has been arrested in any
> one of such jurisdictions either to release the ship or to avoid a threatened arrest, any
> subsequent arrest of the ship or of any ship in the same ownership by the same
> claimant for the same maritime claim shall be set aside, and the ship released by the
> Court or other appropriate judicial authority of that State, unless the claimant can
> satisfy the Court or other appropriate judicial authority that the bail or other security
> had been finally released before the subsequent arrest or that there is other good
> cause for maintaining that arrest.

The 1999 Arrest Convention expressly and clearly specifies the occasions of
re-arrest by Art 5 in the following circumstances:

(1) where, in any State, a ship has already been arrested and released, or security
has already been provided to secure a maritime claim, that ship shall not thereafter be rearrested or arrested in respect of the same maritime claim unless:

    (a) the nature or amount of the security in respect of that ship already provided
in respect of the same claim is inadequate, on condition that the aggregate
amount of security may not exceed the value of the ship; or

    (b) the person who has already provided the security is not, or is unlikely to be,
able to fulfil some or all of that person's obligations; or

    (c) the ship arrested or the security previously provided was released either
upon the application or with the consent of the claimant acting on reasonable grounds, or because the claimant could not by taking reasonable steps
prevent the release;

(2) with regard to any other ship, which would otherwise be subject to arrest in
respect of the same maritime claim, arrest shall not be allowed unless the nature
or amount of the security provided in respect of the same claim is inadequate; or
the provisions of (1)(b) and (c) above are applicable.

2.5.4 Re-arrest and risk management

In most cases in practice, security is provided by agreement and, in consideration of
that agreement, the claimant releases the ship from arrest and promises not to re-
arrest this, or any other ship, in the same ownership, etc. A further arrest would not
only be in breach of the agreement, but would also be against good faith, unless
there were circumstances in which the agreement was rendered inoperative.[66] It is

---

66 *The Christiansborg* (1885) 10 PD 141; see, also, *Westminster Bank Ltd v West of England Association*
(1933) 46 LIL Rep 101, in which it was said that, when there has been a mistake about the
amount of bail, or there is a question of solvency of the surety, the bail question may be re-
opened. Also, when the security given is by way of a personal guarantee which may prove to
be inoperative, further arrest may be allowed.

portant to bear in mind, however, that any agreement, by which the claimant promises not to re-arrest a vessel in return of security, should expressly be made, not only between the claimant and the entity providing the security, but also between the claimant and the shipowner, or demise charterer, as the case may be.[67]

There have been instances in which a ship has been re-arrested in consequence of the bail becoming insolvent.[68] The rule that the bail represents the ship, so there should be no re-arrest, is not without exceptions, as seen earlier. The justification for the rule is, and always has been, to avoid oppression and unfairness.[69] The same would apply where the security given is not bail, but consists of a personal under-taking such as a guarantee. Where proper reasons are shown for it, re-arrest may be permitted.[70] The discretion of the English court is broad and the judges adopt a pragmatic approach, guided by what would be fair and just in the circumstances.

2.6 Appraisement and sale by the court

2.6.1 Sale by the Admiralty Marshal

If there is no acknowledgment of service and/or defence to a claim *in rem* within the time required, the claimant may apply for a judgment in default by filing an application, a certificate proving proper service of the claim form and evidence proving the claim to the satisfaction of the court. There is a presumption of good service if the claim form was served by the court. The property under arrest will be appraised and sold by court order. Appraisement is an official valuation of the property by a court-appointed valuer. An order for sale before judgment may only be made by the admiralty judge.[71]

The Admiralty Marshal can sell either by private treaty or public auction advised by brokers. The effect of sale by him is that all encumbrances, including maritime liens, are extinguished. Private negotiations for sale by the owner, or a third party, after a court order is made will be in contempt of court.

The APJ Shalin [72]

In a dispute arising under a shipbuilding contract, the plaintiffs alleged default in payment under the contract. The defendants' vessel came within the English juris-

---

67 A suggestion made by Clarke LJ in his speech on the subject ('The civil justice reform, its impact on maritime litigation, the maritime industry and London', lecture in memory of Professor Cadwallader, the London Shipping Law Centre, 7 July 1999; the text of the speeches on the CPR can be obtained from the office of the Shipping Law Centre, UCL Law Faculty).

68 *The City of Mecca* (1879) 5 PD 28, per Sir Robert Phillimore.

69 Lloyd LJ, in *The Arctic Star* (1985) *The Times*, 5 February; the same view was held by Steel J, in *The Ruta* [2000] 1 Lloyd's Rep 359.

70 *Westminster Bank Ltd v West of England Steamship Owners' P&I Association Ltd* (1933) 46 LlL Rep 101, per Roche J.

71 PD 61.10, para 9.3.

72 [1991] 2 Lloyd's Rep 62.

diction and the plaintiffs issued a writ *in rem* and arrested her. The defendants applied for the writ and the arrest to be set aside, claiming that the vessel was valueless to the plaintiffs as security because there were other claims ranking in priority to that of the plaintiffs. They also sought an order giving them liberty to sell the vessel privately, subject to the supervision of the Admiralty Marshal. It was held that, without security being given, it would not be right for the court to order the release of the ship against the wishes of the creditor who had properly exercised his right to arrest the ship. The issue of priority was to be determined when all the actions had proceeded to judgment. It was also held that while a ship was under arrest, it was in the custody of the Admiralty Marshal. The shipowners could only sell the vessel, if they could find someone willing to buy her under arrest, but it would remain under arrest. However, where an order for sale was made by the court, there could not be a private sale because such a transaction would be open to abuse.

The Cerro Colorado [73]

The plaintiff lent a substantial amount of money to the defendants, secured by a mortgage upon the ship. They obtained judgment and the court ordered that the ship be appraised and sold by the Admiralty Marshal. Earlier, solicitors for the master and crew of that ship had requested the entry of a caveat against the release of the ship, on the grounds that they had a right of action *in rem* against the ship, pursuant to s 20(2)(o) of the SCA 1981, for various claims for wages, severance pay and interest. A writ had not been issued against the ship on their behalf. When an order for the sale was made, the Spanish Embassy in London sent a note to the effect that a purchaser of the ship would find himself subject to substantial claims by the crew for unpaid wages, which had been incurred by the previous owner. An article in the Lloyd's List, published soon thereafter, contained the same warning. Upon an application by the Admiralty Marshal to the court for directions, it was held that a sale by the Admiralty Marshal gave the purchaser a title free of all liens and encumbrances. It was also held that the articles published could be treated as a contempt of court, tending to interfere with the administration of justice. The master and crew were given 28 days in which to make a claim *in rem* against the ship, or the proceeds of sale if they so wished.

The Admiralty Marshal cannot sell the ship for less than the appraised value without an order of the court.

The Halcyon The Great [74]

The mortgagees of the ship proceeded by an action *in rem*. During the trial, they applied for an order for the appraisement and sale of the vessel. After her appraisal, the Admiralty Marshal invited bids. Even the highest of the bids made was substantially below the appraised value. The commission of appraisement and sale required that the Admiralty Marshal did not sell below the appraised value.

---

73 [1993] 1 Lloyd's Rep 58.
74 [1975] 1 Lloyd's Rep 525.

He applied to the court for an order to sell below the appraised value. The plaintiffs opposed the application and were supported by various creditors and other parties interested in the action. The court considered that there was a risk that there might not even be a bid as good as the one offered at that time, if the application of the Marshal to sell below the appraised value was refused and the ship was re-offered. However, the judge agreed to grant the request made by the plaintiffs and the other parties, on the condition that they undertook to indemnify the court against any loss, which could result from refusing the Marshal's application. On receiving the undertaking, the judge held that the Marshal was, thus, denied liberty to sell the ship for less than the appraised value without further order of the court.

The proceeds of sale will be kept in court until all claimants, who have obtained judgment against the ship, apply to be joined in the list for payment. The court will determine the priorities of the various claimants when it distributes the court fund (see paras 4 & 5 below).

2.6.2 *Sale* pendente lite

Appraisement and sale of the ship may be ordered pending action (*pendente lite*) in certain circumstances.

The Myrto [75]

The plaintiffs were mortgagees of the defendants' vessel. They arrested the vessel for the amount due and owing to them under a registered mortgage. Many other claimants had also entered caveats against release of the vessel. The charterers of the ship intervened in the action claiming that the arrest of the ship was an unlawful interference with their contractual rights. The plaintiffs applied for the appraisement and sale of the vessel *pendente lite*, which was resisted by both the owners and charterers. It was held that, on the evidence, it was unlikely that the owners would have sufficient resources either to pay off the claims against the ship or to complete the voyage, which had been seriously disrupted already by the events that had taken place leading up to the arrest of the vessel. No purpose would be served by releasing the ship from her present arrest. [76]

On the question of whether an order for appraisement and sale of the ship under arrest should be made, the court held that such a situation only arises where there is a default of appearance or defence. If the defendants appear, they usually obtain release from arrest by giving bail or providing security. The court would make such an order (on the plaintiff's application) in a situation where the security of the plaintiff's claim was imperiled to be diminished by the continuing costs of maintaining the arrest to the disadvantage of all those interested in the ship, including the defendants themselves, if there was still a residual interest left to them.

---

75 [1977] 2 Lloyd's Rep 243.

76 For further information on this point, and possible interference with the contractual rights of third parties, see Chapter 9 on mortgages.

Brandon J said:

> I accept that the court should not make an order for the appraisement and sale of a ship *pendente lite* except for good reason, and this, whether the action is defended or not. I accept further that, where the action is defended and the defendants opposed the making of such an order, the court should examine more critically than it would normally do in a default action the question whether good reason for the making of an order exists or not ... It would, in my view, be unreasonable to keep the ship under arrest at great expense for seven months or more, with the result that, if the bank succeeded in their claim, the amount of their recovery would be reduced by the costs incurred. If the owners were prepared to hear or contribute to those costs for the time being in order to prevent a sale, different considerations might apply.[77]

Following this principle, appraisement and sale were permitted *pendente lite* in the circumstances of the following case.

The Gulf Venture[78]

The plaintiffs applied for the appraisement and sale of *The Gulf Venture*. They claimed that the vessel was a wasting asset and ought to be sold for the benefit of all the creditors, as the cost of maintaining her under arrest would exceed £5,000 per month. The owners and the second mortgagees disputed the application. The court considered whether the plaintiffs had a reasonably arguable case, that the defendants would be liable on the claim in an action *in personam*. There was no dispute as to the amount it would cost to maintain the vessel under arrest. The court examined and reaffirmed the principles laid down in *The Myrto*.[79] It was held that the plaintiffs had a probable case on liability and, also, it was probable that if judgment was obtained in their favour, it would not be satisfied by the defendants personally. The plaintiffs would still have to obtain an order for the sale of the ship. Concerning the second mortgagees, it was in their interest that they should intervene to enforce their security at the present time, rather than later, seeing that the security available one year later after the adjudication would be about £60,000 or less. The sale of the vessel was therefore ordered.

The Admiralty Marshal may seek the advice of experts about the condition of the ship and what repairs may be necessary to be carried out on the vessel before it is sold in order to achieve a better price.

The Westport (No 2)[80]

The case concerned the supply of necessaries to the defendants' ship by the plaintiffs who had a claim for the price. The court had already ordered a sale of the vessel *pendente lite*. In a motion for judgment in default of defence, the plaintiffs applied for an order that the feed water pump of the ship was repaired. The brokers advised that it would be good commercial practice to repair the ship, so that she might be sold at a better price than if the pump remained unrepaired. The court held that in

---

77 *The Myrto* [1977] 2 Lloyd's Rep 243, pp 260–61.
78 [1985] 1 Lloyd's Rep 131.
79 [1977] 2 Lloyd's Rep 243.
80 [1965] 1 Lloyd's Rep 549.

order to safeguard the interests of all the claimants, including those of the owners, the advice of the brokers would be taken and the ship was duly repaired.

3 COMPETITION OF CLAIMS BROUGHT IN ADMIRALTY AND COMPANY COURTS[81]

There are occasions when there are company creditors who may petition to the court dealing with company matters (Chancery Division of the High Court) for the winding up of the company. At the same time, maritime claimants may exercise their right *in rem* either by the issue of a claim form or by the arrest of the company's asset, the ship. A question that arises, in such circumstances, is this: which class of creditors should be permitted to proceed with enforcement of their rights against the company's assets? On the one hand, the policy of the insolvency legislation aims to protect the company's assets for the benefit of the company's creditors and, on the other hand, the policy of the Admiralty Court is to protect secured maritime creditors. Secured maritime creditors, such as maritime lien holders and mortgagees, may be allowed to proceed in the Admiralty Court to realise their security, only with the leave of the Companies' Court. Such leave will be given, even if the secured maritime creditors issue their *in rem* claim after the winding up order is made against the company (s 130(2) of the Insolvency Act 1986 and equivalent provisions of the Insolvency Act 2000). Maritime claimants, other than maritime lien holders and mortgagees, are not secured creditors, unless they issue their *in rem* claim form before commencement of the winding up of the company.

Re Aro Co Ltd[82]

An unregistered Liberian shipping company was ordered to be wound up compulsorily in the Commercial Court, following a petition by a P&I club to which the company was indebted to the sum of $134,912.37. The company had no assets in the UK and the only asset it had was the vessel, *Aro*, which had been laid up for years for lack of employment. The vessel's value was only about $300,000 and there were numerous other claims against the vessel, including that of the plaintiffs. The plaintiffs' claim was for damages in respect of damage to cargo of oil carried by the vessel and estimated to be about $60,000. There was also a debt owed to the Admiralty Marshal, incurred after the arrest of the vessel. The plaintiffs had issued a writ in the Admiralty Court with respect to their claim, prior to the commencement of the winding up, but they had not served it, nor had they arrested the vessel because she was already under arrest by S Ltd. They merely entered a caveat against release on the same day, so that, even if the arrest was lifted, the petitioners could not have her removed without notice to the plaintiffs. The plaintiffs applied for leave

---

81　For details of the statutory provisions of the insolvency legislation and how the issue of an *in rem* claim form or the arrest of the ship has been interpreted in the context of that legislation, see Meeson, N, *Admiralty Jurisdiction and Practice*, 3rd edn, 2003, LLP, pp 95–107.

82　[1980] 2 WLR 453.

pursuant to s 231 of the Companies Act (CA) 1948 to continue their action against the vessel and the Liberian company pending in the Admiralty Court, notwithstanding the winding up order. The trial judge held that the plaintiffs remained unsecured creditors because they had not served the writ or arrested the vessel. The Court of Appeal overturned this decision and held that regardless of whether the plaintiffs had invoked the jurisdiction of the Admiralty Court prior to the winding up, they were considered as having the status of secured creditors because, after the issue of the writ, they could have served it and could have arrested *The Aro*, with the result that the vessel would effectively be encumbered with their claim.

Also, that it had been a long-established practice to issue a caveat against release of a vessel under arrest, rather than cause multiple arrests. Relief under s 231 of the CA 1948 could not be confined to a case of a claimant who had served a writ on the ship, as distinct from one who had issued his writ but not served. According to Brightman LJ:

> The service of the writ adds nothing to the status of the claimant vis-à-vis the vessel sued. This is established by the issue of the writ. As between the plaintiff and the defendant, service merely causes time to commence running within which the defendant must enter appearance in order to avoid being a respondent to a motion for judgment by default.[83]

He further said that the rights of a plaintiff suing *in rem* have points of similarity with legal or equitable mortgagees or charges. The similarity has been carried forward by the decision in *The Monica S* where it was held that the burden of the statutory right *in rem* ran with the ship, so as to enable the plaintiff to arrest the ship, notwithstanding the transfer of ownership since the writ was issued.[84]

In this connection, it should be pointed out again that, if the House of Lords in *The Indian Grace* intended to alter this position, it should have done so expressly, as discussed in Chapter 3.

4 PRIORITIES IN PAYMENT OF CLAIMS OUT OF THE COURT FUND

As soon as the arrested ship has been sold by court order, the proceeds of sale remain under the control of the Admiralty Marshal. He will distribute the fund on the basis of established priorities. The court still maintains discretion. Priorities are a matter of procedure and are subject to the law of the forum, *lex fori*. However, some rights, which lie on special powers of arrest and detention, fall outside the scheme of priorities and are considered first below as they affect the order of priorities.

---

83 [1980] 2 WLR 453, p 465.
84 See Chapter 3.

4.1 Statutory powers of port authorities for detention and sale

The Harbours, Docks and Piers Clauses Act (HDPCA) 1847 empowers the port authorities to arrest and sell any vessel or wreck within the precincts of the port for unpaid port dues or damage done to its premises by the ship. The statute grants a statutory right of detention on the ship in favour of the port authority. If the relevant ship comes under the custody of the Admiralty Marshal, two related questions are important here: (1) is the port authority's statutory right of detention of the ship preserved? And (2) is the claim of the port authority transferable to the court fund while retaining its preferential treatment over and above other preferential claims?

4.1.1 Effect of sale by the Admiralty Marshal upon the right of the port authority

The Court of Appeal in *Emilie Millon*[85] held that the claim of the port authority could not be transferred to the court fund; the right of detention should be maintained until the port was paid, regardless of maritime liens. The court could not order the sale and delivery of the ship to the purchaser.

While the ship was in the docks at Liverpool, the master and crew arrested her for unpaid wages earned. Judgment was given and the Admiralty Marshal ordered the sale of the ship by auction. Sale by auction failed and the ship was sold by private treaty. The court was asked to sanction the sale and deliver the ship to the purchaser, free of all encumbrances. At this time, the appellants (the port authority) were asserting their rights under statute to detain the ship until the outstanding port dues were paid. The judge sanctioned the sale and ordered that any right of the port authority to payment of their charges in priority over other claimants be preserved as against the fund in court. The port authority appealed against this order. The Court of Appeal reversed the order on the ground that the judge ignored the right given by the statute to the port authority to detain the vessel until they were paid:

> While the port's dock tonnage rates remained unpaid in respect of any vessel liable, the Board would cause such vessel to be detained until all such rates were paid. Such a right given by the statute was paramount, notwithstanding that the master and crew of the vessel had a maritime lien upon her for wages due before she entered the dock. Therefore, the court could not, in such an action, make an order for the sale and delivery of a ship to a purchaser which would deprive a dock authority of its statutory right of detention without its consent; and that such a right was not transferable to the court fund representing the ship.

This decision was followed by subsequent decisions concerning the same issue of preserving the port authority's statutory right of detention and sale over the Marshal's jurisdiction to deal with the res and the priorities of other claims.

However, even if the statutory power of detention of the port authority is preserved, such power would be of no practical use if the port authority were not able by law to sell the ship free of other encumbrances. A purchaser would not be

---

85 [1905] 2 KB 817.

prepared to buy from the port authority, and the Admiralty Marshal would have to sell the ship.

The courts were faced with this issue in subsequent decisions. Guidance was given by the House of Lords in *The Countess* (para 4.1.2, below) when it had to decide a similar question, namely: whether or not the port's right of detention would serve a practical purpose in circumstances in which the court has to distribute the fund established in court for the purpose of the shipowners' right to limit liability.

In *The Sea Spray*,[86] Dean J resolved the question of priorities between the port authority for their expenses incurred in respect of raising the wreck of this ship (which sank after a collision with a barge) and the claim of the barge for damages suffered due to the collision, by allowing the port authority (who intervened in the action) to sell the ship, pay itself and deposit the balance of the proceeds with the court. The main reason of this decision was that, had it not been for the port authority, which raised the wreck, there would be no *res* for the Marshal to sell. The decision did not deal with the question whether the purchaser from the port authority could buy the ship free from encumbrances. Willmer J, in *The Ousel*,[87] followed *The Sea Spray* by upholding the motion of the Harbour Board as interveners (claiming wreck removal expenses) in the arrest of the ship by salvors exercising their maritime lien on the cargo on board. The Board could proceed with its statutory power of detention and sale and reimburse itself out of the proceeds. The judge did not decide, but accepted, obiter, that the sale by the port authority in the exercise of its statutory power could give title free of encumbrances. The motion requiring the Marshal to withdraw from the arrest was not opposed.

Although the judge did not decide the issue of whether the port authority could give title free of encumbrances, his *obiter* comments in this respect should be disregarded in the light of the following decisions.

In *The Spermina*,[88] again, there was a motion, this time by the Manchester Ship Canal Company, as interveners in a mortgagees' action, requesting that the Marshal be directed to withdraw from possession of the steamer *The Spermina*, or, alternatively, that the warrant of arrest be set aside to enable the interveners to exercise their statutory right of sale of the vessel. Hill J held that, while the Canal Company were in a preferential position to be paid for outstanding dues in priority to the mortgagees' claim, it might be disastrous if the Canal Company sold, because they could not give a clean title, whereas the Marshal could in a sale by him.

In *The Blitz*,[89] the court decided that the port authority could only pass title to a purchaser of the ship free of mortgages but not free of maritime liens.

---

86 [1907] P 133.
87 [1957] 1 Lloyd's Rep 151.
88 (1923) 17 LlL Rep 17.
89 [1992] 2 Lloyd's Rep 441 (see also para 4.1.5, below).

4.1.2 Effect of constituting limitation fund on the right of the port authority

In a similar question, namely whether the statutory claim by the port authority was transferable to the limitation fund set up by the shipowner who was, by statute, entitled to limit his liability, the House of Lords held (by majority of 3:2) in *The Countess*,[90] that the claim by the port authority for damage done to the port by the ship permitted the port to be paid first out of the limitation fund, provided it had exercised its right of detention. Overruling the majority of the Court of Appeal and the President of the Admiralty Court, it held that the Board's claim, having the status of a statutory possessory lien conferred by the statutory power to detain, remained effective against the fund, although the harbour authority parted with possession of the ship. The right was not extinguished. The court, in distributing the statutory amount of the shipowners' liability ratably among the claimants, ought to have regard to the priorities as well as to the amounts of the claims; consequently, the whole of the fund should be paid out to the Board as its special right was not adjunct to the right to participate in the distribution of the limitation fund.

Although the majority of the Lords agreed with the Court of Appeal in *Emilie Millon* that the right of detention of the port authority was paramount, because the authority did not have a charge on the ship or any other protection, it could not see how the problem could be resolved if the port authority was not paid first, but kept the ship under detention.[91]

4.1.3 The Scottish approach

The Scottish Court of Session, in *The Sierra Nevada*,[92] applied the reasoning of the House of Lords in the above case and held that the port authority's right would be transferable to the proceeds of sale where the ship was sold by the court with the consent of the port authority, on the understanding that its priority was preserved. It distinguished the *Emilie Millon* decision on the facts, in that it concerned a private sale and that the harbour authority had intervened before the sale had been sanctioned by the court but, in any event, it criticised the decision as being inconsistent with the view taken of the matter by the majority in the House of Lords in *The Countess*.

Clyde Navigation Trustees in the Scottish case, were, therefore, entitled to enforce their statutory right by its notional transference to the fund in the competition of claims and to enjoy a preference over the first mortgagees in the distribution of the proceeds of sale.

---

90 *Mersey Docks and Harbours Board v Hay* [1923] AC 345.

91 Lord Sumner (dissenting) did not think that the port should have priority over other claimants as the right to detain was not equivalent to an arrest or proceeding *in rem*. If the port continued to detain the ship after the money owed was deposited with the court, the owner would have an action in detinue. Further, he said, that, apart from pressure put upon the owner, detention may lead to nothing.

92 (1932) 42 LlL Rep 309 (Ct Sess).

It seems that there are two conflicting approaches on the issue of transfer of the port authority's claim into the court fund: the approach of the Court of Appeal in *Emilie Millon*, and the Scottish approach in *The Sierra Nevada*. It should be observed that the House of Lords in *The Countess* did not deal with this issue directly but only with the similar issue of transfer of the port authority's claim into the limitation fund. But the definite answer to these issues hangs on the practical question of whether the port authority is able to sell the ship to a purchaser free of all encumbrances, which only the Admiralty Marshal has power to do.

4.1.4 Reconciliation of approaches

Since the House of Lords in *The Countess* did not have to decide whether the Admiralty Marshal can proceed with the sale of the ship, but only dealt with the situation of claims when a limitation fund is constituted and the preservation of the right of the port authority, Brandon J, in ***The Queen of the South***,[93] tried to conciliate the two approaches mentioned above.

If the matter were free from authority, he said, he would have followed the Scottish approach which, as was indicated by Lord Fleming in *The Sierra Nevada*, allows the court to sell, free of rights, while transferring equivalent rights with equivalent priority to the court fund, whether or not the dock or harbour authority consents. However, he recognised that this area was a disputed area in law and he preferred not to express a final decision, since he did not have to, and there was a simpler solution. English authorities, he said, allow the Marshal to incur expenditure on the ship where it is for the benefit of all parties interested in her. So, the court, if it thinks fit for the benefit of all, Brandon J proposed, has power to pay off the claims of the intervening port authority and then include such expenditure to his expenses of sale. In future cases, he suggested, the Marshal could ask all interested parties whether they objected to such a solution; if all interested parties consented, the Marshal would apply to the registrar to give such authority. If, on the other hand, one or more parties objected, the registrar should determine the matter himself or apply to the judge.[94] In the case before him, Brandon J decided:

> In my judgment, on the facts of this case, it would be for the benefit of all those interested in *The Queen of the South* that the interveners' claims for rates should be paid off, so that the marshal can sell the vessel free of the interveners' rights of detention and sale, whether already exercised or capable of being exercised hereafter. If the marshal cannot sell the ship free of such rights, he may be unable either to find a purchaser at all, or at any rate to find one willing to pay a proper price. If the interveners are to be paid off in this way, however, it must be on the basis that they give a written undertaking to the court not to exercise their rights of detention or sale in respect of the rates concerned.[95]

---

93 [1968] P 449; if the port authority does not exercise its power of detention, its right will be lost: *The Charger* [1966] 2 Lloyd's Rep 670.

94 [1968] P 449, pp 462–66.

95 Ibid, p 465.

4.1.5 Port authorities' statutory right
of sale and risk management

In a fairly recent decision, the court held that a sale by the harbour authority will give a purchaser title free only of all mortgages on the ship but not of prior maritime liens.

The Blitz[96]

A mortgage for a loan granted in connection with this ship was duly registered, but the debt remained unpaid. The vessel was arrested for unpaid harbour dues and, pursuant to s 44 of the HDPCA 1847, the harbour authority sold the vessel to the defendant. The mortgagee claimed the money due under the mortgage and the question was whether the sale of the vessel pursuant to s 44 of the HDPCA 1847 was a sale free from encumbrances, so that a bona fide purchaser obtained a title, free of the mortgage, on the ship.

Sheen J held that the harbour authority could give a title free from any mortgage, because the purchaser could not be expected to investigate the registry of interests on the ship before buying from a harbour authority. If the harbour authority was required to find out whether there was a mortgage and advertise for sale subject to that mortgage, it would not be possible to sell the vessel. If that was allowed, the owner of a ship could effectively deprive a harbour authority of its remedy under s 44 by mortgaging the ship for her full value. The risk of non-payment should be borne by the person who, voluntarily and unwisely, lends a large amount on the security of a ship, rather than by a harbour authority, or an innocent purchaser without notice of the mortgage.

The conclusion to be drawn from these decisions is that the port authority is justified by statute to exercise its right of detention for payment of outstanding dues or other charges or a claim for damage caused to its property by a ship, but a sale of the ship by the authority does not have the same effect as the sale by the admiralty Marshal, so as to give a title free from all encumbrances. The port authority should be co-operative to give up its detention of the ship, in lieu of payment by the Marshal, in priority over other claimants, once the proceeds of sale are materialised by a court sale. If it is not co-operative, the court should make an appropriate order in those terms. Purchasers from the port authority should be aware that they will not get a title free from all encumbrances.

4.2 The ship-repairers' lien and risk management

This type of lien arises at common law and commences as soon as the ship enters the yard and continues as long as the yard retains possession of the ship. This means that, provided the yard does not give up possession of the ship, it is entitled to priority of payment of its fees and the cost of repairs over all other claims, except for maritime liens created before it exercised its possessory lien.

---

96   [1992] 2 Lloyd's Rep 441.

The Russland[97]

After being stranded on rocks, *The Russland* was assisted by salvors to get off and was successfully placed in the dock for temporary repairs. The salvors commenced an *in rem* action for payment of salvage. The ship-repairer who carried out the repairs after the salvage claimed that the sum for the repairs due to him should be allowed over the salvors' claim. The court ordered that a ship-repairer's claim ranked after maritime liens already accrued, and there was no basis on which the ship-repairer's claim could be preferred to those of the salvors, even taking into consideration that the repairs benefited the salvors.[98]

The repairer's right to lien is lost if it is not exercised, or if possession of the ship is given up. Even if a ship-repairer enjoys a maritime lien under the substantive law of the country in which the repairs were done, such as in the USA, the ship-repairer, as it will be seen later, ought to consider getting paid before letting the ship leave his yard, in the event of arrest of the ship by the mortgagee in a jurisdiction which applies English law for the enforcement of maritime claims.

If a yard maintains possession of the ship, a line of old authorities show that the English court has recognised and preserved the priority of the possessory lien holder over other maritime claims, even maritime liens that arose after the ship entered the shipyard.

In *The Immacolata Concezione*,[99] there was a competition between claims of a necessaries man, the master and crew, and the shipyard in which the ship had entered before the other claims arose. Some wages for the crew had already accrued. Butt J said:

> But for *The Gustaf*,[100] I should not feel quite clear that [the claim of the repair yard] had not priority over a maritime lien, but, by that decision of Dr Lushington, I am bound. I shall, therefore, give priority to Carter [repair yard] over all the other claimants, except the mariners, so far as regards the claim of the latter for wages [already accrued before the ship entered the yard]. *The Gustaf* is a clear decision to the effect that the claim of the mariners has priority over the shipwrights' common law possessory lien up to the time of the beginning of such lien, and therefore, as I have said, the seamen's wages must have priority over the other claims. With regard to the rest of the wages claim, it will rank after Carter's claim.

Following this principle, the judge held, in *The Tergeste*,[101] that a possessory lien holder who surrenders the ship to the Admiralty Marshal should be put in exactly the same position as if he had not surrendered the ship.

The Italian steamship *The Tergeste* was arrested by the Admiralty Marshal in an action for wages and disbursements brought by the master on behalf of himself and the crew. At the time she was arrested, the ship-repairers claimed to have a common law possessory lien on the ship for work which they had done but surrendered the ship to the Marshal. The ship was sold in the wages action, and, as the proceeds in

---

97   [1924] P 55.
98   See, also, *The Katingaki* [1976] 2 Lloyd's Rep 372.
99   (1883) 9 PD 37, p 42.
100 Cited by Butt J.
101 [1903] P 26.

court were insufficient to meet the total amount of both claims, the question that arose was about the priority of the possessory lien holder.

Phillimore J, relying on previous authorities, stated as follows:

> The view which the Admiralty Court took with regard to conflicting claims by ship-wrights having a possessory common law lien, and claims which have been sustained by process in the Admiralty Court, has been well established . . . It is that it is the duty of the material man not to contend with the Admiralty Marshal but to surrender the ship to the officer of the court, and let the officer of the court, under the order of the court, remove and sell her; but when he has done that, the court undertakes that he shall be protected, and that he shall be put exactly in the same position as if he had not surrendered the ship to the marshal. The court has further decided in the case of *The Gustaf* that the possessory lien of a shipwright is subject to maritime liens attaching prior to the ship being taken into the shipwright's yard. If there is a possessory lien, that possessory lien takes precedence of all maritime liens for claims which accrue after the date when the possessory lien begins. The only doubt that Butt J had in the case of *The Immacolata Concezione* was whether *The Gustaf* was not too favourable to the claimants under a maritime lien. There is no doubt here when the possessory lien began; it began when the ship was put into dry dock. It is perfectly true that for some days there was no money in respect of which the lien would operate; but if Messrs Rait and Gardiner had such possession as to give them a possessory lien at the date when the ship was taken by the Admiralty Marshal, they had it for the price of the whole of the work which they had done up to that time.
>
> It is said that they had no possessory lien, because the master and crew were on board; if that were the rule a great number of shipwrights' liens would be disturbed. That man has a lien who has such control of the chattel as prevents it being taken away from his possession. He may admit other persons or workmen to access to the chattel, and other tradesmen may claim a possessory lien over the chattel or part of it, but if it cannot be got out of the dock or yard without the consent of the owner of the dock or yard, the owner of the dock will have a possessory lien, though perhaps not the only one, on the chattel, which he can enforce, and which the Court has taken upon itself to enforce for him as against subsequent claims. I have no doubt in this case that Rait and Gardiner had an ample possessory lien.

5 DISTRIBUTION OF THE COURT FUND BY THE COURT

The court will determine the distribution following the order of priorities (s 21(6) of the SCA 1981), but questions of priorities cannot be compartmentalised in the form of strict rules of ranking. The court has broad discretionary power, taking into account considerations of equity, public policy and commercial expediency, with the ultimate aim of doing what is just in the circumstances of each case.[102] Payment will be made only to judgment holders as follows:

(a) The Admiralty Marshal's costs.

(b) Claimant's costs.

(c) Maritime lienees.

---

102 *The Ruta* [2000] 1 Lloyd's Rep 359, per Steel J, citing with approval Thomas on Maritime Lines, BSL vol 14 at para 418.

(d) Mortgagees in the order of registration, equitable mortgagees having last priority.

(e) Claimants who become secured creditors by the issue of the *in rem* claim form (statutory liens *in rem*). As between themselves, they run *pari passu*.

(f) Claimants who have obtained a judgment *in personam* against the shipowner of the *res* will be last. For the execution of the judgment, a judgment creditor will seek the issue of a writ of execution, *fieri facias*, and the sheriff will seize any property of the company in England. Since most shipowning companies are foreign, the sheriff will execute such a writ upon a ship when it comes within the jurisdiction. If the sheriff seizes the ship before the issue of an *in rem* claim form by maritime claimants (other than maritime lien holders) and prior to mortgagees, it is likely that the *in personam* creditor will be able to have his judgment executed against the seized ship.[103]

(g) The balance, if any, will be paid to the owner of the ship.

As far as maritime lien holders are concerned, the following examples illustrate how the courts have dealt with priority principles between different maritime lienees when the value of the ship is not sufficient.

Subject to the broad discretionary approach of the court to do what is just in each case, if all liens are in the same category, they rank *pari passu*,[104] except in relation to salvage, where the last in time may take priority on the justification that the ship is saved by the salvor for the benefit of other claimants. Such an approach serves also to encourage salvors to save maritime property. It must be the latest in time of all other liens created (including all other salvage and damage liens)[105] in order to take priority. As regards wages no distinction is made between wages earned before or after salvage; the salvage claim takes priority over wages.

The Lyrma (No 2)[106]

The ship encountered bad weather and began to list. Her master sent out a signal and the ship A responded to the call for assistance. By the time the *A* reached *The Lyrma*, the weather conditions had become worse. After much difficulty, *The Lyrma* was towed with her cargo to safety. The salvors brought an action for remuneration, so the ship and cargo were arrested. The crew of the ship had remained in the service of the ship until quite a long time after this incident and, therefore, brought an action *in rem* against the ship, claiming unpaid wages, emoluments and other disbursements. The owners did not enter an appearance. The court gave an order for the sale of the ship. The master and crew claimed priority for wages, earned before and after the salvage was rendered, and repatriation expenses. It was held that there was no distinction in priorities between wages earned before or after salvage, as against a salvor's claim. It was a long-established principle that a salvor's lien took priority over all earlier liens, including those of wages claimants.

---

103 *The James W Elwell* [1921] P 351. CPR, Sched 1, Ords 46 & 47.
104 *The Steam Fisher* [1926] P 73.
105 *The Inna* (1938) 60 LlL Rep 414.
106 [1978] 2 Lloyd's Rep 30.

The Veritas[107]

The vessel was safely towed into the Mersey Docks by salvors after her engines broke down. Another vessel ran to her assistance, thereafter, and, to prevent her sinking into deep water, second salvors tried to beach her with the result that she came into contact with and damaged a landing stage belonging to the Dock Board. The Board removed the vessel under its statutory powers, as she was obstructing the waterway. The vessel was sold and, after expenses were taken out, the remaining sum was paid into court. The proceeds were insufficient to meet the claims of the two salvors and the Dock Board for the damage done. It was held that the Board's statutory lien took first priority, overriding the prior salvage liens. Between the two salvors, the claim of the second salvor took precedence, being the one that preserved the *res* for the benefit of the earlier claimants.

The issue whether a damage claimant has priority over a wages' claimant or vice versa was decided by the admiralty judge, David Steel, in *The Ruta*[108] in favour of the wages maritime lien. The judge said, in particular:

> Although there was a suggestion in some of the textbooks that there was a rule whereby a damage lien had priority over a wages' lien, it was clear that questions of priority were not capable of being compartmentalised in the form of strict rules of ranking.

The decisive factor in resolving the present issue was the fact that the wages' claimants had no alternative forms of redress; the owners of *The Ruta* were insolvent; and where the only remedy open to the wages' claimants was recovery from proceeds of sale, consideration of public policy justified, according to them, a very high level of priority; any preferment of the damage lien to the wages' lien would encourage crews to refuse to disembark from vessels under arrest so as to try to force other claimants to pay off their claims, and this was likely to exacerbate their plight, at least in the short term, and in any event not be conducive to the efficient dispatch of business when vessels were under arrest.

The maritime lien which attaches to the ship in connection with which the claim arose may lose its normal priority over other claims *in rem*, if a sister ship, and not that ship, is arrested, but the right will remain in the class of the statutory rights *in rem*.

The Leoborg[109]

The plaintiffs, who were the first mortgagees of the ship, applied to the court for a determination of the priorities and payment out of the fund available in court after the sale of *The Leoborg*. The chief engineer of the vessel had a claim for unpaid wages while in service on board *The Leoborg*. He also claimed lien for unpaid wages while serving on *The Leoborg*'s sister ship, *H*. The mortgagees argued that his claim for wages in the service of *H* did not carry a maritime lien because the sister ship of *H* was arrested and, thus, should rank below the mortgagees' claim. The court held

---

107 [1901] P 304.
108 [2000] 1 Lloyd's Rep 359.
109 [1964] 1 Lloyd's Rep 380.

that in order of priorities, the claim for wages for service on board *The Leoborg* took priority over the first mortgagees' claim, while the claim relating to service on *H* came after the mortgagees' claim because the maritime lien for that claim had attached on that ship.

6 APPLICABLE LAW TO MARITIME LIENS AND CONFLICT OF LAWS [110]

The concept of maritime liens, as discussed in Chapter 2, originated from the *The Bold Buccleugh*:[111]

> The claim or privilege travels with the thing, into whosoever possession it may come. It is inchoate, from the moment the claim or privilege attaches, and when carried into effect by legal process, by a proceeding *in rem*, relates back to the period when it first attached.

It has already been seen earlier that a maritime lien attaches on the ship in connection with which the claim arose and cannot be extinguished until a court sale. It follows the vessel even into the hands of a bona fide purchaser for value. Under English law, claims which attract maritime liens are: the damage lien, the salvage lien and crew's accrued wages, master's wages and disbursements.

There are, however, other maritime claims, which are assigned the status of a maritime lien by the law of the country in which they arose or the contract was made. As a ship moves from one jurisdiction to another, there is a risk that the priority of a mortgagee may be affected. This raises a conflict of laws problem when the court has to determine the validity of the foreign lien before it determines priorities of claims for the distribution of the proceeds of sale of a ship.

English law, and the laws of countries following it, recognise the priority of a mortgage over other statutory rights *in rem*, but not over a maritime lien. In the USA, however, there are US contract maritime liens (necessaries) which include repairs to a ship, supply of bunkers, other supplies, stevedores' claims, claims under towage, even damage to cargo carried under US contract and charterers' liens. All these are, in English law, statutory rights *in rem* which become statutory liens *in rem* from the issue of the claim form. In the USA they could have priority even over a US preferred mortgage, only if they entered into before the filing of the mortgage. Foreign ship mortgages that are not guaranteed under Title XI of the Merchant Marine Act 1936 have lower priority to US preferred contract liens.[112]

For the purpose of priorities, a very important question is whether or not the recognition of a maritime lien should be decided by applying the law of the State where the claim arose (the *lex causae*), or the law of the forum deciding the matter of

---

110 See, also, Chapter 9 on mortgages.

111 [1851] 7 Moo PC 267, p 284.

112 See Tetley, W, *Maritime Liens and Claims*, 2nd edn, 1998, pp 872–76; and Tetley, W, *International Conflict of Laws (Common, Civil and Maritime)*, 1994, International Shipping, p 540.

priorities (the *lex fori*). If the maritime lien is regarded as a substantive right, given by the *lex causae*, then it should be enforceable in another jurisdiction where the claims against the vessel are being tried and it should be afforded the priority that it commands by its nature. On the other hand, if it is a mere procedural remedy, then its enforcement will depend on the procedure of the forum of the court that determines priorities.

This issue was decided by the Privy Council (3:2 majority) in *The Halcyon Isle*.[113] The case involved the priority of claims between a mortgagee, an English bank, granted under English law and an American ship-repair yard, which carried out repairs to the vessel in New York. It should be noted that the mortgage at this time was not registered. Knowing that his right of enforcement was protected under US law, the ship-repairer let the vessel sail without payment of his cost of repairs. Later the mortgage was registered. The ship was diverted by the mortgagees to Singapore and was arrested by them. Subsequently, she was sold by the order of the High Court of Singapore. The Singaporean court, in the exercise of its admiralty jurisdiction, applies English law. When the proceeds from the sale were insufficient to satisfy all claims, the question was whether the claim of the mortgagees should take priority over the claim of the ship-repairers. Since the latter's claim gave rise to a maritime lien under US law, the judge decided in favour of the ship-repairer, which was reversed on appeal. Upon further appeal to the Privy Council, the issue was which law should be applied, the *lex loci contractus*, or the *lex fori*.

By a majority of 3:2, it was held that a maritime lien was a remedy and, therefore, subject to the law of the forum, English law, which regarded the claim of the ship repairer as a statutory right *in rem* ranking after mortgages. Lord Diplock (delivering the majority judgment) stated:

> As explained in the passage from *The Bold Buccleugh* . . . any charge that a maritime lien creates on a ship is initially inchoate only; unlike a mortgage, it creates no immediate right of property; it is, and it will continue to be, devoid of any legal consequences unless and until it is 'carried into effect by legal process, by a proceeding *in rem*'. Any proprietary right to which it may give rise is thus dependant upon the lienee being recognised as entitled to proceed *in rem* against the ship in the court in which he is seeking to enforce his maritime lien. Under the domestic law of a number of civil law countries, even the inchoate charge to which some classes of maritime claims give rise is evanescent. Unless enforced by legal process within a limited time, for instance, within one year or before the commencement of the next voyage, it never comes to life. In English law, while there is no specific time limit to a maritime lien, the right to enforce it may be lost by laches.[114]

With respect to Lord Diplock, the above statement has been criticised. There are three flaws in this judicial statement: it cuts through the very essence of maritime liens; it misinterprets the word 'inchoate' used in *The Bold Buccleugh*; it disregards principles applicable to conflict of laws. The recognition of a right created by foreign law should be a matter of substance to be determined by applying that law and not a matter of procedure to be determined according to *lex fori*. Once the

---

113 [1981] AC 221, p 234.
114 Ibid.

validity is determined according to foreign law, then it would be a matter of determining its ranking, the procedure of priorities, in accordance with the law of the forum.

Clearly, this decision was based on policy considerations in order to protect the security of mortgagees by avoiding uncertainty in the law regarding the enforcement of their security rights over the ship. It was thought to be necessary, particularly, because of the law in the USA where more maritime claims than those under English law are treated as giving rise to a maritime lien. This problem was highlighted very succinctly by the minority view in the Privy Council in answering the question: should English and Singaporean laws recognise a foreign maritime lien, where none would exist, had the claim arisen in England or Singapore?

> Whatever the answer, the result is unsatisfactory. If in the affirmative, maritime States may be tempted to pass 'chauvinistic' laws conferring liens on a plurality of claims, so that the claimants may obtain abroad a preference denied to domestic claimants; if in the negative, claimants who have given the ship credit in reliance upon their lien may find themselves sorely deceived. If the law of the sea were a truly universal code, those dangers would disappear. Unfortunately, the maritime nations, though they have tried, have failed to secure uniformity in their rules regarding maritime liens.[115]

In the view of the minority, the balance of authorities, the comity of nations, private international law and natural justice, all answer this question in the affirmative. If this was correct, they said, the *lex fori*, English law, should give the maritime lien created by the *lex loci contractus* precedence over the mortgagees' mortgage. If it were otherwise, injustice would prevail because the American ship-repairer relied on his lien, valid as it appeared to be throughout the world and, unlike an English ship-repairer, who would keep possession of the ship, he gave up his possession. The nature of a maritime lien, therefore, should be determined by the *lex loci contractus* and the priority by the *lex fori*.[116]

A number of commentators have criticised the judgment of the majority.[117] Its correctness has now been seriously undermined by the Rome Convention 1980, which was enacted in English law by the Contracts (Applicable Law) Act 1990 and has been in force since 1 April 1991. The decision has, nevertheless, been followed in other jurisdictions.[118] But, the Supreme Court of Canada, in a case decided prior to *The Halcyon Isle*, had a different view.

---

115 [1981] AC 221, p 244; see, also, Berlingieri, F, 'An analysis of the issues and difficulties involved in the ratification of the International Conventions of Maritime Liens and Mortgages, 1926, 1967, 1993' [1995] LMCLQ 57.

116 Lord Diplock espoused the view of the Bermuda court in *The Christine* (1974) AMC 331.

117 See Jackson, DC, *Enforcement of Maritime Claims*, 4th edn, 2005, LLP, pp 683, 616–718; op cit, Tetley, 1994, fn 112, and Chapter 9, below.

118 See the South African case of *The Andrico Unity* [1987] 3 SALR 794; New Zealand, Australia, Singapore, Malaysia, Cyprus and Israel followed *The Halcyon Isle*; China applies the law of the forum pursuant to its Maritime Code; European countries have their own codified systems, but the Rome Convention 1980 must now be the guide to conflicts. For details of relevant cases in different jurisdictions, see the useful references in op cit, Tetley, 1994, fn 112; also Chapter 9 on mortgages, below.

The Ioannis Daskalelis[119]

The vessel, a Panamanian ship, was subject to a Greek-registered mortgage. Ship-repairers rendered necessary repairs to the vessel in New York. The ship left the shipyard without paying the cost of repairs and was diverted by the mortgagees to a port in Vancouver, Canada, where they arrested her. The question for the Supreme Court of Canada was whether the shipyard's claim had priority over the mortgage. Ritchie LJ quoted with approval from Cheshire's *Private International Law* (8th edn, p 676) thus:

> Where, for instance, two or more persons prosecute claims against a ship that has been arrested in England, the order in which they are entitled to be paid is governed exclusively by English law.
>
> In the case of a right *in rem* such as a lien, however, this principle must not be allowed to obscure the rule that the substantive right of the creditor depends upon its proper law. The validity and nature of the right must be distinguished from the order in which it ranks in relation to other claims. Before it can determine the order of payment, the court must examine the proper law of the transaction upon which the claimant relies in order to verify the validity of the right and to establish its precise nature.[120]

The court recognised the ship-repairer's maritime lien applying US law, because it held that the lien was a substantive right governed by the law of the country in which it was created. Thus, applying its own procedural law on priorities, it held that it had priority over the mortgagee's claim. It relied on the English decision in *The Colorado*,[121] which the Supreme Court interpreted as being the authority for the contention that, where a right in the nature of a maritime lien exists under foreign law which is the proper law of the contract, the English courts will recognise it and will accord it the priority which a right of that nature would be given under English procedure.[122] The German necessary man in this case did not take priority over the French mortgagee, not because the English court disregarded the proper law of the contract, but because the necessaries had been supplied in England and, as such, the claim did not give rise to a maritime lien, while under French law it was accorded the status of a maritime lien.

In the light of the conflict that exists in this area, the mortgagee usually protects its position in the deed of covenants, requiring the owner to provide information about the movements of the ship in case she calls at a port of a jurisdiction where

---

119 [1974] 1 Lloyd's Rep 174; so Canada recognises foreign maritime liens.

120 Ibid, p 177.

121 [1923] P 102.

122 [1974] 1 Lloyd's Rep, pp 177–78. It was also explained that *The Colorado* decision was clouded by the fact that the judges purported to follow the cases in *The Milford* (1859) Swa 362 and *The Tagus* [1907] P 44, which were concerned with foreign seamen's wages and the English court disregarded the proper law of the contract, which restricted their lien to the last voyage only. The Supreme Court of Canada also interpreted *The Zigurda* [1932] P 113, as having been misunderstood, but that a closer examination would reveal that it did not really support the contrary proposition. The German necessary man argued that, if the ship was under arrest in Germany, he would have rights analogous to those given by a maritime lien and, therefore, would rank in priority to other claimants. In fact, on evidence called in proof of German law, it was not shown that his claim would be recognised in Germany as being equivalent to an English maritime lien. In the result, the English court treated him as an ordinary creditor.

The Halcyon Isle has been applied. There is also insurance cover for such a risk. At the time of enforcement of his security, the mortgagee usually considers the jurisdiction in which to proceed, although this necessitates forum shopping. As regards a ship-repairer, he could protect his rights by demanding payment before giving up possession of the ship.

7 EXTINCTION OF MARITIME LIENS AND TRANSFERABILITY

7.1 Extinction

The space in this book allows only a list of the circumstances in which the lien can become extinct:[123]

- immunity from suit (in cases of foreign State immunity and Crown ships, the maritime lien may lie dormant until the ship is transferred out of Government ownership);

- delay of suit to enforce the lien by an *in rem* claim;

- stay of proceedings upon provision of security;

- provision of bail, payment into court, or provision of security by way of an undertaking or guarantee;[124]

- establishment of limitation fund under the Limitation Convention;

- waiver, or general principles of estoppel;

- destruction of the property;

- judgment on liability, although the lien must continue until satisfaction of the claim by arrest of the property;

- judicial sale.

7.2 Transferability by assignment

Whether a lien can effectively be assigned depends on principles of assignment applicable to 'choses in action', which are rights enforceable by litigation. An assignment of a bare right of litigation (for example, not being ancillary to an assignment of a property right or interest, or without a genuine commercial interest of the assignee) is not valid. This principle has been laid down in *Trendtex Trading Corp v Credit Suisse*:[125]

> If the assignment is of a property right or interest and the cause of action is ancillary

---

123 See further Jackson, DC, *Enforcement of Maritime Claims*, 4th edn, 2005, LLP, at pp 501–508.

124 The Canadian court in *The Birchglen* [1990] 3 CF 301, cited in *The Ruta* [2000] 1 Lloyd's Rep 359, held that, whether or not a maritime lien continues, or is revived, or is extinguished when security has been put up, is determined according to the facts of each particular case and the requirements that full justice and equity be applied.

125 [1981] 3 All ER 520, p 531.

to that right or interest or if the assignee had a genuine commercial interest in taking the assignment and in enforcing it for his own benefit, the assignment of a chose in action is valid.

For the purpose of assignment of a maritime lien, however, which is considered to be a chose in action, an assignment of the claim does not mean that it carries with it the maritime lien, if the right reflected in the claim is not assignable.[126]

Wages' lien cannot be renounced by any agreement, as provided by s 39 of the MSA 1995. Could an assignment of the claim to a person who pays the wages voluntarily be seen as falling foul of this section? This question came before the court in Hong Kong, for the first time, in *The Sparti*[127] and the judge considered the equivalent statutory provision to s 39 under the Merchant Shipping (Seafarers) Ordinance, s 93(1).

Briefly, on the facts of this case: the owners of the vessel were in financial difficulties and asked the assignee who was acting as the agent of the vessel in Colombo, to pay the crew. Although the assignee was under no legal duty to do so, he agreed to pay the crew taking appropriate assignments from them. Each of the assignments from the members of the crew was in the same form and provided, inter alia:

> In consideration of the payment by you to me of US . . . in respect of wages and other amounts due for my employment on board *MV Sparti*, I hereby assign to you all my rights against the owners of the vessel or the vessel itself.

No written notice of the assignment was given by the crew or the assignee to the owners of the vessel, so that the assignments were equitable assignments. Both the mortgagee and the agent of the ship obtained judgments for their respective claims against the ship, and the ship was sold by court order. Since the court fund was insufficient to satisfy the claims in full, the issue was one of priorities.

The mortgagee's counsel argued that the assignment was invalid because it meant the renouncement of the maritime lien. The judge disagreed because the assignment of wages to the assignee in this case was not an inequitable agreement and could not be characterized as renouncement of the lien or the remedy for recovery of wages. The owner's obligation to pay wages was not in any way abandoned by the crew granting the assignment. As a matter of construction, the judge held that s 93(1) did not itself present a bar to the transfer of the crew's wages lien by the assignment to the assignee. However, he granted priority to the mortgagee, on the basis that a maritime lien, being personal in nature, was incapable of being transferred in law by an assignment. Nothing could be read in the judgment of Hill J, he said, in *The Petone*,[128] who left the matter of assignability of maritime liens open, indicating otherwise.

---

126 Op cit, Jackson, fn 123.
127 [2000] 2 Lloyd's Rep 618.
128 [1917] P 198.

7.3 Can a maritime lien be transferred by voluntary payment of the claim?

A voluntary payment by a third party of claims to which a maritime lien has attached will not transfer the lien to that party unless the payment is made with judicial consent or is ordered by the court.[129]

This is relevant in particular to payment of crew wages by the ship's agents or mortgagees.

In *The Sparti*,[130] Waung J dealt with this issue as understood by the British and Hong Kong courts. By contrast to Scottish law[131] and US law[132] under which a person, who pays off the crew wages in a foreign port, is put into the shoes of the seaman whose wages he had paid, he held that the weight of English authorities was strongly against this doctrine.

The restrictions or limitations on the exercise of jurisdiction on the merits is examined in the next chapter.

---

129 Ibid.

130 [2000] 2 Lloyd's Rep 618; the decision is important, also, from a comparative perspective because it refers to how the courts in other jurisdictions have dealt with this issue (such as Canada and New Zealand, where the maritime lien is not assignable).

131 *Clark v Bowring* (1908) SC 1168.

132 *The President Arthur* (1928) 25 F (2d) 999, in which public policy applied in favour of the payer of wages.

CHAPTER 5

RULES AND DOCTRINES RESTRICTING THE JURISDICTION OF THE ADMIRALTY COURT TO ADJUDICATE ON THE MERITS OF A CASE

1 INTRODUCTION

Although the jurisdiction of the Admiralty Court is very wide (see Chapter 1), there are some limits and restrictions which the court will consider in exercising its discretion to determine its own jurisdiction. For example, as mentioned in Chapter 1, para 7, the jurisdiction of the Admiralty Court cannot be assumed in circumstances provided by the Crown Immunity Act 1947 and the State Immunity Act 1978. Convention rules or other doctrines also restrict the scope of exercising or maintaining jurisdiction on the merits of a case, as will be seen in this and in the following chapters. On the other hand, the court may, by an anti-suit injunction, restrain a litigant from continuing proceedings commenced in a foreign court if there are grounds for protecting rights, or asserting its own jurisdiction (see Chapter 7).

2 JURISDICTION BASES

There are two broad types of jurisdiction bases under English procedural law: the jurisdiction base by way of 'service of process' and the 'Convention' jurisdiction base. While in both types of asserting jurisdiction a claim form is issued to initiate the proceedings, which is then served, as regards the 'service of process' jurisdiction base there has traditionally been no need for substantive connecting factors between the jurisdiction and the claim. It is sufficient that in claims in *personam*[1] the claim form is served upon the defendant, or as is otherwise provided by the procedure rules, provided the defendant is within the jurisdiction, unless he voluntarily submits to jurisdiction. In collision damage claims, pursued *in personam*, special rules apply (see Chapter 3, para 2). In claims *in rem*, the claim form must be served on the property within the jurisdiction.

However, as far as claims *in personam* are concerned and in cases in which the defendant is not within the jurisdiction, there are exceptions to the general rule of no connecting factors with the English jurisdiction; these are the occasions described by the Civil Procedure Rules 1998 (CPR) for service out of the jurisdiction (Ord 11, now found in Pt 6, section III, rr 6.17–6.31 of the CPR). A substantive connecting factor must be shown for the court to give leave to the claimant to serve the defendant out of the jurisdiction.

As far as claims *in rem* are concerned, once the ship is within the jurisdiction, it provides the link and can be served with the *in rem* claim form.[2] In accordance with

---

1   Governed by CPR, Pt 58 and PD 58.
2   PD 61, para 3.

Convention jurisdiction bases, founding jurisdiction depends on specified substantive links with the jurisdiction required by Conventions, which have been enacted, or reflected, into English law.

In the following paragraphs, the occasions on which the court has discretion whether or not to exercise or maintain its jurisdiction are examined.

3 OCCASIONS WHEN JURISDICTION MAY NOT BE EXERCISED OR MAINTAINED

(a) On an issue of time bars applicable for instituting proceedings.

(b) On grounds relating to service out of the jurisdiction. This applies only to a claim brought *in personam* when the defendant is outside the jurisdiction and the cause of action does not fall within any of the prescribed rules of Ord 11, which would allow the English court to assume jurisdiction.

(c) On the ground of *forum non-conveniens*; when a forum other than England is shown to be more appropriate for the claim which, on balance, has substantive links with the other forum.

(d) On the ground of a foreign jurisdiction agreement.

(e) On the ground of an arbitration agreement.

(f) On the ground of *res judicata* (as seen in Chapters 3 and 4).

(g) On the ground of Convention jurisdiction provisions, which allocate jurisdiction according to special rules of a particular Convention. Some of these rules are mandatory and the court will be bound to decline its jurisdiction, others give the court discretion whether or not to do so.

The topics from (a) to (e) will be examined in this chapter. The topic under (g) (Convention rules) and, in particular, the rules under the Brussels Convention (now the Brussels Regulation) or the Lugano Convention will be discussed in Chapter 6.

3.1 Discontinuance of proceedings on ground of time bars

There are statutory and consensual time limits within which a claim may be brought. Delay in bringing suit may bar the remedy or, in exceptional cases, the claim, unless an extension of time has been obtained, either by agreement or by an order of the court.

The CPR also provide for certain time limits regarding procedures. The court has power to strike out proceedings for failure by the litigants to observe a rule, or practise direction, or a court order. Inexcusable delays may amount to an abuse of process. Once proceedings have started, case management under the new rules[3] is intended to assist the parties in taking the required procedural steps without delay

---

3   CPR, Pt 3.

and has, in a way, curtailed the strict approach of the court to strike proceedings out under the old rules.

As a general rule, under English law, a time bar is a procedural remedy and is governed by the law of the forum, unless the substantive matter is governed by foreign law, when limitation will also be treated as a matter of that law in accordance with the Foreign Limitation Periods Act 1984. In addition, the Contracts (Applicable Law) Act 1990 (which enacted the Rome Convention 1980) has affected the classification of time bars as procedure. It provides that matters of extinguishing obligation, prescription and limitation of action, are matters of the applicable law to the contract.

The general time limits are contained in the Limitation Act (LA) 1980, as amended by the Latent Damage Act (LDA) 1986, which does not apply where other statutes dealing with particular matters prescribe limitation. In maritime claims, particularly for collision damage or salvage or personal injury claims, limitation provisions of Conventions, as enacted into English law, have been consolidated in the Merchant Shipping Act (MSA) 1995, which are referred to below. Limitation of time, with regard to contracts to which the Hague-Visby rules apply by force of law, is governed by those rules.

3.1.1 Cargo claims against the carrying ship or her owners

When there is a contract to which the Hague-Visby Rules (HVR) do not apply, or when they do not apply by force of law but by agreement, there is usually a contractual time limit,[4] which may be extended by agreement. When the HVR apply by force of law, Art III, r 6 provides: 'Subject to para 6 *bis* (referring to indemnity claims) the carrier and the ship shall, in any event, be discharged from all liability whatsoever in respect of the goods, unless suit is brought within one year of their delivery, or of the date when they should have been delivered. This period may, however, be extended if the parties so agree after the cause of action has arisen.'

The wording of this Article makes time bar mandatory and the court does not have power to extend it.[5] The effect of lapse of time, without prior agreement to extend it, is that it extinguishes the claim and no reliance on it can be made, by way of defence, or a set off, in accordance with the view of the majority of the House of Lords in *The Aries*.[6]

Lord Wilberforce clearly stated the effect of Art III, r 6:

---

4   A specifically negotiated clause is likely to take precedence over the merely incorporated, but clear words are required for a time bar, so that, in a case of doubt or ambiguity, the conflict must be resolved in favour of a longer time limit: *Finagra (UK) Ltd v OT Africa Line Ltd* [1998] 1 Lloyd's Rep 622. It should also be noted that, under the Arbitration Act 1996, the arbitrators have power to consider whether a time limit should be extended; s 12(2) limited the right to seek an extension to circumstances 'after a claim had arisen and after exhausting any available arbitral process for obtaining an extension of time'. This new provision postpones formally any right to apply to the court for an extension under any scheme of arbitration giving the arbitrators the right to extend time; it would, therefore, be the arbitrators who may determine whether or not any time bar applied, before deciding whether to grant an extension: *The Seki Rollete* [1998] 2 Lloyd's Rep 638.

5   *The Antares* [1987] 1 Lloyd's Rep 424.

6   [1977] 1 WLR 185 (HL).

This amounts to a time bar created by contract. But, I do not think that sufficient recognition to this has been given by the courts below; it is a time bar of special kind, viz, one which extinguishes the claim . . . not one which, as most English statutes of limitation . . . and some international conventions do, bars the remedy while leaving the claim itself in existence . . . The charterers' claim, (in this case) after May 1974 and before the date of the writ, had not merely become unenforceable by action, it had simply ceased to exist, and I fail to understand how a claim which has ceased to exist can be introduced for any purpose into legal proceedings, whether by defence or (if this is different) as a means of reducing the respondents' claim, or as a set off, or in any way whatsoever. It is a claim which, after May 1974, had no existence in law, and could have no relevance in proceedings commenced, as these were, in October 1974.[7]

The severe consequences of loss of the right to claim by the lapse of the limitation period can occur even if a claim form has been issued within time, but is not served within the time of the validity of the 'claim form'. Under the CPR, r 7.5, a claim form *in personam* is valid for service for four months, unless it is to be served out of the jurisdiction, when it is valid for six months. An application to extend the time of service must be made within the period of service (CPR, r 7.6). If the application is made out of time, the court has discretion to extend the time if the claimant has taken all reasonable steps to serve, but has been unable to do so and if he acted promptly in making the application (r 7.6(3)). In *Pirelli v United Thai*,[8] the court was lenient to extend the time for issuing a concurrent 'writ'[9] under the previous Rules of the Supreme Court (RSC) (Ord 6, r 8), which had not been issued within the validity of the original writ, as provided by the old rules. In order to cure this defect, the original writ was deemed to be extended for six months. An *in rem* claim form is valid for 12 months (CPR, r 61.3(5)(b)).

It should also be noted that an amendment to the claim form would not be permitted, once the time bar has expired, to include a defendant not named in the original claim form, which was issued against another defendant within time.[10]

Under the Gold Clause Agreement (GCA) 1950, as amended in 1977, the time for bringing suit for a cargo claim may be extended. The GCA is an agreement entered into between insurers, certain cargo interests and shipowners. Clause 4 provides that, upon the request of any party representing the cargo, whether made before or after the expiry of the one year period, the shipowners will extend the time for bringing suit for a further 12 months provided notice of the claim, with the best particulars available, has been given within the one year period.

3.1.2 *Indemnity claims for liability to cargo owners*

Allocation of liability for cargo claims, as between owners and charterers (contracted under a New York Produce Exchange (NYPE) time charter which incorporates the Inter-Club NYPE Agreement), in respect of cargo carried on board under

---

7   Ibid, p 188.

8   [2000] 1 Lloyd's Rep 663; the case is also relevant to stay of proceedings on ground of a foreign jurisdiction agreement, discussed at para 3.4, below.

9   Apparently, the CPR do not refer to the issue of a concurrent claim form under Pt 7.

10 *The Jay Bola* [1992] 2 Lloyd's Rep 62.

bills of lading to which the HVR are incorporated, is subject to a two-year time limit.

The HVR, by Art 6 *bis*, also provide that indemnity claims can be brought, even after the expiration of the year provided for in Art 6, if brought within the time allowed by the law of the court seised of the case. However, the time allowed shall not be less than three months commencing from the day when the person bringing such action for indemnity has settled the claim, or has been served with process in the action against himself.

The Privy Council gave the interpretation of this provision in *The Xingcheng and Andros*[11] in which it held that:

> Rule 6 *bis* of Art III created a special exception to the generality of r 6; r 6 *bis*, in a case to which it applied, had a separate effect of its own independently of r 6; the case to which r 6 *bis* applied was a case where shipowner A, being under actual or potential liability to cargo-owner B, claimed an indemnity by way of damages against ship or shipowner C; if that claim was made under a contract of carriage to which the HVR applied, then the time allowed for bringing it was that prescribed by r 6 *bis* and not r 6; there was no requirement in r 6 *bis* that the liability to shipowner A should also arise under a contract of carriage to which the HVR applied and there was no reason why such a requirement should be implied.

3.1.3 Claims for loss of life or personal injury against the carrying ship

Claims for loss of life or personal injury of persons carried on the ship, except when the Athens Convention applies (see para 3.1.4, below), occasioned by negligence are subject to the Fatal Accidents Act 1976,[12] in respect of claims by the dependants of a deceased, and the LA 1980. The time limit against the carrying ship is three years, commencing from the date of the incident, which gave rise to the cause of action. The period may not commence until the claimant has knowledge of the injury.[13]

3.1.4 Claims of passengers carried on passenger vessels

Claims for loss of life or personal injury or loss of luggage of passengers carried on passenger ships are subject to a two-year time limit, commencing from a date as specified by Art 16 of the Athens Convention 1974, when it applies. The commencement date depends on the particular claim made. The date of disembarkation is the relevant date for personal injury claims, or the date of death for loss of life when death occurred after disembarkation of an injured passenger, provided that the time should not exceed three years from the date of disembarkation. The date of disembarkation or the date when disembarkation should have taken place is relevant for damage to, or loss of, luggage. These time limits may be extended either by a written declaration of the carrier or by agreement of the parties after the cause of action has arisen.

---

11   [1987] 2 Lloyd's Rep 210.
12   As amended by the Administration of Justice Act 1982.
13   Limitation Act 1980 (ss 11, 12, 13), as amended by the Latent Damage Act 1986.

3.1.5 Property or personal injury/loss of life claims against another ship at fault

Under s 190(1), (3) of the MSA 1995, the time limit to bring any claim against owners or ship, in respect of damage or loss caused by the fault of that ship to another ship, its cargo or freight, or any property on board it, or for damages for loss of life or personal injury caused by the fault of that ship to any person on board another ship, is two years from the date of the incident causing the damage or loss. This may be extended on grounds of reasonableness.[14]

3.1.6 Claims for contribution

Claims for contribution by one ship against the other ship at fault, in respect of liability to third parties for loss of life or personal injury, are subject to a one year time limit, commencing from the date of payment under s 190(4) of the MSA 1995. But, contribution claims for liability incurred to third parties concerning damage to property are subject to a two-year time limit, commencing from the date of payment under s 1 of the Civil Liability (Contribution) Act 1978.

3.1.7 Salvage claims

Under Art 23 of the Salvage Convention 1989, any claim for payment under the Convention shall be time barred, if judicial or arbitral proceedings have not been instituted within a period of two years. The limitation period commences on the day on which the salvage operations are terminated. The person against whom the claim is made may extend this period by making a declaration to the claimant. An action for indemnity by a person liable may be instituted, even after the expiration of the aforesaid limitation period, if brought within the time allowed by the law of the State where proceedings are instituted.

3.1.8 Claims for wages

The LA 1980 provides for a six-year time limit to bring claims arising from breach of contract, commencing from the date of the breach. This time limit applies to claims of seamen against their employer for unpaid wages.

3.2 No assumption of jurisdiction if a claim *in personam* is not within Ord 11 (CPR Pt 6, Section III)

Order 11 has been incorporated in CPR, Pt 6, Section III (rr 6.17–6.31) and PD 6b (service out of the jurisdiction).

Save for cases where the defendant is within the jurisdiction to be served with the claim form, or he has agreed to submit to the jurisdiction of the court, and for those in which the Brussels Regulation or the Lugano Convention apply (examined in Chapter 6, below), a claimant will need the permission of the court to serve

---

14 *The Berny* [1979] 2 Lloyd's Rep 533.

proceedings out of the jurisdiction. This is only applicable to limited circumstances in which there is a link between the claim and the jurisdiction.[15]

For example, there may be a contractual link if the contract was made here, or is governed by English law. Another link with this jurisdiction will be in cases of claims based on tort, where the alleged tort happened within the jurisdiction.

Granting permission is discretionary. The claimant must state the grounds of the application and show that, in his belief, he has a good cause of action and that there is a real issue to be tried. No permission shall be granted, unless it shall be made sufficiently to appear to the court that the case is a proper one for service out of the jurisdiction.

In circumstances outside the provisions of this order, the court cannot assume jurisdiction if the defendant is foreign, unless there is a convention jurisdiction base, or the parties to a dispute have agreed to this jurisdiction.

It is beyond the scope of this book to deal with this procedural area which requires a book in its own right.

3.3 Stay on the ground of *forum non-conveniens*

Even if English jurisdiction has been properly invoked, the English court has power to exercise its discretion and stay an action before it, when there are grounds of *forum non-conveniens*. For example, when there are connecting factors with the jurisdiction of a foreign court which is amenable to the defendant, the English court will consider, taking also into account all the circumstances of the case, whether that court is more appropriate to determine the matter for the ends of justice and the interests of all parties. The origins and meaning of this doctrine are explained in the following paragraphs. What would constitute connecting factors are explained under para 3.3.5.4, below.

Being originally a Scottish doctrine, *forum non-conveniens* was gradually incorporated into English law in the 1970s. The court's approach before that time is briefly explained below.

3.3.1 Historical perspective and 'the 1936 rule'

Prior to the Judicature Act (JA) 1873, the High Court had power to grant an injunction to restrain proceedings in England. By s 24(5) of the 1873 Act, however, this power to restrain proceedings by an injunction was removed but, in the same subsection, the court's inherent power to stay proceedings, as it thought fit for the purpose of justice, was recognised.

Section 24 of the JA 1873 was later replaced by s 41 of the Judicature (Consolidation) Act 1925. The court's inherent power to stay proceedings was maintained in the new Act, as it had been in the 1873 Act. However, the rule in the new Act added a provision relating to the court's power to stay its proceedings in cases where there

---

15   CPR, Pt 6, Section III, (rr 6.17–6.31) and PD 6B.

was proof of vexation or oppression on the part of the claimant. But, the power was not limited only to those cases. It is important to note that the rule in the 1873 Act contained no reference to vexation or oppression in relation to the court's power to stay.

In the leading case of *McHenry v Lewis*[16] the Court of Appeal, in a matter involving multiple proceedings in England and America, used the word 'vexatious' as an illustration of the provision. In later decisions,[17] the court followed this principle, but without placing too much weight on the words oppressive and vexatious. The emphasis was on whether the defendant would be subjected to such an injustice, that he ought not to be sued in the court in which the action was brought.

This principle was formulated in the *St Pierre* case, known as 'the 1936 rule'. The criteria of injustice, however, as laid down by Scott LJ, were whether the English action would cause an injustice to the defendant that was 'oppressive or vexatious' to him, or an abuse of the process of the court, which he had to prove.

St Pierre v South American Stores[18]

The action brought in this jurisdiction involved a dispute with regard to a lease of land in Chile. The defendants (English companies) had commenced proceedings in Chile, while the plaintiffs commenced proceedings in England. The defendants applied for a stay of the English action, on the ground that Argentina was a more appropriate forum. Scott LJ held that: (1) a mere balance of convenience was not a sufficient ground for depriving a plaintiff of the advantages of prosecuting his action in England when the English action was, otherwise, properly brought; and (2) in order to justify a stay, the defendants had to prove (a) that the continuance of the action in England would cause an injustice that was oppressive or vexatious to him, or would be an abuse of the process of court in some way, and (b) that the stay would not cause an injustice to the plaintiff. The burden of proof in both situations was on the defendant.

Thus, if the plaintiff was not acting vexatiously or oppressively, but genuinely believed that England would be to his advantage (despite there being another more appropriate forum), the court would not grant a stay.

The application of the 1936 rule in subsequent cases, until 1973, operated in such a way as to make it extremely difficult for the defendant to obtain a stay of an action. He could not easily satisfy the court that the continuance of the action would work an injustice to him. This was due to the difficulty of proving that the action was oppressive or vexatious in the opprobrious sense, which was a meaning these epithets were generally regarded as having, in the context in which they were used.[19] Such applications were, invariably, dismissed.[20]

---

16 (1882) 21 Ch D 202.

17 *Peruvian Guano Co v Bockwoldt* (1883) 23 Ch D 225; *Hyman v Helm* (1883) 24 Ch D 531; *Logan v Bank of Scotland* [1906] 1 KB 141.

18 [1936] 1 KB 382 (CA).

19 *The Abidin Daver* [1984] 1 All ER 470, p 481, per Lord Brandon of Oakbrook.

20 *The Janera* [1928] P 55; *The London* [1931] P 14; *The Madrid* [1937] 1 All ER 216; *The Quo Vadis* [1951] 1 Lloyd's Rep 425; *The Monte Urbasa* [1953] 1 Lloyd's Rep 587; *The Lucile Broomfield* [1964] 1 Lloyd's Rep 324.

3.3.2 *Why was the 1936 rule distinct from the doctrine of* forum non-conveniens?

(a) It recognised an exceptional power of the court;

(b) the power could be described by reference to vexation or oppression; and

(c) the court's discretion was general, as is shown in the *Peruvian Guano* case.[21]

An action was brought in this court by an English company against a firm of French merchants for the delivery of the cargoes of certain ships, or in the alternative for damages, and for an injunction and appointment of a receiver.

At the commencement of the action the ships were in British waters, but they had since been removed by the direction of the defendants to ports in France, and the cargoes had been taken possession of by the defendants. Proceedings had been instituted by the plaintiffs in a French court for recovery of the cargoes. The English action comprised a claim for the cargo of one ship which was not claimed in the French action.

A motion, on behalf of the defendants, that the plaintiffs might be ordered to elect whether they would proceed with the English action or with the French proceedings, was refused.

Jessel MR laid down the criteria for a stay, which was rarely granted in those days, as follows:

> It is very important in these cases that the court should clearly see that in stopping an action it does not do injustice. Of course, a man brings an action at the peril of costs if the action does not succeed, and as a general rule that is sufficient to protect defendants from ill founded actions. There is another protection, which is that, where the action is vexatious, it may be stayed. Now it may be vexatious on many grounds. It may be so utterly absurd that the judge sees it cannot possibly succeed, and that it is brought only for annoyance, and then the judge has jurisdiction to stay the action. That is pure vexation. Or, it may be vexatious in another way; that is, the plaintiff not intending to annoy or harass the defendant, but thinking he would get some fanciful advantage, sues him in two courts at the same time under the same jurisdiction – two of the Queen's courts. That is vexatious, because whatever the intention of the plaintiff may be he cannot get any benefit in that way, and the defendant is harassed by two suits . . .

> It may be put, as regards this case, shortly in this way: that it is not vexatious to bring an action in each country where there are substantial reasons of benefit to the plaintiff. He has the right to bring an action, and if there are substantial reasons to induce him to bring the two actions, why should we deprive him of that right? It is very unpleasant, no doubt, to be sued twice – it is unpleasant to many people to be sued once – but still that does not make it vexatious where the plaintiff seeks to get a real substantial advantage.

---

21   *Peruvian Guano Co v Bockwoldt* (1883) 23 Ch D 225.

3.3.3 The gradual incorporation of the
Scottish doctrine into English law

The incorporation of the Scottish doctrine of *forum non-conveniens* into English common law was effectively done by *The Abidin Daver* in 1984, but the process started in 1973 with *The Atlantic Star* and it was refined further in *Macshannon*. The trilogy of these decisions (which will be examined shortly) had a great impact on the change of the attitude of English judges, so that a tendency for jurisdictional chauvinism was gradually diminished. The difficulty of showing that the action in England was oppressive or vexatious was for the first time examined by the House of Lords in the following case.

The Atlantic Star [22]

Pursuant to a collision between a barge and the appellants' (defendants) vessel, *The Atlantic Star*, in Belgian waters, the respondents (claimants), Dutch owners of the barge, arrested *The Atlantic Star* in England. By virtue of the arrest, they founded jurisdiction in the English court and obtained security for their claim. The appellants sought a stay of the action in England on the ground that the Belgian court was the more appropriate forum to deal with the claim. The court surveyor in Belgium had already been called to give evidence in court and the conclusion in his report appeared to point to the opinion that the appellants' vessel was not at fault. Therefore, the chances were that, if the action was tried in Belgium, the respondents would fail. The trial judge had held that, although the balance of convenience was heavily in favour of the Belgian court, and the case had absolutely no connection with England, he felt bound by previous authorities to refuse a stay, since it was not proved that the plaintiffs were acting 'vexatiously' or 'oppressively', or in abuse of the process of the court. His decision was upheld by the Court of Appeal in which Lord Denning MR re-emphasised that access to the Queen's court, even by a foreign plaintiff, must not be lightly refused and said:

> No one who comes to these courts asking for justice should come in vain ... This right to come here is not confined to Englishmen. It extends to any friendly foreigner. He can seek the aid of our courts if he desires to do so. You may call this 'forum shopping' if you please, but if the forum is England, it is a good place to shop in, both for the quality of the goods and the speed of service. [23]

Lord Reid later, in the House of Lords, criticised this statement:

> My Lords, with all respect, that seems to me to recall the good old days, the passing of which many may regret, when inhabitants of this island felt an innate superiority over those unfortunate enough to belong to other races ... There was a time when it could reasonably be said that our system of administration of justice, though expensive and elaborate, was superior to that in most other countries. But, today we must, I think, admit that as a general rule there is no injustice in telling a plaintiff that he should go back to his own courts ... So, I would draw some distinction between a case where England is the natural forum for the plaintiff and a case where the

---

22 [1973] 2 Lloyd's Rep 197.
23 [1972] 2 Lloyd's Rep 446, p 451.

plaintiff merely comes here to serve his own ends. In the former, the plaintiff should not be 'driven from the judgment seat' without very good reason, but, in the latter, the plaintiff should, I think, be expected to offer some reasonable justification for his choice of forum if the defendant seeks a stay . . . I think that a key to the solution may be found in a liberal interpretation of what is oppressive on the part of the plaintiff. The position of the defendant must be put in the scales. In the end, it must be left to the discretion of the court in each case where a stay is sought . . . looking to all the circumstances, including the personal position of the defendant.[24]

Lord Wilberforce reviewed the previous authorities and concluded with regard to 'vexatious and oppressive':

These words are not statutory words; as I hope to have shown from earlier cases, they are descriptive words, which illustrate, but do not confine, the courts' general jurisdiction. They are pointers rather than boundary marks. They are capable of a strict, or technical application; conversely, if this House thinks fit, and as I think they should, they can in the future be interpreted more liberally.[25]

Lord Kilbrandon agreed and added:

There are plenty of earlier examples of the use of the words 'oppressive' and 'vexatious' in this context. But the words have, at all events today, certain shades of meaning which make it difficult to accept an uncritical construction . . . 'Oppressive' is an adjective which ought to be, and today normally is, confined to deliberate acts of moral, though not necessarily legal, delinquency, such as an unfair abuse of power by the stronger party in order that a weaker party may be put in difficulties in obtaining his just rights. 'Vexatious' today has overtones of irresponsible pursuit of litigation by someone who either knows he has no proper cause of action, or is mentally incapable of forming a rational opinion on that topic. Either of these attitudes may amount to abuse of the process of the court, but in my opinion a defendant moving for a stay cannot be compelled to bring the plaintiff's conduct within the scope of these grave allegations.

Thus, the House of Lords rejected the narrow construction of the expressions 'oppressive' and 'vexatious'. It was invited to take the opportunity in this case to bring English law into line with the Scottish doctrine of *forum non-conveniens* and make the plea available in England. It refused to adopt this approach, but upheld the court's residual right to decline to exercise its jurisdiction in appropriate cases. It was for the court to take into account (a) any advantage to the plaintiff in this jurisdiction, and (b) any disadvantage to the defendant by refusing a stay. It was held by majority of 3:2 that the defendants (appellants) had shown that they ought not to be required to litigate in England and the action was stayed.

At this stage, the judgment of Scott LJ in *St Pierre* was still treated as the framework on which the law was built, but the words 'oppressive' and 'vexatious' were no longer to be understood in their natural meaning. However, the House of Lords in the following case eliminated these words from the test.

---

24   [1973] 2 Lloyd's Rep 197, pp 200–01.
25   Ibid, p 209.

Macshannon v Rockware Glass Ltd[26]

The plaintiffs were Scotsmen who brought actions against their employers for damages for personal injury or disabilities suffered in the course of employment in a factory in Scotland. It was alleged that the injuries had been caused by the negligence of the employers. The employers were companies with their head offices in England, but their places of business in Scotland. The plaintiffs brought their actions in England, though there was no connection with it, because they were advised that the English court would be likely to award higher damages and more generous party and party legal costs. The Court of Appeal acknowledged that Scotland was the more appropriate forum for the action, but considered that the *ratio decidendi* of *The Atlantic Star* compelled the court to allow the proceedings to continue in England.

In the House of Lords, Lord Diplock examined the *ratio decidendi* in *The Atlantic Star* and said that, although by the modification of the statement of the law, as had been set down by Scott LJ in the *St Pierre* case, the words 'vexatious and oppressive' were given, by the House of Lords in *The Atlantic Star*, a liberal interpretation, these words still caused problems and should be eliminated to avoid confusion, as in the instant case. He then restated the principle of *St Pierre* as follows:

> In order to justify a stay two conditions must be satisfied, one positive and the other negative: (a) the defendant must satisfy the court that there is another forum to whose jurisdiction he is amenable in which justice can be done between the parties at substantially less inconvenience or expense, and (b) the stay must not deprive the plaintiff of a legitimate personal or judicial advantage which would be available to him if he invoked the jurisdiction of the English court.[27]

No reference was made to the burden of proof. Lord Keith added:

> Where England is the natural forum for the action, in the sense of being that with which the action has the most real and substantial connection, it is necessary for the defendant, in order to establish injustice to him and no injustice to the plaintiff, to show some very serious disadvantage to him which substantially outweighs any advantage to the plaintiff. Where, however, the defendant shows that England is not the natural forum and that, if the action be continued there he would be involved in substantial (that is, more than *de minimis*) inconvenience and unnecessary expense, or in some other disadvantages, which would not affect him in the natural forum, he has made out a *prima facie* case for a stay, and if nothing follows it may properly be granted. The plaintiff may, however, seek to show some reasonable justification for his choice of forum in the shape of advantage to him. If he succeeds, it becomes necessary to weigh against each other the advantages to the plaintiff and the disadvantages to the defendant, and a stay will not be granted unless the court concludes that to refuse it would involve injustice to the defendant and no injustice to the plaintiff.[28]

Thus, the House of Lords examined the advantages of hearing the action in Scotland, viz: the availability of medical and other expert witnesses, who treated

---

26   [1978] 1 All ER 625 (HL).
27   [1978] 1 All ER 625, p 630.
28   Ibid, pp 644–45.

the plaintiffs in Scotland, and all the witnesses to the facts in this matter were living in Scotland. The main disadvantage of hearing the action in England would be the inconvenience, not only for the parties, but for all the witnesses concerned. The plaintiffs alleged that the advantage they would be deprived of, if the action was tried in Scotland, was an unsubstantiated, though perhaps bona fide, belief of their legal advisers on the advantages of English over Scottish legal process. It was held that the advantage to the plaintiff must be a real one, it must be shown objectively and, on balance of probabilities, that it exists. The defendants had shown that Scotland was the only natural and appropriate forum for the actions, where they could be tried at substantially less inconvenience and expense. The plaintiffs had not shown that they would be deprived of any real personal or judicial advantage. The action was stayed.

In the final case of the trilogy, the doctrine of *forum non-conveniens* was firmly established in English law. The existence of *lis pendens* in a foreign jurisdiction was a factor to be taken into account, but alone was not sufficient to tilt the balance.

The Abidin Daver [29]

This involved a collision, in Turkish territorial waters, between a Turkish ship and a Cuban ship. Both vessels sustained damage. The Turkish parties arrested the Cuban ship and started an action in the Turkish court against the Cubans. Three months later, the Cuban shipowners arrested a sister ship of the Turkish vessel in England. The Turkish owners brought a motion to stay the action in England, giving an undertaking to provide security for any cross-claim that the Cubans may decide to make in the Turkish action. The stay was granted by the trial judge, but his order was reversed by the Court of Appeal. The Court of Appeal held that a mere balance of convenience was insufficient to deprive the plaintiffs of pursuing their action in England. It was also held that a situation of *lis pendens* in another jurisdiction was not, in itself, a bar to the plaintiffs' right to proceed in England.

Lord Keith of Kinkel referred to 'natural forum', having already defined it in the *Macshannon* case as 'that with which the action had the most real and substantial connection'. He said that, in this case, the defendant, if he were required to meet the plaintiff's claim in England, would be involved in substantial inconvenience and expense. Lord Diplock, delivering the main judgment, examined all the factors pointing towards Turkey as the forum in which justice could be done at less inconvenience and expense than in England. Neither party had any connection with England. The connecting factors were: (i) the crew and the pilot were Turkish; (ii) the surveyors were appointed in Turkey; (iii) the collision took place in Turkish waters; and (iv) most of the witnesses were Turkish. As far as the Cuban witnesses were concerned, there was little to choose between Turkey and England. Turkey was definitely the natural and appropriate forum for the action, which was already pending there. It was stressed that:

> ... the essential change in the attitude of the English courts to pending or prospective litigation in foreign jurisdictions, that has been achieved step by step during the last 10 years as a result of the successive decisions of this House in *The Atlantic Star*,

---

29 [1984] 1 All ER 470.

Macshannon and *Amin Rasheed*, is that judicial chauvinism has been replaced by judicial comity to an extent which I think the time is now ripe to acknowledge, frankly, that is indistinguishable from the Scottish legal doctrine of *forum non-conveniens*.[30]

Lord Brandon also added:

... the Court of Appeal ... have fallen into error. Mere balance of convenience cannot, of itself, be decisive in tilting the scales; but strong, and *a fortiori* overwhelming, balance of convenience may easily, and in most cases probably will, be so. Similarly, the mere disadvantage of multiplicity of suits cannot of itself be decisive in tilting the scales; but multiplicity of suits involving serious consequences with regard to expense or other matters, may well do so. In this connection, it is right to point out that, if concurrent actions in respect of the same subject matter, proceed together in different countries, as seems likely if a stay is refused in the present case, one or other of two undesirable consequences may follow: first, there may be two conflicting judgments of the two courts concerned; or, second there may be an ugly rush to get one action decided ahead of the other, in order to create a situation, or *res judicata*, or issue estoppel in the latter.[31]

It was also held that there was no evidence that, in Turkey, the plaintiffs would be under any disadvantage compared with a plaintiff in England, nor that they would not obtain justice in the Turkish courts.

Thus, from this point in time, the Scottish doctrine of *forum non-conveniens* became part of English law.

3.3.4 *The application of* forum non-conveniens *principles and service out of the jurisdiction*

Similarities do exist between the doctrine of *forum non-conveniens* and criteria applicable to applications for service out of the jurisdiction. Their differences are examined under para 3.3.6, below, after discussion of the new formula of *forum non-conveniens*, as was encapsulated by Lord Goff in *The Spiliada*.

Amin Rasheed Corp v Kuwait Ins [32]

The plaintiffs were a shipping company incorporated in Liberia having their place of management in Dubai. They sought to litigate their claim in England against their insurers, who had their head office in Kuwait and a branch office in Dubai. The claim was for a constructive total loss of their ship insured under a hull policy against marine and war risks. The form of policy was based upon the Lloyd's (of London) standard form of marine policy, but Kuwait was stated as the place of issue and the place for the payments of claims. There was no provision as to proper law of the contract. In order to bring their action in England, as opposed to in the Kuwaiti court, the plaintiffs had to bring their case within RSC Ord 11 r 1, to obtain leave to serve the writ out of the jurisdiction on the insurers. Both Bingham J and

---

30 Ibid, p 476.
31 [1984] 1 All ER 470, p 485.
32 [1984] AC 50.

the Court of Appeal held that there was no jurisdiction to serve the writ on the defendants in Kuwait under that rule. On appeal to the House of Lords, Lord Diplock said:

> ... the jurisdiction exercised by an English court over a foreign corporation which has no place of business in this country, as a result of granting leave under RSC Ord 11 r 1(1)(f) for service out of the jurisdiction of the writ on that corporation is an exorbitant jurisdiction ... [thus] the judicial discretion to grant leave under this paragraph of RSC Ord 11 r 1(1) should be exercised with circumspection in cases where there exists an alternative forum, viz the courts of the foreign country where the proposed defendant does carry on business, and whose jurisdiction would be recognised under English conflict rules. Such a forum in the instant case afforded by courts of Kuwait.[33]

The House went on to examine whether a Kuwaiti court, in addition to having jurisdiction, was also a *forum conveniens* for the dispute. According to Lord Wilberforce:

> In considering this question the court must take into account the nature of the dispute, the legal and practical issues involved, such questions as local knowledge, availability of witnesses and their evidence and expense. It is not appropriate, in my opinion, to embark upon a comparison of the procedures, or methods, or reputation or standing of the courts of one country as compared with those of another ...[34]

After considering the necessary factors, it was held that the Kuwaiti court was an alternative forum where the defendant had its place of business, and where the contract was made and had jurisdiction over the matter in dispute. The plaintiffs had not shown, either that justice could not be obtained, or that it could only be obtained at excessive cost, delay or inconvenience. Therefore, it was held that this case was not a proper one for service out of jurisdiction under the rule.

Thus, *forum non-conveniens* principles can be considered at the time of the application to obtain leave to serve out of the jurisdiction.

3.3.5 *The present formula of* **forum non-conveniens**

The principles of *forum non-conveniens*, as applied under English law today, were laid down by Lord Goff in the following case.

The Spiliada [35]

The shipowners were a Liberian corporation with part of their management in Greece and the other part in England. Their ship, *The Spiliada*, was chartered to carry a cargo of sulphur from Vancouver to India, the chemicals of which caused damage to the ship. The voyage charter provided for arbitration in London. The shippers and sellers of the cargo carried on business in Canada as exporters of sulphur. The shipowners obtained leave to serve proceedings on the shippers in Vancouver on the ground that it was an action to recover damages for breach of a

---

33 [1984] AC 50, pp 65–66.
34 Ibid, p 72.
35 [1987] 1 AC 460 (HL).

contract governed by English law. According to them, the cargo was wet when it was loaded and, therefore, caused severe corrosion to the holds and tank tops of the vessel. The sellers applied to have the ex parte order discharged on the ground that the case was not a proper one for service out of jurisdiction under Ord 11, r 4(2). The trial judge, who was at the same time hearing the trial of a similar action involving the same sellers and another ship, *The Cambridgeshire*, dismissed the application. He considered that the availability of witnesses, possible multiplicity of proceedings and the experience of counsel and solicitors, derived from their participation in *The Cambridgeshire* action, would save money and time. On appeal by the shippers, the Court of Appeal allowed the appeal and set aside the writ. It thought that it was impossible to conclude that the factors considered by the judge showed that the English court was distinctly more suitable for the ends of justice. On appeal to the House of Lords, it was held that, in order to determine whether a case was a proper one for service out of the jurisdiction under Ord 11, r 4(2) of the RSC, the court had, as in applications for a stay on the ground of *forum non-conveniens*, to identify in which forum the case would be most suitably tried for the interests of all parties and the ends of justice.

After examining the Scottish authorities on *forum non-conveniens*, and the trilogy of cases referred to above, Lord Goff found the opportunity to consolidate and summarise the law concerned with the doctrine of *forum non-conveniens* as derived from the Scottish doctrine. He laid down the general principle and a two-stage test for the court's approach to applications for a stay on this ground.

3.3.5.1 General principle

A stay will only be granted where the court is satisfied that there is some other available forum, having competent jurisdiction, which is the appropriate forum for the trial and in which the case may be tried more suitably for the interests of all parties and the ends of justice.

3.3.5.2 Burden of proof

In general, the burden of proof rests on the defendant to establish that there is another forum, which is clearly, or distinctly, more appropriate than the English forum for the trial. Where a party seeks to establish some evidence to persuade the court to exercise its discretion in his favour, the evidential burden will rest on that party. If the court finds that another forum is prima facie the appropriate forum for the trial, the burden will then shift to the plaintiff to show that there are special circumstances, by reason of which justice requires that the trial should, nevertheless, be held in England.

3.3.5.3 Effect of founding jurisdiction as of right

The fact that the claimant has found jurisdiction as of right in accordance with the law of England and Wales is not in itself an advantage for the claimant that should not be disturbed by the court. However, in cases in which there is no other natural forum (that is, collision on the high seas), the English court will not disturb the jurisdiction so established.

3.3.5.4 Connecting factors (first stage test)

In determining whether there exists another forum clearly more appropriate for the trial, the court will look first to see what factors there are which point in the direction of another forum. It will look at the forum with which the action had the most real and substantial connection. These connecting factors will include, not only those affecting convenience or expense (such as the availability of witnesses), but also other factors, such as the law governing the relevant transaction and the parties' place of residence or business. If the court concludes, at that stage, that there is no other available forum which is clearly more appropriate for the trial, it will ordinarily refuse a stay.

3.3.5.5 Second stage (all the circumstances)

If, however, the court concludes, at that stage, that there is some other available forum which prima facie is clearly more appropriate for the trial, it will ordinarily grant a stay, unless there are circumstances by reason of which justice requires that a stay should, nevertheless, not be granted. In this inquiry, the court will consider all the circumstances of the case, including circumstances which go beyond those taken into account when considering connecting factors with the other forum. One such factor, if established objectively by cogent evidence, can be the fact that the plaintiff will not obtain justice in the foreign jurisdiction.

3.3.5.6 Treatment of a legitimate personal or juridical advantage

Other advantages to the plaintiff proceeding in this jurisdiction may be relevant but not decisive. The key to the solution as to the treatment of a legitimate personal or juridical advantage lies in the underlying fundamental principle, which is where the case may be tried suitably for the interests of all the parties and the ends of justice. Typical examples of such advantages are: the award of higher damages; power to award interest; a more generous limitation period. However, even if the plaintiff were to be deprived of an advantage, such as a higher award of damages, a procedural advantage, time bar, and such like, it would not mean that the action should not be stayed. The most important element would be that the court was satisfied that substantial justice would be done in the available forum.[36]

It was held in the *The Spiliada* that the trial judge, having identified the correct test, considered the relevant factors and that his exercise of discretion should not be interfered with. The existence of *The Cambridgeshire* action was also a relevant factor to be considered in the exercise of the court's discretion.

In a fairly recent case, ***Lubbe v Cape plc Africa and Others***,[37] concerning claims by employees of South African subsidiaries of the defendant (an English-based company) for asbestos-related diseases allegedly caused to workers over a period of 20 to 30 years, the *Lubbe* action was stayed by the judge on the ground that South Africa was clearly a more appropriate forum than England. The Court of Appeal lifted the stay and the defendants appealed to the House of Lords. Thereafter,

---

36 [1987] 1 AC 460 (HL), pp 476–78, 482–84.
37 [2000] 2 Lloyd's Rep 383 (HL) and [2000] 1 Lloyd's Rep 139 (CA).

further actions were commenced on behalf of 1539 claimants (the African writ), neighbours to the South African subsidiaries, who alleged they suffered asbestos-related damage. The defendants applied for a stay, again, in these new actions. Two reasons were submitted by the claimants against a stay: first, that the South African court did not have experience in group actions with multiple claimants and, second, that the claimants would not be able to obtain legal aid there. It was held by Buckley J that, as the circumstances had changed since the last Court of Appeal decision, the African and other actions should proceed as a group in the more appropriate forum, South Africa.

On appeal, the Court of Appeal affirmed the judgment of Buckley J, and Pill LJ described the factors pointing towards South Africa as 'overwhelming':[38]

> It is not disputed that South Africa has a legal system of high repute, both with respect to the quality of its judges and its administration. I am entirely unpersuaded by arguments that the South African High Court would be unable to handle these actions efficiently, either on the ground that there are territorial divisions within South Africa, or because there is at present no procedure expressly providing for group actions. It is common ground that the law potentially to be applied is the same throughout South Africa . . .[39]

> Justice does not in my judgment require the refusal of a stay . . . The general rule is that the court will not refuse to grant a stay simply because the plaintiff has shown that no financial assistance will be available to him in the appropriate forum. It may exceptionally be a relevant factor, but the plaintiff has far from established that substantial justice cannot and will not be done in South Africa. I have already referred to the high repute in which the South African courts are held. There is also in South Africa a legal profession with high standards and a tradition of public service, though I do not suggest that lawyers in South Africa, any more than those anywhere else, can be expected to act on a large scale without prospects of remuneration. While I would not be prepared to apply the second stage of *The Spiliada* test, so as to permit English litigation, even in the absence of evidence that legal representation will be available, I am unable to conclude that in the circumstances it would not become available for claims in the South African courts. Moreover, given the accessibility to the wealth of scientific, technical and medical evidence available in this context, I am confident that it could be made available in a South African court to the extent required to achieve a proper consideration of the plaintiffs' cases. The action would by no means be novel or speculative.[40]

On appeal to the House of Lords[41] by the plaintiffs against the second Court of Appeal decision, the House reiterated the principles thus:

> . . . It is the interest of all the parties, not those of the plaintiff only or the defendant only, and the ends of justice as judged by the court on all the facts of the case before it, which must control the decision of the court. In *Spiliada* it was stated (at page 476):

>> 'The basic principle is that a stay will only be granted on the ground of *forum non conveniens* where the court is satisfied that there is some other available *forum*, having competent jurisdiction, which is the appropriate *forum* for the trial of the

---

38   [2000] 1 Lloyd's Rep 139, p 160.
39   Ibid at p 162.
40   Ibid, p 164.
41   [2000] 1 WLR 1545.

action, ie in which the case may be tried more suitably for the interests of all the parties and the ends of justice.'

In applying this principle the court's first task is to consider whether the defendant who seeks a stay is able to discharge the burden resting upon him not just to show that England is not the natural or appropriate *forum* for the trial but to establish that there is another available *forum* which is clearly or distinctly more appropriate than the English *forum*. In this way, proper regard is had to the fact that jurisdiction has been founded in England as of right (*Spiliada*, page 477). At this first stage of the inquiry the court will consider what factors there are which point in the direction of another *forum* (*Spiliada*, page 477; *Connelly v RTZ Corporation Plc* [1998] AC 854 at 871). If the court concludes at that stage that there is no other available *forum* which is clearly more appropriate for the trial of the action, that is likely to be the end of the matter. But if the court concludes at that stage that there is some other available *forum* which prima facie is more appropriate for the trial of the action it will ordinarily grant a stay unless the plaintiff can show that there are circumstances by reason of which justice requires that a stay should nevertheless not be granted. In this second stage the court will concentrate its attention not only on factors connecting the pro-ceedings with the foreign or the English *forum* (*Spiliada*, page 478; *Connelly*, page 872) but on whether the plaintiff will obtain justice in the foreign jurisdiction. The plain-tiff will not ordinarily discharge the burden lying upon him by showing that he will enjoy procedural advantages, or a higher scale of damages or more generous rules of limitation if he sues in England; generally speaking, the plaintiff must take a foreign *forum* as he finds it, even if it is in some respects less advantageous to him than the English *forum* (*Spiliada*, page 482; *Connelly*, page 872). It is only if the plaintiff can establish that substantial justice will not be done in the appropriate *forum* that a stay will be refused (*Spiliada*, page 482; *Connelly*, page 873).

This is not an easy condition for a plaintiff to satisfy, and it is not necessarily enough to show that legal aid is available in this country but not in the more appropriate foreign *forum*. Lord Goff of Chieveley said in *Connelly* (at page 873):

'I therefore start from the position that, at least as a general rule, the court will not refuse to grant a stay simply because the plaintiff has shown that no financial assistance, for example in the form of legal aid, will be available to him in the appropriate *forum*, whereas such financial assistance will be available to him in England. Many smaller jurisdictions cannot afford a system of legal aid. Suppose that the plaintiff has been injured in a motor accident in such a country, and succeeds in establishing English jurisdiction on the defendant by service on him in this country where the plaintiff is eligible for legal aid, I cannot think that the absence of legal aid in the appropriate jurisdiction would in itself justify the refusal of a stay on the ground of *forum non conveniens*. In this connection it should not be forgotten that financial assistance for litigation is not necessarily regarded as essential, even in sophisticated legal systems. It was not widely available in this country until 1949; and even since that date it has been only available for persons with limited means. People above that limit may well lack the means to litigate, which provides one reason for the recent legalisation of conditional fee agreements.

Even so, the availability of financial assistance in this country, coupled with its non-availability in the appropriate *forum*, may exceptionally be a relevant factor in this context. The question, however, remains whether the plaintiff can establish that sub-stantial justice will not in the particular circumstances of the case be done if the plaintiff has to proceed in the appropriate *forum* where no financial assistance is available.'

In *Connelly* a majority of the House held that the case before it was such an exceptional case. The nature and complexity of the case were such that it could not be tried at all without the benefit of legal representation and expert scientific assistance, available in this country but not in the more appropriate *forum*, Namibia. That being so, the majority of the House concluded that the Namibian *forum* was not one in which the case could be tried more suitably for the interests of all the parties and for the ends of justice.

Thus, the House in the *Lubbe* case (the group action) refused the stay of the English proceedings on the ground that the lack of means of the plaintiffs to prosecute their case in South Africa, in the unusual circumstances of the proceedings, would amount to a denial of justice, since the proceedings could only be handled efficiently, cost-effectively and expeditiously on a group basis and the preparation of the case required the service of professional lawyers. The claimants won in their appeal.

In the appeal brought by the defendants in the earlier action, the House dismissed their appeal against the finding of the Court of Appeal that the defendants had not shown South Africa to be clearly the more appropriate forum.

Whether the issue of delay by the foreign court to deliver judgment would be a factor to be taken into account at the second stage of *The Spiliada* test, Newman J held[42] that the court was not satisfied that substantial justice could not be done in India, although it might well be that it would take longer than if the proceedings had remained in England. In addition, the difference in the level of recoverability of costs was not something that denied substantial justice to parties in India.

It is further interesting to note that to select a forum solely on the basis of the level of damages that could be awarded in a foreign forum, in order to displace the most obvious and convenient forum, will not be looked on favourably by the court.[43]

3.3.6 Order 11[44] and forum non-conveniens *compared*

Lord Goff concluded that, although the general principle of *forum non-conveniens* was remarkably similar to the principle applied to cases of the court's discretionary power under RSC Ord 11, as derived from what Lord Wilberforce said in *Amin Rasheed* (see para 3.3.4, above), he identified three differences:

(a) in Ord 11 cases, the burden of proof rests on the plaintiff, whereas in *forum non-conveniens* cases, it rests on the defendant, at least at the first stage;

(b) in Ord 11 cases, the plaintiff is seeking to persuade the court to exercise its discretionary power to permit service on the defendant outside the jurisdiction. Although statutory authority has specified the particular circumstances in which that power may be exercised by Ord 11, r 1, the court can decide whether to exercise such power in a particular case, by virtue of r 4(2) of Ord 11. Permission shall not be granted, unless it shall be made sufficiently to appear to the

---

42 *Radhakrishna Hospitality Service Private Ltd and Eurest SA v Eih Ltd* [1999] 2 Lloyd's Rep 249.
43 *Bristow Helicopter Ltd v Sikorsky Aircraft Corporation* [2004] 2 Lloyd's Rep 150.
44 Now replaced by CPR, Pt 6, Section III (rr 6.17–6.31) and PD 6B.

court that the case is a proper one for service out of the jurisdiction. Special regard must be had to the fact stressed by Lord Diplock in *Amin Rasheed*, that the jurisdiction exercised under Ord 11 may be exorbitant, meaning extraordinary;

(c) the importance to be attached to any particular ground invoked by the plaintiff may vary from case to case. For example, the fact that English law may be the putative proper law of the contract may be of great importance in some cases, but of little importance in others.[45]

3.3.7 *What change did* The Spiliada *bring to the doctrine of* forum non-conveniens?

(a) It made a coherent statement of the principle as had developed from the previous cases and confirmed its uniformity with the Scottish doctrine;

(b) it provided a clear guideline for judges, by dividing the test into two stages;

(c) it delineated the burden of proof; and

(d) it clarified the treatment of a legitimate personal or juridical advantage.

In subsequent cases, the principle was easy to apply.

In collision cases the appropriate forum would be easily identifiable as the place where the collision occurred, if not on the high seas, as for example in *The Wellamo*,[46] where the collision took place in Swedish territorial waters. The action in England was stayed in favour of the court in Stockholm. However, if the interests of all parties and the ends of justice are not served, the place of the collision will not be the only factor. In *The Vishva Ajay*,[47] despite proof of a natural forum, a stay of the English action was refused. The collision took place in India. However, the circumstances prevailing in India at that time (delay in delivering a judgment, non-realistic award of legal costs) would constitute denial of justice to the plaintiff, who had come to the English courts for justice.[48]

It should be noted, however, that the court has wide discretion and, if it considers that these factors do not deprive the claimant of substantial justice, it may order the stay of the English proceedings as was done in *Radhakrishna Hospitality v Eih Ltd*.[49] The conclusion to be drawn is that the court has wide discretion on the treatment of a juridical advantage of the claimant, which depends on the circumstances of a particular case and the time at which the issue is determined.

Where there is no natural forum the court will refuse a stay.[50]

In *Vishva Abha* (VA),[51] there was a collision in the Red Sea between a sister ship

---

45 *The Spiliada* [1987] 1 AC 460 (HL), pp 480–81.

46 [1980] 2 Lloyd's Rep 229.

47 [1989] 2 Lloyd's Rep 558.

48 See, also, *The Sidi Bishir* [1987] 1 Lloyd's Rep 42.

49 [1999] 2 Lloyd's Rep 249, see para 3.3.5.6, above.

50 *The Coral Isis* [1986] 1 Lloyd's Rep 413; *The Po* [1990] 1 Lloyd's Rep 418 (CA); [1991] 2 Lloyd's Rep 206.

51 [1990] 2 Lloyd's Rep 312.

of VA and Dias. The sister ship sank and VA was served with a writ. The defendants contended that the English court was not the appropriate forum for the hearing of this action and applied for a stay on the ground that they had already commenced proceedings in South Africa where they had arrested the Dias. The limitation fund was much lower in South Africa than in England. The court was not convinced that South Africa was a more appropriate forum. Mr Justice Sheen held that the defendants, Indian shipowners, whose ships were frequently coming to England, would not be put to more inconvenience or expense by having their witnesses attend the English court than they would in attending a court in South Africa. It was mere chance that the defendants found themselves litigating in South Africa. Moreover, it would be a grave injustice to deprive the claimants of their right to litigate in England and instead send them to South Africa, where their chances of recovering damages would be much less than the sum they would recover in this country under English law. The principles of *The Spiliada* were applied.

3.3.8 Forum shopping by way of limitation actions

As has already been seen, prior to 1973, there was an inclination by the English courts towards English jurisdictional chauvinism which culminated with the well-known remark of Lord Denning MR that: 'No one who comes to these courts asking for justice should come in vain provided he acts in good faith . . . You may call this forum shopping . . . but if the forum is England, it is a good place to shop in, both for the quality of the goods and the speed of service.'[52] To which Lord Reid responded in the House of Lords: '. . . that seems to me to recall the good old days, the passing of which many may regret, when inhabitants of this island felt an innate superiority over those unfortunate enough to belong to other races.'[53]

Until then, it was rare for proceedings brought in England to be stayed, or set aside in favour of a foreign jurisdiction, even if it could have been more appropriate for the particular case.

In a limitation action, which is an action brought by a person seeking to limit his liability in respect of maritime claims, consideration is given by that person to the system of law which provides either low limits (such as the law of the countries following the International Convention for Limitation of Liability 1957), or a more difficult test by which the right to limitation may be broken (such as those countries which have adopted the 1976 Limitation Convention).[54] The latter has been ratified by States holding 45% of the world tonnage, while the former applies to 7.6%; the remaining States adhere to limitation of their own national law.

Outside the European Conventions regime (discussed later), there is flexibility for forum shopping and this has been acceptable in practice. This position seems to have been strengthened by recent decisions.

The person seeking to limit liability will usually admit liability when the limitation action is commenced at the forum of his choice. The limitation fund is

---

52 *The Atlantic Star* [1972] 2 Lloyd's Rep 446 (CA), p 451.
53 *The Atlantic Star* [1973] 2 Lloyd's Rep 197 (HL), p 200.
54 These Conventions are examined in Chapter 17.

established and deposited with the court as provided by the relevant Convention which applies in that jurisdiction. It is not unusual to have liability and limitation determined by courts of different jurisdictions, as was decided in the following case.

Caspian v Bouygues [55]

There was a loss of a barge in Cape Town, South Africa, being towed under a towage contract which provided for English jurisdiction. The owners and time charterers of the tug boat brought limitation proceedings in England to determine the limitation of their possible liability to the barge owners under the Limitation Convention 1976. In South Africa the old Convention of Limitation of Liability 1957 applies. The owners of the barge who commenced proceedings on liability in Cape Town contested jurisdiction on the ground that a court in South Africa was the more appropriate forum.

Rix J, having thoroughly reviewed all relevant authorities, held that admission or determination of liability was not a condition precedent to limitation. Limitation of liability for the loss of a barge could be determined here on the basis of the Limitation Convention 1976, prior to liability actions which had commenced in both South Africa and England. Although there was no connection with England, other than that the towage contract provided for English jurisdiction, the advantage to the applicants for limitation here was that it would be harder for limitation to be broken, while under South African law (which applies the 1957 Convention) it would be easier. In accordance with the second stage of *The Spiliada* test, the judge decided in favour of England despite South Africa being the natural forum for the liability issues. There was nothing unusual in determining a limitation action in a forum different from that of liability, Rix J said. The Court of Appeal [56] upheld the decision and allowed the limitation action to continue here; it confirmed that the right to limit was a quite separate issue from the issue of liability. The action for damages, by the owners of the barge against the owners of the tug, its time charterers and the Cape Town port authorities, was allowed to continue in South Africa.

A similar situation arose in ***Caltex Singapore v BP Shipping***. [57]

BP's ship collided with the jetty of the plaintiffs (Caltex oil companies) in Singapore. Liability proceedings against BP were brought in England where the limitation under the 1976 Convention was higher than the plaintiffs' claim. Naturally, BP commenced its limitation action in Singapore, (the natural forum for determination of liability) in view of lower limits applicable there under the 1957 Limitation Convention. There was no issue of apportionment of fault. BP also applied for a stay of the English action. Although Clarke J ruled that the appropriate forum for liability was Singapore, he dismissed BP's application for stay of the English proceedings on the basis of the second stage of *The Spiliada* test. He concluded that the interests of both parties and the ends of justice – viewed objectively – would be better served if the plaintiffs were not deprived of the larger limit, since it was proper to regard the

---

55 [1997] 2 Lloyd's Rep 507; see Chapter 8 for the facts of the case.
56 [1998] 2 Lloyd's Rep 461.
57 [1996] 1 Lloyd's Rep 286.

1976 Convention as representing a widely accepted development, and being part of English law, it could be fairly regarded as part of English public policy.

It was that very reasoning that the judge in Hong Kong found difficult to accept in the subsequent decision, *The Kapitan Shvestov*,[58] basically because the *Caltex* judgment seemed to equate the local public policy (being a subjective value judgment) with objective substantial justice, which was a distinct requirement laid down by *The Spiliada* and *De Dampierre v de Dampierre*.[59]

There were similar facts to the *Caltex* case in *The Kapitan Shvestov*. A collision between a Russian and a Singaporean ship took place in the dredged channel of the Chao Fhraya river in Thailand, but neither of the shipowners wanted proceedings brought in Bangkok (natural forum). Instead, the Singaporean owners commenced an action in Singapore and the Russian owners brought an action in Hong Kong. Both applied for a stay of the respective proceedings of each other. An important factor in the applications was that Singaporean law applied the 1957 Limitation Convention, while Hong Kong applied the 1976 Convention. Waung J stayed the Hong Kong action on the ground that – since the parties had displaced the natural forum of the Bangkok court – Singapore was a more appropriate forum than Hong Kong, on the basis of various connecting factors and, also, because the proceedings in Singapore had reached an advanced stage. There, objectively, substantial justice could be done for the interests of all parties and the ends of justice. The judge thought that in the *Caltex* case undue emphasis had been placed on the loss of the advantage to the plaintiffs if their limitation action in England was stayed, which was not in accord with *The Spiliada* and *De Dampierre* cases.

However, the Hong Kong Court of Appeal, by majority of 2:1, reversed this result and decided in favour of the Hong Kong jurisdiction. The majority thought that, since Singapore was not the natural or appropriate forum, the trial there would deprive the Russian owners of a legitimate juridical advantage and, since the Russian ship was more severely damaged, the limitation fund in Singapore would not be sufficient, particularly if the Singaporean ship was found more to blame. An interesting point was raised by the minority in the Court of Appeal, which supported the judge's decision as regards the result. This was that substantial legal costs had already been incurred in the Singaporean proceedings and, given that the expected burdensome additional legal costs which were likely to be incurred to reach the same level of the proceedings in Hong Kong, the possible shortfall in the limitation figure of US$338,000 could hardly justify a second set of legal proceedings in Hong Kong.

In the subsequent case, *Herceg Novi and Ming Galaxy*,[60] the competing fora were Singapore and England. A collision occurred in the straits of Singapore between the *Ming Galaxy* and *Herceg Novi*, which resulted in the sinking of the latter. The owners of the former began an action *in rem* in Singapore and the owners of the latter commenced an action in England. The motives of the parties to the actions were, again, the differences in the law of each forum with respect to limitation of liability.

---

58 [1998] 1 Lloyd's Rep 199 (HK Court of first instance and CA).
59 [1988] 1 AC 92 (HL).
60 [1998] 1 Lloyd's Rep 167.

The defendants to the English action sought a stay of the action on the ground that England was not the natural or appropriate forum. The plaintiffs' argument was that, were the stay to be granted, they would be deprived of the benefit of the more generous limitation amount under the 1976 Convention. Clarke J was inclined to refuse the stay, bearing in mind this factor, but temporarily granted it until the determination of the liability and quantum issues were resolved in Singapore.

The Court of Appeal[61] chose to discourage forum shopping, on the basis of higher limitation applicable by the law of a forum in which jurisdiction is obtained as of right by arrest of a ship, particularly when there is another forum which is more appropriate by being the natural forum, as was Singapore in this case. It was stressed that as the 1976 Convention has not received universal acceptance, the preference for it had no greater justification than the 1957 regime. The Court of Appeal agreed with the first instance judge in *The Kapitan Shvetsov* and with the dissenting judgment of the Hong Kong Court of Appeal in the same case.

Apparently, there is a conflict between two Court of Appeal decisions, *The Caspian*, which encourages forum shopping, if a party chooses to proceed in a jurisdiction where the higher limit of the 1976 Convention applies, and *The Herceg Novi*, which discourages such an approach. While there may be an opportunity in the future for that conflict to be resolved by the House of Lords, it is submitted that no general principle can be drawn either way. Each case should be looked upon its own circumstances (see *The Western Regent* discussed in Ch 7 para 3.2.2). Where there is a natural forum, the first stage test of *The Spiliada* can easily be satisfied, although this factor alone will not be decisive. As regards the balancing act of advantages and disadvantages at the second stage, the 1976 Convention limit should not weigh heavy, if the court is satisfied that substantial justice could be done in the alternative more appropriate forum. However, better justice could be done if there is a larger fund in court to satisfy the claims and this reason may justify the separation of the liability from the limitation action.

3.4 Stay on the ground of a foreign jurisdiction agreement[62]

The parties to a contract usually agree where and how any disputes arising out of the contract will be adjudicated. Such agreements may provide either for arbitration, or for the jurisdiction of a competent court, English or foreign. There are occasions, however, when one party to the agreement decides to bring suit in a jurisdiction other than the contractual, in breach of the jurisdiction agreement. In the following paragraphs, both the principles and the approach of the English court with regard to proceedings brought in the English courts in breach of a foreign jurisdiction clause (to which the Brussels Convention – now Brussels Regulation – or Lugano Convention does not apply) are examined. With respect to jurisdiction agreements to which the Brussels Regulation or Lugano Convention applies, see

---

61 [1998] 2 Lloyd's Rep 454.

62 The issues involved in this area are analysed in detail by Peel, E, 'Exclusive jurisdiction agreements: purity and pragmatism in the conflict of laws' [1998] LMCLQ 182.

Chapter 6.[63] As far as breach of an English jurisdiction clause or arbitration is concerned, see Chapter 7.

3.4.1 General principle

In contracts the parties usually agree the jurisdiction of the court or the arbitral tribunal to which their dispute can be referred. Invariably, however, one party to the contract may decide to sue the other in a forum other than the one which is provided for by the contract. The aggrieved party will apply for a stay of those proceedings.

When there is a breach of a foreign jurisdiction clause to which the Brussels Convention (now Brussels Regulation) does not apply, the English court, upon the application of the aggrieved party for a stay of the proceedings, is not bound to stay the action, but it has discretion. The court's discretion is exercised in favour of a stay, unless the claimant shows a strong reason or cause for not giving effect to the foreign jurisdiction clause. The English courts have followed this principle consistently.[64] Balancing of all the circumstances of the particular case is required in order to determine in which forum, the chosen or the English, justice will best be served with less inconvenience and expense. The discretion of the first instance judge should not easily be disturbed by the appellate court, if the latter disagrees with it, unless it is shown that the judge made an error in principle, or that he took or omitted to take into account matters which he ought not to, or he evaluated the circumstances wrongly.[65]

The following broad factors have been considered in various cases to have been connecting factors with either forum:

(a) where the evidence is available;

(b) with which country either party is closely connected;

(c) whether the law chosen is different from English;

(d) whether the defendant genuinely desires to proceed in the chosen forum, or only seeks a procedural advantage;

(e) whether there are related actions already commenced in one forum;

(f) whether the plaintiff would be prejudiced in the chosen forum, if the claim was time barred, or if he was deprived of security for the claim, or if there was delay in procedures of administration of justice there.

It will be seen that one of these factors alone may not be sufficient to tilt the balance in favour of not granting the stay. In recent years, a less nationalistic attitude of the English courts and more respect for the parties' choice of forum has been shown.

---

63 The rules applicable under the Brussels Regulation and Lugano Convention are different, as explained at the end of Chapter 6.

64 In *The Cap Blanco* [1913] P 131, p 136, it was said that 'effect must be given, if the terms of the contract permit it, to the obvious intention and agreement of the parties'; *The Fehmarn* [1957] 2 Lloyd's Rep 511; *The Chaparral* [1968] 2 Lloyd's Rep 158; and other, more recent, cases mentioned in this section.

65 *The Nile Rhapsody* [1994] 1 Lloyd's Rep 382; *Reichhold Norway v Goldman Sachs Int* [2000] 1 WLR 173 (the judge had not misdirected himself).

3.4.2 Strong cause or reason for the court to refuse stay of proceedings

Broadly, for the court to refuse a stay of the English proceedings commenced in breach of the foreign jurisdiction clause there must be either expert evidence in the English jurisdiction, or multiplicity of proceedings, or connecting factors such as those described in *The Spiliada* decision. A few examples are shown below.

3.4.2.1 Expert evidence in England would be a strong cause

Evidence of experts appointed in England was regarded as an exceptional factor for not granting a stay. The same judge and the Court of Appeal in the following case decided against a stay. It is worth noting the factors that were decisive in the exercise of their discretion.

The Adolf Warski[66]

The plaintiffs, cargo-owners, started actions *in rem* against the shipowners for damages to cargo carried on two of their Polish ships from South America to England. There were two bills of lading issued which contained similar jurisdiction clauses in favour of the Polish courts and, also, provided that Polish law was to apply. The claims in Poland had, however, become time barred and the defendants had refused to agree an extension of time. The defendants provided security for the claims and applied for a stay of the English proceedings. The plaintiffs objected on the grounds that the receivers were English companies and the evidence was more readily available in England. They pleaded two further important factors: their claim had become time barred in Poland and, if it were necessary to call witnesses from Chile, the port of loading, there could be political difficulties in obtaining visas for them to visit Poland. The trial judge came to the conclusion that the court should exercise its discretion by refusing a stay and allowing the actions to proceed in England. Looking at all aspects of the main evidence necessary to enable claims to be decided justly, there was a strong balance of argument in favour of a trial in England, rather than Poland. The Court of Appeal held that the judge was entitled to exercise his discretion that way. Cairns LJ stated:

> The judge was not satisfied that there was any factor in favour of the plaintiffs arising from their connection with England as against the defendants' connection with Poland. He considered that the jurisdiction clauses were reasonable, but that this did not mean that it would be right to enforce them irrespective of the circumstances . . . There was no evidence of any difference between the English and Polish law, and nothing to show that the English court would have difficulty in applying Polish law. He considered that expert evidence was the most important factor in this case, and as the damaged goods had been surveyed on both sides by English surveyors, and both sides had consulted English experts . . . it would be difficult to put the evidence in a satisfactory form before the Polish court. He attached some, but no great, weight to possible difficulties in calling Chilean witnesses.[67]

On the question as to what made this case exceptional, Cairns LJ said, having

---

66 [1976] 2 Lloyd's Rep 241.
67 [1976] 2 Lloyd's Rep 241, p 244.

approved the judge's approach, that it was the necessity of calling English expert witnesses on a highly technical matter.[68]

Similarly, in *The El Amria*,[69] a stay of the English proceedings, which were commenced despite the Egyptian jurisdiction clause, was refused because, on balance, there was a significant or strong cause shown for refusing the stay. That was, again, the evidence of expert witnesses in England (surveyors and agronomists) who had examined the cargo during and after discharge, and the evidence relating to the slowness of discharge. Such evidence, being at the centre of the dispute, was more readily available in England and there would be considerable difficulty in conveying – through interpreters to the Egyptian judge or court – expert technical evidence which the surveyors and agronomists would be called to give.

3.4.2.2 Multiplicity of proceedings is a strong cause

Another factor, which the Court of Appeal in *The El Amria*, unlike the judge in the same case, found to be not just a matter of convenience, but of great importance, was the existence of another action in this jurisdiction by the same claimant against another party (Mersey Docks and Harbour Company). In this action, many of the issues were the same as the action between the claimants and the defendants with regard to the cargo claim for which a stay was sought in favour of the chosen jurisdiction, Egypt. It would be a potential disaster if these actions were not tried together, because of the inherent risk that the same issues might be determined differently in the two countries, said the Court of Appeal. Although it approved the judge's application of the general principle, it criticised him in three respects for his reasons in refusing the stay: (a) he had misapprehended the potential importance of oral evidence which the defendant might reasonably have wished to call from Egypt; (b) he had failed to take into account the close connection of the defendants with Egypt; and (c) he had taken into account a factor which he should not have, namely a supposed inferiority of the procedures used by the Egyptian court. On the whole, there were strong conflicting considerations in favour of either court. However, the two factors stressed by the Court of Appeal, namely: the expert evidence and the parallel action in England, led it to refuse the stay. In addition, the fact that the defendants did not just ask for a stay merely for a procedural advantage (since security for the claim had been provided) added a weight in favour of England.

Multiplicity of proceedings is, undoubtedly, a strong cause, as has clearly been stated in more recent decisions, *Citi-March v Neptune*[70] and *The MC Pearl*,[71] (see later), in which Colman J and Rix J (respectively) applied *The El Amria*, having considered that the strong cause was the multiplicity of suits in England. This was a paradigm of cases, Rix J said, requiring the concentration of all relevant parties' disputes in a single jurisdiction.

Occasionally, however, there may be a clash of jurisdiction clauses contained in separate contracts, which involve disputes of related issues and may give rise, unintentionally, to multiplicity of proceedings in different jurisdictions. Such a

---

68   Ibid, p 246.
69   [1981] 2 Lloyd's Rep 119.
70   [1997] 1 Lloyd's Rep 72.
71   [1997] 1 Lloyd's Rep 566.

clash arose in a fairly recent case, ***Sinochem v Mobil Sales***,[72] in which Rix J decided in favour of each exclusive jurisdiction clause contained in the individual contracts, which provided for jurisdiction in Hong Kong and England, respectively. The mere possibility of multiplicity of proceedings, when no proceedings had yet commenced in Hong Kong under the separate contract, was not a strong reason why, in the interests of justice, Sinochem London should be relieved of its bargain to litigate disputes under its English contract in England.[73]

The El Amria case, which has been applied by judges in subsequent decisions, insofar as jurisdiction agreements are concerned, represents the school of thought of 'broad judicial discretion'. In particular, in determining whether or not a stay should be granted, it allows judges to consider which would be the appropriate forum (England or the chosen one) for the ends of justice and the interests of parties, which is almost identical to the doctrine of *forum non-conveniens*. Sometimes, the agreement of the parties as to jurisdiction may play, relatively, a less important role. The 'broad judicial discretion' school of thought has, however, been criticised for allowing *forum non-conveniens* principles to assist, instead of preventing, a party to an agreement breaking his bargain. Since *The Angelic Grace*[74] – which involved a breach of an arbitration clause – there has emerged a school of thought supporting the view that there should be a 'narrow judicial discretion' when there is a contractual choice of jurisdiction. In particular, the Court of Appeal, in this case, stressed, in strong terms, that a choice of forum by parties to a contract should be respected. The differences between these two strands are examined in Chapter 7, in the context of anti-suit injunctions.[75]

The English court has, however, recently emphasised[76] that English law applied the same principle whether the contractual forum was England or another country, and it made no difference whether the jurisdiction clause was exclusive or non-exclusive, and the force of the general rule was not in any way weakened where the clause was a standard clause and not one freely negotiated. Unless circumstances had arisen which could not have been foreseen at the time of the contract, release on the ground only of foreseeable matters of convenience was likely to be rare.

3.4.2.3 The Spiliada *connecting factors provide a strong cause*[77]

In the following case, connecting factors, which were important at the first stage of *The Spiliada* case, pointed towards the chosen jurisdiction as being the most appropriate forum, so a stay of the English proceedings was granted. Had the connecting factors existed in relation to the English jurisdiction, they would have

---

72 [2000] 1 Lloyd's Rep 670.

73 See also *Import Export Metro Ltd v Compania Sud Americana De Vapores SA* [2003] 1 Lloyd's Rep 405.

74 [1995] 1 Lloyd's Rep 87; see also *Reichhold Norway v Goldman Sachs* [2000] 1 WLR 173; stay of related proceedings in England was granted pending determination of arbitration in Norway.

75 Consistency in the treatment of foreign and domestic jurisdiction clauses is needed. Other than those cases concerning breach of an arbitration agreement, or a jurisdiction agreement which is within Art 23 of the Brussels Regulation, where special rules apply, all other cases of breach of a jurisdiction agreement, whether the application is for an anti-suit injunction, or for a stay of proceedings, should be treated in the same way: see, further, Chapter 7.

76 See *Import Export Metro Ltd v Compania Sud Americana De Vapores SA* [2003] 1 Lloyd's Rep 405.

77 *The El Amria* [1981] 2 Lloyd's Rep 119.

been taken into account in support of not granting the stay, despite the foreign jurisdiction clause.[78]

The Rothnie[79]

The plaintiffs, an English company, were the demise charterers of the vessel, R. The defendants were an English company carrying on business as a shipyard and ship-repairer in Gibraltar. The parties entered into a contract to repair the vessel in drydock in Gibraltar. The contract expressly provided that 'the agreement shall be governed by and construed in accordance with the laws of Gibraltar and the parties hereto submit to the non-exclusive jurisdiction of the courts of Gibraltar'.

Subsequent to a dispute concerning the work carried out on the vessel, the plaintiffs issued a writ in England on 17 July 1995. The defendants, who had not been paid, served proceedings in Gibraltar, on 19 July 1995, and applied for a stay of the English proceedings. They contended that the effect of the non-exclusive juris-diction clause, by which the parties acknowledged the jurisdiction of the courts of Gibraltar, combined with the defendants' commencement of proceedings there, created a strong prima facie case that the jurisdiction of Gibraltar was an appropri-ate one. The plaintiffs contended that both parties were English companies and jurisdiction had been founded by right in the English High Court. Moreover, the wording of the jurisdiction clause imposed no obligation to litigate in Gibraltar. After summarising the principles laid down by Lord Goff in The Spiliada,[80] the learned trial judge held that the defendants had satisfied the court that there was another available forum which was prima facie the appropriate forum for the trial of the action. The jurisdiction agreement in the parties' contract created a strong prima facie case that the jurisdiction of Gibraltar was an appropriate one. The action had its most real and substantial connection with Gibraltar, having regard to all the relevant factors, such as the place where the work was completed, the law, witnesses resided there, and such like. There were no circumstances by reason of which justice required that a stay should not be granted, after considering all the circumstances of the case.

3.4.3 What would not be a strong cause or reason?

By a process of elimination, the circumstances which have not been regarded as constituting a strong cause or reason by the courts for the purpose of staying the English proceedings, in favour of a foreign jurisdiction clause, are shown in the following examples.

3.4.3.1 Availability of factual evidence in England is not in itself a strong cause

In The Eleftheria,[81] an express jurisdiction clause was contained in the bill of lading, which provided that all disputes arising under it were to be decided in the country

---

78   See further on these issues BP plc v Aon Ltd [2006] 1 Lloyd's Rep 549.
79   [1996] 2 Lloyd's Rep 206.
80   [1987] 1 AC 460 (HL).
81   [1969] 1 Lloyd's Rep 237.

where the carrier had his principal place of business, applying the law of such country. The principal place of business of the defendants, the shipowners, was in Greece. *The Eleftheria* carried wood intended to be discharged in London and Hull. When she arrived at docks in London, there was labour trouble and she could only discharge part of the cargo. She sailed for Rotterdam where she discharged the rest, as was allowed by the contract in the circumstances. The plaintiffs claimed the expenses to transship the cargo back to its destination and arrested the vessel in England, alleging breach of contract. In this court, the defendants confined themselves to the application for a stay of the action on the ground that the Greek courts had jurisdiction by express agreement of the parties, which was not disputed. Considering the fact that the parties had agreed the jurisdiction and the law for their disputes, Brandon J held that the inconvenience to the plaintiffs in having to take witnesses to Greece was not insuperable. It was of substantial importance that Greek law governed the contract and that it would be more satisfactory for the law of a foreign country to be decided by the courts of that country. Therefore, he exercised his discretion by granting the stay. The plaintiffs had not shown a strong cause why they should not be held to their agreement and they would not be prejudiced by having to sue in Greece. All the circumstances in each case need to be taken into account.

In *The Makefjell*,[82] the Court of Appeal upheld the decision of the trial judge, Brandon J, in this case, affirming the same principle. At the time, and after *The Atlantic Star*, a more liberal and less nationalistic attitude was being displayed by the English judges.

The case involved Norwegian shipowners, a Canadian shipper and an English receiver of cargo of cheesecakes, which was loaded on *The Makefjell* in Canada for carriage to London. The bills of lading provided for Norwegian law and jurisdiction in the place of business of the carrier, with respect to any disputes arising under the bills. The cargo arrived in London and was partly discharged. Due to some difficulties in further discharge of the cargo, the rest of it was left in a non-refrigerated shed. Consequently, the cheesecakes thawed. The plaintiffs brought two actions in England, one *in personam* (by serving out of the jurisdiction) and one *in rem* and threatened to arrest a sister ship, which was about to come to England. They also issued summons in the Norwegian court to protect themselves in the event the English action was stayed. The defendants applied for a stay on the ground of the express jurisdiction clause, while the plaintiffs contended that they should not be held to their agreement, because the facts giving rise to their claim arose in England. This, they alleged, was because the factual witnesses were here. As regards the applicable law, Norwegian lawyers who were familiar with English language could give evidence on Norwegian law (which was not materially different from English law).

It was held that the inconvenience of witnesses, if they had to give evidence in the foreign agreed jurisdiction, was not a strong cause to refuse a stay. The existence of factual evidence in England was not, in itself, a decisive factor for not granting a stay.

---

82 [1976] 2 Lloyd's Rep 29.

On the discretion point, the judge (at first instance) thought that English witnesses could very well give evidence in Norway, as it could equally happen the other way around. Two considerations were influential upon exercising his discretion to grant the stay: (a) the key point was, in his view, whether the circumstances that the bulk of the evidence was to be found here, was something of such an exceptional character as to afford strong reasons for allowing the plaintiffs to depart from their contract. The answer to this, in his view, was that, while this may be an important factor, there must also be other factors operating against a stay. Besides, a large number of cargo claims involved evidence which would be found in the country of discharge. If all such cases were treated as exceptional, the rule as to enforcement of jurisdiction clauses would be undermined; and (b) a broader consideration, which the judge took into account, was the tendency of the courts, both in England and the USA, at that time to adopt a more liberal and less nationalistic attitude to questions of choice of jurisdiction. The Court of Appeal, constituted by Cairns and Stevenson LJJ and Sir Gordon Willmer, approved the judge's reasoning and conclusion.

3.4.3.2 *Time bar in the contractual jurisdiction is not in itself a strong cause*

Whether or not the time bar of a claim in the contractual jurisdiction is a strong cause in refusing a stay of the English proceedings has not been treated uniformly by the courts. There are three possible views: it is either a factor against a stay (*The Blue Wave*),[83] or a factor in favour of a stay, or a neutral factor. The judge in *The Adolf Warski*[84] preferred the second view, but it was obiter and the Court of Appeal did not decide the point, although it thought that the time bar might be a neutral factor.

There are a number of interesting recent decisions on the issue. Rix J in **The MC Pearl**[85] chose a robust approach. In this case, the claim in the contractual jurisdiction, South Korea, had become time barred. He considered the authorities and conflicting views on this issue and distinguished cases concerning *forum non-conveniens*. He held that, as regards jurisdiction clauses, the time bar point alone would not have assisted the plaintiff to continue their case here, if he did not have a strong cause for it separately.[86] He was not prepared to find that the existence of a limitation defence in South Korea saved this action, or caused him even to stay it, only on terms that the South Korean limitation defence was waived.[87] Even where the plaintiff did have a strong cause for jurisdiction in England, the fact that he had

---

83 [1982] 1 Lloyd's Rep 151.

84 [1976] 2 Lloyd's Rep 241.

85 [1997] 1 Lloyd's Rep 566.

86 The strong cause was multiplicity of proceedings, of which see later. Previously, Sheen J (in *The Blue Wave* [1982] 1 Lloyd's Rep 151) had decided that a time bar in the contractual jurisdiction would be an important factor for refusing a stay of the English action, unless the plaintiff acted unreasonably and his conduct showed that, without good reason, he deliberately allowed the time limit to expire without instituting alternative proceedings. Lord Goff, obiter, in *The Spiliada* [1987] 1 AC 460, seemed to support that view. The Court of Appeal, in *The Adolf Warski* [1976] 2 Lloyd's Rep 241, thought that it was a neutral factor to considerations of a stay with regard to jurisdiction clauses.

87 [1997] 1 Lloyd's Rep 566, p 576, 2nd col: to that extent he differed from the view expressed by Colman J in *Citi-March v Neptune* [1997] 1 Lloyd's Rep 72.

allowed the time bar to go by default in the contractual jurisdiction always required some consideration or explanation.[88] Although Rix J agreed with Colman J, who stated the law in *Citi-March v Neptune*[89] as derived from previous cases, he stressed his disagreement with the following proposition of Colman J that:

> In a case where, however, but for the time bar, strong cause in favour of England could not be shown, a plaintiff may be able to rely on the prejudice to him by reason of the time bar in the contractual forum if he can show that he did not act unreasonably in failing to issue protective proceedings in order to prevent time running against him . . . At the end of the day, the court must consider whether in the interests of justice it is more appropriate to permit a plaintiff to proceed in England, although he has omitted to preserve time in the contractual forum, and although England is not clearly the more appropriate forum, than to deprive him of all opportunity of pursuing his claim in any forum.[90]

Such a soft approach was not acceptable to Rix J, who preferred a hard-line attitude to deprive a litigant of pursuing his claim, if he let the time limit in the contractual jurisdiction expire.

In some cases, however, a plaintiff may be unable to obtain an extension of time under the law of the country of the chosen jurisdiction, either by waiver, or through the discretion of the court, which would, in effect, result in rendering the exclusive jurisdiction clause invalid. In such a case, the Court of Appeal held in 2000[91] that the action commenced here as protective measures, should not be stayed. It reversed its previous order by which a stay had been granted on ground of *forum non-conveniens* and on the condition that the defendants gave an undertaking to waive the time bar point in the contractual jurisdiction, Pakistan. At this hearing it was shown that it would be very difficult under the local statute to obtain a waiver of the time bar.

A warning to litigants, who deliberately let a time limit lapse in the contractual jurisdiction in order to proceed in another forum, was given in the strongest terms by Godfrey J sitting in the Court of Appeal of Hong Kong, which was cited with approval by Lord Goff at the Privy Council in the same case, ***The Pioneer Container***.[92] Godfrey J said:

> If you find yourself bound to litigate in a forum which is more expensive than the one you would prefer, deliberately to choose the latter rather than the former seems to me . . . to be forum shopping in one of its purest and most undesirable forms. And, if in pursuance of your deliberate decision to litigate here, instead, you let time run out in the jurisdiction in which you are bound to litigate, without taking the trouble (because of the expense) even to issue a protective writ there, you are not, as I think, acting reasonably at all; you are gambling on the chance of a stay being refused here

---

88 [1997] 1 Lloyd's Rep 566, p 576; Rix J thought that this case was on all fours with *Citi-March v Neptune* [1997] 1 Lloyd's Rep 72, in which Colman J summarised the principles derived from previous cases.

89 [1997] 1 Lloyd's Rep 72.

90 Ibid, p 77, 1st col, per Colman J. (The above statement does not seem to be in accord with the general principle stated by Colman J in the previous paragraphs of his judgment.)

91 *Baghlaf Al Zafer Factory Co v Pakistan National Shipping Co (No 2)* [2000] 1 Lloyd's Rep 1.

92 [1994] 1 Lloyd's Rep 593.

and you cannot complain if you then lose that gamble. That may seem to you at the time a justifiable commercial risk to take. But that, in the context of the litigation, does not make your decision a reasonable one.

On a voyage from Taiwan to Hong Kong, the vessel in this case sank off the coast of Taiwan. Despite the Taiwan exclusive jurisdiction clause contained in the bill of lading, the cargo-owners, plaintiffs, allowed the time limit to expire deliberately and commenced an action in Hong Kong. An application for a stay by the defendants, shipowners, was successful on appeal, as it was found that, apart from the time bar point, there was strong connection of the case with Taiwan.

3.4.4 Forum shopping in breach of a jurisdiction agreement and risk management

In the light of these decisions, careful consideration should be given to the circumstances, which have been regarded by the courts to constitute a strong cause, before litigants embark in wasted litigation. The burden of proof is on the claimant to show why a stay of the English proceedings should not be granted in favour of the agreed jurisdiction, by contrast to cases of a stay on ground of *forum non-conveniens* in which the burden of proof, at the first stage of *The Spiliada* test, is on the defendant to show why the stay should be granted. There seems to be, in some respects, a great similarity between the two approaches, with regard to the factors taken into account. For this reason, the courts, in some cases, tend to conflate the principles and assimilate *forum non-conveniens* when considering a stay on the ground of foreign jurisdiction agreements.[93] Such an approach, however, leads to inconsistent results given that, in other cases, the courts have distinguished the doctrine of *forum non-conveniens* per se from considerations applicable to a stay in favour of a foreign jurisdiction agreement and have approached the matter with caution in order to keep the parties to their bargain.[94] This trend has been observed in recent decisions: for example, Colman J in *Konkola Copper Mines Plc v Coromin Ltd*[95] stated:

> The concept that it is not normally open to an overseas defendant seeking to set aside service in the face of a non-exclusive English jurisdiction clause which had been freely negotiated to rely in support of a *forum non conveniens* argument on factors of inconvenience which he ought reasonably to have appreciated might arise when he entered into the jurisdiction agreement presents itself to me as entirely correct in principle. Were it otherwise, it would be open to a defendant to invite the court to exercise a discretion to enable him to escape from his contract for reasons of which he ran the risk of occurrence from the outset.

Whether reasons of judicial comity, ie respect to the jurisdiction of the court chosen, should be taken into account, giving a broader application of the principles as stated in *Patel v Airbus* on issues of anti-suit injunctions, are discussed in Chapter 7.

However, jurisdiction clauses will not be upheld if the HVR apply to the bill of

---

93   *The El Amria* [1981] 2 Lloyd's Rep 119; *The Nile Rhapsody* [1992] 2 Lloyd's Rep 399 and [1994] 1 Lloyd's Rep 382 (CA).

94   *The MC Pearl* [1997] 1 Lloyd's Rep 566; *The Pioneer Container* [1994] 1 Lloyd's Rep 593; *The Angelic Grace* [1994] 1 Lloyd's Rep 168; [1995] 1 Lloyd's Rep 87 (CA) (see Chapter 7).

95   [2006] 2 Lloyd's Rep 446, at p 452.

lading contract by force of law, and the foreign law chosen by the foreign jurisdiction clause confers less liability upon the carrier than the liability under the HVR – unless the defendant undertook to take no advantage of the lower limit.[96] If not, then the foreign jurisdiction will be null and void by virtue of Art 8 of the HVR.[97]

Sometimes, a jurisdiction clause may not be exclusive but optional, or may be obligatory upon one party to the agreement only, or it may not be effective.[98]

An attempt by one party to the agreement to oust the jurisdiction clause, by issuing proceedings in a jurisdiction other than the chosen one on the ground of *forum non-conveniens*, will be futile, if the clause provides for an exclusive jurisdiction which is a question of construction of the agreement.

Whether or not an agreement provides for an *exclusive jurisdiction*, guidance has been given by the courts in further two cases. In the case below, Webster J took the view that a plea of *forum non-conveniens* would not be open to the parties when their agreement was freely negotiated and it was not just a standard term incorporated by reference. Although this case concerned a breach of an English jurisdiction clause, the remedies for which are discussed in Chapter 7, it is relevant in this context as well.

Aerospace v Dee Howard[99]

DHC was a company incorporated and carrying on business in the USA. BAE was an English company carrying on business in England. Both parties entered into an agreement known as TAA, whereby BAE agreed to provide DHC with assistance and information in connection with a re-engineering programme that DHC was undertaking. Their contract provided that the courts in England should have jurisdiction and for each party to provide an address in England for service of documents, in the event of proceedings being commenced. In December 1991, DHC stopped further work on the grounds that BAE had totally failed to perform its obligations under the TAA agreement. DHC commenced proceedings in the Texas court, USA, and service was made on BAE in England. BAE applied to have the Texas proceedings dismissed on the grounds (a) that they were in breach of the jurisdiction clause in the agreement, and (b) *forum non-conveniens*. It was held that whether or not the clause was one of exclusive jurisdiction was a question of construction, irrespective of whether or not the word 'exclusive' is used. The jurisdiction clause stated:

> This agreement shall be governed by and be construed and take effect according to English law and the parties hereto agree that the courts of law in England shall have jurisdiction to entertain any action in respect hereof . . .

It was also held that, since the parties here had expressly agreed on English law, there would be no need to agree expressly that the English courts should have exclusive jurisdiction. The use of the word 'shall' was apposite to create the

---

96   *Pirelli v United Thai* [2000] 1 Lloyd's Rep 663.
97   *The Morviken (sub nom The Hollandia)* [1983] 1 Lloyd's Rep 1 (HL).
98   *Insurance Co Ingosstrakh Ltd v Latvian Shipping Co* [2000] IL Pr 164.
99   [1993] 1 Lloyd's Rep 368.

language of an obligation. Furthermore, the words 'any action' clearly do mean all actions. This clause was, under English law, an exclusive jurisdiction clause. It was not open to the defendant to start arguing about the relative merits of fighting an action in Texas as compared with England, where the factors relied upon would have been eminently foreseeable at the time of the contract. Adopting that approach, he thought it was not permissible to displace England based on such factors as inconvenience of witnesses, the location of documents, timing of the trial, and so on, in favour of Texas.

Sinochem v Mobil Sales[100]

Litigants should also note from this recent case that, while in the context of jurisdiction agreements the party suing in the non-chosen jurisdiction must show a strong cause why he should not be held to the agreement, the judge said that matters of convenience are, at any rate, largely, if not entirely, irrelevant. With regard to the determination of whether or not the clause was an exclusive jurisdiction one, the judge said that, not only did the clause in the Hong Kong contract provide for Hong Kong law to apply, but also that the Hong Kong courts 'are to have jurisdiction to settle any disputes' between the parties and that the parties 'submit to the jurisdiction of those courts'. In the judge's view, such a clause, as well as the clause under the London contract, provided for exclusive jurisdiction. 'It has all the indicia of such a clause,' the judge said. 'It is mutual, it refers to "any disputes" . . . and the language "are to have jurisdiction" . . . is a language of obligation and not an option.'[101]

A clear example of a non-exclusive jurisdiction clause is provided in *RBC v Rabobank*.[102] Although the contract provided that the parties irrevocably submitted to English jurisdiction, if the contract was expressly governed by English law, it did not preclude the parties from bringing proceedings in any other jurisdiction. Proceedings were commenced in New York, where both RBC and Rabobank had business dealings, after a breach of the 'Swap agreement'. On an application by RBC for an anti-suit injunction to prevent Rabobank from taking any step to obtain determination of any issue, Mance LJ held that, if it could be assumed that a non-exclusive jurisdiction clause in the form of this contract could relax the inhibitions which the English court might otherwise feel in interfering with a foreign suit, considerations of comity grew in importance the longer the foreign suit continued and the more the parties and the judge had engaged in its conduct and management. The presence of a non-exclusive jurisdiction clause might have the effect of lightening the burden on the applicant of establishing vexatious or oppressive conduct by the other party in pursuit of parallel proceedings.

By contrast, an exclusive English jurisdiction clause has been upheld in two recent cases: Collins J in *Bas Capital Funding Corporation v Medifinco Ltd*[103]

---

100 [2000] 1 Lloyd's Rep 670, p 677, per Rix J; see, also, *Insurance Co Ingosstrakh Ltd v Latvian Shipping Co* [2000] IL Pr 164 (CA).
101 Ibid, p 676.
102 [2004] 1 Lloyd's Rep 471 (CA).
103 [2004] 1 Lloyd's Rep 652, p 678.

observed that it would require very strong grounds to override a choice of English jurisdiction and that the normal *forum non-conveniens* factors had little or no role to play, especially where it could be inferred from the lack of other connections with England that the parties had chosen the English forum as a neutral forum. He continued that the fact that in some cases the clause was non-exclusive might make it easier to displace the strong presumption in favour of upholding the choice; but that would depend on the circumstances. On the basis of the same reasoning, Colman J upheld the exclusive jurisdiction clause in *Konkola Copper Mines Plc v Coromin Ltd (No 2).*[104]

To the extent that proceedings are brought to obtain security for the claim, the English court has power, under s 26 of the Civil Jurisdiction and Judgments Act (CJJA) 1982, to retain the arrest of a ship until sufficient security is provided to satisfy a judgment of a foreign court of competent jurisdiction, which had been chosen by the parties in their contract to have exclusive jurisdiction.[105]

3.5 Stay on the ground of an arbitration agreement

The intention of the Arbitration Act 1996 is to limit the involvement of the courts, as much as possible, in matters of jurisdiction under an arbitration agreement. In place of such a limitation, the Act has extended the powers of arbitrators.[106]

3.5.1 General principles under s 9 of the Arbitration Act 1996

The stay of court proceedings on this ground is discretionary, with regard to domestic arbitration, and mandatory in respect of non-domestic arbitration.

By s 9(1) of the Arbitration Act (AA) 1996, a party to an arbitration agreement against whom legal proceedings are brought in respect of a matter, which under the agreement is to be referred to arbitration, may (upon notice to the other parties to the proceedings) apply to the court in which the proceedings have been brought to stay the proceedings, so far as they concern the matter. Section 9(4) provides that, upon an application under this section, the court shall grant a stay, unless satisfied that the arbitration agreement is null and void, inoperative, or incapable of being performed.[107]

The grant of a stay in non-domestic arbitration has been mandatory since the previous AA 1975, by s 1, which is reflected in s 9(4) of the 1996 Act. Section 86 of the 1996 Act expressly states that s 9(4) does not apply to domestic arbitration. Although, generally, the intention of the Act is not to distinguish between domestic

---

104 [2006] 2 Lloyd's Rep 446.

105 *The Havhelt* [1993] 1 Lloyd's Rep 523.

106 Details of the Act and Arbitration cases can be found in Merkin, R, *The Arbitration Act 1996: An Annotated Guide*, 2nd edn, 2000, LLP; and Merkin, R, *Arbitration Law* (loose-leaf) LLP, (service issues quarterly).

107 The House of Lords, in *Inco Europe Ltd v First Choice Distribution and Others* [2000] 1 Lloyd's Rep 467, decided whether an appeal lay to the Court of Appeal from a decision of a first instance court made under s 9, which is silent on the point. It held that, where a section was silent about an appeal from a decision of the court, no restriction was intended.

and non-domestic arbitration, the distinction exists with regard to stay of court proceedings, in that the stay is mandatory when a non-domestic arbitration is involved, while in domestic arbitration the court retains a general discretionary power under s 86, which is transitional.[108] Once such a distinction is abolished, s 86, which has not been brought into force with the rest of the Act, will be repealed. The Secretary of State has power under s 88 to repeal or amend s 86.[109]

A significant difference between s 9 and the equivalent s 1(1) of the 1975 Act is that the latter was specifically providing that, if there was in fact no dispute between the parties with regard to the matter referred to arbitration, a stay would not be granted. In such a case, an application under Ord 14 of the old RSC (now Pt 24 of CPR) would be made to the court to give a judgment, where it was shown that there was no arguable defence. The words of s 1(1) of the 1975 Act, referred to above, have been omitted from s 9. If one party to a non-domestic arbitration agreement commences English proceedings, a stay of those proceedings is mandatory by s 9. This is so even when the party who has resorted to the court argues that there is no contract due to alleged bribery, unless the arbitration clause itself has been the subject of improper inducement or fraud (*Fiona Trust Holdings v Yuri Privelor*).[110]

Three very important questions arise in relation to the stay of court proceedings under s 9 of AA, about which there have been some important judicial determinations: first, is there a dispute? Second, is there an arbitration agreement? Third, is the dispute covered by the agreement to arbitrate?

3.5.2 Application of principles for a stay of court proceedings under s 9

3.5.2.1 Is there a dispute?

The question as to whether or not there is a dispute has been the subject of fruitful discussion over recent years. It has long been accepted that there is a dispute until the defendant admits that the sum is due and payable;[111] such an admission would, in effect, amount to an agreement to pay the claim and there would then clearly be no further basis for referring it to arbitration.[112]

However, the expression in arbitration clauses such as 'any dispute' is to be approached simply as one of construction of the relevant arbitration clause. If, for example, one party required the other to make immediate payment and the other

---

108 This reflects s 4 of the repealed Arbitration Act 1950, which was applicable to domestic arbitration and the court had discretion whether or not to stay court proceedings brought in breach of an arbitration agreement.

109 See Merkin, R, *The Arbitration Act 1996: An Annotated Guide*, 2nd edn, 2000, LLP, pp 25 and 120.

110 [2007] EWCA Civ 20. The Court of Appeal confirmed the separability of the arbitration agreement from the main contract.

111 *Ellerine v Klinger* [1982] 1 WLR 1375; *Amec Civil Engineering Ltd v Secretary of State for Transport* [2005] EWCA Civ 291; *Halki Shipping Corp v Sopex Oils Ltd (The Halki)* [1998] 1 Lloyd's Rep 49, Clarke J; [1998] 1 Lloyd's Rep 465 (CA) in which it was held that there was a dispute once money was claimed, unless and until the defendants admitted that the sum was due and payable. If a party refused to pay a sum, which was claimed or denied that it was owed, then, in the ordinary language, there was a dispute between the parties.

112 *The M Eregli* [1981] 2 Lloyd's Rep 169.

refused to do so, they were in dispute notwithstanding that the party refusing to pay had admitted liability.[113]

3.5.2.2 Is there an arbitration agreement and is the dispute covered by the arbitration agreement?

There have been a few very important decisions about the court's approach in applications for a stay under s 9, particularly with reference to s 30 of the AA 1996 and its interrelationship with the CPR. In *Al-Naimi v Islamic Press*,[114] concerning a building contract, the subject matter of the court proceedings was whether the dispute between the parties was covered by the arbitration agreement of the main contract, or arose under a separate oral contract not being subject to arbitration. The Court of Appeal approved the approach of HHJ Humphrey Lloyd QC, in *Birse Construction Ltd v David Ltd*,[115] relating to s 9 applications in a situation in which the dispute was not about whether a clause existed at all but about what the clause precisely covered.[116] It is important, therefore, to refer to extracts of the judge's approach in this case and then add the comments made by Waller LJ in the *Al-Naimi* case.

Per HHJ Humphrey Lloyd QC in *Birse*:

The following courses are open to me:

1   To determine, on affidavit evidence that has been filed, that an arbitration agreement was made between the parties, in which case the proceedings will be stayed in accordance with s 9 of the AA 1996.

2   To stay the proceedings but on the basis that the arbitrator will decide the question of whether or not there is an arbitration agreement since s 30 of the AA 1996 provides: '(1) unless otherwise agreed by the parties, the arbitral tribunal may rule on its own substantive jurisdiction, that is, as to (a) whether there is a valid arbitration agreement . . . (c) what matters have been submitted to arbitration in accordance with the arbitration agreement. (2) Any such ruling may be challenged by any available arbitral process of appeal or review.' This sub-section refers to s 67 of the Act about challenging the award.

3   Not to decide the question immediately but to order an issue to be tried. Under the old procedure rules, RSC Ord 73 r 6(2) provided, 'in a question whether an arbitration agreement has been concluded or whether the dispute which is the subject matter of the proceedings falls within the terms of such agreement, the court may determine that question or give directions for its determination, in

---

113   *Exfin Shipping Ltd v Tolani Shipping Co Ltd* [2006] 2 Lloyd's Rep 389, per Langley J. Unlike the previous cases in which the issue had been whether or not the claim had been admitted, in this case the question, which arose for the first time, was whether or not the failure to make payment admittedly due constituted a dispute arising under a charter party.
      This question had been dealt with, obiter, by Clarke J (as he then was) in *The Halki* (above), in which he commented that, even if the defendant admitted that the sum was due but then refused to pay, there could be an argument that the claimant would be entitled to an award.

114   [2000] 1 Lloyd's Rep 522 (CA).

115   [1999] BLR 194.

116   Although his decision was later reversed by the Court of Appeal, on the point that the parties had failed to make it clear to the judge that he should decide the question on affidavit evidence alone, it was understood that his approach was not disapproved of.

which case it may order the proceedings to be stayed pending the determination of that question'.

4   To decide that there is no arbitration agreement and dismiss the application to stay.

The judge held that the power of the arbitrator under s 30 is not mandatory. The Act does not require a party who maintains that there is no arbitration agreement to have that question decided by the arbitral tribunal. The existence of the power does not mean that the court must always refer a dispute, which concerns whether or not an arbitration agreement exists, to the tribunal whose competence to do so is itself disputed. The judge then referred to another decision (*Azon Shipping Co v Baltic Shipping Co*),[117] which supported the approach that the court ought to decide questions relating to the existence or the terms of the arbitration agreement, for there may, otherwise, be a real danger that there will be two hearings: the first, before the arbitrator under s 30 of the Act, and the second before the court on a challenge under s 67 of the AA 1996.

In the *Al-Naimi v Islamic Press* case, Waller LJ entirely supported the above approach and added:

> If the court decides that it is the court which should determine whether the matters, the subject of the action, are the subject of an arbitration clause, unless the parties were agreed that the matter should be resolved on affidavit, then, if there is a triable issue, directions should be given for trying that issue. . . . It is right to point out that *under the CPR the court has a wider discretion* to rule what evidence it needs to decide any particular point . . . (emphasis added)

> The only other comment I would like to make, so far as the above approach is concerned, is that it must not be overlooked that the court has an inherent power to stay proceedings. I would in fact accept that on a proper construction of s 9 it can be said with force that a court should be satisfied (a) that there is an arbitration clause and (b) that the subject of the action is within that clause, before the court can grant a stay under that section. But a stay under the inherent jurisdiction may in fact be sensible in a situation where the court cannot be sure of those matters but can see that good sense and litigation management make it desirable for an arbitrator to consider the whole matter first.[118]

The English courts have taken a firm stance on the issues of who, the arbitrator or the court, is to determine the validity or the scope of an arbitration clause in a case before them. The cases confirm that the court is more likely to determine either issue to save time and costs, thus removing from the arbitrators the power to determine their own jurisdiction.[119]

---

117 [1999] 1 Lloyd's Rep 68, per Rix, J: that there was an interest in encouraging parties to put their arguments on jurisdiction before the arbitrator himself under s 30; in many cases where there was simply an issue as to the width of an arbitration clause and no issue as to whether a party was bound to the relevant contract in the first place, the arbitrator's view might be accepted; where, however, there were substantial issues of fact as to whether a party had made the relevant agreement in the first place, then, even if there had already been a full hearing before the arbitrator, the court, upon a challenge under s 67, should not be placed in a worse position than the arbitrator, for the purpose of determining the challenge.

118 Waller LJ in *Al-Naimi v Islamic Press* [2000] 1 Lloyd's Rep 522 (CA), p 525.

119 See further decisions in which a stay was refused: *Anglia Oils Ltd v Owners of the Marine Champion* [2002] EWHC 2407; *T & N Ltd v Royal & Sun Alliance plc* [2002] EWHC 2420; *El Nasharty v J Sainsbury plc* [2003] EWHC 2195 (concerning the authority of an agent to enter into a contract).

3.5.3 *The scope of s 11 of the AA 1996*

Section 11 of the 1996 Act re-enacts s 26(1) of the CJJA 1982 insofar as an order for security to be provided and an order to stay the court proceedings in favour of the arbitration clause are concerned.

It has already been discussed[120] that, before the enactment of s 26, when a ship was arrested for the purpose of obtaining security in satisfaction of an arbitration award, the court had a *wide discretion* either to release the ship from arrest by setting aside the warrant of arrest, or to maintain the arrest until security was provided for the arbitration award, if the plaintiff showed that an arbitration award in his favour would be unlikely to be satisfied by the defendant.[121] If the discretion was exercised in favour of ordering security to be provided, the plaintiff would thereafter pursue the action *in rem*, to enforce the security.

Such a wide discretion was abolished by s 26 of the CJJA 1982 and now by s 11 of the AA 1996. Section 26 is, naturally, wider than s 11, in that it empowers the court to make the same orders when the dispute should be submitted to another court, either in the UK or overseas. Both sections provide that, where admiralty proceedings are stayed on the ground that the dispute in question should be submitted to arbitration, and property has been arrested, the court may: (i) order that the property, or security provided, be retained for the satisfaction of the award; or (ii) order that the stay of the proceedings be conditional on the provision of equivalent security for the satisfaction of any such award. The maintenance of arrest is discretionary.[122]

Section 26(2) of the CJJA 1982, which allows the court to attach any other conditions as it thinks fit when it makes the orders referred to in s 26(1) – such as the prompt commencement of the arbitration – has been omitted from s 11 of the AA 1996. This was necessary because its inclusion would have caused difficulties with regard to non-domestic arbitration to which the New York Convention applies, which prevents the grant of a stay being made subject to any conditions.[123]

---

120 Chapter 4, para 2.3, above.
121 *The Rena K* [1978] 1 Lloyd's Rep 545; *The Vasso* [1984] 1 Lloyd's Rep 235 (CA); *The Tuyuti* [1984] 2 Lloyd's Rep 51 (CA).
122 *The Bazias* [1993] 1 Lloyd's Rep 101.
123 See, further, op cit, Merkin, fn 106.

CONVENTION JURISDICTION BASES AND MULTIPLE PROCEEDINGS

1 INTRODUCTION

It has already been explained in the previous chapter that under English procedural law there are two broad types of jurisdiction bases by which the jurisdiction of the court can be invoked on the merits. The one depends merely on service of the proceedings on the defendant, without requiring substantive connecting factors between the claim and the jurisdiction, subject to certain exceptions (see Chapters 3, 4 and 5). The other is known as the 'convention jurisdiction' bases, which depends on jurisdiction rules as provided by International Conventions. Examples of International Conventions relating to maritime claims providing jurisdiction are briefly given in this Chapter, while the main emphasis is placed upon the Council Regulation (EC) 44/2001[1] ('The Brussels Regulation') which replaced the Brussels Convention 1968 on Civil Jurisdiction, Recognition and Enforcement of Judgments in Civil and Commercial Matters. It will be shown below how the jurisdiction of the English court may be restricted to determine the merits of a case and how conflict of jurisdictions is resolved by other Convention rules which are applicable to maritime disputes.

1.1 The Athens Convention 1974[2]

This provides a liability regime for the carriage of passengers and their luggage, which has been directly enacted by the UK. It is included in Sched 6 to the Merchant Shipping Act (MSA) 1995. Article 17 provides for jurisdiction of the court of (a) the place of permanent residence or principal place of business of the defendant; or (b) the place of departure or destination; or (c) the place of the domicile or permanent residence of the claimant, if the defendant has a place of business there and is subject to that jurisdiction; or (d) the place of the contract if the defendant has a place of business there and is subject to the jurisdiction of that State.

1.2 The Convention relating to Contracts for International Carriage of Goods by Road 1956 (CMR)[3]

It deals with liability for contracts of international carriage of goods by road. Article 1 makes the Convention applicable to the whole of the carriage, if the vehicle

---

1   [2001] OJ L 12/1.
2   See Chapter 18.
3   As enacted into English law by the Carriage of Merchandise by Road Act 1965.

containing the goods is carried over part of the journey by sea, rail, inland water-ways, or air and the goods are not unloaded from the vehicle. However, when the loss, damage or delay is caused by an event during the sea transport, and the carrier by road is also the carrier by sea, the carrier's liability is to be determined as if the contract was for the carriage of goods by sea (Arts 2 and 10(2)). By Art 31(1), jurisdiction is allocated to a court of a Contracting State designated by agreement of the parties to a contract. In addition, in the courts of a country where (a) the defend-ant is ordinarily resident, or has principal place of business, or the branch or agency through which the contract of carriage was made; or (b) the place where the goods were taken over by the carrier, or the place designated for delivery is situated; and in no other courts or tribunals.

1.3 The International Convention on Civil Liability for Oil Pollution Damage 1992 [4]

The 1969 Civil Liability Convention for oil pollution damage was enacted by the UK in 1971, and was revised by the 1992 Protocol, known as the Civil Liability for Oil Pollution Damage Convention 1992, which came into force at the end of May 1996. Its provisions have been made part of English law, ss 152–170 of the MSA 1995. Actions for compensation may only be brought in courts of Contracting States where pollution damage occurred or preventative measures were taken to minimise such damage.

1.4 The International Convention Relating to the Arrest of Sea-going Ships 1952

The Arrest Convention was ratified by the UK in 1959 but it was previously partly enacted through s 3 of the Administration of Justice Act 1956 (now ss 20 and 21 of the Supreme Court Act (SCA) 1981.)[5] Article 7 of the Arrest Convention provides that the court of the country where the arrest was made has jurisdiction to deter-mine the case on its merits, if the domestic law of that country gives jurisdiction to that court. It will be seen later how this provision interrelates with the provisions of the Brussels Convention. The Arrest Convention 1999 alters Art 7 but it is not yet in force in the UK.

1.5 The International Convention on Civil Jurisdiction in Matters of Collisions at sea 1952

The International Convention on Certain Rules Concerning Civil Jurisdiction in Matters of Collisions 1952 (the Collision Convention) is not enacted into English law, but the UK is a party to it. Article 1 of the Collision Convention relating to

---

4   See Chapter 19, below.
5   As amended by the Merchant Shipping (Salvage and Pollution) Act 1994 and the MSA 1995.

jurisdiction is reflected in s 22 of the SCA 1981 in relation to jurisdiction in actions *in personam*.

Article 1 provides for the jurisdiction of the court in a country where: (a) the defendant has his habitual residence, or place of business; or (b) the arrest was made; or (c) arrest could have been effected but bail, or other security, has been furnished; or (d) the collision took place. The claimant may choose any of the above bases, unless the parties involved agree the place of jurisdiction, or refer the matter to arbitration (Art 2). Counterclaims or multiple proceedings may be brought in the court first seised (Art 3).

1.6 The European jurisdiction regime in civil and commercial matters

The Brussels Convention on Civil Jurisdiction, Recognition and Enforcement of Judgments in Civil and Commercial Matters 1968 – as amended by the Accession Conventions 1978,[6] and 1989 (the San Sebastian Convention)[7] – was enacted into English law by the Civil Jurisdiction and Judgments Act (CJJA) 1982. It came into force in the UK on 1 January 1987. It was further amended when Austria, Finland and Sweden became parties in 1996. In 2001 the Brussels Convention was superseded by Council Regulation (EC) No 44/2001[8] (hereinunder referred to as 'The Regulation'), except in so far as Denmark is concerned which is not a signatory to the Regulation.

Revision of the Brussels Convention was considered essential for the following reasons: (i) to make the rules of jurisdiction highly predictable; (ii) to clarify the domicile of a legal person, so as to make the common rules more transparent; (iii) to preserve the autonomy of the parties to a contract, save for insurance, consumer and employment contracts in which the parties' autonomy is limited; (iv) to minimise the possibility of concurrent proceedings and to ensure that irreconcilable judgments will not be given in two Member States by providing a clear and effective mechanism for *lis pendens* cases and related actions; (v) to extend the protection given to consumers; and (vi) to ensure effective and swift enforcement procedures.

No later than five years after entry into force, the Commission will present a report on the application and, if need be, submit proposals for adaptation.[9]

In addition, there has been a parallel Convention on the same matters entered into between the members of the European Community (EC) and the then six members of the European Free Trade Association (EFTA)[10] dated 1988 ('the Lugano

---

6   This Accession Convention brought the UK into the Brussels Convention when the UK, Ireland and Denmark joined the EC.

7   The San Sebastian Convention incorporated Spain and Portugal into the scheme of civil jurisdiction and judgments when they joined the EC. When Greece joined the EC, this was done by the Greek Accession Convention, which was signed on 25 October 1982, but made no other changes to the Brussels Convention.

8   [2001] OJ L 12/1.

9   See para 28 of the preamble to the Regulation.

10 Norway, Sweden, Finland, Iceland, Austria and Switzerland. In 1996, Austria, Finland and Sweden, when they joined the European Union, became parties to the Brussels Convention (1997 OJ C 15/1). These states and all other EU members (apart from Denmark) are bound by the Brussels Regulation with effect from March 2002. The Lugano Convention applies to Norway, Iceland and Switzerland.

Convention'). It came into force in the UK on 1 May 1992 and it is to be found in Sched 1 to the CJJA 1991. The Lugano Convention is substantially identical to the post-San Sebastian version of the Brussels Convention (the Conventions), but it is separate from it. Once all the EFTA states join the EU and adhere to the Regulation, the Lugano Convention will become obsolete.

The primary purpose of the Conventions was to give effect to Art 220 of the Treaty of Rome in order to ensure the simplification of formalities governing the reciprocal recognition and enforcement of judgments within the Contracting States. To this end, it was necessary to provide a scheme for determining which courts were to have jurisdiction over what matters, and prevent occasions in which conflicting judgments might be issued if two courts of different Contracting States became involved in the same matter. The basis of the Regulation is Art 65 of the EC Treaty.

Primarily, the aim has been to protect persons, who have their domicile or seat in EU Member States, from being sued in the courts of States other than where their domicile or seat is established. There must be a link between proceedings to which the Conventions or the Regulation apply and the territory of the Member States bound by the Conventions or the Regulation. Thus, common rules on jurisdiction should, in principle, apply when the defendant is domiciled in one of those Member States. In addition to the domicile of the defendant, there are alternative grounds of jurisdiction based on a close link between the court and the action. However, in relation to insurance, consumer contracts and employment, the objective is to protect the weaker party by rules being more favourable to its interests than the general rules provided for by the regime. Thus, well-defined rules provide for various jurisdictional bases, which, in some respects, restrict the jurisdiction of the English courts.

As will be seen later in this chapter, Art 71 of the Regulation (Art 57 of the Conventions) confers jurisdiction to specialised Conventions, such as the Arrest Convention and the Collision Convention, which are relevant to the Admiralty jurisdiction. If those Conventions apply and the jurisdiction of the Admiralty Court is seised in accordance with the provisions of those Conventions, the Admiralty Court shall have jurisdiction. If, however, another court of a Member State had been seised first, the rules of *lis pendens* as prescribed by Art 27 and 28 of the Regulation will apply.[11]

The purpose of this chapter is to focus on those provisions of the Regulation which determine the jurisdiction of the EU Member States and affect the jurisdiction of the Admiralty Court. Thus, reference will be made to the Regulation, save in so far as reference is required to be made to court decisions decided under the Brussels Convention.

---

11   See later Gasser v MISAT, ECJ (Case C-116/02) [2004] 1 Lloyd's Rep 222.

2 COUNCIL REGULATION (EC) 44/2001

The Regulation entered into force on 1 March 2002 (Art 76) and applies to EU Member States, apart from Denmark, which is not a signatory and, therefore, it will continue to be bound by the Brussels Convention.[12] The UK, by virtue of the Civil Jurisdiction and Judgments Order 2001,[13] adopted it.

As from 1 March 2002, the provisions of the Regulation shall apply to all legal proceedings instituted on or after that date, and to documents formally drawn up or registered as authentic instruments (Art 66).

It is now clearly provided in Art 30 that the date of institution of the proceedings is the date of the issue of the proceedings, not of service as had previously been held in *Dresser UK Ltd v Falcongate Freight Management Ltd (The Duke Yare)*[14] decided under the Convention.

The basic provisions are summarised below.

2.1 Application

The Regulation shall apply to civil and commercial matters whatever the nature of the court or tribunal. It shall not extend to revenue, customs or administrative matters (Art 1(1)).

Article 1(2) provides that the Regulation shall not apply to:

(a) matrimonial matters, wills and succession;

(b) bankruptcy and analogous proceedings;

(c) social security; or

(d) arbitration.

'Member State' means an EU Member State with the exception of Denmark.

'Civil and commercial matters' is not to be interpreted by national law. It must be given a Convention meaning.[15] A distinction has been drawn between private and public law matters; for example, an action by a public authority, exercising its public powers, is not within the subject matter of the Convention and this should be the same under the Regulation. An interesting shipping case,[16] in which the Dutch Government had to remove a wreck from the international waterway and tried to recover its cost from the German defendant in the Dutch court, reached the European court. As the removal of the wreck was carried out under the public law powers of the Dutch Government, the Court of Justice decided that the claim did not arise in a civil or commercial matter and therefore it was outside the scope of the Convention.

---

12 See full treatment of the subject in Briggs, A, and Rees, P, *Civil Jurisdiction and Judgments*, 4th edn, 2005, LLP.

13 SI 2001/3929.

14 [1992] QB 502: 'a court was not seised until service had been effected'.

15 *LTV GmbH & Compania KG v Eurocontrol* [1977] 1 CMLR 88.

16 *Netherlands State v Ruffer* [1980] ECR 3807; see further Briggs fn 12 para 2.23.

It is beyond the scope of this book to deal with the individual exceptions,[17] other than considering the exception of arbitration in the context of anti-suit injunctions in the next chapter.

2.2 The domicile rule and allocation of jurisdiction

The basic and fundamental rule of the European jurisdiction regime is that the defendants are entitled to be sued in the courts of their domicile, whatever their nationality.

Article 2 provides:

(1) Subject to this Regulation, persons domiciled in a member state shall, whatever their nationality, be sued in the courts of that member state.

(2) Persons who are not nationals of the member state in which they are domiciled shall be governed by the rules of jurisdiction applicable to nationals of that state.

The Regulation is not limited to claims against defendants domiciled in a Member State; for example, a court of a Member State may have exclusive jurisdiction, regardless of domicile, by virtue of Art 22, which allocates jurisdiction to the court of a Member State where the property is situated with regard to proceedings whose object is rights in immovable property.

The domicile of the claimant is not relevant, as was the case also under the Convention.[18]

The domicile of an individual is to be determined at the time the proceedings are issued by the law of the Member State whose court is seised of the matter.[19] If that person is not domiciled in the Member State whose court is seised of the matter, in order to determine whether the person is domiciled in another Member State, the court shall apply the law of that Member State (Art 59).

By para 9 of Sched 1 to the 2001 Order by which the UK adopted the Regulation, an individual is domiciled in the UK if he resides there and the nature and circumstances of his residence indicate he has a substantial connection with the UK.

Under Art 60 of the Regulation, a company or other legal person or association is domiciled at the place where it has its (i) statutory seat, or (ii) central administration, or (iii) principal place of business. In order to determine the seat, the court shall apply its rules of private international law (Art 22(2)). For the purposes of the UK and Ireland, 'statutory seat' means the registered office or, where there is not such an office anywhere, the place of incorporation.

---

17 For which see Briggs, A, and Rees, P, *Civil Jurisdiction and Judgments*, 4th edn, 2005, LLP, chapter 2.

18 *Oversea Union Insurance v New Hampshire Insurance Co* [1991] ECR I–3317; *Universal General Insurance Co v Groups Josi Reinsurance* [2000] ECR I-5925.

19 Per Lord Steyn in *Canada Trust Company v Stolzenberg (No 2)* [2002] 1 AC 1; the major aim of the Convention is to achieve predictability and certainty at all stages for all concerned.

Article 3 provides:

(1) Persons domiciled in a member state may be sued in the courts of another member state only by virtue of the rules set out in Sections 2 to 7 of this chapter.

(2) In particular the rules of national jurisdiction set out in Annex I shall not be applicable as against them.

Sections 2 to 7 set out the Special jurisdiction in contract and tort cases, limitation actions, insurance, consumer or employment contracts, exclusive jurisdiction, and prorogation of jurisdiction.[20]

Article 4 provides:

(1) If the defendant is not domiciled in a member state, the jurisdiction of the courts of each member state shall, subject to articles 22 and 23, (exclusive jurisdiction, or jurisdiction by agreement) be determined by the law of that member state.

(2) As against such a defendant, any person domiciled in a member state may whatever his nationality, avail himself in that state of the rules of jurisdiction there in force, and in particular those specified in Annex II, in the same way as the nationals of that state.

Thus, if the defendant is domiciled outside the Member States of the Regulation, or those States to which the Brussels Convention still applies (such as Denmark) or the States which apply the Lugano Convention, this Article permits the court to exercise jurisdiction in accordance with its own national law. The effect of this in terms of application of the *forum non-conveniens* doctrine, as far as the UK is concerned, will be seen later.

However, since such jurisdiction is derived from the Regulation, it must be exercised subject to other conditions which are imposed by the Regulation, such as the *lis pendens* rule, explained by *Gasser v MIS AT*,[21] which is considered at greater length later.

The provisions of the Regulation provide when there can be derogation from the domicile rule.

2.3 Mandatory versus optional derogation from the domicile rule

2.3.1 *Mandatory derogation*

The only mandatory exceptions to the general rule of domicile are the following:

(a) Article 22 of the Regulation provides for exclusive jurisdiction of the court of a Member State where the immovable property, the subject matter of the dispute, is situated. The jurisdiction of that court will take priority over the court of a member state where the defendant is domiciled

(b) Article 24 of the Regulation provides that a court of a Member State in which the

---

20   Discussed extensively in Briggs, A, and Rees, P, *Civil Jurisdiction and Judgments*, 4th edn, 2005; LLP.

21   Case C-116/02 [2004] 1 Lloyd's Rep 222.

defendant enters an appearance, which may be other than the court of the Member State where the defendant is domiciled, shall have jurisdiction. This Article, however, will not apply:

– where appearance was entered solely to contest jurisdiction, or

– where another court has exclusive jurisdiction under Art 22.

(c) Article 23 of the Regulation allocates jurisdiction to a court of a Member State where the parties agreed in their contract to resolve their disputes. This consensual jurisdiction, however, is subject to there being a valid agreement by which the parties intended that the jurisdiction of that court would be exclusive. The validity and effect of the jurisdiction agreement is judged by the court first seised.[22] In addition, Art 23 is subject to Arts 22 and 24 (above) and also subject to Art 27 in the case of multiple proceedings in Member States (see later).

2.3.2 Optional derogation

Other Articles provide for optional allocation of jurisdiction; such option being given to the claimant in certain circumstances to sue in a court of a Member State other than that of the defendant's domicile.

The optional derogation from the domicile rule comprises the following categories:

(a) Special jurisdiction of a court of a Member State as provided by Art 5(1) (when there is a specific substantive link with the dispute, such as the place of performance of the obligation by the defendant). Where there are a number of obligations in issue, the court will look at the place where the principal obligation was to be performed.[23]

(b) Regarding a dispute arising out of the operation of a branch or agency, a person domiciled in a Member State may also be sued in another Member State where the branch or agency is established (Art 5(5)).[24]

(c) In matters relating to tort, or delict, the court of the place where the tort, the harmful event, occurred will have jurisdiction (Art 5(3)).

(d) In disputes relating to salvage remuneration claimed in respect of the salvage of cargo or freight, the court where the cargo or freight in question has been arrested to secure such payment, or could have been arrested but bail or other security has been given, will have jurisdiction, provided that the defendant has an interest in the cargo or freight or had such an interest at the time of the salvage (Art 5(7)).

(e) A person domiciled in a Member State may also be sued where he is one of a

---

22 *Coreck Maritime GmbH v Handelsveem BV* [2000] ECR I-9337; *Erich Gasser GmbH v MISAT Srl* (Case C-116/02) [2004] 1 Lloyd's Rep 222.

23 *Union Transport v Continental Lines* [1992] 1 All ER 161.

24 In *Mahme Trust v Lloyds TSB Bank Plc* [2004] 2 Lloyd's Rep 637, the choice of forum allowed to a claimant under Art 5 was to be exercised unfettered by any court order. The claimant was entitled to sue the Bank in England (where the head office was) under Art 2 of the Lugano Convention. The court had no jurisdiction to grant a stay of the English proceedings in favour of Switzerland (where the branch was located in which the trust had been established).

number of defendants in the courts of a Member State where any one of them is domiciled, provided the claims are so closely connected that it is expedient to hear and determine them together to avoid the risk of irreconcilable judgments resulting from such proceedings ('the *Kalfelis* test') (Art 6(1)).[25]

(f) In third party proceedings, a person domiciled in a Member State may also be sued in the court seised of the original proceedings (Art 6(2)).

(g) On a counter-claim arising from the same contract or facts on which the original claim was based, a person domiciled in a Member State may also be sued in the court in which the original claim is pending (Art 6(3)).

(h) In limitation of liability actions, Art 7 of the Regulation provides for an alternative jurisdiction to the domicile of the defendant which shall be the jurisdiction of the court which has jurisdiction for the liability of the defendant arising from the use or operation of a ship. If the defendant, however, has already commenced a limitation of liability action in the court of his domicile and that court is seised first, the rule of *lis pendens* of Art 27 will apply (see later).

(i) Jurisdiction in relation to insurance contracts is provided for by Arts 8–14 of the Regulation.

(j) Jurisdiction over consumer contracts is provided for by Arts 15–17 of the Regulation, while Arts 18–21 concern jurisdiction over contracts of employment.

2.4 Inapplicability of certain national jurisdictional rules

In Annex I referred to in Art 3(2), certain provisions of national procedural law of Member States, which conflict with the basic principles of the Regulation, are declared inapplicable, as against a defendant domiciled in a Member State. In particular, as far as UK law is concerned, the following rules, which would otherwise enable jurisdiction to be founded, are overridden: (a) service upon the defendant during his temporary presence in the UK; (b) the presence of the defendant's property within the UK; and (c) the seizure by the plaintiff of property situated in the UK.

The prohibition of Annex I is lifted when the defendant is not domiciled in a Member State (see Art 4(2)).

It has been seen (in Chapters 2 and 3) that, when a ship is within the English jurisdiction, it can be arrested and the court will be seised of jurisdiction on the merits of the case in accordance with the Arrest Convention 1952. Reading (b) above, it would appear that the Admiralty Court would have no jurisdiction to entertain a suit against a ship which came within the jurisdiction when the person who would be liable for the claim is domiciled in a Member State. However, Art 71

---

25 *Kalfelis v Bankhaus Schroder Munchneyer Hengst & Co* [1988] ECR 5565, at 5584; *Marsi v Consolidated Group SAL (Holding Company) and others* [2006] 1 Lloyd's Rep 391; *Casio v Sayo* [2001] ILPR 43: 'a broad common sense approach is to be adopted, an over-sophisticated analysis is to be avoided'; *FKI Engineering Ltd v Dewind Holdings Ltd* [2007] EWHC 72 (Comm); *Reunion Europeenne SA v Splietthoff's Bevarachtingskantoor BV* [1998] ECR I-6511: claims in contract and in tort are not sufficiently connected to fall within Art 6(1); cf *Andrew Weir Shipping Ltd v Wartsila UK Ltd and Another* [2004] 2 Lloyd's Rep 377, distinguished from the former case.

of the Regulation (to which both Arts 2 and 3 are made subject) permits a court of a Member State to assume jurisdiction in accordance with the rules of specialised Conventions, eg the Arrest Convention, to which the Member State is a party.

Article 71(1) provides that the Regulation shall not affect any conventions to which the Member States are parties and which, in relation to particular matters, govern jurisdiction or the recognition or enforcement of judgments. Article 71(2) provides that this Regulation shall not prevent a court of a Member State, which is a party to a convention on a particular matter, from assuming jurisdiction in accordance with that convention, even where the defendant is domiciled in another Member State which is not a party to that convention. Discussion of this topic will follow later.

It is now made clear, since the decision of the ECJ in Gasser v MISAT, that Art 71 (through which a court of a Member State can assume jurisdiction based on specialised Conventions) is subject to the *lis pendens* provision of the Regulation, Art 27; and, if a court of another Member State is seised first, it will be bound to determine jurisdiction. The second seised court will be bound to stay its proceedings, as will be explained further in this chapter.

2.5 Interpretation of concepts

It is for the ECJ to interpret the following concepts:

(a) civil and commercial matters under Art 1 (see 2.1, above);[26]

(b) *lis pendens* under Art 27 and related actions under Art 28;[27]

(c) exclusive jurisdiction under Art 22;

(d) place of harmful event under Art 5(3);[28]

(e) sufficient time for defence under Art 26, which contains additional paras 3 and 4 dealing with service of judicial documents within Member States; and

(f) the date on which a court is seised, now dealt with by Art 30 and not by national laws.

Other concepts are left to be determined by national laws:

(a) the place of performance of the obligation[29] under Art 5(1); and

(b) the meaning of cause of action.

---

26 *LTV GmbH & Compania KG v Eurocontrol* [1977] 1 CMLR 88.

27 *Gubisch v Giulio Palumbo* [1989] ECC 420; *The Maciej Rataj* [1995] 1 Lloyd's Rep 302 (ECJ).

28 *Kronhofer v Maier* [2005] 1 Lloyd's Rep 284.

29 Where there are many obligations to be performed, the place of performance for the purpose of Art 5(1) is the place of the primary obligation: *Union Transport v Continental Lines* [1992] 1 All ER 161 (HL).

2.6 Multiple proceedings within Member States: *lis pendens* and related actions

2.6.1 *English* lis pendens *versus Regulation* lis pendens

The treatment of *lis alibi pendens* under English law is not uniform, but it depends on the procedural topics in which the issue arises. For example, the law on discretionary stays is different from the law on anti-suit injunctions in matters to which the Regulation or the Convention do not apply. In both areas, however, if the foreign proceedings have reached an advanced stage by the time an application is made either for a stay of parallel English proceedings, or for an anti-suit injunction to prevent the continuance of the foreign proceedings, it may then be appropriate to let the foreign proceedings determine the parties' rights. In the absence of an agreement between the parties to a dispute to submit to the jurisdiction of a certain court or tribunal, an overall consideration in applications of *lis pendens* is the interests of justice.[30]

By contrast, in the context of the Regulation, there is a uniform treatment of *lis pendens* by rigid rules based on the approach of the civil law system. Multiple proceedings are an unavoidable result of the fact that there is more than one jurisdiction base provided by Conventions or other jurisdictional criteria.

2.6.2 *How does the Regulation resolve* lis pendens?

When more than one jurisdiction base is involved, the courts of two Member States may be seised of jurisdiction in the same matter at different times. The Regulation governs *lis pendens* by Arts 27–30 in the same way as the Convention did; thus, the cases decided prior to the Regulation coming into force are good law.

Article 27 (*lis pendens*) provides:

(1) Where proceedings involving the same cause of action and between the same parties are brought in the courts of different Member States, any court other than the court first seised shall of its own motion stay its proceedings until such time as the jurisdiction of the court first seised is established.

(2) Where the jurisdiction of the court first seised is established, any court other than the court first seised shall decline jurisdiction in favour of that court.

2.6.2.1 The 'same cause of action' and 'between the same parties'

The general rule under Art 27 of the Regulation is that the proceedings brought in the courts of two Member States must have the same cause of action and must be between the same parties. It may not be too difficult for the court to ascertain whether a matter of which two courts are seised of jurisdiction concerns the same cause of action. Also, in cases where the cause of action is brought by proceedings *in*

---

30 See, further, op cit, Briggs and Rees, fn 17, para 4.19.

personam in two Member States, the identification of the parties to such proceedings should be of no difficulty.

The issue whether the English action *in rem* and an action *in personam* instituted in a court of a Member State are between the same parties has been resolved by the ECJ in *The Tatry*, and its historical background was extensively discussed in the first edition of this book. It suffices, for the purpose of this edition, to refer only to *The Tatry*, which was decided when the Convention was applicable.

The question was whether, for the purpose of Art 21, an action *in rem* could be between the same parties as an action *in personam*. It was referred to the European Court of Justice (ECJ) by the Court of Appeal. But an earlier Court of Appeal decision had addressed this question, in *The Deichland* (see para 3.1.1 below). It had held that the action *in rem* really aimed against the person interested in defending the claim, who was being sued, from the time of the service, which was confirmed by the ECJ in the following decision. Briefly, the ECJ decided that, for the purpose of the Convention, the special characteristics of the *in rem* claim under national laws are irrelevant. Both the *in rem* and *in personam* proceedings in this case involved the same parties and the same cause of action.

The Maciej Rataj (sub nom The Tatry) [31]

A cargo of soya bean oil was carried aboard *The Tatry*, a vessel belonging to a Polish shipping company. The voyage was from Brazil to Rotterdam for part of the cargo, and then to Hamburg with the rest of the cargo. The cargo-owners complained that the cargo was contaminated during the voyage with hydrocarbons or diesel. They were split in three groups. Group one obtained security from the owners' P&I club in October 1988 and agreed that the Rotterdam court had jurisdiction for their dispute. Groups two and three missed the opportunity to arrest the ship and, although they requested an undertaking for provision of security from the owners' P&I club stipulating for English jurisdiction, their request was ignored. The ship-owners commenced proceedings in Rotterdam on 18 November 1988 for a declaration of no liability in relation to groups one and three cargo. On 15 September 1989, groups two and three located *The Maciej Rataj* (a sister ship of *The Tatry*) in Liverpool and arrested her. Security was, then, provided by the P&I club. On 18 September 1989, the owners brought proceedings in Rotterdam, again, for a declaration of no liability against group two cargo-owners. On 26 October 1990, they initiated proceedings in Rotterdam for limitation of their liability under the International Convention of 1957, and also applied to the English court to decline jurisdiction pursuant to Art 21 (*lis pendens*) or alternatively, pursuant to Art 22 (related actions). The grounds of the application were that, at the date of the English writ, the Rotterdam court was already seised of the proceedings involving the same cause of action and being between the same parties. Alternatively, the Rotterdam court was already seised of related proceedings and it was the appropriate forum.

Sheen J held, inter alia, that *in rem* proceedings did not involve the same cause of action with the declaratory proceedings in Rotterdam. The shipowners only

---

31   [1995] 1 Lloyd's Rep 302.

commenced those proceedings as a pre-emptive forum seeking. However, the Court of Appeal decided this question as follows:

> For the purpose of Art 21, the declaratory proceedings in Rotterdam and the English proceedings had the same cause of action (that is, the same contractual relationship) and the same subject matter, which was the issue whether or not the cargo on *The Tatry* was contaminated. After an acknowledgment of service had been given an action *in rem* continued as a hybrid; the action became *in personam* but it did not lose its previous character of being an action *in rem*. The guidance of the ECJ was needed in order to determine whether a hybrid action could involve the same cause of action as an action *in personam* at another Contracting State for the purpose of Art 21, and whether the actions were between the same parties for the purpose of Art 21.[32]

The ECJ confirmed what the Court of Appeal had held about the proceedings involving the same cause of action, despite the fact that the Rotterdam proceedings were only concerned with an application for a declaration of no liability. On the question of whether they involved the same parties, it was held that:

> ... in Art 21 of the Convention the terms 'same cause of action' and 'between the same parties' have an independent meaning (see *Gubish v Palumpo* [1989] ECC 420). They must therefore be interpreted independently of the specific features of the law in force in each Contracting State. It follows that the distinction drawn by the law of a Contracting State between an action *in personam* and an action *in rem* is not material for the interpretation of Art 21.[33]

Thus, it was held that, where an action *in rem* has subsequently continued both *in rem* and *in personam*, or solely *in personam* (according to the distinctions drawn by the national law of the Contracting State), it did not cease either to have the same cause of action and the same object, or to be between the same parties as a previous action brought *in personam*.

On the scope of Art 57, the ECJ held that Art 57 precluded the application of the provisions of the Brussels Convention only in matters governed by the specialised Convention. It was stated:

> In those circumstances, when a specialised Convention contains certain rules of jurisdiction but no provision as to *lis pendens* or related actions, Arts 21 and 22 of the Brussels Convention apply.[34]

It should be observed that the question put to the ECJ was purely whether a hybrid action (that is, an *in rem* action which has become also *in personam* by the acknowledgment of service by the defendant) was between the same parties as an action *in personam* in another Contracting State. Thus, the ECJ answered this question from a point of view of the Convention, and was not concerned with an action *in rem* in which no acknowledgment of service had been filed. Therefore, the need to answer this last question arose in *The Indian Grace* in the context of *res judicata*.

---

32 It is interesting to note that Sheen J, in both *The Linda* [1988] 1 Lloyd's Rep 175 and *The Kherson* [1992] 2 Lloyd's Rep 261, had decided that the parties of an action *in rem*, in which the defendant had acknowledged service, and of an action *in personam* brought in another Contracting State, were the same. These decisions had been decided before the Court of Appeal had decided *The Tatry*.

33 [1995] 1 Lloyd's Rep 302, p 308.

34 [1995] 1 Lloyd's Rep 302, p 307.

The Indian Grace (No 2)[35]

The plaintiff's cargo consisting of munitions was carried by the defendants' ship, *The Indian Grace*, from Sweden to India. Fire broke out during the voyage in one of the holds which was extinguished by the crew. Some artillery shells had to be jettisoned. The cargo was repackaged and re-stowed at an intermediate port and the vessel arrived at destination to discharge. It was found that the cargo had suffered damage from the heat and from the water used to extinguish the fire. In September 1988, the Union of India, as plaintiffs, started proceedings in India seeking damages for shortage of cargo. While these proceedings were pending, they brought an action *in rem* in England in August 1989 for total loss of the cargo, which had been damaged by heat. A judgment was given in India in December 1989, in the plaintiff's favour. The *in rem* writ was served on a sister ship, *The Indian Endurance*, in May 1990. To avoid her arrest, the owners provided security and submitted to the jurisdiction conditionally. They applied to strike out the English action on various grounds, but the relevant one in this context was that the claim was barred by *res judicata* and relied upon s 34 of the CJJA 1982, which provides:

> No proceedings may be brought by a person in England and Wales or Northern Ireland on a cause of action in respect of which a judgment has been given in his favour in proceedings between the same parties, or their privies, in a court in another part of the UK or in a court of an overseas country, unless that judgment is not enforceable or entitled to recognition in England and Wales.

One of the three main issues was whether the section applied to bar the English proceedings, having regard to the fact that it was an action *in rem*. Clarke J thought it did not since, at the time when the action was brought, it was not between the same parties as the action *in personam* in India. The defendants' application was refused. The Court of Appeal took the opposite view and reversed the decision. It was held that s 34 must have been intended, like Arts 2 and 21 of the Brussels Convention, to prevent the same cause of action being tried twice over between those who were in reality the same parties. The test under s 34 was satisfied and the action was barred. On appeal by the plaintiffs, the House of Lords approved the decision above, saying (p 10):

> For the purpose of s 34 an action *in rem* was an action against the owners from the moment that the Admiralty Court was seised with jurisdiction. The jurisdiction of the Admiralty Court was invoked by the service of the writ, or where a writ was deemed to be served, as a result of acknowledgment of the issue of the writ by the defendant before service. From that moment, the owners were parties to the proceedings *in rem* and s 34 was a bar to the action *in rem*.

However, since the entry into force of the Brussels Regulation, which provides by Art 30 that the date on which the court will be seised is the date of issue of the proceedings, the ruling of the above decision that the jurisdiction of the court is invoked upon service of the proceedings may have to be revisited in cases to which the Regulation applies.

Another important issue which has recently been dealt with by the ECJ is whether an action for liability in damages brought in one court of a Member State

---

35   [1998] 1 Lloyd's Rep 1; see Ch 3 para 3.5 for full discussion of the case.

has the same cause, or subject matter, as an application to a court of another Member State, for the establishment of a liability limitation fund under the Limitation of Liability Conventions. The ECJ decided in *Maersk Olie & Gas v Firma M De Haan & W De Boer*[36] that such actions do not involve the same cause of action nor the same subject matter, within the terms of Art 21, because the action for damages is sought to have the defendant declared liable, while the application to limit liability is designed to ensure, in the event that the person is declared liable, that such liability would be limited. The legal rule which forms the basis of each claim is different. For this reason, the *lis pendens* rule of Art 21 (now Art 27) did not apply. Therefore, a decision ordering the establishment of a limitation of liability fund was a judgment within the meaning of the Convention and it could not be refused recognition in another Contracting State, provided the defendant was notified and had an opportunity to arrange his defence. It is for the court in which enforcement is sought to determine whether notification was effected in the due and proper form and in sufficient time.

The facts were simple. Maersk suffered loss by the damage to its pipeline in Denmark (a Brussels Convention country) caused by a fishing trawler belonging to the defendant shipowner who made an application to limit its liability in Netherlands, the place of registration of the ship. The court made an order fixing the amount of liability, and the decision was notified to Maersk by telex. Later, Maersk brought an action in Denmark claiming damages and appealed against the decision of the Dutch court on the ground of no jurisdiction. Maersk lost in the appeal and it had not submitted a claim in the limitation fund. In the absence of any claims, the fund lodged was returned to the shipowner. The Danish court decided that, being the court second seised, it had to decline jurisdiction in accordance with Art 21, but Maersk appealed and reference was made to the ECJ.

Litigants will appreciate what change this decision has brought to limitation of liability actions which have frequently provided an opportunity for forum shopping. For the purpose of lis pendens, there will no longer be a need to race in issuing limitation proceedings in order to seise the jurisdiction of a court in a preferred Member State, prior to a claimant issuing the liability proceedings to seise the jurisdiction of a court in another Member State, since the *lis pendens* provision of the Regulation does not apply to those proceedings because the basis of each claim is different.

The court, however, stated that its conclusion on Art 21 did not, in principle, preclude the application of Art 22 (related actions, now Art 28), and that applications for limitation of liability are sufficiently closely connected with the liability proceedings as to be capable of being regarded as related within the meaning of Art 22(2), with the result that the court second seised may stay its proceedings. In this case, the court did not have to decide this point because the limitation proceedings had been definitively terminated in the absence of any claims submitted by injured parties, and the lodged fund had been returned to the shipowner. This may be a technique to be deployed by injured parties should they wish to insist on the jurisdiction of the court seised in the action for liability – but, of course, in this case there was only one injured party, Maersk.

---

36 [2005] 1 Lloyd's Rep 210.

The concern of the court was to give effect to the objective of the Convention, that is to prevent parallel proceedings in order to avoid conflicting judgments, as is the intention of the *lis pendens* and related actions provisions. In this context, there is logic in this decision, in that, since the liability and limitation actions do not have the same subject matter, it would not matter for the purpose of irreconcilability if they were each determined by the courts of different Member States. However, that result would conflict with Art 7 of the Regulation, which is discussed under para 4.4 below.

The fact that the limitation proceedings were terminated in this case deprived the court from the opportunity of considering Art 6A of the Convention (now Art 7 of the Regulation) providing that the court which has jurisdiction for the liability arising from the use or operation of a ship shall also have jurisdiction over claims for limitation of such liability. This is linked to the issue of related actions governed by Art 28, and it would be sensible if both liability and limitation actions were decided by the same court for, at least, it will save legal costs, unless of course the party seeking to limit liability admits liability, in which case there will only be one court decision.

It should be noted that proceedings for limitation of liability are different from proceedings seeking a declaration of no liability. The latter has the same cause of action as the proceedings in relation to liability issues, as was decided by the ECJ in *The Tatry*.

2.6.2.2 Power of the court first seised

The decision of the ECJ in *Gasser v MISAT* clarified what a court of a Member State should do, when it is either the court first or second seised. Whether or not the decision will facilitate practical justice remains to be seen.

Erich Gasser GmbH v MISAT Srl[37]

Gasser, registered in Austria, had for several years supplied children's clothes to MISAT, registered in Italy. A dispute arose under the contract and, in 2000, MISAT brought proceedings against Gasser in the Italian courts, seeking a declaration that the contract had been terminated and claiming damages for Gasser's breach of contract.

After eight months, Gasser brought an action against MISAT in the Austrian courts, seeking payment against outstanding invoices. He claimed that the court had jurisdiction because Austria was the place of performance of the contract (Art 5(1) of the Brussels Convention), and also that the Austrian court was the court designated by a 'choice of court' clause in the invoices sent by Gasser to MISAT without the latter having raised any objection to it. Thus, Gasser argued that, in accordance with their practice and the usage prevailing in trade between Austria and Italy, the two parties had agreed to confer jurisdiction on the Austrian courts within the meaning of Art 17 of the Convention.

MISAT contested the jurisdiction of the Austrian court on the grounds that:

---

37   Case C-116/02 [2004] 1 Lloyd's Rep 222.

(i) MISAT was domiciled in Italy (Art 2);

(ii) there was no valid jurisdiction agreement; and

(iii) Misat had already commenced proceedings in Rome in respect of the same dispute.

The Austrian court referred the matter to the European Court for a preliminary hearing on the following question:

> Whether the court second seised may review the jurisdiction of the court first seised if the second court has exclusive jurisdiction pursuant to an agreement conferring jurisdiction under Art 17, or must the second court stay its proceedings according to Art 21, notwithstanding the agreement conferring jurisdiction?

Although Gasser did not involve English parties, the UK Government still submitted written observations on the issues raised.

They submitted that, in cases of exclusive jurisdiction, the court second seised may derogate from Art 21 and proceed to judgment without waiting for the court first seised to determine that it had no jurisdiction. They relied on a previous ECJ decision in *Overseas Union Insurance*,[38] which concerned Art 16 (exclusive jurisdiction), as opposed to Art 17 which was in issue in this case. They further argued that the court designated by the agreement conferring jurisdiction will, in general, be in a better position to rule as to the effect of that agreement by applying the substantive law of that Member State.

Moreover, it was argued that in certain instances it may be viable for a court second seised to make an exception to Art 21 where the claimant has started proceedings in bad faith before a court without jurisdiction, with the aim of blocking proceedings before the courts of another Contracting State, and the court first seised has not decided the jurisdiction question within a reasonable time. The European Court refused to recognise this, and ruled that issues relating to what amounts to reasonable time afforded no reason to derogate from Art 21.

The European Court declared that the purpose of Art 21 was to prevent parallel proceedings taking place in courts of different Contracting States so as to prevent unenforceability of judgments. Therefore, in order to give effect to this, Art 21 would have to be given a broad interpretation:

> From the clear terms of Art 21 it is apparent that, in a situation of *lis pendens*, the court second seised must stay proceedings of its own motion until the jurisdiction of the court first seised has been established and, where it is so established, must decline jurisdiction in favour of the latter.

Furthermore, it held that it is for the court first seised to examine whether a 'choice of court' clause is duly incorporated into any contract and, if so, whether it should be applicable to the proceedings or not.

The ECJ pointed out that, in cases concerned with Art 17 agreements, it was always open to a defendant to enter appearance before the court first seised and decline to invoke the jurisdiction agreement. The ECJ was also concerned to protect

---

38 Case C-351/89 [1991] ECR I-1745.

the weaker contracting party when jurisdiction clauses are incorporated in a contract by one party alone.

This decision interpreted the *lis pendens* provisions broadly so as to cover all situations of *lis pendens* before courts in Member States, irrespective of the parties' domicile. The court first seised is entitled by Art 27(1) of the Regulation, being equivalent to Art 21 of the Convention, to determine its jurisdiction first, while the court second seised must stay its proceedings of its own motion until such time as the jurisdiction of the court first seised has been established. Where it is so established, the court second seised must then decline jurisdiction in favour of the former. For this purpose, no distinction is drawn between the various heads of jurisdiction provided for by the Convention or Regulation. The ECJ further stated that Art 21 of the Convention is based clearly and solely on the chronological order in which the courts involved are seised. The court second seised is never in a better position than the court first seised to determine whether the latter has jurisdiction.

Thus, it is incumbent on the court first seised to verify the existence of the jurisdiction agreement and whether or not the parties actually agreed to designate the court second seised as having exclusive jurisdiction in accordance with Art 17 of the Convention (now Art 23 of the Regulation). If the court finds it is a valid and exclusive jurisdiction agreement, then it must decline jurisdiction (more discussion of this follows under para 5 later).

Article 29 deals with exclusive jurisdiction of several courts:

> Where actions come within the exclusive jurisdiction of several courts, any court other than the court first seised shall decline jurisdiction in favour of that court.

Thus, if the rival court has exclusive jurisdiction by virtue of Art 22, although this point was not before the ECJ for decision in *Gasser*, it was stated obiter that any court, whether it is the court first seised or not, must declare, of its own motion, that it has no jurisdiction.

This would apply even when, following the rule of Art 24, the defendant entered an appearance in the court first seised.

Article 30 deals with the date of when a court is deemed seised and provides:

> For the purpose of this Section (ie *lis pendens* and related actions) a court shall be deemed to be seised:
>
> (1) at the time when the document instituting the proceedings, or an equivalent document, is lodged with the court, provided that the plaintiff has not subsequently failed to take the steps required to have service on the defendant, or
>
> (2) if the document has to be served before being lodged with the court, at the time when it is received by the authority responsible for service, provided that the plaintiff has not subsequently failed to take the steps he was required to take to have the document lodged with the court.

Therefore, all previous decisions which decided that the time of service was the time when the court was seised are no longer good law.

2.6.2.3 Related actions

A problem of irreconcilable judgments may also arise when multiple proceedings are brought in different Member States, which do not have the same cause of action, but they are related. The Regulation prevents this problem from arising by Art 28.

Article 28 provides:

(1) Where related actions are pending in courts of different member states, any court other than the court first seised may stay its proceedings.

(2) Where these actions are pending at first instance, any court other than the court first seised may also, on application of one of the parties, decline jurisdiction if the court first seised has jurisdiction over the action in question and its own law permits the consolidation thereof.

(3) For the purpose of this Article, actions are deemed to be related where they are so closely connected that it is expedient to hear and determine them together to avoid the risk of irreconcilable judgments resulting from separate proceedings.

This Article puts the burden on the court second seised either to stay its proceedings or to decline jurisdiction, as the case may be.

Judicial definition of 'related actions' was given by the House of Lords in the following case, which was decided under Art 22 of the Brussels Convention.

Sarrio SA v Kuwait Investment Authority [39]

The plaintiffs brought two identical actions in England claiming damages in tort for negligent misstatements by the defendants, which allegedly induced them to enter into a contract with companies controlled by the defendants for the sale of the plaintiffs' special paper. A year before, the plaintiffs had filed a claim in Spain for a debt against the defendants concerning unpaid sums under the contract and the defendants had duly been served with the Spanish proceedings. For this reason, the defendants applied to the English court for a stay of the action in England on the basis of Art 22 of the Brussels Convention. Unlike the judge, the Court of Appeal held on this point that the case was outside the scope of Art 22 because the primary issues of fact in the English proceedings were distinct from those raised in the Spanish proceedings and there was, thus, no risk of irreconcilable judgments. In its analysis, it drew a distinction between facts necessary to establish a cause of action and other facts and matters on which conflicting decisions might arise. The House of Lords (having approved the decision of Mance J) rejected this analysis. It held that the simple wide test laid down in Art 22 should be applied in every case. Lord Saville stated, in his analysis of the words used in that article, that:

> The actions, to be related, must be 'so closely connected that it is expedient to hear and determine them together' to avoid the risk of irreconcilable judgments resulting from separate proceedings. To my mind these wide words are designed to cover a range of circumstances, from cases where the matters before the courts are virtually identical (though not falling within the provisions of Art 21) to cases where although this is not the position, the connection is close enough to make it expedient for them to be heard and determined together to avoid the risk in question. These words are required, if 'irreconcilable judgments' extends beyond 'primary' or 'essential issues', so as to exclude actions which, though theoretically capable of giving rise to conflict,

---

39 [1998] 1 Lloyd's Rep 129 (HL).

are not sufficiently closely connected to make it expedient for them to be heard and determined together.[40] There should be a broad common sense approach to the question whether the actions in question are related, bearing in mind the objective of the article, applying the simple wide test set out in Art 22 and refraining from an over-sophisticated analysis of the matter.[41]

The English action was stayed in favour of Spain for the same reasons as held by the judge.

It should be noted that injunction proceedings in England to restrain disposal of assets of the defendant were recently considered as not being so closely connected with parallel proceedings in Germany brought first by the defendant, concerning matters of enforceability of interest provisions in the parties' contract; thus the English court (being second seised) did not have to stay the injunction proceedings.[42]

2.6.2.4 When is there a 'pending action'?

Pending action means 'definitively pending' – without procedural defects.

Grupo Torras[43]

The plaintiffs, a Spanish company and its English subsidiary, claimed damages for conspiracies and monies due for breaches of directors' duties in which the defendants were involved. The defendants applied to the English court to stay the action in favour of the Spanish court on the ground, inter alia, that there were pending proceedings in Spain and the Spanish court was first seised. The English court was urged to decline or stay the proceedings either under Art 21 or 22. Mance J held that, although in any Contracting State the precise procedural formalities reflecting the concept of when proceedings are 'definitively pending' would depend on the national law and be selected by the national court, there must be respect of the general concept of a 'decisive, conclusive, final or definitive' litigation relationship between the court and the litigant. But, which court was first seised of such proceedings was to be decided by a simple test of chronological priority, ignoring any amendments of the cause of action or parties which might otherwise be treated under national law as having retrospective effect.

In *Molins plc v GB SpA*[44] the action was not pending for the purpose of Art 21 when the Italian proceedings had not been served. In *Andrea Mezario Ltd v Internationale Spedition*,[45] relating to the International Carriage of Goods by Road Convention 1956, Art 31(2), it was held that 'pending' means when the proceedings have been served. Further, in *Tavoulareas v Tsavliris*,[46] the action was not pending for the purpose of Art 21 when the Greek proceedings had been served defectively.

---

40   [1998] 1 Lloyd's Rep 129 (HL), p 134.
41   Ibid, p 135.
42   *JP Morgan v Primacom* [2005] 2 Lloyd's Rep 665.
43   [1995] 1 Lloyd's Rep 374.
44   [2000] 2 Lloyd's Rep 234 (CA).
45   [2001] EWCA Civ 61; [2001] 1 All ER (Comm) 883.
46   [2004] EWCA Civ 48; [2004] 2 All ER (Comm) 221.

2.6.3 When does a court of a Member State have an obligation to decline its jurisdiction?

Declining jurisdiction has a more permanent and definite result. An obligation to decline jurisdiction arises under the following Articles:

(a) Art 25 – this provides that, where a court of a Member State is seised of a claim which is principally concerned with a matter over which the court of another Member State has exclusive jurisdiction by virtue of Art 22, it shall declare of its own motion that it has no jurisdiction.

(b) Art 26 – which states that, where a defendant is domiciled in a Member State and is sued in another, provided he has not appeared, that court shall declare of its own motion that it has no jurisdiction, unless its jurisdiction is derived from the provisions of this Regulation.

(c) Art 27(2) just mentioned above – there must be multiple proceedings in different Member States involving the same cause of action and the same parties, whereupon the court second seised must decline jurisdiction once the jurisdiction of the court first seised is established.

(d) Similarly, under Art 29 – where actions come within the exclusive jurisdiction of several courts, any court other than the court first seised shall decline jurisdiction in favour of that court.

2.6.4 When does a court of a Member State have an obligation to stay its proceedings?

(a) Under Art 26(3), (4), the court shall stay the proceedings, so long as it is not shown that the defendant has been able to receive the documents instituting the proceedings in sufficient time to enable him to arrange for his defence. Paragraphs 3 and 4 refer to a previous Council Regulation ((EC) 1348/2000) on service of process of judicial and extra-judicial documents in civil and commercial matters in the Member States, which shall apply if the document instituting the proceedings had to be transmitted from one Member State to another pursuant to this Regulation. Otherwise, if the aforesaid Regulation relating to service of process does not apply, Art 15 of the Hague Convention on the Service Abroad of Judicial and Extra-judicial Documents in Civil and Commercial Matters 1965 shall apply, if the document instituting the proceedings had to be transmitted pursuant to that Convention.

(b) Under Art 27(1) of the Regulation, the court, other than the court first seised of proceedings involving the same cause of action and the same parties, shall, of its own motion, stay its proceedings until such time as the jurisdiction of the first seised court is established.

2.6.5 When does a court of a Member State have discretion to decline or stay its proceedings?

Only under Art 28, where related actions are brought in the courts of different Member States, does any court other than the one first seised have discretion to stay its proceedings, while the actions are pending.[47] It may also decline jurisdiction, on the application of one of the parties, if the law of that court permits the consolidation of related actions and the court first seised has jurisdiction over both actions. In a very complex case of fraud and conspiracy by the supplier of hazelnuts against the lending banks and the purchaser, the English court was seised second in the tort action, for the fraud was committed in England. It held that the contractual claims brought in Italy, being the court first seised for a negative declaratory relief, were not related with the tortious claims brought in England; hence it stayed its proceedings in relation to the contractual claims pursuant to Art 27 of the Regulation, until the Italian court determined its jurisdiction, and maintained the proceedings for the tort claims, although it was reluctant to split the claims in such a way.[48]

3 PERMITTTED JURISDICTION UNDER INTERNATIONAL CONVENTIONS AND *IN REM* PROCEEDINGS

The primary purpose of the Convention or the Regulation is to prevent irreconcilable judgments and, therefore, its rules regulate what is to happen when multiple proceedings have commenced in more than one Member State, as seen earlier. But clash of jurisdictions is sometimes inevitable due to the existence of more than one jurisdictional base under the Regulation.

In this section of the book, the role of Art 71 is examined. This allows specialised Conventions to take precedence over the primary Regulation jurisdiction base of domicile, provided jurisdiction has properly been established under the rules of those specialised Conventions. In a recent decision of the ECJ,[49] in which a court of a Contracting State had jurisdiction under the CMR Convention via Art 57 of the Brussels Convention (now Art 71 of the Regulation), the court interpreted Art 57(2)(a) as meaning that the court of a Contracting State in which a defendant (domiciled in another Contracting State) was sued could derive jurisdiction from a specialised Convention to which the first State was a party as well and which contained rules on jurisdiction. Article 57 introduced an exception to the general rule that the Brussels Convention took precedence over other Conventions signed by the Contracting States on jurisdiction. The purpose of that exception was to ensure compliance with the rules of jurisdiction laid down by specialised Conventions, since when those rules were enacted account was taken of the specific features of the matters to which they related.

It is important to see the interrelationship between Art 71 and other jurisdiction rules and what the courts have held under its predecessor, Art 57 of the Convention.

---

47 Pending actions mean definitely pending without procedural defects: *Grupo Torras* [1995] 1 Lloyd's Rep 374.
48 *Bank of Tokyo-Mitsubishi Ltd v Baskan Gida* [2004] 2 Lloyd's Rep 395.
49 *Nurnberger Allgemeine v Portbridge Transport International BV* Case C-148/03 [2005] 1 Lloyd's Rep 592.

3.1 Delegation of jurisdiction to other Conventions by Art 71 of the Regulation

It is provided in this Article that:

(1) This Regulation shall not affect any conventions to which Member States are parties and which, in relation to particular matters, govern jurisdiction or the recognition of judgments.

(2) With a view to its uniform interpretation, paragraph 1 shall be applied in the following manner:

(a) This Regulation shall not prevent a court of a Member State, which is party to a convention on a particular matter, from assuming jurisdiction in accordance with that convention, even where the defendant is domiciled in another Member State which is not a party to that convention. The court hearing the action shall, in any event, apply Art 26 of this Regulation;

(b) Judgments given in a Member State by a court in the exercise of jurisdiction provided for in a convention on a particular matter shall be recognised and enforced in the other Member States in accordance with this Regulation.

Where a Convention on a particular matter to which both the Member State of origin and the Member State addressed are parties lays down conditions for the recognition or enforcement of judgments, those conditions shall apply. In any event, the provisions of this Regulation which concern the procedure for recognition and enforcement of judgments may be applied.

Save for Art 22 (exclusive jurisdiction) and subject to considerations of the validity and effect of a consensual jurisdiction under Art 23, the jurisdiction obtained on the bases of specialised Conventions via Art 71 prevails over other Regulation jurisdiction. However, since the decision in *Gasser*, if there are multiple proceedings in courts of Member States, the court whose jurisdiction is derived through Art 71 must be the court first seised. Notwithstanding that Art 71 grants jurisdiction to a court of a Member State by the application of the rules of other Conventions, the jurisdiction granted is Regulation jurisdiction. The result of this is that, if the rules of the specialised Conventions do not provide for *lis pendens*, or are not properly invoked, the *lis pendens* provisions of Arts 27–30 will come into operation.[50] Article 71 is like a window, which permits exit from the jurisdiction bases provided by the Regulation and allows entry to other Convention jurisdiction bases, only if that jurisdiction is assumed in accordance with the special provisions of the specialised Conventions. If not, then there will be a return to a jurisdiction base according to the other provisions of the Regulation. There are many international Conventions with regard to maritime claims, which have jurisdiction provisions.[51]

---

50 See, further, op cit, Briggs and Rees, fn 17, para 2.196–2.208.

51 Arrest of Sea-going Ships Conventions 1952, 1999; Collision Convention 1952; Convention on Civil Liability for Oil Pollution Damage 1992 (Protocol 1996) and Fund Convention 1992 (Protocol 1996); Fund Convention 2003 (in force since 1 March 2005); Hague Rules 1924 and Hague-Visby Rules 1968; Hamburg Rules 1978 (not in force in the UK); CMR Convention 1956, to the extent that it is relevant to carriage of goods by sea, Multimodal Convention 1980; Athens Convention 1974 in relation to Carriage of Passengers (note a new Athens Convention 2002, not yet in force); Limitation of Liability Convention for Maritime Claims 1976; Law of the Sea Convention 1982.

The relevant conventions that will be referred to below for the purpose of Art 71 and admiralty jurisdiction are the Arrest Convention 1952, Art 7, and the Collision Convention 1952, Art 1.

3.1.1 Jurisdiction under the Arrest Convention 1952

It was seen in earlier chapters that jurisdiction on the merits under this Convention may be invoked by Art 7, which, insofar as it is material here, provides:

> The courts of the country in which the arrest was made shall have jurisdiction to determine the case upon its merits . . . If the court within whose jurisdiction the ship was arrested has no jurisdiction to decide upon the merits, the bail or other security given in accordance with Art 5 to procure the release of the ship shall specifically provide that it is given as security for the satisfaction of any judgment which may eventually be pronounced by a court having jurisdiction so to decide; and the court or other appropriate judicial authority of the country in which the arrest is made shall fix the time within which the claimant shall bring an action before a court having such jurisdiction.

How Art 7 of the Arrest Convention can effectively surpass the domicile rule (and, by inference, jurisdiction rules other than those conferring exclusive[52] jurisdiction under the European jurisdiction regime) is shown by the following case, which was decided under Art 57 of the Brussels Convention.

The Deichland [53]

In January 1986, the plaintiffs shipped a cargo of steel coils on board *The Deichland* from Glasgow to La Spezia. At the time, the vessel was under a demise charter to a Panamanian corporation, Deich, which had its central management and control in Germany. The plaintiffs alleged that the cargo was damaged on that journey and, therefore, issued a writ *in rem* against the vessel in January 1987. The writ was served on 27 November 1988, but the vessel was not arrested. By this time, the demise charter to Deich had ended and the vessel was in different ownership. The demise charterers, however, acknowledged service of the writ, put up security for the claim, by way of an undertaking from their P&I club, in consideration of the plaintiffs refraining from arresting the vessel. They refused to submit to the English jurisdiction and later applied to the court seeking a declaration that the court had no jurisdiction over them. They argued that they should be sued in Germany, the place of their central management and control, in accordance with Art 2 of the Brussels Convention and s 42 of the Civil Jurisdiction and Judgments Act (CJJA) 1982. The plaintiffs contended that Art 2 of the Convention did not apply, because the jurisdiction of the English court was properly exercised by the service of the writ on the ship, and that such jurisdiction remained unaffected by the Convention because of the effect of Art 57. Even if the domicile rule was to be applied, the place of domicile was Panama (a non-contracting State) and not Germany.

---

52 A possible conflict between Arts 71 and 23 will be seen later. The ECJ decision in *Gasser v MISAT* resolves any doubt that might have prevailed over the hierarchy between Arts 71 and 23.

53 [1990] 1 QB 361.

Sheen J held that the provisions of the CJJA 1982 did not apply to an action *in rem*, when it remained solely *in rem*. The action in the writ was described as an action *in rem* against the ship, *The Deichland*. Therefore, Deich was not a defendant in this action and Art 2 did not apply. The motion was dismissed and the charterers appealed.

In the Court of Appeal, the issues were: (1) whether the provisions of the Brussels Convention incorporated in the CJJA 1982 had any application at all to an admiralty action *in rem*; (2) whether Deich was domiciled in Germany as opposed to Panama; and (3) whether, nevertheless, jurisdiction had been founded under Art 57 of the Convention which gave effect to the provisions of the Arrest Convention. Issues one and three are relevant here – the seat of the corporation (issue two) was straightforward. Neill LJ stated, inter alia, that:

> ... the right approach when one is considering the effect of an international convention is to take account of the purpose or the purposes of the convention. Plainly the 1968 Convention was intended, inter alia, to regulate the circumstances in which a person domiciled in one Contracting State might be brought before the courts of another Contracting State in civil and commercial matters.
>
> Accordingly it seems to me that all forms of proceedings in civil and commercial matters were intended to be covered except insofar as some special provisions such as Art 57 might otherwise prescribe. Furthermore it seems to me that para 7 in Art 5, which confers a special jurisdiction in the case of claims for remuneration in respect of the salvage of cargo or freight, contemplates that this special jurisdiction may be exercised by proceedings either *in rem* or *in personam*.
>
> It is true that in the present case the vessel is no longer chartered to Deich and that jurisdiction to entertain the action *in rem* is based on the provisions of s 21 of the Act of 1981. But looking at the reality of the matter, it is Deich who is interested in contesting liability and against whom the plaintiffs would wish to proceed *in personam* if an appearance is entered ...
>
> In these circumstances, I find it impossible to conclude that on the proper construction of Arts 2 and 3 of the 1968 Convention, Deich is not being 'sued' in these proceedings, even though at this stage the proceedings are solely *in rem*. Deich is liable to be adversely affected by the result of the proceedings and wishes to contest the merits of the plaintiff's claim. By English law an admiralty action *in rem* has special characteristics ... I do not consider, however, that the rules relating to such actions and governing the rights of a plaintiff to levy execution can affect the substance of the matter when the court is faced with an international convention designed to regulate the international jurisdiction of national courts.[54]

On the issue whether the jurisdiction of the English court had properly been invoked in accordance with the Arrest Convention, the operation of which is not affected by the Brussels Convention, the Court of Appeal also held that, on proper construction of the word 'arrest' in Art 7 of the Arrest Convention, an arrest of the vessel is mandatory to found jurisdiction, and mere service of a writ or provision of security is not sufficient. If the ship had been arrested, the English court would have had jurisdiction over the merits.

Mere service of the writ or provision of security without arrest will not suffice to

---

54   [1990] 1 QB 361, pp 373–74.

establish jurisdiction under Art 7 was stressed by Stuart-Smith LJ, as follows:

> If a plaintiff for some reason is determined to litigate in the English Admiralty Court he can easily secure this: either he arrests the ship, or he secures express agreement by the defendant owner or demise charterer to submit to the jurisdiction of the English court to avoid arrest, no doubt at the same time obtaining security. In the present case the plaintiffs did neither of these things.[55]

3.1.2 *How has the trap of* The Deichland *been prevented?*

The words of Stuart-Smith LJ provided sufficient guidance in a subsequent case, *The Anna H*, in which the lawyers acting for the claimants took the appropriate steps to ensure that the English jurisdiction was properly invoked by arresting the ship as required under Art 7 of the Arrest Convention, despite the defendants' attempt to avoid that result by filing a caveat against arrest.

The Anna H[56]

In December 1990, *The Anna H* was loaded with cargo of steel coils at Swansea for carriage to Barcelona. During loading, the coils got wet due to rain. The Spanish cargo-owners (consignees of the bills of lading) alleged that since this happened during loading and stowing of the cargo, the shipowners and demise charterers (both Germans) were responsible for the damage. Their solicitors sought to obtain security from the owners' P&I club in September 1991. The shipowners, anticipating that the ship might be arrested, entered a caveat against arrest of the vessel. At the same time they purported to initiate proceedings in Germany against the cargo-owners for a declaration of no liability, but it turned out that the German court did not become seised of the action. In October 1991, the cargo-owners issued a writ *in rem* and on 11 November arrested *The Anna H* for a few minutes only because of the caveat against arrest.[57] She was released without security having been obtained. Subsequently, the defendants' P&I club executed a bail bond without protest in respect of any judgment that might be given against the shipowners, not just against the ship. The defendants acknowledged service of the writ and sought an order that the English court set aside or stayed its proceedings, or declined jurisdiction in favour of the court of their domicile in Germany. The plaintiffs contested the shipowners' arguments and relied on (a) Art 57 of the Convention, (jurisdiction could be founded by arresting the vessel), and (b) the fact that the defendants had submitted to the jurisdiction of the English court when they filed the praecipe for the caveat against arrest, or when they acknowledged service of the writ and put up bail as security. The defendants contended that, since the CJJA 1982 expressly mentions bail in s 26 and gave the court power to decline jurisdiction where security had been given, the putting up of bail could no longer amount to an irrevocable submission to jurisdiction.

---

55 Ibid, p 385.

56 [1995] 1 Lloyd's Rep 11.

57 A caveat (or caution under the CPR) against arrest of a vessel does not prevent the issue of a warrant of arrest on that vessel.

Clarke J (as he then was) held in favour of the plaintiffs on the ground of Art 57 and that there was submission to jurisdiction by the lodging of the bail bond, which could not be affected by the wording of s 26 of the 1982 Act. The Court of Appeal examined the relationship of the Arrest and Judgments Conventions and paid regard to the *travaux preparatoires* which explained the importance of giving heed to jurisdictional rules imposed by other agreements between state parties. Hobhouse LJ said:[58]

> The two Conventions are to be read together. Their relationship is of the special to the general. Where special provision is made in the special convention, it shall govern. Where no special provision is made, the general provision of the judgments convention apply. Accordingly, within its scope, the Arrest Convention governs the jurisdiction of the Admiralty Court and prevails over the provisions of the judgments convention. There is no reason to impose any implicit restriction on the effect of Art 57 ... Further, it is clear that the intention is that the jurisdiction available under the Arrest Convention should be preserved and that it should continue to apply even though the owner of the ship may be domiciled in another Member State.

He continued:

> The Arrest Convention, in the words of Mr Jennard and Professor Schlosser, 'prevails over' the Judgements Convention. The Arrest Convention qualifies and must be read as part of the Judgements Convention. Any supposed difference of policy must be resolved in favour of the Arrest Convention ... Article 57(2) expressly negatives the inference that the jurisdiction is to be excluded because 'the defendant is domiciled in another Contracting State'.

3.1.3 Submission to jurisdiction and bail

On the issue of submission to jurisdiction, Hobhouse LJ did not have to decide but he said, obiter, that as a defendant can acknowledge service without always submitting to the jurisdiction, should he wish to challenge it, equally, he can put up bail, conditionally reserving the right to challenge jurisdiction.

However, the lodging of bail was thought, at first instance in this case and prior to *The Anna H*, to be a clear submission to jurisdiction by Sheen J in the following case.

The Prinsengracht[59]

The plaintiffs issued a writ *in rem* on 15 April 1991 for damage to their cargo laden on the defendants' ship. It could not be served during the remaining months of that year because the ship did not come within jurisdiction. *The Deichland* had just been decided, so the plaintiffs' solicitors wanted to be cautious and wrote to the defendants' solicitors formally asking for appropriate security for the claim and a letter of undertaking submitting to the jurisdiction. In order to avoid the inconvenience of arrest, the defendants, without waiting for the writ to be served, acknowledged its issue and executed a bail bond. The bond was filed into the Admiralty Court and, a few minutes later, the plaintiffs arrested the ship to avoid the problem of *The Deich-*

---

58 [1995] 1 Lloyd's Rep 11, pp 18, 20.
59 [1993] 1 Lloyd's Rep 41.

land. Thereafter, the ship was released on the same day. The defendants contended that, since they had voluntarily given bail as security for the claim, they had deprived the plaintiffs of the right of arrest; the arrest should be set aside, and they should have been sued in the Netherlands, which was their country of domicile. The question for the court was this: if shipowners were domiciled in a Contracting State and voluntarily gave bail to avoid the inconvenience of arrest of their ship, was the consequence of putting up bail that this court was deprived of jurisdiction (in the sense that the plaintiffs were deprived of the right to arrest) to hear and determine the plaintiffs' claim?

Bearing in mind that bail is an undertaking given to the court, Sheen J answered the question in strong terms:[60]

> Contractual security may be given without submitting, or agreeing to submit, to the jurisdiction of this court (as in *The Deichland*) but bail cannot be given without submitting to the jurisdiction ... Under the old procedure relating to appearance, bail could only be given after appearance ... but the defendant who appeared under protest could put in bail ... Under the current procedure a person who desires to prevent the arrest of his property must acknowledge the issue or service of the writ, as the defendants have done ...

> It would be absurd and it would bring the law into disrepute, if a defendant could procure a bail bond in which there is a solemn undertaking to satisfy a judgment of the court and then say to the plaintiff 'of course you can not obtain a judgment against me because you cannot arrest my ship and I have not submitted to the jurisdiction of the court'. Fortunately that is not the effect of the decision in *The Deichland*. The defendants have, by acknowledging the issue of the writ, shown their desire to take part in the proceedings. They are free to do so.

It was held that the defendants had clearly submitted to the jurisdiction of the court, not only by voluntarily acknowledging the issue of the writ at a time when no action was required of them, but also by putting up bail.

The shipowners in this case fell into two traps: (1) acknowledging issue of the writ; and (2) putting up bail without protest.[61] Apart from obiter comments by the Court of Appeal in *The Anna H*, that it is possible to put up bail under protest, reserving the right to challenge jurisdiction, there are two first instance decisions (*The Anna H* by Clarke J and this one) upholding the view that, by lodging a bail bond, the defendant submits to jurisdiction. Although bail under protest could be a safeguard for the defendant, it would be of no significant effect if the claimant proceeds with the arrest of the ship for a few minutes only to ensure that jurisdiction is established under Art 7 of the Arrest Convention.

---

60 Ibid, pp 45–46.
61 Jackson doubts that the provision of bail which is a provisional measure should cause submission to jurisdiction: op cit, fn 6, at pp 429–430.

3.1.4 The Arrest Convention 1999

Under the Arrest Convention 1999,[62] however, Art 7 has been amended, so that the issues discussed in the above cases will be of no significance if the 1999 Arrest Convention is enacted into English law. Article 7(1) gives jurisdiction to a court of a place where either the arrest has been made or security is provided in lieu of arrest, unless the parties validly agree, or have validly agreed to submit to the jurisdiction of another State, which accepts jurisdiction. However, by para (2), the court which is given jurisdiction, either by arrest or by provision of security to obtain release of the ship, will have power to refuse to exercise that jurisdiction if the law of that State allows it, and the court of another State accepts jurisdiction. The Arrest Convention 1999 will be more in line with the provisions of the Collision Convention 1952, discussed next.

3.1.5 Jurisdiction under the Collision Convention 1952

Article 1 of the Collision Convention states that an action for collision between seagoing vessels can only be introduced:

(a) before the court where the defendant has his habitual residence or a place of business; or

(b) before the court of the place where arrest had been effected of the defendant ship or of any other ship belonging to the defendant which can be lawfully arrested, or where arrest could have been effected and bail or other security had been furnished; or

(c) before the court of the place of the collision when the collision has occurred within the limits of a port or in inland waters.

Article 3 provides that any counterclaims arising out of the same collision can be brought before the court having jurisdiction over the principal action (as per Art 1).

The best illustration of this was provided by the following case.

The Po [63]

The Italian vessel of the defendants, *The Po*, collided with an American ship, *The Bowditch*, belonging to the US Navy (plaintiffs), in Rio de Janeiro while at anchor. The operators of the American ship commenced proceedings in the Brazilian court and the vessel was duly arrested. An undertaking was provided by the P&I club of *The Po* for her release. After an inquiry by the administrative agent in the Port of Rio de Janeiro, the proceedings in the Brazilian court were discontinued. Subsequently, the plaintiffs commenced these proceedings in England. A writ *in rem* was served on *The Po* in Southampton and, in order to prevent her arrest, the owners' P&I club put up security for the second time. In the covering letter, the defendants' solicitors reserved the right to challenge the jurisdiction of the English court on the ground of *forum non-conveniens*.

---

62 For an authoritative commentary on the Arrest Convention 1999, see Gaskell, N and Shaw, R, 'The Arrest Convention 1999' [1999] LMCLQ 470.

63 [1991] 2 Lloyd's Rep 206.

As the decision of the Court of Appeal in *The Deichland* had just been given, the defendants brought a motion asking the court to decline jurisdiction on the ground that under the Brussels Convention the proceedings should have been brought in Italy where the vessel was registered. One of the main questions for consideration was whether this case could be distinguished from *The Deichland*.

The question of whether or not England had implemented the Collision Convention or made it part of English municipal law was immaterial.

According to Lloyd LJ:[64]

> Article 57 of the 1968 Convention does not depend for its beneficial operation on showing that the Contracting States have implemented the special convention. It is enough that the state is a party to the Convention, which the UK is. The High Court indubitably has jurisdiction in accordance with English municipal law in the present case, since the writ *in rem* was properly served on the vessel when she was at Southampton . . . This assumption of jurisdiction was not only not contrary to the Collision Convention, but was positively authorised by it, since the vessel could have been arrested and security was duly offered and accepted. In those circumstances, I cannot see that it matters whether the Collision Convention as such, or the last part of Art 1(1)(b) are part of English municipal law. Since the assumption of jurisdiction was in accordance with the Collision Convention, it is saved from being contrary to Arts 2 and 3 of the 1968 Convention by Art 57.

He distinguished *The Deichland* on the ground that it was a case decided on Art 7 of the Arrest Convention, the wording of which is stricter than the wording of Art 1 of the Collision Convention.

The issue of the first motion in this case (which was a stay on the ground of *forum non-conveniens*) is discussed later. Briefly in this context, the new series of decisions by the ECJ disallow the application of such flexible doctrine (which is foreign to the civil law system), when the defendant is domiciled in a Member State regardless of whether or not the competing court is within a Member State (*Owusu v Jackson*, see later).

3.2 Return to Regulation jurisdiction by operation of Art 27

The rules of the Regulation permit the jurisdiction of a court of a Member State to be assumed on the basis of the provisions of specialised Conventions through Art 71. If, however, such jurisdiction is not properly seised or invoked in accordance with the rules of the specialised Conventions, jurisdiction will be clawed back to another Regulation jurisdiction base.[65]

It has already been seen in *The Tatry* that proceedings by a defendant for a declaration of no liability brought in a court of a Member State (his domicile) prior to the arrest of a ship in England caused the other court to be first seised of the same cause of action and between the same parties. Thus, the Convention rule of *lis pendens* applied in accordance with Art 21 of the Convention (now Art 27 of the Regulation).

---

64   Ibid, p 211.
65   Briggs, A, 'The Brussels Convention tames the Arrest Convention' [1995] LMCLQ 163.

As has been shown in the decisions in *The Deichland*, *The Anna H* and *The Prinsengracht*, if litigants wish the English court to be the court first seised, they must follow the correct procedure provided by the Arrest Convention 1952 to found jurisdiction, which will be upheld by the rules of the Convention or the Regulation for the purpose of *lis pendens*. Jurisdiction would derive from the Arrest Convention only if the vessel had been arrested and not just served with the *in rem* proceeding. The relationship between the Arrest Convention and the Brussels/ Lugano Conventions or the Regulation is that of the special to the general and, in default of the former, the general provisions of the latter shall govern.

It has also been seen that, since those decisions, the ECJ in *Gasser v MISAT* has further clarified *lis pendens* under the Convention or the Regulation. Apparently and ironically, forum shopping is unintentionally encouraged, and litigants will make an even more careful note of dates for invoking jurisdiction in a Member State of their preference.

4 PRINCIPLES OF *FORUM NON-CONVENIENS* AND THE REGULATION

The recent decisions of the ECJ have certainly provided some certainty as to the application of principles with regard to *lis pendens*, related actions and *forum non-conveniens*, but not all situations have been resolved. An attempt is made here to look at various scenarios in order to examine the extent to which there may be situations needing guidance from the ECJ.

4.1 Defendant domiciled in a Member State; natural forum in a non-Member State

The doctrine of *forum non-conveniens*, which is a common law concept, is not known to continental legal systems.[66] It has been held by English courts that the doctrine could be applied through Art 4 of the Convention, when the defendant is not domiciled in a Member State of the Convention and other primary rules of the Convention are not involved. This line of judicial decisions may have to be re-examined in the light of the ECJ decision in *Owusu v Jackson* (discussed later).

Art 4 expressly states that:

(1) If the defendant is not domiciled in a Member State, the jurisdiction of the courts of each Member State shall, subject to Articles 22 and 23, be determined by the law of that Member State.

(2) As against such a defendant, any person domiciled in a Member State may, whatever his nationality, avail himself in that State of the rules of jurisdiction

---

66 Lord Goff explained, in *Airbus v Patel* [1998] 1 Lloyd's Rep 631, the different approaches between the civil law systems and the common law systems in this respect; see Chapter 7, Introduction.

there in force, and in particular those specified in Annex I, in the same way as the nationals of that State.

Since Art 4 permits the court of a Member State – in a case where the defendant is not domiciled in a Member State – to apply its own law, and assuming that that court is in the UK, the doctrine of *forum non-conveniens*, which is part of the UK internal law should apply.

English courts have held that Art 4 grants discretion for staying proceedings on the ground of *forum non-conveniens* although this has been disputed by some writers in the field.[67]

In the recent case of *Owusu v Jackson*,[68] the ECJ ruled out the possibility of a Contracting State declining its jurisdiction founded on Art 2 of the Convention in favour of a non-Contracting State jurisdiction, on the ground of *forum non-conveniens*. The same ruling applies under the Brussels Regulation.

This case concerned a defendant, Mr Jackson, domiciled in the UK, who had let his villa in Jamaica to the claimant, Mr Owusu, a British national domiciled in the UK. The contract had provided that Mr Owusu would have access to a private beach, which was owned and occupied by a management company in Jamaica. Whilst staying at the villa, Mr Owusu waded into the sea and dived into the water. He struck a sand bank and, as a result, fractured his vertebra and was rendered a tetraplegic. He claimed damages against Mr Jackson in the English court for personal injury on the ground of breach of contract, as he alleged that the beach was unsafe. An action was also brought in tort in the English court against the management company of the beach and several other Jamaican companies. Mr Jackson and the companies applied to the English court for a declaration to decline jurisdiction on the ground that Jamaica was the appropriate forum with jurisdiction in which the case might be tried more suitably for the interests of all parties and the ends of justice. Mr Owusu argued that Art 2 of the Convention applied and removed the power of the court to stay its proceedings. The judge refused to stay the proceedings and, on appeal by the defendants to the Court of Appeal, the case was referred to the ECJ.

It should be noted that the competition here was between the jurisdiction of a Contracting and a non-Contracting State, and this is very important to the extent of the implications of this decision.

The question put to the ECJ was this:

1   Is it inconsistent with the Brussels Convention, where a claimant contends that jurisdiction is founded on Art 2 for a court of a Contracting State to exercise a discretionary power, available under its national law, to decline to hear proceedings brought against a person domiciled in that State in favour of the courts of a non-Contracting State:

(a) if the jurisdiction of no other Contracting State under the 1968 Convention is in issue;

(b) if the proceedings have no connecting factors to any other Contracting State?

---

67   Eg; Newton J, '*Forum non-conveniens* in Europe (again)' [1997] LMCLQ 337.

68   Case C-281/02, [2005] 1 Lloyd's Rep 452.

The ECJ confirmed that the Convention precluded a court of a Contracting State from declining its jurisdiction, conferred on it by Art 2,[69] on the ground of *forum non-conveniens*, which – if allowed – would undermine the predictability of the rules of jurisdiction laid down by the Convention and, hence, it would undermine legal certainty. Thus, being consistent with its previous judgments in *Gasser*[70] and *Turner*,[71] the ECJ emphasised the principles of legal certainty and uniform application of Convention rules across all Member States as reasons for rejecting the proposal that Art 2 could be derogated from when principles of *forum non-conveniens* applied. No exception on the basis of the *forum non-conveniens* doctrine was provided for by the authors of the Convention. Article 2 was mandatory in nature and there could be no derogation from it except in cases expressly provided for by the rules of the Convention. Further, the ECJ expressly declared the decision of the Court of Appeal in *Re Harrods (Buenos Aires)*,[72] in which the doctrine of *forum non-conveniens* had been applied in similar circumstances, as bad law.

It seems that the court extended the remit of this decision by pronouncing generally that allowing *forum non-conveniens* in the context of the Convention would be likely to affect the uniform application of the rules of jurisdiction contained therein, since the doctrine allows the court seised a wide discretion. The court also stated that, while the doctrine was only applicable in a limited number of Contracting States, the objective of the Convention was precisely to lay down common rules to the exclusion of national rules. Thus, Art 2 applies to circumstances involving relationships between the courts of a single Contracting State and those of a non-Contracting State, rather than only the courts of a number of Contracting States.

Since the Convention was inspired largely within the civil law system, the flexible discretionary methodology of the common law was disallowed, because it is inconsistent with the objectives underlying the Convention to the effect that jurisdiction should be certain and predictable.

However, it is submitted that the ruling of the ECJ in this case cannot be said to have excluded the doctrine altogether when the defendant is not domiciled in a Contracting State of the Convention or in a Member State of the Regulation. In such cases, the Convention/Regulation permits the court of the Member State seised of the matter to apply its own domestic law and, unless another ECJ decision specifically forbids the application of the doctrine if a UK court is seised of the matter, the UK courts will dare to apply it.

This decision should be strictly limited to the point it decided, namely non-derogation from Art 2 when the defendant is domiciled in a Member State, even if the competing court is in a non-Member State. It is not an authority insofar as Art 4 is concerned.

---

69 See also *Besis SA v Wasserreinigungbau Alfred Kretzschmar GmbH & Co KG* Case C–256/00 [2002] ECR I-1699.

70 See para 2.6.2.2, above.

71 See further, Chapter 7, para 1.

72 [1992] Ch 72.

4.2 Defendant not domiciled in a Member State; proceedings are brought in two Member States

As was seen earlier, Art 4 of the Convention and the Regulation permits the application of national laws if the defendant is not domiciled in a Member State. If, for example, in such a situation the English court is first seised of a matter which is within the scope of the Regulation, English law will be the national law to be applied. Part of English law is also the doctrine of *forum non-conveniens*, and s 49 of the CJJA 1982 provides that:

> Nothing in this Act shall prevent any court in the UK from staying, sisting, striking out or dismissing any proceedings before it, on the ground of *forum non-conveniens* of otherwise, where to do so is not inconsistent with the 1968 Convention or as the case may be the Lugano Convention.

What would be inconsistent with the Convention or Regulation is not absolutely clear. Read now in the light of the judgment of the ECJ in *Owusu v Jackson* it might, in the most liberal interpretation, mean that s 49 may apply only in cases where the defendant is not domiciled in a Member State (as per Art 4 of the Regulation) and where other Regulation rules, such as the provision of exclusive jurisdiction, do not apply. This has been the understanding so far, unless and until the ECJ rules otherwise expressly.

However, applying a strict civil law interpretation and considering the tenor of the recent ECJ decisions, the doctrine may be excluded altogether, even if the defendant is not domiciled in a Member State. For example, if the competing courts are within Member States, following the ruling in *Gasser*, the English court, if it is first seised, will determine that it has jurisdiction rather than decline its jurisdiction in favour of the court of another Member State which may happen to be the natural forum.

In this connection, it should be noted that a caution to litigants had been given by Professor Schlosser in his report,[73] in that they should not waste their time and money risking that the court concerned may consider itself less competent than another, and the choice of the plaintiff should not be weakened by considerations of *forum non-conveniens*.[74]

It could be argued that the *Jackson* case has undermined previous English decisions on the application of the *forum non-conveniens* doctrine decided in the context of the Convention. Let us consider the extent to which the doctrine may or may not be applicable in the following scenarios.

The factual background of **The Sarrio** case illustrates how the English courts approached this issue under the equivalent Art 22 of the Convention.

---

73 On the accession of Denmark, Ireland and the UK to the Brussels Convention [1979] OJ C 59, p. 71.

74 However, both Mance J in *The Sarrio* [1998] 1 Lloyd's Rep 129 (HL), and Clarke J in *The Xin Yang* case [1996] 2 Lloyd's Rep 217 (see later), interpreted this to mean that the discouragement by Professor Schlosser for the application of *forum non-conveniens* was only relevant in the context of jurisdiction exercised on pure Convention grounds under Art 2 or 3, where the Convention lays down a scheme which does not apply to defendants not domiciled in a Convention State.

The Sarrio

The defendants (KIA) were established in Kuwait and through various sub-sidiaries controlled a Spanish company, Grupo Torras (GT) and its subsidiaries. GT was involved in the business of paper packaging. The plaintiffs, Sarrio, a Spanish company, decided to sell off its own special paper business to a subsidiary of GT, Torraspapel (T). Part of the agreement was, inter alia, that the plaintiffs would buy shares in T and other subsidiaries of GT and they were also given a 'put option' to require GT to buy back the shares in T from Sarrio. Having exercised the 'put option', Sarrio made a loss out of the deal because GT did not pay the agreed value, went into receivership, and the subsidiary's value fell sharply. Sarrio filed proceed-ings in Spain against the defendants, claiming sums, which GT, the Spanish subsidiary company of the defendant, had failed to pay under the 'put option'. Subsequently, it also brought two identical actions in England, claiming damages in tort for negligent misstatement made orally during the negotiations which induced it to enter into contracts with these companies controlled by the defendants. The defendants applied for a stay of the action on two grounds. First, under Arts 21 and 22 of the Brussels Convention; secondly, under *The Spiliada* doctrine of *forum non-conveniens*, in that Spain was a more appropriate forum. It was not disputed that the defendants were not domiciled in a Contracting State. The plaintiffs contended that where the choice of forum was between two Contracting States, the English court had no power, even in a case of a defendant domiciled outside the EC, to apply the common law principles of *forum non-conveniens*. Mance J[75] rejected this contention and enunciated the principle as follows:

> In the case of a defendant domiciled within a Contracting State jurisdiction was regulated by the pure convention rules negotiated between such States. The primary rule set out in Art 2 was that suit was to be brought in the court of defendant's domicile. Article 3 referred to situations in which suit may be brought elsewhere and identified a number of national rules which could not as a result survive . . .

> The position in relation to defendants not domiciled within a Contracting State is quite different. Jurisdiction depends upon national rules: see Art 4 of the Brussels Convention. Insofar as jurisdiction or the exercise of jurisdiction by English courts depends on considering whether England is the appropriate forum, there is nothing in the Convention inconsistent with the English court considering this: see s 49 of the CJJA 1982. The obvious qualification is that it would not be consistent for an English court to insist on exercising jurisdiction on the grounds that it was, applying *The Spiliada* principles and apart from the Convention, the appropriate forum, in circum-stances where under Arts 21–23 it would be obligatory or appropriate for it, as the court second seised, to decline or stay the exercise of its jurisdiction.[76]

Evans LJ approved this analysis in the Court of Appeal[77] but, unlike the judge, he did not allow the stay of the English proceedings on the ground that the actions were not related. Upon application of Art 22, however, the House of Lords restored the judge's decision because the Spanish court had been seised first, and, therefore, the House of Lords declined jurisdiction under Art 22(2). It did not have to consider

---

75   [1996] 1 Lloyd's Rep 650.
76   Ibid, at p 654.
77   [1997] 1 Lloyd's Rep 113 (CA); [1998] 1 Lloyd's Rep 129 (HL).

whether the court had discretion under Art 4 to consider principles of *forum non-conveniens* as applied by national law in appropriate cases, because the issue of jurisdiction was resolved on the basis of Art 22.

This decision is consistent with the recent decision of the ECJ in *Gasser*, which emphasised that, as between two Contracting States, the rules are clear: the court first seised will determine jurisdiction, and the court second seised is obliged to stay the proceedings or decline jurisdiction in favour of the court first seised. Therefore, *forum non-conveniens* principles may not come into the equation in cases in which two Member States are seised of jurisdiction. The rules of the Regulation will apply as to *lis pendens* or related actions.

There may be circumstances, however, in which, for example, the appropriate forum is outside Member States, the defendant is not domiciled in a Member State, no court of a Member State has exclusive jurisdiction, and there is no exclusive jurisdiction agreement in favour of a Member State. The English court may, in accordance with Art 4 of the Regulation, apply *forum non-conveniens* principles if it is the court first seised.

It is submitted that such an approach would be justified and would not be inconsistent with the Regulation rules.

4.3 Defendant not domiciled in a Member State; natural forum in a Member State; competing courts in Member States

In the light of the aforesaid ECJ decisions, it is appropriate to consider their effect on the following decisions of the English court.

The Xin Yang[78]

A collision occurred between two foreign ships in Holland, *The Xin Yang* and a moored ship, while she was loading cargo alongside a berth. Damage was caused to both of them and to the jetty. The owners of the moored ship arrested a sister ship of *The Xin Yang* in England claiming damages. Subsequently, the defendant commenced limitation proceedings in Holland (the place of the collision) and applied to stay the English action on the basis of *forum non-conveniens*. Proceedings had also commenced in Holland by the owners of the jetty who arrested *The Xin Yang*, to obtain security for damages to the jetty. Clarke J (as he then was) stayed the English liability action in favour of Holland, although the English court was first seised.

It should be noted that on these facts, and following the recent decision of the ECJ in *Maersk v Firma*,[79] discussed earlier, Art 27 would not apply because the liability proceedings in England and the limitation of liability proceedings in Holland did not have the same cause of action. The actions, however, were related and the court second seised in Holland would have an option, not an obligation, under

---

78 [1996] 2 Lloyd's Rep 217.
79 [2005] 1 Lloyd's Rep 210, see p 209 above.

Art 28 of the Regulation to stay its proceedings although it was the natural forum. Such a conundrum would be capable of being resolved if the English court, albeit first seised, was allowed to apply the *forum non-conveniens* doctrine by virtue of applying its own domestic law as is permitted by Art 4, unless the effect of the ECJ decision in *Owusu v Jackson* has, by implication, put a bar to it.

In this connection the reasoning of the judge in *Xin Yang* is worthy of mention. Clarke J considered that, as the parties were not domiciled in a Contracting State (and since neither Art 16 or 17 of the Convention applied), the court was not prevented by pure Convention rules (such as Arts 2 and 3) from staying the proceedings on the ground of *forum non-conveniens*. Following the reasoning of Mance J, in *Sarrio v Kuwait* (later approved by the Court of Appeal on this point),[80] he relied on Art 4, which expressly permits domestic law to apply if the defendant is not domiciled in a Contracting State. Since English law includes principles of *forum non-conveniens*, there was no sound basis for holding that the Convention intended to restrict the court in the exercise of its jurisdiction to stay the action on those grounds. Furthermore, the power of the court to stay the action was expressly retained by s 49 of the CJJA 1982. In such circumstances, the court, although it was first seised, was entitled to decline to exercise jurisdiction on ground of *forum non-conveniens*, whether or not the alternative forum was the court of a Contracting State.[81] The sensible place, the judge said, for the determination of the quantum between the various claimants would be in the Dutch limitation proceedings. Thus, the appropriate forum for the liability and limitation issues was the place of the collision.

If the English court were not allowed to apply the doctrine as the judge did in this case, and instead decided to maintain its rightful jurisdiction, the question would be whether the result would serve practical justice.

The Happy Fellow [82]

A collision took place near the mouth of the Seine, between *The Happy Fellow* and *The Darfur*. The latter, being blamed for the collision, was arrested at Le Havre by the owners of *The Happy Fellow*. Seven other French claimants also issued proceedings there. Subsequently, the time charterers of *The Darfur* issued proceedings in England against the owners of this ship claiming indemnity. A few days later, a limitation action commenced in England by the owners of *The Darfur* naming as defendants the time charterers and all the other parties who were proceeding in France. A stay of the limitation action in England in favour of the French court was allowed upon application of the operators of *The Happy Fellow* on the ground that the actions 'were related' and Art 22 of the Convention should apply. The Court of Appeal[83] – to prevent a risk of irreconcilable judgments – approved the judge's

---

80 The Court of Appeal in *Haji-Ioannou v Frangos* [1999] 2 Lloyd's Rep 337 was in favour of that view but did not have to decide the point.

81 [1992] 1 Lloyd's Rep 204, p 220.

82 [1997] 1 Lloyd's Rep 130 and [1998] 1 Lloyd's Rep 13 (CA).

83 [1998]1 Lloyd's Rep 13.

decision that the French court would conclude it should deal with limitation issues as well. It disregarded the fact that, before the appeal, the owners of *The Darfur* – hoping to influence the court in exercising its discretion to refuse the stay of the English limitation action – admitted liability in the French proceedings.

The English court, being the second seised, followed the correct approach to stay its proceedings in favour of the French court (the natural forum) on the ground of Art 22 (now Art 28 of the Regulation).

4.4 Limitation of liability actions; defendant not domiciled in a Member State

Invariably, litigants pre-empt an action for limitation of liability (the limitation action) in the court of a State of their preference. If that court were in a Member State and first seised, *Gasser v MISAT* would not apply because the liability and limitation actions do not have the same cause of action, thus the rule of *lis pendens* would not apply as per *Maersk v Firma*, discussed earlier. But limitation and liability actions are related actions and Art 28 will apply in conjunction with Art 7 of the Regulation.

Article 7 of the Regulation (previously Art 6A of the Convention) provides:

> Where by virtue of this Regulation a court of a member state has jurisdiction in actions relating to liability arising from the use or operation of a ship, that court, or any other court substituted for this purpose by the internal law of that state, shall also have jurisdiction over claims for limitation of such liability.

This Article pre-supposes that a court of a Member State has jurisdiction in the liability action by virtue of the Regulation. 'Use or operation of a ship' clearly includes liability arising from collisions between sea-going ships. Jurisdiction may be established in a Member State where the collision occurred, in the place of the harmful event, or the natural forum. Also, by virtue of Art 71, the jurisdiction of a Member State other than the one where the collision occurred may be invoked as provided by Art 1 of the Collision Convention; namely, that Member State may be the one where an arrest of the relevant ship, or a sister ship, is made or where security is provided for the claim.

Once the jurisdiction of a court of a Member State is first seised of the matter, Art 7 of the Regulation contains both a discretionary and a mandatory element. The discretion relates to permitting that court to substitute another court for the claim upon criteria of its internal law.

If the court first seised is English, it may determine to decline jurisdiction only on the basis that another Member State is the appropriate forum, applying *forum non-conveniens* principles according to domestic law, provided the defendant is not domiciled in a Member State. It is submitted that this will not be considered as being inconsistent with the Regulation. What Clarke J said in *The Xin Yang*, namely that it would be permitted by Art 6A of the Convention to substitute the appropriate court for the claim on grounds of *forum non-conveniens*, should be good law, provided the defendant is not domiciled in a Member State.

If the English court is second seised, it may stay its proceedings (as per Art 28), since the action in the court of the other Member State (being first seised) is related.

It is submitted that practical justice can be delivered if the flexible principles of the doctrine are permitted to be applied in appropriate cases within the Regulation regime. Perhaps it is about time that the European civil systems borrowed this good aspect from the common law for the interests of justice.

The obligation imposed by Art 7 (formerly Art 6A) is that the original court, or the substituted one, shall also determine limitation of liability for such claims, so that liability and limitation are determined by the same court. There is, therefore, a restriction upon a defendant to a collision action, who wishes to limit liability, in that the limitation action cannot be split from the liability action, unless he admits liability, and the court which will decide both issues may be the court first seised, but not necessarily so, as explained above.

4.5 Natural forum is in a non-Member State

It is now clear from *Owusu v Jackson* that the application of *forum non-conveniens* will not be permitted if the defendant is domiciled in a Member State, even if the competing court (the natural forum) may be in a non-Member State. It is also declared by the ECJ in the same case that the *Harrods (Buenos Aries)* decision, in which the English Court of Appeal had permitted *forum non-conveniens* to be applied in favour of the natural forum, a non-Member State, is not good law. It had been thought in *Harrods* that the Convention was an agreement as between Member States.

Unfortunately, the decision in *Jackson* is likely to produce odd results, particularly in maritime cases. Let us see how *The Po*[84] (summarised below) would be decided today.

The owners of the ship *The Po* were an Italian company (thus, domiciled in a Contracting State) and the competing courts were in Brazil (a non-Contracting State) and England. *The Po* collided with another ship in the harbour of Rio de Janeiro, Brazil (the natural forum). When she arrived in Southampton, England, she was served with a writ *in rem* and security was put up by her P&I club to prevent arrest. By virtue of Art 57 of the Convention, the jurisdiction of the English court was established under Art 1 of the Collision Convention 1952. The owners of *The Po* (defendants) applied to the court for a stay of the proceedings in favour of Italy, where they should be sued on the basis of their domicile. Both the court below and the Court of Appeal refused to grant a stay.[85]

The defendant's second motion that the English proceedings should be stayed in favour of the natural forum, Brazil, failed too. The Court of Appeal applied the second stage test of *The Spiliada* principles and refused the stay (by majority 2:1) because, although Brazil was the natural forum, if the case was tried there, the

---

84 [1991] 2 Lloyd's Rep 206, decided after *Re Harrods* the latter was reported late.
85 The jurisdiction of the specialised Convention through Art 57 prevailed, being an exception to the general rule of the Convention.

plaintiff would be deprived of an important juridical advantage which he would enjoy in England. That advantage was in relation to the burden of proof; under English law, where a prima facie case of negligence had been made out on the basis of *res ipsa loquitur*, as was in this case, the defendant had to disprove negligence. This was not so under Brazilian law. (Gibson LJ was in favour of the natural forum on issues of evidence.)

Following the *Re Harrods (Buenos Aires)* case, the Court of Appeal thought that it had discretion and was not precluded from applying *forum non-conveniens* principles when the competing forum was not a Contracting State.

Now, following the ruling of the ECJ in *Owusu v Jackson* (that, when the defendant is domiciled in a Contracting State, *forum non-conveniens* is not to be applied even if the competing court is in a non-Contracting State and that *Harrods* is not good law to be followed), the English court would not be able to consider the doctrine albeit that it maintained its jurisdiction on the basis of the second stage of *The Spiliada*.

However, the court would arrive at the same result, if the case was decided today, by applying the principle as stated in *Gasser*, because the English court, being the first seised, would most likely maintain its jurisdiction, assuming that the Italian court, being in a Member State of the defendant's domicile, was also seised (but it was the second seised court).

5 JURISDICTION AGREEMENTS UNDER ART 23

5.1 Interpretation of Art 23

The position is now clearer under the Regulation than it was under the Convention. Art 23 provides expressly that a choice of jurisdiction by the parties shall be exclusive, unless the parties agreed otherwise. Whether or not the agreement provides for an exclusive jurisdiction is a matter of construction of the agreement (*Sohio Supply Co v Gatoil USA*).[86] Furthermore, since *Gasser v MISAT*, it is for the court first seised to determine whether Art 23 applies and whether the agreement is valid, effective and exclusive.

Article 23:

(1) If the parties, one or more of whom is domiciled in a member state, have agreed that a court or the courts of a member state are to have jurisdiction to settle any disputes which have arisen or which may arise in connection with a particular legal relationship, that court or those courts shall have jurisdiction. Such jurisdiction shall be exclusive unless the parties have agreed otherwise. Such an agreement conferring jurisdiction shall be either: (a) in writing or evidenced in writing, or (b) in a form which accords with practices which the parties have established between themselves, or (c) in international trade or commerce in a

---

86 [1989] 1 Lloyd's Rep 588 (CA) (see Chapter 7).

form which accords with a usage of which the parties are or ought to have been aware and which in such trade or commerce is widely known to, and regularly observed by, parties to contracts of the type involved in the particular trade or commerce concerned

(3) Where such an agreements is concluded by parties, none of whom is domiciled in a member state, the courts of other member states shall have no jurisdiction over their disputes unless the court or courts chosen have declined jurisdiction.

Article 23 applies when twofold conditions are satisfied: first, the agreement is between parties one or more of whom are domiciled in a Member State; and, second, the agreement is that a court of a Member State shall have jurisdiction. Both conditions shall be examined by the court first seised,[87] and Member States are not entitled to set their own additional requirements.[88]

In determining whether a forum clause is 'an agreement conferring jurisdiction' within the ambit of Art 23, the court has to treat these words as an independent concept and not simply as referring to the national law of one or other of the Member States.[89] However, the ECJ has not provided guidelines as to the criteria which should be applied in determining whether any particular agreement falls within Art 23. The starting point, therefore, is to consider the meaning of the clause under the law which is the proper law of the contract.[90] What is the proper law of the contract will be determined by the *lex fori* in accordance with its own private international law rules, as the Rome Convention (Art 1(2)(d)) excludes from its scope agreements on choice of court. Conflicts may arise if the *lex fori* rules are different from the *lex fori* of the chosen jurisdiction.

Jurisdiction under Art 23 conferred by the agreement of the parties has been held to be mandatory[91] if (a) the requirements of the Article are fulfilled, (b) the agreement is valid and effective covering the scope of the dispute, and (c) the parties intended that the court chosen shall have exclusive jurisdiction. The effect of this is that the agreed jurisdiction should be given precedence over other jurisdiction bases provided by the Regulation,[92] except the exclusive jurisdiction provided under Art 22.

In some types of contracts, such as insurance policies, there is a reason for providing for non-exclusive jurisdiction. It will be seen from the following insurance cases that the answer depends on the context of the particular case.[93]

---

87 *Coreck Maritime GmbH v Handelsveem BV* [2000] ECR I-9337.

88 *Elefanten Schu GmbH v Jacqmain* [1981] ECR 1671.

89 *Powell Duffryn plc v Petereit* [1992] ECR I-1745.

90 *British Sugar plc v Babbini* [2005] 1 Lloyd's Rep 332.

91 *Lafarge Plasterboard Ltd v Fritz Peters & Co KG* [2000] 2 Lloyd's Rep 689.

92 Per Rix J (as he then was) in *Hough v P & O Containers Ltd* [1999] QB 834 (dealing with precedence of Art 17 over Art 6(2).

93 See, for example, *Evialis SA v SAIT and Others* [2003] 2 Lloyd's Rep 377.

Berisford v New Hampshire [94]

The case concerned a dispute which arose out of two insurance policies taken out by the first plaintiffs (a UK parent company) with the London office of the defendants (insurers, who were incorporated in the USA) through London brokers for the benefit of the second plaintiff (a subsidiary of the first, being incorporated in New York). One policy was made in the usual form used by the Institute of London Underwriters incorporating the Institute Cargo Clauses (A) and expressly bore on its face the words 'This insurance is subject to English jurisdiction'. The other policy covered fidelity risks and there was no jurisdiction clause. The second plaintiffs had been the victims of a series of thefts at their premises and claimed under the policies in England. The defendants applied for a stay of the action on the ground that the courts of New York were the appropriate forum. The issues before the court were: (a) whether the jurisdiction clause was an exclusive jurisdiction clause or merely a permissive one; (b) if there was no exclusive jurisdiction clause, whether the provisions of the Convention had any application; and (c) whether the action should be stayed. Was the clause one that on its true construction obliged the parties to resort to the relevant jurisdiction irrespective of whether the word 'exclusive' is used. According to Hobhouse J (as he then was):

> In the present case, in my judgment, the words used are inapt to create any obligation. If an obligation was intended it could easily have been so stated in clear words ... Under English law where a contract has been placed through brokers it will be very rare indeed that an underwriter will ever have to start an action against an assured. The primary relevance of the clause must be for actions to be brought by the assured against the underwriter. To construe this wording as requiring the assured to sue only in England is to go beyond the natural meaning of the words actually used. Further, to construe the words as declaratory is not to deprive them of significance. It is a statement to the assured, who may be foreign, that the rights that he has under the policy are capable of enforcement in the English courts. Such is an apt interpretation having regard to the legal and commercial relationships created by the document and having regard to the words actually used. Such a clause, even though creating no obligation to sue only in England is a contractual acknowledgment of the jurisdiction of the English courts and a contractual agreement to the invocation of that jurisdiction. [95]

Hobhouse J concluded that the clause was not an exclusive jurisdiction clause. Relying on Art 8, which provides for jurisdiction also of the place where an agency of the insurer is established, he decided that the defendants were deemed to be domiciled in England.

Art 17 (now Art 23) does not apply when the court chosen is in a non-Member State (even if the domicile of one of the parties is in a Member State). In such a case, the English court would apply its own domestic law to exercise its discretion to stay its proceedings in favour of a foreign (non-Member State) jurisdiction clause, unless a good cause is shown not to do so. So held Colman J in *Konkola Copper Mines plc v*

---

94 [1990] 1 Lloyd's Rep 454.
95 [1990] 1 Lloyd's Rep 454, p 458.

Coromin[96] in which he also decided, after careful consideration of the *Jackson v Owusu* case (mentioned earlier), that the ECJ in that case did not disturb the approach of the El Amria as confirmed by *Donohue v Armco* (seen in Chapter 5), since this particular issue had not been addressed in *Jackson v Owusu*.

5.2 *Lis pendens* and jurisdiction agreements

The ECJ in **Gasser v MISAT** has resolved any doubts that might have existed previously with regard to a conflict between the jurisdiction conferred on a court in a Member State by agreement and the jurisdiction of a court in another Member State (see para 2.6.2.2 above). When two courts of different Member States are seised of a civil or commercial matter to which the Regulation applies, it is the court first seised – in accordance with the established rule of *lis pendens* (Art 27) – that will determine whether or not to decline jurisdiction in favour of a court of another Member State which may have jurisdiction pursuant to Art 23 of the Regulation.

To remind readers, the buyers in *Gasser* commenced proceedings in Rome in relation to a dispute that arose under a sale contract. Later, the sellers commenced proceedings in Austria on the ground that the contract contained an exclusive Austrian jurisdiction clause within the meaning of Art 17 of the Convention. The buyers challenged the jurisdiction of the Austrian court. Upon reference of the matter to the ECJ, it was decided that Art 21 in effect trumped Art 17, and the court second seised must stay its proceedings until the question of the jurisdiction of the court first seised had been established and, if it was, the court second seised was to decline jurisdiction. It is the court first seised that will determine the validity and effectiveness of the jurisdiction agreement (and then it may determine to decline jurisdiction).

If it holds that the agreement is valid and effective, the court of the Member State selected by the parties to have exclusive jurisdiction should normally regain its jurisdiction. Courts of Member States should respect a valid and effective exclusive jurisdiction agreement, even if the court first seised has jurisdiction on the basis of the domicile rule. It is the methodology and the approach in the application of an otherwise clear rule of *lis pendens* in Art 21 that the ECJ emphasised in *Gasser*.

Until this decision, English courts were following the Court of Appeal judgment in **Continental Bank NA v Aeakos Compania Naviera SA**,[97] which allowed the English court (being second seised) to give effect to an English exclusive jurisdiction clause, thereby precluding the operation of Art 21 of the Convention. Further to this, the court went so far as to grant an anti-suit injunction to restrain the defendants from proceeding with their claim in the Greek court which was first seised of the proceedings. (Anti-suit injunctions within the scope of the Regulation are now

---

96 [2005] 2 Lloyd's Rep 555; the judge agreed with the view expressed in *Dicey & Morris*, 13th edn, para 12-090.

97 [1994] 1 Lloyd's Rep 505.

clearly forbidden after another recent decision of the ECJ in *Turner v Grovit*,[98] as will be seen in the next chapter.)

The *Continental Bank* case concerned a loan agreement from its Athens branch to several one-ship companies managed in Greece. The borrowers defaulted. The underlying contract contained a jurisdiction clause in favour of the English courts. The borrowers had commenced proceedings in Greece, claiming a wrongful exercise of the bank's contractual rights in breach of its obligation, under Article 919 of the Greek Civil Code, to act in good faith. Given that no equivalent implied obligation exists in English law, the bank was concerned about the prospect of legal proceedings in Greece and promptly applied to the English courts to restrain the Greek proceedings, which was duly granted in the Court of Appeal, affirming the first instance judgment.

Such an approach is now clearly wrong, and the *Gasser* judgment intends to ensure clarity and certainty to the scheme of *lis pendens*. In the future, the English courts, if second seised, will be obliged to stay their proceedings and allow the court first seised to judge if a choice of court clause was valid and that it provided for exclusive jurisdiction in order for the court second seised to determine the dispute.

Therefore, cases such as *Denby v Hellenic Mediterranean Lines*,[99] *Kloeckner v Gatoil* [100] and *Continental Bank v Aeakos Naviera SA* [101] are no longer good law, on this issue.

It was recently decided in *WPP Holdings Italy v Benatti*[102] that the burden of proof in establishing that the agreement satisfied Art 23 was a matter of English law, to which the employment agreement was subject, and the English court was first seised of the matter. However, with regard to who bears the burden and what is the standard of proof in cases where an exception to the jurisdiction is alleged, this has not been settled in a number of first instance decisions of the English courts.

5.3 Resolving conflict between jurisdiction basis conferred by Art 71 and the jurisdiction of Art 23

The decision that brought this possible conflict to attention was *The Bergen*. We know now that when there are proceedings brought in a court of a Member State, which is seised of the matter first under any of the specialised Conventions by virtue of Art 71, and in the court of a Member State which the parties chose for their disputes, the court first seised will determine (by virtue of Art 27) issues as to the validity and scope of the agreement and, subject to that, it may decide to decline

---

98 [2004] 2 LLR 169.
99 [1994] 1 Lloyd's Rep 320.
100 [1990] 1 Lloyd's Rep 177.
101 [1994] 1 Lloyd's Rep 505.
102 [2006] 2 Lloyd's Rep 610.

jurisdiction in favour of the agreed exclusive jurisdiction. Alternatively, it is always open to a party to the jurisdiction agreement to submit to the jurisdiction of the other court (*Gasser v MISAT*).

It is worth seeing whether or not *The Bergen* would be decided in the same way today and for this purpose Art 57 of the Convention is relevant.

Art 57 provided:

(1) This Convention shall not affect any Conventions to which the contracting states are or will be parties and which, in relation to particular matters, govern jurisdiction or the recognition or the enforcement of judgments.

(2) This Convention shall not prevent a court of a Contracting State which is party to a Convention referred to above from assuming jurisdiction in accordance with that Convention, even where the defendant is domiciled in a Contracting State which is not a party to that Convention.

The Bergen [103]

The plaintiffs were the owners of wood carried on the defendants' vessel, B, from the USA to Scotland. The bills of lading contained a jurisdiction clause that any dispute between the parties would be decided in the courts of the carrier's principal place of business, Germany. The plaintiffs claimed for loss and damage to the cargo and arrested the vessel in England. Jurisdiction was founded by virtue of Art 57. The defendants challenged the jurisdiction of the English court relying on the agreed exclusive jurisdiction clause on the basis of Art 17 of the Brussels Convention. The plaintiffs contended that Art 17 had no application because the English court was seised with jurisdiction as was permitted by Art 57. Clarke J (as he then was) held:

> Article 7 of the Arrest Convention is preserved by Art 57 of the Brussels Convention. It confers jurisdiction upon the courts of the State in which the arrest is made to determine the case upon its merits in accordance with the domestic law of that state. In the instant case the vessel was properly served and arrested in England. It follows that the English court has jurisdiction to determine the plaintiff's claim on the merits in accordance with English domestic law. As so far understood the position under English domestic law is that the court retains jurisdiction ... even in case where there is an exclusive jurisdiction clause which provides for the determination of the dispute in a foreign court, but the court has a discretion to stay the action, which it will exercise unless strong cause why it should not do so is shown ...

> If Art 17 applies and is relied upon, the court will be bound to hold that it has no jurisdiction and will have no such discretion. In that event, the court would not be applying English domestic law in accordance with Art 7 of the Arrest Convention.

> It follows that in the absence of authority I would conclude that the plaintiffs are right in their submission that there is a conflict between Art 17 of the Brussels Convention and Art 7 of the Arrest Convention and that, by reason of Art 57 of the Brussels Convention, Art 7 must prevail. That conclusion seems to me to follow logically from the express provisions of Art 57(2).[104]

---

103 [1997] 1 Lloyd's Rep 380.
104 [1997] 1 Lloyd's Rep 380, p 383.

And he held further:

> The effect of Art 17, where it applies, is . . . to deprive the court of original jurisdiction. Accordingly, its effect is not that another court must decline to exercise jurisdiction which it otherwise has, as is the case under Art 21, but that it must decline jurisdiction on the ground that it never had it.[105]

He concluded that Art 17 did not apply, because the English court had jurisdiction by virtue of Art 7 of the Arrest Convention.[106]

Undoubtedly, the court had jurisdiction by virtue of Art 7 of the Arrest Convention, but the question whether or not Art 17 applied was a different one, as seen earlier. It should be noted that, in *The Bergen*, only the English court had been seised of the matter and no proceedings had been brought in the court of the parties' chosen jurisdiction. Nothing would prevent a party from doing so, in order for Art 27 to come into operation to resolve conflict applying the ruling in *Gasser*.

If *The Bergen* was decided today and assuming that proceedings were also brought in the court of the parties' chosen jurisdiction, the English court (being first seised) would have to apply the methodology of Art 27, which is clearly and solely based on the chronological order in which the courts involved are seised. It would have to determine whether or not the jurisdiction agreement was valid, effective and exclusive. If it decided that it was, then it would have to decline its jurisdiction in favour of the chosen exclusive jurisdiction of the parties.

The equivalent to **Art 57**, Art 71 of the Regulation, provides:

(1) This Regulation shall not affect any Conventions to which the member states are parties and which, in relation to particular matters, govern jurisdiction or the recognition or the enforcement of judgments.

(2) With a view to its uniform interpretation, paragraph 1 shall be applied in the following manner:

(a) This Regulation shall not prevent a court of a member state, which is a party to a convention on a particular matter, from assuming jurisdiction in accordance with that convention, even where the defendant is domiciled in another member state which is not a party to that convention. The court hearing the action shall, in any event, apply Art 26 of this Regulation;

(b) Judgments given in a member state by a court in the exercise of jurisdiction provided for in a convention on a particular matter shall be recognised and enforced in the other member states in accordance with this Regulation.

6 RECOGNITION AND ENFORCEMENT OF JUDGMENTS

The recognition and enforcement of judgments provisions have been substantially clarified and tightened by the Regulation.

---

105 Ibid, p 387.

106 In *The Bergen (No 2)* [1997] 2 Lloyd's Rep 710, the same judge accepted that Art 17 applied and he stayed the English proceedings in favour of the agreed forum, Germany, on grounds of *forum non-conveniens*. In the light of the ECJ decision in *Jackson v Owusu* (seen earlier), this decision will no longer be good law.

Briefly, a judgment given in a Member State shall be recognised in the other Member States without any special procedure being required (Art 33). A judgment shall not be recognised if such recognition is manifestly contrary to public policy in the Member State in which recognition is sought (Art 34(1), save that public policy may not be applied to the rules relating to jurisdiction of the court of the Member State of origin (Art 34(3)). Furthermore, a judgment shall not be recognised if it was given in default of appearance, or if the defendant was not served with the proceedings, or if the judgment is irreconcilable with a judgment given in a dispute between the same parties in the Member State in which recognition is sought, or with an earlier judgment given in another Member State (Art 34(2)–(4)).

It should be noted that, as far as English law is concerned, a judgment given in breach of an agreement not to be sued in the country giving judgment will not be recognised or enforced by virtue of s 32 of the Civil Jurisdiction and Judgments Act 1982. Thus, there will be a serious problem in terms of recognition of a judgment, if the court other than the court which is chosen by the parties does not decline its jurisdiction in favour of the court so chosen. And, as seen earlier, the ECJ has not yet given guidelines with regard to the application of common criteria by all Member States' courts in determining whether a forum clause is an agreement conferring jurisdiction within the ambit of Art 23.

The Regulation further provides, by Art 41, that a judgment shall be declared enforceable immediately on completion of the formalities concerning the authenticity of the judgment without any review, at this stage, as provided under Arts 34 and 35. Only upon appeal by the party against whom the judgment is sought to be enforced can grounds of non-enforceability be considered (Arts 43 and 44).

By Art 45, a declaration of enforceability shall be revoked only on grounds specified in Arts 34 and 35. Such grounds have been tightened.

In the next chapter, anti-suit injunctions are reconsidered due to the drastic developments brought about in this area after the first edition of this book, particularly, in the context of cases to which the Convention or the Regulation applies.

CHAPTER 7

ANTI-SUIT INJUNCTIONS

1 INTRODUCTION

An anti-suit injunction is an order obtained from the court to restrain a litigant from continuing court proceedings on the ground that the English court, or an arbitral tribunal, or a court of another forum has jurisdiction on the matter. The principal aim of the injunction is to resolve clash of jurisdictions and prevent irreconcilable judgments or to enforce the parties' agreement to arbitrate. The English court has jurisdiction to grant injunctions on the basis of s 37 of the Supreme Court Act 1981 which provides that: 'the High Court may by an order . . . grant an injunction . . . in all cases in which it appears to the court to be just and convenient to do so'.

Such an injunction can be granted if there is a legal right of the applicant not to be sued in court or in the foreign proceedings. For example, when there is an English exclusive jurisdiction clause or a valid arbitration agreement in the contract, there has been a promise not to be sued other than in the chosen jurisdiction.[1]

The remedy for breach of such a promise has, at common law, been either a stay of the English proceedings, if the breach concerns a foreign jurisdiction agreement, or an anti-suit injunction, if there is a breach of an English jurisdiction agreement and the remedy of damages is not considered to be an adequate remedy.

Where there is no breach of a jurisdiction or arbitration agreement, the English court has considered applications by defendants for anti-suit injunctions when there is unconscionable conduct by the claimant; the court, in order to protect an equitable right of the defendant (applicant), exercises a broad discretion as will be seen under para 3.2 below. Thus, certain principles have been established.[2]

Recently, however, the European Court of Justice (ECJ) prohibited anti-suit injunctions in cases in which the Brussels or Lugano Convention or the Brussels Regulation applies.[3]

But uncertainty still exists as to whether or not an anti-suit injunction will be permitted by the ECJ to restrain proceedings brought in a court of a Member State of the Regulation in breach of an arbitration agreement. The Court of Appeal in *Through Transport Mutual Insurance Association (Eurasia) Ltd v New India Insurance Co Ltd (The Hari Blum)*[4] decided that, since arbitration was excepted from the scope of the Convention (and hence the Regulation), an application for an anti-suit injunction to restrain proceedings brought in breach of a binding arbitration agreement was within the arbitration exception. A subsequent case of the English court, *The*

---

1   *British Airways v Laker Airways* [1985] AC 58 (HL).
2   *Airbus Industrie v Patel* [1998] 1 Lloyd's Rep 631; *Donogue v Armo Inc* [2002] 1 Lloyd's Rep 425, p 432.
3   *Turner v Grovit* [2004] 2 Lloyd's Rep 169.
4   [2005] 1 Lloyd's Rep 67; see facts under para 3.1.1.4 below.

Front Comor,[5] which leapfrogged the Court of Appeal to the House of Lords, has been referred to the ECJ on this point (see para 3.1.1.4 below).

Before entering into further discussion of anti-suit injunctions, an important distinction must be made between two regimes of jurisdiction: the European Civil Jurisdiction regime and the common law system. Lord Goff summarised the salient features of their respective approaches in *Airbus v Patel*:[6]

> This part of the law is concerned with the resolution of clashes between jurisdictions. Two different approaches to the problem have emerged in the world today, one associated with the civil law jurisdiction of continental Europe and the other with the common law world. Each is the fruit of a distinctive legal history and also reflects, to some extent, cultural differences ... In the continent of Europe ... the essential need was seen to be to avoid any such clash between Member States ... A system, developed by distinguished scholars, was embodied in the Brussels Convention, under which jurisdiction is allocated on the basis of well-defined rules. The system achieves its purpose, but at a price. The price is rigidity and rigidity can be product-ive of injustice. The judges of this country ... have to accept the fact that the practical results are, from time to time, unwelcome. This is, essentially, because the primary purpose of the Convention is to ensure that there shall be no clash between the jurisdictions of Member States of the Community.

> In the common law world, the situation is precisely the opposite. There is, so to speak, a jungle of separate, broadly based, jurisdictions all over the world ... But the potential excesses of common law jurisdictions are generally curtailed by the adop-tion of the principle of *forum non-conveniens*[7] – a self-denying ordinance under which the court will stay (or dismiss) proceedings in favour of another clearly more appropriate forum ... The principle is directed against cases being brought in inappropriate jurisdiction and tends to ensure that, between common law jurisdic-tions, cases will only be brought in a jurisdiction which is appropriate for their resolution ... It cannot, and does not aim to, avoid all clashes ... Indeed, parallel proceedings in different jurisdictions are not of themselves regarded as unaccept-able. In that sense, the principle may be regarded as an imperfect weapon; but it is both flexible and practicable and, where it is effective, it produces a result which is conducive to practical justice. It is, however, dependent on the voluntary adoption of the principle by a State in question ... if one State does not adopt it, the delicate balance which the universal adoption of the principle could achieve will, to that extent, break down.

The interpretation of the Brussels Regulation by the ECJ in *Turner v Grovit* has significantly impacted on the common law rules and, instead of flexibility in the approach of resolving clashes of jurisdiction, it has favoured certainty. In addition, the ECJ declared in *Erich Gasser GmbH v MISAT Srl*[8] that the rules of resolving *lis pendens* are clearly provided in the Convention rules and must be strictly applied by Member States to the Brussels/Lugano Convention or to the Brussels Regulation. The ECJ has made it clear that an anti-suit injunction cannot be granted because Art

---

5   *West Tankers Inc v RAS Riunione Adriatica di Sicurta (The Front Comor)* [2005] 2 Lloyd's Rep 257; and [2007] 1 Lloyd's Rep 391 (HL); see facts under para 3.1.1.4 below.

6   *Airbus Industrie v Patel* [1998] 1 Lloyd's Rep 631, p 636, per Lord Goff.

7   It is of interest that it has also been adopted in Japan, whose system has largely been influenced by German law.

8   [2003] ECR I-14693, [2004] 1 Lloyd's Rep 222 (see Ch. 6, above).

27 trumps Art 23 (see Chapter 6). This is compounded by another recent decision of the ECJ in *Jackson v Owusu*,[9] which curtailed the discretion of the English court to apply *forum non-conveniens* principles when the defendant is domiciled in a Member State even if the competing natural forum is in a non-Member State.

Normally, under English law, which has now been affected by the decision of the ECJ in *Turner v Grovit*,[10] discussed later, there have been three remedies in cases of breach of a jurisdiction clause or arbitration agreement:

(1) When there is a breach of a foreign jurisdiction clause or arbitration agreement, an application can be made to the English court by the defendant seeking the stay of the English proceedings.

(2) When there is a breach of an English jurisdiction clause (in a matter which must now be outside the rules of the Brussels Regulation), or a breach of a valid arbitration agreement, the defendant can apply to the English court for an anti-suit injunction. Although arbitration is excluded from the scope of the Convention or the Regulation, whether or not an injunction can be granted in the future in support of an arbitration agreement will depend on the expected decision of the ECJ in *The Front Comor*.

(3) The defendant in either of these proceedings can seek damages for the breach, but this is not usually an effective remedy.

The major issues the courts have had to grapple with, on applications for an anti-suit injunction, have been: (a) whether interference with the foreign court would be justified, in a sense that the injunction might be considered as impeaching the jurisdiction of the foreign sovereignty;[11] (b) whether the injunction would be in breach of rules of public policy of that State,[12] and (c) whether it would be against the provisions of the Human Rights Convention.[13]

The conventional view has been that such an injunction operates only *in personam*, so that the English courts have never regarded themselves as interfering with the jurisdiction of the foreign court.

However, the Court of Appeal in *Philip Alexander Securities v Bamberger*[14] was sceptical about anti-suit injunctions and held that the practice of the courts in England to grant injunctions to restrain a defendant from prosecuting proceedings in another country may now require reconsideration. Leggatt LJ (as he then was) raised a very important issue in this case:

> Where the foreign court regards such injunctions as an infringement of its sovereignty and refuses to permit them to be served, the English court is in a quandary. In cases concerning the European Union, what would best meet the predicament is a directive defining the extent of the recognition which the orders of the courts of each Member State are entitled to receive from the courts of other Member States.

---

9   [2005] ECR I-1383, [2005] 1 Lloyd's Rep 452 (see Ch. 6).

10 [2004] ECR I-3565, [2004] 2 Lloyd's Rep 169.

11 *Philip Alexander Securities v Bamberger* [1997] IL Pr 73.

12 *Akai Pty Ltd v People's Insurance Co* [1998] 1 Lloyd's Rep 90.

13 *OT Africa Line v Hijazy* [2001] 1 Lloyd's Rep 76: the anti-suit injunction was not unlawful under s 6 of the Human Rights Act 1998.

14 [1997] IL Pr 73 (see para 3.1.1.2 below).

As it happened, the ECJ has now resolved this dilemma by stating that such injunctions are forbidden as between courts of Member States of the Convention or the Regulation, for they undermine the mutual trust between such courts. The purpose of this chapter, which inevitably differs from the corresponding chapter in the first edition of this book, is: first, to review the position of anti-suit injunctions, taking into account the prohibition placed upon the jurisdiction of the English court to restrain proceedings brought in another Member State of the Brussels Regulation; and, second, to examine the circumstances in which the injunction may still be granted.

Although there have been a number of cases in this area, some of which are no longer good law, space does not permit to include them all. The reader is given general guidance and an opportunity for further research.

2 PROHIBITION OF ANTI-SUIT INJUNCTIONS WITHIN THE EUROPEAN UNION

2.1 Allocation of jurisdiction by the rules of the Brussels regime

The provisions concerning recognition and enforcement of judgments between Member States embodied in the Brussels/Lugano Conventions and in the Brussels Regulation are of great importance in the context of an anti-suit injunction, as will become apparent from the decision in *Turner v Grovit*[15] (decided under the Convention). The European Court of Justice has ruled that the injunction to restrain foreign proceedings in a court of a Contracting (or, now, Member) State is simply prohibited.

Turner v Grovit

Mr Turner, a solicitor, was domiciled in the UK and was employed by the Chequepoint Group of companies controlled by Mr Grovit. He originally worked for them in London and was then transferred to Spain in 1997. He resigned in 1998 and brought proceedings before the Employment Tribunal in London for constructive dismissal, alleging that he was the victim of efforts to implicate him in illegal conduct. He was awarded damages. Chequepoint brought proceedings against him in Spain for alleged negligence. The conflict of jurisdiction was between the English court (which would have jurisdiction on the basis of Turner's domicile) and the Spanish court.

Objecting to the jurisdiction of the Spanish court, Mr Turner applied to the High Court in London for an anti-suit injunction, seeking to prevent the continuation of the Spanish proceedings on the ground that they were vexatious. There was no jurisdiction clause in this case. The injunction was granted and was upheld by the Court of Appeal, on the ground that the Spanish proceedings were brought in bad

---

15 Case C-159/02, *Turner v Grovit* [2004] 2 Lloyd's Rep 169.

faith in order to vex Mr Turner in the pursuit of his case before the Employment Tribunal. This had the effect of discontinuing the Spanish proceedings. However, the case went on appeal to the House of Lords.[16] Chequepoint disputed the authority of the English courts to issue anti-suit injunctions which had the effect of discontinuing legal proceedings in countries which were covered by the Brussels Convention. Although Lord Hobhouse was inclined to think that the grant of the injunction was justified as being consistent with the Brussels Convention because here there was unconscionable conduct, he referred the matter to the ECJ to rule on the issue. He observed, however, that the terminology of 'anti-suit' injunction was misleading, since it fosters the impression that the order is addressed to and intended to bind another court. He explained that the injunction does not question the jurisdiction of the foreign court, but makes a restraining order only to a party which is before the court on the basis of there being wrongful conduct of that party and binds only that party *in personam*.

Both Mr Turner and the UK Government defended the use of anti-suit injunctions to proceedings which were covered by the Convention on the following grounds: first, an injunction does not encroach upon the jurisdiction of a foreign court, as it is addressed to an individual who brings proceedings in bad faith; second, the fact that an anti-suit injunction is a procedural mechanism of national law, and the Convention does not regulate on procedural matters, means that there is no conflict in its operation; and, third, an anti-suit injunction helps to meet the Convention's objectives since it works to minimise the risk of conflicting decisions and avoid a multiplicity of proceedings.

The ECJ ruled that the use of anti-suit injunctions runs counter to the mutual trust which the Member States gave to each other's legal systems and institutions.[17] Within the principle of mutual trust, it is inherent that the rules of jurisdiction laid down in the Convention are able to be applied and interpreted with equal authority by each Member State's courts. For this reason, and save in a few exceptional cases with regard to recognition of judgments, the Convention itself does not permit the jurisdiction of a court to be reviewed by the court of another Member State, even in cases where the litigant was acting in bad faith. Moreover, an anti-suit injunction undermines a foreign court's jurisdiction to determine a dispute, which cannot be justified by reference to the fact that such an injunction is indirect and intends to guard against abuse. Finally, the use of an anti-suit injunction to determine a jurisdictional dispute is seen as rendering ineffective the *lis alibi pendens*[18] rules under the Convention.

In *Erich Gasser GmbH v MISAT Srl* (referred to in Chapter 6), the ECJ also held that, in cases concerning the same cause of action and the same parties and which involve Member States of the Brussels regime, the court second seised, even if it is

---

16 [2002] 1 WLR 107.
17 Op cit fn 3, para 24. This echoes the reasoning of the ECJ in another recent judgment: *Erich Gasser GmbH v MISAT Srl* (Case C-116/02) [2004] 3 WLR 1070; [2004] 1 Lloyd's Rep 222. For a detailed outline of this case, see Chapter 6, para 2.6.2.2.
18 See, further, Chapter 6.

the forum chosen by a jurisdiction agreement of the parties, must stay the proceedings until the court first seised determines its jurisdiction, even if it takes inordinate delay to rule on its jurisdiction.

Although this decision concerned a breach of a foreign jurisdiction clause, its effect, coupled with the ruling in *Turner v Grovit*, is that, even if the choice of court is English, the English court will be prohibited from issuing an anti-suit injunction to restrain the proceedings brought in another Member State in breach of the English jurisdiction clause. If the English court is first seised, it will determine its jurisdiction on the basis of Art 23, but if it is second seised, it will have to stay its proceedings.

2.2 Allocation of jurisdiction by another Convention and anti-suit injunctions

If jurisdiction is allocated by the Brussels/Lugano Conventions or the Brussels Regulation, anti-suit injunctions cannot be considered within the European Union. In some cases, jurisdiction can be allocated by another Convention which might or might not involve EU States.

In the following case, however, France and England were involved, and although, at the time the case was decided, anti-suit injunctions were not forbidden, the judge did not grant the injunction for reasons of comity towards the French court.

Deaville v Aeroflot Russian International Airlines[19]

It involved a jurisdiction base provided by the Warsaw Convention 1929, Art 28, namely: (a) where the carrier is ordinarily resident or has his principal place of business; or (b) where the carrier has an establishment by which the contract for carriage was made; or (c) at the place of intended destination, respectively. An Aeroflot flight destined for Hong Kong crashed near Siberia killing all passengers and crew. The competing jurisdictions were either Russia or England or Hong Kong. The dependants of the deceased brought proceedings in France against both the manufacturers and Aeroflot. Then, they issued proceedings in England, just to protect time against Aeroflot. Aeroflot challenged the jurisdiction of the French courts and applied here for a declaration that the plaintiffs must comply with Art 28 of this Convention and, since France was not one such jurisdiction, they also applied for an anti-suit injunction.

Brice QC, acting as the judge in the case, exercised his discretion against granting the anti-suit injunction for reasons of comity towards the French court. It was more appropriate, he said, to let the French court determine its own jurisdiction. Comity required a policy of non-intervention.[20]

---

19 [1997] 2 Lloyd's Rep 67.
20 See also *Re Maxwell Communications Corp (No 2)* [1992] BCC 757, p 765, per Hoffmann J.

It should be noted that the French court was seised first and the English court was seised second. Both were Contracting States to the Brussels Convention and are now to the Brussels Regulation.

Were this case to be decided today, granting an anti-suit injunction would be refused on the basis of ECJ decision in *Turner v Grovit*. Considering also that the French court was first seised, it would today be permitted to determine its jurisdiction on the basis of the ECJ decision in *Gasser v MISAT*, which clarified the proper application of the rule under Art 21 of the Brussels Convention (now Art 27 of the Brussels Regulation).

However, this does not prevent the jurisdiction of the English courts from granting anti-suit injunctions in cases where the Brussels/Lugano Convention or the Brussels Regulation does not apply. The rest of this chapter is dedicated to cases involving non-EU jurisdictional issues and arbitration agreements. Arbitration is specifically excluded from the remit of the Brussels Regulation[21] but the issue of anti-suit injunctions to protect arbitration is not yet resolved (as is seen later).

3 ANTI-SUIT INJUNCTIONS OUTSIDE THE SCOPE OF THE REGULATION

Two broad categories of anti-suit injunctions are compared here: (i) the 'breach of contract cases', which are concerned with a breach of a jurisdiction, or an arbitration agreement; and (ii) the 'non-contract cases', those not involving a breach of a contractual jurisdiction, but cases where an injunction may be granted to restrain vexatious or oppressive conduct or, as is now referred to, 'unconscionable' conduct.

The principles applicable to anti-suit injunctions in each of these cases under English law are examined separately, but it is convenient to show how the court recently summarised these principles in **Royal Bank of Canada v Cooperatieve Centrale**,[22] as derived from previous cases, thus:

(i) under English law, a person has no right to be sued in a particular forum, domestic or foreign, unless there is some specific factor that gives him that right, but a person may show such right if he can invoke a contractual provision conferring it on him or if he can point to clearly unconscionable conduct (or a threat of unconscionable conduct) on the part of the party sought to be restrained;

(ii) there will be such unconscionable conduct if the pursuit of foreign proceedings is vexatious or oppressive, or it interferes with the due process of this court;

(iii) the fact that there are such concurrent proceedings does not in itself mean that

---

21 Brussels Regulation, Art 1(2)(d).

22 By Smith J at first instance and approved by the Court of Appeal: [2004] 1 Lloyd's Rep 471 at para 8; see also *Seismic Shipping v Total E & P UK plc (The Western Regent)* [2005] 2 Lloyd's Rep 54 and [2005] 2 Lloyd's Rep 359 (CA).

the conduct of either action is vexatious or oppressive or an abuse of the court, nor does that in itself justify the grant of an injunction;

(iv) however, the court recognises the undesirable consequences that may result if concurrent actions in respect of the same subject matter proceed in two different countries: that there may be conflicting judgments of the two courts concerned, or that there may be an ugly rush to get one action decided ahead of the other in order to create a situation of res judicata or issue estoppel in the latter;

(v) the court may conclude that a party is acting vexatiously or oppressively in pursuing foreign proceedings and that he should be ordered not to pursue them if (a) the English court is the natural forum for the trial of the dispute, and (b) justice does not require that the action should be allowed to proceed in the foreign court; and, more specifically, that there is no advantage to the party sought to be restrained in pursuing the foreign proceedings of which he would be deprived and of which it would be unjust to deprive him; and

(vi) in exercising jurisdiction to grant an injunction, regard must be had to comity, and so the jurisdiction is one which must be exercised with caution.

For present purposes, only leading decisions will be referred to under the broad categories, in order to identify the extent to which the principles stated have been consistently applied and whether there are any common considerations or differences between them.

3.1 The 'breach of contract cases'

These encompass breach of arbitration or an English court choice agreement which are not subject to the Brussels/Lugano Convention or the Brussels Regulation. Arbitration cases are examined first.

3.1.1 Breach of an arbitration agreement

3.1.1.1 The principle of granting an anti-suit injunction under English law

Since the decision of the Court of Appeal in *The Angelic Grace*,[23] the injunction to enforce a London arbitration agreement has been granted, unless there has been a good reason not to do so. A good reason not to grant it has been narrowly interpreted. It could include proof that: (i) the foreign court would stay execution of the judgment on ground of the New York Convention concerning the Recognition and Enforcement of Arbitral Awards 1958;[24] (ii) the arbitration provision in the parties'

---

23 [1995] 1 Lloyd's Rep 87.

24 The French court was not willing to stay its proceedings in favour of the English arbitration clause in *Toepfer v Société Cargill* [1998] 1 Lloyd's Rep 379. But the issue concerned the interpretation of Art 1(4) of the Brussels Convention, which excludes arbitration from the Convention, and the question was whether an injunction could be obtained to restrain the French court from continuing its proceedings on the ground that the French proceedings constituted a breach of the arbitration agreement. This was referred to the European Court of Justice but the case was, in the meantime, settled.

contract did not create a binding agreement to arbitrate in London;[25] (iii) there has been submission to the foreign jurisdiction; or (iv) there has been delay in applying for an injunction.

The facts of this case concerned a dispute between owners and charterers under a charter party which provided for arbitration in London. The owners pre-empted proceedings in England (suspecting that the charterers might proceed in Italy despite the arbitration clause), seeking a declaration that all claims and cross-claims were subject to arbitration in London and the charterers be restrained from commencing court proceedings in respect of such claims. Then the owners commenced arbitration. As expected, the charterers commenced proceedings in Italy and submitted to the English jurisdiction only for the purpose of determining the scope of the arbitration agreement. Despite the final decision of the court that all claims and cross-claims were within the arbitration agreement, the charterers continued the proceedings in Italy. Against this background, Rix J (as he then was) granted the anti-suit injunction, and the Court of Appeal upheld it, stating:

> The time has come to lay aside the ritual incantation that this is a jurisdiction which should only be exercised sparingly and with great caution. There have been many statements of great authority warning of the danger of giving an appearance of undue interference with the proceedings of a foreign court. Such sensitivity to the feeling of a foreign court has much to commend it where the injunction is sought on the ground of *forum non-conveniens* or on the general ground that the foreign proceedings are vexatious or oppressive but where no breach of contract is involved . . . but in my judgment there is no good reason for diffidence in granting an injunction to restrain foreign proceedings on the clear and simple ground that the defendant has promised not to bring them.[26]

Sometimes, the arbitration agreement may not have been properly incorporated into the contract and, in such a case, the foreign proceedings will not be interfered with,[27] or the validity of an arbitration clause may be disputed by one party to it who brings proceedings in another forum. This was dealt with by the English court in *The XL Insurance v Owens Corning*.[28] Toulson J held that, by stipulating for arbitration in London under the provisions of the Arbitration Act 1996, the parties chose English law to govern the matters which fell within those provisions, including the formal validity of the arbitration clause and the jurisdiction of the arbitral tribunal. It is for the arbitral tribunal to rule on the validity of the agreement and its jurisdiction in the event of challenge, unless the matter is referred to the court. He granted the injunction restraining the party in breach of the putative arbitration agreement from continuing with litigation it had commenced in Delaware.

It is now clear from the ECJ decisions (to be seen under paras 3.1.1.2 & 3.1.1.3) that an application for a declaration that the arbitration agreement is valid comes within the exception of arbitration, and hence it is not a matter within the scope of the Convention or Regulation.

---

25 *Philip Alexander Securities & Futures Ltd v Bamberger* [1997] IL Pr 73 (CA); see below.

26 Op cit, fn 23, at 96, Millett LJ.

27 *American International Specialty Lines Insurance Co v Abbott Laboratories* [2003] 1 Lloyd's Rep 267.

28 [2000] 2 Lloyd's Rep 500.

3.1.1.2 The problem of recognition and enforcement

Despite the encouragement received by the Court of Appeal in *The Angelic Grace*, the English courts have been reticent before granting an anti-suit injunction against parties resident in the European Union, even in cases involving breach of an arbitration agreement. The problem concerns recognition and enforcement of an anti-suit injunction in the foreign court. It has been thought that the injunction may involve an infringement of foreign sovereignty, although this is not a widely held view.[29] Yet there has been a dilemma for courts considering the issue of an anti-suit injunction, and such a dilemma was first shown in the *Bamberger*[30] case.

Philip Alexander Securities & Futures Ltd v Bamberger

The dispute involved trading in futures and options by German customers who were recruited in Germany by German brokers to trade through the plaintiff (that is, the applicant for an anti-suit injunction). Liability of the plaintiff for losses in trading was incurred and the customers brought actions in various German courts. The plaintiff's defence was that the dispute should be adjudicated by arbitration in London. While the plaintiff had referred the same matter to arbitration in London and won, some of the German courts gave judgment against him. The plaintiff, therefore, sought interim injunctions and declarations from the English court to restrain the remaining actions in Germany and enforce the arbitration order. Interlocutory injunctions obtained had no effect in restraining the customers from continuing with their actions in Germany. Some German courts refused to serve the orders on the basis that there would be an interference with the German sovereignty. At first instance, Mance J thought that, although it was an appropriate case to grant an injunction, he felt that it was not appropriate to grant it at this stage of the proceedings.

The Court of Appeal held that the rules to which the agreements were subject gave customers the right to elect to arbitrate. But, since some had not so elected, their case could only be litigated. Consequently, the arbitration agreement would be considered by a Contracting State of the New York Convention, in this case Germany, to be inoperative. Different factual situations can give different results.[31] It distinguished *The Angelic Grace* case on the facts, in that the arbitration proceedings in London had commenced before the Italian court proceedings and the foreign parties submitted to the arbitration proceedings. The Italian proceedings were held vexatious and the Italian court would decline jurisdiction. By contrast, it was clear in this case that the German court was offended and took the view that there was no obligation to stay its proceedings under the New York Convention on the basis of the consumer laws being applied in Germany. The citizens, according to German law, had the right, as consumers, to come to German courts.

For these reasons the Court of Appeal regarded it inappropriate to grant the anti-suit injunction.

---

29 As Lord Hobhouse observed in *Turner v Grovit* [2002] 1 W.L.R. 107 (HL), such a view of anti-suit injunctions is based on a misunderstanding.

30 *Philip Alexander Securities & Futures Ltd v Bamberger* [1997] IL Pr 73, [1996] CLC 1757.

31 *Alfred Toepfer International v Molino Boschi* [1996] 1 Lloyd's Rep 510.

Another interesting case highlighting the concerns surrounding anti-suit injunctions was *Toepfer International GmbH v Cargill France SA*.[32] It involved a dispute about the condition of a cargo of soya bean meal pellets sold by the plaintiff to the defendant (the parties in the English proceedings) under a contract incorporating a GAFTA London arbitration clause. The defendant brought first emergency proceedings in France. The plaintiff commenced proceedings in England for a declaration that the defendants were in breach of the arbitration agreement, and also sought an anti-suit injunction to restrain the defendants from continuing the French proceedings. The defendants asserted that, by virtue of Art 21 of the Brussels Convention, the English court, being second seised, should stay its proceedings and the plaintiffs in turn relied on Art 1(4) of the Convention, arguing that arbitration was outside the scope of the Convention. While, at first instance, Colman J decided in favour of the plaintiffs, Phillips LJ (as he then was) in the Court of Appeal referred the matter to the ECJ on the following questions:

(1) Does the exception in Art 1(4) of the Brussels Convention extend to proceedings commenced before the English court seeking (a) a declaration that the commencement and continuation of the proceedings before the French court constitutes a breach of an arbitration agreement; (b) an injunction restraining the appellants from continuing the proceedings before the French court in breach of the arbitration agreement? If not

(2) Do such proceedings constitute the same cause of action as a challenge to the jurisdiction of the French court founded on the same arbitration agreement, so as to require the English court to stay its proceedings pursuant to Art 21 of the Convention?

Unfortunately the parties settled their dispute, and the opportunity of enlightenment on these questions from the ECJ was lost.

The position as to how the ECJ would have decided on these questions remains uncertain, despite the decision in *Turner v Grovit* which can be distinguished, since the proceedings did not concern an anti-suit injunction in support of an arbitration agreement.

Normally, as Phillips LJ stated in *Toepfer* before he referred it to the ECJ, when the New York Convention 1958 on recognition and enforcement of foreign arbitral awards applies, it requires (by Art 11.3) the court of a Contracting State to refer the parties to arbitration, when an action is commenced in disregard of a binding arbitration clause.[33]

3.1.1.3 How does the ECJ view the matter of arbitration?

Support for the aforesaid view is also derived from the decision of the ECJ in *Rich (Marc) & Co AG v Societa Italiana Impianti PA (The Atlantic Emperor)*,[34] in which Marc Rich claimed damages for contamination of cargo bought from Impianti under an FOB contract. Impianti denied liability and commenced proceedings in

---

32 [1998] 1 Lloyd's Rep 379.
33 Ibid, p 386.
34 [1992] 1 Lloyd's Rep 342.

Italy for a declaration of no liability. Marc Rich commenced arbitration in London but Impianti failed to appoint its arbitrator. Marc Rich issued an originating summons for the appointment of an arbitrator and obtained leave from the English court to serve it out of the jurisdiction. Impianti applied to set aside the order on the ground that there was no valid arbitration agreement and hence the dispute fell within the Convention. Hirst J held that the Convention did not apply. The matter proceeded to the Court of Appeal which referred the matter to the ECJ for a preliminary ruling. The primary question for the court was: does the arbitration exception in Art 1(4) of the Convention extend (a) to any litigation or judgment and, if so, (b) to litigation or judgment where the initial existence of an arbitration agreement is in issue?

The ECJ held that:

(1) by excluding arbitration from the scope of the Convention on the ground that it was already covered by international conventions, the Contracting parties intended to exclude arbitration in its entirety, including proceedings brought before national courts; the appointment of an arbitrator by a national court was a measure adopted by the State as part of the process of setting arbitration proceedings in motion, and such a measure came within the sphere of arbitration and was covered by the exclusion contained in Art 1(4) of the Convention;

(2) in order to determine whether a dispute fell within the scope of the Convention, reference had to be made solely to the subject matter of the dispute; if, by virtue of its subject matter, such as the appointment of an arbitrator, a dispute fell outside the scope of the Convention, the existence of a preliminary issue which the court had to resolve in order to determine the dispute could not, whatever that issue might be, justify application of the Convention;

(3) the fact that a preliminary issue related to the existence or validity of the arbitration agreement did not effect the exclusion from the scope of the Convention of a dispute concerning the appointment of an arbitrator; and

(4) the answer to question 1 was that Art 1(4) of the Convention had to be interpreted as meaning that the exclusion provided for therein extended to litigation pending before a national court concerning the appointment of an arbitrator, even if the existence or validity of an arbitration agreement was a preliminary issue in litigation.

Although the statement in this judgment that the arbitration exclusion is broad can be interpreted as encompassing an application for an anti-suit injunction to enforce an arbitration agreement, the recent ECJ decision in *Gasser*, which ruled that in no case is the second seised court in a better position than the court first seised to determine whether the latter has jurisdiction, has overshadowed the issue.[35]

The crucial question is whether or not an application for an anti-suit injunction is an integral part of, or ancillary to, arbitration, so as to be included in the exception from the Convention or Regulation, or whether it is to be regarded as a civil and commercial matter and hence fall within the Convention or Regulation, whereupon the principles of the *Gasser and Turner v Grovit* will apply.

---

35 See commentary on Anti-suit injunctions and Arbitration, *The Front Comor*: LMCLQ May 2006 166 by Professor J Hill.

Some guidance on this issue may be gleaned from *Van Uden Maritime BV v Firma Deco-Line*,[36] which was referred to the ECJ but did not directly concern this issue.

By a contract containing a clause for arbitration in the Netherlands, the plaintiff, Van Uden, a company established in the Netherlands, agreed to make available to the defendant, a company established in Germany, cargo space on vessels operated by the plaintiff, in return for the payment of charter hire. The plaintiff started arbitration proceedings, claiming the payment of invoices allegedly not paid, and later it applied to a court in the Netherlands for the interim payment of a sum representing certain invoices, claiming that the defendant was not showing diligence in the appointment of arbitrators and that the non-payment of the invoices was disturbing its cash flow. The defendant objected to the jurisdiction of the Netherlands court, on the ground that he was domiciled in Germany and the general rule in Art 2 of the Brussels Convention applied. In a reference for a preliminary ruling to the ECJ, a number of questions were posed, relating to Arts 5(1) and 24, whereby an application for provisional measures could be made to a court of a Contracting state. But since the contract contained an arbitration clause, the interpretation of Art 1(4) of the Convention, which excludes arbitration, had to be considered first.

Two arguments were put forward in this regard, predicated on opposite interpretations of Art 1(4) of the Convention.

The first, put forward by the defendant, the UK Government and the German Government, was that the interim relief sought was ancillary to arbitration and, hence, excluded from the Convention.

The second, put forward by the plaintiff and the Commission, suggested that the scope of that exclusion should not be stretched too far.

Since these divergent opinions are very important to the issue under discussion, it is equally important to set out the opinion of the Advocate General before the ruling of the court is laid out.

Far from being convinced by the first argument, that the application for interim relief was ancillary to arbitration, the Advocate General – delivering his opinion – agreed with the Commission and the plaintiff, in that the exclusion of 'arbitration' from the scope of the Convention did not cover the circumstances of this case. He added that, in the circumstances of this case, he saw an advantage in allowing the application of the rules of the Convention, even though the risk of two courts both claiming jurisdiction could not be discounted. If the Convention were not applied, it would be difficult to see how a situation such as that, where arbitration could not be implemented owing to the inertia of one of the parties, could be resolved. In line with the court's judgment in *Marc Rich*, any proceedings for the appointment of arbitrators would, in that case, certainly fall outside the scope of the Convention. He further stated that, if we set out to define the purpose of the exclusion referred to in Art 1(4), as it may be inferred from its logical basis, that provision cannot be attributed the wide scope suggested by the German and UK Governments.

36   [1998] ECR 7091, or [1999] QB 1225.

The reasons for the exclusion are very clear from the report by Mr P Jenard on the Brussels Convention:[37]

> There are already many international agreements on arbitration. Arbitration is, of course, referred to in Article 220 of the Treaty of Rome. Moreover, the Council of Europe has prepared a European Convention providing a uniform law on arbitration, and this will probably be accompanied by a Protocol which will facilitate the recognition and enforcement of arbitral awards to an even greater extent than the New York Convention. This is why it seemed preferable to exclude arbitration.

Thus, the Advocate General concluded on this issue that the objective of the exclusion was to prevent the Brussels Convention from duplicating pre-existing or future international provisions. The purpose of the exclusion can therefore only be to ensure that the matter of arbitration, as regulated elsewhere, remains outside the scope of the Convention. The matters covered by the exclusion are those which[38]

> are ancillary to arbitration proceedings, for example the appointment or dismissal of arbitrators, the fixing of the place of arbitration, the extension of the time limit for making awards or the obtaining of a preliminary ruling on questions of substance ... [such as appeal from the award] ... In the same way a judgment determining whether an arbitration agreement is valid or not, or because it is invalid, ordering the parties not to continue the arbitration proceedings, is not covered by the 1968 Convention ... Nor does the 1968 Convention cover proceedings and decisions concerning applications for the revocation, amendment, recognition and enforcement of arbitration awards.

The ECJ held that, where the parties have validly excluded the jurisdiction of the courts in a dispute arising under a contract and have referred that dispute to arbitration, there are no courts of any State that have jurisdiction as to the substance of the case for the purposes of the Convention. Consequently, a party to such a contract is not in a position to make an application for provisional or protective measures to a court that would have jurisdiction under the Convention as to the substance of the case. In such a case, it is only under Art 24 that a court may be empowered under the Convention to order provisional or protective measures.

It must here be borne in mind that Art 24 of the Convention applies even if a court of another Contracting State has jurisdiction as to the substance of the case, provided that the subject matter of the dispute falls within the scope *ratione materiae* of the Convention, which covers civil and commercial matters. Art 24 may confer jurisdiction on the court hearing the application even where proceedings have been, or may be, commenced on the substance of the case and even where those proceedings are to be conducted before arbitrators.

However, Art 24 cannot be relied on to bring within the scope of the Convention provisional or protective measures relating to matters which are excluded from it.[39] Under Art 1(4) of the Convention, arbitration is excluded from its scope. By that

---

37 [1979] OJ C 59/1, at p 13.
38 See the Schlosser report [1979] OJ C 59/71, at p 93, paras 64, 65.
39 *De Cavel v de Cavel* (Case 143/78) [1979] ECR 1055, p 1067, para 9.

provision, the Contracting parties intended to exclude arbitration in its entirety, including proceedings brought before national courts.[40] The experts' report drawn up on the accession of the Kingdom of Denmark, Ireland and the United Kingdom of Great Britain and Northern Ireland to the Convention[41] specifies that the Convention does not apply to judgments determining whether an arbitration agreement is valid or not or, because it is invalid, ordering the parties not to continue the arbitration proceedings, or to proceedings and decisions concerning applications for the revocation, amendment, recognition and enforcement of arbitration awards. Also excluded from the scope of the Convention are proceedings ancillary to arbitration proceedings, such as the appointment or dismissal of arbitrators, the fixing of the place of arbitration, or the extension of the time limit for making awards.

The Court of Justice further explained that provisional measures are not, in principle, ancillary to arbitration proceedings but are ordered in *parallel* to such proceedings and are intended as measures of support. They concern not arbitration as such but the protection of a wide variety of rights. Their place in the scope of the Convention is thus determined not by their own nature but by the nature of the rights which they serve to protect. Referring to its previous decision in *Reichert v Dresdner Bank*, the Court defined 'provisional and protective measures' within the meaning of Art 24 of the Convention. They are measures which, in matters within the scope of the Convention, are intended to preserve a factual or legal situation so as to safeguard rights the recognition of which is otherwise sought from the court having jurisdiction.

Unlike the opinion of the Advocate General, the Court held that the interim relief sought in this case for interim payment was not considered to be a provisional measure within the meaning of Art 24.

This case cannot be regarded as having given the answer to the question whether or not an anti-suit injunction is covered by the exception of arbitration. The issue here was whether or not the interim relief for payment of a debt was a provisional measure within Art 24, which clearly was not; the ECJ avoided entering into a wider argument as to the extent of the arbitration exception other than following its previous ruling in *Marc Rich*. The ECJ specifically defined protective measures as being required to protect a wide variety of rights which are determined not by their own nature but by the nature of the rights they serve to protect. For example, seeking security to protect the underlying right of a party's claim falls within the meaning of protective measures under Art 24. It is submitted that an anti-suit injunction should not fall within Art 24 (or presently, Art 31 of the Regulation) but should be seen as ancillary to arbitration with the sole purpose of preserving the underlying right to arbitrate and not litigate. Since arbitration is exempted from the Convention or Regulation, the anti-suit injunction should be also – but, at this stage, such a conclusion is uncertain until the ECJ determines the issue in *The Front Comor*.

---

40 *Marc Rich & Co AG v Società Italiana Impianti PA* (Case C-190/89) [1991] ECR I–3855, pp 3900–3901, para 18.
41 [1979] OJ C 59/71, pp 92, 93.

Unless the *Van Uden* case is interpreted as having paved the way for a retreat from the position of the ECJ in *Marc Rich*, which seems unlikely, academic arguments that this decision lends support to the view that an anti-suit injunction is outside the scope of the arbitration exception may be pessimistic.[42]

In the meantime, the opinion of the Advocate General in this case may lead litigants to be prudent. For example, a party claiming breach of an arbitration agreement should commence proceedings in the court of the seat of the arbitration for an appointment of arbitrator, or for a declaration of the validity of the agreement, which will certainly fall within the exception of arbitration and will not be within the Regulation, instead of applying for an anti-suit injunction.

3.1.1.4 Are the English courts encouraged or discouraged?

Further questions were explored in *The Ivan Zagubanski*,[43] a case involving a London arbitration clause incorporated into the bill of lading from the charter party. The cargo interests, some domiciled in Convention countries having lost their cargo due to an explosion of the ship, commenced proceedings in Marseilles. The shipowners applied to the English court for a declaration of the validity of the arbitration clause and also for an anti-suit injunction to restrain the claimants from continuing the proceedings in France. The claimants challenged the principle that the English court could grant an anti-suit injunction against a party domiciled in a Convention state.

It was held by Aikens J that the English proceedings for an anti-suit injunction were outside the scope of the Convention because their principal focus, or essential subject matter of the claim for relief to enforce the arbitration agreement, was within the arbitration exception of Art 1(4) of the Convention. He arrived at this conclusion by relying on the decision of the ECJ in *The Atlantic Emperor* (see above) and he was greatly assisted by the opinion of the Advocate General in that case and by the *Van Uden* decision.

In *The Front Comor*,[44] the ship collided with a jetty of an oil refinery in Syracuse, Italy. The insurers of the refinery paid the insured, the owners of the refinery who were also the charterers of the vessel, for the damage caused by the collision. They then issued proceedings under their subrogated rights against the owners of the ship in Italy. The charter party, however, contained a London arbitration clause, and the charterers commenced arbitration proceedings against the owners, claiming their uninsured losses.

The issues of liability in both the proceedings in Italy and the arbitration were substantially the same. The owners obtained an interim injunction from the English court to restrain the insurers from maintaining the Italian proceedings; they further applied to the Italian court and sought a stay of its proceedings.

---

42   Prof J Hill, op cit, fn 35; A Briggs 'Anti-Suit Injunctions and Utopian Ideals' LQR [2004] 120 (Oct) 529–533; cf 'Arbitration and Interim measures: in the twilight of the Brussels Convention' LMCLQ [2000] 99, by G Petrochilos, discussing an interpretation of the *Van Uden* case and its implications.

43   [2002] 1 Lloyd's Rep 106.

44   op cit fn 5.

One of the issues in the present context was whether the arbitration exception of Art 1(2)(d) of the Regulation encompassed the anti-suit injunction.

Colman J held that, as regards injunctions sought to restrain a breach of jurisdiction clauses, they are no longer permissible following *Turner v Grovit*, but the reasoning in that decision is inapplicable to anti-suit injunctions in respect of cases involving breach of an arbitration agreement which falls outside the scope of the Regulation. The judge found support also in the decision of the Court of Appeal in *The Hari Blum* (below), which confirmed the exclusion of arbitration; but, as far as the anti-suit injunction was concerned, the judge distinguished this case from the case in front of him. The House of Lords, which referred the question to the ECJ, stressed the importance of considering the practical reality of arbitration as a method resolving commercial disputes, which is excluded from the scope of the Regulation. In the opinion of Lord Hoffman, as much as the courts of Member States should trust each other in matters in which the Regulation applies, they should equally trust the arbitrators, or the court exercising supervisory jurisdiction to make orders requiring the parties of a binding arbitration agreement to arbitrate and not to litigate.

The Hari Blum[45]

This case concerned the loss of containerised cargo in transit shipped under a through bill of lading issued by Borneo Maritime Ltd, which eventually filed bankruptcy proceedings. The claim was paid by the insurers of the cargo owner, New India, who became assignees of the claim against the carrier. The insurers of the carrier for cargo liability were Through Transport Mutual (the club) whose terms with their assured contained a London arbitration clause. Because of the bankruptcy of the carrier, New India commenced proceedings against the club in Finland under Finnish law, which gave the claimant the right to proceed directly against the defendant's liability insurer. The club sought a declaration from the English court that New India was bound to pursue any claim in arbitration, because the substance of the claim was one to enforce against the club the right of indemnity which was available to the carrier, the assured with the club. In support of the arbitration agreement, the club sought also an anti-suit injunction to restrain the Finnish proceedings. Moore-Brick J granted the anti-suit injunction. The Court of Appeal (Lord Woolf, LCJ, and Clarke and Rix LJJ) ordered the discharge of the anti-suit injunction, but held that the English court was not obliged to stay its proceedings under Art 27 of the Regulation because the matter was not within the Regulation. It was open to the court to consider whether the arbitration exception applied even if it was the second seised. It further held that the judge was right to hold that the proceedings were outside the scope of the Regulation, because the principal focus of the matter was arbitration, which included, among other things, ancillary assistance to arbitration proceedings. Thus, it concluded that both a declaration that the arbitration agreement was valid and an injunction to restrain proceedings in

---

45 *Through Transport Mutual Insurance Association (Eurasia) Ltd v New India Assurance Co Ltd (The Hari Blum)* [2005] 1 Lloyd's Rep 67.

courts in breach of a binding arbitration agreement were within the exception. However, the club was sufficiently protected by the first declaration that there was a binding arbitration agreement and did not need the anti-suit injunction.

In view of this Court of Appeal decision, the issue of anti-suit injunctions in support of arbitration in *The Front Comor* leapfrogged the Court of Appeal to the House of Lords, which made a reference to the ECJ. Unfortunately, the answer to this question has not been given at the time of finalising the writing of this edition.

3.1.1.5 Questions of enforceability of judgments

Until a final ruling is made by the ECJ on this issue, litigants have to trust that the court seised of the proceedings brought in breach of the arbitration agreement will stay its proceedings. If not, then there will be issues of enforceability of the judgment obtained from the court of a Member State.

Article 34 of the Brussels Regulation concerning recognition and enforcement of judgments (see Chapter 6) requires a stricter test than its predecessor which was Art 27(1) of the Convention; namely, for a judgment not to be recognised, it must be manifestly contrary to public policy of the Member State in which recognition is sought. What would constitute 'manifestly' contrary to public policy will be an issue for interpretation in the context of a particular case.

As public policy varies between legal systems,[46] the English courts have considered that more universal criteria should be taken into account, such as international rules of justice, or the criterion of the interests of justice in a particular case, rather than the public policy of the foreign sovereign.[47]

If the English court has issued an anti-suit injunction, or a declaration that the arbitration agreement is valid, would recognition of the foreign judgment fall within the exception from recognition of Art 34(3)?

If all else fails, the final resort for a party against whom a foreign judgment has been issued in breach of an arbitration agreement would be to seek damages, and such proceedings will not offend the Regulation as they will be issued after the judgment of the court in the Member State is published. It is beyond the scope of this book to speculate on the circumstances in which damages can be sought, as this is a matter for specialised texts.

3.1.2 Breach of an English jurisdiction agreement falling outside the scope of the Regulation

Although in the context of the Regulation, following the decisions of the ECJ in *Turner v Grovit* and *Gasser v Misat*, the decision in *The Aeakos*[48] is no longer good law, it remains good law in respect of actions brought in contravention of an exclusive jurisdiction agreement the parties to which are not both domiciled in an

---

46 *Akai v People's Insurance Co* [1998] 1 Lloyd's Rep 90.

47 See paras 3.2.2 & 3.4 below.

48 *Continental Bank v Aeakos Naviera SA* [1994] 1 Lloyd's Rep 505 (CA). (See Ch 5 para 5.2).

EU country, or the competing courts are not both in Member States. With regard to cases not involving Contracting States to the Brussels or Lugano Convention or Member States of the Brussels Regulation, the principles were summarised in *A/S D/S Svendborg v Wansa*,[49] namely:

(a) there is a clear breach of an exclusive jurisdiction agreement;

(b) damages for that breach would not be an effective remedy; and

(c) the injunction will be granted unless there is a good reason not to do so.

The court has discretion whether or not to grant an anti-suit injunction.

A few decisions are mentioned here to show how the principles have evolved. In the early 1980s, an anti-suit injunction to restrain foreign proceedings in breach of an English exclusive jurisdiction clause would be granted if (a) the foreign proceedings were vexatious and oppressive, in the sense that there was no ground whatever for bringing the foreign proceedings; and (b) the party seeking the injunction would not be adequately protected by an award in damages.[50]

The reference to 'vexatious and oppressive' was made again by Staughton LJ in *Sohio Supply Co v Gatoil (USA) Inc*,[51] in which he held that to proceed in the foreign court in breach of a contract, which provides for an exclusive English jurisdiction, may well in itself be vexatious and oppressive in a given case.[52]

The principles were summarised by Rix J (as he then was) in ***The Angelic Grace***[53] (later approved by the Court of Appeal).[54] In this case (where proceedings were brought in Italy in breach of an English arbitration agreement), the court elaborated more specifically on the criteria of granting an anti-suit injunction. Such criteria must be that:

(a) the foreign proceedings are vexatious;

(b) without an injunction the defendants will be deprived of their contractual rights in a situation in which damages will be manifestly an inadequate remedy; and

(c) the injunction has been sought promptly and before the foreign proceedings are too far advanced.

Further refinement of the principles was made by Clarke J (as he then was) in ***A/S D/S Svendborg v Wansa***[55] (later approved by the Court of Appeal), which is the current law as mentioned earlier. It involved a breach of an English jurisdiction agreement (not being subject to the Brussels or Lugano Convention) and the

---

49 [1996] 2 Lloyd's Rep 559, p 570, affirmed [1997] 2 Lloyd's Rep 87 (CA).

50 *The Lisboa* [1980] 2 Lloyd's Rep 546, in which Italian proceedings had been brought in breach of the English jurisdiction agreement. This case would today fall within the European Union category, and an anti-suit injunction would be prohibited.

51 [1989] 2 Lloyd's Rep 588 (CA), p 592.

52 The Texan court, in this case, was not obliged to decline jurisdiction in the face of the parties' agreement to sue in England.

53 [1994] 1 Lloyd's Rep 168.

54 [1995] 1 Lloyd's Rep 87 (CA), p 96: Millett LJ said that, 'there was no good reason for diffidence in granting an injunction to restrain foreign proceedings on the clear and simple ground that the defendant has promised not to bring them' (see para 3.1.1.1 above).

55 Op. cit, fn 49.

injunction was granted.[56] He held that, where there is an exclusive jurisdiction clause, the parties should be held to their bargain and the court would grant the injunction if:

(a) the application for an injunction has been made promptly; and

(b) there exists no good reason to deny the injunction (such as delay or voluntary submission to the jurisdiction of the foreign court).

This decision shows that the courts have become less concerned with proof of 'vexatious and oppressive' foreign proceedings by the applicant for an anti-suit injunction when there is a breach of a jurisdiction agreement. The conduct of the other party in bringing foreign proceedings in breach of an English jurisdiction agreement may be vexatious in itself. It is for that party to prove a 'good or strong reason' for the court not to give effect to the exclusive jurisdiction clause or not to grant the injunction in cases where there has been a breach of contract. This has been followed in recent decisions: *OT Africa Line Ltd v Magic Sports Wear Corp*[57] (in which the injunction was granted), and by the House of Lords in **Donohue v Armco**,[58] in which, despite the breach of the English exclusive jurisdiction clause, no anti-suit injunction was ordered to restrain the proceedings in New York. There was proof of strong reasons for not giving effect to the exclusive jurisdiction clause and, thus, not granting the injunction because the defendants were victims of fraudulent conspiracy. In the circumstances, the interests of justice would be best served in one forum which was New York, rather than continue partly in England and partly in New York.

The jurisdiction agreement must be exclusive, and the parties must have intended it to be exclusive, thus precluding parallel proceedings elsewhere, unless there was some special reason and mere convenience could not count as a special reason.[59] An example of a non-exclusive jurisdiction can be found in the recent case of *Royal Bank of Canada v Cooperatieve Centrale BA*,[60] in which, although the jurisdiction clause provided for submission to the English court, it also contained a waiver of objections to any proceedings brought in a foreign court; in this case, that court was New York.

3.1.3 Discretion of the judge in 'breach of contract cases' which fall outside the scope of the Regulation

Discretion varies in degree depending on the circumstances of a case. For example, in arbitration cases, the judge will be less cautious in granting it; in other words, he

---

56 Similarly, in *Akai v People's Insurance Co* [1998] 1 Lloyd's Rep 90, the judge was in favour of giving effect to the jurisdiction agreement by an injunction, unless to do so would be contrary to public policy.

57 [2005] 1 Lloyd's Rep 252 and [2005] 2 Lloyd's Rep 170 (CA). The English action was retained pursuant to an exclusive jurisdiction clause and the anti-suit injunction against cargo interests (including their insurers) who pursued their claim against the carriers in Canada was not discharged. The Canadian statute providing for local jurisdiction was not a good reason for the court not to give effect to the contractual jurisdiction.

58 [2002] 1 Lloyd's Rep 425.

59 *Sabah Shipyard (Pakistan) Ltd v Islamic Republic of Pakistan* [2003] 2 Lloyd's Rep 571, in which the Court of Appeal granted the injunction to restrain the proceedings in Pakistan commenced as a pre-emptive strike to prevent proceedings in the agreed jurisdiction, England.

60 [2004] 1 Lloyd's Rep 471 (see under para 3 above).

has limited discretion not to grant it. In all other cases of breach of an English jurisdiction clause, except in cases in which the Brussels Regulation applies (and thus the injunction would be prohibited), the discretion not to grant the injunction is wider and caution is invariably exercised. Comity has a smaller role to play in these cases than in cases in which there is no jurisdiction agreement. The courts uphold party autonomy and regard that the true role of comity in such cases is to ensure that the parties' agreement is respected, unless there is a sufficiently strong reason not to do so. (*OT Africa Line Ltd v Magic Sports Wear Corp.* above).

3.2 The 'non-contract cases' and anti-suit injunctions

These encompass anti-suit injunctions where no breach of contract is involved. The issue of interference with foreign courts has been an acute problem, particularly in the non-contract cases. Therefore, the courts require that there should be proof of sufficient interest or connection with the English jurisdiction for the English court to consider the application.

The broad principle underlying the jurisdiction of a court to grant an anti-suit injunction under this category is that it is to be exercised when the ends of justice require it. However, in exercising its jurisdiction, the court must pay regard to comity, and so the jurisdiction is one which must be exercised with great caution.[61] Thus, the jurisdiction of the court is limited by the respect that should be shown to the jurisdiction of the foreign court in question. But, in certain cases, interference with the foreign court by issuing the injunction may be justified only for the ends of justice.

How this broad principle can be applied was analysed by Lord Goff, in *Airbus Industrie v Patel*,[62] who drew together principles from previous cases; in particular, from his decision in *Société Nationale Industries Aerospatiale v Lee Kui Jak* (the *Aerospatiale* case),[63] and the Canadian decision, *Amchem Products Inc v Workers Compensation Board*.[64]

3.2.1 The principles in the early 1980s

Prior to the *Aerospatiale* case, there were two House of Lords' decisions on anti-suit injunctions[65] of this category which had determined the issue on the basis of *forum non-conveniens* principles, but the jurisdiction was exercised with caution. The doctrine of *forum non-conveniens* applied only if there were two alternative fora having jurisdiction for a particular claim, one of which was England. But different criteria applied where there was only a single foreign forum whose court had competent jurisdiction to determine the merits of a particular claim. In a case of a single forum,

---

61 *Airbus Industrie v Patel* [1998] 1 Lloyd's Rep 631, p 637, per Lord Goff (see para 3.2.2 below).

62 Ibid.

63 [1987] 1 AC 871 (PC) (see below).

64 [1993] 102 DLR (4th) 96.

65 *Castano v Brown & Root* [1981] AC 557 and *British Airways v Laker Airways* [1985] AC 58.

Lord Scarman said in **British Airways v Laker**[66] that the English court would only interfere to restrain the foreign proceedings, if the conduct of the claimant was so unconscionable and unjust that, in accordance with English principles of a 'wide and flexible' equity, such conduct could be seen to be an infringement of an equitable right of the applicant. This equitable right not to be sued abroad, he said, arose only if the inequity was such that the English court ought to intervene to prevent injustice. He further said that such cases of anti-suit injunction must be few, because the court should be guided by caution.

On the facts of this case, which is classed as a 'single forum' case, Laker had sued BA in the US courts for protection of their trading interests. An anti-suit injunction, applied for in the English court by BA to restrain those proceedings, was refused because Laker's conduct was not unconscionable.

On the other hand, the *Aerospatiale* case below belongs to the 'alternative fora' sub-category of the non-contract cases. It is important to summarise the facts of this case for the purpose of comparison with the *Patel* case (see later), which set the general principle.

Société Nationale Industries Aerospatiale v Lee Kui Jak

A helicopter, which had been built in France and was operated and serviced by a Malaysian company, crashed at Brunei and a businessman was killed. His widow sued both the Malaysian company and the French manufacturer in the court of Brunei. In addition, she sued the French manufacturers in France (where the action was later discontinued) and, also, sued both defendants in Texas, under the law of which punitive damages and strict liability apply. The Texas court had jurisdiction over the manufacturers because they carried on business there. The widow's action against the Malaysian company in Brunei was settled eventually, but the French manufacturers issued a contribution notice on the Malaysian company in Brunei. The French manufacturers accepted service of a writ issued in Brunei by the owners and insurers of the helicopter seeking an indemnity. In the meantime, their application to the Texas court for a stay in favour of Brunei on the ground of *forum non-conveniens* was dismissed, despite their undertaking to protect the rights of the plaintiff – which she would have if the action continued in Texas. But the widow had also agreed that she would not pursue punitive damages and strict liability in Texas. In these circumstances, the Court of Appeal of Brunei dismissed the appeal by the French against the refusal by the lower court to grant an anti-suit injunction and held that the Texas court had become the appropriate forum, having regard to the advancement of the proceedings there.

On appeal to the Privy Council,[67] Lord Goff, examining the historical development of the court's jurisdiction with regard to anti-suit injunctions, declined to apply *forum non-conveniens* principles to the determination of whether or not an anti-suit injunction should be granted. He thought that such principles were only appropriate to applications for a stay of proceedings. His reasons were threefold: (i) if *forum non-conveniens* principles were applied, there would be a risk that the

---

66   [1985] AC 58, p 95.
67   [1987] 1 AC 871.

English court could arrogate jurisdiction only on the basis of England being the natural forum; (ii) the injunction would indirectly terminate the jurisdiction of the foreign court; and (iii) the mere fact that Brunei was the natural forum was not enough, of itself, to justify the grant of an injunction. It would only be granted to prevent injustice, which, in the context of this case, meant that the Texas proceedings must be shown to be vexatious or oppressive.

The elements of vexation or oppression, however, had in this case been neutralised by the plaintiff's agreement not to pursue punitive damages or strict liability in Texas. On the other hand, the fact that the defendant had undertaken to preserve the rights of the plaintiff (obtainable in Texas) in the Brunei proceedings was a factor in favour of Brunei. Therefore, since the advantage the plaintiff would have had in Texas would have been maintained in Brunei, a possible element of injustice to her had been eliminated.

At the end, the most important factors in favour of granting the injunction against Texas proceedings were the claims for contribution and indemnity brought in Brunei. Had the Texas proceedings continued, there would have been multiplicity of actions. For this reason the injunction was granted.

3.2.2 The new formula – stricter approach

Lord Goff in *Airbus v Patel* clarified the principle with regard to alternative fora cases, as he had previously formulated it in the *Aerospatiale* case. For the first time, he imposed limitations to the granting of the injunction on grounds of comity upon both categories, the 'alternative fora' and the 'single forum' cases.

Airbus v Patel [68]

The aeroplane in this case belonged to Indian Airlines, which flew from Bombay to Bangalore; it struck the ground and caught fire on landing at its destination. Ninety-two passengers died. The London families of British citizens carried on board (four died and four were injured) sued Airbus in Texas. The defendants sought an injunction from the English court to restrain those proceedings on the ground that they were vexatious and oppressive. Colman J refused to grant it. The Court of Appeal granted it, mainly because India was the natural forum. Applying *forum non-conveniens* principles, it regarded Texas as a non-appropriate forum.

The House of Lords reversed the decision of the Court of Appeal and set out the new formula (below) to be applied to applications for anti-suit injunctions in such cases.

Twofold requirement: the marriage of 'comity' with the 'ends of justice'

There is one general non-rigid rule applicable to both, the 'alternative fora' and the 'single forum' cases, namely: (a) there must be a sufficient interest or connection between the action and England for an intervention with the foreign court by an

---

68 [1998] 1 Lloyd's Rep 631.

anti-suit injunction to be considered (the comity requirement); and (b) such an intervention must be for the ends of justice.[69]

Lord Goff set out the guidelines for the court's approach with regard to 'comity' in each case. In particular:

(a) In the 'alternative fora' cases, where England is the natural forum and the jurisdiction of a foreign court has been invoked, there is sufficient interest to justify an intervention by the English court in order to protect its jurisdiction. On this basis, there would be no infringement of comity. Thus, the court will examine only whether the interests of justice are served, taking into account the claimant's advantage there and the possible loss of advantage for the defendant in the natural forum. It will also consider whether any possible oppression in the foreign court was neutralised. It will seek to ascertain what the foreign court will be likely to do. Would the foreign court stay its proceedings itself observing judicial comity?

(b) In the 'single forum' cases, where there is only one foreign court having jurisdiction, but the jurisdiction of another foreign court is invoked, the question for the English court when an application for an anti-suit injunction is made is this: could the English court be asked to guard the jurisdiction of the single forum by issuing an anti-suit injunction? *In this situation, the role of comity has been prominent* (emphasis added). At first glance, an intervention by the English court would be inconsistent with comity.

Therefore, the court will proceed in two stages. At the first stage, it will examine whether there is sufficient interest or connection with England, which warrants the court's intervention for the ends of justice. Such a connection could be established if the transaction was made here,[70] or there were grounds of public policy. If there is no connection or sufficient interest, the matter will be closed at the first stage by refusing the injunction. If, on the other hand, there was such a connection, the comity requirement would be satisfied, as it would be if England was the natural forum in the 'alternative fora' cases. Then, the court will proceed to the second stage, during which it will examine whether the foreign proceedings against which the injunction was sought were oppressive. If they were, an injunction would be granted, because to allow them to continue would be against the ends of justice.[71]

In a recent decision of the Court of Appeal, *The Western Regent*,[72] limitation of liability proceedings were commenced in England (the limitation action) in respect of collision liability and the liability action was commenced in Texas. The collision occurred in the Shetlands, North Sea. Upon an application for an anti-suit injunction to restrain the Texas proceedings, the court held that the Texas liability proceedings were not unconscionable, although US law did not follow the 1976

---

69 Generally speaking, Lord Goff said, injustice can occur when the foreign proceedings are vexatious and oppressive and, as he had said in the *Aerospatiale* case, these terms, historically, have had different meanings. From the tenor of his judgment in the *Airbus* case, however, he seemed to prefer no reference to these terms.

70 *Midland Bank plc v Laker Airways Ltd* [1986] QB 689.

71 These approaches are inferred from the conclusion of the analysis by Lord Goff [1998] 1 Lloyd's Rep 631, p 642.

72 [2005] 2 Lloyd's Rep 359, op cit fn 22.

Limitation Convention, and refused to grant the anti-suit injunction. Considerations of comity played an important part in the decision. The English limitation proceedings were not stayed. The Texas court had to decide on the effect, if any, of the English limitation decree on the Texas proceedings.

By contrast, indulgence in forum shopping was disapproved of, and an anti-suit injunction was granted, in *Cadre SA v Astra Asigurari SA*[73] in which the defendant, despite the decision of the English court that England was the natural and appropriate forum for the case, continued to seek the determination of the dispute in Romania without any good reason.

3.3 Mixture of 'breach of contract' and 'non-contract' cases

A good example of a situation like this is *Bouygues v Caspian (sub nom BOS-400).*[74] It is a paradigm case of numerous proceedings and court orders, which were issued in two jurisdictions, England and South Africa.

BOS-400

By a towage contract, Bouygues, a French company and owners of the tow, *BOS-400*, engaged the services of the tug, *Tigr*, owned by Caspian, a Russian company. The tug was under time charter to Ultisol, which was managed by a Dutch company. As the tow was approaching Cape Town, the tow lines parted in stormy conditions and it was driven ashore to the rocks becoming a total loss. Bouygues claimed damages against Ultisol, Caspian and the Cape Town port authority, Portner. Proceedings were brought in both England and South Africa. Since, in the towage contract, Bouygues and Ultisol had agreed English jurisdiction, an injunction was granted by Clarke J to Ultisol restraining Bouygues from proceeding in South Africa, while such an injunction was refused to Caspian by Morison J. Both Caspian and Ultisol issued third party notices to join Portner in the English proceedings. Colman J refused to set aside these notices on application by Portner. Rix J granted a declaration sought by Ultisol and Caspian to limit their liability in England, where the 1976 Limitation Convention is applicable, while the 1957 Convention is applicable in South Africa. Walker J refused to set aside the anti-suit injunction granted by Clarke J and to stay the limitation proceedings. There were appeals against the orders of Clarke, Colman, Rix and Walker JJ.

The Court of Appeal discharged the anti-suit injunction, set aside the third party joinder of Portner and stayed the liability proceedings in England, in the light of change of circumstances. Since the time of the order that had been made by Clarke J, the action against Portner was substantially advanced in South Africa (called the Portner factor). Also, the fact that Morison J subsequently refused an anti-suit injunction to Caspian against Bouygues radically altered the possibilities of avoiding multiplicity of proceedings, with its attendant risk of conflicting decisions. Thus, the argument that Bouygues should be kept to its contractual

---

73   [2006] 1 Lloyd's Rep 560.
74   [1998] 2 Lloyd's Rep 461.

bargain with Utisol was counterbalanced. The anti-suit injunction against Bouygues was discharged for a good reason – being widely interpreted – which was the existence of proceedings in South Africa involving the same issues and facts between parties not bound by a contractual jurisdiction. The Portner factor constituted a special countervailing factor (otherwise known as a 'good reason') against the anti-suit injunction.

The English liability proceedings were stayed on the ground of *forum non-conveniens*, as South Africa was the natural forum for the resolution of the disputes regarding liability. The limitation action, which was considered quite separate from the liability actions, was maintained in England.[75]

3.4 Common considerations used in both contract and non-contract categories

3.4.1 The phrase 'vexatious and oppressive conduct' is reconsidered

Historically, since the 19th century, serious consideration has been given by the English courts to whether or not the foreign proceedings were brought to oppress the defendant.

Thus, in most decisions concerning either anti-suit injunctions or stay of proceedings, proof that the foreign proceedings were vexatious and oppressive would lead the judge to exercise its discretion in favour of the anti-suit injunction (to restrain the continuing of the foreign proceedings) or against the stay of the English proceedings.

However, in the cases concerning stay of proceedings on the ground of another forum being the more appropriate, the term 'vexatious and oppressive' was effectively abolished by the House of Lords in the *Macshannon*[76] case. This was because of the moral connotations attached to these words and the difficulty for the defendant to prove that there was something wrong in the character of the plaintiff.

In considering the grant of an anti-suit injunction, different meanings were attributed to the term 'vexatious and oppressive' by the judges in various authorities, concerning either the contract or non-contract cases, depending on the context of a particular case. For example:

(a) In *The Angelic Grace*, it was said that it would be 'vexatious and oppressive' to allow the contract breaker to persist with the breach of contract where damages would be an inadequate remedy;

(b) In *Toepfer v Societe Cargill*,[77] it was said that it would be 'vexatious and oppressive' if the party, who was in breach of an arbitration agreement, was allowed to continue the foreign proceedings. This would be so if there was no proof that

---

75 It should be noted that, since this case did not fall within the ambit of the Brussels Convention, there was no prohibition on separating the limitation from the liability action.

76 *Macshannon v Rockware Glass Ltd* [1978] 1 All ER 625 (see Ch 5).

77 [1998] 1 Lloyd's Rep 379.

the foreign court would stay its proceedings under the mandatory provisions of the New York Convention 1958;

(c) In the case of both *Estonian Shipping Ltd v Wansa*[78] and *Akai Pty Ltd v People's Insurance Co Ltd*,[79] the public interest was balanced against the interest of the parties. It was explained by the court that it would be 'vexatious and oppressive' if multiple proceedings were allowed where the plaintiff resorted to the foreign court in order to evade important policies of the English jurisdiction;

(d) In the context of the Texas cases, the non-contract category, the fact that the Texas jurisdiction was so wide and extra-territorial, so as to be contrary to accepted principles of international law, was 'vexatious and oppressive';

(e) If it was shown that the claim in the foreign court was bound to fail, then the making of such a claim could be seen to be frivolous and vexatious (although a case of this kind was thought to be rare).[80]

In the seminal decisions by Lord Goff concerning the modern approach to anti-suit injunctions, he explained, in the *Aerospatiale* case, that although the words 'vexatious and oppressive' could have different meaning in different contexts, he was inclined, in the *Patel* case, to agree, albeit obiter, with Judge Sopinka in the *Amchem* case, who preferred to use the 'ends of justice' test instead of 'vexatious and oppressive'. Various considerations are taken into account by the court to determine 'the ends of justice' in each case.

The difference between the two terminologies is important, because proof of vexatious and oppressive conduct places a heavy burden on the applicant for an anti-suit injunction in the same way as it had been in applications for a stay of proceedings.

In legal parlance, there is a tendency by lawyers to use the term 'vexatious and oppressive' or 'unconscionable' conduct of the person pursuing the foreign proceedings (who should be restrained) to distinguish applications of anti-suit injunctions concerning non-contract cases from those applications brought to restrain breach of a jurisdiction or arbitration agreement in which the test is proof of a 'good or strong reason' not to grant the injunction.

The legal principles have, however, become clearer in recent years, as confirmed by a number of important decisions and there is emphasis on the interests of justice.[81] The questions for the court are: (i) whether the ends of justice would be met by the grant of the injunction; (ii) whether it would be unconscionable to allow the continuation of the foreign proceedings; and (iii) what degree of caution must be exercised (which is a matter of comity).

---

78 [1997] 2 Lloyd's Rep 183.
79 [1998] 1 Lloyd's Rep 90.
80 *Shell v Coral* [1999] 2 Lloyd's Rep 606.
81 *Airbus v Patel* [1998] 1 Lloyd's Rep 631; *Donohue v Armco* [2002] 1 Lloyd's Rep 425; *Seismic Shipping v Total* (*The Western Regent*) [2005] 2 Lloyd's Rep 359.

3.4.2 The importance of 'comity' in all cases

As has been shown, comity is part of the general principle limiting the jurisdiction of the court to exercise its jurisdiction by granting an anti-suit injunction in the non-contract cases. Comity has also been considered in the 'breach of contract' cases, in which it has been stressed that the court should exercise its discretion with caution for reasons of comity. In cases which are within the ambit of the European Union jurisdiction rules, the concept of comity is looked at now in terms of the mutual trust between Member States. In cases where there is a breach of an arbitration agreement, regard to comity is not negligible, as was pointed out by the Court of Appeal in *The Angelic Grace* although, in a straightforward case, there was little mileage in a 'ritual incantation' of the doctrine of comity.[82] In other circumstances, particularly when there is a question of validity of an arbitration clause under foreign law, comity may require caution.[83] Furthermore, considerations of comity grew in importance the longer the foreign suit continued, and the more the parties and the judge had engaged in its conduct and management.[84]

3.5 Practical considerations and risk management

It is now firmly settled by the ECJ that anti-suit injunctions are prohibited as between Member States to the Brussels/Lugano Conventions or the Brussels Regulation. Even prior to the recent decisions of the ECJ, the German courts were reluctant to recognise anti-suit injunctions issued by the English courts, as they were considered an infringement of the foreign court's sovereignty.[85] This view is strongly rejected by the English courts because the injunction aims to restrain the person from pursuing his case in the foreign court, although it affects the foreign court indirectly and, for this reason, the jurisdiction is exercised with caution.[86] Even if the matter is not between Member States to the Brussels Regulation, litigants should be cautious before they apply for an anti-suit injunction, the proceedings for which will cause unnecessary costs.[87]

There must be a balancing act of the advantages and disadvantages, before an application for an anti-suit injunction is made, and promptness in issuing the application, if the circumstances favour such a procedure, is an important factor, as has been shown in the cases discussed.

There may be an alternative protection for an aggrieved party instead of applying for an anti-suit injunction. The injunction may not be needed if it is possible to

---

82 [1995] 1 Lloyd's Rep 87 (CA), *per* Millett LJ, p 96.

83 This point was explained by Rix J in *Credit Suisse v MLC* [1999] 1 Lloyd's Rep 767, p 781.

84 *Royal Bank of Canada v Cooperatieve Centrale* [2004] 1 Lloyd's Rep 471 (involving a non-exclusive English jurisdiction clause and proceedings in New York which were quite advanced).

85 Harris, J, 'Enforcement of an English anti-suit injunction' (1997) CJQ 283, pp 283–89.

86 *Société Nationale Industries Aerospatiale v Lee Kui Jak* [1987] AC 871, per Lord Goff.

87 *Akai v People's Insurance Co* [1998] 1 Lloyd's Rep 90, *per* Thomas J (on breach of an English jurisdiction clause by proceedings in Australia, the defendant applied for an anti-suit injunction in the Singaporean court instead of England. Although the injunction was granted later by the English court, Akai was ordered to indemnify the other party for its expenses to defend the Singaporean injunctive proceedings).

resist the enforcement of the foreign judgment obtained – in cases in which the Brussels Regulation does not apply – in breach of a jurisdiction agreement.

Another important consideration must be the existence of related multiple actions commenced in various jurisdictions, two of which are contractual, or one is contractual and the other is the natural forum. Interference in such cases may be justified, if there are reasons of justice to restrain the foreign proceedings and determine the related actions in England,[88] or to stay the English proceedings in favour of the natural forum, despite the jurisdiction agreement, particularly when there are parties in the foreign proceedings not bound by any agreement.[89]

3.6 Conclusion

It has been apparent, in all cases, that the judges pondered judicial comity. Leaving aside the cases to which the Brussels or Lugano Convention or the Brussels Regulation apply, anti-suit injunctions may be considered in two situations: (a) in cases of breach of a valid arbitration agreement, or a jurisdiction agreement, in which the injunction may be granted unless there is proof of a strong cause not to grant it; and (b) in non-contract cases in which considerations of comity and ends of justice need to be taken into account before granting the injunction.

The rule in *Airbus v Patel* is sound and straightforward. The basic elements of the *Patel* case are the ends of justice and respect for the other court's jurisdiction (comity). The court makes an inquiry whether the foreign proceedings against which the injunction is sought are unconscionable, and whether the ends of justice would be served if an injunction were not granted.

With regard to that inquiry, the following non-exhaustive list of factors may be relevant: (a) whether the foreign forum is acting oppressively by not staying its proceedings;[90] (b) whether its rules are against international rules of justice[91] or public policy;[92] (c) whether there is unconscionable conduct in the pursuit of the foreign proceedings;[93] or (d) whether in the competing forum there are related actions which must be tried together.[94]

Such factors are also considered by the courts, to some extent, in appropriate cases concerning breach of an English jurisdiction agreement.

---

88   See, eg, *A/S D/S Svendborg v Wansa* [1996] 2 Lloyd's Rep 559, where the Sierra Leone proceedings were restrained because of evidence that the party proceeding there was boasting that he could manipulate the legal system in Sierra Leone to obtain justice in his favour.

89   *BOS-400* [1998] 2 Lloyd's Rep 461; *Credit Suisse First Boston (Europe) Ltd v MLC (Bermuda) Ltd* [1999] 1 Lloyd's Rep 767.

90   As shown in the cases referred to above; see also *General Star International Indemnity v Stirling Cooke Brown Reinsurance Brokers Ltd* [2002] EWHC 3.

91   As in *Société Nationale Industries Aerospatiale v Lee Kui Jak* [1987] 1 AC 871 (PC).

92   *Akai v People's Insurance Co* [1998] 1 Lloyd's Rep 90, but public policy varies between legal systems.

93   *Glencore International AG v Exter Shipping Ltd* [2002] 2 All ER (Comm) 1.

94   *Bos-400* [1998] 2 Lloyd's Rep 461.

PART II

SUBSTANTIVE LAW

OVERVIEW

In this edition, all chapters concerning substantive law based on common law, as affected by Conventions, statutes and International Regulations or EU Directives, appear together in this Part.

It contains nine chapters: Chapter 8 deals with ownership and management of ships, touching upon the significance of flag States in the context of a regulatory regime; it also explores the legal implications of the International Safety Management Code concerning the implementation of safety management systems for ship operations, as imposed by Chapter IX of the International Convention for Safety of Life at Sea (SOLAS) 1974. Chapter 9 highlights important issues of the law relating to ship mortgages. Chapter 10 deals with the general legal principles of shipbuilding contracts, and Chapter 11 with the essential aspects of the law relating to ship sale and purchase. Chapter 12 deals with the Collision Regulations and the law relating to both criminal and civil liabilities arising from collisions between ships. Chapter 13 explores the law of salvage. Chapter 14 analyses the contractual relationship between contracting parties and their liabilities to third parties. Chapter 15 is new in this edition and explains briefly the elementary aspects of general average. Chapter 16 is concerned with the rights and duties of port authorities, as well as with the liabilities of users of port facilities to the port authority.

CHAPTER 8

OWNERSHIP AND MANAGEMENT OF SHIPS; THE INTERNATIONAL SAFETY MANAGEMENT CODE AND LEGAL IMPLICATIONS

1 INTRODUCTION

This chapter begins with the concept of the ship's flag, the regulatory regime, safety and security standards, registration of British ships and ownership principles. It continues with management of ships and examines the effect of the ISM Code upon the liabilities of shipowners and ship-operators. The choice of a flag which a ship flies is of great importance, particularly, with regard to whether or not the international safety regulations are rigorously enforced, as will be seen later.

1.1 Importance and role of the ship's flag [1]

Ships must possess a national character to be allowed to use the high seas freely. They have the nationality of the State whose flag they are entitled to fly, which is the symbol of the ship's nationality. Individual States fix the conditions for the entry of ships in their registries. Connecting factors between a ship and a State, such as the incorporation of the owning company of the ship in that State, provide a test for the ship's nationality. However, some States may not require the ship to be registered in the records of the State where the owning company is registered. The registration of a ship in the public records of a State attributes the national character of that State to the ship and the documents issued to the ship by the competent authority of that State are evidence of the ship's nationality. The registration of a vessel under the flag of a State implies that her operation will be subjected to the laws and fiscal regime of that country. Jurisdiction over vessels on the high seas will reside with that State. The law of the vessel's flag will govern offences committed on the high seas.[2] Nationality of ships enables them to engage in trade, to enter ports and deal with the authorities of other nations. International law lays down rules regulating how the freedom to sail on the high seas should be used. The Geneva Convention on the High Seas 1958 and the United Nations Convention 1982 on the Law of the Sea require States to exercise effective control over ships flying their flag.

With the opening of European Union membership, re-flagging of ships from one European register to another for cheaper labour may attract industrial action by the International Transport Workers' Federation and the national seamen's union in order to ensure payment to seamen at the higher rates. Threatened industrial action

---

1 Coles, R, Ready, N (editors), *Ship Registration: Law and Practice*, 2002, LLP. The editors deal with the subject from a comparative perspective, as between British and other well-known registers.
2 *The Oteri v The Queen* [1977] 1 Lloyd's Rep 105 (PC).

may be lawful in one Member State and unlawful in another, but it imposes restrictions on the freedom of establishment under the EC Treaty. To determine whether or not an injunction to restrain threatened industrial action could be granted was a matter for the ECJ in the recent case of *Viking Line ABP v ITF*.[3]

There are various factors that influence shipowners to choose a flag of a particular State. The most important factors are economic considerations and operating costs.

1.2 Flags of convenience

Maritime nations, historically, required a 'genuine link' between a vessel and the State in which the ship was registered. Market forces and attractions offered by 'open registries' known as 'flags of convenience' brought a significant decline of the traditional ship registries since the 1950s.

Subject to international law, States have had freedom to set their own regulations for ships carrying their flag. Some States have been very liberal in the regulations for entry of foreign ships in their ship registers, making it very convenient and opportune for shipowners to register their ships with them. This gave rise to the proliferation of open registers or flag of convenience States which provided attractive advantages.[4] The most important of such advantages have been: the confidentiality of who is the actual beneficial owner of the ship,[5] the allowance of ownership and control of the ship by non-citizens of that State, no income tax (only a registration fee and annual fees), the freedom of manning of those ships by non-nationals. The tax advantages and the freedom of manning have been the greatest stimuli for shipowners to register under a flag of convenience. In addition, open registries enable the shipowners to distance themselves from the political and economic situation of their country.

The origin of flag of convenience has its roots in the ingenuity of British merchants in the 16th century, who used the Spanish flag to avoid Spanish monopoly restrictions on trade with the West Indies, and later of British fishermen in the 17th to 19th centuries, who tried to avoid fishing restrictions imposed by Great Britain by using either the French or the Norwegian flags. In the early 20th century prohibition laws of the USA preventing the sale of liquor signalled the beginning of the use of open registries. This resulted in the transfer of ships to the Panamanian flag, which at the time had a liberal maritime law to attract foreign tonnage. Another factor contributing to the boost of the Panamanian flag was the worsening of the political situation in Europe in the 1930s and the outbreak of war in 1939. The dissatisfaction with the Panamanian flag, however, was first shown after the Sec-

---

3   [2006] 1 Lloyd's Rep 303.

4   See op cit, fn 1, Coles and Ready, Chapter 2. See, also, Spruyt, J, *Ship Management*, 1990, LLP, pp 50–51.

5   However, with the implementation of the ISM Code and legislation in the USA, transparency of ownership is required by the identification of the entities responsible for the operation and management of the ship, as will be seen later, but this may not necessarily reveal the beneficial ownership.

ond World War, due to political instability in Panama, and this gave rise to other flags of convenience, such as the Liberian flag.[6] Other nations raised such flags of convenience,[7] some of which have been criticised for being lax in preserving high standards in terms of enforcing safety regulations.

However, safety aspects of sub-standard ships linked to flags of convenience and sub-standard labour conditions on board have led to a campaign against those flags for many years. Moreover, in recent years, the fact that incidents of casualties of ships under flags of convenience have outnumbered the casualties of ships under other flags has alerted the international shipping community to action. The safety aspect has a lot to do with the age of ships, as well as construction and lack of a rigorous system of maintenance by regular surveys and repairs. Classification societies play a great role here as well and there has been a move through the International Maritime Organisation (IMO), in co-operation with the International Association of Classification Societies (IACS), to consolidate common rules for the construction of ships.

An attempt to attract European shipowners away from flags of convenience has been pursued by the European Commission, which proposed the establishment of a European Community (EC) ship register (EUROS) in 1989. However, for such a flag to be successful, the incentives offered have to be greater than those offered by the existing flag States.

1.3 The regulatory regime

1.3.1 The flag and port state controls – safety measures

The International Convention on the Law of the Sea 1982, coupled with the International Convention for Prevention of Maritime Pollution (MARPOL 1973/1978), oblige each of its Contracting States to take such measures for ships flying its flag as are necessary to ensure safety at sea and the protection of the marine environment. Further duties are imposed upon flag States by the SOLAS and the STCW (Standards of Training, Certification and Watchkeeping for Seafarers, 1978 as amended in 1995) Conventions. These duties relate to construction, equipment, seaworthiness, manning and training, and are carried out by regular surveys of ships under their flag. The surveys are delegated to classification societies who issue certificates of compliance (see later). Although the major flag States carry out their responsibilities admirably well, others do not, or they are not even signatories to the International Conventions, such as the Law of the Sea Convention or the MARPOL.

The failure of some flag States to exercise effective control on the enforcement of international safety regulations, the slackness of some shipping companies to

---

6   Op cit, Cole and Ready, fn 1, pp 18–19.

7   Algeria, Barbados, Belize, Bulgaria, China, Cuba, Croatia, Cyprus, Egypt, Estonia, Honduras, Iran, Lebanon, Liberia, Lithuania, Malta, Panama, Portugal, Romania, St Vincent and Grenadines, Syria, Vanuatu, Ukraine. The number of flags of convenience has increased, see Cole and Ready at p 17.

observe safety issues, the poor performance of some classification societies to perform their duties properly during inspections, coupled with increased public interest in protecting the marine environment, led to new measures of control. Thus, to counterbalance these deficiencies, the Port State Control (PSC)[8] emerged in Europe first as a second line of defence. Coastal States have had to harmonise their approach to Port State Control by membership of the Paris Memorandum of Understanding (MOU)[9] 1982 which ensures that ships calling in the ports of a port State are inspected and, if they have not complied with international safety standards, may be detained. The MOU established uniformity of Port State Control on regional bases. The success of the MOU in Europe led to the establishment of other regional MOU, eg the Latin America MOU 1992, the Tokyo MOU 1993 covering the Asia/ Pacific region, and the MOU 1996 covering the Caribbean region.

However, before the ISM Code came into operation, the Achilles' heel of the PSC was the lack of risk analysis, as the late Lord Donaldson had stated: 'If ship owners and ship operators undertook a serious risk analysis to prevent detention by the Port State Control, the problem would go away, but, it is a fact of life, that some owners do not'.[10] He had taken an active role in ship safety, and commented that ship safety – and the consequences of any lack of it – is a topic which is as fascinating as it is complex. His recommendations made after the public inquiry on The Braer disaster, which he chaired, are contained in the report *Safer Ships; Cleaner Seas*. The scope of this, he said:

> ... covered every aspect of manning, operation, maintenance, classification and insurance of vessels. It covered Flag State and Port State Controls, surveillance, tracking and identification of vessels. It covered pollution protection and clean-up. It did so in the context of domestic and international law, as well as on a practical, day to day basis.

Remedial action in shipping has to be international in both its application and enforcement. He further said:

> Insofar as there is a regulatory regime, it is to be found in international Conventions evolved through the International Maritime Organisation, a United Nations agency. Primary responsibility for enforcement lies with the States whose flags the vessels fly – Flag State Control. However, coastal States at which vessels call are entitled to take measures to protect themselves from sub-standard shipping – Port State Control. The principal measure consists of detaining ships, which do not come up to the internationally agreed standard . . . But Port and Flag States are not the only players in this battle to raise standards. Classification societies have a major part to play.[11]

---

8   For details of the evolution of the Port State Control system see Kasoulides, G, *Port State Control and Jurisdiction*, 1993, Kluwer and further developments in Ozcayir, ZO, *Port State Control* 2nd edn (2004).

9   Membership of the Paris MOU 1982 includes the UK, Belgium, Denmark, Finland, France, Germany, Greece, the Republic of Ireland, Italy, The Netherlands, Norway, Portugal, Spain and Sweden (in Europe) and Canada. The original countries increased to 25.

10   See Lord Donaldson's paper, 'The ISM Code: the road to discovery?' [1998] LMCLQ 526, delivered at the inaugural lecture in memory of Professor Cadwallader, 26 March 1998, the London Shipping Law Centre, UCL Law Faculty.

11   See Lord Donaldson, 'Safer ships; cleaner seas – full speed ahead or dead slow?', the Donald O'May (annual memorial) lecture at the Institute of Maritime Law, University of Southampton, 12 November 1997 (published in [1998] LMCLQ 170, pp 171, 172).

The Paris MOU, the principle of which has spread worldwide, has taken a more proactive approach to monitoring compliance in recent years, and it works particularly because the new measures include the publication of data and trends of ships which are deficient, as well as the banning of these ships from the region.

However, despite the current trend for implementation by owners and operators of a systematic risk assessment, which primarily derives from the ISM Code's philosophy, not all ship operators have adopted a culture of self-imposed regulation, and there are still sub-standard ships which may avoid visiting ports where control is vigorous. There is a need for close co-operation between flag and port States. If there was more rigorous enforcement of regulations by flag States, the problem of sub-standard ships might be diminished. In response to this, the IMO has commenced a system for flag State voluntary self-assessment, or audit by each other, in order to encourage co-operation between flag States and give assistance to those States where needed in terms of ensuring that the international regulations are properly enforced (see further Chapter 20, below).

If such a system does not work in due course, it may be necessary to take more formal measures, perhaps of a statutory nature.

The ISM Code is examined later.

1.3.2 The role of the ISPS Code for security measures

In addition, there has been the implementation of the International Ship and Port Security (ISPS) Code in view of awareness of the threat of terrorists after September 11, 2001 and concerns that piracy is funding terrorism.

The IMO, by Resolution A.924(22), reviewed measures to prevent acts of terrorism and a brand new Chapter XI–2 (Special measures to enhance maritime security) has been added to SOLAS, which was implemented on 1st July 2004.

This chapter applies to passenger ships and cargo ships of 500 gross tonnage and upwards, including high-speed craft, mobile offshore drilling units and port facilities serving such ships engaged on international voyages. Regulation XI–2/2 of the new chapter enshrines the International Ship and Port Facilities Security Code (ISPFS Code). Part A of this Code is mandatory, and Part B contains guidance on how best to comply with the mandatory requirements.

The Regulation requires Flag administrations to set security levels and ensure the provision of security level information to ships entitled to fly their flag. Prior to entering a port, or whilst in a port, within the territory of a Contracting Government, a ship shall comply with the requirements for the security level set by that Contracting Government, if that security level is higher than the security level set by the administration for that ship.

Both ships and ports are required to comply with this chapter. It should be noted that SOLAS was originally meant to apply to ships only; its application has now been expanded to shipping companies through the ISM and ISPS Codes, and to ports through the ISPFS Code.

SOLAS Regulation XI–2/9.1.1 provides that every ship to which the ISPS Code applies is subject to control when in a port of another Contracting Government by Delegated Ashore Officers (DAOs), who may be the same as those carrying out the functions of Port State Control. Such control shall be limited to verifying that there is onboard a valid International Ship Security Certificate (ISSC) or a valid Interim ISSC which, if valid, shall be accepted, unless there are clear grounds for believing that the ship is not in compliance with the requirements of Chapter XI–2 or Part A of the ISPS Code. The clear grounds will be determined by inspection of general and specific security aspects.

Before entry to a port, ships will be required to supply information, including details of their ISSC, current security level, the name of the last 10 ports visited, their interactions with other ships and ports, along with other practical related security information. Based on this information, the Contracting Government will identify any deficiencies. Where deficiencies exist, the ship may be denied entry if it is considered it presents a serious security threat.

Where no *clear grounds* are established before the ship enters port, the ship may still be subject to control measures. These may be carried out in conjunction with established Port State Control inspections. Where control measures are implemented these will be reported to the flag administration and copied to the Recognised Security Organisation (RSO).

Regulation XI–2/8 confirms the role of the Master in exercising his professional judgment over decisions necessary to maintain the security of the ship. It says he shall not be constrained by the company, the charterer or any other person in this respect. However, safety issues should not be compromised over security issues, which sometimes causes problems in USA ports, where there is a tendency for the authorities to overreact over security issues.

Regulation XI–2/6 required all ships to be provided with a ship security alert system by 2004 and the remainder by 2006. When activated, the ship security alert system shall initiate and transmit a ship-to-shore security alert to a competent authority designated by the administration, identifying the ship, its location and indicating that the security of the ship is under threat or it has been compromised. The system will not raise any alarm on-board the ship. The ship security alert system shall be capable of being activated from the navigation bridge and in, at least, one other location.

Regulation XI–2/10 covers requirements for port facilities, providing among other things for Contracting Governments to ensure that port facility security assessments are carried out and that port facility security plans are developed, implemented and reviewed in accordance with the ISPFS Code.

Other regulations in this chapter cover the provision of information to IMO, the control of ships in port (including measures such as the delay, detention, restriction of operations including movement within the port, or expulsion of a ship from port).[12]

1.3.3 *The role of classification societies in the safety of ships*

Classification societies have two functions: first, they carry out structural surveys on ships which are entered with them and issue certificates that the ships are com-

---

12   See, further, www.imo.org.

plying with the rules and regulations of the particular class; they can also advise shipbuilding yards on the proper construction of ships. The certificates of class are required by the SOLAS Convention and are very important for the trading of ships, but are not certificates of seaworthiness.

Second, classification societies carry out statutory surveys on behalf of flag States to verify that the ships entered with them comply with the international mandatory requirements of SOLAS and MARPOL Conventions. For example, certificates required by SOLAS to be issued by the Flag administrations are: international tonnage certificate, passenger ship safety certificate, cargo ship safety certificate, load line certificates, etc. In addition, classification societies are authorised to carry out formal audits of ships and operating companies, and issue certificates of compliance with the particular requirements of the ISM and ISPS Codes. Such certificates are valid for a certain period of time and can be verified by an intermediate audit.

Classification societies can now be appointed as the Recognised Organisation (RO) of flag States for the above purposes, and are subject to further regulations regarding recognition and responsibilities emanating from the EU.

Some classification societies have over the years shown weaknesses in the performance of their duties regarding structural surveys, mainly because they are not authorised, nor are they regulated by statute for the issue of classification certificates, as is the case with airworthiness certificates issued by statutory bodies in the aviation industry. The lack of a statutory regulatory regime for classification societies permits some of them to be more lenient than their competitors in granting grace periods within which the recommendations of maintenance or repairs can be completed after a survey on structural defects is carried out.

This particular weakness, Lord Donaldson explained,[13] 'has now, to some extent, been cured by the creation of the International Association of Classification Societies (IACS), which imposes and polices the quality of its members' work and prevents owners transferring from one member society to another, simply in order to avoid having to take remedial action required by the first society. However, not all classification societies are members of IACS, although IACS members classify 90% of the world's shipping.

There has been an initiative by the European Commission to tackle these problems by the implementation of a Directive (94/57/EC) on inspection of ships by classification societies, as amended, so that more control is imposed upon the activities of classification societies for corporate responsibility and accountability. Financial liabilities are imposed upon classification societies, but only if a classification society is sued by the relevant flag State for an indemnity, and if it is proved and decided by a competent court that the failure of the classification society was the cause of the loss for which the flag State was made liable (see further developments in Chapter 20, below).

The issue of the liability of classification societies for negligence (under English law) to third parties who suffer economic loss, due to unseaworthiness of a ship

---

13   Op cit, Lord Donaldson, fn 10.

emanating from defects in the ship which the classification society had certified as being in the class required according to its rules, is discussed in the context of sale of ships, in Chapter 11, para 9. Briefly, the classification society does not owe a duty of care to third parties who suffer loss in such circumstances.

Recently, the IACS has been developing the 'Common Structural Rules', which apply to tankers and bulk carriers and are in line with the further initiative by the IMO to implement the 'Goal Based Standards' aiming to achieve uniformity in shipbuilding standards.

1.3.4 The role of the ISM Code[14] in safety

What has the Code sought to do? It superimposes a safety case regime by which risk analysis by owners has become compulsory,[15] whether or not the owners or operators have realised it. It has adopted a new approach to ship operations and management by requiring the shipowners and managers to establish a safety management system (SMS) so that the company's philosophy to safety becomes transparent. It obliges both flag and port States to enforce it and has already had a significant effect on surveillance and control of sub-standard ships.

The Preamble of the Code sets out its purpose, which is to provide an international standard for the safe management and operation of ships and for pollution prevention. By the Assembly of IMO resolution A.443(XI), all Governments were invited to take the necessary steps to safeguard the shipmaster in the proper discharge of his responsibilities with regard to maritime safety and the protection of the marine environment.

By a further resolution, A.680 (17), the Assembly recognised the need for appropriate organisation of management to enable it to respond to the need of those on board ships to achieve and maintain high standards of safety and environmental protection. The Code is based on general principles and objectives and is expressed in broad terms so that it can have a widespread application. Clearly, different levels of management, whether shore-based or at sea, will require varying levels of knowledge and awareness of the items outlined.

It is further stated in the Preamble of the Code that the cornerstone of good safety management is commitment from the top. In matters of safety and pollution prevention it is the commitment, competence, attitudes and motivation of individuals at all levels that determines the end result.

The Objectives of the Code are set out in paragraph 1.2, namely:

(a) To ensure safety at sea, prevention of human injury or loss of life, and avoidance

---

14 See the text of the Code under para 5 below. It has been implemented under Chapter IX of the SOLAS Convention 1974 and has had the force of law in SOLAS States with regard to passenger ships, oil, chemical tankers, gas and bulk carriers and high-speed crafts (all of 500 GRT and over) since 1 July 1998. With regard to ro-ro passenger vessels operating on regular service to and from ports of EU Member States, it has been applied since 1 July 1996. It became enforceable on other cargo ships and mobile offshore drilling units (of 500 GRT plus) since 1 July 2002.

15 Per Lord Donaldson, op cit, fn 10.

of damage to the environment, in particular to the marine environment and to property.

(b) The safety management objectives of the company should include:

    (i)   to provide for safe practices in ship operation and a safe working environment;

    (ii) to establish safeguards against all identified risks; and

    (iii) to continuously improve safety management skills of personnel ashore and aboard ships, including preparing for emergencies related both to safety and environmental protection.

It is further provided in paragraph 1.2 that the safety management system should ensure:

(i) compliance with mandatory rules and regulations; and

(ii) that applicable codes, guidelines and standards recommended by the organisation, administrations, classification societies and maritime industry organisations are taken into account.

The system includes the maintenance of reports of accidents and non-conformities with the Code, which is monitored and supervised by a Designated Person Ashore (DPA). Paragraph 4 specifies the duties of the DPA:

> To ensure the safe operation of each ship and to provide a link between the company and those on board, every company, as appropriate, should designate a person or persons ashore having direct access to the highest level of management. The responsibility and authority of the designated person or persons should include monitoring the safety and pollution-prevention aspects of the operation of each ship and ensuring that adequate resources and shore-based support are applied, as required.

Certificates of compliance with the requirements of such a system are granted by the flag State and delegated authorities, which audit whether the system with regard to the company and each of its ships is in place and fully operative. If compliance is in order, the company is issued with a document of compliance (DOC) and each of its ships with the safety management certificate (SMC). Classification societies, or other bodies, are delegated by the flag States to carry out formal audits to ensure compliance. The underlying purpose of this Code, together with its counterpart, the Standard of Training Certification and Watch-keeping (STCW) Convention 1978, as amended in 1995 and subsequently, is to reduce accidents in which the 'human element' plays a great part.

1.3.5 Further initiatives on safety and security standards

It may be claimed that the ISM Code marked the beginning of a safety culture, or perhaps that was what had been intended. To reinforce a culture of safety, further measures have been taken by industry organisations which aim to further the objectives of the Code in a parallel way. Such measures include:

(i) the initiative by oil majors to require tanker owners to complete the Tanker Management Self Assessment (TMSA) forms, if they wish to trade with the oil majors (see more under para 1.3.6, below);

(ii) the guidelines for best industry practice issued by the International Chamber of

Shipping and supported by the industry organisations, such as Intertanko, Intercargo, Bimco and the International Group of P&I Clubs;

(iii) the international Quality Management Systems established by the International Organisation for Standardisation (ISO): the ISO 9000 series covers the requirements for a quality management system; the 9001:2000 is the internationally recognised Quality Management Standard for all types of organisations and focuses on the management of processes within an organisation. It is the most important quality management standard in use today. It requires the adoption of eight quality management principles which are very similar to those of the ISM Code; these relate to leadership, customer, involvement of people, documented processes, integrated systems, continuous improvement, factual approach to decision making, and mutually beneficial customer relationship. Implementation of those principles aims to control risks. Formal auditing and certification are required;

(iv) in addition, the ISO 14001:2004 relates to management systems that control the impact of a company on the environment, providing for International Environmental Management Standards. These also require auditing and certification, as with any other system of organisational quality, and are supplemented by Guidelines for Quality and Environmental Management Systems Auditing (currently, series 19011);

(v) the OHSAS 18001 provides for a health and safety management standard and has been developed for international use; it is based on the ISO 9001:2000 standard. It enables an organisation to control its health and safety risks and improve its performance; and

(vi) ISO 28001, recently introduced, addresses the subject of supply chain security, an integral part of which is carriage by sea through the world's ports. The standard is based on the risk management principles enshrined in ISO 14001 and recognises the mandatory nature of the ISPS Code as applied to ships and port facilities. Implementation of the standard by each component part of the supply chain, including the shipping company, will significantly reduce the vulnerability of that supply chain to external threats.

Further measures are being taken for the purpose of tackling sub-standard ships, harmonising levels of inspection, and co-ordinating information about the performance of vessels of particular flags, which is monitored and kept in electronic databases. A similar scheme, known as Early Warning System (EWS) for the Baltic Sea, was concluded in 1999. The database information operates through the internet: it is known as the European Quality Shipping Information System (EQUASIS)[16] established by the Paris MOU, in which the names of failing flags and classification societies are recorded. It gives users a wide range of safety related information; it is a tool aimed at reducing sub-standard shipping and facilitating better selection of ships for trading. A database of inspections which have led to detention for serious deficiencies is kept for future targeting.

Parallel to these are the Green Flag Award and the US Coast Guard's 'Qualship 21', which aim to drive standards higher.

---

16 See further www.equasis.org and Chapter 20, below.

1.3.6 The missing link in the equation of safety

The ISM Code and its legal implications will be examined further later (under para 5 below), but the question at this point is this: what can go wrong if the implementation of the Code by ship owners and operators, coupled with the integration of the parallel quality systems, are complied with diligently? It is worth noting what the late Lord Donaldson thought of the probable effect of the ISM Code:

> On the face of it, full compliance [with the code] would at a stroke eliminate all shipping accidents and pollution, save only those brought on by unforeseen perils of the seas and unforeseen defects in safety management policies. Sadly, the answer is that quite a lot can and will go wrong. We live in a wicked world and the greater the financial pressure, the wickeder some of us will become. Shipowners are not more wicked than others, but overcapacity (which hopefully the ISMC will help to eliminate), the international nature of competition within the industry and low or negative margins of profit will lead many shipowners into temptation. A few, it has to be said, need no temptation. It just comes naturally. In practical terms, some Flag States will undoubtedly ignore their responsibilities and will be prepared to certify compliance in the teeth of the evidence or in spite of it . . . Accepting, as I do, that until some form of discipline can be introduced in relation to Flag States by, for example, an International maritime organisation (IMO) resolution withdrawing the right of offenders to issue internationally accepted certificates, the real burden of making this system work will fall upon Port State Control. However, I hope that classification societies, underwriters, charterers and shippers will provide powerful assistance in their own interests, by withdrawing class, by loading premiums or declining to insure and, in the case of shippers and charterers, by becoming much more selective in the shipping which they use.[17]

It is worth exploring this observation further. When Lord Donaldson made this statement, and since the first edition of this book, there have been further moves to monitor safety at sea, as explained above and in Chapter 20, below. While it is impossible to eliminate all accidents from maritime transport, or any transport for that matter, as there are some contingencies, for example of the kind of nature's forces that cannot be controlled and often cause disasters, let us assume that the 'Equation' of safety were to be represented by this mathematical formula: 'Safety = ISM + other supporting systems of safety + unknown factors represented by Y'. The missing link is to find the value of 'Y' for the purpose of this equation.

While ships are the obvious and tangible objects when disastrous casualties occur, their owners or flag States may not always be the operative wrongdoers. They sometimes become the scapegoats for the faults of others who are not easily detectable. Equal efforts must be made to detect those who place ships in a position of danger, either by their chartering practices or by loading dangerous cargoes or by exposing ships to unnecessary risks in dangerous ports. In addition, one should not leave out of the equation the practices of some shipyards, in the construction of ships or in the implementation of repairs, which ought to be made accountable for disastrous accidents. Classification societies, too, some of which fail to observe

---

17 See fn 10.

safety standards must be targeted. If the failing ones happen to be members of IACS, the sanction is now disqualification from membership, unless they follow the rules of quality standards. However, this sanction alone may not be sufficient if the problem stems from those societies which are not members of IACS. An effective sanction worth considering may be to render those classification societies obsolete by international law for safety reasons.

Since the last edition of this book, there have been commendable initiatives taken by both the IMO and the EU to implement ways of controlling the activities of both the flag States and classification societies. The IMO, through the flag State implementation sub-committee, has implemented the voluntary system of self-audit of flag State performance (mentioned in para 1.3.1, above). The EU has implemented the proposals made by the Commission to make classification societies accountable for negligence, or misconduct committed during the performance of their duties in carrying out structural surveys, as well as to audit and monitor the performance of recognised organisations (on which, see Chapter 20, below).

It has also been recognised by the Quality Shipping Campaign that the role of the shippers/cargo-owners is important and that the successful eradication of sub-standard operations and practices in shipping depends on the co-operation of all links in the responsibility chain.[18] But the role of the shippers had been looked at only with regard to whether or not a mechanism could be created by which sanctions can be imposed on them if they engage sub-standard ships. Any monitoring, however, in this direction was rejected on the basis that it would be impracticable and expensive.[19] The questions that had not been asked by the Quality Shipping Campaign were these: (i) to what extent the shippers/cargo-owners and charterers contribute to making ships unsafe and thereby causing pollution at sea?; and (ii) how can they be targeted so that sanctions can be imposed upon them for the consequences of rendering ships unsafe?

At that time, the London Shipping Law Centre held a seminar on 'The missing link in regulations in shipping'[20] examining these issues, and it was concluded that the 'missing link' was a lack of transparency within the industry, as well as a lack of consistency and effective implementation of international Conventions by flag States.[21] It is pleasing to witness that, since then, further initiatives have taken place towards safeguarding safety through the OCIMF by which a voluntary system has been set up by oil companies, supported by the international maritime organisations. This additional safety measure concerns tanker owners and is called the Tanker Management Self Assessment (TMSA), which involves a self-audit of tanker ship owners (mentioned under para 1.3.5, above). Those tanker owners who wish to trade with the oil majors must file the necessary documentation regarding their operations, for the oil majors to be able to evaluate the safety of the tankers. The oil

---

18 Lisbon Conference on Quality Shipping, 4 June 1998.

19 British Maritime Law Association (BMLA) study: On 'the role of cargo-owners/shippers and marine insurers in the Quality Shipping Campaign'; copy available from the office of the London Shipping Law Centre, UCL Law Faculty.

20 The seminar was set as a challenging question to the shipping industry and it was chaired by Lord Donaldson on 18 January 2000; papers are available at the Centre's Office.

21 By Cubbin, A, Director of Policy and Standards, Maritime & Coastguard Agency (ibid).

majors perform an audit of tanker owners for vetting, which provides a tangible commercial incentive for the tanker owners to commit to safety.

For the purpose of furthering the aims of the Quality Shipping Campaign a study was completed by Terence Coghlin, commissioned by the OECD,[22] in which the author – having competently reviewed the available systems of policing sub-standard ships – includes in his recommendations that P&I clubs should take serious measures against sub-standard shipowners and, if they do not do so, perhaps such P&I clubs should be targeted and penalised by the International Group of P&I Clubs to encourage risk selection. P&I clubs are structurally in a better position than the general insurance market to police the quality of operators who enter with them. Some clubs, however, may be sheltered from the full financial effects of their slack risk selection by the comfortable blanket of the International Group. The author admits, however, that there is no 'single instant cure available to us to remove the blot of these remaining sub-standard operators from our seascape'.

As regards quality in shipbuilding, there has been another concerted effort made by the IMO to formulate the 'Goal Based Standards' for ship construction and safety. The International Association of Classification Societies is supporting the scheme with the development of their 'common structural rules'.

In the first edition of this book, the answer to the question: 'what is the value of the unknown "Y" in the equation of safety' could not be given, and it may still be elusive but some answers can be discussed. It is very satisfying that what had been suggested in the first edition seems to have materialised, perhaps coincidentally. The Equasis information system has been expanded and the EU has implemented the Directive on monitoring the movements of ships visiting EU ports (see Chapter 20, below). If all the additional efforts made in recent years to improve safety by targeting the other players involved in shipping (mentioned above) were effective so as to give the answer to the value of Y, the equation of safety might be solved.

In the writer's view, however, there is more to be done on the part of the owners in training their ship and shore personnel not only in navigational and technical issues but most importantly in the importance of the human element in order to approach safety matters more conscientiously. The culture is gradually changing but with continuous training and conscious realisation that this is a risk management era, the ethos in ship operations will change in due course from the top of the hierarchical ladder. To this end, there is still more to be done internationally and by the insurers who can impose upon those who are insured with them, as the oil majors have done commercially, to complete a self assessment form for insurance purposes. Statements made in such a form would have legal implications under the insurance contract; therefore, a code should be internationally imposed upon insurers and their assured to comply with safety standards, in order to prevent evasion from insurance or obtaining insurance from sub-standard insurers. The IMO could invent new systems of flag State surveillance if the voluntary audit system does not prove satisfactory, in the near future.

---

22 The Removal of Insurance from Substandard Shipping (OECD, 2004), see paper delivered at the Donald O'May Lecture organised by the Institute of Maritime Law, University of Southampton, on 17 November 2004; published version 'Tightening the screw on substandard shipping' [2005] LMCLQ 316.

In the recent Cadwallader Memorial lecture of the London Shipping Law Centre, shipping and aviation were compared, and it was shown that there is a lot to be learnt from the performances of each industry in relation to safety issues.[23]

2 STATUTORY OVERVIEW OF OWNERSHIP AND REGISTRATION OF BRITISH SHIPS

2.1 The effect of the Merchant Shipping Acts prior to 1995

In 1988 the British Government launched a new system of ownership and registration of British ships, aiming to encourage foreign investment into British shipping, because the law in Britain concerning ownership of British ships, unlike other foreign laws, was too restrictive to allow foreign capital.

Under s 1 of the previous Merchant Shipping Act (MSA) of 1894, only British subjects (by birth or naturalisation) could own all 64 shares in a British ship. If the owner was a corporation, it should have been registered and have had its principal place of business in Her Majesty's dominion. Although this mechanism permitted foreign capital investment to a certain extent, it was in a way prohibiting, because of the requirement that the company should be established under the laws of some part of Her Majesty's dominions and have its principal place of business there. From a taxation point of view, this was discouraging to investment. Moreover, breach of the statutory provisions would result in forfeiture of the ship to the Crown.[24]

The MSA 1988 brought fundamental changes.[25] First, a new UK shipping register of ships was created which replaced the old British Empire register. The new register stopped the imposition of UK maritime law on old dependent territories.

Secondly, the 1988 Act introduced, for the first time, the registration of ships in the British Registry as entitlement, instead of as an obligation. It allowed, therefore, 'flagging out' to other registers of a ship which, otherwise, would be entitled to be registered as British. As a result, the definition of a British ship changed from one based on ownership to one based on registration, under the provisions of the MSA.

Thirdly, the Act introduced flexibility in ownership, in that only the majority

---

23 See www.london-shipping-law.com.

24 *The Polzeath* [1916] P 241 (CA): a ship registered as British was owned by a company registered as British under the Companies Acts. Doubts having arisen as to the title of the ship to be registered as a British ship, the Commissioners of Customs and Excise, pursuant to the provisions of s 51 of the MSA 1906, directed the plaintiff, the registrar of shipping at the ship's port of registry, to require evidence to be given to his satisfaction that the ship was entitled to be so registered. The evidence adduced established that the affairs of the company, from the time the ship was bought and put upon the register, were directed from Hamburg by the chairman of the board of directors, a naturalised British subject of German origin, who held the majority of the shares and resided at Hamburg, both before and after the outbreak of war between Great Britain and Germany. Accordingly, proceedings for forfeiture were instituted in accordance with the provisions of s 76 of the MSA 1894 – since the principal place of business of the company was not within His Majesty's dominions, the ship, therefore, was forfeit to the Crown.

25 See Gaskell, N, 'The Merchant Shipping Act 1988' [1989] LMCLQ 133.

interest in a ship of 24 metres,[26] or more, in length (instead of all 64 shares in it) had to be British owned. Furthermore, if these persons were not UK residents, then a representative person, being a UK resident, should be appointed, providing the British connection.

Thus, persons qualified to own a British ship, as defined by s 3 of the MSA 1988, are: (i) British citizens; (ii) British Crown dependent territories' citizens; (iii) British citizens overseas;[27] (iv) companies incorporated in the UK, or in any of the relevant overseas territories[28] and having their principal place of business in the UK, or in any such territory; (v) persons who were British subjects under the Nationality Act (NA) 1981; (vi) persons who under the Hong Kong (British Nationality) Order 1986 were British nationals (overseas); (vii) and citizens of the Republic of Ireland.

Section 5 of this Act encouraged the registration of a ship owned by a foreign company registered in any relevant overseas territory to be registered as British, provided there was a representative in the UK.

However, there was a serious irregularity in the Act which caused conflict with European law, and the issue was resolved by the European Court of Justice (ECJ) (see below). The Act invented a rigid system for fishing vessels by setting up a separate British fishing register to prevent fishing 'quota hopping' by non-British ships changing to the British Registry. Under s 14, the legal ownership, management and control of fishing vessels were required to be British. This resulted in great controversy with European fishing competitors, which ended up in the ECJ in *The Factortame*. A change to the statute became necessary later by the Merchant Shipping (Registration, etc) Act (MS(Reg)A) 1993.

Since this case establishes a general principle with regard to resolving a conflict between European law and national law, it is important to refer to it in a short summary.

The Factortame[29]

The applicants, companies incorporated under the UK law and their directors and shareholders, most of whom were Spanish nationals, owned between them 95 deep sea fishing vessels registered as British under the 1894 Act. In the light of the change of the statutory regime of registration by the 1988 Act, vessels registered as British under the previous Act were required to be re-registered. The 95 vessels in question failed to satisfy the conditions for registration under s 14 of the 1988 Act by reason of being managed and controlled from Spain or by Spanish nationals, or by reason of the proportion of the beneficial ownership of the shares in the applicant companies in Spanish hands. The applicants by an application for judicial review sought to challenge the legality of these provisions of the Act on the ground that they contravened the provisions of the EEC Treaty by depriving the applicants of

---

26 Ships below 24 metres were dealt with for registration purposes by the MSA 1983, which provided for a small ships register.

27 Such as in Hong Kong.

28 The Isle of Man, and any of the Channel Islands (included colonies, but that is now out of date).

29 [1991] AC 603 (HL).

Community law rights. They also applied for the grant of interim relief until such time as final judgment was given on their application for judicial review. The trial judge decided to stay the proceedings and apply for a preliminary ruling on the issues of Community law raised from the ECJ. He also ordered that, pending judgment, the application of that part of the 1988 Act be disapplied by way of an interim relief as regards the applicants.

Both the Court of Appeal and the House of Lords held that, under English law, English courts had no jurisdiction to suspend the application of Acts of Parliament by way of interim relief in advance of any decision by the ECJ. The House of Lords referred this matter of interim relief to the European Court, which held that, in a case concerning Community law, if a national court considered that the only obstacle to granting such a relief was a rule of national law, it had to set that rule aside.

Therefore, on reference back to the Lords, it was held that, in considering whether an interim relief should be granted, the court had to consider, first whether there was an adequate remedy in damages and, then, if no such remedy existed, the court had to take into account the interests of the public in general to whom the authority enforcing the law owed a duty. The court had discretion and was not obliged to restrain the public authority from enforcing the law, unless it was satisfied that the challenge to its validity was sufficiently and firmly based to justify that exceptional course being taken. The applicants' challenge to the compatibility of the 1988 Act with Community law was prima facie a strong one in the light of ECJ cases. Since the substantial detriment to the public interest was not sufficient to outweigh the obvious and immediate damage that would continue to be caused to the applicant if interim relief were not granted, interim relief was granted.

The EJC in a subsequent decision[30] struck down Greek legislation with regard to the registration of ships as being contrary to EC law. It held that Member States should not discriminate on grounds of nationality when exercising their powers to define the conditions on which they will grant nationality in respect of vessels, but ensure that there is a genuine link[31] between State and the ship.

2.2 Who can own and register a British ship under the present statute?

2.2.1 Eligibility to own a British ship under the MSA 1995

The provisions of the 1988 Act as to who would be a qualified person to own a British ship were carried forward in the MS(Reg)A 1993,[32] which was accompanied by the Merchant Shipping (Registration of Ships) Regulations 1993 (MS (Reg) Regulations). By reg 7, the categories of qualified persons outlined above were amalgamated into eight broad categories. The qualifications were extended to EC nationals. Regulation 7(1) as amended by the 1998 Regs provided that qualified persons are:

---

30 *Commission v Greece* (Case C-62/96), judgment 28 November 1997.
31 High Seas Geneva Convention 1958, Art 5 and UNCLOS 1982, Art 91.
32 See Gaskell, N, and Clarke, A, 'Sailing towards consolidation' [1994] LMCLQ 146.

British citizens or non-UK nationals exercising their right of freedom of movement of workers or right of establishment (within the meaning of Art 52 of the EEC Treaty); British dependent territories' citizens; British overseas citizens; persons who under the British NA 1981 are British subjects; persons who under the Hong Kong (British Nationality) Order 1986 are British nationals (overseas); bodies corporate incorporated in a EEA State, or in any relevant British possession and having their principal place of business in the UK or in any such possession; and European Economic Interest Groupings, being groupings formed in pursuance of Art 1 of Council Regulation (EEC) 2137/85 and registered in the UK.

A person who is not qualified under para 1 of reg 7 to be the owner of a British ship may nevertheless be one of the owners of such a ship, if:

(a) a majority interest in the ship (within the meaning of reg 8) is owned by persons who are qualified to be the owners of British ships; and

(b) the ship is registered on Pt I of the Register, which covers ships owned by 'qualified persons', excluding fishing vessels (Pt II) and those registered as small ships (Pt III).

The British connection and majority interest is provided by reg 8. A representative person in the UK for service of documents and notices is an essential requirement preserved by the Regulations (regs 8, 9, 18, 19). Thus, subject to having a British connection either by residence, or by a representative in the UK, it became possible for a foreign company incorporated in any of the EU States to own a British ship for the first time.

Upon consolidation of all MSAs by the 1995 Act, which came into force on 1 January 1996, Sched 1 to the MS(Reg)A 1993, concerning British ships their registration and mortgages, was transferred in the new Act, under Pt I & Pt II and Schedule 1. The 1993 MS(Reg) Regulations issued under the previous Act, as amended in 1994 and 1998 are still applicable. The Secretary of State can review and issue new regulations empowered by s 10 of MSA 1995.

Thus, the MS(Reg) Regulations 1993 (reg 2) created a new Central Register of British ships[33] available for public inspection, divided into four parts: (a) the large ships register (Pt I) for ships of 24 metres in length and over; (b) the register of fishing vessels (Pt II); (c) the small ships register; and (d) the bareboat register (Pt IV).

For the first time, by s 7 of the 1993 Act, now s 17 of the 1995 Act, British bareboat charterers became entitled to register a foreign chartered vessel under the British flag under Pt IV of the Registry.[34]

2.2.2 Eligibility to own a British fishing vessel

British citizens or nationals of other EU States (resident and domiciled in an EU State) must wholly own the legal and beneficial title of a fishing vessel (regs 12, 13) Pt IV of MS(Reg) Regulations 1993. If the above requirements are not met, but the

---

33 The register of ships maintained under the 1894 Act, the small ships register maintained under the 1983 Act, and the register of fishing vessels under the 1988 Act were closed by s 1 of the 1993 Act.

34 The formalities of registration are dealt with in Pt X of the 1993 MS(Reg) Regulations.

person has been resident in the UK for a long time, there may be a dispensation of the provisions by the Secretary of State who may determine eligibility (reg 15). In case the owner is a body corporate in any of the EU States, there must be a British connection (reg 14).

2.3 The effect of the reform upon British ship-ownership

The flexibility of registration introduced by the 1988 Act was a noble attempt to encourage the growth of British shipping by lifting the restriction of full British ownership and making registration in the British Registry optional. But, by making registration in the UK optional, the Act permitted flagging out indirectly and the result may have been counter-productive. The lure of foreign registers (even in relevant overseas territories), with a more flexible taxation system than the UK, became an attraction.

The unintended effect of the legislation does not, however, give a full answer to the central question of why British shipping has declined. In the 1850s, the British controlled 82% of the world shipping tonnage, legislation and colonialism having played a great part in this boom.[35] The British islanders of the 20th and 21st centuries seem reluctant to invest in shipping, considering the risks inherent to shipping business, when there are more attractive business opportunities on land. Yet, there must be more to it than just a choice between land and sea. Young people may not regard themselves as belonging to a maritime nation since it does not build ships any longer.

The British Government has offered some reasons for the decline of British shipping, such as unequal competition for the UK shipping industry from flags which offer lower labour costs when ships are crewed with officers from South East Asia and Russia, and the additional costs of operating UK ships stemming from the regulatory regime, globalisation of the world economy and changing patterns in seaborne trade, which have shifted the focus of growth to the Far East. The Government accepts, however, that such reasons have caused a steeper decline to UK shipping than to other traditional maritime nations.[36] The answer to explaining the decline certainly lies in a combination of factors, which are beyond the scope of this book, and deserves a different type of study.[37]

Two obvious factors for lack of growth of British shipping are pointed out here which have been addressed presently by the British Government: (a) the lack of attractions for young people to choose the sea as the area of their profession; and (b) the lack of Government encouragement to cost-effective investment in shipping business. The first has been attended to by the original initiative, the 'Sea Vision', undertaken by the Chamber of Shipping and supported by the shipping industry.

---

35 It is worth reading the book, Davies, M, *Belief in the Sea, State Encouragement of British Merchant Shipping and Shipbuilding*, 1992, LLP.

36 See Department for Trade, *British Shipping – Charting a New Course*, 16 December 1998, www.dft.gov.uk.

37 Harlafis, G, *Greek Shipowners and Greece 1945–1975*, 1993, Athlone, explains from a historical point of view how familial bonds and kinship greatly assisted the development of a close network in Greek shipping and contributed to the success of a strong shipping enterprise: also, by the same author, *A History of Greek-Owned Shipping*, 1996, London: Routledge.

The initiative includes further training of seafarers, awareness amongst the public about the need for promoting seafaring careers, and encouragement of young people to take up a career on board ships, coupled with support for a follow-up career on shore. The second factor, which is linked to the first, has been addressed by the Government with the introduction of the UK tonnage tax.

Following extensive consultation, the tonnage tax – an optional regime for shipping companies – was introduced into the UK tax system as part of the Finance Act 2000. The provisions implementing the regime form part of the Government's wider policy to bring about a reversal in the decline of the UK fleet and have been widely welcomed by the shipping industry.[38]

This new legislation of corporate taxation of shipping companies is based on the net tonnage of vessels operated in the UK. It aims to provide incentives for investment in shipping and boost UK shipping by encouraging shipowners to relocate to the UK because their services are very important to the British economy. A UK-resident shipowning company may either elect for tonnage tax, or be taxed under the normal corporation tax rules.[39] The introduction of the tonnage tax has proved to be effective in boosting British shipping, but more has to be done in relation to British seafaring.

Other countries in Europe had already initiated similar legislation to increase their national shipping tonnage; for example, Norway took this route in 1987. The Norwegian system,[40] which created a second register, the offshore national register, did result in a successful increase of the Norwegian tonnage.[41] However, the Norwegian system is quite different, overall, from the British tonnage tax.

One also hopes that, in this century, the number of open registers will decline considerably because of the pressures brought internationally to promote a safety culture. But this will not be enough to deter sub-standard operators as seen under para 1.3.6 above. The pressure should be applied also by financial institutions and the insurance market which can have a great impact upon deterring sub-standard operators; the trend is now that banks and insurers are more vigilant in selecting ship operators for provision of finance, or insurance.

3 OWNERSHIP PRINCIPLES

Evidence of ownership rests in the documents of registration and executed bill of sale. However, registration of a ship in the ship registry is not conclusive evidence, but provides prima facie evidence of the registered owner being the true owner. The

---

38 Visit www.hmrc.gov.uk/international/tonnage.htm; To accompany the legislation, and in order to clarify how the regime works, the Inland Revenue has issued a comprehensive *Statement of Practice*, and the Inland Revenue's *Tonnage Tax manual ('TTM')* is available online. Further information can be obtained from the British Chamber of Shipping.

39 Moore Stephens, Greiner, R, 'Off-shore and UK shipping structures, tonnage tax, advantages and disadvantages', delivered in the series of Risk Management Papers, the London Shipping Law Centre, 18 October and 22 November 2000.

40 Briefly, it includes: no taxation of foreign owners; minimum registration fee; no nationality requirements in respect of crew; freedom to negotiate wages; the company may be incorporated outside Norway with a representative in Norway.

41 See, op cit, Spruyt, fn 4, pp 48–49.

burden of proof shifts to the person alleging to be the owner. The court has jurisdiction to make a declaration as to which party would be entitled to be registered as the legal owner of a ship.[42] In absence of fraud, execution and registration of the bill of sale give good title.[43] The legal person registered to be the owner would be liable for the negligence of those on board the ship,[44] unless the ship has been chartered to a charterer by demise.

The common and voluntary methods of acquiring ownership are discussed in Chapter 10 (regarding new buildings) and Chapter 11 (regarding the commercial purchase of ships). Ownership can also be acquired involuntarily either by inheritance or bankruptcy, which is known as transmission. It may be acquired by capture of an enemy ship in times of war, or by judicial sale (discussed in Part I, above).

The principles applicable to ownership of chattels[45] apply to ownership of ships. When two or more people own a ship jointly, they own it either as 'joint tenants' or as 'tenants in common'. These phrases bear the meaning attributed to them at common law. There can be joint owners of shares in the ship who have a single joint right to possession of the whole chattel. In the absence of any words to the contrary, when a chattel is transferred to two or more people, they will hold the chattel as 'joint tenants' with a unity of title. Joint tenants do not have an exclusive right to possession as against their co-owners. When one of them dies, his interest in the ship will automatically accrue to the other.

'Tenants in common', on the other hand, own separate shares in the ship with an undivided interest in the whole of their shares and, therefore, they have several rights to possession in the ship, unless it is otherwise agreed between them. There must be an express intention of the co-owners, in such a case, that they should have separate shares in the ship for them to be tenants in common, otherwise they will be joint tenants. Indications of there being 'tenants in common' will be inferred either from the words used in their agreement, for example, 'they are to have separate interests in the ship in equal shares', or, when the joint owners have contributed to the purchase price in unequal proportions. When one of them dies, his interest in the ship passes to his estate or pursuant to the terms of his or her will.

A tenant in common can dispose of his 'interest' in the ship and the assignee or buyer of it will step in his position, becoming a tenant in common with the others.

If a joint tenant disposes of his 'interest' in the ship by a lifetime gift or assignment, the effect of it will be the severance of the joint tenancy, and the third party will become a tenant in common with the other co-owners.

The ownership in the 'whole ship' owned jointly could only be transferred to a third person by the agreement of all co-owners. If one of them purports to sell the absolute interest in the ship without the authority of his co-owners, he cannot pass greater title than he actually has, *nemo dat quod non habet*. So the purchaser will acquire the seller's interest in the ship and become a tenant in common with the other joint owners.

---

42   *The Bineta* [1966] 3 All ER 1007; see Chapter 3, para 3.1, above.
43   *The Horlock* (1877) 2 PD 243.
44   *Hibbs v Ross* (1866) 1 QBD 534.
45   Palmer, N and McKendrick, E (eds), *Interests in Goods*, 2nd edn, 1998, LLP, Chapter 10.

The relationship between co-owners is normally regulated by express agreement. In the absence of an agreement, the rights and remedies between joint owners are governed by common law. For example, if one co-owner wrongfully takes possession of the chattel, or wrongfully disposes of it, or refuses to give it back when demanded, he or she will commit the tort of conversion.[46]

When the co-owners disagree about the employment of the ship, the principle in English law is that the will of the majority must prevail, provided that the interest of the dissenting minority can be protected. The court's power of sale may be exercised, even on the application of a minority, if it is for the interest of all parties.

The Hereward [47]

The majority shareholders of a ship formed a limited company to which they transferred their shares. This had the result that the liability of the minority increased and their shares were rendered non-saleable. In addition, the majority made it impossible for the ship to be employed profitably, unless the minority shareholders joined the company. The minority shareholders applied to the court for 'restraint' of the majority and the sale of the ship. According to Bruce J:

> ... that power may be exercised on the application of a minority of part-owners; and it seems to me that, when part-owners of the ship are unable to agree as to what is to be done with their common property, and there appears to be no way of preventing the sacrifice of the property except by a sale, the court ought to direct a sale.[48]

It was held that the majority of the co-owners had no right to change the character of the ownership without the consent of all parties. Therefore, in the interests of all concerned, the sale of the whole ship was ordered.

All part-owners must consent to a voyage, but when the minority shareholders dissent, they will be excluded from any profits or losses of the voyage.

The right of a part-owner holding a minority of shares in a vessel to institute an action of restraint and arrest the vessel is undoubted. Upon sufficient proof being adduced by the minority shareholder that he/she objects to the manner in which the vessel is being employed, the court is bound to order security to be provided by the remaining part-owners for the safe return of the vessel and in the amount of the plaintiff's interest in the vessel.[49] If the court makes the order for security, the minority, though not liable for the expenses of the voyage on which the vessel is engaged, will not be entitled to any share of the profits of the adventure. The right of the minority to arrest the vessel is in no way affected by the fact that the ship's husband, who negotiated the charterparty to which the minority objects, was appointed by the whole body of the co-owners without objection on the part of the objecting part-owner.[50]

---

46 See *Halsbury's Laws of England*, 4th edn, Vol 45.

47 [1895] P 284.

48 Ibid, p 285; he applied *The Nelly Schneider* (1878) 3 PD 152.

49 *The Appollo* (1880) 1 Hagg 306.

50 *The Talca* (1880) 5 PD 169.

The foregoing principles derive from 19th-century cases and have been applied by the court up to the present day, except where there is an agreement to the contrary.

The Vanessa Ann[51]

The case involved three part-owners of the fishing vessel, *The Vanessa Ann*, which had not yet been registered because of defects of the registration of previous owners. It had been agreed between them that the vessel would be converted to a topsail schooner for use as a pleasure cruiser. In the meantime, one of the part-owners signed a charterparty for the vessel for day cruises from Antigua at $10,000 per week, providing for cancellation of the contract upon 28 days' notice. The length of the charterparty was later varied to last for 12 months. The plaintiff, who had already proposed to the other owners to sell his share to them, opposed to the length of the charter and arrested the ship, thus obstructing the commencement of the charter. He applied to court for sale of the vessel *pendente lite*. The main dispute at this hearing was the employment of the vessel.

Staughton J, taking the interests of all parties into account, exercised his discretion and ordered the defendants: (i) to execute an equitable mortgage of the vessel or of their interest therein containing the usual covenants to secure the plaintiff's claims in a form satisfactory to the plaintiff; (ii) to undertake to the court that they would procure the execution and registration of a statutory mortgage as soon as possible; and (iii) to undertake to the court that they would perform all the covenants. An equitable mortgage,[52] he said, was the best that could be achieved, for the time being, until the registration of the vessel in the names of the parties had been perfected, bearing also in mind that the plaintiff wished to get out of the partnership.

Even if there is a management agreement signed by all co-owners, by which a third party is authorised to carry out the management of the ship, the minority shareholders can still object (subject to any contrary term) to the way the ship is managed. By an action of restraint,[53] they will be entitled to bail in the value of their shares, but they will obtain no profits nor incur any liabilities concerning a particular voyage.[54] Such an action of restraint cannot, however, be sustained if the part-owner is also the mortgagee of the ship who arrests the ship while she is performing a charterparty.[55] Similarly, a purchaser of shares in a ship, which at the time of the sale is on a voyage, will not be entitled to arrest the ship on the ground of objection to the charterparty having already been concluded by the appointed managing owner. The purchaser will be liable for the expenses of the voyage and

---

51 [1985] 1 Lloyd's Rep 549.

52 For what is an equitable mortgage, see Chapter 9, below.

53 Under the MSA 1995, Sched 1, para 6 (previously MSA 1894, s 30), upon an application of any interested person in the ship (who has a proprietary right), the court has power to grant an injunction to prevent, for a specified time, any dealing with a registered ship or a share in it.

54 *The England* (1886) 12 PD 32.

55 *The Innisfallen* (1886) LR 1 A&E 72; see, further, in Chapter 9, below, to what extent a mortgagee may, or may not, interfere with the rights of a charterer of the mortgaged ship.

will be entitled to a share of the freight, but may also be made to pay damages resulting from his wrongful arrest of the ship.[56]

The relationship between co-owners of ships in modern times is primarily governed by agreements, which contain extensive clauses of every aspect of their rights and obligations. The company structures of ownership are complex and they will either be in a form of various limited companies, parent and subsidiaries, each owning one ship, or in the form of public companies, depending on their financial arrangements. One company, for example, in the ownership venture may provide management and operation services, while another may charter the ship on a long bareboat charter and engage chartering brokers for the ship's employment. A different company may deal with the employment of crew, their competence and training, as well as their welfare. As will be shown in para 4, managing companies of a ship or a fleet can be exposed to liabilities and, with the advent of the ISM Code, they also have an obligation to establish the operation of a safety management system. Breach of statutory provisions with regard to safe operation of ships will make them accountable to criminal liabilities.

4 MANAGEMENT OF SHIPS

4.1 General overview

The manager of the ship under English law has been known, from old times, as the ship's husband, who is expressly appointed by an agreement to manage the vessel or vessels of a company for its owners, and he is not a part-owner.[57] The ship's husband is distinct from a managing owner who may be one of the co-owners.[58]

'Shipbrokers and agents' is a term used to represent the owners' managing agents, which are usually incorporated offshore with a representative office in the UK. It may be a subsidiary or a sister company of the owning company, another offshore company. The company of shipbrokers is delegated with various tasks of management, and it may have an equitable interest in the ships owned by the registered owners. The shipbrokers or agents sign contracts on behalf of the owners as agents only.

The growing complexities and competition in shipping since the late 1970s and, in particular, in the 1980s and 1990s have led to management of ships by independent professionals, who may manage their own ships, as well as those of others, or may provide management services for others only. Traditional and experienced owners, however, prefer to keep all management aspects under their control, by setting up their own management company and engaging the necessary expertise in-house or engaging a professional manager as a consultant. In a traditional integrated system, there is a close link between the officers and crew on a ship and the

---

56   *The Vindobala* (1887) 13 PD 42.
57   *The England* (1886) 12 PD 32.
58   *The Vindobala* (1887) 13 PD 42, in which the manager was a managing owner.

owner. In this way, a dual or split loyalty of the master, in particular, between owner and manager is avoided.[59]

As John Spruyt says:

> ... most of the large ship-management companies were shipowners before they became dedicated managers of ships for third parties. Most of these owners made a conscious switch into being managers, rather than doing a bit of management on the side. Few of the current leading managers are shipowners in any significant way, that is, in the sense of being involved in an equity risk in ships.[60]

A broad range of activities are undertaken by managers, if the whole management is delegated to them. For example, they supply all the necessary services on board, they carry out shore supervision, they look after the employment of the ship, arrange for a chain of charterparties, and even provide finance for certain debts. The capital finance of the ship is a risk taken by the owners. Finance, marketing and sales have been separate activities delegated to different expertise. Commercial management has included the marketing and chartering, while the technical operation and manning of ships have been kept separately.[61] Some managers provide only crewing management under special agreements. Professional managers are engaged also by banks when they take over ships from the owner after default under the mortgage agreement.

4.2 The framework of management of ships

Although most of the agreements are tailor-made, the Baltic and International Maritime Council (BIMCO) has drafted a simple and straightforward ship management form (SHIPMAN), which is all embracing on the basic aspects of management. It was first issued in 1988, and updated in 1998 to reflect the changes brought by the ISM Code, with regard to safety aspects of management of ships and contemporary ship management practices. The parties to the contract can agree further details to suit their requirements. The objective of this agreement and the need for its revision in 1998 was highlighted by BIMCO,[62] thus:

> The importance of SHIPMAN as a standard agreement for third-party ship management cannot be under-estimated. The absence of national or international background law covering third party ship management makes the contract clauses increasingly important – not only in providing contractual clarity but also in the setting of standards in an industry where an increasing proportion of the world fleet is being placed under management agreements. The main task of the original sub-committee during the development of SHIPMAN was, therefore, to prepare a document that provided clear contractual provisions striking a fair balance between the rights and obligations of the owners and the managers, thus reducing the risk of

---

59 See Willingale, M (ed), *Ship Management*, 1998, LLP (this is the third edition of op cit, Spruyt, fn 4).

60 Ibid, p 178.

61 Spruyt, op cit, fn 4, and the second edition (1994, LLP) have been drastically updated because of many changes in ship management in the late 1990s and the third edition, ibid, looks very different from the first two (Willingale is the general editor, with other contributors).

62 Visit www.bimco.org for the full text of SHIPMAN.

disputes on interpretation to the extent possible. It would be fair to say that this objective was also successfully achieved.

However, in the intervening time since SHIPMAN was first issued, the shipping industry as a whole has been faced with an increasing regulatory burden – demonstrated most recently by the entry into force of the International Ship Management (ISM) Code. Like all sectors within international shipping, the ship management industry is potentially affected by regulations such as the ISM Code.

There are also two BIMCO standard crew management agreements (CREWMAN A and CREWMAN B) which deal with specific management of crew. It is beyond the scope of this chapter to outline and analyse all management agreement clauses, but some will be mentioned in the appropriate sections later. The standard management agreement broadly includes the following tasks to be performed by the manager:

(a) to engage competent and qualified master and crew for the ship on behalf of he owners;

(b) to provide technical and operational information as required by the owner;

(c) to buy stores and lubricants;

(d) to engage arrange drydocking and surveys for the vessels;

(e) to maintain the ships in class and comply with requirements of class and safety regulations;

(f) to arrange insurance;

(g) to provide chartering services (if not separately provided by the managing owners or shipbrokers);

(h) to provide voyage estimates and accounting;

(i) to subcontract and appoint agents;

(j) to supervise sales and purchases; and

(k) to provide budgeting and keep true accounts.

The standard ship management agreement responds to a need for uniformity. SHIPMAN has a widespread usage, providing a self-contained document which is used as a pro forma for third party management. It contains clear contractual provisions, aiming to strike a fair balance between owners and managers.

The new form divides the management into three main compartments: crew management; technical management; and commercial management (chartering and activities incidental to chartering). Each of these aspects of management can be delegated to one professional managing company or be separated. A general manager may also deal with insurance arrangements, accounting services, sale and purchase, supply of provisions and bunkering. While accounting is part of the duties of any manager, the tasks of insurance, sale and purchase, bunkering and ship's provisions are usually preserved by the managing owner or shipbroker.

An experienced owner has, traditionally, maintained separate companies in his venture structure, each dealing with each aspect of management. Since the advent of the ISM Code and subsequent guidelines for the protection of the environment, however, which require continual improvement and recording of safety matters in the safety management system (SMS), as well as proof of integrated quality management systems, there is a tendency by less sophisticated ship owning companies to engage professional managers rather than preserving control of all management aspects within the ownership structure. Thus, there is now more need for reputable professional managers, particularly as the legal implications of non-compliance with the requirements of the Code (as will be seen at the end of this chapter) may be far reaching for the less experienced owners.

4.3 Authority of ship managers and the ISM Code

The authority of the manager is contained in the management agreement, which provides details of the powers of the manager to bind the owner to contracts with third parties and defines his obligations to the owner. Clause 3 of SHIPMAN 1998 makes it clear that the manager acts as the agent for, and on behalf of, the owner.

The manager must act always within the authority granted to him by the owners in accordance with the management agreement or, as the case may be, additional express authority. When the contract is silent about a specific matter, implied authority will arise only if that matter is reasonably incidental to the execution of the manager's express authority. An example of this can be seen in *West of England Ship Owners Mutual P & I v Hellenic Industrial Development Bank*.[63] The bank took over the ships from the owner following default in payments and appointed HCS as managers, who in the course of their duties enter the bank as a member of the P&I club. When the club claimed the calls being due under the contract from the bank, the latter denied the authority of HCS to bind the bank into a contract with the club. The main issue was whether the bank was bound by the arbitration clause contained in the club's rules. The court held that, on the evidence, HCS had actual express authority to bind the bank as owner of the vessel to pay calls. But, if the correct analysis was that the express actual authority was simply to operate the vessel for the account of the bank and that it was implicit in that arrangement as a matter of Greek law that HCS had authority to bind the club, HCS had implied actual authority to do so.

Clause 3 of SHIPMAN provides: 'The managers shall have authority to take such actions as they may from time to time in their absolute discretion consider to be necessary to enable them to perform this agreement in accordance with sound ship-management practice.'

If the manager exceeds his authority, he will not bind the owner to contracts with third parties, unless the owner later ratifies the contract, and he will be at risk of being sued by the third party for breach of warranty of authority.

In some circumstances, the conduct of the principal may be such as to have held the agent out as having such authority; this would give rise to an agency by estoppel or apparent authority, in that the principal could be estopped from denying that the agent had authority to bind him to the contract.

Difficulties arise when the third party is not aware of the owner's existence. This is particularly so, because the owner of the ship, that is, the registered owner, is

---

63 [1999] 1 Lloyd's Rep 93.

never in the front line. The ship broking company or agent, which is separate from the registered owner, will usually contract on the owners' behalf, who may or may not be named in the contract.

Sometimes, the agent is made a party to the contract and he may sue on it. The question then arises as to what he can recover. In the leading case, *The Albazero*,[64] it was affirmed that the measure of damages for breach of contract is generally the financial loss which the plaintiff has sustained by reason of the defendant's failure to perform the contract according to its terms. The manager, therefore, who does not come within the exceptions of certain classes of people such as trustees or bailees who can recover the loss suffered by the beneficiary or bailor respectively, must prove his own loss.

It is common practice and knowledge that the shipbroker signs contracts on behalf of his principals, always as agent only. In this connection, particular attention must be given when proceedings are about to be issued for a breach of contract signed by the agent for the owners with the third party (defendant). The proceedings must be issued in the name of the registered owner, the contracting party. Otherwise, if they are issued in the name of the agent (who normally gives the instructions), there may be a professional negligence claim against the lawyer by his client owner for the loss suffered by not being able to claim his loss against the defendant, unless the owner takes part in the proceedings later (provided the claim is not yet time barred) and the claim form is amended accordingly.

The professional manager must also make it clear to the third party that he is acting for his principal, the owner. He will not be liable to the third party, if the third party knew that the manager was acting with authority of his principal. It is common practice for the managers to act as agents for the owners, except in certain circumstances when managers act as principals for the engagement of crew. However, for navigational matters, and in so far as third parties are concerned, the crew are the employees of the owner or the demise charterer, as the case may be.

When the owner is disclosed and named, he can enforce the contract against the third party. When he is not named, that is, undisclosed, the intention of the third party becomes important. If, for example, the third party wanted to contract with the manager and no one else, then he is not bound to accept performance by the owner, or, even worse for the owner, he may refuse to pay for the performance. Complex questions frequently arise in this respect as to whether the third party has repudiated the contract if his intention to contract with the agent, instead of the owner, is not sufficiently shown.

It is important to summarise the general principles in this respect:[65]

(a) where an agent enters into a contract, oral or written, in his own name, evidence is admissible to show who is the real principal, in order to charge him or entitle him to sue on the contract;

(b) an undisclosed principal may sue or may be sued on any contract made on his

---

64 [1977] AC 774.
65 See *Bowstead and Reynolds on Agency*, Sweet & Maxwell, 2000, Chapter 8, Art 78, and Chapter 9, below (on relations between agents and third parties).

behalf, or in respect of money paid or received on his behalf by his agent acting within the scope of his actual authority;

(c) an undisclosed principal may also be sued on any contract made on his behalf by his agent, acting within the authority usually confided to an agent of that character, notwithstanding limitations put upon that authority as between the principal and the agent; and

(d) subject to the intervention of the principal, the agent can sue on a contract made with a third party when the principal is undisclosed; he is personally liable and entitled to the benefit of it, provided he can prove his loss.

Whether or not the agent has authority is a question of fact in each case. At common law, the manager may pledge the credit of his co-owners who have appointed him, or have acceded to his appointment, or held him out as having their authority. Registration of the manager in the registry does not, in itself, amount to holding out, as was held by Mr Justice Bowen in *Frazer v Cuthbertson*:[66]

> Shipowners to begin with are not necessarily partners. An owner's liability or non-liability for necessaries supplied to a ship depends on the question whether the person who gave the order had his authority to give it. The register no doubt is evidence of ownership of the vessel and the registered owner, until the contrary is shewn, may be presumed to be the employer of those who have the custody of her, and who are engaged in her navigation. But a part-owner, whether registered or not, has no power to bind the other owners without their assent. The question in each case is one of fact, whether he has had such authority committed to him, or if this is not in fact the case, whether he has been allowed to hold himself out as armed with such apparent authority . . .

> The term managing owner . . . is not defined in the Act of Parliament; it is a commercial and not a legal expression. It is perfectly true that a managing owner is a name which frequently and commonly denotes an owner to whom the other owners have delegated the management of a vessel. But I do not think it follows. . . that every single other owner must be taken to have joined in the adventure merely because there is an owner called a managing owner. There is no magic in the term managing owner which creates him a plenipotentiary for those owners whose agent he is not in fact.[67]

The fact that the defendant had allowed the entry on the register describing W as managing owner to remain unaltered, did not, per se, amount to a holding out of W as his agent, so as to render the defendant liable for the necessaries supplied by the plaintiffs. In as much as W had not, in fact, authority to bind the defendant, the plaintiffs could not recover against the defendant for such necessaries.

Unless the management agreement provides that the manager has authority to engage repairers for exceptional repairs needed on the ship, or a specific authority is given in this respect, the manager is only authorised to debit the credit of the owner for ordinary running repairs. In *Boston Deep Sea v Deep Sea Fisheries*,[68] it was held that the management agreement did not of itself cover authority to carry out exceptional repairs, and the agreement would normally cover ordinary running

---

66   (1880) 6 QBD 93.
67   (1880) 6 QBD 93, pp 97, 98.
68   [1951] 2 Lloyd's Rep 489.

repairs. However, on the facts, there was special and express authority from the defendants to do this work and to pay for it. There was no question that the work was not necessary and that the cost was not reasonable. Even in the absence of special authority, the defendants, on the facts, ratified what had been done.

Normally the management agreement will provide the particular way in which the parties wish to regulate their affairs. Confidentiality clauses and provision for close co-operation are very much in demand at present times.

SHIPMAN 1998 expressly provides, by cl 3.2, for authority of the manager, if the provision of technical management is agreed, to arrange and supervise drydocking, repairs, alterations and upkeep of the vessel, provided that the manager shall be entitled to incur the necessary expenditure to ensure that the vessel will comply with the law of the flag and the recommendations of the classification society. In addition, it has been incorporated in the new form that the manager shall have authority to fulfil the function of development, implementation and maintenance of a safety management system (SMS) in accordance with the ISM Code.

This is a very important new development in the light of the international regulations imposed upon owners and managers to provide a transparent system of safety. These regulations have made the need of professional managers even more prominent. Some owners would now prefer to have the professional managers in the front line, but the owners themselves would also have the obligation to provide a clear line of communication with the manager and define the extent of responsibilities and authority delegated to others.

If the crew management is delegated to a manager, the manager has authority and should make sure that the crew supplied should be competent and well trained and comply with the International Convention on Standards Training Certification and Watchkeeping for Seafarers (STCW) 1995.[69] This is clearly the crew manager's obligation.[70]

If the technical management is also delegated to managers, cl 4.2 of SHIPMAN 1998 provides that they shall procure that the requirements, or the law of the flag of the vessel, are satisfied and they shall, in particular, be deemed to be the 'company'[71] as defined by the ISM Code. They shall assume responsibility for the operation of the vessel and take over the duties and responsibilities imposed by the Code, generally, and, in particular, in respect of the ships' surveys and repairs and whatever is required for their proper maintenance. All incidents must be recorded in the manuals and monitored for the purpose of risk analysis and prevention of accidents.

These two aspects of management (crewing and technical) are the cornerstone of the requirements of the Code for a safe management system. It should be noted,

---

69 In 1995, the STCW 1978 was substantially revised and amended, and entered into force in February 1997. The revised Convention contains explicit new responsibilities for shipping companies and is the 'sister' to the ISM Code.

70 Hilton, C, 'Shipman and crewman revisited' (2000) BIMCO Review 57, pp 57–59.

71 ISMC, para 1.1.2 provides that: 'Company means the owner or any other organisation or person such as the manager, or the bareboat charterer, who has assumed the responsibility for operation of the ship from the shipowner and who, on assuming such responsibility, has agreed to take over all duties and responsibility imposed by the code'.

however, that the fulfilment of the obligations under the Code is a joint operation, between the owner and the manager under the agreement, and depends on what is delegated to the manager.

By cl 5.2 of the agreement, where the managers are not providing technical management, the owners shall procure that the requirements of the law of the flag of the vessel are satisfied and that they, or such other entity as may be appointed by them and identified to the managers, shall be deemed to be the 'company' as defined by the Code, having the responsibilities for the operation, etc. (See further on managers' obligations under the ISM Code in para 4.8, and generally in para 5, below.)

4.4 Duties arising from the management agreement and statute

Generally, an agent is under a contractual duty to perform his obligations under the contract with his principal with reasonable care and diligence in accordance with the terms of the contract and his principal's instructions. Under cl 4 of the SHIP-MAN form, the manager undertakes to use his best endeavours to provide the agreed management services as agent for the owners, in accordance with sound management practice, and to protect and promote the interests of the owners in all matters relating to the provision of services agreed in the contract.

Best endeavours, coupled with emphasis on sound ship-management practice, do not mean less than exercising due care in the performance of the services by the manager, who must do his best in accordance with the skill that he professes to possess. Although the phrase 'best endeavours' usually embraces a subjective element in the standard of the duty, such endeavours are measured against the standard of a reasonable manager possessing the same skill and experience. The yardstick is 'sound management practice', which is an objective standard and does not refer to the manager's personal view of what is sound. For example, if the manager was instructed to insure the ship and he failed to do so, causing loss to his principal, he will be in breach of his duty of care and, hence, be liable in damages.[72] But, if he exercised his best endeavours to find an insurer for the ship and no insurer was willing to insure the particular risk, the manager would not be in breach of his duty. Under-insurance of the ship by the ship manager, which causes loss to the principal when the ship becomes total loss, will be a breach of the manager's duty, as it was in *The Maira*.[73]

The manager will also owe a fiduciary duty to his principal owners. This derives from the nature of the agreement, which is one of trust and confidentiality. It includes the duty of the manager not to take advantage of his position or his principal's property in order to acquire benefit for himself and not to act inconsistently with the interests of the owners. An illustration of such a duty was aptly given in *The Borag*, a ship-management case, in which the question was whether the manager's relationship with the shipowner was one of trustee and beneficiary.

---

72 *Turpin v Bilton* (1843) 5 Man & G 455.
73 [1986] 2 Lloyd's Rep 12.

The Borag[74]

The owners entered into an agreement by which the managers were appointed to act as technical and commercial managers of the vessel, *The Borag*. The agreement provided, inter alia, that the managers were entrusted with the entire and exclusive management responsibility of the owners' tanker, and that the managers undertook to perform the task with the same zeal and energy as if the vessel were their own, watching over the owners' interests in the spirit of close co-operation. In the course of dealings between the parties, the owners paid the managers US$55,000 to cover the vessel's monthly operating expenses, and any balance in favour of the managers would be settled by the owners on receipt of the managers' monthly statement of accounts and vouchers. Disputes later arose between the parties, as regards funds for the drydocking of the vessel, and the manager claimed unpaid balances for one month and advance payment for the other. On the managers' orders, but without the knowledge of the owners, the vessel was secretly sailed into South African territorial waters, were she was arrested by the managers for the sums allegedly owed them by the owners. The vessel was released on the tender of a letter of guarantee. The dispute was referred to arbitration and the umpire stated his award in the form of a special case for the opinion of the court. The owners were claiming that the circumstances of the arrest were such as to constitute breach of contract by the managers. According to the owners, the clause providing for the relationship between the parties had the effect of creating a full relationship of trustee and beneficiary, carrying with it all the incidents attached to such a relationship under English law. The managers claimed that the clause merely stipulated the standard of skill and endeavour they were expected to show, and was not different from any ordinary contract between a manager and a shipowner. Mustill J, as he then was, held that the managers had been in breach of their obligations:

> In my view, its purpose was to prescribe the spirit as well as the letter of the managers' functions. The owners were dependent on the managers' expertise in carrying out the day to day running of the vessel, which had been placed entirely within their control. They were entitled to have confidence in the managers to provide not merely a technically competent performance of their functions, but one which was furnished in a spirit of undivided loyalty to the best interests of the owners. The facts stated in the award make it clear that this confidence was abused. The managers did not, as the contract required, 'watch over' the owners' interests in a 'dedicated' manner. Instead, they watched over their own.[75]

It was also held that the managers could not have been trustees of the vessel in the strict sense, as they had no proprietary interest in the vessel. Although the parties clearly intended to create a fiduciary relationship between them, such a relationship was not identical with that of a trustee and beneficiary. In the light of breach of contract by the managers, the owners would be entitled to claim damages resulting from the provision of the guarantee and wasted running costs and expenses by reason of the vessel's detention if the arrest was wrongful.

A similar case arose recently with regard to breach of the fiduciary duty by the

---

74   [1980] 1 Lloyd's Rep 111.
75   [1980] 1 Lloyd's Rep 111, p 122.

manager in **The Peppy**,[76] which was arrested by the manager for alleged outstanding balance of account. It was held, inter alia, that the conduct of the director of the managing company was dishonest, in that he knew that his company was the exclusive chartering manager and was required to fix the vessel at the most favourable terms and to collect the freight and account for them to the owner. As, on the facts, it was found that there was no outstanding balance at the time of the arrest, because there was a variation of the agreement to defer payments until the vessel was sold, the arrest of the vessel was a repudiatory breach by the managers and the owners suffered recoverable loss by reason of the arrest.

The manager also has statutory duties, as provided by the MSA 1995 and international regulations.

For example, in **Seaboard Offshore Ltd v Secretary of State for Transport**,[77] the question was whether a manager could be criminally liable for acts or omissions of the crew for breach of s 31 of the MSA 1988, now s 100 of the MSA 1995. It was held that s 31 imposed a personal duty on a shipowner. That personal duty involved taking all reasonable steps to secure that the ship was operated in a safe manner, but it did not make him vicariously liable for the omissions of all his employees; where the owner was a limited company, that duty had to be performed by those who managed the company's business; since there were no findings as to how the company was managed, or who was responsible for the failure to operate the ship in a safe manner, liability on the part of the company (managers) had not been established.

Certain duties are also imposed by the ISM Code as incorporated in the management agreement, if the manager is the 'company' which has undertaken the duties prescribed by the Code (see para 4.8, below).

4.5 Consequences of breach of contract by the manager and exclusion or limitation of liability

If the manager fails to perform his obligations under the contract, in accordance with sound ship-management practice, he will be exposed to liability, not only towards his principal, but also towards third parties for negligence.

Clause 11 of the SHIPMAN form regulates the extent of liability of the manager to the owner. *Force majeure* is stated to be a cause excusing both parties from their mutual obligations to each other, if performance is prevented by reason of any cause whatsoever of any nature or kind beyond their reasonable control.

A very interesting case, **Globe Master Management Ltd v Boulus–Gad Ltd**,[78] was decided recently and it should be borne in mind by both managers and owners because it concerned terrorist activities in Israel and this affected Eastern Mediterranean cruises. The management agreement contained a *force majeure* clause and a termination clause. The cruise, and hence the management agreement, had to be terminated by the owners because of warlike hostilities and alleged dangerous

---

76   [1997] 2 Lloyd's Rep 722.

77   [1993] 1 WLR 1025

78   [2002] EWCA Civ 313

security complications. The managers sought to recover their fees and repatriation crew expenses provided under the agreement. The owners relied on the frustration clause of the contract. However, both the court and the Court of Appeal decided against the alleged frustrating event and, thus, the managers succeeded in their claim.

The manager will be liable to the owner for any loss, damage or delay or expense of whatsoever nature, caused due to his negligence, gross negligence or wilful misconduct, or that of his employees, or agents, or subcontractors employed by him in connection with the vessel. He can limit his liability (cl 11.2) provided the loss, etc, did not result from his personal act or omission committed with intent to cause same or recklessly and with knowledge that such loss would probably result. The liability shall not exceed the total of 10 times the annual management fee payable under the agreement (cl 11.2(i)). Such a limit is very low, but it takes into consideration the manager's annual income per ship.[79]

The thinking behind cl 11.2 of the contract is that the managers should be able to limit their liability, so that they can insure it, except in particularly culpable situations. The limit of liability has been related to the level of the annual management fee in order to strike a reasonable balance between the funds received by the managers on the one hand, and their exposure for insurance purposes (and therefore level of insurance premiums) on the other. The circumstances in which the managers should have unlimited liability have been related to the wording in the 1976 Convention on Limitation of Liability for Maritime Claims (see Chapter 17), which is an internationally recognised formula.[80]

If the manager is engaged for crew management, he has an option either to engage the crew as an employer, under BIMCO'S form CREWMAN B 1998, in which case he will be liable to the owner for their negligence, for which he can limit his liability, or to engage the crew as agent for, and on behalf of, the owner under CREWMAN A.

The manager shall not be liable for crew negligence, or gross negligence when the employment contract is signed on behalf of the owner, who will be the crew's employer. He may be liable, however, if he supplied uncertificated crew or failed to ensure that the crew had passed a medical examination or training in compliance with STCW 1995 and flag requirements (cl 11.2(ii)) for which the manager is entitled to limit his liability.

4.6 Indemnity and 'Himalaya' clauses

An indemnity from the owner with regard to liability to third parties incurred by the manager, his employees, agents or sub-contractors in the course of the performance of the agreement is also granted to the manager by cl 11.3. Such indemnity

---

79 Lawford, H (Chapter 6), in op cit, Willingale, fn 59.

80 The SHIPMAN agreement is available at www.bimco.org and the clauses are explained by the ITIC club who insure managers (see para 4.7 below).

refers to liability that might be incurred by the manager to third parties and not to the owner, under cl 11.2.

The protection of the manager under his contract with the owner is extended to his employees, agents and sub-contractors. SHIPMAN includes a Himalaya clause (11.4), which is designed to afford a wide protection of the managers' employees, agents and sub-contractors.

Before the Contracts (Rights of Third Parties) Act 1999, the doctrine of privity of contract prevented third parties to a contact to take the benefit or protection of exclusion or limitation of liability clauses. Common law had invented a way round this situation, basically for policy reasons rather than strict legal principle. If a special clause was incorporated in the contract of the two main parties, the protection of exclusion or limitation of liability afforded to one contracting party would be extended to his employees or agents.[81] Otherwise, the employees, whose negligence invariably causes loss to the other contracting party, could be sued in tort to circumvent the contractual exclusion or limitation of liability. Such a clause became known as the 'Himalaya' clause having taken the name of the ship in a case in which this issue first arose.[82]

The need and reasons for change in the light of the problems that had been created by the privity doctrine, which was seen as undermining commercial contracts, are explained in other recent publications.[83] Now a person, who is not a party to a contract, may, by virtue of this Act, enforce a term of the contract if the contract expressly provides that he may, or the term purports to confer a benefit on him, unless on proper construction of the contract it appears that the parties did not intend the term to be enforceable by the third party.

4.7 Insurance and risk management

Potential exposure of the ship manager, for liability to the owners of the vessel managed and to third parties for loss caused due to his or his employees' negligence, is covered by insurance. For example, with regard to liabilities to

---

81 *New Zealand Shipping Line v Satterthwaite (The Eurymedon)* [1972] 2 Lloyd's Rep 544 (PC); however, it was recently clarified by the Privy Council in *The Mahkutai* [1996] 3 All ER 502, that an exclusive jurisdiction clause did not fall within any of the terms in the bill of lading which purported to confer the benefit of exception or limitation of liability to every servant, agent and sub-contractor.

82 *Adler v Dickson (The Himalaya)* [1954] 2 Lloyd's Rep 267: a passenger of a cruise ship suffered injuries, which were allegedly due to the master's negligence. The contract for the cruise excluded all liability of the shipping company and its employees. The claimant commenced proceedings in tort against the master, who sought to rely upon the exclusion clause in the contract to which he was not a party. The defendant could not rely on the clause. Similarly, in *Scruttons Ltd v Midland Silicones Ltd* [1962] AC 446 (HL), the House of Lords held that the stevedores, by whose negligence the cargo on board the ship was damaged during discharge, were unable to rely upon a contract between the carrier and the consignees by which they had been given immunity from suit at the instance of the consignees; see, also, Chapter 14, below.

83 Recommendations for reform by the Law Commission (Report No 242) which resulted in the passing of the Contracts (Rights of Third Parties) Act 1999; and comments on that report: Burrows, A, 'Reforming privity of contract (Law Commission Report No 242)' [1996] LMCLQ 467. See, also, Merkin, R (ed), *Privity of Contract*, 2000, LLP.

contracting parties of the owner under the contract of carriage which is governed by the Hague-Visby Rules (see para 5.6, below), the duty of the owner to exercise due diligence to make the ship seaworthy before and at the beginning of the voyage is non-delegable. If the manager, in exercising his duties having undertaken full management, has been negligent and the ship is rendered unseaworthy, causing loss to cargo interests, the owner will be liable to his contracting party, if he cannot discharge the burden of proof that he exercised due diligence to make the ship seaworthy. The manager will be responsible under the management agreement to indemnify the owner for the liability incurred to third parties due to such unseaworthiness. He may be sued in tort by the third party.

He needs professional indemnity insurance and protection for such potential liabilities and those arising under statute. The insurance must cover the manager's and his sub-contractors' negligence, breach of warranty of authority and fraud by his employees. The International Transport Intermediaries Club (ITIC) provides professional indemnity insurance of ship agents and shipbrokers. It also covers risks for claims by third parties against the manager when the owner's indemnity is inoperative or the owner has gone into liquidation. It also covers legal costs in defending claims or in pursuing claims against others.

The manager has a separate insurable interest and, in a legal sense, his interest is not a joint interest with that of the owners or disponent owners. He stands in a legal relationship to the ship which he is contracted to manage and he might benefit by its safety or might be prejudiced by its loss. He can be insured for his third party liabilities as a joint assured or joint member. Joint members are fully insured in respect of their interest and are also jointly and severally liable for premiums or calls. Alternatively, the manager can be insured as a co-assured with the owner, under the so called 'umbrella of a member's entry', whereupon there is an extension of the benefit of the cover afforded to the owner member of a P&I club. In such a case, his cover is of a dependent character and exists only as an extension of the cover to the owner (see the construction of the cover in *Newcastle P & I v V Ships*).[84]

The risk of such a cover is that the protection of the manager stands or falls together with that of the owner's protection, and the manager can be vulnerable in cases in which the owner is guilty, for example, of wilful misconduct, or is in breach of other statutory provisions of the MIA 1906, or the rules of the club. Such cover will only respond once, whether to the owners or to the co-assured managers,[85] rather than the managers having a full and separate cover of their own. Accordingly, the managers will only recover from the club to the extent that the owners themselves would have been entitled to recover. If the owners can limit their liability and the managers cannot, the managers may find themselves uninsured for

---

84 [1996] 2 Lloyd's Rep 515; see also issues involving managers, their insurable interest, their authority to insure (on behalf of the owners) and for themselves as co-assured, in *The Martin P*, [2004] 1 Lloyd's Rep 389.

85 See, eg, *The Marion* [1984] 2 Lloyd's Rep 2 (HL), where the actual fault and privity of the managers deprived their principal, the owner, from the right to limit liability under the Limitation of Liability Convention 1957, as contained in the Merchant Shipping Act 1958. As both the managers and owner were co-assured in the same P&I club, no indemnity was pursued.

the amount of the claim beyond the owners' limit. However, the managers will not be held liable for outstanding calls owed by the owners (see cl 6 of SHIPMAN).

The manager needs also to be co-assured with the owner, in the owners' insurance for Hull and machinery of the ship, because of the nature of the duties he undertakes under the management agreement. If the potential risks that might arise from the performance of his duties were insured separately, the premium would exceed the management fee.[86] It is advisable to be insured as a co-assured under the owners' policies and separately with regard to his liabilities to third parties for greater protection, if it is needed.

4.8 Safety aspects and the manager's obligations under the ISM Code

The ISM Code has had a significant impact on the obligations of both owners and managers as well as on their contractual relationship. Although the Code's provisions are set out in para 5, below, certain provisions are summarised here in the context of managers.

4.8.1 General purpose and objectives of the ISM Code

As mentioned under para 1.3.4, above, the *purpose of the Code* is to provide an international standard for the safe management and operation of ships and for pollution prevention. The cornerstone of good safety management is commitment from the top to bottom of the ship owning company.

'Company' under paragraph 1.1.2 of the Code means the owner of the ship or any other organisation or person, such as the manager or bareboat charterer, who has assumed the responsibility for the operation of the ship from the shipowner and who, on assuming such responsibility, has agreed to take over all duties and responsibility imposed by the Code.

The safety management *objectives* of the company under the Code are generally described in paragraph 1.2:

(a) to ensure safety at sea, prevention of loss of life or human injury, protection of the environment;

(b) to improve safety management skills of personnel ashore and aboard ships; to establish safeguards against identified risks and to provide safe practices in ship operation; and

(c) to ensure compliance with mandatory rules and regulations and that guidelines and standards recommended by the flag State, classification societies and the marine industry organisations are taken into account.

4.8.2 Duties and responsibilities of the relevant company under the Code

Such duties and responsibilities are prescribed in various articles of the Code which require owners or managers, in particular:

---

86 Op cit, Willingale, fn 59, Chapter 6, pp 124 and 131.

(a) to establish a safety management system and policy and ensure that the policy is implemented and maintained at all levels of the organisation, ship-based and shore-based (para 2);

(b) to define levels of authority and lines of communication between shore and shipboard personnel, as well as to establish procedures for reporting accidents and non-conformities with the provisions of the code (para 1.4);

(c) to designate a person or persons ashore having direct access to the highest level of management, who should have authority and responsibility to monitor all aspects of safe operation of each ship (para 4);

(d) to define clearly the master's responsibility and issue instructions and orders in a clear and simple manner (para 5) and ensure that the ship's personnel are able to communicate effectively in the execution of their duties under the Code (para 6.7);

(e) to establish procedures to ensure that the ship is maintained in conformity with the provisions of the relevant rules and regulations and that inspections are held at appropriate intervals; to report non-conformities, to take corrective action and to keep record of these activities (para 10);

(f) to establish and maintain procedures to control all documents and data which are relevant to the safety management system (para 11);

(g) to ensure that the ship should be operated by a company which has been issued a document of compliance (DOC) and that every ship is issued with a safety management certificate (SMC) in compliance with the Code (para 13);

(h) if a manager is appointed, the owner must report full details to the flag State administration and document the authority and responsibility of all personnel who manage (para 3, which should be read together with paras 1.1.2 and 12.6: the management personnel should take timely corrective action on deficiencies found).

The 1998 SHIPMAN form has taken into account the provisions of the Code and provides, if agreed between the parties, who will assume direct responsibility under the Code. It has already been noted that, under cl 4.2 of the contract, when the manager undertakes the technical management of the ship, his company will be considered to be the 'company' under the Code, having the duties prescribed by it. On the other hand, if the owner does not delegate the technical management to the manager, cl 5.2 places an obligation on the owner to procure whatever is necessary for this purpose and, accordingly, his company will be the 'company' as defined by the Code.

The implementation of the Code has brought enormous changes in management practices, attitude and the interrelations between managers and owners. It does not require much imagination to appreciate the legal and commercial implications of the Code. It has, indeed, enhanced a safety culture within most serious shipping companies, and it is hoped that its objectives will be seriously applied by all ship operators who wish to remain in business in the future.

The documentation that is required to be maintained by both owners and managers under the Code will provide evidence and will be required to be made available under the court's disclosure rules in litigation. Thus, claims in relation to carriage of goods by sea, or claims by the owner or manager under the insurance contract, or for limitation of liability, may be affected, depending on the particular circumstances. Such issues are explored under the legal implications of the Code in the next paragraphs.

5 LEGAL IMPLICATIONS OF THE ISM CODE AND RISK MANAGEMENT

5.1 General definition, objectives and requirements for safety under Part A of the Code

1.1 **The following *definitions* apply to parts A and B of this Code:**

1.1.1 "International Safety Management (ISM) Code" means the International Management Code for the Safe Operation of Ships and for Pollution Prevention as adopted by the Assembly, as may be amended by the Organization.

1.1.2 "Company" means the owner of the ship or any other organization or person such as the manager, or the bareboat charterer, who has assumed the responsibility for operation of the ship from the shipowner and who, on assuming such responsibility, has agreed to take over all duties and responsibility imposed by the Code.

1.1.3 "Administration" means the Government of the State whose flag the ship is entitled to fly.

1.1.4 "Safety management system" means a structured and documented system enabling Company personnel to implement effectively the Company safety and environmental protection policy.

1.1.5 "Document of Compliance" means a document issued to a Company which complies with the requirements of this Code.

1.1.6 "Safety Management Certificate" means a document issued to a ship which signifies that the Company and its shipboard management operate in accordance with the approved safety management system.

1.1.7 "Objective evidence" means quantitative or qualitative information, records or statements of fact pertaining to safety or to the existence and implementation of a safety management system element, which is based on observation, measurement or test and which can be verified.

1.1.8 "Observation" means a statement of fact made during a safety management audit and substantiated by objective evidence.

1.1.9 "Non-conformity" means an observed situation where objective evidence indicates the non-fulfilment of a specified requirement.

1.1.10 "Major non-conformity" means an identifiable deviation that poses a serious threat to the safety of personnel or the ship or a serious risk to the environment that requires immediate corrective action and includes the lack of effective and systematic implementation of a requirement of this Code.

1.1.11 "Anniversary date" means the day and month of each year that corresponds to the date of expiry of the relevant document or certificate.

1.1.12 "Convention" means the International Convention for the Safety of Life at Sea, 1974, as amended.

1.2 **Objectives**

1.2.1 The objectives of the Code are to ensure safety at sea, prevention of human injury or loss of life, and avoidance of damage to the environment, in particular to the marine environment and to property.

1.2.2 Safety management objectives of the Company should, inter alia:

1.2.2.1 Provide for safe practices in ship operation and a safe working environment;

1.2.2.2 Establish safeguards against all identified risks; and

1.2.2.3 Continuously improve safety management skills of personnel ashore and aboard ships, including preparing for emergencies related both to safety and environmental protection.

1.2.3 The safety management system should ensure:

1.2.3.1 Compliance with mandatory rules and regulations; and

1.2.3.2 That applicable codes, guidelines and standards recommended by the Organization, Administrations, classification societies and maritime industry organizations are taken into account.

1.3 **Application**

The requirements of this Code may be applied to all ships.

1.4 **The functional requirements for a safety management system:**

Every Company should develop, implement and maintain a safety management system which includes the following functional requirements:

1.4.1 A safety and environmental-protection policy;

1.4.2 Instructions and procedures to ensure safe operation of ships and protection of the environment in compliance with relevant international and flag State legislation;

1.4.3 Defined levels of authority and lines of communication between, and amongst, shore and shipboard personnel;

1.4.4 Procedures for reporting accidents and non-conformities with the provisions of this Code;

1.4.5 Procedures to prepare for and respond to emergency situations; and

1.4.6 Procedures for internal audits and management reviews.

5.2 Specific provisions of the Code under Part A

2 **Safety and Environmental-Protection Policy**

2.1 The Company should establish a safety and environmental-protection policy which describes how the objectives given in paragraph 1.2 will be achieved.

2.2 The Company should ensure that the policy is implemented and maintained at all levels of the organization, both ship-based and shore-based.

3 *Company Responsibilities and Authority*

3.1 If the entity who is responsible for the operation of the ship is other than the owner, the owner must report the full name and details of such entity to the Administration.

3.2 The Company should define and document the responsibility, authority and interrelation of all personnel who manage, perform and verify work relating to and affecting safety and pollution prevention.

3.3 The Company is responsible for ensuring that adequate resources and shore-based support are provided to enable the designated person or persons to carry out their functions.

4 Designated Person(s)

To ensure the safe operation of each ship and to provide a link between the Company and those on board, every Company, as appropriate, should designate a person or persons ashore having direct access to the highest level of management. The responsibility and authority of the designated person or persons should include monitoring the safety and pollution-prevention aspects of the operation of each ship and ensuring that adequate resources and shore-based support are applied, as required.

5 Master's Responsibility and Authority

5.1 The Company should clearly define and document the master's responsibility with regard to:

5.1.1 Implementing the safety and environmental-protection policy of the Company;

5.1.2 Motivating the crew in the observation of that policy;

5.1.3 Issuing appropriate orders and instructions in a clear and simple manner;

5.1.4 Verifying that specified requirements are observed; and

5.1.5 Reviewing the safety management system and reporting its deficiencies to the shore-based management.

5.2 The Company should ensure that the safety management system operating on board the ship contains a clear statement emphasizing the master's authority. The Company should establish in the safety management system that the master has the overriding authority and the responsibility to make decisions with respect to safety and pollution prevention and to request the Company's assistance as may be necessary.

6 Resources and Personnel

6.1 The Company should ensure that the master is:

6.1.1 Properly qualified for command;

6.1.2 Fully conversant with the Company's safety management system; and

6.1.3 Given the necessary support so that the master's duties can be safely performed.

6.2 The Company should ensure that each ship is manned with qualified, certificated and medically fit seafarers in accordance with national and international requirements.

6.3 The Company should establish procedures to ensure that new personnel and personnel transferred to new assignments related to safety and protection of the environment are given proper familiarization with their duties. Instructions which are essential to be provided prior to sailing should be identified, documented and given.

6.4 The Company should ensure that all personnel involved in the Company's safety management system have an adequate understanding of relevant rules, regulations, codes and guidelines.

6.5 The Company should establish and maintain procedures for identifying any training which may be required in support of the safety management system and ensure that such training is provided for all personnel concerned.

6.6 The Company should establish procedures by which the ship's personnel receive relevant information on the safety management system in a working language or languages understood by them.

The Company should ensure that the ship's personnel are able to communicate effectively in the execution of their duties related to the safety management system.

7 *Development of Plans For Shipboard Operations*

The Company should establish procedures for the preparation of plans and instructions, including checklists as appropriate, for key shipboard operations concerning the safety of the ship and the prevention of pollution. The various tasks involved should be defined and assigned to qualified personnel.

8 *Emergency Preparedness*

8.1 The Company should establish procedures to identify, describe and respond to potential emergency shipboard situations.

8.2 The Company should establish programmes for drills and exercises to prepare for emergency actions.

8.3 The safety management system should provide for measures ensuring that the Company's organization can respond at any time to hazards, accidents and emergency situations involving its ships.

9 *Reports and Analysis of Non-Conformities, Accidents and Hazardous Occurrences*

9.1 The safety management system should include procedures ensuring that non-conformities, accidents and hazardous situations are reported to the Company, investigated and analysed with the objective of improving safety and pollution prevention.

9.2 The Company should establish procedures for the implementation of corrective action.

10 *Maintenance of the Ship and Equipment*

10.1 The Company should establish procedures to ensure that the ship is maintained in conformity with the provisions of the relevant rules and regulations and with any additional requirements which may be established by the Company.

10.2 In meeting these requirements the Company should ensure that:

10.2.1 Inspections are held at appropriate intervals;

10.2.2 Any non-conformity is reported, with its possible cause, if known;

10.2.3 Appropriate corrective action is taken; and

10.2.4 Records of these activities are maintained.

10.3 The Company should establish procedures in its safety management system to identify equipment and technical systems the sudden operational failure of which may result in hazardous situations. The safety management system should provide for specific measures aimed at promoting the reliability of such equipment or systems. These measures should include the regular testing of stand-by arrangements and equipment or technical systems that are not in continuous use.

10.4 The inspections mentioned in 10.2 as well as the measures referred to in 10.3 should be integrated into the ship's operational maintenance routine.

11 *Documentation*

11.1 The Company should establish and maintain procedures to control all documents and data which are relevant to the safety management system.

11.2 The Company should ensure that:

11.2.1 Valid documents are available at all relevant locations;

11.2.2 Changes to documents are reviewed and approved by authorized personnel; and

11.2.3 Obsolete documents are promptly removed.

11.3 The documents used to describe and implement the safety management system may be referred to as the Safety Management Manual. Documentation should be kept in a form that the Company considers most effective. Each ship should carry on board all documentation relevant to that ship.

12 *Company Verification, Review and Evaluation*

12.1 The Company should carry out internal safety audits to verify whether safety and pollution-prevention activities comply with the safety management system.

12.2 The Company should periodically evaluate the efficiency of and, when needed, review the safety management system in accordance with procedures established by the Company.

12.3 The audits and possible corrective actions should be carried out in accordance with documented procedures.

12.4 Personnel carrying out audits should be independent of the areas being audited unless this is impracticable due to the size and the nature of the Company.

12.5 The results of the audits and reviews should be brought to the attention of all personnel having responsibility in the area involved.

12.6 The management personnel responsible for the area involved should take timely corrective action on deficiencies found.

5.3 Certification and verification under Part B of the Code

13 *Certification and Periodical Verification*

13.1 The ship should be operated by a Company which has been issued with a Document of Compliance (DOC) or with an Interim Document of Compliance (IDOC) in accordance with paragraph 14.1, relevant to that ship.

13.2 The Document of Compliance should be issued by the Administration, by an organization recognized by the Administration or, at the request of the Administration, by another Contracting Government to the Convention to any Company complying with the requirements of this Code for a period specified by the Administration which should not exceed five years. Such a document should be accepted as evidence that the Company is capable of complying with the requirements of this Code.

13.3 The Document of Compliance is only valid for the ship types explicitly indicated in the document. Such indication should be based on the types of ships on which the initial verification was based. Other ship types should only be added after verification of the Company's capability to comply with the requirements of this Code applicable to such ship types. In this context, ship types are those referred to in regulation IX/1 of the Convention.

13.4 The validity of a Document of Compliance should be subject to annual verification by the Administration or by an organization recognized by the Administration or, at the request of the Administration, by another Contracting Government within three months before or after the anniversary date.

13.5 The Document of Compliance should be withdrawn by the Administration or, at its request, by the Contracting Government which issued the Document when the annual verification required in paragraph 13.4 is not requested or if there is evidence of major non-conformities with this Code.

All associated Safety Management Certificates and/or Interim Safety Management Certificates should also be withdrawn if the Document of Compliance is withdrawn.

13.6 A copy of the Document of Compliance should be placed on board in order that the master of the ship, if so requested, may produce it for verification by the Administration or by an organization recognized by the Administration or for the purposes of the control referred to in regulation IX/6.2 of the Convention. The copy of the Document is not required to be authenticated or certified.

13.7 The Safety Management Certificate should be issued to a ship for a period which should not exceed five years by the Administration or an organization recognized by the Administration or, at the request of the Administration, by another Contracting Government. The Safety Management Certificate should be issued after verifying that the Company and its shipboard management operate in accordance with the approved safety management system. Such a Certificate should be accepted as evidence that the ship is complying with the requirements of this Code.

13.8 The validity of the Safety Management Certificate should be subject to at least one intermediate verification by the Administration or an organization recognized by the Administration or, at the request of the Administration, by another Contracting Government. If only one intermediate verification is to be carried out and the period of validity of the Safety Management Certificate is five years, it should take place between the second and third anniversary dates of the Safety Management Certificate.

13.9 In addition to the requirements of paragraph 13.5.1, the Safety Management Certificate should be withdrawn by the Administration or, at the request of the Administration, by the Contracting Government which has issued it when the intermediate verification required in paragraph 13.8 is not requested or if there is evidence of major non-conformity with this Code.

13.10 Notwithstanding the requirements of paragraphs 13.2 and 13.7, when the renewal verification is completed within three months before the expiry date of the existing Document of Compliance or Safety Management Certificate, the new Document of Compliance or the new Safety Management Certificate should be valid from the date of completion of the renewal verification for a period not exceeding five years from the date of expiry of the existing Document of Compliance or Safety Management Certificate.

13.11 When the renewal verification is completed more than three months before the expiry date of the existing Document of Compliance or Safety Management Certificate, the new Document of Compliance or the new Safety Management Certificate should be valid from the date of completion of the renewal verification for a period not exceeding five years from the date of completion of the renewal verification.

14 *Interim Certification*

14.1   An Interim Document of Compliance (IDOC) may be issued to facilitate initial implementation of this Code when:

14.1.1 a Company is newly established; or

14.1.2 new ship types are to be added to an existing Document of Compliance, following verification that the Company has a safety management system that meets the objectives of paragraph 1.2.3 of this Code, provided the Company demonstrates plans to implement a safety management system meeting the full requirements of this Code within the period of validity of the Interim Document of Compliance. Such an Interim Document of Compliance should be issued for a period not exceeding 12 months by the Administration or by an organization recognized by the Administration or, at the request of the Administration, by another Contracting Government. A copy of the Interim Document of Compliance should be placed on board in order that the master of the ship, if so requested, may produce it for verification by the Administration or by an organization recognized by the Administration or for the purposes of the control referred to in regulation IX/6.2 of the Convention. The copy of the Document is not required to be authenticated or certified.

14.2   An Interim Safety Management Certificate may be issued:

14.2.1 to new ships on delivery;

14.2.2 When a Company takes on responsibility for the operation of a ship which is new to the Company; or

14.2.3 When a ship changes flag.

    Such an Interim Safety Management Certificate should be issued for a period not exceeding 6 months by the Administration or an organization recognized by the Administration or, at the request of the Administration, by another Contracting Government.

14.3   An Administration or, at the request of the Administration, another Contracting Government may, in special cases, extend the validity of an Interim Safety Management Certificate for a further period which should not exceed 6 months from the date of expiry.

14.4   An Interim Safety Management Certificate may be issued following verification that:

14.4.1 The Document of Compliance, or the Interim Document of Compliance, is relevant to the ship concerned;

14.4.2 The safety management system provided by the Company for the ship concerned includes key elements of this Code and has been assessed during the audit for issuance of the Document of Compliance or demonstrated for issuance of the Interim Document of Compliance;

14.4.3 The Company has planned the audit of the ship within three months;

14.4.4 The master and officers are familiar with the safety management system and the planned arrangements for its implementation;

14.4.5 Instructions, which have been identified as being essential, are provided prior to sailing; and

14.4.6 Relevant information on the safety management system has been given in a working language or languages understood by the ship's personnel.

15   *Verification*

15.1   All verifications required by the provisions of this Code should be carried out in accordance with procedures acceptable to the Administration, taking into account the guidelines developed by the Organization.

16   *Forms of Certificates*

16.1   The Document of Compliance, the Safety Management Certificate, the Interim Document of Compliance and the Interim Safety Management Certificate should be drawn up in a form corresponding to the models given in the appendix to this Code. If the language used is neither English nor French, the text should include a translation into one of these languages.

16.2   In addition to the requirements of paragraph 13.3, the ship types indicated on the Document of Compliance and the Interim Document of Compliance may be endorsed to reflect any limitations in the operations of the ships described in the safety management system.

5.4 Effect of non-compliance and risk management

The Code itself does not impose liabilities on the owners and managers of ships in the event of breach of its provisions. Breaches, however, will result in the non-certification of the company or the particular non-compliant ship, which, in turn, may have legal implications in the areas discussed here. SOLAS States that implement the Code into domestic legislation may, however, impose penalties, or criminal sanctions, for non-compliance.

By the Merchant Shipping ISMC Regulations 1998 (SI 1998/1561), the UK Government has effectively enacted the Code into domestic legislation. This statutory instrument provides for offences and penalties in the event of breach of the obligations stated therein, which will be discussed later under the sub-paragraph dealing with criminal liability.

Undoubtedly, the Code provides a yardstick of conduct against which the shipowner's or manager's performance in operation of ships can be measured, by the very reason that the Code requires extensive documentation of all incidents and communications between the designated person and senior management of the respective companies.

What is reported in the SMS may, sometimes, carry adverse consequences for those owners or managers who fail to comply with the recommendations made by external auditors, or to follow up the results of their internal risk assessment. Equally, a deficient system with gaps in reporting will give cause for serious questions to be asked.

The message derived from the ISM Code is clear for owners and managers.

First, it is now a foremost obligation of good corporate governance that they must adopt a philosophy of safety culture at all levels; they must set their mission, have the right attitude to safety and commitment, from the top of the hierarchical ladder to the bottom.

Second, they must provide for safe practices through procedures and proper record keeping, ensure competence of the crew by training, both in the handling of equipment and in the understanding of procedures for risk prevention and protection of the environment.

Third, they must strive for continuous improvement by monitoring safety and conducting internal audits to prevent recurrence of faults. Particular attention must be given to the human element in accidents and man/equipment interface.

There are several areas where risk management and the proper implementation of safety management systems as required by the ISM Code can be relevant in litigation. It is only intended here to examine four of them: (1) due diligence under the Hague-Visby Rules (HVR); (2) privity of the assured under s 39(5) of the Marine Insurance Act (MIA) 1906; (3) limitation of liability under the Limitation Conventions; and (4) criminal liability of the company.

These aspects become complicated because the owners or managers are not individuals, but companies, and, in each case, one has to identify the person or persons making the decisions in the corporate structure. Before entering into discussion of each area mentioned in the previous paragraph, it is appropriate at this point to examine the basis on which liability may be attributed to the company, for acts of persons of the company.

5.5 The rules of attribution of liability [87]

The leading authority, redefining the rules of attributing liability to a company, is *Meridian Global Funds Management Asia v Securities Commission*.[88] In a nutshell, the rule was put in the following words:

> Where a company's rights and obligations could not be determined either by the primary rules of attribution, expressed in its constitution or implied by law (for determining what acts were to be attributed to the company) or by the application of the general principles of agency or vicarious liability, the question of attribution for a particular substantive rule was a matter of interpretation or construction of that rule.

Thus, the sub-divisions of the rules of attribution of liability to a company are these:

(a) The *primary rules of attribution* of the company itself, which are to be found in the company's articles of association or its constitution, or the majority decisions of the shareholders, or the board's decisions. One will be able to find how the company has allocated responsibility and authority to certain persons, so that the directing mind and will of the corporation will be identified: thus, this theory is known as the 'identification' theory or doctrine.[89]

(b) The rules of attribution based on general principles of *agency or vicarious liability*

---

87 An analysis of the origins and development of the sub-divisions of the rule of attribution is given in Chapter 17, para 8.

88 [1995] 3 All ER 918 (PC).

89 *Tesco Supermarkets Ltd v Nattrass* [1972] AC 153 (HL); *The Safe Carrier* [1994] 1 Lloyd's Rep 75 and 589 (HL); see, further, previous authorities about the 'alter ego' of a company, which the House of Lords in *Tesco* clarified: *Lennard's Carrying Co Ltd v Asiatic Petroleum Ltd* [1915] AC 705 (HL); *DPP v Kent and Sussex Contractors Ltd* [1944] 1 KB 146; *ICR Haulage Ltd* [1944] KB 551; *Moore v Bresler* [1944] 2 All ER 515; *The Lady Gwendolen* [1965] P 294 (CA); *The Eurysthenes* [1976] 2 Lloyd's Rep 171 (CA).

for determination of liability of a corporation. As was explained by the Privy Council in *Meridian*, the primary rules of attribution are not always enough to enable a company to go out into the world and do business. Not every act on behalf of the company could be expected to be the subject of a resolution of the board, or a unanimous decision of the shareholders. The company, therefore, builds upon the primary rules of attribution by using general rules of attribution, which are equally available to natural persons, namely, the principles of agency. It will appoint servants and agents whose acts, by a combination of the general principles of agency and the company's primary rules of attribution, count as the acts of the company. And, having done so, it will also make itself subject to the general rules by which liability for the acts of others can be attributed to natural persons, such as estoppel or ostensible authority in contract and vicarious liability in tort. This is known as the 'agency or vicarious liability' doctrine.[90]

(c) The *special rule of attribution* which the Privy Council fathomed is this: sometimes, the court, having considered the policy of a statute or Convention (which may be the substantive law applicable to a particular case), may have to devise a special rule of attribution to determine whose act, or knowledge, or state of mind was, for the purpose of that statute or Convention, to be attributed to the company. Knowledge of an act of a duly authorised servant or agent, or the state of mind with which it was done, although such person may not be the 'directing mind and will' of the company, would be attributed to the company only where the policy behind the substantive rule of law so required, upon true construction of the relevant substantive provisions.

In all cases, the Privy Council explained, it was a matter of construction of the underlying rule of law (eg relevant legislation or statute) by the court in order to decide how the substantive rule of law was intended to apply. It may be that the rule of law, either expressly or by implication, excludes attribution of liability to a company on the basis of the general principles of agency; or the court might interpret the law as meaning that liability could apply to a company only on the basis of its primary rules of attribution (that is, if the act giving rise to liability was specifically authorised by a resolution of the board or a unanimous agreement of the shareholders).

However, in some cases, insistence on the primary rules of attribution could, in practice, defeat the intention of the substantive rule of law, thus, the court must fashion a special rule of attribution for the particular substantive rule as a matter of interpretation. It has to ask the question: 'Whose act (or knowledge, or state of mind) was, for this purpose, intended to count as the act, etc, of the company?' The contrast between this case and the *Tesco*[91] case illustrates the difference between the special rule of attribution and the pure identification doctrine.

On the facts of the *Meridian* case, the substantive rule was a statute (New

---

90 *Birmingham and Gloucester Rly Co* (1842) 3 QBD 223; *Great North of England Rly Co* (1846) 9 QBD 315; *Mousell Brothers Ltd v London and North Eastern Rly Co* [1917] 2 KB 836; *Griffiths v Studebakers Ltd* [1924] 1 KB 102 (HL).

91 *Tesco Supermarkets Ltd v Nattrass* [1972] AC 153 (HL); see Chapter 17, below.

Zealand Securities Amendment Act 1988). A chief investment officer of an invest-ment management company and its senior portfolio manager with the company's authority, but unknown to the directors, used funds managed by the company to acquire shares in a public issuer. So, the company became a substantial security holder in that public issuer. Under s 20(3) of the Act, the company ought to give notice of that holding, which it did not do and, therefore, it was in breach of its duty. The Securities Commissioner prosecuted the company and the question for the court was whether the knowledge of the employees, below the level of directors, could be attributed to the company. It was held that:

> Having regard to the policy of s 20 of the Act of 1988, and upon its true construction, the appropriate rule of attribution to be implied was that a corporate security holder knew that it was a substantial security holder in a public issuer when that was known to the person who had acquired the relevant interest with the company's authority, whereupon the company was obliged to give notice under s 20(3). The knowledge of the transaction by the relevant employee was attributable to the com-pany irrespective of whether he could be described in a general sense as its directing mind and will, and so in failing to give notice the company had been in breach of its duty under s 20(3).

If, on the contrary, the primary rules of attribution were applied, by which only the directors' knowledge would be attributed to the company, the policy of the Act which compelled immediate disclosure would be defeated.

This was contrasted with the ruling of the House of Lords in *Tesco Super-markets v Nattrass*[92] (the identification doctrine), in which the substantive law for interpretation was the Trade Descriptions Act (TDA) 1968. Tesco were prosecuted under s 11(2) for displaying a notice that goods were being 'offered at a price less than that at which they were in fact being offered'. The shop manager had failed to notice that he had run out of the specially marked low price packets.

The Act requires reasonable precautions to be taken and due diligence to be exercised by the shop owner to avoid commission of an offence under the Act. But, whose precautions counted as those of the company? For the purpose of the TDA 1968, it was sufficient that the board of the company took the precautions and it had taken them. Therefore, the negligence of the manager, who was personally liable, was not attributed to the company.

It should be noted that Lord Hoffmann (in the *Meridian* case), when formulating the rule of attribution, entered a caveat of caution:

> Their Lordships would wish to guard themselves against being understood to mean that whenever a servant of a company has authority to do an act on its behalf, knowledge of that act would for all purposes be attributed to the company. It is a question of construction in each case as to whether the particular rule requires that the knowledge that an act has been done, or the state of mind, with which it was done, should be attributed to the company.[93]

Following this analysis there are three central questions in the context of the issues raised under para 5.4 above: first, whose acts or omissions could be attributed to the

---

92   [1971] 2 All ER 127.
93   *Meridian Global Funds Management Asia v Securities Commission* [1995] 3 All ER 918, p 928.

ship owning or ship-management company? Second, what is the relevance of the ISM Code to the attribution of liability? Third, what is the role of the delegated person in this respect? Each category of the attribution rules mentioned earlier will be considered in the context of the 'due diligence' provision of the HVR, 'privity' of the assured under s 39(5) of the MIA 1906, limitation of liability, and criminal liability.

5.6 The due diligence provision of the HVR and the role of the ISM Code

5.6.1 The principles

The HVR provide, in Art III, r 1, that the carrier shall be bound before and at the beginning of the voyage to exercise due diligence to:

(a) make the ship seaworthy,

(b) properly man, equip and supply the ship, and

(c) make the holds, refrigerating and cool chambers, and all other parts of the ship in which goods are carried, fit and safe for their reception, carriage and preservation.

The standard to be applied, as established by common law,[94] is that the vessel must be fit to encounter the ordinary perils of the voyage, and must have that degree of fitness which an ordinary and careful owner would require his vessel to have at the commencement of her voyage, having regard to all the probable circumstances of it.

The courts have further held that the due diligence provision is not delegable but personal.[95] This means that there would be no defence to a cargo claim by the owner if the ship was negligently repaired by independent contractors, or if the classification society inspected the ship before sailing, but still the ship was unseaworthy, unless it is shown that no other professional could have detected the defect.[96] The obligation imposed on the shipowner is one of due diligence in the work of repair by whomsoever it might be done, even when the work is delegated to the independent contractor for his technical or special knowledge or experience and the negligence is not apparent to the shipowner. If competent professionals conducted repairs, the owner may be able to discharge the burden of proof that he exercised due diligence, provided there is no doubt in the evidence heard by the court.[97]

---

94 See for example: *Mcfadden v Blue Star* [1905] 1 KB 697.

95 *The Muncaster Castle* [1961] AC 807 (HL), p 836, per Viscount Simonds; see further: *The Antigoni* [1991] 1 Lloyd's Rep 209 (no proof of latent defect in engine; owner not able to discharge burden); *The Apostolis* [1997] 2 Lloyd's Rep 241 (holds not intrinsically unsafe); *The Fjord Wind* [2000] 2 Lloyd's Rep 191 (latent defect but there was no clear evidence to indicate other than lack of due diligence by delegated agents); *The Happy Ranger (No 2)* [2006] 1 Lloyd's Rep 649.

96 *The Hellenic Dolphin* [1978] 2 Lloyd's Rep 336, 339–344 (seawater entered hold through leaking seam; undetected defect during surveys by classification society; owner able to discharge burden); cf *The Toledo* [1995] 1 Lloyd's Rep 40 (no proper system of maintenance; classification society did not warn).

97 *The Amstelslot* [1963] 2 Lloyd's Rep 223, 233–35 (HL) (fatigue cracks not detected by reasonable diligence; professionals had inspected ship; no negligence found).

When the cargo carried on the ship is damaged, the cargo-owner has the burden of proving not only that the ship was unseaworthy, but that the unseaworthiness caused the loss.[98] The burden then shifts on the shipowner to show that he exercised due diligence before and at the beginning of the voyage to make the ship seaworthy, as is required by the Rules.[99]

Since attribution of liability to the owner of the ship for unseaworthiness, as far as the HVR are concerned, has been firmly settled, the next questions are: what is the relevance of the ISM Code; and how may the role of the designated person affect the position?

It is apparent that the policy behind the HVR is not to ask whose fault it was if the ship is unseaworthy. The law assumes that the responsibility is upon the owner personally (the ego of the company) to ensure that due diligence was exercised by him in whatever was necessary to be done to make the ship seaworthy. The substantive rule of law about the nature of the carrier's obligation is clear, and it does not need further interpretation. The legal obligation of the carrier's personal duty to make the ship seaworthy, before and at the beginning of the voyage, has not been changed by the regulatory regime imposed by the ISM Code.

However, the ISM Code and the documentation that is required to be available will have evidential effect on establishing, first, that the ship was unseaworthy and, second, that the owner might have failed to exercise the required due diligence. Any failings of the system of operations, selection of crew,[100] or management, which render the ship unseaworthy, will now be more apparent from the safety management manual (SMM). Equally, any equipment failure will be apparent from the documentation, if it has been properly kept, as required by the ISM Code. This will supply ammunition to cargo claimants to show a causative link between the cargo damage and the unseaworthiness, just as it will make the position of the carrier more difficult in discharging his burden of proof.

Incidents that occur on the ship which are likely to render her unseaworthy will now have to be reported. Thus, the examples of cases such as *The Apostolis*[101] (in which there were no contemporaneous documents showing when the welding to the ship, which was alleged to have been the cause of the fire, took place) and *The Toledo*[102] (failure to have proper systems in place for inspecting and maintaining the vessel) ought to be borne in mind. On the other hand, if the system is not transparent enough, the owner will be taking a gamble because he will not be able to explain why the documents are not kept. It will be no excuse to say that he had delegated

---

98 *The Yamatogowa* [1990] 2 LLR 39; *The Torenia* [1983] 2 Lloyd's Rep 210 (most probable cause was un/seaworthiness, corrosion; sinking raised inference of un/seaworthiness); *The Theodegmon* [1990] 1 Lloyd's Rep 52 (failure of steering gear caused the stranding of the ship, not pilot failure); *The Toledo* [1995] 1 Lloyd's Rep 40 (no proper system of maintenance; classification society did not warn).

99 See Art IV, r 1; *The Glendarroch* [1894] P 226 (laid down the principle of how the burden of proof shifts from the cargo owner to the shipowner in cases of unseaworthiness); *The Hellenic Dolphin*, op cit, fn 96; *The Polessk* [1996] 2 Lloyd's Rep 40.

100 *The Makedonia* [1962] 1 Lloyd's Rep 316 (inefficient chief engineer rendered the ship unseaworthy).

101 [1996] 1 Lloyd's Rep 475 and [1997] 2 Lloyd's Rep 241 (CA).

102 [1995] 1 Lloyd's Rep 40.

the tasks of monitoring deficiencies for the purpose of the ISM Code to the designated person (who is supposed to inform the senior management) or that the company responsible for the ISM requirements was the third party ship manager.

Some examples below demonstrate the use of the ISM Code to cargo claimants in appropriate cases, although there have not as yet been cases in which the ISM Code was directly in issue.

The Eurasian Dream[103] was not a case to which the ISM Code applied mandatorily at the time, but the facts and comments by the judge are very important for future reference.

The ship and its cargo of cars on board caught fire, due to jumpstarting by stevedores while there was refuelling side by side. The fire spread on the ship, it could not be contained by the crew and caused damage to the cargo. The alleged unseaworthiness concerned defective equipment, incompetence of the crew and inefficiency of the master. The fire drill training was deficient and the master was not properly qualified for command of his ship, nor was he familiar with the obligations under the SMS. The owners were sloppy and not supportive. There was voluminous documentation without clear instructions. Viewed from the perspective of the owners' obligations under the ISM Code, the system had been taken off the shelf and it was confusing. All these deficiencies were held to have a cumulative effect on the unseaworthiness, and the owner could not discharge the burden of proof that he exercised due diligence.

By contrast, in *The Torepo*,[104] the ISM Code evidence assisted the owners in proving that they had exercised due diligence. They were able to show that they had proper manuals, procedures and standing orders and instructions which had been read by the crew. In addition, the master kept records of his meetings with his navigation officers to communicate and brief them.

In *Isla Fernandina*,[105] although the ISM Code was not at that time relevant to the case, the facts should be borne in mind for risk management purposes, should a similar case reach the scrutiny of the court in the future, whereupon the ISM Code will be relevant. The third officer was inexperienced in radar plotting and put the vessel aground. The master was not on the bridge to supervise him when entering port and had not made a passage plan. There was a lack of procedures for ongoing navigational training and with regard to watch keeping. Although the court held that the grounding was due to navigational error, the owner today would have to show evidence of training and compliance with the ISM Code in order to discharge his burden of proving that he exercised due diligence when unseaworthiness is proved to have been the cause of the loss.

5.6.2 The position of the ship manager

Since the duty of due diligence is non-delegable, the significance of this for ship managers is that the owner, who may be found liable to third parties due to

---

103 [2002] 1 Lloyd's Rep 719.
104 [2002] 2 Lloyd's Rep 535.
105 [2000] 1 Lloyd's Rep 15.

negligence of the manager, would seek an indemnity or damages against the manager for breach of the management contract, if the failings rendering the ship unseaworthy were due to the latter's negligence.

However, since the manager is normally co-assured with the owner for third party liabilities under the same P&I insurance cover, the consequence will be that the owner's P&I club will pay the claim to the third party and it will not sue its other member (under its subrogated rights). As has been seen earlier (para 4.7, above), a co-assured has parasitic rights and is dependent on the rights that the main assured has under the policy.

An example of this was in *The Marion*[106] case (seen later under limitation of liability), in which the ship-managing company failed to make sure that old charts on the ship were destroyed and up-to-date ones provided. As a result, the master of the ship – who followed an old chart – caused the fouling of the ship's anchor, resulting in damage to an oil pipe line in berth. Both manager and owner were insured with the same P&I club, under the same policy, and, since the owner could not limit his liability due to the manager's actual fault or privity, which is the test for breaking limitation under the 1957 Limitation of Liability Convention (see Chapter 17), the P&I insurer paid the third party's claim in full (unlimited). The insurer could not sue (under its subrogated rights) its other assured (the manager) for a claim the owner might have had against him. The reason for this is to avoid circuity of action; thus, there is an implied term in a policy that an insurer cannot exercise rights of subrogation against a co-assured who has the benefit of cover protecting against the very loss which forms the basis of the subrogated claim.[107]

If, on the other hand, the manager has independent professional indemnity insurance covering liabilities to third parties and to the owner, the P&I club can sue that other insurer under its subrogated rights for the indemnity the owner would have against the manager under the management contract.

As far as breaking limitation of liability under the HVR is concerned, the test is the same as under the 1976 Convention discussed under para 5.8.1, below.

5.7 Privity of the assured under s 39(5) of the MIA 1906 and the role of the ISM Code

5.7.1 *The principles*

What is said here assumes some knowledge of the subject. In a claim by the assured under an insurance policy contract against the underwriters for an indemnity in respect of a loss or damage to the ship (hull and machinery insurers), or liability to third parties (P&I insurance), the insurers may raise the defence of s 39(5). The burden of proof is on the insurer to show that: (i) the ship was unseaworthy when she was sent to sea; (ii) the assured had positive knowledge of her unseaworthiness

---

106 [1984] 2 Lloyd's Rep 1.

107 *National Oilwell (UK) Ltd v Davy Offshore Ltd* [1993] 2 Lloyd's Rep 582; *Petrofina (UK) v Magnaload* [1984] QB 127; *Stone Vickers v Appledore Ferguson Shipbuilders* [1991] 2 Lloyd's Rep 288.

or had turned a 'blind eye'[108] to the facts, which rendered her unseaworthy; and (iii) the loss was attributable to that unseaworthiness of which the assured was privy[109] (causation).

Privity is concerned with the assured's state of mind. In a case of a company, the identification[110] of the natural persons who had the relevant state of mind in relation to unseaworthiness is necessary. It is the state of mind of the head man that is taken into consideration, or whoever may be considered to be the *alter ego* of the company, or the directing mind and control of the company.[111] Constructive knowledge of the condition of the ship on the part of the directors of the owning or managing company is not sufficient, as is shown in the case discussed below.

In decided cases, it has been difficult for the insurers to discharge this burden, even in *The Star Sea*,[112] the factual background to which, one would have thought, ought to have assisted the insurers to succeed in discharging the burden of proof on the privity point. However, the events happened before the implementation of the ISM Code. It is important, therefore, to look at this case in the light of the Code.

The ship had some history of deficiencies and, in 1990, the Belgian port authority surveyor had found, *inter alia*, that the emergency fire pump was not working. The master was instructed to rectify this and other deficiencies before departure. The chief engineer tried to repair the pump, but failed. In the course of his efforts to do so, he cut the suction pipe passing through the forepeak ballast tank to a non-return valve in the ship's side. The emergency fire pump was, in due course, repaired, but the cut pipe was never repaired. The ship sailed for her next voyage fully loaded. As she approached the Panama Canal, a fire started in the engine room, which spread to other parts and was not finally put out for several days, by which time the vessel had become a constructive total loss (CTL). Two other vessels in the same ownership, the *Centaurus* and the *Kastora*, had become CTL by fire in similar circumstances. When the owners claimed under the insurance policy, the insurers denied liability relying on breach of the duty of utmost good faith and on s 39(5). Only the second defence is relevant here, the grounds of which were the following: (i) by reason of the cut pipe, the emergency fire pump was useless when the vessel was laden; and (ii) there was ineffective sealing of the engine room; and (iii) the master was incompetent in that he was unaware of the need to use the CO_2 system as soon as he realised that the fire could not be fought by any other means and that he did not know how to use it.

Tuckey J (as he then was) held that the ship was unseaworthy by reason of the

---

108 Eg, if a man is suspicious of the truth and turns a blind eye to it, and refrains from inquiry so that he should not know it for certain: see *The Eurysthenes* [1976] 2 Lloyd's Rep 171, p 179, per Lord Denning MR. In addition, the House of Lords held in *The Star Sea* [2001] 1 Lloyd's Rep 389 that 'blind eye knowledge . . . requires a conscious reason for blinding the eye. There must be at least a suspicion of a truth about which you do not want to know and which you refuse to investigate', per Lord Clyde.

109 *The Eurysthenes* [1976] 2 Lloyd's Rep 171; *Thomas v Tyne and Wear Steamship Insurance Association* (1917) 117 LT 55.

110 The 'identification' theory (see, further, Chapter 17, below).

111 *The Eurysthenes* [1976] 2 Lloyd's Rep 171, p 179, per Lord Denning MR.

112 *The Star Sea* [1995] 1 Lloyd's Rep 651 (1st inst), [1997] 1 Lloyd's Rep 360 (CA), [2001] 1 Lloyd's Rep 389 (HL).

cut pipe and the fact that the master was incompetent in not knowing how to use the CO_2 system, which was the most potent weapon in fire-fighting. On the issue of privity of the assured under this section, the judge held that the directors of the company, the alter ego, had a 'blind eye' knowledge of the relevant facts of the ship's unseaworthiness. In particular, he said that:

> With the message staring them in the face that the CO_2 system on *Centaurus* and *Kastora* had not been used so as to prevent those ships from becoming constructive total losses, the assured took no effective steps to ensure that this would not happen again. The incompetence of the master and the state of the safety equipment for sealing the engine room, essential to the effectiveness of the CO_2 system on *Star Sea* show only too clearly how ineffective those steps were and how inadequately equipped she was to fight a fire effectively. The assured did not want to know about the competence of the master to use the CO_2 system effectively.[113]

Thus, the assured's claim failed. However, the Court of Appeal thought differently on the issue of privity. Leggatt LJ held that:

> However negligent it may have been not to learn lessons from the previous fires on *Centaurus* or *Kastora*, or to fail to give proper instructions in fire-fighting or whatever, what the defendant underwriters had to establish was a suspicion or realisation in the mind of at least one of the relevant individuals that *Star Sea* was unseaworthy in one of the relevant aspects, and a decision not to check whether that was so for fear of having certain knowledge about it. Thus, on this aspect, and to be precise, to succeed the underwriters would have to establish that one or other of the individuals . . . suspected that the master was incompetent in lacking the knowledge as to how to use CO_2 and that that rendered *Star Sea* unseaworthy, but that he decided not to check for fear of having certain knowledge and allowed the ship to go to sea anyway. The judge made no such finding. Indeed his finding in this area comes down simply to a finding of negligence, albeit negligence in a high degree.[114]

The Court of Appeal found that the relevant directors of the management company of the assured were involved in the decision-making process required for sending the ship to sea. But Leggatt LJ drew a distinction between an allegation that 'they ought to have known' (as the judge thought) and an allegation that 'they suspected or realised but did not make further enquiries'. The former indicates constructive knowledge, while the latter would amount to 'blind eye' privity.

The House of Lords[115] affirmed the decision of the Court of Appeal. Lord Scott explained 'blind eye' knowledge by giving a vivid example: 'Nelson at the battle of Copenhagen made a deliberate decision to place the telescope to his blind eye in order to avoid seeing what he knew he could see if he placed it to his good eye.' Lord Scott continued: 'It is, I think common ground – and if it is not, it should be – that an imputation of blind eye knowledge requires an amalgam of suspicion that certain facts may exist and a decision to refrain from taking any step to confirm their existence.'

So, how does the ISM Code help the position of the underwriters in discharging the burden of proof under s 39(5)? The House of Lords has now confirmed that the

---

113 *The Star Sea* [1995] 1 Lloyd's Rep 651, p 664.
114 [1997] 1 Lloyd's Rep 360 (CA), p 377.
115 [2001] 1 Lloyd's Rep 389.

knowledge of the owner with regard to unseaworthiness of the ship must be actual and not constructive. Since the test of 'privity' is subjective, the knowledge of other people in the company who are not classed in the category of the ego or the alter ego[116] of the company will not do, nor would it be sufficient if the underwriter proved that the facts shown ought to have been known to the owner.

However, *The Star Sea* is a very significant decision with respect to the application of the duties of the owners and managers under the ISM Code. At the time of the casualty, the Code was not yet in existence. The factual position of this case is the very situation that the Code intends to prevent. The directors of the managing company, or the owners, have to make sure that the master is competent in using any systems on the ship, as well as to ensure (by an efficient risk assessment) that previous incidents in any of the ships of the group do not recur. Documenting, monitoring and making a risk analysis of all previous incidents, which must be recorded in the company's SMM, can achieve this objective. Such information will be of assistance to the insurers in future cases, to the extent that the SMS and SMM may lead to information by which the insurer may be able to show actual or 'blind eye' knowledge of the assured in so far as the unseaworthiness of the ship is concerned.

5.7.2 The role of third party ship manager

Would the owner be able to hide behind the third party manager, if the duties under the ISM Code were delegated to him? In other words, would he be able to say: 'I did not have any knowledge of the situation, as the third party manager was the "company" for the purpose of the ISM Code'? At first glance, the answer to this would seem to be in the affirmative, since the test for proving privity under s 39(5) is subjective, eg it is what the owner actually knew or consciously realised of the truth and did not take steps to find out for certain. However, if the owner and manager are co-assureds for hull and machinery risks, they will stand or fall together and, in any event, the owner's responsibilities under the Code are not absolved by delegating to the manager the technical management and presenting the manager to the authorities as the company for the purpose of ISM certification. It should be remembered that para 3.2 of the Code provides that:

> the company should define and document the responsibility, authority and interrelation of all personnel who manage, perform and verify work relating to and affecting safety and pollution prevention

There must be, therefore, interaction between the personnel of both manager and owner while monitoring safety matters, and the relevant directors of the owning company should be privy to the information.

5.7.3 The role of the designated person

The next question is: what is the role of the designated person ashore (DPA)? By Art 4 of the Code, the DPA has a duty to report to the highest management (see the

---

116 See *Tesco v Nattrass* in Chapter 17, below, for an analysis of the 'identification' doctrine.

Code set out above). It is frequently asked whether, for the purpose of s 39(5), the knowledge of the DPA of deficiencies in the SMS, which he failed to report to the senior management, could be attributed to the company.[117] Although this may be a 'catch 22' situation for the owners, in that a failure by the DPA to report could be, if proved, a failure of the SMS of the company in some cases, it is submitted that knowledge of the DPA could not be imputed to the company, unless DPA is made, by the primary rules of attribution, a member of the board of directors. However, the directors of the company are now, at least by implication, under an increased obligation by the Code to ask questions, to make clear what reports they expect from the DPA, and make an enquiry of what the DPA knows.

For the purpose of s 39(5), it is not what the directors ought to have known, but what they suspected or consciously realised by the reported events and did not make further inquiries (*The Star Sea*, CA). The point in law made by Leggatt LJ and the House of Lords in this case is that, if the insurers could show only constructive knowledge by the directors of the company of the relevant facts, it will not be sufficient for the discharge of the burden of proof under s 39(5).

5.7.4 Other provisions under the insurance contract

If the insurer fails to discharge the burden under s 39(5), there is an alternative way in which he can be discharged from liability. The Institute Clauses for Hull Insurance 1995 contain a special contractual classification warranty. The warranty in effect side-steps the difficulty of s 39(5). It requires strict compliance by the assured with matters of class and maintenance of seaworthiness during the duration of the policy, failing which the insurer will be discharged from liability as from the date of the breach. The documentation under the ISM Code will assist in the collection of evidence and make owners and managers more vigilant about management practices and incidents, which have or ought to have been reported to class, which, in turn, will assist the insurers to catch the recalcitrant assured under this warranty, if not under s 39(5).

Similarly, the amendment to the Inchmaree clause in the 1995 Clauses (unlike the new Hull Clauses of 2002) makes the insured risks under this clause (including crew negligence) subject to the exercise of due diligence not only by the owners and managers, but also by the superintendent and the assured's shore management. If, for example, a loss is caused due to the negligence of the master or crew, this will be a covered peril, provided due diligence had been exercised by the persons mentioned in the clause, not only in the selection procedures of the ship's personnel but also in their supervision and training. The documentation required under the Code may enable the insurers to support their defence to a claim made by the assured under the policy.

In any event, since the implementation of the Code, the Hull and Machinery insurers insert a clause in the policy expressly requiring the assured to comply with the provisions of the Code, spelling out that the consequences of breach will be no

---

117 For relevant questions raised when the ISM Code was first published, see Mandaraka-Sheppard, A, 'The ISMC in Perspective' (1996) 10 P & I International Journal, LLP (the name of this Journal has changed to 'Maritime Risk Management International').

cover. Similarly, P&I clubs have taken care to include an ISM compliance clause in their rules in the nature of a condition that the owner shall not be entitled to any recovery under the policy in respect of claims arising during the period when the assured was not fulfilling the requirements of certification under the Code.[118] But the latter condition relates only to breaches which result in non certification under the Code.

5.8 Limitation of liability and the role of the ISM Code

5.8.1 From an English law perspective

Limitation of liability is examined in Chapter 17. Only brief reference will be made here to general principles, for the purpose of considering the likely effect of the ISM Code on the right of the owner or manager to limit liability.

Under the Limitation Convention 1957, following which s 503 of the MSA 1894 was amended by the subsequent MSA 1958, the shipowning company could limit its liability, if there was no 'actual fault or privity' of the owner. The burden of proof was upon the owner seeking to limit liability. 'Breaking' limitation was relatively easy. English law now applies the 1976 Limitation Convention, but some maritime nations still apply the 1957 Convention.

To make a brief contrast between the two, it suffices to mention that, under the old system of limitation, the owner, even if he had delegated the duty of management to a manager, could not limit his liability if the 'actual fault' of the managing director of the managing company was the cause of the casualty. Such fault was imputed to the owner. So, it was held in *The Marion*,[119] by the House of Lords, in which the managing director of the managing company had failed to give proper instructions to his subordinates during his absence and to ensure that adequate supervision was exercised over the master of the ship (see, further, Chapter 17).

In *The Lady Gwendolen*,[120] the owners were unable to limit liability because the fault of a superintendent was traced upwards to the board of directors for a series of faults in the operating manuals and for not having adequately supervised the operation. In *The Garden City*,[121] again, the owners could not limit liability under the 1957 Convention, as they failed to discharge the burden of proof that the accident was without their fault or privity. The top management of the owning company had failed to ensure that a senior superintendent should be responsible for supervising the quality of navigation and that the vessels in the fleet should be regularly inspected with checklists and written reports.

The facts of these cases echo the philosophy behind the ISM Code. Where the

---

118 See, eg, the new cl 5K of the UK Club Rules, which is a provision subject to the directors' discretion. Similarly, r 29 of the North of England P&I Club.
119 [1984] 2 Lloyd's Rep 1 (see, further, Chapter 17).
120 [1965] 1 Lloyd's Rep 335 (see case summary in Chapter 17).
121 [1982] 2 Lloyd's Rep 382.

1957 Convention still applies, any failures by the owner or manager in keeping an SMS under the Code will provide the evidence of fault or privity, but even prior to the implementation of the Code, it was not that difficult under this Convention for the right to limit to be broken.

By contrast, the 1976 Limitation Convention has a rigid rule of impeaching the right to limit liability. First, the burden of proof is upon the claimant resisting limitation, instead of upon the owner, as it was under the old law. The claimant needs to prove: (i) that the loss claimed resulted from a personal act or omission of the legal persona of the shipowner, and (ii) that it was committed, either with intent to cause such loss, or recklessly and with knowledge that such loss would probably result (Art 4 of the Convention).

In other words, the legal persona of the company must have anticipated the likelihood or probability of the loss or damage, but, nevertheless, acted or failed to act regardless of that probability. So, it is not a question of simple fault, nor is it sufficient for the act or omission to be that of servants or agents,[122] but it is required to be the personal act or omission of the person who seeks to limit. (It would not be enough that the fault was that of a DP unless he was a director.) The loss must be the very loss actually anticipated.[123]

Instead of privity, as was necessary under the old English system of limitation, proof of intent to cause such loss is needed, or proof of recklessness coupled with knowledge that such loss would probably result. Since it is hard to discharge the burden required by this new rule, it has been difficult to break limitation.[124] As a *quid pro quo* to bargaining away a test by which it was not previously difficult to break limitation, a much higher limitation figure per ship's ton is provided by this Convention. In applying the rules of attribution (explained earlier) for the purpose of Art 4 of the 1976 Convention, it is submitted that it would be a violation of its wording and the policy behind this substantive rule of law, if the act or failure to act by an employee (such as the DP) was allowed to be taken into account – unless such a person had been made a member of the board of directors.

If, however, the evidence showed that the highest level of management ignored certain facts reported to them by the DP in relation to deficiency of the system leading to non-conformity with the Code, then such evidence would point strongly to recklessness by the legal persona of the company. A person acts recklessly when he acts in a manner which indicates a decision to run the risk or a mental attitude of indifference to its existence.[125] But in the context of the Convention, for the purpose of breaking limitation, the claimant must also prove that the legal persona of the company seeking limitation acted with knowledge that such loss would probably result[126] from such non-conformity with the Code.

---

122 Unlike Art 4 of the 1976 Convention, Art 25 of the Warsaw Convention, as amended, providing a bar to limitation of liability of airlines, includes acts or omissions of 'servants or agents'.

123 *The Leerort*; *The MSC Rosa M*: see Chapter 17.

124 For details of cases that have construed the wording of this rule, see Chapter 17, below.

125 *Goldman v Thai Airways International* [1983] 1 WLR 1186, p 1194, per Eveleigh LJ.

126 These words were construed by the Court of Appeal, in *Goldman* (ibid and [1983] 3 All ER 693), as requiring a higher standard than mere recklessness.

This would involve proof of either (i) a high degree of subjective realisation (actual knowledge) that damage would probably result from non-conformities with the Code, or (ii) a deliberate shutting of the eyes to a means of knowledge derived from the SMS which, if used, would have produced the same realisation (an amalgam of suspicion that certain facts exist and a decision to refrain form taking any steps to confirm their existence).[127] Falling short of that test, constructive knowledge of the directors of the company, in a sense that they ought to have known that damage would probably result from what the DPA knew about non-conformities with the Code, would not be in line with the policy behind the respective statutes dealing with limitation of liability and having the wording analysed above.

However, in the light of the Code, the person seeking limitation is likely to be questioned as to why he did not make inquiries to ensure that all was in order. Were it to be shown that he made a decision to run the risk and shut his eyes to a means of knowledge staring him in the face by virtue of the information documented in compliance with the ISM Code, which, if used, would have produced a conscious realisation that such loss would probably result, the test of Art 4 would be met.

In each case it will be a question of fact with regard to the extent and degree of faults in the SMS of the relevant company, and whether a non-corrective approach to those faults amounted to recklessness with knowledge that the kind of loss claimed would probably result.

5.8.2 From a US perspective

A very appropriate example in terms of factual background in this respect is provided by an American decision, *The Merchant Patriot*,[128] although the facts surrounding the case arose prior to the implementation of the Code. The issue in this decision was limitation under USA law, in particular, the Limitation of Liability Act 1851, 46 USC paras 183–89. So, the test was one of knowledge or privity of the loss-causing negligent act, or unseaworthy condition by the owners or the owners *pro hac vice* of the vessel. The facts of this decision may be relevant in considering the role of the DP and the impact of the ISM Code so it is important to look at the history of the ship and the quality of its management in relation to the casualty.

The ship was carrying steel products worth $10 million, which were lost during the voyage. The problem started with the deteriorated and wasted condition of certain pipes in the seawater circulating system, which caused the flooding of the engine room, the contamination of the lube oil and, eventually, the shutdown of the main engine which resulted in the abandonment of the ship and the loss of the cargo.

The ship, which had been built in Scotland in 1980 and classed with Lloyd's Register, was bought in 1988 and the management of it was transferred to V Ships, who also managed other vessels of the same owner as agents without ownership

---

127 Per Lord Scott in *The Star Sea*, op cit, fn 115, there has recently been a little doubt about the 'blind eye' knowledge in the context of limitation but not decided; see, further, Chapter 17, below.

128 (2000) transcript of the US District Court of Georgia, 17 February, kindly provided to the author by Herry Lawford of the UK P&I Club.

rights in the ships. V Ships were not charterers but hired and managed the crew, operated the ship and oversaw her maintenance on an annual budget. The owners paid crew wages, running expenses of the ship and repair costs. The principal of the owners spoke to V Ships personnel about the ships under their management, during every given day, and was meeting with the managing and operations' directors frequently to discuss the status of the ships. V Ships provided the owners with several types of reports pertaining to the condition of the vessels, and the principal of the owners was, interestingly, described as 'a hands-on owner' who would personally attend the vessels and perform his own repairs. V Ships performed their duties through a Safety and Quality Management System, which set out in a series of manuals, policies and procedures what should be followed. The maintenance to the vessels was to be a joint effort by the ship's staff and the office personnel of V Ships who were to conduct periodic inspections of the vessel's structure and systems including the engine room piping, together with V Ships' fleet Superintendents.

V Ships, apparently, had a very similar system of safety management in place to that required now by the ISM Code, but it was not as structured and vigorously enforced as the one required by the Code. So, what did go wrong? It was the corroded state of the pipes internally and externally. When the principal of the owners and every senior person in V Ships saw the status of the pipes, it was admitted – with hindsight – that the condition was unacceptable and the pipes ought to have been renewed. Why, then, had they not been renewed? The senior fleet superintendent of V Ships did not call for any renewal or replacement during the vessel's drydocking in April 1997, although six months earlier, when he had performed an inspection, he commented in his report that some engine pipes and valves required replacement, indicating that that should be done at the upcoming drydocking. However, the chief engineer, at about the same time, had reported after conducting visual inspection and hammer tests that the engine room piping was satisfactory. Was this due to human error, incompetence or superficiality in inspection, or due to inadequate mechanical equipment used for the inspection?

This background has significant implications on how things can be prevented under the systems imposed by the ISM Code. The use of old methods of hammer tests at inspections will be insufficient to satisfy the requirements of the Code.

The court found that the ship was unseaworthy and both the owners and V Ships were privy to the condition that caused the casualty, which could have been averted if those, having managerial responsibility of the vessel, including the fleet superintendents, the managing directors of the companies and the principal of the owning company, had taken reasonable action. The court pointed out the critical acts and omissions of the owners and V Ships which established privity and are important to be summarised here by way of illustrating how such acts and omissions can be averted under the ISM Code system:

(a) There was no effective system for creating an historical record of critical information about the seawater pipes and ensuring that those responsible for maintenance were provided with that information. The fleet superintendent had not seen reports of previous failures nor was he aware of them.

(b) There was no planned system in effect for the inspection and maintenance of the seawater pipes. V Ships kept no written records of pipe inspections. The techniques to prevent galvanic corrosion were not employed on the vessel.

(c) No programme was implemented to identify and renew pipes prior to their failure, although there was knowledge possessed by the managing director of V Ships that ferrous seawater pipes fail after five years of service.

(d) There was a failure to effect a permanent repair to the patched aft pipe after more than three years and intervening drydocking. This demonstrated, the court said, either an ineffective follow-up system, or a conscious decision to leave the pipe in place.

(e) The corrosion reports put the owners and the managers on notice that galvanic corrosion was a significant problem with regard to seawater piping.

(f) The type of inspection that the owners and managers employed was insufficient and unreasonable. They conducted only a visual examination of the seawater piping, while the implementation of additional procedures for the inspection and replacement of them was feasible.

(g) Nothing was done to impede the progress of corrosion or galvanic corrosion.

In conclusion, the court found the owners liable for the damage to the cargo on the ground of their failure to exercise due diligence to make the ship seaworthy at the commencement of the voyage, which caused the casualty. The owners could not discharge the burden of proof required under the US limitation statute that they lacked knowledge or privity with regard to unseaworthiness.

Under USA law, constructive knowledge of the top management of the owners counts for the purpose of limitation. In other words, 'knowledge is not only what the shipowner knows but what he is charged with discovering in order to apprise himself of conditions likely to produce or contribute to a loss',[129] or knowledge and privity includes constructive knowledge, or what the vessel owner could have discovered through 'reasonable inquiry'.[130] The belief of V Ships that they had an efficient system was not accepted by the court. What mattered was that the system, in fact, was inefficient to detect the defects in the piping system.

5.9 Resume of the relevance of the ISM Code and the role of the DP

The court's finding, in this case, seems to have been the prelude to the ISM Code and the safety system which must be in place, which has to be monitored and supervised by the designated person who is the link man between the top management and those on board. In this connection, it is relevant to refer to what Lord Donaldson said at the first Cadwallader Memorial Lecture,[131] considering the role of the DP:

> I regard this as not only one of the central pillars of the code, but also as the errant shipowners Achilles' heel. The 'blind eye' shipowner is faced with a 'catch 22' situation. If he hears nothing from the designated person, he will be bound to call for reports, for it is inconceivable there will be nothing to report. If the report is to the

---

129 *Hercules Carriers Inc*, cited in the judgment of *The Merchant Patriot* (2000) transcript of the US District Court of Georgia, 17 February, p 28, see fn 128.

130 *Suzuki of Orange Park Inc v Shubert* [1996] 86 F 3d 1060, p 1064 (11th Cir).

131 Op cit, Lord Donaldson, fn 10.

effect that all is well in a perfect world, the shipowner would be bound to enquire how that could be, as the safety management system is clearly intended to be a dynamic system which is subject to continuous change in the light, not only of the experience of the individual ship, and of the company as a whole, but also of the experience of others in the industry. So, there will always be something to report. Quite apart from this, the shipowner can, at any time, be called upon to produce documentary evidence of his internal audit of every area of his system including the work of the designated person.

This observation suggests that any mistakes or personal inattention of the DP will be caught up, if the owner or manager is rigorous in the enforcement of the Code. It also suggests that the Code is capable of reversing the fallibility of human beings! It has been realised in the industry that the 'human element' in accidents is a very significant factor, and the provisions of the Code aim to tackle this important issue. To a great extent, it is correct to say that a 'catch 22' situation has been created by the Code for owners and managers, but the writer is still sceptical about the extent to which, in reality, all will become transparent in the SMS. There are still a lot of issues in the enforcement aspects of the Code that need to be looked at. There are no strict controls yet in relation to the formal audits, and there is a long time gap regarding the verification of the ISM certificates.

It is certain, however, that during cross-examination of witnesses in court, many relevant deficiencies of the implementation of the Code will be revealed.[132]

In the light of what was shown in the previous paragraphs about the possible effect of the ISM Code upon an owner's ability to discharge the burden of proof regarding due diligence in cases of unseaworthiness, the role of the Code and of the DP in insurance claims and in limitation of liability, caution should be exercised, so that the Code is properly implemented. The very significant effect of the Code has been to raise awareness that risk assessment and analysis are now a must. It is only a matter of further time that is required to persuade some owners, their managers and crew to change their attitude and look at the Code as a constructive way of implementing safety and not as just another administrative and regulatory burden.

5.10 Criminal liability and the role of the ISM Code

It should be noted again that the ISM Code does not itself impose criminal liability. It is up to each individual State, which implements the Code, to legislate the extent to which criminal liabilities for breach of the Code by the owner, or manager, or officers delegated with ISM Code responsibilities can arise. In this part, the matter is looked upon from the point of view of English law. Criminal sanctions for the unsafe operation of ships had already been imposed by the MSAs 1988 and 1995, before the ISM Code was implemented by statutory instrument, SI 1998/1561. Separate criminal sanctions for breaches of the obligations under the Code are now imposed under this statutory instrument (see para 5.10.2, below). The offences provided by the SI and the MSA 1995 are clearly defined. In the next paragraph, the

---

132 The London Shipping Law Centre has constructed and run a series of 'Mock' Trials, in which the cross-examination of witnesses was very enlightening for owners and DPs.

relevant offences under the MSA are briefly examined, followed by the SI enacting the ISM Code into English law and the offences prescribed by it. In the last part of this chapter, developments in the law with regard to corporate manslaughter are examined and how relevant the ISM documentation might be.

5.10.1 Statutory offences under the MSAs

The MSA 1995 contains various statutory offences, some of which are relevant here. By s 77, every British ship must keep an official logbook on board (that is an obligation of any ship of any nationality). Destruction of, or obliteration of, entries of the logbook by anyone is a criminal offence punishable with a fine on summary conviction.

Section 98, which replaced s 30 of the MSA 1988, makes the owner and master of a dangerously unsafe ship, or any other person who has assumed the responsibility for safety matters (under a charterparty or a management agreement), guilty of an offence liable on summary conviction to a fine up to £50,000, or, on conviction on indictment, to imprisonment for up to two years.

'Dangerously unsafe' is defined in s 94, as amended by the Merchant Shipping and Maritime Security Act 1997:[133] a ship in port is dangerously unsafe if it is unfit to go to sea without serious danger to human life. A ship at sea is dangerously unsafe, if, having regard to the nature of the service for which it is being used, or intended, the ship is, by reason of the matters mentioned in sub-s (2), either unfit to remain at sea without serious danger to human life, or unfit to go on a voyage without serious danger to human life.

Incidents of unsafe condition include the unsuitability of machinery or equipment, undermanning, overloading or unsafe loading.

The only defence under this provision is proof by the accused that, at the time of the offence, arrangements had been made to ensure the ship's fitness before she was sent to sea.

Section 100, which replaced s 31 of the MSA 1988, imposes a duty upon the owner, demise charterer or manager of a ship to take all reasonable steps to ensure that the ship is operated in a safe manner, failing which it shall be a criminal offence punishable on summary conviction or on indictment. By contrast to s 98, this section does not extend the liability to the master.

The first decision on unsafe operation of a ship under the predecessor to s 100 was *The Safe Carrier*,[134] which is worth mentioning in some detail to see the extent to which the SMS of the ISM Code is likely to prevent the same, or similar, incidents from happening and, if they do, whether the SMM will provide the evidence required for conviction of the owner or manager under this section.

The ship-managers were charged with an offence for failing to ensure that the vessel was operated in a safe manner, particularly by allowing the chief engineer less than three hours to familiarise himself with the ship before sailing. Usually, he

---

133 See Sched 1, para 1.
134 [1994] 1 Lloyd's Rep 589 (HL).

would need three days for a newly converted ship. During the next 24 hours, the engines broke down, leaving the ship in total black-out drifting at sea. The service tanks had run dry, because the fuel purifier throughput was inadequate to meet the engine demand. The justices for the city of Newcastle upon Tyne convicted the managers but stated a case for the opinion of the Divisional Court of the High Court, which quashed the conviction. The Secretary of State for Transport appealed to the House of Lords.

The issues were these: (i) whether the principle of the *Tesco v Nattrass* case (that the corporation was criminally liable only for the conduct of those representing its directing mind and will) applied; (ii) whether s 31 provided for strict liability; and (iii) whether there was vicarious liability under the section on the part of the manager, if any of his employees failed to comply with the requirements of the section, or was there a crime only if the manager himself or someone whose omission was to be attributed to him failed to comply.

It was held by the House of Lords that, to secure a conviction under s 31, the prosecution must prove beyond reasonable doubt that the accused owner, charterer or manager of a ship had failed to take all reasonable steps to secure that the ship was operated in a safe manner. The fault of an employee other than senior management in putting the ship to sea with an engineer insufficiently familiar with the ship could not be attributed to the company (the Tesco principle applied). There was no evidence as to how it came about that the engineer was only allowed very little time to get familiar with the ship. It further held that it was not helpful to categorise the offence as being or not being one of strict liability. The section provides simply for failure to take steps, which by an objective standard must be reasonable. It is a personal duty and the owner, charterer or manager will not be criminally liable for the acts or omissions of his subordinate employees if he had himself taken all such steps, which were 'reasonable to him'.

Undoubtedly, there should be evidence in the future in the ISM Code documentation to show how the engineer of *The Safe Carrier* was allowed only such a short time to become familiar with the ship and who ordered the ship to sail. In any event, if the company is complying with both the ISM Code and the STCW Convention, which specifically require that sufficient familiarisation of new personnel on the ship should be given, a casualty such as *The Safe Carrier* should not occur again.

There are also other statutory offences under the MSA 1995 for breach of the collision regulations, which are referred to in Chapter 12, and for breach of the statutory provisions in relation to pollution damage, examined in Chapter 19. The EU Criminalisation Directive is examined in Chapter 20.

In connection with the criminal liabilities under the Act, s 277 refers to offences by officers of corporations. It makes a director, manager, secretary or other similar officer of the body corporate or any person who was purporting to act in such a capacity, as well as the body corporate, guilty of the relevant offence punished accordingly, if it is proved that the offence was committed with the consent or connivance of, or attributable to any neglect on the part of any of them. This will be relevant in the interpretation of offences under the SI enacting the ISM Code below, in particular para 5.10.2.2.

5.10.2 Criminal liability under SI 1998/1561 enacting the ISM Code into English law

5.10.2.1 Substantive provisions of the 1998 Regulations

Extracts of the Statutory Instrument are set out here because the duties and requirements are more clearly defined than in the Code, but space does not permit to include the preamble and definitions of these Regulations which can be found in the text of the Code; only the following definitions of these Regulations are set out:

'audit' means a systematic and independent examination to determine whether the safety management system is suitable to meet the objectives set out in section 1 of the Code, and, so far as the system has been operated, that the system has been implemented effectively. Such audits shall take into account the Guidelines on the Implementation of the ISM Code by Administrations, adopted by IMO pursuant to Assembly Resolution A. 788(19);

'authorised person' means a person authorised by the Secretary of State to carry out inspections and audits for the purpose of these Regulations and includes any surveyor of ships appointed under section 256 of the Merchant Shipping Act 1995;

The Regulations apply to all ships and every Company as provided by the Code; in particular to:

(a) United Kingdom ships wherever they may be; and

(b) Other ships while they are within United Kingdom waters.

Duty to comply with the ISM Code

4. Every company shall comply with the requirements of the ISM Code as it applies to that company and to any ship owned by it or for which it has responsibility.

Duty to hold certificates

5. (1) No company shall operate a ship unless that company holds a valid Document of Compliance.

(2) No company shall operate a ship unless there is in force in respect of that ship a valid Safety Management Certificate.

(3) No United Kingdom ship shall be operated unless:

(a) the company holds a Document of Compliance issued or accepted by the Secretary of State; and

(b) there is in force in relation to the ship a Safety Management Certificate issued by the Secretary of State.

(4) For the purposes of this regulation a Document of Compliance or Safety Management Certificate is not valid if it has not been endorsed, in the circumstances required by the ISM Code, showing, in the case of a Document of Compliance satisfactory annual audits, or in the case of a Safety Management Certificate, a satisfactory intermediate audit.

Duty to carry certificates

6. It shall be the duty of every company to ensure that a valid Safety Management Certificate and a copy of the Document of Compliance is carried on board each ship to which these Regulations apply.

Duty of master

7.   The master of every ship shall operate his ship in accordance with the safety management system on the basis of which the Safety Management Certificate was issued.

Designated Person

8. (1) The company shall designate a person who shall be responsible for monitoring the safe and efficient operation of each ship with particular regard to the safety and pollution prevention aspects.

(2) In particular, the designated person shall-

(a) Take such steps as are necessary to ensure compliance with the company safety management system on the basis of which the Document of Compliance was issued; and

(b) Ensure that proper provision is made for each ship to be so manned, equipped and maintained that it is fit to operate in accordance with the safety management system and with statutory requirements.

(3) The company shall ensure that the designated person-

(a) Is provided with sufficient authority and resources; and

(b) Has appropriate knowledge and sufficient experience of the operation of ships at sea and in port, to enable him to comply with paragraphs (1) and (2) above.

Issue of Document of Compliance and Safety Management Certificate

9. (1) If the Secretary of State is satisfied that a company operating United Kingdom ships complies with the requirements of the ISM Code he may issue it with a Document of Compliance valid for a period not exceeding five years.

(2) If the Secretary of State is satisfied that a ship is operated by a company to which he has issued a Document of Compliance and that the company and its shipboard management operate in accordance with the safety management system he has approved, he shall issue in respect of that ship a Safety Management Certificate valid for a period not exceeding five years.

(3) Where a company operating ships which are registered in more that one country, but at least one of which is registered in the United Kingdom, complies with the requirements of the ISM Code the Secretary of State may accept a Document of Compliance issued by the government of one of those countries to which SOLAS applies, if prior to the issue of that document he has agreed to accept it. Conditions for acceptance may include completion of a satisfactory audit of the company by an authorised person.

(4) Where a company newly registers a ship in the United Kingdom, the Secretary of State may accept a Document of Compliance issued by the government of a country to which SOLAS applies in which ships operated by the company are registered. Conditions for acceptance may include completion of a satisfactory audit by an authorised person.

(5) If the Secretary of State is satisfied that a United Kingdom ship is operated by a company which has a Document of Compliance accepted by the Secretary of State under paragraph (3) or (4) above and that its shipboard management operates in accordance with a safety management system which complies with ISM Code he shall issue in respect of that ship a Safety Management Certificate valid for a period not exceeding five years.

Interim certificates

10. (1)(a) Where a company is newly established, or the company assumes, for the first time, the responsibility for operating a ship type not covered by a Document of Compliance the company already holds, an interim Document of Compliance the company already holds, an interim Document of Compliance may be issued to facilitate implementation of the ISM Code.

    (b) An interim Document of Compliance, valid for no more than 12 months, may be issued to a company following a demonstration that the company has a safety management system that meets the objectives of section 1.2.3 of the ISM Code. The company shall demonstrate plans to implement a safety management system meeting the full requirements of the ISM Code within the period of validity of the interim Document of Compliance.

    (2)(a) An interim Safety Management Certificate, valid for not more than six months, may be issued in respect of a new ship on delivery, when a company takes on the responsibility for the management of a ship which is new to the company or when a ship is transferred between flag states. The Secretary of State, may, as he considers appropriate, extend the validity of the interim Safety Management Certificate for a further six months.

    (b) An interim Safety Management Certificate shall only be issued when the Secretary of State is satisfied that–

      (i) The Document of Compliance, or the interim Document of Compliance, is relevant to that ship type;

      (ii) The safety management system provided by the company for the ship includes all key elements of the ISM Code and has been assessed during the audit for issuance of the Document of Compliance or issuance of the interim Document of Compliance;

      (iii) The master and relevant senior officers are familiar with the safety management system and the planned arrangements for its implementation;

      (iv) Instructions which have been identified as essential to be provided prior to sailing have been given;

      (v) Plans for audit, by the company, of the ship within three months exist; and

      (vi) The relevant information on the safety management system is given in a working language or languages understood by the ship's personnel.

Issue and endorsement of Safety Management Certificate by another government

11. The Secretary of State may request, through a proper officer or otherwise, the government of a country to which SOLAS applies–

    (a) To conduct an audit of the safety management system operated onboard a United Kingdom ship, and

    (b) If satisfied that the requirements of the ISM Code are complied with, to issue to the ship a Safety Management Certificate or authorise such issue or, where appropriate, endorse such certificates in accordance with the requirements of SOLAS after intermediate audit. A certificate issued in accordance with such a request shall contain a statement that it has been so issued and shall have the same effect as if it was issued by the Secretary of State.

Issue of certificates on behalf of other governments

12.   The Secretary of State may, at the request of a government of a country to which SOLAS applies, audit the safety management systems of companies and ships registered in that country and, if satisfied that the requirements of the ISM Code are complied with, and that the audit has been satisfactorily completed in accordance with this Regulations, issue to the company a Document of Compliance or, in respect of the ship a Safety Management Certificate, or, where appropriate, endorse such certificates in accordance with the requirements of SOLAS after annual or intermediate audits. A certificate issued in accordance with such a request shall contain a statement that it has been so issued and shall have the same effect as if it was issued by that government and not by the Secretary of State.

Annual audit of Document of Compliance

13.   The Secretary of State shall carry out an annual audit of the safety management system of every company to which he has issued a Document of Compliance, within three months of the anniversary date of the Document of Compliance.

Intermediate audit of Safety Management Certificate

14.   The Secretary of State shall carry out an intermediate audit of each ship, to ensure that the conditions for the continued validity of the Safety Management Certificate are being met, between the second and third anniversaries of the Safety Management Certificate issued by him, and at other times if he thinks fit.

Renewal of certificates

15.   Before the renewal of any certificate the Secretary of State shall carry out a renewal audit of the company or ship during the six month period preceding the expiry date of the Document of Compliance or Safety Management Certificate as the case may be, to ensure that compliance with the requirements of the ISM Code is maintained.

Powers of audit, inspection, suspension of service and detention

16. (1)(a) Any authorised person may audit the safety management system of any company.

      (b) If an authorised person considers that a company, notwithstanding that it holds a Document of Compliance, is unable to operate ships without creating a risk of–

         (i) Serious danger to safety of life; or

         (ii) Serious damage to property; or

         (iii) Serious harm to the environment, or that the company does not hold a Document of Compliance, he may suspend the operation of ships by that company until such time as any such risk is removed or a valid Document of Compliance is held.

      (c) Where a service is to be suspended pursuant to sub-paragraph (b) above the authorised person shall serve on the company a notice stating that the operation of the service specified in the notice shall be suspended.

(2)(a) Any authorised person may inspect any ship, and any such inspection may include an audit of its safety management system.

(b) If an authorised person is satisfied on inspecting a ship that there is a failure to comply in relation to that ship with the requirements of regulation 4 or 5 he may detain the ship.

(c) In any case where a ship is liable to be detained, section 284 of the Merchant Shipping Act 1995[10] (which relates to the detention of the ship) shall have effect in relation to the ship subject to the modification that as if for the words "this Act" wherever they appear, there were substituted "the Merchant Shipping (International Safety Management (ISM) Code) Regulations 1998."

(d) Where a ship is detained in relation to a failure to comply with a requirement of these Regulations sections 96 and 97 of the Merchant Shipping Act 1995 shall apply to the notice of detention as they apply to a detention notice under section 95, and as if for references to the ship being dangerously unsafe there were substituted references to it being in breach of these Regulations.

(3) An authorised person exercising functions under this regulation shall have the powers conferred on an inspector by section 259 of the Merchant Shipping Act 1995.

Exemptions

17. The Secretary of State may grant exemptions from all or any of the provisions of these Regulations (as may be specified in the exemption) for classes of cases or individual cases on such terms (if any) as he may specify, and may, subject to giving reasonable notice, alter or cancel any such exemption.

Suspension or cancellation of Documents of Compliance and Safety Management Certificates

18. (1)(a) The Secretary of State may by notice in writing suspend or cancel any Document of Compliance or Safety Management Certificate issued by him or at his request under these Regulations where he has reason to believe that:

(i) The certificate was issued on false or erroneous information; or

(ii) Since any audit required by these Regulations, the management structure of either the company or ship has changed substantively, or where any audit of a company or ship has revealed a failure to comply with regulation 4.

(b) Any such notice shall contain the grounds for the suspension or cancellation of the certificate.

(c) A notice shall not be given unless the holder has been given the opportunity to make representations, except where the Secretary of State considers that urgent safety or pollution prevention considerations require the notice to be given immediately.

(2) The Secretary of State may require that any Document of Compliance or Safety Management Certificate, issued by him under these Regulations, which has expired or has been suspended or cancelled, be surrendered as directed.

(3) No person shall:

(a) Intentionally alter a Document of Compliance or Safety Management Certificate;

(b) In connection with any audit conducted pursuant to these Regulations, knowingly or recklessly furnish false information;

(c) With intent to deceive, use, lend or allow to be used by another, a Document of Compliance or Safety Management Certificate;

(d) Fail to surrender a Document of Compliance or Safety Management Certificate required to be surrendered under paragraph (2); or

(e) In Scotland forge any Document of Compliance or Safety Management Certificate.

Offences and penalties

19. (1) Any contravention of regulations 4, 5, or 8 by a company shall be an offence punishable on summary conviction by a fine not exceeding the statutory maximum, or on conviction on indictment by imprisonment for a term not exceeding 2 years, or a fine, or both.

(2) Any contravention of regulation 6 by the company shall be an offence punishable on summary conviction by a fine not exceeding level 3 on the standard scale.

(3) Any contravention of regulation 7 by the master of a ship shall be an offence punishable on summary conviction by a fine not exceeding the statutory maximum, or on conviction on indictment by imprisonment for a term not exceeding 2 years, or a fine, or both.

(4) Any contravention of regulation 8(2) by the Designated Person shall be an offence punishable on summary conviction by a fine not exceeding the statutory maximum, or on conviction on indictment by imprisonment for a term not exceeding 2 years, or a fine, or both.

(5) Any company which operates a ship on a service when the service is suspended under regulation 16(1)(b) above shall be guilty of an offence and liable on summary conviction to a fine not exceeding the statutory maximum, or on conviction on indictment, to imprisonment for a term not exceeding 2 years, or a fine, or both.

(6) Any contravention of regulation 18(3) shall be an offence, punishable on summary conviction by a fine not exceeding the statutory maximum, or on conviction on indictment by imprisonment for a term not exceeding 6 months, or a fine, or both.

Defence

20. It shall be a defence for a person charged with an offence under these Regulations to show that he took all reasonable precautions and exercised all due diligence to avoid the commission of the offence.

5.10.2.2 Interpretation

This statutory instrument was issued under the powers given to the Secretary of State by s 85 of the MSA 1995. Its regulations apply to UK ships, wherever they may be, and to other ships while they are within UK waters.

Regulation 19 of the SI sets out offences, which may be committed by the

Thus, the law of manslaughter as it applies to companies is parasitical upon the offence which applies to individuals, and the guilt or innocence of the company is entirely dependent on the guilt or innocence of the individual.

The *Herald of Free Enterprise*[146] provides the immediate and much-debated example. Briefly, what caused the disaster were these facts:

(a) the assistant bosun failed to close the bow doors of the ferry before it sailed;

(b) the chief officer failed to check that the bow doors were shut;

(c) the master, who set off at a maximum speed in an overcrowded boat, was responsible for the safety of the ship, but he had followed the system approved by the senior master;

(d) the senior master failed to co-ordinate practices of different crews on board and to enforce such orders as had been issued; and

(e) the board of directors did not appreciate their responsibilities for the safe management of their ships and did not apply their mind to safety issues. In addition, the management had not acted upon reports of previous open door incidents.

This is the area that the ISM Code is now taking care of, but the question still remains whether the company can be convicted for involuntary manslaughter under the present law.

A jury must find a culpable state of mind in order to convict a corporation and that state of mind must be of someone in the senior management of the company.[147]

As seen earlier, the vicarious liability doctrine usually applies in relation to statutory offences when that is the intention of the particular statute.[148] In *The Safe Carrier*, it was elaborated by both the Divisional Court[149] and the House of Lords that it was not the intention behind s 31 of the MSA 1988 (which was enacted to prevent the recurrence of situations like the *Herald* case) to make the company criminally liable for breach of duty of an employee, below the board of directors, as that was not intended by Parliament, regardless of whether or not the section imposed strict liability.

In the *Herald* case, *R v HM Coroner for East Kent ex p Spooner*,[150] Bingham LJ noted that:

> A company may be vicariously liable for the negligent acts and omissions of its servants and agents, but for a company to be criminally liable for manslaughter . . . it is required that [culpability for] manslaughter should be established not against those who acted for, or in the name of the company but against those who were to be identified as the embodiment of the company itself.

---

146 *R v HM Coroner for East Kent ex p Spooner and Others* (1989) 88 Cr App Rep 10 and *R v P&O European Ferries (Dover) Ltd* (1990) 93 Cr App Rep 72; see, also, summary in Chapter 12, para 2.3.

147 See, further, Wells, C, *Corporations and Criminal Responsibility*, 1993, OUP; Sullivan, GR, 'The attribution of culpability to limited companies' (1996) 55(3) CLJ 515, pp 515–46; *AG's Reference (No 2 of 1999)* [2000] IRLR 417, or [2000] 3 All ER 182 (CA).

148 HSWA 1974; *British Steel plc* [1995] 1 CR 586.

149 [1994] 1 Lloyd's Rep 75, pp 80–82.

150 (1989) 88 Cr App R 10.

The identification doctrine became the established route to the imposition of corporate criminal liability. However, there are major problems with this doctrine and, over the past decade, there has been a growing realisation that it simply does not reflect modern corporate practice, particularly in larger companies.[151]

In the *Herald* case, it could not be proved that the risk of open door sailing was obvious to any of the crew and to others who testified, nor to any of the senior managers.[152] Accordingly, no *mens rea* could be attributed to the company and it was not acceptable to the court to aggregate the faults of each of those liable. Turner J acquitted P&O[153] in the criminal proceeding brought against the company, although Sheen J, who chaired the public inquiry, was considerably critical about the conduct of everyone in the company.

Despite this decision, the Crown, in the trial of Great Western Trains over the Southall train disaster in 1998, tried to argue that the identification doctrine should no longer apply, and that it was possible to consider the conduct of the 'company' as a whole rather than the conduct of an individual being the 'controlling mind' of the company. The trial judge held that:

> There is, I accept, some attraction in the fact that gross negligence manslaughter, involving as it does an objective test rather than *mens rea* in the strict sense of the expression, is in some ways closer to statutory offences of the kind in the cases relied on by Mr Lissack than it is to the ordinary run of criminal offences. But I do not think this is a good reason for no longer having to look for a directing mind in the company to identify where the fault occurred. In my judgement it is still necessary to look for such a directing mind and identify whose gross negligence it is that fixes the company with criminal responsibility.

Accordingly, he concluded that the doctrine of identification which was both clear, certain and established was the relevant doctrine by which a corporation may be fixed with liability for manslaughter by gross negligence'. Following this ruling, the Attorney General asked the Court of Appeal for clarification of the law on this point. In *Attorney General's Reference No 2/1999*,[154] the court held that the trial judge was correct and confirmed that:

> . . . the identification principle remains the only basis in common law for corporate liability for gross negligence manslaughter.

The conclusion is that the identification doctrine is unworkable in proving the required mental element of the offence of involuntary manslaughter, because it requires the prosecution to prove that one of the controlling officers of the corporation was personally guilty of gross negligence in respect of his duty of care, in order for the offence to be attributed to the corporation. Considering that directors delegate tasks to subordinates, it is very difficult for the prosecution to succeed in

---

151 Clarkson CMV, 'Kicking corporate bodies and damning their souls' (1996) 59(4) MLR 557, p 561; see, also, a very clear analysis of the law in this area in the Law Commission's Report No 237, 1996.

152 At the time of the prosecution, the courts were still applying the recklessness test of criminal liability, ie failure to appreciate an obvious and serious risk of injury, as derived from *The Lawrence* [1982] AC 152, prior to the test of gross negligence of *The Adomako* [1995] 1 AC 171.

153 In *R v P&O European Ferries (Dover) Ltd* (1990) 93 Cr App Rep 72.

154 [2000] EWCA Crim 10.

discharging the burden of proof. This has been evident in the four unsuccessful prosecutions against corporations: P&O Ferries, Great Western Trains, Network Rail, and Balfour Beatty.

In the context of shipping, there remains the main question: are the implications of the ISM Code such as to impute the gross negligence of the designated person to the company for the purpose of convicting the company for involuntary manslaughter? From the above analysis of English law, it can be concluded that the identification of the designated person, whose conduct may amount to gross negligence for the purpose of involuntary manslaughter, will not suffice to attribute that liability to the shipowning company, unless he has been included in the board of directors and represents the embodiment or ego of the company, or he is delegated with specific authority and has full power of discretion so as to be the alter ego of the company.

However, the matter is not as simple as that, as was shown in the *Herald* case, because it will be difficult to ascertain whether it was the act of the DP alone that caused the death. If he is not a director, he may be personally exposed to the risk of conviction, if the required mental element is proved and his gross negligence caused the death, but the duties under the ISM Code are not performed by him alone, unless death resulted clearly from his act or omission.

Generally, however, it may now be easier for the prosecution, through the documentation required by the Code, to collect evidence. Whether or not the prosecution will be able to ascertain that the criminal negligence was that of the directing mind and will of the company (so as to impute that criminal negligence to the company) will still be elusive. The Code does not require the DP to take full charge of ISM and safety matters. It only requires the DP to have access to the highest management. Whether or not he tells them the whole story will depend on his efficiency or on whether the company directors instruct him to tell them everything. But what the ISM Code achieves is to create a trail of documents which facilitates further investigation. What is necessary for possible success in prosecutions is to base the test of gross failure on the management systems and not on individuals, which is examined next.

5.10.3.3 *The future of corporate manslaughter*

In its report the Law Commission in 1996[155] proposed reform in corporate killing and set out in its recommendations three separate offences:

(a) Corporate killing when there is management failure (as opposed to operational negligence of employees), in circumstances in which the conduct of the corporation falls significantly below what might reasonably be expected. Such management failure must have caused the death. There is no requirement to show that the risk was obvious, or that the company was capable of appreciating the risk.

(b) Reckless killing.

---

155 Law Commission Report No 237 (*Involuntary Manslaughter*, 1996).

(c) Killing by gross negligence, which does not require proof that a duty of care was owed to the victim and it would apply to prosecution of directors and officers of companies personally.

All three offences were proposed as a replacement for the common law crime of gross negligence manslaughter for breach of duty of care.

Clarkson had commented on this proposal that the implementation of these offences would make the conviction of companies a real possibility, and perhaps the damning of their corporate souls might stimulate the development of a few more consciences in those companies that have the lives and safety of others on their hands.[156]

There had been some criticisms of the Law Commission's proposal, in that it did not deal with grievous bodily harm, and that, perhaps, the Australian approach should have been adopted, which takes into account the corporate policy or culture test.[157] Another critic of the Law Commission's proposal commented that the approach applicable under the HSWA 1974, which relies on the 'vicarious liability' doctrine, is strong, flexible and tested. Therefore, it should be adopted across the board instead of resorting to new untested concepts of 'management failure'.[158]

The Law Commission's recommendations for a statutory offence of corporate killing were considered by the Government which published its first consultation document in 2000. It has taken a long time since then for the Bill to go through the various stages and there have been many amendments to the original proposal.[159]

Rail crash victims have pressed the Government to fulfil its 1997 commitment to introduce a corporate manslaughter offence. Home Secretary David Blunkett, in March 2003, gave details of a draft Bill on corporate killing, with a timetable for legislation.

Since the first edition of this book, the Government published in March 2005 a draft Bill to reform the law of manslaughter. The period of consultation finished in June 2005.

A Bill titled 'The Corporate Manslaughter and Corporate Homicide Bill'[160] was issued in October 2006, which unfortunately includes the element of 'breach of the relevant duty of care'.

As seen in the analysis made by the House of Lords in *The Adomaco* case, the requirement of breach of duty of care by the common law offence 'gross negligence manslaughter for breach of duty of care' caused problems in the past in the burden of proof as to whether or not the accused owed a duty of care. However, the Bill

---

156 Op cit, Clarkson, fn 151, p 572.

157 Bergman, D, 'Manslaughter and corporate immunity' (2000) 150 NLJ 316.

158 Smith, I, 'Manslaughter and corporate immunity' (2000) 150 NLJ 656.

159 To find out about the stages which proposed legislation goes through in both the House of Commons and the House of Lords, visit www.parliament.uk/about/how/laws/stages.cfm; to follow the progress of the Bill and comments, visit www.corporateaccountability.org/manslaughter/reformprops/main.htm.

160 'Corporate manslaughter' will be an offence under the law of England and Wales, while 'corporate homicide' will be an offence under the law of Scotland.

states that a prosecution can only take place if there is a 'relevant' duty of care – which is defined in cl 3 of the Bill.

At the proceedings of Standing Committee B, the Parliamentary Under-Secretary of State for the Home Department, Gerry Sutcliffe, stated:

> The Bill will create a new offence to deal adequately with the gross organisational failings that cause death, and employees and service users in both the public and the private sectors will be protected by its provisions. It also addresses the imbalances between small and large companies; in practice, the current law is truly effective only against small companies. It puts the public and private sectors on an equal footing, and it penalises companies that seek to gain competitive advantage by cutting costs on health and safety.

The Committee believed that merely making additions to the regulatory framework for health and safety would not be good enough.

The offence in cl 1:

(1)   An organisation to which this section applies is guilty of an offence if the way in which any of its activities are managed or organised by its senior managers

    (a)   causes a person's death, and

    (b)   amounts to a gross breach of a relevant duty of care owed by the organisation to the deceased

(2)   The organisations to which this section applies are

    (a)   a corporation

    (b)   a department or other body listed in Schedule 1

    (c)   a police force

    In this Act 'Corporation' includes any body corporate whenever incorporated.

(3)(c)   A breach of duty of care by an organisation is a 'gross' breach if the conduct alleged to amount to a breach of that duty falls far below what can reasonably be expected of the organisation in the circumstances.

The definition of 'gross breach' was borrowed from the Law Commission's proposal. The other terms are defined below.

Clause 2: Meaning of 'senior manager'

A person is a 'senior manager' of an organisation if he plays a significant role in

(a)   the making of decisions about how the whole or a substantial part of its activities are to be managed or organised, or

(b)   the actual managing or organising of the whole or a substantial part of those activities.

Apart from directors of the organisation, this definition also specifically includes managers who may not be on the board of directors to make decisions but just manage activities. The significance here is that, if a manager does not organise the whole of the activities, he should organise or manage a substantial part, which will include managers of units of an organisation if they represent a substantial part of overall activities. Failings at a junior level are not intended to be included. The focus of identifying management failure is intended to be at the organisation as a whole, targeting the strategic management of the organisation, rather than aggregating the conduct of individuals to identify a gross management failure.

Clause 3 defines the 'relevant duty of care'

(1) A 'relevant duty of care' in relation to an organisation, means any of the following duties owed by it under the law of negligence

  (a) a duty owned to its employees or to other persons working for the organisation or performing services for it

  (b) a duty owed as occupier of premises

  (c) a duty owed in connection with

     (i) the supply by the organisation of goods or services (whether for consideration or not),

     (ii) the carrying on by the organisation of any construction or maintenance operations,

     (iii) the carrying on by the organisation of any other activity on a commercial basis, or

     (iv) the use of keeping by the organisation of any plant, vehicle or other thing.

The section goes on to define what is 'construction or maintenance operations'. While the duty owed by employers to employees, or the duty owed by occupiers of premises, will not cause any problems regarding the persons to whom such duty is owed, there will be problems in finding to whom an organisation owes a relevant duty of care in connection with its activities of a commercial nature, or in connection with supplying goods or services. Perhaps the area of such activities needs further elaboration.

There is an important exclusion in cl 4 in favour of public authorities, in connection with their making public policy decisions or performing exclusively public functions and statutory inspections, where it is stated that, if any duty of care is owed, it is not a 'relevant duty of care'. There are similar exclusions in favour of the police, law enforcement agencies, prisons (cl 6), and emergency services of public authorities, such the fire brigade (cl 7). In effect, this means that, for the purpose of this offence, a public body does not owe a duty of care to those who may be affected by the public policy decision-making; this embraces a wide scope of activities, including detentions on behalf of the State during which the detainee may die.

Factors for the jury: cl 9

The Bill further deals with factors for the jury to take into account in relation to 'gross breach'.

Once it is established that an organisation owed a relevant duty of care (this is the first hurdle), it will fall to the jury to decide whether there was a gross breach of that duty (the second hurdle).

As seen in cl 1(3)(c), conduct alleged to amount to a breach of that duty will be gross if it falls far below what can reasonably be expected of the organisation in the circumstances. In other words, the way in which the organisation is organised and managed will be looked at and, drawing on the Law Commission's original proposal, 'management failures' are the central focus rather than the negligence of an individual employee.

Clause 9 further provides that the jury will be guided to consider whether the evidence shows that the organisation failed to comply with any health and safety legislation that relates to the alleged breach, and if so

(a) how serious that failure was, and

(b) how much of a risk of death it posed.

An important provision of this clause is that the jury may also consider the extent to which the evidence shows that there were attitudes, policies, systems or accepted practices within the organisation that were likely to have encouraged any such failure, as is mentioned in sub-cl (2), or to have produced tolerance of it. The jury will also have regard to any health and safety guidance that relates to the alleged breach.

Such information will be found in the safety management systems of an organisation and, in this respect, the SMS of the ISM Code will provide the evidence as far as shipping organisations are concerned.

Of course, it will be necessary to establish that the death was caused by the way the activities were managed or organised by the senior managers; the strategic management will be relevant.

It is strange that the Bill does not deal with penalties or sentencing, although the heading of cl 14 is 'Procedure, evidence and sentencing', and it leaves it up to the Secretary of State to make such provisions by an Order. The only provision which specifies a penalty of a fine concerns the offence by an organisation committed by failing to comply with remedial orders, eg to take steps to remedy a breach (cl 10).

Proceedings for an offence of corporate manslaughter may not commence without the consent of the Director of Public Prosecutions (cl 16).

Once the Bill becomes an Act, it will apply to England and Wales, Scotland and Northern Ireland (cl 23). The offence will apply if the harm resulting to death is sustained in the UK or within the seaward limits of the territorial sea adjacent to the UK (thus, it will apply to foreign ships which are within these waters if a death occurs); or on a British-registered ship, or on a British-controlled aircraft or hovercraft.

The proposed Act will not apply to individuals (cl 17). Once the Act is in force, the common law offence of manslaughter by gross negligence for breach of duty of care will be abolished.

The Criminal Justice Act 2003 is proposed to be amended to include reference to the offence under this Act; the Coroners Act 1988 will also be amended by inserting 'corporate manslaughter' and, inter alia, that there will be no finding of guilt at coroner's inquest (Sched 2).

The Act will come into force on such a date as the Secretary of State may appoint by order (cl 22).

At the time of writing, the Corporate Manslaughter and Corporate Homicide Bill 2006 had passed through all stages of the House of Commons but it was seriously criticised for inadequacies by senior lawyers.[161]

Upon consideration of the Bill by the Grand Committee in the Lords, it was returned to the Commons requesting amendments to the effect that prisons and the police are not entitled to the exclusions incorporated in the Bill. Since then, there have been various proposed amendments by the Commons which are being rejected by the Lords as not being satisfactory. This is the current status of the Bill as at the end of June 2007, and it may take another 10 years before it becomes an Act!

---

161 Peter Thornton QC, Francis Fitzgibbon, of Doughty Street Chambers, dated 5 January 2007; see also comments to the Lords Committee by the Centre for Corporate Accountability: www.corporateaccountability.org/index.htm.

CHAPTER 9

THE LAW OF SHIP MORTGAGES

1 INTRODUCTION

The lender is known as the mortgagee, and the borrower as the mortgagor.

Unlike lenders for the purchase of land, the inherent risks involved in a floating object of security necessitated the ship mortgagees seeking special protective measures, that is, insurance cover and collateral securities. The loan agreement contains covenants regulating the conduct of the borrower; the mortgage creates a preferential security interest of the lender on the ship; insurance to protect the interest of the mortgagee on the ship must be obtained in addition to the borrower's insurance against perils of the sea; assignment of the insurance proceeds of the ship, in the event of loss, is provided, as well as assignment of the earnings of the ship. Apart from the risk of accidental loss of the ship, mortgagees are protected by law in the enforcement of their security on the ship and are given priority over other maritime creditors, save for those who claim maritime liens. Given this limitation to their security, mortgagees may seek to obtain personal and corporate guarantees, a general charge over the company's assets, or a pledge on the company's shares. The development of ship mortgages, therefore, is based on these unique characteristics of the nature of the subject matter and the business in which it is used. The main concern of the financier is to balance the risks involved in the trading of ships with the expected return on capital.

Ship mortgages are today distinctive contractual transactions, with voluminous documentation including the loan agreement, the mortgage, deed of covenants, assignments of earnings, assignments of insurance policies, guarantees, pledges or charges on other assets and the like depending on the circumstances of a particular transaction. The sophistication of their development has reached a level, which requires special expertise in financial markets.[1]

The most straightforward transaction is a loan supported by a mortgage on a ship, based on a satisfactory valuation with an assignment of earnings and insurance. The flag State in which the ship is registered is very important to the mortgagee. Most financiers will insist on a flag that has a good reputation in the enforcement of international regulations of safety. They will also consider the law of the flag State, which will govern the validity of the mortgage.

With new orders of shipbuilding, a 'project finance' transaction may be suitable in which the assets are the new buildings and the source of repayment of the loan is the cash flow generated by the assets. The construction may be financed through a

---

1   Goldrein, I (ed), 'Financing ships and shipping companies', in *Ship Sale and Purchase*, 4th edn, 2003, LLP, Chapter 5.

tax-based scheme (offshore) or through the capital markets; the ships are chartered to a reputable charterer of substance from delivery.

This chapter examines the legal nature of a ship mortgage, the rights and obligations of the mortgagor and mortgagee, the methods of protection of the mortgagee's rights in enforcing his security under statute and common law, conflict of laws in relation to enforcement, and the legal position of third parties, particularly charterers, who have contractual rights in the trading of the ship being subject to a mortgage.

2 WHAT IS THE NATURE OF A SHIP MORTGAGE IN ENGLISH LAW?

There have been two theories about the nature of a ship mortgage, which are worth mentioning in order to understand the principles that derive from each.

2.1 The property transfer theory

A ship is a chattel. Prior to the Merchant Shipping Act (MSA) 1854, which introduced the form of a statutory charge on a ship for the protection of the mortgagee, the law of land mortgages applied also to mortgages of chattels.[2] This meant that a mortgage on a chattel involved a transfer of the legal title in the chattel to the mortgagee, and this was effected by delivery. The transfer of the legal title in a registered ship was done by the delivery of a bill of sale to the mortgagee, who took steps to register his ownership interest in the ship under the statutes for the Registration of British Vessels 1823–1825. This method was, however, changed by the MSA 1854 and the subsequent Bills of Sale Act 1878, which regulated the mortgages on chattels, other than ships. Ships were excluded from this Act.

Thus, traditionally, at common law, the chattel mortgage was regarded as a property transfer by way of security,[3] whereby legal ownership was transferred to the mortgagee and, upon payment of the loan amount with interest, was re-transferred to the mortgagor.

According to this traditional property transfer analysis, the first ship mortgagee acquired legal title regardless of whether or not the mortgage was registered.[4] The registered owner of the ship retained, during the mortgage, an equitable right of redemption. All other subsequent mortgages were necessarily equitable, because the shipowner did not have legal ownership to pass to another lender. Once the first mortgage was discharged, the second in line of creation would become legal.

---

2   *Reeves v Capper* (1838) 132 ER 1057.

3   *Santley v Wilde* [1899] 2 Ch 474 (CA). For an historical account of the evolution of mortgage, from a pledge to a transfer by way of security, see Bagias, A, 'Legal aspects of ship mortgages in English and Greek Law', unpublished thesis, 1996, Gonville and Caius College, University of Cambridge.

4   About the procedure and effect of registration, see para 3, below.

This theory derived in particular from the judgment of Lindley J in *Keith v Burrows*,[5] although the case was decided after the MSA 1854. Lindley J said:

> The mortgage to the plaintiffs was in the statutory form, and by it the ship was 'mortgaged' to them. The word 'mortgage' is a well-known word, and signifies a transfer of property by way of security ... A mortgage is a transfer of all the mortgagor's interest in the thing mortgaged: but such transfer is not absolute; it is made only by way of security; or, in other words, it is subject to redemption. Unless, therefore, there is any statutory enactment to the contrary, the plaintiffs in this case acquired by their mortgage the whole of the mortgagor's interest in the ship, or, in other words, the legal title to the ship as a security ...
>
> The conclusion, then, to be drawn from the mortgage and the statute, is, that the mortgagee of a ship, like the mortgagee of any other property, acquires an ownership in the ship, viz, such ownership as the mortgagor has to give. A first mortgagee will, thus, acquire the whole ownership in the ship, but only of course as a security for his money. Second and other mortgagees will only acquire the interest left in the mortgagor, or, in other words, his right to redeem. That right will be legal or equitable ... as the time for paying off the first mortgage has not yet arrived or has passed.

The mortgage in this case was unregistered, as to which the judge said:

> ... the only consequence of not registering a mortgage is to postpone it to a subsequent mortgage or transfer which is registered before it.[6]

There is, however, a contradictory element between the first and second quotations from the judgement. It appears that the judge conflated the principles of the nature of a mortgage derived from the law prior to the MSA 1854 with the principles as derived from statutory registration. While in his opinion the first created mortgage was a legal mortgage, he, nevertheless, stated that a subsequent mortgage would take priority over the legal mortgage, if it was registered prior to the first created mortgage, according to statutory requirements. The result of this is that a subsequent registered mortgage, which in the judge's view would have been equitable, if the time for paying off the first mortgage had not arrived and, thus, the mortgagor would not have been able to pass a title that he did not have, would, nevertheless, take priority over the first legal mortgage by reason of it being registered.

The judge further said:

> The mortgagee, however, is not to be deemed the owner of the ship, except so far as may be necessary for making her a security for the mortgage debt (s 70 of the MSA 1854). This section was inserted for his protection against liabilities which might have attached to him by reason of his interest in the ship; see *Dickinson v Kitchen*; and would have been quite unnecessary if the mortgage transferred no interest in the sense of ownership in her to him; or, in other words, if it created a mere charge on her in his favour.[7]

---

5 (1876) 1 CPD 722, pp 731–33; (1887) 2 App Cas 636 (HL): no comment was made on this issue by the House of Lords, which decided the rights of a mortgagee in possession of the ship. However, what Lord Cairns said on the rights of a mortgagee before possession (pp 645, 646) seems to impinge upon the very foundation of the judge's view of the nature of a mortgage.

6 (1876) 1 CPD 722, p 734. It is submitted that this case would not have been decided in the same way today.

7 MSA 1854, s 70 (equivalent to s 34 of the 1894 Act) is now MSA 1995, Sched 1, para 10.

This decision has been doubted. The judge's view was obiter and the language used, by its own contradictions, shows ambivalence of the application of the transfer of property theory on ships. The decision was overruled on other grounds by the Court of Appeal, whose decision was subsequently upheld by the House of Lords, but the judge's analysis was not considered as it was not directly relevant to the issues before the higher courts. Reading what Lord Westbury and Lord Cairns[8] said, however, generally about the mortgagor's rights of ownership, strongly indicates an implicit disapproval of the judge's view.

The MSA 1854 provided that the mortgagee shall not by reason of his mortgage be deemed to be the owner of the mortgaged ship, nor shall the mortgagor be deemed to have ceased to be the owner, except in so far as may be necessary for making the ship available as a security for the mortgage debt.[9] Applying this provision in *Collins v Lambort*,[10] the Lord Chancellor held that the statute was intended to reverse the result of earlier statutes whereby the mortgagee became, upon registration, the owner of the property and the owner being treated as his quasi agent. Under the new statute, the owner/mortgagor was to be deemed to be the owner, unless the mortgagee's security was impaired whereupon the mortgagor's authority ceased.

The nature of a ship mortgage under general English law was examined during the last decade in **Downsview v First City Corp**,[11] in which Lord Templeman said:

> A mortgage, whether legal or equitable, is security for repayment of a debt. The security may be constituted by a conveyance, assignment or demise or by a charge on any interest in real or personal property. An equitable mortgage is a contract which creates a charge on property, but does not pass a legal estate to the creditor. Its operation is that of an executory assurance, which, as between the parties, and so far as equitable rights and remedies are concerned, is equivalent to an actual assurance, and is enforceable under the equitable jurisdiction of the court. All this is well settled law and is to be found in more detail in the textbooks on the subject and, also, in *Halsbury's Laws of England* (4th edn, 1980, Vol 32, p 187, paras 401ff).

> The owner of property entering into a mortgage does not by entering into that mortgage, cease to be the owner of that property any further than is necessary to give effect to the security he has created. The mortgagor can mortgage the property again and again. A second or subsequent mortgage is a complete security on the mortgagor's interests subject only to the rights of prior encumbrances.

Various other authors[12] have disputed the transfer of property theory as an appropriate theory applicable to mortgages of ships, and support the theory advanced below.

---

8 See para 8.3 of this chapter.

9 Very similar provisions are to be found in the present MSA 1995, Sched 1, paras 9 and 10, referred to later.

10 (1864) 11 LT 497; see later in relation to the mortgagee interfering with a charter party preceding the mortgage para 10.2 below.

11 [1993] AC 295 (PC), p 311.

12 Bowtle, G. and McGuinness, K. *The Law of Ship Mortgages*, 2001, LLP, chapter 3, para 3.16; Meeson, N. in his 3rd edition, 2003, *Admiralty Jurisdiction and Practice*, LLP, chapter 10, para 10.46, states that the property transfer theory is no longer appropriate to a registered statutory mortgage. A registered ship mortgage is better regarded as a *sui generis* form of statutory security perfected by registration, agreeing with the view of the author below, fn 13.

2.2 The theory of a statutory nature of a ship mortgage perfected by registration

The modern and prevailing view of the nature of a ship mortgage is that registration under the Merchant Shipping Acts (MSAs) has created a *sui generis* statutory security perfectible by registration.[13] It is a form of security created by a contract which confers a property interest to the mortgagee and it comes to an end upon the performance of agreed obligations by the mortgagor. Mortgages under the MSAs have ceased to be a property transfer. Ownership still remains with the mortgagor as is reflected in MSA 1995 (Sched 1, para 10, being formerly s 34 of the MSA 1894).[14] There are authorities supporting this view. A couple of examples are given below:

Barclays Bank v Poole[15]

The managing owner of a ship contracted to sell his shares in the ship to other part-owners who agreed: (i) to apply the purchase money in discharging the vendor's debt to the ship; and (ii) to pay the balance to him. The shares were transferred to the purchasers by a registered bill of sale. After the contract and transfer, but before the purchase money had been paid, the purchasers received notice of an unregistered mortgage existing prior to the contract. The mortgagees applied to court to stop the money being transferred to the seller. Section 56 of the MSA 1894 had given the registered owner absolute power, not only to dispose of his interest in the ship in a manner provided by the Act, but also to give effectual receipts for the purchase money. It was held, therefore, that the seller could give effectual receipts for it and direct how the money should be used. The purchasers had acquired a valid title to the shares, being a registered interest, and their contractual right had priority over the previous unregistered mortgage.

The Two Ellens[16]

The registered vessel was mortgaged to B as security for the repayment of a $5,000 debt. The mortgage was duly registered under the MSA 1854. Subsequently, in February 1868, by order of the master who was also a part-owner of the vessel, ship-repairers did work and provided supplies to the vessel to put her in a seaworthy condition. In July 1868, B transferred the mortgage to C in the prescribed form. This transfer was made without valuable consideration and was not registered.[17] C took possession of the vessel on behalf of B, the registered mortgagee. The ship-repairers instituted an action against the ship to recover the amount due to them for the necessaries supplied and work done on the ship. C (the assignee of the mortgagee)

---

13 Clarke, A, 'Ship mortgages', in Palmer, N and McKendrick, E (eds), *Interests in Goods*, 2nd edn, 1998, LLP, Chapter 26; she provides a most comprehensive study and a critique of the traditional view of the nature of ship mortgages.

14 Op cit, Clarke, fn 13.

15 [1907] 2 Ch 284.

16 (1872) LR 4 PC 161.

17 The effect of this assignment being made for no valuable consideration ought to have been questioned as to whether it defeated the right of the original registered mortgagee.

intervened. At the time, however, the vessel was already under arrest by the crew for unpaid wages. When the vessel was sold by court order, the proceeds were insufficient to pay off the mortgage and the debt to the ship repairer. The question was which of the unsatisfied claims took priority: the assignee of the mortgagee or the necessaries man (the ship-repairer)?

The Privy Council, affirming the judgment of the court below, held that the assignee of the mortgagee was entitled to have his mortgage debt satisfied before the ship-repairer, who did not have a maritime lien, was paid out. Moreover, the assignee of the mortgagee was not liable to the ship-repairer for the necessaries supplied to the ship because the master, who instructed the ship-repairer, was not acting as his agent, but as the agent of the mortgagor who remained the owner of the vessel under the MSA 1854.

The point made in this case was that registration of a mortgage according to statutory provisions created a legal mortgage[18] as opposed to an unregistered one, which is regarded under English law to be equitable. This should not be confused with the unregistered mortgage of an unregistered ship which is discussed later.

As explained earlier, the British ship mortgage originated as a property transfer security and was executed by a bill of sale, which was registered and was subject to a covenant for re-transfer of the ship back to the mortgagor upon the payment of the loan.[19] The transformation of a modern ship mortgage into a statutory form of security came with the passing of the MSA 1854, which introduced a statutory scheme of registration of a mortgage form. The bill of sale was no longer used. This was maintained by the MSA 1894 and was re-enacted by the present MSA 1995. This statutory system has undoubtedly changed the nature of the ship mortgage, which is now more accurately described as a statutory security perfectible by registration.[20]

> If registration in the Shipping Registry perfects title so that mortgagors have legal title by virtue of being registered owners, and all legal mortgages are legal by virtue of registration, it is difficult to see how the registered ship mortgage can realistically be described as a property transfer mortgage.[21]

The purpose of the registered mortgage is to give the mortgagee a right against the property of the debtor so he is not left only with a personal remedy against him. The effect of the mortgage is that the mortgagee, when he needs to enforce his security, can exercise owner-type rights on the mortgaged property, subject to rights of previous registered mortgages, or maritime liens, to meet the debt, and such rights are given by statute and contract.

---

18 However, it may be doubtful whether the subsequent assignment, which was made without valuable consideration and was not registered, was capable of conferring the same rights to the assignee in this case.

19 *Thompson v Smith* (1815) 1 Madd 395.

20 Op cit, Clarke, fn 13.

21 Op cit, Clarke, fn 13, p 672. She explains the origins of the property transfer theory as existed before the passing of the MSA 1854 and, sensibly, proposes at p 674 some reasons why, bearing in mind the reality of modern ship mortgages, the traditional view ought to be jettisoned.

Owner-type rights of a ship-registered mortgagee stay dormant until it becomes necessary for him to take possession and exercise his powers given under statute and contract. These rights are not exercised if the debt is paid as agreed.

The Merchant Shipping Act 1995 allows the registration of second and subsequent mortgages and gives them the same legal consequences as a first registered mortgage being subject to priorities between themselves in accordance with the date of their respective registration.

2.3 The property subject to the mortgage

The ship and all articles necessary for the navigation are included. The word 'appurtenances' is used in the mortgage documents and the prescribed form. The word means, broadly, a thing belonging to another and, in the case of mortgages, it indicates that anything on board the ship, being necessary for the voyage and the adventure, is included as belonging to the owner and it is thus part of the security.[22] But whether or not particular equipment has become an appurtenance to the ship is a question of fact.[23] For example, containers are not part of the ship as they are not necessary for its operation.[24] Bunkers on board the ship are not always part of the security. Fuel is not part of the ship, but it could be included in the mortgage by a collateral agreement if fuel is the property of the owner. Normally, charter parties provide for the charterer to pay for all bunkers on board the ship,[25] and it is common practice for the fuel to be the property of the time charterers.[26] The cargo on board the ship is not part of the security, unless the mortgagor has an interest in it and the mortgage provides that it attaches to that interest.[27] With regard to freight earned by the ship, the mortgagee does not have a right to earn freight until he enters into possession to realise his security.[28] The freight is not part of the security unless there is a special assignment of earnings to the mortgagee by a separate agreement.[29]

3 EFFECT OF THE STATUTORY SCHEME OF REGISTRATION

As mentioned earlier, the transfer of ownership in the ship to the mortgagee by a bill of sale was abolished by the MSA 1854. Instead, a special mortgage form as prescribed by the statute created the security on the ship and was the instrument to

---

22   *The Dundee* (1823) 1 Hagg 109; *Coltman v Chamberlain* (1890) 25 QBD 328.

23   *The Mabel Vera* [1933] P 109.

24   *The River Rima* [1987] 2 Lloyd's Rep 106 (CA), aff'd by HL [1988] 2 Lloyd's Rep 193; see also Chapter 2, above.

25   *The Saetta* [1994] 1 All ER 851.

26   *The Eurostar* [1993] 1 Lloyd's Rep 106, P 111; *The Pan Oak* [1992] 2 Lloyd's Rep 36; see, further, cases in Chapter 2, above.

27   *Langton v Horton* (1842) 66 ER 847(CP).

28   *Liverpool Marine Credit Co v Wilson* (1872) LR 7 Ch 507, P 511.

29   *Wills v Palmer* (1860) 141 ER 847 (CP).

be produced for registration of the mortgage. The subsequent statute, MSA 1894, followed the same statutory scheme and, in particular, s 31 provided:

(1) A registered ship or a share therein may be made as a security for a loan or other valuable consideration, and the instrument creating the security (in this Act called a mortgage) shall be in the form marked B in the First Schedule to this Act ... and on the production of such instrument the registrar of the ship's port registry shall record it in the register book.

(2) Mortgages shall be recorded by the registrar in the order in time on which they are produced to him for that purpose, and the registrar shall by memorandum under his hand notify on each mortgage that it has been recorded by him, stating the day and the hour of that record.

A slightly amended version of this wording made only for linguistic purposes – leaving the substance unchanged – was carried forward in the MSA 1988 and later in the Merchant Shipping (Registration etc) Act (MS(Reg)A) 1993, which was supplemented by the Merchant Shipping (Registration of Ships) Regulations 1993,[30] as amended in 1994 and 1998.[31] These Regulations have modernised the registration system and apply only to British ships registered under the Acts.[32]

The MSA 1995[33] (the consolidating Act), Sched 1 (Private Law Provisions for Registered Ships), provides by para 7:

(1) A registered ship, or share in a registered ship, may be made a security for the repayment of a loan or the discharge of any other obligation.

(2) The instrument creating any such security (referred to in the following provisions of this Schedule as a 'mortgage') shall be in the form prescribed by or approved under registration regulations.

(3) Where a mortgage executed in accordance with sub-para (2) above is produced to the registrar, he shall register the mortgage in the prescribed manner.

(4) Mortgages shall be registered in the order in which they are produced to the registrar for the purpose of registration.

A mortgage of a British ship owned by a company registered in England and Wales also requires registration under s 395 of the Companies Act 1985.

Paragraph 8(1) of Sched 1 (MSA 1995) deals with priorities of registered mortgages. Their respective priority is determined by the order in which the mortgages were registered (and not by reference to any other matter). Paragraph 8(2) permits the intending mortgagee to give a priority notice to the Registrar in the form prescribed by reg 59 of the 1993 Regulations. The purpose of the priority notice is to record and thus protect the interest of an intending mortgagee on the Register for

---

30 SI 1993/3138.

31 Merchant Shipping (Registration of Ships) (Amendment) Regulations 1994, SI 1994/541 and Regulations 1998, SI 1998/2976.

32 See Chapter 8 on the registration of British ships, para 2.

33 The Act is supplemented by the 1993 Registration Regulations issued pursuant to the MS(Reg)A 1993, the provisions of which have been consolidated by the 1995 Act. These provisions have substantially re-enacted the mortgage provisions of the MSA 1894. They enable proprietary interests on ships to be recorded on the Register. MSA 1995, Sched 1, paras 7, 8 and 10 have replaced ss 31, 33 and 34, respectively, of the MSA 1894.

the interim period until proper registration takes place. The notice is valid for 30 days and the protection lapses at the end of the period, unless the notice is renewed for a further 30 days at the end of each period. The effect of the notice would be to give priority to the intended mortgagee in accordance with para 8 of Sched 1 from the date of the notification, as if the mortgage had been registered at the time when the relevant entry was made.

Paragraph 9 deals with the mortgagee's power of sale when the money falls due:

(1) Subject to subparagraph (2) below, every registered mortgagee shall have power, if the mortgage money or any part of it is due, to sell the ship or share in respect of which he is registered, and to give effectual receipts for the purchase money.

(2) Where two or more mortgagees are registered in respect of the same ship or share, a subsequent mortgagee shall not, except under an order of a court of competent jurisdiction, sell the ship or share without the concurrence of every prior mortgagee.

Paragraph 10, titled 'Protection of registered mortgagees', is important in the scheme of the statutory provisions and provides:

Where a ship or share is subject to a registered mortgage then (a) except so far as may be necessary for making the ship or share available as a security for the mortgage debt, the mortgagee shall not by reason of the mortgage be treated as owner of the ship or share; and (b) the mortgagor shall be treated as not having ceased to be owner of the ship or share.

This paragraph clarifies that the mortgagee, by reason of the exercise of his statutory powers, which give him owner-type rights for the limited purpose of realising his security, shall not be treated as owner. The heading indicates that the mortgagee is protected from being exposed to owner-type liabilities during his possession of the ship.

It is also relevant to quote, at this point, para 1 of Sched 1,[34] which affirms the most fundamental rights of the registered owner of the ship:

(1) Subject to any rights and powers appearing from the register to be vested in any other person, the registered owner of a ship or of a share in a ship shall have power absolutely to dispose of it provided the disposal is made in accordance with this Schedule and registration regulations . . .

(3) The registered owner of a ship or of a share in a ship shall have power to give effectual receipts for any money paid or advanced by way of consideration on any disposal of the ship or share.

Such rights will, of course, be subject to the terms of the mortgage.

Paragraphs 11 and 12 deal with transfer and transmission of the registered mortgage respectively. Paragraph 13 provides for the de-registration of a mortgage upon its discharge:

Where a registered mortgage has been discharged, the registrar shall, on production of the mortgage deed and such evidence of the discharge of the mortgage as may be

---

34 It has replaced ss 56 and 57 of the MSA 1894.

prescribed, cause an entry to be made in the register to the effect that the mortgage has been discharged.

4 UNREGISTERED SHIPS AND STATUS OF AN UNREGISTERED MORTGAGE

The prescribed form of a ship mortgage applies only to mortgages granted on registered ships. There is no prescribed form for a mortgage of an unregistered ship, which does not come within the provisions of the MSA. Therefore, the common law on chattel mortgage will be relevant to determine the status of such a mortgage. As discussed earlier, the nature of the common law mortgage[35] is simply a transfer of the mortgagor's interest in the chattel mortgaged by way of security and is subject to redemption on payment of the debt. However, the mortgage is not an outright disposition but only by way of security. The words used in the transaction will be relevant in construing whether it has been intended to be a security transaction. The courts will examine, by allowing extrinsic evidence, the true nature and not the form of the transaction.[36]

Unregistered ships are not common nowadays, but the following case is an example of the risk to an innocent purchaser who may buy an unregistered ship which may be subject to an unregistered mortgage because there is no public register for it.

The Shizelle[37]

The operative words were 'hereby mortgages to BCT all that the vessel . . . as security for repayment of the said loan'. The plaintiffs (P) were a finance company who lent money to M to finance purchase of the vessel *The Shizelle*. The loan agreement contemplated that the vessel would be registered under the 1894 Act, but neither the vessel nor the mortgage was ever registered. On 18 March, M sold the vessel to D 'free from any encumbrances' and D never had reason to believe that there was a mortgage on the vessel. D was a bona fide purchaser without actual or constructive knowledge of the mortgage. On 9 April, D registered the vessel under the Merchant Shipping (Small Ships Register) Regulations 1983, but this did not have the same effect as the 1894 Act. On 2 February 1992, P wrote to D advising him of the outstanding mortgage. D contended that the mortgage was invalid against him as he was a bona fide purchaser of the vessel without notice. P arrested the vessel. It was held that nothing prevented the mortgage executed between the parties from being a legal mortgage, as opposed to an equitable one at common law. The non-registration of the vessel and, hence, of the mortgage did not reduce the legal mortgage to an equitable one. Mr Adrian Hamilton QC stated that: 'I therefore

---

35 (1876) 1 CPD 722, p 731.
36 *Re Watson, ex parte Official Receiver in Bankruptcy* (1890) 25 QBD 27.
37 [1992] 2 Lloyd's Rep 444.

cannot find anything in the 1894 Act, which affects a common law mortgage of an unregistered ship.'[38]

The mortgagee had acquired, by the mortgage, the whole of the mortgagor's interest in the ship by way of security. This was a legal mortgage of an unregistered ship. On the question of the effect on a bona fide purchaser without notice of the mortgage, it was held that a legal mortgage at common law was enforceable against such a purchaser, but an equitable mortgage would not be.

It should be noted that only the first mortgage against an unregistered ship can be a legal one in the sense of a common law mortgage. Any subsequent mortgages will be equitable and will be secured on the mortgagor's equity of redemption and not on the legal title to the ship.

Since the MSA has not made any provisions regarding mortgages of unregistered ships, such mortgages cannot be statutory. This lacuna in the law ought to be rectified for the protection of innocent purchasers of unregistered ships,[39] although such a situation is not very common.

5 COMPARISON OF A SHIP MORTGAGE WITH OTHER TYPES OF SECURITY

5.1 Charge

A mortgage under the MSA 1995 is different from a charge on a property in that the latter is recognised in equity as an appropriation of property as security for a debt. The chargee can realise his security by judicial process either by appointment of a receiver or court sale. Being equitable, it ranks below legal registered interests, hence, a registered mortgage, and the chargee, unlike the mortgagee, does not have a right to take possession. A charge may be fixed on a specific asset of the debtor, which cannot be disposed of without the permission of the chargee, or payment of the debt. Alternatively, it may be floating on stocks-in-trade, which are changeable. When a default occurs, a floating charge crystallises, in other words, it becomes fixed. A charge is always equitable.

A charge on a ship is not registrable as it does not come within the statutory scheme of the MSA 1995.

A distinction between a mortgage under general law and a charge in equity was made by Buckley LJ, in *Swiss Bank Corp v Lloyds Bank Ltd*:[40]

The essence of any transaction by way of mortgage is that a debtor confers upon his creditor a proprietary interest in property of the debtor, or undertakes in a binding

---

38 Ibid, p 449.

39 The lacuna arises from the fact that all ships are excluded from the scope of the Bills of Sale Act 1878. Although the Act makes provision for registration of certain agreements, ship mortgages fall outside its scope. So, there is no means of discovering an unregistered mortgage of an unregistered ship, which does not come within the statutory provisions of the MSA 1995.

40 [1982] AC 584 (HL), p 595: in which the House of Lords approved the judgment and repeated it in this report.

manner to do so, by the realisation or appropriation of which the creditor can procure the discharge of the debtor's liability to him, and that the proprietary interest is redeemable, or the obligation to create it is defeasible, in the event of the debtor discharging his liability. If there has been no legal transfer of a proprietary interest but merely a binding undertaking to confer such an interest, that obligation, if specifically enforceable, will confer a proprietary interest in the subject matter in equity. The obligation will be specifically enforceable if it is an obligation for the breach of which damages would be an inadequate remedy. A contract to mortgage property, real or personal, will, normally at least, be specifically enforceable, for a mere claim to damages or repayment is obviously less valuable than a security in the event of the debtor's insolvency. If it is specifically enforceable, the obligation to confer the proprietary interest will give rise to an equitable charge upon the subject matter by way of mortgage.

Under the Law of Property Act (LPA) 1925, which deals with mortgages on land, the phrase 'charge by way of legal mortgage' is used in ss 85(1) and 87(1). A legal mortgage on land is created by a deed expressed to be by way of a legal mortgage. The charge is registrable and the chargee will enjoy the protection of the Act and have the statutory powers of sale and appointment of a receiver, as provided by s 101 of this Act. The charge under the LPA 1925 is different from a charge in equity.

A charge under English law should not be confused with the charge under civil law, which is known as *hypotheque* and is registrable. A hypothecation under civil law gives the mortgagee the same rights as the statutory English mortgage exercisable when a default event occurs but excludes the power of the mortgagee to sell the ship, otherwise, than by a court sale.[41] A hypothecation under English maritime law was effected in the past by way of a bottomry bond (charge on the ship) or respondentia (charge on the cargo). Both are, however, now obsolete.

5.2 Pledge

Pledge is the oldest and most fundamental form of chattel security.[42] It arises whenever a person (the pledgor) transfers the possession of goods actually, or constructively by an atttornment or by transferring the means of control, or symbolically by the delivery of documents of title to another person as security for a debt.[43] It is to be distinguished from the other three forms of security relating to chattels, namely the mortgage, the charge and the lien.

By contrast to a mortgage, possession is essential to a pledgee for the creation of the right, while a mortgagee may enter into possession when his security is impaired. The mortgage is regulated by statute and it is perfected by registration. While foreclosure by the mortgagee (which would operate to defeat the

---

41 Under Greek law, there is, in addition, another type of ship mortgage, the 'preferred ship mortgage' perfected by registration, which is founded by a special statutory instrument (SI 1958/3899) issued pursuant to the Code of Private Maritime Law. This gives the mortgagee practically the same powers as the English ship mortgage, under the statutory provisions of the MSA 1995.

42 Palmer, N, *Bailment*, 2nd edn, 1991, LLP, Chapter 22.

43 Palmer, N and Hudson A, 'Pledge', in Palmer and McKendrick, op cit, fn 13, Chapter 24, p 621 and fn 6.

mortgagor's right of redemption) would be another difference between mortgage and a pledge, foreclosure is not consistent with the statutory type mortgage and, besides, the MSAs do not refer to such a right.[44]

Examples of a pledge as an additional security for a mortgagee of a ship are a pledge or charge over the shares in the shipping company, which is common with a single ship company (shares security). When the shares are bearer shares, however, this effectively means that whoever has the bearer shares owns the company and, thus, the ship.

5.3 Common law possessory lien

This resembles the pledge, in that it depends on possession until the debt is satisfied. But the lien holder does not have a right of sale in the event of default and he will lose his security right if he delivers the chattel, while the pledgee may redeliver the chattel to the pledgor temporarily without losing his security.[45]

6 PRIORITIES OF MORTGAGES

The importance of priorities between various maritime claimants and mortgagees has been discussed in Chapter 4 and will also be seen in the context of conflict of laws in para 7, below.

6.1 Priorities between mortgages

A mortgage is valid from the date of its creation and not from the date of registration, but priorities of mortgages are determined by the date of registration. In *Keith v Burrows*, see para 2.1 above, the statutory provision of priorities of registered mortgages among themselves and over unregistered ones was shown by the judgment.

The series of events leading up to the issue of priorities that arose in this case are worth summarising:

(a) On 1 December, M, the registered owner of the ship, mortgaged his ship to the plaintiff (P) for a loan plus further advances. The mortgage was not registered.

(b) On 4 January and 22 February, the defendants (D) advanced money to M upon an equitable assignment of the cargo by way of security, without notice of P's mortgage which had not been recorded on the registry. It was arranged that D should sell the cargo and receive the proceeds on account of M.

(c) On 2 February, M again mortgaged the ship to P for further advances.

(d) On 26 February, D was assigned the freight of the ship as security for their advances.

---

44 Op cit, Clarke, fn 13, p 690.
45 Op cit, Palmer and Hudson, fn 43, p 622.

(e) On 2 March, M mortgaged the ship to Harold (H) who registered his mortgage on 3 March.

(f) On 6 March, P registered his mortgage.

(g) On 13 April, the ship arrived and H and P took possession. H's claim was satisfied with the security on the ship, therefore, he did not claim freight.

On the question of priorities and entitlement to freight, it was held that P had not lost priority over D by virtue of non-registration. By the MSA 1854, an unregistered mortgage was not void, its priority was only postponed to a subsequent registered mortgage.

The effect of H's mortgage was that it had statutory priority, being registered, and could receive freight. However, since H's claim was satisfied, he would hold any surplus for the benefit of subsequent encumbrances. P's mortgage was prior in date to the assignment to D, and P could, thus, take possession and freight against anyone except the registered mortgagee, H.

A registered mortgage takes priority over an earlier unregistered interest even if the registered mortgage had notice of the unregistered interest.

Black v Williams[46]

Debentures were issued by the company in statutory form under a trust deed executed by the mortgagors on 8 November 1889. Mortgages, also in statutory form, were created on three steamers and then registered, on 15 June 1891. Later, two remaining steamships, mortgaged under the debenture deed were transferred to company M and registered. Mortgages were created subsequently in favour of the company M and registered. In accordance with the agreement (debenture deed), the company executed mortgages of the vessels in favour of the trustees. The mortgages, given or transferred to the corporation M, were all registered before the mortgages given to the trustees. It was held that the mortgage in the statutory form, which had been registered, was to be preferred to the title of the debenture holders. The debenture holders had a prior equitable title and were entitled to get that converted into a legal title in the statutory form and be registered, but they had chosen not to do so. Vaughan Williams J gave the rationale of the law as it stood:

> The Act of Parliament was passed for the benefit of commerce, and in order that English ships might be easily dealt with by English shipowners. The legislature has recognised that occasions arise when it is to the interest of the whole community that people should be able to raise money on ships by sale or mortgage, and, in the interests of the general public, it has, therefore, provided that registered titles in the statutory form shall have a priority, thus, enabling those who are disposed to purchase or lend money upon ships to do so with perfect confidence that their titles will not be overridden by priority being obtained by equitable unregistered titles which happen to be prior in point of time, and which for reasons of their own, the owners of those equitable titles have not thought fit to convert into legal form, or to register in the way pointed out by statute.[47]

---

46 (1895) 1 Ch 408.
47 Ibid, p 421.

Registration is essential to priority. In an old case, *Barclay v Poole*,[48] which is unlikely to happen today, a managing owner of a ship mortgaged his share to his bankers, who did not register the mortgage, being persuaded by the owner not to do so. Subsequently, the managing owner sold his share to his joint owners, who were not aware of the mortgage. The bill of sale was duly registered. The mortgagee having an unregistered prior mortgage did not have priority over the purchasers.

The MSA 1995, Sched 1, para 8 states:

(1) Where two or more mortgages are registered in respect of the same ship or share, the priority of the mortgages between themselves shall, subject to sub-para (2) below, be determined by the order in which the mortgages were registered (and not by reference to any other matter).

(2) Registration regulations may provide for the giving to the register by intending mortgagees of 'priority notices' in a form prescribed by or approved under the regulations which, when recorded in the register, determine the priority of the interest to which the notice relates.

A scheme of priority notices is provided by reg 59 of the Merchant Shipping (Registration of Ships) Regulations 1993. By this regulation, a mortgagee may register his intention to register a mortgage and, if he subsequently does register such a mortgage within 30 days (which may be renewed for a further period) of the priority notice, his mortgage is deemed to have been registered at the date of entry of the priority notice.

If no registration takes place within the notice period and, in the meantime, another mortgagee registers his mortgage granted subsequently to the first, the mortgage, which is registered first, takes priority. Registered mortgages, of course, take priority over unregistered ones but, as between unregistered mortgages (otherwise equitable ones), priorities are determined by equitable principles, that is, by the date of creation.

6.2 Further advances

As a general rule, known as the ***Hopkinson v Rolt***[49] rule, advances made by the first mortgagee, whose mortgage is taken to secure future advances, cannot take priority over a second mortgagee when such advances were made after he had notice of the second mortgage. Lord Chelmsford stated this rule succinctly as follows:

As the first mortgagee is not bound to make the stipulated further advances, and with notice of a subsequent mortgage he can always protect himself by inquiries as to the state of the accounts with the second mortgagee, if he chooses to run the risk of advancing his money with the knowledge, or the means of knowledge, of his position, what reason can there be for allowing him any priority? ... But, on the other hand, if it be held that he is always to be secured of his priority, a perpetual curb is imposed on the mortgagor's right to encumber his equity of redemption.

---

48 [1907] 2 Ch 284, cf The Shizelle under para 4 above.

49 (1861) 9 HLC 514 (HL); concerning a shipbuilder who granted a mortgage to a bank and, subsequently, to the plaintiff. The bank made the further advances with knowledge of the plaintiff's mortgage.

It follows that, if the first registered mortgagee does not have knowledge of the second mortgage, the priority of his further advances is not affected.[50] However, it is understood from an earlier decision that the advances must have been made under the registered mortgage and not under a separate unregistered instrument.[51]

In a non-shipping case, the Court of Appeal subsequently held that the doctrine of *Hopkinson v Rolt* applies to further advances made in pursuance of an obligation or covenant on the part of the first mortgagee entered into at the time of the first mortgage.[52]

6.3 Harbour authority claims and risk management by the mortgagee

It is appropriate at this point to refer to what was said about priorities of maritime claims in Chapter 4, above, that a mortgagee may find himself bound to take his security subject to a harbour authority's right of detention and sale. Moreover, the harbour authority, in exercising its statutory right, may sell the ship and can pass a title to a purchaser of the vessel free of the mortgage, even though the mortgage had been registered.

The Blitz [53]

A loan of £10,000 was secured by mortgage on the vessel and the mortgage duly registered in 1989.

In 1991, the vessel was arrested for unpaid harbour dues and pursuant to s 44 of the Harbours, Docks and Piers Clauses Act 1847, the harbour owners sold the vessel to the defendant. The purchaser was unaware of the mortgage. The question was whether the sale was one free of encumbrances, or whether the mortgagee could enforce his mortgage against the ship after she had been sold by the harbour authority. Sheen J held that a purchaser of the ship from the harbour authority could not be expected to investigate the register, which may be in some foreign land, and a harbour authority could not be expected to clear any unsatisfied mortgage affecting a ship pursuant to his right under s 44. The risk of non-payment should be borne by the person who voluntarily lends an unwisely large amount on the security of a ship, rather than a harbour authority or an innocent purchaser without notice of the mortgage. The claim of the mortgagee failed.

The decision is based on a construction of a statutory provision and may be correct as a matter of both law and policy. From the point of view of risk management by the mortgagee, he may prevent a sale by the harbour authority from happening by stepping in to pay off the authority's claim, assuming that the value of the ship is sufficient to cover his security and the additional advance.

---

50   *Liverpool Marine Credit Co v Wilson* (1872) 7 Ch App 507, p 512.
51   *Parr v Applebee* (1855) 7 De GM&G 585.
52   *West v Williams* [1899] 1 Ch 132 (CA).
53   (1992) 2 Lloyd's Rep 441.

7 CONFLICT OF LAWS

There are two major issues on the question of conflict of laws:

(a) what law determines the validity of the mortgage; and

(b) priorities between foreign liens and mortgages.

7.1 Law governing the mortgage and law of the agreement to grant a mortgage

Prior to the Rome Convention 1980, the proper law of the mortgage was the law of the place of registration of the ship or the law of the flag,[54] unless another choice of law had been expressly stated in the mortgage deed.

Mortgages of foreign land or ships would, prima facie, be governed by the law of the situs or flag, in the absence of contrary evidence or choice of law (express or implied) by the parties. The following case (decided prior to the Convention) is a good example of which law governed the mortgage. Here there was a conflict between the law of the country in which the mortgage was supposed to be registered and the law of the country in which the agreement to grant the mortgage was reached.

The Angel Bell[55]

The owners of the ship, a Panamanian company, approached G for a loan to purchase vessels. In February 1974, it was agreed that G would be granted a mortgage for payment of the loan and have the marine policies assigned to them. The mortgage was granted and was provisionally registered under Panamanian law, which fixed all questions of priority by reference to the date of the registration, provided that there was a definite registration within six months. Time expired without final registration of the mortgage. The vessel sank with all cargo belonging to the plaintiff, who brought an action in England, obtained a Mareva injunction against the insurance proceeds restraining the defendant from dealing with his assets within the jurisdiction, or removing them out of the jurisdiction. G intervened in the action on the basis that they were: (a) originally assured under one set of insurance policies; (b) designated loss payees; (c) assignees under another set of insurance policies; or (d) assignees under the notices of assignment endorsed on the policies. The issue was whether G was a secured creditor and, a related question to this issue, was: which law governed the mortgage?

It was held by Donaldson J that, although it was possible to have an English contract for a mortgage of foreign land which would result in the mortgage being

---

54 The law of the flag is unsuitable, as a rule, today because of flags of convenience which render the flag a questionable contact in terms of conflict of laws. It can only be one indicator of contact, among many, in determining the law of the contract: see Tetley, W, *International Conflict of Laws (Common, Civil and Maritime)*, 1994, International Shipping, p 224.

55 [1979] 2 Lloyd's Rep 491.

governed inter partes by English law, prima facie, mortgages either of foreign land or ships would be governed by the law of their *situs* or flag, in this case – Panamanian law. There was no contrary evidence to displace that presumption. Thus, the failure of G to register the mortgage under Panamanian law reduced its effectiveness, in that it conferred no *in rem* rights against the ship, but only rights *in personam* against the borrower because Panamanian law does not have the concept of equitable mortgages.

One of the agreements, however, which concerned the granting of a mortgage to G, was governed by English law, meaning that G were equitable mortgagees under English law. Under that agreement, G could, therefore, rely upon the 'loss payable' clause in the insurance policy, under which money received by the assured would be received on behalf of G. Also, G were held to be assignees of the policies under the notices of assignment. Therefore, G were creditors of the borrower, secured on the proceeds of the hull and machinery policies.

Since this case, the Rome Convention on the Law Applicable to Contractual Obligations 1980 clarified and settled the conflict of laws rules. The Convention was implemented in the UK by the Contracts (Applicable Law) Act 1990, and applies to English contracts entered into after 1 April 1991. The Convention provides that its rules shall apply to contractual obligations in any situation involving a choice between the laws of different countries, whether or not it is the law of a Contracting State. Essentially, the rules of the Convention will apply to all cases brought in UK courts, provided the dispute falls within the scope of the Convention, save for certain exceptions provided by it.[56] Priority is given to the law chosen by the parties to a contract who can select the law applicable to the whole, or part of it, when the contract is severable (Art 3(1)). The validity of the law chosen is to be determined by the law so chosen (Arts 3(4), 8(1), 9(4)).[57] In the absence of choice, Art 4(1) provides that, to the extent that the parties have not chosen a law to govern the contract, the law of the country with which the contract is most closely connected shall govern the contract. This is to be determined by reference to presumptions contained in the article, such as characteristic performance, habitual residence, central administration, and principal place of business.[58]

7.2 Priorities between foreign liens and mortgages

This is an issue involving conflict of laws. The question is whether recognition and enforcement of foreign maritime liens or claims that have arisen against a ship are a matter of substance or procedure. For the adjudication of the existence of such claims, different laws may apply pursuant to their underlying contracts.

There is a universally admitted rule that matters of procedure are governed by the *lex fori*, which is the domestic law of the country in whose courts legal proceedings are taken. On the other hand, matters of substance are governed by the law to

---

56 See Benjamin's Sale of Goods, 7th edn, 2006, Sweet & Maxwell.
57 Ibid.
58 Ibid. And, further, see Dicey and Morris, *The Conflict of Laws*, 13th edn, 2000, Sweet & Maxwell.

which the court is directed by its choice of law rule, namely the *lex causae*. Sometimes, particularly in the past, English courts might have been tempted to extend the meaning of 'procedure' in order to evade an unsatisfactory choice of law rule. But this has now fallen into disfavour because it tends to frustrate the purpose of choice of law rules. The distinction between procedure and substance is by no means clear-cut.[59]

There is as yet no uniform international approach to the problem of recognition and enforcement of maritime liens granted by foreign law and attached to a vessel before it leaves the jurisdiction of the law where such liens were created. Therefore, different jurisdictions may attach different legal consequences to the same type of claim in terms of recognition and enforcement. This raises a conflict of laws problem when determining priorities in the distribution of the ship's fund to the various creditors.

The principle that the priorities between claimants to a limited fund which the court will distribute are governed by the lex fori was well established by the Privy Council in *The Halcyon Isle*,[60] but it is not a universal one.

The problem was aptly summarised by Lord Diplock:

> In the case of a ship, however, the classification of claims against her former owners for the purpose of determining priorities to participate in the proceeds of her sale may raise a further problem of conflict of laws, since claims may have arisen as a result of events that occurred, not only on the high seas, but also within the territorial jurisdictions of a number of different foreign States. So the *lex causae* of one claim may differ from the *lex causae* of another, even though the events which gave rise to the claim in each of those foreign States are similar in all respects, except their geographical location; the *leges causarum* of various claims, of which, under English conflict rules, the 'proper law' is that of different States, may assign different legal consequences to similar events. So, the court distributing the limited fund may be faced, as in the instant case, with the problem of classifying the foreign claims arising under differing foreign systems of law in order to assign each of them to the appropriate class in the order of priorities under the *lex fori* of the distributing court.

There was no English authority directly relating to maritime liens and mortgages at the time. There were only cases in which similar incidents had arisen involving other foreign rights.[61]

The decision of the Privy Council in The Halcyon Isle

In this case, the mortgagees were an English bank with a mortgage created in April 1973 and registered in London in May 1974. In March 1974, American ship-repairers carried out repairs to the vessel in New York, and under US law, they were entitled to a maritime lien for the repairs done. The vessel sailed from New York and was later arrested and sold by the order of the High Court of Singapore. When the proceeds from the sale were insufficient to satisfy all claims, the question was whether the claim of the mortgagees should take priority over the claim of the

---

59   Op cit fn 58, Chapter 7.
60   [1981] AC 221 (PC), p 230.
61   See *The Colorado* [1923] P 102 (discussed in Chapter 4, para 6).

necessaries (repair) men, the latter's claim giving rise to a maritime lien under US law. The practice and procedure of the Singaporean court, in the exercise of its admiralty, jurisdiction applies English law, and such a claim would not give rise to a maritime lien if the event had occurred in England. The court had two options, viz: (1) to accord the claim the legal consequence that would have attached to that event if it had occurred in England, or in Singapore (the *lex fori*); or (2) to accord the claim the legal consequence that would be accorded to it under the *lex causae* (USA).

The question was, thus, whether the maritime lien, which arose by reason of the events in the foreign jurisdiction, was enforceable in the court distributing the fund. Would English law, in circumstances such as these, recognise the maritime lien created by the law of the USA, the *lex loci contractus*, where no such lien existed by its own internal law? English choice of law rules provide that, for a substantive right, the *lex loci contractus* governs the transaction, while for a procedural right, the *lex fori* would govern. It was concluded that the legal nature of the maritime lien was procedural or remedial both under English and Singaporean law, therefore the claim would be classified according to the *lex fori*. Lord Diplock stated:

> ... in principle, the question as to the right to proceed *in rem* against a ship, as well as priorities in the distribution between competing claimants of the proceeds of her sale in an action *in rem* in the High Court of Singapore, falls to be determined by the *lex fori*, as if the events that gave rise to the claim had occurred in Singapore.[62]

This meant that the mortgagee's claim took priority over that of the ship-repairers. The court was not ready to extend the classes of claims recognised in English law (and Singaporean law) as giving rise to maritime liens.[63] Lord Diplock, in particular, stated that:

> As a matter of policy, such a claim might not unreasonably be given priority over claims by holders of prior mortgages, the value of whose security had thereby been enhanced. If this is to be done, however, it will, in their Lordships' view, have to be done by the legislature.[64]

The dissenting minority, Lords Salmon and Scarman, held that:

> The question is: does English law, in circumstances such as these, recognise the maritime lien created by the law of the USA, that is, the *lex loci contractus*, where no such lien exists by its own internal law? In our view, the balance of authorities, the comity of nations, private international law and natural justice, all answer this question in the affirmative. If this be correct, then English law (the *lex fori*) gives the maritime lien created by the *lex loci contractus* precedence over the mortgagee's mortgage. If it were otherwise, injustice would prevail. The ship-repairers would be deprived of their maritime lien, valid as it appeared to be throughout the world, and without which they would obviously never have allowed the ship to sail away without paying a dollar for the important repairs upon which the ship-repairers had spent a great deal of time and money and from which the mortgagees obtained substantial advantages.[65]

---

62 [1981] AC 221, p 235.

63 The International Convention 1993 relating to maritime liens and mortgages has not been ratified. For its contents and scope, see Berlingieri, F, 'The 1993 Convention on Maritime Liens and Mortgages' [1995] LMCLQ 57.

64 [1981] AC 221, p 242.

65 [1981] AC 221, pp 246–47.

And they continued, comparing a maritime lien with a mortgage as security rights:

> A maritime lien is a right of property given by way of security for a maritime claim. If the Admiralty Court has, as in the present case, jurisdiction to entertain the claim, it will not disregard the lien. A maritime lien validly conferred by the *lex loci* is as much part of the claim as is a mortgage similarly valid by the *lex loci*. Each is a limited right of property securing the claim. The lien travels with the claim, as does the mortgage; and the claim travels with the ship. It would be a denial of history and principle, in the present chaos of the law of the sea governing the recognition and priority of maritime liens and mortgages, to refuse the aid of private international law.[66]

The decision of the majority has been criticised by academic writers,[67] particularly as the following decision is regarded by most commentators to be correct in the application of principles of international private law.[68] It should be noted, however, that since the Rome Convention 1980 is binding upon the UK, if a ship were arrested today in the UK in circumstances of *The Halcyon Isle*, the result might be different in that the UK court would be obliged by the Rome Convention to apply USA law. This is because of Arts 3 and 4 of the Convention (mentioned earlier). Thus, 'much of the air has been taken out of *The Halcyon Isle* balloon', as Professor Tetley has put it. He further states that the law of the flag, in respect of contractual liens, seems inconsistent with the basic conflict rules of Arts 3 and 4 of the Rome Convention, which call for the law expressly or implicitly chosen by the parties, or the law having the closest connection with the contract.[69]

By contrast, the following decision is consistent with private international law rules.

The Ioannis Daskalelis[70]

The Canadian Supreme Court was faced with a similar kind of situation as that in *The Halcyon Isle*. The vessel was mortgaged to the defendants in December 1961. In March 1963, the plaintiffs rendered necessary repairs to the vessel in New York, but the sum due to them remained unpaid. The vessel sailed to Canada and she was arrested in June 1964. She was sold by a court sale and the question arose again whether the plaintiffs' claim in respect of the repairs had priority over the defendants' mortgage. The ship-repairers were entitled to a maritime lien under US law, but not under the law of Canada, the distributing court. Firstly, the court established that it had jurisdiction. Ritchie J then summarised the law of England (also the applicable law in Canada in this case) and quoted a passage from *Cheshire's Private International Law* (8th edn, p 676) as follows:

> The validity and nature of the right must be distinguished from the order in which it ranks in relation to other claims. Before it can determine the order of payment, the

---

66 Ibid, p 250; see, also, Chapter 4, para 6.

67 See Chapter 4, para 6.

68 Lord Salmon and Lord Scarman, applying those principles, delivered dissenting judgments in *The Halcyon Isle*.

69 Op cit, Tetley, fn 54, Chapter XVII, pp 580–81.

70 [1974] 1 Lloyd's Rep 174.

court must examine the proper law of the transaction upon which the claimant relies in order to verify the validity of the right and to establish its precise nature.

The court also followed *The Strandhill*,[71] where the principle was clearly established that a maritime lien, acquired under the law of a foreign State, would be recognised and enforced in Canada. On the question of priorities, the court followed *The Colorado*,[72] which was taken as authority for the contention that, where a right in the nature of a maritime lien exists under foreign law, which is the proper law of the contract, the English courts will recognise it and accord it the priority which a right of that nature would be given under English procedure. It was held that the ship-repairer's lien took priority over the mortgagee's claim.

However, in the following case, the South African court followed *The Halcyon Isle*.[73]

The Andrico Unity[74]

The South African court had to consider similar circumstances in a case involving the supply of bunkers to a vessel in Argentina. In a bid to justify the arrest of the vessel, the supplier contended that a 'privileged credit' in the nature of a maritime lien attached to his claim under Argentinean law, and he was therefore entitled to enforce it by an action *in rem* against the vessel. The South African court was required by its law to apply the law which the High Court of Justice of England and Wales would have applied on 1 November 1983. Following *The Halcyon Isle*, the court held that a notional High Court of England would have declined to recognise the Argentinean lien. Marais J discussed the difference between the nature of a maritime lien and a mortgage as follows:

> . . . when, therefore, a court dealing with competing claims to priority in the distribution of a limited fund is asked to recognise a foreign maritime lien which would not arise under the court's own system of law, it is being asked to supplant its own law in that regard by a foreign law. When a court is asked to recognise a foreign mortgage, it is not being asked to go as far. It is merely being asked to enforce a contract of mortgage, which the parties have entered into in a foreign jurisdiction.[75]

Marais J saw no conflict between *The Halcyon Isle* and the prior English authority (*The Colorado*). *The Halcyon Isle* was described, simply, as a decision based on readily understandable considerations of policy. In a more recent decision, the South African court followed *The Halcyon Isle* again.[76]

The lack of uniformity in the law of liens between maritime nations still continues.

---

71   [1926] 4 DLR 801.

72   [1923] P 102.

73   *The Halcyon Isle* has also been followed in Cyprus, Singapore, Malaysia, Australia; see further authorities in op cit, Tetley, fn 54, Chapter XVII.

74   (1987) 3 SALR 794.

75   Ibid, p 812.

76   *Banco Exterior de Espana SA v Government of Namibia* [1999] 2 SA 434.

7.3 Proposed solutions and risk management issues

Unless the Rome Convention applies, matters relating to the creation and perfection of a mortgage will usually be governed by the law of the State of registration, as the legally attributed *situs* of the ship. Matters relating to enforcement will be controlled by the law of the State of enforcement. Priorities under the conflict rules of some countries are treated as substantive and, therefore, are governed by the law of the place of registration, while, in others, will be regarded as procedural and be determined by the *lex fori*.[77]

Could there be a solution to conflicting judicial decisions from different jurisdictions in this area by the ratification of the 1993 Convention on Maritime Liens and Mortgages to ensure certainty and uniformity in the law and prevent forum shopping, or is this issue a political matter reflecting a protectionist approach of individual national interests?

Is there a likelihood that a compromise can be reached? The same questions have been asked since the drafting of the very first Convention for unification of the law in this area in 1926 (which was ratified by non-common law jurisdictions) and later by the subsequent Convention in 1967. The 1993 Convention, which is an improvement of the previous two, remains the thorny issue between ship-repairers and mortgagees. It is unlikely to come into force, because its authors (against strong advice) did not take into account consideration of special legislative rights of various nations. The world needs a proper Convention of international maritime liens and mortgages as well as a proper international Convention on conflict of laws.[78] The problem can only be solved by the legislators, as Lord Diplock pointed out in *The Halcyon Isle*.

As nothing has changed in the area of ratification of the 1993 Convention on Maritime Liens and Mortgages since the first edition of this book, the protection of foreign maritime lien holders would still depend on their taking the necessary steps to enforce the remedies available to them under the law of their contract without delay. Thus, ship-repairers, for example, whose interests would be likely to be affected adversely by the arrest of the ship in an unfavourable jurisdiction, should well be advised to exercise their possessory lien before the ship leaves the shipyard. A mortgagee may be able to control the jurisdiction to which the ship may proceed to, in order to enforce its security there, while the ship-repairer will lose his possessory lien rights once the ship leaves his yard.

---

77 Goode, R (Sir), 'Battening down your security interests: how the shipping industry can benefit from the UNIDROIT Convention on International Interests in Mobile Equipment', [2000] LMCLQ 161.

78 Tetley W, *Maritime Liens and Claims*, 2nd edn, 1998, Blais, p 214.

8 OBLIGATIONS AND RIGHTS OF THE MORTGAGOR

8.1 The mortgagor is bound by contractual covenants

The rights and obligations of the parties are largely governed by the terms of their contract, which are contained in the deed of covenants. There is usually a long list of covenants stipulating the mortgagor's obligations.

In practice, ship mortgages have developed into a sophisticated system of extensive contractual terms to cover every aspect of the parties' legal relationship, so as to avoid the uncertainties created by common law principles. When there is no deed of covenants, which is unlikely nowadays, the parties' relationship will be governed by the provisions of Sched 1 to the MSA 1995 and the 1993 Regulations (as amended by the 1998 Amendment Regulations). Where there are gaps in the statutory provisions, common law and equity step in.

Broadly, the covenants include the following provisions.

8.1.1 An obligation to insure

A hull and machinery (H&M) insurance against the physical loss of or damage to the mortgaged ship, third party liability for collision, general average contributions and other losses caused by insured perils must be procured by the mortgagor. Separate war risks cover may be obtained, in circumstances where the ship is likely to enter a war zone. The mortgagor must also ensure that third party liabilities are insured with a P&I club. He is required to pay all premiums and comply with insurance warranties. The mortgagee's interest must be noted in the insurance policies as an assignee, as a co-assured, or as a loss payee. The mortgagor must obtain a letter of undertaking from the insurers confirming the status of the insurance and that the mortgagee will be informed in the event the insurance is suspended or terminated for breaches of the insurance contract by the mortgagor.[79]

Lord Hoffmann, in *Colonial Mutual General Insurance Co Ltd v ANZ Banking Group (New Zealand) Ltd*, illustrated the legal effect of the insurance covenant, thus:[80]

> The purpose of a covenant for insurance is to ensure that, if the value of the security should be depreciated by the occurrence of a fire or other insurable risk, the proceeds of the policy will provide a fund to make up the shortfall. This purpose can be achieved only if the covenant gives the mortgagee an interest by way of charge, and no more than an interest by way of charge, in the proceeds. Standard insurance covenants contain various provisions designed to ensure that the mortgagee will be able to retain control of the insurance policy and its proceeds. Insisting that the mortgagee has the right to approve or nominate the insurer, take custody of the insurance policy, be shown receipts for premiums . . . are some of the cumulative techniques used for this purpose. So is the requirement that the insurance be effected in the name of the mortgagee. But all these provisions are, in their Lordships' view,

---

79 The reader is referred to specialist books on marine insurance.
80 [1995] 2 Lloyd's Rep 433 (PC), p 436.

intended to protect the mortgagee's interest by way of charge over the proceeds of the policy rather than to create it. That such an interest exists is a fundamental assumption of the covenant. It cannot be destroyed by the mortgagor's failure to comply with one or other of the protective terms.

The insurance covenant is paramount, but it has its limitations. If the assured mortgagor is in breach of the insurance contract (that is, of the duty of 'utmost good faith' under the Marine Insurance Act (MIA) 1906,[81] which will entitle the insurer to avoid the contract *ab initio*, or in breach of a warranty,[82] which will discharge the insurer of liability from the date of the breach), the mortgagee will not be able to recover the assigned insurance proceeds. The mortgagor may be guilty of wilful misconduct, whereupon it may be proved that the loss of the ship was not proximately caused by a peril insured against.[83]

8.1.2 *An obligation to maintain the ship in good condition and repair*

Obviously, the mortgagee is concerned not only that its security is not devalued by the deterioration of the ship, but also that accidents are prevented by maintaining the ship in good condition. In addition, this covenant protects the mortgagee from the risk of the ship being detained in a port for breaches of the International Safety Management (ISM) Code, which may result in the impairment of his security and prejudice the insurance cover. Connected with this covenant is the covenant to maintain the ship registered and in class. Keeping the vessel always in class by following class recommendations for repairs, complying with the international requirements for the safety of ships and safe management (the ISM Code compliance) are also paramount obligations for insurance purposes as well. Were the assured, however, unable to recover for the loss of the ship under the insurance for hull and machinery, the mortgagee, as assignee, would not be able to recover either.

In practice, the mortgagee takes out a separate insurance, the mortgagee's interest insurance, to cover himself for any of these eventualities. The law of mortgages is, thus, very much linked to marine insurance law and the reader is referred to specialist books on the subject.[84]

8.1.3 *An obligation to notify the mortgagee*

Notification to the mortgagee with regard to the movements of the ship is required, in case the ship sails either in war zones, where the security will be exposed to a higher risk or loss, or in jurisdictions in which the law may be unfavourable to the priority enjoyed by the mortgage over other maritime claims, which are not recognised as maritime liens under the law of the mortgage.

---

81 See *Pan Atlantic Insurance Co Ltd v Pine Top Insurance Co Ltd* [1994] 2 Lloyd's Rep 427 (HL); *Manifest Shipping Co Ltd v Uni-Polaris Shipping Co Ltd (The Star Sea)* [2001] 1 Lloyd's Rep 389 (HL).

82 See *The Good Luck* [1991] 2 Lloyd's Rep 191 (HL).

83 *Samuel v Dumas* [1924] AC 431 (HL).

84 See Colinvaux & Merkin's *Insurance Contract Law*, loose-leaf, quarterly updated, (2005) Sweet & Maxwell; and C Bowtle & K McGuinness, *The Law of Ship Mortgages*, LLP, 2001, Chapter 5.

Giving information to the mortgagee about any accidents the ship has experienced, which may affect the security, are also included in the covenants as obligations of the mortgagor.

8.1.4 An obligation to discharge claims or liens

In parallel with the previous covenant, the mortgagor has an obligation to discharge all debts and liabilities, which may encumber the ship and can be enforced against the security by arrest, as discussed in Chapter 2. If the ship is arrested, the mortgagor has an obligation to provide security and procure its release.

To pay dues to port authorities and any debts, which may affect the priority of the mortgagee's security, also form part of the covenants.

8.1.5 An obligation not to sell or grant a charge on the ship

During the duration of the mortgage, the mortgagor covenants not to sell, or grant a mortgage or charge to any person without first discharging the debt to the mortgagee.

8.1.6 An obligation of legal trading

Illegal trading will prejudice the insurance policy for breach of the implied warranty of legality under s 41 of the MIA 1906. Furthermore, it will result in detention or confiscation of the ship.

8.1.7 A covenant as to charterparties

Although a long time charter agreed on favourable terms will be a source of revenue for discharging the debt to the mortgagee, the mortgagor may be required to inform the mortgagee prior to engaging the ship for a long term, in case the terms of the charterparty prevent the mortgagee from exercising his rights in case of default by the mortgagor.

The mortgagor must employ the ship in a prudent manner so that the earnings will provide income for payment of the instalments. Assignment of earnings is a collateral security.

8.2 The mortgagor's statutory obligations

It is implicit in the statute (paras 9 and 10 of Sched 1 to the MSA 1995) that, unless the mortgagor repays the loan, as agreed, or if he is in breach of contract, impairing the security, the mortgagee may take steps, as empowered by the statute, to make the ship available as a security. The statute does not provide for any other obligations leaving the parties to agree the details in their contract, by the deed of covenants.

8.3 The mortgagor's right of ownership of the mortgaged ship

From paras 1 and 10 of Sched 1 to the Act (see above), the ownership rights of the mortgagor are confirmed.

Lord Westbury, in *Collins v Lamport*[85] as far back as 1864, described the position under the statute as follows:

> In my judgment, under the statute, so long as the mortgagee of a ship does not take possession, the mortgagor, as the registered owner, subject to the mortgage, retains all the rights and powers of ownership, and his contracts with regard to the ship will be valid and effectual, provided that his dealings do not materially impair the mortgagee's security.

The mortgagor's rights of ownership are restricted only when the mortgagee takes possession for the purpose of making the ship available to satisfy the mortgaged debt. Apart from that incident, were the owner not to have retained his powers and rights of ownership, he would be acting as an agent for the mortgagee on the basis of the property transfer theory. Lord Westbury in the same case continued:

> Under earlier statutes the mortgagee, upon the making and registration of the mortgage, became in the eye of the law, the owner of the property, the mortgagor being treated as his quasi agent. The result was, that the mortgagee frequently found himself bound either by the contracts of the mortgagor, or, at all events, by the necessary expenditure and outgoings of the vessel, a result seriously injurious and inconvenient to mortgagees, and one which interposed considerable difficulty in the way of persons desirous of raising money upon this species of security.[86]

It is clear from this statement that the property transfer theory was already a spent force upon the reform of the ship mortgage by the 1854 statute.[87] The mortgagor has all the ordinary incidents of ownership while he is in possession, including the payment of expenses, provision of insurance, entitlement to freight, and the right to enter into contracts which do not materially impair the mortgagee's security. The manner in which he wishes to employ his asset, subject, of course, to his obligations to the mortgagee under the deed of covenants, is up to him.

In this connection, the famous dictum of Lord Cairns, in *Keith v Burrows*,[88] is in sharp contrast to the property transfer theory advanced by the judge at first instance in the same case:

> The question arises with regard to the rights of the mortgagee of the ship taking possession, both generally and also under the circumstances of this case. My Lords, with regard to the general rights as between mortgagor and mortgagee of a ship there cannot, I think, at this time of day be any real controversy. The mortgagee of a ship does not, ordinarily speaking, or by a mortgage such as existed in the present case, obtain any transfer by way of contract or assignment of the freight, nor does the

---

85   (1864) 4 De GJ&S 500.

86   (1864) 4 De GJ&S 500, p 503.

87   It is submitted that references to Lindley J's judgment in *Keith v Burrows* (1876) 1 CPD 722, after what Lord Westbury said, serve only to confuse matters, and the case should be taken as having been implicitly overruled.

88   (1887) 2 App Cas 636, p 645.

mortgagor of a ship undertake to employ the ship so as to earn freight at all. The mortgagor of a ship may allow the ship to lie tranquil in dock, or he may employ it in any part of the world, not in earning freight, but for the purpose of bringing home goods of his own for his own benefit ... All these acts would be the ordinary incidents of the ownership of the mortgagor, who remains the *dominus* of the ship with regard to everything connected with its employment, until the moment arrives when the mortgagee takes possession. If the mortgagee is dissatisfied with the amount of authority which the mortgagor possesses by law, it is for him to put an end to the opportunity of exercising that authority by taking the control of the ship out of the hands of the mortgagor.

Lord Westbury in *Collins v Lamport*[89] summed up the mortgagor's rights to enter into contracts in relation to his ship in the light of the statutory provisions:

> Every contract, therefore, entered into by the mortgagor remaining in possession, is a contract which derives validity from the declaration of his continuing to be the owner, but at the same time, every such contract is a contract into the benefit of which the mortgagee may at any time enter by giving notice to the person who under that contract is to pay to the mortgagor, that he requires the payment to be made to him, the mortgagee.[90]

8.4 The mortgagor's right to redeem the ship

The equitable right of the mortgagor to redeem his property upon payment of the loan is central to the essence of a ship mortgage. The right exists from the time of the inception of the mortgage irrespective of default and it does not depend on a contractual term to confer it. Moreover, the court has inherent equitable jurisdiction to interfere in all ship mortgages in which the terms are unconscionable, or constitute a 'clog or fetter' on the mortgagor's right of redemption. The Court of Appeal defined the extent of the court's intervention in **Knightsbridge Estates Trust Ltd v Byrne**[91] concerning a mortgage of real property, in which Sir Wilfrid Greene MR said:

> ... equity may give relief against contractual terms in a mortgage transaction, if they are oppressive or unconscionable, and in deciding whether or not a particular transaction falls within this category the length of time for which the contractual right to redeem is postponed may well be an important consideration ...

> But equity does not reform mortgage transactions because they are unreasonable. It is concerned to see two things – one that the essential requirements of a mortgage transaction are observed and, the other, that oppressive or unconscionable terms are not enforced. Subject to this, it does not, in our opinion, interfere ...[92]

> ... In our opinion the proposition that a postponement of the contractual right of redemption is only permissible for a 'reasonable' time is not well-founded. Such a postponement is not properly described as a clog on the equity of redemption, since it is concerned with the contractual right to redeem. It is indisputable that any

---

89   (1864) 4 De GJ&S 500.
90   Ibid, p 504.
91   [1939] Ch 441.
92   Ibid, p 457.

provision which hampers redemption after the contractual date for redemption has passed will not be permitted. Further, it is undoubtedly true to say that a right of redemption is a necessary element in a mortgage transaction and, consequently that, where the contractual right of redemption is illusory, equity will grant relief by allowing redemption.[93]

If the mortgagee refuses the mortgage money offered, the court will protect the mortgagor's equity of redemption. An action in damages against the mortgagee would lie, if it were no longer possible to redeem the mortgaged property.

Fletcher & Campbell v City Marine Finance Ltd[94]

The defendants in this case were the mortgagees of the ship for a loan granted to the first plaintiffs (the mortgagor). The deed of covenants provided for repayment of the loan in monthly instalments. There was default in payment and the mortgagees wanted to take possession, refusing to accept payment from the second plaintiffs, who were the beneficial owners of the ship, and insisting that the mortgagor should pay on unconditional terms. Although an offer was made by the second plaintiffs for payment by the mortgagor, the mortgagees sold the vessel a few days thereafter, depriving the mortgagor of his right to redeem. It was held that the tender of the sum due was a proper tender, and the defendants had acted unreasonably by refusing to accept it. The mortgagor was entitled to recover damages, because his right to redeem was prevented by the wrongful action of the mortgagee. Roskill J quoted from p 16 of Benjamin Constant's book:

> It should be explained that an essential characteristic of a mortgage is the right of the mortgagor to redeem his property at any time after the date named in the mortgage as the date for repayment of the mortgage debt until the mortgage is foreclosed, or the property is sold, and a term, whether in the mortgage itself or in an independent agreement, which impedes or prevents the mortgagor in the exercise of this right may be a clog on the equity of redemption, and therefore invalid and unenforceable.[95]

The judge further commented that the courts would not, however, intervene in every case of interference with a due exercise of a mortgagor's right to redeem and continued, referring to another relevant passage from the book of the above author:

> Although a mortgagor retains, even after the date specified in the mortgage as that for the repayment of the mortgage debt, an equitable right to redeem his property, he can do so only by giving the mortgagee six month's notice of his intention or by paying him six month's interest in lieu of notice . . . But, where the mortgagee has himself demanded the repayment of his debt, or has taken other steps to realise his security, no question of notice arises, and the mortgagee must accept a tender of his principal with interest to the date of repayment.

Roskill J concluded in this case:

> Accordingly, in my judgment, there is, as a matter of English law, a right in the mortgagor of a ship to recover damages against his mortgagee, if his right to redeem

---

93 [1939] Ch 441, p 456.
94 [1968] 2 Lloyd's Rep 520.
95 Ibid, pp 535, 536.

is prevented by the wrongful act of the mortgagee. I do not think it matters whether one makes the necessary implication into the collateral deed as a matter of law, or whether one makes the implication therein as arising from the other express terms of the deed or whether one arrives at the same result by the application of basic principles of equity.[96]

A clog on the equity of redemption would be void where the clog was imposed as part of the original transaction of a mortgage, in which it had been arranged between the mortgagor and the transferee that the transferee, in return for the loan, should have an option to purchase part of the mortgaged property. The option to purchase part of the mortgaged property, unless it is given by a separate transaction, would be void as a clog on the equity of redemption for, if it was exercised, it would prevent the mortgagor from recovering the part of the property to which it applied. The court looks at the substance of the matter and not the form in which the bargain was carried out, and inquires into the object and purpose with which the documents were executed.[97]

If the mortgagee has a right under the contract to accelerate his power of sale without notice, even if there is no financial default, such a clause, normally, would be a 'clog' on the right to redemption, if the mortgagee exploited his bargaining strength at the time of the agreement.

There is, therefore, prohibition to contract out of the right of redemption known as a 'clog' or 'fetter' on the mortgagor's right, which means that any term impeding the right will be repugnant to the right of redemption.[98]

Although there is freedom of contract, permitting the parties to agree their terms and how to deal with specific events, a power of sale without notice may, in certain circumstances, violate the right of the mortgagor to redeem his property.[99]

In exceptional circumstances, however, the courts may adopt a non-interventionist approach if, upon true construction of the relevant clause in the deed of covenants, the parties had expressly agreed that the mortgagee should have power to sell the vessel in the event of a non-financial default, even though no sum of money had become due under the loan agreement. The mere possibility that the power of sale could be exercised in an unlawful manner without notice, so as to defeat the mortgagor's right of redemption, did not invalidate the power of sale conferred in the following case.

The Maule [100]

The plaintiffs lent money to the defendants. As security for the performance of their obligations under the loan agreement, the defendants granted to the plaintiffs a mortgage over their vessel, which was registered in Cyprus. The deed of covenants provided that upon the occurrence of any of the events of default specified in the loan agreement the plaintiffs would be entitled, forthwith, to exercise all the powers

---

96 [1968] 2 Lloyd's Rep 520, p 538.
97 *Lewis v Love* [1961] 1 WLR 261; *Reeve v Lisle* [1902] AC 461 (HL); *Samuel v Jarrah Timber and Wood-Paving Corp Ltd* [1909] AC 323 (HL).
98 *Santley v Wilde* [1899] 2 Ch 474 (CA).
99 *The Maule* [1997] 1 WLR 528 (PC).
100 Ibid.

possessed by them as mortgagees of the vessel. One such power was to sell the ship, with or without prior notice to the owners and the sale would be deemed to be within the mortgagees' power. Amongst the events of default in the loan agreement was the failure by the borrower to sell a vessel belonging to the group, *The Foresight Driller II*, within 60 days after notice by the mortgagees had been given, in the event that no employment could be found for her. The ship was not sold within the required time limit. Although no instalment was outstanding and the lender had not exercised its power to accelerate repayment of the loan, the defendants' vessel, *The Maule*, was arrested in Hong Kong. *The Foresight Driller II* was eventually sold and its proceeds were used to reduce the indebtedness of the owners in the group to the lender.

The judge held that a power of sale under a mortgage could only be exercised when money was due. The Court of Appeal of Hong Kong dismissed the plaintiffs' appeal. The plaintiffs appealed to the Privy Council and the issue was, whether they were entitled to arrest *The Maule* in the circumstances. If they were not, the shipowners were claiming damages for wrongful arrest. As the ship was registered in Cyprus, the applicable statute was the same in all material respects as the MSA 1894, the relevant sections of which have now been consolidated in the MSA 1995.

The Privy Council, allowing the appeal, held that the rights and duties of the parties to the mortgage of a ship were primarily governed by the contract. On true construction of the relevant clause in the deed of covenants the plaintiffs were not obliged to give notice accelerating repayment of the loan before exercising their power of sale. The mere possibility that the power of sale could be exercised in an unlawful manner without notice, so as to defeat the borrowers' right of redemption, did not invalidate the power conferred in this case. Therefore, the plaintiffs were entitled to arrest the vessel pursuant to their power of sale conferred by the contract.

While the Privy Council confirmed the principle derived from the previous case,[101] that any sale without notice would be unlawful and give rise to a claim in damages, it distinguished that position from the facts of the case in question. In this case, the borrowers were aware of the proposed sale and they could seek assistance from the contract under which they could give seven days notice to repay and thereby redeem the ship.[102] It seems that the decision will have a limited application, but it reinforces, save for the right of redemption, freedom of contract in the loan agreement. It allows the parties to bargain the power of sale beyond the classic events of default known in practice and in law. Skilful drafting, however, would have prevented the borrowers from finding themselves in such an unfavourable situation, unless the bargaining power weighed heavily on the side of the mortgagee.

---

101 *Fletcher & Campbell v City Marine Finance Ltd* [1968] 2 Lloyd's Rep 520.

102 Clarke, A, in her commentary on this case, [1997] LMCLQ 329, p 337, concluded that: 'Any uncertainties about the power of sale left unresolved by *The Maule* can be avoided by competent drafting'.

9 MORTGAGEE'S RIGHTS AND OBLIGATIONS

The mortgagee's rights derive from the contract, the statute and common law. Unless it is otherwise specified in the contract, normally a default in payment will trigger the right of the mortgagee to enforce his security. He should first give immediate notice of the default to the mortgagor, requiring remedy of the default, depending on what the contract provides. He may demand payment of the whole debt, which is triggered by a default, but he must specify a reasonable time for the mortgagor to do so. This is known as acceleration of debt, and it is not void as a penalty if it provides for payment of the unpaid principal amount secured by the mortgage and not for future interest that would have been payable.[103] If the default is minor, he may decide to waive it, or give time to the mortgagor to rectify the default. In the event the mortgagor does not pay the amount due, the mortgagee can seek enforcement of his security, either by taking possession and then exercising his power of sale, or arresting the ship and proceeding for a judicial sale.

Once the mortgagee enters into possession of the ship, if the occasion arises for the realisation of his security, he has owner-type rights conferred on him by statute or contract, but only such rights as are necessary for the enforcement of his security. They are exercisable only to the extent that it is necessary for that purpose. The rights and remedies of a registered mortgagee are conferred by statute, essentially by paras 9 and 10 of Sched 1 to the MSA 1995. Paragraph 10 not only defines the mortgagee's rights but also regulates their exercise.

9.1 The right to take possession

The statute does not expressly confer to the mortgagee a right to take possession; there is no express reference in Sched 1 to the MSA 1995 that the mortgagee has such power. But such right is conferred by common law independently of express provisions in the contract. Express provisions in the deed of covenants will specify when the mortgagee can enter into possession. At common law the mortgagee can enter into possession when there is default in payment of capital or interest, or a threat to his security. In addition, he can rely on the statutory rights given by the MSAs.

In particular, para 10 of Sched 1 to the 1995 Act seems to imply a right of possession, in that it protects the registered mortgagee, only insofar as it is necessary for making the ship or share available as a security for the mortgage debt, to exercise ownership rights. In pursuance of such rights, he can interfere with the mortgagor's possession, control and operation and, insofar as it is necessary to make the ship available as a security, he may be treated as owner. Ownership rights include possession.

The mortgagee has no right to take possession of the ship unless there has been default in payment or a threat to his security in a sense that the security would be impaired. If the mortgagee enters into possession in the absence of either of these

---

103 *The Angelic Star* [1988] 1 Lloyd's Rep 122 (CA).

circumstances, or express contractual provisions, he may be liable to the mortgagor for costs and substantial damages.[104]

9.1.1 What would amount to default?

Default in payment of instalments of the capital and interest will entitle the mortgagee to take possession, but the totality of the circumstances will be looked at in the context of the contract. Paragraph 9 of Sched 1 to the MSA 1995 provides for when the mortgagee could sell the ship and, by implication, he may enter in possession before sale. Before such power can be exercised, para 9 puts a condition that there must be money or any part of it due. In the absence of a variation in the contract, once the date of payment has passed, technically, the mortgagee will be able to exercise his statutory power. The statute does not specify any other default or the extent of default, but gives only a general event of money being due, leaving the parties to agree other reasons of default and any maximum or minimum non-payment. In The Cathcart,[105] for example, while the date for payment had passed, the parties had agreed to postpone repayment until freight had been paid. When the mortgagee arrested the ship for non-payment, despite the fact that he had full knowledge that the vessel was about to commence a profitable charterparty, the court held him liable in damages.

9.1.2 When would the security be impaired?

Other than default in payment of instalments by the due date, there may be various events which indicate that, at the end of the day, the ship's value may be diminished to an extent that it will not be sufficient for the mortgagee to cover his security, thus a threat to the security may be imminent.

One question that has frequently faced the courts is this: when could it be said that the mortgagee's security is being endangered, or that his security is likely to be impaired? The answer to that question depends on the circumstances of each case and it is a question of fact.[106] The courts usually consider a certain number of factors before coming to the conclusion that the mortgagee was justified in taking possession, if his security was indeed impaired or likely to be impaired, in the absence of default of payment. Examples of some of these circumstances have been an impecunious mortgagor[107] and the prospect of the vessel remaining burdened with maritime liens coupled with financial difficulties of the mortgagor. (This may mean that the vessel remains unrepaired for a long time or uninsured.)[108] An unprofitable charterparty with onerous terms and provisions, which may greatly affect the mortgagee's right to recover his security, may amount to impairment.[109] Sometimes,

---

104 *The Cathcart* (1867) LR 1 A&E 314, per Dr Lushington; *The Blanche* (1887) 6 Asp MLC 272; *The Manor* [1907] P 339.

105 (1867) LR 1 A&E 314.

106 *The Myrto* [1977] 2 Lloyd's Rep 243.

107 *De Mattos v Gibson* (1858) 4 De G&J 276.

108 *Laming & Co v Seater* (1889) 16 Ct of Sess Cas (4th ser) 828.

109 See *The Myrto* [1977] 2 Lloyd's Rep 243; cf *The Maxima* (1878) 4 Asp MLC 21; *The Fanchon* (1880) 5 PD 173.

the mere presence of one of these factors may not be sufficient to entitle the mort-gagee to enter into possession, but a combination of them will.[110] Some examples given below illustrate those circumstances.

The Manor[111]

The borrower was in breach of a covenant to pay premium with respect to insur-ance. (It had been agreed that the mortgagees would pay part of the premium.) In addition, the borrower had incurred debts, such as unpaid wages to the crew and master, canal dues, dues for coal. A lot of money was needed for the repair of the vessel. The liabilities would exceed the amount expected to be earned from freight out of a nine-month voyage. Time for the repayment of the mortgage amount was imminent and the mortgagee took possession of the ship. The issue for the court was whether the mortgagee's security would be materially impaired if the ship were left under the control of the mortgagor. The judge came to the conclusion that, on the facts, there was not sufficient impairing of the security to justify the mort-gagee in taking possession. The Court of Appeal held that a set of circumstances existed, which did, in fact, impair the security and the mortgagee was entitled to take possession. In particular, Fletcher Moulton LJ said:

> It may well be that to allow a ship to become subject to a maritime lien may not be an infringement of the rights of the mortgagee, even though that maritime lien ranks above claims of the mortgagee . . . But, there is an obvious difference between allow-ing a ship to become burthened with a maritime lien, and allowing her to remain burthened with such a lien, without the power to discharge it, for, to that extent, you have, as in this case, substantially diminished, that is to say, impaired the value of the mortgage security.[112]

Law Guarantee and Trust Society v Russian Bank of Foreign Trade[113]

The plaintiffs were trustees of a debenture trust deed. The deed was entered into by the defendants, British shipowners, to secure the holders of debentures of the ship-owning company. By an undertaking of the company, all its property was assigned to the plaintiffs as a security for the payment of the debentures. Three steamships of the company were the 'mortgaged premises'. Mortgages on the steamers were exe-cuted in the statutory form and were registered. The trust deed provided that the trustees might enter into possession of the mortgaged premises upon the happen-ing of certain events. In 1904, when Russia was at war with Japan, the defendants entered into charterparties for carriage of cargoes of coal from Barry to Vladivos-tock in Russia in their three steamers. However, they signed fictitious documents with the knowledge of the charterers, purporting to carry the goods to the neutral ports of Manilla and Shanghai, because there was great risk of the vessels being captured, as Russian ports were blockaded by the Japanese. It was not disputed that the Russian Government was interested in the coal. Insurance premiums against

---

110 *The Manor* [1907] P 339, per Moulton LJ; *The Myrto* [1977] 2 Lloyd's Rep 243, per Brandon J.
111 [1907] P 339.
112 Ibid, pp 361–62.
113 [1905] 1 KB 815.

war risks for vessels going to Russian ports were very high at the time, so to insure them for war risks would have left little or no profit on the charterparties. Lord Alverstone CJ, agreeing with the learned judge in the lower court, stated that the mortgagor was not justified to enter into these charterparty contracts, which were, in themselves, such as to imperil the security of the mortgagee and, therefore, the latter was not bound by those charterparties according to the rule in *Collins v Lamport*. Making reference to his previous judgment in *The Heather Bell*,[114] he clarified the issue of whether or not there would be an impairment of the security if there was no proper insurance in place for ordinary perils of the sea, and said:

> ...I did not mean to say [in that case] that non-insurance was not a matter to be considered in connection with such cases, but merely that, if the charterparty was otherwise binding on the mortgagee, the fact that the ship was not properly insured against ordinary perils of the sea might not of itself be sufficient to prevent the charterparty from being binding upon him.[115]

Whether or not the security would be impaired if the ship sailed to a jurisdiction where the mortgagee would find it difficult to enforce his security, he referred to a previous case and said:

> The mere fact that the ship is about to sail in a jurisdiction in which it may be more difficult for the mortgagee to enforce his security is not a factor in itself to allow the mortgagee to take possession.[116]

The modern deed of covenants in ship mortgages provides extensively for the circumstances in which the mortgagee can enter into possession.[117]

9.2 Mode of exercising his powers

The mortgagee may recover his debt, either by instituting an action *in rem* under s 21 of the Supreme Court Act 1981, or by taking actual or constructive possession of the vessel. He may take actual possession by putting his own representative on board the vessel, and constructive possession by simply giving notice to the mortgagor and all interested parties, like insurers, charterers and bill of lading holders.[118] When he takes possession, he must take sufficient steps to indicate his intention to enter into possession, which must be clear and unambiguous to the interested parties.[119]

9.3 Mortgagee's rights and obligations in possession

When the mortgagee takes possession of the vessel, he becomes responsible for the mortgagor's contractual obligations under pre-existing binding contracts. Thus, he

---

114 [1901] P 272.
115 [1905] 1 KB 815, pp 825 and 826.
116 *The Highlander* (1843) 2 W Rob 109.
117 See, eg, *The Maule* [1997] 1 WLR 528.
118 *Rushden v Pope* (1868) LR Ex 269.
119 *Benwell Tower* (1895) 8 Asp MLC 13.

will be liable to pay the expenses, but he will also enjoy the benefits of such contracts. Once he has taken possession of the vessel, he is entitled to freight, which is being earned.

9.3.1 Right to freight

A mortgagee of the ship, having taken possession of her before any freight had become payable from the charterers to the owners, is entitled to the freight. He takes it in priority to an assignee of freight, who took an assignment with knowledge of the mortgage.[120]

Liverpool Marine Credit Co v Wilson [121]

The owners of the ship executed and registered a mortgage in favour of the plaintiffs, the first mortgagee. Two days later, a second mortgage was executed in favour of the defendants, the second mortgagee, and it was later registered. The owners then gave a lien on the accruing freight to a third party, to which the first mortgagee signed a written consent that this advance would have priority over their own mortgage. As additional security to the second mortgagee, the owners granted them a lien on accruing freight. The first mortgagee, with no notice of the second mortgagee's lien on the freight, made further advances to the owners on the security of another mortgage, including all freight already earned, or to be earned under any charterparty entered into during the continuance of the mortgage. The first mortgagee's second mortgage was unregistered. All parties who were given a lien on the freight subsequently gave notice of their charge to the charterers. The first mortgagee (plaintiffs) took possession of the vessel and claimed priority over the second mortgagee to the net proceeds of the sale and to the freight (subject to the sum payable to the third party) for the satisfaction of their second mortgage. The second mortgagee contended that the first mortgagee was not entitled to the freight as a separate fund in the discharge of their first mortgage. It was held that:

> The first registered mortgagee of a ship, by taking possession of her before the freight is completely earned, obtains a legal right to receive the freight, and to retain thereat not only what is due on his first mortgage, but also the amount of any subsequent charge which he may have acquired on the freight, in priority to every equitable charge of which he had no notice; and it makes no difference that a subsequent incumbrancer was the first to give notice to the charterers of his charge on the freight.

On the right of the mortgagee to the freight, Sir WM James LJ stated:

> It is to be observed that the MSA nowhere deals with charges on freight. They were long before the passing of the Act securities well known in the shipping world, and of ordinary occurrence. And the right of a mortgagee in respect of freight had also been long settled and well recognised. But it was not thought fit to provide by that Act either with respect to the priorities of charges on freight, or with respect to the rights of mortgagees to freight. These were left to be dealt with according to the ordinary principles of law and equity, and the rules and doctrines established by the decisions of the courts. Now, the right of the mortgagee in respect of freight was well

---

120 *Brown v Tanner* (1868) LR 3 Ch 597 (CA).
121 (1872) LR 7 Ch 507.

established and clear, but somewhat peculiar. He had no absolute right to the freight as an incident to his mortgage; he could not intercept the freight by giving notice to the charterer before payment; but, if he took actual possession, or, according to a recent decision in the Court of Exchequer, if he took constructive possession of the ship before the freight was actually earned, he, thus, became entitled to the freight as an incident of his legal possessory right, just as a mortgagee of land taking actual possession of the land before severance of the growing crops would have the right to sever and take the crops.[122]

His position was like that of the legal mortgagee of any other kind of property who made further advances on the property itself without notice of any intervening equitable interests.

If the mortgagee, however, takes possession before the freight has become payable and, at the time of the possession, still remains unpaid, he will not be entitled to the freight.[123]

9.3.2 Obligation during operation and management

Although the statute does not specifically stipulate this, it should be implicit that when a mortgagee exercises his owner-type rights by taking possession, he may like to continue the operation of the ship and earn the profits to satisfy his security, particularly, if there is a profitable charterparty ongoing. He is not obliged to exercise his power of sale once he enters into possession. As the mortgagee, usually, does not have the expertise to operate or manage ships, he will appoint a professional manager. The operation of a ship will entail liabilities and, in practice, it is rarely the case that a mortgagee would wish to get involved in such an exposure, unless the circumstances warrant profitable returns.

Should he decide to trade her, he must use her as a prudent man would use her. Lord Campbell, in *Marriott v The Anchor Reversionary Co*,[124] stated as follows:

> I cannot concur in the unlimited right of the mortgagee to use the ship as the owner might do . . . Nor can I lay down the strict rule that the mortgagee can never lawfully employ the ship to earn freight, or that, after taking possession, he must allow her to lie idle till he may prudently sell her . . . But, although there may be great difficulty in defining the limits of the power of the mortgagee to use the ship, this, I think, may be laid down with perfect safety and confidence, that if the mortgagee does take possession he can lawfully use the ship as a prudent man would use her, if she were his own property.

A mortgagee has an equitable duty to manage the ship with due diligence, so that he trades her profitably (see para 9.5, below).

---

122 Ibid, p 511.
123 *Anderson v Butler's Wharf Co Ltd* (1879) 48 LJ Ch 824.
124 (1861) 2 Giff 457.

9.4 Power of sale

9.4.1 Source of power

As already mentioned, para 9 of Sched 1 to the MSA 1995 is the key to this statutory power. It has slightly varied the power of its predecessor, s 35 of the MSA 1894, in that it specifically requires that there must have been some default in payment. A second or subsequent registered mortgagee cannot exercise the power of sale without the concurrence of every prior mortgagee, except when the order is made by a court of competent jurisdiction (Sched 1, para 9(2)).

An additional source of the mortgagee's power of sale is the contract. Whether or not he takes possession of the ship, he can exercise this power by having the ship arrested and sold by the court.

9.4.2 Role of the mortgagee in the sale of the ship and extent of his power

In exercising his power of sale, the mortgagee is not a trustee of the power of sale for the mortgagor. Salmon LJ restated the principle of the mortgagee's role in the sale of the ship in *Cuckmere Brick Co Ltd v Mutual Finance Ltd*,[125] in which he said:

> It is well settled that a mortgagee is not a trustee of the power of sale for the mortgagor. Once the power has accrued, the mortgagee is entitled to exercise it for his own purposes whenever he chooses to do so. It matters not that the moment may be unpropitious and that by waiting a higher price could be obtained. He has the right to realise his security by turning it into money when he likes. Nor, in my view, is there anything to prevent a mortgagee from accepting the best bid he can get at an auction, even though the auction is badly attended and the bidding exceptionally low. Providing none of those adverse factors is due to any fault of the mortgagee, he can do as he likes. If the mortgagee's interests, as he sees them, conflict with those of the mortgagor, the mortgagee can give preference to his own interests, which of course he could not do were he a trustee of the power of sale for the mortgagor.[126]

A mortgagee is at all times free to consult his own interests alone as to whether or not to exercise his power of sale.[127]

The mortgagee's decision is not constrained by reason of the fact that the exercise or non-exercise of the power will occasion loss or damage to the mortgagor.[128]

It does not matter that the time may be unpropitious and that, by waiting, a higher price could be obtained: he is not bound to postpone in the hope of obtaining a better price.[129]

The mortgagee is entitled to sell the mortgaged property as it is. He is under no

---

125 [1971] Ch 949.
126 Ibid, p 965.
127 *Raja v Austin Gray* [2002] EWCA Civ 1965, para 95 per Peter Gibson LJ.
128 *China and South Sea Bank Limited v Tan Soon Gin* [1990] 1 AC 536.
129 *Tse Kwong Lam v Wong Chit Sen* [1983] 1 WLR 1349, p 1355B.

obligation to improve it or increase its value. There is no obligation to take any such pre-marketing steps to increase the value of the property.[130]

With regard to any surplus of value fetched by the sale after satisfaction of the debt to him, he will hold the sum as a constructive trustee,[131,132] for any subsequent mortgagees and for the mortgagor.

9.4.3 Nature of duty of the mortgagee in the exercise of his power of sale

The question that has frequently arisen, particularly in land property cases, is whether the mortgagee, in the exercise of his power of sale, owes a duty of care to the mortgagor, in the same way as the duty owed by a trustee of a power of sale to the beneficiary of the property,[133] or whether he just has an obligation to act in good faith. In other words, does the duty lie in tort or in equity? This issue is of great importance because, if the mortgagee is in breach of a duty of care in tort, he will be made liable in damages suffered by the mortgagor due to such negligence, while, if he is only required to act in good faith, he will be liable in damages only if he acted dishonestly, recklessly, or fraudulently. If the duty is just a duty in equity, and not in tort, he will only have to account to the mortgagor and to others interested in the equity of redemption, not just for what he actually received but for what he should have received.[134] When the sale is tainted by fraud, provided relief is sought promptly, the court may, depending on the circumstances of the particular case, set aside the sale.[135] However, the court will also consider the position of the purchaser; if the purchaser had notice of the breach, setting aside the sale may be an appropriate order,[136] but if the purchaser was innocent, damages to the mortgagor may be an alternative remedy.

The following decisions illustrate how the courts have approached the issue of the mortgagee's duty to the mortgagor when he exercises the power of sale. A recent Court of Appeal decision (explained later) clarifies the position that the duty lies in equity.

In *Farrar v Farrars Limited*,[137] the Court of Appeal held that the mortgagee must act bona fide for the purposes of realising his security and must take reasonable precautions to secure a proper price.

There were three mortgagees involved. One of them was a solicitor and acted for the other mortgagees. He negotiated a sale in principle and agreed a price with intended purchasers. He subsequently took shares in a company formed by the purchasers to carry the sale into effect. The plaintiffs contended that the sale was by

---

130 *Silven Properties Ltd v Royal Bank of Scotland Plc* [2003] EWCA Civ 1409.

131 *Banner v Berridge* (1881) 18 Ch D 254.

132 *Den Norske Bank v Acemex Management (The Tropical Reefer)* [2004] 1 Lloyd's Rep 1. In case of a surplus in the price after payment of the loan to himself, he is in a fiduciary relationship to hold the surplus in trust for the mortgagor.

133 See *Kennedy v De Trafford* [1896] 1 Ch 762 (CA), p 772, [1897] AC 180 (HL), p 185.

134 *The Tropical Reefer* [2004] 1 Lloyd's Rep 1.

135 *Haddington Island Quarry Co Ltd v Alden Wesley Huson* [1911] AC 722 (PC).

136 *Tse Kwong Lam v Wong Chit Sen* [1983] 1 WLR 1349.

137 (1888) 40 Ch D 395.

the mortgagee to himself and others, under the guise of a sale to a limited company. On the nature of a mortgagee's power of sale, Lindley LJ stated:

> A mortgagee with a power of sale, though often called a trustee, is in a very different position from a trustee for sale. A mortgagee is under obligations to the mortgagor, but he has rights of his own, which he is entitled to exercise adversely to the mortgagor. A trustee for sale has no business to place himself in such a position as to give rise to a conflict of interest and duty. But every mortgage confers upon the mortgagee the right to realise his security and to find a purchaser if he can, and, if in exercise of his power, he acts bona fide and takes reasonable precautions to obtain a proper price, the mortgagor has no redress, even though more might have been obtained for the property if the sale had been postponed.[138]

There was no impropriety in this case and the mortgagee's solicitor did his best to get the best price.

However, other decisions were not consistent on the issue. The Court of Appeal in the *Cuckmere*[139] case, mentioned above, summarised the conflicting authorities, and Cairns LJ was in favour of the view that there was a duty owed by the mortgagee to take reasonable care to obtain a proper price:

> I find it impossible satisfactorily to reconcile the authorities, but I think the balance of authority is in favour of a duty of care. That there is such a duty was certainly the view of Kekewich J and of the Court of Appeal in *Tomlin v Luce* (1889) 41 Ch D 573; (1889) 43 Ch D 191; also, of the Judicial Committee in *McHugh v Union Bank of Canada* [1913] AC 299. It also appears to have been the view of Lindley LJ at the time of his judgment in *Farrar v Farrars Ltd* (1888) 40 Ch D 395. That judgment was so interpreted by the judge of first instance in *Kennedy v de Trafford*, but, on the appeal, in that case, Lindley LJ said ([1896] 1 Ch 762, p 772) that, when he had referred in Farrar's case to a mortgagee's duty to take reasonable precautions, he had meant merely that the mortgagee must not act fraudulently or wilfully or recklessly; and, in the House of Lords, [1897] AC 180, p 185, Lord Herschell said that he thought it would be unreasonable to require the mortgagee to do more than act in good faith, that is, not wilfully or recklessly to sacrifice the interests of the mortgagor. These expressions of opinion in the Court of Appeal and in the House of Lords were, however, not necessary to the decision. Lindley LJ said, [1896] 1 Ch 762, p 772, that the mortgagees 'acted from first to last in an honourable and businesslike manner, without in the least sacrificing the interests of the mortgagor'.
>
> Lord Herschell said, [1897] AC 180, p 185: 'My Lords, it is not necessary in this case to give an exhaustive definition of the duties of a mortgagee to a mortgagor, because it appears to me that, if you were to accept the definition of them for which the appellant contends, namely, that the mortgagee is bound to take reasonable precautions in the exercise of his power of sale, as well as to act in good faith, still in this case he did take reasonable precautions.'
>
> I, therefore, consider that *Tomlin v Luce* (1889) 43 Ch D 191 is the stronger authority and I would hold that the present defendants had a duty to take reasonable care to obtain a proper price for the land in the interest of the mortgagors.

Salmon LJ dissented, only to the extent of the need to establish a yardstick with

---

138 (1888) 40 Ch D 395, pp 410–11.
139 *Cuckmere Brick Co Ltd v Mutual Finance Ltd* [1971] Ch 949, pp 977–78.

regard to the value to be obtained on sale; he preferred to use the phrase 'the true market value' instead of 'proper price':

> ... both on principle and authority, the mortgagee, in exercising his power of sale, does owe a duty to take reasonable precautions to obtain the true market value of the property at the date on which he decides to sell it.[140]

In 1993, it was explained by the Privy Council in the *Downsview Nominees* (below) that the duty to take reasonable precautions was limited to obtaining a proper price for the mortgaged property, and that the *Cuckmere* decision was not an authority for any wider proposition. This was the correct interpretation of the case.

Downsview Nominees v First City Corp[141]

The nature and extent of the duties owed by a mortgagee and his receiver or manager to subsequent encumbrancers and the mortgagor was examined. The first debenture holder (also the first defendant) appointed the second defendant as receiver for the sole purpose of disrupting the receivership under the second debenture belonging to the first plaintiff. The first plaintiff offered to buy the first debenture from the first defendant at a price equivalent to the amounts outstanding and secured under the debenture, but the first defendant refused. There was subsequently gross mismanagement on the part of the defendant's receiver resulting in considerable losses. The question was whether the first debenture holder and his receiver owed any duty to subsequent encumbrancers (the plaintiff) and to the company. The judgment of the Privy Council was delivered by Lord Templeman, who said, with regard to the duty, that it is primarily an equitable duty:

> If a first mortgagee commits a breach of his duties to the mortgagor, the damage inflicted by that breach of duty will be suffered by the second mortgagee, subsequent encumbrancers and the mortgagor, depending on the extent of the damage and the amount of each security ...
>
> ... when a receiver and manager exercises the powers of sale and management conferred on him by the mortgage, he is dealing with the security; he is not merely selling or dealing with the interests of the mortgagor. He is exercising the power of selling or dealing with the mortgaged property for the purpose of obtaining repayment of the debt owing to his mortgagee. The receiver and manager owes these duties to the mortgagor and to all subsequent encumbrancers in whose favour the mortgaged property has been charged ...[142]
>
> The general duty of care said to be owed by a mortgagee to subsequent encumbrancers and the mortgagor in negligence is inconsistent with the right of the mortgagee and the duties which the courts, applying equitable principles, have imposed on the mortgagee. If a mortgagee enters into possession he is liable to account for rent on the basis of wilful default; he must keep mortgage premises in repair; he is liable for waste. Those duties were imposed to ensure that a mortgagee is diligent in discharging his mortgage and returning the property to the mortgagor. If a mortgagee exercises his power of sale in good faith for the purpose of protecting his security, he is not liable to the mortgagor even though he might have obtained a higher price and

---

140 Ibid, p 968.
141 [1993] AC 295.
142 Ibid, pp 311–12.

even though the terms might be regarded as disadvantageous to the mortgagor. *Cuckmere Brick Co Ltd v Mutual Finance Ltd* [1971] Ch 949 is Court of Appeal authority for the proposition that, if the mortgagee decides to sell, he must take reasonable care to obtain a proper price, but is no authority for any wider proposition. A receiver exercising his power of sale also owes the same specific duties as the mortgagee. But that apart, the general duty of a receiver and manager appointed by a debenture holder, as defined by Jenkins LJ in *In re B Johnson & Co (Builders) Ltd* [1955] Ch 634, p 661, leaves no room for the imposition of a general duty to use reasonable care in dealing with the assets of the company. The duties imposed by equity on a mortgagee and on a receiver and manager would be quite unnecessary if there existed a general duty in negligence to take reasonable care in the exercise of powers and to take reasonable care in dealing with the assets of the mortgagor company.[143]

The receivership of the second defendant was inspired by improper purposes and carried on in bad faith, verging on fraud. Lord Templeman continued:

A mortgagee owes a general duty to subsequent encumbrancers and to the mortgagor to use his powers for the sole purpose of securing repayments of the moneys owing under his mortgage and a duty to act in good faith. He also owes the specific duties which equity has imposed on him in the exercise of his powers to go into possession and his powers of sale. It may well be that a mortgagee who appoints a receiver and manager, knowing that the receiver and manager intends to exercise his powers for the purpose of frustrating the activities of the second mortgagee or for some other improper purpose or who fails to revoke the appointment of a receiver and manager when the mortgagee knows that the receiver and manager is abusing his powers, may himself be guilty of bad faith, but in the present case this possibility need not be explored.[144]

Such duty in equity was recently further confirmed by the Court of Appeal in the following case.

The Tropical Reefer [145]

A loan facility agreement for US$6 million was reached between the bank, Den Norske, and three companies, the borrowers, for the purchase of three vessels, one of which was *The Tropical Reefer*. The security for the loan included mortgages on the three vessels and was subject to the law of Cyprus. A personal guarantee was also given by the defendants in this case, the guarantors, as a further security, which was subject to English law. There were various events of default under the mortgage agreement and *The Tropical Reefer*, which was laden with a cargo of perishable bananas, was arrested by the mortgagee in Panama. The vessel's P&I cover had been withdrawn due to non-payment of premiums. The bank demanded payment of the outstanding indebtedness from the guarantors in the English courts. The defendants resisted the claim on the ground of breach of duty of care in equity owed by the bank to the defendants. The breach, as alleged, was committed by the arrest of the vessel while laden with perishable cargo which deteriorated due to the

---

143 [1993] AC 295, p 315.
144 Ibid, p 317.
145 *Den Norske Bank ASA v Acemex Management Co Ltd* (*The Tropical Reefer*) [2004] 1 Lloyd's Rep 1, CA.

arrest of the ship. Hence, costs of disposing the cargo were incurred which diminished the sale proceeds of the ship. The proceeds were also encumbered by a lien for the damage to cargo. In those circumstances, it was argued that the bank was unable to proceed against the defendants under the guarantee.

The Court of Appeal, relying on its previous decision in *Silven Properties and Chart Enterprises Ltd v Royal Bank of Scotland plc*,[146] held:

> a mortgagee had an unfettered discretion to sell when he liked to achieve repayment of the debt which he was owed, and his decision was not constrained by reason of the fact that the exercise or non-exercise of the power would occasion loss or damage to the mortgagor; he was entitled to sell the mortgaged property as it was, and was under no obligation to improve it or increase its value; when and if the mortgagee did exercise the power of sale, he came under a duty in equity (and not tort) to the mortgagor and all others interested in the equity of redemption to take reasonable precautions to obtain 'the fair' or 'the true market' value of or the 'proper price' for the mortgaged property at the date of the sale, and not the date of the decision to sell; he had to take proper care to obtain the best price reasonably obtainable at the date of sale; the remedy for breach of that equitable duty was not common law damages, but an order that the mortgagee account to the mortgagor and all others interested in the equity of redemption, not just for what he actually received, but for what he should have received; and a mortgagee was entitled to sell the property in the condition in which it stood without investing money or time in increasing its likely sale value.

It decided against the defendants, the guarantors, and stated:

> The defendants' argument that if, in the course of carrying out the sale of a mortgaged ship, the mortgagee impaired the value of the ship, he was in breach of his duty to obtain the best reasonably obtainable price for the ship, would be rejected on the facts of the present case; first, the submission fell foul of the many statements that the mortgagee was entitled to decide the time at which he sold without regard to the interests of the mortgagor; secondly, the bank was in any event entitled to take the view that releasing the vessel from arrest and permitting her to travel to Germany with her cargo on board was fraught with risk.

However, the mortgagee is not entitled to act in a way which unfairly prejudices the mortgagor by selling hastily at a knock-down price sufficient to pay off his debt. He should not act in an arbitrary manner.[147]

There is no fixed rule that a mortgagee exercising his power of sale might not sell the mortgaged property to a company in which he is interested, but he must show that he had made the sale in good faith and had taken reasonable precautions to obtain the best price reasonably obtainable at the time. However, he must not sell to himself as an individual.

---

146 [2003] EWCA Civ 1409, [2004] 1 WLR 997 (the court distinguished the duty of the mortgagee from the duty of the receiver; the receiver has no right to remain passive if that course would damage the interests of the mortgagor or mortgagee); *Standard Chartered Bank v Walker* [1982] 1 WLR 1410, p 1416B (Lord Denning MR accepted that, although the mortgagee can choose his time for sale, he added that these dicta from previous cases did not mean that the mortgagee could sell at the worst possible time and that, in choosing his time, he must exercise a reasonable degree of care).

147 *Palk v Mortgage Services Funding Plc* [1993] Ch 330; there are numerous other cases in property law (which go beyond the scope of this book) emphasising the same principle.

Tse Kwong Lam v Wong Chit Sen [148]

The mortgagee, in exercise of his power of sale under a charge, arranged for the property to be sold by public auction. The auction was advertised and at the auction, the mortgagee instructed the auctioneer that the reserve price was to be $1.2 million. Meanwhile, the mortgagee and his wife were directors of a company of which his children were the shareholders. It had been agreed at a directors' meeting of this company that the wife would bid for the property, on behalf of the company, up to $1.2 million. His wife was the only bidder at the auction and, at a bid of $1.2 million, the property was sold to the company. The borrower/mortgagor applied to have the sale set aside. The court held that, because of the close relationship between the mortgagee and the company, a heavy onus lay on the mortgagee to show that, in all respects, he had acted fairly to the borrower, and used his best endeavours to obtain the best price reasonably obtainable for the mortgaged property.

The Judicial Committee of the Privy Council stated thus:

> In the result, their Lordships consider that in the present case the company was not debarred from purchasing the mortgaged property but, in view of the close relationship between the company and the mortgagee and in view in particular of the conflict of duty and interest to which the mortgagee was subject, the sale to the company for $1.2 million can only be supported if the mortgagee proves that he took reasonable precautions to obtain the best price reasonably obtainable at the time of sale. [149]

In this case, the mortgagee had made no effort to discharge this burden, and there was insufficient evidence to show that this particular auction produced the true market value of the property. However, the sale was not set aside, in view of the borrower's delay in pursuing his claim.

The mortgagee can sell to the mortgagor, as there is no fiduciary relation between them during the sale. The mortgagee stands in a fiduciary position only when he holds a surplus of the value after the sale. If there is a single mortgagor, he can simply redeem his property by paying the principal, interest and costs. Where there are several mortgagors and one of them agrees to buy from the mortgagee, there is nothing to prevent him. The mortgagors are tenants in common and the mortgagee is at liberty, under his power of sale, to sell to any one of the mortgagors for his own benefit, without any notice to or consent of the co-mortgagors, provided the sale is made under a proper and bona fide exercise of the power of sale. [150]

In conclusion, as is shown in the recent authorities, the duty of the mortgagee to the mortgagor and other mortgagees during the exercise of his power of sale is to act in good faith when he deals with the asset of the mortgaged property. [151] He does not have a duty to achieve the best price on sale; he should use his best endeavours to obtain the market price. [152] If he does not, the remedy for the mortgagor may be to

---

148 [1983] 1 WLR 1349.

149 [1983] 1 WLR 1349, p 1356.

150 *Kennedy v De Trafford* [1896] 1 Ch 762.

151 See, also, *China and South Sea Bank Ltd v Tan Soon Gin* [1990] 1 AC 536 (PC).

152 *Tse Kwong Lam v Wong Chit Sen* [1983] 1 WLR 1349.

obtain an injunction from the court to prevent the sale at a low value. The duty lies in equity and not in the tort of negligence.[153] The sale may be set aside only in case of fraud of which the purchaser had notice.

9.4.4 Effect of sale by the mortgagee

A purchaser of the ship from the mortgagee will obtain good title. However, a private sale will have the effect of extinguishing only such encumbrances on the ship that arose after the mortgage, including mortgages taken with notice of the prior mortgage.[154] Sale by the mortgagee privately does not extinguish maritime liens created at any time. In the light of this disadvantage, which would make it difficult for the mortgagee to find a buyer willing to take such risk, the mortgagee seeks the assistance of the Admiralty Court by arresting the ship, so that the sale can be made by a court order, the effect of which is to extinguish all encumbrances.

9.5 Appointment of a receiver

There may be occasions when the mortgagee does not wish to undertake the liabilities, which would be inherent from his position in possession of the ship or from the exercise of his power of sale. The deed of covenants normally contains an express provision for an appointment of a receiver by the mortgagee who will be deemed to be the agent of the mortgagor.[155] If the deed of covenants does not provide for appointment of a receiver, the mortgagee can apply to court for such an appointment, where the mortgagor is in default or the mortgagee's security is threatened. Where a prior mortgagee has already taken possession of the ship, a subsequent mortgagee may apply to court for the appointment of a receiver subject to the right of the first mortgagee. The court may appoint a receiver in cases where there has been gross mismanagement on the part of the first mortgagee in possession. The function of the receiver is to collect the earnings of the mortgaged property (freight or hire), and pay the necessary expenses until the realisation of the security, or an order from the court.

The nature of the duties owed by a receiver and manager appointed by a debenture holder to act bona fide were summarised in the case of *Downsview Nominees v First City Corp* (see above). In the more recent Court of Appeal decision, *Medforth v Blake*,[156] it was held that the extent and scope of any duty of the receiver or manager additional to that of good faith depended on the facts and circumstances of the particular case. While his primary duty in the exercise of his powers of management was to try to bring about a situation in which interest on the secured debt

---

153 *Den Norske Bank v Acemex Management (The Tropical Reefer)* [2004] 1 Lloyd's Rep 1).
154 *Black v Williams* [1895] 1 Ch 408.
155 *Gaskell v Gosling* [1896] 1 QB 669 (CA), p 679, per Lord Esher MR, concerning appointment of a receiver by a trustee. The receiver negligently bought goods from the plaintiff after a winding-up order of the company. The receiver acted as agent of the company and was not liable himself to the plaintiff.
156 [1999] 3 WLR 922.

could be paid and the debt itself repaid, the receiver owed a duty to manage the property with due diligence.

9.6 Foreclosure

Foreclosure under the general law means the taking over of the property by the mortgagee, who becomes absolute owner of it in consideration of the mortgage debt. It extinguishes the equitable right of redemption of the mortgagor and, therefore, it is contradictory to that right protected by equity. For this reason, only the court can order it.

With regard to ship mortgages, the MSAs have not envisaged such a right, and it is doubtful whether the right exists with regard to registered mortgages of registered ships, because it would be inconsistent with the statutory nature of the ship mortgage. It has been argued that foreclosure is, essentially, the remedy of a property transfer mortgage. So, in principle, it ought not to be available on the statutory security analysis, since the MSAs, by virtue of which the mortgagee has been a registered mortgagee and not a registered owner since 1854, do not provide for it. By contrast, in a genuine property transfer-type mortgage, the mortgagee is already owner, and foreclosure is achieved merely by a court of equity declaring that the mortgagor's equity of redemption is at an end. But, even in land mortgages, foreclosure is now obsolete.[157]

10 EFFECT OF MORTGAGEE'S EXERCISE OF RIGHTS UPON THIRD PARTIES

10.1 The issues

It has been stated, in the authorities discussed earlier, that the mortgagor as owner in possession is free to employ his vessel in any way in which he wishes provided that his acts do not impair the mortgagee's security, which will necessitate the mortgagee to take possession. This derives from para 10 of Sched 1 to the MSA 1995, as discussed earlier. It follows that the mortgagor can enter into charterparty contracts while in possession, and such contracts will be binding on the mortgagee, provided they do not materially impair his security.

For a charterparty contract between the owner and a charterer to be binding upon the mortgagee, a distinction has been made by authorities between charterparties entered into after the mortgage was granted and those entered into prior to the mortgage.

It is a well-established principle, as will be seen in the following authorities, that, where the charterparty contract is subsequent to the mortgage, the mortgagee may only enter into possession and interfere with the charterparty where his secur-

---

157 Op cit, Clarke, fn 13, p 690.

ity is threatened, or is materially impaired. But, if the charterparty contract precedes the mortgage, the issue of whether or not the mortgagee had notice of the charterparty becomes important in determining whether or not the mortgagee can exercise his rights under the mortgage, which will interfere with the continuation of the charterparty. If he had actual knowledge of the charterparty and its terms, the charterparty will be binding on him and he will not be entitled to interfere with it, unless circumstances have changed since then.

Against this background of general principles, the question that has arisen before the courts is this: has the charterer of the ship any rights himself to restrain the mortgagee from interfering with the performance of the contract after the mortgagee entered into possession to realise his security? Being a third party vis-à-vis the mortgagee, can common law or equity assist him? The authorities discussed below demonstrate that, if the mortgagee commits a wrong by unjustified or wrongful interference, in cases where either his security is not threatened or when he had actual knowledge of the charterparty, that wrong will be actionable either on the ground of the tort of knowing interference with a contract between two other parties, or in equity. At least, an injunction can be granted to prevent the mortgagee from further interference. In appropriate cases, damages may also be an additional remedy and, if the ship has been arrested, an order for its release will be granted.[158]

In the following paragraphs, some examples of leading authorities of the two categories of charterparties (subsequent to or preceding the mortgage) illustrate the complexities in this area. The principles of the tort of knowing interference with contractual rights are also explained.

10.2 A post-mortgage charterparty: the impairment factor

It has been seen that the mortgagor has a right to deal with the mortgaged property, until it becomes necessary for the mortgagee to make the ship available as security (para 10 of Sched 1 to the MSA 1995). Under the deed of covenants, the mortgagor is obliged to inform the mortgagee of the terms of the employment of the ship under a charterparty. The mortgagee can only interfere with the performance of such a charterparty if there is a serious impairment of his security. If there is no impairment of the security, then the mortgagee will wrongfully interfere with the contractual rights between the mortgagor and the charterer, inducing breach of contract. The charterer's remedy to restrain him from doing so by way of an injunction is both an equitable remedy and a remedy at common law, based on the tort of wrongful interference.[159] If he suffered loss, by reason of the tort, which was reasonably foreseeable, he would have a claim in damages against the mortgagee.[160] No such remedies will be available if the security is in fact impaired, as the mortgagee will be committing no wrong by interfering with the charter to enforce his legal rights.

---

158 *The Myrto* [1977] 2 Lloyd's Rep 243.

159 *Collins v Lamport* (1864) 4 De GJ&S 500 and *The Myrto* [1977] 2 Lloyd's Rep 243.

160 *Kuwait Airways Corp v Iraqi Airways Co (No 7)* [2001] 1 Lloyd's Rep 161, pp 248–53 (concerning the test for causation and remoteness of damages in cases of wrongful interference with goods).

Collins v Lamport [161]

After a registered mortgage had been granted on the ship, her owner, who was contemplating the sale of the vessel, chartered her to the prospective buyer's nominee. The mortgagee also contracted to sell the vessel to another buyer free from the charterparty. An application of an injunction to restrain the mortgagee from interfering with the charterparty was made to the court. The question was whether the MSAs gave the mortgagee the power to interfere, at will and at any time, with everything done by the mortgagor and to take possession of the ship, stripping her entirely of any contract or engagement. Lord Westbury stated:

> As long . . . as the dealings of the mortgagor with the ship are consistent with the sufficiency of the mortgagee's security, so long as those dealings do not materially prejudice and detract from or impair the sufficiency of the security comprised in the mortgage, so long as there is parliamentary authority given to the mortgagor to act in all respects as owner of the vessel, and if he has authority to act as owner he has, of necessity, authority to enter into all those contracts touching the disposition of the ship which may be necessary for him to get the full value and benefit of his property. But, whenever a mortgagee can shew that the act of the mortgagor prejudices or injures his security, he ceases to be bound by the Parliamentary declaration as to the ownership of the mortgagor, and can claim the full benefit of and exercise the rights given to him by his mortgage.[162]

An injunction was granted to restrain the mortgagees from interfering with the performance of the charterparty, as it was not shown that it would prejudicially affect the sufficiency of their security.

The Heather Bell [163]

The defendant was the former owner of the vessel and also the holder of a mortgage on the vessel, being a collateral security for purchase money owed to him, as mortgagee. The new owners of the vessel (mortgagors) entered into an agreement with the plaintiffs (charterers) to run her on specified daily excursion trips for about six weeks, dividing the profits between themselves after deduction of expenses. The mortgagor was to insure the vessel and the charterers were to have a charge and lien on the boat ranking, in the highest position that the owners were able to fix, for money advanced. When an instalment to the mortgagee fell due, the defendant (mortgagee) seized the vessel, alleging that the agreement between the charterers and the owners was not binding upon him, as it postponed his rights as mortgagee and depreciated the saleable value of the vessel. The charterers applied to the court seeking an injunction against the mortgagee. It was held that the agreement was binding upon the mortgagee as it was not prejudicial to the security created by the mortgage,[164] nor was there proof of fraud between the owner and the plaintiff. Lord

---

161 (1864) 4 De GJ&S 500.

162 Ibid, p 504.

163 [1901] P 272.

164 Contrast *The Law Guarantee & Trust Society v Russian Bank of Foreign Trade* [1905] 1 KB 815, in which the mortgagee's security was impaired by the fact that the ship, being uninsured, was at risk of being captured by the Japanese during the war between Russia and Japan; see also *The Manor* [1907] P 339, in which the ship was burdened with maritime liens which the insolvent owner had no means of discharging.

Alverstone did not believe that the agreement to run the boat at half profits was, under the circumstances, impinging upon the rights of the mortgagee. There could still be an honest expectation that there would be profits and the contract, therefore, could not be considered as materially impairing the security of the mortgagee. The mortgagee could restrain her from going to sea, if she was not fully insured against perils of the sea, but that alone would not justify him to set aside the charterparty.

Where a profitable charterparty has been entered into by the mortgagor, the mortgagee cannot object to the charterparty being carried out simply upon the ground that the effect of it would be to remove her out of the jurisdiction of the court and to render it difficult for him to enforce his security.[165]

The following decision of Brandon J set down a broad principle of the circumstances in which the mortgagee could exercise his rights without being bound by the charterparty, and it is worth looking at the various issues that arose, particularly as they provide a guide for risk management purposes.

The Myrto [166]

The vessel was bought and registered in Liberia. The bank had advanced money to the owners to buy the vessel and it was agreed that the debt was to be secured by a first mortgage on the vessel. The mortgage was executed and, then, the vessel was transferred to the Greek Registry, when it was provisionally registered in Greece. The bank lent further sums to the owners secured by a second mortgage executed under Liberian law, but registered in Greece. The owners then let their vessel on a voyage charterparty. Default of payments under both mortgages occurred and the mortgagees arrested the vessel and applied for her appraisement and sale. One of the grounds on which the owners applied for the release of the vessel was that the arrest was an unlawful interference with their rights to continue with the charterparty.

It was held that the owners had dealt with the vessel in such a manner as to impair the mortgagee's security for the following reasons: (i) the charterparty contract was speculative and improvident; (ii) the mortgagors were impecunious and there was every possibility that the expenses of completing the voyage would exceed the funds expected from the freight; (iii) the vessel had already been under arrest for three weeks at the suit of a creditor in respect of a substantial debt; and (iv) the mortgagors had numerous other accrued debts and liabilities, the most important being a large debt to the crew carrying a maritime lien having priority over the bank's mortgages. Brandon J summarised the general principles:

(1) the owner is entitled subject to one exception to deal with the ship as he would be entitled to do if the ship were not mortgaged, that includes employing her under contracts with third parties;

(2) the one exception is that the owner is not entitled to deal with the ship in such a way as to impair the security of the mortgagee. The question whether the contract is such as to impair the mortgagee's security is a question of fact;

---

165 *The Fanchon* (1880) 5 PD 173.
166 [1977] 2 Lloyd's Rep 243.

(3) when a contract with a third party is not such as to impair the security of the mortgagee and the owner is both able and willing to perform the contract, the mortgagee is not entitled to interfere with the performance of the contract;

(4) the mortgagee is, however, entitled to exercise his rights under the mortgage without regard to any such contract where:

   (i) The contract is of such a kind and/or the performance of that contract would result in the impairment of the mortgagee's security, or

   (ii) Where the owner is unwilling and/or unable to perform the contract. This is a question of fact;

(5) Where the mortgagee exercises his rights in circumstances other than these, he commits a tort or actionable wrong in the nature of interfering with the contractual rights of a third party. In such cases, the remedy available to the third party – depending on the mortgagee's actions – includes: (a) an injunction restraining the mortgagee from selling the ship; or (b) an order for the release of the ship if he has arrested it in an action *in rem*; (c) further or alternatively to (a) or (b), damages;

(6) it is open to a court as a matter of law to find as a fact that a particular contract is such as to impair the mortgagee's security, if evidence shows that the owner is impecunious and that he can only perform the voyage to which the contract relates, if at all, on credit and that the ship is already subject to pressing liabilities and charges.

10.3 A pre-mortgage charterparty: the knowledge factor

If there was a pre-mortgage charterparty, the mortgagee would, normally, take his security with knowledge of the charterparty. In practice, the distinction between actual and constructive knowledge may be academic because the mortgagee's lawyers ought to have inquired about any pre-existing charterparty and studied its terms. If they did not, they would be exposed to a potential claim in negligence. Assuming that the mortgagee was so advised, it would follow that he could not later turn round and say to the mortgagor or to the charterer: 'I do not like the terms of this charterparty now because it impairs my security,' unless the circumstances in relation to the performance of the charter have changed, or important side letters between the owner and the charterer varying the terms of the charter had not been disclosed to the mortgagee.[167]

Save as aforesaid, the charterer will have an equitable remedy based on the principle of *De Mattos v Gibson* to obtain an injunction against the mortgagee, if the latter, having full knowledge of the charter's terms, attempts to terminate the charter.[168] The injunction would be an appropriate remedy in equity, if the mortgagee took the mortgage with full knowledge of the charterparty.[169] Evidence of actual

---

167 *The Odenfeld* [1978] 2 Lloyd's Rep 357.

168 The mortgagor may also be able to rely on an equitable estoppel by way of a defence if the mortgagee, having taken the mortgage with knowledge of the charterparty, interferes with the performance of the contract by arresting the ship.

169 See, also, Clarke '*De Mattos v Gibson* again' [1992] LMCLQ 448.

knowledge of the terms of the charter would be sufficient ground for the injunction to be granted. It seems that the risk is placed on the mortgagee, when he enters into the loan transaction with knowledge of the circumstances, unless cumulative factors of the mortgagor's inability to perform would justify an order for sale of the ship by the court, as was decided in *The Myrto*.

De Mattos v Gibson[170]

The plaintiff had chartered a ship from its owner, Curry, who subsequently charged the ship to Gibson. Gibson had actual notice of the charterparty and its terms. Curry got into financial difficulties and was unable to continue the voyage. Gibson sought to enforce his security by taking possession of the ship and diverted her to another port to sell her. The plaintiff (charterer) claimed an injunction against Gibson restraining him from interfering with the charterparty. The judge refused to grant it. Lords Justice Knight Bruce and Turner granted an interim injunction on appeal, but on full hearing, Lord Chelmsford LC affirmed the judge's decision that the injunction ought to be refused, only because the owner was unable to perform the charter.

After considering the issue of specific performance against the owner of the ship, the Court of Appeal turned to the main issue whether the mortgagee was justified to do what he did. It was held that the mortgagee had not, in any way, interfered with the performance of the charterparty, until it was evident that Curry was wholly unable to perform it. It was clear that, if the vessel had remained in the possession of the owner (Curry), no repairs would have been effected and without them, the vessel could not put to sea. The actual performance of the contract, as between the plaintiff and Curry, was virtually at an end when Gibson took possession of the vessel and repaired her, Curry being utterly unable to perform the contract.

The well-known and much-quoted statement of Lord Justice Knight Bruce is said to have established a general principle of law applicable even outside the context of ship mortgages:

> Reason and justice seem to prescribe that, at least as a general rule, where a man, by gift or purchase, acquires property from another with knowledge of a previous contract, lawfully and for valuable consideration made by him with a third person, to use and employ the property for a particular purpose in a specified manner, the acquirer shall not, to the material damage of the person, in opposition to the contract and inconsistently with it, use and employ property in a manner not allowable to the giver or seller. This rule, applicable in general, as I conceive, to moveable and immoveable property, and adopted, as I apprehend, by English law, may, like other general rules, be liable to exceptions arising from special circumstances . . .[171]

The remedy of an injunction, suggested in *De Mattos v Gibson*, is equitable and is generally applied in cases where the charterparty precedes the mortgage. In such cases, if the security was impaired, the mortgagee's interference to protect his rights would not be a wrong at common law, that is why the charterer would not have a

---

170 (1858) 4 De G&J 276.
171 Ibid, p 282.

legal basis to sue the mortgagee in tort for an injunction or damages. But he would have a remedy in equity and actual knowledge of the charter party by the mortgagee is important for the court to grant the remedy of an injunction. Thus, for the mortgagee to be bound by the charterparty and, consequently, to be unable to interfere with it, he must have notice of it and its terms, the effect of which should be that the mortgagee had the opportunity to foresee whether or not his rights under the mortgage would be likely to be impaired.

10.4 Exception to the *De Mattos* principle

The outcome of the decision in *De Mattos v Gibson* was that, although the mortgagee had actual knowledge of the contractual obligation imposed under the charterparty, he was not prevented from dealing with the ship otherwise than in accordance with the charterparty, because there was evidence that the mortgagor was not himself in a position to perform his contractual obligation under the charterparty. Thus, the exception to the principle of *De Mattos v Gibson* is that, when there is an accumulation of factors pointing towards inability of performance of the charterparty by the mortgagor, the mortgagee can exercise his statutory rights under his security.[172] In theory, the charterer should look upon his contracting party for enforcement of his rights and remedies. However, demand for performance will be of no practical use, if the mortgagor is unable to do so. Under those circumstances, the charterer could not, by an injunction, prevent the mortgagee from exercising his rights just because the charterparty would be interfered with. The charter would have been at an end, in any event, because of the inability of the mortgagor to perform, regardless of the mortgagee's action. If the mortgagee satisfies his security from the sale proceeds of the ship, when there is one ship company, the charterer will be left without any material recourse against a bankrupt owner. That is a risk to be borne by the charterer.

The Celtic King[173]

This involved a sale of the mortgaged ship being subject to a charterparty. While the steamer was being built, the shipowner entered into an agreement with the defendants (charterers) by which he undertook to fit her for a particular trade and run her for five years, as one of the defendants' line. After completion of building and registration of the vessel, the shipowner mortgaged the vessel to the first mortgagees, who had no notice of the agreement with the defendants. A second mortgage was subsequently granted to the plaintiff, who had notice of the agreement between the shipowner and the defendants. After the charterparty had been running upwards of two years in the defendants' line, and was temporarily laid up, her owner died having made default in payment of instalments under the first mortgage. The first mortgagees took possession of the vessel and sold her to the plaintiff

---

172 In such a situation, Brandon J was right to conflate the principles as derived from both *Collins v Lamport* (1864) 4 De GJ&S 500 and *De Mattos v Gibson* (1858) 4 De G&J 276 in *The Myrto* [1977] 2 Lloyd's Rep 243.

173 [1894] P 175.

(second mortgagee) who, at the time of purchase, had notice of the contents of the agreement between the owner and the defendants. The plaintiff (second mortgagee, who by this time was the owner of the ship) entered into a contract of sale of the ship with a third party and demanded the certificate of registration, which was in the hands of the defendants (the charterers). The defendants denied the plaintiff's right to the certificate, except on condition that the plaintiff was restrained from dealing with the ship in derogation of the existing charter party, and applied for an injunction.

Barnes J held that the certificate was a separate issue from the possible right of the charterer for an injunction to restrain the plaintiff from dealing with the ship without being bound with the charterparty. It was ordered that the certificate should be handed over to those entitled to it, that is, the plaintiff.

In considering the application for an injunction against the plaintiff (second mortgagee), it was held that the first mortgagees, having no notice of the prior agreement, were not bound by its terms at the time of their mortgage. That meant that they could sell the ship, free of it, if they chose to enforce their security. On the issue of whether the mortgagee could pass his title free from the charterparty to a purchaser who had notice of it, Barnes J stated:

> . . . decisions in equity cases have been cited to me which shew that a purchaser with notice is entitled to rely upon the title of his vendor without notice, because otherwise that vendor would be restricted in his powers of sale.[174]

The main concern of the judge, on the facts of this case, was that the charterparty contract was not an ordinary one. It was such that it would have depreciatory effect on the mortgagee's security, because it was a contract binding the ship for a very long period with various clauses making it difficult for anybody to purchase a ship tied to these terms. Although, it was argued that, since this particular buyer was aware of the terms of the contract and was buying the ship burdened with it, what was significant, the judge thought, was that the vendor, first mortgagee, was not aware of it and he ought to be able to sell the ship free from an onerous contract. Otherwise, he would be unable to sell to the plaintiff, if he was the best purchaser available, and this definitely constituted a fetter in the vendor's right to realise his security. Bearing in mind that the original owner had by then died, it was not certain whether his estate would, in any event, be prepared to continue with this contract and the best remedy for the charterer would be to seek damages from the estate of the deceased.

On those facts, this case was quite unusual. It involved one mortgagee who had no knowledge of the pre-dated charterparty and a subsequent mortgagee with knowledge of it and of its terms (the *De Mattos v Gibson* point). The judge based his decision on the fact that the first mortgagee had no knowledge of the charterparty, thus, he was entitled to deal with the ship free from the contract.

---

174 [1894] P 175, pp 188–89.

10.5 Sale of the ship under charter and the issue of knowledge

The issue of knowledge also arose in the context of the sale of a ship which is subject to a charter party. In the following leading decisions, the question was whether an injunction could be granted against a new purchaser of a ship upon the application of the charterer. They are important in this context of mortgages because the courts clarified whether or not the buyer of the ship should have actual or just constructive knowledge for an injunction to be granted. Unlike in the case of a mortgagee, a purchaser of a ship does not have statutory rights against the ship but only contractual rights.

Lord Strathcona Steamship Co Ltd v Dominion Coal Co Ltd[175]

The owners of a steamship entered into a charterparty with Dominion for 10 consecutive St Lawrence seasons, with an option for continuing for a further period of at least five more seasons. Later, the ship was transferred to various successive owners; all had notice of the terms of the charterparty agreement and undertook to accept all responsibilities there under. The appellants, Lord Strathcona, who were the new owners of the vessel, refused to perform the charterparty. Following the case of De Mattos v Gibson, it was held that an injunction could be granted in such circumstances to compel one who obtains a conveyance, or grants sub-conditions, from violating the condition of his purchase to the prejudice of the original contractor. The Privy Council further stated that the purchaser of a ship who has notice of the terms of a charterparty, entered into for its employment, is in the position of a constructive trustee, and he can be restrained, at the suit of the charterers from employing the ship in a way inconsistent with the charterparty. In order to get the injunction, the plaintiff ought to have a continuing interest in the property, but that, also, a bare contractual right, as opposed to a property interest, was a sufficient interest for this purpose.

Port Line Ltd v Ben Line Steamers Ltd[176]

In this case, Diplock J, sitting then as a judge, thought that The Lord Strathcona was wrongly decided on the point of constructive trusteeship.

In this case, the dispute was between Port Line (the plaintiffs and charterers) and Ben Line (the defendants, new owners), over a sum paid by the British Government to Ben Line when the vessel, which was subject to a time charter to Port Line, was requisitioned during the Suez crisis in 1956. Ben Line, who had purchased the vessel from Silver Line while she was on time charter to Port Line, were aware of the time charter although they had not seen it. Port Line had consented to the sale of the ship to the defendants, provided the previous owners, Silver Line, maintained all control of the vessel by the grant of an immediate demise charter to Silver Line from the defendants. This demise charter contained a clause providing that, if the Government requisitioned the vessel, this charter (the time charter) would expire.

---

175 [1926] AC 108 (PC); Lorenzen v White Shipping Co Ltd (1943) 74 LlL Rep 161 followed it.
176 [1958] 2 QB 146, [1958] 1 Lloyd's Rep 290.

When the vessel was requisitioned, she was put at the Crown's disposition, and an agreement was entered into between Ben Line (the new owner) and the Ministry of Transport providing for rates of hire, as compensation during the period of requisition. Port Line claimed they were entitled to recover the compensation, or part of it, received by Ben Line for the requisition on the ground that there was a subsisting contract between them and Silver Line and, under the Compensation Act 1939, such compensation should be paid to the person entitled to possession or use of the ship. Therefore, Ben Line, to whom the compensation was paid, was deemed to act as a trustee for Port Line under this Act and the principle laid down in *The Lord Strathcona*. Ben Line denied that Port Line were entitled to any compensation, and contended that the requisition operated as a cancellation of the time charter between Port Line and Silver Line. They also argued that *The Lord Strathcona* had been wrongly decided, or if not, it applied only when the subsequent purchaser had express notice of the terms of the subsisting charter.

Deciding against compensation, the judge did not follow *The Lord Strathcona* on the constructive trusteeship point. The ground for his decision in refusing the remedy was that actual, as opposed to constructive, notice of the terms, and not just of the existence of the charter by Ben Line, was necessary in such a case.

In the following decision, **Swiss Bank v Lloyds Bank**,[177] Browne-Wilkinson J, at first instance,[178] having examined previous authorities, summarised the principles regarding the existence of the court's jurisdiction to grant an injunction on the basis of the tort of interference with a pre-existing contract, as follows:

(1) The principle stated by Knight Bruce LJ in *De Mattos v Gibson*, is good law and represents the counterpart in equity of the tort of knowing interference with contractual rights.

(2) A person proposing to deal with property in such a way as to cause a breach of a contract affecting that property will be restrained by injunction from so doing, if when he acquired that property he had actual knowledge of that contract.

(3) A plaintiff is entitled to such an injunction, even if he has no proprietary interest in the property: his right to have his contract performed is a sufficient interest.

(4) There is no case in which such an injunction has been granted against a defendant who acquired the property with only constructive, as opposed to actual, notice of the contract. In my judgment, constructive notice is not sufficient, since actual knowledge of the contract is a requisite element in the tort.[179]

When the case was decided, it had already been recognised at common law that it was a legal wrong or tort for someone to interfere with the contractual rights of

---

177 [1982] AC 584 (HL); the appeal to the House of Lords was concerned with competing claims to a fund of approximately £800,000 held on deposit by Lloyds Bank (Lloyds). It represented proceeds of sale of securities issued by a company incorporated in Israel, FIBI Holdings Ltd, to the respondent, Israel Financial Trust (IFT). There were three issues in the appeal: (1) whether the appellants, Swiss Bank, had a charge over or a proprietary interest in the FIBI securities and, if so, what was the nature of that charge or interest; (2) whether a charge created by IFT over the FIBI securities in favour of Lloyds was valid; and (3) (depending on the answers to (1) and (2)) whether the interest of the Swiss Bank had priority over the charge to Lloyds.

178 [1979] 3 WLR 201.

179 Ibid, p 226.

others.[180] It was subsequently established, the judge said, that equity would intervene to restrain such a tort, and such jurisdiction has frequently been exercised in recent times.[181] It follows that, if at the date of the Lloyds charge, Lloyds had had actual notice of the plaintiff's (Swiss Bank) rights in relation to the FIBI securities, the plaintiff could, in my judgment, have obtained an injunction restraining Lloyds from taking the charge since, by so doing, they would have been committing the tort.[182]

On the facts, however, the judge did not find that Lloyds had actual knowledge, which is an essential ingredient of the tort and, therefore, committed no legal wrong. It is to be noted that the judge regarded the principle of *De Mattos* as the counterpart in equity of the tort of knowing interference with contractual rights at common law.

10.6 The tort of wrongful interference with a contract

This tort is about inducing breach of a contract existing between two parties. For the tort to be committed, not only must there be inducement, absence of justification and substantial damages suffered, but also knowledge of an existing contract.[183]

When a mortgagee, or a purchaser, takes over a ship, with actual knowledge of the terms of the contract between the mortgagor and the charterer, he may find that he has committed the tort, if he wrongfully and unjustifiably interferes with its performance. In practice, no wise mortgagee or purchaser would fund, by loan or purchase, a ship without investigating its precise history and its owners' contractual relationships with third parties. Thus, an issue of impairment of the mortgagee's security would rarely arise. In both equity and common law, an injunction against the mortgagee or purchaser would be a just and practical result for the protection of the charterer, who could not have recourse against his contracting party if that party was not in breach of the charterparty.

In a decision of the House of Lords, **Merkur Island Shipping Corp v Laughton**,[184] albeit in a different shipping context, ITF officials boycotted the performance of a towage contract by persuading the servants of the tugowner, who was performing towage services to assist the ship out of the dock, to stop working in protest at low wages to the ship's crew. The shipowners applied for an injunction on the basis of the common law tort of wrongful interference with the performance of a contract. The contract interfered with was the charterparty and, in turn, the series of charters in the chain. The form of interference was the immobilisation of the ship in port (Liverpool). The judge granted the injunction requiring ITF to lift the blacking of the ship. His decision was approved by both the Court of Appeal and the House of

---

180 *Lunley v Gye* (1853) 2 E&B 216.
181 *Sefton v Tophams Ltd* [1965] Ch 140.
182 *Swiss Bank v Lloyds Bank* [1979] 3 WLR 201, p 223, per Browne-Wilkinson J.
183 *Halsbury's Laws*, 1999, Vol 45(2), para 691.
184 [1983] 2 All ER 189 (HL).

Lords. Lord Diplock, in his decision, summarised the development and extension of this tort and approved the statement of principle, as had been enunciated by Lord Denning MR, previously, at the Court of Appeal in 1969, in *Torquay Hotel Ltd v Cousins*:[185]

> ... there must be interference in the execution of a contract. The interference is not confined to the procurement of a breach of contract. It extends to a case where a third person *prevents or hinders* one party from performing his contract, even though it be not a breach. (Lord Denning's emphasis)

This statement of principle, Lord Diplock said, resolved pre-existing doubts, if any, in this matter.

A different but related question arose in a decision of the Court of Appeal, *Edwin Hill and Partners v First National Finance Corp plc*,[186] which is of importance in this context. It concerned a legal charge on a freehold property as security for the indebtedness of a developer to the bank. The developer was unable to repay the loan or raise further finance to complete the development, for which the plaintiffs had been appointed as architects. The bank agreed to provide the necessary finance, on condition that the plaintiffs were replaced by other architects. So, the developer dismissed the plaintiffs, who sued the bank claiming damages against it for procuring breach of contract. Both the judge and the Court of Appeal decided against the plaintiffs on the ground that the bank's interference with the plaintiffs' contract was justified as being in defence and protection of an equal or superior right of the bank, under the legal charge to be repaid. This case should be distinguished from a case of a ship mortgagee who is in a position to investigate the terms of a pre-existing charterparty before he lends money.

In a more recent case, *The Tropical Reefer*,[187] mentioned under para 9.4.3 above) the mortgagee arrested the ship with perishable cargo on board. An action was brought by the cargo interests against the bank for damages on the ground of wrongful interference with the performance of the bill of lading contract. It was held that if Panamanian law applied to the mortgage, a bill of lading holder whose cargo was damaged or lost on account of a valid arrest of the ship had a right to sue the arresting party, if the arrest was carried out in bad faith. Bad faith had not been alleged here and there was no evidence that the bank intended to harm the claimant. If the applicable law was English, the court applied the principles derived from previous cases and held—distinguishing Edwin Hill (above)—that: a mortgagee was not to be regarded as enjoying a right equal or superior to that of a bill of lading holder so as to interfere with the bill of lading contract, provided his security was not impaired. On the facts of this case, there was a long history of default and there was no realistic sign of immediate payment to the bank or restoration of the P&I cover. The bank's security would have been impaired if the vessel had been allowed to sail without P&I club cover to the discharge port, Hamburg. The court further

---

185 [1969] 2 Ch 106, p 138.
186 [1989] 1 WLR 225.
187 *Anton Durbeck GMBH v Den Norske Bank ASA* (*The Tropical Reefer No 2*) [2006] 1 Lloyd's Rep 93 (see summary of fact) in the action by the Bank against the owner under 9.4.3 above.

distinguished mortgages of ships from mortgages of land following *Brown v Tanner*.[188]

10.7 Conclusion

In conclusion, in cases of a charter party being subsequent to the mortgage, if the mortgagee exercises his statutory right to enforce his security when it is impaired, he will be committing no wrong. If the third party charterer suffers loss in consequence thereof, his cause of action should be against his contracting party, whose conduct with regard to the mortgaged ship gave cause to the mortgagee to take possession and control of the ship. Thus, the charterer should claim damages against his contracting party, the ship owner, for breach of contract. Specific performance would not be possible in the circumstances when the mortgagee has taken possession. On the other hand, if the mortgagee enters into possession unjustifiably, the charterer could either restrain him by seeking an injunction from the court, and/or claim damages for his loss on the basis of the tort of wrongful interference with his contract.

In a case in which the mortgagee took the mortgage with full knowledge of the terms of the charter, an injunction to protect the charterer, third party, will be available in equity to prevent interference by the mortgagee because he should have full knowledge of the facts of the ship's employment when he entered into the mortgage, unless the circumstances of that employment changed. The equitable right of the third party, charterer, for a remedy by an injunction is equivalent to the right in tort in cases of wrongful interference with contractual rights when there is prior actual knowledge of a contract between two parties.

11 RISK MANAGEMENT AND INSURANCE ISSUES OF THE MORTGAGEE

There is an infinite variety of risks that attach to the mortgagee's interest in the ship, which has been financed. The risks are inherent to the mobility of the mortgaged property and, hence, its exposure, not only to perils that it may encounter on the sea, but also to being exposed to the law and jurisdiction of other nations, which may apply a wide range of maritime liens, or submit the ship to political or war risks, or cause the detention of the ship for any reason. The mortgagee, therefore, will be concerned to balance such possible risks by taking into account the charterparty commitments of the vessel, the reputation of the owners and managers and their respective compliance with the ISM Code and other international regulations, the value and condition of the ship, the experience and nationality of the crew and their relations with the owners.

In order to manage or minimise such risks, the mortgagee will seek a

---

188 (1868) 3 Ch App 597 (a shipowner can bind the mortgagee by a charter party being to that extent in a different position from the mortgagor of real property who cannot bind his mortgagee by a lease).

combination of contractual, insurance and security mechanisms. He will arrange to obtain as much protection as possible contractually in the deed of covenants (discussed at para 8.1, above).

He will obtain sufficient insurance both as a co-assured with the owner by way of assignment and separately by taking a mortgagee's interest insurance (MII), which is designed to protect the mortgagee from the mortgagor's breaches under the insurance contract of which the mortgagee is an assignee or loss payee. But, the MII has its limitations based on its wording and exclusions from liability. The Institute Mortgagee's Interest Clauses 1997 enumerate the perils insured which relate to conduct of the mortgagor for which the underwriters of the H&M or the P&I policies would decline to pay. Indemnity under the MII would not be recoverable, however, if the mortgagee were privy to that conduct of the mortgagor. Similarly, the MII would not cover the event of termination of the hull or P&I insurance for non-payment of premium. A mortgagee's additional perils (MAP) policy can be obtained to cover exposure of mortgagees to pollution risks, particularly in jurisdictions such as the USA, where the tort law enables third parties to acquire a priority lien over a vessel for liabilities incurred from oil pollution exceeding the convention limits. Pre-existing liens on the ship can also be covered by insurance.

CHAPTER 10

SHIPBUILDING CONTRACTS[1]

1 INTRODUCTION

In recent years, the shipbuilding market has shown a major shift towards the East, particularly Japan, Korea and China (the last two having attracted a large shipbuilding capacity since the mid–1990s). This movement has prompted the European Commission to issue a proposal for a Council Decision on the signing and conclusion of an International Agreement between the European Community and the Republic of Korea relating to assistance of the world shipbuilding market (Com/2000/263, 3 May 2000 and Com/2000/0130, 26 May 2000). With the ban on single-hull tankers (see Chapter 20), there has been a boom in orders for building new double-hull tankers in the last six years. Furthermore, since the first edition of this book, there have been initiatives to improve the quality of new ships. The IMO has recently developed standards for shipbuilding called 'the goal based standards' and, in addition, there has been a tripartite dialogue between ship owners, shipbuilders and classification societies, through IACS, to discuss their mutual interest in ensuring that ships are fit for purpose. The discussions relate to shipbuilding standards, contractual relationships and yard capacity.

Shipbuilding contracts are, usually, made in the English language and provide for English law and jurisdiction. The contracts are on standard terms led by the shipyards. Recognising that such contracts are not serving the interests of both parties equally, there has been a new initiative by BIMCO which has produced a draft of a standard wording of shipbuilding contracts to be used across the industry and help in facilitating the business process. The objectives of this proposed contract is to provide clarity in the terms and balance between the respective liabilities of the parties, so that the parties can easily identify their rights and obligations and reduce the risk of disputes on matters of interpretation of contractual terms. This is a welcomed initiative but, at the time of writing this edition, the proposed draft contract was being circulated for consultation purposes and, therefore, it is not considered appropriate to comment on its terms in this edition.

Thus, in this chapter, the basic principles of English law pertaining to standard terms of existing shipbuilding contracts are explained, with examples of leading cases including recent developments.

---

1   There are three authoritative books in this area: Clarke, M, *Shipbuilding Contracts*, 2nd edn, 1992, LLP; Curtis, S, *The Law of Shipbuilding Contracts*, 3rd edn, 2002, LLP; Goldrein, I (ed), *Ship Sale and Purchase*, 4th edn, 2003, LLP.

2 NATURE OF SHIPBUILDING CONTRACTS

The contract involves both the construction and the sale of the ship. The question that has frequently arisen in some cases is whether the contract can be categorised as a building contract, or one of sale of goods. The answer to this question is of importance to the extent that, if the contract is one of sale, only the ordinary rules relating to the sale of goods will apply. If it is classified as a building contract, the rules relating to construction and the supply of work and materials will apply, which in many respects are similar to those applying to sale of goods contracts, but they place emphasis on the means of production.

Historically, in older cases, English law treated the shipbuilding contract as one for the sale of goods. For example, in *Lee v Griffin*[2] it was held that:

> ... if the contract be such that, when carried out, it would result in the sale of a chattel, the party cannot sue for work and labour; but if the result of the contract is that the party has done work and labour which ends in nothing that can become the subject of a sale, the party cannot sue for goods sold and delivered.

Diplock J, in *McDougall v Aeromarine*,[3] followed the same view and said:

> ... it seems well settled by authority that, although a shipbuilding contract is, in form, a contract for the construction of the vessel, it is in law a contract for the sale of goods.

Naturally, the intention of the parties to the contract was and is always relevant and the result may vary from contract to contract. In **Sir James Laing & Sons v Barclay, Curle & Co Ltd**,[4] the issue was whether the property in a ship under construction, for which payment was by instalments, passed to the buyer bit by bit, at each period of construction and as soon as the work had been inspected by the buyer. The House of Lords considered this question:

> Where it appears to be the intention of the parties to a contract for the building of a ship that the vessel is not to be delivered and finally accepted until after an official trial of a foreign coast, and until after conditions of the contract have been fulfilled as to speed, consumption of coal, capacity, etc, the property in the ship does not pass to the purchaser while the vessel remains uncompleted, although the contract contains stipulations for the price to be paid by instalments at certain periods of construction.

The respondents, a Glasgow firm of shipbuilders, agreed to build two ships for an Italian firm, according to certain specifications and under the superintendence of an agent appointed by the Italian firm, for a certain amount payable by instalments at specified stages of construction; but delivery of the ships was not to be considered to be completed until they had passed trials at Greenock and off the Italian coast. Before the ships were fully constructed, but after several instalments had been paid,

---

2   (1861) B&S 272.
3   [1958] 2 Lloyd's Rep 345, p 355: concerning the issue whether the buyer could reject the ship when she was tendered for delivery on the ground of unmerchantable quality. The question whether the ship had become the property of the buyer after payment of an instalment was relevant to the issue of rejection. Since the buyer had not yet become the owner of the ship, his rejection right was not affected.
4   [1908] AC 35.

the appellants, an English firm of shipbuilders, arrested the ships in Scotland for a debt alleged to be due to them by the Italian company, but on a petition to the First Division of the Court of Session the arrestments were recalled.

> Affirming the decision of the First Division, it was held that no intention was shown in the contract to make delivery of or to pass the property in the ships, before they were completed and that the arrestments were properly recalled.

Whether the contract is one for sale of goods, or a contact for construction and sale, the crucial issue concerns the determination of the parties' accrued rights. This involves three separate questions: (a) does the buyer have a property right to the partly constructed hull? (this is relevant when a third party, that is, a claimant of the buyer, or a receiver appointed to arrange the affairs of the shipbuilder, arrest the semi-constructed ship); (b) could a buyer claim a property right on the material, which had been approved by him but had not yet been made part of the hull?; and (c) what is to happen to accrued rights of the parties upon cancellation of the contract?

The answer to these questions can be found in the following authorities. The first (concerning buyer's property right to the partly constructed hull) was dealt with by the House of Lords (Sc) in *Seath v Moore*,[5] in which, although Scottish law applied to the contract of a shipbuilding in Scotland, Lord Blackburn illuminated the issue involved by comparing English with Scottish law, thus:

> The law of England does differ from the civil law and those laws founded on it, including the Scotch law, as to what is sufficient to pass the property in a moveable chattel. A contract for a valuable consideration, by which it is agreed that the property in a specific ascertained article shall pass from one to another, is effectual according to the law of England to change the property. It may be that the party who has sold the article is entitled to retain possession till the price is paid, if that was by the contract to precede delivery, but still the property is changed.

> It is essential that the article should be specific and ascertained in a manner binding on both parties, for unless that be so it cannot be construed as a contract to pass the property in that article. And in general, if there are things remaining to be done by the seller to the article before it is in the state in which it is to be finally delivered to the purchaser, the contract will not be construed to be one to pass the property till those things are done.

> But it is competent to parties to agree for valuable consideration that a specific article shall be sold, and become the property of the purchaser as soon as it has attained a certain stage: though if it is part of the bargain that more work shall be done on the article after it has reached that stage, it affords a strong prima facie presumption against its being the intention of the parties that the property should then pass . . . It is, I think, a question of the construction of the contract in each case, at what stage the property shall pass; and a question of fact, in each case whether that stage has been reached.

> As I understand the civil law, the property is not transferred without delivery, and, consequently, unless there was an actual, or perhaps a constructive delivery, the property remained the property of the seller, and his creditors might seize it.

---

5   (1886) 11 App Cas 350 (HL), p 370; see, also, *Re Foster v Blyth Shipbuilding and Drydocks* [1926] Ch 494 (see para 10.1.1, below).

Lord Watson added:[6]

> The English decisions to which I have referred appear to me to establish the principle that, where it appears to be the intention, or in other words the agreement, of the parties to a contract for building a ship, that at a particular stage of its construction, the vessel, so far as then finished, shall be appropriated to the contract of sale, the property of the vessel as soon as it has reached that stage of completion will pass to the purchaser, and subsequent additions made to the chattel thus vested in the purchaser will, *accessione*, become his property. It also appears to me to be the result of these decisions that such an intention or agreement ought (in the absence of any circumstances pointing to a different conclusion) to be inferred from a provision in the contract to the effect that an instalment of the price shall be paid at a particular stage, coupled with the fact that the instalment has been duly paid, and that until the vessel reached that stage the execution of the work was regularly inspected by the purchaser, or some one on his behalf.

Although this case was decided prior to the Sale of Goods Act (SOGA) 1893, it was made sufficiently clear that, under English law, it is the intention of the parties to the contract of sale of ascertained goods that determines, upon construction of the contract, when the property passes to the purchaser. The parties can agree in their contract whether property can pass as soon as it has attained a certain stage. In a shipbuilding contract, the agreement may provide whether property in the ship being under construction can pass before completion.

Whether property in the materials can pass to the buyer before completion (referring to the second question raised above), clear and unambiguous words must be used specifically stating the stages and requirements of appropriation.[7]

For example, a clause in a shipbuilding contract purporting to pass the property in the material to the purchaser as the construction of the vessel proceeded was construed by the House of Lords in *Reid v Macbeth & Gray*[8] against the purchaser, as the parties had failed to express a clear intention to that effect. Since the material had not been affixed to the ship at the time of the bankruptcy of the builder, it could not be regarded as appropriated to the contract.

In *Re Blyth Shipbuilding and Drydocking Co*,[9] Romer J held, on the facts of this case, that although a receiver and manager of the shipbuilder's estate had no right to retain the partly constructed hull, the property of which had passed to the purchaser, he could retain both the unworked and worked material intended for the vessel. The latter portion of that decision was appealed. The Court of Appeal approved the judge's decision and affirmed that certain worked material lying on the yard ready to be incorporated into the hull of the vessel and approved by the purchaser's surveyor, had not been 'appropriated for her' so as to become the property of the purchaser. Thus, in relation to the issue of appropriation of property, although the ship had not been completed, the

---

6   (1886) 11 App Cas 350, p 380.
7   Such a clause can be found in *Workman, Clarke & Co Ltd v Lloyd Brazileno* [1908] 1 KB 968, in which it had been agreed that the property in the material was to pass to the purchaser from payment of the first instalment.
8   [1904] AC 223 (HL).
9   [1926] Ch 494.

property in the uncompleted ship excluding the non-affixed material was the property of the purchaser.

The modern view of the nature of a shipbuilding contract is that it has a hybrid nature. The answer to the third question (that is, what is to happen to the parties' accrued rights upon cancellation of the contract) arose in the *Hyundai* cases.[10] The House of Lords declined to apply a rule that there were no accrued rights to be enforced after termination of the contract. There would be no accrued rights if the contract were solely one of sale.[11] The buyer in *Hyundai v Papadopoulos*[12] defaulted in the second instalment, and the builder exercised his right under the contract to terminate it. The issue was whether the second instalment was payable by the guarantor. It was held by all courts that it was. Viscount Dilhorne commented that:

> ... in this case the contract was not just for the sale of goods ... It was a contract to 'build, launch, equip and complete' a vessel and 'to deliver and sell' her. The contract price included 'all costs and expenses for designing and supplying all necessary drawings for the vessel ...'. It was a contract which was not simply one of sale but which, so far as the construction of the vessel was concerned, the contract resembled a building contract.[13]

Particular rights of the parties to the contract will be determined, depending on the circumstances of a case, and the issue in question will be addressed by applying either sale or construction principles as may be appropriate, upon proper construction of a particular agreement. A large part of a shipbuilding contract is directed towards the regulation of a substantial and complex construction project in which each party assumes long term obligations to the other and bears significant commercial risks. Although the ultimate purpose of the contract is to transfer the legal title in the ship upon payment of the price, to categorise the contract as belonging to the one or the other category would be misleading.[14]

In a more recent decision, *Stocznia Gdanska SA v Latvian Shipping Co*,[15] Clarke J said that the shipbuilding contract in question was for the construction and sale of the hull. In the same case, the House of Lords, affirming the decision of the judge and reversing the Court of Appeal's decision, answered the question, whether or not an accrued instalment was payable to the yard after termination of the contract, as follows:

> The present case cannot, therefore, be approached by asking the simple question whether the property in the vessel or any part of it has passed to the buyers. That test would be apposite if the contract in question was a contract for the sale of goods (or, indeed, a contract for the sale of land) *simpliciter*, under which the consideration for the price would be the passing of the property in the goods (or land). However,

---

10 *Hyundai Shipbuilding Heavy Industries Co Ltd v Pournaras* [1978] 2 Lloyd's Rep 502 (HL) and *Hyundai v Papadopoulos* [1980] 2 Lloyd's Rep 1 (HL).

11 Benjamin's *Sale of Goods*, 5th edn, 2000, Sweet & Maxwell: '... in ordinary circumstances, unless the contract otherwise provides, the seller on rescission following the buyer's default, becomes liable to repay the part of the price paid.'

12 See para 10.1.6 for the facts of this case.

13 *Hyundai Heavy Industries Co Ltd v Papadopoulos* [1980] 2 Lloyd's Rep 1, p 5, per Viscount Dilhorne (HL).

14 See, also, op cit, Curtis, fn 1, p 1.

15 [1995] 2 Lloyd's Rep 592; [1996] 2 Lloyd's Rep 132 (CA); [1998] 1 Lloyd's Rep 609 (HL).

before that test can be regarded as appropriate, the anterior question has to be asked: is the contract in question simply a contract for the sale of a ship or is it rather a contract under which the design and construction of the vessel formed part of the yard's contractual duties, as well as the duty to transfer the finished object to the buyers? If it is the latter, the design and construction of the vessel form part of the consideration for which the price is to be paid, and the fact that the contract has been brought to an end before the property in the vessel or any part of it has passed to the buyers does not prevent the yard from asserting that there has been no total failure of consideration in respect of an instalment of the price which has been paid before the contract was terminated, or that an instalment which has then been accrued due could not, if paid, be recoverable on that ground.

I am satisfied that the present case falls into the latter category. This was what the contracts provided in their terms. Moreover, consistently with those terms, payment of instalments of the price was geared to progress in the construction of the vessel. That this should be so is scarcely surprising in the case of a shipbuilding contract, under which the yard enters into major financial commitments at an early stage, in the placing of orders for machinery and materials, and in reserving and then occupying a berth for the construction of the vessel.[16]

Thus, by these two House of Lords' decisions (*Hyundai v Papadopoulos* and *Stocznia*), the issue of the nature of the shipbuilding contract has now been settled as being a hybrid contract of construction and sale of a ship.

The preamble to the standard form of the Shipbuilders' Association of Japan (SAJ) form states that the builder shall 'build, launch, equip and complete' the vessel and, thereafter, 'sell and deliver' her to the buyer. It is a special agreement to sell a ship by description after construction, which is regulated by the specific terms of the contract and the SOGA 1979, as amended by the Sale and Supply of Goods Act (SSGA) 1994.[17] Under the SOGA 1979, contracts for sale are divided into 'sales' outright, in which property in the goods passes to the buyer from the time of the conclusion of the contract (s 2(3)), and 'agreements to sell' (which usually concern future goods). Under an agreement to sell, the property passes to the buyer at a future time or when a condition has been fulfilled (s 2(4)). It is undisputed that shipbuilding contracts relate to the sale of future, rather than existing, goods.[18]

3 PRE-CONTRACT STAGE

This stage is particularly important to both parties and it can be time consuming and expensive. The nature of shipbuilding contracts is such that it entails the need of negotiations in great detail between the buyer and the builder before an agreement can be reached about the form, the substance of the contract and the ship's specification. A very important factor for the buyer in his choice of a builder would be previous business dealings with the shipbuilding yard. Expertise in commercial,

---

16 [1998] 1 Lloyd's Rep 609, pp 619, 620, per Lord Goff.

17 The Sale of Goods (Amendment) Act 1995 concerns only the amendments to the law relating to the sale of unascertained goods forming part of an identified bulk and the sale of undivided shares in goods.

18 *Behnke v Bede Shipping Ltd* [1927] 1 KB 649.

technical and legal terms is needed for the success of a building project. Shipbrokers and naval architects are usually crucial at this stage, who may be instructed to approach various shipbuilding yards to obtain information about pricing, timing and specific designs. The shipbuilder may be able to supply a ready made specification, known as Principal Particulars. In other cases, the buyer may already know what he wants and submit to various shipbuilders his own specification and summary of proposed contract terms to obtain competitive bids. This is known as 'an invitation to tender'. If the first method (that is, the builder's specification) is followed, the next stage of negotiations will be less time consuming, while if the second is chosen (that is, the buyer's specification) the builder will need some time to prepare the technical requirements of the tender. Once these have been completed, the parties will execute a 'letter of intent',[19] which is not usually intended to be legally binding unless such an intention is derived from it. It is useful in order to set out the parties' mutual understanding of the proposed project and it imposes a moral rather than a legal obligation. It is an agreement to negotiate in good faith and it is usually made subject to the terms of the shipbuilding contract.

This is the crucial time, which will determine whether or not the parties will proceed to contract. That decision will depend on the ability of the buyer to obtain appropriate finance for the project. Assuming that a willing bank becomes interested in financing the project, an interim or 'bridging' contract may be concluded at this stage so that the builder is assured that the buyer is serious before he engages in substantial work. By the bridging contract, the builder agrees to provide design and technical services for the development of the project in return for a fee.[20]

After the design is submitted, final negotiations take place about the details of the contract and specification. There are standard forms of contract reflecting the strength of the particular shipbuilding yard. The SAJ form 1974 has been widely used and has formed the basis of other standard contracts used by other yards, such as South Korea, Taiwan and China. There is also the AWES (Association of West European Shipbuilders) form 1972, the MARAD form 1980 of the US Department of Marine Administration, and the form of the Association of Norwegian Marine Yards 1981.[21]

4 SIGNIFICANCE OF REPRESENTATIONS DURING NEGOTIATIONS

It is naturally common for commercial people to use legitimate means and persuasive skills during negotiations to make the other party accept the deal offered. What is not allowed, however, is to make representations, which the party making them knows are not true and, by making them, induces the other party to enter into the contract. This is distinguished from mere puffs or expressions of opinion.

---

19 For the effect of letters of intent see: *Wilson Smithest & Cape (Sugar) Ltd v Bangladesh Sugar & Food Industries Corp* [1986] 1 Lloyd's Rep 378, concerning sale of goods (c&f (cost and freight) terms).

20 See further op cit, Curtis, fn 1.

21 These can be found in op cit, Goldrein, fn 1, Appendices.

Control of what negotiating parties state during negotiations leading up to a contract is provided by the Misrepresentation Act (MA) 1967, which imposes an absolute duty on the negotiating parties not to state facts which the representor could not later show that he had reasonable ground for believing.

Section 2 of the MA 1967 states:

(1) Where a person has entered into a contract after a misrepresentation has been made to him by another party thereto and as a result thereof he has suffered loss, then, if the person making the misrepresentation would be liable to damages in respect thereof had the misrepresentation been made fraudulently, that person shall be so liable notwithstanding that the misrepresentation was not made fraudulently, unless he proves that he had reasonable ground to believe and did believe up to the time the contract was made that the facts represented were true.

Breach of the provisions of this Act may entitle the other party to damages, which will be assessed as if the misrepresentation were fraudulent.[22] The consequences of negligent misstatements are discussed in the next chapter in the context of sale and purchase of used ships, which will equally apply in this context as well.

5 THE MAKING OF A SHIPBUILDING CONTRACT AND RISK MANAGEMENT

Like any other contract, there must be a binding agreement – an offer and an unconditional acceptance, intention to create a legal relationship, and consideration. Consideration under English law requires that each party has given something of value in return for the other party's promise. There must also be certainty of terms, which define clearly the extent of the duties of each party, particularly as shipbuilding contracts are complex and contain many clauses of technical jargon. For a contract to be binding, there must be no inconsistent or uncertain terms, and matters of substance must not be left to be agreed at a later stage.[23] Shipbuilding contracts are most challenging for lawyers, both in the drafting and in trying to make sense of what others have drafted when the matter has reached litigation. It cannot be stressed too strongly that this is an area which requires skilful legal risk management at the stage of negotiations, drafting and at the stage of performance of the contract when, frequently, a need to renegotiate the terms arises. A simple example of such problems may be offered by the decision of Lord Denning MR in *Okura & Co Ltd v Navara Shipping Corp SA*.[24]

The original contract for shipbuilding was between Okura (Japanese contractors) and Navara. But the shipbuilder was Ujina dockyard. Navara were to pay a considerable amount of money by instalments in advance, coming to nearly half

---

22 *Howard Marine & Dredging Co Ltd v Ogden & Son (Excavations) Ltd* [1978] 2 WLR 515 (CA); *Royscot Trust v Rogerson* [1991] 2 QB 297 (CA); *Avon Insurance v Swire Fraser* [2000] 1 All ER 573.

23 *Fast Ferries v Ferries Australia* [2001] 1 Lloyd's Rep 534); see also *Thoresen (Bangkok) Ltd v Fathom Marine Co* [2004] 1 Lloyd's Rep 622: (recap e-mail provided 'otherwise basis Saleform 93 sub-details suitably amended to reflect also the above terms'; held: no binding contract.

24 [1982] 2 Lloyd's Rep 537 (CA).

the price as the ship was being built. Navara fulfilled that provision. Although the vessel was to be built in 12 months, that time could be extended by reason of *force majeure*, if causes of delay were beyond the builder's control. Another provision in the contract allowed the buyer to cancel the contract and claim repayment of the instalments with interest, if the delivery was delayed by more than 150 days after delivery date. Okura did not manage to keep to the delivery date, because it ran into financial difficulties. Not only were many items unfinished, but also the first trials revealed serious defects in the engines. Navara gave their notice of cancellation. So, this contract came to an end. New negotiations commenced for a new contract. This contract was on a tripartite basis between the shipbuilders under the head contract (Ujina), the Japanese contractors (Okura) and the buyers (Navara). The proposal was that the buyers should take the ship as it was, and do remedial work on the defects in the engines. The shipbuilders should make good the listed unfinished items. But the buyers were not to be bound by the contract until after sea trials had been completed. It was contemplated that there would be a written contract drawn up and signed after the telex sent setting out the telephone negotiations. The issue for the court was whether these negotiations as contained in the telex resulted in a binding contract or were merely the basis for a future agreement. It was a question of construction. Two points arising from the telex were crucial to the construction: (a) it referred to all other terms and conditions as contained in the previous shipbuilding contract to apply in full. The original contract stated that, 'the contract shall become effective as from the date of fulfilment and realisation of all conditions'. Such conditions included the signing of the contract by the buyer and the contractor; and (b) it had also been stated in the telex that its items would be incorporated in a memorandum of agreement (MOA) in mutually acceptable manner. It was, therefore, contemplated that an MOA was to be drawn up and the parties conducted themselves on that footing. The buyer's solicitors did draft the MOA reflecting the telex, but included a new clause:

> The parties hereto agree that there shall be no extension of time for delivery of the vessel due to *force majeure* and that the provision of Art III(1) of the contract shall not apply to this agreement.

That clause was inconsistent with the telex by which the parties intended to incorporate all other terms and conditions of the previous contract. In effect, what the buyers were saying was that they wanted absolute compliance with the delivery date, while the builders were saying they wanted an extension of time for *force majeure*. As the parties could not reach agreement about this clause, Navara gave an ultimatum that, unless the builders agreed to it, by a certain time, Navara would withdraw from the contract and ask that all money held by the builders be released. On the other hand, if the builders agreed to this clause, Navara were prepared to wait for another week for the contract to be signed. The builders did not accept the clause, so no MOA was signed up and the money was refunded to Navara. The builders sold the vessel elsewhere, but that was not the end of the matter. Later Navara claimed that there was a binding contract, which was repudiated by the builders. The latter issued a writ seeking a declaration that there was no contract, which the buyers contested.

The judge held that there was a binding contract. The Court of Appeal reached a unanimous decision on the issue, reversing the judge.

The reasoning of Lord Denning MR was that, upon construction of the documents, the agreement was provisional; the parties were not to be bound unless and until they signed a contract. In addition, the parties did not treat the telex as a binding agreement because all sorts of matters had to be arranged. The refund was requested and was made to Navara.

An interesting recent decision demonstrates the importance of paying attention to what the contract means before taking steps which will expose a party to damages for repudiation. In *Covington Marine Corp v Xiamen Shipbuilding Industry Co Ltd*,[25] the contract was made subject to certain conditions to be fulfilled within certain time after execution of the contract, failing which the contract would be automatically rescinded, unless the party to whom performance was due agreed otherwise. Such conditions referred to in the contract were: agreement about the supplier of the engine; receipt by the buyer of the letter of guarantee; receipt by the buyer of evidence of the validity of the contract; specifications and all government licences; and receipt by the builder of the first instalment. Three weeks after entering into this contract, the builders signed contracts to build three of the same vessels for another buyer and refused to perform this contract. The buyers accepted such conduct as repudiation and claimed damages. The dispute was referred to arbitration. The builders alleged that there was no binding contract and challenged the jurisdiction of the arbitrators. The arbitrators decided that the binding effect of the contract depended on the parties being able and willing to reach an agreement as to the supplier of the engine and the other conditions within the prescribed time. Since the parties were not able to agree the supplier of the engine, there was no binding contract. The buyers appealed to the court under s 69 of the Arbitration Act 1906. The issue turned on whether or not the exchanges between the parties constituted a firm offer and acceptance, which should be viewed objectively to determine whether the parties intended to be bound. The court held that the contract was made subject to conditions subsequent, not conditions precedent, and it was an agreement to agree. It was a binding agreement subject to automatic rescission. The court found that the arbitrators were wrong to conclude that there was no agreement as to the supplier of the engine. The builders repudiated the contract and were liable to damages.

Other essential terms of the shipbuilding contract, without which a contract may not be complete, are the following:

(a) ship's description and dimensions with dead weight capacity (DWC); the ship is given a hull number during construction, which is not, however, regarded as an essential part of her description;[26] the class must also be specified; details of description and class may be inserted later;

(b) speed and fuel consumption;

(c) price and method of payment;

(e) inspection of work in progress;

(f) modification of agreed description;

---

25 [2006] 1 Lloyd's Rep 745.

26 *The Diana Prosperity* [1976] 2 Lloyd's Rep 621 (HL).

(g) nature and conditions of trials;

(h) time and place of delivery;

(i) transfer of title and risk with insurance arrangements; and

(j) rectification of defects.

The description, modification of description and transfer of title are the most essential terms of the contract for it to confer the necessary certainty. It can be agreed that the details of other terms may be filled in later. If the parties need more time to consider their position, they can agree provisionally on a draft which is made 'subject to contract',[27] which is understood to mean that there is no binding contract until a formal written contract is drawn up or this condition is withdrawn or waived.

The contract may be subject to conditions to be fulfilled by either party before the commencement of the construction. The effect of conditions on the contract depends on the type of condition. If a condition is to the effect that one party has to do something before the commencement of the contract (condition precedent), there will be no contract until that condition is met. If the condition requires one party to the contract to do something within a certain time after the commencement of the contract (condition subsequent), (see *Covington Marine*, above) the non-fulfilment of that condition will operate to discharge the parties from an existing contract. If the condition suspends the operation of the contract until a subsequent agreement on the details or upon the buyer obtaining finance, there is a contract, but its operation is suspended until the condition is met (see *Fast Ferries*, in which it was held that the parties proceeded on the assumption that approval of finance was a formality; the parties were agreeing in the exchanges to treat the contract as effective, but subject to termination if the assumption was unjustified).[28]

The contract will state that the vessel is to be built according to a specification, which is an integral part of the making of the contact.

6 THE FRAMEWORK OF THE CONTRACT

Taking as an example the SAJ shipbuilding contract, which is more widely used, the basic express terms of the contract are divided into 21 articles and include the following broad provisions:

Article I: description, dimensions, characteristics, classification (rules and regulations), subcontracting and registration.

Article II: contract price, currency, terms and method of payment.

Article III: delivery, speed, fuel consumption, dead weight.

Article IV: approval of plans and drawings, appointment of buyer's representative, inspection by him, liability of builder and responsibility of the buyer.

---

27 This phrase has been explained in cases concerning conveyance of land: see *Keppel v Wheeler* [1927] 1 KB 577 (CA); *Law v Jones* [1974] Ch 112 (CA).

28 For the construction of such a condition in the context of the parties' exchanges, see *Fast Ferries One SA v Ferries Australia Ltd* [2000] 1 Lloyd's Rep 534.

Article V: modification of specification, change in class, substitution of materials.

Article VI: trials and notice, weather conditions, method of trials; method of acceptance or rejection, effect of acceptance.

Article VII: time and place of delivery, when the buyer has fulfilled his obligations, documents to be delivered to the buyer, tender of the vessel, title and risk.

Article VIII: delays and extension of time, notice of delay, defining what is permissible delay, right to rescind for excessive delay.

Article IX: warranty of quality, notice of defects, remedy of defects, extent of builder's responsibility.

Article X: rescission by the buyer, notice, refunds by builder, discharge of obligations.

Article XI: buyer's default, what is default, interest and charge, effect of default, sale of vessel.

Article XII: builder's obligation to insure and extent of coverage, recoverable losses.

Article XIII: dispute and arbitration (the printed form stipulates for arbitration in Tokyo, but it is usually the case that parties agree London as the seat of arbitration, hence the relevance of English law).[29]

Article XIV: deals with prohibition of assignment of the contract unless prior consent of the other party and approval from the Japanese government are obtained.

Articles XV and XVI: deal with taxes and duties in Japan, patents trademarks, copyright, etc.

Article XVII: regulates supplies by the buyer and his responsibility for them.

The remaining four articles deal with address of notices, effective date of contract, law and interpretation of the contract, and the guarantee in the event of default by the buyer.

7 TYPES OF CONTRACTUAL TERMS

7.1 General

The contract will contain other important terms, some of which may be conditions, the breach of which under English law will entitle the other party to treat the contract as at an end. Other terms may have been agreed to be warranties, the breach of which will sound in damages only, but will not entitle the other party to treat the breach as terminating the contract.[30] There may be other terms, known as intermediate or innominate; the effect of breach of such a term depends on whether the breach goes to the root of the contract, so that the other party is entitled to treat

---

29   The printed form of NSF 1993 provides for English law and arbitration.

30   Contrast 'warranties' under insurance contracts, breach of which discharges the insurer of liability as from the date of the breach (*The Good Luck* [1991] 2 Lloyd's Rep 191 (HL)).

himself as discharged. It will depend on the nature and consequences of the breach.[31] Whether a term is a condition or a warranty or an innominate term does not depend on the use of those words in the contract, but on the construction of the contract as a whole. In the absence of clear words, a term will not be interpreted as a condition, if the result of doing so would be unreasonable.[32] The term 'shipped in good condition' in a sale of goods contract was held by Lord Denning MR in *The Hansa Nord*[33] not to be a condition, but an intermediate term and the buyer would not be discharged from the contract, unless there was a serious and substantial breach of this term.

7.2 Implied terms under the SOGA 1979

Sometimes, the court may imply a term if it is necessary to give business efficacy to the contract and if both parties could reasonably have intended such a term, although they did not expressly say so.

7.2.1 Compliance with description (the law before 3 January 1995)

Other important terms are implied by statute. Section 13 of the SOGA 1979 provides that, where there is a contract for the sale of goods by description, there is an implied condition that the goods will correspond with the description.

As it was mentioned earlier, a shipbuilding contract is a contract for the construction and sale of a ship by description. If the relevant terms in the description do not conform with the vessel when it is eventually delivered, the buyer is entitled to reject the ship for non-compliance.

An important question, with regard to non-conformity of delivered goods with the contractual description is this: would any non-conformity of whatsoever nature entitle the purchaser to reject the goods whether or not the non-conformity would have caused him loss had he accepted them? Contract law lawyers would say that, historically, English law has treated the term of description strictly. This was emphasised by the decision of the House of Lords in *Arcos Ltd v Ronnasen*.[34]

Arcos Ltd v Ronnasen

Agents for the sale of Russian timber agreed to sell to English buyers a quantity of staves of Russian redwood and whitewood, required by the buyers for making cement barrels. The price was to include cost, freight and insurance from Archangel to the River Thames. With respect to the length, breadth, and thickness, the agreement contained stipulations, which allowed some variation in the length and in the

---

31 *Hong Kong Fir Shipping Co Ltd v Kawasaki Kisen Kaisha* [1961] 2 Lloyd's Rep 478 (CA); *Bunge Corporation v Tradax Export SA* [1981] 2 Lloyd's Rep 1 (HL), p 7, per Lord Scarman; *The Aktion* [1987] 1 Lloyd's Rep 283, concerning sale of a ship, see Chapter 11.

32 *The Hansa Nord* [1975] 2 Lloyd's Rep 445 (CA): read Roskill LJ, p 457.

33 Ibid, p 451.

34 [1933] AC 470 (HL).

breadth of the staves, but none in the thickness, which in all cases was specified as half an inch. When the goods arrived in London the buyers claimed to reject them on the ground that they did not conform to the description in the contract, in that they were not of the thickness of half an inch.

In an arbitration under the contract, an umpire made an award in the form of a special case for the opinion of the King's Bench Division, in which he found that, in thickness, none of the staves was less than half an inch; about 5% were half an inch; a large proportion were over half an inch, but not more than an inch. The umpire found that the staves were fit for making cement barrels and that, when shipped, they were commercially within and merchantable under the specification in the contract.

Wright J in his judgment decided in favour of the buyers, upon the ground that the difference in the sizes was not of such a trivial character as would justify its being disregarded by the court; that the finding as to measurement showed that the goods were not those contracted to be sold and that it was those goods, and not their commercial equivalent, that the buyers were entitled to demand.

The Court of Appeal affirmed his decision. The House of Lords also held that the buyers were entitled to demand goods answering the description in the contract, and were not bound to accept the goods tendered merely because they were merchantable under that description.

This strict approach to the construction of description clauses by old authorities was questioned by the House of Lords in the 1970s when Lord Diplock adopted a more flexible approach in *Ashington Piggeries Ltd v Christopher Hill Ltd*:[35]

> It is open to the parties to use a description as broad or narrow as they choose. But ultimately the test is where the buyer could fairly and reasonably refuse to accept the physical goods proffered to him on the ground that their failure to correspond with that part of what was said about them in the contract makes them different goods from those he had agreed to buy.

The trend since then has been that the shortcoming of the goods must have been a substantial ingredient of the description of the goods, so that a reasonable person would regard the goods as distinct from what he contracted for. The description must also be seen in the context and purpose of the particular contract. The House of Lords, in the following case, did not regard the number of the hull of the ship delivered under a long term charterparty as a matter entitling the charterers to reject the newly constructed ship when it was delivered to them for chartering services.

The Diane Prosperity [36]

It concerned a charterparty, entered in Shelltime 3 form, with respect to a new building of a tanker constructed in Japan. At the time of construction, the oil market was strong. The description of the vessel was referred to by the owners in the charterparty and in the documents as being built by Osaka Shipbuilding Co (a

---

35 [1972] AC 441, pp 503–04 (HL).
36 [1976] 1 WLR 989 (HL).

reputable Japanese builder) with the hull number 354. Due to some difficulties at the Osaka yard the vessel was actually built at Oshima yard (a company in which Osaka owned 50% of shares) and with the hull number 004. All other physical attributes of the vessel corresponded with those required under the charterparty. At the time of delivery to the charterers, the oil market had fallen sharply and the charterers rejected the vessel, contending that the vessel tendered did not correspond with that on the documents. It was held that the hull number of the vessel had no special significance for the parties, so as to raise it to a matter of fundamental obligation. The words 'hull number 354' were not intended to be part of the description of the vessel. The vessel contracted for was the vessel tendered.

The purpose of the hull number in the context of this contract was without a significant meaning, other than to identify the vessel, which had not been constructed nor did it have a name at the time of fixing the charter. Lord Wilberforce said that he was not prepared to accept that the authorities as to 'description' in the sale of goods cases should be extended or apply to the contract in question. He rather thought they ought to be re-examined:[37]

> Some of these cases either in themselves, for example, *Moore v Landauer*,[38] or as they have been interpreted, for example, *Behn v Burness*,[39] I find excessively technical and due for fresh examination in this House.[40]

In his view, the question of importance was whether a particular item in a description of goods – whether in sale of goods, or in other contracts – constituted a substantial ingredient of the 'identity' of the thing and, only if it did, he was prepared to treat it as a condition. He absolutely agreed with what Roskill LJ said in *The Hansa Nord*:[41]

> In principle it is not easy to see why the law relating to contracts for the sale of goods should be different from the law relating to the performance of other contractual obligations, whether charterparties or other types of contract. Sale of goods law is but one branch of the general law of contract. It is desirable that the same legal principles should apply to the law of contract as a whole and that different legal principles should not apply to different branches of that law.

Lord Wilberforce further stressed that the general law of contract had developed along much more rational lines, and, in particular, after the *Hong Kong Fir* case,[42] it has no longer been necessary to adhere to rigid categories of breach which do or do not automatically give right to rescind. It is rather a question of attending to the nature and gravity of a breach, he said. However, it might have been a different matter, if the parties to a construction contract had intended that a particular yard, and no other, should build the ship.

---

37 [1976] 1 WLR 989 (HL), p 998.

38 [1921] 2 Lloyd's Rep 519.

39 (1863) 3 B&S 751.

40 Following the same lines of argument, Lord Glaisdale and Lord Kilbrandon commented that the cases on the sale of goods may call for reconsideration.

41 [1975] 2 Lloyd's Rep 445, p 458.

42 *Hong Kong Fir Shipping & Co Ltd v Kawasaki Kisen Kaisha* [1961] 2 Lloyd's Rep 478.

7.2.2 The 'taming' of the SOGA 1979 by the SSGA 1994

In view of extreme consequences that might result, even if the breach is slight, it was thought appropriate to amend the 1979 Act. By s 4 of the Sale and Supply of Goods Act (SSGA) 1994, s 15A was inserted in the 1979 Act. It relates to modification of remedies for breach of a condition in non-consumer contracts and provides:

(1) where in the case of a contract of sale (a) the buyer would, apart from this subsection, have the right to reject goods by reason of a breach on the part of the seller of a term implied by ss 13, 14 and 15 . . . but (b) the breach is so slight that it would be unreasonable for him to reject them,

. . . then, if the buyer does not deal as consumer, the breach is not to be treated as a breach of condition but be treated as a breach of warranty.

This section applies unless a contrary intention appears in, or is implied from, the contract; the burden of showing that a breach fell within the above subsection is upon the seller. The test is that of a reasonable purchaser.

The new Act came into force on 3 January 1995, so only contracts entered into after that date are affected by it.

7.2.3 The demise of 'merchantable quality'

7.2.3.1 The law until 3 January 1995

Section 14(2) of the SOGA 1979 provided that, where the seller sold goods in the course of a business, there was an implied condition that the goods supplied under the contract were of merchantable quality, except that there was no such condition as regards defects specifically drawn to the attention of the buyer. Goods of any kind would be of merchantable quality within the meaning of this Act,[43] if they were as fit for the purpose or purposes for which goods of that kind were commonly bought, as was reasonable to expect having regard to any description applied to them, the price (if relevant) and all the other relevant circumstances (s 14(6)). The implied condition would be broken, if the defect was so serious that a commercial man would have thought that the purchaser was entitled to reject them. Thus, 'merchantable' quality was made synonymous with 'fitness for purpose', and other aspects of quality were left ambiguous.

7.2.3.2 The law after 3 January 1995

As mentioned in para 7.2.2, s 4 of the SSGA 1994 modified the effect of the consequences of breach of implied terms under the 1979 Act and, by the insertion of s 15A in the 1979 Act, a non-consumer buyer will not have the right of rejection if the breach is slight.

Also, in recognition of the difficulties created in the interpretation of the term 'merchantable quality', s 1(1) of the SSGA 1994 introduced the term 'satisfactory quality' and substituted s 14(2) of the 1979 Act with the following:

---

43   The definition was adopted from the Supply of Goods (Implied Terms) Act 1973, s 7(2).

Where the seller sells goods in the course of his business, there is an implied term that the goods supplied under the contract are of satisfactory quality. For the purpose of this Act, goods are of satisfactory quality if they meet the standard that a reasonable person would regard as satisfactory, taking into account of any description of the goods, the price (if relevant) and all the other relevant circumstances.

For the purpose of this Act, the quality of the goods includes their state and condition and the following (among others) are in appropriate cases aspects of the quality of the goods:

- the fitness for all the purposes for which goods of the kind in question are commonly supplied;
- appearance and finish;
- freedom from defects;
- safety and durability.

All other references to 'merchantable quality' in the 1979 Act have been substituted, accordingly, by the term satisfactory or unsatisfactory, as the case may be.

But, if the goods are sold second hand, then the buyer must judge what is satisfactory for him considering the price he pays, unless there is something radically wrong with them.[44] Whether a defect renders the vessel unsafe or unable to operate in the market for which she was built will be judged in the view of a commercial man. Defective electrical wiring has been considered by the court to be a serious defect affecting the vessel's quality (see *The Raspora*, para 7.3, below).

7.2.4 Fitness for purpose

As much as the description and the quality of the goods, the purpose for which the goods are bought is equally important to the commercial man's decision to purchase the particular goods. Again, when the breach of this implied term is slight there will be no right of rejection by the buyer, by virtue of the new s 15A of the SOGA 1979, as mentioned earlier.

Section 14(3) of the SOGA 1979 provides that:

> ... where a seller sells goods in the course of a business and the buyer, expressly or by implication, makes known ... any particular purpose for which the goods are being bought, there is an implied condition that the goods supplied under the contract are reasonably fit for that purpose, whether or not that is a purpose for which such goods are commonly supplied, except the circumstances show that the buyer does not rely, or that it is unreasonable for him to rely, on the skill or judgment if the seller.

7.2.4.1 Reliance on the skill and judgment of the seller

The extent of reliance upon the skill and judgment of the seller was in issue in the following House of Lords' case.

---

44 *The Hansa Nord* [1975] 2 Lloyd's Rep 445 (CA), p 452.

Cammell Laird & Co Ltd v The Manganese Bronze and Brass Co Ltd[45]

A firm of shipbuilders agreed to build for and sell to the UM Company, two sister ships (A and B) designed for carrying petroleum or molasses, with main propelling diesel engines, each ship to be classed A1 at Lloyd's.

The shipbuilders entered into a contract with the MB and B Company, who were makers of ships' propellers out of manganese bronze prepared by a special process, for the manufacture of two propellers for these ships, to be of special Parsons manganese bronze, of a specified diameter, and pitch, each with four blades of a specified total developed area and of a maximum brake horsepower at a specified number of revolutions per minute. Each propeller was to be finished, chipped, and polished in style of the highest class, with boss bored, faced, and keyway cut to the shipbuilders' template, with edges brought up to fine lines, to be true to pitch; all in accordance with the shipbuilders' blue print, to be ready for fitting to the shaft on delivery; and to be to the entire satisfaction of the UM Company's representative and the shipbuilders themselves. They were to be delivered on a certain agreed date. The working drawings gave the information necessary to enable the work to be carried out, including the thickness required along the medial lines of the blades; but beyond this and apart from the direction that the 'edges' were 'to be brought up to fine lines', further details as to the thickness of the blades were left to the skill and judgment of the MB and B Company.

On trials, the propeller fitted onto vessel A made so much noise that the vessel could not be classed A1 at Lloyd's. The propeller which had been fitted onto B, the second vessel, was tried on A and it worked satisfactorily. Without prejudice to the rights of the parties, a second propeller was made for A to the correct specifications and free from fault in other respects, but proved equally unsatisfactory as the first. Finally, a third propeller was made for A (also without prejudice to the rights of the parties) and this one worked quite silently. The shipbuilders sued the engine constructors for delay in executing the work and the expenses incurred as a result of delay. It was found that nothing in the specification or plan could account for the trouble in the propellers or the engines. It seemed reasonable to infer that the problems lay with the finishing which was a matter left to the discretion of the builders and not given in the plan and particulars.

The House of Lords held that the agreement was a contract of sale of future goods under s 14(1) of the SOGA 1893. Inasmuch as the buyers had made known to the builders (sellers) the purpose for which the propeller was required, and relied upon their skill and judgment, it was not necessary, for the purposes of this subsection, that the buyer should rely totally and exclusively on the skill and judgment of the seller for every detail in the production of the goods. It was sufficient, if reliance was placed on the skill and judgment of the seller to some substantial extent. In the present case, with regard to that part of the work which was left to the skill and judgment of the sellers, there was a breach of the implied condition that the propeller should be reasonably fit for the purpose for which it was required.

---

45 [1934] AC 402 (HL).

7.2.4.2 Idiosyncrasy of the subject matter

By contrast, there will be no breach of the implied condition of fitness when the failure of the goods to meet the intended purpose arises from an abnormal feature or idiosyncrasy not made known to the seller. *Slater v Finning*[46] is a House of Lords' decision on this issue.

The defendants were dealers in marine engines. The plaintiffs were owners of a fishing vessel, *Aquarius 11*, which functioned on a caterpillar diesel engine and presented some problems. They called the defendants to replace a new camshaft to the engine of *Aquarius 11*, but the first replacement was not a success. Subsequently, two other camshafts were fitted to the engine, none of them was a success and the engine continued to have problems. Therefore, the plaintiffs sold the engine and installed a new engine with a different design.

The old engine, after an extensive overhaul, but with no replacement to the camshaft by the new owner in South Africa, was fitted into another vessel, *The Ocean Spray*, and it worked for long periods without any problems. The plaintiffs instituted an action against the defendants for breach of the implied condition under s 14(3) of the 1979 Act, contending that the camshafts which were bought for *Aquarius 11* were not reasonably fit for the purpose of her engine, and the defendants had known that the camshafts were to be fitted into *Aquarius 11*.

The House of Lords rejected the plaintiffs' argument and held that there was no breach of the implied condition. It had been found that *Aquarius 11* had an unknown and unusual characteristic, a tendency to create excessive torsional resonance in camshafts. The particular purpose for which the camshafts were required was that of being fitted in the engine of a vessel which suffered from a particular abnormality or idiosyncrasy. The defendants, not being aware of that tendency, were not in a position to exercise skill and judgment for the purpose of dealing with it. Lord Keith stated:

> As a matter of principle, therefore, it may be said that where a buyer purchases goods from a seller who deals in goods of that description there is no breach of the implied condition of fitness where the failure of the goods to meet the intended purpose arises from an abnormal feature or idiosyncrasy, not made known to the seller, in the buyer or in the circumstances of the use by the buyer. That is the case whether or not the buyer is himself aware of the abnormal feature or idiosyncrasy.[47]

In the context of a shipbuilding contract, whether or not there has been a breach of the implied term of 'fitness for purpose' will depend on the particular circumstances of the contract. A breach of fitness may be an aspect of quality, thus, it will fall within the previous sub-paragraph. In any event, contracts entered into after 3 January 1995 will be subject to the amendment of the 1979 Act by the SSGA 1994, by which the breach must not be so slight as to be unreasonable for the buyer to reject the ship.[48]

---

46 [1996] 2 Lloyd's Rep 353.
47 [1996] 2 Lloyd's Rep 353, p 358.
48 See, further, op cit, Curtis, fn 1, pp 102–03.

7.3 Exclusion clauses and the Unfair Contract Terms Act 1977

The Act does not apply to international supply contracts as defined by s 26 of the Act. The Act by s. 27(1) limits the operation of the controls in the Act if the law applicable to the contract is, by choice of the parties, the law of the UK and apart from that choice the contract would be governed by the law of another country. This limitation on the controls of the Act applies on the assumption, or proof, that the foreign law which, otherwise, would apply to the contract is different from the UK law of choice.[49] On the other hand, the Act does not permit a party to a contract to impose a term providing for the application of foreign law whose main purpose, as appears to the court or arbitrator, is to evade the operation of the Act (s 27(2)).

Where the Act applies, it provides a statutory prohibition of exclusion or limitation of liability clauses for death or personal injury resulting from negligence. Otherwise, it does not prohibit exclusion or limitation of liability clauses[50] relating to other forms of loss or damage provided they satisfy the test of reasonableness (s 2(1), (2)).

Insofar as consumer contracts of sale of goods are concerned, s 6(2) prohibits exclusion or limitation of liability for breach of the statutory conditions implied by ss 13, 14 and 15 of the SOGA 1979 and s 1 of the SSGA 1994 (referring to description, quality and fitness for purpose). Insofar as non-consumer contracts are concerned, s 6(3) makes such exclusion or limitation subject to the requirement of reasonableness.

The 1977 Act obviously plays a very important role in protecting vulnerable consumers from the effects of draconian contract terms. But it does not interfere with contracts between parties of equal bargaining strength, who would generally be considered capable of being able to make contracts of their choosing, allocate the risks between themselves and expect to be bound by their terms. However, a blanket exclusion of any liability whatever would, *prima facie*, be unreasonable.[51]

In the following case, the building of a powerboat was classed as a consumer contract; it did not fall within the category of an international supply of goods.

Rasbora v JCL Marine[52]

The contract was for the building and sale of a powerboat and included a clause excluding the application of any implied condition or warranty, and liability 'for any loss, damage, expense or injury howsoever arising' except as accepted under the terms of the warranty certificate. Although the builders agreed to build the boat for a private buyer in England (A), the contemplated purchaser was a company

---

49 Dicey & Morris, *Conflict of Laws*, 13th edn, 2000, para 33–108, Sweet & Maxwell. For the application of sections 26 & 27 of the Act, see *Balmoral Group Ltd v Borealis* [2006] 2 Lloyd's Rep 629.

50 *The Zinnia, Stag Line Ltd v Tyne Shiprepair Group Ltd* [1984] 2 Lloyd's Rep 211.

51 Tuckey LJ in *Granville Oil & Chemicals Ltd v Davis Turner & Co Ltd* [2003] 2 Lloyd's Rep 356, p 362; in *Balmoral v Borealis*, fn 49, Borealis did not satisfy the court that their conditions of sale which excluded the statutory implied terms of satisfactory quality and fitness for purpose, and liability for any loss or damage arising from any defect in the goods, satisfied the test of reasonableness.

52 [1977] 1 Lloyd's Rep 645.

registered in Jersey, which was wholly owned by A – this was to avoid paying UK tax. After the sale was completed, the vessel caught fire during a cruise and the plaintiffs, who had now been substituted for the original buyers, claimed damages from the sellers for breach of the implied condition under s 14(2) of the SOGA 1979, that the boat was not of merchantable quality. They contended that the fire was caused by defective electrical installations on the boat. The sellers sought to rely on the exclusion clause.

It was held that by novation, the company, as plaintiffs, were party to the contract originally made between A and the defendants. The substitution was amply supported by consideration. By s 55 of the SOGA 1979, contracting out of the implied term of merchantability was prohibited except in the case of international sales of goods, and in the case of non-consumer sales where the test of reasonableness would be applicable. This was clearly a consumer sale and did not involve an international sale of goods. Therefore, the implied condition could not be excluded when the boat was not of a merchantable quality. It was further held that the sellers could not rely on the exclusion clause in the contract because the seller's breach and the consequences of the breach were fundamental in character.

The majority of shipbuilding contracts, however, are undertaken outside the UK and the contract may not have any connection with the UK. Being characterised as international contracts, the Unfair Contract Terms Act 1977, or ss 2 to 7 and 16 to 21 of the Act will have no application, even if the parties choose English law as the law of the contract (s 27(1)). In the absence of express or implied choice of law by the parties, the Rome Convention 1980 will apply the law of the country with which there is closest connection.

8 THE SPECIFICATION

A significant part of the contract is the specification, which comprises the second part (the first being the terms of the contract). It covers the details of how the ship is to be constructed and includes the following general items:

(a) a detailed description of the type of ship, her hull and equipment, including the builder's scale plan and drawings;

(b) the materials to be used, depending on the wish of the buyer and the cost he is prepared to pay;

(c) the way in which the ship is to be constructed, configuration of engine and fittings, details of officers' cabins, details of the piping system, method of welding, etc;

(d) the specification must meet mandatory regulations of the country of the ship's intended registration, as well as international regulations of safety imposed by conventions (for example, the International Convention for Safety of Life at Sea 1974) and the regulations of the ship's intended classification society; and

(e) sea trials and how they will be carried out.

The specification is of equal significance to the main contract but, in the event of a conflict between the two, in the absence of express agreement, the contract will prevail.

9 INCREASE IN PRICE

The contract must address the risk of price fluctuation in costs of labour and materials.

A cost escalation clause may be included in the contract, where extra costs incurred by the builder with respect to fluctuation in prices for labour and materials may make it necessary for the builder to pass on such costs to the buyer. Such clauses are otherwise known as 'contract price adjustment clauses' or 'fluctuation clauses'. For those representing either the buyer's interests or those of the builder, careful drafting of such a clause is needed. The builder will require as wide a clause as possible, while the buyer must be cautious and restrict the width of such a clause with clear words for a cut-off point. At the end, it will depend on market forces, inflation and the parties' respective bargaining powers.

If there is no such a clause and the builder unilaterally attempts to increase the price in the course of the building, exercising pressure upon the buyer and threatening to discontinue performance unless the extra price is agreed, he will be faced with the risk of the agreement being unenforceable for lack of consideration, or be set aside for economic duress. Each of these situations is briefly explained, and it is hoped that the parties to a contract will bear in mind the issues involved for the purpose of risk management.

9.1 Lack of consideration and risk management

The agreement may be legally unenforceable for lack of consideration if the builder undertook to perform nothing more than that which he was obliged to perform under the existing agreement. By analogous application of the principle, in *Stilk v Myrick*,[53] it could be said that the performance of a pre-existing obligation under a building contract could not be held to constitute good consideration so as to justify increase of the contract price.

In this case, two members of the crew deserted the ship before the return voyage commenced. The captain promised to reward the remaining crew with extra wages if they sailed the vessel safely home. The issue was whether the crew were entitled to that reward. It was held that the deserting two members of the crew made no difference to the duties required of the remaining crew. The latter were performing their obligations under the pre-existing contract of employment, being members of the ship's crew, and had done no extra work to have earned any extra pay. Although the captain had made a promise of extra pay, on which the crew had relied, the court was reluctant to support what was implicitly a form of blackmail or extortion.

In the context of *Stilk v Myrick*, the principle clearly emerges that something further is required of one contracting party in order to merit extra payment. The principle of this case, however, having stood for almost 200 years, underwent a radical development in the following Court of Appeal decision from 1990.

---

53   [1809] 2 Camp 317.

Williams v Roffey Bros & Nichols [54]

The defendant (main builder) sub-contracted with the plaintiff to carry out carpentry work in a block of 27 flats for an agreed price of £20,000. The plaintiff got into financial difficulty because the agreed price was too low for him to operate satisfactorily and at a profit. The main building contract contained a time penalty clause and the builder worried lest the plaintiff did not complete the carpentry work on time. He, therefore, agreed orally with the plaintiff to pay him an additional sum of £10,300, at the rate of £575 for each flat. Approximately seven weeks later, when the plaintiff had substantially completed eight more flats, the defendants made only one further payment of £1,500, whereupon the plaintiff ceased work on the flats. The plaintiff then sued the defendants for the additional sum promised. The judge held that the agreement for payment of the additional sum was enforceable and did not fail for lack of consideration, because the defendant received a commercial advantage. He gave judgment for the plaintiff.

The Court of Appeal affirmed the judgment and held:

> ... that where a party to a contract promised to make an additional payment in return for the other party's promise to perform his existing contractual obligations and as a result secured a benefit or avoided a detriment, the advantage secured by the promise to make the additional payment was capable of constituting consideration thereof, provided that it was not secured by economic duress or fraud;

The consideration was avoidance of the detriment of delivering the flats late, which would result in having to pay penalties to the purchasers of the flats, or to buy further building materials and employ labour for the flats to be completed on time.

The refinement and limitation of the principle in *Stilk v Myrick* has gained acceptance in other recent cases. It is worth mentioning an unusual shipbuilding case, which can be of practical use to both buyers and shipbuilders.

Anangel Atlas Compania Naviera v Ishika Heavy Industries Co Ltd (No 2) [55]

The Angelicoussis group was a long standing customer of a Japanese shipbuilding yard and ordered some new buildings through their agent, a naval architect. During the shipping slump in 1984–85, he and other customers of the yard obtained substantial price reductions for their buildings. Mr Angelicoussis, being a loyal customer, obtained a variation of the original contract and letters were exchanged in which it was stated that the group would be entitled to 'most favoured customer treatment'. The group agreed to take early delivery of the new building, although it did not have to, which would encourage other reluctant customers of the yard to follow suit. However, it was later found out that a friend of Mr Angelicoussis, Mr Goumas, another customer of the yard, had obtained a better reduction in the price from the yard than the reduction granted to his group, and sued the yard for price differential or damages. The issue was whether the aforesaid letters constituted a binding contract. Hirst J held, on the consideration issue, applying *Williams v Roffey*, that whoever provides the services, where there is a practical conferment of benefit

---

54 [1991] 1 QB 1 (CA).
55 [1990] 2 Lloyd's Rep 526.

or a practical avoidance of detriment for the promisee, there is good consideration, and it is no answer to say that the promisor was already bound. The yard got a clear benefit, or avoided a detriment, since their best customers accepted an early delivery, so that the other customers followed suit.

Similarly, in *The Atlantic Baron*,[56] Mocatta J (see fully below) had held 11 years earlier that the parallel increase of the letter of credit (refund guarantee provided by the builder to the buyer as security) being equivalent to the demanded increase of the contract price to counterbalance the devaluation of the dollar was not merely fulfilling a pre-existing contractual obligation, but an 'increased detriment' constituting good consideration.

9.2 Economic duress and risk management

The principle derived from the aforesaid trilogy of cases, however, will not suffice to save the contract, if the agreement is founded on economic duress or fraud, when it may be vitiated by the buyer at his option. In the event that the builder exercises undue pressure on the buyer to pay the extra price, his conduct may amount to economic duress, thus, being subject to the common law rule that the agreement may be held by the court to be voidable (see also Chapter 13 para 7.2.1).

The Atlantic Baron

Hyundai shipbuilding company entered into a contract by which they agreed to build a tanker for shipowners for a fixed price in US dollars, payment to be made in five instalments. The company agreed to open a letter of credit to provide security for repayment of instalments in the event of their default in the performance of the contract. After the owners had paid the first instalment, the US dollar was devalued by 10%, upon which the company put forward a claim for an increase of 10% in the remaining instalments. The owners, asserting that there was no legal ground on which the claim could be made, paid the second and third instalments without the additional 10%, but the company returned both instalments. The owners suggested that the company should subject their claim to arbitration, but the latter declined to do so, and requested the owners to give them a final and decisive reply to their demand for an increase by a certain date, failing which they would terminate the contract. The owners, who at that time were negotiating a very lucrative contract for the charter of the tanker, replied that, although they were under no obligation to make additional payments, they would do so 'without prejudice' to their rights, and requested that the company arranged for corresponding increases in the letter of credit. The company agreed to do so and the owners remitted the remaining instalments, including the 10% increase, without protest. After eight months, the owners commenced arbitration claiming the return of the overpayments on two grounds: lack of consideration and economic duress. The arbitrators stated a special case for the opinion of the court.

---

56 *North Ocean Shipping Co Ltd v Hyundai Construction Co Ltd (The Atlantic Baron)* [1979] QB 705, [1979] 1 Lloyd's Rep 89.

Mocatta J gave a judgment in favour of the builder on the consideration point (see earlier) and in favour of the owners with respect to economic duress, but for the delay to bring the claim. In particular, he held that:

> ... the company's threat to break the contract without any legal justification unless the owners increased their payments by 10% did amount to duress in the form of economic pressure and, accordingly, the agreement for extra payments was a voidable contract which the owners could either affirm or avoid; that, since there was no likelihood that the company would resile from the contract to build the tanker at the time she was due for delivery, the owners, by making the final payments without protest and, also, by their delay from November 1974 until July 1975 before making a claim for the return of the extra payments, had so conducted themselves as to affirm the contract and, accordingly, their claim failed.

This is a good example for owners to bear in mind in the future, for the purpose of risk management, should they find themselves in the same situation of making extra payments to the builder under economic duress. However, mere commercial pressure and use of bargaining power by one party to the contract negotiated at arms length will not suffice for the court to declare the contract voidable for economic duress. The Privy Council, in *Pao v Lau Yiu Long*,[57] said that: although the defendants had been subjected to commercial pressure, the facts disclosed that they had not been coerced into the contract of guarantee and, therefore, the contract was not voidable on the ground of duress; in the absence of duress, public policy did not require a contract negotiated at arm's length to be invalidated because a party had either threatened to repudiate an existing contractual obligation, or had unfairly used his dominant bargaining position in negotiating the agreement.

Economic duress was revisited in *Huyton v Cremer*,[58] in which the court redefined its ingredients. These are: illegitimate pressure and deflection, rather than coercion of the will of the innocent party. Mance J said that relief must depend on the court's assessment of the qualitative impact of the illegitimate pressure objectively assessed. He rejected the argument advanced that there was a third essential ingredient of economic duress: that is, 'no practical, alternative course open to the innocent party'. However, he said, relief may not be appropriate if the innocent party decides, as a matter of choice, not to pursue an alternative remedy, which any and, possibly, some other reasonable persons in his circumstances would have pursued.

Examples of factors that may lead the court to find economic duress may be: evidence of the builder's knowledge that the buyer has a charterparty to commence on the date of delivery and, thus, cannot afford to have the ship delivered late; or the builder's knowledge of the buyer's circumstances, by which the latter would have no option but to agree to a sudden price increase.

---

57   [1980] AC 614 (PC).
58   [1999] 1 Lloyd's Rep 620.

10 BASIC RIGHTS AND OBLIGATIONS OF THE PARTIES

The relationship between the buyer and the builder is governed by the terms of contract provided for in the standard form contract. The seller has agreed to build a ship for a fixed price made to specification, to perform trials and to deliver on time. The buyer has agreed to pay the contract price by instalments during the process of building, the full agreed price being payable upon satisfactory completion to specification, and to accept delivery of the ship on time.

10.1 Payment, transfer of title and protection of the builder in the event of non-payment

The builder's primary concern is to be paid for the job done. The contract provides details of payment and when property and risk pass to the buyer. Payment by instalments is necessary in this type of contract to commit the buyer more and more to the building of the ship.

10.1.1 Title and risk

The contract provides when property and risk shall pass to the buyer. Article VII.5 of the SAJ form stipulates that the title and risk for loss of the vessel shall pass to the buyer only upon delivery and acceptance thereof, having been completed, as stated in the contract. Until such time, it is expressly stated that title to the vessel and risk for her loss or her equipment shall be in the builder, excepting risks of war, earthquake and tidal waves.

In the absence of express or clear provision in the contract with regard to transfer of title, the usual contract rule in English law concerning specific goods is that the property in them is transferred at such a time as the parties to the contract intend it to be transferred. By s 17(2) of the SOGA 1979, the intention of the parties is ascertained from the terms of the contract, the conduct of the parties and the circumstances of the case.

The rules of ascertaining intention are specified in s 18 of the SOGA 1979. Where there is a contract for the sale of future goods by description, as is the case in the construction and sale of a ship, the property does not pass until the goods are in a deliverable state and are appropriated to the contract, either by the seller with the assent of the buyer or by the buyer with the assent of the seller (s 18 r 5). However, bearing in mind the hybrid nature of a shipbuilding contract, even if the ship is uncompleted, the property in it (but not in the materials which have not been appropriated to her) may, in some circumstances, pass to the buyer, if the parties have clearly stipulated it in their contract.[59]

---

59 See *Re Blyth Shipbuilding and Drydocks Co Ltd* [1926] Ch 494 (para 2, fn 9 above).

guarantee. The defendants contended that, by exercising the right to rescind before the writ was issued against them, liability to pay instalments which had become due and had not been paid ceased and was replaced by a claim, not in debt, but in damages. The cancellation deprived the builder of his accrued right to payment of the unpaid instalment either from the buyer or the guarantor.

The House of Lords (and the courts below) held unanimously that it was difficult to believe that commercial men could have intended that the guarantors were to be released from their liability for payments already due and in default just because the plaintiff, builders, had used his remedy of cancelling the shipbuilding contract for the future.

The default of the buyer was the very event that gave rise to the liability of the defendants under the letter of guarantee. The buyers' promise that they would forthwith make the payment in default showed that the obligation arose immediately upon their default and was not merely an obligation to pay any deficiency brought about in the final accounting. The buyers could not be released from their liability for payments already due, just because the builders exercised their rights of cancellation under the contract. It was also held that the cancellation by the builders did not release the buyers of their liability under the second instalment. The builders could rely on their remedies at common law.

Viscount Dilhorne, who stressed that the shipbuilding contract is not just a contract for sale, said – distinguishing cases of sale of land or goods, or in which there is total failure of consideration – that the law has been that cancellation or rescission of a contract, in consequence of repudiation, did not affect accrued rights for the payment of instalments of the contract price, unless the contract provided that it was to do so.

These and similar issues came before the House of Lords again in the following case.

Stocznia v Latvian Shipping Co[74]

Contracts were agreed for the construction and purchase of six refrigerated vessels. Under the contracts, payment was structured into four instalments so that: (a) 5% of the contract price was to be paid seven banking days after receipt by the buyer of the bank guarantee to be furnished by the builder; (b) 20% was to be paid within five banking days after the yard had given notice to the buyer of keel laying; (c) 25% was to be paid within five banking days after the builder had given notice of the successful launching of the vessel; and (d) the balance of the contract price (50%) was to be paid upon delivery of the vessel. The first instalment was paid for all six vessels. Thereafter, the owners began to have financial problems because of downturn in the reefer market and proposed to the builder a 20% reduction in the price for each vessel, together with a five year deferral of payment of the new reduced price and delayed delivery. Otherwise, the buyers informed the builder during these negotiations that, although they wanted the vessels, taking delivery of them

---

74   [1998] 1 Lloyd's Rep 609.

would be impossible. However, the proposal would have disrupted the yard's cash flow and work programme.

The yard did not treat that as repudiation, but completed the keel laying of the first vessel, and served notice claiming the second instalment. The money was not paid and the yard gave notice that they were treating the contract as repudiated. The same thing happened with the second vessel. The keel was laid, the second instalment was demanded, but remained unpaid and the builder served notice treating the contract as being repudiated. Later, the builder brought an action claiming instalments of the remaining four vessels on the basis of repudiation by the buyer.

The issues for the House of Lords were these: (1) whether the yard acquired accrued rights to the second instalments of the contract price in respect of vessels 3–6; (2) what was the impact of the yard electing for contractual rescission on the yard's right to recover the second instalments of the price; and (3) whether the yard's action to recover the second instalments of the price should fail because, if recovered, they would have to be immediately repayable on the ground of total failure of consideration.

With regard to the first and second issues, it was held that, by exercising the right of rescission under the contract, the yard did not express an intention that they abandoned their right at common law to recover, as a debt, unpaid instalments of the price, which had already accrued and were due. This right at common law was not inconsistent with the contract terms, and the yard was entitled to recover accrued and unpaid instalments.[75]

As regards the third issue, the fact that the contract had been brought to an end before the property in the vessel or any part of it had passed to the buyers did not prevent the yard from asserting that there had been no total failure of consideration in respect of an instalment of the price, which had been paid before the contract was terminated. An instalment which had then accrued could not, if paid, be recoverable on that ground. (*Hyundai Heavy Industries Co v Papadopoulos* was applied.)

It was further held that the yard did not have any rights under the contract with respect to non-accrued instalments. The yard was entitled to make an alternative claim in damages for anticipatory repudiation in relation to contracts for vessels 1 and 2.

10.1.7 Liquidated damages, acceleration in payment, and penalty clauses

Liquidated damages

In some circumstances, the builder may demand that the payment under the contract is accelerated, or the contract may provide for liquidated damages in favour of the builder in the event of buyer's default.

The level of such damages must not amount to a penalty clause.[76] The rule of

---

75 The decision of the Court of Appeal was reversed on both points.

76 Whether increase in default interest amounted to penalty so as to be an invalid reason for taking possession, see *First Commercial Bank v Mandarin Container* [2004] Hong Kong (unreported), see a summary at www.dmconline.co.uk.

public policy is that the court will not enforce a penalty clause so as to permit a party to a contract to recover a sum greater than the measure of damages entitled at common law. Liquidated damages agreed in favour of either party to the contract must be a genuine pre-estimate of damages. For agreed liquidated damages to amount to a penalty, there must be unconscionable, oppressive or extravagant conduct by the party seeking to enforce the provision. [77]

The principles enunciated by Lord Dunedin in *Dunlop Pneumatic Tyre Co Ltd v New Garage Motor Co Ltd*[78] are that:

> the question whether a sum stipulated is penalty or liquidated damages is a question of construction to be decided upon the terms and inherent circumstances of each particular contract, judged as of at the time of making the contract, not as at the time of the breach.

Whether a clause is a liquidated damages provision or a penalty, is explained in *Philips Hong Kong Ltd v Attorney General of Hong Kong*.[79] Lord Woolf, giving the advice of the Privy Council, cited with approval what was said by Dickson J in the Supreme Court of Canada in *Elsey v JG Collins Insurance Agencies Ltd*:[80]

> It is now evident that the power to strike down a penalty clause is a blatant interference with freedom of contract and it is designed for the sole purpose of providing relief against oppression for the party having to pay the stipulated sum. It has no place where there is no oppression.

Lord Woolf went on to observe that such views are in accord with those expressed by Diplock LJ in *Robophone Facilities Ltd v Blank*:[81] the 'court should not be astute to descry a penalty clause in every provision of a contract which stipulates a sum to be payable in the event of breach'. Lord Woolf concluded:

> Except possibly in the case of situations where one of the parties to the contract is able to dominate the other as to the choice of the terms of the contract, it will normally be insufficient to establish that a provision is objectionably penal to identify situations where the application of the provision could result in a larger sum being recovered by the injured party than his actual loss. Even in such situations so long as the sum payable in the event of non compliance with a contract is not extravagant, having regarded to the range of losses that it could reasonably be anticipated it would have to cover at the time the contract was made, it can still be a genuine pre-estimate of the loss that would be suffered and so a perfectly valid liquidated damage provision.

A liquidated damages clause is not meant to apply to trifling breaches or losses; if it is held to apply, there is a danger that the whole clause might be struck down as a penalty clause.[82] Furthermore, if the contract provides for liquated damages in the

---

77   Ibid, and *Clydebank Engineering & Shipbuilding Co Ltd v Don Jose Ramos* [1905] AC 6 (HL).
78   [1915] AC 79, p 86.
79   (1993) 61 BLR 41 at 59 (PC).
80   (1978) 83 DLR, p 15.
81   [1966] 1 WLR 1428, p 1447.
82   *Cenargo Ltd v Izar Construcciones Navale SA* [2002] EWCA Civ 524 C. L. C. 1151 (CA).

event of delay, such damages will not be awarded if the delay is due to the conduct of the party claiming the damages.[83]

Acceleration in payment

In *The Angelic Star*,[84] the plaintiffs, Swedish shipbuilders, agreed to build, sell and deliver this ship to Angelicos Company. The payment of 20% of the contract price was payable in advance and the remaining 80% on delivery by a 'delivery credit', which was to be repaid over eight years by 16 semi-annual instalments and it bore a fixed rate of interest at 8.5%. Upon delivery of the vessel, the buyer was to deliver to the builder 31 bills of exchange covering the capital and interest. By way of security to the builder, the buyer was required to execute a mortgage of the vessel. For this purpose, the shipbuilding contract included complex loan conditions; the relevant condition in this context was the event of default in payment of the loan. This clause provided that:

> The loan together with all other monies due to the lenders by the owners shall immediately become payable and the lender shall forthwith be put in funds to cover all existing and future liabilities under the bills of exchange drawn in connection with the loan, and the security for the loan and such monies shall become enforceable . . . if . . . (a) the owners fail to make payments of capital or interest . . . on due dates.

The buyer failed to make payments of capital and interest, and the issue was whether the above clause was enforceable or whether it amounted to a penalty clause.

The Court of Appeal, following the decision of the House of Lords in *Dunlop Pneumatic Tyre Company Ltd v New Garage and Motor Co Ltd*,[85] held:

> Clearly, a clause which provided that, in the event of any breach of contract a long term loan would immediately become repayable and that interest thereon for the full term would not only be still payable but would be payable at once, would constitute a penalty as being 'a payment of money stipulated as *in terrorem* of the offending party' . . . But I do not so read condition 13. 'The loan' is the capital sum. 'All other monies due to the lenders by the owners' cannot be construed as 'all other monies which would otherwise become due by the owners in the future'. It means 'all other monies due at the time of the happening of an event of default'. The mere fact that the capital sum becomes immediately repayable upon a failure to comply with the conditions upon which credit was extended cannot constitute a penalty. The provision that the lenders shall forthwith be put in funds to cover all existing and future liability under any outstanding bills drawn in connection with the loan is intended to safeguard the shipbuilders against their potential liability as drawers, should the bills have been negotiated and the purchaser, as acceptor, fail to honour the bills upon maturity . . . This again is not a penalty provision.[86]

As regards the justification of non-sanctioning a penalty clause, Gibson LJ said:[87]

---

83 *The Cape Hatteras* [1982] 1 Lloyd's Rep 518.

84 [1988] 1 Lloyd's Rep 122.

85 [1915] AC 79 (HL).

86 [1988] 1 Lloyd's Rep 122 at p 125, per Lord Donaldson MR.

87 Ibid, pp 126–27.

... it seemed clear to me that there was no basis for holding that the provision for acceleration of capital must be regarded as unenforceable or as excluded from the contract. The doctrine relating to penalties is not a rule of illegality: it is a rule by which the court refuses to sanction legal proceedings for recovery of a penalty sum, a rule which the court had produced and maintained for purposes of public policy: see per Lord Radcliffe, *Campbell Discount Company Ltd v Bridge* [1962] AC 600, p 622. The rule is, in my judgment, not designed to strike down any more of a lawful contract than is necessary to give effect to the court's purpose of applying public policy; and, moreover, the rule should be applied so as to interfere as little as possible with the proper enforcement of a lawful contract according to its terms. Parties to a contract are free expressly to stipulate not only the primary obligations and rights under the contract but also the secondary rights and obligations, that is, those which arise upon non-performance of any primary obligation by one of the parties to the contract: see per Diplock LJ (as he then was): *Robophone Facilities Ltd v Blank* [1966] 1 WLR 1428, p 1446B.

10.2 Builder's guarantee, trials and risk management

Sea trials are an important part of the contractual terms. The purpose of the sea trials is to test whether the performance and condition of the ship are satisfactory and in accordance with the contract. Trials give the opportunity to the buyer to verify whether the builder has complied with the specification. The standard forms of contract, SAJ and the Norwegian forms, oblige the buyer either to accept that the ship complies with the specification and requirements of the contract, or to reject her within a specified period of time after the completion of the trials.

In this context, the builder's guarantee that certain characteristics and condition of the ship will be met on delivery is very important. Failure by the builder to meet the minimum guaranteed characteristics might cause delay in delivery resulting in loss of profit to both parties. The guarantee is usually linked to a provision for liquidated damages in favour of the buyer as a pre-estimate of the buyer's loss, which will preclude him from relying on common law damages. A neat example of this is provided by the House of Lords' decision in the *Cellulose Acetate*[88] case.

A contract for delivery and erection of an acetone recovery plant provided that, if the work were not completed within a certain time, the contractors should pay to the purchasers by way of penalty a sum of 20*l* for every week that they were in default. The contractors were 30 weeks late in completing the work. In an action by them against the purchasers for the contract price, the defendants counterclaimed 5,850*l*, the actual loss they had suffered through the delay.

It was held that the sum of 20*l* a week was the full amount that the plaintiffs agreed to pay towards compensation to the defendants for delay in completing, and that they were liable for 600*l* and no more.

The fact that a precise pre-estimate is almost impossible will not prevent the sum being liquidated damages.[89]

---

88 *Cellulose Acetate Silk Co v Widnes Foundry Ltd* [1933] AC 20 (HL).
89 *Clydebank Engineering v Don Jose Ramos Yzquierdo Castaneda* [1905] AC 6 (HL).

A builder's guarantee usually provides that, following acceptance by the buyer, if defects in materials and/or workmanship are discovered within 12 or 24 months, the builder shall remedy the defects at his own expense. But, if defects have not been discovered within the guarantee period, there is no remedy for the buyer. The contract expressly exempts the builder's liability for any other defects whatsoever. A recent example of the construction of a guarantee clause and the extent of builder's liability is provided by *The Seta Maru*.[90]

The Seta Maru

Art IX.1 of the guarantee provided that:

> ... the builder for a period of 12 months following acceptance by the buyer of the vessel, guarantees the vessel, her hull and machinery ... which are manufactured, furnished or supplied by the builder ... against all defects in material and/or workmanship on the part of the builder.

Art IX.3 (extent of builder's liability) excluded the builder's liability for any defects discovered after the expiration of the guarantee period and for any defects what-soever, other than the defects specified under Art IX.1. Any other indirect con-sequential, or special, losses, damages or expenses were also excluded.

Three ships were built by China shipbuilding and were delivered to the buyer. After the expiration of the guarantee period, two of them appeared defective in the erection welding, as result of which they suffered a casualty, involving ingress of water through the shell plating. Following the discovery of these defects, the third vessel was inspected within the guarantee period and the same defects were dis-covered and corrected by the builder. With regard to the defects in the other two ships the buyer commenced arbitration and claimed from the builder the costs of repairs and depreciation in value as damages.

On a preliminary issue before the arbitrators, it was decided that in view of non-compliance by the builder of the notification procedures for acceptance of the ves-sels, the terms of the contract did not exempt the builder from liability for the breaches. The builder appealed to the court, which was asked to construe IX.3 Art excepting the builder's liability after the guarantee period.

Thomas J held that Art IX.3 was a comprehensive provision forming part of what was a complete code for dealing with defects discovered after the delivery of the vessel. The terms of Art IX provided a guarantee for defects discovered after the buyer accepted delivery of the vessel. Art IX.3 excluded liability for defects, arising from breaches of the express terms beyond the liability expressly assumed under the guarantee terms. The sending by the builder of a telex notification of readiness was not a condition precedent to the operation of the clause. He remitted the case to the arbitrators.

Naturally, the buyer suffered loss here, which arose mainly from an unfavour-able drafting in the contract. In the light of this risk that defects may, and frequently do, appear after the 12-month guarantee period, the buyer could perhaps protect

---

90 *China Shipbuilding Corp v Nippon Yusen Kabukishi Kaisha and Galaxy Shipping PTE Ltd (The Seta Maru)* [2000] 1 Lloyd's Rep 367.

his position by seeking to obtain a longer guarantee period. If this cannot be achieved at the stage of negotiations, particularly if the builder is in a stronger bargaining position, the buyer ought to inspect the vessel during the guarantee period for any defects that might exist in the vessel, which could be remedied by the builder under the guarantee, as was done in this case with respect to the third ship.

Ordinary insurance cover may not always protect the buyer to indemnify his loss. It will depend on the type of loss and the construction of the insurance contract,[91] unless the buyer obtains special cover for building defects.

The builder also obtains insurance for guarantee risks, but he must ensure that the period of insurance adequately covers the 12-month period of the guarantee, which sometimes may be overlooked if an attachment for cover of such risks is made to the main policy covering construction risks.[92]

10.3 Default by builder – the buyer's right to reject the ship or rescind the contract

The buyer's remedies are provided for in the standard shipbuilding agreement forms. These are supported by statutory rights and rights at common law. He may reject the ship, or reject and demand remedial work, and/or damages, or claim specific performance.

The buyer's right to reject the vessel may arise in two situations. First, he may reject the ship after the trials, pointing out that there are various defects which need to be remedied.

Second, he may reject the ship where there has been a serious breach of the contract by the builder. In such a situation, the buyer may accept the conduct of the seller/builder as a repudiation and sue in damages.

A breach by the builder does not necessarily mean that the breach amounts to repudiation of the contract by him. It will depend on the magnitude of the defect and its consequences. In *McDougall v Aeromarine*,[93] it was held that, if the defect was one that could be remedied within a time, which would still permit the builder to deliver within the period of delivery permitted by the contract, the buyer would not be entitled to treat the contract as repudiated. The buyer could recover damages for delay in the delivery. The SAJ form provides for liquidated damages as a remedy for delay.

An interesting question arose recently in a dispute between the builders and the buyer, which was resolved by arbitration; it concerned whether the price escalation clause could be rendered inoperative if the builder was in breach of the delivery provision. The buyer alleged that, since the builder was in breach and delivered the ship late, he could not benefit from his own wrong doing and claim the escalation of

---

91 See *The Caribbean Sea* [1980] 1 Lloyd's Rep 338.

92 *Heesens Yacht Builders v Cox Syndicate Management Ltd (The Red Sapphire)* [2006] Lloyd's Rep IR 103.

93 [1958] 2 Lloyd's Rep 345.

the price shown in Clarkson's Clean Indexes for the period. The arbitrators decided that the yard could not be said to be seeking to benefit from its wrongdoing unless it was shown that the benefit of the price increase was in fact brought about by its own wrongful acts or omissions. The yard had no influence of or control over the factors dictating market movements. The price escalation and the delay in delivery were separate incidents. The builders had to pay liquidated damages for late delivery and were awarded the contractual price increment.[94]

If the delay has been caused partly by the buyer, he will not be entitled to recover damages. The principle that no liquidated damages for delay can be claimed, if completion was in part delayed by conduct of the employer, would be applicable.[95]

Invariably in shipbuilding contracts, the buyer may be the victim of vague drafting of contractual terms. However, in a shipbuilding boom era, as it has been in the last decade, shipbuilders have been in a strong position.

The contract in *Ravennavi SPA v New Century Shipbulding Co Ltd*[96] is an example of alerting buyers to the risk of possible incompatibility between an option agreement clause and the so-called 'Entire Agreement' clause in a shipbuilding contract, if the drafting is not clear.

There was a preliminary issue in this case as to the interpretation of an option agreement and a shipbuilding contract. The shipyard (the builder) had entered into an option agreement with the claimant, the buyer. The option agreement gave the buyer an option to require the yard to build two vessels, and also provided by cl 4(ii) that, if the yard could do so, it would grant the buyer 'the earlier delivery position for the optional vessel(s)'. The consequence of the exercise of the option was said to be that a shipbuilding contract would automatically come into effect, although that was not absolutely clear. The buyer exercised the option in respect of the two optional vessels, and two shipbuilding contracts were entered into between the yard and the buyer. The shipbuilding contracts contained an entire agreement clause. The buyer claimed damages against the yard on the basis that the latter was in breach of cl 4(ii) of the option agreement because it had contracted with third parties to deliver other tankers on dates falling earlier than the dates for delivery of the buyer's two vessels.

Referring to the entire agreement clause of the contract and to a couple of previous cases concerning this subject, Gloster J held that the effect of the entire agreement clause, read together with the express provisions of the contract relating to delivery and payment dates, was to replace the provisions of the option agreement once the option was exercised. She also held that the effect of the entire agreement clause in the shipbuilding contracts was to exclude any obligation on the builder to accelerate the delivery dates, once the final agreements had been entered into. There was a business justification for the option agreement to lapse under the entire agreement.

---

94 London Arbitration 21/6/2006, LMLN 3, 27/12/2006, 707.
95 *The Cape Hatteress* [1982] 1 Lloyd's Rep 518, p 526: the delay to the repairs of the ship had been caused by the conduct of the defendants.
96 [2006] 2 Lloyd's Rep 280.

The Court of Appeal,[97] approving the decision, held that: a shipyard's obligation under an option agreement to make available an earlier delivery date for a vessel, should one become available, was not intended to be a continuing obligation but only obliged the shipyard to offer the purchaser any earlier date for delivery that might become available prior to the exercise of the option. In this case there was a complex option agreement.

It should be noted that, in the proposed draft of BIMCO's shipbuilding contract, the drafting of the option clause seems to be much clearer and compatible with the entire agreement.

10.4 Delay in delivery and *force majeure*

Events beyond the builder's control frequently occur during the construction of the contract and become a cause of delay in delivery. The builder needs protection and, although it is possible to manage such risks by insurance, it is also sensible to limit his liability for delay in delivery by an exclusion clause in the contract with regard to a range of events, which would be beyond his control. The contract provides a protection for the builder in this respect by the *force majeure* clause (Art VIII of the SAJ form). It enumerates 35 specific events, which may be beyond the builder's control and prevent the work. Upon the occurrence of any of such events, the clause provides that the time for the delivery is extended for certain days, not exceeding the total accumulated time of all such delays, after the builder has given notice to the buyer of any *force majeure* event.[98] The burden of proof is upon the builder to show that such an event has occurred and it is within the clause.

Most common events include act of God, fire, flood, hurricanes, storms or other weather conditions not included in normal planning, earthquakes, intervention of government authorities, war, blockade, strikes, lockouts, labour shortage, explosions, shortage of materials, defects in materials, machinery, equipment (which could reasonably be expected by the builder to be delivered), delays in transportation, delays in the builder's other commitments. There is a sweeping up provision at the end of the clause providing: '. . . or due to other causes or accidents beyond the control of the builder, its sub-contractors or supplier of the nature whether or not indicated by the foregoing words, irrespective of whether or not these events could be foreseen at the day of signing this contract.'

Industrial action during the building of a ship is the most common incident of delay. However, as the builder may sometimes be able to control the happening of strikes and labour disturbances, this incident may become the cause of a dispute between the builder and the buyer, if the latter considers that the event does not come within the protection of the *force majeure* clause. For example, if the builder acted unreasonably in dealing with the workforce and, therefore, failed to prevent

---

97 [2007] EWCA Civ 58.

98 For details of *force majeure* and shipbuilding contracts, see McKendrick, E (ed), *Force Majeure and Frustration of Contract*, 2nd edn, 1995, LLP, Chapter 7 (by Curtis), particularly, as to the effect of *force majeure* events, and his comments on the lack of clarity in Art VIII of the SAJ form about the extent of delay.

the strike or mitigate its consequences, it will not be regarded as being beyond his control.[99]

With regard to shortage of materials or equipment, the clause restricts the protection of the builder to circumstances in which the builder at the time of ordering could reasonably expect their delivery. Failing delivery, despite the builder's reasonable conduct in ordering from a certain supplier in whom the builder could reasonably rely and expect timely delivery, the question is whether the builder would be obliged to buy in from other sources. Were he obliged to do so, should he do so, instead of relying on the *force majeure* clause, even if the price was much dearer? The House of Lord has held in a non-shipping case that, provided a shortage of supply has been proved, the defendants were entitled to rely on the clause, notwithstanding the existence of an alternative source of supply. But, a mere increase in price would not be sufficient to establish a shortage in supply.[100]

The clause, in para 4 of Art VIII of the SAJ form, provides that the buyer may or may not elect to cancel the contract if the delay exceeds beyond a certain period.[101]

Invariably, a *force majeure* event has a knock-on effect, so that delay of completion of one vessel caused by *force majeure*, may affect completion of other vessels, as was shown in the following case.

Matsoukis v Priestman[102]

The defendants agreed to build and deliver a steamer to the plaintiff on or before 28 February 1913. The contract contained the following exceptions clause: 'If the said steamer is not delivered entirely ready to purchaser at the above mentioned time, the builders hereby agree to pay to the purchaser for liquidated damages, and not by way of penalty, the sum of 10 pounds Sterling for each day of delay and in deduction of the price stipulated in this contract, being excepted only the cause of *force majeure*, and/or strikes of workmen of the building yard where the vessel is being built, or the workshops where the machinery is being made, or at the works where steel is being manufactured for the steamer, or any works of any sub-contractor.'

As a result of a general coal strike of 1912, the works from which the defendants obtained their materials for other ships they were building got behind. The ship in turn to be built, before the plaintiff's ship, occupied the berth much longer than otherwise she would have done. The same berth was intended to be occupied by the plaintiff's ship. Consequently, the plaintiff's steamer was late in being laid down. The steamer having been delivered after the contract date, the plaintiff claimed damages.

The court held that the general dislocation of the business of the defendants and of those from whom they obtained materials operating indirectly on the completion of the plaintiff's steamer, by preventing the completion of the vessel prior in turn,

---

99 *Channel Island Ferries Ltd v Sealink Ltd* [1988] 1 Lloyd's Rep 323 (CA).
100 *Tennants (Lancashire) Ltd v CS Wilson and Co Ltd* [1917] AC 495.
101 *Harland & Wolff Ltd v Lakeport Navigation Co Panama SA* [1974] 1 Lloyd's Rep 301.
102 [1915] 1 KB 681.

constituted a case of *force majeure* within the meaning of the exceptions clause and, therefore, excused the defendants in respect of the delay so caused.

It further held that, apart from delay due to bad weather, the delay due to breakdown of machinery was covered by the exception of *force majeure*.

10.5 Effect of buyer's rescission for builder's default; imbalance of remedies

It can be observed from Art X (buyer's rescission) and Art XI (builder's rescission) of the SAJ form, as well as from the equivalent provisions of the AWES form (cll 10 and 11 respectively), that there is an imbalance of contractual remedies between the buyer and the builder. Upon rescission by the buyer for builder's default, the buyer is only entitled to a refund of all instalments paid in advance, plus interest, and is discharged from any further obligations. But the contract expressly excludes any claim in damages for losses incurred. The builder, on the other hand, has a contractual right to claim damages for loss of profit due to buyer's default, or damages that he would have had at common law. The Norwegian form is silent about this issue, so presumably the parties' rights at common law are preserved.

The refund to the buyer must be paid promptly. The refund guarantee is construed as a first demand guarantee, and the obligation is expressed to be an irrevocable and unconditional undertaking. The words 'subject to arbitration' in cl 11 did not make the buyer's option under this clause to make a demand under the refund guarantee.[103]

Apart from the refund that the buyer is entitled to claim, the effect of the buyer's rescission is to terminate the parties' further primary obligations under the contract. If the buyer has provided supplies, they presumably remain the property of the buyer and are therefore returnable, unless the contract stipulates otherwise.

In the event that title in the vessel has passed to the buyer, if the contract provided that it would pass in stages during the building after payment of the first instalment, the buyer has two options: (i) either to re-vest the title in the builder upon reimbursement of the pre-paid instalments; or (ii) to remove the ship from the yard and terminate the builder's contractual entitlement to continue the completion of the ship. If the builder is in liquidation, however, this issue will have to be decided in accordance with the *lex situs*.[104]

In some contracts, it may be provided that the buyer has the right to complete the building work at his own risk and expense. Such a clause usually provides that the buyer has the option, by giving notice to the builder, to take possession of the vessel in its unfinished state and complete the vessel in accordance with the contract and the specification, whether at the builder's yard or elsewhere, at the owner's option. If such option is exercised, the instalments provided for in the contract remained due, but subject to the right of the owner to set off liquidated

---

103 *Gold Coast Ltd v Caja de Ahorros del Mediterraneo & others* [2002] 1 Lloyd's Rep 617, CA (buyer declared builder in default for delay in delivery under terms of the contract).

104 op cit, Curtis, fn 1, p 164.

damages already accrued; and also subject to the builder being liable to pay, on demand, the excess of the costs of completion over the amounts of the outstanding instalments. So it was held by the Court of Appeal in *BMBF (No 12) Ltd v Harland & Wolff Shipbuilding & Heavy Industries Ltd;*[105] the court further held that the entitlement of the owner under such a clause is linked to a positive obligation to complete the ship in accordance with the contract and, thus, the owner was liable to pay the instalments due, if the cost of completing the ship was less than the outstanding instalments including the delivery instalment.

In the light of the risk involved for the buyer in case of rescission and the contractual prohibition against claiming his losses, which may inevitably be loss of bargain, or expenses thrown away, the buyer manages those risks by obtaining insurance cover in the event of delayed delivery or cancellation of the contract.

10.6 Can specific performance be ordered?

Specific performance is a discretionary remedy under English law when a party to a contract does not wish to bring the contract to an end by exercising his option to rescind the contract for breach by the other party. He may seek, therefore, to obtain a remedy of specific performance ordered by the court or tribunal, particularly when an award in damages would not be an adequate remedy to compensate the victim of the breach.[106] Such remedy is available under s 52 of the SOGA 1979 and applies to sale of ascertained goods. The ship under construction, although not yet completed, is ascertainable, insofar as the agreement provides for the end product. It concerns the sale of a future ship and the order of specific performance would be relevant only to the extent that it would be possible for it to be completed for delivery to take place. In this context, therefore, an order for specific performance obtained by the buyer may be useless, if the builder has been unable to complete for financial reasons and his company is in liquidation. Even if he is not in liquidation, there may be problems of enforcing such a court order, if the building is taking place in a foreign yard. Usually, an order for specific performance would not be granted where the remedy required detailed supervision by the courts.

In *Gyllenhammar & Partners Int Ltd v Sour Brodogradevna Split,*[107] the defendants (builders) entered into a shipbuilding contract with the plaintiffs (buyers) which was subject, inter alia, to the defendants declaring by telex to the buyer that all necessary permissions and approvals had been obtained. The approvals were to be obtained within 30 days of signing the contract, without which, the contract would be null and void, unless otherwise agreed by both parties. On failing to obtain the necessary approvals, the defendants notified the plaintiffs asserting that the contract had become null and void. The plaintiffs sued them arguing that the defendants were debarred from relying on this clause because, in

---

105 [2001] 2 Lloyd's Rep 227.
106 *The Ore Chief* [1983] 2 Lloyd's Rep 509.
107 [1989] 2 Lloyd's Rep 403.

their view, the necessary approvals were not obtained by reason of (i) the defendants' non-compliance with this clause, and (ii) the defendants' failure to use their best endeavours to obtain the necessary permission. They claimed specific performance of the contract, or damages in lieu of that.

Holding that the defendants were entitled to rely on the clause, the court went on to examine the plaintiff's request for specific performance (merely for academic purposes). Hirst J said:

> Here, I need say no more than that the voluminous specification shows that this is a very complex contract requiring extensive co-operation between the parties on a number of matters, in particular modifications, optional variations, and, perhaps most important of all, matters of detail (some by no means unimportant) left undefined in the specification. In my judgment, these factors, coupled with the consideration that the work would take place in a foreign yard outside the court's jurisdiction, would tell strongly against an order for specific performance being in principle appropriate in the present case.[108]

11 INSURANCE AND MANAGEMENT OF RISKS

Unless otherwise agreed in the contract, the builder retains property and risk in the ship until delivery. Even if property is agreed to pass to the buyer gradually during the stages of construction, the risk of total loss of the ship in the yard remains with the builder. He has an insurable interest to insure the ship for damage or loss during construction, under a shipbulders' all risks policy on the vessel, either as owner, or as bailee as the case may be. He has a duty under the contract to insure. The buyer will be a co-assured and he should be named as an additional assured in the policy.

The insurance may be the other way round, and the buyer may be required by the building contract to include the builder as co-assured. It is very important for risk management purposes, not only as regards the builder but also the insurance broker, that the builder is named in the category of 'additional assureds', as this recent case demonstrates.

Talbot Underwriting Ltd v Nausch Hogan & Murray Inc (The Jascon 5)[109]

Shipowners (C) placed a contract with a shipyard (S) for completion works to a vessel. The contract provided that the yard would be responsible to C and idemnify C for any losses or damage. C instructed N to obtain a shipbuilders' all risks policy of insurance on the vessel's hull and machinery in respect of the period of the completion work on behalf of various interested parties, including S as co-assured. Forty per cent of the risk was placed on the London market but S was not named as a co-assured in the London policy. The vessel sustained damage in drydock. The damage was repaired by S, who made a claim under the insurance against the London insurers. The claim was rejected on the basis that S was not one of the assureds. S claimed against C and N for failing to procure the necessary insurance.

---

108 [1989] 2 Lloyd's Rep 403, p 422.
109 [2006] 2 Lloyd's Rep 195.

S and C settled their claim and assigned their rights to the London market insurers (T) who agreed to pay a sum to S and C. T brought proceedings in the names of S and C against N for breach of duty of care. N's defence was that S was a co-assured under the policy, either because it was an 'additional assured' or because it was entitled to enforce the policy as C's undisclosed principal, and that in any event neither C nor S had suffered any loss as a result of the failure to include S as a named co-assured. The judge rejected those contentions.

On appeal by the brokers, it was held that the clause in question was not intended to embody a self-contained provision providing for the extension of the policy to persons other than those referred to in the section dealing with the assured. The parties presumably had an 'additional assureds' clause in mind, but none had been identified or included. On true construction of the policy, S was not an assured. The question whether S could sue as undisclosed principal depended on whether T had demonstrated unwillingness to contract with anyone other than the person or persons identified as the assureds in the slip. The omission of any reference to S or its subcontractors in the slip was not neutral, but had to be regarded as a positive indication that T were not willing to contract with them. Accordingly, both S and C had suffered loss from N's failure to include S as a co-assured under the policy.

The buyer can also insure separately for other risks in the event of rescission of the contract and the consequential losses, which he will be unable to recover from the builder, if a claim for damages at large is excluded, as is normally the case under shipbuilding contracts. Most importantly, the buyer should obtain cover for any latent defects in the ship which may be discovered after the guarantee period and which will be excluded from the obligation of the builder under his guarantee to correct them, as was shown earlier in *The Seta Maru*.

12 MANUFACTURER'S OR BUILDER'S LIABILITY TO THIRD PARTIES FOR DEFECTIVE PRODUCTS

English law is well settled with regard to liability of a manufacturer in tort for physical injury on the one hand, and for pure economic loss to remote owners of chattels on the other hand. With regard to loss resulting from the physical damage to property caused by construction defects in a ship, the manufacturer or shipyard will be joined as a third party in proceedings brought against the owner of the ship for an indemnity with regard to the loss or damages caused to the property of a third party.[110]

With regard to pure economic loss claims, the House of Lords, in *Murphy v Brentwood DC*,[111] re-examined the principles. In this case, the claim was brought in tort by the purchaser of a defective building against the Council which had approved the plans of the building before construction. It was concluded that

---

110 See, for example, *The Manchester Courage* [1973] 1 Lloyd's Rep 386.
111 [1991] 1 AC 398.

remote purchasers of a defective building had no claim in tort for economic loss against the Council.

In particular, Lord Bridge stated the principle:[112]

> If a manufacturer negligently puts into circulation a chattel containing a latent defect which renders it dangerous to persons or property, the manufacturer, on the well-known principles established by *Donoghue v Stevenson* [1932] AC 562, will be liable in tort for injury to persons or damage to property which the chattel causes. But, if a manufacturer produces and sells a chattel which is merely defective in quality, even to the extent that it is valueless for the purpose for which it is intended, the manu-facturer's liability at common law arises only under and, by reference to the terms of any contract to which he is a party in relation to the chattel, the common law does not impose on him any liability in tort to persons to whom he owes no duty in contract but who, having acquired the chattel, suffer economic loss because the chattel is defective in quality. If a dangerous defect in a chattel is discovered before it causes any personal injury or damage to property, because the danger is now known and the chattel cannot safely be used unless the defect is repaired, the defect becomes merely a defect in quality. The chattel is either capable of repair at eco-nomic cost, or it is worthless and must be scrapped. In either case, the loss sus-tained by the owner or hirer of the chattel is purely economic. It is recoverable against any party who owes the loser a relevant contractual duty. But, it is not recoverable in tort in the absence of a special relationship of proximity imposing on the tortfeasor a duty of care to safeguard the plaintiff from economic loss. There is no such special relationship between the manufacturer of a chattel and a remote owner or hirer.

While there is a duty of care owed by a manufacturer or builder to third parties for a reasonably foreseeable physical injury to a person or property caused by a danger-ous defect in a chattel, with regard to economic loss, as a general rule, there is no such duty on the part of the manufacturer, unless there is a special relationship of proximity imposing a duty on the manufacturer to safeguard a third party from economic loss. A special relationship of proximity would exist, if the defendant had voluntarily assumed a responsibility to act in the matter by involving himself in the claimant's affairs, or by choosing to speak.[113] For example, in the celebrated case of *Hedley Byrne*,[114] the defendant chose to speak and was taken to have assumed responsibility from that fact alone. Reliance by the claimant on the defendant's act or advice would be relevant in determining whether there was an assumption of responsibility and causation.

How can these principles apply in the context of shipbuilding? There is no doubt that, if a dangerously defective part, such as an engine, of a new building (whether it be a ship or an aircraft), causes explosion resulting in death, it will give rise to tortious liability. If the ship, or aircraft, is not new, however, it will be a matter of evidence whether the dangerous equipment, which caused an accident, was due to bad maintenance or developed from a latent defect.

---

112 Ibid, p 475.

113 *White v Jones* [1995] 2 AC 207 (HL).

114 *Hedley Byrne & Co v Heller & Partners* [1963] 1 Lloyd's Rep 485 (HL).

Insofar as economic loss is concerned, the application of the principles is best explained by the decision of the Court of Appeal in the case below.

The Rebecca Elaine [115]

The claimants owned a number of fishing vessels and contracted with boat builders to build what became *The Rebecca Elaine*. Because of their good experience with Gardner engines, the appellants decided that the new vessel should be fitted with such an engine. The manufacturers did not sell engines direct and there was a chain of contracts between them and the boat builders. The new vessel was commissioned and her new Gardner engine was accompanied by a one-year manufacturer's warranty against defects in workmanship or material and a manual which stated that its 'pistons would run for 20,000 hours or more without dismantling and before replacement is necessary'.

Later, the manufacturers of the engine sold their business to the defendants in this action. The sale was of the entire undertaking, property and assets of the business as a going concern, together with the buyers' right to represent that they were carrying on the business in continuation of, and in succession to, the manufacturers. Two years after the building of the boat, the defendants began to receive reports that pistons in Gardner engines had broken or cracked before they should have done. The pistons concerned had all been manufactured by an independent contractor, Wellworthy Ltd. These pistons, as the judge found, were liable to fail after only about one third of the running time stated in the manual. On the judge's unchallenged finding, the defendants were on notice of a very real problem affecting the Wellworthy pistons which they realised might cause major engine failure, or worse. However, despite this knowledge the defendants chose not to warn those with engines fitted with such pistons, which the judge held they could have done by contacting known customers, authorised distributors and service agents, or by advertising in trade journals.

When *The Rebecca Elaine* was four miles south west of the Needles, the pistons failed prematurely and the engine seized. Fortunately, the vessel was towed to safety and the only loss was the damage to the engine itself, which cost £25,972 to repair, and loss of earnings, which the judge assessed at £21,344.

The claimants' case could not be made in contract since the warranty had expired and any claim against the boatbuilders would have been successfully met by an exclusion clause in the boatbuilding contract and/or the fact that the defendants did not rely on the boatbuilders' skill or judgment in the supply of the engine. The case against the defendants was put solely in negligence. The essence of the claimants' complaint was that, knowing there was a problem with the Wellworthy pistons, the defendants did nothing to warn operators/owners to carry out inspections more frequently, so as to confine any damage to the pistons themselves and avoid major engine failure of the kind suffered by *The Rebecca Elaine*.

The judge found that, if the defendants had been under a duty to warn, they were in breach of duty and that this was the cause of the claimants' loss because, if they had been given a warning, they would have acted on it.

---

115 [1999] 2 Lloyd's Rep 1.

After a full review of the authorities, the judge concluded that, for the claimants to establish a duty of care owed to them by the defendants, they had to show a special relationship of proximity which involved both an assumption of responsibility by the defendants and reliance upon it by the claimants.

He held that the defendants had not assumed any responsibility to safeguard the claimants against suffering economic loss, although they might have assumed responsibility to avoid physical damage to persons or property.

The Court of Appeal approved the first instance decision and considered further whether in such cases there is duty to warn.

Tuckey LJ said:[116]

> Under English law I do not think that there is any basis for putting failure to warn of a known danger into a category of its own . . . My review of the authorities shows that the general rule is that a manufacturer in the position of the respondents owes no duty of care to avoid economic loss. Exceptionally, he may be under such a duty if he assumes responsibility to his customers in a situation, which is akin to contract. That duty may include a duty to warn, but it would be much more difficult to infer in the case of mere silence than in the case of misrepresentation.[117] Reliance by the customer is relevant to whether there has been an assumption of responsibility and essential as to causation.[118]

This chapter examined the principles of construction and sale of new ships. The next chapter deals with the sale of second hand ships. Although the core principles of sale of goods, as seen in this chapter, apply, there are, inevitably, different obligations upon the seller of an already used ship.

---

116 [1999] 2 Lloyd's Rep 1, pp 6, 7.

117 *Banque Keyser Ullman SA v Scandia (UK) Insurance* [1988] 2 Lloyd's Rep 514 (CA): the court had to consider whether the underwriter of the defendant (insurers), who knew that a broker had issued a false cover note to the plaintiff bank, owed a duty of care to warn the bank which lent large sums of money on the security of the cover. Slade LJ, giving the judgment of the court, said, at p 559: 'Can a mere failure to speak ever give rise to liability in negligence under *Hedley Byrne* principles? In our view it can, but subject to the all important proviso that there has been, on the facts, a voluntary assumption of responsibility in the relevant sense and reliance on that assumption. These features may be much more difficult to infer in the case of mere silence than in the case of misrepresentation.'

118 In a Canadian case, *Can-Arc Helicopters v Textron*, cited by Tuckey LJ in *The Rebecca Elaine* [1995] 2 Lloyd's Rep 1, the British Columbia Supreme Court found the manufacturers liable for economic loss for a failure to give adequate warning of a defect in a service bulletin, which they knew their customers relied on.

CHAPTER 11

SHIP SALE AND PURCHASE CONTRACTS

1 INTRODUCTION

The sale and purchase of used ships involves various stages of preparation before a contract is signed and before delivery of the ship to the buyer takes place. These stages can be grouped into three main ones: the negotiations and contract stage; the inspections stage; and the completion stage.

At the negotiation stage, which is usually carried out by brokers appointed by the respective parties (buyer and seller), there will be telex exchanges with the seller's brokers making an invitation to offer. The parties are mainly concerned initially with the price, the particulars of the ship and lay-days, to decide whether the transaction is worthwhile. Price bargaining and negotiations of the main terms of the contract usually follow this initial approach, which may be prolonged or may be quick-fire exchanges between professional brokers, having experience of many previous dealings and commercial knowledge of the trade. If the parties agree on the basic terms, a recap telex recapitulating the terms discussed is exchanged, being made subject to details to be agreed later. A large number of negotiations can, therefore, be split into negotiation and agreement of the main terms, followed by a similar process regarding details. The 'main terms' and 'details' are, usually, separated by the recap telex setting out the main terms agreed. The question often arises, as will be seen later, whether or not there is a contract at the time of the recap telex.[1] In this respect, the role and experience of the brokers engaged are crucial.

Provided the details are agreed, which may involve numerous back and forth communications, a formal contract for the sale of the ship is later drawn up. This is known as the Memorandum of Agreement (MOA), which usually incorporates a standard form contract like the Norwegian Sale Form, otherwise known as the NSF. Sometimes, the final agreement of the parties may be made conditional upon the drawing or the incorporation of the sale form. Invariably, the contract may still be subject to certain details such as obtaining approvals from directors or shareholders, or licences, or being subject to satisfactory inspection and other checks. It will be seen later in more detail that these 'subjects' indicate that the parties intend to have a conditional contract.

A deposit of 10% of the agreed price is paid by the buyer to commit him to the contract, which is held at an escrow account in the joint names of the parties.

The inspections stage involves: first, the inspection of documents, such as the ship's class records, certificates of compliance with regulations, etc; and second, the physical inspection of the ship afloat, as provided for in the contract, by the buyer or his representative surveyor. The physical inspection is usually a superficial one

---

1   See Jamieson, A, *Shipbrokers and the Law*, 1997, LLP.

of the ship and its logbook, unless the parties have agreed otherwise. After inspection, the buyer may confirm his commitment to buy by accepting the ship, or he may refuse her.

The third stage, known as the completion stage, involves pre-delivery matters, including inspection of underwater parts by the classification society,[2] delivery of documents, and the physical delivery of the ship upon payment of the balance of the contract price. There are also post-delivery matters to be taken care of at this stage.

Documents and physical delivery usually occur at different places, depending on where the ship is. The final inspection in drydock, at the port of delivery, is conducted by the surveyor of the classification society, who checks the ship's bottom and underwater parts, so that a clean certificate of class can be given. He may recommend some repairs to be effected at the seller's expense before delivery. Sometimes, in lieu of a drydock inspection, the buyer may appoint a diver, approved by the classification society, to carry out the underwater inspection while the ship is afloat.

The MOA specifies the procedures necessary for the closing meeting. The necessary documents are prepared. Such documents include: the closing memo, minutes of a meeting of the seller's directors and shareholders, a certificate of good standing, power of attorney, the bill of sale, certificate of class, any consents or licences required by Government authority, and a certificate by the registrar of the ship's registry permitting the sale. The seller must also arrange for the deletion of his name from the registry and the deletion of the ship from her existing flag, if the buyer wishes to change flag. He also cancels the insurance cover, pays off the mortgage and other debts, and arranges for the repatriation of his crew from the vessel. When the seller is ready, he serves an advance notice of delivery, Notice of Readiness, on the buyer. If the ship is, indeed, ready, the buyer arranges for payment of bunkers and stores on board, as has been agreed, and instructs his bank, or financial institution, to make arrangements for payment on the actual delivery date.

These broad three stages are examined in turn under Sections A, B and C.

SECTION A: THE NEGOTIATIONS AND CONTRACT STAGE

2 THE MAKING OF THE CONTRACT AND GOOD FAITH

Unlike non-common law systems, which recognise and enforce an overriding principle of good faith in both the making and during the performance of contracts, there is no such principle under English law. Bingham LJ, (as he then was) in

---

2   The role of the classification societies is to ensure that the ship inspected complies with the structural rules of the society and will not be a danger to life or property at sea. Regular surveys of ships entered with a society aim to enhance safety by making recommendations for repairs. Rules and technical standards vary from society to society, but societies which are members of the IACS apply, by and large, similar practices. Since the 1st edition of this book, efforts have been made through IACS to make these rules more uniform.

Interfoto Picture Library Ltd v Stiletto Visual Programmes Ltd[3] (concerning the validity of a power granted under a purported power of attorney), contrasted the two systems, thus:

> In many civil law systems, and perhaps in most legal systems outside the common law world, the law of obligations recognises and enforces an overriding principle that, in making and carrying out contracts, parties should act in good faith. This does not simply mean that they should not deceive each other, a principle which any legal system must recognise; its effect is perhaps most aptly conveyed by such metaphorical colloquialisms as 'playing fair', 'coming clean' or 'putting one's cards face upwards on the table'. It is in essence a principle of fair and open dealing . . . English law has, characteristically, committed itself to no such overriding principle, but has developed piecemeal solutions in response to demonstrated problems of unfairness. Many examples could be given. Thus, equity has intervened to strike down unconscionable bargains. Parliament has stepped in to regulate the imposition of exemption clauses and the form of certain hire purchase agreements. The common law has also made its contribution by holding that certain classes of contract require the utmost good faith, by treating as revocable what purports to be agreed estimates of damage but are, in truth, a disguised penalty for breach, and in many other ways.

In a later case, *Walford v Miles*,[4] the House of Lords confirmed in stronger terms that good faith during the negotiation stage of a contract is not compatible with the adversarial position of the parties:

> . . . the concept of a duty to carry on negotiations in good faith is inherently repugnant to the adversarial position of the parties when involved in negotiations. Each party to the negotiations is entitled to pursue his (or her) own interest, so long as he avoids making misrepresentations, and to advance those interests they must be entitled, if they think it appropriate, to threaten to withdraw from further negotiations, or to withdraw in fact, in the hope that the opposite party might seek to reopen the negotiations by offering improved terms.

If one party has, however, undertaken to use his best, or reasonable, endeavours to negotiate an agreement with the other party in good faith, it is possible to infer a collateral contract. Then, the good faith aspect will have a legal effect representing an undertaking.[5] If the party who undertook to negotiate in good faith withdraws, his withdrawal may amount to a breach of that collateral contract, hence – subject to issues of causation – he may be liable to the other party in damages.

However, this is distinguishable from a clause providing purely for each party to 'use its reasonable endeavours' to do what is necessary and to carry out the intent and effect of the agreement. Any attempt to imply a term of good faith into the contract would not succeed, because it would be inconsistent with the express terms.[6]

---

3   [1988] 1 All ER 348, pp 352–53.
4   [1992] 2 AC 128, p 138.
5   *The Mercedes Envoy* [1995] 2 Lloyd's Rep 559, p 565.
6   *Bernhard Schulte GmbH & Co KG v Nile Holdings Ltd* [2004] 2 Lloyd's Rep 352.

3 THE PARTIES' OBLIGATION TO AVOID MISREPRESENTATIONS

There is no general duty of disclosure, and the parties are free to make their own investigations about each other's position and the ship intended to be purchased. The *caveat emptor* principle applies in this respect,[7] which means 'let the buyer beware', before he enters into a transaction of purchasing property. But *caveat emptor* will not protect a seller if he has done a dishonest act before exchange of contracts for sale of property.[8] There are statutory controls to prevent the seller from inducing the buyer to enter into the contract by making material representations which he knows are not true. Under the old doctrine of *caveat emptor*, and before controls were brought by statutory law as to implied terms of quality of goods and fitness for purpose and as to misrepresentations, the buyer could not recover from the seller for defects on the property. The only exception was if the seller actively concealed defects that were not obvious. Now, statutory law provides for implied warranties of fitness and satisfactory quality, and forbids misrepresentations, but beyond that a buyer must take care to make his own investigations about the property.

Statements or assurances made during negotiations leading to a contract may be either 'terms', which form the express terms of the contract, or 'statements', which are not intended to be part of the contract, but help to induce the contract. If they are untrue, they are misrepresentations. Mere 'puffs', as, for example, when the broker makes a comment that, if he had the money he would buy that ship, would be so vague as to be without effect.

Depending on whether an untrue statement became a contractual term, or whether it was only intended to induce the innocent party to enter into the contract, and it did so, different remedies are available to the innocent party.

3.1 Untrue statements forming express terms of the contract

If an untrue statement is made an express term of the contract, it will result in a breach of contract. The innocent party may either rescind the contract or claim damages and, depending on the breach, he may elect for both. Unlike the situation of a misrepresentation, which is not part of the contract (see below), the claim for damages on the ground of an untrue statement forming an express term of the contract does not depend on fraud or negligence. If the term is fundamental, or the

---

7   The principle of *caveat emptor* does not apply to the making of a partnership agreement, and each party has a duty to disclose all material facts of which he has knowledge and of which the other negotiating parties might not be aware: *Conlon v Simms* [2006] EWCA Civ 1749; *caveat emptor* does not apply to insurance contracts which are contracts of uberrima fides; but, as to opinions or honest belief, see *Economides v Commercial Union Assurance Co plc* [1998] Lloyd's Rep IR 9: an honest representation of belief in an insurance context must have some basis, but there is no implied representation that there exist reasonable grounds for making it. If insurers wish their clients to obtain independent valuations of their goods, then that must be made a term of the contract.

8   *Taylor v Hamer* [2003] 1 P & CR DG 6, distinguished in *Sykes v Taylor-Rose* [2004] 2 P & CR 30.

seriousness of its breach goes to the root of the contract, the innocent party may treat the contract as repudiated by the other party and elect to terminate it, as well as claim damages.

3.2 Mere representation inducing the contract

By s 2(1) of the Misrepresentation Act (MA) 1967, where a person has entered into a contract after a misrepresentation has been made to him by the other party and as a result he has suffered loss, the person making the misrepresentation would be liable in damages, as if the misrepresentation were made fraudulently, unless he proves that he had reasonable ground[9] for believing, and did believe up to the time the contract was made, that the facts represented were true. Where there is room for exercise of judgment by the other party, a misrepresentation ought not to be too easily found. The test is whether the representation was substantially correct. For a representation to have induced the contract, there must be material contribution to the decision made by the other party, not just mere support or encouragement.[10]

In the present context, for example, an issue may arise concerning the effect of a representation made by the seller's agent that the vessel is in class. Would that be a representation as to the condition of the vessel? It was held by Phillips J in *The Morning Watch*[11] that such a representation amounted to no more than a statement of the classification status of the vessel, and did not constitute any implicit representation by the maker as to the actual condition of the vessel. (The class records are inspected by the buyer anyway at the inspection stage.)

Under s 2(2) of the MA 1967, the innocent party would have a right to rescission in lieu of damages, if he entered into the contract in reliance upon an innocent or negligent misrepresentation. The right to rescission may be lost if the innocent party, upon learning of the misrepresentation, declares to perform the contract, or actually performs some act from which such an intention can be inferred, or where he fails to rescind for a considerable time after discovering the falsity.

Apart from the case of fraudulent misrepresentation, the court is given power by s 2(2) to grant damages in lieu of rescission, if it is equitable to do so having regard to the nature of the misrepresentation, the loss that would be caused if the contract were upheld, and the loss that the rescission would cause to the other party. On the other hand, where the misrepresentation was fraudulent and, as a result of it, the innocent party entered into the contract, the remedy will be both damages and rescission. The principle of measure of damages in such a case is that

---

9   The absolute obligation, imposed under the Act, not to state facts which the representor could not show he had reasonable grounds for believing in their truth was stressed in *Howard Marine & Dredging Co Ltd v Ogden & Sons (Excavations) Ltd* [1978] 2 WLR 515. The capacity of barges was misrepresented by the barge-owner before a charterparty was concluded. The charterer had a right in damages under the Act.

10   *Royscot Trust v Rogerson* [1991] 2 QB 297 (CA); *Avon Insurance v Swire Fraser* [2000] 1 All ER 573.

11   [1990] 1 Lloyd's Rep 547. For an interesting decision on negligent misstatement and other issues relating to a shipbuilding conversion and statements as to 'plate thickess' required, see *Kellog Brown Inc v Concordia Maritime AG and others* [2006] EWHC 3358, [2006] All ER 349 referring to principles of interpretation of contracts as set by leading authorities.

the claimant must be put in the same position he would have been in, had the tort not been committed. In other words, had the misrepresentation not been made, the particular contract would not have been entered into, as it was held on the facts of *The Siben (No 2)*.[12] The recoverable loss is the loss directly caused by the misrepresentation, whether it was foreseeable or not (being subject to mitigation).[13]

In the event that someone other than the contracting party or his agent makes the misrepresentation, the innocent party will not be able to rely on the statutory protection afforded by the above MA 1967. His remedy, however, will lie at common law in damages, if he can establish that the person who made the misrepresentation owed a duty of care to him by reason of a special relationship that existed between them. For a special relationship to exist, in accordance with the negligent misstatement principle, under *Hedley Byrne v Heller & Partners*,[14] three requirements must be fulfilled: (i) that the innocent party relied on the skill and judgment of the representor that he would make careful inquiries; (ii) that the representor knew, or ought reasonably to have known, that the innocent party was relying on his advice or representation; and (iii) that it was reasonable in the circumstances for the innocent party to rely on the representor.

Alternatively, he may sue the other party on the ground of the tort of deceit (see *The Kriti Palm*, distinguishing deceit from mere fallibility).[15]

3.3 Brokers' role and risk management

Brokers play a significant role in the negotiations and will use their skills and persuasion to conclude a contract on best terms for their principals. They must be aware, however, of their potential exposure to liability for misrepresentation, if they overstep the mark in their excitement to conclude the contract and induce the other party by false statements. A broker owes a duty of care to his principal. Unless a special relationship of the Hedley Byrne type exists between the broker and the third party, the broker does not owe a duty of care to the latter. However, in the event that the buyer is induced to enter into the contract having relied on a misrepresentation made by the seller's broker about the ship, the broker's principal will suffer loss, if the buyer chooses to rescind the contract or claim damages. The principal could claim damages against his broker to recover his loss, if the latter, without the authority of his principal, gave untrue information about the ship in order to induce the contract.

If the broker is a sole broker for both seller and buyer, he will be in a precarious situation of conflict of interest, as he will owe a duty of care to both principals. In

---

12 *The Siben (No 2)* [1996] 1 Lloyd's Rep 35.

13 *Smith New Court Securities v Citibank* [1997] AC 254 (HL).

14 [1963] 1 Lloyd's Rep 485 (HL).

15 *AIC Limited v ITS Testing Service (UK) Limited (The Kriti Palm)* [2005] EWHC 2122 (Comm), by Cresswel J: 'The representation that "the certificate (which stated 'Fuel meets Specification') was and remained a good and valid certificate", was a false representation made by Mr Lucas who was reckless as to its truth', but was reversed by the CA: [2007] 1 Lloyd's Rep 555, which held that there was no deceit; more muddle and fallibility than fraud.

such circumstances the principles applicable to insurance brokers would apply.[16] It is beyond the scope of this book to unravel these issues here.

Another issue which is of importance to brokers' liability is liability arising from a broker having exceeded the limits of his authority. Agency principles have been examined elsewhere in this book,[17] but it is important to note in this context the parameters of authority as set out by Lord Goff in *The Ocean Frost*.[18]

Briefly, the buyers (the plaintiffs) had appointed a broker to negotiate the purchase of *The Ocean Frost* from the sellers, the defendants, on the basis that the ship was to be chartered back to the defendants. The chartering manager of the sellers accepted a bribe from the broker and told him that he had authority to complete the agreement for the sale with a three-year charter. The sale was completed and the sellers became the charterers. Believing that they had a 12-month charter, the charterers redelivered the ship at the end of the period. The plaintiffs claimed breach of contract. It was held that the chartering manager exceeded his authority; he did not have any general authority to enter into a three-year charter party, and he could not, in the absence of any representation by the defendants as to his authority, reasonably believe to have specific authority to notify the other contracting party that the defendants' consent had been obtained and thereafter to complete the agreement. An employer whose servant, having made a fraudulent representation which has caused loss to an innocent party contracting with him, could be liable to bear the loss by reason of having, by words or conduct, induced the innocent party to believe that the servant was acting in the course of the employer's business. Such circumstances did not exist where such belief, although present, had been brought about through misguided reliance on the servant himself, in particular: when the servant was not authorised to do what he was purporting to do; when what he was purporting to do was not within the class of acts that an employee in his position was usually authorised to do; and when the employer had done nothing to represent that the servant was authorised to do it. Accordingly, the defendants were not vicariously liable for the chartering manager's deceit.

This result, obviously, causes injustice to the innocent party, whose remedy must then lie against the broker and the managing charterer of the seller personally. The peculiar fact in this case was that the chartering manager of the seller had a senior position, vice-president, in the seller's company, but the buyer's broker offered the bribe!

This decision, however, alerts both buyers and sellers to the fact that they must exercise great care in choosing their representatives in sale and chartering transactions and in making the boundaries of their authority very clear.

Brokers protect themselves for risks under a special insurance cover for errors and omissions, or under mutual liability insurance for professional negligence, as well as for risks arising from breach of warranty of authority, but not for fraudulent conduct.

---

16 The court has condemned a broker for acting in a dual capacity in a manner contrary to the interests of his principal, in this case the assured: *Vesta v Butcher* [1989] 1 Lloyd's Rep 331 (HL); see, also, *Anglo-African Merchants v Bayley* [1970] 1 QB 311 and *Eagle Star Insurance Co v Spratt* [1971] 2 Lloyd's Rep 116.

17 See Chapter 8, para 4.3.

18 *Armagas Ltd v Mundogas SA (The Ocean Frost)* [1986] AC 717; see further Chapter 12 para 3.2.1 employers' liability for wrongful acts of employees.

4 ON THE MAKING OF A BINDING CONTRACT AND RISK MANAGEMENT

4.1 Express your intention clearly

The negotiations stage is the stage during which the parties must exercise care and prevent possible risks, either of not having a firm agreement, or of being found bound to an agreement to which they did not yet wish to be bound.

Generally, in all contractual transactions, the court looks for a firm offer and an unconditional acceptance in determining whether or not a binding contract exists between the parties. It examines the intention of the parties from what they said and the surrounding circumstances.

The striking feature of sale and purchase transactions is that, sometimes, the brokers may have expressed themselves as if there was a final agreement but, upon true construction of their telex exchanges, it may transpire that either one or both parties did not objectively have such an intention. For example, they may not have completed the agreement because they have not agreed some details, or the terms may not have been sufficiently certain. If parts of the agreement, which are considered important by the parties, are left for further negotiations, or are so ambiguous that the ambiguity cannot be resolved by reference to the rest of the contract, the court or arbitrator will not complete an incomplete bargain by adding what might be considered reasonable. Conversely, if both parties believe that there is an agreement, when they have had previous dealings and have left out what would be considered by them as familiar gaps, the court will not destroy a commercial bargain.[19]

The general principles to be applied in deciding whether there has been a concluded contract were summarised by Cresswell J, in *The Bay Ridge*,[20] as derived mainly from the judgments of Bingham and Lloyd LJJ in **Pagnan SPA v Feed Products Ltd**.[21] It is important to set out extracts from the summary for guidance particularly to brokers:

1   The court's task is to review what the parties said and did and from that material to infer whether the parties' objective intentions as expressed to each other were to enter into a mutually binding contract. The court is not concerned with what the parties may subjectively have intended.

2   There will be some cases where continued negotiations after a contract has

---

19   See also Goldrein, I (ed), *Ship Sale and Purchase*, 4th edn, 2003, LLP, Chapter 2.

20   [1999] 2 Lloyd's Rep 227, p 240. This case is very important from the point of view of risk management, in terms of choosing an experienced broker for the negotiations and a good solicitor for the litigation, if things have gone wrong. The judge's comments in this respect are very interesting; see facts of this case under para 4.4, below.

21   [1987] 2 Lloyd's Rep 601 (CA), pp 610, 611, 619. With regard to relevant principles of the modern approach to interpretation of contracts see further leading decisions: *Investors Compensation Scheme v West Bromwich Building Society* [1998] 1 WLR 896, per Lord Hoffman; *BCCI v Ali* [2002] 1 AC 251, per Lords Hoffman and Bingham; *The Tychy* [2001] 2 Lloyd's Rep 403, per Lord Phillips MR; *Sirius International Insurance Co. v FAI General Insurance Ltd* [2004] UKHL 54, per Lord Steyn. There has been a shift from literal methods of interpretation towards a more commercial approach.

allegedly been made will lead to the inference that the parties never in truth intended to bind themselves ... This will more obviously be so where a term raised by one or other party early in the negotiations had not been the subject of agreement at the time of the alleged contract.

3   Where the parties have not reached agreement on terms which they regard as essential to a binding agreement, it naturally follows that there can be no binding agreement until they do agree on those terms ... But just as it is open to parties by their words and conduct to make clear that they do not intend to be bound until certain terms are agreed, even if those terms (objectively viewed) are of relatively minor significance, the converse is also true. The parties may by their words and conduct make it clear that they do intend to be bound, even though there are other terms yet to be agreed, even terms which may often or usually be agreed before a binding contract is made ... The parties are to be regarded as masters of their contractual fate. It is their intentions which matter and to which the court must strive to give effect.

4   Even if the parties have reached agreement on all the terms of the proposed contract, nevertheless they may intend that the contract shall not become binding until some further condition has been fulfilled. That is the ordinary 'subject to contract' case. Alternatively, they may intend that the contract shall not become binding until some further term or terms have been agreed ... Conversely, the parties may intend to be bound forthwith even though there are further terms still to be agreed or some further formality to be fulfilled ... If the parties fail to reach agreement on such further terms, the existing contract is not invalidated unless the failure to reach agreement on such further terms renders the contract as a whole unworkable or void for uncertainty.

5   The relevant principles of the law of contract are of universal application, but the proper inference to draw may differ widely according to the facts of the particular case. One case may concern a protracted negotiation, perhaps conducted in writing through lawyers, between parties who have had no dealings of any kind before. Another may concern a series of quickfire exchanges between professionals, both of them practitioners of the same trade, both having had many previous dealings, and with a wide measure of common experience, knowledge, and understanding between them. One could not sensibly approach these cases in the same way. Inferences which it would be appropriate to draw in one case might be quite inappropriate in the other. But the court's task remains essentially the same: to discern and give effect to the objective intention of the parties.

6   The courts recognise that business terminology and practices may differ from one market to the next. The courts recognise the efficacy of the maritime variant of the well known 'subject to contract'. The expression 'subject to details' enables owners and charterers to know where they are in negotiations and to regulate their business accordingly. The assumption of those in the shipping trade that it is effective to make clear that there is no binding agreement at that stage ought to be respected.[22]

---

22   As in *The Junior K* [1988] 2 Lloyd's Rep 583, p 588, and *The CPC Gallia* [1994] 1 Lloyd's Rep 68, p 74.

4.2 The effect of non-signing a formal document upon the validity of the contract

Sometimes, an agreement may not be binding until a formal contract has been drawn up. It is, however, important for the parties to use phrases like 'subject to contract', to make it clear to the court and each other that they did not intend to be bound by a firm contract at that stage.

In *The Blankenstein*,[23] Goff LJ said:

> ... the court has to decide on the construction of the relevant documents, considered in the light of the surrounding circumstances, whether it was the intention of the parties that the negotiations were not to have contractual force until a formal document was signed.

In this case, the buyer's brokers entered into negotiations with the sellers for the purchase of three vessels, after which a contract was concluded containing all terms of the sale including the price of the vessels. The only detail that was left for a later stage was the name of the purchasing company which was to be nominated in due course. An MOA was drawn up in the NSF for and on behalf of the buyer yet to be nominated. The buyer was required to pay a deposit at 10% of the contract price. By cl 13 of the agreement, the sellers had a right to cancel the contract, and a right to keep the deposit if the purchase did not go through. The MOA was not signed, and later on, when the buyer's company was nominated, a new MOA was drawn up. By the cancelling date, the agreement was still not signed and no deposit had being paid. The sellers elected to treat the contract as repudiated by the buyers, claimed damages and retained the deposit.

It was held that there was a binding contract between the parties, irrespective of the fact that the MOA had not been signed. Fox LJ said:

> I see nothing in the present case to lead me to the conclusion that the parties contemplated the execution of the MOA as a prerequisite to the conclusion of a contract. That they contemplated and indeed agreed upon the execution of a written memorandum I accept. But that, of itself, is not conclusive. It is open to parties to agree to execute a formal document incorporating terms, which they have previously agreed. That is a binding contract. In the present case, on 8 July all the terms of the sale were agreed. And, it seems to me, that all the indications are that they were not intended to be subject to the execution of the memorandum.[24]

Similarly in *The Great Marine (No 2)*.[25] The sale was confirmed by a recap telex, which was not made subject to signing of the MOA. The price was agreed and the contract was to incorporate the terms of the standard form NSF 1987 in the MOA. The vessel was to be delivered on completion of her then voyage, but was delivered outside the agreed period. The buyers claimed damages for breach of contract. One of the issues for the judge was whether a binding agreement had been reached

---

23 [1985] 1 Lloyd's Rep 93 at 104 (CA).
24 [1985] 1 Lloyd's Rep 93, p 97.
25 [1990] 2 Lloyd's Rep 250 (1st inst).

upon the exchange of telexes. It was held that, at the time of the recap telex, the parties were *ad idem* and, having manifested an intention to create binding legal relations, an oral agreement had been reached. The fact that the terms of the standard form of agreement were to be incorporated into the contract did not prevent a binding agreement being reached. The signing of the form was not a condition precedent to the contract. The buyers were entitled to insist on delivery of the vessel at the requisite time.

The phrase, commonly used, 'otherwise NSF to be mutually agreed and to incorporate agreed terms/conditions' was construed in the context of *The Bay Ridge*.[26] The buyer's opening offer was expressed to be a firm offer in a sense that it was based on main terms, but subject to agreement of further terms and conditions. It was held that, until all further terms and conditions had been agreed, there was no concluded agreement.

4.3 The effect of 'buyer to be nominated' on the validity of the contract

Usually, a buyer has to form the corporate vehicle by which the ship can be bought. A company may already exist for this purpose, but often, when an opportunity arises for the purchase of a ship, a buyer may not yet be certain about the outcome of negotiations. Thus, the buying interests may not wish to incur the expense of incorporating a company until agreement has been reached. In such circumstances, the contract will permit the subsequent nomination of the buyer, whereupon the contract between the original parties will be novated. The nominated company will enter the contract in substitution for the original buyer. By the method of novation, all contractual rights and obligations of the original buyer are transferred to the nominated one and the original buyer is discharged. Novation, however, requires formal consents to be obtained by the sellers and the novated company. The sellers, in addition, may require a specific time by which the nomination can be made and a guarantee to be given by the original buyer that the substituted buyer will perform. The following two cases highlight problems that can arise with novation.

The Blankenstein[27]

The sellers entrusted the task of selling their three vessels, *The Blankenstein*, *The Bartenstein* and *The Birkenstein*, to their broker Mr Nebelsiek, while the broker of intending buyers was Mr Panas. Following negotiations between the brokers, a telex was sent on 4 July 1977, containing what was described as an official firm offer for all three vessels at $2 million. The offer was made on behalf of Messrs Raftopoulos and/or for company or companies to be nominated by them in due course.

On 8 July 1977, a concluded contract was reached in which all the terms and conditions of the sale and the price of $2,365,000 were agreed, save for the name of the purchasing company or companies, which had yet to be disclosed.

---

26 [1999] 2 Lloyd's Rep 227.

27 *Damon Compania Naviera v Hapag-Lloyd International SA (The Blankenstein)* [1985] 1 Lloyd's Rep 93.

There was a further exchange of telexes between the brokers and, on 13 July 1977, an MOA was drawn up between the sellers and the buyers, Raftopoulos, for and on behalf of companies still to be nominated. The memorandum was on the NSF, and provided that the buyers were to pay a deposit of 10% of the purchase money on signing the contract. By cl 13, it was provided inter alia that:

> Should the purchase money not be paid ... the sellers have the right to cancel this contract in which the amount deposited shall be forfeited to the sellers.

The memorandum was not signed by the Raftopoulos brothers or by any company or other person nominated by them.

On 1 August 1977, Mr Panas sent another telex to Mr Nebelsiek in which he stated that the buyers nominated as purchasing company Damon Compania Naviera SA, and requested a new MOA to be issued in which the buyers would be Damon. However, at that time, the Raftopoulos brothers had not acquired the shares in Damon, and it was not until after the nomination that this occurred. The new MOA, recording Damon as buyers, was sent to the buyer's broker, but neither was the agreement signed nor was the deposit paid by the time required. The sellers withdrew from the contract, reserving all their rights, and claimed damages against Damon, which the arbitrator awarded, stating a special case for the court. Damon challenged the award on the ground that the purported novation was never ratified and was ineffectual.

The lower court and the Court of Appeal decided that there was an agreement, of which payment of the deposit was a fundamental term. Although the Raftopoulos brothers became directors of the company after the nomination, it was highly likely that, at the time of the nomination, they had authority to make the nomination. It was always understood, Fox LJ said, that the Raftopoulos brothers were not buying the ships in their own name, but that they would eventually nominate a company. But the contract could not be forced on Damon without its agreement. The issue was whether Damon accepted such nomination between the time of the nomination and the repudiation of contract. The Lords Justice accepted that, on the evidence, there was acceptance of the nomination by Damon on the footing that the nomination was ratified by two subsequent telexes, sent by one of the brothers with full power to do so, on behalf of Damon. In any event, on the facts, either the original nomination was authorised, or it was ratified afterwards.

By contrast, in the following case, the nomination was ineffectual and the original buyers failed to show that the nomination was validly accepted by the nominated company.

The Action[28]

Briefly, by an MOA on the NSF, Action Maritime, as sellers, and Kasmas, as buyers, agreed on the sale of *The Action*. The MOA described the buyers to be nominated by Kasmas and later a purported nomination of Lagonissi was made. The deposit was duly paid by Kasmas. At the time of signature of the MOA, the ship was on the high seas. She proceeded to Lisbon and, shortly thereafter, the sellers served notice of

---

28   [1987] 1 Lloyd's Rep 283.

readiness of the vessel to the buyers. After inspection by the buyers, defects were found in the vessel, which were notified to the sellers. The latter, in the spirit of good co-operation, were willing to put them right, although they regarded such defects of minor significance. The buyers still insisted that the defects had not been put right and refused to take delivery. After many exchanges between the parties, the buyers cancelled the contract and the sellers accepted buyers' conduct as repudiation claiming damages and the forfeiture of the deposit against Kasmas, as the original party, against Lagonissi as the substituted party, and against three Kasmas brothers individually as being the company's undisclosed principals at the time of signing the MOA. Kasmas alleged, inter alia, that after the nomination of Lagonissi, the latter became the sole contracting party and Kasmas were absolved of any further obligations under the contract, and were also retrospectively relieved of their former obligation, so that they were entitled to be repaid the deposit.

It was held that the original buyers remained the contracting party.

The truth of the matter was that the buyers wanted to get out of this contract because of the falling market, but they were caught being themselves in a repudiatory breach. This case is relevant also later on, but the point to be made here is what was the effect of the cancellation by the buyers on the purported novation. The facts of *The Blankenstein* were distinguished. The court rejected the submission of the defendants that novation takes place at the moment of the nomination, whatever the nature and the circumstances of the contract. The terms of the contract in this case undermined any possibility of novation prior to the transfer of the vessel. Also a strong factor against Kasmas was that all the telex exchanges, including the cancellation one, were despatched by Kasmas. Since the transfer of the vessel was forestalled by the buyer's cancellation, the Kasmas company remained the contracting party, and novation of Lagonissi never in fact occurred.[29]

In terms of risk management, the buyers could well have been better off had they not cancelled the contract. They thought that, by cancelling the contract, they would obtain the advantage of the falling market. The result of having to pay damages (the difference in market value) to the sellers and legal costs to defend the case, as well as the costs of the winning party, must have cost them more than the amount they thought they would have saved by getting out of this contract.

4.4 What do 'subjects' mean?

Where the main terms have been agreed, but there are subsequent details to be discussed, there will be no legally binding agreement until those details have been agreed upon. It is, at best, a conditional agreement. If the recap telex is made 'subject to contract', it is clearly understood that there is no binding agreement, yet. Frequently, however, the parties use the expression 'subject details' or 'subrecon', and other similar expressions with which both chartering and sale/purchase brokers are familiar. The question that has arisen in quite a number of chartering and sale of ship cases is whether or not the parties have made their intention to be bound to the contract clear to each other.

---

29 Ibid, at p 310.

The general principle was stated in *Pagnan SPA v Feed Products Ltd*,[30] in which Lloyd LJ (as he then was) said:

> It is for the parties to decide whether they wish to be bound and if so, by what terms, whether important or unimportant. It is the parties who are, in the memorable phrase coined by the judge, 'the masters of their contractual fate'. Of course, the more important the term is, the less likely it is that the parties will have left it for the future decision. But there is no legal obstacle which stands in the way of the parties agreeing to be bound now while deferring important matters to be agreed later.[31]

He added that the distinction between essential and non-essential terms was misleading.

Bingham J (as he then was) stated at first instance, which was endorsed by the Court of Appeal, that the court's task is to review what the parties said and did and, from that material, to infer whether the parties' objective intentions, as expressed to each other, were to enter into a mutually binding contract. The court was not concerned with what the parties subjectively had intended.

It was recently confirmed by Langley J in *Thoresen & Co (Bangkok) Ltd v Fathom Marine Co Ltd*[32] that the words 'subject details' had a recognised meaning when used in the context of the sale of ships: there was no binding agreement until all the details or the proposed formal agreement had been agreed.

The factual circumstances of the following examples illustrate how the principle has been applied by the courts. More importantly, the cases illustrate how careful the parties and their brokers must be, at the negotiation stage of either the sale or the chartering of a ship, in recording their agreement precisely and in expressing in clear terms whether or not they wish, at that stage, to be bound by a final contract.

The Gladys (No 2)[33]

The buyer's broker, acting on behalf of the Indian Government, indicated acceptance of a firm offer for the purchase of this vessel for scrap. The understanding was that the broker would be supplied with an MOA on the NSF, blank as to details of the vessel, the price and other conditions requiring completion and, without additional clauses added, such blanks and clauses were left for the broker to draft before final agreement and signature. The buyers later withdrew. The sellers claimed that there was a binding contract and, by appointing an arbitrator as provided by the contract, claimed a declaration to that effect and damages for breach, while the buyers disputed the existence of an agreement and, consequently, of the validity of the arbitration agreement. The issue for the court was the construction of the contemporary documents and correspondence between the parties. The court came to the conclusion – having examined the parties' previous dealings – that, on this occasion, no final agreement had been reached. It further held that, it was clear from the facts, an oral agreement had been reached only in terms which plainly

---

30 [1987] 2 Lloyd's Rep 601 (CA), p 610.

31 Ibid, p 619.

32 [2004] 1 Lloyd's Rep 622: (Recap email provided: 'otherwise basis Saleform 93 sub-details suitably amended to reflect also the above terms').

33 [1994] 2 Lloyd's Rep 402.

contemplated that there were further terms to be agreed, albeit only matters of detail, before a binding contract was made.

An important point to bear in mind, and which arose during the negotiations in this case, was that, on the basis of previous dealings between the Indian Government (which was determining what vessels to buy through a committee) and the owners (sellers) of the vessels, some deals were indicated by the committee to be 'subject of a firm offer' and others 'subrecon'. With respect to this particular vessel, there was an exchange of telexes from which the court inferred that the parties had not come to a firm agreement about the price, date of delivery, and whether the terms would be on the basis of the sale of previous ships. Thus, the deal was on the basis of 'subrecon', despite the brokers' failure to spell this out in the telex. Just before the final agreement was communicated to the committee, the latter withdrew because, in the meantime, the committee had found out that the ship was a reefer, and reefers were not within the purchasing policy of the Indian Government. Although this might have been a matter of detail, particularly with regard to the purchase of a ship for scrap, the buyer was entitled to make its inquiries to check whether the information previously supplied proved to be significantly in error.[34]

The Junior K[35]

This case concerned negotiations to fix a charter party. These were concluded by the despatch and receipt of the recap telex in which it was stated that the fixture was 'sub details'. The terms agreed were set out, ending with the words 'sub dets Gencon CP', meaning subject to the details of a Gencon charterparty standard form, the details and alternative provisions of which require exercise of choice by the parties. The principal issue was whether there was a binding contract. It was held that no contract had been concluded, in this case, at that stage, since the parties had not made a positive selection of the desired alternative provisions of the form, and no discussion had taken place about these options. Against this background, it was clear that the words used conveyed that there was a fixture conditional upon agreement being reached about the details of the Gencon form. Steyn J stated:

> The expression 'subject to details' enables owners and charterers to know where they are in negotiations and to regulate their business accordingly. It is a device which tends to avoid disputes and the assumption of those in the shipping trade, that it is effective to make clear that there is no binding agreement at that stage, ought to be respected.[36]

In the following decisions the term 'subject to details' was construed in the same way.

---

34 Ibid, p 409.

35 [1988] 2 Lloyd's Rep 583.

36 Ibid, p 588: the judge referred to previous authorities; *The Solholt* [1981] 2 Lloyd's Rep 574 and *The Nissos Samos* [1985] 1 Lloyd's Rep 378, in which there had been some observations, albeit that they did not form part of the *ratio decidendi*, about the meaning of this expression to the effect that there was no contract until the subsidiary terms were agreed. In the USA, however, the judge commented, the details were regarded as unimportant if the parties can go back to the printed form. However, it was observed that there has been no uniform approach by the judiciary and arbitrators there.

The CPC Gallia[37]

This case concerned the carriage of a jet foil from Kobe to Las Palmas under a Conline booking note 'subject to details/logical amendments'. The precise form of the booking note became later the subject of a dispute, particularly a clause with regard to substitution of the vessel and transshipment. CPC line took the view that there was a contract while the shipper CTM held the opposite view. The court held, in favour of the shippers, that the term 'subject to details', despite the additional words 'logical amendments', meant that a contract had still to be drawn up on the basis of the booking note. If the parties intended to restrict the customary effect of the term by the additional words, the words of limitation ought to be made clear in their content and context. 'Logical amendments', therefore, were interpreted as an illustration rather than a limitation.[38]

Granits SA v Benship International Inc[39]

In this contrasting factual situation, C entered negotiations with S for S to charter its ship to C for the carriage of a cargo of wheat to Bangladesh. C sent a telex proposing terms, including 'otherwise Synacomex terms'. There was a telephone conversation whose terms were disputed. S claimed only to have agreed 'subject details', but C denied that there had been any such qualification. C sent a recap telex which made no reference to the phrase, but included two matters which S later disputed. It stated that it was S's responsibility to have the vessel accepted by the receivers and also incorporated the Synacomex strike clause. It later became clear that there might be significant delays in Bangladesh, and S claimed that no fixture had been agreed. The issues were (i) whether there was a consensus, but 'subject details', and (ii) if there was no express reference to 'subject details', were there important terms still to be agreed between the parties, or had a concluded agreement been reached? It was accepted that, if the words had been used, there could be no binding agreement. It was held that there was a binding contract, as there was no express mention of the words 'subject details' in the telephone conversation. Although there were blanks in the Synacomex form, which needed to be filled in, and a number of clauses in which specific choices would have to be made, it was not suggested that these would have presented any difficulty. The court would be slow not to uphold what was intended to be a binding bargain just because there were minor matters in relation to which there would be no difficulty at all to be ironed out once the formal charterparty was drawn up.

Messina v POL[40]

Different words were used in this case, namely: 'subject to appropriate amendments to be mutually agreed'. The central issue here was the construction of the

---

37 [1994] 1 Lloyd's Rep 68.
38 On the other hand, in *The Mercedes Envoy* [1995] 2 Lloyd's Rep 559, where the fixture telex contained 'subject to logical alterations', and there were other 'subjects' which had been lifted, these words did not prevent a binding contract from being formed.
39 [1994] 1 Lloyd's Rep 526.
40 [1995] 2 Lloyd's Rep 567, and, in particular, pp 578–81.

various exchanges between the parties and, in particular, the words that 'the terms of the NSF were subject to appropriate amendments to be mutually agreed'. Clarke J, as he then was, held that there would be no agreement until such amendments were agreed. This was supported by the fact that the NSF contained 15 printed clauses, many of which have gaps which have to be filled in. In particular, he stated:[41]

> These negotiations were approached in the usual way. There were exchanges between the brokers during which different terms were agreed in principle at different times. Once all the terms were agreed, it was contemplated that the board [of the sellers] would give approval and that an MOA would be drawn up setting out all of the agreed terms. I would not expect the parties to have intended that there be a legally binding agreement until then. That conclusion seems to me to be borne out by the terms of the NSF condition, namely that the terms were to be subject to 'appropriate amendments to be mutually agreed'. If one asks what was to happen if there was no mutual agreement, the natural answer is that no NSF would or could be agreed and, if no NSF was or could be agreed, there would be no agreement for the sale of the vessels unless the parties intended that there should be an agreement of sale notwithstanding the absence of an MOA on the terms of the NSF. Yet, I do not see how it could be held that the parties intended that there should be a legally binding contract for the sale of the ships in those circumstances, when the agreement expressly provides that, otherwise, the terms of the NSF subject to appropriate amendment are to be mutually agreed ... A term such as the NSF condition is recognised among brokers as meaning, in effect, that the agreement is subject to contract in the sense that, there is to be no binding agreement, until the MOA is signed.

In this case, the facts that determined that there was no binding agreement were that the NSF was subject to appropriate amendments, and not the fact that the form had not been signed, which in itself would not be a reason to hold that there was no agreement.[42]

The Bay Ridge[43]

The words for construction were a combination of 'approvals' and 'subjects'. Briefly, the sellers and the buyers negotiated the sale of this ship through their respective brokers. The exchanges and telephone communications culminated in the recap telex. The buyers alleged that one of the 'subjects' was 'sellers warrant vessel approved by all major oil companies', which the sellers disputed.

There were also two further 'subjects': 'buyers' inspection and approval of classification records' and 'buyers' inspection and approval of onboard condition survey'. In addition, there was a statement in the recap concerning 'buyers' right to place two representatives on board *after conclusion/confirmation of sale by telex/fax'*.

The first issue was whether there was a binding agreement (another issue was whether the sellers' brokers had authority).

---

41 Ibid, pp 578, 579.
42 See *The Blankenstein* [1985] 1 Lloyd's Rep 93 and *The Great Marine (No 2)* [1991] 1 Lloyd's Rep 421 (CA), above.
43 [1999] 2 Lloyd's Rep 227.

The judge concluded that there was no binding agreement, on the following grounds:[44]

There was a good commercial sense in seeking to agree main terms first. If main terms could not be agreed there was no point in going further. If main terms were agreed the parties would, thereafter, proceed to seek to agree further terms and conditions (by way of amendments, additions and deletions to NSF-87). There would be no concluded agreement until all further terms and conditions had been agreed ...

The recap at the end of the day recorded what had been agreed to date as to certain main terms. There was good commercial sense in recording the position reached at the end of the day, but the objective intentions of the parties were that negotiations would continue until all further terms and conditions had been agreed ...

The words in the recap fax 'otherwise per NSF-87 mutually agreed ...' meant in context 'otherwise per NSF-87 to be mutually agreed ...'

The words, 'We are pleased to confirm the sale of the above vessel as follows: ...' must be construed in context. Amendments, additions and deletions to NSF-87 remained to be agreed. The fact that there was no concluded contract of sale at the end of the day ... is confirmed by the words ... of the recap, *'after conclusion/ confirmation of sale by telex/fax'* ... (emphasis added)

The common understanding was that this would take place after 28 June. All oral exchanges between the brokers on 28 June proceeded on the basis that main terms would be agreed first (and embodied in a recap to the extent that the same were agreed) and that negotiations would follow as to appropriate amendments, additions and deletions to NSF-87. Thus, the position reflected in para 8 of Oceanbulk's opening offer, ('Otherwise NSF-87 to be mutually agreed and to incorporate agreed term/conditions'), continued throughout. At no stage did these inexperienced brokers consider the detailed provisions of NSF-87. This was to be left to a later stage ...

On June 28 the parties sought to establish agreement on main terms. There was no intention to create legal relations at the time of the recap. The question of oil majors approval (which had been accorded the status of a main term by Oceanbulk) was still being negotiated at the end of the day. The mutual agreement of amendments, additions and deletions to NSF-87 had yet to take place.

He further held that:

... without agreement of the details, the right of buyers to place divers for the underwater inspection would be unworkable. Since the first issue was decided in favour of the sellers, there was no need to consider the remaining issues about the brokers' authority and the possibility of breach of warranty of authority.

The case history in this area demonstrates that the words 'subject to' can mean different things in different contexts; they may incorporate a term of the contract, or may prevent a contract arising. For example, the words 'subject to superficial inspection' was held in *The Merak*[45] not to negative contractual intent; and 'subject to satisfactory survey' was commented on by Lord Denning MR in the same case to mean that there was an implied obligation on the seller to permit a survey and on

---

44   See pp 242–43.
45   [1976] 2 Lloyd's Rep 250.

the buyer to make it; the buyer would only be excused if the surveyor's report was unsatisfactory.[46]

5 CLASSIFICATION OF TERMS OF A CONTRACT AND THEIR IMPORTANCE

5.1 At common law

Although the terms of a contract were explained in the previous chapter, it is pertinent to summarise their significance in the context of this chapter as well. The terms of a contract under English common law are divided into three categories: conditions, warranties, and innominate or intermediate terms. Breach of the first will amount to repudiation entitling the innocent party to elect either to terminate the contract and also claim damages, or to go on with the contract and claim damages only. A breach of a warranty (except in insurance contracts, in which the insurer is automatically discharged from liability from the date of the breach) does not entitle the innocent party to terminate the contract, but to claim damages. The consequences of a breach of an intermediate or innominate term (lying between a condition and a warranty)[47] will depend on the nature and seriousness of the breach.[48]

Even if the parties describe a term as a condition, it does not mean that it is a condition, and it will depend on the construction of the term in the context of the whole contract.[49] An apt example, in this context, is the term which was in dispute in *The Action*.[50] The ship was to be delivered in the same physical condition as she was when she was inspected. The buyers alleged that there were defects when notice was given to them for delivery. Although the sellers agreed to make repairs, the buyers cancelled the contract before the sellers completed the repairs. The court construed the term of the condition of the ship on delivery as an innominate term and not as a condition precedent. If the parties wanted to make it a condition, they should expressly set out in the contract the right to cancel in the event of a breach of a term. There was judgment for the sellers.

In principle, contracts are made to be performed and not to be avoided according to the whims of market fluctuations and, where there is a free choice between two constructions, the court should tend to prefer that construction which will ensure performance and will not encourage avoidance of contractual obligations.[51]

---

46 He doubted the correctness of the decision in *Astra Trust v Adams* [1969] 1 Lloyd's Rep 81, where it had been held that there was no binding contract.

47 *Bunge Corporation v Tradax Export SA* [1981] 2 Lloyd's Rep 1 (HL).

48 *Hong Kong Fir Shipping v Kawasaki Kisen Kaisha* [1961] 2 Lloyd's Rep 478 (CA).

49 *Schuler v Wickham Machine Tools Sales Ltd* [1973] 2 Lloyd's Rep 53, [1974] AC 235 (HL).

50 [1987] 1 Lloyd's Rep 283.

51 *Cehave NV v Bremer (The Hansa Nord)* [1975] 2 Lloyd's Rep 445 (CA), p 457, per Roskill LJ.

5.2 Under the Sale of Goods Act 1979[52]

Similarly, the Sale of Goods Act (SOGA) 1979 provides, in s 11(2), that where a contract of sale is subject to a condition to be fulfilled by the seller, the buyer may waive the condition, or may elect to treat the breach of the condition as a breach of a warranty and not as a ground for treating the contract as repudiated.

In s 61(1), the Act defines a warranty as a term the breach of which gives rise to a claim for damages, and not to a right to reject the goods and treat the contract as repudiated. Whether a stipulation in a contract of sale is a condition or a warranty, depends in each case on the construction of the contract; and a stipulation may be a condition, though called a warranty in the contract (s 11(3)).

The SOGA 1979, by s 10, does not regard a stipulation as to time of payment as a term of essence of a contract of sale, unless a different intention appears from the terms of the contract. Whether any other stipulation as to time is or is not of essence of the contract depends on the terms of the contract.

5.2.1 Sale by description

It has already been seen in the previous chapter that the strict rule under the SOGA 1979, concerning the implied terms that goods sold by description should comply with that description, has been amended by s 4 of the Sale and Supply of Goods Act (SSGA) 1994. The effect of the amendment is that, where goods have been sold commercially, ie not to a consumer, a breach of description, or quality, or fitness for purpose will not be treated as a breach of a condition but as a breach of a warranty, if the breach is so slight that it would be unreasonable for the buyer to reject the goods (ship).

It has also been seen in the shipbuilding chapter (Chapter 10) that the SSGA 1994 has replaced the term 'merchantable quality' with the new implied condition of 'satisfactory quality', although this change may not be so relevant to the sale of second-hand ships, which will depend on what the parties agreed.

But, is it necessary to describe the ship adequately in the sale contract? The preamble to the sale form contains the classification of the ship, the year in which she was built, the builder, flag, call sign, register number, place of registration and register tonnage. There may not be a misdescription of the ship's year of building or registration if it falls within the *de minimis* rule, and the certificate of registry, as well as the builder's certificate, provide prima facie evidence of the year in which the ship was built.[53]

5.2.2 The passing of property

By s 17(1) of the SOGA 1979, where there is a contract for the sale of specific or ascertained goods, the property on them is transferred to the buyer at such time as

---

52 The Act was amended by the Sale of Goods (Amendment) Act 1994, the Sales of Goods (Amendment) Act 1995 and by the Sale and Supply of Goods to Consumers Regulations 2002 (SI 2002/3045) implemented in 2003.

53 *The Troll Park* [1988] 1 Lloyd's Rep 55, approved by CA [1988] 2 Lloyd's Rep 423.

the parties to the contract intend it to be transferred. Section 17(2) provides that, for the purpose of ascertaining the intention of the parties, regard shall be had to the terms of the contract, the conduct of the parties and the circumstances of the case.

By s 18, unless a different intention appears, the intention of the parties as to the time at which the property in the goods is to pass to the buyer is ascertained in accordance with five rules, depending on the circumstances of the case. Two of these rules are mentioned below, by way of a contrast, the second of which is relevant to the sale of second-hand ships.[54]

Rule 1: where there is an unconditional contract for the sale of specific goods in a deliverable state, the property in the goods passes to the buyer when the contract is made, and it is immaterial whether the time of payment or the time of delivery, or both, is postponed. [This rule is relevant to the first category of sale contracts made by s 2 of the SOGA 1979, namely, the sale contract and not the agreement to sell. Section 61(5) defines a 'deliverable state' as being such a state that a buyer would be bound to take delivery under the contract.]

Rule 2: where there is a contract for the sale of specific goods and the seller is bound to do something to the goods for the purpose of putting them into a deliverable state, the property does not pass until the thing is done and the buyer has notice that it has been done. [This rule refers to an agreement to sell, the second category under s 2 of the Act, where the property passes at a future date.]

The sale of second-hand ships is normally an agreement to sell, in which the parties provide in the saleform that, in the event of deficiencies found at the inspection stage, the seller will be obliged to carry out repairs and put the ship in a deliverable state. Before notice of delivery, the ship is not yet in a deliverable state, and the parties' intention is that property shall pass upon payment on the day of delivery. Property cannot pass when the contract is made, unless the agreement is for a sale 'as is where is', which means that the buyer has chosen an 'outright' sale, if he had already inspected her before the contract was concluded. In such a case, the seller is not required to carry out repairs on the ship after the conclusion of the contract, but, even in this situation, property shall pass when the parties intended it to pass.

Naamlooze Vennootschap Stoomvaart Maatschappij 'Vredoobert' v European Shipping Co Ltd[55]

An agreement for sale of five second-hand ships provided that buyers were to 'buy now'. Before any part of the purchase price had been paid, one of the vessels was sunk by a collision, and the insurance company paid the seller on the policy. The buyer claimed that property had passed to him, and he was, therefore, entitled to the benefit of the insurance policy.

The House of Lords, affirming the decision of the Court of Appeal, held that the words 'buy now' did not mean an immediate transfer of property. This was an agreement to sell and not a sale. Viscount Dunedin remarked that:

> ... using the phraseology of the SOGA 1979, I look on this contract as a 'contract to

---

54 The second rule is also relevant to shipbuilding contracts (see Chapter 10).

55 (1926) 25 LlL Rep 210.

sell' and not a 'sale' . . . in determining whether a contract is a sale or an agreement to sell, is to see whether there remains something to be done. Now, here there was certainly something to be done.[56]

6 CONTRACTUAL TERMS UNDER STANDARD FORMS OF THE SALE CONTRACT

The sale contract most frequently used is the NSF 1987, its predecessors being dated 1983 and 1966. The latest edition of NSF, however, is Saleform 1993. The parties must specify at the outset which form is going to be used. Another sale contract of second hand ships is the Nipponsale 1993, which is used by Japanese sellers. Both types of forms concern an absolute sale,[57] which comprises physical possession and transfer of property at the same time, in exchange for payment of the contract price. It is not within the scope of this book to examine all contracts and all their clauses.[58] Only clauses that have presented problems are examined. Comparisons between clauses of the various forms are made where a situation warrants drawing a comparison.

6.1 When is the deposit payable?

As stated earlier, the buyer is required to pay a deposit of 10% as security for the due performance of the contract. Clause 2 of both NSF forms (1987 and 1993) provides for the payment of deposit as follows:

> As a security for the correct fulfilment of this contract, the buyers shall pay a deposit of 10% of the purchase money within . . . banking days from the date of this agreement. This amount shall be deposited with [a bank] and held by them in a joint account for the sellers and the buyers. Interest, if any, to be credited to the buyers. Any fee charge for holding said deposit shall be borne equally by the sellers and the buyers.

Payment of the deposit is a fundamental term of the contract, breach of which entitles the seller to cancel the contract and recover his loss as damages.[59] What is the measure of damages depends on the contract terms. Clause 2 must be read together with cl 13, which has been amended (see para 7.1.1, below). If the buyer fails to pay the purchase money, the seller will be entitled to cancel the contract, and the buyer will forfeit his deposit and all the interest that has accrued on it. In *The Blankenstein*,[60] the contention made by the buyers was that, since cl 2 of the NSF provided for payment of the deposit 'on signing' the contract, the deposit never became payable, as the contract was never signed. According to Fox LJ, the

---

56 (1926) 25 LIL Rep 210, p 212.

57 Other types of sale are by instalments, or by credit, which may involve a mortgage on the ship granted to the seller as security, or by hire purchase, or judicial sale.

58 Reference will be made to op cit, Goldrein, fn 19.

59 *The Selene G* [1981] 2 Lloyd's Rep 180.

60 [1985] 1 Lloyd's Rep 93.

situation that existed in this case was that a binding contract had already been entered into, the consequence being that:

(a) the parties became bound to sign the MOA incorporating the agreed terms within a reasonable time; and

(b) the purchaser became bound, upon signing the memorandum, to pay the deposit.

The Court of Appeal also held that the plaintiff (seller) was entitled to recover the amount of the deposit by way of damages for breach of contract, in which cl 13 of the 1966 NSF (which was used in this case) did not specify the kind of damages in case of non-payment of the deposit. It will be seen at para 7.1.1, below, that cl 13 of the 1987 NSF has been amended.

The payment of the deposit is linked to the right of the buyer, as provided by a new cl 15 of the 1993 NSF, to place two representatives on board the ship for familiarisation purposes and as observers, but without interfering with the operation of the vessel.

Where there is a sale and a sub-sale, the head-buyer may use the sub-sale deposit to pay the seller, but the sale and sub-sale must be back to back. Problems may arise if the buyers' lawyers omit to reconcile the delivery date under both contracts, as is illustrated by the following case.

The Ranger[61]

The contract between the sellers and the head-buyers required the buyers to put up a deposit of 10% of the purchase price and gave the buyers a right to cancel the contract if the vessel was not delivered by 30 June. Upon failure of delivery on the due date by the sellers, the deposit and accrued interest would immediately be released to the buyers. The head-buyers sub-contracted to sell the vessel to the second defendants for the same price and on the same terms, but the delivery and cancelling date for this agreement was 31 May of the same year. The deposit for the first contract was funded by the deposit paid under the second contract, and the amount was paid into an interest bearing account in the joint names of the second defendants (the buyers under the sub-sale) and the head-sellers' agent. Upon non-delivery of the vessel under the sub-sale by the cancelling date, the second defendants cancelled the sub-contract on 1 June. On 13 June, the head-sellers tendered the ship for delivery under the head-contract to the buyer but the latter refused to accept the vessel. Treating the buyers' conduct as a repudiation, the head-sellers cancelled the contract and sought the release of the deposit. The second defendants refused.

It was held that, since the second defendants had consented to the use of their names as one of the two parties to the opening of the joint account, the second defendants were ratifying its use as agents for the head-buyers. Therefore, as the head-sellers were entitled to the deposit as against the head-buyers, the sub-buyers had no claim to the deposit as against the head-sellers.

For risk management purposes, the mistake that was made in this case was that

---

61 [1970] 1 Lloyd's Rep 32.

By comparison with the equivalent clause of the 1993 Saleform, an alternative is provided by the later edition to reflect market practice. The first part provides for inspection by the classification society's surveyor, to be done at the seller's expense, if defects are found, while the second alternative provides that the vessel shall be delivered without drydocking. However, a diver appointed by the buyers, upon the approval of class, may carry out the underwater inspection at the buyer's expense. The extent and conditions under which this inspection is performed shall be to the satisfaction of class. If the diver (under the diver's inspection) discovers any damage, which cannot be repaired afloat, the sellers must arrange for the ship to be drydocked at their own expense. This new clause is very long and detailed.

If the classification society surveyor decides that the ship is in acceptable condition, the buyer will be bound by that decision. If the classification society makes recommendations for repairs, the seller must make repairs at his own expense; if he does not, he cannot tender the vessel for delivery and could be held in repudiatory breach of contract. The seller's obligation in such circumstances is to make such repairs to the satisfaction of the classification society.

The Great Marine (No 2)[64]

Instead of the provision of cl 6 in the NSF 1987, the parties had agreed by an additional clause to have a joint inspection by a diver approved by ABS (the classification society). If the diver found damage to the ship's hull or underwater parts below the summer load line, leading to a condition of class being placed on the ship, cl 6 would be reinstated and the ship would be drydocked. Clause 11 provided that the ship would be delivered and taken over 'as she is at the time of inspection fair wear and tear excepted . . . with present class free of recommendations'. The same clause obliged the sellers to notify ABS of any matters coming to their knowledge prior to delivery which would lead to the withdrawal of the ship's class or to imposition of recommendations relating to her class. In addition, cl 18 provided that the sellers should deliver the ship free of average damage affecting class.

When the underwater inspection was done, the diver discovered that the propeller was seriously damaged. The buyers attempted unsuccessfully to persuade the sellers to report the damage to the classification society, but the sellers contended that the damage did not affect the class of the ship. The buyer's attempt to inform the society of the damage also failed since the society claimed that, prior to delivery, it kept contact with the seller only. However, the buyers took delivery, repaired the propeller themselves and claimed damages against the sellers.

The court gave judgment for the buyers, holding the sellers in breach of their obligation under cll 11 and 18 to notify the classification society and deliver the vessel free of any average damage affecting class. Recoverable damages were the costs incurred by the buyer to make the propeller's damage good by the heating and fairing method. While the sellers accepted they were in breach of their obligation, they disagreed on the method of repairs and, hence, the amount of damages. They appealed. The Court of Appeal held that the sellers' obligation was to deliver

---

64 [1991] 1 Lloyd's Rep 421 (CA).

the ship with clean certificate from the classification society and that was the contractual measure of quality. The buyers were to be put in the same position as if the sellers had performed their obligations; that was as if the sellers had reported the damage, ABS had made its recommendations and the vessel had been drydocked for carrying out the necessary work to obtain a clean certificate from ABS. Clause 6 required the seller to carry out repairs to the satisfaction of the ship's classification society without qualification.

The standard of repair required was that which would preserve a clean certificate of class; by cropping and grinding in a workshop the sellers would have done what was required of them under the contract, irrespective of whether a loss of efficiency of the propeller resulted. The sellers won by majority of 2:1, so the buyers could not recover their heating and fairing expenses; Lloyd LJ, however, agreed with the judge.

While fair wear and tear is excluded from the requirement of the ship's condition at delivery, what could affect class was interpreted in *The Alfred Trigon*:[65]

> The words 'affecting class' . . . meant damage of such a character as either to prevent the vessel being in class or to result in the surveyor, on his becoming aware of the damage, imposing some qualification on class by way of recommendation.[66]

> 'Average damage affecting class' was not just any damage affecting class but damage affecting class of a certain kind and meant damage occasioned by a peril ordinarily covered by insurance as opposed to defects through wear and tear or general old age.[67]

6.4 Notice of readiness and risk management

The notice of readiness is linked to arrangements for payment of the balance of the contract price. Therefore, the seller is anxious to give notice of readiness as soon as he considers that the ship might be ready by the end of the notice period. Sometimes, it may not be ready pursuant to the contract and problems usually arise.

Clause 3 of the NSF 1987 provides:

> The said purchase money shall be paid free of bank charges to . . . on delivery of the vessel, but not later than three banking days after the vessel is ready for delivery and written or telexed notice thereof has been given to the buyers by the sellers.

> The notice period for payment expires at midnight of the third day.[68] Banking day is taken to be the business working day for both the principal financial centre in the country of the currency in which the money is payable and the place where the financial closing of the sale is to take place.[69]

The clause is essentially dealing with the buyer's obligation to pay the purchase

---

65 *Piccinini v Partrederiet Trigon II (The Alfred Trigon)* [1981] 2 Lloyd's Rep 333.

66 [1981] 2 Lloyd's Rep 333, p 336.

67 Ibid, p 338.

68 This is also the position of payment of hire under a time charterparty: *The Afovos* [1983] 1 Lloyd's Rep 335.

69 See, op cit, Goldrein, fn 19.

money within a time limit after the seller has given notice that the ship is ready for delivery. Whether the clause requires the seller to give notice only when the ship is in a deliverable state at the time of the notice, or whether prospective readiness would be sufficient, has caused concern in practice and in law. In *The Action*, Hirst J held that it does not. In particular, he said:

> The suggestion that it is necessary for the vessel to be in a fully deliverable state at the time of the notice, as contrasted with the time of delivery, has an air of marked commercial unreality, seeing that it is of no consequence whatsoever to the buyers whether or not the vessel is in a deliverable state at the earlier date, so long as it is at the latter.[70]

As a matter of construction of the contract, he said, there was no prerequisite to the validity of the notice of readiness that the vessel was actually in a deliverable state on the date it was given.

At first glance, it seems that such a construction of cl 3 would be correct, but the wording of the clause creates uncertainty. One would expect that the seller's obligation to have the ship in a deliverable state – save for details and preparation of documentation – on the date of the notice would be a natural prerequisite to the buyer's obligation to make arrangements for payment of the balance of the contract price. If the ship were not ready, there would be little or no time to correct any outstanding matters of the ship's condition in three days, unless such matters were trivial. The buyer would be exposed to risks by releasing his money when the ship might not, practically, be ready by the end of the notice period. The ship's non-readiness would have practical and legal consequences. Such risks the buyer could properly have managed if thought had been given at the stage of negotiations and the drafting of this clause. Bearing in mind that this is the most important part of completion of the parties' respective obligations under the contract, the clause ought to have been drafted in clear and unambiguous language. The notice obligation of the seller ought to be in a separate clause.

In the following case, however, cl 3 of the NSF 1987 was given a different construction from that given in *The Action*. The contract had been varied by the parties with the addition of other notice provisions.

Zegluga Polska SA v TR Shipping Ltd (No 2)[71]

The NSF 1987 was used with additions and amendments. But the contract concerned a new building of a bulk carrier, so, in addition to the printed notice of readiness (cl 3), there was added another clause of notices to be given by the sellers to suit the requirements of this contract. Clause 5 provided: 'The sellers shall give the buyers three months and one month approximate notice and a seven days definite notice of readiness for delivery of the vessel.' The sellers did comply with these notices, but the buyers refused to accept the seven days definite notice of readiness contending that the grabs, which formed part of the specification of the vessel, were not in accordance with the specification. They refused to pay the balance of the contract price and obtained an ex parte injunction restraining the sellers

---

70 [1987] 1 Lloyd's Rep 283, p 295.
71 [1998] 2 Lloyd's Rep 341.

(who had already given notice of cancellation of the contract) from disposing of the vessel. Colman J ordered specific performance and maintained the injunction until then. On appeal by the sellers, the issue was: when, on the proper construction of the contract, did the buyers become obliged to make payment?

It was held that, on a natural reading of cl 3, the notice must be of actual readiness for delivery, when the notice was given, not of any prospective readiness. The notices required under the other clauses were prospective notices. Under cl 5, in particular, it was not required that the vessel should be actually ready for delivery when the seven days' definite notice was given, all that the notice appeared to require was a notice by the sellers that the vessel definitely would be ready for delivery after seven days. The giving of actual notice of readiness, if properly given, acted as a trigger and left no room for doubt when the three days began and ended, and could not begin to run from any date earlier than the expiry of the seven days' notice. The buyers, therefore, were entitled to insist on the vessel being ready.

It should be noted that the Court of Appeal commented on the construction of cl 3 given by Hirst J in *The Action*, that any support of the view held by the judge would be profoundly uncommercial.[72]

In the light of the problems created by the drafting of the notice provisions in the NSF 1987, which became apparent from the decision in *The Action*, the notice provision in the next edition of the NSF has been amended.

The obligation of the buyer to arrange for the purchase money after notice has been given, and the obligation of the seller to give notice when the ship is ready, are provided in two separate clauses in the 1993 NSF. Clause 3 of the 1993 form provides:

> The said purchase price shall be paid in full free of bank charges to . . . on delivery of the vessel, but not later than three banking days after the vessel is *in every respect physically ready for delivery* in accordance with the terms and conditions of this agreement and notice of readiness has been given in accordance with cl 5. (emphasis added)

Clause 5 provides:

> When the vessel is at the place of delivery and *in every respect physically ready for delivery* in accordance with this agreement, the sellers shall give the buyers a written notice of readiness for delivery. (emphasis added)

The separation of each party's obligations at delivery is achieved by these two clauses, and it seems that by linking the two, the trigger of the buyer's obligation to instruct his bank for payment is the fulfilment by the seller of his obligation to give notice when the ship is in every respect physically ready for delivery. This is emphasised by stressing the obligation of the seller in cl 5 that he shall give notice when the vessel is in every respect physically ready for delivery at the place of delivery. There is no room for construction that there can be prospective readiness. In addition, the consequences of the seller's failure to comply with this obligation are spelt out in cl 14 of the NSF 1993, which provides:

> Should the sellers fail to give Notice of Readiness in accordance with cl 5 or fail to be

---

72 [1998] 2 Lloyd's Rep 341, pp 344–45.

ready to validly complete a legal transfer by the date stipulated in line 61 the buyers shall have the option of cancelling this agreement provided always that the sellers shall be granted a maximum of three banking days after Notice of Readiness has been given to make arrangements for the documentation set out in clause 8. If after Notice of Readiness has been given but before the buyers have taken delivery, the vessel ceases to be physically ready for delivery and is not made physically ready again in every respect by the date stipulated in line 61 and new Notice of Readiness given, the buyers shall retain their option to cancel. In the event that the buyers elect to cancel this agreement the deposit together with interest earned shall be released to them immediately.

Should the sellers fail to give Notice of Readiness by the date stipulated in line 61 or fail to be ready to validly complete a legal transfer as aforesaid they shall make due compensation to the buyers for their loss and for all expenses together with interest if their failure is due to proven negligence and whether or not the buyers cancel this agreement.

Clause 14 of the 1993 NSF has considerably expanded the same clause of the 1987 NSF. It makes it to be understood that the three days after notice is given are intended for the preparation of the necessary documentation by the seller and not for making the vessel physically ready, which, as derived from cll 3 and 5, should be in every respect physically ready at the date of the notice. The clause also caters for the eventuality that the ship may cease to be physically ready after notice has been given and before delivery, in which case the seller is obliged again to make her physically ready by the date stipulated in the contract. Although the clause requires the seller to give new notice of readiness in such a case, it does not seem to grant a grace period to the seller to make the ship ready again from the date of the new notice. It is inferred from this drafting that the only occasion the seller can deal with the physical aspects of the ship's readiness during the three-day period after notice has been given is when something happens to the ship affecting her physical readiness after the date of the notice of readiness. Unless the parties vary this provision to give the seller another three days from the date of the new notice to make the ship physically ready definitely and, also, suspend the buyer's obligation to transfer the purchase money accordingly, it can be inferred from this drafting that the seller has an absolute obligation to rectify any new physical defects by the agreed date of delivery. This is so because the clause expressly provides that the buyer's right of election to cancel is retained. It may, however, be argued that the clause just intends to place the control on the buyer, who may decide to give extra time to the seller, if he wishes, instead of exercising his option to cancel.

6.5 Essential documentation for exchange at delivery

Clause 8 of the 1987 Saleform stipulates:

In exchange for payment of the purchase money the sellers furnish the buyers with legal bill of sale of the said ship free from all encumbrances and maritime liens or any other debts whatsoever, duly notarially attested and legalised by the ... consul together with a certificate stating that the ship is free from registered encumbrances. On delivery of the ship the sellers shall provide for the deletion of the ship from the registry of ships and deliver a certificate of deletion to the buyers. The deposit shall be placed at the disposal of the sellers as well as the balance of the purchase money, which shall be paid as agreed together with payment for items mentioned in cl 7 (bunkers and spares).

The sellers shall, at the time of delivery, hand to buyers all classification certificates as well as all plans, etc, which are on board the ship. Other technical documentation which may be in the sellers' possession shall promptly upon the buyers' instructions be forwarded to the buyers. The sellers may keep the logbooks, but the buyers to have the right to take copies of same.

Clause 8 of the 1993 Saleform improves on cl 8 of the 1987 form, being clearer about the required documents to be delivered by the sellers. It provides for:

(a) closing meeting ashore;

(b) delivery protocol;

(c) documents for delivery at completion;

(d) documents to be delivered on board.

The form of the bill of sale is determined by the ship's flag State.[73]

The gist of this clause is the obligation of the seller to furnish a bill of sale of the said ship, free from all encumbrances, which is linked with the sellers' warranty provided by cl 9 (see later).

It is clear from the clause what are the important documents to be delivered by the sellers in exchange for receiving the balance of the purchase price. The duties of the buyers under this clause are to release the deposit to the seller, to pay the balance, and to pay for bunkers, lubricants and other items on board.

6.6 Sellers' obligations under clause 9

6.6.1 Sellers' undertaking

Clause 9 of the NSF 1987 stipulates:

The sellers warrant that the vessel, at the time of delivery, is free from all encumbrances and maritime liens or any other debts whatsoever. Should any claims, which have been incurred prior to the time of delivery be made against the vessel, the sellers hereby undertake to indemnify the buyers against all consequences of such claims.

Clause 9 of the NSF 1993 is a variation of cl 9 of the 1987 form:

The sellers warrant that the vessel, at the time of delivery, is free from all charters, encumbrances, mortgages and maritime liens or any other debts whatsoever. The sellers hereby undertake to indemnify the buyers against all consequences of claims made against the vessel which have been incurred prior to the time of delivery.

This amended clause is, in effect, the same as under the 1987 NSF, but for the addition, in the first sentence, of the words 'charters' and 'mortgages'. The second sentence is effectively reversed. However, the difficulties in the construction of cl 9,

---

73 Insofar as British ships are concerned, see Chapter 8.

which will become apparent upon careful reading and which arose in the case to be discussed below, have not been removed by the amendment.

6.6.2 Construction of clause 9

It seems that the clause provides for two separate remedies for the buyer under each sentence. Liability for damages will arise in the event of breach of the warranty provided in the first sentence regarding incidents of encumbrances attached on the ship. A liability to indemnify the buyer will arise when the latter incurs losses by reason of claims brought against the ship. What is unclear in the clause is this: what is meant by the phrase 'any other debts whatsoever' in the first sentence, and is there an overlap between the two sentences by the words 'all consequences of claims' used in the second sentence?

The Barenbels[74]

The ship was sold under the NSF 1966, in which cl 9 was broadly similar to cl 9 of the 1987 form, except that it provided for a guarantee, instead of a warranty, in the first sentence, to deliver the ship free from encumbrances, maritime liens or any other debts whatsoever. Prior to delivery, the sellers owed large sums of money to their agents in Qatar in respects of debts. After delivery of the ship to the buyer, the agents commenced proceedings in the court of Qatar for the purpose of recovering the money due to them from the sellers, and the court ordered the detention of the vessel in Qatar. The detention was allowed under Qatar law even though the ship had been transferred to a new owner and no proceedings had been issued against the ship before the transfer. The buyers, having failed to persuade the sellers to provide security or to settle the claim, provided security in the form of a guarantee furnished by their P&I club for the release of the vessel. The buyers then claimed damages against the sellers for breach of the guarantee under the first sentence of cl 9, or alternatively an indemnity against the consequences of the arrest under the second sentence of the clause.

The arbitrators, by a unanimous award, decided against the claim for damages on the ground that the claim did not fall within encumbrances and maritime liens; they construed 'any other debts', of the same sentence, as inappropriate to embrace indebtedness arising otherwise than in relation to the vessel. With regard to the indemnity claim, they held that the language in the second sentence of the clause was insufficiently clear to embrace a conservatory arrest ordered by the court in Qatar, and the buyers could not show that the claim was a claim against the vessel. The buyers appealed.

Sheen J found in favour of the buyers. He construed the word 'encumbrances' as referring to claims, liens and liabilities attaching to the ship. As to 'any other debts whatsoever', he said, the draftsman had in mind the personification of the ship when claims are made against her. So, the words meant that the sellers guaranteed that, at the time of delivery, the vessel would be free from the risk of being arrested in respect of any debts of the sellers. (Under English law, this risk would

---

74 [1985] 1 Lloyd's Rep 528.

arise if a writ or claim form had been issued against the ship or a sister ship before the transfer of the ship to the buyer.) On the issue of indemnity under the second sentence, he disagreed with the arbitrators that a conservatory arrest was not embraced within the indemnity provision. The sellers appealed.

The Court of Appeal (with Goff LJ, as he then was, delivering judgment) held that the two sentences of the clause contain separate obligations. The second sentence is not intended merely to express a remedy available to the buyer in the event of breach of the guarantee contained in the first sentence:

> The first sentence is concerned with a guarantee relating to the vessel at the time of delivery, whereas the second sentence is concerned with an indemnity in respect of claims made against the vessel which are plainly intended to refer to claims so made after the delivery of the vessel though incurred prior to the time of delivery.[75]

Then Goff LJ proceeded to construe the effect of the words contained in the two sentences. In the first sentence, 'encumbrances' referred to proprietary and, possibly, possessory rights over the ship. The sellers' debt to their agents in Qatar at the time of delivery did not constitute an encumbrance.

On construction of the phrase 'free from . . . any other debts whatsoever', in the context of the first sentence, he held that:

> . . . this should be read as relating to any other debts, which at the time of delivery, had given rise to *actual existing rights affecting the property in, or the use of, the ship.*[76] (emphasis added)

These words were not wide enough to include debts, which would be capable of rendering the ship liable to be arrested in the future, because this was intended to be covered by the second sentence. On this construction, the debt owed by the sellers to Qatar National (the agent) was not within the guarantee provision under the first limb.

Turning to the indemnity provision, it was held that the claim by the Qatar agents in respect of debts owed to them by the sellers was a claim in respect of liabilities, which had been incurred prior to the time of delivery, and the claim was indeed against the ship.

6.6.3 Comments on the wording of clause 9 in the 1987 and 1993 NSF

Careful reading of the words used in the first sentence by Goff LJ reveals the following: the first sentence is referring to proprietary rights in the ship (that is, title in, use or possession of the ship), which are truly *in rem*, actual and existing at the time of delivery. The second sentence includes claims other than the above, which may arise in the future for pre-delivery debts that may render the ship liable to be arrested. Since the clause in the previous form did not include in the first sentence the word 'mortgages', which was added to the 1993 form, the additional phrase 'any other debts whatsoever' was justified in the 1987 NSF. The use of the same phrase in the 1993 NSF can be justified only for the purpose of avoiding any doubt

---

75   [1985] 1 Lloyd's Rep 528, p 532.
76   [1985] 1 Lloyd's Rep 528, p 533.

with regard to proprietary claims. The insertion of the words 'free from any charters' in the first sentence may be intending to cover the situation in which a charterparty existed at the time of delivery of which the buyer had no notice. If he had notice, he would be bound by it,[77] but that presupposes that he bought the ship with actual knowledge of the charter and its terms.

6.6.4 Judicial interpretation of clause 9 of the NSF 1993

The second sentence of cl 9 of the 1993 NSF became the subject of a dispute and was determined by the Court of Appeal recently. The issues arose because of grammatical problems in its drafting, which had already been commented upon by both the judge and the Court of Appeal in *The Barenbels*. The parties can prevent such litigation risks from arising by making amendments to the standard form. It is unfortunate that cl 9 still remains problematic, even after its amendment in the 1993 NSF. It is hoped that, in a future amendment of the NSF, the draftsman takes into account the issues raised in the following case, so that a clear and unambiguous clause results.

Rank Enterprises v Gerrard [78]

The buyers had been able to obtain a company guarantee as a security for breach of cl 9 by the seller. After delivery, claims were made against the vessel, which the seller denied as being invalid and spurious. The issue was the construction of the words, 'should any claims which have been incurred prior to the time of delivery be made', and the meaning of 'claims against the vessel' in both cl 9 and the company guarantee. At first instance, the judge – adopting the expanded version of the clause as interpreted in *The Barenbels* – construed these words as meaning claims in respect of any liability incurred (actual or contingent) prior to delivery, which resulted in a later claim against the vessel. The words did not include the consequences of claims against the vessel such as costs and expense in defending them. He then construed 'claims against the vessel' as involving a demand which carried with it a threat of seizure of the vessel and that the threat must be real and present, but there was no need for there to have been proceedings, or an order of arrest, before there could be said to be a claim against the vessel.

There was an appeal by the buyers and a cross-appeal by the sellers. The issue on appeal was whether the second sentence of cl 9 referred only to claims in respect of which the sellers were actually liable. Liabilities in respect of any claim or demand under the expanded version of the sentence, Mance LJ said, may embrace 'liabilities actual or alleged'. It did not have to be actual or contingent liabilities. One paraphrase of the clause, which seemed to be appropriate, was that the sentence applied to 'any claims exposure, which was incurred prior to delivery and was made against the vessel after delivery'.[79] It was common ground that the clause intends to protect the buyer against adverse consequences, for example, costs and

---

77 See similar issues arising when the mortgagee of a ship exercises his right to possession, Chapter 9, para 10.
78 [2000] 1 Lloyd's Rep 403.
79 Ibid, p 409.

expense of valid claims, but the question was whether it covered such costs and expense resulting from spurious claims. The answer to this was that, if cl 9 was read as covering the adverse consequences of claims, good or bad, generated by pre-delivery events, the buyers would be assured of indemnity, provided they acted in a reasonable and business-like way in dealing with such claims. The buyers, in reality, as a matter of elementary self-protection and prudence, usually inform the sellers on receipt of any claims and try to co-operate, seeking information and assistance from the sellers, although the clause does not contain any such provision. In conclusion, Mance LJ said:

> ... the judge took too limited a view of the scope of the second sentence of cl 9. The sentence, in my judgment, addresses claims made, the exposure to which stems from pre-delivery events, whether the liability asserted by such claims may prove to exist or not.

The buyers' appeal was allowed and the cross-appeal was dismissed.

6.6.5 Risk management in drafting and safeguarding against breach of clause 9

(a) Clause 9 ought to be redrafted, as has already been pointed out. The difference between the two sentences ought to be spelt out. Goff LJ criticised the clause, that it was not grammatically correct in the second sentence, but the same problems of construction, unfortunately, still appear in cl 9 of the 1993 NSF.

(b) It would be more meaningful if the obligation under the first limb of the clause was made a condition entitling the buyer to terminate the contract, if he became aware of the breach at delivery. In some contracts, the parties amend the clause to that effect. While the buyer can find out from the ship's registry whether a registered ship is subject to a registered mortgage,[80] there is no public record for maritime liens. In what ways can the buyer protect himself against such risks? He could examine the accident history of the ship from the logbook to find out whether the ship had caused damage by collision, or received salvage services, or there was any other incident, which would have given rise to a maritime lien. He could question the crew if they have been remunerated. An ownership or possessory right on the ship could be discoverable from the ship's registry.

(c) The buyer could seek to negotiate, at the stage of the formation of the contract, that security is provided in the event of breach. An unconditional and irrevocable guarantee, backed up by a bank guarantee, could be obtained by which the seller, or the guarantor in default of the seller, would guarantee to pay the buyer on demand for any loss or damages and expenses incurred by him in consequence of a breach of cl 9.[81] A provision for the non-release of the deposit to the seller at the delivery stage, in the event of a breach of cl 9, would be the minimum safeguard for the buyer by way of a self-help remedy, but this would

---

80 By contrast, there is no means of registering a mortgage of an unregistered ship (see, eg, *The Shizelle* [1992] 2 Lloyd's Rep 444, Chapter 9, above).

81 This was achieved in *Rank Enterprises v Gerrard* [2000] 1 Lloyd's Rep 403.

only be useful when encumbrances or claims are discovered at the time of delivery.

(d) In the event of a claim for indemnity under the second sentence, by virtue of the nature of such a claim, the buyer will only be able to claim his loss after he had defended the claim made by the third party against the ship for liability incurred by the seller prior to delivery. By that time, however, the risk the buyer runs is that the seller may no longer be in existence. He may negotiate to amend this part of the clause either by obtaining the seller's agreement to take over the claim brought by any third party against the ship after delivery, or by seeking security for such a claim from the seller at the time of the contract by way of a company guarantee backed up by a bank guarantee to be activated if and when a claim by a third party is brought. This is essential as a risk management exercise, particularly, because there is no means of knowing whether there are outstanding claims for debts or liabilities of the seller for which the ship might be arrested unless *in rem* proceedings have been issued in England, which are registered in the admiralty book in court.[82] If, after delivery of the vessel, the buyer is put in a position to have to defend a claim against a third party, the possibility of losing the opportunity of enforcing an indemnity against a dissolved one-ship company, the seller, will not be a light risk to take.

6.7 Condition of vessel on delivery and risk management

Clause 11 of the 1987 NSF provides:

> The vessel with everything belonging to her shall be at the sellers' risk and expense until she is delivered to the buyers, but subject to the conditions of this contract, she shall be delivered and taken over as she is at the time of inspection, fair wear and tear excepted.

The second sentence of cl 11 of the 1993 NSF has significantly been amended in the following respects:

> ... her class maintained without condition/recommendation free of average damage affecting the vessel's class, and with her classification certificate and national certificates, as well as all other certificates the vessel had at the time of inspection, valid and unextended without condition/recommendation by class or the relevant authorities at the time of delivery. 'Inspection' in this cl 11, shall mean the buyers' inspection according to cll 4(a) or 4(b), if applicable, or the buyers' inspection prior to the signing of this agreement. If the vessel is taken over without inspection, the date of this agreement shall be the relevant date.

This additional provision requires the vessel to be delivered with present class, free of recommendations. The sellers shall notify the classification society of any matters coming to their knowledge prior to delivery which, upon being reported to the classification society, would lead to the withdrawal of the vessel's class, or to the imposition of a recommendation relating to her class.

---

82 See Chapter 3, above.

There are three obligations of the seller under this clause:

(a) to deliver the ship in the same condition as she was at the time of inspection – fair wear and tear excepted;

(b) to deliver the ship with her present class maintained, free of recommendation;

(c) to notify the class of any matters within their knowledge prior to delivery which would lead to withdrawal of class or to recommendation relating to class.

The first obligation is an obligation to reconcile the condition at delivery with the condition at the time of inspection. There is an exception for fair wear and tear to the extent that the class of the ship and normal maintenance matters are not affected.

Naturally, the risk of loss or damage until delivery is still on the seller, whose insurance will cover damage or loss caused by an insured peril. The seller's insurance is cancelled immediately post-delivery.

The second obligation means that the ship's certificates must be valid and free from conditions or recommendations. This can simply be satisfied by the seller delivering an original class status certificate to the buyers issued within a few days prior to delivery.

The additional words in the second part of the clause of the 1993 Form, 'free of average damage', are for clarification and they are usually added to the same clause of the 1987 Saleform, when it is used.

The phrase has been held, in *The Alfred Trigon*,[83] to mean:

> ... 'average damage affecting class' is not just any damage affecting class. It is damage affecting class of a certain kind, and means damage occasioned by a peril ordinarily covered by insurance as opposed to defects arising through wear and tear or general old age.[84]

The words 'class maintained' mean that the vessel had to be in class; 'affecting class' means damage of such a character as either to prevent the vessel being in class or to result in the surveyor, on his becoming aware of the damage, imposing some qualification on class by way of recommendation.[85]

It is to be observed that, under the 1987 Saleform, the seller has an obligation to notify the classification society of any matter coming to their knowledge, prior to delivery, which may lead to a recommendation against class. This obligation was introduced in the 1983 revision of the NSF as a direct consequence of the gap in the wording, which was considered in *The Buena Trader*.[86] The sellers' obligation to notify class has, however, been deleted from cl 11 of the 1993 form (see above). With the deletion of this obligation under the 1993 Saleform, the buyer's position is weakened as it reverts back to the position before 1983. This duty will not be implied into the contract as was held in *The Buena Trader*. It is important to examine this development.

---

83 [1981] 2 Lloyd's Rep 333.

84 Ibid, p 338, *per* Goff J; see, also, *The Star of Kuwait* [1986] 2 Lloyd's Rep 641, and *The Great Marine (No 2)* [1990] 2 Lloyd's Rep 250.

85 *The Andreas P* [1994] 2 Lloyd's Rep 183.

86 [1978] 2 Lloyd's Rep 325.

The Buena Trader

Negotiations by telex for the sale of a vessel were concluded in accordance with the provisions of the NSF 1966. It provided that, '. . . the vessel shall be delivered charter free, class maintained free of recommendation, free of average damage affecting class with all trading certificates clean and valid at the time of delivery': also that, '. . . the vessel is to be delivered with continuous machinery survey cycle up to date at time of delivery'.

The buyers refused to accept delivery of the vessel on the ground that, among other matters, the continuous machinery survey was not up to date and that the vessel had suffered wear and tear damage, known to the sellers, affecting the maintenance of the vessel's class. They contended that the sellers were, therefore, under an implied obligation to notify the classification society of this fact. The breach of this implied obligation entitled them to refuse to accept delivery of the vessel. The dispute was referred to arbitration.

The arbitrator decided in favour of the sellers and found that 'up to date' only meant that each item would have been examined some time within the last five years. Relying upon evidence as to practice of Lloyd's surveyors, he said that it did not matter that the whole cycle was not evenly spread. He stated a special case for the court to decide the issue whether the buyers were liable to the sellers in damages for their refusal to accept the vessel.

The judge came to the opposite view in that, pursuant to the rules of the class, 20% of the items ought to be examined each year, so that the cycle was evenly spread. Seeing that far fewer were examined, and that the cycle was not up to date, he held in favour of the buyers. The sellers appealed.

Lord Denning MR agreed with the arbitrator, insofar as the interpretation of the rules of the classification society were concerned and, further, considered whether there was an implied term in the contract that the sellers ought to notify the class about wear and tear items. He held that:

> In those circumstances it seems to me that there was no implied term that the owners were to notify Lloyd's of any of these items of wear and tear, which might affect class. As we all know, no terms are to be implied unless they are necessary to carry out and give business efficacy to the contract.[87]

There was no obligation, therefore, upon the sellers to do anything other than do the repairs, which were recommended and outstanding. The ship was delivered as she lay at the time of delivery. Thus, the 1966 form had a serious deficiency. Even if the sellers were aware of defects or damage affecting the ship's class, which arose after the buyer's inspection, they were not obliged to report them to the classification society, or to make them known to the buyer. The latter had to rely on the statutory protection if he could prove breach of merchantable quality or fitness for purpose.

To avoid the problems of The Buena Trader, the notification obligation was introduced in 1983 and was repeated in the amendment of the form in 1987.

---

87 [1978] 2 Lloyd's Rep 325, pp 329–30.

The questions that arose after the amendment of the clause have been, as follows. What matters does it refer to? What is the position with matters that already existed at the time of the buyer's afloat inspection? What is the earliest date when the existence of these matters is of relevance to the sale contract?

In *The World Horizon*,[88] under a contract of sale drawn on the 1983 Saleform, the plaintiffs were the buyers and the defendants were the sellers of the vessel *The World Horizon*. Clause 11 of the form provided for the delivery of the vessel with her present class maintained free of recommendations and free of average damage affecting class. It also provided that the sellers shall notify the classification society of any matters coming to their knowledge prior to delivery which upon discovery would lead to the withdrawal of the vessel's class or the imposition of a recommendation. When the vessel was delivered, it was contended that the sellers were in breach of their obligation under cl 11 because they had failed to notify the classification society of two matters which they knew prior to delivery, and which would affect the class of the vessel. These matters were that the spare main/engine piston rod was not yet on board the vessel, and the clamps and supports for the deck piping were in need of repair.

It was found that both these matters were old, as they had existed since the inspection by the buyers and the classification society, and the society had made no recommendations on them. The Court of Appeal held that the obligation under cl 11 related to matters coming to the knowledge of the sellers from the date of the last survey by the classification society or the last inspection by the buyers.

The leading decision is now *The Niobe*,[89] in which this question was directly in issue. It was held by the Court of Appeal that the obligation referred to matters coming to the sellers' knowledge from the date of the contract. 'Coming' looks to the future from the date of the contract. It reversed the decision of Gatehouse J who had held that it was from the date of the last survey by the classification society before the contract. However, the House of Lords[90] chose a more flexible approach than the two earlier Court of Appeal decisions. The question put to the House of Lords was whether the sellers were under an obligation to notify their classification society prior to delivery of matters that affected class and which came to their knowledge, as from (1) the date of the contract, or (2) the date of the last survey of the equipment in question, or (3) from some other date and, if so, what date. The Lords unanimously held that the obligation covered all matters affecting class, whenever such matters might have come to the sellers' knowledge before or after the contract and it did not only refer to the future. According to Lord Mackay of Clashfern LC:

> Grammatically, the phrase 'coming to their knowledge' is an adjectival present principle governing the word 'matters' . . . Of course, the phrase may take colour from its context, and in some contexts point only to the future . . . But in the present context the adjectival phrase is as apt to cover knowledge acquired before the contract as after. Like 'within their knowledge', it means matters known to the sellers: neither more nor less. It follows that there is no *terminus a quo*, and the sellers are obliged

---

88 [1993] 2 Lloyd's Rep 56, p 57.
89 [1994] 1 Lloyd's Rep 487.
90 [1995] 1 Lloyd's Rep 579.

under the contract to inform the classification society before delivery of all matters affecting class whenever such matters may have come to their knowledge. In practice however, it will not usually be necessary to go back beyond the last relevant survey.[91]

From a risk management point of view, the protection afforded to buyers by cl 11 of the 1987 form should not lightly be bargained away. If the 1993 form is used, then an appropriate reinstatement of the reporting requirement should be negotiated.

Sellers' knowledge does not include constructive knowledge, for example, that possessed by the sellers' agents, but it ought to include a 'turning a blind eye knowledge' when a person, suspicious of the truth, deliberately refrains from inquiring and turns a blind eye to the truth.[92]

There are, however, still difficulties in practice as to how the buyer can prove that the sellers knew about defects, since there is no duty of good faith. Presumably, the standard of a reasonable seller would apply depending on the particular case, that is, what a reasonable person in the position of a seller would have suspected, or believed, to be the situation.[93]

6.8 The closing meeting

It has already been mentioned that all documents need to be ready for exchange at this meeting, which invariably takes place at a different location from the place of the physical delivery, but simultaneously. Representatives of the buyer and seller on board the ship will communicate with the lawyers of the parties at the place of the financial closing, once the pre-delivery inspection is completed and the buyer's representative is satisfied with the condition of the ship. This is the time when either matters go smoothly and the buyer's bank is instructed to release the balance of the money, or heated arguments may ensue if the seller has failed to comply with his obligations discussed previously.

From a risk management aspect, the timing is very important. If the money has already been released and the buyer's representative communicates that the ship should not be accepted, the buyer's lawyers should be on the alert to obtain a freezing injunction against the seller to refrain him from removing the money out of the jurisdiction. At what point in time this can be done will be seen under para 8.2, below.

If the closing proceeds smoothly, the next step is for the seller to communicate with the registrar of the ship's registry to discharge the mortgage and deliver to the buyer the ship's certificates and other documents. An executed discharge of the mortgage would have been lodged with the ship's registry in advance. Upon payment of the money, the seller will transfer title in the ship to the buyer. The buyer

---

91 [1995] 1 Lloyd's Rep 579, p 583.

92 *The Eurysthenes* [1976] 2 Lloyd's Rep 171 (CA), in the context of s 39(5) of the Marine Insurance Act 1906.

93 This test derives from what the Court of Appeal said, in *The Star Sea* [1997] 1 Lloyd's Rep 360, about privity of the owners or managers in relation to the unseaworthiness of a ship.

will register the ship under the new flag and the buyer's mortgagee will instruct the registrar to register the new mortgage.

The seller must also deliver additional documents, such as minutes of the directors' and shareholders' meeting approving the sale, the company's constitutional documents, and an original certificate of the seller's good standing. An original power of attorney, an original certificate of the ship's classification society, an original certificate of the ship's registry stating that the ship is free from all registered encumbrances and any governmental approvals or consents, that might be needed, must also be delivered. A protocol of delivery with a commercial invoice and an original inventory of the ship's parts, together with the ship's manuals and plans, form part of the essential documents for delivery at this stage.

6.9 Post-delivery matters

After the closing meeting, the remaining matters for completion to be finalised are: the cancellation of insurance by the seller, and the issue of a new insurance policy in the name of the buyer; the delivery to the buyer of the certificate of permanent deletion from the ship's registry; the issue of a new class certificate by the classification society; and the registration of the ship, or the conversion of a preliminary registration to a permanent one by the buyer. Finally, the new crew boards the ship.

7 THE PARTIES' RESPECTIVE REMEDIES FOR DEFAULT

7.1 Buyer's default

7.1.1 The seller's contractual remedies

It has been seen earlier that, under cl 2, the buyer is obliged to establish the deposit within a stated time as a security for his commitment to the contract. This clause does not specify the consequences for breach.

Clause 13 of the NSF 1987 deals with buyers' default in payment, either of the deposit or the purchase money, and stipulates the consequences of non-payment. It provides:

> Should the deposit not be paid as aforesaid, the sellers have the right to cancel this contract, and they shall be entitled to claim compensation for their losses and for all expenses incurred together with interest at the rate of 12% per annum.

> Should the purchase money not be paid as aforesaid, the sellers have the right to cancel this contract, in which case the amount deposited together with interest earned, if any, shall be forfeited to the sellers. If the deposit does not cover the sellers' losses, they shall be entitled to claim further compensation for their losses and for any expenses together with interest at the rate of 12% per annum.

Clause 13 of the 1993 NSF provides the same, apart from omitting a fixed rate of interest which leaves discretion with the arbitrators to fix it according to market rates, if the parties adjudicate their dispute by invoking the arbitration clause of the contract.

Prior to the 1987 NSF, the 1966 form did not provide for compensation in respect of the seller's loss and for his expenses incurred by reason of the buyer's failure to pay the deposit. In *The Blankenstein*[94] (decided in 1985), failure to pay the deposit was held to be a repudiatory breach of the contract, entitling the sellers to recover the amount of the deposit by way of damages for breach of contract, even though the amount of the deposit exceeded the amount of their loss (that is, the fall in market price). No doubt because this was felt to be an unfair 'windfall' for the sellers, what is now the first paragraph of cl 13 was added to the 1987 Saleform, giving the sellers the option to cancel the contract and claim compensation for their losses.

Whether the first paragraph of cl 13 – having regard to the second paragraph of the same – precludes the sellers from recovering the deposit as part of 'their losses', if the buyer withdraws from the sale before payment of the deposit, was adjudicated by London arbitrators.[95] The argument in the arbitration was that the ordinary measure of the sellers' loss would be to put them in the same position as if the deposit had been paid. If that were correct, the deposit could be forfeited. The arbitrators decided that the second paragraph of cl 13 is intended to prescribe the only situation in which the deposit can be forfeited. When the deposit has not been paid in breach of cl 2, then the deposit does not exist and, therefore, it cannot be forfeited or claimed as part of the sellers' damages for the buyers' repudiation. Their measure of loss is now spelt out in the first paragraph of cl 13.[96]

As regards the second paragraph of the clause, it simply refers to failure by the buyer to pay the purchase price. However, the buyer may rightfully not pay because of default by the seller to deliver the ship free of defects. It must be implied in the clause that the sellers' right of cancellation arises from a wrongful refusal by the buyer to pay. An example of this has been seen in *The Action*:[97] the list of 12 defects presented to the seller by the buyer's representative were eventually repaired – nevertheless, the buyers withdrew from the contract just before the rectification of the last defect and were held to have wrongfully withdrawn from the contract.

7.1.2 The seller's statutory remedies

Equally, the SOGA 1979 affords protection to the seller should the buyer fail to pay the purchase price. Section 50(1) provides that 'where the buyer wrongfully neglects or refuses to accept and pay for the goods, the seller may maintain an action against him for damages for non-acceptance'. Sub-section (2) states that 'the measure of damages is the estimated loss directly and naturally resulting, in the ordinary course of events, from the buyer's breach of contract'. In particular, sub-s (3)

---

94 [1985] 1 Lloyd's Rep 93.

95 Unreported; arbitration awards are not published because of confidentiality unless the parties to the reference consent.

96 See, also, op cit, Goldrein, fn 19.

97 [1987] 1 Lloyd's Rep 283, see fn 50 under 5.1 above.

provides that 'where there is an available market for the goods in question the measure of damages is prima facie to be ascertained by the difference between the contract price and the market or current price at the time or times when the goods ought to have been accepted'. This section will apply when the parties have not dealt with damages expressly in the contract. If the parties use either the 1987 or the 1993 NSF, cl 13 stipulates the amount recoverable.

The right to cancel and claim damages must be exercised within a reasonable time by the sellers. What is a reasonable time will depend on the circumstances of a case, but in *The Great Marine (No 1)*[98] the sellers delayed for over a week and that was held to have been too long.

7.2 Seller's default

7.2.1 Delay in delivery or non-delivery as per contract

Clause 14 of the 1987 NSF deals with default of the seller and provides:

> If the sellers fail to execute a legal transfer or to deliver the ship with everything belonging to her in the manner and within the time specified in line 38, the buyers shall have the right to cancel this contract in which case the deposit in full shall be returned to the buyers together with interest at the rate of 12% per annum. The sellers shall make due compensation for the losses caused to the buyers by failure to execute a legal transfer or to deliver the ship in the manner and within the time specified in line 38, if such are due to the proven negligence of the sellers.

The effect of cl 14 is twofold:

(a) the buyer has a right to elect to cancel and claim the deposit back with a fixed rate of interest, if the ship is not delivered as provided by the contract irrespective of negligence by the seller (no fault provision);

(b) in addition, the buyer has a right to claim compensation if it is proved that the seller's failure to deliver the ship according to the contract and within the contractual date was due to his negligence, which caused losses to the buyer[99] (proven negligence provision).

The clause has been made clearer in cl 14 of the amended NSF 1993, which provides:

> Should the sellers fail to give Notice of Readiness in accordance with cl 5 or fail to be ready to validly complete a legal transfer by the date stipulated in line 61 the buyers shall have the option of cancelling this agreement provided always that the sellers shall be granted a maximum of three banking days after Notice of Readiness has been given to make arrangements for the documentation set out in cl 8. If after Notice of Readiness has been given but before the buyers have taken delivery, the vessel ceases to be physically ready for delivery and is not made physically ready again in every respect by the date stipulated in line 61 and new Notice of Readiness

---

98 [1990] 2 Lloyd's Rep 245.

99 *Linett Bay Shipping Co Ltd v Patraicos Gulf Shipping Co SA (The Al Tawfiq)* [1984] 2 Lloyd's Rep 598.

given, the buyers shall retain their option to cancel. In the event that the buyers elect to cancel this agreement the deposit together with interest earned shall be released to them immediately.

Should the sellers fail to give Notice of Readiness by the date stipulated in line 61 or fail to be ready to validly complete a legal transfer as aforesaid they shall make due compensation to the buyers for their loss and for all expenses together with interest if their failure is due to proven negligence and whether or not the buyers cancel this agreement

As explained under para 6.4 (above), this clause must be read together with cll 5 and 3 providing for the seller's obligation to give notice of readiness and the buyer's obligation to arrange for payment of the balance of the purchase money respectively when the ship is in every respect physically ready for delivery.

Apart from the clarification in this new clause with respect to the seller's obligation to have the ship actually physically ready and not just prospectively ready when he gives notice of readiness, there are two further differences between the 1987 and the 1993 clauses: (i) when the buyer elects to cancel the contract under the first paragraph of the 1993 clause and claims the deposit, the interest rate is not fixed; presumably, the arbitrators will determine the interest rate; and (ii) when the ship is not ready due to proven negligence by the seller, under the second paragraph of the clause, the buyer can claim compensation, not only for losses so caused, but also for his expenses, whether or not he elects to cancel the contract.

For other breaches, the buyer will be entitled to rely on remedies provided either in other terms of the contract or under the general law.

7.2.2 *Other breaches by the seller*

Generally, and if the contract does not otherwise provide, the buyer would have protection under common law or the provisions of the SOGA 1979 and/or the SSGA 1994 as discussed in the beginning of this chapter and in Chapter 10. Such protection is afforded for a total or partial failure by the seller to perform. If it is a partial failure, the buyer's remedy will depend on whether the breach is one of a condition of the contract or a statutory condition under the SOGA 1979 and/or the SSGA 1994. If it is a breach of a condition, the buyer has the right to elect either to cancel the contract and claim damages for repudiation or to affirm the contract and claim damages caused by the breach. If it is a breach of a warranty, his remedy will be in damages only, and, if it is a breach of an innominate term, his remedy will depend on the seriousness of the breach.

7.3 Causation and remoteness of loss

Generally, the principle applicable to causation and remoteness for breach of contract derives from *Hadley v Baxendale*:[100]

Where two parties have made a contract which one of them has broken, the damages which the other party ought to receive in respect of such breach of contract should be

---

100 (1854) 9 Exch 341.

such as may fairly and reasonably be considered as either (a) arising naturally, that is, according to the usual course of things, from such breach of contract itself, or (b) such as may reasonably be supposed to have been in the contemplation of both parties, at the time they made the contract, as the probable result of the breach of it.

For many years, it had been thought that the principle contained two separate rules under (a) and (b) above which were mutually exclusive and this had led, on occasions, to a degree of rigidity in the application of the principle. Only until recently was it clarified in *The Achilleas* (a case of a late redelivery of a ship under a time charter) that the rule was composite with two limbs not exclusive of each other, as derived from the House of Lords decisions first in *Hall v Pim* and subsequently in *The Heron II* (cited by C. Clarke J in **The Achilleas**.[101]

The judge summarized the principle of *Hadley v Baxendale*, as had been interpreted by Lord Reid in *The Heron IT*. He said that (a) the mere fact that the type of loss is foreseeable is not, in itself, sufficient to make it recoverable; (b) a claimant would, however, be entitled to recover damages in respect of a foreseeable result on two occasions: (i) when the result would happen in the great majority of cases, or (ii) when, on the facts known or available to the defendant, the chances of the result happening might be less than evens but the occurrence would not be very unusual. [To use Lord Reid's words, a reasonable man in the position of the defendant would have realized that such loss was sufficiently likely to result from the breach to make it proper to hold that the loss flowed naturally from the breach or that loss of that kind should have been within his contemplation. However, a type of damage, which – although foreseeable as a substantial possibility – would only happen in a small minority of cases and, therefore, would be very unusual, should not be regarded as having been in the parties' contemplation.]

The owners in *The Achilleas* were awarded damages for the loss of profit they suffered resulting from the late redelivery of the vessel by the charterers. The damages were not based just on the difference between the market rate of hire and the charter-party rate for the overrun period (as has been the usual method of calculating damages in similar cases), but on the basis of the reduced sum of hire per day agreed between the owners and the next charterers for the whole period of the next charter-party. The reduction in the daily rate of hire had been agreed by the owners to prevent cancellation of the next charter in view of the delay in redelivery of the ship by the previous charterers. Such step should be regarded as reasonable in order to mitigate their loss. Had the owners lost the next fixture by reason of the late redelivery, it would not, perhaps, have been unusual – subject to the owners having mitigated their loss by finding another fixture – to be awarded the loss of profit which they would, otherwise, have earned by the lost fixture, less the profit which they might have made from the subsequent fixture. This is, in essence, the effect of The *Achilleas* decision. Considering the significant factor in this case, which was the existence of a profitable fixture, the case ought to be distinguished from previous authorities, which have decided damages for late redelivery on the basis of the

---

101 *Transfield Shipping Inc v Mercator Shipping Inc (The Achilleas)* [2007] 1 Lloyd's Rep 19; *R & H Hall Ltd v W H Pim (Junior) & Co Ltd* (1928) 30 Ll L Rep 159; *Czarnikov Ltd Koufos (The Heron II)* [1967] 2 Lloyd's Rep 457 or [1969] 1 AC 350.

difference between the market and the current charter hire rates, if the market rate is higher.

Buyers and sellers of ships are probably aware that the recoverable loss for breach of contract is the loss that arises naturally, in the usual course of things, from the other party's breach, and this is judged objectively. In addition, there may be a loss which, at the time of the contract, was in the reasonable contemplation of the parties as likely to result from the breach. For example, the seller ought to bear in mind that the buyer, at the time of the contract, might have already fixed the ship for a charterparty to commence at the time of delivery under the sale contract. He may also have been put on notice by the buyer why the latter may need the ship delivered punctually on the date agreed. Conversely, the buyer ought to bear in mind that if he wrongfully withdraws from the contract, the seller might be likely to miss another good buyer, or that the price may fall later.

In particular, in the event of non-delivery by the seller, if there is an available market for the particular ship, the measure of damages for non-delivery of, or failure to transfer the title in, the vessel is *prima facie* the difference between the contract price and the market price, or the current price of the ship at the time when it ought to have been delivered (s 51(3) of the SOGA 1979). If there is no market for this type of vessel, the measure of damages is the estimated loss directly and naturally resulting, in the ordinary course of events, from the seller's breach of contract (s 51(2).

In addition, in the event of loss of profit from not having the use of the ship for employment in the meantime, until a substitute is found, such loss of profit can be added to the difference between the contract and the market price.

This interesting point arose in *The Ile aux Moines*,[102] in which the buyers' lawyers had only pleaded damages under s 51(3) in the arbitration. When the case was referred to the court, as a special case on a point of law, namely whether the buyer could claim both the difference in the market price and the loss of use suffered in the meantime, the answer was in the affirmative. However, it was by then too late to recover both, because the award had already been made final!

In this case, such loss of profit (applying Lord Reid's test, above) was sufficiently likely to result from the breach and it would have been in the reasonable contemplation of the parties at the time of the contract.

Loss of a lucrative charter, however, cannot be claimed, unless the seller was aware of the intended use of the particular ship.[103]

If the buyers accept the ship late, they could claim loss of profit being measured on the basis of what they would have been likely to earn during the gap between the specified delivery date and the actual delivery. The buyers are to be put in the

---

102 [1974] 2 Lloyd's Rep 502.

103 *Victoria Laundry (Windsor) v Newman Industries* [1949] 2 KB 52 8 (CA), leading authority on remoteness and measure of damages for breach of contract: the defendants, an engineering company, with knowledge of the nature of the plaintiffs' business, having promised delivery by a particular date of a large and expensive plant, could not reasonably contend that they could not foresee that loss of business profit would be liable to result to the purchaser from a long delay in delivery; that although the defendants had no knowledge of the dyeing contracts which the plaintiffs had in prospect, it did not follow that the plaintiffs were precluded from recovering some general, and perhaps conjectural, sum for loss of business in respect of contracts reasonably to be expected.

same financial position as if the sellers had performed the particular obligation in question.[104] Applying the decision of *The Achilleas*, unless it is reversed on appeal, if the charter rate of an agreed fixture is reduced by reason of the ship's delay to commence the charter, the buyer may be able to recover the difference between the original charter rate and the agreed one after the reduction, provided the terms and the length of the charter party are not unusual.

7.4 Mitigation of loss by the buyer

The Solholt[105]

The question of mitigation of loss arose in *The Solholt*. The contract for sale of this vessel was on the NSF. The purchase price was US$5 million. The contract provided for a specified delivery date being 'not later than 31 August 1979'. In the event of default by the sellers for reasons for which they were responsible, cl 14 gave the buyers the right to cancel, claim the deposit with interest of 5% and compensation for their losses so caused. Fearing late delivery, as the vessel had to complete a charterparty at the time, the sellers sought an extension of time from the buyers, but the latter refused. The vessel arrived at the port for inspection and she was late by only two days. Her market price was $5 million, but the buyers cancelled the contract. It was agreed that the buyers were entitled to cancel the contract and to recover their full deposit ($500,000). The question was whether they were entitled to a remedy in damages in addition to the return of their deposit, that is, the increase in the market value, and whether the buyers had mitigated their loss.

The judge and the Court of Appeal held that the direct loss of the buyer from the sellers' breach was $500,000, but since there was evidence that the sellers would be prepared to accept an offer from the buyers to buy the ship at the original price, the buyers failed to take reasonable steps to mitigate their loss.

Lord Donaldson MR said with respect to mitigation:

> A plaintiff is under no duty to mitigate his loss, despite the habitual use by the lawyers of the phrase 'duty to mitigate'. He is completely free to act as he judges to be in his best interests. On the other hand, a defendant is not liable for all loss suffered by the plaintiff in consequence of his so acting. A defendant is only liable for such part of the plaintiff's loss as is properly to be regarded as caused by the defendant's breach of duty.[106]

7.5 Currency of loss

The currency in which the loss is claimed may make a significant difference. However, the currency must appropriately reflect the recoverable loss. Disputes arising under sale of ships contracts are expressly made subject to arbitration in London,

---

104 *The Great Marine (No 2)* [1990] 2 Lloyd's Rep 250.
105 [1983] 1 Lloyd's Rep 605 (CA).
106 Ibid, p 608.

so, by inference, English law would apply. For the purpose of assessing the currency of loss for breach of the contract, however, it would not matter if the proper law of the contract were English law. If neither of the parties to the contract, nor the contract itself, nor the claim, had any connection with sterling, it would be a prima facie case for giving judgment in a foreign currency.

In this connection it is relevant to quote what Lord Wilberforce said in **The Despina R and The Folias** (a collision case, but the principle is broadly the same in breach of contract cases):[107]

> My Lords, in *Miliangos v George Frank (Textiles) Ltd* [1976] 1 Lloyd's Rep 201; [1976] AC 443, this House decided that a plaintiff suing for a debt payable in Swiss francs under a contract governed by Swiss law could claim and recover judgment in this country in Swiss francs. Whether the same, or a similar, rule could be applied to cases where (i) a plaintiff sues for damages in tort, or (ii) a plaintiff sues for damages for breach of contract, were questions expressly left open for later decision. These questions were regulated before *Miliangos* as to tort by *SS Celia (Owners) v SS Volturno (Owners) (The Volturno)* (1921) 8 LlL Rep 449; [1921] 2 AC 544 and as to contract by *Di Ferdinando v Simon, Smits & Co Ltd* [1920] 3 KB 409, which decided that judgment in an English court could only be given in sterling converted from any foreign currency as at the date of the wrong. Now these questions are directly raised in the present appeals.

In the first appeal, the issue of the currency in which damages were payable arose when the plaintiff sued in tort for collision damage. The award made for the repairs was held to be in the currency in which the loss was sustained. In the second appeal, the same issue arose from breach of contract. This time the charterers sued the owners of the ship to recover their loss for money paid in French francs to the cargo-receivers. Lord Wilberforce observed:

> A decision in what currency the loss was borne or felt can be expressed as equivalent to finding which currency sum appropriately or justly reflects the recoverable loss. This is essentially a matter for arbitrators to determine. A rule that arbitrators may make their award in the currency best suited to achieve an appropriate and just result should be a flexible rule in which account must be taken of the circumstances in which the loss arose, in which the loss was converted into a money sum, and in which it was felt by the plaintiff. In some cases the 'immediate loss' currency may be appropriate, in others the currency in which it was borne by the plaintiff. There will be still others in which the appropriate currency is the currency of the contract.[108]

The Court of Appeal stated, in 2004, in a case involving breach of contract, **Virani Ltd v Manuel Revert Y Cia SA**,[109] that the proper approach was to enquire which currency most truly expressed the claimant's loss. The relevant test was to ascertain which currency would as nearly as possible compensate the claimant in accordance with principles of restitution, and whether the parties must be taken reasonably to have had that in contemplation.

---

107 [1979] 1 Lloyd's Rep 1 at p 4; see also *Transoceanic Francesca and Nicos V* [1987] 2 Lloyd's Rep 155, Chapter 12, para 3.12.5.

108 Ibid, p 9.

109 [2004] 2 Lloyd's Rep 14; see also *The Texaco Melbourne* [1994] 1 Lloyd's Rep 473 (HL) and Chapter 12 para 3.12.5 below.

8 LEGAL AND COMMERCIAL RISK MANAGEMENT FOR THE BUYER

8.1 Considerations before exercising the option to reject the ship

First, the buyer should consider whether the breach amounts to failure to perform and whether the contract or statutory provisions give him the right to cancel. He should also consider whether the seller's failure is capable of being remedied, and whether the seller is willing to rectify the breach within a reasonable time. If he purports to cancel the contract when the seller is willing to rectify the breach within a reasonable time, the buyer may be in repudiation of contract. Assuming that he has the right to cancel, foremost consideration for the buyer before electing to cancel the contract will be, whether he would be likely to recover damages from the seller, and whether the market for this type of ship has risen. The buyer may have already been committed to perform a charterparty. He should consider whether the consequence of his waiting until the defects are remedied would be the cancellation of the charter; also, whether he could recover his consequential damages from the seller, who may not be in existence after the delayed transfer of the ship.

8.2 Considerations before applying for a freezing injunction against the purchase money

8.2.1 The underlying principles

The nature of a freezing injunction and what it purports to achieve has already been discussed in Chapter 2, para 5, above. Briefly, it assists a claimant – by obtaining a court order – to prohibit a defendant from disposing of his assets, which are within the jurisdiction or worldwide, until a judgment or arbitration award is obtained. The injunction does not, however, give a security interest to the claimant as against the assets over which the injunction has been granted, nor priority over other creditors of the defendant.

> Such principles were restated by Lord Bingham in **Fourie v Le Roux & others**:[110]
>
> Mareva (or freezing) injunctions were from the beginning, and continue to be, granted for an important but limited purpose: to prevent a defendant dissipating his assets with the intention or effect of frustrating enforcement of a prospective judgment. They are not a proprietary remedy. They are not granted to give a claimant advance security for his claim, although they may have that effect. They are not an end in themselves. They are a supplementary remedy, granted to protect the efficacy of court proceedings, domestic or foreign: see Steven Gee, *Commercial Injunctions*, 5th ed (2004), pp 77–83.[111]
>
> In recognition of the severe effect which such an injunction may have on a defendant, the procedure for seeking and making Mareva injunctions has over the last three

---

110 [2007] UKHL 1 or [2007] 1 WLR 320.
111 See also Gee, S. First Supplement to the 5th edn (2007).

decades become closely regulated. I regard that regulation as beneficial and would not wish to weaken it in any way. The procedure incorporates important safeguards for the defendant. One of those safeguards, by no means the least important, is that the claimant should identify the prospective judgment whose enforcement the defendant is not to be permitted, by dissipating his assets, to frustrate. The claimant cannot of course guarantee that he will recover judgment, nor what the terms of the judgment will be. But he must at least point to proceedings already brought, or proceedings about to be brought, so as to show where and on what basis he expects to recover judgment against the defendant.

The main ground of the application by Le Roux to the court seeking the discharge of the order which had been granted was that there was no jurisdiction to make the order because, at the time the order was made (which was before the extension of jurisdiction by the CJJA 1982 order 1997) there had been no subsisting proceedings to which the freezing order could be ancillary and no undertaking to commence any such proceedings had been offered by Mr Fourie. The order was discharged.

Since 1997, it has been possible to obtain a 'free standing' freezing injunction. Before 1997, such an injunction could not be granted by the English court unless it had jurisdiction to determine the main substantive issues of a case for which the order was sought. As regards foreign defendants, leave to serve a defendant out of the jurisdiction could not be granted by reference only to the need to obtain the order, but only if the cause of action was within the provisions of RSC Ord 11, r 1. In other words, the cause of action should be triable in England, and the application for the injunction was not itself sufficient to obtain leave to serve out of the jurisdiction. This was known as 'The Siskina rule'.[112] There was one exception to this rule after the enactment of the Civil Jurisdiction and Judgments Act 1982, s 25, which permitted this interlocutory remedy, if the substantive proceedings were in a court of a Contracting State to the Brussels Convention, as amended. With regard to proceedings in a court of any other State in the world, the restriction was also lifted in 1997 by a statutory instrument.[113] In addition, s 44(2)(e) and (3) of the new Arbitration Act 1996 allows such an interim relief to be granted by the court to preserve assets for the purpose of, and in relation to, arbitral proceedings anywhere.

The general requirements for obtaining such an order must first be satisfied: there must be a good arguable case; it must be shown that there is a real risk that the seller will dissipate the assets or remove them from the jurisdiction;[114] the buyer must make a full and frank disclosure of all material facts in his statement of truth; and it must be just and convenient that the order should be granted. The buyer must be prepared to give an undertaking to pay damages to the defendant for any loss suffered by reason of the order, as well as an indemnity to third parties in respect of costs and liabilities reasonably incurred by them in complying with the order.

---

112 [1978] 1 Lloyd's Rep 1 (HL).

113 SI 1997/302.

114 The test for risk of dissipation is objective: *Harrison Partners Construction Pty v Jevena Pty Ltd* (2005) ALR 369; and solid evidence of risk of dissipation must be shown: *Laemthong International v ARTIS* [2005] 1 Lloyd's Rep 100.

8.2.2 Limits of granting such an injunction to a buyer of a ship

Frequently, buyers are in a dilemma whether or not to part with their money when they believe that there might be some defects in the ship on delivery, which the seller, upon receiving full payment, may not be willing to rectify and – being a one-ship foreign company – there may be a risk that the only asset of the seller (the purchase money) will be dissipated or removed from the jurisdiction.

Being sympathetic to such a dilemma of buyers of ships, the court, before *The Veracruz* case in 1992 (see below), invented a conditional injunction.

Saville J was in favour of a conditional injunction in the *A v B* case.[115]

The buyers in this case entered into a contract to buy a vessel from the defendants and paid the deposit into an account in their joint names. Subsequently, the buyers suspected that, on delivery, the vessel might not be in the order and condition stipulated by the contract. The defendants had no assets within the jurisdiction, and the buyers applied for a Mareva relief to freeze the sums in the joint account until an arbitration award was obtained. The buyers intended to commence arbitration proceedings against the sellers but, at the time of this application, they did not have a cause of action.

It was held that, if the material produced to the court satisfied the court that it would be appropriate to grant a Mareva relief when the cause of action arose, there was no good reason why the court should not grant relief, in advance, to take effect at that moment. If a conditional Mareva injunction was granted, it would give effect to the court's view that it would be appropriate to freeze the sums involved, provided nothing in the order came into effect until the moment of delivery. Thus, a conditional injunction was granted.

Although the English courts have recognised that a freezing injunction against the seller may be appropriate and just in some cases, they have, since this case, imposed some restrictions on the granting of this discretionary relief. First, there must be an accrued cause of action and, second, the buyer must notify the seller of the application, if the court has attached such a requirement in the order. These are examined next.

8.2.2.1 An accrued cause of action

The buyer cannot obtain the order for an anticipatory breach by the seller, but only for an existing cause of action.[116] It must be an actual or threatened invasion of rights or breach.[117] For example, he cannot apply to the court in advance of the delivery of the ship in anticipation that the seller will be in breach of contract. He must make out an arguable case of breach by the seller when he makes the ex parte application. Until the ship is delivered, unless there is already a late delivery and therefore a breach, the buyer does not have the right to sue for damages in case the ship is delivered in a defective condition.

---

115 A v B [1989] 2 Lloyd's Rep 423.

116 This is the third and still prevailing rule derived from *The Siskina*, op cit, fn 112: the rule establishes that the injunction has an ancillary nature to a substantive cause of action.

117 *Zucker v Tyndall Holdings Plc* [1992] 1 WLR 1127.

The Veracruz I[118] is a very good example of these issues. The ship bought by the plaintiff was under a bareboat charter. Repairs were necessary in the amount of $3 million, and a dispute arose between the owners (sellers) and charterers as to who would pay this sum; that dispute was referred to arbitration in Norway. The ship was not ready for delivery on the agreed date. The buyers referred this dispute to arbitration in London.

The buyers were concerned that the purchase price, which would be paid to the sellers in London, would be the sellers' only asset within the jurisdiction and that the latter, fearing an adverse award in the London arbitration, would remove the purchase money out of the jurisdiction. The buyers' concern was that there would be no assets against which to enforce the arbitration award. Consequently, when the sellers gave a new notice of intention to deliver the vessel, the buyers applied ex parte for a Mareva injunction to restrain the sellers from dealing with the purchase money when it was paid over, which was granted. The injunction was not to come into effect until after delivery and payment. The buyers' claim was for damages for late delivery and for damages in respect of defects, as they believed that the repairs had not been fully carried out. On handing over the purchase money, the buyers advised the sellers that it was subject to the injunction.

On appeal inter partes, Hobhouse J held that, although the plaintiffs had no accrued cause of action for damages for defects in the vessel at the time of the ex parte application, they had an accrued cause of action for damages for delay in delivery; and, to the extent that the plaintiffs could show an arguable claim for defects which, they expected, would be present on delivery, the court had jurisdiction to grant an anticipatory Mareva injunction. He also held that, despite the buyers' misrepresentation of the factual position pertaining to communications between the charterers, the owners and the classification society, when applying for the ex parte injunction, which was culpable, this did not, in the circumstances, justify a total discharge of the injunction, but a reduction of the sum over which the injunction was originally granted.

On further appeal, although the Court of Appeal agreed with the judge that the order should not be discharged completely, it felt bound by the decision of the House of Lords in *The Siskina* that the right to obtain an interlocutory injunction was not a cause of action in itself, but it could only stand in relation to a pre-existing cause of action.

Thus, on the issue of the feared defects, the Court of Appeal held that the learned judge was wrong to grant so much of the relief as related to the plaintiffs' claim to damages for defects which they feared would be present when the vessel was delivered; the plaintiffs could not, before delivery, by means of a Mareva injunction, secure a retention, in whole or in part, of the purchase price against feared defects; on this issue the defendants' appeal would be allowed.

As regards delayed delivery, the Court of Appeal confirmed the continuation of the injunction.

Beldam LJ rejected the approach of Saville J in the *A v B* case and said:

---

118 [1992] 1 Lloyd's Rep 353.

Though it may be convenient to the applicant to obtain an order which anticipates his cause of action, the court has to balance any such convenience against the obvious inconvenience to the other party. The defendant seller, obliged by the terms of the contract to carry out repairs to put the ship in a deliverable state, may depend upon the assurance of receiving the purchase price to secure finance to carry out the repairs. The prospect that they may be deprived of the whole or a substantial part of the price by a surreptitious application to the court could impede or prevent them obtaining the means to do so.[119]

This case re-affirms the general principle that a buyer may obtain such an injunction, provided (i) he could show that he has a good arguable case that a breach has already been committed by the seller, (ii) he makes a full and frank disclosure of all material facts to the court;[120] and (iii) he shows that there is a real risk of dissipation of assets (an inference of an intention to dissipate assets, from the fact that the defendant is short of money, would not be enough, unless there is proof of dishonesty[121]). This is in conformity with the test for granting an injunction whenever it is just and convenient.[122]

Prior to the Court of Appeal decision in *The Veracruz* in 1992, commercial court judges were following the approach of Saville J, because it was expedient to grant the injunction in cases such as the sale of used ships where the accrual of the cause of action was both imminent and, in practical terms, inevitable. The approach by Saville J was a common sense approach in the interests of justice. Thus, in special cases, judges were prepared to introduce an exception to the general *Siskina* rule applicable to injunctions if, in reality, there was a high probability that the seller had committed a breach, which would, inevitably, be effective on the day of delivery. The buyer's difficulty has been that he is not able to show, before the delivery date, that his cause of action has certainly accrued. It is a matter of a technical jurisdiction. This problem was, in fact, recognised by Sir John Megaw in *The Veracruz*; but, in agreement with Nourse LJ, he said that the court's difficulty was that it was not free to deal with the question of jurisdiction without the constraint of binding authority (meaning *The Siskina*). He, nevertheless, regarded the approach of Saville J in *A v B* as being a sensible and desirable approach in commercial cases. He saw no valid reason, in logic or practical convenience in the interests of justice, why jurisdiction should not exist in such cases provided the court order was made on the condition, which Saville J applied, that the injunction should not operate unless and until the anticipated cause of action arose. In the end, he felt precluded by authority from so deciding on the question of technical jurisdiction.[123]

Perhaps the House of Lords, or legislation, may, in due course, vary the third rule of *The Siskina* (as has been done with its other two rules discussed earlier) and

---

119 Ibid, p 358.

120 See, also, on similar issues *The Giovana* [1999] 1 Lloyd's Rep 867: an inchoate right and non-full and fair disclosure disbarred the cargo interests from obtaining the injunction against the owners of the ship.

121 *Midas Merchant Bank Plc v Bello* [2002] EWCA Civ 1496.

122 *Rasu Maritima SA v Pertamina* [1977] 2 Lloyd's Rep 397, per Lord Denning MR, applying the principle laid down by the House of Lords in *American Cyanamid v Ethicon* [1975] AC 396; *The Niedersachsen* [1983] 2 Lloyd's Rep 660.

123 *The Veracruz* [1992] 1 Lloyd's Rep 353, p 361.

make a distinction between the general rule applicable to the granting of injunctions and a possible exception to the rule that ought to apply in the cases of sale of ships for the interest of justice. This could perhaps be done by giving guidelines to judges for the exercise of a wider discretion in these cases, such as was exercised by Saville J in *A v B*. Until such time, buyers should bear in mind what Nourse LJ said in *The Veracruz* in connection with applications for such an injunction:

> If there is no cause of action, the want of jurisdiction cannot be supplied by suspending the operation of the injunction until one exists.[124]

What the buyers can do to overcome this difficulty is to have the application ready, and apply to the court at the same time as the delivery of the vessel, provided that they can show that the anticipated breach has indeed become actionable.

Ninemia Corp v Trave (The Niedersachsen)[125]

It was held at first instance and on appeal that the buyer seeking a Mareva injunction must show, on the evidence as a whole, a good arguable case that he will succeed at trial, and that the refusal of an injunction will involve a real risk that a judgment or award in his favour will remain unsatisfied. On a dispute over a contract for the purchase of a ship, the buyer alleged defects, in the boiler tubing and other defects on evidence from a surveyor. Since the application was made before delivery of the ship and there was no cause of action yet, the application for an injunction was refused. However, immediately after the delivery of the ship and payment of the price, the buyer was not deterred and applied again. In view of the change of the circumstances, the injunction was granted. On the seller's application to discharge the injunction, the injunction was discharged on the ground that there was no evidence before the court from which a prima facie inference could be drawn that there was a risk of the seller disposing of his assets before an arbitration award could be enforced. The Court of Appeal confirmed the decision.

Buyers and their lawyers should also bear in mind the judgment in **Laemthong International v Artis and Others**,[126] in which three freezing injunctions were discharged on grounds of failure to show a good arguable case, failure to prove risk of dissipation of assets, and failure to comply with the obligation of full and frank disclosure, respectively.

Perhaps, there may be a possibility for the buyer to obtain the injunction if he is able to show a threatened breach the day before the delivery of the ship by providing solid evidence of existing defects in the ship. This should substantiate a potential action. The order could be granted to take effect on the day of delivery.[127]

For example, in **The Assios**,[128] the buyers knew from the drydock inspection that the ship's bottom had a good deal of indentation which would require repairs;

---

124 Ibid, p 360.
125 [1983] 2 Lloyd's Rep 600.
126 [2005] 1 Lloyd's Rep 100.
127 Support for this proposition is derived from *Zucker v Tyndall Holdings Plc* [1992] 1 WLR 1127.
128 [1979] 1 Lloyd's Rep 331.

Loan Receipt
Liverpool John Moores University
Library and Student Support

Borrower Name: Umar,Hussaini
Borrower ID: **********0111

Modern maritime law :
31111013958051
Due Date: 18/01/2013 23:59

Total Items: 1
11/01/2013 22:25

Please keep your receipt in case of
dispute.

although the injunction was granted at the time, it was discharged later for want of disclosure (see later).

8.2.2.2 Notification of the application to the seller prior to delivery

Apart from the issue of the cause of action, the courts had been uneasy from the early days of the Mareva jurisdiction about making the order ex parte in cases of ship sales. This had been expressed aptly by Mr Justice Leggatt in *The Great Marine (No 1)*.[129]

> The sellers . . . have an understandable sense of disappointment if not of grievance, that having been led to expect that they would receive an unfettered right to deal with the whole of the purchase monies as they saw fit, they found themselves deprived of the right to deal with . . . it . . . Provided that the court is told the facts, it can then decide whether to grant an injunction subject to an undertaking that notice of the intention to serve it will be given to the sellers before completion of the sale so that they may consider, before there are assets of theirs within the jurisdiction to which the injunction can apply, whether there are grounds open to them for not completing the sale.
>
> Although such an order may be appropriate in some cases, in others it may seem more just to allow the trap to be laid so that a one-ship foreign company is not enabled to divest itself not only of the ship but also of the proceeds of sale before a bona fide claim advanced against it can be satisfied.[130]

The words of Lord Denning MR in *The Niedersachsen* (above) remain entirely appropriate today. Thus, in addition to the requirement that the buyer must have an accrued cause of action based on an actual or threatened breach, he must also disclose to the court all the circumstances, so that the court can determine whether or not the buyer should undertake to notify the seller of the injunction prior to the closing meeting. The court has wide discretion as to whether or not to order the buyer to notify the seller in advance, which depends on the circumstances of a case.[131]

The buyer's failure to make full and frank disclosure in the statement of truth, or failure to comply with his undertaking given to the court to notify the seller in advance, will result in the discharge of the injunction. In *The P*,[132] the plaintiffs were not justified in making the application ex parte; having taken it upon themselves to make the application without notice to the defendants, the plaintiffs undertook a heavy duty of disclosure which should be stringently enforced.

In *The Assios*, the injunction was discharged on the ground that the buyer had not made proper disclosure to the court that the injunction was intended as a trap for the seller to be presented with it at the closing meeting, particularly bearing in mind that the seller had, in any event, undertaken not to remove the deposit out of the jurisdiction except upon giving the buyer two clear days' notice. Lord Denning

---

129 [1990] 2 Lloyd's Rep 245.

130 Ibid, p 250.

131 *Petroleum Investment Co Ltd v Kantupan Holdings Co Ltd.* [2002] 1 All ER (Comm) 124.

132 *The P* [1992] 1 Lloyd's Rep 470: in any event, the injunction was discharged for want of an accrued cause of action; Evans J was bound by *The Veracruz* [1992] 1 Lloyd's Rep 353.

MR thought that the defendants would be entitled in such a case at least to delay delivery to some extent.

Conversely, if the defendants were not entitled to delay delivery, then by definition the plaintiffs had nothing to lose by giving advance notice. It was even to their advantage to have this issue, if it was to be raised, decided before delivery took place (per Evans J in *The P*).

In *A v B*, Saville J required the buyers to give the sellers notice of the injunction immediately and the buyers did give an advance notice.

Commercial judges, however, are realistic about the risk involved for the buyer when notice of the injunction is given to the seller in advance of delivery, particularly with regard to one-ship companies.

Buyers may negotiate with the seller to obtain an undertaking that the money will not be removed from the jurisdiction without prior notice to the buyer. To a great extent, however, such co-operation will depend on the reputation of the seller.

9 CIVIL LIABILITY OF CLASSIFICATION SOCIETIES TO BUYERS AND OTHER THIRD PARTIES

The role of classification societies was looked at in Chapter 8, in connection with their functions in enhancing safety of life and property at sea. This is purported to be achieved by each classification society when it surveys ships entered as members of the particular society in order to verify whether they comply with the society's own technical rules and regulations with regard to structural matters. Such rules may vary from one society to another but, by and large, societies which are members of the International Association of Classification Societies (IACS) aim to apply the same rules. The approach of each classification society varies in overseeing whether the class rules are complied with and this, invariably, causes problems.

A classification society issues or renews the classification certificate, or may make recommendations to member owners to carry out repairs, either straight away or within a certain time, and may impose certain conditions shown on the certificate. Unlike in the aviation industry where the relevant authority empowered under statute may issue a certificate of airworthiness in relation to an aircraft, the classification certificate issued by a classification society is not a certificate of seaworthiness. There is usually a misunderstanding by the public that the classification society is responsible to make sure that a ship is seaworthy. That obligation is upon the shipowner, who has a non-delegable duty to make his ship seaworthy.

As explained in Chapter 8, the additional work of classification societies relates to carrying out surveys to verify whether ships comply with the international and statutory provisions under SOLAS and MARPOL.

From the aforesaid, it would seem to an outsider that it is intrinsic in the function of surveying ships to verify whether or not they are compliant with the classification society's technical rules and regulations, or with the statutory provisions, that issues of seaworthiness are embraced and, undoubtedly, they are. However, issues of unseaworthiness depend on many other factors.

When a classification society performs its classification or statutory work, it does not design, build, install, supervise, own, control, manage, operate, repair, maintain, or derive the commercial benefits from the ship it surveys. For a ship to be seaworthy, or safe, it has to be substantially sound, but it also has to be properly crewed, maintained, operated and navigated. These factors fall outside the scope of classification.[133]

There is a contract between a shipowner and the classification society that surveys the ships entered with it. There would be a breach of contract if the society did not perform its contractual duties but, if the owner made a claim against the society for a loss suffered and allegedly caused by the negligence of the society's surveyor, the outcome would depend on causation. Invariably, there is a year gap between one survey to another, thus, maintenance of the ship in a good condition during the year is the owner's responsibility which would affect causation.

An important question which reached the House of Lords[134] was whether a classification society of a vessel owes a duty of care to third parties, who may suffer economic loss, when a vessel being in class causes damage to property on board. The same question has arisen in the context of purchase of ships when buyers – relying on a clean class certificate – suffer economic loss by reason of defects in the ship. Since there is no contractual relationship between a buyer of a ship and its classification society, which acts independently and is, normally, appointed by the seller, the matter has to be examined in tort. The general principles of tortious liability, as developed in recent years, are briefly summarised below.

Since 1990,[135] the English courts have applied a three-stage incremental approach to the question whether a duty of care exists. This is comprised of three ingredients: (i) foreseeability of damage; (ii) a relationship of proximity between the parties; and (iii) that in all circumstances it is fair, just and reasonable to impose a duty of care upon the defendant. With regard to liability of classification societies, there has been a trilogy of cases.

The Morning Watch [136]

The owners requested that the classification society carried out a special survey of their yacht which was to be sold early in the next season. A full time senior yacht surveyor of the defendants (the classification society) carried out the special survey and issued an interim certificate. The vessel passed the special survey, subject to listed repairs, which were duly effected by the owners. The vessel was later purchased by the plaintiffs. The plaintiffs contended that the vessel proved to have serious defects that rendered her unseaworthy and that these defects should have been discovered by the defendant's surveyor. They claimed against the classification society (Lloyd's) damages for economic loss suffered as a consequence of relying on the misstatements made by the society's surveyor negligently.

---

133 Extracts from a paper delivered by Harrison, J, of Lloyd's Register, 'Accountability of classification societies', seminar held by the London Shipping Law Centre, 21 February 2001.

134 *Marc Rich and Co AG v Bishop Rock Marine Co (The Nicholas H)* [1995] 2 Lloyd's Rep 299, [1996] AC 211 (HL).

135 *Caparo Industries plc v Dickman* [1990] 2 AC 605 (HL); *Murphy v Brentwood DC* [1991] 1 AC 398 (HL).

136 [1990] 1 Lloyd's Rep 547.

The court examined the principles and cases in this area under English law and held: a duty of care would only arise where: (1) it was reasonably foreseeable to the defendant that the plaintiff was liable to rely upon his statement; (2) there was the necessary proximity between the plaintiff and the defendant; and (3) it was just and reasonable in all circumstances to impose a duty of care on the part of the defendant to the plaintiff.

On the facts, since Lloyd's had been informed that the plaintiff was interested to buy the vessel after the survey was carried out, the first requirement was established.

However, the court was not prepared to accept the general proposition that Lloyd's owed a duty of care to those who would be likely to suffer economic loss in consequence of reliance on the negligent classification of a vessel. To accept such a proposition, it would be to make a substantial further advance in the law of negligence. Therefore, the plaintiffs had failed to show that the defendants owed them a duty of care, either when the special survey was carried out or on the issue of the interim certificate.

While Phillips J (as he then was) accepted the plaintiff's submission that Lloyd's deliberately maintained a system whereby parties other than the owners of classified vessels would be likely to rely on the fact that a vessel was maintained in class, and that this system provided an assurance that the vessel was maintained in good condition, he made the following observation:

(i) The primary purpose of the classification system is, as Lloyd's rules make plain, to enhance the safety of life and property at sea, rather than to protect the economic interests of those involved, in one role or another, in shipping.

(ii) Insofar as negligence in relation to classification is liable to harm economic interests, I can see no general ground for distinguishing between the economic interests of the charterer, the mortgagee and the purchaser. All are foreseeably liable to rely upon the class status of the vessel – often to the extent of making the maintenance of class a contractual obligation – and all are at risk of being caused economic loss if classification surveys are not carried out with proper skill and care.

Does English law impose a duty of care upon a classification society towards those whose economic interests are likely to be harmed?[137]

Referring to *Caparo v Dickman*, he considered the relationship between the classification society and purchasers of ships, and stated:

The relationship does not reflect any statutory scheme to protect purchasers . . . There is no relationship akin to contract. There is no voluntary assumption of responsibility to potential purchasers of shares . . . There is no greater proximity between Lloyd's and a potential purchaser than between Lloyd's and the bank that may advance the purchase price on the security of a mortgage on the vessel . . .[138]

Applying the three stages of the incremental approach, the second and third requirements were not satisfied in the circumstances. In effect, the third requirement that it must be fair, just and reasonable in all circumstances has restricted the

137 Ibid at, p 559.
138 Ibid, p 560.

law of negligence, unless the principle to be applied is clearly that of assumption of responsibility.[139]

The three-stage approach is now to be applied universally in cases concerned with the recovery of damages for either economic loss or physical damage, for example, whatever is the nature of the harm sustained by a plaintiff. It is an over-arching formula within which can be found all cases of recognised duties of care.[140] However, recognition is given to some categories in which it is obvious that, as a matter of common sense and justice, a duty should be imposed. The difference between categories lies in the fact that it may be more difficult to satisfy the three-stage test in cases of pure economic loss than in straightforward cases of physical damage.[141]

Furthermore, the duty of care was not imposed upon a classification society for physical damage to cargo on board a ship and consequential economic loss, mainly for policy considerations, by the majority of the House of Lords in the following decision.

The Nicholas H [142]

The vessel was loaded with the plaintiffs' cargo of lead and zinc for a voyage from Chile to Italy and the USSR. She had to deviate and call at a port in Europe because a crack was found in her hull. Further cracks later developed. A surveyor from the vessel's classification society boarded her and recommended permanent repairs at the nearest port with such facilities. The owners, however, persuaded the surveyor that temporary repairs should be carried out at anchor because permanent repairs would have involved drydocking and unloading of the cargo. The surveyor then reversed his initial recommendation, allowed temporary repairs and the vessel proceeded to the discharge port where the repairs would be further examined after discharge. The next day, while on the voyage, the welding of the temporary repairs cracked. Six days later, the vessel sank with the loss of all cargo. The cargo claim was settled between the cargo interests and the shipowner at the limitation amount in accordance with the Hague-Visby Rules which were applicable to the contract of carriage. The cargo interests claimed the balance of their claim against the classification society on the ground of breach of duty of care owed to them, which caused the loss to their cargo.

The case reached the House of Lords on a preliminary point: assuming there was negligence of the surveyor (which the classification society denied), did a classification society owe a duty of care to a third party – the owners of the cargo laden on the vessel – for the careless performance of a survey resulting in the vessel being allowed to sail and subsequently sink with her cargo? Counsel for the cargo-owners contended that, since the case involved physical damage to property in

---

139 As developed by *Hedley Byrne v Heller* [1964] AC 465.

140 *The Nicholas H* [1995] 2 Lloyd's Rep 299 (below).

141 See also a paper delivered by Gross, P (QC), at a lecture held by the London Shipping Law Centre, March 1997, available at the Centre's office.

142 *Marc Rich and Co AG v Bishop Rock Marine Co (The Nicholas H)* [1995] 2 Lloyd's Rep 299, [1996] AC 211 (HL).

which the plaintiff had a proprietary or possessory interest, the only requirement was proof of reasonable foreseeability and, therefore, the additional requirements of proximity and considerations of whether it was fair, just and reasonable to impose a duty of care were inapplicable.

The House of Lords by a majority rejected this argument. It was held that the elements of foreseeability, proximity, fairness, justice and reasonableness were relevant to all types of harm sustained by the plaintiff. The majority of their Lordships considered that there was a sufficient degree of proximity to fulfil the requirement for the existence of a duty of care. However, it was held that the recognition of a duty would be unfair, unjust and unreasonable based on considerations of policy. Lord Steyn stated:

> I conclude that the recognition of a duty would be unfair, unjust and unreasonable as against the shipowners who would ultimately have to bear the cost of holding classification societies liable, such consequence being at variance with the bargain between shipowners and cargo-owners based on an internationally agreed contractual structure. It would also be unfair, unjust and unreasonable towards classification societies, notable because they act for the collective welfare and, unlike shipowners, they would not have the benefit of limitation provisions. Looking at the matter from the point of view of cargo-owners, the existing system provides them with the protection of the Hague Rules or Hague-Visby Rules. But that protection is limited under such rules and by tonnage limitation provisions. Under the existing system any shortfall is readily insurable. In my judgment, the lesser injustice is done by not recognising a duty of care.[143]

Unlike the judge at first instance, who did not think that there were any considerations of policy which would justify the application of the criterion of 'fair, just and reasonable', both the Court of Appeal and the House of Lords dismissed the claim on application of this criterion. However, Lord Lloyd (dissenting) agreed with the judge and said:

> We are not here asked to extend the law of negligence into a new field. We are not even asked to make an incremental advance. All that is required is a straightforward application of *Donoghue v Stevenson* . . .

> In physical damage cases, proximity very often goes without saying. Where the facts cry out for the imposition of a duty of care between the parties, as they do here, it would require an exceptional case to refuse to impose a duty on the ground that it would not be fair, just and reasonable. Otherwise, there is a risk that the law of negligence will disintegrate into a series of isolated decisions without any coherent principles at all, and the retreat from *Anns v Merton* will turn into a rout.[144]

However, the majority were influenced by three important factors: (a) the assumed negligence of the class surveyor had not involved the direct infliction of the physical damage to the cargo; (b) the class played a subsidiary role in matters of seaworthiness as compared to the shipowner; and (c) a recognition of a duty would cause an imbalance with the Hague-Visby Rules. It would be a different situation if the classification society assumed a responsibility towards a third party, for

---

143 [1995] 2 Lloyd's Rep 299, pp 316–17.
144 Ibid, p 309.

example, a buyer of a ship by giving advice on which the buyer relied and the society knew, or ought reasonably to have known, that the buyer would rely on their advice before he/she decided to buy the ship.[145]

The trilogy of English decisions in this area is completed by the following decision: *Reeman v DOT and Others.*[146]

It concerned the certification of a fishing vessel by a surveyor of the Department of Trade (DOT) performing regulatory functions under the Merchant Shipping Acts (MSAs). The DOT was sued by a buyer of a fishing vessel claiming economic loss.

Statutory certification of fishing vessels was required by the Safety Provisions Act 1970 and the Regulations 1975 designed to ensure their seaworthiness. The vessel was inspected by a surveyor appointed by the DOT and a certificate was issued, the validity of which was extended twice every four years. No British-registered fishing vessel could put to sea unless she carried a certificate issued by the DOT.

When the claimants bought the fishing vessel, she carried such a certificate, but it was based on an erroneous stability calculation made by the DOT's surveyor, which was discovered after the purchase. The certificate was then withdrawn, as the expenditure required to be incurred by the purchasers to rectify the faults, improve her stability and satisfy the minimum statutory requirements, was beyond their means. They sued the DOT for breach of the common law duty of care alleged to be owed to them and claimed damages for the economic loss suffered. The issue was whether the DOT owed a duty of care to purchasers of fishing vessels when issuing certificates of compliance.

The judge held that the requisite degree of proximity between the plaintiffs and the DOT was established taking into consideration the following factors:

(a) there was a virtual certainty that the certificate would be communicated to prospective purchasers such as the plaintiffs;

(b) there was an extreme likelihood that such prospective purchaser would rely on the certificate in deciding whether to purchase;

(c) there was overwhelming probability that the purchaser would do so without independent verification; and

(d) these facts were all facts known actually or inferentially by the DOT.

In addition, the plaintiffs did not appear to have a remedy against anyone other than the DOT; applying the criteria of fairness, justice and reasonableness, it was possible to set an acceptable limit or control mechanism which substantially

---

145 On the basis of the *Hedley Byrne v Heller* principle; in a case involving duty owed by auditors of a company to third parties, *Galoo Ltd v Bright Grahame Murray* [1994] 1 WLR 1360, the Court of Appeal held that, although mere foreseeability that a potential bidder for shares in, or lender to, a company might rely on the company's audited accounts did not impose on the auditor a duty of care to the bidder or lender, such a duty would arise if the auditor were expressly made aware that a particular bidder or lender might rely on them or other statements approved by the auditor without independent inquiry and intended that he should so rely; that, since it was not alleged that the defendants knew or intended that the third plaintiff would rely on their accounts for the purpose of making loans, or for the purpose of calculating the purchase price under the supplemental share purchase agreement, the pleaded facts disclosed no cause of action against the defendants on those issues.

146 [1997] 2 Lloyd's Rep 648 (CA).

avoided the mischief in question; this would be to confine the duty to persons who actually purchased the relevant vessel during the currency of the certificate. The DOT appealed.

The Court of Appeal reversed this decision because it thought that the judge had made a significant extension to the ambit of the tort of negligence. With regard to the relationship of proximity, it said:

> When a British fishing vessel certificate was issued those who might in the future place reliance on that certificate when deciding whether to purchase the vessel did not form part of a class that was capable of definition and delimitation by identifiable characteristics; not only did potential future purchasers not form an identifiable class when the certificate was issued, the certificate was not issued for the purposes of providing information to assist them in deciding whether or not to purchase the vessel; and foreseeability that the information might, or probably would be relied on by others than those for whom it was provided did not suffice to constitute such persons part of a class in a proximate relationship with those providing the information.

It would always be open to a party entering into a commercial transaction in relation to a certificated vessel to take steps such as surveying the vessel, or stipulating for contractual warranties, that would provide protection against the risk that the certificate did not reflect the true condition of the vessel.

With regard to the third characteristic of the test whether a duty of care should be imposed, the Court of Appeal said:

> The statutory framework was one designed to promote safety at sea. The protection of those whose commercial interests might foreseeably be affected by unseaworthiness of vessels formed no part of the purpose of the legislation and no part of the purpose for which the fishing vessel certificates were issued.

It would not be fair, just and reasonable to impose a duty of care on a body like the DOT, charged with the duty of certifying with a view to promoting safety at sea; the DOT, when performing its regulatory functions under the MSAs, performed a similar role to that of classification societies, that is, they existed for the purpose of further safety at sea rather than for the protection of commercial interests; and the learned judge erred in finding that the DOT had owed a duty of care to the purchasers, Mr and Mrs Reeman. The appeal was allowed.

The American approach to liability of a classification society towards third parties for economic loss is similar to the English approach. In the following case, a claim in damages was made by the owner of a ferry which was converted into a cruise ship and was approved by the classification society appointed by the flag State in accordance with the International Convention for Safety of Life at Sea (SOLAS) 1974. It is important to note that the court held that the classification certificate was not a guarantee to the owner of the ship that the ship has been safely constructed; the responsibility for maintenance and seaworthiness remains with the owner, who has a non-delegable duty in this respect.

The Sundancer [147]

Sundance bought a passenger car ferry and converted it into the luxury cruise ship, named *The Sundancer*. The vessel was registered in the Bahamas.

Under the Bahamian MSA the vessel required, inter alia, a safety certificate representing compliance with the SOLAS 1974 Convention and a certificate showing compliance with the Load Line Convention.

The defendant classification society, ABS, was nominated under the Bahamian Regulations as one of six classification societies authorised to perform surveys on behalf of the Bahamian Government. ABS undertook SOLAS and load line surveys of *The Sundancer*.

Acting on behalf of the Bahamian Government, ABS issued a five-month provisional load line certificate and a SOLAS passenger ship safety certificate to the vessel. Shortly thereafter, ABS issued a provisional classification certificate to the vessel.

The Sundancer struck an underwater rock off the coast of British Columbia. Her hull was breached below the waterline and, while only two watertight compartments were initially flooded, progressive flooding of other compartments occurred. As a result of the progressive flooding, the vessel listed heavily and eventually sank at a nearby pier. There had been some violations of SOLAS regulations and ABS rules, neither of which had been reported by ABS. No lives were lost. The buyer sued ABS for negligence and/or gross negligence for the loss of the ship.

It was held that:

A shipowner was not entitled to rely on a classification certificate as being a guarantee to the owner that the vessel was soundly constructed; the great disparity between the fee charged by ABS for its services and the damages sought by Sundance was strong evidence that such result was not intended by the parties. The shipowner, and not ABS, was ultimately responsible for and in control of the activities aboard ships; Sundance had full responsibility for the conversion and repair and maintenance of the vessel and their ongoing responsibility was supplemented by the requirement that the shipowner had a non-delegable duty to furnish a seaworthy vessel; ABS could not be said to have taken over such obligations by agreeing to inspect and issue a classification certificate. The purpose of a classification certificate was not to guarantee safety, but merely to permit the owner to take advantage of the insurance rates available to a classed vessel.

Had there been loss of life in the aforesaid case, caused by violation of the SOLAS regulations by the classification society, the question under English law would have been whether a duty of care ought to be imposed upon the class. A comparison with the regulatory regime applied to the air industry for the certification of aircraft is discussed in the next case.

Perrett v Collins [148]

It concerned physical injury of a passenger of an aircraft. Both the judge and the Court of Appeal decided in favour of the plaintiff, who was injured while flying as a passenger in an aircraft which had been certified as fit to fly.

---

147 [1994] 1 Lloyd's Rep 183.
148 [1998] 2 Lloyd's Rep 255.

Mr Collins, the first defendant, purchased an aircraft construction kit from which he constructed the aircraft. During construction, he exchanged the gearbox provided with the kit with another, which was not suitable. The second defendant, an inspector of the Popular Flying Association (PFA), certified that the aircraft was fit to fly and issued the certificate of fitness for flight, valid for one month. Mr Collins took the aircraft on a test flight from Rochester Airport. The plaintiff was his passenger. The first flight was very short, consisting only of taking off, flying to a height of about 20 feet, and then landing. On the second flight, the aircraft was taken up to 150 feet. As it descended, it went out of control and hit the ground, with the result that the plaintiff was injured.

The plaintiff's case was that the personal injuries that he suffered when the aircraft crashed were caused by the negligence of one or more of the defendants, and alleged that the aircraft had a propeller which did not match the gearbox fitted to the engine of the aircraft. The preliminary issue for decision was whether (a) the third defendants (PFA), being approved by the Civil Aviation Authority (the CAA)/the Authority), pursuant to Art 110 of the Air Navigation Order 1989, as qualified to furnish reports to the Authority in connection with flying permits, owed a duty of care in tort to the plaintiff; and (b) the second defendant, being a person to whom the third defendant had delegated the inspection of the aircraft with a view to enabling it to furnish such a report, owed a duty of care to the plaintiff.

It was held by both the judge and the Court of Appeal that it was foreseeable that, if the second and third defendants granted a certificate of fitness to fly in respect of this aircraft with an inappropriate gearbox, there was likely to be an accident, and they ought reasonably to have had in contemplation a person travelling as a passenger on the test flight in the aircraft as being so affected when they were directing their minds to the acts or omissions which were called into question. Also, it was foreseeable that greater injustice would be done to a person injured in circumstances such as those that arose in this case, by not imposing a duty on those responsible for issuing a fitness to fly certificate, than would result to the defendants in imposing such a duty; the first and second defendants had undertaken to discharge the statutory duty for the protection of the public, and no injustice was done by imposing such a duty on them in respect of a negligent act. The regulatory framework provided by the Civil Aviation Act 1982 was designed, at least in substantial part, for the protection of those who might be injured if an aircraft was certified as being fit to fly when it was not.

This was a case of a personal injury in which it was obvious that, as a matter of common sense and justice, as well as because of a statutory duty, a duty of care was imposed. The balance of justice came down firmly on the side of imposing a duty, and members of the public would expect to be protected from injury by careful operation of the regulatory system and to be compensated for injury sustained by its negligent operation. Hobhouse LJ (as he then was) said, in refusing to apply *The Nicholas H* to this case:

> What the second and third defendants seek to achieve in this case is to extend decisions upon 'economic' loss to cases of personal injuries. It represents a

regulation and the collision must be established, whether the breach was partial or the sole cause of the collision and the damage resulting from it. In addition, s 1 of the MCA 1911 established the division of loss rule in proportion to the degree to which each vessel was at fault, instead of 50/50 as was the position previously in every case of joint fault. The MCA 1911 was passed to implement the Brussels Convention on Collisions, in 1910, relating to collisions and salvage, and survived the passage of time until the enactment of the MSA 1995.

1.3 The law and regulations at present

Section 4 of the MCA 1911 made a significant amendment by abolishing the arbitrary rule of presumption of fault contained in s 419(4) of the 1894 Act.

In the middle and latter part of the 20th century, with continuous advancements in technology affecting ships and specialist craft, there were three sequential amendments to the Collision Regulations. The 1910 regulations were superseded by the 1948 regulations, then by the 1960 regulations and, finally, by the 1972 regulations.

The International Regulations for Preventing Collisions at Sea (Colregs) 1972 – adopted under the auspices of the International Maritime Organisation (IMO) – revised the 1960 Collision Regulations. The British Parliament adopted them in 1977. Since then, the 1972 Regulations have had the force of law with regard to all British ships on the high seas and all waters connected therewith navigable by sea-going vessels and to foreign ships coming within the UK territorial waters. These regulations were subsequently amended in 1983, 1989, and 1991. The amendments were necessary due to an increased number of accidents, particularly with regard to breaches of the Traffic Separation Schemes. The current UK Merchant Shipping Regulations of 1996 revoked and replaced the Merchant Shipping (Distress Signals and Prevention of Collisions) Regulations of 1983, 1989 and 1991. They are subject to the MSAs which have been consolidated by the MSA 1995. The Regulations were further amended in November 2003 to make it clear that an action by ships to avoid a collision must follow the steering and sailing rules. The amendment also deals with low-flying aircraft, 'wing in ground' (WIG) carrying heavier loads than normal and flying only a few feet above the ground.

By s 306 of the MSA 1995, the Secretary of State has power to make regulations, orders or rules exercisable by statutory instrument, and such instrument shall be subject to annulment pursuant to a resolution of either House of Parliament. With regard to collisions, he may make regulations as to the steps to be taken to prevent any collision involving a ship (s 85(3)(k), or a collision between seaplanes on the surface of water and between ships and seaplanes (s 85(4)).

1.4 Ships being subject to the Collision Regulations

The Collision Regulations (Colregs) apply to all British ships wherever they may be and to all foreign ships within UK waters. Her Majesty's ships are exempt from the provisions of the MSA 1995 to which the Collision Regulations are subject (s 308(1)), but obedience to Collision Regulations by the Royal Navy is provided by the Queen's Regulations, which are broadly the same as the Colregs and are published to the world at large, not being only a matter of departmental discipline.[3] In old cases, war ships did not have to carry lights, but these are now dealt with by special rules requiring ships of war to display lights and signals.

The current regulations, by reg 1(c), now allow the Government of any State to make special rules regarding signal lights, shapes or whistle signals for ships of war and vessels proceeding under convoy, so that these lights, shapes or signals cannot be mistaken for any others authorised under the rules. Also, by reg 1(e), compliance with the Collision Regulations is excused, if a Government so determines for special construction vessels for which other provisions can be made so as to provide for the closest possible compliance by them with the rules.

Non-naval Government ships are not subject to the regulations, but power is given by s 308 of the MSA 1995 for such ships and any ships held for the benefit of the Crown, that they might, by Order in Council, be registered as British ships, so that the Act will apply. Hence, the Collision Regulations being subject to it will also apply with exceptions and modifications, as the Order in Council may provide. Section 309 extends the application of such Order in Council to ships in the service of the government by a demise charter to the Crown. No orders have yet been made under these provisions. Nevertheless, the prevailing view is that, as a matter of good seamanship, such ships, which are not obliged by statute to comply with the regulations, will conform to them.

As has been seen in the first part of this book, no action *in rem* may be brought against Crown vessels (s 29 of the Crown Proceedings Act 1947), but only an action *in personam* against the relevant Government department as is provided by s 24(2) of the Supreme Court Act 1981.

1.5 Definition of vessel and ship

The rules define a vessel as including every description of water craft, including non-displacement craft and seaplanes,[4] used or capable of being used as a means of transportation on water (reg 3(a)). The Merchant Shipping (Distress Signals and Prevention of Collisions) Regulations 1996 (reg 2(2)) provides that 'ship' includes hovercraft; reg 2(1) provides for the application of the Collision Regulations to seaplanes registered in the UK and on the surface of water anywhere, and to other seaplanes on UK waters. Special provisions are made for lights and shapes to be exhibited by seaplanes.

Section 313 of the MSA 1995 defines a ship as including every description of vessel used in navigation.[5] Section 310 makes the Act applicable to

---

3   *HMS Truculent* [1951] 2 Lloyd's Rep 308 and, also, *The Albion* [1953] 1 Lloyd's Rep 239.

4   'Seaplane' includes a flying boat and any other aircraft designed to manoeuvre on the water (Civil Aviation Act 1982, s 97(6)).

5   Judicial interpretation of what constitutes a vessel has been given in various decisions; see, op cit, Marsden, fn 1, paras 1-6, and 1-19 and 6-92 with regard to mobile offshore drilling units; see, also, Chapter 1, above.

in the prevailing circumstances and conditions, for *The Eleni V* a safe speed would have been 6 knots and, for *The Roseline*, 8 knots.

There are numerous examples of collisions cases which have occurred due to unsafe speed. It suffices for the purpose of this book to mention two more. In *The Coral I*,[18] a collision occurred on a clear night with an anchored vessel due to high speed of the proceeding vessel in a crowded anchorage area with lack of a straight passage. The judge found that half manoeuvring speed ought to have been maintained in those circumstances. In *The ER Wallonia*,[19] the fault of the colliding vessels lay in their respective failure to reduce speed when visibility began to be restricted.

Regulation 7: risk of collision

(a) Every vessel shall use all available means appropriate to the prevailing circumstances and conditions to determine if risk of collision exists. If there is any doubt such risk shall be deemed to exist.

(b) Proper use shall be made of radar equipment if fitted and operational, including long range scanning to obtain early warning of risk of collision and radar plotting of equivalent systematic observation of detected objects.

(c) Assumptions shall not be made on the basis of scanty information, especially scanty radar information.

This rule suggests a sensible approach to determining the risk of collision which might exist. The second part of the rule is new. What is a proper use of radar was explained in *The Roseline* (above). In determining if risk of collision exists, para (d) of the rule gives guidelines to be considered: (i) if the compass bearing of an approaching vessel does not appreciably change; and (ii) even if an appreciable bearing change is evident, a risk may exist when approaching a very large vessel or a tow or when approaching a vessel at close range.

A remarkable situation arose in a collision between *Selat Arjuna* and *Contship Success*,[20] in which the latter performed a major and wholly unexpected alteration to starboard when the vessels were starboard-to-starboard passing. Her master thought that he saw an echo on the radar on his port bow, which was in fact false. By altering to starboard, he placed the other vessel ahead and, becoming more confused, proceeded to alter more and more to starboard, whereupon he collided with and sank the other ship. *Contship Success* was found wholly to blame.

A recent example of a situation of danger is illustrated in *The Bow Spring v Manzanillo II*,[21] a collision between a chemical tanker and a hopper dredger, in which the hopper dredger left the tanker in doubt as to her intentions in the channel. The tanker overreacted and grounded, resulting in significant consequences in damages.

Situations of danger commonly arise when a vessel fails to make an effective turn around the bends of a narrow channel.[22]

---

18 [1982] 1 Lloyd's Rep 441.
19 [1987] 2 Lloyd's Rep 485.
20 [2000] 1 Lloyd's Rep 627.
21 [2004] 1 Lloyd's Rep 647.
22 *The Siboeva and Vitastar* [2002] 2 Lloyd's Rep 210.

Regulation 8: action to avoid collision

The gist of the six paragraphs of this rule is that any action to avoid a collision shall be positive, made in ample time and with due regard to observance of good seamanship, and the provisions of regs 5 and 6 shall be observed in avoiding collision.

Regulation 9: narrow channels

(a) A vessel proceeding along the course of a narrow channel or fairway shall keep as near to the outer limit of the channel or fairway which lies on her starboard side as is safe and practicable.

The remaining six paragraphs of this rule give guidelines on safe crossing in narrow channels or fairways, limit the scope of overtaking unless necessary to permit safe passage with appropriate sounding signals, stress the need of particular alertness and caution when navigating near a bend, and prohibit anchoring in a narrow channel.

A few examples illustrate this rule.

The Toluca[23]

A channel about 18 km long had been dredged through the mud in order to enable vessels to get to the city of Bangkok by river, situated about 25 miles above the mouth of Mae Chao. No local rules relating to the navigation of the channel had been passed, therefore, for every vessel navigating the channel, reliance had to be placed on the Colregs, the 1960 version. Regulation 25 of those rules provided that:

> In a narrow channel every power driven vessel when proceeding along the course of the channel shall, when it is safe and practicable, keep to that side of the fairway or mid-channel which lies on the starboard side of such vessel.

The Visahakit 1 loaded with petroleum products was heading for Bangkok, while The Toluca was leaving Bangkok laden with cargo. The Toluca was 3 ft longer than the longest ship normally permitted to enter the port of Bangkok so that she had to obtain special permission to enter. At night, in excellent visibility, a collision occurred between the vessels resulting in slight damage to The Toluca, but heavier damage to The Visahakit 1. It was found that the collision took place in the middle of the eastern half of the main channel, therefore, both vessels were bound to comply with reg 25 governing navigation of vessels in narrow channels. The admiralty judge held that, on the balance of probabilities, The Toluca was hampered by the limits of the channel and the effect of her speed. There was no fault on the part of Visahakit 1, even in starboarding at the last minute, as that was a decision made in the 'agony of the moment' in an attempt to avoid the collision, for which the master could not be blamed. The Court of Appeal affirmed the decision and added:

> Toluca was not entitled to expect Visahakit 1 to wait for her to come round the bend; Toluca was negligent in respect of her speed in approaching the bend and in her reduction of speed at the bend; the way in which the accident could have been avoided was by Toluca keeping on her own side of the channel as Visahakit 1 had done . . .

---

23 [1984] 1 Lloyd's Rep 131.

In particular, Slade LJ said:

> There is no dispute that *Toluca* would have had to go into the centre of the channel when rounding the bend. This would risk a collision if *Visahakit 1* was on the bend at the same time. In my opinion in these circumstances *Toluca* should have given way so that the two vessels passed in part of the channel that was straight. But *Toluca* did not slow down to avoid this situation, she approached the bend at 10 knots and it was too late to slow down when she realized that she was going to meet *Visahakit 1* on the bend. In answer to a question from us our assessors were of opinion that *Toluca* should have approached the bend at 6 knots and indeed that her speed should not have exceeded 6 knots in this channel. I agree with and accept this opinion. In my opinion the judge came to a correct conclusion and I would dismiss this appeal.[24]

Therefore, *The Toluca* was solely to blame for the damage caused.

In *The Koningin Juliana*,[25] the collision with *The Thurokini* occurred in Harwich harbour, when the former was outward bound and the latter inward bound. The pilot of *The Koningin* having misunderstood that *The Thurokini* was not moving, created a crossing situation. The issue was whether *The Thurokini* was in the correct position on the dividing line to starboard and this depended on the meaning of mid-channel; did it mean the centre line of the whole navigable channel or of the dredged channel? The answer – confirmed by the Court of Appeal – was that 'narrow channel' meant the whole width of the navigable water and that, in Harwich harbour, the line to starboard of which each vessel shall keep is the centre of the dredged channel. Both ships were at fault.

In *The Sitarem and Spirit*,[26] less emphasis was placed upon the definition of 'narrow channel'. Instead, Mr Justice Steel placed reliance upon the rule that 'dictates good seamanship' which requires vessels to observe the regulations at all times. There was a significant breach of the traffic regulations, total absence of any lookout, and the resultant failure to give way.

Regulation 10: traffic separation schemes[27]

This rule regulates opposing streams of traffic and vessels passing along the entire length of the scheme by establishing traffic lanes. The rule is new and has been amended by the recent amendments to the Colregs. The improvements have been based on examination of collision incidents and indeed have reduced the number of these incidents, particularly in the Dover Straits.

The *The Hagieni and Barbarossa*,[28] a fairly recent example of a breach of reg 10 occurred in Bosporus where *The Hagieni* (a bulk carrier proceeding southward) and *The Barbarossa* (a chemical tanker, proceeding northward) collided. *The Barbarossa* was largely at fault, failing to keep her position in her own northbound lane. In addition, she increased her speed and caused confusion to the other vessel, and her

---

24 [1984] 1 Lloyd's Rep 131, p 136.
25 [1974] 2 Lloyd's Rep 353, and [1975] 2 Lloyd's Rep 111 (HL).
26 [2001] 1 Lloyd's Rep 107.
27 For full details and interpretation of the individual paragraphs of this scheme, the reader is referred to op cit, Marsden, fn 1, paras 6-257–6-305.
28 *The Hagieni and Barbarossa* [2000] 2 Lloyd's Rep 292.

lookout was defective. The collision occurred at an angle of 80 degrees where the bow of *The Barbarossa* struck the starboard side of *The Hagieni*.

It was held by the admiralty judge that *The Hagieni* failed to cope with the embarrassment of *The Barbarossa*'s approach. Her alteration to port was, however, an imprudent and unannounced close-range option. But, the overriding consideration in this case was that *The Barbarossa* was at all material times persisting in navigating in the southbound lane or separation zone. She created a situation of danger and inevitably instilled the maximum of confusion as to her intentions. Therefore, she was 80% to blame.

1.6.3 Conduct of vessels in sight of each other (Part B, Section II)

While Section I (regs 4–10) apply in any condition of visibility, regs 11–18 of Section II deal with conduct of vessel in sight of one another, and reg 19 of Section III applies to conditions of restricted visibility.

In particular, reg 12 refers to sailing vessels when they are approaching one another and which of them should keep out of the way to avoid a risk of collision. For example, the vessel which has the wind on the port side shall keep out of the way of the other.

Regulation 13 deals with overtaking situations, stressing that any vessel overtaking any other shall keep out of the way of the vessel being overtaken.

Regulation 14 gives guidelines when vessels are on a head-on situation, whereupon each shall alter her course to starboard so that each shall pass on the port side of the other.

The rule provides, in particular, that:

When two power driven vessels are meeting on reciprocal or nearly reciprocal courses so as to involve risk of collision each shall alter her course to starboard so that each shall pass on the port side of the other.

Such a situation shall be deemed to exist when a vessel sees the other ahead or nearly ahead and by night she could see the masthead lights of the other in a line or nearly in a line and/or both sidelights and by day she observes the corresponding aspect of the other vessel.

When a vessel is in any doubt as to whether such a situation exists she shall assume that it does exist and act accordingly.

An illustration of such a situation is given in the following case.

The Argo Hope [29]

The Argo Hope was outward bound from Runcorn, partly laden, navigated along the Manchester Ship Canal by a pilot, while *The Bebington* was bound from Stanlow to Manchester. They collided port-to-port at a 30 degree angle in the Manchester Ship Canal. The vessels were in a head-on situation and would have passed side by side if they had kept their correct headings. It was found that *The Argo Hope* was not

---

29 [1982] 2 Lloyd's Rep 559.

navigated with caution, the immediate cause of the collision being that she suddenly changed her heading to port. She was found 85% to blame. The master of *The Bebington* was also at fault for having misjudged the speed of *The Argo Hope* and did not keep well on the starboard side.

Regulation 15: crossing situation

> When two vessels are crossing so as to involve risk of collision, the vessel which has the other on her own starboard side shall keep out of the way and shall, if the circumstances of the case admit, avoid crossing ahead of the other vessel.

The Nowy Sacz [30]

The Olympian and *The Nowy Sacz* were both proceeding northwards parallel to each other in the Atlantic Ocean, when a collision occurred between them at night in fine weather and good visibility. The vessels had been in sight of each other for a considerable period of time before the collision occurred. The plaintiffs, owners of *The Olympian*, contended that the crossing rules applied, and that under them, it was the duty of *The Nowy Sacz* having *The Olympian* on her starboard side, to keep out of the way of *The Olympian*. The defendants, however, owners of *The Nowy Sacz*, said that the overtaking rules applied and it was the duty of *The Olympian* under those rules, as the overtaking ship, to keep out of the way of *The Nowy Sacz*. The judge held on the facts that the two ships were in sight of one another, and that the risk of collision between them had already arisen. The situation in this case (being subject to the 1960 rules) was a crossing situation and not an overtaking one. Therefore, it was the duty of *The Nowy Sacz* to keep out of the way of *The Olympian*, and the duty of *The Olympian* to keep her course and speed. Also, *The Nowy Sacz* was at fault in failing to take early and positive action to keep out of the way of *The Olympian*, and in failing to reduce her speed in good time so as to allow *The Olympian* to pass ahead of her.

Regulation 16: action by give-way vessel

Every vessel which is directed to keep out of the way of another vessel shall, so far as possible, take early and substantial action to keep well clear.

In a collision between **The Mineral Dampier and Hanjin Madras**,[31] the latter failed to take correct avoiding action as a give-way vessel in a crossing situation as soon as the vessels came into sight of one another. She should have altered her course to starboard. When it appeared clear to *The Mineral Dampier* that she did not turn to starboard, *The Mineral Dampier* turned to port in desperation and the bow of *Hanjin Madras* struck her aft starboard side at an angle of 50 degrees leading aft on *The Mineral Dampier*. The apportionment of blame was 80% and 20%, respectively.

Regulation 17: action by stand-on vessel

> Whether one of two vessels is to keep out of the way, the other shall keep her course and speed.

---

30 [1976] 2 Lloyd's Rep 682.
31 [2001] 2 Lloyd's Rep 419.

The latter vessel may however take action to avoid collision by her manoeuvre alone, as soon as it becomes apparent to her that the vessel required to keep out of the way is not taking appropriate action in compliance with these Rules.[32]

The mutual obligations imposed upon both the give-way vessel and the stand-on vessel under this regulation provide a good illustration of the way in which the courts apportion liability. In a collision between *The Topaz and Irapua*,[33] the former failed to take correct avoiding action when it became apparent that the give-way vessel was not taking any action. It was found that the officer on watch had been observing the latter vessel for some time, but had made the decision to take avoiding action under this regulation too late in time. The action subsequently taken was also incorrect, with the alteration in course too little in the circumstances. As a result, although *Irapua* was to blame for breaches of regs 5, 7, 8 and 15 of Colregs, the breach of *Topaz* in not altering her course sooner under reg 17(a)(ii) led to an apportionment of 80% and 20% in favour of *Topaz*.

Regulation 18: specifies responsibilities between vessels

For example, a power driven vessel shall keep out of the way of a vessel not under command, or restricted in her ability to manoeuvre, or engaged in fishing or sailing.

1.6.4 Conduct of vessels in restricted visibility (Pt B, s III)

Regulation 19

(a) The rule applies to vessels not in sight of one another when navigation in or near an area of restricted visibility.[34]

(b) Every vessel shall proceed at a safe speed adapted to the prevailing circumstances and conditions of restricted visibility. A power driven vessel shall have her engines ready for immediate manoeuvre.

(c) Every vessel shall have due regard to the prevailing circumstances and conditions of restricted visibility when complying with the rules of s I of this part.

(d) A vessel which detects by radar alone the presence of another vessel shall determine if a close quarters situation is developing and/or risk of collision exists. If so, she shall take avoiding action in ample time, provided that when such action consists of an alteration of course, so far as possible the following shall be avoided: (i) an alteration of course to port for a vessel forward of the beam, other than for a vessel being overtaken; (ii) an alteration of course towards a vessel abeam or abaft the beam.

(e) Except where it has been determined that a risk of collision does not exist, every vessel which hears apparently forward of her beam the fog signal of another vessel, or which cannot avoid a close quarters situation with another vessel forward of her beam, shall reduce her speed to the minimum at which she can be

---

32 See *The Estrella* [1977] 1 Lloyd's Rep 525 and *The Angelic Spirit* [1994] 2 Lloyd's Rep 595.

33 [2003] EWHC 320 (Admiralty), [2003] 2 Lloyd's Rep 19.

34 This paragraph extends the rules applicable to vessels navigating in restricted visibility to vessels navigating near an area of restricted visibility too (see op cit, Marsden, fn 1, para 6-390).

kept on her course. She shall if necessary take all her way off and on any event navigate with extreme caution until the danger of collision is over.

The Ercole [35]

A collision occurred between *The Embiricos* and *The Ercole*. The ships were approaching each other in opposite directions.

Each ship was observed by the other on the radar during the approach period. *The Ercole* was steering 230 degrees. and substantially making good that course at 13 knots. *The Embiricos* was on a course of 40 degrees doing about 15 knots. The visibility was restricted. The second officer, on watch on *The Embiricos*, first saw *The Ercole* at 18 miles some two to three degrees on the starboard bow. *The Ercole* then changed slowly to six degrees at eight miles and to eight degrees at five miles, when she ceased to be visible because of rain. The second officer estimated that, if the two ships maintained their courses, they would pass each other on parallel courses at about one mile and switched from automatic to manual steering. Meanwhile, the master of *TheErcole* first saw *The Embiricos* on radar on the 24-mile range bearing six degrees at 20 miles on her port bow. As she approached, he changed to the 12-mile range and, when *The Embiricos* was some three miles distant, her echo disappeared into the clutter round the centre of the radar screen and he formed the view that the two ships would pass port to port at one to two miles. He altered course 10 degrees to starboard when some three miles distant. He next saw a group of white lights from *The Embiricos*, but before seeing her side lights he put *The Ercole* hard to starboard. *The Embiricos'* wheel was put hard to port and the collision then took place.

It was held that both ships were at fault.

On the above findings, *The Embiricos* was at fault in two respects: first, as regards defective appreciation of the situation on the radar; and, second, for not reducing her speed substantially when the visibility lessened. *The Ercole* was at fault in four respects: first, as regards defective appreciation of the situation on the radar; second, for not stopping her engines and then navigating with caution when she lost the echo of *The Embiricos* in the clutter; third, for altering course 10 degrees to starboard at an improper time; and, fourth, for going hard to starboard at the last instead of putting her engines full astern, and all these faults on either side were causative.

Brandon J commented on the situation:

If plotting is necessary in order to enable a navigator to ascertain correctly the course of an approaching ship, then either he should make a plot, or he should not draw conclusions about the course of that ship which are unwarranted without one.

1.6.5 Lights and shapes (Part C)

Regulations 20–27

Regulation 20: applies to all weather conditions between sunset and sunrise and in

---

35   [1977] 1 Lloyd's Rep 516.

restricted visibility and in addition when the use could reasonably be considered necessary.[36]

Regulation 21: defines each type of light.

Regulation 22: explains a new rule about visibility of lights.

Regulation 23: specifies the type of lights to be exhibited by power driven vessels underway.

Regulation 24: covers the situation of lights during towing.

Regulations 25 and 26: provide the requirements for sailing vessels, vessels under oars and fishing vessels.

Regulation 27: covers lights for ships not under command.

In *The Djerada*,[37] the judge said in relation to these rules:

> First, as to lookout. I find that the lookout on *The Djerada* was extremely bad, as a result of which the lights of *The Ziemia* were not properly observed, nor her course and speed properly appreciated, during the period of 45 minutes leading up to the collision.

> Second and third, as to lights. I find that *The Djerada* was not justified in carrying not under command lights and should in any case not have carried a white masthead light as well as such lights. I find that she was in both these respects in breach of reg 1(b) of the Collision Regulations, which forbids the exhibition of lights other than those prescribed by such rules.

The Albion[38]

A collision between the plaintiff's steamship, *The Maystone*, and an uncompleted aircraft carrier, *The Albion*, occurred in a southerly gale, at night, in the North Sea. *The Albion*, with skeleton crew on board, was being towed northwards by three tugs and *The Maystone* was southward bound. While the tugs of *The Albion* safely passed by *The Maystone* port to port, there was an impact between the stem of *The Maystone* and port side aft of *The Albion*, at approximately a right angle. *The Maystone* sank after unsuccessful manoeuvres to clear *The Albion*. An action was brought by the owners of the sunk ship against the admiralty, as owners of *The Albion*, and against SH (shipbuilders) who until acceptance by the admiralty, were responsible for the care and efficient protection of the vessel and against FF (tugowners) who had contracted with SH to be responsible for the tow.

It was held:

> ... that the port light of *Albion* was defective and that no blame attached to *Maystone* for failing to see *Albion* lying across her course; that the number and disposition of the tugs, the failure to obtain a long range weather forecast, and the absence of warnings issued by *Albion* to shipping in the vicinity, together constituted a negligent failure to conduct the towage in a seamanlike manner; in addition, *The Albion* had suffered an accident and she was not in command, therefore she should display the 'non-under command lights'.

---

36   See *The Coral* [1982] 1 Lloyd's Rep 441.
37   [1976] 1 Lloyd's Rep 50.
38   [1953] 1 Lloyd's Rep 239.

Regulations 28, 29, 30 and 31 specify the type of lights to be shown by vessels constrained by their draught, pilot vessels, anchored vessels and vessels aground, as well as seaplanes, respectively.

1.6.6 Sound and signals (Part D)

After definitions of sound signals, reg 34 deals with manoeuvring and warning signals, reg 35 with signals for restricted visibility, reg 36 with signals to attract attention, and reg 37 with distress signals. Part E exempts vessels under construction from displaying certain lights.

SECTION B

2 CRIMINAL LIABILITY

2.1 General

Maritime offences have been dealt with by the MSAs and are now to be found in the MSA 1995 as well as in regulations. By s 85, the Secretary of State has power to make regulations relating to safety and health on ships, which may provide that a contravention of those regulations shall be an offence punishable on summary conviction by a fine or on indictment by imprisonment for a term not exceeding two years and a fine.

Intentional or reckless damage to property of another, without lawful excuse, is covered by the Criminal Damage Act (CDA) 1971, which also includes endangering or threatening the life of another. Where a collision between ships or between a ship and a fixed or floating object is caused deliberately or recklessly, this criminal behaviour will now fall to be dealt with under the offences applicable generally to wilful damage of property.[39]

Apart from specific offences created by statute, the general principles of criminal law would apply in cases of loss of life by criminal gross negligence. A brief account of statutory offences under the MSA 1995 is given below. Then, criminal liability for involuntary manslaughter is briefly looked at, but the reader is also referred to Chapter 8.

---

39 See op cit, Marsden, fn 1, p 723; as to an offence of criminal damage committed by a British subject on a foreign ship on the high seas, see *R v Kelly, The Winston Churchill* [1981] 3 All ER 387 (HL).

2.2 Statutory offences under the MSA 1995

2.2.1 Disobeying the Collision Regulations

Failure to comply with Colregs, whether the breach causes a collision or not, has been made a criminal offence under the MSAs.

Section 419 of the MSA 1894 was the first statutory provision which made the infringement of a collision regulation a criminal offence, if the infringement was caused by the wilful default of the master or owner of the ship. The effect of s 419(2) was that the offence was not absolute.[40] So the prosecution had to prove wilful default. If any damage occurred from non-observance, there was a deeming provision that the damage was caused by the wilful default of the person in charge of the deck of the ship at the time, unless it was shown that a departure from the regulation was made necessary by the circumstances. This offence was amended by the amendments to the Colregs in 1983, 1989 and 1991.[41]

The current Merchant Shipping (Distress Signals and Prevention of Collisions) Regulations 1996, provide as follows.

Regulation 5

(1) Where any of these regulations is contravened, the owner or the vessel, the master and any person for the time being responsible for the conduct of the vessel shall each be guilty of an offence, punishable on conviction on indictment by imprisonment for a term not exceeding two years and a fine, or on summary conviction:

  (a) in the case of any infringement of reg 10(b)(i) (duty to proceed with traffic flow in lanes of separation schemes) of the international regulations[42] and by a fine not exceeding £50,000; and

  (b) in any other case by a fine not exceeding the statutory maximum.

(2) It shall be a defence for any person charged under these regulations to show that they took all reasonable precautions to avoid the commission of the offence.

In addition, the vessel may be detained by any commissioned naval or military officer, any officer of the Department of Transport, any Customs and Excise Officer and any British Consular Officer, under s 284 of the MSA 1995.

There are two differences between this offence and that under s 419:

(a) first, no longer is it required that the prosecution proves wilful default of the master or owner of the ship. For example, the prosecution of the master for

---

40 *Bradshaw v Ewart-James (DC)* [1983] QB 671.

41 These were issued by the Secretary of State pursuant to his powers given under the then MSAs – the MSA 1894, s 418 and, subsequently, by the MSA 1979, s 21, which has now been repealed and replaced by the MSA 1995, s 85. Statutory instruments made under the MSA 1894, s 418 continue to be in force until superseded by new regulation made under the MSA 1995, s 85.

42 This offence corresponds to the offence under the MSA 1894, s 419(2).

breach of the traffic separation scheme in *The NF Tiger*,[43] when he had delegated the task of bridge watch to the chief engineer, was unsuccessful, since the prosecution could not prove the requirement of the offence under s 419 of *mens rea*. The offence was not an absolute criminal offence. This case necessitated the change of the law and the requirement of proof by the prosecution of wilful default has been eliminated; and

(b) second, the current provision includes any other person responsible for the conduct of the vessel at the time that can be prosecuted, and also that the master and the owner of the ship will not be exonerated from being prosecuted for that offence, even if the task of the watch on the bridge is delegated to another person, who commits the breach. For the owner to avoid conviction, he must show that he took all reasonable precautions to choose a competent master and that there was a system to supervise the master and ensure that he knew the regulations.[44]

However, this may not be sufficient now, bearing in mind the international regulations imposed on shipowners to ensure maritime safety. In particular, the adoption in July 1995 of substantial amendments to the International Convention on Standards of Training, Certification and Watchkeeping for Seafarers (STCW) together with the International Safety Management Code (ISMC) system of transparency of the company's practices will provide evidence as to whether the master and crew had been sufficiently trained and qualified in accordance with international standards.

As shipowners are corporate bodies, the corporation as well as the director, manager, secretary or similar officer may be found guilty of an offence, if it is proved that the offence has been committed with the consent or connivance of, or is attributable to any neglect on the part of, a director, manager, secretary or other similar officer of the body corporate or any person purporting to act in such a capacity (s 277 of the MSA 1995).

2.2.2 Not giving assistance to vessels after collision or to vessels or persons in distress

Section 92 of the MSA 1995 (which replaced s 422 of the 1894 Act) provides that:

(1) In every case of collision between two ships, it shall be the duty of the master of each ship, if and so far as he can do so without danger to his own ship, crew and passengers (if any)—

(a) to render to the other ship, its master, crew and passengers (if any) such assistance as may be practicable and necessary to save them from danger caused by the collision, and to stay by the other ship until he has ascertained that it has no need of further assistance.

(b) to give to the master of the other ship the name of his own ship and the names of the ports from which it comes and to which he is bound.

---

43 [1982] 2 Lloyd's Rep 564; in *The Nordic Clansman* [1984] 1 Lloyd's Rep 31, the court applied *The NF Tiger*, but the master was convicted on proof of *mens rea*.

44 *The Lady Gwendolen* [1965] 2 All ER 283.

Although failure to do so does not raise any presumption of law that the collision was caused by his wrongful act, neglect or default, such failure is a criminal offence, which applies to masters of British ships and to masters of foreign ships when in UK waters. In case of failure to comply with sub-s (1)(a), without reasonable excuse, he is liable (i) on summary conviction, to a fine not exceeding £50,000 or imprisonment for a term not exceeding six months or both; or (ii) on conviction on indictment, to a fine or imprisonment for a term not exceeding two years or both. In case of failure to comply with sub-s (1)(b), he is liable to a fine. In either case, his certificate may be cancelled or suspended upon inquiry on his conduct.

By s 93(1), (2) of the MSA 1995 (which derived from s 22(1), (2) of the Merchant Shipping (Safety Convention) Act 1949), the master of a ship has a duty – upon receiving a signal of distress at sea or information from any other source that a ship or aircraft is in distress – to proceed at all speed to the assistance of the persons in distress, unless he is unable, or in special circumstances of the case considers it unreasonable or unnecessary to do so, or unless he is released from this duty in case of requisition as provided by sub-ss (4) and (5). Failure to do so is a criminal offence punishable on summary conviction to a term not exceeding six months or to a fine (not exceeding the statutory maximum) or both; on conviction on indictment up to two years' imprisonment, or to a fine or both. Compliance by the master with these provisions shall not affect his right or the rights of others to salvage.

2.2.3 Breach of documentation and reporting duties

Section 77 of the MSA 1995[45] provides that, except as required by regulations under this section, an official logbook shall be kept in every UK ship. Regulations made under this section may prescribe the particulars to be entered in the official logbooks, and may require the production or delivery of official logbooks in circumstances as may be specified. They may also provide for exceptions of some ships from such requirements. Regulations under this section may make a contravention of any provision of this section an offence punishable with a fine. If a person intentionally destroys or mutilates or renders illegible any entry in an official logbook they shall be liable on summary conviction to a fine.

Section 90[46] requires charts and other information to be carried on board when a ship goes to sea, as may be required by rules made by the Secretary of State under this section. If a ship goes to sea or attempts to go to sea without copies of charts, directions or information, which it is required to carry by rules under this section, the master or the owner shall be liable on summary conviction to a fine.[47]

Section 91[48] requires the master of any UK ship to report dangers to navigation to ships in the vicinity and to authorities on shore, otherwise he shall be liable to a fine.

---

45 Section 77 derives from the MSA 1970, s 68 and the Criminal Justice Act 1982, Sched 6, Pts III, IV, para 4 and s 46(2).

46 Section 90 derives from the MSA 1970, s 86 and the MSA 1979, Sched 6, Pt III.

47 *The Huntingdon* [1974] 1 WLR 505.

48 This section derives from the Merchant Shipping (Safety and Load Line Convention) Act 1932, s 24, which was enacted after concerns caused by *The Titanic* disaster; the MSA 1964, s 16 added the information which has to be sent.

2.2.4 Dangerously unsafe ships and unsafe operation of ships

The MSA 1995 regulates the consequences of operating dangerous or unsafe ships in ss 94–107. Section 94 (which derived from s 30 of the MSA 1988, as amended by the Merchant Shipping Maritime Security Act 1997) defines when a ship is 'dangerously unsafe' (see Chapter 8, para 5.6.1).

Section 95 gives power to the inspecting officer of an UK port to detain such a ship, whether she is British or foreign.

The provisions, which are relevant to the prevention of collisions, are contained in ss 98 and 100. Under s 98 (which derived from s 30 of the MSA 1988), both the master and the owner of a dangerously unsafe ship (or any other person who has assumed responsibility for safety matters, such as charterers and managers) shall be guilty of an offence.[49] A defence to such an offence is specified under s 98(4), (5), (6) which states broadly that the accused must prove that, at the time of the offence, arrangements had been made to ensure the ship's fitness to go to sea as required.

Under s 100 (being equivalent to s 31 of the MSA 1988), a duty is imposed upon the owner of any UK ship, or any ship registered under the laws of any other country and which is within the UK waters, to take all reasonable steps to ensure that the ship is operated in a safe manner. If the owner of such a ship fails to discharge such a duty, he shall be liable on summary conviction to a fine (up to £50,000), on conviction on indictment to imprisonment for a term up to two years or a fine, or both. In the event that the ship is chartered by demise or is managed, either wholly or in part, by any person other than the owner, the same duty is imposed on such a person, as the case may be.

By contrast to s 98, this offence does not extend to the master of the ship.

With regard to officers of corporate bodies, reference should be made again to s 277 of the Act.

The first case that was decided on the application of the former equivalent to this section was *The Safe Carrier*.[50] The ship-managers were charged with an offence for failing to secure that the vessel was operated in a safe manner when the chief engineer was given less than three hours to familiarise himself with the machinery. Within the next 24 hours, the engine broke down and the vessel drifted at sea requiring the assistance of towage, but no damage occurred. Although the Court of Appeal held that the section has created a strict liability offence and no criminal state of mind was required, the House of Lords held that it was not helpful to categorise the offence as either one of strict liability or not. The prosecution must prove that the accused owner, manager, or demise charterer had failed to take all reasonable steps (which must be reasonable to him sub-s (4)(iii)) to ensure that the ship was operated in a safe manner. Although the test is objective, it has a subjective element. The fault of the employee below the senior management level was not to be taken into account for attributing liability to the corporation. The act or omission must have been of the directing mind and will of the relevant corporate owner or

---

49 The details of this long section should be read from the Act.
50 [1994] 1 Lloyd's Rep 589 (HL).

manager following the direction in the *Tesco v Nattrass* case.[51] The duty imposed is personal to the owner or charterer or manager.[52] The senior manager who has failed to operate a safe system will also be charged with the offence, in accordance with s 277. Under the requirements of the ISMC, it will be easier to show that the senior management failed to operate a safe system, particularly as it requires that new personnel should be given sufficient time to familiarise themselves with the ship.[53]

The defective condition of hull or equipment, or the improper loading or undermanning of a lighter or a barge which is used or is permitted to be used in navigation by any person, endangering human life by its unsafety, is made an offence by s 99 of the MSA 1995. Equally, the Act contains provisions for the manning, qualification of officers and seamen, equipment and management of vessels, the infringement of which carries penalties.

Relevant to danger to or safety of ships is the Dangerous Vessels Act 1985 which, by s 1, authorises the harbour master to direct the removal from the harbour of any vessel, the condition of which or the nature/condition of anything it contains might involve, in his opinion, a grave and imminent danger to the safety of any person or property; or it might involve a grave and imminent risk of preventing or seriously limiting the use of the harbour by its sinking or foundering.

2.2.5 *Conduct endangering ships, structures or individuals*

This offence was originally created by s 220 of the MSA 1894, as amended by s 27 of the MSA 1970, and was substituted by s 32 of the MSA 1988. The amendments by s 32 became necessary after the sinking of *The Herald of Free Enterprise* (see later). It now appears in s 58 of the MSA 1995. It refers to the master or any seaman of a UK ship, or a foreign ship being within UK waters.

Section 58(2) provides that, if such a person is on board the ship or in its immediate vicinity and does any act which causes or is likely to cause loss or destruction of or serious damage to his ship, machinery, navigational or safety equipment, or to any other ship, or the death of or serious injury to any person, he shall be guilty of an offence. The act must have been deliberate or have amounted to a breach or neglect of duty; or the master or seaman was under the influence of drink, or drugs at the time (sub-s (3)).

The same applies to an omission by such a person to preserve his ship, etc, from being lost, destroyed or seriously damaged; or to preserve any person on board from death or serious injury; or to prevent his ship from causing loss or destruction or serious damage to any other ship or any structure, or the death of or serious injury to any person not on board his ship.

The offence extends, by sub-s (4), to a situation in which the person performs his

---

51 The identification theory; see, further, in Chapter 8, paras 5.2 and 5.6.1, above.

52 It should be noted that other statutory offences may not be worded in the same way as s 100, so as to make the duty personal to the senior management of a company, and the special rule of attribution, as applied in *Meridian Global Funds Management Asia v Securities Commission* [1995] 3 All ER 918 (PC), may apply to attribute liability to the company when an employee below the senior management is found guilty of the offence; see, further, Chapter 8.

53 See Chapter 8.

duties in relation to operation of his ship in such a manner as to cause, or to be likely to cause, any such loss, destruction, death or injury as mentioned above; also, when he fails to discharge any of his duties, or to perform any such function, properly to such an extent as to cause, or to be likely to cause, any of those things.

The offence is punishable on summary conviction by a fine, or on conviction on indictment by imprisonment (two years' maximum) (sub-s (5)).

There is a defence available to the accused as provided by sub-s (6) that he took all reasonable steps to discharge the duty imposed by sub-s (2), or that he was under the influence of drugs medically prescribed and he had no reason to believe that the drug might have the influence it had. In the case of an offence under sub-s (4), proof of reasonable precautions taken and exercise of due diligence to avoid committing the offence will excuse the accused.

While there is no defence when the act or omission was deliberate, there is a further defence under both subsections if the avoidance of the offence would involve disobeying a lawful command, or that in all the circumstances the loss, damage, death or injury in question could not reasonably have been foreseen or avoided by the accused.

It should be noted that, under the original provision, there was no defence and the court had to consider the gravity of the conduct in order to determine whether or not the offence had been committed. But the words of the previous statutory provision did not include neglect of duty, for example, want of proper care in the discharge of the master's or seaman's duty. So, in the collision between *The Gladys and The Prome*[54] which resulted in the sinking of *The Prome* with her crew, poor lookout due to simple negligence of the master did not amount to a criminal offence. After this case, there were no further criminal prosecutions until 1980, when the court in *The Harcourt*[55] reached a decision (confirmed on appeal) which widened the scope of s 27 of the MSA 1970. The master was ill in bed, but had left an experienced mate with instructions to keep watch during the night. While his vessel was anchored off the main navigational channel in the Hull West Roads, the mate left an experienced deckhand on watch after sunset, who omitted to turn on the forward anchor light, creating a potentially dangerous situation. The mate noticed this when he returned for watch before midnight. The master was made aware of the event by police officers when they boarded the vessel a few days later. Having accepted responsibility, he was found guilty.

It seems from this decision that the master' duty is non-delegable. He will only discharge his responsibilities under the statute if he checks personally whether or not those delegated by him carried out their responsibilities properly and the same will apply under the present statute, s 58. In addition, it follows from this decision that actual loss need not occur by reason of breach of the provisions of the statutory offence.

A further offence is provided by s 59 of the MSA 1995 in relation to disobedience of lawful commands and neglect of duty by seamen.

---

54 [1911] 1 KB 571.
55 [1980] 2 Lloyd's Rep 589.

2.2.6 Breach of statutory duty with regard to life-saving regulations

There is a statutory duty to ensure the safety of ships and persons on them and protect their health under the Merchant Shipping (Life-Saving Appliances) Regulations 1980,[56] made under the MSA 1979 and consolidated in the MSA 1995, s 85. The duty is absolute. This applied in a recent decision[57] when a ship engineer was seriously injured while taking part in a drill. The cause of the accident was the failure of a link caused by stress corrosion cracking. The claimant, who was injured when a suspension chain holding a lifeboat failed, succeeded in his claim against the defendant, who was responsible for the vessel, for breach of statutory duty under the Act.

2.2.7 Offence in relation to lighthouses, buoys or beacons

In addition to the general criminal law offences for damage to property provided by the Criminal Damage Act (CDA) 1971, the MSA 1995 includes specific offences in relation to criminal damage to lighthouses. Section 219 is worded in similar language to s 1 of the CDA 1971 and makes it an offence when a person, without lawful authority, intentionally or recklessly damages any lighthouse, or its lights or buoy or beacon, or removes, casts adrift or sinks, conceals or obscures any of the same. A person who is guilty of such an offence shall, in addition to being liable for the expenses of making good any damage so occasioned, be liable, on summary conviction, to a fine. Further, s 220 gives power to the lighthouse authority to issue and serve 'a prevention notice' upon any person who exhibits a light on a place in such a manner as to be liable to be mistaken for a light proceeding from a lighthouse. If the person who is served with such a notice fails, without reasonable excuse, to comply with the directions contained in the notice, he shall be liable, on summary conviction, to a fine.

2.2.8 Breach of duty to give directions after shipping casualties

Under the MSA 1995, criminal sanctions attach also to oil pollution incidents which extend beyond pollution incidents arising out of collisions. Section 136 imposes a duty upon the owner or master of a ship to report the occurrence of discharge of oil mixture from a ship into a harbour in the UK waters, or escape of oil from a ship into any UK waters, to the harbour master or authority. Failure to comply with such a duty shall be punishable, on summary conviction, by a fine.

In addition, by s 137, the Secretary of State has wide powers to issue directions when an accident occurs to or in a ship and, in the opinion or the Secretary of State, oil from the ship will or may cause pollution on a large scale in the UK waters.

It will be an offence if a person to whom a direction is duly given under s 137 contravenes, or fails to comply with, any requirement of the direction (s 139).

---

56 SI 1980/538.
57 *Ziemniak v ETPM Deep Sea Ltd* [2003] 2 Lloyd's Rep 214 (CA).

2.3 Involuntary manslaughter for breach of duty

A breach of the Colregs, or of the provisions of the MSA 1995 relating to danger-ously unsafe ships (ss 94, 98) and unsafe operation of ships (s 100 (seen earlier)), which might result in loss of life, will give rise to a prosecution for manslaughter by criminal negligence involving a breach of duty, if the elements of the offence, as stated at common law, exist. The principles of criminal negligence were re-examined in the following case.

R v Adomako [58]

The appellant was the anaesthetist in charge during an eye operation in Mayday Hospital. During the operation, the supply of oxygen to the patient had been dis-connected, but the appellant did not notice until the patient had a cardiac arrest a few minutes later and died. It was admitted that the appellant had been negligent, but the question was whether his actions were criminal. A jury convicted him of manslaughter after the death of the patient. The Court of Appeal (Criminal Division) dismissed his appeal, and the same question was referred to the House of Lords. The question was stated as follows: in cases of manslaughter by criminal negligence not involving driving but involving a breach of duty, is it sufficient direction to the jury to adopt the gross negligence test without reference to the test of recklessness, as defined in *R v Lawrence*, or as adapted to the circumstances of the case? The House of Lords considered the authorities on the point, and Lord Mackay, delivering the judgment, said:

> In my opinion the ordinary principles of the law of negligence apply to ascertain whether or not the defendant has been in breach of a duty of care towards the victim who has died. If such breach of duty is established the next question is whether that breach of duty caused the death of the victim. If so, the jury must go on to consider whether that breach of duty should be characterised as gross negligence and there-fore as a crime. This will depend on the seriousness of the breach of duty committed by the defendant in all the circumstances in which the defendant was placed when it occurred. The jury will have to consider whether the extent to which the defendant's conduct departed from the proper standard of care incumbent upon him, involving as it must have done a risk of death to the patient, was such that it should be judged criminal. [59]

Therefore, in reply to the question posed to the House, he stated:

> In cases of manslaughter by criminal negligence involving a breach of duty, it is sufficient direction to the jury to adopt the gross negligence test set out by the Court of Appeal in the present case following *R v Bateman* (1925) 19 Cr App R 8 and *Andrews v DPP* [1937] 2 All ER 552, [1937] AC 576 and it is not necessary to refer to the definition of recklessness in *R v Lawrence* [1981] 1 All ER 974 ... although it is perfectly open to the trial judge to use the word 'reckless' in its ordinary meaning as part of his exposition of the law if he deems it appropriate in the circumstances of the particular case. [60]

---

58 [1994] 3 All ER 79.
59 Ibid, pp 86–87.
60 Ibid, p 88.

In the case of corporations, however (as discussed in Chapter 8), it has been difficult to convict the corporation itself for criminal negligence, unless it is found that the individuals, who can be identified as the 'directing mind and will' of the corporation, are themselves guilty of gross negligence. It is worth repeating in this context the case in which this problem was illustrated.

Herald of Free Enterprise (R v East Kent Coroner ex p Spooner and Others) [61]

The vehicle ferry ship, *The Herald of Free Enterprise*, capsized outside Zeebrugge harbour, resulting in loss of life of a large number of passengers. A formal investigation carried out, pursuant to s 55 of the MSA 1970, by Sheen J, confirmed that the immediate cause of the vessel's loss was that she sailed with her bow doors open and trimmed by the head. In addition, it was found that the capsize was caused by the negligence of the assistant bosun, the chief officer, the master, the superintendent and the directors of the company, who did not appreciate their responsibilities for the safe management of the ship (the company, from top to bottom, was criticised for sloppiness).

The incident was subsequently considered by a coroner, Turner J, who directed the jury that, as a matter of law, there was insufficient evidence to convict the individuals. As regards the company, he said that, as a matter of law, a corporate body could not be guilty of manslaughter, unless one of the individual defendants who could be identified with the company could have been guilty of manslaughter. He ruled against the adoption of the principle of aggregation of the faults of the individuals involved in order to convict the company. He said that, where the acts or omissions of employees or managers of a corporate body were not sufficient to render them guilty of manslaughter, those acts or omissions could not be aggregated so as to render the corporate body guilty.

On an application for judicial review of the decision, Bingham LJ in the Queen's Bench (Divisional Court) held that:

> ... on appropriate facts the *mens rea* required for manslaughter can be established against the corporation. I see no reason in principle why such a charge should not be established. [62]

He further stated that:

> Whether the defendant is a corporation or a personal defendant, the ingredients of manslaughter must be established by proving the necessary *mens rea* and *actus reus* of manslaughter against it or him by evidence properly relied on against it or him. A case against a personal defendant cannot be fortified by evidence against another defendant. The case against a corporation can only be made by evidence properly addressed to showing guilt on the part of the corporation as such. On the main substance of his ruling I am not persuaded that the coroner erred. [63]

After *The Herald of Free Enterprise*, a new statutory offence was created by s 31 of the MSA 1988, making the owner, demise charterer or the ship-manager of a ship (upon whom responsibility for her safe operation lies at a particular time) criminally liable

---

61 (1989) 88 Cr App R 10.
62 (1989) 88 Cr App R 10, p 16.
63 Ibid.

for unsafe operation, punishable upon summary conviction with a fine up to £50,000 or, on indictment, with two years' imprisonment. This offence is now repeated in s 100 of the MSA 1995, mentioned previously.

This section applies also to non-UK ships which are within UK territorial waters, to take reasonable steps to ensure that the ship is operated in a safe manner, but it is not applicable to non-UK ships if they only came within the UK territorial waters for shelter due to bad weather or unavoidable circumstances.

However, the problems in relation to involuntary manslaughter may only be resolved by enacting the proposed Bill 2006 based on gross management failures, rather than a finding of guilt of gross negligence committed by individuals (see Chapter 8).

SECTION C

3 CIVIL LIABILITY

3.1 Introduction

It was explained in Section A of this chapter that there is no longer a presumption of fault by the mere breach of the Colregs. To establish civil liability resulting from a collision between ships or between a ship and another object, the burden of proof is on the claimant to prove the facts that have given rise to liability incurred due to negligence or want of good seamanship. Breach of the Colregs will be part of the evidence to be adduced by the claimant for the court to make an assessment of the blameworthiness of the defendant and evaluate the causative potency of the fault.

The principles of the law of negligence will be applicable (apart from one instance where no proof of negligence is required under s 74 of the Harbours, Docks and Piers Clauses Act (HDPCA) 1847, which creates strict liability for damage to a harbour's property by a vessel). In all other instances, the claimant must establish that there was a duty of care, there was a breach of that duty by the defendant, which caused the collision, and also that the breach caused the damage claimed, which is subject to the remoteness rule.

For the court to identify whether there is a duty of care in negligence cases, a three-stage test was developed in 1990.[64] These are: reasonable foreseeability of damage; a relationship of proximity between the parties; and that in all circumstances it was fair, just and reasonable to impose a duty of care upon the defendant. Although the three-stage test applies universally to all cases whether the claim is for physical damage or economic loss, the proximity requirement of the test varies according to the circumstances and the type of damage claimed.

In straightforward cases of direct infliction of physical injury by the act of the defendant, the three-stage test is easily satisfied. There may be no need to look

---

64 *Caparo Industries plc v Dickman* [1990] 1 All ER 568, [1990] 2 AC 605 (HL).

beyond the foreseeability test in order to establish that the defendant had been in a 'proximate' relationship with the claimant.[65] In most claims in respect of physical damage to property or to a person, the question of the existence of a duty of care does not give rise to any problems, because it is self-evident that such a duty exists and the contrary view is unarguable.[66] This is applicable to collision cases in which it is self-evident that a duty of care exists by a vessel towards other vessels navigating the same seas.[67] The same applies to consequential financial or economic loss resulting from the inflicted physical damage.

The duty owed to other vessels at sea is based on the principles of the tort of negligence and, as early as 1823, Lord Stowell in *The Dundee*[68] stated the essential elements of actionable negligence in collision cases:

> Want of that attention and vigilance which is due to the security of other vessels that are navigating the same sea, and which, if so far neglected as to become, however unintentionally, the cause of damage of any extent to such other vessels, the maritime law considers as a dereliction of bounden duty, entitling the suffered to reparation in damages.[69]

When a claim is for pure economic loss, it is more difficult to satisfy the second and particularly the third stage tests of the *Caparo* decision. This aspect is examined in the context of damages, and it relates in particular to claims for financial loss by time or voyage charterers of the one ship colliding with the other, which in such a case is pure economic loss.[70]

Since a duty of care exists in determining civil liability of a defendant in collision cases for physical and consequential financial loss, the other elements of the burden of proof are examined under para 3.3 below.

There are special rules for division of loss in collisions at sea, which became statutory by the MCA 1911. These are now consolidated in the MSA 1995, s 187 (see para 3.7).

---

65 *Murphy v Brentwood DC* [1990] 2 All ER 908, [1991] AC 398 (HL), pp 486–87.

66 *The Hua Lien* [1991] 1 Lloyd's Rep 309 (PC); contrast *The Nicholas H* [1994] 1 WLR 1071 (HL), in which proof of foresight and proximity were not enough in a physical damage case where the claim was for economic loss. Instead, the third stage test, namely whether it would be fair, just and reasonable to impose such a duty, restricted the possibility of recovery by cargo-owners who sued the classification society of the ship, which was allowed to sail before permanent repairs to some defects had been carried out. The cargo on board the ship was lost when the ship sank due to unseaworthiness; (see, further, the analysis of decisions in this area in Chapter 11, para 9).

67 As developed originally by the landmark decision of *Donoghue v Stevenson* [1932] AC 562 (HL).

68 [1823] 1 Hagg Ad 109.

69 Ibid, p 120.

70 See *The Mineral Transporter* [1986] AC 1 (PC).

3.2 Who may be liable?

3.2.1 *The employer of the wrongdoer* in personam

The employers of those on board whose negligent act caused the collision will be vicariously liable for the collision. The employer may be either the owner of the ship or the charterer by demise, who takes possession and control of the ship and employs the crew. A charterer under a time or voyage charter does not normally employ the crew. The act, or omission, giving rise to negligence must be that of the servant acting within the scope of his employment. In collision cases it will be the negligent act in navigation.

An interesting question arising in the context of vicarious liability is whether an employer or principal can be held vicariously liable to an innocent party when damage is caused due to a malicious, or criminal, act of the employee, or agent. In an old decision, *The Druid*,[71] the master of the ship deliberately rammed another vessel and caused damage to it when the master of the other ship refused to engage *The Druid* into a towage contract. The judge held the employer not liable for the criminal act of his employee because the act was not within the scope of the master's employment.

In subsequent, non-admiralty, cases, however, concerning a fraudulent act of an agent,[72] or a theft of goods held under bailment by an employee of the bailee,[73] it was held that the agent, or the employee, acted in the course of his agency or his employment and, therefore, the principal or employer was liable. On the facts of these cases, it was the duty of the principal or the employer to exercise due care to see that no fraud or theft was committed.

Similarly, in the context of the duty owned to the public by police authorities, the Privy Council held[74] that:

> When entrusting a police officer with a gun the police authorities owed to the public at large a duty to take reasonable care to see the officer was a suitable person to be entrusted with such a dangerous weapon lest by any misuse of it he inflicted personal injury, whether accidentally or intentionally, on other persons; that, therefore, a duty of care was owed to the claimant; and that, in view of the relaxed and surprisingly casual response of senior officers to the two earlier incidents involving the officer, there had been a sufficient breach of that duty to found liability in negligence.

In a decision of the House of Lords, *Credit Lyonnais Bank Nederland v Expert Credits*,[75] it was held that, before there can be vicarious liability, all the features of the wrong which are necessary to make the employee liable have to have occurred

---

71 (1842) 1 W Rob 391.

72 *Lloyd v Grace Smith* [1912] AC 716 (HL); *Uxbridge Permanent Benefit Building Society v Pickard* [1939] 2 KB 248 (CA).

73 *Morris v CW Martin & Sons Ltd* [1966] 1 QB 716 (CA); *Port Swettenham Authority v T Wu & Co* [1979] AC 580 (PC).

74 *Attorney General of the British Virgin Islands v Hartwell* [2004] UKPC 12.

75 *Credit Lyonnais Bank Nederland v Export Credits Guarantee Department* [2000] 1 AC 486 (HL).

in the course of the employment. But the employer will not be liable for acts of an employee committed in the course of his employment which were not in themselves tortious and only became so when linked to other acts outside the course of his employment. What is meant by the words 'occurred in the course of employment' is that the employee or agent had authority to do certain things on behalf of his employer or principal.

The law seems clearer in recent years than in the past, but not absolutely; the answer will depend on the facts of individual cases. As a general rule, it is now well established that an employer could be held vicariously liable for an employee's deliberate wrongdoing, but vicarious liability cannot be established simply because the 'guilty' servant did have, by reason of his employment, the opportunity to commit the wrongdoing in question. More than a mere opportunity to commit the wrong has to exist. There has to be a close connection between the work the servant has been employed to do and the wrongdoing. In cases in which the servant is entrusted with the safety of premises, as in *Frans Maas (UK) Ltd v Samsung Electronics (UK) Ltd*,[76] the answer will not be difficult, but in other cases the question of connection between employment and the wrongdoing may be more difficult to answer.

The cases of bailment mentioned earlier, or the cases in which a fiduciary duty is owed, differ from other cases because it is within the terms of bailment, or the fiduciary relationship, that due care should be exercised to employ honest servants, or to safeguard against the wrong.

Considering the facts of *The Druid* (above), the malicious act of the master, committed in a fit of temper, might have not been within the scope of his employment because it did not derive from actual or implied authority of his employer (but see *Ocean Frost* later and the authorities cited in fn 79). The authors of *Marsden* argue that the decision may not be good law today.[77] Support for the proposition that the violence used by the master in *The Druid* was not within the scope of his employment can be derived from the decision, **Mattis v Pollock (trading as Flamingos Nightclub)**,[78] involving violence used by the club's doorman. The Court of Appeal defined the scope of employment in terms of what the employer expects of his employee, and held:

> (T)he established test for vicarious liability, including where an employer/employee relationship was under consideration, required a broad approach to the determination of the question whether the employee's action was so closely connected with what the employer authorised or expected of him in the performance of his employment that it would be fair and just to conclude that the employer was vicariously liable for the damage sustained by the claimant as a result of the employee's act; that, where the employee was expected to use violence while carrying out his duties, the likelihood of establishing that an act of violence fell within the broad scope of his employment was greater than it would be if he were not.

---

76 [2004] 2 Lloyd's Rep 251.
77 See, op cit, Marsden, fn 1, para 12-04.
78 [2003] 1 WLR 2158.

In a different context, in *The Ocean Frost*,[79] the House of Lords distinguished cases which involve reliance by the claimant on a representation made by the servant of the defendant from cases involving intentional or negligent physical act by the servant. It held that the chartering manager of the owner of the ship did not have ostensible authority to deceive the agent of the buyer of the ship into believing that he had authority to enter into a three-year charter party. What he was purporting to do was not within the class of acts that an employee in his position was usually authorised to do, and the employer had done nothing to represent that he was authorised to do it. Lord Goff distinguished cases concerning physical violence from cases involving reliance by the innocent party on the misrepresentation of the opponent's servant, as a matter of policy of the law:

> For where the servant's wrong consists of a misrepresentation upon which the plaintiff relies, if that misrepresentation is not within the ostensible authority of the servant, the plaintiff is placing reliance on a statement by the servant which, as I have already indicated, either does not fall within the class of acts which a person in his position is usually authorised to perform, or is a statement made in circumstances where the plaintiff has notice that his authority is limited. In either case, in my judgment, the plaintiff is placing his reliance exclusively upon the servant; and it is understandable that it should be the policy of the law in those circumstances, not merely that the unauthorised act should not be imputed to the master, but also that the master should not be vicariously liable for the servant's wrong.

> On this basis, those torts which involve reliance by the plaintiff upon a representation by the servant should be distinguished from other wrongs, for example those which involve intentional or negligent physical acts by the servant. In the latter class of case, the ostensible authority of the servant does not provide the criterion of the master's vicarious liability: see, in particular, *Bugge v Brown* (1919) 26 CLR 110, 116, et seq, per Isaacs J and, at p 132, per Higgins J. So where a servant is authorised to carry on a certain dealing or transaction with the plaintiff and reinforces his approach to the plaintiff with an (unauthorised) physical assault upon him, his master may be vicariously liable for the assault: see *Dyer v Munday* [1895] 1 QB 742; but where the servant induces the plaintiff to enter into an authorised transaction by means of a fraudulent misrepresentation which is not within his ostensible authority, the master will not be vicariously liable for the fraud. It also follows that there are acts of a servant for which a master may be vicariously liable, although they are not within the servant's ostensible authority; so that the conclusion which I have reached on the authorities is not inconsistent with the dictum of Denning LJ in *Navarro v Moregrand Ltd* [1951] 2 TLR 674, 680.

The difficulty in this case, however, is that the chartering manager had been appointed as Vice President of the company (the seller), and his acts could be

---

79 [1986] AC 717; contrast *Navarro v Moregrand Ltd* [1951] 2 TLR 674, p 680, that a master or principal is 'responsible in tort for all wrongs done by the servant or agent in the course of his employment, whether within his actual or ostensible authority or not'. Furthermore, there is authority that, where a servant is authorised to do a certain act and while doing that act he assaults the plaintiff, he may be held to have committed the assault in the course of his employment if it is an improper mode of carrying out that which he was employed to do (see *Dyer v Munday* [1895] 1 QB 742); and there is also authority that, where an agent bribes the clerk of the plaintiff in order to obtain information concerning the plaintiff which he was employed to obtain by legitimate means, the action of the agent in bribing the clerk may likewise be held to be committed within the course of his employment: see *Hamlyn v John Houston & Co* [1903] 1 KB 81.

considered as the acts of the company, the ego the company, subject to what the articles of association or board decisions provided.

In considering the question of what acts or omissions of employees can be attributed to a company, the rules of attribution of liability are explained in Chapters 8 and 17.

3.2.2 Persons responsible for the management and operation of the ship

Liability of a shipowner, or charterer by demise, or manager of the ship, for collision damage may arise from negligent management and operation of the ship and it is distinct from vicarious liability. Failure in ensuring that the ship is in a condition that she may be navigated safely by being properly equipped, manned and maintained, by reason of which the collision occurs, is negligence for which the persons responsible for the management will be answerable.

If the ship is properly maintained by the shipowner, or demise charterer, or the manager, but due to defective repairs, for example, in the steering gear, a collision occurs causing damage to a third party, the relevant person (shipowner, charterer by demise, or manager) will have to show in detailed particulars that: (a) he exercised due care to appoint competent repairers; (b) due attention had been given to any signs of possible malfunctioning of the steering gear, or defective equipment; and (c) no reasonable care and skill could have discovered the defect. In such circumstances, the repairer or supplier of the defective equipment will be joined as a second defendant, or as a third party to the proceedings under s 1 of the Civil Liability (Contribution) Act (CLCA) 1978 for contribution to liability, which may be a complete indemnity.[80]

The employer, shipowner, or demise charterer, will be liable to their own employees who may be injured on board the ship due to defective equipment. Under s 1 of the Employer's Liability (Defective Equipment) Act 1969, the employer is liable to any employee who suffers personal injury in the course of his employment in consequence of a defect in equipment provided by his employer, even if the defect is attributable to the fault of a third party, whether identified or not. A ship for this purpose is 'equipment'.[81] The Act provides for a right of contribution against the third party, who is really at fault. The third party, however, may not exist or may not be worth suing, so this is another policy reason behind the statutory liability of the employer, that is, for the protection of employees.

In practice, liability insurers will indemnify the relevant assured under the respective insurance policy for liability incurred by the collision to third parties.

3.2.3 Liability attaches to the ship

Leaving personal liability aside, liability *in rem* attaches to the ship for the damage caused by the collision, since damage caused by the ship is a maritime lien. This is irrespective of the fact that her owner may not be the employer of the master and

---

80 See para 3.11, below.
81 *The Derbyshire* [1987] 3 All ER 1068; see, also, discussion of the case in Chapter 2.

crew at the time of the negligence, if the ship is under a demise charter. It is the voluntary entrusting of the possession of the vessel to the demise charterer, for a temporary period, that has been held not to relieve the ship from being arrested as security by the claimant, even though her owner would not be in such a case vicariously liable for the negligence of those employed by the demise charterer.[82]

3.2.4 Master and crew

The wrongdoer by whose negligence the collision occurred will also be liable. This includes any person in control of navigation, the master, pilot, seaman on watch, and the helmsman, who might have directed a wrong course resulting in the collision. The master is not vicariously liable for the wrongdoing of the crew, without fault of his own, but he may be liable if he gave negligent instructions to a helmsman, or if he allowed the pilot who was under the influence of drink to take charge of the ship. The master and crew can, under the 1976 Limitation of Liability Convention, limit their liability being included in the persons who can limit.[83] The pilot, who may be negligent during navigation of the ship, could limit his liability either under the 1976 Convention because he is treated as the employee of the owner or manager and operator *pro tempora*, or under s 22 of the Pilotage Act (PA) 1987.

3.2.5 Tug or tow

Under a towage[84] contract, it is common to have an express term that the master and crew of the tug are deemed to be the servants of the hirer of the tug. Although the effect of this clause is to impose vicarious liability on the hirer for negligent acts or omissions of the tug, such a provision regulates only the liabilities of the parties to the contract.[85]

The question whether the tug or the tow will be liable for a collision to a third party depends on who was in control of navigation at the time of the act or omission which caused the collision. The theory that the tow and the tug always comprise one unit, so as to render the tow always liable for negligence of the master or crew of the tug, has been implicitly overruled by *The Devonshire*,[86] in which the House of Lords explained the concept of the control theory.[87] Whether or not the tug is solely in control of the tow for all aspects of navigation is a question of fact.

The tug in this case was towing a dumb barge when a collision between the barge and *The Devonshire* took place due to negligence of the tug and *The Devonshire*. When the tow, which on the facts was an innocent party, sued the owners of *The Devonshire* for the collision damage, the defence of contributory negligence was raised on the ground of the tug's negligence – being considered as the negligence of

---

82 *The Lemington* (1874) 2 Asp MC 475, and *The Father Thames* [1979] 2 Lloyd's Rep 364.
83 See Chapter 17, below.
84 For definition and nature of a towage contract, see Chapter 14, below.
85 See, eg, *The President Van Buren* (1924) 19 LlL Rep 185 and other authorities referred to in Chapter 14, below.
86 [1912] AC 634 (HL).
87 See Chapter 14, para 8.2.2, below.

the tow on application of the 'unit' theory. The defence failed because the tow in this case had no control in navigation.

An instance of sole control by the tug arises when the tow is unmanned or in a condition in which she is incapable of navigation. In most situations, however, navigation will be shared between the two, whereupon the tug and the tow will each be responsible for their respective negligent acts or omissions which may cause or contribute to a collision and resulting damage thereof.[88] It will all depend on whose fault caused the collision.

Similarly under US law, in third parties' claims, the fault of the tug and the tow are considered separately in proportion to their individual fault. But, as regards navigation rules a tug and a tow are considered one vessel that must observe the rules as a unit. When damage is caused by a casualty involving the tow or the whole flotilla, the courts employ the concept of 'dominant mind' to place liability on the tug and to absolve the tow from liability. The rule is not absolute, however; at best it is only a presumption that the tug in control is responsible as the dominant mind.[89]

3.2.6 Salvors

Salvors are independent contractors and invariably take full control of navigation depending on the state of the vessel to be salved. They owe a duty of care not only to the salved property, but to third parties as well. Breach of such a duty during the salvage operation, resulting in damage, will expose them to liability. They can limit such liability under the provisions of the Limitation Convention 1976, as enacted by the MSA 1995.[90] As regards liability towards the salved property, an award of damages for negligence will be a set-off against the salvage award earned.[91]

3.2.7 Pilots

Pilots are professionals and act as independent contractors although a port authority licenses them. Mere licensing does not create liability of the port authority, s 22(8) of the PA 1987. Sometimes, a port authority may employ a pilot, but even so, the authority will not be vicariously liable for his fault in navigation of the ship.[92] Section 16 of the PA 1987, replacing s 15 of the PA 1913, has been construed as rendering a shipowner vicariously liable for negligent acts or omissions of the pilot on board his ship. The pilot, whilst on board a ship, is considered to be the employee of the shipowner, *pro tempora*, whether pilotage is compulsory or voluntary.[93] However, a port authority may be liable for its own faults, for example, by not providing for the attendance of sufficient and experienced pilots according to

---

88 *The Panther and The Ericbank* [1957] P 143, see Chapter 14, below.
89 See Schoenbaum, TJ, *Admiralty and Maritime Law*, 4th edn, 2004, Thomson/West vol 2 p 62.
90 See Chapter 17, below.
91 See Chapter 13, below.
92 *The Esso Bernicia* [1988] 2 Lloyd's Rep 8 (HL).
93 *The Cavendish* [1993] 2 Lloyd's Rep 292, see Chapter 16, below.

by-laws. The shipowner will have a cause of action to sue the pilot or the port authority, each for their own faults, but their respective liability is limited, by s 22 of the PA 1987, to £1,000 plus whatever dues the pilot was to earn on the relevant assignment.

3.2.8 Port authority

A port authority may incur liability to ships using its facilities if it has been careless in providing navigational safety in breach of its statutory duties. There is also a common law duty of care to make the port safe for users. Obstructions may cause ships to collide or strike an unlit object. When a ship sinks and becomes a wreck, there are statutory obligations imposed by the MSA 1995, local Acts and by-laws upon the authority to take certain steps in order to ensure the prevention of accidents.[94]

The question that frequently arises is whether the owner or the port authority will be liable for damage caused to third parties by a sunken wreck. It was held in *The Utopia* (below) that the owner's liability would depend on whether or not he divested himself from possession or control of the wreck.

Port or harbour authorities are given wide statutory powers to deal with sunken ships in their area. It is only when the port authority has, under its statutory powers, taken possession and control of the vessel, that the shipowner may be absolved from liability. But the Court of Appeal[95] has held that this only applies to cases where the shipowner or his servants were not negligent at common law. A defendant cannot avoid his common law liability for negligence, which cannot be wiped out by abandoning the thing that caused damage. Mere abandonment of the vessel after a collision for which the ship was at fault will not relieve her owner from liability; nor will mere delegation of control to a third party relieve the owner from liability.[96] The Privy Council, however, in *The Utopia*, placed the blame on the port authority on the facts of the case.

The Utopia [97]

Subsequent to a collision with *HMS Anson*, *The Utopia* sank and lay with her hull submerged in the Gibraltar Bay. Her owners lighted the wreck at each masthead. The acting captain of the Port of Gibraltar then complained to the manager of *The Utopia* that the lights were not sufficient, and were not properly looked after. He instructed a boarding officer to have a hulk moored in the vicinity of the wreck in order to warn vessels in accordance with the Board of Trade Regulations. The regulations required that these marking vessels, when so employed and fitted, should not show the ordinary riding light. The hulk was accordingly placed in a position near the wreck exhibiting the lights described in these instructions. It was the duty of those employed by the port to see that the positions of the lights relative

---

94 See Chapter 16, para 3.2, below.
95 See, later, *Dee Conservancy Board* [1912] AC 634.
96 *The Snark* [1900] P 105.
97 [1893] AC 492 (PC).

to the wreck were preserved. *The Primula,* entering the bay, claimed to have only seen two lights visible on board of the hulk before the collision. Therefore, they were ignorant that they were approaching *The Utopia* till they saw her masts and funnel, and so came into collision with her. In proceedings brought by the owners of the steamship *The Primula,* it was held that the port authority, and not the owners of the wreck, was liable for the collision which ensued. The control and management of the wreck insofar as it related to the protection of other vessels from her, had legitimately been transferred by the owners to the port authority, acting within the apparent scope of its powers.

Thirty-five years later, the Court of Appeal stated the respective duties of a port authority and of the owners of the wreck in the following case, and commented upon the ruling of the Privy Council in *The Utopia.*

Dee Conservancy Board v McConnell [98]

The first plaintiffs, the conservators, sued the defendants for expenses incurred in the removal of the defendants' ketch, which sunk in the river alongside the second plaintiffs' wharf. The wreck had been caused by the negligence of the defendants' servants. Immediately after the sinking of the ketch, the defendants had given notice of abandonment to their underwriters who refused the notice. Both plaintiffs paid for the removal of the ketch, as it became an obstruction to operations in the river. In the Court of Appeal, Sankey LJ, relied on the case of *Brown v Mallet* (1848) 5 CB 599 and *White v Crisp* (1854) 10 Ex 312 to lay down the duties of the ketch owners and the duties of the port authority respectively. The duty of the defendants was to use their vessel (of which they had control and management) on the navigable river; to use reasonable skill and care to prevent mischief to others; this liability was the same whether their vessel was in motion or stationary, floating or aground. The port authority, on the other hand, was under a duty at common law to take reasonable care, so long as they kept the port open for the public use of all who chose to navigate it, that the public could do so without danger to their lives or property. The Court of Appeal held that the defendants, who by their negligence had sunk their vessel, which obstructed the navigation, were liable at common law for the expenses for its removal. They could not escape liability by abandoning the wreck. Sankey LJ explained the decision in *The Utopia* by stating that, in that case, although the owner of the wreck remained in possession, the port authority undertook the duty of indicating its position so as to ensure that other ships do not suffer damage by collision. The owners were, therefore, not liable for the resulting collision, because they had legitimately transferred that duty to the port authority, and duly indicated to the latter the position of the wreck. The Court of Appeal, however, questioned the *dictum* of Sir Frances Jeune in *The Utopia* where he had stated, at p 498:

> ... the owner of a ship sunk whether by his default or not, has not, if he abandons the possession and control of her, any responsibility either to remove her or to protect other vessels from coming into collision with her.

Thus, it is not the mere abandonment of the wreck after a collision by its owner that will absolve him of a subsequent liability incurred to third parties by the wreck. It is

---

98 [1928] 2 KB 159.

only when the port authority has clearly undertaken to deal with it, and take care of safety precautions, that the owner may be found not liable.

It is the duty of those in charge of a vessel sunk in the fairway to mark its position according to regulations. Thus, the owner of a wreck, who has given notice to an authority having power to remove wrecks, will not be liable for a collision caused by reason of an unlit wreck.[99]

An omission by a port authority to raise a wreck sunk in their jurisdiction, which results in other vessels colliding with the wreck, is regulated by statute and common law principles. Section 252 of the MSA 1995 gives powers to the authority to deal with the wreck for the protection of those using the area. Section 2(2) of the Occupiers' Liability Act 1957 imposes a duty of care to occupiers (including port or harbour authority) of premises to see that the premises are reasonably safe to visitors.[100] If the port is not safe for any reason, a warning notice should be displayed.[101]

Sufficient mooring at a port or harbour for vessels using it is within the province of the authority, and proper typhoon precautions must be taken.[102] If damage is sustained or done by a vessel by going adrift due to insufficiency or parting of the moorings, the authority would be in breach of its duty of care in this respect and, hence, wholly or partially liable.

A port, harbour or dock authority may also be vulnerable to potential liability if their servants are negligent in navigation when a harbour or dock master directs the movements of a ship in the harbour or dock as empowered to do so by statute.[103] They may be found wholly or partially liable for damage done to or by the ship.[104]

3.2.9 Shipbuilders and ship-repairers

As mentioned earlier, defects in the building of or repairs to a ship, or defective equipment, by reason of which a collision or death or personal injury occurs, will amount to liability for negligence under common law, or by statute (under s 2 of the Consumer Protection Act 1987, covering liability of manufacturers and repairers for defective products). As far as pure economic loss caused by manufacturer's defective products is concerned, see Chapter 10, para 12.

3.3 Breach of the duty of care

As there is no absolute presumption of fault by mere breach of the Colregs, since s 4 of the MCA 1911, which repealed the deeming provision of fault of s 419(4) of the MSA 1894, and has now been replaced by s 187(4) of the MSA 1995, a breach of the

---

99 *The Douglas* (1882) 7 PD 151; contrast *The Snark* [1900] P 105. If the owner does not abandon a sunken wreck but employs independent contractors to raise her, he will be liable for the fault of the contractor, even if he exercised due care in selecting him.

100 *St Just SS v Hartlepool Port Harbour Commissioners* (1929) 34 LlL Rep 344.

101 *The Moorcock* (1889) 14 PD 64; *The Bearn* [1906] P 48.

102 *The Hua Lien* [1991] 1 Lloyd's Rep 309 (PC).

103 See Chapter 16.

104 See *The Zeta* [1893] AC 468; and *Mersey Docks Trustees v Gibbs* (1866) LR 1 HL 93.

Colregs is only one factor to be taken into account in determining fault, and no civil liability will arise by a mere breach, unless the infringement was causative of the collision. The question to be asked in each case is essentially this: did the failure to observe the particular regulation set in motion or contributed to a chain of circumstances which resulted in the collision, or was there an intervening factor which broke this chain and that factor was in fact the real cause of the collision incident? The onus of proof[105] is on the party alleging negligence to discharge three elements of the burden in order to establish liability of the defendant, namely:

(a) breach of duty of care;

(b) that the breach caused or contributed to the collision (causation in fact); and

(c) it caused the damage claimed, which must not be too remote (causation in law and remoteness of damage).

These elements are examined in the following paragraphs.

3.3.1 Standard of care and burden of proof

A defendant would have fulfilled his duty of care if he behaved in accordance with the standard expected of a reasonable and careful person. It is an objective standard and disregards the idiosyncrasies or the opinion of the defendant. If there is a breach of that duty, it will be the servants of a shipowner, or demise charterer, who ought reasonably to have foreseen that carelessness on their part would be likely to cause harm to those navigating the same seas.

Prior to s 4 of the MCA 1911 (which is now found in s 187(4) of the MSA 1995), and even until 1939, it had been held by the President, Sir Boyd Merriman, in *The Aeneas*[106] that it was for the defendant, who had been in breach of a Colreg, to exonerate himself and show affirmatively that his default did not contribute in any degree to the collision, or to the resulting damage.

The defendants' vessel, A, while tying up to the bank in the Suez Canal to allow the plaintiffs' vessel B to pass, was exhibiting lights, which were more consistent with her not having finally been tied up than with that operation having been completed so as to enable B to pass in safety.

In answer to the plaintiffs' allegation that they were misled by the lights, the defendants contended that, if B had kept a better lookout, she would not have been misled.

The court held that the mere fact that if the B had been keeping a better lookout, she might have appreciated the situation sooner, was not sufficient to exonerate the defendants; that the burden was on the defendants, who had broken, not indeed one of the international regulations, but a rule of an accepted code laid down for canal pilots, to prove not only that the breach ought not to have misled the B, but that it did not in fact mislead her; and the court, being of opinion that the B was to some extent misled, found the A one-fifth to blame and the B, which was coming too fast and took drastic helm and engine action causing her to sheer into the A, four-fifths to blame.

---

105 *Heranger v Diamond* [1939] AC 94 (HL), per Lord Wright.
106 [1935] P 128.

A few years later, however, this case was overruled by the House of Lords in *Heranger v Diamond*.

Heranger v Diamond[107]

In an action arising out of a collision in the Thames between *The Diamond* and *The Heranger*, Bucknill J and the Court of Appeal (Scott LJ dissenting) held that *The Diamond* was the more seriously to blame, but that *The Heranger* was also to blame by failing to take effective action earlier by reducing her speed, and was, therefore, liable in the proportion of one-third. *The Diamond* was a small steamship in ballast and failed to comply with the Port of London river by-laws. *The Heranger* was a twin-screw motor vessel, partly laden, and bound down the river in charge of a Trinity House pilot. The collision occurred at night at a point where the width of the river was about half a mile. *The Diamond* was expected to show her red light around the bend, but she did not do so and, thus, confused *The Heranger*, which did not take action sufficiently early to avoid the collision.

On appeal to the House of Lords by the owners of *The Heranger*, the defendant, it was argued that *The Diamond* was solely to blame.

The court held that *The Heranger* left it too late to reverse her engines and thus reduce her speed, and was, therefore, in part liable for the collision. Two important issues were resolved by the House of Lords (per Lord Wright): (a) that the question whether a vessel is justified in maintaining her speed and relying on another vessel taking action to avoid the possibility of collision is a question of fact and not of law; and (b) that, whatever the admiralty law on the matter was before the MCA 1911, it is now clear that the onus is on the party setting up a case of negligence to prove both the breach of duty and the damage. This, the ordinary rule in common law cases, is equally the rule in admiralty.[108]

The decision of the courts below were affirmed.

Thus, the same rule of common law pertains also in admiralty that the claimant has to make out, by adducing evidence, a prima facie case of negligence by the defendant.

There are some situations, however, in which the burden of proof will shift to the defendant, when the facts speak for themselves and there is a prima facie evidence of negligence (as is shown below).

3.3.2 Res ipsa loquitur

Sometimes, the claimant may not have difficulty in discharging the burden of proof that there was a breach of duty because it may be obvious from the facts that there was a breach. In these situations, the facts provide a prima facie evidence of negligence, and the rule of *res ipsa loquitur* ensures that the burden of proof shifts to the defendant. It is then upon the latter to rebut that presumption of fault by adducing strong evidence that no amount of reasonable care and skill would have prevented

---

107 [1939] AC 94.
108 Ibid, p 104.

the collision. Nothing short of the defence of inevitable accident will suffice to relieve him from liability. The test is that of reasonable explanation.

This was emphasised in *The Merchant Prince*.[109]

In broad daylight, the plaintiff's steamer was lying at anchor in the Mersey, when *The Merchant Prince*, belonging to the defendants, which was coming down the river, struck the plaintiff's steamer a heavy blow doing considerable damage to her. According to the defendants, the collision and damage were caused by a latent defect in the steering gear, leading to the jamming of the wheel, so that the collision could not be avoided. In the Court Appeal, the Master of the Rolls, Lord Esher, stated the plain rule laid down by the courts after long experience:

> Unless you can get rid of it, it is negligence proved against you that you have run into a ship at anchor . . . the only way for a man to get rid of that which circumstances prove against him as negligence is to shew that it occurred by an accident which was inevitable by him – that is, an accident the cause of which was such that he could not by any act of his have avoided its result. He can only get rid of that proof against him by shewing inevitable accident, that is by shewing that the cause of the collision was a cause not produced by him, but a cause the result of which he could not avoid.[110]

It was found that a probable cause of the accident was that the chain that goes around the leading wheel had stretched and become too loose. Therefore, the chain failed to respond and resulted in the wheel jamming. The Court of Appeal held that the defendants had not discharged the burden to support the defence of inevitable accident.[111] The stretching of the chain was something which they could have foreseen. They had not shown that they took measures to prevent the accident by making provision for the immediate use of hand, instead of steam, steering gear. To discharge the burden of proof of inevitable accident the defendants must show all the possible causes of the effect produced and, further, with regard to every one of these possible causes, that the result could not have been avoided. Inevitable accident means that which cannot be avoided by the exercise of ordinary care and caution and maritime skill. Therefore, the cause of this accident was one which could have been avoided.

In a later case, *The Kite*,[112] it was explained by Langton J that the defendant must give a reasonable explanation of the cause of the accident which, if it were accepted, would be an explanation showing that the accident happened without his negligence. He did not even need to go so far as that, because, if the reasonable explanation was equally consistent with the accident happening without his negligence as with his negligence, the burden of proof would shift back to the plaintiff to show that it was the negligence of the defendant that caused the accident.[113]

The plaintiffs' goods, while on board one of the lighterers' barges, which with others was in tow of a tug, were damaged through the barge colliding with one of the abutments of Cannon Street railway bridge. The plaintiffs brought an action

---

109 [1892] P 179.
110 Ibid, pp 187–88.
111 See para 3.7.1, below.
112 [1933] P 154.
113 Ibid, p 170.

against the tugowners, framing it entirely in tort. There being a prima facie case of negligence against the tug, the plaintiffs called no evidence on this point, and the defendants called one witness only, the master in charge of the tug, who did not see the actual contact but heard the blow and saw the barge 'flared out', owing, in his opinion, to the breast rope not having been properly made fast by the lighterers' servants and not the tug's servants:

Held, that there was no greater probability that the accident happened through negligence on the part of the tugowners' servants than on the part of the lighterers' servants, and that, following Lord Dunedin's *dictum* in *Ballard v North British Rly Co* 1923 SC (HL) 43, p 54, that '. . . if the defenders can show a way in which the accident may have occurred without negligence . . . the pursuer is left as he began, namely, that he has to show negligence'. The plaintiffs failed on the issue of fact.

In a recent decision concerning a collision between *The Global Mariner and The Atlantic Crusader*[114] while the latter was at anchor, the former was found solely to blame although the anchored ship was at fault in failing to control her yaw and sway by anchoring to an open moor and by the use of helm, but it was found on evidence that such failure was not causative.

The discussion of this topic is inevitably linked to causation and to what defences the defendant can raise, of which there will be more examples below.

3.4 Causation in fact

Once the claimant proves breach of duty of care by the defendant, he must also prove that the breach caused the collision. In other words, the collision would not have happened but for the defendant's breach.[115] Nautical assessors, who explain technical evidence, assist the judge in matters of navigation.[116]

The Humbergate[117]

In the middle of the river, just above the Ocean Lock, were situated two sunken wrecks substantially blocking the navigable channel. In accordance with the 'Notice to Mariners' issued by the Conservation Authority, the dock master gave a light signal which signified that the plaintiff's vessel *The Haskerland* was leaving the

---

114 [2005] 1 Lloyd's Rep 699; an important recent development shown in this case, following the CA guidance in *Bow Spring* and *Manzanillo II* [2005] 1 Lloyd's Rep 1, is that the expert evidence offered by the nautical assessors to the court in navigational matters (being independent, in that they are not appointed by the parties) must be made open for the parties to have the opportunity to comment. Such practice is necessary in order to be compatible with Art 6 of European Convention for the Protection of Human Rights and Fundamental Freedoms 1950 (as set out in Sched 1 to the Human Rights Act 1998).

115 The principle is most aptly explained under the general law in *Barnett v Chelsea and Kensington HMC* [1969] 1 QB 428: the hospital was held not liable although the doctor employed by it had breached his duty of care to the plaintiff's husband by having failed to examine him, but the breach was not causative of his death, as he would have died by arsenic poisoning even if the doctor had examined him.

116 CPR, r 61.13.

117 [1952] 1 Lloyd's Rep 168.

Ocean Lock and entering the tideway. In such circumstances, no other vessel was allowed to pass into a certain prescribed area. The defendant's vessel, *The Humbergate*, in spite of the unlocking signal, had entered and was proceeding through the prescribed area, rapidly getting closer to *The Haskerland*, as the latter was making her way. A wreck marking vessel (a barge) restricted the navigable channel and *The Humbergate* attempted to pass through between *The Haskerland* and the wreck-marking vessel. A collision resulted at that point between the two vessels. It was held that, although the 'Notices to Mariners' did not have any apparent statutory effect, they should nevertheless be taken into account when considering the dictates of good seamanship. On the facts, the breach of duty by *The Humbergate* was causative of the collision and she was to blame for not holding back. But for her negligence, the collision would not have happened. No negligence was found against *The Haskerland*.

The House of Lords, in **The Statue of Liberty** (see facts later), distinguished causative from non-causative faults and held, on the facts of this case, that the failure to keep a proper lookout was not causative of the collision.

The Andulo was at fault in not taking more accurate observations at an earlier stage but that fault had no causative effect and should be left out of account in the assessment of blame.

There are many other cases exemplifying the point that the breach must have caused the collision; for example, in **The Estrella**,[118] the fact that one vessel was travelling the wrong way in the traffic separation zone was left out of account as it was not causative of the collision. Similarly, in **The Tempus**,[119] failure by the defendant's vessel to blast a sound signal on turning her helm to port at the last minute, to avoid collision, was held to be non-causative, as the collision would have happened even if the signal had been given.

In **The Homer**,[120] the negligence of the pilot of the other ship to take a swift action to avoid a collision danger in a crossing situation was found to be non-causative to the collision. *The Homer* was solely to blame.

In **Selat Arjuna v Contship Success**,[121] in which the latter made an unexpected turn to starboard when the ships were passing starboard to starboard, sinking the former, she was found solely to blame. While *Selat Arjuna* might have gone hard to port, failure to do so was not characterised as negligent or in breach of duty of care. Her master could not have known what *Contship Success* would or might do, and while he should have appreciated earlier than he did that *Contship* was altering to starboard, even if he had, he would not be blamed for standing on. Similarly, in **The Hagieni and Barbarossa**,[122] the fault of *The Hagieni* ordering half-ahead had minimal causative significance. She failed to cope with the embarrassment of *Barbarossa*'s approach, which created a situation of danger and instilled confusion as to her intentions. The apportionment was 80/20 in favour of *The Hagieni*.

---

118 [1977] 1 Lloyd's Rep 525.
119 [1913] P 166; see, also, *The Stella Antares* [1978] 1 Lloyd's Rep 41.
120 [1973] 1 Lloyd's Rep 501.
121 [2000] 1 Lloyd's Rep 627.
122 [2000] 2 Lloyd's Rep 292.

Even if the claimant establishes that the defendant was negligent, it is rarely the case in a collision between two or more ships that the collision occurred just by the fault of one ship. The court, therefore, will evaluate the blameworthiness of the fault of each vessel and deduce their causative potency.

The Statue of Liberty [123]

A collision occurred at about 2 am between *The Statue of Liberty* and *The Andulo* some miles off Cape St Vincent while both vessels were on crossing courses. There were breaches of duty on the part of both vessels. It was the duty of *The Andulo* to maintain her course and speed when she saw *The Statue of Liberty* some miles away on her port bow. *The Statue of Liberty* was guilty of gross negligence for, amongst other things, not giving way to *The Andulo*. The learned trial judge had apportioned 70% of the blame to *The Statue of Liberty* and 30% to *The Andulo*. The Court of Appeal varied the proportions to 85% and 15%, respectively. On appeal to the House of Lords, the appellants claimed that *The Andulo* was not to blame at all, while the respondents sought to have the apportionment made by the learned trial judge at first instance restored. The House of Lords evaluated the blameworthiness of each party's fault. It was held that the fault of *The Andulo*, in not taking more accurate observations at the earlier stage when *The Statue of Liberty* was sighted some miles away, had no causative effect and would be left out of account in the final assessment of the degree of blame. It was held, however, that *The Andulo* could not be totally absolved from blame because, according to the assessors, it was bad seamanship on her part to change her course to port, the way she did, after she had seen the green light of *The Statue of Liberty*. Lord Reid said:

> One must consider both the 'causative potency' and the blameworthiness of the faults. I must confess that I find some difficulty in assessing causative potency in terms of percentages. But it is sufficient here to adopt the view of Brandon J at first instance that the failure by *The Statue of Liberty* to give way early was, to my mind, by far the most causative fault on either side . . .[124]

In *The Devotion II*,[125] the Scottish Court of Session held that the collision was caused by the failure of both skippers to keep even a minimal lookout, and liability was equally apportioned.

On causative potency, the Court of Appeal will not normally disturb the judge's finding. While altering course to port at a distance of about 9 miles was wrong, the Court of Appeal said in *The Maloja II*,[126] such fault would only have added a small percentage to her share of the blame and the judge's assessment should not be disturbed.

An illustration of evaluating blameworthiness and apportioning fault can be found in *The Mineral Dampier*[127] (which sank with all her crew after a collision and

---

123 [1971] 2 Lloyd's Rep 277.
124 Ibid, p 282.
125 [1979] 1 Lloyd's Rep 509.
126 [1994] 1 Lloyd's Rep 374.
127 [2000] 1 Lloyd's Rep 282.

was only 20% to blame) and in a recent decision **The Bulk Atlanta and The Forest Pioneer**[128] (if the lookout had been sharper and there had been a more vigorous alteration to starboard, the collision would have been avoided and the damage reduced).

While irrelevant factual causes are eliminated with the 'but for' test, this test does not apply where there are several successive causes of the accident, to which other rules apply. Invariably, in collision cases, the claimant himself, or a third party, may have contributed to the collision, or there may have been an intervening cause, which broke the chain of causation of the defendant's negligence. When there are multiple successive causes, the view taken by the courts is to look at which of these was the most probable cause, either solely or in operation with other causes.

3.5 Causation in law

After the elimination of irrelevant factual causes, the court has then to ascertain which of the relevant causes is to be regarded as the cause in law for the loss or the damage suffered. In other words, it has to answer the question whether the defendant is legally liable. For example, in **The Panther and The Ericbank**,[129] The Ericbank failed to signal to her tug that they were passing another vessel, The Trishna, and the tug without orders from the tow made a manoeuvre resulting in a collision with The Trishna. The tug's propeller, which was improperly left revolving, struck The Trishna repeatedly, after which The Trishna sank. It was found that the damage done to both vessels by the actual collision was minimal, but the cause of the eventual damage to The Trishna was the continuous revolving of the tug's propeller.

Furthermore, when subsequent, or successive, damage occurs after the first incident of collision by another cause, which is not related to the previous negligence, the defendant, whose fault caused the collision, may be able to escape liability, if the damage caused by his fault is subsumed by the subsequent damage. This rule was laid down in **The Carslogie**[130] by the House of Lords, although the case is more relevant to measure of damages.

A ship damaged in a collision through the fault of another ship received temporary repairs, which rendered her seaworthy, but on the way to a port where permanent repairs were to be effected she encountered heavy weather and thereby suffered damage rendering her unseaworthy and requiring immediate repair. Both sets of repairs were effected concurrently, the work occupying 30 days. Ten days would have been required for the collision damage if executed separately: it was held that the owners of the ship at fault in the collision were not liable for damages in respect of the 10 days' detention, since the heavy weather damage was not a consequence of the collision. The owners of the damaged ship sustained no loss of profitable time by reason of the fact that, for 10 out of the 30 days occupied in

---

128 [2007] EWHC 84, 26 Jan 2007.
129 [1957] P 143.
130 [1952] AC 292; see also under para 4.3.4, below.

repairing the heavy weather damage, she was also undergoing repairs necessitated by the collision.

On the facts of this case, the 10 days of detention needed to repair the collision damage were also needed to repair the heavy weather damage (see later on measure of damages). The heavy weather causing the subsequent damage was an independent cause.

Another example that the loss or damage to ship and her cargo by the ingress of water was not proved to have been caused by the collision is shown in *The Fedra* and *The Seafarer I*.[131]

There can, however, be cases in which the subsequent damage would not have occurred had it not been for the first accident, the effect of which continued for some time (see, for example, *The Calliope* later).

Various scenarios of causation (both factual and legal) are examined below while considering the defences that may be available to the defendant. Principles of remoteness of damage are examined under para 3.12.

3.6 Defences available to the defendant

The defences are inextricably linked to questions of both causation in fact and in law.

3.6.1 The defence of inevitable accident

An inevitable accident is one which the party charged with the damage could not possibly prevent by the exercise of ordinary care, caution, and maritime skill.[132]

The claimant must first make out a prima facie case of negligence or of want of good seamanship, and then the burden shifts on to the defendant.[133]

The defendant pleading inevitable accident must show that the proximate cause of the accident was some external event, which was totally unavoidable. The question is not whether all that could be done was done as soon as the danger of the collision arose, but whether sufficient precautions had been taken much earlier. Any negligence at any time will override the defence of inevitable accident. The burden of proof for this defence is heavy and has been successful only in a few cases.

The Marpesia[134]

In this case, a collision took place between *The Marpesia* and *The America* in the morning, but in such dense fog that the vessels could only discern each other at a very short distance. One vessel was proceeding up the Irish Channel and the other

---

131 [2002] 1 Lloyd's Rep 453.
132 *The Virgil* (1843) 2 W Rob 201.
133 *The Marpesia* (1872) LR 4 PC 212.
134 Ibid.

down the Irish Channel. Only about a minute elapsed between the vessels' sighting of each other and the collision. It was found that *The Marpesia* had failed to execute the proper manoeuvre which, after sighting *The America*, it was competent for her to have executed. The defence relied on by the appellants was that the collision was the result of inevitable accident.

The judge (Sir Robert Phillimore) held that *The Marpesia* was solely to blame, as she ought to have hauled aft her head sheets and let go all the lee braces, and he pronounced *The Marpesia* to blame for the collision.

The appeal from this decree was to the Judicial Committee, which reversed the decision, after considering the facts and the circumstances of the case. It was stated that:

> Here, we have to satisfy ourselves that something was done or omitted to be done, which a person exercising ordinary care, caution and maritime skill, in the circumstances, either would not have done or would not have left undone, as the case may be ... Considering the admitted time which elapsed after the two vessels had sighted each other to have been not more than a minute, and the state in which *The Marpesia* was, in attempting to go about, (we) have failed to come to the conclusion that the Captain was to blame for having omitted to do that which the judgment seems to find that he might have done. It is a question entirely of navigation ... the nautical assessors confirmed ... that the time was so short that the omission to do that which has been said ought to have been done with the rigging and the sails cannot be imputed as negligence, or anything approaching to negligence, in the master of *The Marpesia*.[135]

The defence succeeded.

After a prima facie case of negligence is made out, Fry LJ said in *The Merchant Prince*[136] that:

> The defendants had failed to sustain the plea of inevitable accident, as it was necessary for them either to shew what was the cause of the accident, and that though exercising ordinary care, caution, and maritime skill, the result of that cause was unavoidable, or to enumerate all the possible causes, one or other of which might have produced the effect, and shew with regard to every one, that the result was unavoidable.

That the defendants were liable, as they had not satisfied the burden of proof, for, in order to support the defence of inevitable accident, and disprove the prima facie evidence of negligence, it was necessary for them to show that the cause of the accident was one not produced by them, and the result of which they could not avoid, but the defendants knew of the tendency of new chain to stretch, and, therefore, that an accumulation of links at the leading wheels might possibly cause jamming, and, considering the crowded condition of the river where the accident occurred, the use – or readiness for immediate use – of hand, instead of steam, steering gear, was a means by which the result could have been avoided.

This should not be misunderstood as altering the rule that the burden of proving fault lies on the person alleging it. It rather seems to elaborate that the

---

135 (1872) LR 4 PC 212, p 220.
136 [1892] P 179.

defendant will have a difficult task in discharging the burden of proof to succeed in the defence of inevitable accident.

Inevitable accident – which implies no negligence – will not work as a defence in the event of damage to a harbour's property, being caught by the statutory strict liability provision of s 74 of the HDPCA 1847. Even an act of God would be irrelevant to such liability, unless the ship was not under the control of human agency.[137]

3.6.2 The defence of contributory negligence

At common law, in non-admiralty cases, there was a rule until 1945 that the defence of contributory negligence on the part of the claimant disallowed recovery of damages from the defendant. The Law Reform (Contributory Negligence) Act (LR(CN)A) 1945 changed this common law rule and, since then, contributory negligence has been taken into account in the assessment of damages.[138]

By contrast, in admiralty cases concerning collisions, the defence of contributory negligence was taken into account and, when two or more ships were found at fault, the Court of Admiralty applied the rule of equal division of loss by s 25(9) of the Judicature Act 1873. In considering the contributory negligence defence, the equal division of loss was changed by the Maritime Conventions Act (MCA) 1911 to division of loss in proportion to the fault of each ship (known as the proportionate fault rule, which is linked to this defence, see under para 3.7, below).

The statement of principle of the rule of contributory negligence in admiralty was expounded by Viscount Birkenhead LC in the *Admiralty Commissioners v SS Volute*:[139]

> I think that the question of contributory negligence must be dealt with somewhat broadly and upon common sense principles . . . And while no doubt, where a clear line can be drawn, the subsequent negligence is the only one to look to, there are cases in which the two acts come so closely together, and the second act of negligence is so much mixed up with the state of things brought about by the first act, that the party secondly negligent, while not held free from blame . . . might, on the other hand, invoke the prior negligence as being part of the cause of the collision so as to make it a case of contribution. And the MCA with its provisions for nice qualifications as to the quantum of blame and the proportions in which contribution is to be made may be taken as to some extent declaratory of the admiralty rule in this respect.

As issues of contributory negligence by the claimant are inextricably linked with issues of intervening causes, which may break the chain of causation giving rise to the collision by the defendant's negligence, it is necessary to look at examples of cases involving considerations of the effect of negligence by the claimant, either during or subsequent to the collision.

---

137 See *The Mostyn* [1928] AC 57 (HL); and *River Wear Commissioners v Adamson* (1877) 2 App Cas 743 (HL); see Chapter 16, Section A on port authorities.

138 This Act intended to bring the common law rules regarding contributory negligence broadly in line with the admiralty rules: *Davies v Swan Motor Co* [1949] 2 KB 291, p 319, per Evershed LJ.

139 [1922] 1 AC 129, at 144 (HL).

3.6.3 The defence of actus novus interveniens

When the claimant's servants act reasonably in response to an accident for which the defendant was at fault, any negligence of the former in trying to mitigate the loss will not break the chain of causation.

The City of Lincoln [140]

A collision took place between a steamer and a barge, the steamer being alone to blame. The steering compass, charts, log and log glass of the barge were lost through the collision. Her captain made for a port of safety, navigating his ship by a compass which he found on board. The barge, while on her way, without any negligence on the part of the captain or crew, and owing to the loss of the requisites for navigation, grounded, and was necessarily abandoned. The Court of Appeal held that the grounding of the barge, without any intervening independent moving cause, was a natural and reasonable consequence of the collision, and that the owners of the steamer were liable for the damages caused thereby.

What is a reasonable act by the master and crew whose vessel suffers damage from a collision accident is a question of fact depending on the circumstances of a case, for example, in *The Oropesa*.[141]

The MR and *The Oropesa* collided. Although *the MR* was badly damaged, her master thought that she could be salved. He sent five of his crew in lifeboats to *The Oropesa* and, about an hour and a half after the collision, he decided himself to board *The Oropesa* to confer with her master on the measures to be taken. He embarked with 16 of his remaining crew another lifeboat. The weather was rough and getting worse and, before the boat could reach *The Oropesa*, it capsized. Nine of his men, including the sixth engineer, were drowned. *The MR* subsequently sank. The owners of *The MR* and the parents of the deceased sixth engineer sued the owners of *The Oropesa*. It was argued that the master of *The MR* was negligent and his negligence broke the chain of causation. The Court of Appeal, affirming the decision of Langton J below, held (i) that the master of *The MR* had acted reasonably in the emergency, and (ii) that the death was not the result of his action, but it was caused by the collision.

This defence will succeed if there is a break in the chain of causation, where-upon the defendant will cease to be liable for what could otherwise be regarded as the consequence of his fault. Lord Wright stated the law precisely in *The Oropesa*:[142]

> To break the chain of causation it must be shown that there is something which I will call ultroneous, something unwarrantable, a new cause which disturbs the sequence of events, something which can be described as either unreasonable or extraneous or extrinsic.

Similarly, in *The Hendrick*,[143] when a trawler sank after a collision, there were

---

140 (1889) 15 PD 15.

141 [1943] P 32 (CA).

142 (1943) 74 Ll L Rep 86, p 91.

143 [1964] 1 Lloyd's Rep 371, p 379.

criticisms of her crew by the defendant that they were inactive in seeking to preserve the trawler which was flooding with water due to the collision damage. Hewson J said, about judging what was reasonable in the circumstances:

> Placed suddenly in the situation in which they found themselves, the French crew must not be too harshly judged, and they must certainly not be judged in the light of theories, but in the light of the conditions and circumstances at the time. In reflecting upon that I must have in mind their lack of training in damage control and the absence of effective damage control gear on board their vessel. It may well be that a trained salvage crew, provided with all the necessary equipment ready at hand, would have prevented the inflow of water and probably saved the vessel; but this French crew, or any trawler crew, must not be judged by that standard. They must not be too critically examined from an armchair.

In a further example, *The Guildford*,[144] the decision of the master to await tugs for assistance after a collision, instead of accepting assistance from the colliding vessel, was on the facts of this case justified because there was no change for the worse in the situation of *The Guildford* during the waiting time. Accordingly, the sinking of *The Guildford* was a consequence of the collision, in respect of which she was entitled to recover her loss caused by the proportionate fault of the other vessel.

By contrast, this defence was successful in the following case.

Fritz Thyssen [145]

Mitera Marigo (MM), which was fully loaded with cargo, collided with *Fritz Thyssen* off the north-west coast of France. The collision was quite severe and MM suffered serious damage. Immediately after the collision, water was entering in her two double bottom tanks. Pumps were used continuously to pump water out. A salvage tug was called from Falmouth to assist MM by which time the water had reached about four or five feet in the No 1 hold. Her master, however, refused the assistance of the tug, merely engaging the tug as an escort. The vessel safely arrived at the Falmouth harbour, but a few hours later began to sink. The master called for the assistance of the tug, which had been standing by, but it was too late and MM sank in deep water. In an action brought against the owners of *Fritz Thyssen*, the defendants alleged that the loss of MM was wholly due to the negligence of her own master. The trial judge held that it was for the defendants to prove that the sinking was due to a *novus actus interveniens*. That involved proving first that MM omitted some precaution required by good seamanship, and second that, if that precaution had been taken, the loss of the ship would probably have been averted. The Lords Justice in the Court of Appeal agreed with the judge's conclusions that the negligence of the master had broken the chain of causation. Willmer LJ emphasised the need not to judge the situation on the basis of hindsight in the light of what was now known, but to view the situation as it would have appeared to the master of MM himself in the emergency with which he was faced. It was held that the master's omission to accept salvage assistance was a reckless gamble putting at risk a

---

144 [1956] 2 Lloyd's Rep 74.
145 [1967] 2 Lloyd's Rep 199.

vessel and cargo worth about £800,000, the loss of which was attributable to that negligence.

Not infrequently are there situations in which there is a collision between A and B – for which either A is solely to blame, or they are both to blame – and there is further collision, taking place at a different time or place, involving a third ship which may or may not be a consequence of the first incident. The claimant's subsequent negligence may or may not break the chain of causation.

In 1927, the House of Lords, by majority of 3 : 2, held that the claimant's sub-sequent negligence broke the chain of causation. The claimant's negligence was not even considered to amount to contributory negligence.

The Paludina [146]

The Paludina (P), *The Singleton Abbey* (SA) and *The Sara* (S) were moored by their sterns to the quay in Valletta Harbour, Malta. There was a strong wind blowing and there was a swell in the harbour. P dragged her anchors and the fore part of the vessel fell down upon SA. In endeavouring to get free from her, she broke away from her moorings, struck SA further, causing the parting of her moorings. In turn, SA fell down upon S and cast her adrift. SA and S then manoeuvred in the harbour under their own steam to keep away from the shore. Twenty minutes later, S got under the starboard quarter of SA, when the revolving propeller of SA struck S, with the result that the latter sank. P was clear of both ships at the time. In an action by SA against P, the latter was found liable for the earlier collisions. The only question at issue was whether she was also liable for the final collision between SA and S. The President, acting on the advice of two of the Elder Brethren of the Trinity House, found that the final collision was directly caused by the negligence of P, but his decision was reversed on appeal.

On further appeal, Lord Sumner, Lord Carson, Lord Blanesburgh, held (Viscount Dunedin and Lord Phillimore dissenting) that the final collision was not directly caused by the negligence of P but that the action of S constituted a *novus actus interveniens*. At the point in time of the second collision, the ships which had broken away were free agents and, having not being in the 'agony of the moment', they could have taken reasonable steps to avoid the collision. The majority distinguished the facts of this case from those in *The City of Lincoln* [147] with regard to the actions of her captain, in which, it was said: 'The hand of the original wrongdoer was still heavy on his ship and his own navigation was not the sole human agency determining her fortune.' The majority did not find that *The Paludina*'s negligence was still operating.

The dissenting minority thought that there was no break in the chain of

---

146 [1927] AC 16 (HL).

147 In *The City of Lincoln* [1890] P 15, the defendant's vessel negligently collided with and caused damage to the plaintiff's vessel, whose master attempted to reach port in safety. But the vessel grounded accidentally before he did so, and was lost. In the absence of negligence by the master, the defendants were liable not merely for the collision damage, but for the subsequent loss.

causation from the original negligence of *The Paludina*, which obliged the other ships to adopt the alternative of a dangerous leap, or to remain at certain peril.[148]

Invariably, however, difficult questions arise when further damage occurs by a separate and successive cause of damage, following an earlier incident of collision. The courts consider whether either the strength of the subsequent event or lapse of time has interrupted the connection between the original collision and the subsequent damage.

The Calliope [149]

The Calliope collided with *The Carlsholm* in the river Seine, ran aground and was damaged. In view of the damage caused by the collision and the time lost, the master of *The Calliope* decided to proceed up river to Villequier and to lie there over the ebb tide. Next day, whilst executing a turning manoeuvre in the river, she grounded twice at different times and collided with a tug which was assisting her, sustaining further damage. In the liability action between the parties, *The Carlsholm* was found 45% at fault and *The Calliope* 55% for the collision; the damage sustained by *The Calliope* as a result of the first grounding was a direct consequence of the collision. The question of law was whether the damage caused by the subsequent grounding was too remote or whether it was caused by both the original collision and the subsequent negligence; if that was so, could the court make further sub-apportionment of liability in respect of that head of damage?

Brandon J observed that the question was interesting and difficult, but at the same time it was of some general importance in the law of tort, not only in maritime cases. It involved the interrelationship between the doctrines of contributory negligence and remoteness of damage.'[150] He held that:

(i) It was open to the court as a matter of law to find that the alleged consequential damage was caused partly by the original casualty and partly by the claimants' own intervening negligence and to make a further apportionment or sub-apportionment of liability accordingly;

(ii) On the facts, the two later groundings were not caused solely by the negligence of *The Calliope* in executing the turning manoeuvre, but partly by such negligence and partly by the joint negligence of that vessel and *The Carlsholm*, which led to the collision the effect of which was still continuing when the two later groundings took place.

(iii) The question in a situation like this was not whether the negligence, which caused the collision, was continuing, but whether the effect of the collision – which such negligence caused – was continuing.

---

148 [1890] P 15, p 32.

149 [1970] 1 Lloyd's Rep 84.

150 Ibid, p 96. Of particular interest was the judge's reference to older cases which were conflicting on the issue of whether subsequent damage was recoverable without sub-apportionment. In all but 3 of the 13 cases he mentioned, the court had found that there was no causative intervening negligence. It followed that the claim for consequential damage succeeded wholly, and there was no question of apportionment. The three cases in which there was causative intervening negligence were: *The Glendinning* (1943) 76 LlL Rep 86 (concerning subsequent grounding); *The Egyptian* [1910] AC 400; and *The Fritz Thyssen* [1968] P 255 (where the ship later sank). In these cases, the claim for consequential damage failed.

The effect of the collision was obviously continuing in one sense in that, but for the collision, *The Calliope* would never have been at Villequier at all. But that is not, of course, enough. It is necessary to consider whether it was continuing in the further sense, that, at the time when the chief officer was negligent, the hand of the negligent navigator on board *The Carlsholm* was still heavy on *The Calliope*; or that those on board *The Calliope* were not, by reason of the hard necessities imposed on them by the collision, free agents; or that those on board *The Calliope* were still in the grip of the collision.

> Approaching the questions of causation which arise in this case from that point of view, I have reached the conclusion that the groundings were not caused solely by the negligence of *The Calliope* in executing the turning manoeuvre, but partly by such negligence and partly by the joint negligence of the plaintiffs and the defendants, which led to the collision and the effect of which was still continuing when the groundings took place.[151]

How can the judgment of Brandon J, who adopted an intermediate approach, be reconciled with two previous House of Lords' decisions, which had opted for the all or nothing approach?[152] Brandon J treated the matter as not being expressly decided previously, as a matter of law. The reasons for this, he said, were, in his view: (i) that the development of the concept of multiple causes of damage, and the elimination of the last opportunity rule, had been part of an historical process, which extended over many years. The process was greatly accelerated by the passing of the LR(CN)A 1945; and (ii) that in certain cases, the facts pointed towards the 'no recovery option' when there was an *actus novus interveniens*. Thus, where there is a substantial time interval between a casualty and alleged consequential damage, and intervening events occur which include further causative negligence of the party making the damage claimed, the case for finding on the facts that such further negligence was the sole cause of the damage tends to be very strong.

In a later decision, ***The Vysotsk***,[153] Sheen J held that the negligence of the vessel, which largely caused the first collision, set in motion a chain of events which led to the second collision with a third vessel. As this chain had not been broken by an intervening negligence, the parties would be liable for the damage caused by the second collision in the same proportion as for the first.

3.6.4 The defence of alternative danger or 'agony of the moment'

Such a defence may arise when the claimant's master has acted under the stress of circumstances forced upon him by the defendant's servants, whereupon he may do some act which brings about the collision. It would then be open to the party pleading 'alternative danger' or 'agony of the moment', as a counter-defence to contributory negligence, to show how the danger arose. The alternative danger plea is also available where the actions of the claimant's master or crew force the

---

151 Ibid, p 102.
152 *The Paludina* [1927] AC 16 (albeit not a unanimous decision) and *The Metagama* (1928) 29 LlL Rep 253 (HL).
153 [1981] 1 Lloyd's Rep 439.

defendant to act in the agony of the moment to avert a peril resulting from the negligence of the claimant's servants.

The sound rule is, that: a man in charge of a vessel is not to be held guilty of negligence, or as contributing to an accident, if in a sudden emergency caused by the default or negligence of another vessel, he does something which he might, under the circumstances as known to him, reasonably think proper; although those before whom the case comes for adjudication are, with a knowledge of all the facts, and with time to consider them, able to see that the course which he adopted was not in fact the best.[154]

Where one ship has, by wrong manoeuvres, placed another ship in a position of extreme danger, that other ship will not be held to blame if she has done something wrong, and has not been manoeuvred with perfect skill and presence of mind.

Brett LJ in *The Bywell Castle*[155] put the reasoning behind this as follows:

> I am of the opinion that when one ship by her wrongful act suddenly puts another ship into the position of difficulty of this kind, we cannot expect the same amount of skill as we should under other circumstances. The captains of ships are bound to show such skill, as persons of their position with ordinary nerve ought to show under the circumstances. But any court ought to make the very greatest allowance for a captain or pilot suddenly put into such difficult circumstances, and the court ought not, in fairness and justice to him, require perfect nerve and presence of mind enabling him to do the best thing possible.[156]

On the facts of the case, *The Princess Alice*, a paddle-wheel steamer, had come up the river and was struck on the starboard bow by *The Bywell Castle*, in consequence of the porting of the helm of the latter. *The Princess Alice* soon afterwards sank. More than 500 of her passengers and many of the crew, including the captain, were drowned.

It was found in the lower court that *The Princess Alice* was navigated in a careless and reckless manner, without due observance of the regulations with respect to lookout and speed and that *The Bywell Castle* appeared to have been navigated with due care and skill until very shortly before the collision.

The evidence certainly established that, having seen the green light of *The Princess Alice*, *The Bywell Castle* put hard to port. There was no doubt that this was not only obviously a wrong manoeuvre, but the worst which she could have executed. The only defence offered for it was that it was executed so very short a time before the collision.

It was held at first instance that, although *The Princess Alice* was to blame for the collision, *The Bywell Castle* made a wrong manoeuvre for which she would carry some blame. Had the wrong manoeuvre not been made by *The Bywell Castle*, *The Princess Alice* would still have received some injury, but would not have sunk and would not have lost so many lives. The Court of Appeal overruled that *The Bywell Castle* was to blame at all. It held that *The Princess Alice* was solely to blame, and said that a ship has no right by its own misconduct to put another ship into a situation

---

154 *The Bywell Castle* (1879) 4 PD 219, p 228, per Cotton LJ.
155 Ibid.
156 Ibid, pp 226, 227.

of extreme peril, and then charge that other ship with misconduct. James LJ stated:

> My opinion is that if, in that moment of extreme peril and difficulty, such other ship happens to do something wrong, so as to be a contributory to the mischief, that would not render her liable for the damage, inasmuch as perfect presence of mind, accurate judgment, and promptitude under all circumstances are not to be expected.[157]

3.6.5 The defence of necessity

This may avail the defendant to escape liability in circumstances in which an action, which would otherwise have amounted to actionable negligence, might have been justified because of necessity to choose between two perilous situations, either in the interest of its own ship or in the interest of third parties.[158] The Colregs, by reg 2(b), also provide for departure from them in cases of necessity. But the defendant cannot avail himself of this defence if the necessity was brought about by his own fault.[159]

3.6.6 Time bar defence[160]

Section 190 of the MSA 1995 provides for a period of two years within which any claim or lien can be enforced against a ship or her owners. It covers all claims for property damage or loss caused by the fault of that ship to another ship, its freight, or any property on board. It also covers claims for damages for loss of life or personal injury caused by the fault of that ship to any person on board another ship.

The section, which derives from s 8 of the MCA 1911, does not apply when the collision is not between ships, but between a ship and another object.[161] In the latter case, the normal six years' time limit provided under the Limitation Act (LA) 1980 applies to property damage claims. In this connection, the importance of defining a ship becomes apparent, as was discussed in Chapter 1.

As regards claims for personal injury or loss of life of persons on board the carrying ship, such claims are not covered by s 190 (which refers in sub-s (1)(b) to claims by persons on board another ship – the non-carrying ship). These are subject to the normal three years' time limit as provided under the LA 1980, as amended by the Latent Damage Act 1986; or, if the Athens Convention applies, a two years' time limit is provided by Art 16.

The time commences from the date of the incident (that is, when the damage or loss was caused or the loss of life or injury was suffered) and stops running from the date of the issue of the claim form.

---

157 *The Bywell Castle* (1879) 4 PD 219, p 223.

158 See *The Koursk* (1920) 2 LlL Rep 244 (HL): the defence that a reversing action would be fatal and, hence, the thrust to port helm saved the ship, succeeded; in *The Hessa* (1921) 9 LlL Rep 271, the defence succeeded: what is demanded of a man who has to choose between two perils is to exercise judgment as a prudent seaman.

159 *Southport Corp v Esso Petroleum Ltd* [1954] 2 QB 182.

160 This is a procedural type of defence, the time may be extended by agreement. For other procedural defences, such as res judicata or issue estoppel, see, op cit, Marsden, fn 1, pp 458–463.

161 See *The Nlase (formerly Erica Jacob)* [2000] 1 Lloyd's Rep 455.

In sub-ss (5) and (6) of s 190, it is provided that any court having jurisdiction may, in accordance with rules of court, extend the period allowed for bringing proceedings to such extent and on such conditions as it thinks fit. In addition, if any such court is satisfied that there has not been – during the period allowed for bringing proceedings – any reasonable opportunity of arresting the ship within the jurisdiction of the court, or the territorial sea of the country to which the plaintiff's ship belongs, or in which the plaintiff resides or has his principal place of business, it shall extend the period allowed for bringing proceedings to an extent sufficient to give a reasonable opportunity of so arresting the ship. It should be noted that, when the claim form has been issued, the time limit is interrupted but, because the validity of the *in rem* claim form lasts for one year,[162] it will need to be extended if the ship does not come within the jurisdiction within the year to be arrested. So, the provision under s 190(6) is useful with regard to renewal of the *in rem* claim form.

3.7 The proportionate fault rule

Lord Stowell stated, in **Woodrop Sims**,[163] that there are four possibilities in which a collision may occur:

(a) without the blame being imputable to any party to it, that is, by a storm or without human error – in such a case the loss is borne by the party upon whom it happens to fall;

(b) both parties are to blame for want of due diligence and skill, whereupon the loss will be apportioned in accordance to the proportion of fault;

(c) misconduct of the suffering party only, who must bear his own loss;

(d) fault of the ship which ran the other down – the innocent party is entitled to recover compensation.

The second category concerns us here. The MCA 1911 enacted the Brussels Convention on Collisions 1910 and, by s 1, the equal division of loss rule was altered to proportionate fault, meaning that blame was attributed according to the degree of each ship's fault, even in cases where a vessel was to blame in a small proportion.

Now, the applicable statute enshrining this rule is s 187 of the MSA 1995 (which replaced s 1 of the MCA 1911). Section 187(1)(a) states:

> Where, by the fault of two or more ships, damage or loss is caused to one or more of those ships, to their cargoes or freight, or to any property on board, the liability to make good the damage or loss shall be in proportion to the degree in which each vessel was in fault.

3.7.1 When and how does the rule apply?

(a) The apportionment of loss pursuant to this rule applies only to damage or loss caused by the fault of two or more ships. Apportionment applies only to those vessels at fault and their cargo on board. Thus, when there is a collision between

---

162 CPR, r 61.3(5)(b), modifying rr 7.5 and 7.6 (general provision of extension of time by the court).
163 (1815) 2 Dod 83, p 85.

a ship and a non-ship, s 187 does not apply for apportionment of loss; the rule of contributory negligence under the Law Reform (Contributory Negligence) Act 1945 will apply.

(b) The ships at fault do not have to be in actual collision with each other. It will suffice if, by the fault of ships A and B, for example, a collision occurs between B and C.[164] If C sues B, the latter will join A in the proceedings, and the faults of all will be apportioned by assessing the faults of each, so that B can recover from A the adjudged proportion of what she has to pay C as well as her own damage.

(c) No liability will be attached to a ship whose fault has not contributed to the loss or damage at all (sub-s (4)).

In apportioning liability, there are no strict rules, but there exist some guidelines for the court to take into account. For example, the court will look at the nature and quality of faults rather than their number; it will also look at the seriousness and extent to which such faults contributed to the collision and damage. Furthermore, the court will distinguish a fault-creating danger from a fault which was a reaction to danger. Ships embarking on a deliberate action bear a greater degree of fault.[165] The tendency of the courts is to deal with apportionment in a fairly broad way, and the most usual division of blame has been 60/40 or 70/30 or 75/25,[166] or 80/20,[167] or sometimes 50/50,[168] and very rarely 100%.[169] Further apportionment or sub-apportionment for a subsequent head of damage may be made in appropriate cases, which may be adjudged on a 50/50 basis of the original apportionment.[170]

Section 187(2) allows an equal division of loss only in cases where it is not possible to establish different degrees of fault. But the effect of sub-s (1) is mandatory. The judge should not decide too readily that the vessels are equally to blame, as is seen below, merely because it is difficult to assess the degree of blame of each ship. Only when it is not possible to establish different degrees of fault, having regard to the circumstances of the case, will the liability be apportioned equally.

The Anneliese [171]

A collision occurred in the English Channel, in daylight, between *The Arietta S Livanos* (*The Arietta*) and *The Anneliese*. *The Arietta* was on a course of 050 degrees with engines at stand-by. *The Anneliese* was on a course of 235 degrees with engines at full ahead (15 knots) when *The Arietta* was sighted (visually and by radar) bearing ahead distant about six miles. *The Arietta* was, thereafter, watched visually and by radar. Four minutes later, *The Anneliese* altered course to 239 degrees bringing *The Arietta* fine on port bow, distant about four miles. Three minutes later, visibility

---

164 *The Cairnbahn* [1914] P 25; *The Betavier III* (1925) 42 TLR 8.
165 *The Bywell Castle* (1879) 4 PD 219.
166 *The Sitarem and The Spirit* [2001] 2 Lloyd's Rep 107.
167 *The Topaz and The Iraqua* [2003] 2 Lloyd's Rep 19.
168 *The Pearl and The Jahre Venture* [2003] 2 Lloyd's Rep 188.
169 *The Contship Success* [2000] 1 Lloyd's Rep 627; *The Navios Enterprise and The Puritan* [1998] 2 Lloyd's Rep 16.
170 See *The Calliope* [1970] 1 Lloyd's Rep 84.
171 [1970] 1 Lloyd's Rep 355.

deteriorated and *The Anneliese* altered course to 250 degrees to increase passing distance between vessels. Half a minute later, *The Arietta* disappeared from view and *The Anneliese* commenced fog signals. Two minutes later, *The Anneliese* altered to starboard over a period of about two minutes until on a course of 267 degrees. During this time, *The Anneliese*, realising from her radar that *The Arietta* was altering to port, stopped her engines and, seeing *The Arietta* visually distant half to a quarter of a mile and bearing 45 degrees on the port bow, put her wheel hard-a-port and ordered engines emergency full astern, sounding a two-short-blast signal and then a three-short-blast signal.

The Arietta's case was that visibility was restricted by fog to about three-quarters to one mile and she was sounding regulation signals. Her relative motion radar was on eight-mile range and the echo of *The Anneliese* was seen distant about eight miles bearing five degrees on the starboard bow. A little later, when *The Arietta* saw that *The Anneliese* had altered to starboard, *The Arietta's* wheel was put hard-a-port. *The Arietta* saw *The Anneliese* visually distant a quarter to one half of a mile bearing 60 degrees on starboard bow, and sounded two-short-blast signals. *The Arietta's* wheel was ordered hard-a-starboard, but collision occurred between stem of *The Anneliese* and starboard quarter of *The Arietta* at angle of about 59 degrees leading forward on *The Arietta*.

Both vessels were criticised for not keeping a proper lookout and for using excessive speed in those conditions. Brandon J, at first instance, found it difficult to apportion different degrees of fault and ordered that the liability should be apportioned equally. He expressed his approach to the MCA 1911 thus:

> ... on the whole, I have come to the conclusion that with such serious faults on both sides, it is impossible to say that there is any clear preponderance of blame on *The Arietta* ...[172]

The expression 'clear preponderance of blame' was derived from Lord Atkinson in *The Peter Benoit*,[173] where he had said that a clear preponderance of culpability must be proved. Since then, the courts had used that approach. But Davies LJ in his judgment in *The Anneliese* (on appeal) stated, thus:

> With the greatest respect to the learned Lord, the section does not say that there must be proved a clear preponderance of culpability. What it says is: ... the liability to make good the damage or loss shall be in proportion to the degree in which each vessel was in fault, subject of course to the proviso that if, having regard to all the circumstances of the case, it is not possible to establish different degrees of fault, the liability shall be apportioned equally ... Now that section, as I read it, is mandatory. It does not say that the liability shall be apportioned equally unless different degrees of fault are shown. It is the other way round. It says that the court must apportion the liability in proportion to the degree in which each vessel was at fault unless it is impossible so to do. Of course, the different degrees of fault must be proved, like anything else in a court of law.[174]

It was held that it was possible to distinguish between the degrees in which each

172 [1969] 2 Lloyd's Rep 78, p 93.
173 (1915) 13 Asp MLC 203, p 207.
174 [1970] 1 Lloyd's Rep 355, p 363.

vessel was at fault. *The Anneliese* was not at fault in making a succession of alterations to starboard nor was she at fault in failing to react more promptly to *The Arietta*'s turn to port. Thus, *The Arietta* was two-thirds to blame and *The Anneliese* one-third.

The Appeal Court will not normally interfere with the actual apportionment of blame fixed by the trial judge, who will have made his judgment having heard all the evidence and assisted by nautical assessors and the Elder Brethren, unless there is mistake in law.

As mentioned earlier, for the assessment of fault it is not necessary for there to be a physical impact between two vessels, nor navigational fault.[175] In the event that one vessel responds foolishly to a deliberate action of another, the latter vessel may bear a greater degree of fault than the one which responded foolishly. This is illustrated in *Miraflores v Abadesa*.

Miraflores v Abadesa [176]

The George Livanos was proceeding up the river Scheldt behind *The Miraflores*. *The Abadesa* was proceeding down the river at the same time. When the vessels reached the narrows on the river, *The Abadesa* negligently failed to hold back to give way to *The Miraflores*. As a result, *The Miraflores* could not deal properly with the difficulties she met owing to a cross-current present at the time. She reacted foolishly, steering first to starboard and then to port and continued to port until she was hit by *The Abadesa*. Both vessels, blocking the channel at the time, caught fire due to the leakage of burning oil. *The George Livanos*, being behind *The Miraflores*, acted rather in a confused way and did not take immediate action to avoid danger; she ran aground and sustained damage. The owners of *The Miraflores* brought an action against the owners of *The Abadesa* in respect of the collision, and the owners of *The George Livanos* brought a separate action against the owners of both *The Miraflores* and *The Abadesa* in respect of her grounding. The actions were heard together by Hewson J, who held in respect of the collision action that *The Miraflores* had been one-third and *The Abadesa* two-thirds to blame for the collision. In respect of the grounding action, he held that *The George Livanos* had herself been negligent. He treated the negligence which led to the collision as 'one unit', and the negligence of *The George Livanos* in respect of the grounding as the other unit. He found it impossible to distinguish between the degrees of fault of the two units and, therefore, held that *The George Livanos* was 50% to blame for the grounding and entitled to recover the remaining 50% from *The Abadesa* and *The Miraflores* in the proportions of two-thirds and one-third, respectively. The Court of Appeal varied the apportionment of liability, attributing 45% to *The Abadesa*, 30% to *The Miraflores* and 25% to *The George Livanos*.

On appeal to the House of Lords, Lord Wilberforce held that, in investigating 'fault' under s 1(1) of the Act, the 'unit approach'[177] was wrong, since it might be misleading to substitute, for a measurement of the individual fault of each

---

175 *The Norwhale* [1975] 1 Lloyd's Rep 610.

176 [1967] AC 826.

177 The 'unit approach' did not require assessment of the degree in which each vessel was at fault. Such an approach was disapproved by the House of Lords again in *The Koningin Juliana* [1975] 2 Lloyd's Rep 111, in which, also, a mathematical 'composite faults' approach was rejected.

contributor to the accident, a measurement of the fault of one against the joint fault of the other two.

It was further held that, on the evidence, the same proportions of fault as between *The Miraflores* and *The Abadesa* fixed by the judge in respect of the collision should be adhered to in respect of the grounding, but the proportion of fault attributable to *The George Livanos* should be altered, the final proportions being assessed at two-fifths to *The Abadesa*, two-fifths to *The George Livanos* and one-fifth to *The Miraflores*.

> A person who embarks on a deliberate act of negligence should, in general, bear a greater degree of fault than one who fails to cope adequately with the resulting crisis thus thrust upon him; and further:
>
> . . . the driver who deliberately goes round a corner on the wrong side should, as a rule, find himself more harshly judged than the negligent driver who fails to react promptly enough to the unexpected problem thereby created. For all humans can refrain from deliberately breaking well known safety rules; but it is not in mortals to command the perfect reaction to a crisis; and many fall short at times of that degree which reasonable care demands.[178]

The alteration of apportionment of loss from the finding of the trial judge was made with great caution and was stressed, repeating the rule of *The MacGregor* case[179] that, in matters of apportionment, even more than as regards finding of fact generally, the decision of the trial judge should be interfered with only where some clear error of law or principle can be shown to have influenced his decision.

3.7.2 Exceptions to the proportionate fault rule

If both vessels are at fault, it will be right to apportion the blame. The rule will not apply in the following circumstances.

3.7.2.1 When the defence of alternative danger or 'agony of the moment' succeeds

As seen earlier, such a defence will be taken into account when the claimant's master has acted under the stress of circumstances, forced upon him by the defendant's servants, to avoid a further danger, whereupon he may do some act which brings about the collision. His ship will not be held to blame. In the agony of that moment, it cannot be expected from masters of ships to show the same amount of skill as should be expected under other circumstances, as Brett LJ put it in *The Bywell Castle*:[180]

> The captains of ships are bound to show such skill, as persons of their position with ordinary nerve ought to show under the circumstances. But any court ought to make the very greatest allowance for a captain or pilot suddenly put into such difficult circumstances, and the court ought not, in fairness and justice to him, require perfect nerve and presence of mind enabling him to do the best thing possible.[181]

It must, however, be shown how the danger arose.

178 [1967] AC 826, p 848, per Lord Pearce.
179 [1943] AC 197 (HL).
180 Ibid.
181 Ibid, pp 226, 227.

3.7.2.2 When a clear line can be drawn between two separate negligent acts

Section 187 of the MSA 1995 provides that nothing in the section shall operate so as to render any vessel liable for any loss or damage to which her fault has not contributed.

For example, if it is the act of the claimant, unprotected by the alternative danger plea, which is the direct/proximate cause of loss, the defendant may escape liability. Most times, however, it is difficult to establish a clear line rule as to when the second negligent act was sufficiently removed from the first to enable the party first at fault to escape liability, as was shown in *The SS Volute*. The courts consider whether the negligence of both parties is contemporaneous or whether the act of the claimant was in fact much later in time. A usual consideration is whether there is sufficient separation of time, place or circumstance between one negligent act and the next. However, strong evidence is required to show this separation.

Admiralty Commissioners v SS Volute[182]

The Volute was the leader of a convoy under the charge of two destroyers, *The Radstock* and another (*The Radstock* being on the starboard hand). She had instructions when to alter her course and, being responsible for the alteration, she was to sound the necessary short-blast helm signals when altering course. She was directed to alter course to port a little before midnight, and she starboarded her helm and blew the appropriate signal of two blasts, which was answered as intended by the other vessels of the convoy, and the course was altered without mishap. On this altered course, the vessels then proceeded till a particular bearing, when it would be right for the course to be altered about seven points to starboard. While doing so, *The Volute* ought to have signified this very striking alteration by the blowing of a short blast of her whistle. Whether she did so was a serious matter in dispute at the trial. The night was dark, and no lights were being carried except that each vessel in the convoy carried a shaded stern light. *The Radstock*, whose officer and crew said that they heard no whistle, did not alter course when *The Volute* ported her helm and the result was that a position of danger arose. Only the master of those on board *The Volute* was examined, and he, though awake and in the chart room, was not on the bridge till the last moment. On discovering *The Volute*'s change of course to starboard, *The Radstock* went hard a-port, but her helm jammed, and she then increased her speed from 8 to 18 knots, with the result that a collision occurred, notwithstanding that *The Volute* stopped and reversed her engines. In the opinion of the House of Lords on the evidence (reversing the finding of the trial judge), *The Volute* did not sound the appropriate helm signal before porting.

It was held that the collision was caused partly by *The Volute*'s omission to signal and partly by *The Radstock*'s going full speed ahead after the position of danger brought about by *The Volute*'s negligence, and that both vessels were to blame.

The decision of the Court of Appeal holding *The Radstock* alone to blame was reversed.

---

182 [1922] 1 AC 129 (HL).

3.7.2.3 When an innocent third ship claims against one of the tortfeasors

Section 187 of the MSA 1995 is applicable to a situation when two or more ships involved in a collision are at fault. When an innocent third ship is involved in a collision which is caused by the fault of two other ships, it can proceed to recover its damage from one of the tortfeasors. The common law rule will apply and the innocent party can claim the whole of his damage from either or both joint tortfeasors.[183] The paying tortfeasor can claim contribution, under the CLCA 1978, from the other tortfeasor for any excess amount – over and above his proportion of liability – paid to the innocent party, or alternatively their respective liability can be apportioned as between themselves in accordance with s 187. If only one tortfeasor is sued, the other can be joined as a third party, or as a second defendant later (see, further, para 3.10, below).

3.7.2.4 The rule does not apply when the collision is between a ship and a non-ship

Whilst contributory negligence and the rule of apportionment in a collision between ships is governed by s 187 of the MSA 1995, by which their respective faults are apportioned, contributory negligence in the event of collision between a ship and another object is governed by the LR(CN)A 1945. The purpose of this Act has been to bring the rules of common law more or less in line with those of admiralty. However, unlike the admiralty rule, where there is an individual assessment of each fault of each ship for damage caused to each other or to a third ship,[184] the 1945 Act does not require individual assessment when there are multiple faults. The claimant's conduct is contrasted with the totality of the defendants' conduct (the 'unit approach') in the liability proceedings in which the claimant's contributory negligence is taken into account. Then, apportionment of contribution between the defendants *inter se* is determined in the contribution action under s 2 of the CLCA 1978, which may be joined with the main action or be determined in separate proceedings, as is shown below.

Fitzgerald v Lane [185]

A plaintiff successfully sued more than one defendant for damages with regard to personal injuries. Contributory negligence by the plaintiff was established in the liability proceedings. Apportionment of liability between the plaintiff and the defendants, pursuant to s 1 of the LR(CN)A 1945, was kept separate from apportionment of contribution between the defendants *inter se* under s 2 of the CLCA 1978. Assessment of the plaintiff's share in the responsibility for the damage he had sustained did not involve the determination of the extent of the individual culpability of each of the defendants:

> In the contribution proceedings, whether or not they are heard during the trial of the main action or by separate proceedings, the court is concerned to discover what contribution is just and equitable, having regard to the responsibility between the

---

183 *The Devonshire* [1912] AC 634; *The Cairnbahn* [1914] P 25; see further analysis in Chapter 14, paras 8.2.2–8.2.4.

184 As opposed to a 'unit approach' assessment: *Miraflores v George Livanos* [1967] 1 AC 826.

185 [1988] 3 WLR 356 (HL); also, op cit, Marsden, fn 1, paras 14–17.

tortfeasors *inter se*, for the damage which the plaintiff has been adjudged entitled to recover. That damage may, of course, have been subject to a reduction as a result of the decision in the main action that the plaintiff, by his own negligence, contributed to the damage which he sustained.[186]

In cases where no contribution between tortfeasors is involved, the apportionment of fault is determined in the liability proceedings.

The Ellen M[187]

The Ellen M was moored alongside other vessels head up river. The bridge master of the Haven Bridge had verbally informed the master of *The Ellen M* that the bridge would be opened for those vessels at 0735 hours. A good lookout was being kept on *The Ellen M*. All aft moorings of *The Ellen M* were cast off and a blue flag was exhibited indicating that the bridge was about to be opened to allow vessels to proceed northward. A strong gust struck *The Ellen M*, catching her port bow and turning her to starboard, whereupon her rudder was put hard-a-port and her engines were worked variously ahead and astern in an attempt to straighten her on to an up-river heading. Despite those manoeuvres, *The Ellen M*, under the influence of wind and tide, was carried across the river angled to starboard. Very shortly afterwards, as a result of her port quarter being in contact with another vessel, she straightened up to an up-river heading, from which position she could have been safely manoeuvred up river and through the open bridge.

When she was about to proceed towards and through the bridge, the bridge was seen to begin to close to river traffic. Immediately afterwards, the starboard anchor of *The Ellen M* was let go and three short blasts were sounded on her whistle in accordance with local practice to indicate to those operating the bridge that the bridge should be kept open. The arms of the bridge stopped at an angle of about 45 degrees from the upright, apparently indicating that the bridge was going to reopen, whereupon the engines of *The Ellen M* were put full ahead. However, the arms of the bridge again began to lower, closing the bridge, whereupon the starboard anchor chain of *The Ellen M* was again veered, her engines were stopped and her wheel was put hard-a-starboard in an attempt to turn her round to starboard. Her engines were worked variously ahead and astern in an attempt to keep her stern clear of a coaster moored up river and her bows clear of craft moored at Town Hall Quay. Nothing further was or could be done to prevent *The Ellen M* from colliding in quick succession with the offside of a motor cruiser moored alongside, and other craft at Town Hall Quay closer to the bridge.

In proceedings by the owners of *The Ellen M* against the owners of the bridge, it was alleged that the collision was caused by the defendant's negligent operation of the bridge. The defendants alleged that the collision was caused by *The Ellen M* allowing herself to get out of control.

It was held by Brandon J: (1) that the bridgemaster was negligent in closing the bridge; (2) that *The Ellen M* was negligent in reversing her turning manoeuvre and

---

186 Ibid, p 362, per Lord Ackner.
187 [1967] 2 Lloyd's Rep 247.

attempting to pass through the bridge in belief that it was opening again; and (3) that the negligence of *The Ellen M* was an immediate cause of casualty; that, although the bridgemaster's negligence would not have caused the casualty without the subsequent negligence of *The Ellen M*, no clear line could be drawn between earlier negligence of the bridgemaster and later negligence of *The Ellen M*. Accordingly, both acts of negligence were causative, and both parties were equally to blame. Brandon J explained (at p 258):

> It seems to me that the second act of negligence was so close to the first and so mixed up with the state of things brought about by the first that both acts of negligence should be regarded as causative, and I so hold.

> That leaves me with the task of apportioning the blame between the two sides. Apportionment of blame in a case of this sort is governed by the LR(CN)A 1945. Under that Act, the same principles are to be applied as under the MCA 1911, that is to say, the court is to take account of both culpability and causative potency. I do not find this an easy case in which to apportion the blame. The original trouble was due to the negligence of the bridgemaster; the subsequent negligence of the master of *The Ellen M* was committed in the situation of difficulty caused by that original negligence and allowances must obviously be made for that. But, after making all allowances for that, I consider that the master's decision to reverse his turning manoeuvre in order to make for the bridge again was a rash decision. It was the duty of the master of *The Ellen M* to put the safety of his ship first in a crisis of that kind and not to 'chance his arm', as I think he did. On the whole I have come to the conclusion that the fair apportionment in this case is to hold both sides equally to blame.

There may be occasions when a ship strikes an object, that is, a pier, as a consequence of taking an evasive action to avoid a collision with another ship, which is at fault. If they are both at fault, s 187 of the MSA 1995 will apply between the two ships for apportionment of fault, even if there had been no actual physical contact between them.

An example of such a situation is shown below, although on the facts of this case only one ship was found to have been at fault.

The Belle Usk [188]

The Brittania was in collision with a pier in her manoeuvre to avoid a collision with *The Belle Usk*. The latter had been lying on at the passenger pontoon to which *The Brittania* was bound. She was, however, required to move out from the pontoon. *The Brittania* was a passenger vessel and, as she approached her berth, *The Belle Usk* was seen to be moving out. Both vessels seemed to be safely clear of each other. However, *The Belle Usk* suddenly came ahead across the path of *The Brittania*, causing *The Brittania*, in an attempt to avoid a collision, to stop her engines, suddenly, and put full speed astern, her wheel being turned to starboard. In an attempt to regain her position, so that she could still make it into the berth, *The Brittania* got caught by the westerly wind and a slight set of tide, and was carried against bullnoses, causing damage both to herself and the pier. It was held that the damage was due to the bad

---

188 [1955] 2 Lloyd's Rep 421.

seamanship of *The Belle Usk* in crossing ahead of *The Brittania* rendering collision with the pier inevitable. Therefore, *The Belle Usk* was alone to blame, and had to recompense *The Brittania* for the damages paid to the pier owner.

The risk of contact between arriving or departing vessels and shore cranes is a matter of notoriety, particularly when ships berth in close proximity to each other and under the influence of a cross wind. *The Maersk Colombo*[189] came into contact with a shore crane by the overhang of her bow while berthing and caused the crane to topple over and collapse. The admiralty judge found that, although *The Maersk Colombo* created a situation of danger by trying to berth in cross wind without yet having the tug made fast forward, the crane manager and the berth master were negligent also. In accordance with regulations, cranes should be positioned close to midships for a vessel manoeuvring on and off a berth. In this case, however, there was not enough time to move the crane when *The Maersk Colombo* arrived. Bearing in mind also the negligence of the berth master, the contributory negligence of the crane owners amounted to 15%.

3.7.2.5 *The rule does not apply to claims for personal injury or loss of life*

Section 187 expressly provides for division of loss concerning property damage, while ss 188 and 189 deal with this category of claims, as shown below.

3.8 Claims for loss of life and personal injury

The rule of division of loss in s 187 of the 1995 MSA does not apply to cases of liability for death or personal injury. Sections 188 and 189 of the Act deal with such liability.[190] In particular, s 188 provides:

> Where loss of life or personal injuries are suffered by any person on board a ship owing to the fault of that ship and of any other ship or ships, the liability of the owners of the ships shall be joint and several.

That means that the claimant may claim his full damages from any one of the tortfeasors.

The origin of this rule lies at common law. In *The Bernina*,[191] there was a collision with *The Burshire*, and a crew member and a passenger of the latter were drowned. The collision was due to the fault of the masters of both ships.

The representatives of the deceased brought actions *in personam* against the *The Bernina*'s owners for negligence under Lord Campbell's Act (9 & 10 Vict c 93). It was held that, since the deceased persons had nothing to do with the navigation of *The Burshire*, their representatives could maintain the actions and could recover the whole of their damages. The admiralty rule as to half damages was not applicable.

If one of the joint tortfeasors bears all the loss, he has a right to contribution

---

189 [1999] 2 Lloyd's Rep 491.
190 MSA 1995, ss 188, 189 have substantially reproduced the MCA 1911, ss 2 and 3.
191 (1888) 13 App Cas 1 (HL).

against the other for the excess of the proportion in which the ship was in fault, as provided under s 189. Nothing in this section authorises the recovery of any amount which could not, by reason of any statutory or contractual limitation of, or exemption from, liability, or which could not for any other reason have been recovered in the first instance as damages by the persons entitled to sue (sub-para (3)).

A claim to enforce any contribution under ss 187–89 may be brought by way of an action *in rem* and must be brought within one year from the date of payment to the claimant (s 190(4)).[192]

As mentioned under para 3.6.6, when the claimant for personal injury or loss of life sues the non-carrying vessel, the action must be commenced within two years of the incident. This derives from s 190(1)(b). The time may be extended. The court has a discretion to grant the extension, which may be exercised depending on the length of the delay, or on whether the delay was excusable and beyond the party's control, or on whether justice would be done if the extension was granted. The time limit to bring an action for this type of claims against the carrying ship is three years.[193]

Where persons are killed, their estates have an action against the vessel at fault and her owners under the LR(MP)A 1934, and their dependants have an action under the FAA 1976,[194] as amended by the Administration of Justice Act 1982.

3.9 Contrast claims in relation to cargo damage

At common law today, the position for recovery of loss or damage suffered by an innocent third party due to the fault of two joint tortfeasors is that he can recover the whole of his loss against either tortfeasor. As has been discussed under para 3.7.3.3, this common law rule applies to an innocent third ship involved in a collision and to claims for personal injury or loss of life.

By contrast, the admiralty law rule of division of loss applies to all property claims including the claims of the innocent cargo-owner, whose cargo is damaged or lost on board the carrying ship due to a collision between this ship and another for which both ships are at fault. Students of shipping law usually question this rule because the cargo owner should be regarded also as an innocent third party. An explanation as to the justification of the rule can be found in the following case.

The Drumlanrig[195]

Tongariro, laden with cargo, collided with the steamship *The Drumlanrig*, and it was not disputed that both vessels were to blame. The cargo owners claimed against the owners of *The Drumlanrig* for the whole of the damage to their goods sustained by

---

192 Previously, the MCA 1911, s 8.
193 The limitation period provided for by the LA 1980 applies to this type of claim.
194 See *The Esso Malaysia* [1974] 2 Lloyd's Rep 143.
195 [1911] AC 16 (HL).

the collision. The question for the court as to damages was whether the plaintiffs could recover the whole of their loss from the owners of *The Drumlanrig*, or only 50% of it; (at the time, the rule in admiralty was about equal division of loss between the two guilty ships).

Sir Samuel Evans (President) held that they were entitled to a moiety only of the limitation fund lodged in court by the defendants. This decision was affirmed by the Court of Appeal. On further appeal, the House of Lords affirmed the decisions of the lower courts. The following extracts from the judgment help to understand the development and justification of the rule.

Lord Loreburn LC:[196]

Under the JA of 1873, s 25, sub-s 9: 'In any cause or proceeding for damages arising out of a collision between two ships, if both ships shall be found to have been in fault the rules hitherto in force in the Court of Admiralty, so far as they have been at variance with the rules in force in the courts of common law, shall prevail.'

In order to apply this statutory direction, let me first see what is the rule at common law. In 1873, when the Act was passed, the supposed rule was that the owner of goods in such a case could recover nothing at all, because he was imagined to be identified with the ship in which his goods were stowed, and, she being in fault, he also was disabled by her disability. There was really nothing to say either in principle or good sense for this metaphysical view, and it was finally exploded by the decision of this House in *The Bernina*,[197] which decided that so far from recovering nothing the owner of cargo could recover the full amount of his loss.

The law of admiralty was different. In admiralty, the rule had been for a long time that, in case of collision between two ships where both were to blame, each shipowner could recover from the other one half his loss. In 1861, in *The Milan*,[198] Dr Lushington directly decided that the owner of cargo in one of the ships could in like manner recover only one half of the loss from the other ship. And he expressly repudiated the supposed doctrine of common law, relying upon the uniform practice in admiralty. How old that practice may have been in regard to cargo is not quite certain . . . That practice as to the cargo-owner only receiving one half his loss may have been based upon the similar and long settled practice as to shipowners. Perhaps the analogy was a false one and the practice not really fair. Indeed . . . I should be very glad if I could award to these plaintiffs the full amount of their claim. But we must obey the Act of Parliament, and when once it is made good that the rule as to recovering one half only was in 1873 'hitherto in force', we have no choice. If this state of the law is to be remedied, the remedy must be provided by the legislature.[199] It is no valid argument to say it ought not to have been ever established.

---

196 Ibid, pp 18, 19.
197 (1888) 13 App Cas 1 (HL), concerning loss of life on board a ship.
198 (1861) Lush 388.
199 The subsequent MCA 1911 and the present statute, MSA 1995, s 187, however, have perpetuated this rule.

Lord Atkinson:[200]

My Lords, the sole question for decision in this case is this: whether the rule of law in force in the Courts of Admiralty in this country in the year 1873, to the effect that when two ships collide, each being found to blame, the innocent owner of the cargo carried by one of them is only entitled to recover half the damages he has sustained from each ship in default, is still in force. This again depends upon two considerations – first, whether this rule is in reality based on the principle that the cargo carried is identified with the ship which carries it, according to the principle laid down in the case of *Thorogood v Bryan*, and second, whether, even if this be so, the rule is stereotyped and continued in force by the provision of s 25, sub-s 9 of the JA 1873. Your Lordships, in the case of *The Bernina*, undoubtedly held that the case of *Thorogood v Bryan* was wrongly decided, and that the principle laid down in it was erroneous in law, and Sir Robert Finlay ... contends that because of this the rule of law based upon the principle so held to be erroneous must, in the construction of the above-mentioned provision of the JA, be treated as non-existent ...

I shall presently consider whether Sir Robert Finlay's contention as to the foundation of this rule be sound or not; but, even assuming that it is sound, I do not think that the rule, however erroneous, can be thus got rid of. The words of the sub-section are: 'The rules hitherto in force in the Court of Admiralty, so far as they have been at variance with the rules in force in the courts of common law, shall prevail.' ... The words 'so far as they have been' ... point apparently to the past, and it certainly would appear to me that both these phrases have been introduced in order to stereotype and perpetuate the rules of law in force in the Court of Admiralty.

The question remains, is this rule in reality based upon the principle of *Thorogood v Bryan*? ... Well, in the first place the cargo is not completely identified with the ship that carries it, for its owner, though he, like the owner of that ship, is only entitled to recover half the damage sustained from the owner of the other ship, is entitled to recover the other half from the owner of the carrying ship. Again, Dr Lushington in *The Milan* case discusses this rule, first, from the point of view of its abstract justice, and, secondly, from that of the principles on which the admiralty practice is founded. As to the first, he says: 'The only inference I can draw from this view of the matter is that beyond all doubt an action would be maintainable by the owners of cargo against the owners of either vessel, but to what extent damages should be recoverable against one party only is left an open question.'

He then proceeds to deal with the rule of the Admiralty Courts, and, after pointing out that *Hay v Le Neve*, decided that the owner of the cargo is only entitled to recover half the damages from the ship which does not carry it, he says: 'Abstract justice might give a remedy to the owner of the cargo against the owner of each vessel in proportion to the culpability of each. ...' He then proceeds to repudiate in most explicit terms the authority of *Thorogood v Bryan* and refuses to be bound by it. He says: 'It is difficult to conceive how it can be contended that he, that is, the owner of the cargo, is *particeps criminis* when he is not so either as principal or agent. It is argued that he shall be so considered, and deprived of his remedy because he himself or his agent selected the ship by which his goods were carried. But there is, in my judgment, in the mere selection of the ship for the conveyance of his cargo, none of the ingredients which constitute any kind of responsibility for a collision, for I cannot conceive a responsibility for an act done where the individual has not, either by himself or his agent, any power of interference or control.'

---

200 [1911] AC 16, pp 21–25.

This would appear to me to be the precise line of reasoning which led the Court of Appeal and your Lordships' House in the case of *The Bernina* to decide that *Thorogood v Bryan* was wrongly decided, and to overrule it . . .

It would appear to me, therefore, that the rule applied in *The Milan* case is not based upon the principle of *Thorogood v Bryan* at all, and was not so regarded, but that it is based rather on some supposed principle of equity and justice to the effect that, as the innocent owner of the cargo suffered by the negligence of each of the ships found to blame, each should compensate him for a portion of his loss.[201]

Lord Shaw:[202]

Dr Lushington lays down, and I think he rightly lays down, that it has become the admiralty practice. He suggests a very plausible reason for it . . . that the Court of Admiralty looked upon the two ships as two tortfeasors, and divided the responsibility equally between them so that the owner of cargo recovered one half from one ship, and the other half from the other ship . . . I do not think that the rule started with the judgment of Dr Lushington in *The Milan* case. It was affirmed in *Hay v Le Neve*,[203] decided in 1824, and applicable not to ship alone, but also to cargo.

As explained in this decision, whether the rule of division of loss proportionately to the fault of each ship with regard also to the cargo carried on board each ship is fair or not, it has been a uniform practice in the Admiralty Court since 1789 and it has been incorporated in the legislation of the 20th century. The purpose of this rule was to establish several (not joint) liability for the proportion of the damage to, or loss of, cargo carried on board any of the ships at fault.[204] Most maritime nations, which have ratified the Brussels Collision Convention 1910, apply this rule. The way of recovering is by suing each ship for the proportion of the loss caused by the fault of each. In seeking to recover from the carrying ship, however, the cargo owner will be subject to the contractual provisions of the contract of carriage, which includes exception from liability for negligent navigation, if proved.[205] The respective liabilities of both ships, as well as exceptions from liability, will be adjusted during the apportionment of damages to each other in order to give effect to the 1910 Convention.

By contrast, in the USA, where the Brussels Collision Convention 1910 has not been ratified, the rule is joint and several liability, and the cargo-owners can recover in full from the non-carrying ship in US courts. Then, the non-carrying ship may recover from the carrying ship the amount which is proportionate to the latter's degree of fault.[206] This circumvents the right of the carrying ship to rely on the exceptions from liability against the cargo claimant under the contract for errors in navigation.[207]

---

201 The equal division of loss was made by the MCA 1911, s 1 as an alternative option only if assessment of proportionate faults cannot be established

202 [1911] AC 16, pp 28, 29.

203 (1824) 2 Shaw's Scotch Appeals 395.

204 See *The Giacinto Motta* [1977] 2 Lloyd's Rep 221, in which the purpose of the 1911 Act was explained.

205 *The Giacinto Motta* [1977] 2 Lloyd's Rep 221.

206 *The Sucarseco* (1935) 51 LlL Rep 238 (US Sup Ct).

207 Hague-Visby Rules, Art IV, r 2(a), but not under the Hamburg Rules.

To rectify this anomaly created by US law, a clause known as a 'both to blame' collision clause is inserted in charterparties and bills of lading. The effect of this clause is that, if the carrying ship has paid to the non-carrying ship the proportionate amount of the loss in respect of the cargo carried on board the latter, it can claim back that amount from the cargo owners. The cargo underwriters, who usually agree to indemnify their assured under a 'both to blame' collision clause, which is also inserted in the insurance contract, will refund its assured the amount paid to the shipowner, provided they are given the opportunity to defend their assured against a claim under such clause. A further complication, however, is that, in the USA, the 'both to blame' collision clause in bills of lading has been regarded as invalid.[208]

3.10 Contribution between joint tortfeasors[209]

3.10.1 The common law rule

Under common law, in non-admiralty cases, the liability of joint concurrent tortfeasors is joint and several. Payment by one in full and final settlement bars the claimant from making a claim against the other tortfeasors. The cause of action for damages is extinguished against all of them.[210] Contribution between joint tortfeasors was not permitted until the Law Reform (Married Women and Tortfeasors) Act 1935, which was subsequently superseded by the CLCA 1978. These Acts provided that, if one tortfeasor had paid damages in full, or more than the damages caused by his fault, to the injured party, he could later claim (in a separate action) contribution from the other guilty party.

3.10.2 The admiralty rule in property claims

As has already been seen, when damage or loss occurs concurrently through the fault of two or more wrongdoers, the wrongdoers are joint concurrent tortfeasors. In admiralty law, where there is property damage through the fault of two or more ships, there is division of loss and apportionment of liability by assessing the blameworthiness and causative potency of the faults of each wrongdoer. Each wrongdoer contributes to the loss caused to each other's property, including the property carried on board, and to consequential losses, in proportion of its fault. This right of contribution existed at common law for admiralty claims only[211] and was later made statutory by s 1 of the MCA 1911,[212] now enshrined in s 187 of MSA 1995.

---

208 See details of this in *O'May on Marine Insurance*, 1993, Sweet & Maxwell, pp 185, 186.
209 See further Chapter 14, paras 8.2.3, 8.2.4.
210 *Jameson and Another v Central Electricity Generating Board* [2000] 1 AC 455 (HL).
211 *The Frankland* [1901] P 161.
212 See Chapter 14, para 8.2.4, *The Cairnbahn* [1914] P 25.

3.10.3 The admiralty rule in non-property claims

The common law rule of joint and several liability also applied to admiralty claims for personal injury or loss of life. This became statutory in admiralty cases by the MCA 1911. Section 2 governed joint and several liability, and s 3 the right of contribution between joint tortfeasors. These are now found in ss 188 and 189 (respectively) of the MSA 1995.

3.10.4 When the common law rule applies in admiralty

Where there is an innocent third ship, which suffered damage due to the fault of two other ships, the innocent third party is entitled to recover his damage or loss in full[213] from either tortfeasor. The liability is joint and several; the common law rule applies.[214] If one of the tortfeasors paid the whole damage to the innocent party, his right of contribution against the other tortfeasor would be based on the CLCA 1978. This Act is available as an alternative right of contribution to the MSA 1995.

In some cases, the 1978 Act may be beneficial to the party entitled to claim contribution in two respects. First, the time limit to claim contribution is two years, commencing from when the claimant either is held liable, or he agrees to pay the innocent party, while the time limit under s 190(4) of the MSA 1995 is one year. Second, the 1978 Act, s 1(4), prevents the defendant in contribution proceedings from challenging the issue of the plaintiff's liability to the original claimant.[215]

3.11 Damages and the rule of remoteness of damage

Even if the claimant discharges the burden of proof that the negligence of the defendant caused the collision (causation in fact, see para 3.5 above) and also that that negligence was the cause, or one of the causes, of the damage (causation in law, see para 3.6 above), the claimant must also prove that the damage suffered is not too remote.

The first and earliest rule of the common law was that the defendant was liable for damage which 'in the ordinary course of things would flow from' his wrongful act.[216] It was also recognised, however, that the law was concerned with what were called direct, rather than remote, consequences; otherwise, the defendant could be held liable for increasingly remote consequences stretching indefinitely into the future.[217] It was wrong to hold that the defendant in a tort claim would be liable for all consequences.

---

213 Since the innocent ship is not at fault, MSA 1995, s 187, will not apply to it.

214 See *The Devonshire* [1912] AC 634.

215 See, also, op cit, Marsden, fn 1, paras 14-33, 14-34.

216 *The City of Lincoln* [1890] P 15, p 18, per Lindley LJ, quoting from *Mayne on Damages*.

217 As Lord Wright said in *Liesbosch Dredger v SS Edison* (1933) 45 LlL Rep 123 (HL), p 129; [1933] AC 449, p 460.

3.11.1 General principle

Since 1960, the general rule which has been accepted about 'remoteness' of damage is that the defendant would only be liable if he could reasonably have foreseen the kind of damage suffered by the claimant. The claimant must prove, therefore, that the breach of duty by the defendant caused the kind of damage claimed, which must not be too remote. The breakthrough for the establishment of this rule, started with *The Wagon Mound (No 1)* [218] (decision of the Privy Council).

Prior to this decision, however, the Court of Appeal had decided in *Re Polemis* [219] that the defendant would be responsible for the direct consequences resulting from his negligence, whether or not the actual damage sustained was reasonably foreseeable.

Readers familiar with English law are, of course, well aware of the distinction. For the benefit of those who are unfamiliar, it is important to summarise and compare these two cases.

Re Polemis

Under a time charterparty contract between the shipowner and the charterer, damage caused by fire, either to cargo on board or to the ship, was exempted.

Besides other cargo, the charterers loaded a quantity of benzine and/or petrol in tins in cases. During the voyage the tins leaked and, in consequence, there was a considerable quantity of petrol vapour in the hold. When the ship called at a port, it became necessary to shift some of the cases of benzene. Stevedores, employed by the charterers, placed a number of heavy planks at the forward end of the hatch-way, which they used as a platform, for transferring the cases from the lower hold to the 'tween deck. Due to the negligence of the stevedores, when the sling containing the cases of benzine was being hoisted up, it knocked a plank into the hold. The fall was immediately followed by a rush of flames, the result being the total destruction of the ship.

The shipowners claimed the value of the ship as damages from the charterers. The charterers disputed liability, and the dispute was referred to arbitration under a clause in the charterparty. The arbitrators found that: the ship was lost by fire; the fire arose from a spark igniting the petrol vapour in the hold; the spark was caused by the falling board coming into contact with some substance in the hold; and the causing of the spark could not reasonably have been anticipated from the falling of the board, though some damage to the ship might reasonably have been anticipated. The arbitrators awarded that the owners were entitled to recover from the charterers a sum assessed by the arbitrators.

On appeal to the court, the judge affirmed the award and the charterers appealed to the Court of Appeal.

---

218 [1961] AC 388 (PC).
219 [1921] 3 KB 560 (CA).

The charterers contended: (1) that they were protected from liability by the exception of 'fire' in the charterparty; and (2) that the damages were too remote, as it could not reasonably have been anticipated that the falling of the board would have caused a spark.

It was held, (1) that the exception clause did not protect the charterers against loss by fire caused by the negligence of their servants, there being no express stipulation to that effect; and (2) that, as the fall of the board was due to the negligence of the charterers' servants, the charterers were liable for all the direct consequences of the negligent act, even though those consequences could not reasonably have been anticipated; and they were, therefore, liable for the loss of the ship by fire.

Referring to previous authorities, the principle applicable was summarised by Scrutton LJ as follows:

> To determine whether an act is negligent, it is relevant to determine whether any reasonable person would foresee that the act would cause damage; if he would not, the act is not negligent. But, if the act would or might probably cause damage, the fact that the damage it in fact causes is not the exact kind of damage one would expect is immaterial, so long as the damage is, in fact, directly traceable to the negligent act, and not due to the operation of independent causes having no connection with the negligent act, except that they could not avoid its results. Once the act is negligent, the fact that its exact operation was not foreseen is immaterial.[220]

It should be noted that the claim in *The Polemis* case was made for breach of contract based on negligence committed in the performance of contractual obligations, namely the negligence of the servants of the charterers, the stevedores. The case was, in particular, concerned with the construction of the exemption clause in the charterparty contract.[221] The conduct of the stevedores in the course of their employment was in question in determining whether their principals, the charterers, should be held liable for the actual damage caused. The case reached the Court of Appeal, as a special case. Warrington LJ said that it was clear that the act causing the plank to fall was, in law, a negligent act, because some damage to the ship might reasonably be anticipated. If this was so then the charterers were liable

---

220 [1921] 3 KB 560 (CA), p 577.

221 The distinction of *The Polemis* case had carefully been pointed out by the appellants' counsel (Ashton Roskill QC) in *The Wagon Mound (No 1)* who said: 'The first submission on *Polemis* is that the issue was one of contract, namely, the construction of the exceptions clause in a time charterparty ... If that be so, it is difficult to regard the case as a satisfactory authority on the tort of negligence or on what constitutes a cause of action in negligence. That submission may be elaborated under three heads. First, negligence is read by implication into the exceptions clause: it does not, in the context of the exceptions clause, mean the same as the tort of negligence. The exceptions clause means that the charterers were not responsible for the fire unless caused by their carelessness. It is doubtfully correct to say, as Warrington LJ said, that the claim was based on the tort of negligence ...' (p 393). It is tentatively submitted that, for this reason, *The Polemis* case has caused confusion, and in any event it is misleading to refer to it as a decision against the stevedores, as it is also not stated in op cit, Marsden, fn 1, para 15-08.

for the actual loss that being the direct result of the falling board on the arbitrators finding.[222]

What, then, did *The Polemis* decide? That was the question posed by Viscount Simonds in *The Wagon Mound (No 1)*, discussed next. He said that their Lordships did not propose to spend time in examining whether the issue there lay in breach of contract or in tort. That might be relevant for a tribunal for which the decision was a binding authority but, for their Lordships, it was not. It may, however, be observed, he said, that in the proceedings there was some confusion. The case arose out of a charterparty and went to arbitration under a term of it, and the first contention of the charterers was that they were protected from liability by the exception of fire in the charterparty. But it was clear from the pleadings and other documents that alternative claims for breach of contract and negligence were advanced, and it was clear, too, that before Sankey J and the Court of Appeal, the case proceeded as one in which, independently of contractual obligations, the claim was for damages for negligence. It was upon this footing that the Court of Appeal held that the charterers were responsible for all the consequences of their negligent act even though those consequences could not reasonably have been anticipated. The negligent act was nothing more than the carelessness of stevedores (for whom the charterers were assumed to be responsible) in allowing a sling or rope by which it was hoisted to come into contact with certain boards, causing one of them to fall into the hold. The falling board hit some substances in the hold and caused a spark: the spark ignited petrol vapour in the hold: there was a rush of flames, and the ship was destroyed. The special case submitted by the arbitrators found that the causing of the spark could not reasonably have been anticipated from the falling of the board, though some damage to the ship might reasonably have been anticipated. They did not indicate what damage might have been so anticipated.

As it seemed that the decision of the Court of Appeal in *The Polemis* might have stated a general principle to the effect that when a defendant – being sued in tort – is guilty of negligence he is liable for all the consequences, whether reasonably

---

222 Aspects of causation and remoteness in contract, in clams for indemnity and in the tort of negligence were contrasted by Evans LJ in *The Sivand* [1998] 2 Lloyd's Rep 97 (CA), p 105 (see para 3.11.5, below): 'These two situations [breach of contract and indemnity] have in common what a claim in tort does not, namely, a pre-existing legal relationship, almost invariably contractual, between the parties. It must follow, therefore, that the legal aspects of causation and remoteness must depend upon that legal relationship also. For example, the basic rule that the wrongdoer is liable for the "direct and natural" consequences of his act is applied by reference to a person situated as the contracting parties were when the contract was made, rather than to a reasonable man at the time of the wrongdoing. The same considerations arise, in my judgment, in relation to the questions whether the liability of the wrongdoer is affected by negligence of the other party (the same duty to mitigate damage arises) or of a third party. In the indemnity cases, such negligence, far from breaking the "chain of causation", may be the very event against which the promise to indemnify was given . . . The present case resting solely in tort, it is unnecessary for present purposes to consider these questions further.' (*The Sivand*, p 105.) See, also, how Staughton LJ contrasts issues of causation and remoteness in claims for breach of contract, claims for indemnity and in tort: *Total Transport Corporation v Arcadia Petroleum Ltd (The Eurus)* [1998] 1 Lloyd's Rep 351 (CA), a breach of contract case: 'Although the foreseeability test is a handmaiden of the law, it is by no means a maid-of-all-work. To my mind, it cannot serve as the true criterion when the question is, how was the damage caused? It may be a useful guide, but it is by no means the true criterion' (p 362). See, also, Treitel, GH, *The Law of Contract*, 11th edn, 2003, Sweet & Maxwell, p 976, and clarification of the remoteness of damages rule in contract by Clarke, C. J in *The Achilleas* [2007] 1 Lloyd's Rep 19, Ch 11 above, para 7.3.

foreseeable or not, the Privy Council disapproved of it in *The Wagon Mound (No 1)*. The events of this case are seen below.

The Wagon Mound (No 1)[223]

The plaintiffs were ship-repairers and owned the Sheerlegs Wharf in Sydney for their business. The defendants were demise charterers of the vessel *The Wagon Mound*, an oil-burning vessel which was moored 600 ft from Sheerlegs Wharf and was taking in bunkering oil in Sydney harbour. A large quantity of the oil was, through the carelessness of the defendants' servants, allowed to spill into the harbour. During that and the following day, the escaped furnace oil was carried by wind and tide beneath the wharf owned by the plaintiffs, at which was lying a vessel which they were refitting, and for which purpose their employees were using electric and oxyacetylene welding equipment. Some cotton waste or rag on a piece of debris floating on the oil underneath the wharf was set on fire by molten metal falling from the wharf. The flames from the cotton waste or rag set the floating oil afire either directly, or by first setting fire to a wooden pile coated with oil. Thereafter, a conflagration developed which seriously damaged the wharf and equipment on it.

In an action by the shipbuilders to recover compensation from the defendants for the damage by fire, it was found by the trial judge, on the evidence, that the defendants 'did not know and could not reasonably be expected to have known that the furnace oil was capable of being set afire when spread on water'. Apart from the fire damage, the plaintiffs had also suffered some damage from the fact that the oil had congealed upon and interfered with the use of their slipways.

The judge concluded, however, that on the basis of the decision in *In Re Polemis v Furness Withy & Co*, the defendants were liable for all damage suffered because it was the direct consequence of their negligence. On the defendants' appeal to the Full Court of the Supreme Court of New South Wales the main heads of appeal were, first, that *The Polemis* was wrongly decided, and, secondly, that if it was right, the damage by fire was not the direct consequence of the defendants spilling the oil. The judgment of the Full Court contained a critical analysis of the decision in *The Polemis*, and the conclusion was reached that it would not be proper to regard that decision otherwise than as binding on them. Manning J, however, giving the judgment of the court, said that it would be a gross understatement to say that he was able to apply that decision with any degree of confidence, and he expressed the hope that the House of Lords, or the Judicial Committee of the Privy Council, would pronounce on it in the near future.

The Supreme Court of New South Wales allowed an appeal by the defendants (the appellants) to the Privy Council. Their Lordships were concerned to displace the proposition that 'unforeseeability is irrelevant if damage is direct'.

Viscount Simond, commenting on *The Polemis* case, said:[224]

> Before turning to the cases that succeeded it, it is right to glance at yet another aspect of the decision in *Polemis*. Their Lordships, as they have said, assume that the court

---

223 [1961] AC 388.
224 [1961] AC 388 (PC), p 419.

purported to propound the law in regard to tort. But up to that date, it had been universally accepted that the law in regard to damages for breach of contract and for tort was, generally speaking, and particularly in regard to the tort of negligence, the same. Yet *Hadley v Baxendale* was not cited in argument nor referred to in the judgments in *Polemis*. This is the more surprising when it is remembered that in that case, as in many another case, the claim was laid alternatively in breach of contract and in negligence. If the claim for breach of contract had been pursued, the charterers could not have been held liable for consequences not reasonably foreseeable ... Their Lordships refer to this aspect of the matter not because they wish to assert that in all respects today the measure of damages is in all cases the same in tort and in breach of contract, but because it emphasises how far *Polemis* was out of the current of contemporary thought. The acceptance of the rule in *Polemis* as applicable to all cases of tort directly would conflict with the view theretofore generally held.

Examining all relevant authorities, they came to the conclusion that *The Polemis* case should not be applied and the test of foreseeability was re-instated.

It was held that, on the footing that the damage was the direct result of the escape of the oil, and applying the test of foreseeability, the defendants (appellants), who could not reasonably be expected to have known that the oil would catch fire, were not liable for the damage.

In particular, Viscount Simonds stated:

There is not one criterion for determining culpability (or liability) and another for determining compensation; unforeseeability of damage is relevant to liability or compensation – there can be no liability until the damage has been done; it is not the act but the consequences on which tortious liability is founded ...[225]

... the essential factor in determining liability is whether the damage is of such a kind as the reasonable man should have foreseen. This accords with the general view, thus, stated by Lord Atkin in *Donoghue v Stevenson* ...[226]

It is a departure from this sovereign principle, if liability is made to depend solely on the damage being the 'direct' or 'natural' consequence of the precedent act. Who knows or can be assumed to know all the processes of nature? But if it would be wrong that a man should be held liable for damage unpredictable by a reasonable man because it was 'direct' or 'natural', equally, it would be wrong that he should escape liability, however 'indirect' the damage, if he foresaw or could reasonably foresee the intervening events which led to its being done ... thus, foreseeability becomes the effective test – the 'direct' consequence test leads to nowhere but the never-ending and insoluble problems of causation.[227]

The defendant escaped liability for the fire damage caused to the wharf in Sydney harbour, because on the judge's finding of facts, the fire damage was not reasonably foreseeable, although it was a direct damage from the defendant's negligence. The damage, which was foreseeable, was the fouling of the harbour by the escaped oil.

In the sequel to this decision, *The Wagon Mound (No 2)*,[228] the Privy Council

---

225 Ibid, p 425.
226 Ibid, p 426.
227 [1961] AC 388 (PC), p 426.
228 *Overseas Tankship (UK) Ltd v The Miller Steamship Co* [1967] 1 AC 617 (PC).

explained in great detail the application of the foreseeability test and applied the same to both cases of nuisance and negligence claims.

In this case, the claimants were the owners of the two vessels undergoing repairs at the wharf in Sydney harbour. They sued the demise charterers of *The Wagon Mound* for damages, on the basis of negligence and nuisance.

Walsh J, in the Supreme Court of New South Wales, accepted that the most probable explanation of the fire was that a hot piece of metal fell on some object supporting a piece of inflammable material in the oil-covered water which was ignited. He found that the damage to the claimants' vessels was 'not reasonably foreseeable by those for whose acts the defendants were responsible.' Further findings were that reasonable people in the position of officers of *The Wagon Mound* would regard furnace oil as very difficult to ignite upon water and that if they had given attention to the risk of fire from the spillage they would have regarded it 'as a possibility, but one which could become an actuality only in very exceptional circumstances'. Having made these findings, Walsh J held that liability in nuisance did not depend on forseeability and that the defendants were liable in nuisance but not in negligence. Judgment was accordingly given for the claimants on the claim based upon nuisance and for the defendants on the claim based on negligence. The defendants appealed against the judgment based on nuisance, and the claimants cross-appealed, on the issue of negligence.

It was held by the Privy Council that:

(1) creating a danger to persons or property in navigable waters (equivalent to a highway) fell in the class of nuisance in which foreseeability was an essential element in determining liability, and it was not sufficient that the injury suffered by the respondents' vessels was the direct result of the nuisance if that injury was, in the relevant sense, unforeseeable; and

(2) on the facts, a reasonable man having the knowledge and experience to be expected of the appellants' chief engineer would have known that there was a real risk of the oil on the water catching fire, and the fact that the risk was small did not, in the circumstances, justify no steps being taken to eliminate it. Accordingly, both the appeal on the claim based on nuisance and the cross-appeal upon the claim based on negligence would be allowed.

Lord Reid, who delivered the judgment, distinguished *The Wagon Mound (No 1)* from the findings in this case by saying:[229]

> In *The Wagon Mound (No 1)* the finding on which the board proceeded was that of the trial judge: 'the defendant did not know and could not reasonably be expected to have known that [the oil] was capable of being set afire when spread on water.' In the present case, the evidence led was substantially different from the evidence led in *The Wagon Mound (No 1)* and the findings of Walsh J are significantly different. That is not due to there having been any failure by the plaintiffs in *The Wagon Mound (No 1)* in preparing and presenting their case. The plaintiffs there were no doubt embarrassed by a difficulty which does not affect the present plaintiffs. The outbreak of the fire was consequent on the act of the manager of the plaintiffs in *The Wagon Mound (No 1)* in resuming oxyacetylene welding and cutting while the wharf was sur-

---

229 [1967] 1 AC 617, pp 640–44.

rounded by this oil. So, if the plaintiffs in the former case had set out to prove that it was foreseeable by the engineers of *The Wagon Mound* that this oil could be set alight, they might have had difficulty in parrying the reply that this must also have been foreseeable by their manager. Then there would have been contributory negligence and at that time contributory negligence was a complete defence in New South Wales.

The vital parts of the findings of fact (in the present case) which have already been set out in full are (1) that the officers of *The Wagon Mound* 'would regard furnace oil as very difficult to ignite upon water' – not that they would regard this as impossible; (2) that their experience would probably have been 'that this had very rarely happened' – not that they would never have heard of a case where it had happened; and (3) that they would have regarded it as a 'possibility, but one which could become an actuality only in very exceptional circumstances' – not, as in *The Wagon Mound (No 1)*, that they could not reasonably be expected to have known that this oil was capable of being set afire when spread on water. The question which must now be determined is whether these differences between the findings in the two cases do or do not lead to different results in law.

Further extracts from his judgment illuminate the issues involved in defining the words 'reasonably foreseeable', by comparison to facts of other cases:

> In *The Wagon Mound (No 1)* the board were not concerned with degrees of foreseeability because the finding was that the fire was not foreseeable at all. So Lord Simonds had no cause to amplify the statement that the 'essential factor in determining liability is whether the damage is of such a kind as the reasonable man should have foreseen'. But here the findings show that some risk of fire would have been present to the mind of a reasonable man in the shoes of the ship's chief engineer. So, the first question must be: what is the precise meaning to be attached in this context to the words 'foreseeable' and 'reasonably foreseeable'?

> Before *Bolton v Stone*,[230] the cases had fallen into two classes: (1) those where, before the event, the risk of its happening would have been regarded as unreal either because the event would have been thought to be physically impossible or because the possibility of its happening would have been regarded as so fantastic or far fetched that no reasonable man would have paid any attention to it – 'a mere possibility which would never occur to the mind of a reasonable man' (per Lord Dunedin in *Fardon v Harcourt-Rivington*)[231] – or (2) those where there was a real and substantial risk or chance that something like the event which happens might occur, and then the reasonable man would have taken the steps necessary to eliminate the risk.

> In *Bolton v Stone*, a member of a visiting team drove a cricket ball out of the ground onto an unfrequented adjacent public road and it struck and severely injured a lady who happened to be standing in the road. That it might happen that a ball would be driven onto this road could not have been said to be a fantastic or far fetched possibility: according to the evidence it had happened about six times in 28 years. And it could not have been said to be a far fetched or fantastic possibility that such a ball would strike someone in the road: people did pass along the road from time to time. So, it could not have been said that, on any ordinary meaning of the words, the fact that a ball might strike a person in the road was not foreseeable or reasonably

230 [1951] AC 850 (HL).
231 (1932) 146 LT 391 (HL).

foreseeable – it was plainly foreseeable. But the chance of its happening in the fore-seeable future was infinitesimal. The House of Lords held in *Bolton v Stone* that the risk was so small that, in the circumstances, a reasonable man would have been justified in disregarding it and taking no steps to eliminate it.

But, it does not follow that, no matter what the circumstances may be, it is justifiable to neglect a risk of such a small magnitude. A reasonable man would only neglect such a risk if he had some valid reason for doing so, for example, that it would involve considerable expense to eliminate the risk.

In the present case, there was no justification whatever for discharging the oil into Sydney Harbour. Not only was it an offence to do so, but it involved considerable loss financially. If the ship's engineer had thought about the matter, there could have been no question of balancing the advantages and disadvantages. From every point of view, it was both his duty and his interest to stop the discharge immediately.

It follows that in their Lordships' view the only question is whether a reasonable man having the knowledge and experience to be expected of the chief engineer of *The Wagon Mound* would have known that there was a real risk of the oil on the water catching fire in some way: if it did, serious damage to ships or other property was not only foreseeable but very likely. Their Lordships do not dissent from the view of the trial judge that the possibilities of damage 'must be significant enough in a practical sense to require a reasonable man to guard against them' but they think that he may have misdirected himself in saying:

> '. . . there does seem to be a real practical difficulty, assuming that some risk of fire damage was foreseeable, but not a high one, in making a factual judgment as to whether this risk was sufficient to attract liability if damage should occur.'

In this difficult chapter of the law decisions are not infrequently taken to apply to circumstances far removed from the facts which gave rise to them and it would seem that here too much reliance has been placed on some observations in *Bolton v Stone* and similar observations in other cases.

In their Lordships' view, a properly qualified and alert chief engineer would have realised there was a real risk here and they do not understand Walsh J to deny that. But he appears to have held that if a real risk can properly be described as remote it must then be held to be not reasonably foreseeable. That is a possible interpretation of some of the authorities. But this is still an open question and, on principle, their Lordships cannot accept this view. If a real risk is one which would occur to the mind of a reasonable man in the position of the defendant's servant and which he would not brush aside as far fetched, and if the criterion is to be what that reasonable man would have done in the circumstances, then surely he would not neglect such a risk if action to eliminate it presented no difficulty, involved no disadvantage, and required no expense. (emphasis added)

In the present case, the evidence shows that the discharge of so much oil onto the water must have taken a considerable time, and a vigilant ship's engineer would have noticed the discharge at an early stage. The findings show that he ought to have known that it is possible to ignite this kind of oil on water, and that the ship's engineer probably ought to have known that this had in fact happened before. The most that can be said to justify inaction is that he would have known that this could only happen in very exceptional circumstances. But that does not mean that a reasonable man would dismiss such a risk from his mind and do nothing when it was so easy to prevent it. If it is clear that the reasonable man would have realised or foreseen and prevented the risk, then it must follow that the appellant is liable in damages. The learned judge found this a difficult case: he says that this matter is 'one upon which different minds would come to different conclusions'. Taking a rather different view of the law from that of the judge, their Lordships must hold that the respondents (claimants) are entitled to succeed on this issue.

3.11.2 The kind of damage

It derives from the decision of the Privy Council that no matter how small the foreseeable risk seems to be, it is the kind of damage that a defendant should put his mind to as a possibility of happening, if he continued his act. So, the limitation of recovery imposed by its previous decision in *The Wagon Mound (No 1)* was explained in terms of different findings of fact stated by the judge in each case.

By later decisions, which adopted the principle of *The Wagon Mound*, foreseeability is said to be relevant to the kind of damage and not to the exact way in which it occurred. Lord Pearce, in the well-known case of the House of Lords, *Hughes v Lord Advocate*,[232] put it succinctly that to demand great precision on the test of foreseeability would be unfair to the pursuer since the facts of misadventure are innumerable. The defendants are, therefore, liable for all the foreseeable consequences of their neglect. When the result is of a different type or kind from anything that a defendant could have foreseen, he is not liable for it.

The following shipping case is a good example showing that the exact way in which the damage could occur is irrelevant to the test of foreseeability.

The Trecarrell [233]

The motor vessel *The Trecarrell* was undergoing specialist repairs at a ship-repairers' yard. The work involved was coating her deep tank with vinyl lacquer. This work was to be carried out by specialist contractors. While the contractors' employees were transferring drums of the highly inflammable vinyl lacquer from the drydock to the ship, one of them dropped a drum which fell on and cut a temporary electric cable. As a result, the drum broke, the lacquer escaped and was ignited by sparking caused by a short circuit. Both the ship and the yard were damaged by the fire.

The shipowners sued the contractors, who joined the ship-repairers as a third party. The latter counterclaimed in third party proceedings against the contractors.

Brandon J held that the employee of the contractors could reasonably have foreseen that dropping the drum would create a fire hazard, even if he could not reasonably have foreseen the particular source of ignition; that, therefore, in a situation where a high degree of care was needed, the employee was negligent and that negligence caused the fire.

Judgment was given for the shipowners and the repair yard in the third party proceedings.

Foreseeability depends on the facts of each case. In *The Daressa*,[234] the kind of damage suffered was in question.

---

232 [1963] AC 837 (HL), p 857.
233 [1973] 1 Lloyd's Rep 402.
234 *The Daressa* [1971] 1 Lloyd's Rep 60, pp 63, 64.

Brandon J said:

I accept that a question of reasonable foreseeability is a question of fact, but it does not follow that a court always needs evidence to decide it. If the question arises in a field of common human experience, such as crossing a road or driving a motor car, a court can plainly decide it without evidence. If, on the other hand, the question arises in a technical field, as in *The Wagon Mound* cases, evidence is equally plainly needed. In between these two extremes there are intermediate cases where, although evidence might well assist a court by supplementing its own knowledge and experience, it is not essential to enable the court to reach a conclusion.

The master of *The Daressa* could reasonably have foreseen that any ship with which he collided might be operating with the assistance of a Government operating subsidy and that such operating subsidy might be lost during detention of the vessel for repairs.

3.11.3 Extent of damage

It does not matter if the extent of the damage resulting from the negligent act is greater than expected, provided the consequences were foreseeable. This, however, may lead to extreme results, but it is a matter of common sense and experience of the courts as to what extent of damage may be awarded.[235] For example, the defendant may not be found liable for all damage if there was contributory negligence on the part of the claimant, or not liable at all if the chain of causation was broken by a *novus actus interveniens*.

In *The City of Lincoln*,[236] the defendant's vessel negligently collided with and caused damage to the plaintiff's vessel, whose master attempted to reach port in safety. But the vessel grounded accidentally before he did so, and was lost. In the absence of negligence by the master, the defendants were liable not merely for the collision damage but for the subsequent loss.

In *The Metagama*,[237] the House of Lords approved and adopted the same approach as Lindley LJ in *The City of Lincoln*. The defenders admitted liability for a collision in which the pursuers' vessel was damaged, but they alleged that the damage was increased by the improper handling of the vessel by those in charge of her after the collision had taken place. It was held by the majority that those responsible for the damaged vessel were not guilty of negligence, and it followed that the defenders were liable for the whole of the damages claimed.

In *The Oropesa*,[238] the Court of Appeal, presided over by Lord Wright, adopted the same approach. Two vessels came into collision. The master of one of them launched a lifeboat so that he and some others could go across to the other vessel to confer with her master, despite the rough weather conditions. The lifeboat capsized

---

235 It may appear, from the decision of *Warren v Scruttons* [1962] 1 Lloyd's Rep 497, that the extent of the damage awarded was rather remarkable, namely for the eye infection of the claimant, which resulted from blood poisoning after his finger was pricked by a poisonous wire due to defendant's negligence. It was said by Paull J, p 499, that: 'It is sufficient to say that one of the consequences of getting his finger poisoned was that he got a further ulcer in his eye, and the result of having that further ulcer in his eye is that the eye has become far more misty . . .'

236 [1890] P 15.

237 (1928) 29 LlL Rep 253; [1928] SC 21 (HL).

238 (1943) 74 LlL Rep 86; [1943] P 32.

and some of the crew members were drowned, including the sixth engineer, whose parents claimed damages from the owners of the other vessel, which was partly responsible for the collision. The owners of the other vessel alleged that the master's act was *novus actus interveniens*. This was rejected. The master's actions were reasonable. Lord Wright said: '. . . the hand of the casualty lay heavily on [his vessel] and the conduct of the master and of the deceased was directly caused by and flowed from it.'[239]

In *The Sivand*[240] (see para 3.11.5, below), the physical condition of the soil in a seabed, having been damaged by the colliding tanker, which subsequently caused the capsize of a barge (belonging to contractors who were repairing the harbour works) was not a *novus actus interveniens*. Evans LJ said:

> . . . 'reasonable foreseeability' does not limit the extent of damages when the kind or type of damage could be reasonably foreseen. This is, in effect, for the purposes of legal analysis a 'thin skull' type of case. The factor which increased the cost of repairs and therefore the amount of damages cannot be regarded as an independent, supervening cause. It follows that the reasonable cost is recoverable in full.[241]

3.11.4 Mitigation of loss or damage

It has commonly been expressed by lawyers and judges in old judgments that there is a duty upon a claimant to mitigate his loss if he can reasonably do so. In *The Metagama*,[242] Viscount Dunedin stated the issue as follows:

> But it is always the duty of the person who is damaged to do his best to minimise his loss. This is really the same thing as to say that, if he might reasonably have avoided any part of the damage he has suffered, to that extent the damage is not such as arises directly from the act complained of. In many cases, the question is stated as to whether, after the original fault which started matters, there has been a *novus actus interveniens* which was the direct cause of the final damage.

This is not the case now as will be seen later. The test is how a prudent uninsured would have acted following the collision. The master and crew must take reasonable steps to minimise the damage[243] and preserve the ship, cargo or passengers on board from further loss. There are many cases on this issue, some of which are already discussed earlier in the issues of causation. Other cases are linked to the assessment of damages (see later).

Clarification of the principle of mitigation of loss in cases of damage suffered by a claimant due to breach of duty of care by a defendant was made by the Court of Appeal in *The Sivand* (see 3.11.5, below) and, in cases of breach of contract, in *The Solholt*, (see Ch 11 para 7.4). In these cases, it is explained that the claimant does not have a **duty** to mitigate his loss, as long as he takes reasonable steps to minimize the damage suffered by the defendant's breach. Foreseeability is not an issue in

---

239 Ibid, p 92; p 37.
240 [1998] 2 Lloyd's Rep 97 (CA).
241 Ibid, p 106.
242 (1928) 29 LlL Rep 253 (HL), p 256.
243 *The Egyptian* [1910] P 38.

mitigation of damages as will be seen in *The Sivand*. The burden of proof is on the defendant to show that the claimant failed to mitigate his loss.

3.11.5 The idiosyncrasy of the claimant, remoteness and mitigation of damages

Sometimes, a claimant in a collision case may suffer further loss, which may be due to his financial inability to mitigate damages.

Under common law, the defendant must take his victim as he finds him (the 'thin skull' rule).[244] The principle applies, in particular, to personal injury cases, in which the claimant's physical characteristics at the time of the injury may have the effect of increasing the scale or extent of physical damage caused to him by the defendant's negligence.[245] This principle has been recently confirmed by the House of Lords in *Lagden v O'Connor*,[246] in which their Lordships found the opportunity to overrule a previous decision of the House of Lords in *The Edison*. It is important to consider *The Edison*[247] at this point in order to explain the recent and correct development in the law.

The Edison and The Liesbosch

Lord Wright had held:

> The appellants' financial disability was not to be compared with that physical deli-cacy or weakness which may aggravate the damage in the case of personal injuries, or with the possibility that the injured man in such a case may be either a poor labourer or a highly paid professional man. The former class of circumstances goes to the extent of actual physical damage and the latter consideration goes to interfer-ence with profit-earning capacity; whereas the appellants' want of means was, as already stated, extrinsic.[248]

The vessel, *The Edison*, fouled the moorings of a dredger, *The Liesbosch*, which was carried out to sea and thereafter she sank. The owners of *The Edison* were solely liable for the loss. The dredger had been engaged in construction work with the Patras Harbour Commissioners. There was evidence that one or more dredgers were available in Holland for purchase by the appellants to replace the lost one, but they did not have the money, as most of their liquid resources were engaged in the contract of dredging. As a consequence of the loss of *The Liesbosch*, the Patras har-bour authorities threatened to cancel the contract and forfeit the deposit unless it was replaced within a certain time. It was therefore necessary for the appellants to hire one, and they did hire *The Adria* from Italy. The rate of hire was very high

---

244 *Smith v Leech Brain & Co Ltd* [1962] 2 QB 405 (HL), where Lord Parker, CJ, re-asserted the common law rule that the defendant takes the plaintiff 'as he finds him'. This is exemplified by 'thin skull' cases.

245 A feature of 'thin skull' cases is that the plaintiff's physical characteristics are already in existence when the negligence occurs. The defendant cannot seek to reduce the damages on the ground that the extent of the claimant's injury was unforeseeable; see *McGregor on Damages*, 17th edn, 2003, Sweet & Maxwell, paras 6-085–6-092.

246 [2004] 1 AC 1067 (HL).

247 [1933] AC 449 (HL).

248 Ibid, p 461.

because she was somewhat larger than *The Liesbosch* and more expensive to work. Along with her, and due to her size, the appellants were compelled to take on hire a tug and two hopper barges.

The appellants claimed all their losses from the owners of *The Edison*. Both the registrar and the judge awarded all damages, but the Court of Appeal disagreed and reversed the judgment.

On appeal to the House of Lords, Lord Wright, affirming the Court of Appeal decision, held:

> The respondents' tortious act involved the physical loss of the dredger; that loss must somehow be reduced to terms of money. But the appellants' actual loss insofar as it was due to their impecuniosity arose from that impecuniosity as a separate and concurrent cause, extraneous to and distinct in character from the tort; the impecuniosity was not traceable to the respondents' acts, and in my opinion was outside the legal purview of the consequences of these acts. The law cannot take account of everything that follows a wrongful act; it regards some subsequent matters as outside the scope of its selection, because 'it were infinite for the law to judge the cause of causes', or consequences of consequences.[249]

Subsequently to this case, the Court of Appeal in *The Sivand* had difficulty in reconciling the principle of *The Edison* and, since it was bound by it, it found a way of distinguishing it from the facts of the case before it. The case is relevant to both causation and remoteness of damages, including mitigation.

The Sivand[250]

Evans LJ restated the principles, thus:

> The defendant to a claim in tort was liable for what the law regarded as the consequence of his wrongful act, identifying its consequences on a common sense basis and distinguishing in particular between what had caused rather than provided the occasion of the plaintiffs' loss, subject to reasonable foreseeability of the particular kind of loss and subject also to loss which resulted from negligence of the plaintiff or those to whom he was responsible in breach of his duty to mitigate his loss; when it was alleged that the loss had been caused by the intervening act of a third party, or other *novus actus interveniens*, then the inquiry was whether there was such an independent cause, not limited to whether the third party's act was negligent or not.[251]

---

249 [1933] AC 449 (HL), p 460.

250 *The Sivand* [1998] 2 Lloyd's Rep 97 (CA).

251 Ibid at p 105. Comparing cases of breach of contract and indemnity claims he further said: 'These two situations have in common what a claim in tort does not, namely, a pre-existing legal relationship, almost invariably contractual, between the parties. It must follow, therefore, that the legal aspects of causation and remoteness must depend upon that legal relationship also. For example, the basic rule that the wrongdoer is liable for the "direct and natural" consequences of his act is applied by reference to a person situated as the contracting parties were when the contract was made, rather than to a reasonable man at the time of the wrongdoing. The same considerations arise, in my judgment, in relation to the questions whether the liability of the wrongdoer is affected by negligence of the other party (the same duty to mitigate damage arises) or of a third party. In the indemnity cases, such negligence, far from breaking the "chain of causation", may be the very event against which the promise to indemnify was given (cf *The Island Archon* [1994] 2 Lloyd's Rep 227, pp 234–36). The present case resting solely in tort, it is unnecessary for present purposes to consider these questions further.'

On the facts of this case, the defendants' vessel damaged the harbour installations belonging to the plaintiffs. The latter engaged contractors to carry out repairs. While carrying out the work of reconstructing one of the dolphins, the contractors encountered unforeseen conditions in the soil strata of the seabed; this caused the legs of the jack-up barge, which was at the time being used as a platform from which to transfer a concrete soffit onto one of the dolphins, to sink into the seabed and capsize the barge. The condition of the seabed was unforeseen and could not reasonably have been foreseen by an experienced contractor. There had been no intervening negligence on the part of the contractors.

Under cl 12 of the standard form contract conditions in the contract between the plaintiffs and the contractors, the contractors were entitled to, and recovered, extra payment from the plaintiffs for unforeseen physical conditions, as in this case. The plaintiffs, in turn, sought to recover the amount they had paid to the contractors from the defendants. The other costs for repairs were paid, but there arose a dispute concerning this extra payment.

The defendants contended that the extra payment was the result of extra loss caused by an unforeseen event, the nature of the soil, and that, therefore, the capsize of the contractors' barge did not constitute foreseeable damage resulting from their own initial negligence. They alleged that there was in law an intervening event (a *novus actus*) which broke the chain of causation.

On the issue of causation, Evans LJ distinguished *The Edison* (*Liesbosch Dredger*) on the ground that, in that case, there was an extraneous cause.[252] The repair costs arising out of the contract here were not an extraneous cause.

> In my judgment ... the answer to the submission is that causation is established in the present case ... and that 'reasonable foreseeability' does not limit the extent of damages when the kind or type of damage could be reasonably foreseen. This is, in effect, for the purposes of legal analysis, a 'thin skull' type of case. The factor which increased the cost of repairs and therefore the amount of damages cannot be regarded as an independent, supervening cause. It follows that the reasonable cost is recoverable in full.[253]

On the issue of mitigation and remoteness of damages, he stated:

> Where the plaintiff acted in mitigation of his loss the sole relevant criterion was the reasonableness of the steps which he took in mitigation; provided he had acted reasonably he was entitled to recover the cost of mitigation as the correct measure of his loss; the defendants owed the plaintiffs a duty of care not to damage their property and it was at all times reasonably foreseeable that if they did so, the damage might need to be repaired and that contractors might be engaged to do the necessary work on an ICE form of contract; and the learned judge was right to find that it was foreseeable that the cost of repair might include the payment of remuneration which covered the risk of the relevant contractor encountering unforeseen physical conditions which added to the cost of the work and that all this was within the risk created by the defendants' negligence.

The point to be borne in mind from what Evans LJ said is that a defendant in such

---

252 His reasoning, in the light of the House of Lords' decision in *Lagden v O'Connor*, is now wrong.
253 Ibid, p 106.

CHAPTER 13

THE LAW OF SALVAGE

The maritime law of salvage is based on principles of equity.

(Lord Wright in *The Kafiristan.*)

This of course does not mean that a sort of 'justice under the palm tree' or 'justice under the mast' is to be substituted for legal principles.

(Salmon LJ in *The Tojo Maru.*)

1 INTRODUCTION

Not infrequently, ships find themselves in need of assistance at sea due to various incidents that might affect their safe navigation alone. Assistance may be required whether or not a ship is in danger. An engine breakdown, for example, may be serious enough to put a ship in danger so as to call for a salvage tug and, if the other prerequisites of salvage exist, the special admiralty law rules of salvage will apply, which are different from those applicable to rescuers in land. If there is no danger but, nevertheless, a ship needs some assistance to reach its destination, a tug engaged for this purpose will be contracted under special terms of a towage contract (see Chapter 14). When reaching or leaving a port, a ship needs guidance from a harbour master or a pilot to navigate through other ships or obstructions, for berthing or departing. Harbour owners or administrators of public ports are under statutory obligations to keep the ports safe from any obstructions to navigation and provide pilotage and other services, which are regulated by specialised statutes and by-laws (see Chapter 16). These three areas of the law are interlinked.

The opportunity is taken again in the following chapters to discuss risk management, particularly in relation to towage contracts, and the services that port authorities offer. It transpires, from cases discussed, and from developments with regard to ports, that risk management should be viewed as a new way of proactive thinking in any business activities.

The law and practice of salvage used to be very simple in olden times, but mammoth developments have occurred in this area of law in recent years. For a century the principle of 'no cure no pay', enshrined in the Lloyd's Open Form (LOF) agreements, ensured that success in saving property was generously rewarded but failure could even leave salvors out of pocket. There had been a widespread acceptance of these forms, but that was so at times when ships were not so sophisticated as they are today and professional salvors had not emerged. The advent of very powerful modern tugs, standing by ready to assist in disasters, has meant time and money for the salvors, particularly with the rise of concern in recent years about environmental damage and pollution to marine life which might occur after major casualties. Thus, it has been recognised that salvors should be encouraged, even if no property was saved by their efforts, when minimisation or prevention of damage to the environment was successful. These developments will be discussed at the end of this chapter. It is first important to state the basic principles of salvage.

Two comprehensive 'bibles' exist on the law of salvage in our times, those of Brice[1] and Kennedy.[2] The scope of this book does not permit the same indulgence into the details of salvage as have been admirably analysed in the successive editions of these works. The intention in this chapter is to state the basic principles as supported by leading decisions. This way, the reader has the option to glance first at the basics and then use the 'bibles' as reference guides for further research.

2 THE CONCEPT OF SALVAGE UNDER MARITIME LAW

Brice[3] defines salvage as a right in law, which arises under English law when a person, acting as a volunteer (that is, without any pre-existing contractual or other legal duty so to act) preserves or contributes to preserving at sea any vessel, cargo, freight or other recognised subject of salvage from danger. This is known to be the 'civil salvage' as opposed to military, which is the rescuing of property from the enemy at a time of war for which a reward is made by the Court of Admiralty sitting as a Prize Court.

In Kennedy,[4] salvage is defined as a service which confers a benefit by saving or helping to save a recognised subject of salvage when in danger from which it cannot be extricated unaided, if and so far as the rendering of such service is voluntary in the sense of being attributable neither to a pre-existing obligation, nor solely for the interests of the salvor.

The origins of salvage are ancient and exist in ancient legal systems. Its fundamental principles were established in the early part of the 19th century. It was then recognised that there was a need to administer justice and to proceed according to equitable principles of fairness in the varying and unsettled cases that had arisen when property at sea was in danger. These principles were continually refined and developed by judges of the Admiralty Court. But, not until 1910, were these principles unified by the first salvage Convention to apply internationally.

The right of an award, rather than remuneration, arises from the fact that salvage is a mixed question of a private right and public policy. Its purpose is not merely to compensate the salvor for the benefit he has conferred to the salved property. It is also to provide a positive incentive to seafarers to take risks for the purpose of assisting others in danger. Although the parties involved may regulate, if they wish, the rendering of salvage services by agreement, the right to be rewarded for salvage at sea under common law is based both on equitable principles and

---

1   Brice, G, *Maritime Law of Salvage*, 4th edn, 2003, Sweet & Maxwell.
2   Steel, DW and Rose, FD, *Kennedy's Law of Salvage*, 6th edn, 2002, Sweet & Maxwell.
3   Op cit, Brice, fn 1, p 1.
4   Op cit, Kennedy, fn 2, p 8.

public policy and is not contractual in origin.[5] The law seeks to do what is fair and just both to the owners of property and to the salvor. Each interest that has received a benefit from the salvage services provided must contribute.

In *The Five Steel Barges*,[6] the underlying concept was put succinctly:

> The jurisdiction which the court exercises in salvage cases is of a peculiarly equitable character. The right to salvage may arise out of an actual contract; but it does not necessarily do so. It is a legal liability arising out of the fact that property has been saved, that the owner of the property who has had the benefit of it shall make remuneration to those who have conferred the benefit upon him, notwithstanding that he has not entered into any contract on the subject.

Also, Sir John Nicholl in *The Industry*[7] examined the policy underlying the amount of the salvage reward:

> ... there are various facts for consideration – the state of the weather, the degree of damage and danger as to ship and cargo, the risk and peril of the salvors, the time employed, the value of the property; and when all these things are considered, there is still another principle – to encourage enterprise, reward exertion, and to be liberal in all that is due to the general interests of commerce, and the general benefit of owners and underwriters, even though the reward may fall upon an individual owner with some severity.

Thus, the foundation of salvage is necessity when the subject of salvage has been in danger and services are rendered, even without request, in circumstances that a reasonably prudent owner would have accepted them.

3 SALVAGE UNDER CONTRACT

In old times, salvage used to be rendered by persons or ships using personal skill and efforts chancing their lives in undertaking to rescue property from danger without a specific contract. The salvor did not assume any obligation to continue the services and he could withdraw at any time, yet claim a reward if his services had contributed to the successful saving of the ship. Before 1875, professional salvage contractors did not exist and express contracts were unknown.

When, near the end part of the 19th century, there was an increase in steamships, salvage was rendered under agreements on a 'no cure no pay' basis, which developed into LOF. In the latter half of the 20th century, most salvage services, other than that of 'standing by' a vessel in distress, are performed by professional salvors under a salvage agreement in LOF.[8]

With the availability of powered tugs, modern means of communication and more readily available facilities for salvage, salvage is rendered more commonly by professional salvors under contract, with each party having rights and duties governing the relationship. Under it, the salvage contractor undertakes a continuing

---

5   Goff (Lord) and Jones, G, *On Restitution*, 6th edn, 2002, Sweet & Maxwell, Chapter 18, pp 478–480.
6   (1890) 15 PD 142, p 146.
7   (1835) 3 Hagg 203, p 204.
8   *The Tojo Maru* [1971] 1 Lloyd's Rep 341 (HL), p 362, per Lord Diplock.

obligation, until the ship is brought to a safe port, to use his best endeavours to salve her and to provide the equipment and labour which, in the circumstances, it would be reasonable for him to use for this purpose. These professional salvors keep tugs and equipment, waiting for an opportunity to provide assistance and earn large salvage reward.

Contracts are usually entered into on the LOF (1980, 1990, 1995 and now the 2000 LOF). Under these contracts, the salvors receive no salvage award in cases where no property is salved. However, the concept of special compensation to recover expenses for efforts made to prevent or minimise damage to the environment with an increment of those expenses in the event of succeeding to prevent or minimise such damage, whether or not property is saved, has developed in recent years.[9] This was a major reason for the new International Salvage Convention 1989.[10]

4 THE SALVAGE CONVENTIONS[11]

4.1 Historical development of the revision of salvage law

As was earlier mentioned, the first attempt to unify the principles on the law of salvage was the Brussels Convention 1910, on the initiative of the International Maritime Organisation (IMO). It was enacted only in part into English law by the Maritime Conventions Act (MCA) 1911. The Convention was amended by the Brussels Convention on Salvage of Aircraft 1938, to extend the law of salvage to salvage by or to seaborne aircraft.

The provisions of the 1910 Convention, however, proved to be inadequate to cover the needs of modern times, particularly with regard to problems arising from big disasters which resulted in damage to the marine environment.[12] There was a need, therefore, to encourage salvors with some incentive to prevent or minimise such losses. The first initiative to this effect was an inclusion in the LOF 1980 of a novel concept providing for an 'enhanced award', when the salvor, in addition to saving property, also prevented pollution from oil tankers, and for a 'safety net' in a form of compensation for the salvor's expenses in the event that he failed to earn an award because the tanker sunk, but he prevented pollution to the coastline. In effect, the safety net was a deviation from the general principle of 'no cure no pay' but it provided an incentive to salvors to undertake salvage involving oil tankers. The enhanced award was part of the 'property salvage' (payable by the under-writers of the ship and cargo) but the safety net became known as the 'liability salvage' (payable by the protection and indemnity (P&I) insurers of the shipowners).

---

9   See, further, under paras 7 to 16, below.
10   For an historical background to LOFs 1980 and 1990 and the reasons behind the 1989 Convention, see Darling, G (QC) and Smith, C, *LOF 90 and the New Salvage Convention*, 1991, LLP.
11   See commentary on the 1989 Convention by Shaw, R, [1996] LMCLQ 202.
12   Such as *The Torrey Canyon*, *The Amoco Cadiz* and *The Exxon Valdez*.

At this point, it is helpful to refer to what Lord Mustill said in *The Nagasaki Spirit* [13] about the underlying reasons for the revision of the common law salvage:

> The reward for successful salvage was always large; for failure it was nil. At first, the typical salvor was one who used personal efforts and property to effect a rescue. As time progressed, improvements in speed, propulsive power and communications bred a new community of professional salvors who found it worth while to keep tugs and equipment continually in readiness, and for much of the time idle, waiting for an opportunity to provide assistance and earn a large reward.
>
> This arrangement served the maritime community and its insurers well, and the salvors made a satisfactory living. It was, however, an expensive business and in recent years the capital and running costs have been difficult for the traditional salvage concerns to sustain. A number of these were absorbed into larger enterprises, less committed perhaps to the former spirit, and unwilling to stake heavy outlays on the triple chance of finding a vessel in need of assistance, of accomplishing a salvage liable to be more arduous and prolonged than in the days of smaller merchant ships, and of finding that there was sufficient value left in the salved property at the end of the service to justify a substantial award.
>
> At about the same time, a new factor entered the equation. Crude oil and its products have been moved around the world by sea in large quantities for many years, and the risk that cargo or fuel escaping from a distressed vessel would damage the flora and fauna of the sea and shore, and would impregnate the shoreline itself, was always present; but so long as the amount carried by a single vessel was comparatively small, such incidents as did happen were not large enough to attract widespread attention.
>
> This changed with the prodigious increase in the capacity of crude oil carriers which began some three decades ago, carrying with it the possibility of a disaster whose consequences might extend far beyond the loss of the imperilled goods and cargo. Such a disaster duly happened, at a time when public opinion was already becoming sensitive to assaults on the integrity of the natural environment. Cargo escaping from the wreck of *Torrey Canyon* off the Scillies caused widespread contamination of sea, foreshore and wild life. The resulting concern and indignation were sharpened when *Amoco Cadiz* laden with 220,000 tons of crude oil stranded on the coast of France, causing pollution on an even larger scale, in circumstances which rightly or wrongly were believed to have involved a possibly fatal delay during negotiations with the intended salvors.
>
> To this problem the traditional law of salvage provided no answer, for the only success which mattered was success in preserving the ship, cargo and associated interests; and this was logical, since the owners of those interests, who had to bear any salvage award that was made, had no financial stake in the protection of anything else. This meant that a salvor who might perform a valuable service to the community in the course of an attempted salvage, by, for example, moving the vessel to a place where the escape of oil would be less harmful, would recover nothing or only very little, if in the end the ship was lost or greatly damaged. Something more was required to induce professional salvors, upon whom the community must rely for protection, to keep in existence and on call the fleets necessary for the protection of natural resources in peril. Some new form of remuneration must be devised. It is with an important aspect of the scheme worked out during long and

---

13   [1997] 1 Lloyd's Rep 323 (HL), pp 326–28.

hard fought negotiations between the shipowning and cargo interests and their insurers on the one hand and representatives of salvors on the other, with participation by governmental and other agencies, that the present appeal is concerned.

It is important to make clear that the solution devised in the 1980s was not to create a new institution: a kind of free standing 'environmental salvage'. The services performed remain, as they have always been, services to ship and cargo, and the award is borne by those standing behind ship and cargo. The difference is that the sum payable to the salvor may now contain an additional element to reflect the risk of the environment posed by the vessel for which the services are performed. . . .

The move towards the evolution of what has been called a 'safety net', designed to provide an additional incentive for salvors to keep fleets on station, began during the late 1970s with two parallel initiatives. These first bore fruit in the 1980 revision of the Lloyd's Open Form, so as to make cl 1(a) read as follows:

> 'The contractor agrees to use his best endeavours to salve the [vessel] . . . and/or her cargo bunkers and stores and take them to . . . or other place to be hereafter agreed or if no place is named or agreed to a place of safety. The contractor further agrees to use his best endeavours to prevent the escape of oil from the vessel while performing the services of salving the subject vessel and/or her cargo bunkers and stores. The services shall be rendered and accepted as salvage services upon the principle of "no cure no pay" except that where the property being salved is a tanker laden or partly laden with a cargo of oil and without negligence on the part of the contractor and/or his servants and/or agents (1) the services are not successful or (2) are only partially successful or (3) the contractor is prevented from completing the services the contractor shall nevertheless be awarded solely against the owners of such tanker his reasonably incurred expenses and an increment not exceeding 15% of such expenses but only if and to the extent that such expenses together with the increment are greater than any amount otherwise recoverable under this agreement. Within the meaning of the said exception to the principle of 'no cure no pay' expenses shall in addition to actual out of pocket expenses include a fair rate for all tugs, craft, personnel and other equipment used by the contractor in the services and oil shall mean crude oil fuel oil heavy diesel oil and lubricating oil.'

Within a few months of the *Amoco Cadiz* disaster the International Maritime Organisation (IMO) had taken the matter in hand and prepared an initial report. The problem was also addressed by the Comité Maritime International (CMI) which agreed to co-operate in a study of the private law principles of salvage. The outcome was the establishment of a sub-committee under the chairmanship of Professor E Selvig, which prepared a draft convention accompanied by a report. These documents were placed before a conference of CMI in Montreal during May 1981, by which time LOF 1980 with its safety net provision had come into force. The debates at Montreal led to a final draft, together with a report by Mr B Nielsen. For a time, there was little further progress, but eventually a diplomatic conference led to the agreement of the International Convention on Salvage 1989.

The 1989 Salvage Convention (referred to as 'the Convention' in this chapter) replaced the Brussels Convention for the Unification of Certain Rules of Law Relating to Assistance and Salvage at Sea 1910. The concepts of enhanced award and safety net, enshrined in the 1980 LOF, were adopted by the new Convention. The former is taken into account when the assessment of the award is made by the arbitrators under Art 13(1)(b), and the latter is known as the 'special compensation' provision under Art 14. They apply, not only to environmental damage from oil pollution, but also to substantial physical damage to human health, or to marine life, or resources in coastal or inland waters or areas adjacent thereto by pollution generally, contamination, fire, explosion or similar major incidents (Art 1(d)).

The Convention came into force internationally on 14 July 1996, but, in the meantime, the UK enacted it into English law by the Merchant Shipping (Salvage and Pollution) Act (MS(SP)A) 1994 and it came into force in the UK on 1 January 1995. With the consolidation of the Merchant Shipping Acts (MSAs) by the MSA 1995, the 1994 Act was repealed, and the Convention is found in Sched 11 to the MSA 1995.[14]

The substantive changes to salvage law brought by the Convention were first incorporated in the LOF 1990. However, before the Convention had the force of law, these changes – as incorporated in the LOF 1990 – had only a contractual effect. Once the Convention became part of English law by statute,[15] its provisions have the force of law since 1 January 1995, whether or not the parties enter into a contract, unless the parties to the LOF choose to contract out of some provisions of the Convention.

It should also be noted in this context that the International Convention on Oil Pollution, Preparedness, Response and Co-operation 1990 (OPPRC Convention) was concluded at a diplomatic conference in London at the IMO in November 1990. The OPPRC Convention is in force internationally and provides for salvage policy, contingency plans and reporting of casualties. Briefly, it requires harbour authorities and ships to have oil pollution emergency plans and provides for oil pollution reporting procedures, including national contingency plans, as well as exhorting international co-operation to take action on receiving information about oil pollution incidents. Pursuant to powers under s 128(1)(d) of the MSA 1995 to give effect to the OPPRC Convention, the Merchant Shipping (OPPRC) Order 1997 enables the OPPRC Convention to be given effect by the making of regulations, the Merchant Shipping (OPPRC) Regulations 1998 (SI 1998/1056).

4.2 Application of the 1989 Convention

By Art 2, the Convention shall apply whenever judicial or arbitral proceedings relating to matters dealt with in this Convention are brought in a State party.

Article 6(1) provides that the Convention shall apply to any salvage operations save to the extent that a contract otherwise provides expressly, or by implication. Therefore, parties are free to contract out of the Act, or parts of it, by an express term in their contract.

There is an exception with regard to salvage operations controlled by public authorities. Article 5 provides that this Convention shall not affect any provisions of

---

14 For a detailed exposition of English statutes, historically, which have affected the law of salvage see: op cit, Brice, fn 1, pp 12–14.

15 First by the MS(SP)A 1994, s 71(1), and now by the MSA 1995, s 224(1), the provisions of the Convention (Pt I, Sched 11) shall have the force of law in the UK.

national law or any international convention relating to salvage operations by or under the control of public authorities, although salvors carrying out such salvage operations shall be entitled to avail themselves of the rights and remedies provided for in this Convention. The extent to which a public authority, being under a duty to perform salvage operations, may avail itself of the rights and remedies provided for by the Convention shall be determined by the law of the State where such authority is situated.

Subject to Art 5, the Convention shall not apply to warships or other non-commercial State-owned vessels, unless a State party decides to apply the Convention to warships (Art 4).

5 PRECONDITIONS OF SALVAGE

Before examining the essential elements of salvage, this chapter looks at the geographical limits in which salvage can take place and the subject matter of salvage, as some important changes have been made by the Convention.

5.1 The relevant waters for salvage prior to the Salvage Convention 1989

For the services rendered to be considered as salvage services there was a precondition that the salvage should have occurred in tidal waters.[16] That requirement was an essential ingredient of the cause of action of salvage, and had its basis in s 546(1) of the MSA 1894 (now repealed), which provided:

> . . . a salvor had a right to remuneration for salvage services rendered to any vessel wrecked, stranded or in distress at any place on or near the coast of the UK or any tidal water within the limits of the UK.

Section 742 of the same Act defined tidal waters as meaning any part of the sea and any part of a river within the ebb and flow of the tide at ordinary spring tides, and not being a harbour.

The problem created by this statutory definition became apparent in the amusing factual situation of *The Goring*, a notorious case, which reached the House of Lords, but now belongs to the past.

The Goring[17]

The Goring, a passenger vessel owned by the respondents, broke free of her moorings before midnight, 14 September 1984, in the river Thames, up-river of Reading bridge. Being unmanned, she began to drift towards other vessels, which were moored close by, and she was at risk of colliding with these vessels, or of being

---

16   Although the Salvage Convention 1910, by Art 1, provided that all salvage services in whatever waters the services had been rendered were subject to that Convention, this provision had not been enacted into English law.

17   [1988] 2 WLR 460; [1988] AC 381 (HL).

otherwise carried away. The appellants, employees or members of the Bohemian Club, which was situated on an island in the middle of the river, were enjoying themselves. With the help of the club's ferry boat, they managed to get someone on board *The Goring*, thereby making it possible to get a line from her to the island and to haul her to a vacant mooring where she was made fast. They claimed salvage reward, which was at first instance granted to them by Sheen J. All the elements of salvage being present, the question for decision in the House of Lords was whether the appellants were entitled to salvage, bearing in mind that the Thames above Reading bridge is not tidal.

Lord Brandon of Oakbrook said:

> Section 458 (of the 1854 Act) is important because in it the legislature for the first time prescribed the places in which it was necessary for services to a ship, her cargo or her apparel to have been rendered in order to qualify as salvage services within the UK. It was necessary that they should have been rendered on the shore of any sea or tidal water in the UK. If the legislature had intended that services rendered in non-tidal inland waters of the UK should also qualify as salvage services, it would surely have expressly so provided. It did not do so, however, and the inference which I draw is that the legislature did not have that intention.[18]

> The definitions of the expressions 'harbour' and 'tidal water' in s 742 create a problem when applied to ascertain the meaning of the expression 'tidal water' in s 546. The result of applying the very wide definition of 'harbour' to the definition of 'tidal water', and then applying the definition of 'tidal water' so produced to interpret s 546, is to exclude from the meaning of 'tidal water' in that section numerous localities which might be expected to be included in it. It is fortunately not necessary to solve this problem in this appeal. The significance of s 546 is the same as that of s 458 of the MSA 1854. It prescribes the places in which services must be rendered in order to qualify as salvage services in the UK, and does so in such a way as to exclude non-tidal inland waters.[19]

It was held that there was no cause of action for salvage in respect of services rendered to a ship in danger in navigable non-tidal inland waters. The provisions of the statute had the effect of limiting the scope of salvage to tidal waters and extension of that scope should be left to the legislature. Therefore, the appellants were not entitled to salvage.

As a result of this decision, there was later an attempt to amend s 546(2), by the MSA 1988 (Sched 5, para 3) which defined tidal waters[20] as follows:

(a) any water within the ebb and flow of the tide at ordinary spring tides; or

(b) the waters of any dock which is directly, or (by means of one or more other docks) indirectly, connected with any such waters.

It was meant to extend salvage to events which occurred in harbours, by redefining tidal waters as including the waters of any dock directly or indirectly connected

---

18 Ibid, p 465.

19 [1988] 2 WLR 460, p 466.

20 Despite that amendment, s 255(1) of the 1995 Act defines tidal waters as meaning 'any part of the sea and any part of a river within the ebb and flow of the tide at ordinary spring tides, and not being a harbour', thus perpetuating the anomaly of the old s 742 of the 1894 MSA.

with tidal waters. In the following case, the question was whether there could be a right to salvage when services were rendered in a harbour.

The Powstaniec Wielkopolski[21]

The vessel laden with cargo at the time was moored in Gravesend Reach, within the port limits of the Port of London (which was tidal) awaiting a berth. During the evening, her moorings began to part and later she drifted to the north side of the river and was obviously in danger of colliding with other vessels moored along her side. Although she made no call for assistance, three tugs set off to assist her. Subsequently, the tugowners together with officers and crew brought an action *in rem* against her for salvage remuneration. The defendants contended that on the facts, as the services were rendered within a harbour, they did not give rise to salvage. Salvage was governed by s 546, and since it requires salvage to occur in tidal waters, the latter should be construed in accordance with s 742.

Section 742 of the Act of 1894 provided:

> In this Act, unless the context otherwise requires, the following expressions have the meanings hereby assigned to them; (that is to say) . . . 'harbour' includes harbours properly so called, whether natural or artificial, estuaries, navigable rivers, piers, jetties, and other works in or at which ships can obtain shelter, or ship and unship goods or passengers; 'tidal water' means any part of the sea and any part of a river within the ebb and flow of the tide at ordinary spring tides, and not being a harbour . . .

The problem obviously arose from the last sentence of this section.

Sheen J held that, in the reality of things and bearing in mind previous cases in the last 94 years which had recognised salvage in harbours, it would be absurd to require that the word 'harbour' in the definition of 'tidal water' under s 742 should be given the meaning assigned to it by this section. Instead, the word 'harbour', where it appears in the definition of tidal waters, must be given its ordinary and natural meaning and a tidal harbour was not excluded from being a place in which salvage could occur. The place where the services were rendered was tidal. It was unnecessary for him to decide the meaning of tidal waters in s 546 because of the amendment by the 1988 Act mentioned earlier. Therefore, the plaintiffs were not precluded from claiming a salvage award based on a geographical limitation.

Despite the problem created by s 742 above, s 255(1) of MSA 1995 repeats the definition of tidal waters as was defined in s 742, but the amendment to s 546 by the MSA 1988 is carried forward in para 2(1) Part II of Sch 11 to MSA 1995, as shown below.

5.2 'Relevant waters' under the salvage Convention 1989

The place of relevant waters where salvage operations can be awarded salvage, if successful, has been expanded by the Convention. Article 1(a) defines that, for the purpose of the Convention, salvage operation means any act or activity undertaken

---

21 [1988] 3 WLR 723.

to assist a vessel or any other property in danger in navigable waters, or in any other waters whatsoever.

Although the Convention encompasses salvage which takes place in any waters, contracting States are permitted, by Art 30 of the Convention, to reserve the right not to apply the provisions of the Convention when the salvage operation takes place in inland waters. The UK has made such a reservation. Paragraph 2(1), Pt II of Sched 11 to the MSA 1995 stipulates that the provisions of the Convention do not apply to:

(a) salvage operations which take place in 'inland waters' of the UK and in which all the vessels involved are of inland navigation, and

(b) to a salvage operation which takes place in 'inland waters' of the UK and in which no vessel is involved.

It is thereafter stated that 'inland waters' do not include any waters within the ebb and flow of the tide at ordinary spring tides or the waters of any dock which is directly, or indirectly, connected with such waters (that is, tidal waters).

It is unfortunate that the UK adopted the reservation instead of following the provision of the convention by which salvage is permitted in any waters. However, should there be a need for salvage in the UK inland waters, the parties may agree to contract out of this provision, or to have the services rendered on the basis of a contract for engaged services.

5.3 What is a recognised subject of salvage?

Traditionally, maritime law salvage recognises as its subject the property in danger that is a ship or craft, cargo on board, freight payable pursuant to the contract of carriage, and bunkers carried on board the ship. The concept of property has been expanded by the Convention (see below). The Convention also recognises saving life as an independent subject of salvage, regardless of whether or not the life salvors saved the property in danger. The Convention also recognises as subject of salvage the protection of the marine environment. Although skill and effort by salvors exerted successfully to protect the environment is taken into account in calculating the award for property salvage, protecting the environment is treated separately from property salvage by special compensation, as will be seen later.

The problem under maritime law salvage and under the Merchant Shipping Acts[22] before the MSA 1995[23] was the definition of ship or craft as a subject of salvage.[24] In recent years, the definition of a ship for the purpose of maritime law has been clarified (as discussed in Chapters 1 and 12).

---

22 A vessel or craft had to qualify as a ship before it was recognised as a subject of salvage. Section 742 of the MSA 1894 defined 'vessel' as any ship or boat, or any other description of vessel used in navigation; and 'ship' as including every description of vessel used in navigation not propelled by oars.

23 For more details, see Chapter 1; by the Merchant Shipping (Registration etc) Act 1993, an amendment to s 742 dropped the phrase 'not propelled by oars'.

24 *The Gas Float Whitton (No 2)* [1897] AC 337.

5.3.1 Ship, craft or property under the Convention

The subject of salvage is broader. However, unfortunately, neither the 1989 Convention nor the MSA 1995 has greatly improved the definition of a ship.

Section 313(1) of the MSA 1995 defines 'ship' as including every description of vessel used in navigation.

A vessel used in navigation is confined to a vessel which is used to make ordered progression over the water from one place to another, although it is not a necessary requirement that it should be used in transporting persons or property by water to an intended destination. Craft that are simply used for having fun on the water without the object of going anywhere, such as jet skis, are not 'used in navigation' and are, accordingly, excluded from the definition of 'ship or vessel'.[25]

By s 311 of the MSA 1995, the Secretary of State has power to decide that a thing designed or adapted for use at sea is or is not to be treated as a ship for the purposes of the provisions of the Act.

The Convention, by Art 1(a), defines 'salvage operations' as including services rendered to vessels, or to any other property in danger.

Article 1(b) defines a vessel as meaning 'any ship or craft, or any structure capable of navigation'.

As far as English law is concerned, the definition of 'ship' or 'craft' will be borrowed from s 313 of MSA 1995, which requires the ship to be used in navigation and common law has defined these words, as seen earlier.

As regards any other structure, it is expressly stated that it must be 'capable of navigation'; a structure may not necessarily be a ship in the strict sense, but it could be any other property having the essential characteristic of being capable of navigation, provided it is not permanently and intentionally attached to the shoreline (as per Art 1(c)).

'Property' means any property not permanently and intentionally attached to the shoreline, and includes freight at risk (Art 1(c)).

'Shore line' is defined in the *Oxford English Dictionary* as the line where shore and water meet. So, if a vessel or a buoy were attached to the seabed or moored at sea, it would not be included in the definition of 'property'.[26]

Could a sunken ship, or wreck, come within the meaning of Art 1 of the Convention? Section 255(1) of the MSA 1995 states that a wreck includes jetsam, flotsam, lagan and derelict found in or on the shores of the sea or any tidal water. At common law, a wreck has been held to be a subject of salvage.[27]

A wreck could come within Art 1(a) of the Convention, 'vessel or any other property in danger', provided it is still in danger itself, apart from the fact that it causes danger to navigation. Although a wreck may still be a ship, or structure, for the purpose of Art 1(b), it will no longer be capable of navigation, unless the Con-

---

25   *R v Goodwin* [2006] 1 Lloyd's Rep 432; see, further, about 'what is a ship' in Chapters 1 and 12.
26   Op cit, Brice, fn 1, p 224.
27   *The Gas Float Whitton (No 2)*, op cit, fn 24.

vention does not require the ship or craft to be capable of navigation,[28] or unless its original use of being used in navigation prior to becoming a wreck is taken into account in order to fall within Art 1(b). Failing the above, it is submitted that a wreck will come within art 1(c), 'property' not permanently and intentionally attached to the shoreline, and it will be a subject of salvage. (The Wreck Removal Convention 2007 is briefly discussed at the end of Ch 16, below.) A wreck which contains treasures may be a subject of salvage, provided there is no reservation made by contracting States as to archaeological finds, as is allowed by Art 30(1)(d) of the Convention.

The Convention does not apply to fixed or floating platforms or mobile offshore drilling units when they are on location engaged in the exploration, exploitation or production of seabed mineral resources (Art 3). This suggests that oil rigs and offshore installations which are not fixed or floating on location, or are not engaged in activities described above, would probably be recognised subjects of salvage. The mere fact that 'navigation' is incidental to some more specialised function, such as dredging or the provision of accommodation, does not take oil rigs, if they are capable of and used in navigation, outside the definition.[29]

Gas floats and landing stages not attached to the shoreline[30] may well be included under Art 1(c) of the Convention.

All merchandise being carried on the vessel could be subject to salvage, except personal effects of the crew, master and passengers.[31]

By Art 4, the Convention does not apply to warships or non-commercial vessels owned or operated by the State and entitled, at the time of salvage operation, to sovereign immunity under international law, unless that State decides otherwise.

Section 230 of the MSA 1995 deals with salvage claims against and by the Crown.

5.3.2 Hovercrafts/aircraft

The Hovercraft Act 1968, ss 1(1)(h)(ii)[32] and 2(2) provide that rules of law relating to ships apply to hovercrafts as if references to ship included reference to hovercraft. Also, by Art 8 of the Hovercraft Order 1972, salvage services to hovercraft are treated as if they were salvage services to a ship. Similar provisions are made in s 87 of the Civil Aviation Act 1982, extending salvage to aircraft.[33]

---

28 As Brice suggests, op cit, fn 1, at p 223, that the use of comma after 'craft, may indicate that the requirement 'capable of navigation' is applicable only to structures.

29 *Perks v Clark* [2001] 2 Lloyd's Rep 431 (CA); *The Key Singapore* [2005] 1 Lloyd's Rep 91 was a jack-up rig and was subject to salvage.

30 The gas float in *The Gas Float Whitton* was permanently and intentionally attached to the shore bed. It was not a proper subject of salvage.

31 See op cit, Brice, fn 1, Chapter 3, for further details of salved property.

32 The MSA 1995 applies to enactments and instruments with respect to which provision may be made by Order in Council pursuant to the Hovercraft Act 1968, s 1(1)(h).

33 Thus, *Watson v Victor* (1934) 22 LlL Rep 77, where a claim for salvage of cinematography equipment from a wrecked seaplane failed, is now not good law after the Civil Aviation Act 1982.

5.3.3 Bunkers

Save when the ship is on time charter, when the bunkers will be the property of the charterers, the bunkers are usually a valuable element of the salved value. The House of Lords, in *The Span Terza*,[34] has made it clear that the position of the shipowner in relation to the bunkers, when the ship is time chartered, is that of a bailee and the charterers remained the owners of the bunkers until re-delivery.

5.3.4 Cargo

Property in Art 1 of the Convention naturally includes goods or merchandise being carried on the vessel excluding personal effects of the crew or master and passengers' luggage. Salvors removing cargo during the course of salvage are in a position of bailees of the cargo-owners.[35]

5.3.5 Freight

Article 1(c) of the Convention refers to freight at risk. Freight in this context is the remuneration due and payable for the carriage of cargo and not hire for the use of the ship.[36] Obviously, it does not cover freight paid in advance. The freight may be at the risk of the shipowner or charterer.[37]

5.3.6 Life salvage

Prior to the 1989 Convention, there was no pure life salvage as such, but it depended on whether property was salved. If there was no property salved, remuneration for mere life salvage was not recoverable in the Admiralty Court. The MSA 1854 (ss 458–60) provided for liability to pay a reasonable amount of salvage to life salvors by the owners of cargo as well as the owners of the ship, but such liability was limited to the value of the property saved from destruction. There should have been something more than life saved by salvors for the property to contribute to life salvors' award. In *Cargo ex Sarpedon*,[38] while the cargo owners whose cargo was salved together with 88 people on board the abandoned ship paid for salvage remuneration, the owners of the ship, which was not capable of salvage, were not ordered to pay a portion of the sum awarded to salvors.

By contrast in *Cargo ex Schiller*,[39] the court abandoned a strict construction of the statutory provision in order to remedy the injustice created by existing law and practice, and held that it was immaterial whether or not the property saved from destruction had been saved by the salvors who saved the lives on board. The salvors who saved 15 people from a sinking ship were awarded; divers were later instructed to raise part of the sunken cargo.

---

34 [1984] 1 Lloyd's Rep 119.
35 *The Winson* [1982] 1 Lloyd's Rep 117.
36 Op cit, Brice, fn 1, pp 235–237.
37 *The Pantanassa* [1970] 1 Lloyd's Rep 153.
38 (1877) 3 PD 28.
39 (1877) 2 PD 145.

Despite this decision, which established a judicial recognition of independent life salvage, uncertainty still existed due to a lack of clear statutory provisions to encourage the saving of life at sea by rewarding life salvors. Thus, a Mercantile Fund was established by s 544 of the MSA 1894 and voluntary organisations, such as the Royal National Lifeboat Institution (RNLI) and the HM Coastguard, were formed to help those in danger at sea.

The MS(SP)A 1994 repealed the relevant sections of the MSA 1854, and by Sched 2, s 6(3)(b), saving life was included in salvage services.

Life salvage has now become independent of saving property by the Convention and is dealt with by Art 16 (Sched 11, Pt I of the MSA 1995). The article provides that no remuneration is due from persons whose life is saved but leaves national laws unaffected on this subject (Art 16(1)). It further provides that a salvor of human life is entitled to a fair share of the payment awarded to the salvor for saving the vessel or other property or preventing or minimising damage to the environment (Art 16(2)).

In Pt II of Sched 11, para 5 provides for resource for life salvage payment where services are rendered wholly or in part in UK waters in saving life from a vessel, and the vessel is either destroyed or the sum under Art 16(2) is less than a reasonable amount for the services rendered in saving life; the Secretary of State, if he thinks fit, may pay the salvor an additional sum.

The Admiralty Court has jurisdiction to entertain claims for life salvage under s 20(2)(j) of the Supreme Court Act (SCA) 1981.

6 ELEMENTS OF SALVAGE

There are four elements that must exist for the right of salvage reward to arise, namely: (i) there should be a recognised subject matter; (ii) the object of salvage should be in danger at sea; (iii) the salvors must be volunteers; and (iv) there must be success by either preserving or contributing to preserving the property in danger.

Since what is a recognised subject of salvage is dealt with under para 5.3 above, the three central elements of salvage are examined below.

6.1 Danger

6.1.1 General principles

There must be some real danger, which is likely to expose the property to destruction or damage. An apprehension of danger will suffice, as long as it is not a fanciful danger, and it does not need to be immediate or absolute. The following examples illustrate these points.

The Phantom[40]

> I am of the opinion that it is not necessary that there should be absolute danger in order to constitute salvage service; it is sufficient if there is a state of difficulty, and reasonable apprehension.

In **The Charlotte**,[41] Dr Lushington said:

> According to the principles which are recognised in this court in questions of this description, all services rendered at sea to a vessel in danger or distress are salvage services. It is not necessary, I conceive, that the distress should be actual or immediate, or that the danger should be imminent and absolute; it will be sufficient if, at the time the assistance is rendered, the ship has encountered any damage or misfortune which might possibly expose her to destruction if the services were not rendered.[42]

The vessel was proceeding on a voyage from Bombay to Liverpool. The master of the vessel missed the harbour he was aiming for and the vessel was caught up in a violent gale, with fog and rain, which drove the ship towards the rocks. After a day of effort to board her, the salvors took the ship in tow with great exertion and labour having to force their way through a heavy sea before they could get the vessel towed in. Then, they claimed salvage remuneration. The owners' defence was that no salvage services had been rendered because during the whole time of the towing of the ship, the weather was fine and that there was an agreement for towage at the cost of 20 shillings each. It was held that, on the facts, it was undisputed that the vessel's masts and all her sails had been cut away, and that in her dismasted state she was towed into Long Island Channel, and that, prima facie, salvage services had been rendered.

It does not matter if the danger is slight, but it is important that danger can be said to exist. The extent of the danger is only relevant in determining the extent of the award.

The Helenus,[43] fully laden, was to sail for Rotterdam, but the voyage was cancelled as a gale began with mighty and forceful winds that afternoon. It gradually became stronger, causing the stern ropes of The Helenus to part. Her master made a call for assistance. The vessel, surging under the influence of the wind and tide, came into collision with The Motagua which was lying close to The Helenus. As a result, The Motagua rendered her own moorings. Both vessels drifted north and rubbed up against The Imichil pushing that vessel's bows to port pressing it up against a large dockyard crane. The crane was lifted off its feet on one side, so that it was leaning over dangerously. This was the dangerous position the vessels were in when the tugs arrived. The tugs made fast to The Helenus and pulled her away. They were unable to reach The Motagua but, once The Helenus was removed, The Motagua was in a less dangerous situation and was assisted to her berth. A salvage award was claimed. Sheen J examined the dangers in the circumstances:

> ... having regard to the fact that it was night, there was a very high wind; they were in a very confined space; the tide was ebb; there were dangers of damage to the side

---

40   [1866] LR 1 A&E 58, p 60, per Dr Lushington.
41   (1848) 3 W Rob 68.
42   Ibid, p 71.
43   [1982] 2 Lloyd's Rep 261.

of the vessel from ranging against *The Motagua* and the danger to both vessels from that source. There was the possibility, if they tried to move, of fouling other vessels or doing more damage or even possibly damaging their propellers if they got too close to the wharves.[44]

It was held that salvage services had been rendered to *The Helenus*, but the services rendered to *The Motagua* was to be treated as a comparatively minor service.

Whether a temporary difficulty would amount to danger was examined in **The North Goodwin (No 16)**.[45]

The defendants' light vessel *The North Goodwin* was being towed by *The Mermaid*. It was anticipated that the light vessel would be handed over to the tugs *Northsider* and *Ironsider* so that she might be taken to dock. The tugs were employed under the UK Standard Conditions for towage. Gale force winds caused such a heavy swell that *Northsider* moved up-river. When the tugs arrived, the pilots considered the weather conditions too bad to allow the pilot cutter to leave the harbour entrance, but *Northsider* continued through the piers and turned to the north, towards *The Mermaid*. *The Mermaid* decided to take the light ship into the river and hand over to *Northsider* when the vessels had protection from the piers. While *The Mermaid* was engaged in turning to starboard, the towing rope parted and the light vessel was free to drift down wind. *Northsider* seeing what had happened immediately went to the assistance of the light vessel and managed to pass a towage connection to those aboard and then towed her to an anchorage about a mile and a half from the coasts.

Sheen J held that, although the light vessel was drifting downwind, she was equipped with three anchors and, if *Northsider* had not reacted so promptly to the parting of the tow rope, *The Mermaid* would have been alerted to the danger presented by the lee shore and given orders for an anchor or anchors to be let go which would have held the light vessel, until *The Mermaid* could have manoeuvred to put a line aboard; and, if *Northsider* had come up with the light vessel and offered her services on salvage terms, there was no doubt that that offer would have been declined and the light vessel was not in danger.[46]

In the light of the assumptions made by the judge disregarding the real difficulty and danger presented to the light ship in rough weather, this authority may be disputed. However, the point made by the judge was that *Northsider* was employed under a towage contract.

6.1.2 *Future or contingent danger*

This aspect was examined in **The Troilus**[47] which has become known as 'The Troilus danger'. It illustrates what kind of future danger the court will be prepared to take into account in assessing the existence of danger, but each case will be judged on its own facts. There is no rigid rule about it.

---

44 Ibid, p 265.
45 [1980] 1 Lloyd's Rep 71.
46 [1980] 1 Lloyd's Rep 71, p 74.
47 [1951] AC 820.

The vessel was carrying cargo from Australia to Liverpool. She fractured her tail shaft and dropped her propeller in the Indian Ocean, but, otherwise, she was unimpaired. She was towed to Aden where she anchored. This admittedly constituted salvage services. There being no facilities for repairs, nor for storage of cargo at Aden, the damaged ship was towed by another vessel to the UK, since repair in the Mediterranean would have been difficult and would have involved considerable delay. The cargo-owners contended that this constituted ocean towage, not salvage services, since the ship was in perfect safety when she reached Aden.

The court held that, although the ship and cargo were in physical safety at Aden, the services in question were salvage services. The master of a damaged ship must do his best to preserve the ship and cargo and bring them to their destination as cheaply and as efficiently as possible, bearing in mind expense and the effect of delay on both and considering the possibility of transshipment or of repair at some convenient port. Salvage lasts so long as the master acts reasonably for the combined benefit of ship and cargo. A salvage award held to be reasonable in the case of a ship would be held reasonable in the case of the cargo also, unless it were established that the master neglected its interests.

The decision of the Court of Appeal was affirmed and Lord Porter added:

> The solution of the question whether a ship and cargo have reached a place of safety must, I think, depend upon the facts of each case, one of which is the possibility of safely discharging and storing the cargo and sending it on to its destination and the danger of its deterioration. It is not a sufficient answer to say that she can lie in a particular position of physical safety. It must be remembered that in every voyage of a merchant ship carrying cargo the interests of both ship and cargo have to be borne in mind.[48]

> In the present case the whole of the facts and law were carefully considered by the learned President, and, unless the appellants could establish that salvage services always end where the ship can be in physical safety and where the cargo also can remain at least for some time without danger or damage, he appears to me to have reached the right conclusion upon ample and adequate grounds. He carefully considered the opportunities for repair at each port on the voyage, the risks and delay involved and the possibilities of safe towage. Amongst others, he had in mind those of drydocking *The Troilus* without discharging her cargo and the imprudence of tipping a Liberty ship sufficiently to fit a propeller. On the last two points the Court of Appeal took the advice of their assessors, who thought that either expedient would be unsafe, and your Lordships' assessors took the same view.[49]

Therefore, the services still constituted salvage services.

It has been confirmed in recent years that there could be a reasonable future apprehension of danger even when the swing of the ship by the wind had stopped temporarily.[50]

---

48 Ibid, p 830.
49 Ibid, p 836.
50 *The Hamtun and St John* [1999] 1 Lloyd's Rep 883.

6.1.3 Effect of danger on a towage contract[51]

The existence of danger is a question of fact. The master's decision that the ship is in danger must be reasonable. If his decision was unreasonable, there would be no danger for salvage, no matter how honestly his decision was made. It is not unusual for danger to arise during performance of a towage contract.

Towage may be converted to salvage (see next chapter) if the circumstances that occurred had not reasonably been contemplated by the parties when they entered into the towage contract.

In *The Aldora*,[52] Brandon J laid down the general principle governing claims for salvage by a pilot engaged to pilot a ship, or a tug engaged to render towage services:

> ... they are only entitled to claim salvage if, first, the ship is in danger by reason of circumstances which could not reasonably have been contemplated by the parties when the engagement to pilot or tow was made, and, secondly, risks are run, or responsibilities undertaken, or duties performed, which could not reasonably be regarded as being within the scope of such engagements. This principle is, in my view, a continuing principle in the sense that, where a salvage situation arises by reason of the existence of the two factors referred to above, it only remains in being so long as those factors continue to exist to some extent at least.[53]

It was standard practice for ships of *The Aldora*'s size to be met at the harbour by a pilot and tugs to help her navigate into her berth. Due to a misunderstanding about the time of her arrival, the tugs and pilot were not yet at the buoy when *The Aldora* arrived. The master of the vessel decided to proceed out to sea again when, due to the master's error, the ship ran aground on a sandbank outside the dredged channel leading to the harbour. Four tugs were engaged to help to refloat her. With the help of these tugs and the ship's own engines, and under the direction of the pilot, the vessel was refloated. Thereafter, she was taken up the channel and into the harbour and to her berth with the help of the pilot and the tugs. The tugowners and crew and the pilot claimed salvage remuneration from the defendants – owners of *The Aldora*. The latter contended that the refloating of the vessel constituted salvage, but the subsequent service of assisting the ship back to the harbour was towage. The pilots and tugowners contended that they were entitled to a salvage award and that the salvage services were completed when the vessel was safely berthed in the harbour.

It was held that *The Aldora* was exposed to dangers which could not reasonably have been contemplated within the scope of the original engagements of the pilot and tugs. But, having refloated her and returned her to the dredged channel, the ship was no longer in any unexpected danger, and the responsibilities of the pilot and tugs were exactly the same as those to be undertaken under their original engagements.

The Convention provides, by Art 17, that no payment is due under the provisions of the Convention unless the services rendered exceed what can be reasonably considered as due performance of a contract entered into before the danger arose.

---

51 See definition and details of towage contracts in Chapter 14, below.
52 [1975] 1 Lloyd's Rep 617.
53 Ibid, p 623.

6.1.4 Threat or danger to the environment

What if there is a threat of damage to a third party? Article 8 of the 1910 Convention considered only the danger run by the salved vessel, her passengers, crew and cargo as a criterion for fixing salvage remuneration. By contrast, Art 13(1)(b) of the 1989 Salvage Convention lists the relevant factors for the assessment of the award, amongst which is 'the skill and efforts of the salvors in preserving or minimising damage to the environment'. Also, Art 14 allows special compensation to salvors who prevent or minimise damage to the environment. The 'safety net'[54] concept of LOF 1980 was very different from the special compensation under Art 14 of the present Convention:

> Damage to the environment means substantial physical damage to human health or to marine life or resources in coastal or inland waters or areas adjacent thereto, caused by pollution, contamination, fire, explosion or similar major incidents. [Art 1(d)]

This aspect of salvage will be considered later (under para 12).

6.2 Voluntary services

'Voluntary' means that the services are not rendered under a pre-existing agreement or under official duty, or purely for the interests of self-preservation. As long as the persons are recognised in law as volunteers and they render salvage services, they are entitled to salvage remuneration. Subject to this rule, there is no limit to the class of persons that can be considered as volunteers. Clarke J in *The Sava Star*[55] said:

> There are no rigid categories of salvor. They include any volunteer who renders services of a salvage nature.

The 1989 Convention does not refer to voluntariness, but states in Art 17 that no payment is due under the Convention unless the services rendered exceed what can be reasonably considered as due performance of a contract entered into before the danger arose.

6.2.1 Pre-existing agreement preventing salvage

This relates to agreements entered into prior to the time of the existence of danger. It includes the ship's master and crew who have pre-existing employment agreements with the shipowner and, therefore, have a duty to preserve the ship and cargo. They cannot convert themselves into salvors,[56] although it is not impossible.

In *The Neptune*,[57] it was held that a salvor is a person who, without any particular relation to a ship in distress, confers useful service and gives it as a volunteer

---

54   See Brice, G, 'Safety net' [1985] 1 LMCLQ 33.

55   [1995] 2 Lloyd's Rep 134, p 141.

56   Contrast the situation in *The Telemachus* [1956] 2 Lloyd's Rep 490, where the master and crew of a ship owned by the same owner as *The Telemachus* received a salvage reward for valuable personal services.

57   (1824) 1 Hagg 227.

adventurer without any pre-existing covenant connected with the duty of employing himself for the preservation of the ship.

Lord Stowell explained:[58]

> ... the crew of a ship cannot be considered as salvors. What is a salvor? A person, who without any particular relation to a ship in distress, proffers useful service, and gives it as a volunteer adventurer without any pre-existing covenant that connected him with the duty of employing himself in the preservation of that ship; not so the crew, whose stipulated duty it is (to be compensated by payment of wages) to protect that ship through all perils, and whose entire possible service for the purpose is pledged to this extent. Accordingly, we see in the numerous salvage cases that come to this court, the crew never claim as joint salvors although they have contributed as much as (and perhaps more than) the volunteer salvors themselves.

In *The North Goodwin (No 16)*, Sheen J said:

> ... the master and crew of *Northsider* were not volunteers in that they were employed to work aboard *Northsider* whenever the tug was rendering towing services as she was on this occasion.[59]

Sometimes, the master of a ship which is facing imminent danger may order the crew to abandon ship to protect their lives. Could the crew be volunteers if they later boarded the ship and saved her from danger?

In *The Albionic*,[60] Lord Greene MR held that the mere order of the master to abandon the ship was not enough to constitute abandonment. Whether or not there had been abandonment, depended on the facts of each individual case. He agreed with the trial judge that, on the facts shown below, the master did not give an order in the ordinary sense of the word, but he gave 'a piece of advice' in a state of panic.

During bad weather and rough sea, the vessel caught fire and was completely out of control. The master shouted for all hands to jump overboard in the lifeboats, which had been made ready to pick them up. Some of the crew and the master did so, but the chief officer, who had now taken control, forbade the rest of the crew from abandoning the ship. Those who remained on board rendered valuable assistance in getting the ship to port and keeping the fire under control. The wireless operator of the ship claimed salvage for the services rendered after half the crew had left the ship. He contended that the circumstances in which they left the ship amounted to abandonment.

Here, there was not complete abandonment but conflicting orders given to the crew by senior officers. It was, therefore, not an order which the men were bound to obey, or by which their contract of service was terminated. The conclusion was that those who remained on the ship did so in the ordinary discharge of their duty and were not entitled to any salvage.

6.2.2 Volunteers in exceptional circumstances

Despite a pre-existing agreement, there are circumstances in which a salvage award may be allowed either because there had been an effective abandonment of the ship

---

58 Ibid, p 236.
59 [1980] 1 Lloyd's Rep 71, p 74.
60 [1942] P 81.

by the crew, or because the circumstances that arose were not contemplated by the parties to a contract. There are also cases in which assistance is rendered in compliance with statutory duties and can qualify for a salvage reward.

6.2.2.1 When there is a reasonable abandonment of the ship by her crew

The San Demetrio [61]

The vessel, S, was proceeding with a convoy from Halifax to a UK port heavily loaded with petrol, when an enemy warship attacked the convoy. The ships in the convoy were hit, some sunk, or left disabled. S was severely damaged and her captain gave orders to abandon the ship. In contrast to the facts of *The Albionic*, the crew in this case left in three boats, one of which was manned by the plaintiffs. S was hit again and burst into flames. Two days later, the plaintiffs' boat, still at sea, spotted S which was still in flames. Everything on her was destroyed except her engines. There were no navigational instruments whatsoever. The plaintiffs got on board, extinguished the fires and, after many days, with the help of tugs, took the vessel to Clyde safely with 10,000 tons of cargo still on the ship. Langton J found that the four requisites laid down by Dr Lushington in *The Florence* [62] to justify a reasonable abandonment of the ship had been fulfilled. The ship was properly abandoned under the orders of her master. (Contrast *The Albionic* above.) It was held that the plaintiffs had rendered a magnificent service and a salvage award was given.

6.2.2.2 When the services rendered by the tug are not contemplated by the towage contract

The obligations of a tug contemplated under a towage contract (see Chapter 14) normally prevent the rise of salvage for the services rendered by the tug to the tow, unless there are exceptional circumstances not contemplated by the contract.

In what circumstances, then, if any, could tugs engaged in towage claim salvage? [63]

Hill J in *The Homewood* [64] outlined the circumstances in which a towage contract can be converted into salvage:

> To constitute a salvage service by a tug under contract to tow two elements are necessary: (1) that the tow is in danger by reason of circumstances which could not reasonably have been contemplated by the parties; and (2) that risks are incurred or duties performed by the tug which could not reasonably be held to be within the scope of the contract. [65]

The following case provides an example of circumstances, which, in the view of the Court of Appeal, did not qualify for salvage.

---

61 (1941) 69 LlL Rep 5.
62 (1852) 16 Jur 572.
63 See *The Aldora* [1975] 1 Lloyd's Rep 617.
64 (1928) 31 LlL Rep 336; see Chapter 14, below, on towage for full facts.
65 Ibid, p 339.

The Texaco Southampton [66]

As a result of a switchboard fire, the defendants' vessel *The Texaco Southampton* was without power and was drifting in a westerly direction. The master of the vessel requested Fenwicks, who were Texaco's sole suppliers of tugs, to place tugs on standby. The tugs were supplied under a towage document. Fenwicks sub-contracted with another company, Wallace Tugs Pty, to place tugs on standby. *The Kembla 11* tug was supplied. *The Texaco* was disabled, and the crew of *The Kembla 11* had little experienced of towing a disabled tanker. Although they were paid wages and overtime allowances for their effort, both the ship and they claimed salvage remuneration. The defendants contended that, since their services had not been voluntary, the plaintiffs were not entitled to salvage remuneration. It was held that the work performed by the plaintiffs did not go outside the scope of their normal duties and exposed them to no risks, which were not within the contemplation of their contract of employment. The fact that the tug had been sub-contracted made no difference to the conclusion.

Article 17 of the Convention provides:

> No payment is due under the provisions of this Convention unless the services rendered exceed what can be reasonably considered as due performance of a contract entered into before the danger arose.

In the above case, the services rendered would probably be considered under the provisions of the Convention as qualifying for salvage (see, for example, a recent decision of Steel in *The tug 'Sea Tractor'*).[67] The same would apply in the following cases concerning pilots.

6.2.2.3 When the services of pilots are exceptional

Pilots are in a different situation but these, too, cannot claim salvage, unless the services rendered were exceptional – that is, not within the normal services expected from the pilot. The following cases show the exceptional circumstances in which such an award can be made.

The Sandefjord [68]

The defendants' motor vessel, *The Sandefjord*, being in charge of a pilot, was stranded on Goodwin Sands after a breakdown of the steering gear. Lifeboats and tugs were standing by. Upon recommendation by the pilot that tugs should not be engaged, a kedge anchor was laid out by lifeboats and the ship was refloated by hauling on the anchor.

Willmer J held, that although the courts would never encourage a pilot (in possible anticipation of big reward) to take undue risks in advising against the use of tugs, in the particular circumstances of this case the pilot took no more than a fair risk as, with tugs standing by, there would still have been time for them to have

---

66 [1983] 1 Lloyd's Rep 94.

67 *The tug 'Sea Tractor', her master, officers and crew v Owners of the ship 'Tramp'* [2007] All ER 88.

68 [1953] 2 Lloyd's Rep 557.

been engaged before the position became critical, and that the pilot was entitled to a substantial award, though not approaching a sum which might have been awarded to tugs had they been employed – salved values £655,500, award £500.

> He brought his personal knowledge of the local conditions and his seafaring skill to bear on the problem created by the grounding of *The Sandefjord*; He gave the master advice (which events proved to be good advice); and he gave one more thing of a rather intangible nature, as to which I have had an opportunity of forming some judgment, having seen him in the witness box: he gave, I have no doubt, a great deal of encouragement to this foreign master, whose ship was stranded in waters with which he was not familiar.[69]

In an exceptional case, *The Akerblom v Price*,[70] Brett LJ put it rhetorically: would a fair owner have insisted in requiring the necessary services for ordinary pilotage fees, or even a higher rate of pilotage payment? Would a fair pilot have refused to perform the necessary services, unless upon the terms of a salvage reward? The question, thus, turned on whether the acts of the pilots, by reason of the weather and the position of the ship, were so different in danger or responsibility from the ordinary acts of service of pilots, so that no fair and reasonable owner would have insisted on requiring such service for other than a salvage award. The rule of law was held to be as follows:

> ... in order to entitle a pilot to salvage reward he must not only shew that the ship is in some sense in distress, but that she was in such distress as to be in danger of being lost, and such as to call upon him to run such unusual danger or incur such unusual responsibility, or exercise such unusual skill, or perform such an unusual kind of service, as to make it unfair and unjust that he should be paid otherwise than upon the terms of salvage reward.[71]

The vessel in this case was driven by the violence of the wind and sea to dangerous sands. The locality was strange both to her captain and crew, and therefore she was in danger of being lost. Seeing the peril, the pilots put to sea to assist her. By preceding and signalling to her, they led her to a safe anchorage in the bay. The question put to the Court of Appeal was whether the amount paid to the pilots was only for pilotage services, or was it to be treated as payment for salvage services.

It was held that the payment to the pilots ought to be considered as payment for salvage.

Another good example of a pilot rendering exemplary salvage services is *The Hudson Light*.[72] While the ship was lying at anchor, there was a strong ebb tide and, shortly before evening hours, she began to drag her anchor under the influence of the tide. Despite attempts to combat the drag, she continued to move down river and eventually went aground. Efforts to refloat her with her engines were unsuccessful. Tug assistance was called, and in response, five tugs came to her rescue, but were unable to move her as she was aground on the bottom of sand and gravel covered by a thick layer of mud. A pilot was requested and he took charge of

---

69   Ibid, p 561.
70   (1881) 7 QBD 129.
71   (1881) 7 QBD 129, p 135, per Brett LJ.
72   [1970] 1 Lloyd's Rep 166.

the operations for refloating the ship, giving instructions to each of the tugs. He displayed a very considerable degree of skill both in planning and executing the refloating operation. The ship was eventually refloated and safely moored at a buoy, at about midnight. The pilot claimed a salvage reward for his services contending that a high degree of skill and care was needed bearing in mind especially the congested area of the operation. The defendants, rejecting the claim, argued that only ordinary skill and care were needed and that the method to be used for refloating the vessel was obvious.

It was held that, not only did the pilot display considerable skill, but the responsibility which he undertook in rendering the services and running the risks involved was commendable. He was entitled to salvage reward. It was also held that, in assessing the reward, it was necessary to consider the merits of the contribution made by him to what were in effect joint services rendered by the tugs and him.

6.2.2.4 Could cargo-owners claim a salvage award for services rendered?

Prior to *The Sava Star*,[73] there had been no authority that the owners of cargo on board a ship in need of salvage, who render assistance and advice as to how a particular cargo on board should be handled and, therefore, contribute in the salvage of ship and cargo, could claim salvage. The issue before the court was whether or not cargo-owners should be entitled to a salvage award; the owners of the salved ship argued that they should not, since their services were rendered out of self-interest or for self-preservation.

This interesting point was dealt with by Clarke J (as he then was) as a preliminary issue, and it deserves drawing attention to the particular facts of the case.

The plaintiffs were the owners of complex fertiliser NPK in bulk, which was being carried on board the defendants' vessel, *The Sava Star*, from Heroya in Norway to Immingham in England. The charterers of the vessel under the voyage charterparty were the plaintiffs' parent company.

The master noticed smoke and gas escaping from the holds. On finding that the cargo was decomposing, the master called the charterers who gave practical advice over the telephone regarding cooling of the cargo. The master had further contact with the charterers overnight. The decomposing cargo could not be discharged overboard. The plaintiffs were informed of the incident and, thereafter, they initiated a crisis plan which included, inter alia, contacting the Humberside Fire Brigade, arranging a helicopter overnight to make an inspection, constructing fire lances and providing chemists to take gas tests on the north and south banks of the Humber.

The plaintiffs' general manager gave advice to the dock master at Hull and to the Skuld P&I surveyor. United Towing Ltd (they later became contractors under Lloyd's Form of Salvage Agreement) were informed of the casualty and decided to mobilise one fire-fighting tug. The contractor's tug departed carrying eight firemen, the plaintiffs' technical manager (Mr Martin) and their chief fire fighting officer (Mr Hay), together with specialised fire-fighting equipment provided by the plaintiffs. A meeting took place on board the contractors' tug and the plaintiffs' representatives advised on the use of fire lances and the need to avoid breathing the

---

73 [1995] 2 Lloyd's Rep 134.

fumes released by the burning cargo. After preparations and briefings, the crew of *The Sava Star* and Mr Hay, directed by the salvage master fought the decomposition using water lances and thermocouples provided by the plaintiffs.

In consultation with the salvage master, Mr Martin and Mr Hay recommended that one of the two fire-fighting tugs use their fire monitors to set up a water curtain in an attempt to knock the fumes down to the sea water so that some of the noxious gases might be absorbed. Mr Martin and Mr Hay also identified that the fire monitor might be used to cut through the encrusted product and reach the seat of decomposition. The fire-fighting team monitored the condition of the cargo overnight with the salvage master and Mr Hay, extinguishing one instance of decomposition. The salvage of vessel and cargo was completed within two days and the plaintiffs claimed salvage remuneration, although, admittedly, cargo-owners had not historically claimed salvage, presumably because the occasion had not arisen.

The defendants contended that neither principle nor authority supported the proposition that cargo-owners were or should be permitted to claim salvage from owners of the ship carrying the cargo. Cargo-owners were not within the recognised categories of salvor and they were bound up in the maritime adventure with the shipowners; as such they owed a duty to render such assistance as they could to salve ship and cargo. Further, or alternatively, a cargo-owner who rendered what would otherwise be salvage service acted in self preservation of his own property and as such ought not to be treated as a volunteer. Considerations of public policy pointed to the exclusion of cargo-owners as salvors.

Clarke J held that the submission that cargo-owners were not volunteers would be rejected and stated that the reason why persons with contractual duties or persons like the master and crew of the ship cannot recover salvage award is because they are performing services ordinarily to be expected of them.

He reviewed the principles of cases with regard to salvage services rendered to sister ships, where the owner of the salving tug and the owner of the salved are the same, and salvage had still been rewarded against both the salved ship and the cargo on board her. The judge concluded, thus:

> I have reached the clear conclusion that there is no reason based in principle or authority why cargo-owners should not be able to claim salvage from shipowners in an appropriate case. Considerations of public policy support that conclusion. Moreover, I doubt whether this conclusion will open any floodgate. In any event, cargo-owners may now be able to render valuable salvage services in circumstances where they would not have been able to do so in the past. For example, a large oil company might own tugs or tankers. I can see no reason why salvage services rendered by such tugs or tankers should not attract a salvage award from the owner of the salved ship. In order to qualify, the services would have to be in the nature of salvage services and voluntary in the sense that they were not rendered pursuant to a duty owed to the shipowners and not part of what might ordinarily be expected of a cargo-owner such as providing advice about the characteristics of the cargo. For these reasons, my answer to the question posed at the outset, namely whether on the assumed facts the plaintiffs are entitled to salvage remuneration from the defendant shipowners, is in the affirmative.[74]

---

74   [1995] 2 Lloyd's Rep 134, p 144.

Although the facts of this case were unusual, there might be occasions when a chemical cargo on board necessitates special expertise for handling it by the provider, the shipper, but the terms of the bill of lading or charterparty ought to be checked, in case the shipper has an obligation under contract to assist.[75]

6.2.3 Duties arising under statute or official duty and salvage entitlement

6.2.3.1 Duty to assist after a collision

It has been discussed in Chapter 12 that the MSA 1894, s 422, now replaced by s 92 of the MSA 1995, imposes a duty upon the master of a ship involved in a collision to stand by and render assistance after the collision. Failure to comply with such a duty without reasonable excuse is a criminal offence: s 92(4).[76] The issue whether compliance with such a duty bars the mariners from claiming salvage award was for the first time considered by the House of Lords in the following case.

The Melanie v The San Onofre[77]

In a collision between S and M in the Bristol Channel, on a foggy morning in December 1916, S struck M on her starboard side and made a large hole in her, with the result that the engine room and one of the holds filled with water. The master of M – believing that he was in immediate danger of sinking – boarded S with most of his crew. The rest of the crew boarded U, an armed steam trawler which was escorting S. As M did not sink, the master of S proposed, with the assistance of U, to tow her to Barry, and the crew of M returned to her, lashed her to S on the starboard side and to U on the port side. After towing for three-quarters of an hour, all three vessels accidentally grounded on a ledge of rocks near the shore. S and U got off soon after and left M on the rocks. When the tide fell, the water in M drained out of her, and the master, by closing a watertight door between the hold and the engine room, was able to prevent the water coming into the hold. Both S and M were badly damaged by the grounding. M was successfully towed to Barry by two tugs on the following day.

A series of litigation resulted from the incident. First, it was found in the collision action that M was solely to blame for the collision. Later, this action was brought by the owners of S claiming salvage against M, which was disputed on the ground that M was left abandoned on the rocks after the grounding and, thus, in a greater danger than she was originally. In any event, she was ultimately saved by other tugs.

Bailhache J, acting on the advice of his assessors, decided that the towage had not materially contributed to the ultimate safety of M and dismissed the claim, but the Court of Appeal, on the advice of their assessors, came to the contrary conclusion.

---

75   See Commentary on Current Statutes, the MSA, Chapter 21, Art 17 of the Convention.
76   See Chapter 12.
77   [1925] AC 246 (HL).

The House of Lords reversed the Court of Appeal and restored the judge's decision on the ground that the services rendered were not meritorious.[78]

Lord Phillimore stated, on the point of the duty of mariners to assist after a collision:

> This is, I believe, the first opportunity which this House has had of pronouncing upon a question which has, I imagine, long been treated as settled in the courts below. Ever since the judgment of Sir Robert Phillimore in *The Hannibal* and *The Queen* accepted, I think, in the Privy Council, though there was another ground on which the decision was confirmed – it has been taken as law that the duty cast by the MSAs upon one of the two colliding vessels to stand by and render assistance does not prevent that vessel, if she renders assistance, from claiming salvage. That particular judgment was given upon the construction of the MSA of 1862; but there is no material difference in the section which must govern this case. I am glad that your Lordships have the opportunity of giving your adhesion to this doctrine.[79]

Even when the fault of the vessel, which stands by after the collision, was causative of the collision, that might not prevent her from earning salvage.[80]

6.2.3.2 Duty to assist others in distress

In addition to the statutory duty to stand by after a collision, there has also been a duty upon masters of ships to help others being in distress or danger at sea. This was first imposed by Art 11 of the Brussels Convention 1910. The provision was enacted into English law by s 6 of the MCA 1911, which was replaced by the MS(SP)A 1994 (Sched 2, para 2). It is now found in the consolidating statute, s 93 of the MSA 1995.

Article 10 of the Salvage Convention 1989 reinforces that duty by providing that every master is bound, so far as he can do so without serious danger to his vessel and persons thereon, to render assistance to any person in danger or being lost at sea. State parties shall adopt measures to enforce that duty; but the owner of the vessel shall incur no liability for a breach of the duty by the master of his ship.

By s 93,[81] a master of a ship is obliged to give assistance to persons in distress, upon receiving information that a ship or aircraft is in distress, and failure to do so is a criminal offence (s 93(6) and Sched 11, Pt II, para 3 of the MSA 1995).

However, it has expressly been stated in s 93(7), and in its predecessor, that compliance with this provision shall not affect his right, or the right of any other person, to salvage. An example is provided by the following decision.

The Tower Bridge [82]

The *TB* got into an ice field and she was totally surrounded by a pack of ice, being in a very dangerous situation with the possibility of sinking. An SOS message was

---

78 See para 6.3, below.
79 [1925] AC 246, p 262.
80 See *The Kafiristan* [1938] AC 136, at para 9.3, below.
81 Previously, the Merchant Shipping (Safety Convention) Act 1949, s 22 (repealed).
82 [1936] P 30.

sent out and *The Newfoundland* (N) hastened to her assistance. She had just contrived to get out of the ice herself earlier on. It was, however, found that the *TB* was not in so desperate a position as it had seemed, and by the time the *N* came in sight of the *TB*, she had managed to get things under control to an extent. The *TB*, thus, requested that the *N* merely stand by and see the *TB* into port. The captain of the *N* thought this was unnecessary, and intimated that he was not ready to stand by, indefinitely. Instead, he gave the chief officer of the *TB* definite information on what to do to get into clear water. In compliance with the advice, the *TB* got out of the ice field. It was held that a very material service was rendered by the *N*. One of the arguments put forward by the *TB* was that the master had not, in fact, rendered any salvage service as he was only complying with his duty under the statute. It was held that the provision of the then Merchant Shipping (Safety and Load Line Conventions) Act 1932 clearly stated that compliance by the master with the provisions of this section shall not affect his right, or the right of any other person, to salvage.

6.2.3.3 *Salvage by officers under orders of a naval commander of the Royal Navy*

Confusion may arise as to whether salvage is earned when the services are rendered under orders of a naval commander, which are rendered under an official duty. Exclusion from salvage would arise if the duty were owed to the vessel to be salved[83] and not when the duty was to obey orders of a naval commander. The test of voluntariness in these situations was laid down in *The Sarpen*:[84]

> The test of voluntariness is only applicable between salvor and salved, and if the services are voluntary in relation to the salved, that is, not rendered by reason of an obligation towards him, it is quite immaterial that the salvor has been ordered by someone who has control of his movements to render them.

Prior to 1947, officers of the Royal Navy were regarded as being under a duty by standing orders to carry out salvage services. The courts did not favour claims by them for salvage, but only for special services rendered of substantial importance at personal risk outside their normal duties.

Since s 8(2) of the Crown Proceedings Act (CPA) 1947, there has been no bar on claims for salvage by or against the Crown in relation to services in the nature of salvage rendered by or to the Royal Navy. This position has been confirmed and clarified by s 230(1), (2) of the MSA 1995. Save for the exclusion of *in rem* proceedings against the Crown, salvage claims against or by Her Majesty's ships shall be subject to the same law as with respect to any other private person. However, s 230(3) provides that no claim for salvage by the commander or crew of any HMS vessel shall be finally adjudicated upon without the consent of the Secretary of State.

> In *The American Farmer*[85] the crew of an RAF aircraft was awarded salvage, although the services were not considered meritorious because the ship in danger would have

---

83   In *The Carrie* [1917] PDA 224, the crew of two HM trawlers claimed salvage successfully for saving cargo of munitions belonging to the allies from a German submarine, which was about to sink the carrying ship. Although they had a duty to the allies, they did not owe an official duty to the ship itself.

84   [1916] P 306, p 315.

85   (1947) 80 LlL Rep 672.

been found by the other tugs sent for help, nevertheless, the action to send an aircraft across was not a usual risk to be taken by Royal Air Force planes.

6.2.3.4 Salvage operations controlled by public authorities

Article 5 of the Salvage Convention, Sched 11, Pt I of the MSA 1995, states that the Convention shall not affect any provisions of national laws or any international convention relating to salvage operations by or under the control of public authorities (Art 5(1)). The extent to which a public authority under a duty to perform salvage operations may avail itself of the rights and remedies provided for in this Convention shall be determined by the law of the State where such authority is situated (Art 5(3)). For example, English law by statute forbids a Fire Brigade Authority, which may assist in fire fighting in salvage, to charge for its services (s 3(4) of the Fire Services Act 1947).

The port authorities perform various duties under statute. For example, s 252 of the MSA 1995 (replacing s 530 of the MSA 1894) gives the harbour authority the power to remove any vessel sunk, stranded or abandoned in water under the control of the harbour authority, where the vessel is likely to be or is an obstruction or danger to navigation. Harbour authorities have a common law duty to ensure that the harbour is safe for navigation. The authorities also have a statutory charge for recovering their expenses in respect of the removal of wrecks. They may not be entitled to salvage remuneration unless they did more than what is expected of them under their statutory power.

The Gregerso[86] The ship grounded in port obstructing navigation to and from the port. She called for assistance and a tug of the port authority was sent. The dock and harbour masters had to spend the whole night on board her because the tug could not free the ship by towage that night as the tide had fallen. In the morning, when the tide was higher, the vessel was freed without much difficulty. The tug rendered further assistance by getting her a short distance down the river to a position where she could proceed safely on her own. The port authority, the dock and harbour masters and the master and crew of the tug claimed salvage from the owners of the ship.

It was held that it was in the interest of the port to clear the channel from the obstruction created by the casualty. The authority and its employees were not entitled to salvage because their services were not voluntary but in discharge of duties. The corporation owed a duty to all users of the port and to the owners of this ship, which duties could only be performed through its employees. Considering the circumstances, there was nothing exceptional in terms of difficulty or danger in the work done by their tug. It was also held that the port authority, when exercising its statutory powers, had no power to deal with the situation by entering into an LOF contract to salve the vessel.

However, Brandon J made an obiter observation that nothing in his judgment was intended to throw doubt on the power or the right of a port authority or its servants to recover salvage for assisting a vessel in situations which did not call for the exercise by the authority of its statutory power of removal of wrecks. This was

---

86 [1971] 1 All ER 961.

relied upon by the South African court in *The Mbashi*,[87] in which salvage remuneration was granted to the port authority which sent two of its tugs to a ship in great distress, having lost all its power after a fire on board. Article 5 of the Convention was relied upon, and the court referred to English decisions.

In the English court, a salvage claim was successful in the circumstances of *The Mars*.[88]

This was a salvage claim by three employees of the Port of London Authority, the crew of *The Boy Mark*, a motor patrol vessel, who claimed to have rendered salvage services to 11 drifting dumb barges in Northfleet Hope, River Thames. The barge owners contended that the services were rendered in the ordinary course of the claimants' employment by the Authority, to whom the barge owners had paid a sum for the services, and that, therefore, there could be no claim for salvage.

It was held that the mere existence of the statutory duty imposed by statute upon the Port of London Authority did not, of itself, automatically exclude the possibility of a claim for salvage, and that where, as here, the claimants rendered services which went beyond their ordinary every day duties as servants of the Port of London Authority, they were entitled to an award; the claim being in respect of personal services, the award would be small.

In a recent interesting example, *The Star Maria*,[89] one harbour authority tug engaged under LOF was unable to assist in rough weather *The Star Maria*, which had suffered damage to her steering gear after a collision; subsequently, a chartered tug by the coastguard engaged also under LOF, sought the assistance of another tug belonging to the harbour to assist in the task of bringing the casualty into the harbour. This engagement was understood to be a towing service, which was expected to be remunerated on the terms of the board's commercial tariff rate. Due to the great difficulties in the bad weather conditions, the towage connection with the coastguard tug parted and the casualty was in danger of grounding. The captain of the harbour tug exerted great skill and effort to prevent grounding, which was not a risk reasonably foreseeable when the tug was instructed to assist. The risks incurred and duties performed during this period could not be reasonably held to be within the scope of her contractual duty to act as a steering tug, and therefore it was entitled to salvage under common law. The original LOF between the first harbour authority tug and the master of the casualty had been terminated.

6.2.3.5 Salvage operations and HM coastguards

Section 250 of the MSA 1995 provides for the remuneration of coastguards for services rendered in watching or protecting property at sea, payable by the owner of the property on a scale fixed by the Secretary of State. Being part of the marine division of the Department of Environment and Transport, they perform a public duty and are, therefore, unlikely to be able to claim salvage award, unless they render services far and above those duties expected of them. However, the owners

---

87 [2002] 2 Lloyd's Rep 602.
88 (1948) 81 LlL Rep 452.
89 [2003] 1 Lloyd's Rep 183.

of tugs chartered to the coastguard as emergency towing vessels can enter into a salvage agreement with the casualty's master.[90]

6.2.3.6 Salvage by lifeboat crews of the RNLI

The duty of a lifeboat crew is to go out and save lives and the RNLI rewards them on a scale basis provided they make no claim for salvage. The RNLI is supported by voluntary contributions. Lifeboat crew are not supposed to render services to save property, if other vessels are on the spot. If no other vessel is standing by, then the crew may accept salvage engagement whereupon they become hirers of the lifeboat and, if they succeed, they must pay to the RNLI expenses incurred in respect of the boat in accordance with the RNLI's regulations.

A good example of the courts' attitude towards lifeboat crews is provided in the decision of Hewson J, in *The Viscount*.[91]

Services were rendered by a crew member of the RNLI lifeboat *Henry Blogg* to the defendants' motor vessel, *The Viscount*, which ran aground on the Norfolk coast. *Henry Blogg* arrived at 10.00 hours and stood by until the tide began to make, when she went along the starboard side of *The Viscount*. While she was manoeuvring on to *The Viscount*'s port quarter, a carton of 200 cigarettes was thrown on board from *The Viscount*. *Henry Blogg* was asked to come back and take a rope in an hour, but as the tide was setting strongly to the SE, the lifeboat crew insisted on taking the rope then (15.15 hours). *The Viscount* was refloated in a few minutes. A claim was made for salvage award, but *The Viscount* denied that *Henry Blogg* rendered any material assistance and contended that the plaintiffs agreed to render any assistance necessary for 200 cigarettes. The salved values were not insignificant.

Hewson J held that, although there was little danger, *Henry Blogg* acted as an 'animated drogue' in helping to hold up *The Viscount*'s stern against the flood tide, and those services were rendered at the critical few minutes between the time she became lively and the time she went astern into deep water; that cigarettes were not accepted as prepayment for assistance which was requested; and that, therefore, the plaintiffs were entitled to salvage award of £250. The judge added a general comment:

> In making this award I want to make it quite clear that the primary duty of lifeboat-men manning lifeboats owned by the RNLI is the saving of life. It must be clearly understood that in the course of standing by to save life this court is giving no encouragement to lifeboatmen to get a line on board a disabled vessel at all costs; but, nevertheless, they must be encouraged to stand by and to give such assistance, without unduly risking their craft, when necessary.[92]

The weight of judicial opinion with regard to crews of RNLI lifeboats has been to favour an award for personal risk, local knowledge and highly meritorious

---

90 *The Star Maria* [2003] 1 Lloyd's Rep 183, in which, apart from two harbour tugs engaged in salvage, a chartered tug to the coastguard was also engaged under LOF.
91 [1966] 1 Lloyd's Rep 328.
92 [1966] 1 Lloyd's Rep 328, p 333.

services by those men, for which they should be rewarded for future encouragement.[93]

6.3 Success

Having dealt with the first and second elements of salvage, ie voluntariness and danger, the third element is that the services must either succeed in, or contribute to the success of, saving the property.

6.3.1 Meritorious services

Without success or meritorious services, there will be no award. The cause of action of salvage, which is available in the Admiralty Court, is quite distinct from a *quantum meruit* available in the common law courts.

The principle was laid down by Dr Lushington in *The India*:[94]

> ... unless the salvors by their services conferred actual benefit on the salved property, they are not entitled to salvage remuneration.

Article 12 of Sched 11 to the consolidating MSA 1995 provides that a salvor will be entitled to a reward if the salvage operations had a useful result. The exception to this is contained in Art 14, which gives salvors the right to recover special compensation for salvage services rendered to a vessel, or its cargo, when by itself or its cargo threatened damage to the environment.[95]

Lord Diplock in *The Tojo Maru*[96] examined certain characteristics of salvage contracts which differentiate them from ordinary contracts for work and labour:

> The first distinctive feature is that the person rendering the salvage services is not entitled to any remuneration unless he saves the property in whole or in part. This is what is meant by 'success' in cases about salvage.[97]

The following examples illustrate what would not amount to 'success'. If, after the service is actually rendered, the ship is in as grave a danger as it was originally, then no award will be given. Also, services which rescue a vessel from one danger but end by leaving her in a position of as great, or nearly as great, a danger, though of a different kind, are held not to contribute to the ultimate success and are not entitled to salvage reward.

The Cheerful[98]

On her way from London to Liverpool, *The Cheerful* (C) lost her propeller in the English Channel. The *H* came to her rescue and proceeded to tow her to port when

---

93   *The Boston Lincoln* [1980] 1 Lloyd's Rep 481; *The Africa Occidental* [1951] 2 Lloyd's Rep 107; *The Geertjie K* [1971] 1 Lloyd's Rep 285.

94   (1842) 1 Wm Rob 406.

95   See, later, para 12.

96   [1972] AC 242 (HL).

97   Ibid, p 293.

98   (1855) 11 PD 3.

both the hawsers parted and C got into a position of considerable danger in adverse weather conditions. In an attempt to get the hawser on board again, H got out of command, became unmanageable and eventually collided with C, causing damage to both vessels. Eventually, H left C, as she was in danger herself. Two tugs finally came to the assistance of C and towed her to Portland roads in safety. H claimed salvage alleging that, at the time she came to C's rescue, the weather was bad, that there was a heavy sea with squalls and gale and that C was in danger of going on to the coast and becoming a total wreck if no vessel had come to her rescue. The owners of C argued that she was in no immediate danger and that H had by her actions left C in a worse position than she was originally and should not be awarded salvage. They also counterclaimed for damages for the injury done to C as a result of the negligence of H at the time they were attempting to get the hawser on board again. Since no actual benefit was conferred on C by the services of H, no salvage was awarded. In the opinion of the Elder Brethren, however, H was not negligent in her actions or omissions, therefore, the counterclaim for injury to C due to H's negligence failed.

In *The Melanie v The San Onofre*,[99] the defendants claimed that the plaintiffs had left M in a position of greater comparative danger than she was in before S began to tow her, and, therefore, no salvage was due. It was held that services which rescue a vessel from one danger, but end by leaving her in a position of as great, or nearly, as great danger, though of another kind, do not contribute to the ultimate success and do not amount to salvage. The mere fact that the claimant has brought the ship to a position or spot where the ultimate salvor has found her does not of itself show that bringing her to that spot was a contribution to the ultimate success.

Where many vessels were involved in the salvage operation of a ship, only those vessels that could be considered as having 'materially assisted' the rescue of the ship or cargo would be entitled to any salvage reward.

In *The Killeena*,[100] Sir Robert Phillimore quoted a passage from *The Undaunted* (1860) Lush 90, which summarises the principles of law applicable to the question whether *The Nora* in this case was entitled to a salvage reward:

> Salvors who volunteer, go out at their own risk for the chance of earning reward, and if they labour unsuccessfully, are entitled to nothing. The effectual performance of salvage service is that which gives them a title to salvage remuneration. But if men are engaged by a ship in distress, whether generally or particularly, they are to be paid according to their efforts made, even though the labour and service may not prove beneficial to the vessel.

The Killeena had been abandoned by her master and crew during a heavy gale which affected the vessel badly. She drifted about in the Atlantic till she was sighted by *The Nora*, a Norwegian vessel. The crew of *The Nora* boarded *The Killeena* until they became frightened. They decided to abandon the vessel and hoisted an ensign union down. This attracted the attention of those on board *The Beatrice*, which, with the assistance of another tug, brought *The Killeena* into Falmouth. The court held that the master and crew of *The Nora* were not entitled to any salvage reward.

---

99 [1925] AC 246, see para 6.2.3.1 for a summary of the facts.
100 (1881) 6 PD 193.

Sir Robert Phillimore added:[101]

> Now, there is no doubt that where a set of salvors have done some acts which tend to
> the ultimate salvage of a vessel they are usually entitled to some remuneration, but
> there is a circumstance in this case most material to consider. The four men and the
> boy who were put on board from *The Nora* . . . abandoned and deserted *The Killeena*.
> It appears to me, therefore, that *The Killeena* was again a derelict vessel. . . . It appears
> to me that it would be contrary to the principles upon which salvage remuneration is
> awarded, to allow *The Nora's* people to appear as salvors in this case, inasmuch as
> they were, according to the evidence, turning their backs and running away from the
> danger to which the vessel was exposed. The men from on board *The Beatrice* had as
> much reason to be alarmed, but they persevered, and their courage deserves to be
> rewarded. I am clearly of opinion that the owners, master, and crew of *The Nora* are
> not entitled to claim salvage.

6.3.2 Salvage services by standing by a vessel in danger

Meritorious services can also be rendered merely by standing by as long as the
property is ultimately saved.

In **The Tower Bridge**,[102] it was held that the N rendered most valuable assistance
in showing the *TB* how to get out of the ice field. It was not necessary to define the
precise moment at which the service began or to quantify the moral support
afforded to the *TB* when the only available ship in the North Atlantic came plough-
ing her way through the ice. Each separate item of the proceedings could not be
regarded in isolation. The whole of the circumstances that existed at the time must
be looked at.

6.3.3 Salvage and engaged services

Before the emergence of sophisticated salvage agreements, there used to be salvage
services rendered at request – as contrasted with volunteer salvors – and, even if
there was no contribution to success, there would be salvage remuneration, as an
exception to the general rule that the right to salvage accrues only upon success.
That exception was affirmed by Dr Lushington, in **The Undaunted**:[103]

> There is a broad distinction between salvors who volunteer to go out, and salvors
> who are employed by as ship in distress. Salvors who volunteer, go out at their own
> risk for the chance of earning reward, and if they labour unsuccessfully, they are
> entitled to nothing; the effectual performance of salvage service is that which gives
> them a title to salvage remuneration. But if men are engaged by a ship in distress,
> whether generally or particularly, they are to be paid according to their efforts made,
> even though the labour and service may not prove beneficial to the vessel. Take the
> case of a vessel at anchor in a gale of wind, hailing a steamer to lie by and be ready to
> take her in tow if required; the steamer does so, the ship rides out of the gale safely
> without the assistance of the steamer: I should undoubtedly hold in such a case that
> the steamer was entitled to salvage reward . . .

---

101 (1881) 6 PD 193, p 198.
102 [1936] P 30, see para 6.2.3.2, above.
103 (1860) Lush 90, p 92.

A later example of engaged services was seen in *The Alenquer and Rene.*[104] *The Alenquer*, having done the thing she was asked to do by *The Rene* (that is, to respond to a distress signal and stand by *The Rene*), would have been entitled to an award, had it not been for her negligence which deprived her right to it.

There have been a few other cases in which salvage was awarded on those bases, but, in modern times of salvage requirements and facilities available, such services will either be covered by a specific agreement for towage or salvage, or will be considered as salvage operations falling within the definition of Art 1(a) of the Convention.

7 SALVAGE AGREEMENTS

7.1 General

Ordinary salvage arises out of the fact that aid has been given voluntarily at the time of danger and if there has been benefit to the subject of salvage from the services rendered to the subject matter, an award will be made. There is no need for an actual contract between the parties. Unless the parties expressly agree to contract out of the Act, all salvage operations will be governed by the statute (Art 6(1) of Sched 11 to the MSA 1995).

If the services were already rendered prior to any agreement, a subsequent agreement will cover only future action. The salvor has vested rights prior to the agreement.[105]

Similarly, the Convention and the 1995 Act protect salvors in respect of any salvage operations with a useful result (Art 12).

Formal salvage agreements came to be used in the late 19th century, with the first standardised form dated 1892, on the basis of 'no cure no pay'. Professional salvors render services under an agreement entered into at the time of danger. These agreements are made on the 'no cure no pay' basis, on the Lloyd's (of London) Open Form (LOF), and the remuneration is fixed by arbitration. The parties to the agreement retain their common law rights. There have been a series of LOFs over the years: after the LOF 1980 and since the Salvage Convention, the forms commonly in use have been the 1990 and 1995; in recent years, there is the LOF 2000, which became operational in September 2000 (see para 15, below).

Both the 1990 and 1995 forms were long, including procedural rules about the conduct of arbitration, and incorporated most articles of the Convention, either directly or by reference. By contrast, LOF 2000 is made simple and contains only the most essential terms, corresponding to LOF 1995, in one sheet excluding the procedural provisions, which are separately provided in the Lloyd's Standard Salvage and Arbitration Clauses and are incorporated by reference.

As will be seen later, problems of salvors' compensation for protecting the

---

104 [1955] 1 Lloyd's Rep 101.
105 See *The Inchmaree* [1899] P 111, pp 116–17.

environment from pollution which arose from difficulties in the interpretation of Art 14 of the Convention (see under paras 12 and 13, below) led to commercial pressure being exerted by the salvage community for improvement of the wording of Art 14. After consultation and negotiations between the International Salvage Union, property underwriters and P&I clubs, there has been the birth of a new clause, known as the SCOPIC (Special Compensation of Protection and Indemnity Clause) (see under para 14, below). This, in fact, is a form of guaranteed remuneration to salvors for protecting the environment, payable by the P&I club of the shipowners whose vessel needs salvage, to encourage the salvor to proceed to a casualty, whether or not there is a threat of damage to the environment. It can be incorporated into any LOF, if the salvors so choose (of which see later). The previous LOFs may still be used if the parties so desire.]

Unless the parties wish to contract out of some of the provisions of the Convention, or, as far as English law is concerned, the provisions of the MSA 1995, which incorporates the 1989 Salvage Convention, the Convention shall apply. If there is no contract, the rules of the Convention shall apply to all salvage operations, save where the law applicable to a salvage operation is of a State that has not ratified the Convention.

The contract is for supply of services. Therefore, the Supply of Goods and Services Act 1982, ss 13–16 would apply, particularly regarding implied terms concerning reasonable care and skill, to provide a tug fit for the purpose and complete the services within a reasonable time.]

The Unfair Contract Terms Act 1977, apart from s 2(1) regarding no exclusion of liability for death or personal injury, has no application to marine salvage contracts, but there is an exception in case the owner of the salved property is dealing as a consumer, and this could arise if there is a salvage of a private yacht.

There may be salvage agreements with fixed amounts for specific services, as mentioned earlier; but, with the passing of the Salvage Convention, the scope of these contracts has been limited. If the amount is not agreed upon, the remuneration will be adjudged by the court, which has jurisdiction under s 20(2)(j) of the SCA 1981. [There is, however, a lump sum agreement, the 'Salvom' International Salvage Union Agreement, with detailed clauses about the parties' rights and obligations.

7.2 Court's intervention

Unlike ordinary contracts under English law, the courts can re-open salvage contracts, even in the absence of economic duress, misrepresentation or operative mistake. This is more common where the contracts are fixed-sum salvage agreements, where the courts may intervene to determine the rate of remuneration.[106]

The 1989 Convention, Art 7, provides that a contract may be annulled or modified if it has been entered into under undue influence or the influence of danger and

---

106 See, eg, *The Mark Lane* (1890) 15 PD 135; *The Crusader* [1907] P 15; *The Westbourne* (1889) 14 PD 132.

its terms are inequitable, or if the payment under the contract is in an excessive degree, too large or too small, for the services actually rendered.

The LOF 2000 expressly prohibits undue influence prior to entering into the agreement.

Common law principles will apply to such situations, and examples of economic duress, misrepresentation and mistake are shown below.

7.2.1 Economic duress, or overbearing conduct by the salvor

Both at common law and in equity, a party cannot be held to its contract if its consent has been obtained by unjustified threats, or duress. The Privy Council, in *Pao On v Lau Yiu Long*,[107] held that duress is a coercion of the will so as to vitiate consent, but commercial pressure is not enough to do so. Material questions for the inquiry of the existence of coercion will be whether or not: (i) the innocent party protested; (ii) he had an alternative course open to him; (iii) he was independently advised; and (iv) he took steps to avoid the contract after having entered into it.

In *Huyton SA v Peter Cremer*,[108] the court, reviewing the authorities on economic duress, stated that it was the deflection rather than the coercion of the will of the innocent party that the court will be looking for, in considering whether the contract is voidable. The illegitimate pressure must be a significant cause, which must have induced the innocent party to enter into the contract, but the court will take into account other possible choices available to the victim and assess them objectively.

In salvage contracts, it is in the nature of salvage that agreements have to be entered into quickly and under pressure because of the danger to the property involved, and there will be very rare cases in which the master of the property in danger has other courses open to him, or even time to take independent advice.

On the other hand, the fact that there is not equal bargaining power, or the fact that the parties to an agreement for salvage services about to be performed on the high seas have not contracted on equal terms, will not in itself invalidate such an agreement; but if, in addition to the master of the vessel about to be salved being at a disadvantage, the sum insisted upon by the intending salvor is, in the opinion of the court, exorbitant, the necessary elements exist for setting aside the agreement as inequitable.[109]

The Port of Caledonia [110]

When *The Port of Caledonia* (POC) was in great difficulty during a southwesterly gale, her anchor was dragging towards another ship, the *A*. Both were heading to the wind, were fully exposed to the ground swell and in danger of fouling one

---

107 *Pao On v Lau Yiu Long* [1980] AC 614 (PC); see also *Occidental Worldwide Investment Corp v Skibs A/S Avanti* [1976] 1 Lloyd's Rep 293; *North Ocean Shipping Ltd v Hyundai Construction Co Ltd* [1979] 1 QB 705; and *Universe Tankships Inc of Monrovia v ITWF* [1983] 1 AC 366 (HL) see also Ch 10 para 9.2.

108 [1999] 1 Lloyd's Rep 620.

109 *The Rialto* [1891] P 175.

110 [1903] P 184.

another. The master of POC called for a tug and pilot and the *S*, being close by, responded to the signal asking '£1000' for the service. When the master of POC offered to pay £100, the master of *S* rejected the smaller offer, whereupon the master of POC, being in great difficulty, accepted to pay the greater amount and hailed *S* to take the tow. *S* towed POC to a safe berth and claimed the sum of £1000, as well as a reasonable sum for salvage from *A*. The learned judge considered the value of the services to be less than £1000, and the question was whether the bargain was so inequitable and unreasonable that the court could not allow it to stand. It was held that, as one party was in a position to insist upon his terms, and the other party had to put up with it being in a desperate situation, the agreement was inequitable, extortionate and unreasonable.

7.2.2 *Misrepresentation and non-disclosure*

The general principles of common law and statute will apply, if either party to the agreement has misrepresented the true facts so as to cause prejudice to the other party's position, who relied on the facts as represented.[111] Liability in damages may lie under the Misrepresentation Act 1967, s 2(1).[112]

In addition, the Admiralty Court has inherent jurisdiction to interfere with salvage agreements, and the following case is an example of the court's approach when the salved had misled the salvor about the danger.

The Kingalock[113]

At the entrance of the river Thames, *The K* met with extremely bad weather and suffered considerable damage. Her master entered into an agreement with the master of a steamer to tow *The K* to London for a fixed sum of £40, but he did not disclose the fact that *The K* had encountered such difficulty before and had been damaged. A short time after the towage began, the hawser broke, and the master of the steamship discovered what had previously happened. He immediately declared the agreement at an end, but, nevertheless, towed the vessel to London, as though no agreement had been made. With much difficulty, the vessel was towed safely to London. The salvors claimed a salvage reward, but the owners of *The K* contended that the original agreement was still valid and subsisting. Dr Lushington stated, thus:

> An agreement to bind two parties must be made with a full knowledge of all the facts necessary to be known by both parties; and if any fact which, if known, could have any operation on the agreement about to be entered into is kept back, or not disclosed to either of the contracting parties, that would vitiate the agreement itself. It is not necessary, in order to vitiate an agreement, that there should be moral fraud; it is not necessary, in order to make it not binding, that one of the parties should keep back any fact or circumstance of importance, if there should be misapprehension,

---

111 *The Unique Mariner* [1978] 1 Lloyd's Rep 438 (see also Chapter 10 (para 4) and 11 (para 3.2).

112 See, also, *Howard Marine and Dredging Co Ltd v A Ogden & Sons Ltd* [1978] QB 574 (CA); *The Unique Mariner* [1978] 1 Lloyd's Rep 438, pp 454–55, per Brandon J; and see Chapter 14, para 4.4.

113 (1854) 1 Spinks E&A 265.

accidentally or by carelessness; we all know that there may be what, in the eye of the law, is termed equitable fraud.[114]

It was held that the omission to state the undisclosed facts would vitiate the agreement because those facts would have affected the service to be performed. The lack of ground tackle on the ship may have been important, particularly during weather as tempestuous as this was. This might have to a certain extent governed the manoeuvres of the steamer. Therefore the agreement was null and void *ab initio*. The owner of *The K* was ordered to pay an additional sum suitable in the circumstances because the tug had been misled that this was an ordinary towage. Dr Lushington stressed that if there had been an agreement for extraordinary towage, with full knowledge of the state of the vessel, no addition would have been made.

7.2.3 Operative mistake

This is a very debatable issue, and there have been many court decisions, which can be found in contract law texts. The general principle to be drawn is that, for an agreement to be annulled due to mistake, there must have been a fundamental (mutual) mistake between the parties as to an essential factor underlying the agreement. The effect of such a mistake at common law is to render the contract void.[115] If the parties have been at cross-purposes, which has to be viewed objectively, there will be no agreement at all.

In salvage cases, in which third party tugs are, invariably, engaged, there can be instances where there is a mistake between the parties as to the location of the casualty or the tug, or the time of expected arrival of the tug, or a mistake about the instructions as to which tug had been sent to the casualty, or a misunderstanding as to the appreciation of danger. In reality, salvage requires swift action, and the parties do not have time to seek the assistance of the court but they try to find their own practical solutions. However, disputes may arise afterwards, particularly because the salvor has to subcontract other craft and equipment, and mistaken information may affect his decision resulting in him being liable either to the party needing assistance or to the third party (tug owner) under their respective contracts.

The salvor's main concern is to assist, as soon as possible, the property in danger. But does the law help him, so that he is not left in a worse position than before he gets involved, considering that he is working under different conditions from those in which parties to ordinary contracts do? If the constraints of common law principles do not help, could or should equity help? An answer is given by the following decision which is of general importance.

The Great Peace[116]

The salvor (Tsavliris) contracted on LOF basis to salve *The Cape Providence*, which had suffered serious structural damage in the Indian Ocean. There was a danger that the ship might sink with loss of life if there was a delay for a tug to

---

114 Ibid, p 265.
115 *Bell v Lever Brothers Ltd* [1932] AC 161.
116 [2002] 2 Lloyd's Rep 653 (CA).

arrive. Tsavliris, through brokers, subcontracted *The Great Peace* on the basis of misinformation about its locality, but both parties to this subcontract believed that the tug was close to the casualty. Following the fixture, the real distance of the *Great Peace* from the casualty was discovered, which was about 410 miles away, instead of 35 miles as was originally believed. The salvor immediately sought a tug which was nearer to the casualty, and then cancelled the agreement with *The Great Peace*. The owners of *The Great Peace* sought to recover damages for five days' hire due under the charter party.

The salvors argued that the effect of the mistake was to deprive the contract from the underlying consideration on which it was based, in that it was essentially and radically, or fundamentally, different from the performance contemplated by the parties, therefore the contract was rendered void; they relied on the House of Lords' decision in *Bell v Lever Brothers* which set the principle of mutual mistake at common law.[117] In the alternative, they relied on *Solle v Butcher*,[118] and argued that the effect of the mistake was to make the contract voidable in equity, giving the salvors the right of rescission in equity, because the mistake concerned a fundamental matter to the agreement. Denning LJ, in the latter decision, had held that a contract which did not satisfy the strict test of *Bell* could be voidable and be set aside, if the parties were under a common misapprehension either as to facts or to their relative and respective rights, provided that the misapprehension was fundamental and the party seeking to set it aside was not himself at fault.

The judge at first instance was harsh on the salvors, and interpreted their conduct in making the decision to hold on to the contract with *The Great Peace*, until they found a replacement, as a factor indicating that they did not regard it as void as soon as they discovered its true position. He disregarded the extreme condition of danger in which the salvor had to save life and for this reason was holding on to this tug, which should be distinguished from the position of parties endeavouring to save life in land.

The Court of Appeal agreed with the judge, and commented on the decision in *Solle v Butcher* that it dramatically extended the jurisdiction of the court by introducing a category of equitable mistake where the contract was not void at common law, whereupon making it difficult to reconcile it with *Bell v Lever Brothers*. Thus, the Court of Appeal decided that there was no judicial basis for allowing equity to grant rescission in cases where common law did not make the contract void.

As to the question of mistake at common law, the Court of Appeal held that the fact the vessels were considerably further apart than the defendants had believed did not mean that the services the vessel was in a position to provide were essentially different from those which the parties had envisaged when the contract was concluded.

The decision undoubtedly contributes to the clarity of the general law in this area, and it is worth reading the careful analysis of the principles. However, it is respectfully submitted that more leniency should be allowed in situations of salvage, even if third parties are involved who should be themselves aware of the

---

117 Op cit, fn 115.
118 [1950] KB 671 (CA).

salvage contingencies which may not allow their tug to be ultimately engaged, if the consideration of danger to lives is the primary concern of the salvor, who takes extra risks and not just commercial ones. In such situations, a remedy in equity would not be inconsistent with the principles applicable to salvage law.

As the law stands, however, salvors can, for risk management purposes, protect themselves by negotiating an appropriate cancellation clause to be included in the contract with sub-contractors. Such a clause can stipulate events which would trigger cancellation of the contract without the salvors having to pay a cancellation fee.

8 THE MASTER'S AUTHORITY TO ENTER INTO SALVAGE AGREEMENTS

The master of a ship has authority to act on behalf of the owners in various circumstances arising from being in command of the ship. Such authority is derived mainly from his contract of employment and it is actual authority, express or implied, depending on the circumstances. Actual authority will exist in most cases when the owner issues standing orders, or gives such authority through wireless communications. Implied authority derives from the nature of the contract of employment in respect of acts which are necessary to be done in the performance of that contract and fall within the usual scope of his position, as for example the act of signing bills of lading, or engaging other agents to provide necessary materials and provisions for the running of the ship. On some occasions, the authority may be implied by the operation of law, as for example when the master acts as an agent of necessity. While it is not difficult to trace the root of the master's authority vis-à-vis the owner of the ship through the principles of agency law, a problem had arisen in the past as to whether the master had authority to bind the owners of the cargo carried on board the ship, in the contract with the salvors, by signing the salvage agreement.

Prior to the Salvage Convention 1989, the issue was dealt with in accordance with the principle of agency of necessity, but this proved to be problematic in certain circumstances where the criteria of that agency were not satisfied. Although the Convention has resolved the issue of authority of the master of the ship in danger, when agreeing to accept the assistance of salvors on behalf of both his principal and third parties, and in that respect the parties to a salvage contract are not allowed to contract out of Art 6(2), it is important to explain the problem at common law, which led to the need for this matter to be settled by the Convention.

8.1 Master's authority at common law

The essential characteristic of agency is the power of the agent to affect the legal position of the principal as regards third parties.[119] In a situation of salvage, the master of the ship will be acting as agent of the owners of the properties to be

---

119 Markesinis, B and Munday, R, *An Outline of the Law of Agency*, 3rd edn, 1992, Butterworths, pp 52–54.

salved, with a view to binding them into an effective contract of salvage with the third party, the salvors. There are two sets of triangular relationships to be examined: first, as between the master, his employers, and the salvors; and, second, as between the master, the owners of cargo (or of other property on board), and the salvors.

8.1.1 The basis of the master's authority to bind his principal to a salvage contract[120]

It has been established that the master of a ship, which needs salvage assistance, has implied actual authority to bind his principal, the shipowner, to the contract of salvage.[121]

The Unique Mariner (No 1)[122]

When his vessel ran aground, the master signed an LOF salvage agreement in the mistaken belief that a tug which approached him had been sent on behalf of his principal. He later discovered that his principal had retained another tug and, in the light of this, he dismissed the first tug in favour of the latter. The question before the judge was whether a signed LOF was a valid contract binding on the owners. Counsel for the owners contended that, although the master had implied actual authority to accept the services of a tug, such authority did not extend to his entering into a special contract, such as the LOF. Brandon J stated:

> The implied actual authority of a master, unless restricted by such instructions lawfully given, extends to doing whatever is incidental to, or necessary for, the successful prosecution of the voyage and safety and preservation of the ship.[123] . . . .

> I do not think that the implied actual authority of the master of a stranded ship to accept the services of a suitable tug is limited to his accepting them subject to the ordinary maritime law of salvage. I think, on the contrary, that it extends to accepting such services on the terms of any reasonable contract.[124]

It was held that the LOF had been used and accepted as being reasonable and fair.

8.1.2 The basis of the master's authority to bind cargo interests to a salvage contract[125]

The master could bind the cargo owners to the contract as an agent of necessity, if the means of communication in the time available to respond to an emergency would put his ship and cargo on board at a greater risk. The same would apply in case of freight being at charterer's risk.[126]

---

120 See, also, Chapter 14, para 4.1, below.

121 *The Unique Mariner (No 1)* [1978] 1 Lloyd's Rep 438.

122 [1978] 1 Lloyd's Rep 438, as the ship was in ballast there was no issue of the master's authority vis-à-vis cargo-owners.

123 Ibid, p 449.

124 Ibid, p 450.

125 See, also, Chapter 14, para 4.2, below.

126 *The Pantanassa* [1970] 1 Lloyd's Rep 153.

Agency of necessity arises by operation of law in certain circumstances where a person is faced with an emergency in which the property or interests of another person are in imminent jeopardy and it becomes necessary, in order to preserve the property or interests, to act for that person without his authority.[127]

There exist four elements for the agency to arise:

(i) an emergency;

(ii) inability to obtain instructions, or failure by the cargo interests to give any instructions when appraised of the situation;[128]

(iii) the master must act bona fide for the interest of all; and

(iv) it is reasonable for the master or shipowner to enter into the particular contract.[129]

The court in the following case examined the agency of necessity in the context of salvage, together with principles of bailment.

The Winson [130]

The Winson, a bulk carrier, was chartered by the Food Corporation of India (the cargo-owner) to carry full cargo of wheat from US Gulf ports to Indian ports under a voyage charterparty. In the course of the voyage, she stranded in the South China Sea. Professional salvors (China Pacific) were quickly on the scene and a salvage agreement in the LOF was entered into, signed by the master on behalf of the shipowner and cargo-owner. During the salvage operations, it was necessary to lighten the vessel by off-loading part of her cargo into barges provided by the salvors and carrying it to a place of safety. This was done, and some 15,429 tonnes of wheat were off-loaded and carried to Manila which was a proper place of safety. The carriage was in six separate parcels that arrived in Manila at various dates between 10 February and 20 April 1975. The salvage operations at the site of the stranding were temporarily suspended on 15 April 1975, owing to fighting in the vicinity having broken out between the forces of North Vietnam and South Vietnam. On 24 April 1975, the shipowner gave notice to cargo interests that he had abandoned the chartered voyage. By that date, it was obvious that the completion of the carriage of the cargo in *The Winson* to its destination under the charterparty, even if it were to become physically possible (which, in the event, it was not), would involve such long delay as would frustrate the contract.

It was not disputed that it never became practicable thereafter to resume the salvage operations and, on 20 May 1975, the salvors gave formal notice of termination of their salvage services. *The Winson*, with the remainder of the cargo of wheat still on board her, eventually became a total loss.

Upon arrival of each parcel of salvaged wheat at Manila, where the salvors had no storage premises of their own, it became necessary for it to be stored in suitable accommodation under cover, until a decision was reached what to do with it. The

---

127 *Bowstead and Reynolds on Agency*, 18th edn, 2005, Sweet & Maxwell.

128 Lloyd J at first instance in *The Winson* [1982] AC 939 (HL) thought that the first element of the agency of necessity was inability by the master to obtain proper instructions.

129 The fourth criterion was added by Slade LJ in *The Choko Star* [1990] 1 Lloyd's Rep 516 (see below).

130 [1982] AC 939 (HL).

salvors arranged for the storage of part of the wheat in a vessel, *The Maori*, lying in Manila Harbour, and as to the remainder in a bonded warehouse ashore. In doing so, they incurred expenses for stevedoring and charter hire of *The Maori* and warehouse charges ashore. The stored wheat was held to their order by those in whose vessel and warehouse it was stored ('the depositaries'). These expenses which the salvors became personally liable to pay under the contracts that they made as principals with the depositaries continued to be incurred by them until the cargo-owner had completed taking possession of the wheat – which did not happen until 5 August 1975.

The storage expenses incurred after the termination of the contracted voyage (24 April 1975) were paid by the cargo-owners. The salvors brought this action against the cargo-owners to recover the storage expenses up to that date. The cargo-owners contended that by virtue of the contract of carriage, the immediate right to possession of the goods before it was terminated rested with the shipowner, and the salvors were, thus, under a duty to deliver the cargo to the shipowner. They did not dispute the payment from 24 April, but they did dispute payment of expenses incurred before the termination of the contract of carriage. They argued that it was the shipowner that was liable to reimburse the salvors for those expenses. Such a proposition was rejected by Lloyd J at first instance, but accepted by the Court of Appeal.

The decision of the House of Lords

Apart from the importance of this decision on issues of bailment, the relevant issue in this context was the legal nature of the relationship between the master of the ship and the owner of the cargo when the salvage contract was signed. The issue of payment of the salvors' expenses was solved on the basis of bailment.

It was held that, where in the course of salvage operations cargo is off-loaded from the vessel by which the contract of carriage was being performed and conveyed separately to a place of safety, the direct relationship of bailor and bailee is created between the cargo-owner and the salvor as soon as the cargo is loaded on vessels provided by the salvor to convey it to a place of safety. All the mutual rights and duties attaching to such a relationship at common law become binding. The relationship continues to exist until the cargo-owners take possession of the cargo from the warehouse. The cargo-owner, therefore, had to pay for all expenses incurred.

It is important to quote how Lord Diplock analysed the problem:

> My Lords, it is not suggested that there is any direct authority on the question of law that is posed in this appeal. In my opinion the answer is to be found by applying to the unusual circumstances of the instant case well known and basic principles of the common law of salvage, of bailment and of lien.[131]

> ... with modern methods of communication and the presence of professional salvors within rapid reach of most parts of the principal maritime trade routes of the world, nearly all salvage of merchant ships and their cargoes nowadays is undertaken under a salvage contract in Lloyd's Open Form. The contract is one for the

---

131 [1982] AC 939 (HL), p 957.

rendering of services; the services to be rendered are of the legal nature of salvage and this imports into the contractual relationship between the parties to the contract by necessary implication a number of mutual rights and obligations attaching to salvage of vessels and their cargo under common law, except insofar as such rights and obligations are inconsistent with express terms of the contract.

Lloyd's Open Form is expressed by cl 16 to be signed by the master '. . . as agent for the vessel her cargo and freight and the respective owners thereof and binds each (but not the one for the other or himself personally) to the due performance thereof'. The legal nature of the relationship between the master and the owner of the cargo aboard the vessel in signing the agreement on the latter's behalf is often though not invariably an agency of necessity. It arises only when salvage services by a third party are necessary for the preservation of the cargo. Whether one person is entitled to act as agent of necessity for another person is relevant to the question whether circumstances exist which in law have the effect of conferring on him authority to create contractual rights and obligations between that other person and a third party that are directly enforceable by each against the other. It would, I think, be an aid to clarity of legal thinking if the use of the expression 'agent of necessity' were confined to contexts in which this was the question to be determined and not extended, as it often is, to cases where the only relevant question is whether a person who without obtaining instructions from the owner of goods incurs expense in taking steps that are reasonably necessary for their preservation is in law entitled to recover from the owner of the goods the reasonable expenses incurred by him in taking those steps. Its use in this wider sense may, I think, have led to some confusion in the instant case, since where reimbursement is the only relevant question, all of those conditions that must be fulfilled in order to entitle one person to act on behalf of another in creating direct contractual relationships between that other person and a third party may not necessarily apply.

In the instant case, it is not disputed that when the Lloyd's Open Form was signed on 22 January 1975, the circumstances that existed at that time were such as entitled the master to enter into the agreement on the cargo-owner's behalf as its agent of necessity. The rendering of salvage services under the Lloyd's open agreement does not usually involve the salvor's taking possession of the vessel or its cargo from the shipowner; the shipowner remains in possession of both ship and cargo while salvage services are being carried out by the salvors on the ship. But salvage services may involve the transfer of possession of cargo from the shipowner to the salvors, and will do so in a case of stranding as respects part of the cargo, if it becomes necessary to lighten the vessel in order to refloat her. Where in the course of salvage operations cargo is off loaded from the vessel by which the contract of carriage was being performed and conveyed separately from that vessel to a place of safety by means (in the instant case, barges) provided by the salvor, the direct relationship of bailor and bailee is created between cargo-owner and salvor as soon as the cargo is loaded on vessels provided by the salvor to convey it to a place of safety; and all the mutual rights and duties attaching to that relationship at common law apply, save insofar as any of them are inconsistent with the express terms of the Lloyd's open agreement.

On parting with possession of cargo to the salvor the shipowner loses any possessory lien over it to which he may have been entitled for unpaid freight, demurrage or general average. Whether the lien in respect of liabilities of the cargo owner that had already accrued due at the time of parting with possession would revive upon the shipowner's recovering possession of the cargo for on-carriage to its contractual destination is a question on which there appears to be no direct authority; but it does not arise for decision by your Lordships in the instant case. The shipowners neither obtained nor even sought repossession of any part of the salved wheat after it had been off loaded from The Winson into the barges provided by the salvors on and before 24 April 1975 . . .[132]

My Lords, as I have already said, there is not any direct authority as to the existence of this correlative right to reimbursement of expenses in the specific case of a salvor who retains possession of cargo after the salvage services rendered by him to that cargo have ended. . . .

In the instant case the cargo-owner was kept informed of the salvors' intentions as to the storage of the salved wheat upon its arrival in Manila; it made no alternative proposals; it made no request to the salvors for delivery of any of the wheat after its arrival at Manila, and a request made by the salvors to the cargo-owner through their solicitors on 25 February 1975, after the arrival of the second of the six parcels, to take delivery of the parcels of salved wheat on arrival at Manila remained unanswered and uncomplied with until after notice of abandonment of the charter voyage had been received by the cargo-owner from the shipowner.

The failure of the cargo-owner as bailor to give any instructions to the salvors as its bailee although it was fully apprised of the need to store the salved wheat under cover on arrival at Manila if it was to be preserved from rapid deterioration was, in the view of Lloyd J, sufficient to attract the application of the principle to which I have referred above and to entitle the salvors to recover from the cargo-owner their expenses in taking measures necessary for its preservation. For my part, I think that in this he was right and the Court of Appeal, who took the contrary view, were wrong. It is, of course, true that in English law a mere stranger cannot compel an owner of goods to pay for a benefit bestowed upon him against his will; but this latter principle does not apply where there is a pre-existing legal relationship between the owner of the goods and the bestower of the benefit, such as that of bailor and bailee, which imposes upon the bestower of the benefit a legal duty of care in respect of the preservation of the goods that is owed by him to their owner.[133]

Lord Simon agreed with Lloyd J, the judge at first instance, that, when the LOF was signed, the circumstances that existed were such as to have entitled the master to enter into the agreement on the cargo-owner's behalf as its agency of necessity. On the issue of agency of necessity, Lord Simon commented:

One of the ways in which an agency of necessity can arise is where A is in possession of goods the property of B, and an emergency arises which places those goods in imminent jeopardy: If A cannot obtain instructions from B as to how he should act in such circumstances, A is bound to take without authority such action in relation to the goods as B, as a prudent owner, would himself have taken in the circumstances. The relationship between A and B is then known as an 'agency of necessity', A being the agent and B the principal. This was the situation descried by Lloyd J and denied by the Court of Appeal.

Issues as to agency of necessity generally arise forensically when A enters into a contract with C in relation to the goods, the question being whether B is bound by that contract. The purely terminological suggestion that, in order to avoid confusion, 'agent of necessity' should be confined to such contractual situations does not involve that other relevant general incidents of agency are excluded from the

---

132 [1982] AC 939 (HL), pp 958–59.
133 Ibid, p 961.

relationship between A and B. In particular, if A incurs reasonable expenses in safeguarding B's goods in a situation of emergency, A is entitled to be reimbursed by B. . . .

To confine 'agent of necessity' terminologically to the contractual situations is justified by the fact that the law of bailment will often resolve any issue between alleged principal and agent of necessity, as it has done here. But, sometimes, the law of agency will be more useful: for example, if available here it would obviate any problem about the correlation of performance of a duty of care with a claim for reimbursement, since an agent is undoubtedly entitled to an indemnity for expenses incurred reasonably to benefit his principal.

However, I respectfully agree with the Court of Appeal [1981] QB 403, p 424, that:

> 'The relevant time, for the purpose of considering whether there was a necessity, or an emergency . . . is . . . the time when the existence of the supposed emergency became apparent. The emergency would be the arrival, or expected arrival, of salved cargo at Manila, with no arrangements for its off loading or for its preservation in proper storage having been made or put in hand. There never was, so far as one can ascertain from the evidential matter here, such an emergency.'

In addition to the factual difficulty in treating the case as one of agency of necessity, there are legal difficulties in the way of the salvor. For an agency of necessity to arise, the action taken must be necessary for the protection of the interests of the alleged principal, not of the agent; the alleged agent must have acted bona fide in the interests of the alleged principal: *Bowstead on Agency*, 14th edn, 1976, p 668: *Prager v Blatspiel, Stamp and Heacock Ltd* [1924] 1 KB 566, pp 571, 572, 573. . . . In view of the opinion I have formed on the rights arising by implication from the Lloyd's Open Form and from the common law bailment, it is unnecessary to come to any conclusion on these issues . . .[134]

Although the general principle of what is required for agency of necessity to arise is clear, in practice, even if there might be a possibility for the master to communicate with the cargo interests before signing a salvage contract, there may be pressures to respond quickly to protect the interests of his ship and property on board. The problem of the master's authority to bind the cargo interests to a salvage contract came to a head, in what is regarded as wasted litigation, a few years later.

The Choko Star[135]

The ship was on charter from ports in the Argentine to Italy; she grounded in the river Parana and was stranded. At the time, she was loaded with cargo consisting of soya beans and sun seeds in bulk. As the master could not refloat the vessel without assistance, he entered into a salvage agreement in the LOF 1980, whereupon the vessel was successfully refloated and the salvors claimed salvage remuneration. The shipowner settled their part of the remuneration, but the cargo-owners contended that the master had no authority to engage salvors on their behalf. After arbitration, they paid the amount due, though under protest. They commenced proceedings against the salvors claiming restitution of the monies on the ground

---

134 [1982] AC 939 (HL), pp 965–66.
135 [1990] 1 Lloyd's Rep 516.

that the salvage contract was not done in their own best interests and that it was also unreasonable because the salvors employed were European instead of local ones, who would have been better equipped, and would have had more experience of that river. The issue was the master's authority to bind them to the salvage contract.

The question was whether the master would have authority to bind the cargo-owners by contract in circumstances where it was reasonably practicable to communicate with cargo-owners and obtain their instructions before signing the contract on their behalf. (The master here had not so communicated with the cargo interests in this case.) Would the law imply a term in the contract of carriage binding the cargo-owners, even though the circumstances that existed did not give rise to an agency of necessity?

The learned trial judge held that, when cargo was loaded on a ship, the cargo-owners must recognise that circumstances may exist in which the ship or cargo would require salvage services. Therefore, if the master had implied authority to enter into salvage agreements on behalf of the shipowner, he must also have implied authority to enter into the same reasonable contract on behalf of the cargo-owner. The master's implied authority arose out of the contract of carriage and was not given by necessity. It was being necessarily implied. On appeal by the cargo-owners, the Court of Appeal was not convinced that it was necessary to imply such a term in order to give the contract of carriage business efficacy.[136] Slade LJ stated, thus:

> Until an emergency arises, such as to give rise to an agency of necessity, there is no question of the shipowner or master being an agent for the cargo-owners. Accordingly, it is not possible to spell out authority for either of them to bind the cargo-owners to a salvage contract, as merely incidental to his pre-existing general authority as an agent . . .

> Merely because the authority conferred by shipowners on their agent, the master, is deemed to extend to engaging salvors on reasonable terms on behalf of the shipowners, it does not follow that the master has the like implied authority to bind cargo-owners to salvage contracts, in the absence of circumstances giving rise to an agency of necessity.[137]

Regardless of the correctness of statement of principle of the incident of agency in those circumstances, this decision caused confusion in practice, particularly because of the invidious situation masters of a ship found themselves in when there was an emergency, whereupon quick decisions had to be made to save his ship and cargo on board. Unnecessary haggling over reaching an agreement invariably caused more problems in saving a ship and its cargo from danger. Now, in the light of the Convention, such problems have been resolved.

However, problems may still arise with regard to a master's authority in particular circumstances, when the law of a country which has not ratified, or enacted, the Convention applies to the contract.[138]

---

136 In the sense laid down by the House of Lords in *Liverpool v Irwin* [1977] AC 239.

137 [1990] 1 Lloyd's Rep 516, pp 525–26.

138 See op cit, Brice, fn 1, pp 334–35.

The Pa Mar,[139] in which the events occurred before the Convention had the force of law, provides a good example of the considerations that should be borne in mind by both a shipowner and a salvor when the master signs a salvage agreement to bind the cargo interests.

The generators of *The Pa Mar* had failed in the Red Sea. Her master signed LOF 1990 engaging the tug *Leopard* to tow his ship to a place of safety. That contract was subsequently varied by the managers of *The Pa Mar* ('Kappa') on behalf of her owners. The variation concerned the place of delivery of the properties after salvage. The contractors under the LOF, both in its original form and as varied, were Tsavliris Salvage International Ltd ('Tsavliris'). It was common ground that both the master and Kappa purported to contract on behalf of the owners of *The Pa Mar*, her cargo, freight, bunkers, stores and other property on board her. However, at a comparatively early stage, before the vessel left Singapore and while security was being negotiated, the owners of the cargo took the point that neither the master nor Kappa (or, indeed, the shipowners) had any authority to contract on their behalf. The principal question for decision in these actions was whether the owners of cargo were bound by the LOF apparently entered into on their behalf, either in its original form or as varied.

It was held by Clarke J:

> The evidence showed that no towage assistance was available on commercial terms so that unless the vessel and her cargo were to be left indefinitely immobilised prudence dictated the engagement of the tug on LOF; it was true that the vessel was at anchor in the Red Sea and that her anchor was not dragging, but she could not fairly be said to be in a place of safety; she was exposed to both the winds and the swell and her exposed position together with the fact that she was indefinitely immobilised was sufficient to satisfy the requirement that it was necessary to take salvage assistance; Tsavliris had shown that it was necessary for the master to take salvage assistance.

> In entering into the original contract, that is, without a Dubai/Colombo option, the master and indeed Kappa were acting reasonably; the master was acting both bona fide and reasonably in the interests of both ship and cargo when he entered into the unamended LOF on 9 June; and the cargo-owners were bound by the contract in that form.

However, as to the variation of the agreement with regard to final destination, the judge held that:

> No reasonable shipowner would have committed the owners of cargo to a LOF which involved a long tow on salvage terms without carrying out further investigations; Tsavliris had failed to discharge the burden of proving on the balance of probabilities that Kappa acted bona fide and reasonably in the interests of cargo in agreeing to a variation of the LOF by adding the Dubai/Colombo option.

What was needed was that the owners should have asked both the ship's classification society and the Salvage Association surveyor to investigate the position at the first stop, Aden.

---

139 [1999] 1 Lloyd's Rep 338.

It would be prudent if owners and salvors did bear this in mind in future similar cases, when the Convention does not apply.

8.2 Master's authority under the Convention

The practical problems arising from these decisions led to recognition that the question of the master's authority to bind the cargo interests to a salvage contract ought to be solved by an international Convention. Article 6(2) of the 1989 Convention brought the most significant change (alongside Art 14) to salvage law and clearly provides that:

> The master shall have the authority to conclude contracts for salvage operations on behalf of the owners of the vessel. The master or the owner of the vessel shall have authority to conclude such contracts on behalf of the owner of the property on board the vessel.

Before the Convention had the force of law, this provision had been inserted in the LOF 1990, cl 14, but it had only contractual force, and there were still questions as to whether the consent of the cargo owners was necessary to be obtained expressly. Since 1 January 1995, however, when the provisions of the MS(SP)A 1994 came into force giving effect to the Salvage Convention 1989, the authority of the master was clothed with statutory force insofar as English law was concerned. The subsequent LOF of 1995 incorporated Arts 1, 6, 8, 13 and 14 of the Convention on the back for information. To avoid any doubt, cl 16 of LOF 1995 restated the master's authority to bind the respective owners of the properties to be salved to the agreement which he signs on their behalf.

It can be inferred from the wording of Art 6(2) of the Convention, 'the master shall have the authority', that it is obligatory. It does not allow the parties to provide otherwise in the contract, as the previous para 6(1) does.[140] The policy reason behind it is to prevent delays in signing the contract for the interests of the salved property.

LOF 2000 expressly provides not only that English law shall apply to the contract, but it also defines the scope of the master's authority, namely, cl K provides:

> The master or other person signing this agreement on behalf of the property identified in the contract enters into this agreement as agent for the respective owners thereof and binds each (but not the one for the other or himself personally) to the due performance thereof.

9 DUTIES AND CONDUCT OF SALVORS

The 1989 Salvage Convention, unlike its predecessor, stipulates the duties of both the salvors and the owner of the property in danger; there is, in fact, no change in

---

140 Cf Gaskell, N, 'LOF 1990' [1991] LMCLQ 104.

the law but codification of the common law duty of care throughout the salvage operations. In addition, the contract also provides that the salvor shall use his best endeavours to complete the salvage and to prevent or minimise damage to the environment.

Under ordinary maritime law of salvage, there is no obligation on the salvor to complete salvage. He can discontinue the salvage services without incurring any liability. Under Lloyd's standard forms and the Convention, there are certain obligations upon the salvor, which are examined next.

9.1 Best endeavours

All LOFs, 1980, 1990, 1995 by cl 1(a) and LOF 2000 by cl A, provide that the contractor (salvor) shall use his best endeavours to salve the property and take it either to a place agreed or to a place of safety. In addition, LOF 1990, 1995, cl 1(a)(ii), and 2000, cl B, provide that, while performing salvage operations, the contractor shall also use his best endeavours to prevent or minimise damage to the environment.

There is no absolute obligation of success but that 'the contractor will do his best, not second best'.[141] There has been no definition of 'best endeavours' in salvage cases.[142] The phrase has been defined in a few cases concerned with obtaining a licence for sale of goods. It has been held that, whatever phrase is used, the seller must show that he has done his best,[143] and that the practice of other exporters will be taken into account in determining whether the seller exercised due diligence in obtaining an export licence.[144] By analogy, it would seem that in salvage cases it could equally be said that to determine whether a salvor exercised his best endeavours the standard of reasonable diligence should apply. The standard of reasonableness is that of a prudent salvor acting properly in the interests of the salved property, and his duty is what can reasonably be done in the circumstances.[145] Whether there is an element of subjectivity, in other words what the salvor believes, in his capacity, to be reasonable in the circumstances, is not clear. It is submitted that, if the practice of other salvors possessing the same expertise possessed by the salvor in question is taken into account, the standard is an objective one. Support that there should be an objective standard may be gained from cl G of LOF 2000, which grants a right to both the salvor and the owner of the vessel to terminate the salvage when there is no longer a reasonable prospect of useful result. In the 1990 and 1995 LOFs such right is given only to the owner of the vessel (see para 10.2, below).

---

141 Op cit, Brice, fn 1, p 547.

142 In the glossary to *Current Statutes*, MSA 1995, Chapter 21, para 21–390, it is said that the difference between 'best endeavours' and 'due care' may be that a higher standard is required by the former phrase and that the salvor under LOF 1995 may not be excused if he decides to continue an uneconomic salvage, for commercial reasons, that it may not be worthwhile continuing.

143 *Oversea Buyers Ltd v Granadex SA* [1980] 2 Lloyd's Rep 608, per Mustill J (as he then was).

144 *Malik Co v Central European Trading Agency Ltd* [1974] 2 Lloyd's Rep 279, per Kerr J, applying the principle in *Anglo Russian Merchant Traders Ltd v Batt (John) & Co Ltd* [1917] 2 KB 679.

145 *Terrell v Mabie Todd & Co* [1952] 2 TLR 574.

On proof that best endeavours were not used, there would be a breach of contract.

9.2 Due care

Under the Convention, Art 8(1)(a), (b), it is provided:

1   The salvor shall owe a duty to the owner of the vessel or other property in danger:

   (a) to carry out the salvage operations with due care;

   (b) in performing the duty specified in sub-paragraph (a) to exercise due care to prevent or minimise damage to the environment.

Not only does the salvor owe a duty to the owners of the property in danger to carry out the salvage operations with due care, but also to exercise due care to prevent or minimise damage to the environment. The salvor also has a duty under Art 8(c), (d) – when circumstances reasonably require – to seek assistance from other salvors, and to accept intervention of other salvors, when requested to do so by the owner or master of the vessel or the property in danger.

The reason why the term 'due care' has been used in the Convention may be that it is easily understood internationally.[146] The standard to be applied to due care is that of reasonableness taking into account the standards applied by the salvage industry.

Article 8 has been incorporated into LOF 1990 by reference (see cl 2) while it has been incorporated into LOF 1995 fully as information. If there is a different standard to be applied to 'best endeavours' and to 'due care', there will be a potential conflict in the LOF 1990 and LOF 1995 which incorporate Art 8, unless, as discussed earlier, the objective standard of reasonableness applies to both terms. It may be questioned why both terms 'best endeavours' and 'due care' are necessary if they both aim at performance of duties by the salvor with reasonable diligence. A plausible explanation for that is that 'best endeavours' relates to the completion of the salvage successfully, while 'due care' is emphasising the common law duty of care not to cause damage to the property in danger and to the environment when carrying out the salvage operations.

The LOF 2000 does not expressly include what are the duties of the contractor, while it expressly includes the duties of the property owner. However, the fact that cl J provides expressly that the contract shall be governed by English law, the duties of the salvor will be found in Art 8 of the Convention, as incorporated into English law.

9.2.1 Remedy for negligent misconduct of salvors under the Convention

Article 8(1) of the 1989 Convention imposes a duty of care on salvors, but it does not address the issue of damages. The Salvage Convention 1910 did not do either.

---

146 However, in Art 21, 'best endeavours' is used in relation to the obligation of the owner of the vessel to ensure that security is provided to the salvors by the cargo interests before the cargo is discharged. This raises the question why this term was incorporated in the Convention if consistency was intended, assuming that both terms mean reasonable care.

While Art 8 does not provide for the consequences of breach of the duty of care, common law will assist in this respect (see below).

Article 18 provides for the consequences of salvors' misconduct, in that the salvors may be deprived of the whole or part of the payment due under the Convention to the extent that the salvage operation has become necessary or more difficult because of fault or neglect on his part, or if the salvor has been guilty of fraud or other dishonest conduct.

This article may be dealing only with negligence before salvage and when the salvage becomes more difficult due to the negligence of salvors. If, on the other hand, the intention of the draftsman was that this article should have a broader application, a potential conflict would arise between the consequences provided under common law, eg damages for breach by the salvor, and Art 18 of the Convention.

The conflict is this: if, for the conduct described in Art 18, the draftsman of the Convention regarded it as sufficient to deprive the salvor of part or the whole of the award, there could be a valid argument that to allow common law damages for negligence of the salvor causing damage to the property in danger would be inconsistent with the spirit of the Convention, in particular since the Convention is silent about allowing damages to be awarded, unless this is implied from the duty imposed by Art 8.

As is apparent from the next paragraph, it would be better if the Convention dealt with the lacuna in Art 8, in the interests of certainty in the law.

9.2.2 Negligent misconduct under common law

The English courts have for many years recognised that negligence of salvors who respond to an emergency of a ship in distress at risk to themselves should be judged leniently. It was considered that deduction from the award of an assessed sum of the damage done would be sufficient,[147] or in more serious cases of negligence the deduction would be in proportion to the misconduct,[148] or the misconduct could forfeit the award.[149] Until *The Tojo Maru* case (see later), the courts had been reluctant to award damages against salvors, even in cases in which the misconduct had led to the loss of the ship.[150] Mistake or misconduct, other than criminal, which diminishes the salved value, used to be taken into account in the amount of the award; but wilful or criminal misconduct would result in forfeiture of the entire award.[151]

---

147 *The Dwina* [1892] P 58; *The Queenforth v Royal Fifth* (1923) 17 LlL Rep 204.

148 *The Cape Packet* (1848) 3 W Rob 470; *The Perla* (1857) Swab 230; *The Magdalen* (1861) 31 LJ (Adm) 22, the reduction of the award to one salvor of the two who was negligent was said to be not by way of punishment but it was treated as a means of indemnifying the owner.

149 See *The Neptune* (1842) 1 W Rob 297; *The Kendal* (1948) 81 LlL Rep 217.

150 *The Yan-Yean* (1883) 8 PD 147, due to salvor's negligence the ship sank, but was later raised by her owners. No award of salvage was made nor of damages. As the loss arising from the misconduct of the salvors was probably equal to that from which the Y was first rescued, no salvage reward was due. If the Y had been ultimately saved, such misconduct would have worked as a partial reduction of the reward only. It was laid down by the Privy Council in *The Duke of Manchester* (1847) 6 Moo PC 91 that, if by the negligence of the salvors a ship is led into peril as great as that from which she has been rescued, all claim to salvage is forfeited.

151 *The Atlas* (1862) Lush 518.

The question whether or not a salvor should be liable in damages to the owner of the property arose in 1874 in the **CS Butler**[152] case, where *The Butler* responded to a distress signal sent by *The Baltic* and agreed to tow her upon a fixed sum. During the services, *The Butler* came into collision with *The Baltic* three times, causing much damage to her, but eventually *The Butler* brought her to a place of safety. The concept of *crassa negligentia* was adopted by Sir Robert Phillimore, who stated:

> . . . gross want of proper navigation, which certainly would, in my judgment, render her liable for damage that she, thus, caused, notwithstanding that she was acting as salvor.

The Baltic recovered damages assessed in the usual way, and *The Butler* was awarded the amount agreed upon as salvage remuneration.

In the 20th century, the courts have been more robust in considering awarding damages to the owner of the salved property for a salvor's negligence. In **The Delphinula**,[153] the Court of Appeal (reversing the first instance decision) held that, if the salvor is guilty of misconduct, not only may a reduction in value of the salved property caused by his negligence be taken into account in assessing the award, but also a counterclaim or cross-claim, or an independent action for damages, will lie. In **The Alenquer**,[154] no salvage award was made, but the damage claim had to be paid in full, although the judge adhered to the general principle of policy by saying:

> It seems to me that I have to pay regard to the general principles of policy in relation to salvage which have been laid down over the years by this court. Those general principles of policy require that this court, in judging the conduct of salvors, should err, if anything, on the side of leniency towards salvors insofar as their behaviour is criticised . . . if the result of the decisions of this court were such as to discourage salvors from taking risks and showing enterprise when rendering services at sea. The matter is summed up in a passage in Kennedy LJ's book on the *Law of Civil Salvage* (3rd edn), to which I was referred in the course of the argument. There, at p 162, the learned author says:
>
> > 'In considering whether a salvor has shown such a want of reasonable skill and knowledge as ought materially to affect the court's award, or is guilty only of an error of judgment, the court will incline to the lenient view, and will take into favourable consideration any special circumstances which tend to exonerate the salvor from blame, such as, for example, a request for help, the suddenness of the emergency, or the absence of more efficient means of succour.'

> That appears to me to be the correct approach to the matter, and I gladly adopt that paragraph as part of my judgment.

In 1971, the House of Lords in the following case affirmed that a claim in damages will lie against the salvors for their negligence by way of a counterclaim, independently of merely taking salvors' negligence into account in the assessment of the salvage award.

---

152 (1874) LR 4 A&E 178, p 183.
153 *Anglo-Saxon Petroleum Co Ltd v The Admiralty (The Delphinula)* (1947) 80 LlL Rep 459.
154 [1955] 1 Lloyd's Rep 101, p 112.

The Tojo Maru[155]

Subsequent to a collision with an Italian ship in the Persian Gulf, *The Tojo Maru* entered into a salvage agreement under the standard LOF, 'no cure no pay' basis, with the respondents. In order to cover the large crack caused by the collision to the hull of the ship, a large plate had to be bolted to the hull. This had to be done by firing bolts to the hull, but the adjoining tank had to be made gas-free first, for safety reasons. The chief diver of the respondents (salvors), however, contrary to the orders he had received, fired a bolt through the shell plating of the vessel. The result was an explosion which caused extensive damage and caused a fire on the vessel. Eventually, after obtaining additional help to put out the fire and make the vessel seaworthy, she was towed to Singapore and then Kobe where she was repaired.

The salvors claimed a salvage award in the salvage arbitration, and the owners counterclaimed damages suffered due to the salvors' negligence. They argued that the salvors had by the contract undertaken to 'use their best endeavours' to salve the vessel, but in breach of that contract, they had negligently caused damage to the vessel, and were therefore liable in damages for the loss caused to the owners by their negligence.

The salvors argued that the rules of maritime law were that a successful salvor could not be liable in damages to the owner for the result of any negligence on his part, but such negligence would only allow the court to reduce or forfeit the salvage award and, thus, did not give rise to a claim for damages. The reason, they said, was that the salvage services resulted in an overall benefit to the owner. That is, that the salvor has done more good than harm and no counterclaim in respect of the harm is possible.

On the facts, the arbitrator found that the salvors were negligent and the owners were entitled to recover damages. He took the net salved value after deduction of the damage suffered by the owners and on the basis of that figure he calculated the salvage award. Then he deducted the amount of the award from the damage amount (which was higher) leaving a balance to be paid by the salvors to the owners. But, then he applied, on this balance, limitation of liability based on the tonnage of the salvor's tug, diminishing the amount of damages due from £206,767 to £10,725.

The issues of whether the owners were entitled to a counterclaim, and whether the salvors could limit their liability, were referred to appeal as a special case. Willmer LJ sitting as a judge agreed with the arbitrator with regard to the counterclaim for damages, but disagreed with him on the limitation of liability issue because, at that time, the limitation of liability statute, s 503 of the MSA 1894, did not apply to salvors.[156]

On appeal to the Court of Appeal,[157] the then Master of the Rolls, Lord Denning, analysed the previous relevant authorities in depth and concluded that the issue

---

155 [1972] AC 242, [1971] 1 Lloyd's Rep 341 (HL).

156 Analysis of this principle, together with the present law on limitation, is examined in Chapter 17. Suffice to mention that, under the present law, the salvors would be able to limit in the circumstances that arose in this case.

157 *The Tojo Maru* [1969] 2 Lloyd's Rep 193 (CA).

whether the owners were entitled to full damages could not strictly be determined by the common law of England but only by the maritime law of the world which the English Admiralty Court had done so much to form. Where there was more good than harm done by the salvors, the principle established by the authorities[158] shows that:

> In assessing the amount of salvage remuneration, the conduct of the salvor is a material consideration. He is rewarded highly for great service, poorly for bad service. If he has behaved in a violent or overbearing manner, it may diminish the amount of his reward, even though he has done no damage (*The Marie* (1882) 7 PD 203). So also if he has been negligent and, by so doing, damaged the vessel he is seeking to save, it may diminish the amount of the reward, according to how much he is to blame; but not necessarily to the full extent of the damage done.[159]

Save for three authorities,[160] which were distinguished by Lord Denning because (on their facts) there was more harm than good done by the salvors, he further said:

> The long line of cases represents the maritime law of England and of the world on this subject. They apply whenever the salvor has done much good in saving a vessel in distress, but, in the course of the salvage operation, has damaged her somewhat by his negligence. The damage is taken into account in two ways: first, the salvage award is calculated on the salved value and is, therefore, less on account of the damage; second, it may be further reduced by deducting some part of the damage, or even the whole of it, from the salvage reward. But, save to this extent, the salvor is not liable for the damage done. In particular, he is not liable to a counterclaim for damages.[161]

Lord Denning MR distinguished *The Delphinula* on the basis that the comments made there by the Court of Appeal were obiter dicta and, in any event, he disagreed with that decision in which English common law was applied instead of English maritime law, which was quite different.

In effect, what Lord Denning proposed was in line with the spirit of both maritime law salvage and the present Salvage Convention, Art 18. It does not appear from his dicta that he supported an exoneration of salvors for their negligence causing damage to the property in danger but, drawing support from relevant authorities, he was convinced that the proper approach for dealing with the issue was the maritime law approach and not that of the common law principles applicable to damages for negligence, which can dangerously produce different results and discourage salvors from undertaking difficult salvage operations.

To the lucid judgment of Lord Denning, Salmon LJ added most persuasively why *The Delphinula* was different from the present case. First, it was not a claim for salvage but for damages, as the vessel – having stranded in port at the time – blew up due to the negligence of the superintendent of salvage operations at the port.

---

158 *The Cape Packer* (1848) 3 W Rob 122; *The Perla* (1857) Swab 230; *The Atlas* (1862) Lush 518; *The Yan-Yean* (1883) 8 PD 147; *The Dwina* [1892] P 58; *The Queenforth v Royal Fifth* (1923) 17 LlL Rep 204 (these cases established that the most grave misconduct, gross negligence or wilful, would only forfeit the award, while other negligence would just diminish it).

159 *The Tojo Maru* [1969] 2 Lloyd's Rep 193 (CA), per Lord Denning MR, at p 199.

160 *The Thetis* (1869) LR 2 A&E 365; *The Butler* (1874) LR 4 A&E 178; *The Alenquer* [1955] 1 Lloyd's Rep 101.

161 [1969] 2 Lloyd's Rep 193 (CA), p 200.

The case was for damages because the salvors conferred no benefit. He did not read the judgment of Scott LJ in *The Delphinula* as meaning that, if at the end of the day the ship had been saved, the owners might successfully have claimed a sum due to the salvor's negligence.

Salmon LJ drew a dichotomy of two categories derived from previous authorities, although none was binding on the Court of Appeal. The first category was cases in which the ship had been in dire danger of becoming a total loss and was saved from that danger, but due to salvor's negligence some damage was done (the 'dire danger' cases). In all such cases, negligence by the salvors has been taken into account in assessing the salvage reward, the effect of which has been a reduction in the amount of the reward to the extent of the negligence. The second category was where the 'total loss danger' did not exist and in which no benefit was conferred by reason of negligence by the salvor (the 'non-dire danger' cases). In this second category, he said, the owners, at the end of the day, were worse off than they would have been, but for the salvors' negligence. In such circumstances, an award in damages would not be inconsistent with the principle of public policy applicable to salvage cases, namely:

> On grounds of public policy it is of the greatest importance for the safety of shipping that salvors should come to the assistance of vessels in distress and especially that professional salvors should be encouraged to invest capital and incur expenses in maintaining salvage tugs and services to enable them to come to the assistance of ships in distress.[162]

As regards limitation of liability, although the salvors were not entitled to limit under s 503 of the MSA 1894, the Court of Appeal, unlike the House of Lords (see below), dealt with the question as to when limitation should be applied, that is, before or after a set-off. In its opinion, there would be no set-off before limitation was applied. If, on the other hand, the salvors were not entitled to limit, the salvage reward should first be calculated as if no damage had been done by their negligence; then the counterclaim should be calculated on the cost of repairs, delay and loss of profit; then a balance should be struck.[163]

The House of Lords reversed the decision of the Court of Appeal on the main issue of the owners being entitled to counterclaim damages, but it did not deal with the limitation issue; so it is presumed, in the absence of another decision, that the decision of the Court of Appeal on how limitation should be approached (namely by applying limitation before a set-off) would stand. With regard to the reasons of the House of Lords in support of their decision, it is worth considering some dicta of Lord Reid and Lord Diplock. Both relied heavily on established principles of negligence by professionals at common law, rejecting that any special rule on the basis of 'more harm than good' or 'more good than harm' had been firmly established in the maritime law of salvage. It is hopeful, however, that since this case was unusual in its facts, it could be distinguished in the future, or perhaps another decision of the House of Lords may take a different view on the issue of damages, or clarify the application of this case.

---

162 Ibid, p 205.
163 Ibid, pp 203, 207.

Lord Reid explored the principles:

It is said that public policy requires and always has required that every proper encouragement should be given to salvors. With that I agree. In older times, it was highly desirable to encourage the master and crew of any vessel which encountered another in distress to do their utmost to save that other vessel. And, today, it is equally desirable to encourage professional salvors to maintain salvage vessels in a wide variety of situations. Just as courts are very slow to hold that errors of judgment in emergencies amount to negligence, so too courts are slow to impute negligence to salvors. But, here the arbitrator has found against them on that matter and the respondents do not seek to challenge his finding.

It is said that it will be most discouraging to salvors if they have to contemplate the possibility of heavy awards of damages against them by reason of their vicarious liability for their employees, and that it is not easy for them to cover their liability by insurance. But the rule for which the respondents contend would not prevent such awards. *The rule [of 'more good than harm'] is only said to apply where the salvage has been successful* (emphasis added). It is not disputed that if, by reason of the negligence of the salvors' employees, a ship which they are trying to salve is lost, then the salvor can be sued for that negligence and he must pay damages. To serve the public interest the encouragement of salvors must operate on their minds before they begin salvage operations. But, at that stage, the salvor cannot know whether, if negligence of his employees occurs in the course of salvage operations, it will merely cause damage, or will cause total loss of the vessel. I could understand a rule that a salvor can never be liable for the damage caused by negligence in trying to salve a vessel. . . . But the rule for which the respondents contend would not be a satisfactory solution of the problem viewed as a whole.

. . . (T)here is a second argument which was accepted by the Court of Appeal. It was said that the salvors' operations should be considered as a whole. We should consider the position when the salvors began their operations. If the actual salved value, notwithstanding the damage done by the salvors' negligence, exceeds the value which the vessel had in its perilous and damaged condition when the salvors began their operations, then the salvors have done more good than harm to the owners and they ought not to have to pay damages. It may be proper to forfeit any award of salvage but it would be unjust to go farther.

There is little or no authority for such a principle. But this case presents some novel features, and I would not reject this approach merely because it is new. There would be much to be said for it in certain circumstances. This is not only a question of maritime law.

Lord Reid compared volunteers who save land property from danger with professional salvors, contrasting the effect of their respective negligence, and continued:

Suppose a house is on fire. It contains a valuable collection of, say, china. There is little or no hope of saving the collection but a passer-by, with or without the consent of the owner, goes in and brings most of the collection to safety. But owing to some gross negligence on his part some of the china is smashed. On land, a person who interferes to save property is not in law entitled to any reward. But it would be most unjust in my view if, although he benefited the owner by saving the bulk of the property, he were held liable for his negligence in destroying the rest. Of course, in such a case the court would be very slow to find that the rescuer was guilty of negligence, but the circumstances might be such that such a finding could not be avoided. Similarly, if a passing ship lends assistance to a vessel in dire distress, when without such assistance the vessel would almost certainly be lost, and the salvor succeeds in saving the vessel but by gross negligence causes much unnecessary damage to it, it might be quite proper to forfeit any salvage award, but I would think it most unjust that the salvor should have to pay damages. Taking the salvor's operations as a whole he would have done much more good to the owner than harm. Could it be right that the owner need not even say thank you for the good, but should recover damages because the ship which, without the salvor's efforts he would never have seen again, is of less value when returned to him than it would have been if the salvor had not caused damage by negligence?

But any such exception from the general rule would have to be confined within reasonable limits. Take the volunteer who saves property from the burning house. The case would look very different if others on the spot would almost certainly have saved all the property if the volunteer had not officiously interfered. Or suppose that there is no immediate emergency. The owner of a house is advised that it is likely to collapse soon and he engages professional removal contractors to remove the contents. If they do damage to the furniture by their negligence they could not possibly be allowed to plead that if nothing had been done the furniture would have been destroyed when the house fell a week later.

Even if such a principle were accepted I do not think it could be applied in this case. This was not a case of a sudden emergency. There is nothing to suggest that *The Tojo Maru* would have become a total loss if the respondents' tug had not offered her services. The respondents offered their services as professional salvors, time was taken to arrange a contract, then they made elaborate preparations to do the necessary repair work before the vessel could be towed away and it was only several weeks later in the course of that repair work that the negligence of the diver caused this damage. It would require a very strong case to convince me that in such circumstances it is unjust to apply the ordinary law.[164]

Four essential points can be drawn from what Lord Reid said:

(1) of course, the courts look leniently to negligence of salvors which causes damage to the property in danger during salvage operations and will judge their efforts as a whole.

(2) it was not disputed that there can be a claim for damages when the ship is lost due to salvors' negligence, depending on the circumstances of a case.

(3) the same standards of care should apply in judging the conduct of professional salvors as those applicable to other professionals, save that public policy issues applicable to maritime salvage carried out in an emergency will be taken into account by the court. On the facts of this case, however, there was no emergency and the damage was caused several weeks later, during the repairs of the salved property.

(4) the proposed exception to the common law negligence principle, eg that of 'more good than harm', had not been established, but it could conceivably apply in very exceptional cases when a passing vessel offered assistance to a ship in distress and there was no hope that the property could be saved without assistance.

Lord Diplock was more robust in his conviction that the general rule of negligence applicable at common law should apply to both professional salvors and to those passing vessels which volunteer assistance. Comparing salvage contracts with contracts for work and labour, Lord Diplock said:

---

164 [1972] AC 242 (HL), pp 267–69.

The first distinctive feature is that the person rendering the salvage services is not entitled to any remuneration unless he saves the property in whole or in part. This is what is meant by 'success' in cases about salvage . . . In my view there is nothing in it which ought in principle to displace the general law as to the liability of a party to a contract for work and labour for negligence in the performance of it.[165]

He then phrased the ordinary rule of English law to be, thus:

The special characteristics of salvage remuneration payable for salvage services whether rendered under Lloyd's standard form of salvage agreement with professional salvage contractors, or volunteered by a passing vessel and accepted without any express contract, would not appear in themselves sufficient to oust the ordinary rule of English law that a person who undertakes for reward to do work and labour upon the property of another owes to the owner of the property a duty to exercise that care which the circumstances demand and, where he holds himself out as carrying on the business or profession of undertaking services of that kind, to use such skill in the performance of them as a person carrying on such a business may reasonably be expected to possess.[166]

Lord Diplock thought that there was no justification for treating salvage services as excluded from the general principles of English law of liability for negligence[167] as it has developed in the twentieth century. He further said:

It is not in this but in an entirely different situation that the converse of the concept of 'more harm than good' has previously been applied in salvage law. That is: where one salvor has performed salvage services to a vessel in distress but has not completed her rescue and she has been ultimately brought to a place of safety by a different salvor. The right of the first salvor to share in the salvage reward depends upon his showing that he has contributed to the saving of the vessel. This has often turned upon whether, when his own services ended, he had left the vessel in less peril than that in which he found it, that is, whether his services had done 'more good than harm' . . . I have endeavoured to show that the conclusions sought to be drawn from judgments given in the mid–19th century cases, upon which this proposition is founded, are based upon a misunderstanding of the historical use of the expression 'negligence', upon a failure to take into account of the supposed limitations upon the jurisdiction of the Court of Admiralty and upon a misapprehension of the kind of situation in which it was relevant to inquire whether a salvor had done more good than harm.[168]

Thus, the House of Lords rejected the approach of the Court Appeal that damages would be recoverable from the salvors only if the measure of the harm done by the salvors exceeded the measure of the good. Such a principle was not to be found in any of the previous authorities.[169]

---

165 Ibid, p 293.

166 [1972] AC 242 (CA), p 293.

167 The general principle of negligence had been applied in *Anglo Saxon Petroleum Co v Lords Commissioners of the Admiralty (The Delphinula)* [1947] KB 794 (CA), (1947) 80 LlL Rep 459, which was criticised by the Court of Appeal as being inappropriate to salvage cases.

168 *The Tojo Maru* [1971] 1 Lloyd's Rep 341 (HL), p 367.

169 This principle was deduced by the Court of Appeal from old decisions, which reflected justice and fairness in the cases of salvage in which well-established principles of maritime law had been applied for a long time. It was accepted that these authorities were not binding upon the Court of Appeal as none had reached the House of Lords but, nevertheless, they had not been wrongly decided.

Therefore, reversing the Court of Appeal decision, it was held permissible to entertain the owners' counterclaim for damages, which could be offset against the award. It was stressed, however, that damages would be allowed only by a counter-claim to a claim for an award with respect to successful salvage services. If there was no success, there would be no award. The House of Lords did not decide whether there could be a separate claim in damages for negligence against the salvors if there was no success. It could be inferred from the judgment, however, albeit obiter, that such a claim could be brought if the ship was lost due to the salvors' negligence.

Thus, the arbitrator's decision was restored except with regard to the method of assessment of the salvage award. Lord Diplock objected to the arbitrator's assessment of the salvage award on the basis of her damaged state, the effect of which would be to account for the salvor's negligence twice, and he remitted the award to the arbitrator to make the adjustment.

As regards the measure of damages, their Lordships held that the owners should be put in the same position they would have been in had there been no negligence. In particular, had the salvage operation been conducted without negligence the owners would not have had to spend money for repairs and would not have suffered loss. On the other hand, they would have to pay salvage. The proper measure of damages was the difference between what would have been the value of the ship upon completion of the salvage if there had been no negligence (undamaged salved value) and her actual value at the place of termination in the state in which she was as a result of the negligence. With regard to the salvage remuneration, it was held that it was to be assessed on the assumption that there had been no negligence (no deduction of costs for repairing the damage). Then, the figures arrived at would be set off against each other.[170] The result would seem to be that either a salvage award would be due to the salvor, or an award for damages would be due to the shipowner depending on which figure was the highest.

9.2.3 Unresolved issues

In the light of this decision, and the fact that the Convention does not deal with the issue of damages, there are some unresolved issues concerning salvors' negligence. Brice[171] has been critical of the decision and of the formula of assessment of damages, which may not be appropriate in all cases:

(a) In *The Tojo Maru*, there was an isolated incident of negligence by the diver of the salvors causing damage to the ship during the salvage services, which were otherwise competently performed.

(b) He questioned the way salvage remuneration was proposed to be assessed, which might not be appropriate particularly in cases where the whole planning and execution of a salvage operation was negligent. Perhaps, he suggested, in those cases the 'no cure no pay' principle should be applied and the damages should be assessed on the actual damage done; a fictional state of affairs as

---

170 [1971] 1 Lloyd's Rep 341, pp 355, 367, 368.
171 Paper given at a debate on salvage held by the London Shipping Law Centre on 19 June 1997.

proposed by the House of Lords and an assumption that a successful service was rendered could not be contemplated.

(c) On the assumption that there were two salvors and the ship, although saved, was of little value due to the negligence of the one, for the purpose of arriving at an award for damages against the negligent salvor in accordance with the formula of *The Tojo Maru*, his salvage remuneration would have to be assessed on a notional ship value. The non-negligent salvor, however, would receive no reward as this would be the consequence of the negligence of the other. It would be absurd, he said, if the assessment of damages with regard to the negligent salvor were arrived at on the basis of the formula of *The Tojo Maru*. Presumably, he pondered, the non-negligent salvor would have a cause of action in tort against the negligent one.

In his book, Brice[172] proposes a solution and compares American with English law on the question of salvors' negligence. American salvage law is, in general, the same as English law, and the Salvage Convention applies in both systems. There is, however, a significant difference in approach. It is interesting to note that American courts, Brice says, have developed the doctrine of a liability restricted to 'distinguishable and independent damage'. A distinguishable damage is other than that which the salved would have suffered, had the salvors' efforts not been undertaken. In *The Tojo Maru*, for example, the damage was 'distinguishable', in that it was not the type which was inherent in the situation. He concluded that, perhaps, the English courts may consider to adopt the American approach of distinguishable and independent damage done by salvors, in cases where they assisted a ship in dire peril. Considering that the property would have been lost in any event, but for the salvors' services, the proper approach would have been that the salvor would be made liable for damages only if the damage was distinct and independent of the immediate peril, that is, it would not have occurred in the absence of assistance. The court, he proposes, should exercise greater leniency in cases where the salvors are not professionals and also in cases where the circumstances are very perilous for the would-be rescuer. (This proposal is close to what Lord Reid was prepared to accept.) But, in the more run-of-the-mill cases, he says, the degree of leniency would be less and the ordinary principles for recovery of damages in tort or breach of contract should apply.

It seems that this solution is similar to the two categories (the 'dire danger' and the 'non-dire danger' cases) distinguished by Salmon LJ in the Court of Appeal in *The Tojo Maru*. Brice urges that there should be flexibility in application of the general rule of negligence at common law to salvage cases, since salvage is a distinct area of the law and, historically, is not just only part of common law.

Whether limitation of liability by the salvor should apply before or after the set-off was left unanswered by the House of Lords. Thus, one may assume that the answer given by the Court of Appeal on this issue, albeit obiter, that limitation of liability must be applied first to the damages award before the set-off between the damages and the salvage awards, should be good law, but these dicta were not essential to the decision, since limitation was refused.

---

172 Op cit, Brice, fn 1, p 531.

9.3 Negligence occurring before salvage services were rendered

This can occur when there is a collision between two ships, and salvage services are rendered afterwards to the one ship, which has been put in danger by the fault of the other ship. It has already been seen that there is a statutory duty upon masters and crew of colliding ships to offer assistance to each other after the collision, and that that duty is no bar to earning a salvage award. The House of Lords decided in *The Melanie v The San Onofre*[173] that the vessel at fault can earn a salvage award if the services are meritorious. The outcome will depend on the facts of each case.[174] The Convention, in Art 18, provides that the salvor may be deprived of the whole or part of payment if the salvage operations have become necessary because of his negligence.

In *The Key Singapore*,[175] in which tugs were engaged to tow a jack up rig, in extreme weather conditions, the tow line parted frequently but the rig was eventually brought to safety. The towage had been converted to salvage, and the question was whether the tugs deserved a salvage award or whether the situation of danger was created by their negligence, so as to deprive them of any award. The appeal arbitrator found the tugs 50% at fault and reduced the arbitrator's award due to the tugs to $1 million. On appeal to the court, Steel J upheld the award made by the appeal arbitrator. With regard to Art 18, he held that, to assess the extent to which the salvage operations had become necessary due to the fault or neglect of the salvor, it was necessary to assess the causative potency and blameworthiness of the salvor's faults relative to the causative potency and blameworthiness of the rig's faults. Both tugs and tow had fallen short of their duties.

In Beaverford v Kafiristan,[176] the issue was slightly different. It raised the question whether a sister ship of a colliding ship, whose fault necessitated salvage, could claim salvage award for the successful salvage services rendered to the other colliding ship. *Kafiristan* collided with *The Empress*, which stood by until her sister ship, *Beaverford*, came for assistance and towed *Kafiristan* for about 10 miles, when she handed *Kafiristan* over to other tugs. The tugs brought her to safety. *Beaverford* claimed salvage remuneration.

The House of Lords held that there is no principle in law that prevents a ship from obtaining a salvage award, merely because she belongs to the same owners whose vessel caused, or was partly responsible for, the damage giving rise to the necessity for the salvage services.

Lord Wright said:

---

173 *The Melanie v The San Onofre* [1925] AC 246, p 262 (HL): *dictum* of Lord Phillimore: 'the duty cast by the MSAs upon one of the two colliding vessels to stand by and render assistance does not prevent that vessel, if she renders assistance, from claiming salvage'.

174 In *The Duke of Manchester* (1846) 2 Wm Rob 470, a claim for salvage was dismissed on the ground that the salvors put the vessel in danger by towing her aground; see similarly *The Robert Dixon* (1979) LR 5 PD 54.

175 [2005] 1 Lloyd's Rep 91.

176 [1938] AC 136 (HL); *The Glengaber* (1872) LR 3 A&E 534 approved; *Cargo ex Capella* (1867) LR 1 A&E 356 distinguished.

Where . . . both colliding vessels are to blame, the fixing of the salvage remuneration would seem to be a necessary step in setting off the items of damage on the one side or the other so as to ascertain the final balance of account. It is true that the owners of the other colliding vessel are in law responsible for the damage caused by negligence of their servants including the amount of any salvage awarded to the salving vessel which they also own, but the equities are best worked out by making the salvage award without regard to the fact of common ownership, leaving the incidence of what is awarded to depend on the relative proportions of blame.[177]

It is, I think, in accordance with the ideas of maritime law to treat in a case like this for purposes of salvage the vessels concerned as separate entities and to disregard at that stage the aspect of common ownership and the consequences of the rule of vicarious liability. Thus, the owner of the salving ship is dissociated from himself as owner of the wrongdoing ship.[178]

Lord Atkin added:

As far as the agreement is concerned at this stage after the accident the question of fault seems to be irrelevant. Is it possible to imagine the master of the injured vessel saying to the master of the proposed salvor, I want you to agree to do your best to salve me? You may have to risk your own ship and cargo and to deviate from your voyage and delay your adventure; but it is understood that if either you or any vessel of your owners is in any degree responsible for any damage you will get nothing. The obvious result would be no agreement, no attempt at salvage, other than the ordinary assistance given from humane motives, or sense of statutory duties under the MSA.[179]

The 1989 Convention expressly states, in Art 12(3), that the provisions of the Convention shall apply notwithstanding that the salved vessel and the vessel undertaking the salvage operations belong to the same owner.

It is implicit from these decisions that the rule of common law, namely 'no man will profit from its own wrong', which was applied in this case by the trial judge and the Court of Appeal, is applied flexibly in salvage cases in which the salvage is necessitated by the negligence of the salvor.

10 THE POSITION OF SEVERAL SALVORS

10.1 Dispossession of one salvor by another under maritime law salvage

Under maritime law salvage, the master of the vessel is the sole judge of whether or not to accept salvage services. If, after the master has accepted the services of a salvor, a subsequent salvor supersedes the first against the wishes of the master, he will earn no remuneration. Thus, the principle at common law is that, unless there are special circumstances,[180] a subsequent salvor is not entitled to dispossess a prior

---

177 [1938] AC 136, p 148.
178 Ibid, p 149.
179 Ibid, p 141.
180 *The American Farmer* (1947) 80 LlL Rep 672.

salvor, provided that the prior salvor has a reasonable prospect of accomplishing the salvage service himself and is not endangering the safety of the salved property.[181]

10.2 Dismissal of a salvor under contract by the master of the vessel being salved

Dispossession of a salvor by way of dismissal by the master of the ship being salved has different consequences under (a) maritime law salvage where there is no contract, and (b) where there is a salvage contract. (The consequences of dismissal under the Convention are set out in para 10.3, below.) The contrast between these situations is illustrated by the following case, the facts of which are not uncommon.

The Unique Mariner (No 2) [182]

During a voyage from Malaysia to Indonesia, *UM* ran aground. All attempts to refloat her were unsuccessful. Her owners arranged through agents for a suitable tug to be despatched from Singapore. The agents sent a telegram to the master informing him that a tug was being despatched. In the meantime, the captain and crew of the tug *Salvaliant* noticed *UM* aground in the vicinity and offered salvage assistance. The master, mistakenly believing that *Salvaliant* was the tug which had been sent from Singapore, signed a salvage agreement under the LOF. While *Salvaliant* was preparing to refloat *UM*, the master of *UM* received a further telegram from the agents about the other tug and realised his error. Consequently, he instructed the master of *Salvaliant* to stop work immediately. Her crew got off *UM*, and *Salvaliant* stood by. The tug hired by the agents arrived the following day and finally succeeded in refloating *UM* and then towed her to Singapore. The owners of *Salvaliant* claimed damages for breach of contract and/or salvage remuneration under the LOF in arbitration. They contended that, had their tug not been dismissed, she would have made a refloating attempt by towage and would probably have been successful.

The arbitrator awarded the contractors US$75,000. The shipowners appealed against this award, and the appeal arbitrator allowed the appeal, reducing the award to $35,000, on the ground that the original arbitrator had erred in his approach to the assessment of the sum to which the contractors were entitled.

There was an appeal to the court. The question was how to assess the award for salvage services which had been wrongfully interrupted by the master and whether the contractors were, in addition to an award, entitled to *restitutio in integrum* as compensation, or as damages for breach of contract, or both. The contractors contended that, as superseded salvors, the compensation should be assessed at an amount which they would have earned by way of salvage remuneration, had they been allowed to complete their services successfully, less deductions for risks not

---

181 *The Fleece* [1850] 3 W Rob 278.
182 [1979] 1 Lloyd's Rep 37.

run, expenses not incurred and operating time saved, including an allowance of a discount for the possibility that they might have been unable to complete the services successfully, even if they had been allowed to do so.

Brandon J stated the general principles applicable to: (1) salvage under the general maritime law (where there is no salvage contract); and (2) salvage under contract, to be as follows:

Salvage under maritime law:

Under maritime law salvage, the owners of the property to be salved were under no obligation to allow the salvors to complete their services but were entitled if they wished to dismiss them and supersede them by other salvors.

However, if the salvors were later dismissed by the master of the ship and superseded by other salvors, they were entitled to remuneration in the nature of salvage (a) as a reward for the services which they had actually rendered before they were superseded and (b) by way of some compensation for the loss of opportunity to complete their services.

The justification for the compensation, he said, was to be found on reasons of public policy referred to by Lord Merriman P in *The Hassel*, and was implicit in the passage from Kennedy, *Law of Salvage*, adopted as a correct statement of the law by Willmer J in *The Loch Tulla*. The reasons of public policy were the encouragement of salvors to be willing and ready to render salvage services even though they may, after entering upon them, be deprived, as a result of being superseded, of the opportunity to complete them successfully.[183]

He concluded that salvors, in such cases, were not entitled to full compensation, assessed like damages, for breach of contract or duty, on the basis of *restitutio in integrum*; and the right to compensation for being superseded was not dependant on any prior benefit having been conferred.

Salvage under contract:

By contrast, where the salvors were engaged under an express salvage agreement in the terms of Lloyd's form, as was in the present case, it was an implied term that the owners of the property to be salved would not act in such a way as to prevent the salvors from performing the services, so long as they (the salvors) were willing and able to do so. The obligation not to act in such a way so as to prevent performance included an obligation not to dismiss or supersede.

With particular reference to the facts of this case, he held that: As the appeal arbitrator had found that the salvors were willing and able to perform the services which they had undertaken and the act of the master of *Unique Mariner* in superseding *Salvaliant* with *Asiatic Gala* was a breach of contract, such a conduct was a breach of obligation of such a character as to constitute a repudiation of the contract which was accepted on behalf of the salvors.

On the basis that the shipowners repudiated the salvage agreement and the

---

183 [1979] 1 Lloyd's Rep 37, pp 50–52; *The Hassel* (1959) 2 Lloyd's Rep 82. *The Loch Tulla* (1950) 84 Ll.L Rep 62.

salvors accepted such repudiation, the salvors were entitled to the usual remedy in damages, which a party to a contract had in such a case. However, they were not also entitled to recover payment for services they had actually rendered.

Summary of the principles

(a) Under ordinary maritime law salvage, there is no obligation not to dismiss. There will be payment for salvage rendered and some compensation for lost opportunity.

(b) Under contractual salvage the master of the salved has a duty not to prevent salvors from doing their work and a dismissal by him will be breach of contract answerable in damages for repudiation of the contract. No award in this case would be due.

Both LOF 1990 and 1995 contain a new provision (not being in the Convention) in cll 18 and 4, respectively, about termination of the agreement by the owner of the vessel, when there is no longer any prospect of a useful result leading to salvage reward in accordance with Art 13, by giving reasonable notice to the contractors. Clause G of LOF 2000 grants a right to termination to both the owners of the vessel or the contractor by giving reasonable prior written notice to the other, when there is no longer any reasonable prospect of a useful result in accordance with Arts 12 and 13 of the Convention.

The expression 'useful result', which is borrowed from Art 12 of the Convention, has not been defined, although in obvious cases it may be easily understood. There are potential problems, however, if there is no agreement between the parties to the contract concerning whether the ship is economically salvable where repair costs have not been properly assessed.[184]

10.3 The position of several salvors under the Salvage Convention 1989

Article 8(1)(c) imposes a duty on a salvor, whenever circumstances reasonably require, to seek assistance from other salvors; and Art 8(1)(d) imposes a separate duty on a salvor to accept the intervention of other salvors when reasonably requested to do so by the owner or master of the vessel or other property in danger; provided, however, that the amount of his reward shall not be prejudiced should it be found that such a request was unreasonable.

Thus, prior salvors cannot refuse assistance from subsequent ones, nor exclude them. Any misconduct by a salvor will be taken into account to reduce the award or, depending on the seriousness of the misconduct, deprive him of any payment under the Convention (Art 18). The Convention does not deal, however, with whether the salvor will be liable in damages if such conduct causes damage to the property being subject to salvage. The problems arising from such an omission were discussed under paras 9.2.1 and 9.2.2, above.

---

184 Buckley, M, 'Salvage: LOF 2000' (2000) *International Maritime Law*, May, p 99.

There is also a general duty imposed by Art 8(2)(a) on the owner and master of the vessel, or the owner of other property in danger, to co-operate fully with the salvor during the course of the salvage operations. No provision for remedies to the salvor is found in the Convention in the event that his success is impeded by the non-co-operation of those in charge of the property to be salved. Thus, as far as English law is concerned, principles of common law will apply, of which see next.

11 DUTIES OF THE OWNER OF PROPERTY IN DANGER

11.1 Duty to co-operate

Under common law, the master and owner of the ship in danger have a duty to co-operate with the salvor and not to mislead him.[185] In the event of breach of this duty, ordinary principles of common law will apply to provide a remedy, as was held by Hill J in *The Valsesia*.[186]

When V ran aground, two tugs were engaged to render her assistance upon an agreed sum. After some hours of work, V grounded again due to negligence of her crew in having failed to slip the cable at the time agreed between the masters of the respective parties. The tugs were, therefore, unable to complete the salvage operation and V grounded again. She was then in a worse position than she was before the tugs got hold of her. The tugs claimed damages from the owners of V, on the ground that they were deprived of the opportunity to complete the salvage due to the negligence of V's servants. They contended that, since the tugs had performed the services except for completing the salvage, they should be treated as if they had performed the contract and were, thus, entitled to recover the stipulated salvage sum.

Hill J held:

> In my view this case falls to be decided according to the ordinary principles of common law and no question peculiar to the law of salvage is involved. I think there was a mutual obligation implied in such an agreement as this, at least, to act with ordinary skill and care in carrying out the respective parts in the combined work. It was the duty of the tugs to obey the orders of those who were in command of the ship and to use skill and care in the handling of the tugs, and it was equally the duty of those in charge of the ship to use ordinary skill and care in carrying out their part of the contract, which was the slipping of the cable at the right time. This, indeed, was the essential part which the ship was to play in the combined operation . . .[187]

> I find a difficulty in saying that anybody can recover a lump sum to be paid in respect of a completed work, when in fact, that work has not been completed. But if the plaintiffs were prevented from completing it by the negligence of those on board the ship, and if they were thereby deprived of the opportunity of earning the stipulated sums, then they are entitled to damages for the breach . . . and in this case the damages would be exactly commensurate with the stipulated sums because the

---

185 *The Kingalock* (1854) 1 Spinks E&A 265.
186 [1927] P 115.
187 Ibid, p 118.

plaintiffs had in substance completed the whole of what they had undertaken to do.[188]

Under Art 8(2)(a) of the Salvage Convention 1989, there is an express duty upon the owner of the property in danger and the master of the vessel to co-operate fully during the course of the salvage operations.

The article states:

The owner and master or the vessel or the owner of other property in danger shall owe a duty to the salvor:

(a) to co-operate fully with him during the course of the salvage operations;

(b) in so doing, to exercise due care to prevent or minimise damage to the environment; and

(c) when the vessel or other property has been brought to a place of safety, to accept re-delivery when reasonably requested by the salvor to do so.

The previous Salvage Convention did not provide that a duty of care was owed by either the salvor or the salved to each other during salvage operations, but common law principles applied.

Nothing is said, however, about recoverable damages in the event of breach, thus relevant national law would apply.

Under LOF 1990 and 1995, both contracts provide, by cl 3, that the owners, their servants and agents shall co-operate fully with the contractor in and about the salvage, including entry to a place named or the place of safety. The equivalent clause of LOF 2000 'duties of property owners' is more extensive; in particular, cl F spells out in detail what the co-operation is about:

(i) the contractors may make reasonable use of the vessel's machinery gear and equipment free of expense provided that the contractors shall not unnecessarily damage abandon or sacrifice any property on board;

(ii) the contractors shall be entitled to all such information as they may reasonably require relating to the vessel or the remainder of the property provided such information is relevant to the performance of the services and is capable of being provided without undue difficulty or delay;

(iii) the owners of the property shall co-operate fully with the contractors in obtaining entry to the place of safety stated in the contract or agreed or determined in accordance with the contact.

11.2 Obligation to provide security to salvors

The Convention, by Art 21, and both LOFs 1990 and 1995, by cll 4 and 5, respectively, impose a dual obligation on the owner of the salved vessel: first to provide satisfactory security for the salvage claim, including interest and costs in respect of the vessel and, second, to use their best endeavours to ensure that the cargo-owners provide satisfactory security including interest and costs before the cargo is

---

188 Ibid, p 119.

released.[189] It is submitted that 'best endeavours' in this context also, as under cl 1(a) of LOFs 1990 and 1995 (discussed under para 9.1, above), means the exercise of due diligence. The salved property shall not be removed from the port or place of arrival after completion of salvage without the consent of the salvor, until such security is provided.

A provision for salvage security is included as an important notice in the LOF 2000. It states:

> As soon as possible the owners of the vessel should notify the owners of other property on board that this agreement has been made. If the contractors are successful the owners of such property should note that it will become necessary to provide the contractors with salvage security promptly in accordance with cl 4 of the Lloyd's Standard Salvage and Arbitration (LSSA) clauses. The provision of general average security does not relieve the salved interests of their separate obligation to provide salvage security to the contractors.

Common law principles will apply as to the amount of the security, which must be reasonable.

In *The Tribels*,[190] it was held that it is an implied term of the salvage contract that the contractor would not ask for unreasonably high security. The salvors were entitled to demand security for a sum that would secure payment of a top-level award, which they could reasonably anticipate to obtain including the arbitration costs. In the event of excessive security demanded by the salvor in this case, the owners applied for and were granted an injunction to restrain the salvor from demanding security above £1 million.

The Convention expressly provides, by Art 20, that nothing shall affect the salvor's maritime lien under any international convention or national law, but that the salvor may not enforce his maritime lien when satisfactory security for his claim, including interest and costs, has been duly tendered or provided.

12 ASSESSMENT OF THE AWARD AND SPECIAL COMPENSATION

The Convention provides (Art 12(1), (2)) that if the salvage operations have had useful result the salvor will be rewarded and, except as otherwise provided, no payment is due under the Convention if there is no useful result. Article 13 refers to the assessment of award for property salvage, Art 16 is relevant to life salvage, and Art 14 deals with special compensation (liability salvage), which is not meant to be environmental salvage.[191]

Services rendered, notwithstanding the express and reasonable prohibition of

---

189 When satisfactory security for the salvor's claims is duly provided or rendered, including interest and costs, the salvor may not enforce his maritime lien (Art 20(2)).

190 [1985] 1 Lloyd's Rep 129.

191 As Lord Mustill stressed in *The Nagasaki Spirit*; at the time of writing, the International Salvage Union, in collaboration with other industry bodies, is working on developing the concept of environmental salvage.

the owner or master of the vessel or the owner of any other property in danger which is not and has not been on board the vessel, shall not give rise to payment under the Convention (Art 19).

Every interest salved contributes according to its salved value (Art 13(2)). The rewards, exclusive of interest and recoverable legal costs, shall not exceed the salved value of the vessel and other property.

Both Arts 13 and 14 are incorporated in the LOFs 1990 and 1995 by reference. LOF 2000 is made subject to English law.

12.1 The criteria for assessing the salvage award and special compensation

Criteria for assessing the award are set out in Art 13(1) and reflect the common law position. Article 13(1)(b) gives allowance for increasing the award in the event of efforts made by the salvors to protect the environment.

Relevant factors under the Convention (Art 13(1)) are:

(a) value salved: every interest salved contributes according to its salved value;

(b) the skill and efforts of the salvors in preventing or minimising damage to the environment;

(c) the measure of success obtained by the salvors;

(d) the nature and degree of danger;

(e) salvor's skill, effort in salving the vessel, other property and life;

(f) the time used and expenses and losses incurred by the salvors;

(g) the risk of liability and other risks (including equipment) run by salvors or their equipment;

(h) the promptness of the services rendered;

(i) the availability and use of vessels and equipment intended for salvage operations;

(j) the state of readiness and efficiency of the salvor's equipment and the value thereof.

Criteria for special compensation

Article 14(1)

If the salvor has carried out salvage operations in respect of a vessel which by itself or its cargo threatened damage to the environment and has failed to earn a reward under Art 13 at least equivalent to the special compensation assessable in accordance with this article, he shall be entitled to special compensation from the owner of that vessel equivalent to his expenses as herein defined.

Article 14(2)

If, in the circumstances set out in para 1, the salvor by his salvage operations has prevented or minimised damage to the environment, the special compensation payable by the owner to the salvor under para 1 may be increased up to maximum of

30% of the expenses incurred by the salvor. However, the tribunal, if it deems it fair and just to do so and bearing in mind the relevant criteria set out in Art 13(1) may increase such special compensation further, but in no event shall the total increase be more than 100% of the expenses incurred by the salvor.

Article 14(3)

'Salvor's expenses' for the purpose of paras 1 and 2 means the out of pocket expenses reasonably incurred by the salvor in the salvage operation and a fair rate for equipment and personnel actually and reasonably used in the salvage operation, taking into consideration the criteria set out in Art 13, para 1(h), (i), (j).

Article 14(4)

The total special compensation under this article shall be paid only if and to the extent that such compensation is greater than any reward recoverable by the salvor under Art 13.

Article 14(5)

If the salvor has been negligent and has thereby failed to prevent or minimise damage to the environment, he may be deprived of the whole or part of any special compensation due under this article.

Article 14(6)

Nothing in this article shall affect any right of recourse on the part of the owner of the vessel.

Skill and efforts to minimise damage to the environment will be taken into account in assessing property salvage by way of an enhanced award (Art 13(1)(b)). In addition to the enhanced award, the salvor will get his expenses paid by way of special compensation, under Art 14(1), if he made efforts to protect the environment. He will even get his expenses regardless of whether property was saved or whether his efforts to minimise or prevent damage to the environment were ultimately successful. But, he will not get Art 14 compensation if the award under Art 13 is higher than the total special compensation (Art 14(4)). In particular, Art 14(1) provides for special compensation being equivalent to the salvor's expenses, in the event he has not earned an award under Art 13 at least equivalent to special compensation, when the vessel, or its cargo, threatened damage to the environment. In addition, if the salvor has, in fact, prevented or minimised such damage, the special compensation will be increased up to 30% of the expenses incurred by the salvor. Such compensation may be further increased, taking into account the factors under Art 13, but no more than 100% of the expenses incurred (Art 14(2)). Negligence on the part of the salvor will deprive him of the whole, or part, of any special compensation under this article (Art 14(5)).

In Part II, para 4 of Sched 11 to MSA 1995 (common understanding), it is stated that, for fixing a reward under Art 13 and assessing the special compensation under Art 14, the court or arbitrator is under no duty to fix a reward under Art 13 up to the maximum salved value of the vessel and other property before assessing the special compensation to be paid under Art 14.

12.2 The decision in *The Nagasaki Spirit*

The principal issue in *The Nagasaki Spirit* was concerned with the definition of 'expenses' in Art 14(3) (above) and, in particular, that part of it which refers to 'fair rate for equipment'. In other words, the point was whether, in assessing a 'fair rate' for the salvor's own craft, equipment, personnel, etc, it was permissible to include a market or profitable rate, or whether the salvor was entitled solely to reimbursement of expenditure.

The case involved a collision between *The Nagasaki Spirit*, laden with crude oil, and the container ship, *The Ocean Blessing*, in the northern part of the Malacca Straits. Following the collision, about 12,000 tonnes of crude oil escaped from *The Nagasaki Spirit* into the sea and a fire resulted. Both vessels were engulfed in the fire, and all crew on *The Ocean Blessing* lost their lives. Two members of the crew on board *The Nagasaki Spirit* survived. The next day, professional salvors agreed to salve *The Nagasaki Spirit* and her cargo under the LOF 1990, which contained Arts 13 and 14 of the 1989 Convention. They provided craft, personnel, equipment and consumables. With the help of a number of tugs, the fire on *The Nagasaki Spirit* was extinguished. Her cargo was transhipped and the vessel was safely redelivered to her owners.

The award was made on the basis of Art 13, and the arbitrator, in fixing special compensation, stressed the need for encouragement. In order to arrive at a fair rate, he took into account some contribution to future investment so that professional salvors were encouraged to stay in business.

The appeal arbitrator, Mr Willmer QC, disagreed; he increased the award under Art 13 and took a different line on Art 14, taking into account the type and scope of the job in assessing the fair rate, which would be reflected in the costs to the salvors. Since his assessment of the award was higher than that of the special compensation, no compensation under Art 14 was payable.

The admiralty judge, on appeal from the award, concluded that, although fair rate imported the idea of remuneration, which would normally include an element of profit, the appeal arbitrator was right to reject this. The words read in their context meant recompense for expenditure, because the Convention drew a distinction between remuneration or reward and compensation.

The Court of Appeal agreed with the judge and, reading Art 14 in context with Art 13(1), concluded that fair rate means a rate of expenses, which is to be comprehensive of indirect or overhead expenses and taking into account the additional costs of having resources instantly available. So, fair rate, in the view of the Court of Appeal, was not to be a salvage reward, or anything like it. Article 14 does not refer to skill and effort of the salvors, etc, as does Art 13(1).[192]

Evans LJ dissented only to the extent that these expenses did not necessarily exclude any profit element and, in this respect, he preferred the approach of the appeal arbitrator:

I agree with the judgment of Staughton LJ on the 'fair rate' issue in rejecting the

---

192 [1996] 1 Lloyd's Rep 449, p 455, per Staughton LJ.

concept of salvage remuneration or reward and in limiting the salvor's claim under Art 14(3) to the expenses which he has incurred. I would not go on to hold, however, that these expenses necessarily exclude any profit element or that they are confined to costs, including overheads, as the learned judge held. The appeal arbitrator, Mr JF Willmer QC adopted an approach which is distinct both from that of the arbitrator, Mr RF Stone QC, and that of the judge. In summary, I would hold that the judge was wrong to exclude altogether a possible 'profit' element and that Mr Stone erred in assessing the 'fair rate' as if it was a form of remuneration or reward. Broadly speaking, in my judgment, Mr Willmer was correct to have regard to commercial or, where relevant, market factors as well as to the salvor's costs.[193]

The House of Lords, with Lord Mustill delivering judgment, held that 'fair rate', under Art 14(3), meant fair rate of expenditure and did not include any element of profit. The first half of Art 14(3) covered out-of-pocket expenses and the second half covered overhead expenses. The word 'rate' was the appropriate word to use when attributing or apportioning general overheads to equipment and personnel reasonably and actually used in the particular salvage operation. 'Expenses' denoted amounts either disbursed or borne, not earned as profits. The fact that Art 14(3) requires fair rate to be added to the out-of-pocket expenses made it clear that it contained no element of profit. Also, Art 14(2) twice makes use of the expression 'expenses incurred' by the salvor. The word 'incur' obviously showed that it is not something that yielded him profit. Lord Mustill concluded that Art 14(3) was not concerned with remuneration and described the intention of the legislation, thus:

> Furthermore, and in my view decisively, the promoters of the Convention did not choose, as they might have done, to create an entirely new and distinct category of environmental salvage, which would finance the owners of vessels and gear to keep them in readiness simply for the purpose of preventing damage to the environment. Paragraphs 1, 2 and 3 of Art 14 all make it clear that the right to special compensation depends on the performance of 'salvage operations' which, as already seen, are defined by Art 1(a) as operations to assist a vessel in distress. Thus, although Art 14 is undoubtedly to encourage professional salvors to keep vessels readily available, this is still for the purpose of a salvage for which the primary incentive remains a traditional salvage award. The only structural change in the scheme is that the incentive is now made more attractive by the possibility of obtaining new financial recognition for conferring a new type of incidental benefit. Important as it is, the remedy under Art 14 is subordinate to the reward under Art 13, and its function should not be confused by giving it a character too closely akin to salvage.[194]

12.3 Article 14 does not provide for environmental salvage

The long-standing principle in salvage law of 'no cure no pay' changed, at first, with the introduction of the novel concept of 'safety net' by the LOF 1980, the purpose of which was to encourage salvors to do their best to protect the environment from oil pollution. But this concept related only to steps taken to protect the environment from oil pollution.

---

193 Ibid, p 457.
194 [1997] 1 Lloyd's Rep 323, pp 332–33.

Following the concept of the 'safety net', the Salvage Convention 1989 introduced the concept of 'special compensation'. This new concept widened the scope of encouragement to salvors, in that it applies to prevention of any pollution, not just oil pollution. However, damage to the environment is limited to substantial physical damage to human health or to marine life or resources in coastal or inland waters or areas adjacent thereto (Art 1(d)), and not further than these waters.

Since salvors will recoup at least their expenses if they take steps to protect the environment, even if there is no success in salving the property in danger, there is no longer 'no cure no pay' salvage because of the fallback on Art 14, as Lord Mustill stated in *The Nagasaki Spirit*; but, he added, no profit is allowed by it; the Convention has not introduced a 'pure environmental salvage'. Article 14(3) is not concerned with remuneration, which implies a profit element, but with reimbursement of reasonable incurred expenses and overheads. Giving the words used in this article their natural meaning, and considering its context as a whole, Art 14 is subordinate to Art 13. It provides for an uplift to Art 13, only if the compensation under Art 14 is higher than the award under Art 13.

Its novelty lies in the provision for compensation in respect of expenses incurred by reason of the efforts made during salvage operations to protect the environment, even though no property is saved, or even when damage to the environment is not prevented (Art 14(1)).

However, not all problems were resolved by the Convention and perhaps more were created, as will be seen below. For example, under LOF 1980, the safety net was applicable even if the salvor's efforts to minimise or prevent damage to the environment took place on the high seas, as opposed to near coastal or inland waters or areas adjacent thereto only (Art 1(d)).

A solution has now been found for these problems by the SCOPIC (see para 14 below), which can be incorporated into any LOF, but it will become operative only when the salvor opts to invoke the clause.

In practice, there are insuperable problems that salvors are faced with, particularly when there is a risk to the environment. A marine casualty becomes a political matter as has been witnessed in some major casualties such as *The Erika*, *The Prestige* and *The Castor*. Only recently has there been a move, particularly after these incidents, to oblige coastal States to render assistance to salvors by providing places of refuge (see Chapter 20).

13 PROBLEMS ARISING FROM THE DRAFTING OF ART 14 OF THE CONVENTION

Professional salvors reacted strongly to the decision of the House of Lords in *The Nagasaki Spirit*. From their point of view, the decision disregarded the loss suffered by salvors in maintaining sophisticated tugs and equipment (which invariably may have to be made available by borrowing a large capital) in readiness during salvage operations until the danger to the environment is eliminated. Such advance capital provision cannot be compensated, in their opinion, without allowance of an element of profit in the 'fair rate' of Art 14.

In reply to this, Lord Mustill defended his judgment – at a debate held by the London Shipping Law Centre on 19 June 1997 – that 'he was only the pianist who had to perform the music composed by someone else', referring to the draftsmen of the Convention being the composers.

During the same debate, the appeal arbitrator of the decision, John Willmer QC, highlighted the problem arising from the drafting of the Convention and, in particular, with regard to special compensation, as follows.[195]

13.1 Territorial limits

Unlike LOF 1980, which provided for the 'safety net' to apply in cases in which the casualty occurred on the high seas and the salvor exerted efforts to protect the marine environment, the Convention has restricted special compensation to coastal or inland waters or areas adjacent thereto.

Article 1 provides:

For the purpose of this Convention: . . .

(d) Damage to the environment means substantial physical damage to human health or to marine life or resources in coastal or inland waters or areas adjacent thereto, caused by pollution, contamination, fire, explosion or similar major incidents.

Considerable concerns had been expressed by professional salvors as to the territorial limits of Art 1(d). If salvage of a major disaster on the high seas was required, Art 14 would not apply. Undoubtedly, oil or other chemicals would be transported to the coastal areas but, unless a special agreement was reached between the owners' liability insurers to cover the expenses of salvors as they would be covered had Art 14 applied, there would be no incentive for salvors to act.

It might be possible, however, in a given case, Mr Willmer said, to prove that, having regard to the prevailing wind and current, a ship spilling thousands of tons of oil or noxious chemicals, even though far out to sea, nevertheless threatened damage to marine life or resources in coastal waters or areas adjacent thereto. Questions would, however, arise as to the meaning of coastal waters. Could they be equated to the economic zone? Should the waters over the continental shelf be regarded either as coastal or adjacent waters? Unless these questions were authoritatively answered, uncertainty would prevail for salvors and P&I clubs as to the ambit of the special compensation provision.

13.2 Substantial physical damage

The second difficulty arising from the wording of Art 1(d) has been that the damage must be substantial and physical. Minor damage to a tourist beach or mere economic loss would not be enough. The historical context in which the provisions of

---

195 The paper delivered at the seminar is available from the office of the London Shipping Law Centre, UCL Law Faculty.

the Convention have to be construed, said Mr Willmer, indicated that the word 'substantial' had to be considered to be meaning 'seriously' and must mean something more than 'not trifling'. However, he continued, the imprecision of the word 'substantial' would be likely to lead to continued argument as to its application to the facts in particular cases.

13.3 Threatened damage

The next drafting ambiguity for the application of special compensation has been the word 'threatened' in Art 14(1). Lloyd's arbitrators treat it as indicating that for the salvor to succeed in a claim for special compensation there ought to be reasonable apprehension, rather than actual danger of damage to the environment. The main reason for that approach, he said, was that the incentive or encouragement to salvors intended by the Convention would not be promoted by too rigid an interpretation of this word. To wait until it could be seen that there was actual danger would increase the risk that help would arrive too late.

In this connection, Brice[196] had commented that the distinction between the two words used by the Convention, 'danger' in Art 13, and 'threatened' in Art 14, was significant. This was because there might be cases when a threat of damage to the environment may not materialise as, for example, when there was change in wind force and direction. However, this approach was not universally acceptable by P&I clubs and it was important that parties to a salvage agreement knew where they stood.

13.4 Fair rate

How the arbitrator was to ascertain the fair rate has posed a real practical problem. Staughton LJ in the Court of Appeal (*The Nagasaki Spirit*) concluded that this was a matter of judgment for the tribunals of fact and not necessarily the result of any mathematical calculation. Lord Mustill said, in the same case, that:

> Your Lordships were pressed with a submission that the meaning given to Art 14(3) by the judge and the Court of Appeal would be unworkable in practice. I cannot accept this, for it seems to me that the ascertainment of the fair rate must necessarily be performed with a fairly broad brush, albeit not so broad as the fixing of the reward under Art 13, and the uplift under Art 14(2). Quite sufficient information for such purposes could be derived from the salvor's books, as indeed became clear when reference to materials from that source was made in the course of argument.[197]

Mr Willmer explained during this debate that, from his experience as an appeal arbitrator, the real problem here was that professional salvors were very reluctant to disclose books which they would regard as highly confidential. Involvement of accountants would increase the costs of the arbitration and delay matters.

---

196 Op cit, fn 1, at p 427.
197 [1997] 1 Lloyd's Rep 323, p 333.

13.5 The increment

Another problem mentioned in this debate, which has frequently arisen in arbitration with regard to the salvor's entitlement to increment under Art 14(2), was whether or not the salvor has to prove that, had it not been for the services performed, an escape of oil would have occurred and would have caused the substantial damage. Mr Willmer disagreed with such a construction, which would be illogical in the context of the Convention.

13.6 Security for special compensation

The last point of difficulty raised during this debate was the issue of security for special compensation. Under the Convention, Art 21, there is an obligation upon the owner of the ship to provide security. However, if there was no ship salved, it could be difficult to enforce this obligation under the Convention. Even if the ship was salved, there would be no maritime lien attached to the ship for special compensation. An arrest of the ship in this jurisdiction is allowed to enforce the claim, but there will be other claims in priority of payment. The co-operation of liability insurers (P&I clubs) would be required in order to obtain security for special compensation.

14 THE SOLUTION PROVIDED BY THE SCOPIC

14.1 The initiative

The marine salvage industry, represented by the International Salvage Union (ISU), having discussed the problems outlined above with the International Group of P&I Clubs (IGP&I), the London property underwriters and the International Chamber of Shipping, appointed a committee of experts which worked for two years from 1997 and proposed a new solution, the Special Compensation of Protection and Indemnity Clause (SCOPIC), which was finalised in August 1999 and was amended in 2000. It is kept under annual review by the Salvage Liaison Committee.

This clause leaves the fundamental principles of special compensation unchanged, but gives the option to the parties to use the SCOPIC in place of Art 14; the clause puts in place a more workable framework for calculating remuneration, which is based on pre-agreed rates for vessels, personnel and equipment. It provides a greater financial security to salvors. It dispenses with the problematical special 'triggers' required under Art 14. Instead, the salvor may invoke SCOPIC at any stage during a salvage operation, but only in appropriate circumstances, including high-risk, low-value cases. So, it reinforces the salvor's ability to deliver a swift response.[198]

The implementation of the SCOPIC was the result of lengthy negotiations and required 'give and take' on the part of all interested parties; it represents a balance

---

198 Walenkamp, H (President to International Salvage Union), 'SCOPIC: a new solution now available for us' (2000) 14(7) P&I International, July, p 166.

of everyone's interests. The clause has 15 sub-clauses and three appendices. It is backed up by two Codes of Conduct: one between the ISU and the IGP&I, and the other between the London property underwriters and the IGP&I; these codes are not legally binding but are basically a gentlemen's agreement.

The parties to a salvage contract may agree to incorporate SCOPIC into any LOF contract by reference, thereby contracting out of Art 14 of the Convention.

14.2 The sub-clauses

Substitution of Art 14

Clause 1 of the SCOPIC provides that the clause is supplementary to a 'no cure no pay' LOF, and that the method of assessment of special compensation under Art 14 shall be substituted by the method set out in the SCOPIC. The clause clears up the problems arising from Art 14 discussed earlier.[199]

Invoking Scopic (cl 2)

Whatever the circumstances, even if there is not a threat of damage to the environment, the contractor may, by giving written notice to the shipowner, invoke the provisions of the clause at any time of his choosing. The assessment of the SCOPIC remuneration begins from the time of the written notice, and there will be no SCOPIC remuneration for services rendered before that time. If services to protect the environment have already been rendered prior to the written notice, the compensation will be assessed under Art 14. Therefore, it is important for the salvor to exercise his option as soon as possible in order to maximise his recovery.[200]

Security (cl 3)

Shipowners shall provide security in the sum of $3 million within two days of the contractor invoking SCOPIC. If at any time the security is too great or too little, it shall be reduced or raised on application, and any disputes as to the amount of security shall be determined by the arbitrator.

The P&I clubs agree through the Code of Conduct (mentioned earlier) to provide (on behalf of their member ship-owner) any security required for SCOPIC remuneration by a Standard Guarantee Form ISU 5.

Withdrawal (cl 4)

If security is not provided within two days, the contractor has the option to withdraw from SCOPIC entirely and revert to Art 14. Such right can be exercised at any time before security has been provided.

---

199 See Brice, G, 'Salvage and the role of the insurer' [2000] LMCLQ, February, pp 26–41.

200 Browne, B, 'Salvage – LOF and SCOPIC' (1999) *International Journal of Shipping Law*, June, Pt 2, pp 113, 120.

Tariff Rates (cl 5)

SCOPIC remuneration shall be assessed by applying tariff rates to personnel, tugs, and equipment used, adding a bonus assessed generally at 25% of the sum of the tariff rates and out-of-pocket expenses. The rates are reviewed annually.

The out-of-pocket expenses mean money paid by the contractor, or on his behalf, to third parties for hire of men, tugs, other craft and equipment, as well as other expenses reasonably necessary for the operation. These expenses may be agreed at cost, or on tariff rates if the hire is from another ISU member.

Relationship with Art 13 award (cl 6)

The assessed SCOPIC remuneration is payable by the shipowner only to the extent that it exceeds the total Art 13 award payable by all salved interests, even if the Art 13 award or any part of it is not recovered.

Discount (cl 7)

If the SCOPIC is invoked and the SCOPIC remuneration proves to be less than the Art 13 award, the Art 13 award will be discounted by 25% of the difference between the Art 13 award and the amount of the SCOPIC remuneration that would have been assessed. This would, in effect, be the consequence of opting for SCOPIC when it was perhaps not necessary, for example, if there were prospects of an adequate salvage award.[201]

Payment of SCOPIC remuneration (cl 8)

If there is no potential of an Art 13 award, payment is due within one month of presentation of the claim. (The liability is that of the shipowner and his P&I club.) If there is to be an Art 13 award, 75% of the difference between the SCOPIC remuneration and the Art 13 security is payable within one month and the balance when the Art 13 award is assessed.

Termination (cl 9)

(i) The contractor can terminate SCOPIC and the LOF if the cost of his services exceeds the value of all property salved and the likely SCOPIC remuneration.

(ii) The owners can also terminate the SCOPIC (but not the LOF) at any time after SCOPIC has been invoked, provided that the contractor shall be entitled to at least five clear days' notice of such termination.

(iii) The above provisions shall not apply if the contractor is restrained from demobilising by the Government or local Authority (this is likely to be so if there is a threat to the environment).

This provision may give rise to difficulties for salvors, whose security may prove not to be sufficient to maintain his services. It has been suggested that cl 9(i) be amended, so as to provide flexibility and enable the contractor to obtain further security should the circumstances of cl 9(iii) arise.

---

201 Op cit, Brice, fn 193, p 31.

In a recent case, *The Sea Angel*,[202] sub-clause 9(iii) of the SCOPIC was relevant. The ship laden with light crude oil grounded near the approaches to the port of Karachi and subsequently broke into two. There was a major pollution incident. Tsavliris contracted with the owners of the property to salve the ship under LOF 2000, incorporating the SCOPIC. The salvor subcontracted a ship – belonging to the claimant – under a time charter-party to lighten the casualty by off-loading part of the cargo. The subcontracted vessel, after completing the transfer of the cargo, could not be redelivered by the salvors (as charterers) to its owners because the Karachi Port Authority refused to issue the relevant certificate, resulting in the salvor having to continue payment of hire. To determine whether or not there was a frustrating event which absolved the salvor from paying further hire to the sub-contracted vessel, sub-clause 9(iii) of the SCOPIC was relevant. The court had to consider whether the detention gave rise to a fundamental change of the obligation by Tsavliris under the time charter contract. Despite the prolonged delay, Gross J held that the detention was not a frustrating event. Apart from being important with regard to frustration law, this case is also significant for the purpose of clause 9 of the SCOPIC. At the time of writing, the case reached the Court of Appeal, which approved the decision of Gross J that the detention which caused the delay was not a frustrating event. Rix LJ stated in para 128 of the transcript: 'The foreseeability of this general risk [detention by port authorities], recognised within the industry, and provided for in its well-known terms of trade (SCOPIC), provides a special and highly relevant factor against which the issue of frustration needs to be assessed. However, like most factors in most cases, it must not be exaggerated into something critical, excluding, preclusive: for if, on the special facts of a particular case, the charter is frustrated, then the obligation to reward the salvor under SCOPIC goes – despite his inability to demobilise his equipment.' In the light of this case the salvor has, therefore, to ensure that his security under SCOPIC covers his expense of payment of hire during the period of detention.

Duties of the contractor (cl 10)

The duties and liabilities of the contractor remain the same as under the LOF, namely to use his best endeavours throughout the salvage operations to salve the vessel and property thereon and, in so doing, prevent or minimise damage to the environment.

He must show that he did his best, which will be determined on the basis of standards applicable to other salvors possessing the same expertise.

Shipowners' casualty representative (SCR) (cl 11)

Once the SCOPIC has been invoked, the owners may at their sole option appoint an SCR to attend the salvage operation in accordance with the terms and condition set out in Appendix B.

Thus, the P&I clubs have the opportunity to get involved in the salvage operations through their member's representative.

---

202 *Edwinton Commercial Corp v Tsavliris Russ (Worldwide Salvage & Towage) (The Sea Angel)* [2006] 2 CLC 600, and EWCA (comm) 12/6/7.

Special representatives (cl 12)

At any time after the SCOPIC has been invoked, the hull and machinery under-writers may appoint a special hull representative, and the cargo underwriters may appoint a special cargo representative.

The salvage master, the shipowners and the SCR are obliged to co-operate with the special representative (Appendix C).

Pollution prevention (cl 13)

The assessment of SCOPIC remuneration shall include the prevention of pollution as well as the removal of pollution in the immediate vicinity of the vessel, in so far as this is necessary for the proper execution of the salvage but not otherwise.

General average (cl 14)

The SCOPIC remuneration shall not be general average expense to the extent that it exceeds the Art 13 award. Any liability to pay such SCOPIC remuneration shall be that of the ship owner alone.

Sub clause 15

This sub-cl refers any disputes arising out of the SCOPIC or the operations hereunder to arbitration, as provided under the main agreement (LOF).

The SCOPIC provides a bridge between salvage and wreck removal, and the salvage property contributes towards the overall cost of wreck removal.

There has been an attempt by the International Salvage Union to introduce a new concept, called environmental salvage, in order to encourage salvors to protect the environment by rectifying the defects of Art 14 of the Convention. At the time of writing, this proposal was faced with objections from the International Group of P & I clubs, which considers that the SCOPIC provides adequate encouragement to salvors.[203]

15 GOVERNMENT INTERVENTION

15.1 The SOSREP

The Convention provides, by Art 9, that nothing in this Convention shall affect the right of coastal States concerned to take measures in accordance with generally recognised principles of international law to protect its coastal line or related inter-ests from pollution or the threat of pollution following upon a maritime casualty, or acts relating to such a casualty, which may reasonably be expected to result in major harmful consequences, including the right of a coastal State to give directions in relation to salvage operations.

---

203 For details of the proposal, see papers presented at the event of the London Shipping Law Centre, 'Environmental Salvage', 17th January 2007.

Immediately after the SCOPIC was completed, the Government accepted Lord Donaldson's proposal in his report – 'Review of Salvage, Intervention, Command and Control' – for a Government official (SOSREP) to represent the Secretary of State in maritime emergency situations in UK territorial waters. While the SOSREP will not intervene when he accepts the salvage plan, he has power to resume operational control and determine the salvage plan with the salvage master. The idea to limit the control to two key persons developed after the disaster of *The Sea Empress* spill, at Milford Haven, in which miscommunication between port master and the pilot contributed to the exacerbation of damage caused to the environment. This system has proved to work very well, and other countries are adopting the idea of the SOSREP.

Also, the Merchant Shipping and Maritime Security Act 1997, which amends the MSA 1995, extends the powers of the Secretary of State and of fire authorities to deal with emergencies and safety at sea. In particular, there are: powers of intervention where a shipping accident threatens pollution; powers of intervention in cases of pollution by substances other than oil; and powers of fire authorities to use fire brigades and equipment at sea (amending s 3 of the Fire Services Act 1947).

Furthermore, the Marine Safety Act 2003 provides for powers of intervention and directions to the SOSREP, and this includes powers in relation to places of refuge.

The SOSREP, being the representative of the Secretary of State, acting in the public interest, can order a salvor or harbour master to take action, which may contravene s 85 of the Water Resources Act (WRA) 1991, concerning letting polluting matters to enter controlled waters. If the salvor or harbour master refuses to comply, he will be in breach of s 139 of the MSA 1995; if he does comply, he will be in breach of s 85 of the WRA 1991. This is linked to the general concerns of salvors about lack of protection or immunity from prosecution when they are involved in salvage operations, including protecting the environment from pollution damage.

The potential exposure of salvors and port authorities to criminal prosecution was highlighted by the successful prosecution, under the WRA 1991, of the Milford Haven port authority in *The Sea Empress* case, following her grounding and subsequent extensive pollution. A fine of £4 million was imposed on the port authority. The Act imposes strict liability on anyone who may have caused oil pollution, irrespective of whether that cause was the principal cause and irrespective of whether there was any fault on the part of the party being prosecuted. The salvors are potentially exposed unless the Act is amended, or protection is provided through other legislation,[204] and internationally through the IMO, for responder immunity, otherwise the risk to the environment will be greater if salvors are deterred from taking action.

---

204 Brice, G, writes on maritime salvage, op cit, fn 1, at p 447, that through the 'channelling provision' of s 156(2)(d) of the MSA 1995, which enacted the pollution liability convention, the salvors are protected, provided their involvement in salvage operations is with the consent of the owner of the ship or on the instructions of a competent public authority. This, however, would not protect them if they were involved prior to obtaining consent, or if their assistance is rejected but they nevertheless continue their efforts; for an American perspective, see also 'Responder immunity for salvors' by Shirley, J., Holand & Knight www.hklaw.com.

15.2 Places of refuge

Work on this highly debated issue commenced in 2002 at the IMO level, particularly after the incidents of *The Castor* and *The Prestige*. In May 2002, the Maritime Safety Committee (MSC) at its 75th session approved, in principle, the proposed general framework concerning future work on places of refuge developed by the Sub-Committee on Safety of Navigation (NAV).

Future work placed high priority on the safety of all involved in any operation concerning the provision of places of refuge,[205] with due attention to all environmental aspects associated with these operations.

In November 2003, the IMO Assembly adopted two resolutions addressing the issue of places of refuge for ships in distress – an important step in assisting those involved in incidents that may lead to the need for a place of refuge to make the right decisions at the right time.

Resolution A.949(23) (Guidelines on places of refuge for ships in need of assistance)

These guidelines are intended for use when a ship is in need of assistance but the safety of life is not involved. Where the safety of life is involved, the provisions of the SAR Convention should continue to be followed.

The guidelines recognise that, when a ship has suffered in a casualty, the best way of preventing damage or pollution from its progressive deterioration is to transfer its cargo and bunkers, and to repair the casualty. Such an operation is best carried out in a place of refuge. However, to bring such a ship into a place of refuge near a coast may endanger the coastal State, both economically and from the environmental point of view, and local authorities and populations may strongly object to the operation.

Therefore, granting access to a place of refuge could involve a political decision which can only be taken on a case-by-case basis. In so doing, consideration would need to be given to balancing the interests of the affected ship with those of the environment.

Resolution A.950(23) (Maritime assistance services (MAS))

This resolution recommends that all coastal States should establish a maritime assistance service (MAS). The principal purposes would be: to receive the various reports, consultations and notifications required in a number of IMO instruments; monitoring a ship's situation if such a report indicates that an incident may give rise to a situation whereby the ship may be in need of assistance; serving as the point of contact if the ship's situation is not a distress situation but nevertheless requires exchanges of information between the ship and the coastal State; and serving as the point of contact between those involved in a marine salvage operation undertaken by private facilities if the coastal State considers that it should monitor all phases of the operation.[206]

---

205 See also Van Hooydonk, E, 'The obligation to offer a place of refuge to a ship in distress', in the Work of CMI, Part II, 2004.

206 Extracts from the IMO website, www.imo.org; see also Chapter 20, below.

In addition, the IMO has issued guidelines on places of refuge and the EU has adopted the European Traffic Monitoring Directive (see, further, Chapter 20, below). However, as Van Hooydonk concluded in his study of the subject matter:[207]

> At present there is still not entirely unambiguous reply to the question of whether ships in distress have the right to enter a place of refuge. The liability rules applicable to coastal States and ports are uncertain and lack any international uniformity. Ports have no reasonable incentive to admit ships in distress. The matter is dominated by legal uncertainty and this increases the risk of disasters occurring with 'maritime lepers' ... an attempt should be made to arrive at an international convention that does justice to the concerns of all interested parties and encourage them to take a more positive view of new cases of ships requiring assistance.

The UK's approach to places of refuge is summarised here:[208]

(1) Places of refuge are locations into which a ship which is in need of assistance can be brought, so that its condition can be stabilised – through repair or transshipment of cargo – and further damage to the ship (and consequential pollution damage to the seas and coasts) averted.

(2) In the UK system, the Marine Safety Act 2003 provides powers of intervention and direction to the Secretary of State's Representative for Maritime Salvage and Intervention (SOSREP), working with the MCA's Counter-Pollution and Response Branch.

(3) SOSREP oversees all incidents in UK waters where there is significant risk of pollution, and he or the MCA directs vessels to places of refuge when he judges it appropriate.

(4) Anywhere around the UK's coasts could be a place of refuge and we would consider it unwise to pre-emptively rule anywhere in or out as a potential place of refuge.

(5) The Government considered that there can be no pre-conceived list or ranking of places of refuge. This is because each incident has its own unique, transient and varied nature.

(6) When a ship in need of assistance requires a place of refuge, the SOSREP inevitably takes account of all the factors which relate to the specific incident, such as the weather, the geographical whereabouts of the incident and the type of threat posed by the vessel and its cargo, with a view to determining the most appropriate place of refuge, minimising adverse consequences.

(7) However, in making this judgement, the SOSREP necessarily builds on information which has been assembled pre-event. This information takes the form of a partial inventory of the UK's coast, providing a generic analysis of locations which could lend themselves to becoming a place of refuge for ships. This information is assembled and kept up to date by the MCA.

A good recent example of the implementation of places of refuge policy in the UK was the *MSC Napoli* containership which was in great distress during severe weather conditions in January 2007, on the South Coast of the UK, and was ordered by

---

207 Op cit, fn 205.
208 Extracts from MCA's website, www.mcga.gov.uk (Maritime Coastguard Agency).

the SOSREP to take refuge in Lyme Bay. The way in which the SOSREP handled the incident was much admired by the representatives of the European Commission, which welcomed the effectiveness of the action taken by the UK authorities to assist the *MSC Napoli*. This was based on independent decisions taken following an objective analysis of the situation, making it possible to avoid a major disaster. The incident illustrated the need to expedite the proposals made by the European Commission to improve safety at sea in European waters. One of the Commission's proposals is aimed at tightening up the requirements of the existing directive on vessel traffic monitoring, in order to improve the provision of places of refuge for ships in distress. The proposal establishes the principle that ships in distress must be provided with a place of refuge on the basis of an assessment of the situation by the competent authority, and seeks to ensure that a decision is taken by an independent authority acting in the general public interest and not subject to local pressure, the aim being to reduce the risk of serious pollution affecting the coastline of several Member States (see Chapter 20).

16 LOF 2000 OVERVIEW[209]

LOF 2000 is meant to be used with the SCOPIC. In this context, it is appropriate to give an overview of its clauses: clauses A and B provide that the contractor agrees to use best endeavours to salve the property and to prevent or minimise damage to the environment. By cl C, the SCOPIC provisions may or may not be included. Clause E expressly states that services rendered prior to the agreement are included, and cl F spells out the duties of the property owners.

The right of termination under cl G depends on whether there is no prospect of useful results, but the right is given to both parties, the contractor and the shipowner.

The deeming provision of a place of safety, where the services could be terminated, as in LOF 1990, has been clarified by inserting an agreed place of safety in LOF 2000. The duty of co-operation by the owners of the property has been clarified in cl F by stating what kind of information the salvors should expect from the owners.

In practice, salvors have been frequently faced with a situation when local authorities of a port, where the salved property was taken, demanded a large sum of money as a security for alleged, or possible contamination of the territorial waters. Salvors have been put into a position of having either to negotiate terms or to seek to protect their interests by obtaining insurance cover in the event their efforts to salve failed due to delays ensued by reason of such demands. Clause H is a novel clause which could protect salvors in such situations, by providing for a deemed performance of the services. The clause states:

> . . . the contractors' services shall be deemed to have been performed when the property is in a safe condition in the place stated or agreed . . . in accordance with cl A. For the purpose of this provision, the property shall be regarded as being in safe condition notwithstanding that the property (or part thereof) is damaged or in need of maintenance if (i) the contractors are not obliged to remain in attendance to satisfy the

---

209 See also para 7.1, above.

requirements of any port or harbour authority . . . and (ii) the continuation of skilled salvage services from the contractors or other salvors is no longer necessary to avoid the property becoming lost or significantly further damaged or delayed.

Unfortunately, the wording under proviso (i) may still cause problems for salvors in some ports, because it does not define what kind of requirements and in what circumstances the requirements of the port authority would be satisfied; it is not uncommon that some port authorities abuse their powers (as, for example, the authorities involved in the detention of the *Sea Angel*, above, did abuse their power.)

The LOF 2000 is supplemented by the LSSA clauses and procedural rules which are incorporated by reference (cl I).

The governing law is English (cl J), but even so, cl K reiterates the master's authority to sign the contract on behalf of all respective owners of the property. Inducement to sign the agreement is prohibited by cl L.

17 APPORTIONMENT AND PAYMENT

Article 15(1) of the Convention provides that the apportionment of the reward under Art 13 between salvors shall be made on the basis of the criteria contained in that article, in accordance with the parties' contribution to salvage. Article 15(2) provides that the apportionment between the owner, master and other persons in the service of each salving vessel shall be determined by the law of the flag of that vessel. If the salvage has not been carried out from a vessel, the apportionment shall be determined by the law governing the contract between the salvor and his servants.

The LOF 1995 contains provision for the protection of rights of subcontractors (cl 18), by which the head salvors can claim salvage and enforce any award on their behalf (unless the sub-contractor acts in performance of public duty, for example, fire brigades). A similar provision is incorporated in cl 13 of the procedural rules of the LOF 2000.

The Convention further provides for interim payments by Art 22. The tribunal having jurisdiction over the claim of the salvor may, by interim decision, order that the salvor shall be paid on account such amount as seems fair and just, and on such terms including terms as to security where appropriate, as may be fair and just according to the circumstances of the case. In the event of an interim payment under this article the security provided under Art 21 shall be reduced accordingly.

The interest on any payment due under the Convention shall be determined according to the law of the State in which the tribunal seised of the case is situated (Art 24).

18 JURISDICTION

Under the LOF contracts, the parties submit to the jurisdiction of a Lloyd's arbitrator to determine the award.[210] But salvage is also a remedy that arises independently of contract.

The Admiralty Court has both an inherent jurisdiction to protect the interests of salvors during the course of salvage operations,[211] and a statutory jurisdiction under s 20(2)(j) of the SCA 1981 for any claims under the Salvage Convention 1989, or any contract in relation to salvage services, or in the nature of salvage (not falling within the above). Also, a claim by salvors against the shipowner for breach of the clause in the LOF contracts in relation to his obligation to use his best endeavours to ensure that the cargo interests provide security before the discharge of the cargo comes within sub-s (2)(j).[212] Section 20(6) defines the terms used in s 20(2)(j).

A salvage claim, outside the LOF arbitration agreement, can be brought in the Admiralty Court, and it is defined under CPR r 61.1(2)(f) to mean:

(i)   for or in the nature of salvage;

(ii) for special compensation under Art 14;[213]

(iii) for the apportionment of salvage; and

(iv) arising out of or connected with any contract for salvage services.

The claim is enforceable *in personam* (s 21(1)) and *in rem* (s 21(3), (4)). The ship or a sister ship can be arrested to enforce the claim.

A property salvage attracts a maritime lien against all property salved, but the liability salvage (special compensation under Art 14) does not. The Convention, by Art 20(1), does not affect the salvor's maritime lien on the property under national or international law. As far as liability salvage under Art 14 is concerned, in practice the salvors' right to compensation depends on the co-operation of the liability insurer, the P&I club, and his right can be protected by obtaining security for such claims from the liability insurer. The intention behind the SCOPIC is that such co-operation will be forthcoming, and it has been in most cases in which the SCOPIC has been invoked in practice.

A sister ship arrest under s 21(4) is available if the requirements are satisfied, but

---

210 In *The Lake Avery* [1997] 1 Lloyd's Rep 540, the issue was whether there was an effective agreement to arbitrate, and this depended on whether the salvage services were rendered under LOF 1995, which the defendants disputed. The salvors had appointed an arbitrator, and applied to the court to confirm that there was a valid appointment. If there was a valid agreement, there would be no issue as to the validity of the appointment of the arbitrator; the proceedings were ancillary to arbitration proceedings, so Art 1(4) of the Brussels Convention applied and the case was outside the Brussels Convention which does not apply to arbitration (*The Atlantic Emperor* [1992] 1 Lloyd's Rep 342, applied); see, further, Chapters 6 and 7.

211 *The Tubantia* [1924] P 78.

212 Contrast *The Tesaba* [1982] 1 Lloyd's Rep 397; Chapter 2, paras 3.9, above.

213 The Arrest Convention 1999 provides for arrest of a ship with regard to the enforcement of special compensation.

the maritime lien is not transferable to the sister ship. A maritime lien enjoys certain priorities.[214]

A claim against salvors for negligence is within paras (e), (j) and (h) of s 20(2) of the SCA 1981.[215]

19 TIME LIMITS

Article 23(1) of Sched 11 to the MSA 1995 provides for a two-year time limit for claims in relation to payment under the Convention within which to commence arbitral or judicial proceedings. The limitation commences on the date on which the salvage operations are terminated. The person against whom a claim is made may, at any time during the running of the limitation period, extend that period by a declaration to the claimant. The period may in the like manner be further extended (Art 23(2)). An action for indemnity by a person liable may be instituted, even after the expiration of the limitation period of the preceding paragraphs, if brought within the time allowed by the law of the State where proceedings are instituted (Art 23(3)).

It would seem, from the wording of Art 23(1), that the time limit applies only to claims for payment under Arts 13 and 14 and not to claims for damages.[216] However, since claims for damages against the salvors for negligence can be brought by way of a counter-claim, a wide meaning of the word 'payment' ought to be given.

If the ship is not saved but lost due to the salvor's negligence and an action is brought against the salvor, the time limit that applies in claims based on the tort of negligence will apply, if such an action is sustainable (see discussion under para 9.2.2, above).

---

214 See Chapter 4, paras 4 and 5, above.
215 See *The Eschersheim* [1976] 1 WLR 430; [1976] 2 Lloyd's Rep 1 (HL), discussed in Part I, Chapter 2 para 3, above.
216 See, also, commentary in *Current Statutes*, MSA 1995, Chapter 21, p 426.

CHAPTER 14

TOWAGE CONTRACTS

1 INTRODUCTION

Towage is known in shipping parlance as the service provided, usually by special tugs, to assist the propulsion, or to expedite the movement, of another vessel (the tow) which is not in danger. Danger is an element of salvage, as discussed in the previous chapter. Tugs can range from ocean-going ships to coastal or harbour tugs that are designed with special equipment to push or pull the tow.

The purpose of this chapter is to examine the basic principles relating to the operations of tug and tow under a towage contract governed by English law. Particular attention is given to areas where the law seems to be unsettled. With the evolution of the standard form contracts, the relationship between the parties is primarily governed by the terms and conditions contained in those contracts. Standard form contracts are: the United Kingdom Standard Towage Conditions of 1986 (UKSTC); the Baltic and International Maritime Council (BIMCO) forms designed for International Ocean Towage (Towcon and Towhire); and the BIMCO Supplytime 1989 Form.[1] While the UKSTC is heavily in favour of the tugowner, Towcon and Towhire contain more balanced terms of division of liability, as between tow and tug and their respective liability to third parties. Major issues are dealt with by express terms of the contract. Common law principles and principles derived from relevant statutes will apply to fill the gaps in the contract. A comparison is made in this chapter between common law principles and contractual terms where appropriate. Examples of drafting problems in certain clauses of contracts are shown for the purpose of risk management.

2 DEFINITIONS

Unlike salvage, which does not always depend upon a contract, towage services are always rendered under a contract concluded between a tug and tow for specific services or purpose at a fixed price. It is a contract for services.

Therefore, like any other contracts, towage is governed by the basic principles of contract law, but its particular features have led, over the years, to it being regarded as a specialised maritime law subject.

Towage was defined in *The Princess Alice*[2] as:

---

1 For a detailed treatment of the subject, see Rainey, S, *The Law of Tug and Tow*, 2nd edn, 2004, LLP; for American law, see Parks, A and Cattell, E, *The Law of Tug, Tow and Pilotage*, 3rd edn, 1994, Cornell Maritime Press, and Schoenbaum, T, Thomson. *Admiralty and Maritime Law*, 4th edn, 2004, West.

2 [1849] 3 W Rob 138.

... the employment of one vessel to expedite the voyage of another, when nothing more is required than the accelerating of her progress.

The UKSTC 1986, cl 1(b)(i) defines 'towing' as:

(i) ... any operation in connection with the holding, pushing, pulling, moving, escorting or guiding of or standing by the hirer's vessel and the expressions 'to tow', being towed' and 'towage' shall be defined likewise;

(ii) 'vessel' shall include any vessel, craft, or object of whatsoever nature (whether or not coming within the usual meaning of the word 'vessel') which the tugowner agrees to tow or to which the tugowner agrees at the request, express or implied, of the hirer, to render any service of whatsoever nature other than towing;

(iii) 'tender' shall include any vessel, craft or object of whatsoever nature which is not a tug but which is provided by the tugowner for the performance of any towage or any service;

(iv) the expression 'whilst towing' shall cover the period commencing when the tug or tender is in a position to receive orders direct from the hirer's vessel to commence holding, pushing, pulling, moving, escorting, guiding or standing by the vessel, or to pick up ropes, wires or lines, or when the towing line has been passed to or by the tug or tender, whichever is the sooner, and ending when the final orders from the hirer's vessel to cease holding, pushing, pulling, moving, escorting, guiding or standing by the vessel or to cast off ropes, wires or lines has been carried out, or the towing line has been finally slipped, whichever is the later, and the tug or tender is safely clear of the vessel.

Dr Lushington, in *The Kingalock*,[3] gave the definition of ordinary and extraordinary towage:

... there are two species of agreement that may be entered into by a vessel whose usual occupation is to tow vessels from one place to another. One is, where she meets with a vessel disabled, and ... undertakes for any sum agreed upon between the parties to perform the service of bringing the vessel from one port to another or place of safety. This may be called extraordinary towage ... ordinary towage is that which takes place for the purpose of expediting a vessel on her voyage either homeward or outward.

3 TOWAGE VERSUS SALVAGE

Although towage is distinguishable from salvage because a salvor is generally a volunteer, sometimes there seems to be an overlap or, as has been seen in the previous chapter, the towage may be converted into salvage in exceptional circumstances.

Article 17 of the 1989 Salvage Convention makes it clear that:

No payment is due under the provisions of this Convention unless the services rendered exceed what can be reasonably considered as due performance of a contract entered into before the danger arose.

---

3   (1854) 1 Ecc & AD 264.

Also, cl 6 of the UKSTC 1986 provides:

> Nothing contained in these conditions shall limit, prejudice or preclude in any way any legal rights which the tugowner may have against the hirer including, but not limited to, any rights which the tugowner or his servants or agents have to claim salvage remuneration or special compensation for any extraordinary services rendered to vessels or anything aboard the vessels by any tug or tender . . .

By comparison, cl 15 of Towcon and Towhire does not expressly provide for a possible right of the tugowner to claim salvage, but it should be implied in the first sentence (see below) that any services, which are not contemplated by the agreement and are beyond reasonable efforts to reconnect the towline (which is an obligation under the towage contract), will qualify for salvage. This is reinforced in the second paragraph, which deals mainly with a warranty of authority given by the tow (hirer) when it is necessary for the tug to accept or seek salvage assistance from other vessels. In particular, the clause provides:

> Should the tow break away from the tug during the course of the towage service, the tug shall render all reasonable services to reconnect the towline and fulfil this agreement without making any claim for salvage.

> If at any time the tugowner or the tugmaster consider it necessary or advisable to seek or accept salvage services from any vessel or person on behalf of the tug or tow, or both, the hirer hereby undertakes and warrants that the tugowner or his duly authorised servant or agent including the tugmaster have the full actual authority of the hirer to accept such services on behalf of the tow on any reasonable terms.

At common law, the issue of when a towage contract is converted into salvage has been analysed in decided cases, some of which have been discussed in the previous chapter. The general principles, as have been established in those decisions, are summarised in the following examples.

The *dicta* of Lord Kingsdown in *The Minnehaha*[4] illustrate when towage can become salvage:

> . . . if in the discharge of this task, by sudden violence of wind or waves, or other accidents, the ship in tow is placed in danger, and the towing vessel incurs risks and performs duties which were not within the scope of her original engagement, she is entitled to additional services if the ship be saved, and may claim as a salvor, instead of being restricted to the sum stipulated to be paid for mere towage . . . In the cases on this subject, the towage contract is generally spoken of as superseded by the right to salvage . . .

> . . . they [the tugowners] must show that, the ship being in danger from no fault of theirs, they performed services which were not covered by their towage contract, and did all they could to prevent the danger.

Sir Samuel Evans considered the same issue in *The Leon Blum*:[5]

> Where salvage services (which must be voluntary) supervene upon towage services (which are under contract) the two kinds of services cannot co-exist during the same space of time. There must be a moment when the towage service ceases and the salvage service begins; and, if the tug remains at her post of duty, there may come a moment when the special and unexpected danger is over, and then the salvage

---

4   (1861) 15 Moo PC 133 (HL), pp 153, 158.
5   [1915] P 90.

service will end, and the towage service would be resumed. These moments of time may be difficult to fix, but have to be, and are, fixed in practice.

This, however, raises the question as to how the tugmaster is supposed to know when salvage has superseded towage and what to do in circumstances where there is uncertainty as to whether the duties to be performed are within the contemplation of the parties to the contract.

In *The Annapolis*,[6] the learned judge laid down the rules that may assist the parties involved to recognise the situation in which there may be a conversion from towage to salvage as follows:

> . . . a contract for mere towing does not include the rendering of any salvage service whatever. If it happens by reason of unforeseen occurrences in the performance of the contract to tow that new and special services are necessary, the contract is not at once rendered void, nor is the tug at liberty to abandon the vessel, for that would be most detrimental; nor, on the other hand, is the tug bound to perform the new service for the stipulated reward agreed for the original service; but the law requires performance of the service and allows salvage reward.[7]

And Hill J, in *The Homewood*,[8] considered the elements that should exist for the tug to be able to claim salvage:

> To constitute a salvage service by a tug under contract to tow two elements are necessary: (1) that the tow is in danger by reason of circumstances which could not reasonably have been contemplated by the parties; and (2) that risks are incurred or duties performed by the tug which could not reasonably be held to be within the scope of the contract.[9]

In this case, the steamship had previously been in tow of the tug under a towage contract. Due to bad weather, she broke away and drifted. The crew were rescued and taken off by a lifeboat. The vessel was lying in an exposed position with no one on board. The tow was an empty shell with no means of propulsion and could not anchor. The tug resumed towage services without knowledge of the tow's crew. When the tug claimed remuneration for salvage, the question was whether the events that arose during the towage were within the contemplation of the contract.

It was held that the risk of interruption and prolongation by bad weather, the possibility of the hawser parting, and the fact that there was a need to anchor the tow were reasonably within the scope of the contract. However, the contract did not contemplate that the lifeboat would take off the crew or that the vessel would be let at anchor with no one on board. The element of danger to the tow was present. The crew of the tug was, therefore, entitled to remuneration for salvage.

Similarly, the facts of *The Aldora*[10] are worth noting, for the purpose of defining the boundary between towage and salvage.

The defendants' ship, *The Aldora*, was on a voyage with a full cargo to be

---

6   (1861) Lush 355.
7   Ibid, p 361.
8   (1928) 31 LlL Rep 336.
9   Ibid, p 339.
10   [1975] QB 748.

delivered at a terminal in Blyth Harbour, which was approached from the sea by a dredged channel the seaward limits of which were marked on the north side by a buoy. It was standard practice at the harbour for a ship of *The Aldora*'s size to be met outside the harbour and to be navigated into her berth in the harbour by a pilot with the assistance of four tugs. Due to a misunderstanding as to the time, *The Aldora* arrived earlier than had been anticipated by the pilot, or the tugs which had been engaged to render assistance to her at a position about two miles from the buoy, and *The Aldora* continued on her inward journey towards the buoy at reduced speed, expecting to be met by the pilot and the tugs at any moment. On reaching the buoy and finding that the pilot and the tugs had still not arrived, the master of *The Aldora* turned her around in order to proceed out to sea again. In the process of that operation, the ship ran aground on a sandbank. The pilot and the tugs arrived soon afterwards and succeeded in refloating the ship. Thereafter, the pilot, with the assistance of the tugs, navigated *The Aldora* to her berth in the harbour.

The plaintiffs, the pilot, and the tugowners, masters and crew brought an action *in rem* against the owners of *The Aldora*, claiming remuneration for salvage services and contending that such services lasted until *The Aldora* was safely berthed in the harbour. Brandon J held that the salvage services terminated near the buoy before the ship proceeded inward into the harbour and that, thereafter, the plaintiffs were entitled to be paid for towage services only.

This part of their service was contemplated by the towage contract.

A contrast between *The Albion* and *The North Goodwin* (below) can further illustrate the boundary between towage and salvage: In **The Albion**,[11] the contract simply provided for towage. While the towage services were being performed and after a temporary anchoring of the tow, a strong gale rose which forced the tug to seek shelter nearby. The gale blew the tow into sea resulting in the loss of equipment and anchors. Upon moderation of the weather, the tug went searching for the tow. After considerable effort, the tow was found and was towed back to safety. The tug was awarded salvage for her efforts to find the tow and tow her back.

By contrast in **The North Goodwin**,[12] this lightship was in tow of *The Mermaid*. Having reached close to the River Tyne, about a mile distance, it was anticipated that two other tugs, *The Northsider* and *The Ironsider*, would take over the towage under the UKSTC. However, gale force winds caused heavy swell and it was considered dangerous to allow the pilot boat to leave the harbour. Despite this blowing gale and swell, *The Northsider* went out to meet the tow, being still under tow of *The Mermaid*, which was trying to bring the lightship into the river for more protection and then hand her over to the other tugs. At this point, the towing hawser parted and the lightship drifted away, whereupon *The Northsider* went immediately to her assistance and managed to pass a towage connection and tow her to an anchorage about a mile from the coast. The owners, master and crew of *The Northsider* claimed salvage in respect of these services. Sheen J held that there was no salvage in these circumstances:

---

11 (1861) Lush 282.
12 [1980] 1 Lloyd's Rep 71.

It is implied in all such contracts that the tug will do her duty in case of accident and do all she can to take care of and protect the ship. From time to time towing ropes do part. If *Northsider* had already taken the light vessel in tow and the tow rope had parted in precisely the same position as that in which it parted, and thereafter *Northsider* had made fast again, I do not think it would have been arguable that the tow was in danger by reason of circumstances which could not reasonably have been contemplated by the parties, or that risks were incurred or duties performed by the tug which could not reasonably be held to be within the scope of the contract. In these circumstances, it being conceded that *Northsider* had come out of the protection of the piers pursuant to the terms of her contract, I do not think it can properly be said that risks were incurred or duties performed which were not within the scope of the contract.[13]

Although each case must be looked upon on its own facts, the facts of this case indicate that it ought to be regarded as a borderline case, and perhaps another judge may have held a different view. A clearer case than this, on the issue that there was no immediate danger other than some unexpected difficulty in the performance of the towage, was **The Glaisdale**.[14] This involved an engine defect that developed unexpectedly in the tow after the engagement of towage. The weather conditions were not such as to impose danger. It was held that there was nothing to indicate that the circumstances were so different and the risk to the ship such that the towage contract should be changed retrospectively into a salvage service.

In a recent case, **The Key Singapore**,[15] in which tugs were engaged to tow a jack up rig, in extreme weather conditions, the tow line parted frequently but the rig was eventually brought to safety. The towage was converted to salvage despite the negligence of the tug in the performance of the towage contract.

4 THE MAKING OF A BINDING CONTRACT

Towage contracts are invariably entered into directly between the owner of the tow and professional tug-owning companies. There are, however, circumstances where the master of the ship may have to sign the contract as an agent of the owners and, if there is cargo on board, as an agent for the cargo-owners, provided the requirements of agency of necessity are met. It is necessary first to examine how the master's authority to bind these parties to the contract arises.

4.1 Authority of the master to bind the shipowners

The basic principles of principal and agent and the sources of authority are to be found in Bowstead,[16] from which the following extract illustrates the position of principal and agent by way of a general definition:

---

13   Ibid, p 74.
14   (1945) 78 LlL Rep 403.
15   [2005] 1 Lloyd's Rep 91.
16   Bowstead, FMB, and Reynolds, W, *Bowstead and Reynolds on Agency*, 18th edn, 2005, Sweet & Maxwell.

Agency is the fiduciary relationship which exists between two persons, one of whom expressly or impliedly consents that the other should act on his behalf so as to affect his relations with third parties, and the other of whom similarly consents so to act or so acts. The one on whose behalf the act or acts to be done is called the principal. The one who is to act is called the agent. Any person other than the principal and the agent may be referred to as a third party. In respect of the acts which the principal expressly or impliedly consents that the agent shall so do on the principal's behalf, the agent is said to have authority to act; and his authority constitutes a power to affect the principal's legal relations with third parties. Where the agent's authority results from a manifestation of consent that he should represent or act for the principal expressly or impliedly made by the principal to the agent himself, the authority is called actual authority, express or implied. But the agent may also have authority resulting from such a manifestation made by the principal to a third party; such authority is called apparent authority.[17]

By virtue of his employment contract, the master of a ship has an implied actual authority to enter into towage contracts, only when it is reasonably necessary and the terms are reasonable. This is an additional authority to what is necessary for, or incidental to, effective execution of his express authority in performing his duties for the preservation of the ship and safe prosecution of voyages. The general principle was laid down in *The Ocean Steamship v Anderson*,[18] per Brett MR, when he said:

A captain cannot bind his owners by every towage contract which he may think fit to make: it is binding upon them only when the surrounding circumstances are such as to render it reasonable to be made, and also when its terms are reasonable.

Brandon J referred to this authority in **The Unique Mariner**,[19] holding that the implied actual authority of the master, unless it is restricted by instructions lawfully given by his principal, extends to doing whatever is incidental to, or necessary for, the successful prosecution of the voyage and the safety and preservation of the ship. Although actual implied authority is distinct from ostensible or apparent authority, they can co-exist or overlap only when the restriction of the actual implied authority is not brought to the attention of a third party who deals with the agent, in this case the master. This was the situation in *The Unique Mariner*.[20]

With the modern means of communication, however, the master will normally be able to communicate with his principals (unless he genuinely misunderstands instructions) and an express authority may be given to him. Sometimes, when the third party (the tugmaster) enters into the contract of towage with the apparent agent of the owner of the tow, the latter may be estopped[21] as against the tugowner

---

17 Ibid, para 1-001.

18 (1883) 13 QBD 651, p 662.

19 [1978] 1 Lloyd's Rep 438, pp 443, 449; see, also, Chapter 13.

20 Ibid, pp 450–51; see, also, *Freeman and Lockyer v Buckhurst Park Properties* [1964] 2 QB 480, p 503; and op cit, Bowstead and Reynolds, fn 16, p 105 ('ostensible or apparent authority is the authority of an agent as it appears to others'); and discussion of ostensible and actual implied authority in Markesinis, B, and Munday, R, *An Outline of the Law of Agency*, 4th edn, 1998, Butterworths.

21 Op cit, Bowstead and Reynolds, fn 16, p 101 and para 8-029: 'Ostensible or apparent authority is merely a form of estoppel, indeed, it has been termed agency by estoppel, and you cannot call in aid an estoppel unless you have three ingredients: (i) a representation; (ii) a reliance on the representation; and (iii) an alteration of your position resulting from such reliance.'

from denying that the master of the tow acted as his agent. If, in fact, the master had no actual authority, he may be liable for breach of warranty of authority,[22] unless his principal ratifies the contract.

In circumstances in which the hirer is not the owner of the tow, there is an express warranty of authority given by the hirer to the tug in all standard terms towage contracts that the hirer has such an authority to bind the owner of the tow to the contract. In particular, cl 2 of the UKSTC (and cl 22 of the Towcon and Towhire) provide:

> If at the time of making this agreement or of performing the towage or of rendering any service other than towing at the request, express or implied, of the hirer, the hirer is not the owner of the vessel referred to therein as the 'hirer's vessel', the hirer expressly represents that he is authorised to make and does make this agreement for and on behalf of the owner of the said vessel subject to each and all of these conditions and agrees that both the hirer and the owner are bound jointly and severally by these conditions.

Another type of agency, agency of necessity, which arises by the operation of law, is referred to below but it has also been discussed in Chapter 13, para 8.

4.2 Authority of the master to bind the cargo-owners

The relevance of the authority of the master in this respect is with regard to binding the cargo-owners to pay to the owners of the carrying vessel their pro rata proportion of the towage costs, if the towage comes properly within the provisions of general average.[23] Unless there is agency of necessity,[24] the master would not have authority to bind the cargo-owners to the towage contract, except when the cargo-owners give express authority to him. Neither the owners of the ship nor their master have authority to bind the goods or the owners of the goods by any contract.[25] The master is always the agent of the ship and, in special cases of necessity, the agent of the cargo.[26]

---

22 Op cit, Bowstead and Reynolds, fn 16, para 9-065.

23 See the York-Antwerp Rules 1994. General average is part of the law of carriage by sea. It arises when sacrifices are made or expenditure is incurred for the preservation of ship, freight and cargo, the loss of which is insured under marine insurance policies. Section 66(1) of the Marine Insurance Act 1906 defines a general average loss as a loss caused by or directly consequential on a general average act. It includes a general average expenditure as well as a general average sacrifice. Section 66(2) states that there is a general average act where any extraordinary sacrifice or expenditure is voluntarily and reasonably made or incurred in time of peril for the purpose of preserving the property imperilled in the common adventure. Rule A of the York-Antwerp Rules 1994 has extended the definition of general average act, thus: 'there is a general average act when, and *only when*, any extraordinary sacrifice or expenditure is *intentionally* and reasonably made or incurred for the common safety for the purpose of preserving *from peril* the property involved in a common adventure' (emphasis added to indicate differences). Rule D is important because it makes the rights to contribution in general average independent of fault of one of the parties to the adventure. This rule, however, does not prejudice any remedies or defences that the other party may have against the party guilty of fault. The rules specify events that will qualify as general average. See, generally, Rose, F, *General Average – Law and Practice*, 2nd edn, 2005, LLP, and Chapter 15, below.

24 See Chapter 13, para 8.1.2, above.

25 *Anderson v Ocean Steamship* (1884) 10 App Cas 107, p 117, per Lord Blackburn.

26 *The Onward* (1874) LR 4 A&E 38, p 51.

Agency of necessity has been discussed in the previous chapter but it would be useful to repeat its elements here as well. It has been defined by Bowstead[27] in the following terms:

A person may have authority to act on behalf of another in certain cases where he is faced with an emergency in which the property or interests of the other are in imminent jeopardy and it becomes necessary, in order to preserve the property or interests, so to act. In some cases this authority may entitle him to affect his principal's legal position by making contracts or disposing of property. In others it may merely entitle him to reimbursement of expenses or indemnity against liabilities incurred in so acting, or to a defence against a claim that what he did was wrongful as against the person for whose benefit he acted.

Following the decision in *The Winson*[28] defining this type of agency, the principle was elaborated more extensively in ***The Choko Star***[29] in relation to salvage:

Until an emergency arises, such as to give rise to an agency of necessity, there is no question of the shipowner or master being agent for the cargo-owners. Accordingly, it is not possible to spell out authority for either of them to bind the cargo-owners to a salvage contract, as merely incidental to his pre-existing general authority as an agent.

It derived from these authorities that the rules applicable to the exercise of this authority must be in circumstances when it would be impossible or impracticable to communicate with the principal in question. This could include situations where there are too many principals to consult (for example, owners of cargo shipped under bills of lading on liner terms). The agent must have acted bona fide in the interests of the principal; the action must be necessary for the benefit of the principal, and the authority could not prevail against the express instructions of the principal.[30]

4.3 Authority of the tugmaster

A tugmaster of a professional tug company will be acting within the scope of his employment contract when he enters into a towage contract and his authority will be actual, express or implied to do what is necessary and reasonable to bind his employers to the contract. In cases where the master of a merchant ship decides to tow a vessel without the express authority of his employer, it could not be said that he could bind the owners of his ship to a towage contract because the scope of his usual employment would not encompass entering into such contract. Only if the circumstances of a case are such as to justify him to assist a vessel in distress by towing, it could be held that the master would have implied authority to bind his principals, but this situation would be more likely to amount to salvage services.[31]

---

27   Op cit, Bowstead and Reynolds, fn 16, p 145.
28   See Chapter 13, above.
29   [1990] 1 Lloyd's Rep 516, pp 525–26, per Slade LJ.
30   See Chapter 13, above, on salvage.
31   *The Thetis* (1869) LR 2 A&E 365.

In some circumstances, a professional tug company may charter in tugs from another company to perform a towage contract. Whether this third party is entitled to the benefits of the contract of towage between the tug company and the tow is dependent on there being actual, express or implied authority on the tug company to bind the third party.

In *The Borvigilant and Romina G*,[32] the tug company, National Iranian Oil Company (NIOC), entered into a contract of towage with the owners of a tanker, Monsoon Shipping. Clause 7 of the contract provided that:

> The Company shall have the right to perform their obligations under this contract by using a tug or tugs not owned by themselves but made available to the Company under charterparties or other arrangements. In such circumstances ... the Hirer agrees the Owners or Charterers of such tug or tugs have the benefit of and being bound by these conditions to the same extent as the Company.

Subsequently, NIOC chartered a berthing tug from Borkan, which collided with Monsoon's tanker during the towage operation, causing the total loss of the tug. The question was whether Borkan was entitled to the benefit of the contract, even though they were not expressly mentioned and their services were requested after the contract between NIOC and Monsoon Shipping was created. Lord Justice Clarke in the Court of Appeal found that NIOC had implied actual authority to bind Borkan to the contract. Further, it was found that both NIOC and Monsoon Shipping must have intended NIOC to make the contract on behalf of itself and the owners of any tug used in performing the contract. Clause 7 expressly provided that Borkan should have the benefit of and be bound by the conditions of the contract to the same extent as NIOC.

Perhaps the most interesting aspect of the case was the finding that, following traditional agency principles as laid down by the House of Lords in *Midland Silicones Ltd v Scruttons Ltd*,[33] there would have been no implied authority for NIOC to bind Borkan to the contract. The House of Lords in that case considered circumstances in which stevedores appointed by one party to the contract might have been able to take advantage of provisions in a bill of lading contract to which they were not a party but which were intended to benefit them. Lord Reid said that there was a possibility of success of the agency argument if: first, the bill of lading made it clear that the stevedore was intended to be protected by the provisions in it which limit liability; second, that the bill of lading made it clear that the carrier was also contracting as agent for the stevedore; third, the carrier had authority from the stevedore to do that, or there was perhaps a ratification later by the stevedore; and, fourth, that any difficulties about consideration moving from the stevedore were overcome.

While it was common ground that the first and fourth requirements were satisfied in this present case, the issue for the court was whether the second and third requirements were met. Lord Justice Clarke found that the drafting of the contract between NIOC and Monsoon Shipping was largely based upon UKSTC 1986, which therefore justified applying the commercial common sense interpretation of

---

32 [2003] EWCA Civ 935; [2003] 2 Lloyd's Rep 520 (CA).
33 [1962] AC 446.

cl 7. The approach of the court, he said, was consistent with the approach approved by the Privy Council in other authorities regarding the interpretation of the Himalaya clause[34] since *Midland Silicones*.

Another interesting decision concerning express or implied authority arose in *Targe Towing Ltd v Marine Blast Ltd*.[35] Marine Blast agreed with Noas, the owners of a dredger, *Von Rocks*, to charter her for operations in Scotland. By a towage contract, on terms of the Towcon 1994, Marine Blast as hirer and Targe as tugowner, Targe agreed to tow *Von Rocks* from Sweden to Scotland. During the course of the towage, *Von Rocks* capsized and became constructive total loss. Noas was indemnified pursuant to its insurance contract with its hull insurers, who claimed against Targe. The latter settled the claim and issued proceedings in the English court, claiming indemnity from Marine Blast (the hirer) under the Towcon terms providing for such indemnity in respect of liability incurred by the tugowner to third parties. Marine Blast asserted that, as Noas was a party to the towage contract, Targe would have had a complete defence against the claim by Noas. The preliminary issues for the court were: (i) whether Noas was a party to the towage contract; and (ii) if so, whether, on the true construction of the contract, Targe could maintain its claim against Marine Blast.

Targe's case was that, if Marine Blast had no authority from Noas, then Noas constituted a third party for the purpose of the indemnity clause.

It was held by the court, and approved by the Court of Appeal, that there was no evidence that Marine Blast had express authority from Noas to enter into the towage contract on their behalf; as far as implied authority was concerned, Marine Blast had not discharged the onus of proof that Noas was a party to the contract. That meant that Noas was a third party, so Targe, as the tugowner who paid damages for loss to that third party, would be entitled to rely on the indemnity clause to seek redress from Marine Blast.

4.4 Pre-contractual duties

Under English contract law, the governing principle is that negotiating parties are under a duty not to mislead each other by positive misrepresentation of fact. There is no pre-contractual obligation or positive duty upon the parties to make full and frank disclosure of all material facts. The parties are free to make their own investigations (see further Chapter 11, para 3, above). However, there are limited classes of contracts known as contracts of *uberrimae fidei* (utmost good faith). For example, contracts of insurance are contracts of utmost good faith, which impose upon the negotiating parties the additional duty to disclose all material facts (which are, or ought to be known, by a party to the contract and are material to the formation of the contract). A party to a contract of insurance is also under the ordinary duty to avoid making material misrepresentations before the contract is concluded. Sections 17–20 of the Marine Insurance Act 1906 have codified these principles. Failure

---

34   *The Eurymendon* [1975] AC 154 (PC); *The New York Star* [1980] 2 Lloyd's Rep 317 (PC); *The Mahkutai* [1996] AC 650 (PC).

35   [2004] 1 Lloyd's Rep 721 (CA).

to comply with the duty of utmost good faith by one party entitles the other to avoid the contract.[36]

Whether contracts for salvage or towage fall within the class of contracts of *uberrimae fidei* was discussed in *The Unique Mariner*, in which the contractor argued that they did. Reference was made to *The Kingalock*, decided over 100 years earlier.

The Kingalock[37]

In this case, a tug came to the assistance of *The Kingalock* and entered into an agreement to tow her from Newfoundland to London for £40. In the course of the towage, the hawser broke and the master of the tug discovered for the first time that the tow had previously suffered heavy weather damage. He declared the contract at an end and continued to tow her as if no contract had been made. He brought her safely to port and claimed salvage remuneration, which was resisted on the ground that there was an agreement to tow for £40. Dr Lushington decided in favour of the tug holding that the towage agreement was null and void *ab initio*, because the master of *The Kingalock* had failed to disclose the weather damage to the master of the tug before the agreement was made, which was material to the arduousness and difficulty of the towage. He dealt with the claim on the basis of salvage and rewarded the tug salvage remuneration of £160, explaining thus:

> An agreement to bind two parties must be made with full knowledge of all the facts necessary to be known by both parties; and if any facts which, if known, could have any operation on the agreement about to be entered into is kept back or not disclosed to either of the contracting parties, that would vitiate the agreement itself. It is not necessary, in order to make it not binding, that one of the parties should keep back any fact or circumstance of importance, if there should be misapprehension, accidentally or by carelessness; we all know that there may be what, in the eye of the law, is termed equitable fraud.

However, as was accepted by Brandon J in **The Unique Mariner**[38], *The Kingalock* is not an authority which establishes a general principle that all contracts relating to salvage services are contracts of *uberrimae fidei*. This case was just one example of the exercise by the Admiralty Court of its equitable power to treat that kind of salvage agreement as invalid on the ground of serious unfairness. The Admiralty Court has always exercised an equitable jurisdiction to declare invalid, and refuse to enforce, an agreement of this kind if it considers that the agreement, in all the circumstances of the case, is seriously inequitable to one side or the other. There is no reason why these contracts, which are commercial contracts for work and labour, should be regarded as contracts *of uberrimae fidei*. Insofar as misrepresentation is concerned, Brandon J did not see any reason why the ordinary principles of law relating to rescission of contracts for fraudulent or innocent misrepresentation (including the relevant provisions of the Misrepresentation Act (MA) 1967) should not apply to contracts for the rendering of salvage services, including contracts on the terms of Lloyd's form, in exactly the same way as they apply to all other contracts. Thus,

---

36 See Merkin, R, *Insurance Contract Law*, 2000, Kluwer, loose-leaf, Section A5; and, for the test of materiality, *Pan Atlantic Insurance Co v Pine Top Insurance Co Ltd* [1994] 3 All ER 581 (HL).

37 (1854) 1 Spinks E&A 265.

38 *The Unique Mariner* [1978] 1 Lloyd's Rep 438, pp 454–55.

there should be no reason for the exercise by the Admiralty Court of any additional equitable jurisdiction to treat such contracts as invalid by reason of misstatement.

4.5 Unfair contract terms

Towage contracts are usually entered into between commercial companies with fairly equal bargaining power. The provisions of the Unfair Contract Terms Act (UCTA) 1977 generally do not apply to any contract of marine salvage or towage, unless the tow-owner (of small boats or a yacht) is dealing as a consumer. However, the Act imposes, by s 2(1), a total ban in all contracts on exception clauses which exempt liability for death and personal injury.[39] The Act applies to contracts when the owner of the tow is dealing as a consumer and prohibits exception clauses for negligence (by the tug) if the clauses are unreasonable. If they are, they may be struck down. There may be occasions when a yacht owner or a small boat owner will need towage or salvage and enter into such contracts as individuals and not in the course of business (s 12(1)). An additional protection for consumer yacht owners may be found in the EC Directive on unfair contract terms, which was given statutory force in the UK by the Unfair Terms in Consumer Contracts Regulations 1994, in force from 1 July 1995, which have now been superseded by 1999 Regulations. There is, however, very little that this Directive can add to the UCTA 1977, as far as English law is concerned. An interesting variation introduced by this Directive is that a term would be unfair (if it has not been 'individually negotiated', that is, the consumer was not able to influence its substance), when it is contrary to the requirements of good faith. As such, it causes a significant imbalance in the rights and obligations of the parties to the detriment of the consumer, taking into account the nature of the services and the circumstances in the making of the contract. As it is not within the scope of this chapter to analyse its complex provisions, the reader is advised to look at the standard contract law textbooks.

5 COMMENCEMENT OF TOWAGE, INTERRUPTION AND TERMINATION

5.1 Commencement

At common law, the towage contract commences when the ropes have been passed between the vessels. Under the UKSTC 1986, commencement can occur at an earlier stage, when the tug is ready to receive orders from the hiring vessel. The Towcon and Towhire contracts specify the place from which the contract commences.

The duration of the towage operation under the UKSTC is written in much wider terms than at common law. For the purpose of the UKSTC 1986, cl 1(b)(iv) provides that:

---

39 Cases dated prior to the Act, in which exclusion clauses from liability for loss of life or personal injury were held to be valid, are no longer good law, eg, towage contracts, even on the basis of standard forms, contained such clauses, see *Great Western Rly Co v Royal Norwegian Government* (1945) 78 LlL Rep 152. As a result, neither the exclusion from liability clause nor the indemnity clause of the UKSTC 1986 contain a reference to loss of life or personal injury.

The expression 'whilst towing' shall cover the period commencing when the tug or tender is in a position to receive orders direct from the hirer's vessel to commence holding, pushing, pulling, moving, escorting, guiding or standing by the vessel or to pick up ropes, wires or lines, or when the towing line has been passed to or by the tug or tender, whichever is the sooner, and ending when the final orders from the hirer's vessel to cease holding, pushing, pulling, moving, escorting, guiding or standing by the vessel or to cast off ropes, wires or lines has been carried out, or the towing line has been finally slipped, whichever is the later, and the tug or tender is safely clear of the vessel.

It is very important to know when a towage contract commences, how long it lasts, and when it is interrupted or terminated, since the liabilities and obligations of the contracting parties, as well as the operation of exception clauses or indemnity, will be determined accordingly.

The following examples of cases illustrate the different wording of clauses with regard to commencement and their effect on the operation of exemption from liability of the tug in the event of negligence, or indemnity from the tow to the tug for liability incurred by the tug.

The Clan Colquhoun [40]

Clause 1 of the agreement provided:

> ... the towage or transport shall be deemed to have commenced when the tow-rope has been passed onto the tug and to have ended when the tow-rope has been finally slipped.

The two vessels *Beam* and *Sirdir* belonged to the plaintiffs (the Port of London Authority). They contracted with the defendant to tow the vessel *Clan Colquhoun* (*CC*). *Sirdir* was ahead of *CC* while *Beam* was behind. As they went through the lock into the dock, *Beam* was struck by the revolving propeller of *CC*, and was damaged. The collision was due to the negligence of those on board the tug *Beam*. The plaintiffs contended that, by cl 4 of the towage contract, the defendants were obliged to pay for any damage to their property arising from collision, even though it was due to the contributory negligence of the plaintiffs' tugs. The defendants contended that the clause was inapplicable, as the towage contract had not commenced because, under cl 1 of the agreement, the contract was deemed to commence when the tow-rope had been passed. As the ropes had not yet been passed to the tug *Beam*, the contract had not commenced.

It was held that cl 1 could fairly be interpreted as meaning that the towage shall be deemed to have commenced when the tow-rope or ropes have been passed to each of the two tugs asked for by the owner of the tow. This provision not having been satisfied, the plaintiffs could not take advantage of the terms and conditions of the agreement. Thus, the exception clause did not apply at the time of the collision.

The Uranienborg [41]

The 'commencement' clause in this case stated that:

---

40   [1936] P 153.
41   [1936] P 21.

For the purpose of these conditions, the phrase 'whilst towing' shall be deemed to cover the period commencing when the tug is in a position to receive orders direct from the hirer's vessel to pick up ropes or lines or when the tow-rope has been passed to or by the tug, whichever is sooner . . .

The towage contract was to commence at 11 am. The tug arrived a few minutes earlier, but was proceeding so fast that she was unable to reverse her engines in time. As a result, she struck and damaged the tow. At the time of the collision, the crew of the tow were not ready to give orders as they were still discharging the ship. Also, the crew of the tug were not expecting such orders. The question was whether the towage conditions had begun to apply to enable the tug to take advantage of the exemption provisions.

It was held that 'in a position to receive orders' does not refer to physical readiness. It means, not only that the vessel is within hailing distance, but that the tug is ready in herself to receive orders and the tow is ready to be towed, which was not. Sir Boyd Merriman said:

I doubt whether the word 'position' is only used in the sense of local situation, I think it involves also the conception of the tug being herself in a condition to receive and act upon orders. But, however, that may be, the orders which she is to be in a position to receive are orders to pick up ropes or lines, not orders generally, but those specific orders, and I think that that must have some reference to the intention of those on board the ship to give those orders, and to the readiness of those on board the tug to receive them.[42]

By contrast, in *The Glenaffric*,[43] upon construction of the same clause, towage had commenced on the facts of this case. The agreement was subject to the UKSTC, cl 1 of which provided:

For the purpose of these conditions, the phrase 'whilst towing' shall be deemed to cover the period commencing when the tug is in a position to receive orders direct from the hirer's vessel to pick up ropes or lines, or when the tow-rope has been passed to or by the tug whichever is the sooner . . . Clause 3 provided: the tugowner shall not whilst towing, bear . . . damage of any description done . . . to the tug and the tugowner shall not, whilst at the request expressed or implied of the hirer rendering any service other than towing, be held responsible for any damage done to the hirer's vessel and the hirer shall indemnify the tugowner against any claim by a third party . . .

The tugs, in performance of the agreement, approached early morning within 20 or 30 feet of the steamship which was at anchor with her anchor lights burning. Those in charge of *The Glenaffric* hailed the tug, *Standard Rose*: 'We are not ready. Clear away or keep away.' The master of the tug dropped astern, but kept his engines working to stem the tide until he saw the anchor lights of the steamship replaced by the navigation lights. He then steamed within about 20 ft of the steamer. He was then hailed: 'Don't want you yet. Wait till we get in a bit.' The tug stood off again, and when the steamer had drawn nearer to the dock, it approached again all ready to receive ropes or lines and take the ship in tow. The tug master was told that no

---

42 Ibid, p 27.
43 [1948] P 159, [1948] 1 All ER 245 (CA).

rope would be passed then and was ordered to take a message to the dockmaster to say that the ship would not dock in that tide. In dropping astern to obey that order his tug struck the ship and sustained damage to herself, for which the tugowners claimed to be indemnified under the conditions of the towage agreement.

It was held that, on the true interpretation of the agreement and the application of it to the facts of the present case, the plain meaning of the words in cl 1 were not susceptible of modification by implying the additional words: 'and the ship is ready to give orders'. It was expressly provided that 'whilst towing' was deemed to cover a period of time before the towing proper actually began. The tug was in that position and the plaintiffs were entitled to be indemnified in respect of damage to the tug by virtue of the provision of cl 3 of the conditions.

Scott LJ distinguished the judgment of Sir Boyd Merriman in the previous case, which was the only one on the same point. He said:[44]

> That was quite a different case. There the tug was employed to go to a wharf in the Thames where the vessel was discharging, in order to tow her from her wharf after discharge or to assist her in her passage from the wharf by towing. The tug arrived before the vessel was ready, at a time when the discharging was still going on. In my view, one answer to the question, which was raised in that case indirectly, is that the primary condition precedent to the whole business of towing, namely, that the ship was ready to be towed, had not come into operation, and the learned President so held. He deals, on p 28 of his judgment, with an additional reason which I think I ought to read . . . Mr Bateson argues that *The Tanga* quite plainly was in a position to receive orders to pick up ropes or lines. This is true in the sense that she was within 300 ft and within hailing distance, but in no other sense; she knew that the time was not ripe and was acting accordingly. There is not a shred of evidence from *The Kenia* that anybody, from the master downwards, was even thinking in terms of ropes and lines at the material time. Certainly, they had come there in order to be available for the towing whenever the towing began.

A wide commencement clause used in *The Ramsden*,[45] 'whilst tug is in attendance upon or engaged in any manoeuvre for the purpose of making fast', was held to cover the negligence of the tugmaster when he was proceeding towards the tow in order to make fast.

The criteria of when a tug is ready to receive orders were laid down in *The Apollon*.[46] The usual commencement clause provided that:

> . . . the period commencing when the tug is in a position to receive orders direct from the hirer's vessel to pick up ropes or lines or when the tow-rope has been passed to or by the tug, whichever is the sooner . . .

The owners of *The Apollon* had ordered two tugs. The first tug commenced towing. While the second tug was manoeuvring towards *The Apollon*, she struck a dock gate and sustained damage. The tugowners claimed an indemnity under the conditions providing for the hirer to pay for damages sustained whilst towing.

Brandon J laid down the general principles extracted from the earlier cases:

---

44   [1948] P 159, p 166.
45   [1943] P 46.
46   [1971] 1 Lloyd's Rep 471.

It seems to me that, for a tug to be in a position to receive orders direct from the hirer's vessel to pick up ropes or lines, three conditions must be fulfilled. The first condition is that the situation is such that those on board the tug can reasonably expect the ship to give the tug an order to pick up ropes or lines. The second condition is that the tug is ready to respond to such orders if given. The third condition is that the tug should be close enough to the ship for the order to be passed direct: in other words, that the tug should be within hailing distance.[47]

It was held that all three conditions had been fulfilled in this case, even though the tug had to make a further manoeuvre in order to carry out the pilot's instructions. She was, nevertheless, in a position to receive that order.

In *The Blenheim v The Impetus*,[48] there was no need for the tug to be able to perform at the time the orders were given provided she was ready to receive the orders. When the collision occurred after orders had been given, but before they were carried out, the tug was protected by the exclusion of liability clause.

5.2 Interruption of towing

Where the towage is interrupted, the principle is that it is the tug's duty to return to the tow and resume towage, or if this cannot be done, it must not leave the tow until she is safe or other assistance is sought. If neither of these duties is performed, the towage terms will cease to operate, as there will be an interruption of the towage amounting to a breach of contract. The protection of the tug by the contractual exception from liability applies only while the tug is performing its duties, e.g. 'while towing' (see also paras 9.1 & 9.2, below).

The Refrigerant[49]

The towage contract provided that:

> During the towage service the master and crew of the tugboat become the servants of the owners of the vessel in tow, and are under the control of the master or person in charge of the vessel in tow, the company only providing the motive power. The company will not be liable for any damage or loss to or occasioned by the vessel in tow. . . or any damage or loss to any person or property whatsoever, although such damage or loss may be caused or contributed to by the acts or defaults of the master or crew of the tugboat, or by any defect in or breakdown of or accident to the . . . equipment or towing gear of the tugboat.

It was also expressly stated that the tugowners (the plaintiffs) would provide a towing hawser sufficient for the purpose, and that the tow should have steam available.

During the towage, the hawser parted when the weather was bad. The tug left the tow and went to Falmouth in search of a new rope. The master of the tug sent another tug to assist the tow, but the tow refused assistance, unless the master of the new tug was ready to make an agreement. Eventually, the tow had to hire and pay

---

47 Ibid, p 480.
48 [1959] 2 All ER 354.
49 [1925] P 130.

for the services of another vessel up to Plymouth, before the plaintiffs returned and completed the towage. When the plaintiffs claimed remuneration, the tow counter-claimed for the amount paid to the other vessel. The tugowners sought to rely on the terms of the contract excluding liability for losses or damage to the tow, or any person or property during the towage service.

It was held that the tugmaster had acted improperly by leaving the tow, as the master ought to have stood by the tow throughout. Bateson J stated that:

> In my opinion the words 'during the towage service' mean while the service is being conducted – not while it is being interrupted, in the sense that the master of the tug leaves the ship altogether and goes into port and sends out somebody else to do his work.[50]

The judge in this case relied on the *dictum* of Lord Sterndale in *The Cap Palos* (see below), and held that the exceptions from liability in the contract did not apply to an interruption of towage, but were confined to a time when the tugowner was doing something in the actual performance of the contract, and not when he had abandoned his duties.

The Cap Palos[51]

The plaintiffs entered into contract with the defendants for the latter to tow their vessel on a round voyage. A very wide exception clause was agreed to protect the defendants for damage done, otherwise than by collision to the vessel being towed, or having been towed, by reason of the default of the tugowner. The defendants got another tug to assist in the towing. Both tugs lost their hawsers during the tow. The plaintiff's vessel could not make her way out of the bay, and the defendants' tugs left her there, at which time, a moderate breeze was rising. The defendants errone-ously thought that the Salvage Association would provide tugs to assist the tow, but three days later, still unable to get out, she drifted onto the rocks and became a constructive total loss. When the plaintiffs brought an action for loss of their vessel, the defendants pleaded the exception clause under the contract. The question was whether the exception could cover the period of time when the defendants had left the tow, in breach of their obligations under the contract. Lord Sterndale MR, in the Court of Appeal, reversing the judge's decision, said:

> I think that the whole clause points to the exceptions being confined to a time when the tugowner is doing something or omitting to do something in the actual perform-ance of the contract, and do not apply during a period when, as in this case, he has ceased even for a time to do anything at all and has left the performance of his duties to someone else. In other words, I think the exception extends to cover a default during the actual performance of the duties of the contract, and not to an unjustified handing over of those obligations to someone else for performance.[52]

---

50 Ibid, pp 140–41.
51 [1921] P 458.
52 Ibid, p 468.

5.3 Termination of towing

The towage operations will terminate upon the occurrence of one of the following events: either (i) when the final orders by the tow to cease holding, pushing, pulling, moving, escorting, guiding or standing by, or to cast off ropes wires or lines have been carried out; or (ii) when the towing line has been finally slipped. The latest of either of these events will be taken into account, provided the tug is safely clear of the tow. Whether the lines have been finally slipped does not refer to accidental parting of the towline.

In *The Walumba*,[53] which involved the refloating of a grounded vessel outside Melbourne, the tug, engaged under the UKSTC, was carried away by the tide and the tow-line parted, whereupon the tug's propeller was fouled and the tug obtained salvage assistance. When the costs of the salvage were claimed from the owners of the tow by way of an indemnity pursuant to cl 3(b) of the UKSTC (which provides for an indemnity to the tug for any loss or damage and any claims of whatsoever nature, or howsoever arising or caused (whilst towing) suffered or made against the tugowner), the issue was whether the clause applied. It was argued on behalf of the tow that since the towage had been terminated when the tow-line parted, the clause did not apply. The judge of the Supreme Court of Victoria, Australia, held that the word 'slipping' of the tow-line in the clause did not refer to accidental parting of the line, and up to the time of fouling of propeller there was no question of abandoning towing operation; therefore, fouling of propeller occurred 'whilst towing' and the liability incurred by the tugowner for salvage services, when in peril, was a direct consequence of damage sustained whilst towing. Thus, cl 3(b) did apply. An appeal to the High Court of Australia by the owners of the tow was dismissed.

6 DUTIES OF THE TUGOWNER

The mutual relations of tug and tow are governed by the express terms of the contract and, in the absence of express terms, certain terms will be implied provided they are not inconsistent with the express terms or have not been expressly excluded.

6.1 Fitness of the tug for the purpose for which she is required

This obligation is usually an implied term of the contract, but contracts of standard terms provide expressly for the obligation. It includes an obligation that the crew, tackle and equipment are what might reasonably be expected of a vessel of the particular class.

What is the nature of the obligation of the tugowner to provide a fit tug for the services, in the absence of an express term? Is it an obligation that amounts to an implied absolute undertaking or warranty – like the undertaking given by the

---

53 *The Walumba (Owners) v Australian Coastal Shipping Commission* [1965] 1 Lloyd's Rep 121.

common carrier to provide a seaworthy ship in a carriage of goods contract?[54] Or is it just a duty to exercise reasonable care to make the tug fit? If it is the former, a breach of it which causes damage to the tow will deprive the tugowner from relying on the exception from liability provisions in the contract, and the tow owner will not have to prove negligence of the tug. The burden of proof will shift on to the tugowner to show that there was no breach, the tug was fit, and the damage was caused by an 'act of God'. In other words, this analysis would make the obligation amount to strict liability, in that the tug shall be fit.

If the obligation is a duty to exercise reasonable care to make the tug fit, the tow owner will have to prove negligence on the part of the tug in failing to exercise reasonable care. A breach of this duty which causes damage to the tow would be answerable in damages for negligence. The remedy would be subject to the contractual exceptions from liability, and it would be a matter of construction of the contract if the parties intended to exempt liability of the tug despite the breach.

The issue has not been definitively decided. Judgments decided before the Court of Appeal decision in *The West Cock* (see below) seemed to favour the view that it was an absolute warranty or undertaking.

6.1.1 Cases in favour of an absolute warranty of fitness

Butt J in *The Undaunted*,[55] in which the tug had insufficient coal for the voyage, said:

> ... there being an implied obligation on the tugowners to supply an efficient tug, that is to say, one properly equipped and properly supplied with coal, and as I have found that the tug was deficient in the latter respect, the plaintiffs would be liable. Notwithstanding the exception contained on the card ... the plaintiffs had not properly fulfilled their contract.

In *The West Cock*[56] (at first instance), the decision of the President is important, not only because it was confirmed by the Court of Appeal as to the result, but also because the comments made by the Court of Appeal disapproving the view of the President as to an implied warranty of fitness in towage contracts were only *obiter*, so the President's view still confuses some lawyers on this issue.

The defendant's tugs were engaged to tow the plaintiff's vessel to Liverpool. During the towage, the towing gear of one of the tugs carried away and fell overboard, causing the plaintiff's vessel to be driven against the knuckle of the pier head at the entrance to the dock. The plaintiff's vessel was damaged. It was found that the accident was due to weakness, fatigue and a defective condition in the rivets of

---

54 *Steel v State Line Steamship Co* (1877) 3 App Cas 72 (HL); Lord Blackburn said, p 86: 'I take it, my Lords, to be quite clear, both in England and in Scotland, that where there is a contract to carry goods in a ship, whether that contract is in the shape of a bill of lading, or any other form, there is a duty on the part of the person who furnishes or supplies that ship, or that ship's room, unless something be stipulated which should prevent it, that the ship shall be fit for its purpose. That is generally expressed by saying that it shall be seaworthy; and I think also in marine contracts, contracts for sea carriage, that is what is properly called a warranty, not merely that they should do their best to make the ship fit, but that the ship should really be fit.'

55 (1886) 11 PD 46, p 48.

56 [1911] P 23, pp 30–34; [1911] P 208 (CA).

the tug, resulting in the tug's inefficiency to perform the towage services contracted for. Also, that this inefficiency could have been ascertained by the reasonable care, skill and attention on the part of the tugowners, but they had made no proper inspection of the tug before the towage contract was entered into. The defendants relied on an exemption in the contract, under which they were not responsible for any damage to the tow arising from accidents of the seas, rivers 'or arising from towing gear (including consequences of defects therein or damage thereto)'.

The President, Sir Samuel Evans, at first instance, made the following findings of fact:

> Without going in further detail into the evidence, I will state the conclusions at which I have arrived as to the cause of the accident. I find that the accident was due to the weakness, fatigue, and defective condition of the eight rivets, and that at the time of the contract, and of the commencement of the towing operations, the tug *West Cock* was inefficient on this ground to perform the towage services which the defendants contracted to perform ... I further find upon the evidence ... that this inefficiency could have been ascertained by reasonable care, skill, and attention on the part of the tugowners; that no proper inspection of the tug was made by them or their servants before the towage contract was entered into; and that the last inspection before the contract was only an ordinary and perfunctory one, and did not extend to an examination of the rivets or fastenings between the towing gear and the bulkhead casing.

He referred to authorities that he thought supported his view that there was a warranty of fitness:

> The primary obligation of a tugowner under a towage contract may be described as a duty to provide a tug which, at the time of the contract or at the commencement of the operations of towage under the contract, is efficient to perform the towage services which the tug undertakes to perform in circumstances reasonably to be expected; or as a representation, or an engagement, or a contract, or an implied engagement that the tug is reasonably efficient for that purpose. If my findings of fact in this case are justified, it matters not whether this primary obligation is an absolute one, so as to amount to a warranty of fitness or efficiency, or whether the obligation is satisfied by the tugowner proving that the unfitness or inefficiency was not discoverable or preventable by any care or skill, or by his proving that he was not aware of the unfitness or inefficiency, and that it could not be discovered by an ordinary inspection ...

> In my opinion it is not sufficient for a tugowner in an action like the present to prove that he was not aware of any unfitness or inefficiency or that it could not be discovered by an ordinary inspection. At the lowest, I think his obligation is to prove that the unfitness or inefficiency was not preventable or discoverable by care and skill. But is not the obligation at the outset greater than this? Is it not an obligation which is absolute and which, therefore, amounts to a warranty? I think it is. It is well established that the obligation under a charterparty or a bill of lading to provide a vessel which is 'seaworthy', in the commercial and legal sense, is an absolute one and amounts to a warranty of seaworthiness; and this obligation has been described as 'a representation and an engagement – a contract – by the shipowner that the ship ... is at the time of its departure reasonably fit for accomplishing the service which the shipowner engages to perform' (per Lord Cairns in *Steel v State Line Steamship Co*); and as 'a duty on the part of the person who furnishes or supplies the ship ... unless something be stipulated which should prevent it, that the ship shall be fit for its purpose. That is generally expressed by saying that it shall be seaworthy; and I think also in marine contracts, contracts for sea carriage, that is what is properly

called a "warranty", not merely that they should do their best to make the ship fit, but that the ship should really be fit . . .'

It is as important that a tug which undertakes to tow a vessel in some cases for long distances and in varying circumstances, with lives and property at risk, should be efficient for the accomplishment of its work, as it is that a cargo laden ship should be seaworthy, and in this sense fit for the purposes of the services undertaken under a charterparty. The foundation of the obligation is the same in either case, namely, the fitness of the tug or the ship for the purpose of the services to be performed . . .

In *The Minnehaha*, Lord Kingsdown, in giving the decision of the Privy Council, said:

> 'When a steamboat engages to tow a vessel for a certain remuneration from one point to another, she does not warrant that she will be able to do so, and will do so, under all circumstances and at all hazards; but she does engage that she will use her best endeavours for that purpose, and will bring to the task competent skill, and such a crew, tackle, and equipments, as are reasonably to be expected in a vessel of her class. She may be prevented from fulfilling her contract by a *vis major*, by accidents which were not contemplated, and which may render the fulfilment of her contract impossible, and in such a case, by the general rule of law, she is relieved from her obligations. But she does not become relieved from her obligations because unforeseen difficulties occur in the completion of her task; because the performance of the task is interrupted, or cannot be completed in the mode in which it was originally intended, as by the breaking of the ship's hawser.'

This, I think, means, or at any rate is consistent with the construction, that there is, in a towage contract, first a warranty that at the outset the crew, tackle and equipments are efficient, and afterwards an implied obligation that competent skill and best endeavours should be exercised in the performance of the work.

I see no reason whatever why the same kind of obligation as to efficiency or fitness should not attach to a marine contract of towage as attaches to a marine contract of carriage. But whether the ordinary contract be (as I think it is) a warranty of fitness, or an implied obligation to provide a tug in a fit and efficient condition, so far as skill and care can discover its condition, a serious question remains, namely, whether, under the special terms of exemption in the contract in this case, the defendants are relieved from liability. Whatever the exact obligations of the tugowners may be, there are exceptions under which they seek to avoid, restrict, or minimise those obligations, and they must clearly make out that they are protected by these conditions. I think that the canon of construction to be applied is similar to that which has so frequently been applied in 'seaworthiness' cases.

Before looking at the reasoning of the Court of Appeal in *The West Cock*, which belongs to the next category (that is, not in favour of a warranty of fitness), it is important to see how Sir Samuel Evans had dealt with the same issue in his next decision, decided in the same year, although he was there more concerned with whether the tug would be entitled to salvage.

The Marachal Suchet [57]

The contract was to tow the vessel from Falmouth to London by a tug to be supplied by the plaintiffs. The vessel while in tow of the tug took the ground. This was

---

57 [1911] P 1.

due to a strong wind encountered, which caused the tug and the tow to drift. The vessel remained aground for several days until lifeboats, boatmen and other tugs belonging to the plaintiffs, came to her assistance. Claims for salvage awards by all parties involved were separately considered. With regard to the owners, master and crew of the tug engaged under the towage contract, it was held that the owners had failed to prove that they had supplied a tug efficient for the purpose for which she was engaged. The President, Sir Samuel Evans, said:

> The contract . . . was for the towage of *The Marachal Suchet* by a tug to be supplied by the plaintiffs. This being so, the owners of the tug must be taken to have contracted that the tug should be efficient, and that her crew, tackle, and equipment should be equal to the work to be accomplished in weather and circumstances reasonably to be expected; and that reasonable skill, care, energy, and diligence should be exercised in the accomplishment of the work. On the other hand, they did not warrant that the work should be done under all circumstances and at all hazards, and the failure to accomplish it would be excused if it were due to *vis major* or to accidents not contemplated, and which rendered the doing of the work impossible.[58]

Scrutinising the claim for salvage, he stated that:

> The burden of proof is upon the plaintiffs [tugowners]. It is a twofold burden. They must shew that they were not wanting in the performance of the obligations resting upon them under the towage contract; and they must also account for the stranding of the vessel by shewing something like *vis major*, or an inevitable accident.[59]

The plaintiffs proved neither of these.

Having failed in the towage contract, the tugowners could not in the circumstances claim as salvors. It was also held that, while the special conditions in the towage contract could not avail the plaintiffs in the salvage claim, they had a defence to the counterclaim for damages for breach of contract. The court was left in doubt as to whether the accident (as a matter of causation) was due solely to the inefficient condition of the tug and its equipment. Thus, it cannot be said that this decision directly deals with the issue of whether or not the obligation to provide a fit tug amounts to an absolute warranty.

In 1992, the Court of Appeal in Hong Kong decided the issue in *The Sumi Maru 9001*,[60] by preferring the comments of the President in *The West Cock* that there was an implied absolute warranty as to fitness of the tug and adopting what he said.

The Sumi Maru

The respondents (tugowners) undertook the towage of tow vessels belonging to the appellants from Eleusis Bay, Greece, to Taiwan at an agreed price of $530,000 in four instalments, the first being paid in advance. The contract contained a very wide exception clause (which will be discussed later). The tugowners were obliged to provide bunkers and all necessary provisions. Due to an increase in bunker prices, the tugowners were unable to pay for them at the increased price and after

---

58 Ibid, p 12.
59 Ibid, p 12.
60 *Wiltops (Asia) Ltd v Owners of the Tug Sumi Maru 9001* [1993] 1 SLR 198.

negotiations the appellants agreed to pay the second instalment, although it was not yet due. In return, the tugowners agreed to commence towing on 9 July 1979, but, in fact, did on 25 August. Thereafter, the tugowners pressed for early payment of the third and fourth instalments and a further bunkers surcharge. The third, and part of the fourth, were paid, but the rest was refused. At Cape Town, the tugowners failed to provide bunkers for the next stage of the voyage and were only provided after the appellants agreed to an increase of $170,000 towage fee on a 'no cure no pay' basis of which $60,000 was paid, together with the balance of the fourth instalment. The tug, however, deviated to Mauritius (instead of sailing direct to Singapore) because it did not have sufficient bunkers. En route, she encountered bad cyclonic weather and the tugowners demanded a further sum of $103,500 as demurrage for delays, which was refused by the appellants. The cyclonic conditions worsened and the portside main wire snapped, resulting in the parting of the tug from the tows on 28 January. She did not retrieve the tows, but sailed for Colombo to begin another assignment. Subsequently, the tugowners went into liquidation.

The Lords Justice held that there was an implied absolute obligation in the towage contract, on the part of the tugowner, to provide a tug efficient for the operation of the towage at the commencement of each stage of the voyage in the same way as in contracts of affreightment.[61] They considered that the implied obligation was fully consistent with the obligations of a tugowner, as laid down by Lord Kingsdown in *The Minnehaha*,[62] and disregarded the obiter comments made by the Court of Appeal in *The West Cock* (see below).

The factual position, however, in this case speaks for itself, and the conduct of the tugowner, the level of pressure exerted upon the tow and their final abandonment of the tows, was very bad conduct, albeit that it also amounted to economic duress. On the issue in question, no general principle can be drawn from the decision of the Hong Kong Court of Appeal with regard to the nature of the tug's obligation to provide a tug fit for the purpose, for the following reasons:

First, this was a case of deliberate conduct by the tugowner. Not only did he not meet the standard of reasonable skill and care expected of him, but he received all instalments by exercising undue pressure and still abandoned the contract, the company finally becoming insolvent. Second, it is doubtful whether the same principle can be found in *The Minnehaha*, which dealt with the issue whether or not there was a warranty by the tug to complete the services. Third, the analogy drawn from the contracts of carriage of goods authorities is misplaced, because these are different contracts from the contracts of towage and, in any event, the law with regard to seaworthiness has moved on since those old cases.[63] Fourth, the owner of the tug is

---

61 *Thin & Another v Richards & Co* [1892] 2 QB 141; *The Vortigern* [1899] P 140 (CA); *Northumbrian Shipping Co v Timm* [1939] AC 397 (HL).

62 (1861) 15 Moo PC 133, pp 152–55: when a steamship engages to tow a vessel for a certain remuneration from one point to another, she does not warrant that she will be able to do so and will do so under all circumstances and at all hazard, but she does engage that she will use her best endeavours for that purpose, and will bring to the task competent skill, and such a crew, tackle and equipment as are reasonably to be expected in a vessel of her class.

63 Cf *Hong Kong Fir Shipping Co Ltd v Kawasaki Kisen Kaisha Ltd* [1962] 2 WLR 474, the obligation to provide a seaworthy ship is an innominate term.

not a bailee of the tow, nor is he a bailee of the cargo carried aboard the tow. The rights and duties between the parties are governed by the law of towage, being a unique blend of the law of contract and tort, and the common carrier rules of liability do not apply.[64]

It is submitted that the correct approach should be that there is no absolute warranty as to the tug's fitness, but the tug should be reasonably fit for the service required, as far as reasonable care and skill can make her.[65] The obligation may be modified by express or appropriate terms in the contract. Such was the view held by the Court of Appeal in *The West Cock*, referred to next.

6.1.2 *The view that there is no absolute warranty of fitness of the tug*

The West Cock (Court of Appeal)[66]

Although the Court of Appeal (Vaughan Williams, Farwell, and Kennedy LJJ) affirmed the decision in the court below that the defendants were liable, on the basis of different reasons from the judge, it implicitly disapproved of the President's view that the obligation to provide a fit tug was an absolute one. The reason the tugowner was liable in this case was that the defective condition of the rivets of the tug was not covered by the exemptions in the contract, the conditions of which only applied in circumstances occurring after the commencement of, and during, the towage, and not to the state of things existing before the towage began.

On the issue of fitness, both Farwell and Kennedy LJJ did not wish to extend the common law absolute warranties to towage contracts. Although the Court of Appeal did not have to decide the point, it is important to state the views expressed (albeit obiter) in the course of the judgment on this issue.

Williams LJ said[67] that the President, Sir Samuel Evans, referred to his own decision in *The Marachal Suchet* and claimed that his observations there were based upon the House of Lords' decision in *The Ratata*.[68] However, both *The Ratata* and the Privy Council's decision in *The Minnehaha*, on which the President relied, pointed the other way, rather than supporting the statement that there was a common law warranty or condition of fitness at the commencement of the risk. As regards all other cases claimed by the President to support his proposition, they were cases dealing with different contracts entirely, namely contracts of carriage. Williams LJ did not agree that the same principle applying to contracts of affreightment should also apply to towage.

The question as to what is the liability of the tugowner was answered by

---

64   See also *op cit*, Schoenbaum, fn 1.
65   The same view is suggested by op cit, Rainey, fn 1.
66   [1911] P 208 (CA).
67   [1911] P 208 (CA), p 225.
68   [1898] AC 513 (HL), p 517. Lord Halsbury said: 'The fact that it was an inefficient tug . . . is proved by the defendants themselves, when they shew how on other occasions it had properly and efficiently performed its functions. If it was suggested that it was some extraordinary and unusual event, and as this was not a contract of warranty, the defendants would have been entitled to insist on that as a defence; it was for the defendants to prove it.'

Farwell LJ, quoting Lindley J in *Hyman v Nye*,[69] which dealt with a contract of carriage by coach and horses. He paraphrased the test of that case – which was a test of reasonable care and skill – and adapted it to the situation of tug hire:

> His duty appears to me to be to supply (a tug) as fit for the purpose for which it is hired as care and skill can render it; and if whilst (the tug) is being properly used for such purpose it breaks down, it becomes incumbent on the person who has let it out to shew that the breakdown was in the proper sense of the word an accident not preventable by any care or skill . . . As between him and the hirer the risk of defects in (the tug), so far as care and skill can avoid them, ought to be thrown on the owner of (the tug). The hirer trusts him to supply a fit and proper (tug), the lender has it in his power not only to see that it is in a proper state, and to keep it so, and thus protect himself from risk, but also to charge his customers enough to cover his expenses.[70]

Although Kennedy LJ reserved his final opinion, he was inclined to support[71] the law as laid down in *Hyman v Nye* and the alternative view pointed out by the President, which was:

> . . . an implied obligation to provide a tug in a fit and efficient condition so far as skill and care can discover its condition.

Since the Court of Appeal did not have to decide the issue, and the comments made by the Lords Justice were only obiter, lawyers are none the wiser as to the answer to this problem. However, if one takes the President's alternative view (stated above) to be the correct law, that will be consistent with contractual terms which provide for an obligation on the part of the tugowner to exercise reasonable care to provide a seaworthy tug, as is seen next.

6.1.3 Contractual terms of standard towage contracts on tug's fitness

Clause 4(c)(i) of the UKSTC provides that the exceptions from a tug's liability under cl 4(a), and the indemnity given by the tow to the tug under cl 4(b), shall not apply to the following:

> All claims which the hirer shall prove to have resulted directly and solely from the personal failure of the tugowner to exercise reasonable care to make the tug or tender seaworthy for navigation at the commencement of the towing or other service. For the purpose of this clause the tugowner's personal responsibility for exercising reasonable care shall be construed as relating only to the person or persons having the ultimate control and chief management of the tugowner's business and to any servant (excluding the officers and crew of any tug or tender) to whom the tugowner has specifically delegated the particular duty of exercising reasonable care and shall not include any other servant of the tugowner or any agent or independent contractor employed by the tugowner.

The duty of the tugowner under this contract is to exercise reasonable care to make the tug seaworthy for navigation at the commencement of the towing. The duty is personal upon the persons having the ultimate control and chief management of

---

69   [1881] 6 QBD 685, p 687.

70   *The West Cock* [1911] P 208 (CA), p 227.

71   Ibid, p 232.

the business eg the directors (the 'ego' of the company). The duty may be specific-ally delegated by the directors of the tugowner to any servants, other than the officers and crew of the tug, granting them full authority to deal with seaworthiness issues of the tug, thus, for this purpose, they will be the 'alter ego' of the company.[72] To that extent, only, the duty is delegable but it is still within the personal responsi-bility of the tugowner (its 'ego', or 'alter ego') who cannot delegate it to independ-ent contractors or any other servant or agent employed by him. Therefore, the rule of *The Muncaster Castle*,[73] which is applicable to contracts of carriage of goods by sea to which the Hague-Visby Rules (HVR) have been incorporated, applies. The duty is equivalent to the duty of the carrier under AA III r. 1 of the HVR. Personal failure to exercise reasonable care to make the tug seaworthy will contractually deprive the tugowner from relying on the clause exempting him from liability for negligence, or relying on the indemnity provision with respect to claims which have directly and solely resulted form such personal failure. The burden of proof for breach of this obligation and that such breach was the sole and direct cause of the claim is upon the hirer. Then the burden will be on the tugowner to show that he personally exercised reasonable care to meet his obligation.

If loss or damage to the ship or tug or the personnel of either is caused by the negligence of the tug, the tugowner is protected by the terms of the contract, unless such loss is caused by want of reasonable care on the part of the tugowner to make the tug seaworthy.[74] (See further para 9 below).

Similarly, cl 13 of the Towcon and Towhire provides that:

> The tugowner will exercise due diligence to tender the tug at the place of departure in a seaworthy condition and in all respects ready to perform the towage, but the tugowner gives no other warranties, express or implied.

This clause again reduces the obligation of the tugowner to that of reasonable care, but it is silent as to whether or not the obligation is personal to the tugowner, although this may be implied upon proper construction of the clause.

6.2 The position of fitness when a specific tug is requested

When a particular tug is known in the market for its strength and specific equip-ment, a tow-owner may request it for an ocean towage. Whether or not, in such a case, there is an implied absolute obligation on the tugowner to provide a fit tug, the position is not clear. There are again two strands of judicial view.

6.2.1 One school of thought: no warranty of fitness

It is said that there is no warranty of fitness and no implied contract that the tug shall be reasonably fit for the purpose because, if the tow-owner chose the tug, he would not be able to argue that he had relied on the skill and judgment of the

---

72 See the definition of 'ego' and 'alter ego', or how liability is attributed to a company, in Chapters 8 and 17.

73 [1961] 1 Lloyd's Rep 57.

74 *The Borvigilant and Romina G* [2003] 2 Lloyd's Rep 520.

tugowner to choose a suitable tug. It is said, in those cases, that the tow-owner would have assumed the risk of a possible inefficiency of the specific tug chosen and the consequential damage or loss arising thereof. In this connection, there are some *dicta* in old cases, but in those times it was assumed that, generally, there was a warranty of fitness of tug, as discussed earlier, and the exception was when a particular tug was requested.

Robertson v Amazon Tug and Lighterage Co [75]

The plaintiff, a master mariner, contracted with the defendants to take a steam tug, *The Villa Bella*, belonging to the defendants, to tow six sailing barges for a lump sum. The steam tug had just been bought by the defendants but, unbeknown to both parties, the tug had been kept sunk in water for some time and her boilers and engines were damaged and out of repair. She performed the voyage very slowly, costing the plaintiff more than usual because he had to pay the crew and make provisions for all on board for the duration of the journey. The plaintiff alleged that there was an implied contract that *The Villa Bella* should have been reasonably fit for the purpose for which she was hired. By a majority of 2:1, the Court of Appeal did not consider that there was such an implied requirement in the contract when there was a named tug, which the hirer had an opportunity to inspect, and he, therefore, took the risk of its fitness. Reversing the first instance judgment, Brett LJ said:

> The larger vessel, *The Villa Bella*, was named to the plaintiff at the time of the contract, and, although I do not think it is material, the plaintiff had an opportunity of seeing it. That at once makes the contract a contract with regard to that specific vessel.

> Now the plaintiff, being a skilled mariner and master, undertook by this contract to take the command of the expedition to the Brazils, and to conduct the large tug, *The Villa Bella*, and the barges across the sea. He was to be supplied of course with the means of working the large tug and also the smaller vessel, but he undertook amongst other things to provision the crews, and further, he undertook to conduct this expedition for a fixed sum. It, therefore, was most material to him to calculate what would be the time in which he should in all probability perform the voyage. The larger tug, *The Villa Bella*, at the time when the contract was made, had been kept during the winter in a state which is not infrequent, that is to say, sunk in the water, which may not be so bad for the vessel itself, but it certainly is very deleterious to the engines. She was, in fact, a vessel with engines considerably damaged, but she was the vessel, which the plaintiff undertook to conduct across the Atlantic. [76]

> ... when there is a specific thing, there is no implied contract that it shall be reasonably fit for the purpose for which it is hired or is to be used. That is the great distinction between a contract to supply a thing which is to be made and which is not specific, and a contract with regard to a specific thing. In the one case you take the thing as it is, in the other the person who undertakes to supply it is bound to supply a thing reasonably fit for the purpose for which it is made ...

> If there had been evidence in this case that, after the contract was made, the machinery from want of reasonable care by the defendants had become in a worse condition than it was at the time of the contract, I should have thought that there would have been a breach of contract for which the defendants would have been

liable. But I find no such evidence. The only misfortune about the tug was that the machinery at the time the contract was made was in such a condition that the vessel was not reasonably fit for the purpose of taking these barges across the Atlantic. Therefore, the misfortune which happened was the result of a risk which was run by the plaintiff, and of which he cannot complain, and consequently he has no cause of action as regards *The Villa Bella*.[77]

Cotton LJ, following the same line of argument, added:

> This inefficiency was attributed to the fact that the boilers of *The Villa Bella* were not sufficiently powerful for the engines, and principally to the fact that the boilers were in a bad condition . . .

> The evidence shewed that at the time of the contract the defendants were proposing to send out *The Villa Bella*, and that this was known to the plaintiff. The contract must, therefore, be dealt with as one made with reference to an ascertained steam vessel. Though the contract contains no warranty in terms, the question remains whether there are in it expressions from which, as a matter of construction, any such warranty as that relied on by the plaintiff can be inferred. In my opinion this is not the case . . .

> If the vessel were not at the time of the contract ascertained and known to both parties, probably the contract would imply such a warranty as relied on by the plaintiff. But a contract made with reference to a known vessel, in my opinion, stands in a very different position. In such a case, in the absence of actual stipulation, the contractor must, in my opinion, be considered as having agreed to take the risk of the greater or a less efficiency of the chattel about which he contracts . . . He may examine the chattel and satisfy himself of its condition and efficiency. If he does not and suffers from his neglect to take this precaution, he cannot, in my opinion, make the owner liable. He must, in my opinion, be taken to have fixed the price so as to cover the risk arising from the condition of the instrument which he might have examined if had thought fit so to do.[78]

The two Lords Justice relied upon no authority. However, Bramwell LJ, dissenting, relied on common sense, thus, he said:

> The plaintiff's complaint was that he had agreed upon a lump sum to take this vessel towing several lighters to the Brazils, that it was important to him that the vessel and apparatus should be efficient, as the faster he went the more he gained, and the slower he went the less he gained or the more he lost. He proved as a fact that the boilers were out of order, that they were sufficient in themselves, but needed repairs, and that in consequence it took him much longer to perform his undertaking than it otherwise would have done. The defects, the want of repair, were obvious – obvious to anyone who had looked at or tried the boilers.

> The question is, if this gives a cause of action. I am of opinion that it does. The contract of the defendants was to deliver to the plaintiff the tug and barges, with and in relation to which he was to perform a certain work, or bring about a certain result, for the profitable doing of which the efficiency of the tug was all important. The case seems to me the same as a contract of hiring, and as all contracts when one man furnishes a specific thing to another which that other is to use. The man so letting and furnishing the thing does not, except in some cases, undertake for its goodness

---

77   Ibid, pp 606–07.
78   (1881) 7 QBD 598 (CA), pp 607–09.

or fitness, but he does undertake for the condition being such that it can do what its means enable it to do. Thus, if a man hired a specific horse and said he intended to hunt with it next day, there would be no undertaking by the letter that it could leap or go fast; but there would be that it should have its shoes on, and that it should not have been excessively worked or unfed the day before. If I am asked where I find this rule in our law, I frankly . . . cannot discover it plainly laid down anywhere. But it seems to me to exist as a matter of good sense and reason, and it is I think in accordance with the analogous authorities. I am afraid that the nearest is the *dictum* of Lord Abinger in *Smith v Marrable*: 'No authorities were wanted'; 'the case is one which common sense alone enables us to decide'.[79]

It is submitted that this analysis should be the law.

How did later decisions treat this case?

The Privy Council in *The Mary Francis Whalen*[80] preferred to support the view of the majority in the *Robertson* case, in an appeal from the Supreme Court of Canada arising out of an action brought against this tug, which caused the loss of the tow (a scow) and its cargo on board by abandonment.

The Mary Francis Whalen had been described by its owners to the tow-owners as exactly the same as another tug known to them. On evidence, it was found that this tug was insufficient and lacked capacity to accomplish the task undertaken by it in the weather encountered. Without giving much thought to the issue, the Privy Council held that:

> . . . it was a contract for a named vessel, which brings the case within the authority of *Robertson v The Amazon*, followed by Kennedy in *The West Cock*, and excludes any implied warranty.

The *ratio decidendi* for their decision of no liability of the tug was, however, based on the fact that it had not been explained to the tugowner that the 'scow' would be so difficult to tow as it was, so the decision does not help to clear the confusion in the law.

In another towage case, *Fraser & White Ltd v Vernon*,[81] it was held by the judge that, since the contract was one for the supply of specific tugs, there was, accordingly, no implied warranty as to the fitness of the tugs. The hiring over the telephone of two named and specific tugs was distinguished from the case where there was a general contract for towage services.

No general rule can be drawn from these decisions and, it is submitted, that the common sense approach followed by Bramwell LJ in *Robertson* (above) should be applied.

6.2.2 Second school of thought: there can be no general rule about absence of a warranty of fitness

There is another string of cases, where the hire of a chattel was treated the same as the hire of a tug, in which a general rule as to the absence of a warranty of fitness without qualification was disapproved of. The Court of Appeal in *Yeoman Credit Ltd*

---

79   Ibid, p 603.
80   (1922) 13 LlL Rep 40 (PC).
81   [1951] 2 Lloyd's Rep 175.

v Apps[82] (concerning a hire purchase agreement of a car which was unusable) was surprised at the decision of the majority in the *Robertson* case and did not feel bound by it. It held, instead, that in the ordinary hiring agreement of a specific chattel there was an implied obligation that the chattel should be fit for the purpose for which it was hired, except in the case where the defect was apparent to the hirer and he did not rely on the skill and judgment of the owner. The Court of Appeal relied on its previous decision, *Karsales (Harrow) Ltd v Wallis* and approved *Reed v Dean*, in which it was held that the implied warranty of fitness was subject to the exercise of reasonable skill and care.[83]

6.2.3 Tug fitness and risk management

The apparent conflict between the decisions discussed is unsatisfactory. It appeals to common sense that the proper rule to be applied to such cases should be that the tug or chattel should be fit for the purpose for which it is hired, as far as skill and care can make it. *The Robertson* case may be limited to its own factual situation, which was unusual. The only exception to the rule 'reasonably fit for the purpose' should be when the tow-owner has actual knowledge of the condition of a specific tug which he knows and has requested for hire accepting it as it is, recognising that, if there is an apparent defect, there may be a risk which might arise from that condition. In such a situation, there would be a conscious commercial decision made about allocation of risk between the parties, matched with an appropriate price for the service. A distinction between a contract to perform towage services and a contract for the hire of a specific tug may be artificial and cause more confusion than it offers by way of a solution.[84]

It is important that parties who engage the services of a tug bear these issues in mind and, because the law is unsettled, make it clear in their contract what they expect from the tugowner as to fitness of the tug or tugs and services to be provided.

6.3 To use best endeavours to complete the towage

The UKSTC 1986 form of contract does not mention that the tugowner will use best endeavours to complete the towage, but common law will fill this gap.

In *The Minnehaha*,[85] Lord Kingsdown laid down the principle governing the duty of a tug to complete the towage services by his well-known statement in this case:

> When a steamboat engages to tow a vessel for a certain remuneration from one point to another, she does not warrant that she will be able to do so and will do so under all

---

82 [1962] 2 QB 508.

83 *Karsales (Harrow) Ltd v Wallis* [1956] 1 WLR 936; *Reed v Dean* [1949] 1 KB 188. (It concerned the hire of a named motor launch. Due to an unexplained cause the launch caught fire. The defendant's failure to provide proper fire-fighting equipment was a breach of the implied warranty of fitness, which was subject to the exercise of reasonable skill and care.)

84 See, also, op cit, Rainey, fn 1.

85 (1861) 15 Moo PC 133, p 153.

circumstances and at all hazards; but she does engage that she will use her best endeavours for that purpose, and will bring to the task competence, skill, and such a crew, tackle and equipment as are reasonably to be expected in a vessel of her class.

She may be prevented from fulfilling her contract by a *vis major*, by accidents which were not contemplated and which may render the fulfilment of her contract impossible; and in such case, by the general rule of law, she is relieved from her obligations.

. . . but she does not become relieved from her obligations because unforeseen difficulties occur in the completion of her task; because the performance of the task is interrupted, or cannot be completed in the mode in which it was originally intended, as by the breaking of the ship hawser.

Best endeavours means that the tug did its best (reasonable efforts)[86] in the circumstances to complete the towage. The tug will only be excused by the intervention of unforeseen incidents, which were not contemplated when the contract commenced and which rendered the fulfilment of the contract impossible. But it will not be excused if an unforeseen event made the contract more difficult than expected.

Other standard forms, such as the Towcon, may expressly provide for the tug to use best endeavours, as well as to proceed in the voyage with proper dispatch, as was provided in a sub-Towcon contract, and the same term was implied in the head Towcon contract, in the recent decision in *Ease Faith Ltd v Leonis Marine Management Ltd*.[87]

6.4 The duty to exercise proper skill and diligence throughout

Unless the contract specifies otherwise, ss 13 and 15 of the Supply of Goods and Services Act (SGSA) 1982 apply to the towage contracts which are contracts for supply of goods and services. Section 13 provides:

In a contract for the supply of a service where the supplier is acting in the course of a business, there is an implied term that the supplier will carry out the service with reasonable care and skill.

Section 14 deals with the time for the service to be carried out if it is not fixed by the contract. There is an implied term to carry out the service within a reasonable time; what is a reasonable time is a question of fact.

In fact, these implied terms existed at common law prior to the statute. The Privy Council, in an old case, had given a comprehensive analysis of these duties.

The Julia[88]

A steam tug entered into an engagement to tow a vessel. By the misconduct of the master and crew of the vessel in tow, who acted contrary to the directions of the

---

86 See Chapter 13, para 9.1, above, that the suggested standard to be applied is objective, ie proof of exercise of reasonable diligence. See also *The Kismet* [1976] 2 Lloyd's Rep 585: the tug failed in their best endeavours to supply the water required by the water supply services contract, but this was not the cause of *The Kismet* having to be towed subsequently by the same tug to Durban.

87 [2006] 1 Lloyd's Rep 673.

88 (1861) 14 Moo PC 210.

pilot on board the vessel, a collision occurred whereby the tug received damage. In an action by the owner of the tug for negligence, it was held that the collision and damage had, indeed, been caused by the negligent acts of the tow, and the tugowners were entitled to recover damages. On the issue of fault and liability, Lord Kingsdown stated:

> If, in the course of the performance of this contract, any inevitable accident happened to the one without any default on the part of the other, no cause of action could arise. Such an accident would be one of the necessary risks of the engagement to which each party was subject, and could create no liability on the part of the other. If, on the other hand, the wrongful act occasioned any damage to the other, such wrongful act would create a responsibility on the party committing it, if the sufferer had not by any misconduct or unskilfulness on her part contributed to the accident.

On the duties of both parties to the contract, he summarised the principle:

> When the contract was made, the law would imply an engagement that each vessel would perform its duty in completing it; that proper skill and diligence would be used on board of each; and that neither vessel, by neglect or misconduct, would create unnecessary risk to the other, or increase any risk which might be incidental to the service undertaken.[89]

In line with this principle was the House of Lords' decision in *The Ratata*,[90] in which Lord Halsbury had stated:

> My Lords, no written contract between the parties has been put in evidence, but your Lordships are invited to infer what the contract was from the ordinary course pursued between shipowners and contractors for towage. Looking at the facts, I should infer that, while on the one hand there is no warranty by the contractors that the vessel shall arrive in time to avoid grounding, on the other hand, I think it is clear that they undertook to exercise reasonable care and skill in the performance of the obligation which they have taken upon themselves for hire and reward in conducting the business of the towage to its consummation. Looking at the nature of the thing to be done, I should say they were bound to have reasonable knowledge of the state of the tide, inasmuch as they are to give the signal for the starting of the operations; reasonable care and skill in conducting the operation itself; . . . and reasonable care in providing adequate steam power to accomplish the object in question.

7 DUTIES OF THE TOW

7.1 Duty to specify what is required and to disclose the condition of the tow

As discussed earlier (at para 4.4), under pre-contractual duties, the tow-owner ought to give all necessary information about the tow before the contract commences, so that the tug can make the appropriate arrangements for the towage services required. The court has an equitable jurisdiction to open agreements, which were entered into without full knowledge of the condition of the tow, if, for

---

89 Ibid, p 230.
90 [1898] AC 513, p 516.

example, a non-disclosure of material facts would render the job of the tug more difficult than was contemplated and reflected in the remuneration. The court may award damages for breach of contract, or fix a price that would be fair in the circumstances.

Elliot Steam Tug Co v New Medway Steam Packet [91]

The defendants called the plaintiff's tug company to tow an 800-ton concrete lighter from the mudbank where she was lying. Nothing was disclosed to the plaintiffs showing that this was anything other than an ordinary towing job. But, in fact, the lighter had been lying in mud for some years and the berth was not easy to get to unless the vessel was very small. It was not, therefore, in a position in which the plaintiff's tug could reach it. Consequently, the tugmaster abandoned the tow attempt. The parties entered into a second agreement, whereby the plaintiffs supplied a smaller tug. However, they were still unable to shift the lighter. The plaintiffs claimed damages for breach of contract. It was held that the defendants were in breach of their duty to put the lighter in a position where she could be reached, and in not disclosing that the contract was anything but a simple towage contract.

Any untrue representation of material facts about the tow would be subject to the provisions of the MA 1967. In a recent decision, *Easy Faith v Leonis Marine Management*,[92] there was no misrepresentation of the condition of the tow, when she was described as being 'light ballast condition'.

7.2 The condition of the tow

Whether the tow should be in a seaworthy condition for towage will depend on the circumstances which have necessitated the towage. There can be no general rule that there must be an implied obligation on the part of the tow-owner to provide the tow in a seaworthy condition to be towed, as some cases seem to be taken as suggesting.[93]

In *Elliot Steam Tug Co Ltd v Chester*,[94] Hill J commented that, under a contract for the towage of an obsolete ship, there must be an implied obligation on the part of the tow that she is in a reasonably fit condition to be towed. This case did not decide that the tow should be 'seaworthy' in the strict sense of the word, but to be 'fit to be towed', which is different.

In *The Smjeli*,[95] the contract was about transporting cargo of sections of a steel oil rig on a barge under tow. The sections of the steel oil rig were lost due to negligence of both tug and tow in making the arrangements for the towage of the barge. Sheen J said that there was a common law duty upon both tug and tow in this case to use

---

91   (1937) 59 LlL Rep 35.
92   [2006] 1 Lloyd's Rep 673.
93   See op cit, Rainey, fn 1, pp 47–48.
94   (1922) 12 LlL Rep 331.
95   [1982] 2 Lloyd's Rep 74.

reasonable care to send their vessels to sea in a seaworthy condition. This case, however, was clearly about transportation of cargo with the assistance of a tug, and the obligation of the tow-owner to carry the cargo on a seaworthy barge was an important obligation owed to the owner of the cargo for this purpose.

Provided the position and condition of the tow has been made clear, towage services may be needed because the tow has run into difficulties and may not be considered seaworthy to reach her destination in a damaged condition.[96]

The Towcon form, in cl 12 which has the title 'Tow-worthiness of the tow', provides that:

> (a) The hirer shall exercise due diligence to ensure that the tow shall at the commencement of the towage be in all respects fit to be towed from the place of departure to the place of destination. (b) The hirer undertakes that the tow will be suitably trimmed and prepared and ready to be towed at the time when the tug arrives at the place of departure and fitted and equipped with such shapes, signals, navigational and other lights of a type required for the towage.

The obligation of the tow-owner under this clause is that of exercising due diligence to make the tow 'tow-worthy'. In other words, the tow must be fit with reference to the requirements of the towage needed and is assessed at the commencement of the towage.

As evidence of the tow's tow-worthiness, the clause further requires that the hirer shall supply to the tugowner or the tugmaster on arrival of the tug at the place of departure an unconditional certificate of tow-worthiness issued by a recognised firm of marine surveyors, provided always that the tugowner shall not be under any obligation to perform the towage until, in his discretion, he is satisfied that the tow is in all respects trimmed, prepared, fit and ready for towage. The tugowner shall not unreasonably withhold his approval. (See further *The Salviva* under para 9.3 below.)

7.3 Duty to exercise due care and skill during the towage

This is an implied term in the contract and has been explained in *The Julia* case (summarised at para 6.4, above) but situations in towage vary and, in some instances, it may be that the tow is powerless to do anything depending on who is in control of towage, as will be seen later. However, even if the tow is not in control of navigation, there is still a duty of care and skill to be exercised in the planning of towage, in navigation, and in co-operating with the tug throughout towage, unless the tow is an unmanned barge.[97]

7.4 To pay remuneration to the tug

Towage is a service contract. Therefore, payment is done on completion of the service. Failure to perform towage, which has been fixed for a lump sum on arrival,

---

96   *Gamecock Steam Towing Co Ltd v Trader Navigation Co Ltd* (1937) 59 LlL Rep 170.
97   Eg, see *The Devonshire* [1912] P 21 (HL); *The Abaris* (1920) 2 LlL Rep 411; *Minnie Sommers* (1921) 6 LlL Rep 398; *The Valsesia* [1927] P 115.

will result in no remuneration. If the contract provides for payment 'per running day', then the tug, which has used best endeavours to complete, but failed to do so, will be remunerated for the work actually completed.

If, on the other hand, the contract is frustrated by an unforeseen and supervening event which had not been anticipated by the parties, but payment was made before the time of discharge as a result of a contractual obligation to pay, such sum shall be recoverable. Sums payable after the time of discharge shall cease to be payable. If the tugowner, however, had incurred expenses for the performance of the contract before the time of discharge, the court may, if it considers it just to do so, allow the tugowner to retain or recover the whole or part of the sum so paid or payable (s 1(2) of the Law Reform (Frustrated Contracts) Act 1943).[98]

In a recent case of a slightly different context, *The Sea Angel*,[99] the Court of Appeal approved the judgment of Gross J that the detention of the tug by the port authorities in Karachi was not a frustrating event to render the charter party frustrated, although the delay was inordinate. The judge thought the detention was an ordinary incident of salvage operations, particularly when pollution risk is involved. Rix LJ held that the foreseeability of detention by port authorities was recognised within the industry and provided for in the SCOPIC. It was a highly relevant factor against which the issue of frustration needed to be assessed.

8 RELATIONHIP BETWEEN TUG AND TOW AND THEIR LIABILITIES TO THIRD PARTIES

8.1 Tug and tow

The obligations and liabilities between the tug and tow are governed by express or implied terms of the contract. In standard form contracts, it is usually provided that the crew of the tug are deemed to be the servants of the tow. For example, cl 3 of the UKSTC states:

> Whilst towing or whilst at the request, express or implied, of the hirer, rendering any service other than towing, the master and crew of the tug or tender shall be deemed to be the servants of the hirer and under the control of the hirer and/or his servants and/or his agents, and anyone on board the hirer's vessel who may be employed and/or paid by the tugowner shall likewise be deemed to be the servant of the hirer and the hirer shall accordingly be vicariously liable for any act or omission by any such person so deemed to be the servant of the hirer.

This clause effectively transfers the risks – arising from the negligence of a tug's officers and crew, or other employees of the tugowner – whilst towing (see cl 1(b)(iv)) or whilst rendering any other services at the request of the hirer, upon the tow. Under ordinary common law principles, an employer is, by law, vicariously liable for the negligence of his servants under the principle of 'responder superior'.

---

98 Generally, as to principles of frustration and *force majeure* clauses, see McKendrick, E (ed), *Force Majeure and Frustration of Contract*, 2nd edn, 1995, LLP.

99 [2006] 2 CLC 600 and [2007] EWCA (comm) 12.6.07 (CA) (see chapter 13, above, para 14.2).

In towage situations under UKSTC, the tow will be vicariously liable also for the negligence of the tug's master or crew during towage, because they are temporarily made the servants of the tow by agreement.

However, this contractual provision is only relevant between the parties to the contract. For example, if damage occurs to the tow due to the negligence of the tug's servants, the tow-owner cannot claim, against the tugowner, damages sustained by the tow (cl 4(a)). Moreover, if damage occurs to the tug due to the negligence of those on board it, the tow-owner will be liable to the tugowner for such damage (cl 4(b)). (Clause 4(a), (b) relating to the extent of exception from liability clauses, is discussed under para 9.1, below).

In *The President Van Buren*,[100] decided before the use of the UKSTC, a similar clause in the contract was construed to have the foregoing effect.

S was one of the tugs engaged to tow the American steamship belonging to the defendants. A collision occurred between S and *The President Van Buren*. The defendants alleged that the collision was the result of the negligence of the tug, S. The plaintiffs claimed that by the terms of the contract, they were not liable for any damage done by reason of the negligence of those in charge of S, but that, on the contrary, they were entitled to claim against the defendants for the damage done to their own vessel, S. It was held that the clause in the contract achieved what it set out to do, which was to make the master and crew of the tug the servants of the owners of the tow for the purposes of towage and for all other purposes connected thereto. It was also clear from the contract that the owners of the tow undertook to pay for any damage caused to property belonging to the tugowner.

By contrast to the 'blanket' exception from all liability of the tugowner under the UKSTC, the Towcon provides for a balanced distribution of risk and back-to-back indemnity in cl 18(1): first, for liabilities in relation to deaths or personal injuries occurring during the towage to those engaged in the towage services; and, second, by cl 18(2), the contract allows each party to bear its own loss in respect of loss of or damage to each other's property, as well as to third parties, caused by their respective negligence.

8.2 Tug, tow and third parties

Third parties who may suffer damage or loss due to negligence of the tug's master or crew will not be concerned with the allocation of risk between the contracting parties by their contractual terms. Clause 3 has no effect upon third parties' rights to claim for damage or loss caused by the negligence of the servants of either tug or tow. The usual rules of liability, arising from breach of duty of care at common law, will apply as between third parties and tow or tug. The tow and tug are seen as separate or joint tortfeasors.

The principle was set by the House of Lords' decision in *Mersey Docks and Harbour Board v Coggins and Griffiths*[101] that, as against a third party who is injured by the act of a servant of the tug, the question which of two possible masters is

---

100 (1924) 19 LlL Rep 185.
101 [1947] AC 1 (HL).

liable (the regular employer or the temporary employer to whom the servant is loaned) does not depend on the terms of the contract made between the respective employers; it depends upon which employer has the right to control the servant, not only as to what he is to do, but as to the way he is to do it.

Ultimately, liability will depend on who was in control of navigation or of the towage operations when the cause of action arose, which is a question of fact. Should it be found, on the facts, that the tug had been in control at the time of the incident, and liability to the third party is adjudged against it, then the tug can invoke the indemnity clause of the contract (cl 4 of UKSTC) to recover from the tow in respect of its liability to the third party (*The Atlantic and The Wellington*).[102]

Under the Towcon, whoever is liable to a third party will pay the third party and bear the loss. Both the tugowner and the hirer will be entitled to an indemnity from each other in respect of liability incurred by the fault of the other and adjudged to be due to the third party (cl 18).

8.2.1 Tug in control of a particular manoeuvre

The Panther and The Ericbank [103]

The steam barge *The Trishna* came into collision with the tug of *The Ericbank* as she was proceeding inward-bound up the Manchester Ship Canal. *The Ericbank* failed to signal to her tug that they were passing *The Trishna*, and the tug, without orders from the tow, made a manoeuvre resulting in a collision with *The Trishna*. The tug's propeller, which was improperly left revolving, struck *The Trishna* repeatedly, after which *The Trishna* sank. The contract between *The Ericbank* and her tug deemed the crew of the tug to be the servants of the tow. It was found that the damage done to both vessels by the actual collision was minimal, but the cause of the eventual damage to *The Trishna* was the continuous revolving of the tug's propeller. The tugowners sought to rely on the contractual term in order to escape liability to the third party.

Willmer J stated the effect of the House of Lords' decision in *Mersey Docks and Harbour Board v Coggins and Griffiths* [104] to be as follows:

> ... as between themselves, these parties agreed that the crew of the tug should be deemed to be the servants of the owners of the tow. But, as against a third party who is injured by the act of a servant, the question which of two possible masters is liable (the regular employer or the temporary employer to whom the servant is loaned) does not depend on the terms of the contract made between the respective employers; it depends upon which employer has the right to control the servant, not only as to what he is to do, but as to the way he is to do it. Moreover, it has been held that where the servant of one employer is temporarily loaned to another, it requires cogent evidence to prove that the latter has acquired such a degree of control over the servant as to render him, rather than the regular employer, liable in the event of negligence on the part of the servant.[105]

---

102 (1914) 30 TLR 699; see para 9.2, below.
103 [1957] P 143.
104 [1947] AC 1 (HL).
105 [1957] P 143, p 147.

He stated further:

> Here, however, the faulty manoeuvre of failing to stop the port propeller in time was a matter which concerned the tug alone and not the tow, and in such circumstances, I hold that the liability for the negligence of the mate of *The Panther* [the tug] rests with his regular employers, the owners of *The Panther*.[106]

8.2.2 Contrast between the 'unit' and the 'control' theories

Under common law, there had been two theories on the question of liability of tug and tow to third parties: the 'unit' and the 'control' theories. Under the unit theory, both tow and tug were regarded as being one unit, so that the faulty navigation of the tug was attributable to the tow, in any event, in accordance with the rule of undivided command. The control theory is based on which of the two is in control of the particular act of navigation resulting in the damage, as seen in the case above.

The unit and control theories have been explained in Chapter 12, but it is appropriate to refer to them briefly here in the context of towage.

8.2.2.1 The unit theory (the notion of identity)

Cases decided on the basis of this notion produced peculiar results. For example, in *The Singuasi*,[107] in which the tug negligently caused a collision by turning to port without orders from the pilot on board the tow, the tow was held liable because the tug was regarded as a unit with the tow. This concept was elaborated in the following leading authority.

The Niobe[108]

The tug, *The Flying Serpent*, while towing The Niobe, came into collision with *The Valetta* resulting in severe damage and ultimate sinking of *The Valetta*, with two members of her crew being drowned. *The Niobe* also collided with *The Flying Serpent*, but no damage resulted from that collision. It was found that the collision was partly caused by a bad lookout, on the part of *The Niobe*, and her failure to warn the tug that she was on a collision course. It was held that the collision was due to the fault of both the tug and *The Niobe*. The latter had failed to keep a lookout and guide her tug.

At first instance, Sir James Hannen applied the control theory test:

> But it appears to me that the authorities clearly establish that the tow has, under the ordinary contract of towage, control over the tug. The tug and tow are engaged in a common undertaking, of which the general management and command belongs to the tow, and in order that she should efficiently execute this command it is necessary that she should have a good lookout and should not merely allow herself to be drawn, or the tug to go, in a course which will cause damage to another vessel.[109]

---

106 Ibid, p 149.
107 (1880) 5 PD 241.
108 (1888) 13 PD 55 (HL).
109 Ibid, p 59.

He later stated that:

> If it had been shewn that *The Flying Serpent* had, by some sudden manoeuvre, which those on board *The Niobe* could not control, brought about the collision, I should have held *The Niobe* blameless.[110]

In the House of Lords,[111] the owners of *The Niobe* sought to recover under their insurance policy. The insurance provided that, if the insured vessel came into collision with any ship, and the insured became liable to pay persons interested, the assured would be indemnified by the insurer a certain proportion of the sum so paid. The owners of *The Niobe* paid the owners of *The Valetta* and sought to recover this from their insurers. One of the underwriters refused to pay, on the ground that the insurers would only be liable if the damage arose from a 'collision' with *The Niobe* itself. They contended that the words in the policy imported the meaning that there must be contact between *The Niobe* and the other ship, not just a collision between the tug and the other ship.

The majority of the Lords held that *The Niobe* was, in the contemplation of the law, one and the same ship with her tug, for all purposes of their joint navigation. Therefore, within the meaning of the insurance policy, the collision between the tug and *The Valetta* must be taken to have been a collision of *The Niobe* with *The Valetta*. The underwriters were liable.

Although the judge in the collision action had found the tow liable, on the ground that it was in control of the towage operation, the House of Lords in the insurance claim arrived at the same conclusion by applying the notion of the 'unity' between tug and tow. The House of Lords found the opportunity, 20 years later in *The Devonshire* (below), to analyse the position of tug and tow liability to third parties by taking into consideration which of the two, on the facts, was in control of navigation at the particular time. The artificial notion of a unity between tug and tow, regardless of who was in control, was rejected. The question of who was in control would be a question of fact in each case.

8.2.2.2 *The control theory*

The control theory emerged from a pragmatic view of towage situations, and allows the court to look upon the facts of each case, instead of ascribing control to the tow as a matter of presumption for reasons of expediency and avoidance of a divided command. In the following leading authority, reference is made to old authorities which are useful in explaining the judicial acceptance of this theory.

The Devonshire [112]

The tug was towing a dumb barge, *The Leslie*, which had no propelling apparatus, the control and management of the navigation being entrusted to the tug. *The Leslie* sank after coming into collision with another ship, *The Devonshire*. The owners of *The Leslie* sued the owners of *The Devonshire* claiming damages. It was found that the collision was caused by the faulty navigation of both the tug and *The Devonshire*.

---

110 Ibid, p 60.
111 [1891] AC 401.
112 [1912] AC 634.

The owners of the barge were neither actually nor constructively to blame. The tug was in sole control of the navigation, and her crew were not in the position of servants to the owners of the barge. Lower courts held that the dumb barge – being an innocent ship – could recover the whole of her loss from either one of the two other ships that had caused the collision. The owners of *The Devonshire* were, therefore, ordered to make good the whole of the damage in accordance with the common law rule of no contribution between joint tortfeasors, as was applicable at that time. On appeal to the House of Lords by the owners of *The Devonshire*, one of the questions was whether the tow was to be regarded as being one entity with the tug and, therefore, guilty by reason of the tug's faulty navigation (see further para 8.2.3, below).

Viscount Haldane LC, in enunciating the control theory, relied on the judgment of Butt J, and Sir James Hannen in the case of *The Quickstep*.[113]

This case involved the paddle steamer, *The Charles Dickens*, which was proceeding down the River Tees. When she was almost off the graving dock entrance, she saw the masthead and red light of *The Quickstep*, which, with the hopper barge in tow, was heading up the river, having come out from the buoys on the south shore with the intention of straightening down. Owing to the absence of a second masthead light to indicate that *The Quickstep* was towing, *The Charles Dickens* came into collision with the hopper barge, and sustained such injuries that she had to be beached. The hopper barge carried a proper light, had two men on board, and had a rudder. It was admitted that there was no interference by those on board the hopper barge with the navigation of the tug.

The county court judge found that the collision was caused by the negligence of those on board the tug, *The Quickstep*, and that there was no negligence on the part of those in charge of *The Charles Dickens*, or of the hopper barge; but he held the owners of the hopper barge, as well as the owners of *The Quickstep*, liable on the ground that those on board *The Quickstep* were, as a matter of law, at the time of the collision the servants of the owners of the hopper barge.

Butt J, in the Divisional Court, said:[114]

> No doubt in many cases of towage the negligence relied on as making the owners of the vessel in tow liable for a collision has been the negligence of those on board the tug; and where, as in most of such cases, the navigation was under the direction of those on board the vessel being towed, such negligence has been rightly held to be in law the negligence of her owners. In one or two cases in the Court of Admiralty, Dr Lushington seems to have intimated that the inexpediency of having a divided command and direction of the vessels would in itself be a sufficient reason for attaching liability to the vessel in tow. In all such cases, however, the real question is whether or not the relation of master and servant exists between the defendants, the owners of the vessel towed, and the persons in charge of the navigation of the steam tug. Unless that relation exists, considerations of expediency cannot avail to impose liability on the owners of the vessel in tow . . .

> The truth is, no general rule can be laid down. The question whether the crew of the tug are to be regarded as the servants of the owner of the vessel in tow must depend upon the circumstances of each case . . .

---

113 (1890) 15 PD 196.
114 (1890) 15 PD 196, 199–201.

It would be a hopeless task to attempt to reconcile the numerous decisions bearing on the subject in our English courts. Nor are the American cases more uniform in their result. We think the right view of the law is that stated by Lord Tenterden and Littledale J, in the case of *Laugher v Pointer* adopted and approved by the Court of Exchequer in *Quarman v Burnett*. Both those cases were actions for negligence in driving a carriage. In the earlier case, Lord Tenterden said:

> 'If the temporary use and benefit of the horses will make the hirer answerable, and there be no reasonable distinction between hiring them with or without a carriage, must not the person who hires a hackney coach to take him for a mile, or other greater or less distance, or for an hour, or longer time, be answerable for the conduct of the coachman? Must not the person who hires a wherry on the Thames be answerable for the conduct of the waterman? I believe the common sense of all men would be shocked if anyone should affirm the hirer to be answerable in either of these cases . . .'

Adopting this reasoning, Viscount Haldane LC said in *The Devonshire*:

> In the case of *The Quickstep*, Butt J, . . . laid down that, where a tug and its tow came into collision with an innocent ship, the question whether the owners of the latter can recover damages against the owners of the tow depends on whether the relation of master and servant obtains between the owners of the tow and those of the tug. Unless this relation is established, he said that there was no liability on the part of the tow. I think that, as the doctrine of identification as enunciated in *Thorogood v Bryan* has now been swept away, the principle so laid down was right, and that it is a simple application of the rule established in the well known case of *Quarman v Burnett*. No relation such as that of master and servant was established in the present case, and the tow was therefore an innocent ship, and its owners are at common law entitled to recover the whole of their damage from the owners of *The Devonshire*.[115]

Furthermore, Lord Atkinson,[116] having reviewed some important relevant authorities, resolved the issue of identity between tug and tow once and for all:

> On the question of the identity of the tow with the tug it is only necessary, I think, to refer to two additional authorities; the first preceded *The Quickstep* in date, and the second was quite recent. The first is the case of *Union Steamship Company v Owners of the Aracan*, decided by the Privy Council in 1874.

> There, a disabled steamer, *The Syria*, was being towed . . . by another steamer, *The American*. Both belonged to the same owners. On the voyage, *The American* came into collision with and sank the sailing vessel named *The Aracan*, belonging to the plaintiffs. The learned judge of the Admiralty Court said that, in fact, neither of the crews of *The Syria* or *The Aracan* were to blame, but that the crew of *The American* was solely to blame; . . . notwithstanding these findings, *The Syria* must, he thought, be pronounced to blame on the ground that she must in intendment of law be treated as one vessel with *The American*. The Privy Council, after considering several American authorities, reversed this decision, on the ground that there was no evidence of *The American* having been hired by the captain of *The Syria* or having acted in any way under the control of the latter; that on the contrary it appeared that the governing power was wholly with *The American*.

> The second is the case of the lightship *Comet* (*The WH No 1 and The Knight Errant*).

---

115 [1912] AC 634, p 645.
116 Ibid, pp 653–57.

There the lightship, moored at the mouth of the Mersey, was run into and sunk by a hopper barge, *WH No 1*, which was coming up the river in tow of the tug *Knight Errant*. The owners of the lightship sued both the owners of the barge and the owners of the tug for the damages caused by the negligent navigation of the tug and tow, or alternatively of one of them. The then President, Lord Mersey, held that both the tug and tow were in fact to blame. He treated them, he said, expressly as joint tortfeasors, each being liable for all the damages that followed from their wrongful act. The owners of the hopper barge alone appealed. On behalf of the appellants, *The Quick-step* was relied upon, and it was urged that, as the barge had no motive power of its own, the crew of the tug were necessarily in sole control of the navigation, that the crew of the tug were not, therefore, the servants of the owners of the barge, and the crew of the latter not, in fact, guilty of any negligence.

The Court of Appeal, consisting of Lord Halsbury and Fletcher Moulton and Farwell LJJ, came to the conclusion that the crew of the hopper barge was not, in fact, guilty of any negligence, and allowed the appeal with costs. The plaintiff appealed to this House, when it was again held that the crew of the barge was not, in fact, guilty of negligence, and the appeal was dismissed on this ground.

It must therefore, I think, now be taken as conclusively established that the question of the identity of the tow with the tug that tows her is one of fact, not law, to be determined upon the particular facts and circumstances of each case.

In the recent case of ***The Key Singapore***,[117] in which both the tugs and tow were found jointly at fault in failing to heave to in due time, there was an apportionment of liability between them, and the judge held that there was nothing in the authorities relied upon by the claimants to support the proposition that overall command of a towage convoy imported with it an enhanced degree of fault in circumstances where both tug and tow had fallen short of their mutual duty to take care.

8.2.2.3 *Application of the control theory for risk management*

When a contract, such as the UKSTC, provides that, whilst towing, the master and crew of the tug will be deemed to be the servants of the tow, the question of control is answered by the terms of the contract as between the tug and tow. As regards third parties, who may suffer damage or loss caused by a collision between either the tug or the tow or both and another vessel, the question of control will be determined by the court judging from the circumstances of the particular case. The principle that derives from *The Devonshire* is as follows:

(a) when a tug has undertaken towage of an unmanned boat or craft and there is a collision between either the barge or the tug and a third vessel, the tug, which must, in such circumstances, have been in control of the situation, will be responsible, if it can be established that the negligence of those on board the tug caused or contributed to the collision;

(b) when the tow has officers and crew on board, they should be able to be in control of navigation and warn the tug of dangers in compliance with the collision regulations and seamanship skill. Equally, those on board the tug will have a duty to exercise due care in navigation and will be in control of towage

---

117 [2005] 1 Lloyd's Rep 91.

operations depending on the circumstances. To determine which of the two was in control of a particular manoeuvre, which caused a collision, will be a question of fact and the particular circumstances in each case;

(c) a third innocent party who has suffered damage due to the negligence of the other two can sue either of them for the whole loss. This issue is explained further below.

The Collision Regulations of 1972 apply to tugs and tow, and both have a duty to observe them.[118] In addition to the regulations which apply generally to all vessels, there are special provisions dealing with towage situations, eg reg 21 deals with 'towing lights'; or reg 27 specifies additional lights to be displayed by certain towing vessels.[119] Although there is no presumption of fault for breach of these regulations by any vessel, failure to observe the regulations constitutes evidence on which the plaintiff may rely in showing breach of the duty of care owed to other vessels at sea.[120]

8.2.3 Joint tortfeasors (the common law rule)

At common law, prior to 1935 (that is, the Married Women and Joint Tortfeasor's Act, which was later replaced by the Civil Liability (Contribution) Act 1978), there was no contribution between joint tortfeasors, and each was liable for the entire damage inflicted on an innocent third party by their joint wrong. By contrast, in admiralty, there has been the rule of division of loss between two ships at fault.

The question put to the House of Lords in *The Devonshire* was whether the admiralty law rule as to division of loss was applicable to cases involving two tortfeasors and an innocent third party.[121]

The owners of *The Devonshire* contended that they could only be held liable for half of the loss. Also, since the tow had entrusted its navigation to the tug, it could not be treated as a wholly innocent ship. The submission was that *The Leslie* should be precluded from recovering more than half of its damage from the owners of the other delinquent ship (*The Devonshire*). The House of Lords considered whether there was an admiralty rule displacing the common law rule, and Lord Atkinson analysed the issue, referring to some relevant previous authorities and explained, thus:

> [In *The Niobe*] the contest in the Court of Admiralty was as to whether *The Niobe* was to blame. The tug admitted her liability, but the significance of the decision in relation to the general principle contended for in the present case is that full damages were awarded against tug and tow jointly, and the rule as to the limitation of damages applicable in admiralty cases where the ship of the plaintiff collides with the ship of the defendant, and both are to blame, was not applied. The two tortfeasors

---

118 There are numerous cases of breach of the Collision Regulations (lookout rule, speed, warning on danger, etc): see, eg *The Basis* (1950) 84 LlL Rep 306, when both tug and tow were in breach of the duty to obey those regulations. See further Chapter 12, above.

119 For a more detailed discussion of collisions involving tugs and tows, see Kovats, LJ, *The Law of Tugs and Towage*, 1980, Chichester and London: Barry Rose.

120 See Chapter 12, above.

121 See Chapter 12, paras 3.2.5, 3.7, 3.7.2.3, 3.10, above.

were held liable for all the damage caused as they would have been in a court of common law.[122]

In the following year, 1891, the case of *The Avon and Thomas Joliffe*[123] came up for decision. In that case *The Avon*, while in tow of tug, came into collision with another vessel named *The Thomas Joliffe*. The crews of both the tug and tow were held to have been to blame, and the crew of *The Thomas Joliffe* was held to have been blameless. Sir Charles Butt was pressed to divide the damages between the two wrongdoers on the authority of two American cases, *The Sterling and The Equator* and *The City of Hartford and The Unit*. He refused to do so on the distinct ground that the rule of limitation of damages only applies in admiralty law to cases where the ships of the plaintiff and the defendant have been in collision and have both been found to blame.[124]

In the several cases subsequent in date to 1891 referred to in the judgment of the learned President in the present case, the same principle appears to have been acted upon, and no instance has been found where it was departed from in this country. . . .

Now, in the present case, the President has on the authority of *The Quickstep* found that the owners of the barge were neither actually nor constructively to blame; in other words, that the tug was in sole control of the navigation, and that her crew were not in the position of servants to the owners of the barge . . . This case resolves itself into one where two vessels belonging to two different persons, not being plaintiff and defendant respectively in a suit, both ships having been negligently navigated, have inflicted damage on a third vessel by and through their joint wrongful act. In my view the appellants have wholly failed to shew that there ever was any general principle of law administered in the Court of Admiralty, according to which the owners of the vessels in default were, in such circumstances, not treated in the same way as joint tortfeasors are treated at common law, and each made liable for all the damage he helps to inflict.[125]

The House of Lords stressed that this type of case was different from cases in which two or more ships collide and all are found to be at fault. Only in those cases would the admiralty law rule of division of loss apply pursuant to s 25(9) of the Judicature Act (JA) 1873, which was applicable at the time. A couple of years later, when the admiralty law rule was by then enacted in the Maritime Convention Act (MCA) 1911, the division of loss rule applied between two vessels at fault in an action for contribution after payment had been made to the innocent third party by the one wrongdoer (*The Cairnbahn*, below).

8.2.4 Contribution between joint tortfeasors by statute

The Cairnbahn[126]

This case was concerned with an action between two tortfeasors for contribution. A collision took place between an innocent barge in tow of a tug and a steamship (*The*

---

122 That was the result of applying the unit theory in that the tow and tug were one unit and hence the tow was found to blame for the negligence of the tug.

123 [1891] P 7.

124 Thus, the division of loss rule under admiralty law could not apply as between two colliding ships where one of them was innocent, but only where the two ships were at fault.

125 [1912] AC 634, pp 653–57.

126 [1914] P 25.

Cairnbahn). The steamship and the barge were damaged. The collision was due to the fault of the tug (*The Nunthorpe*) and the steamship (*The Cairnbahn*). The barge recovered the whole of her damage against the steamship. The owners of the steamship sought to recover half of the damage from the tugowners. The question was whether the admiralty rule as to division of loss applied between the two vessels at fault. It was contended on behalf of the owners of the steamship that the tug, *The Nunthorpe*, would have to bear half the loss sustained by the owners of the steamship, including half the amount of damage sustained by the owners of the barge, which had been paid by the owners of the steamship. The owners of *The Nunthorpe* contended that, as both the steamship and the tug were at fault, the owners of the steamship were not entitled to call upon the owners of the tug to bear any share of the loss, because the two vessels were in the position of joint tort-feasors. Therefore, they argued, the common law principle, that there could be no contribution between joint tortfeasors, governed the case.

It was further argued that, as the two vessels at fault were not 'colliding vessels', the admiralty rule, preserved by s 25(9) of the JA 1873, would not have applied before the MCA 1911 came into operation and that the Act did not alter the law in this respect.

However, the President, Sir Samuel Evans, held that:

> The wording of s 1(1) of the 1911 Act is quite different from that of the repealed sub-section. Its language, appears to me to be quite plain. Reading the words of the section which are applicable to the circumstances of this case, it enacts that, where by the fault of two vessels damage or loss is caused to one or to both of those vessels, the liability to make good the damage or loss shall be in proportion to the degree in which each vessel was in fault (subject, of course, to the proviso). There is nothing in the section about the two vessels in fault being themselves in collision with each other. Translate the words into the facts of this case, then the enactment would read thus: 'Where by the fault of the tug *Nunthorpe* and the steamship *Cairnbahn* damage or loss was caused to *The Cairnbahn*, the liability to make good such damage or loss shall be in proportion to the degree in which the tug *Nunthorpe* and the steamship *Cairnbahn* were in fault, namely, in equal degree.' As has been said, the damage or loss caused to *The Cairnbahn* was admitted to include the sum which *The Cairnbahn* was adjudged to pay to the innocent barge, as well as the damage caused to the steamship herself.[127]

On appeal, the Court of Appeal upheld the view that s 1 of the MCA 1911[128] applies, even where the damage to be apportioned does not arise from a collision between the vessels at fault. Lord Parker of Waddington said:

> The section, then, being applicable to the present case, we have to consider its true meaning and effect. It provides for the apportionment in a certain way of the 'liability for the damage or loss' referred to, that is to say, the damage or loss caused by the fault of two or more vessels to one or more of those vessels, to their cargoes or freight, or to any property on board.

> Before the passing of the Act there was at common law no liability on the part of anyone to make good the damage caused to *The Cairnbahn*, both she and *The*

---

127 Ibid, p 29.
128 Now, see the MSA 1995, s 187 (Chapter 12, above).

Nunthorpe being to blame, and, according to the admiralty rule referred to in s 25, sub-s 9, of the JA 1873 (if such rule were applicable), the only liability to make good this damage lay on *The Nunthorpe,* but to the extent only of a moiety thereof. Having regard to the strange results which would otherwise follow, I think that the section must be construed not as apportioning any existing liability, but as providing that the whole of the damage or loss referred to is to be borne in proportion to the degree in which each vessel is in fault, and if it be impossible to establish different degrees of fault, then equally. . . .

Further, I think that though the section refers to damage or loss caused to one or more of the vessels in fault, to their cargoes or freight, or to any property on board, *this is only a figurative way of referring to the damage or loss caused to the persons interested in the vessels, their cargoes or freight, or any property on board.*[129] (emphasis added)

It was made clear that the MCA 1911 dealt with the question from the point of view of the guilty parties only. The rights of the innocent party were not in issue in this case, as they were in *The Devonshire* because this case was for contribution between the tortfeasors in a separate action.[130]

9 EXCLUSION FROM LIABILITY AND INDEMNITY CLAUSES (RISK MANAGEMENT ISSUES)

At common law, the tugowner will be liable for damage to the tow caused by the tug's negligence. Under the UKSTC 1986, the tugowner is protected by an exemption from such liability, as well as by an indemnity for liability that might be incurred by negligence of the tug to third parties. It has been explained earlier that the UCTA 1977 does not apply to towage contracts, except insofar as the tow owner deals as a consumer. By contrast, the Towcon form of contract places the parties on an equal footing, and each one will bear its own loss. There is also a mutual indemnity provision for liability incurred to third parties.

The parties' respective liabilities to each other and to third parties are insured. Collision cross-liabilities with regard to damage caused to tug and tow respectively are insured up to three-fourths by hull and machinery (H&M) insurers and one-fourth by the protection and indemnity mutual insurance (P&I clubs), depending on the particular rules of the club to which the owner is a member. Physical damage to or loss of the tug or tow under towage will be covered by their respective insurers (under the Institute Marine clauses for H&M), who will be subrogated to the rights of their assured against the other party or third parties once payment under the insurance contract has been made (see insurance issues and collisions in Chapter 12).

Liabilities to third parties, such as cargo damage on board the tow or loss of life or personal injury, are covered by the P&I insurance of the tow. The P&I insurer will be subrogated – after payment to its assured – to any rights the tow might have in

---

129 [1914] P 25, pp 30–31.
130 See, further, Chapter 12, paras 3.7, 3.7.2.3 and 3.10, above.

respect of such liability against the tug (subject to the terms of the towage contract) or against a third party who caused or contributed to such liability.

9.1 The ambit of the exception from liability clauses

Exclusion from liability clauses must be drafted in clear terms. Vague and wide clauses will be construed against the person claiming benefit from them, under the rules of construction of contract terms. Careful drafting is essential to managing the risks the parties wish to prevent from happening. Moreover, an exception clause will not assist the tugowner if it aims to exclude the very thing the tugowner was contracted to do (*The Cap Palos*), or if it attempts to negate the object of the contract (*The Sumi Maru*).

In *The Cap Palos*,[131] the exception clause in the towage contract provided that the tugowner would not be responsible (inter alia) for 'any damage or loss that may arise to any vessel or craft being towed, or about to be towed, or having been towed ... whether such damage arise from or be occasioned by any accident or by any omission, breach of duty, mismanagement, negligence, or default of the steam tugowner, or any of his servants or employees ...'.

The defendant contracted to tow the plaintiffs' schooner, *CP*, on a round voyage. Due to negligence of the defendant's tugmaster the vessels got into a bay, the tugs grounded and lost their hawsers and *CP* came to anchor. The tugs got afloat on the early morning and left the *CP* in the bay with a rising north east wind. *CP* remained in there making vain attempts to get out, when eventually she drifted onto the rocks and became a constructive total loss. Although the defendant had ordered another tug to go to *CP*, he cancelled the order, as he thought (erroneously) that the Salvage Association had sent tugs to her assistance. In an action by the plaintiffs for the loss of their vessel by reason of the defendant's breach of contract or duty, the defendant pleaded the exception clause.

It was held by the Court of Appeal, reversing Hill J, that, as the defendant had, at any rate temporarily, given up any attempt to continue the towage and had left the performance of his duty to others, he could not avail himself of the words 'default of the steam tugowner', which only extended to cover defaults during the actual performance of the duties of the contract. It was not clear enough to exclude liability for 'not doing the thing contracted for in the way contracted for'.

In *The Sumi Maru*,[132] the exclusion of liability clause was very wide, and it is important to quote it in full:

> Tugowners shall not be responsible for any loss, damage or delay whatsoever to the tow or any of the cargoes on board or for failure to undertake and/or complete the towage services however caused whether due to any unseaworthiness or defect in or breakdown of the tug or to the unfitness of any gear employed, shortage of fuel, bunkers from whatever cause, or other unforeseen circumstances or to the act of God, perils of the sea, fire, snow, ice barratry or negligence of the master or crew,

---

131 [1921] P 458 (CA); see, also, para 5.2, above.
132 1993 1 SLR 198; see, also, para 6.1.1, above.

arrest or restraint of princes, rulers or people, strikes, labour disturbances or civil commotion, explosion, bursting of boilers, breakage of shafts, or any latent defect in hull, machinery, gear or appurtenances, collision, stranding or other accidents of navigation even when occasioned by the negligence, default or error in judgment of the pilot, master or crew of the tug or any other servants of tugowners or for any personal injury or loss of life to persons on the employ of contractor or any third party; and contractor shall relieve tugowners from and indemnify them against all such loss, damage, injury or liability and against all claims whatsoever arising out of or in respect of such matters including any costs, charges or expenses which tugowners may incur or may be put to in defending any such claims.

The Court of Appeal held that the clause should not be construed in such a way as to render the whole contract nugatory, or defeat the object which both parties had in view, or to make the contract become nothing more than a statement of intent.

Failure to undertake and/or complete the towage services, however caused, cannot possibly extent to and include an intentional and deliberate failure or refusal to perform an obligation under the contract.

In *The Carlton*,[133] the terms of the towage contract between the plaintiff and the port authority (the defendants) contained a clause stating:

. . . the owners of the ship . . . so being towed or transported hereby agree and undertake to indemnify and hold harmless the Port Authority against all claims for or in respect of . . . loss or damage of any kind whatsoever and howsoever or wheresoever arising in the course of and in connection with the towage or transport, and whether such loss, injury or damage be caused or contributed to by any negligence, default or error in judgment on the part of any officers or servants whatsoever of the Port Authority . . .

The plaintiff's steamship suffered damage when in tow by the defendant port authority's tugs, due to wrong signals negligently given by the defendants' lock foreman. The lock foreman had signalled to the plaintiff's ship in tow of the defendants' tugs to enter into the Cutting. About the same time, he also signalled to another tug to enter the Cutting from the opposite end. In an attempt to avoid a collision, the plaintiff's steamship made a wrong move. As a result, she got out of position and struck the walls of the Cutting and suffered damage. When sued by the plaintiff, the port authority sought to rely on the above clause alleging that if their servants were guilty of negligence, they were under no liability to the plaintiffs. They counterclaimed for the damage done to the side of the Cutting.

It was held by Bateson J that the defendants' lock foreman was negligent. The clause was not an indemnity against party and party claim, but only against third party claims. Also, that the damage did not arise in connection with the towage or transport and that accordingly the plaintiffs were entitled to recover the amount of the damage caused by the negligence of the defendants' servant. Clearer terms would be required in the contract to protect the authority from such negligence.[134]

A very clumsy clause, purporting to exempt the tugowner from all liability

---

133 [1931] P 186.
134 *The Carlton* was later approved by the Court of Appeal in *The Lindenhall* [1945] P 8.

whatsoever and howsoever caused, is shown in *The Devonshire and The St Winifred*, which is examined under indemnity clauses para (9.2, below).

The UKSTC have a wide and fairly clear clause of exclusion of liability. Clause 4(a) provides:

> Whilst towing, or whilst at the request, either expressed or implied, of the hirer rendering any service of whatsoever nature other than towing:
>
> (a) the tugowner shall not (except as provided in cl 4(c) and (e) hereof) be responsible for or be liable for
>
> (i) damage of any description done by or to the tug or tender, or done by or to the hirer's vessel or done by or to any cargo or other thing on board or being loaded on board or indented to be loaded on board the hirer's vessel or the tug or tender or to or by any other object or property; or
>
> (ii) loss of the rug or tender or the hirer's vessel or of any cargo or other thing on board or being loaded on board or indented to be loaded on board the hirer's vessel or the tug or tender or any other object or property; or
>
> (iii) any claim by a person not a party to this agreement for loss or damage of any description whatsoever;
>
> arising from any cause whatsoever, including (without prejudice to the generality of the foregoing) negligence at any time of the tugowner his servants or agents, unseaworthiness, unfitness or breakdown of the tug or tender, its machinery, boilers, towing gear, equipment, lines, ropes or wires, lack of fuel, stores, speed or otherwise.

Although cl 4(a) has a very broad spectrum, it is not ambiguous. The question whether a serious breach of the contract by the tugowner will render exception clauses inoperative depends on the construction of the contract as a whole.[135]

It was once thought that a fundamental breach gave the court power to declare that such a breach overrode express contractual terms, exempting the guilty party from liability under the contract. Such a rule was overruled by *Photo Production v Securicor* and, since 1980, it has been definitively settled that there is no such a thing as a fundamental breach, which is not excludable by an exception clause. The parties are free to put what they like into their contract provided the exclusion clause does not defeat the object of the contract, as seen in *The Sumi Maru* (above). If they agree that a breach should not be actionable, the agreement is binding. The rule now, briefly, is that the court should look at the intention of the parties, as it can be deduced from the wording of the clause viewed in the context of the contract. The construction of exclusion clauses in some old decisions, for example *The Refrigerant*, *The Cap Palos*, *The Carlton* (discussed also under para 5.2), would be in line with the present principle.

The parameters of the exception in cl 4(a) of UKSTC are, however, limited by the first two lines of the clause, and the tugowner must show that the incident took place 'whilst towing' or 'whilst at the request'.

In *The Impetus*,[136] when the tug had come along on a parallel course to the tow for the purpose of receiving the tow lines, a collision occurred. The argument was

---

135 *Photo Production Ltd v Securicor Transport Ltd* [1980] AC 827 (HL).
136 [1959] 1 Lloyd's Rep 269, it applied *The Glenaffric* (1948) 81 LlL Rep 174; see para 5.1, above.

that it was not ready to receive orders so the exception from liability did not cover the tug as the collision was outside the scope of 'whilst towing'. It was held that the tug was in a position to receive orders. The fact that no orders were given until after the collision occurred was irrelevant. Therefore, the tug was protected by the exception clause.

The wording of the clause shows fairly clearly what the parties intended to exclude from liability. If there is an interruption of towage, the question whether or not the exclusion from liability will avail the tugowner will depend on whether he can show that he did not abandon the tow, (that is, that he did not stop doing what he had been contracted to do) as in *The Cap Palos* and para 5.2 (above).

Clause 4(b) deals with indemnity of the tug by the tow (see para 9.2, below).

Clause 4(c) qualifies cl 4(a), and renders the tug liable in certain limited situations (see para 9.3, below and para 6.1.3 above).

Clause 4(d) stipulates that the tugowner shall under no circumstances whatsoever be responsible for, or be liable for any loss or damage caused by or contributed to or arising out of delay or detention of, the hirer's vessel or of the cargo on board.

Clause 4(e) prohibits the tug's exception from liability for death or personal injury.

Clause 7 also contains a sub-clause exempting the tugowner from liability for the consequences of war, riots or other unforeseen conditions or delays of any description even if caused by the negligence of the tugowner or his servants.

9.2 Indemnity clause

In all contracts, the importance of using clear language in the drafting has been stressed throughout this book. This is more so with respect to exception or indemnity clauses. Parties claiming the benefit of such clauses may find themselves victims of ambiguous drafting if they do not express their intentions clearly. Before the standard terms of towage contracts, there had been very wide exception clauses, and the following case illustrates why the tugowner was unable to recover an indemnity from the tow owner for the liability incurred to a third party due to the negligence of the tug's servants.

The Devonshire and The St Winifred [137]

A laden barge whilst in tow of a tug, owned by the Manchester Ship Canal Company, was sunk in the Mersey after a collision with a steamship, and the owners of the lost cargo commenced an action for damages against the steamship and the tug. The tugowners brought in the owners of the barge as third parties. They claimed a declaration that they were entitled to be indemnified by the barge owners under the terms of a 'towage requisition' in respect of any sum to which they (the tugowners) might be liable to a third party, the cargo owners.

---

137 [1913] P 13.

The 'towage requisition' contained a long clause excepting the tugowners from any liability and provided:

> The tugowners were not to be responsible or liable for damage or injury to any ship vessel or craft, or the persons or goods on board any ship vessel or craft, of which the company may undertake the towage or docking in the river Mersey ... or which may be piloted by any of their servants to or from any place in the river Mersey ... or for any loss sustained or liability incurred by any one by reason of such damage or injury, or for any loss or liability incurred in consequence of any such ship, vessel, or craft colliding with or otherwise damaging any other vessel or thing, or for any loss or liability of any kind whatsoever arising from the towing, docking or piloting whatever may be the cause or causes of such damage, injury, loss or liability, or under whatever circumstances such damage, injury, loss or liability may have happened or accrued, even though arising from or occasioned by the act, omission, incapacity, negligence or default, whether wilful or not, of the company's servants or agents or any other persons, or any defect, imperfection, or insufficiency of power in or any delay, stoppage or slackness of speed of any tug or vessel, her machinery or equipment engaged in towing or docking any ship, vessel or craft, whether such defect, imperfection or insufficiency of power be in existence at the beginning of or during the said towing or docking.

The argument for the tugowners was that they were relieved by the contract from all liability and from all loss, however incurred or caused, while the towing was carried out; and that consequently there was in their contract with the barge owners an implied term that they should be indemnified from all liability and loss whatsoever. Authorities like *Hamlyn v Wood*,[138] *The Moorcock*,[139] and *Kruger & Co v Moel Tryvan Ship Co*[140] were relied upon.

Sir Samuel Evans held:[141]

> In my view the contract in this case is an ordinary business contract which speaks for itself, and which does not require any implied term to give it efficacy, or to give it the effect which was intended by the parties. Dealing with contracts of indemnity and third party procedure, Bowen LJ in *Birmingham and District Land Co v London and North Western Rly Co*.[142] says as follows:
>
> > 'I think it tolerably clear that the rule' – that is, the third party rule – 'when it deals with claims to indemnity, means claims to indemnity as such either at law or in equity. In nine cases out of 10, a right to indemnity, if it exists at all as such, must be created either by express contract or by implied contract: by express contract if it is given in terms by the contract between the two parties; by implied contract if the true inference to be drawn from the facts is that the parties intended such indemnity, even if they did not express themselves to that effect, or if there is a state of circumstances to which the law attaches a legal or equitable duty to indemnify, there being many cases in which a remedy is given upon an assumed promise by a person to do what, under the circumstances, he ought to do. I say in nine cases out of 10, for there may possibly be a 10th. Thus, there might be a statute enacting that under certain circumstances a person should be

---

138 [1891] 2 QB 488.
139 (1889) 14 PD 64.
140 [1906] 2 KB 792, [1907] AC 272.
141 [1913] P 13, pp 19–20.
142 [1886] 34 Ch D 261, p 274.

entitled to indemnity as such, in which case the right would not arise out of contract, and I do not say that there may not be other cases of a direct right in equity to an indemnity as such which does not come within the rule that all indemnity must arise out of contract express or implied.'

The contract in this case is between A (the tugowners) and B (the barge owners). It means that A is not to be responsible or liable to B for damage, injury, or loss however occasioned: not that A is not to be responsible or liable to any one. In the circumstances of this case A was responsible and liable to, and suffered judgment at the suit of, other persons, namely, the cargo-owners, for the negligence of A.

A seeks to say, not merely 'I shall not be responsible or liable to you, B, for any damage, injury, or loss, which may in any way arise out of the towage', but, further, 'You, B, are responsible and liable to me, A, for any such damage, etc, for which I may be responsible or liable to the rest of the world'. The contract does not say so.

I do not believe that the parties intended that it should impliedly mean that. To make such an implication is not in any sense necessary for the efficient performance of the contract. To introduce such an implied term would, I think, be to make a wholly different contract from that which was made, or which the parties intended to make.

An attempt was made therefore by cl 4(b) of UKSTC 1986 to define the circumstances in which the tugowner can claim an indemnity from the hirer. Clause 4(b) of UKSTC provides:

The hirer shall (except as provided in cl 4(c) and (e)) be responsible for, pay for, and indemnify the tugowner against and in respect of any loss or damage and any claims of whatsoever nature or howsoever arising or caused, whether covered by the provision of cl 4(a) hereof or not, suffered by or made against the tugowner and which shall include, without prejudice to the generality of the foregoing, any loss of or damage to the tug or tender or any property of the tugowner even if the same arises from or is caused by the negligence of the tugowner his servants or agents.

This express indemnity clause is very wide and covers liabilities incurred by the tugowner to third parties, as well as damage to or loss of the tug, or any other property of the tugowner, regardless of his servant's negligence. It is an unfair bargain for the tow, but the parties (engaged commercially) are free to agree their terms. The words 'claims of whatsoever nature or howsoever arising' include a salvage claim brought by third party contractors for their efforts to save the tug or tow if, due to the tug's negligence, such salvage assistance became necessary.[143]

By contrast, an equal bargaining is struck by the Towcon contract in which neither the tugowner nor the hirer will have recourse against each other for either damage or loss to themselves or damage or loss to third parties caused by the negligence of their respective servants or agents, as provided by cl 18.

9.3 Limitations to exclusion and indemnity clauses

As has been seen (under paras 9.1 and 9.2, above), the risk of towage under the UKSTC, for accidents, negligence, delay, and any damage of whatever nature

---

143 In *The Walumba* [1965] 1 Lloyd's Rep 121, a salvage claim was recoverable under the indemnity clause which provided to indemnify the tugowner against all consequences thereof.

caused to either tow or tug or third parties howsoever arising, is put on the tow, provided such risks occur 'whilst towing', as defined in cl 1(b)(iv) (see para 5.1, above).

The benefit of exclusion from liability and indemnity provisions in favour of the tugowner is, however, restricted by cl 4(c), which provides:

The provisions of clause 4(a) and 4(b) hereof shall not be applicable in respect of any claims which arise in any of the following circumstances:

(i) All claims which the hirer shall prove to have resulted directly and solely from the personal failure of the tugowner to exercise reasonable care to make the tug or tender seaworthy for navigation at the commencement of the towing or other service. For the purpose of this clause the tugowner's personal responsibility for exercising reasonable care shall be construed as relating only to the person or persons having the ultimate control and chief management of the tugowner's business and to any servant (excluding the officers and crew of any tug or tender) to whom the tugowner has specifically delegated the particular duty of exercising reasonable care and shall not include any other servant of the tugowner or any agent or independent contractor employed by the tugowner.

This is straightforward in disallowing the tugowner from relying on the protective clauses of the contract for any damage caused to the tug or tow or third parties, upon proof that he failed to exercise reasonable care to make the tug seaworthy. A recent example of this can be found in *The Borvigilant and Romina G*.[144]

The fault must be personal to those who represent the ego of the company, having ultimate control and chief management, or the alter ego of the company (who are specifically delegated the particular duty). This sub-clause helpfully defines who these people might be and who will not be included in the category of those who must exercise reasonable care. Since it is the personal duty of those in top management to take care to make the tug seaworthy, the rule of *The Muncaster Castle* (as discussed under para 6.1.3, above) should apply, in that the tugowner would not be able to disclaim liability arising from the tug's unseaworthiness by the fact that he delegated the duty to independent contractors. The duty is not delegable. The relevant time of seaworthiness is the time of commencement of the towage, and not if the tug became unseaworthy afterwards. Thus, if, by the fault of servants of the tugowner, the tug becomes unseaworthy during the performance of the towage, such incident will not be caught by cl 4(c)(i).

The second sub-paragraph of clause 4(c) provides:

The provisions of clause 4(a) and 4(b) hereof shall not be applicable in respect of any claims which arise in any of the following circumstances:

(ii) All claims which arise when the tug or tender, although towing or rendering some service other than towing, *is not in a position of proximity or risk* to or from the hirer's vessel or any other craft attending the hirer's vessel *and is detached from and safely clear of any ropes*, lines, wire cables or moorings associated with the hirer's vessel. Provided always that notwithstanding the foregoing, the provisions of cl 4(a) and (b) shall be fully applicable in respect of all claims which arise

---

144 [2003] EWCA Civ 935, [2003] 2 Lloyd's Rep 520 (CA).

at any time when the tug or tender is at the request, whether express or implied, of the hirer, his servants or his agents, carrying persons or property of what-soever description (in addition to the officers and crew and usual equipment of the tug or tender) and which are wholly or partly caused by, or arise out of the presence on board of such persons or property or which arise at any time when the tug or tender is proceeding to or from the hirer' s vessel in hazardous condi-tions or circumstances. (Emphasis added)

This is a confusing clause and should be re-drafted to express the intention clearly.

The following conditions must be satisfied in determining whether this clause applies, so as to render the exception from liability and indemnity clauses inoperative for all claims:

(a) the tug must not be in a 'position of proximity or risk to or from the hirer's vessel or any other craft attending' at the critical point in time in which a liability arose; *and*

(b) it must be detached from and safely clear of any ropes, etc;

The phrase 'although towing or rendering some services other than towing' at the beginning of Ch 4 (c)(ii) is contradictory to the above conditions, unless the clause means that the provisions of clause 4(a) and 4(b) shall not apply when there is just interruption of towage (see para 5.2 above).

If that is the correct interpretation, the exception from liability and the indem-nity provisions of cl 4(a), (b) will not apply during such interruption, provided the conditions of the second paragraph of the clause do not exist; these are:

(a) at the time when claims arise, the tug is, at the request, express or implied, from the tow or his agents, carrying persons or property or equipment for the hirer and such claims arise wholly or partly by, or out of, the presence of persons or property on board the tug, or

(b) such claims arise at any time when the tug or tender is proceeding to or from the hirer' s vessel in hazardous conditions or circumstances.

In effect, the last two conditions, if they are satisfied, are the exceptions to the exceptions of cl 4(a) and (b), thus the tugowner will be protected by cl 4(a), (b), notwithstanding the conditions of the first paragraph of cl 4(c)(ii).

It is fairly easy to imagine the difficulties involved in interpreting such a clause. In practical terms, the situations that would be likely to be covered by the exception to the exception might be very limited.

Clear and plain language would greatly assist in establishing what the contracting parties intend to exclude by this clause.

An example of criticism by the Court of Appeal concerning bad drafting is provided by *The Salviva*,[145] in which Parker LJ said: 'The dispute between the parties arises out of an unusual and very ill drafted towage.'

That contract, being under the Norwegian ocean towage form, provided, principally, for the towage of APA's crane barge *Montasser* from Kegoya, Japan, to Alexandria, Egypt, by Goliath's ocean-going tug, *The Salviva*.

---

145 [1987] 2 Lloyd's Rep 457.

Clause 10 provided who would be responsible for the seaworthiness of the tow:

The tow to be prepared for towage by the tugowner and to the satisfaction of the tugowner and/or their master and provided with the necessary documents required for towage issued by a competent classification society [or Nippon Kaiji Kentei Kyokai]. If the tow becomes unseaworthy during the voyage for any reason whatsoever the seaworthiness to be re-established by the company and a new seaworthy certificate to be issued on tugowner's request.

Clause 17 dealt with liabilities as follows:

Damage and loss

Provided the tugowners shall exert due diligence to prepare the tug before departure from Kegoya in a fit, seaworthy and perfect condition in all respects to perform the voyage and provided the tugowner prepares the tow for this towage in accordance with [Nippon Kaiji Kentei Kyokai's] surveyor's requirements the tugowner shall not be responsible for any loss, damage or delay whatsoever to the tow or any of the cargoes on board or for failure to undertake and/or complete the towage services however caused whether due to any unseaworthiness or defect in or breakdown of the tug or to the unfitness of any gear employed, shortage of fuel bunkers from whatever cause or other unforeseen circumstances or to the act of God, perils of the sea, fire, snow, ice, barratry or negligence of the master or crew, arrest or restraint of princes, rulers or people, strikes, labour disturbances or civil commotion, explosion, bursting of boilers, breakage of shafts, or any latent defect in hull, machinery, gear or appurtenances, collision, strandings or other accidents of navigation even when occasioned by the negligence, default or error in judgment of the pilot, master or crew of the tug or any other servants of the tug, tugowner or for any personal injury or loss of life to persons in the employ of the company or any third party, and the company shall relieve tugowner from and indemnify them against all such loss, damage, injury, loss of life or liability against all claims whatsoever arising out of or in respect of such matters including any costs, charges or expenses which tugowners may incur or may be put to in defending any such claims.

The tug and tow departed from Kegoya and shortly thereafter it deviated from her course to avoid the typhoon Gay. The deviation lasted for 3 days. In respect of this, Goliath claimed US$5000 per day for three days' extra steaming time, pursuant to cl 24 of the contract. The learned judge upheld this claim.

Some time later, the crew of the tug inspected the tow and found that some of the sea fastenings consisting of steel wire had loosened during the voyage and that they and other sea fastenings had suffered damage. As a result it was necessary to put in to Singapore for repairs. The repairs were carried out at a cost of US$84,027.18 and were paid for by Goliath, who in turn claimed this sum plus demurrage amounting to US$110,310.41 in respect of the time spent in Singapore. The judge upheld both claims. APA contended that he erred in so doing.

Between Singapore and Port Said the sea fastenings and lashings suffered further damage necessitating the carrying out of further repairs in Port Said. In respect of the cost of those repairs no claim was made, for they were paid by APA's insurers. Goliath, however, claimed demurrage amounting to US$50,821.90 in respect of the time spent in Port Said while repairs were being effected. This claim was also upheld by the learned Judge. APA contended that in so doing he also erred.

APA's basic case was that under the terms of the contract, express or implied, Goliath warranted the tow-worthiness of the tow. In other words, it warranted that the materials and workmanship of the sea fastenings were reasonably fit. They were not so fit because steel wire was used for the primary lashings, such lashings would inevitably stretch in foreseeable weather conditions and, having stretched, would allow movement which would set up loads leading to damage and the necessity for repairs.

APA contended in the alternative that Goliath contracted to prepare the crane barge for towage and to procure her survey. Although they were entitled and expected to sub-contract the work of preparation, they were vicariously liable for any negligence on the part of the sub-contractor or surveyor. It was, they submitted, negligent to use wire lashings.

Goliath, on the other hand, contended that under the contract their obligation was merely to procure and pay for the preparation of the tow for towage to the reasonable satisfaction of themselves and/or the tugmaster, to comply with the recommendations of the towage approval surveyor, and to obtain a certificate of fitness to tow from such surveyor. With those obligations they complied and, having done so, they were, under the terms of the contract, entitled to recover the amount claimed.

They further contended that there was nothing wrong with the steel wire lashings as such. They were unstretched, but the plan did not provide for stretched wire. There was nothing wrong with the workmanship of Kegoya in applying the lashings.

APA's case was simply that wire should not have been used at all, but that, instead, chain, or structural steel rods or tie bars should have been employed.

Parker LJ, on the appeal, proceeded to construe the contract, and said:

Clause 17 and other clauses throw light upon the meaning and intent of the opening words of cl 10 . . .

The two provisos upon which the wide relief accorded to the tugowner depend are of considerable significance. So far as the tug itself is concerned, the exercise of due diligence to make it seaworthy must be shown, but with regard to the tow it is sufficient to show that it has been prepared in accordance with, in the event, NK3's requirements. If cl 10 imposes on the tugowner not merely an obligation to exercise due diligence in the preparation of the tow, but a positive unqualified warranty of seaworthiness and suitability of materials and workmanship, it appears to me unlikely in the extreme that APA would have agreed to relieve the tugowners from all loss, damage or delay to the tow, and indemnify the tugowner against all such loss and damage on the mere proof that the tow had been prepared in accordance with NK3's requirements, albeit that such requirements were insufficient to produce a seaworthy tow, provided for unsuitable materials and were grossly negligent. If the second proviso stood alone, it would in my view point strongly to the mutual intent of the parties that the tugowner's obligation under cl 10 being the limited one found by the learned judge. The indication is even stronger when the second proviso is contrasted with the first proviso. Mr Sumption submits that to derive a limited meaning to cl 10 from the wording of cl 17 is to cut down by an exemption clause the extent of the obligation in cl 10, but this submission in my view fails for two reasons: first, because the problem is to find out by reference to the contract as a whole what is the meaning of cl 10; secondly, because it is of the essence of an exemption clause that it should cut down a liability that would otherwise exist.[146]

The lesson to be learned from this case is that ill drafting results in expensive litigation, and it is essential that the intention of the parties, particularly with regard to exception clauses, ought to be made clearer than having long convoluted clauses such as this and cl 4(c) (ii) of UKSTC (just discussed).

It is surprising that, in this case, however, the court allowed the exception clause to stand.

The second part of clause 17 contained an all-embracing exception from liability, which was made subject to the tugowner having satisfactorily discharged the duty imposed by the first part of the clause. Considering the facts of the case, the lashing broke more than once. Either the quality and type of the lashing, or skill and care to lash properly, had been wanting, which could, conceivably, have led to the conclusion that the tugowner had failed to fulfil the obligation stated in the first part of this clause.

10 THE SUBSTITUTION AND HIMALAYA CLAUSE OF THE UKSTC

10.1 Substitution of tugs, authority to subcontract and transfer of benefits

In particular, cl 5 of UKSTC provides that:

> The tugowner shall at any time be entitled to substitute one or more tugs . . . for any other tug . . . or tugs . . . The tugowner shall at any time . . . be entitled to contract with any other tugowner . . . to hire the other tugowners's tug or tender and . . . it is hereby agreed that the tugowner is acting . . . as the agent of the hirer, notwithstanding that the tugowner may in addition, if authorised . . . act as agent of the other tugowner at any time and for any purpose including the making of any agreement with the hirer . . . It is hereby agreed that such contract is and shall at all times be subject to the provisions of these conditions so that the other tugowner is bound by the same and may as principal sue the hirer thereon and shall have the full benefit of these conditions in every respect expressed or implied herein.

It purports to give authority to the tug to act as an agent of the tow and, at times, of another tugowner for the purpose of substituting another tug, if necessary, binding the tow and the substituted tug to the terms of the contract.

This provision was drafted as a result of the circumstances that existed in the case below.

---

146 [1987] 2 Lloyd's Rep 457, p 461.

The Conoco Arrow[147]

In this case, the substitution clause stated as follows:

> The tug may substitute one tug for another and may sub-let the work, wholly or in part to other tugowners who shall also have the benefit of and be bound by these conditions.

P & Sons, tug supplies company, agreed to supply tugs to the defendants under the then applicable UKSTC. The contract also contained an indemnity provision in favour of the tugowner. The tug let to the defendants belonged to the plaintiffs and not to P & Sons. A collision occurred between the tug and the defendant's vessel (the tow) as a result of which the tug sank. The plaintiffs (owners of the tug) claimed damages from the defendants in tort and also in contract based on the agreement between P & Sons and the defendants. They contended that, under the UKSTC agreement, P & Sons had sub-let the work of supplying tugs to them, and that they were therefore entitled to the same remedies by way of indemnity as P & Sons would have been. The admiralty registrar struck out the claim based on contract. On appeal to the High Court, Brandon J held that the admiralty registrar had rightly struck out the alternative claim based on contract. Without any evidence of agency or trusteeship, the plaintiffs could not obtain rights under a contract between the defendants and the head contractors.

The claim at that time would be bound to fail in the Court of Appeal and House of Lords unless the House of Lords was inclined not to follow its earlier decisions holding that a party could not succeed upon a claim based on a contract to which he was not a party. This problem was eventually resolved by the invention of the so-called 'Himalaya' clauses and, more recently, by statute (see below).

10.2 The Himalaya provision and the Contracts (Rights of Third Parties) Act 1999

The doctrine of privity of contract under English law has meant that third parties can neither take the benefit of, nor be imposed with obligations arising under, a contract made between two other parties.[148] However, invariably, a contract and its performance can affect third parties. This had caused difficulties, over many years, particularly with regard to the extent to which third parties may benefit from exclusion or limitation of liability clauses in a contract for loss or damage arising through their negligence. Civil law systems provide in their codified law that, in some circumstances, rights or obligations under a contract may be conferred on third parties. Although vicarious immunity was accepted by the House of Lords in *Elder, Dempster Co Ltd v Paterson, Zochonis Co Ltd*,[149] demonstrating a desire by the

---

147 [1973] 1 Lloyd's Rep 86.

148 For example, in the towage context, when a towage contract had been entered into between the time charterers and the tug, no claim of indemnity could be enforced against the owners of the vessel: *The Basis* (1950) 84 LlL Rep 306.

149 [1924] AC 522 (HL).

judiciary to find ways around the doctrine of privity, the majority of the House of Lords later, in *Midland Silicones Ltd v Scruttons Ltd*,[150] did not accept that a general principle could be drawn from the *ratio decidendi* in its previous decision. To over-come this problem, parties to a contract have used techniques to enable third parties to take the benefit of exclusion clauses when the circumstances require that third parties involved in the performance of the contract should be protected.

Such clauses have been known as 'Himalaya'[151] clauses, and encouragement for their use was given by the majority of the Privy Council in *The Eurymedon*.[152]

This involved the performance of unloading of goods from a ship by stevedores, who sought to rely on the exclusion from liability clause in the contract of carriage agreed between the shipper and the carrier for the latter's benefit. Lord Wilberforce said:

> [The contract] . . . brought into existence a bargain initially unilateral but capable of becoming mutual, between the shipper and the [stevedores], made through the car-rier as agent. This became a full contract when the [stevedores] performed services by discharging the goods. The performance of these services for the benefit of the shipper was the consideration for the agreement by the shipper that the [stevedores] should have the benefit of he exceptions and limitations contained in the bill of lading.[153]

Although this decision was criticised for providing an artificial analysis, the policy reason behind it was to discourage actions against the servants, agents or independent contractors in order to get round the exceptions in the contract. The Privy Council, in *The New York Star*,[154] re-affirmed the principle of *The Eurymedon*, and stressed that it should not be confined to its own facts. Lord Goff, at the Privy Council, reviewed the function of Himalaya clauses in *The Mahkutai*.[155] Following this decision, Himalaya clauses were regarded as developing towards becoming a fully fledged exception to the doctrine of privity.[156]

The UKSTC, cl 5 (shown under para 10.1, above) combines the substitution of a tug with a Himalaya clause, and effectively shows the intention of the parties that a substituted tug will enjoy the benefits of, and be subject to, the obligations for the performance of the contract, the conditions of which should be binding between the substituted tug and the hirer.

In addition, for extra protection of the servants and agents of the tugowner, or any tugowner whose tug has been sublet to the hirer, the hirer undertakes by cl 8 of

---

150 [1962] AC 446 (HL).

151 It derived the name from the name of the vessel in *Adler v Dickson* [1955] 1 QB 158 (CA), which involved a claim by passengers of a ship against the master of the ship, in tort, in order to avoid the limitation of liability clause in a passenger ticket (see, also, Chapter 8, contracts of management of ships (para 4.6) BIMCO SHIPMAN 98).

152 [1975] AC 154 (PC).

153 Ibid, p 167.

154 [1981] 1 WLR 138.

155 [1996] 3 WLR 1; he did not accept that the principle extends to exclusive jurisdiction clauses.

156 For a full review and analysis of the privity doctrine, as well as the 1999 Act, see Merkin, R, *Privity of Contract*, 2000, LLP (Himalaya clauses, p 158).

UKSTC (the non-suit clause) not to bring proceedings against them in respect of any negligence, breach of duty, or other wrongful act.

In a recent case, **The Borvigilant and Romina G**,[157] the tug company, National Iranian Oil Company (NIOC), entered into a contract of towage with Monsoon Shipping, the owners of the tanker, *Romina G*. There was a tug requisition form signed by the master of *Romina G*, which contained very similar clauses to those of the UKSTC. The contract provided, inter alia, the right to subcontract by cl 7, thus:

> The Company shall have the right to perform their obligations under this contract by using a tug or tugs not owned by themselves but made available to the Company under charterparties or other arrangements. In such circumstances. . . . .the Hirer agrees the Owners or Charterers of such tug or tugs have the benefit of and being bound by these conditions to the same extent as the Company.

Romina G arrived at Kharg Island to load crude oil at NIOC's terminal. NIOC owned its own tugs but they engaged a tug, *Borvigilant*, from the claimants (Borkan) to assist in berthing *Romina G*. During the course of berthing, this tug collided with *Romina G*. There was loss of life and of the tug. Borkan claimed against Monsoon (the owners of *Romina G*) in contract and in tort, and Monsoon claimed in tort for its losses. Borkan relied on the conditions contained in the tug requisition form and argued that, by cl 7, they could take the benefit of the contract under traditional agency principles. Each party argued that the collision was caused by the fault of the other and, in addition, Monsoon contended the collision was caused by the unseaworthiness of the tug. The preliminary issues were: (i) whether Borkan was entitled to rely on the benefit of the conditions in the tug requisition form; and, if so, (ii) whether Borkan was exempt from liability.

It was held by the Court of Appeal that it was not necessary that the tug requisition form should expressly state that NIOC was contracting as agent for Borkan; cl 7 expressly provided that Borkan should have the benefit of, and be bound by, the conditions of the tug requisition form to the same extent as NIOC. As to the second issue, the effect of the exclusion of the indemnity provision for loss of and damage to the tug, and loss of life of the tug's crew caused by want of reasonable care to make the tug seaworthy, was that Borkan (the tugowner) could not rely on the protective clauses of the contract.

The Towcon expressly regulates the rights of the tug's servants or agents to rely on the exceptions, defences, immunities, limitation of liability, indemnities, privileges and conditions granted or provided by the main agreement between the tugowner and the hirer by a separate Himalaya clause (cl 19).

It should be noted, briefly, that the doctrine of privity was reformed at the initiative of the Law Commission, which published its report on *Privity of Contracts: Contracts for the Benefit of Third Parties* in 1996,[158] as a result of which the Contracts (Rights of Third Parties) Act (C(RTP)A) 1999 received Royal Assent on 11 November 1999. Section 10(2) provided for it to come into force six months thereafter, so

---

157 [2003] EWCA Civ 935, [2003] 2 Lloyd's Rep 520 (CA).

158 See Law Commission Report No 242, *Reforming Privity of Contract* [1996] LMCLQ 467, p 468, for the background to the problems existing by reason of the doctrine of privity.

contracts made before 11 May 2000 are not subject to the Act, while contracts made after that date are.

One of the reasons why the reform was required was said (by the Law Commissioner, Andrew Burrows)[159] to be injustice to third parties. In particular, he put it that:

> The privity rule causes injustice to a third party where a valid contract has engendered in the third party reasonable expectations of having the legal right to enforce (as it does, for example, where the contract contains an express term to that effect). The injustice is heightened where the third party has relied on the contract to regulate his or her affairs or has accepted it by communicating assent to the promisor. Indeed, where such heightened injustice is present, we believe that it outweighs the general right of the contracting parties to change their original intentions. That is, the parties' right to vary or cancel the contract should be overridden once the third party has relied on, or accepted, the promise.

Where English law applies to a towage contract, the 1999 Act enhances the protection of third parties intended to be protected by the terms of the contract, providing an alternative to the Himalaya clauses. Section 1 of the Act grants to a third party the right to enforce a term of a contract if either the contract expressly provides he may, or if the term purports to confer a benefit upon him. Section 1(5) of the Act stipulates the enforcement of rights of third parties (as provided by s 1): 'There shall be available to the third party any remedy that would have been available to him in an action for breach of contract if he had been a party to the contract.'

11 LIMITATION OF LIABILITY[160]

The 1976 Limitation of Liability Convention was enacted by the MSA 1979. This Act has been repealed and its provisions have been incorporated in the MSA 1995. Article 1 of the 1976 Convention provides for the parties who can limit liability: shipowners and salvors. Shipowner includes owners, charterers, managers and operator of a sea-going ship. This means that both shipowners (of the tow and of the tug) involved in the towage contract can limit their liability by reference to the tonnage of their vessel. Liability is limited by reference to a limitation fund calculated on the basis of the vessel's tonnage (Arts 11–14). The interpretation of Art 2(1) of the Convention is examined in Chapter 17, below.

In this connection, Rix J in **Caspian Basin**[161] had to consider whether a claim for loss of a tow arising partly out of misrepresentation as to the tug's bollard pull and bhp was a claim occurring within the meaning of Art 2(1)(a), and he concluded that the words 'indirect connection with the operation of the ship' provide the necessary linkage between loss or damage on the one hand and the ship in respect of which the claim to limit is made on the other.

---

159 Ibid.
160 For an outline of the principles of limitation of liability, see Chapter 17, below.
161 [1997] 2 Lloyd's Rep 507.

One main issue dealing with limitation of liability in relation to tugs and tows has been whether or not their tonnage should be aggregated in order to provide higher limitation fund. The question of aggregation is usually referred to as 'the flotilla issue'.[162] If the theory that tug and tow is one unit were correct, the aggregated tonnage of the two might be considered for purpose of limitation. In most collision cases under towage contracts, however, a collision is caused by the faulty navigational manoeuvre of the one that has been in control. That may be either the fault of the tug, or of the tow, or of both. In accordance with the control theory, the limitation fund will be calculated on the basis of the tonnage of the particular vessel or vessels at fault. This is of particular concern to claimants who may have suffered loss caused by the negligent navigation of a small tug towing a great liner. The small tug has comparatively small value and it would have a correspondingly low measure of liability if limitation were to be calculated on the basis of its tonnage alone, as opposed to calculation based on an aggregate tonnage of both tug and tow.

In the following cases, only the tug's tonnage was taken into account for the calculation of the limitation fund.

The Bramley Moore [163]

M and another dumb barge were in tow of *The Bramley Moore* when a collision occurred between M and a motor vessel, E. M brought an action against E and the tug (*The Bramley Moore*) as third party. The trial judge found the vessel E and the tug equally to blame, and entered judgment against the owners of E. He also entered judgment for E against the owners of the tug for half of the damage. The owners of the tug brought a limitation action, and claimed to limit their liability by reference to the tonnage of their tug alone. They contended that the calculation would be based on combined tonnage only if the tug and tow had common ownership. The counter-argument was that the limit should be calculated by reference to the combined tonnages of the tug and one or both of the barges, whether or not they belonged to the same owners. The trial judge held that the tugowners were entitled to limit, based on the tonnage of the tug alone. The Court of Appeal held that, after the MSA 1958, which amended the limitation provisions of the MSA 1894, where damage was caused by a tow owing to the negligence of those on the tug and not of those on the tow, the damage was caused by the negligence of the person on board the tug, and the tugowners could limit their liability according to the tonnage of the tug alone. The flotilla was not to be taken as a unit.

Even when both the tug and the tow belonged to the same defendant, the calculation of limitation was not done on the basis of the aggregate tonnage.

The Smjeli [164]

A tug towing a dumb barge, both belonging to the defendants, damaged the groynes of the District Council of Shepway, which claimed damages against the

---

162 Op cit, Rainey, fn 1.
163 [1963] 2 Lloyd's Rep 429.
164 [1982] 2 Lloyd's Rep 74.

defendants, tugowners. The defendants contended that they were entitled to limit their liability pursuant to s 503 of the MSA 1894, as amended by the 1958 Act. The plaintiffs, however, contended that, if the defendants were entitled to limit their liability, the amount was to be calculated by reference to the aggregate tonnage of both vessels belonging to the defendants. Sheen J held that, as the plaintiffs' claim depended solely on an allegation that there was negligence in the navigation of the tug, so the limit of the defendants' liability must be calculated by reference to the tonnage of the tug alone.

Issues and principles of limitation of liability are examined in Chapter 17. In the next chapter, the rights and liabilities of port authorities and pilots are explained.

CHAPTER 15

PRINCIPLES OF GENERAL AVERAGE

1 INTRODUCTION

This chapter is intended to provide a concise overview of the principles applicable to general average. It sets out only the elementary principles which derive from maritime law, equity and public policy. It is rather a *sui generis* subject, and is relevant to contracts of carriage of goods by sea, and the losses that result from a general average act are insurable as provided by the Marine Insurance Act 1906. Space does not permit a detailed treatment of general average in this book, which can be found in specialist texts on the subject.[1]

To gain an insight into general average, readers are specifically referred to the bible of Carver.[2] In his introduction to the subject, he begins by explaining the difference between general average loss and particular average, the latter being a partial loss sustained by individual interests, being exposed to particular risks; such particular loss, or average, which is not a loss sustained for the preservation of the whole common adventure, 'lies where it has fallen'. By contrast, if an interest of the common adventure is sacrificed to avert a danger which threatens the whole adventure, and the sacrifice is intentional for the benefit of the remainder, 'the whole burden of the loss occasioned is not left on the interest upon which it has fallen. It is imposed upon that and all those others for whose benefit the sacrifice has been made, rateably, in proportion of the saved values'. That is why the loss is said to be a general average loss, 'and the contributions made to it by those benefited are general average contributions'.

As a principle, therefore, general average applies where the common adventure is at risk and an interest of it is sacrificed, or extraordinary expenditure is incurred, in order to preserve that property and other interests involved in the same maritime adventure. The expenditure or sacrifice is the general average act and must be voluntary (meaning intentional) and reasonable. The result is an entitlement to a general average contribution by the person whose property has been sacrificed, or the expenditure incurred, against the other interests which are saved. The word 'average' means 'loss'. Such loss is claimed back as a rateable contribution ('the general average contribution') of the saved values of those interests which have benefited as a result.

The obligation to contribute does not depend so much upon an implied term of a particular contract, since there are many interests involved other than those of the

---

1 One should consult the leading authority in this field, Wilson, DJ, and Cooke, JHS, *Lowndes & Rudolf: The Law of General Average and the York-Antwerp Rules*, 12th edn, 1997. See also a more recent text by Rose, FD, *General Average Law and Practice*, 2nd edn, 2005.

2 13th edn, 1982, vol 2, para 1345.

contracting parties, but it depends upon a general rule of maritime law, as a matter of natural justice.[3]

The concept of general average is very ancient, having its roots in Rhodian law, being adopted into the 'Digest of Justinian', and it is said that its origins date back to at least 1000 BC.[4] Its justification is based mainly on equity as well as mercantile custom, common law, public policy and natural justice.[5] These grounds are the same as in salvage. There are also some common elements between salvage and general average, as they both arise in situations of necessity, and there is a benefit conferred to the property in danger. Unlike in incidents of salvage, however, where a volunteer, being a third party to the adventure, saves property in danger (see Chapter 13, above) the rights and obligations in general average arise only between those who are involved in the 'common maritime adventure'.

The ancient law of general average was, during the Christian era, incorporated into a number of national legal systems. In the course of this process, it received a number of differing interpretations. Therefore, in the 19th century enthusiasm for internationalisation, efforts were made to impose on its interpretation some measure of uniformity. This resulted in what have become known as the York-Antwerp Rules (YAR). These Rules do not form an international convention, but are incorporated by reference into contracts of carriage. This process has in fact imposed a quite remarkable measure of uniformity on the basis of average adjustments around the world.

There have been various sets of YAR over the years; the most commonly known have been the 1890, the 1924, the 1950 Rules, and the most recent editions, which have modernised general average, are YAR 1974 (as amended in 1990), the 1994 and 2004 YAR.

Most general average adjustments are today drawn up on the basis of the YAR 1994, although some are still prepared according to the YAR 1974 (as amended in 1990). The most recent set of Rules, dated 2004, were the result of pressures imposed by cargo insurers. They have therefore found little favour with the remainder of the maritime community, and are seldom encountered in contracts of carriage.

1.1 The York-Antwerp Rules (YAR)

The fact that a general average act can occur in any international waters, or on the high seas, raises the questions of which law and jurisdiction should apply to the

---

3   *Simonds v White* (1824) 2 B & C 805, 811, per Abbott CJ; *Burton v English* (1883) 12 QBD 218, p 200, per Brett LJ; cf Lord Bramwell in *Wright v Marwood* (1881) 7 QBD 62 said that, to judge from the way in which contribution is claimed in England, 'it would seem to arise from an implied contract inter se to contribute by those interested.' And in *Strang Steel v Scott* (1889) 14 App Cas 601, p 608, PC: 'whether the rule ought to be regarded as matter of implied contract, or as a canon of positive law resting upon the dictates of natural justice, is a question which their Lordships do not consider it necessary to determine. The principle upon which contribution becomes due does not appear to them to differ from that upon which claims of recompense for salvage services are founded. But, in any aspect of it, the rule of contribution has its foundation in the plainest equity'.

4   Op cit, Rose, fn 1, p 1; see also an interesting article: John Macdonald 'General Average, Ancient and Modern' [1995] LMCLQ 480.

5   Op cit, Rose, fn 1, pp 6–8.

general average adjustments. But, if the Rules are incorporated into the contract, they will govern the adjustment of general average. They provide a complete code and, by the general rule of interpretation, they 'shall apply to the exclusion of any law and practice inconsistent with them', if the parties to a contract have adopted them.

These Rules consist of a set of lettered rules, followed by a set of numbered rules. The lettered rules from A to G state the general principles, while the numbered rules (I to XXIII) are specific and deal with commercial practicability; they qualify the general principles.

Where the lettered rules do not mention a specific item, but the numbered rules deal with it, the question arose in *Vlassopoulos v British and Foreign Marine Insurance Co (Makis)*[6] whether or not the circumstances that gave rise to the expenditure was general average. The underwriters argued that, since the event which resulted in the expenses at the port of refuge was not covered by the lettered rules, the specific numbered rules had no application. The shipowners, on the other hand, argued that the particular rules should prevail over the general. The judge rejected both arguments, and said at pp 196, 198:

> This is a matter of construction, and in my view the true construction of these Rules, general and particular, is not precisely what either of the contending parties has contended for. In my view those who drew up the Rules intended to provide a complete code which is to govern the law of general average for anybody who adopts it . . . It may be that there are omitted cases not covered by the general or by the specific Rules. That I do not decide. Nor do I decide any question as to the law apart from the Rules, because there is a finding that the parties by their contract intended that the code which should govern their rights and obligations should be the York-Antwerp Rules of 1924, and I treat that as conclusive for the present purpose and the common law of this or any other country as being outside the scope of my consideration and my decision . . .

> (The parties) may choose a self-contained code, and of this code, it may be observed, that although the general Rules are not identical with the law of England, they approach much more nearly to the law of England than they do to the laws of many other countries, and that is not perhaps surprising, having regard to the known and admitted predominance that this country holds in maritime matters. But when that has been done, and a general set of Rules provided laying down the general principles which are to operate, then the Rules go on to deal with certain specific cases, and I am satisfied on the true construction of the Rules that those cases are dealt with not by way of mere illustration, but in order to make definite and certain what the Rules decide about certain cases which are on the border line, and which might be held to be on one side or the other of the line which is to be drawn under the general Rules.

Thus, in construing the 1974 York-Antwerp Rules, the judge held that the lettered rules enunciate the general principles, and the numbered rules settle how the general principles are to be applied in what might, otherwise, be doubtful cases. Roche J further stated:

> The York-Antwerp Rules, 1924, are framed in order that the parties, if they choose to

---

6   [1929] 1 KB 187.

adopt the Rules by way of contract, may not be troubled with any question as to what, if any, general law is to apply ... The Rules must be read together and as a whole, and not as two codes one of which may contradict the other.

In any question of a lacuna in the lettered rules, therefore, or an issue of conflict between the lettered and the numbered rules, the rules should be read as a whole, and the result in a particular case will be a matter of construction of the rules in the context of the circumstances. Whether a literal and purposive approach of interpretation, or a strict interpretation of the rules should be adopted, would depend on the circumstances of a case.[7]

Since the lettered rules enshrine the principles and the numbered rules enshrine commercial practicability, if 'principle and commercial practicability are found to conflict, practicability should be preferred'.[8] It should be noted that the scheme of the rules is governed by the rule of interpretation which, in the 1974 Rules, provides that 'except as provided by the numbered rules' the lettered rules shall be applied.[9] A rule paramount has been added to the 1994 and the 2004 Rules, requiring the principle of reasonableness to apply in any sacrifice or expenditure that might be incurred, which is not required in the 1974 Rules (see para 2.3 below). Thus, the rule of interpretation, in both the 1994 and 2004 Rules, has been amended and reads: 'except as provided by the Rule Paramount and the numbered Rules, general average shall be adjusted according to the lettered Rules'.

A difficult point of construction arose in *The Bijela*.[10] The issue was whether the owners of *The Bijela* could claim general average contribution in respect of the cost of temporary repairs carried out in the course of a voyage before the ship reached destination, in India. Hobhouse J's view, at first instance,[11] was that the repairs in dry dock were not 'necessary for the safe prosecution of the voyage', thus the cost of discharging, storing and reloading the cargo at Providence was not allowed in general average. The majority of the Court of Appeal, Hoffmann LJ dissenting, agreed.

The question in the appeal by the owners to the House of Lords turned on the construction of the second paragraph of Rule XIV of the YAR 1974.

On the facts, the shipowners' vessel was chartered for the carriage of cargo from Providence, Rhode Island, to the West Coast of India, under a charterparty which provided that general average was to be settled in London according to the York-Antwerp Rules 1974. Whilst still in Rhode Island Sound, the vessel grounded and sustained damage. She put into the port of Jamestown, where it was discovered that she could not safely reach New York, the nearest port where permanent repairs could be carried out in dry dock, without discharging the whole of her cargo. The shipowners elected to carry out temporary repairs in Jamestown, at a cost of US

---

7   *The Bijela* [1993] 1 Lloyd's Rep 411 (CA), reversed [1994] 1 WLR 615 (HL) indicating a combination of a literal and purposive approach; for the strict approach, see *The Trade Green* [2000] 2 Lloyd's Rep 451.

8   Macdonald, op cit, fn 4, at 493.

9   *Corfu Navigation Co v Mobil Shipping Co Ltd (The Alpha)* [1991] 2 Lloyd's Rep 515, p. 518.

10 Op cit, fn 7, and [1994] 2 Lloyd's Rep 1 (HL).

11 [1992] 1 Lloyd's Rep 636, p 644.

$282,606. The cost of discharging, storing and reloading the cargo to allow perman-ent repairs in New York would have exceeded $535,000. The vessel having com-pleted her voyage to India, the shipowners declared a general average loss. The adjusters did not allow the cost of the temporary repairs. The shipowners instructed a second firm of adjusters, who included the cost of the repairs in general average as being less than the expense which would have been incurred and allowed if the temporary repairs had not been effected, within rule XIV of the Rules of 1974. The cargo owners refused to pay their contributions and the shipowners issued a writ for their recovery. The judge dismissed the claim on the ground, inter alia, that rule X(b) of the Rules only allowed for the cost of discharging and storing cargo in respect of repairs "necessary for the safe prosecution of the voyage;" and that since repairs in dry dock had not been necessary, the cost of handling and storing the cargo in New York would not have been allowed in general average and there had been no saving in expense. The Court of Appeal, by a majority, dismissed the shipowners' appeal.

On appeal by the shipowners, the House of Lords held, allowing the appeal, that rule XIV of the York-Antwerp Rules 1974 was to be applied on the assumption that the temporary repairs had not been effected, and that assumption was to be carried through when applying rule X of the Rules; that if the temporary repairs had not been carried out, the shipowners' vessel would have been required to discharge its cargo and go into dry dock in New York for the repairs necessary to enable the vessel to proceed to India; and that, accordingly, since, on that assumption, such repairs would have been necessary, within the meaning of rule X(b) of the Rules, for the safe prosecution of the voyage, the shipowners had shown that the cost of handling and storing the cargo would have been allowable in general average.

Apparently the judge and the Court of Appeal misinterpreted the meaning of Rule X(b) and Rule XIV which have to be read together. Unfortunately, the drafters of the 2004 Rules made Rule XIV(b) almost incomprehensible. The Rules generally are not easy to follow, and their drafting leaves a lot to be desired.

As said earlier, the York-Antwerp Rules are voluntary. Therefore, where they are not incorporated into a charterparty or bill of lading, they do not apply. The question therefore arises as to which jurisdiction a general average act falls within, where no mention is made of the York-Antwerp Rules.[12] The authorities in this area are supportive of the view that, in the absence of any contrary agreement, general average is governed by the law of the place where the maritime adventure ends,[13] although the parties can agree a different place.

1.2 Definition

The York-Antwerp Rules define general average in Rule A uniformly, thus:

There is a general average act when, and only when, any extraordinary sacrifice or

---

12   Although, in practice, most parties insert rider clauses into their charterparties which provide for the application of the York-Antwerp Rules, there can be instances where this does not happen.

13   *Simonds v White* (1824) 2 B & C 805.

expenditure is intentionally and reasonably made or incurred for the common safety for the purpose of preserving from peril the property involved in a common maritime adventure.

Where there is general average there is, of course, insurance to cover the losses that have resulted from a general average act. Thus, the principle was codified in s 66 of the Marine Insurance Act 1906:

General Average Loss

(1) A general average loss is a loss caused by or directly consequential on a general average act. It includes a general average expenditure as well as a general average sacrifice.

(2) There is a general average act where any extraordinary sacrifice or expenditure is voluntarily and reasonably made or incurred in time of peril for the purpose of preserving the property imperilled in the common adventure.

(3) Where there is a general average loss, the party on whom it falls is entitled, subject to the conditions imposed by maritime law, to a rateable contribution from the other parties interested, and such contribution is called a general average contribution.

It can, therefore, be said that there are four elements to satisfy for a general average act to occur: (1) a danger, or peril, to the common adventure; (2) extraordinary sacrifice or expenditure; (3) voluntarily or intentionally and reasonably made; and (4) preservation of the property involved in the danger. Before these elements are examined under para 2, below, it is important to look at the issue of authority to act in general average.

1.3 Authority to act in general average

For an act to be considered as a general average act, the test was set by the court in *Athel Line Ltd v Liverpool & London War Risks Ins Assn Ltd*[14], by Tucker J:

> The rule (A) I think, clearly envisages the exercise by someone of his reasoning powers and discretion applied to a particular problem with freedom of choice to decide to act in one out of two or more possible ways, and the language is quite inappropriate to describe the blind and unreasoning obedience of a subordinate to the lawful orders of a superior authority.

On the facts of this case, there was no general average act when the commodore of a convoy ordered the convoy to a port of refuge under the orders of the admiralty in order to protect British ships from enemy acts.

On the point as to who should have ultimate authority to decide the act of sacrifice, the judge did not decide the issue, but expressed his opinion that there was no clear authority as to whether the act giving rise to a general average claim must be the act of the master, or some other member of the crew in case of his incapacity or unavoidable absence, or whether the act may, in exceptional circumstances, be that of a stranger.

---

14 [1994] KB 87, p 94.

This raises an interesting question in a situation when a SOSREP orders the ship to a port of refuge for the safety of the common adventure. Expenditure incurred by the parties to the adventure on account of salvage, whether under contract or not, for the purpose of preserving the common adventure from peril is allowed in general average (Rule VI), including expenses incurred at the port of refuge (Rule X). The SOSREP has statutory powers and he takes control of a casualty; for this reason, it is submitted, his authority should be the authority of a proper person to act. In the recent casualty, *MSC Napoli*, which was ordered to a port of refuge by the SOSREP, there was unfortunately no general average declared, presumably because of the very many items of cargo carried on board for various individuals, and the nature of the casualty.

In ordinary circumstances, the master's authority in cases of necessity, in which he has to act for the interests of all parties, and where there is no superior power involved, has not been doubted for an act of general average to arise, and it was confirmed by the House of Lords in *Morrison v Greystoke Castle (The Cheldale)*:[15]

> The shipowner through the master has imposed upon him other and super-added duties causing him to act as agent for all the persons whose interests are endangered.

He is the person, according to the test stated earlier, to apply his reasoning and discretionary powers to a particular problem of danger, and he has the authority to take reasonable steps in the circumstances, provided his steps are for the interests of all parties involved in the adventure.[16]

As to whether strangers can act, the view according to the principle of agency of necessity is that the master, who is generally authorised to act on behalf of the ship owner and cargo interests, should be consulted.[17]

2 CONDITIONS GIVING RISE TO GENERAL AVERAGE

The subject matter of general average includes all the interests of the common adventure which are at risk. Such interests are physical, namely the ship, the cargo, the bunkers, stores, personal effects; but there are also those interests which are dependent on the safety of the physical property, such as the freight, time charter hire (which are earned upon the safe carriage of the cargo), and any other property involved which is at risk during a maritime common adventure. The definition of general average, given above, identified four elements to be satisfied in order for a general average act to occur. These elements are examined in more detail below, including how the YAR treat the incidents of general average.

---

15 [1947] AC 265, p 281, per Lord Roche.

16 See further *Papayianni v Grampian Ltd* (1896) 1 Com Cas 448; *Price v Noble* (1811) 4 Taunt 123; Rose, op cit, fn 1, discusses other possibilities of intervention at 31–35.

17 Goff & Jones, *The Law of Restitution*, 6th ed, 2002; *The Winson* [1982] AC 939.

2.1 Danger or peril to the common adventure

Danger or peril

Under s 66(2) of the Marine Insurance Act 1906, no recovery can be made in general average unless there exists a peril. The danger or peril must affect the whole adventure and not only one interest.[18] English law has given a strict interpretation to this phrase in requiring such peril to be real and not imaginary.[19] Even a belief reasonably held will be insufficient for recovery.

The wording of Rule A of the York-Antwerp Rules does not include the phrase 'in time of peril'. It refers instead to 'preserving from peril'. It is doubtful whether, in practice, there is any difference between the two phrases; the latter expresses the purpose of a general average act, while the former indicates the trigger of a general average act.

There are difficulties of degree when it comes to deciding whether property is in peril. What should be the extent of the peril, which threatens the common property, before the response to it can qualify as a general average act? Although it is a requirement under English law that the peril must be real,[20] it need not be immediate, in the sense of actually pressing at the moment, but it may be imminent. Indeed, English law allows for the recovery in general average of taking precautionary measures that avert an imminent peril.[21] However, it is also clear that such peril must be substantial and not negligible.[22]

It is worth referring to the facts of the *Vlassopoulos* case (see also under 1.1 above) as it shows the degree of danger required for an act to qualify as a general average act.

A ship was in the port of Bordeaux for the purpose of loading a cargo. While she was so engaged, the foremast broke and fell on to the main deck doing damage, and in consequence of the breakage a derrick, which was attached to the foremast, fell into a hold and was damaged. The casualty was an accidental and fortuitous occurrence, and the ship was not in consequence, thereof, at any time in any danger. The ship was then moved into a wet dock for the purpose of repairs. After being repaired, the ship proceeded on her voyage to her destination. While at sea she fouled some submerged wreckage and damaged the blades of her propeller, and was thereby rendered unfit to encounter the ordinary perils of the sea, and accordingly she put into Cherbourg for inspection and repairs, this being necessary for the common safety of the ship, cargo and freight. Both the charterparty and the policy of insurance in respect of the ship provided that average was to be adjusted according to the York-Antwerp Rules 1924. A dispute arose between the shipowner and the underwriters with regard to liability for certain expenses incurred, and payments made by the owner in the ports of Bordeaux and Cherbourg in connection

---

18 *Nesbitt v Lushington* (1792) 4 TR 783, where a mob took the corn loaded on board by threats to the master of the ship.

19 *Joseph Watson v Fireman's Fund* [1922] 2 KB 355.

20 *Vlassopoulos v British and Foreign Marine Insurance Co (The Makis)* [1929] 1 KB 187, p 199.

21 *Lawrence v Minturn* (1854) 17 How 100; *Société Nouvelle d'Armement v Spillers & Bakers Ltd* [1917] 1 KB 865.

22 *The Makis*, op cit, fn 20.

with the two casualties, namely wages and provisions of master, officers and crew during the time the ship was being repaired; coal consumed in shifting the ship in and out of dock; handling cargo on board; discharging cargo; towage in and out of port, mooring expenses and port charges. The dispute was referred to arbitration, and the arbitrator held that none of these expenses was the subject of general average contribution, but stated a case for the opinion of the High Court. It was held that:

(1) none of the above mentioned items of expenses incurred at the port of Bordeaux in connection with the first casualty came within Rules X, XI or XX of the York-Antwerp Rules, 1924, and therefore they were not recoverable in general average, because they were not incurred for the common safety for the purpose of preserving from peril the property involved in a common maritime adventure, and Rule X did not apply to a case of the repair of accidental damage and the shifting of cargo thereby caused where the ship was in no danger; (2) but that the above mentioned items of expenses incurred at the port of Cherbourg in connection with the second casualty were recoverable in general average under Rules X and XI, because they were expenses incurred for the common safety for the purpose of preserving from peril the property involved in the common maritime adventure.

Threat

Another question that troubles the interpreters of the Rules is whether or not a general average act should be a response to a physical threat to the property, or could a commercial threat to the completion of the voyage qualify for the act to be a general average act? It is suggested that the Rules embody both threats, physical and commercial, and the costs of releasing the common property from the solely commercial threat should form the proper subject of a general average contribution.[23]

The distinguishing feature of general average is that the danger must be threatening to the common adventure; there must be at least two interests[24] exposed to danger, regardless of whether or not such interests belong to the same owner. The danger to the common adventure will end when the property is brought to a safe place. Ideally, that place should be the place where the delivery of the cargo was stipulated by the contract of carriage. But sometimes the cargo may have to be taken off prior to reaching that place, and the ship may have to be taken to a safe place. Once the cargo is taken off, it should not, in principle, be obliged to contribute to general average, or be entitled to general average contribution, unless its removal formed part of complex salvage operations,[25] but this goes beyond the scope of this chapter.

---

23 Macdonald, J, op cit, fn 4, at 483–487; this is indicated by the scope of Rules X, XI and XIV, relating to ports of refuge expenses and temporary repairs to the ship for the purpose of enabling it to continue the adventure.

24 If there is only one interest in danger, this is known as 'particular average loss' which is not a general average loss (s 64(1), MIA 1906); expenses incurred by the assured to preserve the subject matter insured, other than general average and salvage charges, are called particular charges (s 64(2), MIA 1906).

25 See some old authorities in Rose, op cit, fn 1, at 25.

Common maritime adventure

The 1994 and 2004 YAR define, in Rule B, 'common maritime adventure' as including circumstances when one or more vessels are towing or pushing another vessel or vessels, provided that they are all involved in commercial activities and not in salvage operation. It further provides that a vessel is not in common peril with another vessel or vessels if, by simply disconnecting from the other vessel or vessels, she is in safety; but, if the disconnection is itself a general average act, the common adventure continues.

Throughout the successive editions of the Rules, 'adventure' has been used in a way which naturally describes the common enterprise represented by the carriage of goods by sea in which ship and cargo are both involved, while 'voyage' has been used to refer to the passage of the vessel from her first loading port to her final discharging port.[26]

2.2 Extraordinary expenditure or sacrifice

The ship-owner's obligation to perform the voyage under the contract of affreightment is to deliver the cargo safely to the port of destination upon payment of the agreed freight. He must have complied with his obligation to provide a seaworthy ship at the commencement of the voyage.[27] Contribution for general average, when incurred for the common safety, does not absolve the parties from their contractual rights and obligations. Only when the sacrifice or expenditure is beyond the contractual duties will it be allowed in general average.[28]

The term 'extraordinary' is of more relevance when looking at general average expenditures. This is because a charterer or the holder of a bill of lading will have already paid freight in return for the shipowner bearing the costs and expenses that are incidental to the voyage and which safeguards both the ship and the cargo.

The classic examples of an extraordinary sacrifice that will be allowed in general average is the jettisoning of part of the cargo (Rule I); or causing damage to the ship or cargo for the purpose of making a jettison (Rule II); or pouring water into the holds to extinguish a fire on board a ship and thereby damaging the cargo carried in such holds, including damage by beaching or scuttling a burning ship (Rule III); or voluntary stranding (Rule V); or damage done to machinery or boilers when the ship is aground (Rule VII); or ship's materials and stores burnt for fuel for the common safety (Rule IX).

The above are subject always to the operation of the York-Antwerp Rules. For example, Rule I of YAR states that: 'No jettison of cargo shall be made good as general average, unless such cargo is carried in accordance with the recognised custom of the trade'. Similarly, damage to the ship's machinery or boilers shall only

---

26 See *The Trade Green*, op cit, fn 7.

27 For a recent example of no general average contribution to the ship owner, because of his actionable fault in failing to provide a seaworthy ship as required by the contract, see *Sunlight Mercantile Ltd v Ever Lucky Shipping Co Ltd* [2004] 2 Lloyd's Rep 174.

28 *The Bijela* [1993] 1 Lloyd's Rep 411.

be allowed as general average where such damage is occasioned in attempting to refloat her (Rule VII).

Generally, expenditure that will be allowed as general average will come under one of the following examples:

- Additional expenses which would not normally be allowed as general average, but which replace expenses that would normally be classed as general average (Rule F)

- Expenses incurred in saving the ship and cargo from loss or damage. Classic examples include: the engagement of salvage services following a stranding; the cost of employing lighters to transfer cargo in order to lighten the vessel; and the employment of towage services (Rule X)

- Expenses incurred in lightening the ship when ashore (Rule VIII)

- Expenses for wages etc in port of refuge (Rule XI)

- Expenses for temporary repairs either at the port of loading or a port of refuge (Rule XIV)

- Port of refuge expenses.[29]

2.3 Voluntary, or intentionally and reasonably made

The rule paramount which is found in YAR 1994 and 2004 (but not in the 1974 Rules) provides that: 'In no case shall there be any allowance for sacrifice or expenditure unless reasonably made or incurred'.

The word 'voluntary', in s 66 of the Marine Insurance Act 1906, has been replaced with the term 'intentionally' in Rule A of the York-Antwerp Rules.[30] This emphasises the fact that, just because a decision was made under extreme pressure, when there was no effective alternative, this will not of itself be enough for the act to lose its voluntary nature.

The requirement of intention means that the general average act must be made or incurred with the sole objective of preserving the interests involved from peril.[31]

The requirement of reasonableness is a fetter on the master's discretion as to what action to take in times of peril. However, this fetter is not wide-ranging and would only bite when the master makes a decision that fails to benefit the common adventure as a whole. He has complete freedom to choose which action to take in order to benefit the common adventure. For example, the master will be able to enter into a contract for towage or salvage services on standard terms which are widely used in practice.[32] Such action will be reasonable. Even if the master enters into a contract for the provision of services on particularly onerous terms, such

---

29 Many expenses that are incidental to port of refuge expenses are expressly provided for in Rules X and XI of the York-Antwerp Rules.

30 This appears in all three recent York-Antwerp Rules revisions: 1974, 1994 and 2004.

31 *Athel Line Ltd v Liverpool & London War Risks Ins Assn Ltd* [1994] KB 87, p 94.

32 See further commentary on standard form towage contracts (at Chapter 14, above) and salvage contracts (at Chapter 13, above).

losses flowing from this action will be recoverable in general average, provided there was no reasonable alternative open to the master.[33]

The fetter on the master's discretion is examined in the context of having to make his choices in time of danger for the ship and property on board for the purpose of preserving the common adventure.

It should be noted that Rule D provides that rights of contribution in general average shall not be affected if the event giving rise to the sacrifice or expenditure is due to the fault of one of the parties to the adventure, but this shall not prejudice any remedies or defences which may be open against or to that party in respect of such fault.[34]

But the question of actionable fault will depend on the terms of the contract and, if the Hague Rules or Hague-Visby Rules are incorporated, negligence in navigation or management of the ship is an excepted peril (Art IV, r (2)(a)).

However, if in the course of taking action for the purposes of general average, there is negligence in carrying out the operation, which causes damage to the property on board, it may be actionable in a claim for breach of contract.[35] In addition, such negligence may break the chain of causation between the general average act and the loss, and the expenditure may not be recoverable in general average.

For example, whether the master was negligent, in *The Alpha* case,[36] in putting the ship aground in the first place and in dealing with the resultant situation, whereupon he caused damage to the engine of the ship, was irrelevant. He was criticised, however, for acting unreasonably in many respects, when he was trying to refloat the vessel after grounding. The defendants, cargo owners, who were sued by the owners of the ship for general average contribution, argued that either what the master did could not be general average, or that the element of unreasonableness broke the chain of causation between the general average act and the damage. The court held that, on the evidence, the risk of damaging the engine had been appreciated by the master and the damage arose from an actual intention of the master to try to refloat the vessel at risk of such damage. Therefore, the owners recovered general average contribution for the damage to the engine.

The requirement of reasonableness appears in Rule A of YAR. However, if a general average act falls within one of the numbered rules that does not impose a requirement for reasonableness, it follows that such losses that are incurred will be recoverable in general average, even if such action that is taken is unreasonable.[37] Such possible conflict has been remedied by the introduction of the rule paramount,

---

33 *Australian Coastal Shipping Commission v Green* [1971] 1 QB 456, p 483, per Lord Denning MR.

34 *Goulandris Brothers v B Goldman & Sons* [1957] 2 Lloyd's Rep 207: the objects of Rule D were to keep all questions of alleged fault outside the adjustment and to preserve, unimpaired, the legal remedy at the stage of enforcement.

35 See also *The Oak Hill* [1975] 1 Lloyd's Rep 105: breach of contract was proved in handling the cargo carelessly during discharge and storage after the vessel's accident. See also *The Hector* [1955] 2 Lloyd's Rep 218: the fact that the master acts as agent of necessity does not relieve him of his duty to exercise reasonable care in the preservation of the cargo; see also *Goulandris Brothers*, op cit, fn 34.

36 See *Corfu Navigation Co v Mobil Shipping Co Ltd (The Alpha)* [1991] 2 Lloyd's Rep 515.

37 Ibid. The rule of interpretation in the York-Antwerp Rules 1974 provides that, where the numbered and lettered rules conflict, it is the numbered rules that prevail.

in the York-Antwerp Rules 1994 and 2004 (mentioned above), which prevents recovery for sacrifice or expenditure unless reasonably made or incurred. (See further about the rule of construction of the Rules under para 1.1 above.)

2.4 To preserve property imperilled

This requirement relates to the subject matter relating to general average recovery. Traditionally, general average concerns the preservation of property involved in the 'common adventure', ie the ship,[38] bunkers, her cargo and freight (see para 2, above).

In order to be liable to contribute in general average, the freight has to be at the carrier's risk. Therefore, once freight has been earned, it does not contribute as an interest since it is no longer at risk to the carrier. However, the cargo for which the freight has been earned will still be liable to contribute.

3 CAUSATION IN GENERAL AVERAGE AND FAULT

Rule C of the YAR states that only such losses, damages or expenses which are the direct consequence of the general average act shall be allowed as general average; and Rule E provides that the onus of proof is upon the party claiming in general average to show that the loss or expense claimed is properly allowable as general average. Section 66(1) of the Marine Insurance Act 1906 allows recovery in general average for losses 'caused by or directly consequential to' a general average act.

Thus, the claimant has to prove that his loss was a direct consequence of a general average act to recover contribution. The defendant has the burden of showing a break in the chain of causation.[39] The right of contribution in general average shall not be affected if the event giving rise to the sacrifice or expenditure is due to the fault of one of the parties to the adventure, but this shall not prejudice any remedies or defences which may be open against or to that party in respect of such fault (Rule D and *Goulandris v Goldman* under para 2.3 above).

In addition to the obvious sacrifices and expenditures incurred in general average, other losses resulting from general average acts may qualify for recovery in general average. Whether they can or not is dependent upon whether such losses are a direct result of the general average act. Should the loss have been foreseen, or would it be enough if the loss was foreseeable to the general average act?

In *Australian Coastal Shipping v Green*,[40] there were two vessels in peril. The ship owner contracted for two tugs to tow both vessels to safety, contracting on UKSTC terms. In both cases, the towing line broke, rendering one tug a total loss, with the other tug claiming salvage expenses. Under the UKSTC, the ship owner

---

38 The equipment on board the ship also qualifies as 'property' in general average.
39 Eg *The Alpha*, op cit, fn 36.
40 [1971] 1 QB 456.

was liable to indemnify the towage company for all losses and expenses suffered. The shipowner contended that these losses were recoverable by him in general average. Lord Denning MR in the Court of Appeal held that they were, stating:

> If the master, when he does 'the general average act', ought reasonably to have foreseen that a subsequent accident of the kind might occur – or even that there was a distinct possibility of it – then the subsequent accident does not break the chain of causation . . . If, however, there is a subsequent incident which was only a remote possibility, it would be different.[41]

As discussed under para 2.3 above, an intervening negligence during the general average act may or may not break the chain of causation between the act and the loss.

Rule C of the 1974 and 1994 YAR specifically excludes losses caused by delay or loss of market. In addition to these excluded losses, the 2004 YAR also excludes loss and expenses incurred with respect to damage to the environment or connected with the escape or release of pollutant substances from the property involved.

4 WHEN THERE WILL BE NO LIABILITY TO CONTRIBUTE

As noted earlier, the rights and liabilities of the parties in general average are dealt with independently of fault of the parties to the adventure, even if that fault brought about the event which gave rise to the expenditure or sacrifice. But this shall not prejudice any remedies or defences which may be open against or to the claiming party in respect of such fault (Rule D).

In Rule I, it is stated that no jettison of cargo shall be allowed as general average, unless such cargo is carried with the recognised custom of the trade. Thus, if deck cargo is carried with the consent of the parties in accordance with the custom of the trade, general average contribution will be allowed.

In *Strang Steel v Scott*,[42] the Privy Council expounded the exceptions to general average contribution:

> There are two well-established exceptions to the rule of contribution for general average, which it is necessary to notice.

> When a person who would otherwise have been entitled to claim contribution has, by his own fault, occasioned the peril which mediately gave rise to the claim, it would be manifestly unjust to permit him to recover from those whose goods are saved, although they may be said, in a certain sense, to have benefited by the sacrifice of his property. In any question with them he is a wrongdoer, and, as such, under an obligation to use every means within his power to ward off or repair the natural consequences of his wrongful act. He cannot be permitted to claim either recompense for services rendered, or indemnity for losses sustained by him, in the endeavour to rescue property which was imperilled by his own tortious act, and which it was his duty to save. *Schloss v Heriot* is the leading English authority upon the point. In that case, which was an action by the shipowner against the owners of cargo for contribution in an average loss, a plea stated in defence, to the effect that

---

41 Ibid, 482.
42 (1889) 14 App Cas 601, pp 608, 609.

the ship was unseaworthy at the commencement of the voyage, and that the average loss was occasioned by such unseaworthiness, was held to be a good answer to the claim by Chief Justice Erle, and Willes and Keating, JJ.

The second exception is in the case of deck cargo. The reason why relief by general contribution is denied to the owners of goods stowed on deck, when these are thrown overboard in order to save the cargo under hatches, is obvious. According to the rules of maritime law, the placing of goods upon the deck of a seagoing ship is improper stowage, because they are hindrances to the safe navigation of the vessel; and their jettison is therefore regarded, in a question with the other shippers of cargo, as a justifiable riddance of incumbrances which ought never to have been there, and not as a sacrifice for the common safety. But the owner of deck goods jettisoned, though not entitled to general contribution, may nevertheless have a good claim for indemnity against the master and owners who received his goods for carriage upon deck; and the exception does not apply, either (1) in those cases where, according to the established custom of navigation, such cargoes are permitted, or (2) in any case where the other owners of cargo have consented that the goods jettisoned should be carried on the deck of the ship.

If the ship deviated from the voyage route without the consent of the contracting party, or without waiver of the breach, and the deviation caused the general average act, there will be no general average contribution to the owner.[43]

As was stated earlier in *Strang v Scott*, a fault of the claimant which gave cause to the danger (and would give the party from whom contribution is sought a cause of action against the claimant) will disentitle the claimant from recovering contribution, on the basis of the principle that the claimant should not recover for the consequences of his own wrong,[44] for example when the ship was unfit for the voyage at the outset.[45]

A few examples illustrate how the ship owner can be deprived of general average contribution.

In *The Evje No 2*,[46] the ship was found unseaworthy at the beginning of the voyage because there were insufficient bunkers or because the bunkers were of the wrong quality and the unseaworthiness was the cause of the casualty, when the fuel ran out and the ship needed towage. No general average contribution was due to the owners from the charterers.

In *The Kasmar Voyager*,[47] the ship was carrying a cargo of soya beans under a contract of carriage evidenced by a bill of lading, which was subject to the Hague Rules. Engine problems arose during the voyage, and the vessel was immobilised, needing towage services to reach a repair port. Investigations revealed that there was a defect in manufacture of the piston skirt which developed into a crack in the life of the piston. The major damage to the engine had been caused after a spare

---

43 *Hain SS Co Ltd v Tate & Lyle Ltd* (1936) 41 Com Cas 350.

44 The rule against recovery is known as 'equitable defence': *Goulandris Brothers Ltd v B Goldman & Sons Ltd* [1958] 1 QB 74.

45 *Schloss v Heriot* (1863) 14 CB (NS) 59 (improper stowage).

46 [1976] 2 Lloyd's Rep 714; see also *The Aga* [1968] 1 Lloyd's Rep 431: ship had stability problem before she left port, resulting in heavy listing, which necessitated beaching her.

47 [2002] 2 Lloyd's Rep 57.

piston had been fitted whose dimensions were not compatible with the main engine. Upon a claim by the owners against the cargo insurers for general average contribution, the claim was resisted on the ground of the owners' failure to exercise due diligence to make the ship seaworthy before and at the beginning of the voyage. On evidence, it was found that the service of the cylinder had been postponed, and the routine maintenance prescribed had not been followed. The vessel was unseaworthy and the owners could not discharge the burden of proof that they, or their agents, exercised due diligence before and at the beginning of the voyage.[48] Thus, the general average expenditure was caused by their actionable fault and they were unable to recover general average contribution from the cargo interests.

By contrast, in *The Torepo*,[49] where the ship grounded due to various navigational faults and sought the assistance of salvage, the ship was not found unseaworthy, even with the finding of discrepancy in the charts (being not causative of the grounding). The owners were protected by the exception in Art IV, r 2(a) of the HVR (negligence in navigation). Therefore, upon a claim by cargo interests against the owners to recover the amount they were obliged to pay to salvors and for the return of their general average security, their claim failed.

As discussed in causation earlier, the defendant must show a causal link between the fault and the event giving rise to the general average act and to the loss, as is shown in *The Evje* and *The Kasmar Voyager*, unless the claimant of general average contribution proves that his liability for the fault is excluded.[50]

Similarly, when the shipper ships goods that he knows to be dangerous, which results in the jettison of the cargo for the safety of the common adventure, he will not recover general average contribution.[51] Rule XIX also provides that 'undeclared or wrongfully declared cargo' loaded without the knowledge of the ship owner or his agents, or goods wilfully mis-described at the time of shipment, shall not be allowed as general average, if damage or loss is caused to them, but such goods shall remain liable to contribute, if saved.

5 THE CAUSE OF ACTION FOR GENERAL AVERAGE CONTRIBUTION AND TIME LIMIT

The cause of action for contributions in general average under contractual provisions, which did no more than require general average to be adjusted according to

---

48 *The Muncaster Castle* [1961] 1 Lloyd's Rep 57 was applied.

49 [2002] 2 Lloyd's Rep 535; see also *The Isla Fernandina* [2000] 2 Lloyd's Rep 15; *The Lendoudis Evangelos* II [2001] 2 Lloyd's Rep 304.

50 *Milburn & Co v Jamaica Fruit Co* [1900] 2 QB 540 (CA), approved by the House of Lords in *Louis Dreyfus & Co v Tempus SS Co* [1931] AC 726.

51 *Greenshields, Cowie & Co v Stephens & Sons* [1908] AC 431: in this case, the owners of the coal were entitled to claim against the ship contribution in general average in respect of the sacrifices voluntarily made for the common advantage of all, the fire having been caused by the inherent qualities of the coal, or, in other words, by spontaneous combustion, without default on the part of the shippers.

York-Antwerp Rules, accrues at the time when each general average sacrifice is made or general average expense is incurred.[52]

It was stated by the Privy Council in *The Potoi Chau* that:

The general average clause incorporated in a bill of lading creates a contractual liability on the part of the consignee as indorsee of the bill of lading to pay general average contribution, if there be any chargeable on the cargo shipped, whether it was he, the shipper or some intermediate indorsee of the bill of lading, who happened to be owner of the goods, at the time when a general average sacrifice took place, or a liability for a general average expenditure was incurred. Since this liability arises under a simple contract, the period of limitation is six years from the accrual of the cause of action; but the clause is intended to regulate, and to transfer to whoever acquires title to the consignment of cargo under the bill of lading, what would otherwise be a common law liability of the owner of the cargo at the time of the general average act.[53]

6 SECURITY

At the time of the 'Digest of Justinian', the obligation was upon the master of the vessel to have a general average, arising on the voyage, adjusted. In modern times, this responsibility has devolved upon the ship owner. In order to protect the rights of general average creditors, he is obliged[54] to obtain reasonable security from contributing interests. The law assists him in this by allowing him to exercise his right of the common law possessory lien on the property until such security is given. The general average act gives rise to a possessory, not maritime, lien on the property. The owner, therefore, through the master, may withhold delivery of property at the destination until reasonable security has been provided.

Such reasonable security is usually construed as consisting of the following:

(i) an average bond signed by the consignee, *and*

(ii) *either* an average guarantee signed by the insurer of the cargo, *or*,

(iii) if the cargo is uninsured or the particular cargo insurer is not acceptable to the ship owner, a general average deposit[55] – of an amount which is usually recommended by the average adjuster, which amount will be held by the average adjuster, pending the completion of his adjustment.

Where, during the course of the contracted voyage, cargo is forwarded by some other vessel or conveyance, the ship owner will usually require that a non-separation agreement forms part of the average bond and the average guarantee. If the contract of carriage provides that general average is to be adjusted according to the York Antwerp Rules 1994 or 2004, a non-separation agreement wording will automatically apply. A non-separation agreement provides that, although cargo has

---

52 *The Potoi Chau* [1983] 2 Lloyd's Rep 376 (PC); *Chandris v Argo Insurance Co Ltd* [1963] 2 Lloyd's Rep 65 approved.

53 *The Potoi Chau*, p 379.

54 *Crooks v Allan* (1879) 5 QBD 38.

55 Such cash deposits are provided for by YAR, Rule XXII.

been separated, by forwarding, from the rest of the maritime adventure, its contribution to the general average will be calculated as though it had not, but had remained with the carrying vessel until its delivery. The agreement is between the ship owner and the cargo owner, and enables the ship owner to recover his general average expenses as if the cargo had remained on board.

The average bond, as backed by an insurer's guarantee or a cash deposit, is a new contract, being independent from the contract of affreightment, between the ship owner and the owner of the other interest. The consideration provided is the release of the possessory lien on the cargo by the ship owner and, as far as cargo interests are concerned, the consideration is the assumption of personal liability to pay when the adjustment is presented. Usually the parties agree the law and the jurisdiction to which the security will be subject for adjudication of any disputes that might arise between the parties under the terms of the security.

The contractual obligation assumed by the cargo interests under the security is to make payment of a liquidated sum at a future date, which will not arrive until the general average statement has been completed by an average adjuster appointed by the shipowners. That is the earliest date at which the shipowners' cause of action against the consignees under the average bond for payment of general average contribution arose.[56]

Rule XXIII of YAR 2004 provides that a claim for general average contribution, including any rights to claim under general average bonds and guarantees, shall be extinguished, unless an action is brought by the party claiming such contribution within a period of one year after the date upon which the general average adjustment was issued. In no case shall such an action be brought after six years from the date of termination of the common maritime adventure. The period may be extended upon the agreement of the parties after the termination of the common maritime adventure.

At the end of the day, it is the insurers (for hull or cargo) of the respective parties involved in the common adventure that pay for general average contributions which the parties can recover by way of indemnity under their respective insurance contracts. This falls within the scope of marine insurance, and so detailed consideration is outside the scope of this book.

---

56 *The Potoi Chau*, op cit, fn 52, pp 382–383.

CHAPTER 16

THE LAW OF HARBOURS AND PILOTAGE

INTRODUCTION

With the ever-increasing demands for safer ships, cleaner seas and prevention of environmental damage in coastal waters by marine casualties, the role of harbour authorities in ensuring that such demands are met is very important. It is equally important for them to maintain their ports in a safe condition and with adequate facilities, so that accidents to ships using them can be prevented. Manoeuvring in or out of a port can be quite difficult without the guidance of expert pilots, or harbour masters, who know local waters. There are various statutes and by-laws, which regulate the rights and obligations of harbours in making ports safe, preventing accidents and dealing with dangerous or unsafe ships, taking care of environmental safety and performing many other functions. Not only has the British Government charted a new course on port marine operations[1] – which includes accountability of port authorities, risk assessment and management, contingency plans and emergency response, management of navigation and pilotage – but parallel proposals towards a coherent policy on ports and maritime infrastructures have also been made by the European Commission.[2]

The Secretary of State is given powers of intervention by s 137 of the Merchant Shipping Act (MSA) 1995, as amended by s 2 of the Merchant Shipping and Maritime Security Act (MSMSA) 1997, when an accident has occurred to, or in, a ship and, in the opinion of the Secretary of State, oil from the ship will, or may, cause significant pollution on a large scale in the UK, the UK waters, or a part of the sea specified by virtue of s 129(2)(b) of the MSA 1995. For the purpose of preventing, or reducing, oil pollution, he, or his representative, may give directions as respects the ship, or its cargo, or the risk of oil pollution, to the owner of the ship, master, salvor and to the harbour master, or to the harbour authority. The Secretary of State, through his representative, the SOSREP,[3] is able to override the powers of harbour masters and harbour authorities where this is necessary in order to prevent, or minimise, pollution.

---

1 See 'A guide to good practice on port marine operations', 30 January 2001, which supports 'The Port Marine Safety Code', and 'Review of trust ports', following *The Future of Transport* White Paper; further, see The Government's Port Policy Review, May 2006, and MEHRA 2006: www.dft.gov.uk.

2 Proposal for a Directive 2004/0240 (COD)) on Market Access to Port Services; and Directive 2001/96/EC (OJ 2002 L13/09) to harmonise procedures for the safe loading and unloading of bulk carriers. This Directive has been implemented in the UK by the Merchant Shipping (Safe Loading and Unloading of Bulk Carriers) Regulations 2003 (SI 2003/2002); see Chapter 20, below; further progress at EU level is the EU Green Paper which is at the consultation stage by EU Member States.

3 The SOSREP is now always involved in maritime emergency situations in UK territorial waters, as proposed by Lord Donaldson in his report 'Intervention powers, command and control', March 1999, www.dft.gov.uk; see also Chapter 13, above.

The Merchant Shipping (Oil Pollution Preparedness, Response and Co-operation Convention) Regulations 1998 (implementing the OPPRC Convention 1990) require the harbour authorities to have approved oil pollution emergency plans.[4]

A port State, whose port a ship enters voluntarily, must ensure that international conventions, with regard to protecting the marine environment from ship-source pollution, are complied with. The Port State Control (PSC) has undergone many reviews, and is now part of an international regulatory regime.[5] It monitors observance of international standards and inspects ships entering its ports, reports to the flag State, if there are any deficiencies, and may impose penalties. In Europe, a unique system of Port State Control emerged from the Paris Memorandum of Understanding (MOU) 1982 under which 15 States originally agreed, on a co-operative basis, to inspect vessels entering their ports and check whether they complied with the requirements of international conventions. Its purpose is to ensure that sub-standard ships of whatever flag do not enter or leave ports with consequent risk to safety of life, the preservation of property and the protection of the environment. Its role is like a police force that provides an effective deterrent to those owners who might, otherwise, have considered too lightly the risks involved in allowing a 'rust bucket' to leave a port and endanger lives at sea.[6] It became necessary in the light of evidence that the flag States were failing to enforce compliance with international conventions rigorously enough.[7] The MOU has been adopted by States in other regions as well.

This chapter concentrates on duties, rights and liabilities of harbour authorities and pilots, as well as on the legal relations between pilots and ship's master, the question of who employs the pilot when on board the ship and liabilities to third parties. It is not within the confines of this book to examine all aspects of this topic, the treatment of which can be found in other works.[8] First, the law relating to harbours' duties and liabilities is examined (Section A) second, the law of pilotage (Section B), and, third, a brief account is given to the Wreck Removal Convention 2007 (WRC) which is recently adopted (Section C).

---

4   The Secretary of State, in exercise of the powers conferred by art 2 of Merchant Shipping (OPPRC) Order 1997 (SI 1997/2567), issued the 1998 Regulations (SI 1998/1056). This implemented the Oil Pollution Preparedness, Response and Co-operation Convention (OPPRC) 1990 (as amended by OPPRC Protocol 2000) and came into force on 14 June 2007. It is about salvage policy, contingency plans and reporting of casualties; see, further, Chapters 13 above and 19 below.

5   For its origin and the background to it, see Kasoulides, M, *Port State Control and Jurisdiction*, 1993, Kluwer. See, also, Chapters 8 and 20 of this book, where recent developments of the regulatory regime in its totality are discussed in context.

6   Sir Anthony Clarke 'Port state control or sub-standard ships: who is to blame? What is the cure?' [1994] LMCLQ 202.

7   See further developments in this respect, and initiatives taken by the European Commission, in Chapter 20, below.

8   Douglas, R, Lane, P, and Peto, M, *Douglas and Geen on the Law of Harbours, Coasts and Pilotage*, 5th edn, 1997, LLP.

SECTION A – ASPECTS OF LAW AFFECTING HARBOURS

1 SOURCES OF POWERS AND DEFINITIONS

1.1 Statutes and regulations regulating harbours' powers

Legislation about harbours and pilots is very important to harbour authorities, so that they can regulate their affairs and the activities of other persons using the harbours. There exist numerous statutes and local legislation, some of which have been repealed by subsequent legislation. Reference is made to statutory provisions, which have caused problems in their interpretation. The following statutes are the basic applicable statutes at present:

(a) The Harbours, Docks and Piers Clauses Act (HDPCA) 1847 (10 Vict c 27), which is 'the mother statute' containing a comprehensive code of operational powers of the authorities governed by statute, and sections of it are usually incorporated in special legislation of harbour authorities;

(b) The Harbours Act (HA) 1964 was passed after recommendations of the Rochdale Report and was the first Act concerned with the central organisation of harbours. It included provisions for subordinate legislation;

(c) The Docks and Harbours Act 1966, which conferred some new powers on the harbour authorities, including power to carry out harbour operations;

(d) The Local Government Act 1972, s 237, replaces s 83 of the HDPCA 1847, relating to by-laws;

(e) The Medway Ports Authority Act 1973 (relates to raising wrecks);

(f) The Health and Safety at Work Act 1974;

(g) The Transport Act 1981;

(h) The Dangerous Vessels Act (DVA) 1985;

(i) The Pilotage Act (PA)1987, as amended in 2003;

(j) The Environmental Protection Act 1990;

(k) The Aviation and Maritime Security Act 1990;

(l) The Water Resources Act (WRA) 1991;

(m) The Ports Act 1991 provides for the privatisation of port trusts;

(n) The Transport Works Act 1992, basically amends some parts of the HA 1964;

(o) The Environment Act 1995;

(p) The MSA 1995 consolidated all the previous MSAs and some provisions of the HA 1964; it is relevant in this context with respect to wrecks, lighthouses, pollution and relevant powers of port authorities;

(q) The MSMSA 1997 contains important provisions in relation to environmental protection and emergency situations in UK territorial waters. It includes powers of the Secretary of State to make regulations. A representative of the Secretary of State (SOSREP) is appointed to perform the functions of the Secretary of State under the MSA 1995 (s 293) in relation to marine pollution;

(r) The Maritime Safety Act 2003, providing for powers of intervention and directions to the SOSREP;

(s) The Planning and Compulsory Purchase Act 2004.

(t) The Terrorism Act 2006.

The following regulations are also relevant:

- The Dangerous Substances in Harbour Areas Regulations (DSHA Reg) 1987;
- The MS (Dangerous Goods and Marine Pollutants) Regulations 1990;
- The Management of Health and Safety at Work Regulations 1992;
- The MS (Reporting Requirements for Ships Carrying Dangerous or Polluting Goods) Regulations 1995;
- The MS (Port State Control) Regulations 1995;
- The MS (Prevention of Pollution) Regulations 1996;
- MS (Dangerous Goods and Marine Pollutants) Regulations 1997;
- The MS (Port Waste Reception Facilities) Regulations 1997;
- The Fire Precautions (Workplace) Regulations 1997;
- The MS (Prevention of Pollution by Garbage) Regulations 1998;
- The MS (Oil Pollution Preparedness, Response and Co-operation) Regulations 1998;
- The Control of Major Accident Hazards (COMAH) Regulations 1999;
- The MS (Carriage of Cargoes) Regulations 1999;
- The Pilotage (Recognition of Qualifications and Experience) Regulations 2003, amending the Pilotage Act 1987;
- The Control of Major Accident Hazards (Amendment) Regulations 2005, amending COMAH 1999; they implement Council Directive 96/82/EC, known as the Seveso II Directive, as amended by Directive 2003/105/EC.

Harbour authorities have a duty to make proper use of powers to make bylaws, and to give directions (including pilotage directions) to regulate all movements in their waters. The powers should be exercised in support of policies and procedures developed in the authority's safety management system. They should have clear policies on the enforcement of directions and should monitor compliance.[9]

1.2 Definitions

A 'harbour' is defined by s 313 of the MSA 1995 for the purposes of this Act as including 'estuaries, navigable rivers, piers, jetties, and other works in, or at which, ships can obtain shelter, or ship and unship goods or passengers'.

In relation to pollution matters, the Act, in Chapter II, Pt VI, defines harbour in the UK as meaning 'a port, estuary, haven, dock or other place the waters of which are within the UK national waters and, in respect of entry into or the use of which by ships, a person or body is empowered by an enactment (including a local enactment) to make any charges other than charges in respect of navigational aids or pilotage'.

---

9   DETR, *Guide to Good Practice on Port Marine Operations*, 20 January 2001, Section 8, 'Management of navigation'.

The definition of harbour by s 57(1) of the HA 1964 for the purpose of this Act is wider, including, 'any harbour, whether natural or artificial, and any port, haven, estuary, tidal or other river or inland waterway navigated by sea-going ships, and includes a dock, wharf, and in Scotland a ferry or boat slip being a marine work ... Dock is a dock used by sea-going ships and wharf is any wharf, quay, pier, jetty or other place at which sea-going ships can ship or unship goods or embark or disembark passengers'.

The PA 1987 and the Ports Act 1991 adopt this definition, so it is very relevant to the discussion in this chapter.

'Harbour operations' are defined by s 57(1) of the HA 1964 as:

(a) the marking or lighting of a harbour or any part thereof;

(b) the berthing or drydocking of a ship;

(c) the warehousing, sorting, weighing or handling of goods on harbour land or at a wharf;

(d) the movement of goods or passengers within the limits within which the person engaged in improving, maintaining or managing a harbour has jurisdiction, or on harbour land;

(e) in relation to a harbour (which expression for the purposes of this paragraph does not include a wharf);

(f) the towing, or moving of a ship which is in or is about to enter or has recently left the harbour;

(g) the loading or unloading of goods, or embarking or disembarking of passengers, in or from a ship which is in the harbour or the approaches thereto;

(h) the lighterage or handling of goods in the harbour; and

(i) in relation to a wharf, the towing or moving of a ship to or from the wharf, the loading or unloading of goods, or the embarking or disembarking of passengers at the wharf in or from a ship.

2 TYPES OF HARBOUR AUTHORITIES

Harbours may be classified by the type of functions they perform and by the nature of their organisation. Most major ports perform the following broad categories of functions:

(a) provision and maintenance of harbour facilities and pilotage services;

(b) carrying out harbour operations and taking precautions about navigational safety;

(c) regulating the movement and berthing of ships and preventing pollution.

The major ports in the UK are either Port Trusts,[10] created by statute for the management of a harbour without share capital, or statutory companies created by local Acts of Parliament. A number are managed by local authorities (municipal port authorities), while others are re-constituted under the name 'Associated British

---

10 The Government has proposed the 'Review of Trust Ports', *A New Deal for Transport, Better for Everyone*, 1999, White Paper, www.dft.gov.uk.

Ports' by virtue of the Transport Act (TA) 1981, and they are controlled by a company. The TA 1981 allowed the investment of private capital in the development of harbour facilities. Nationalised ports (that is, ports serving the British railway system, south and east coasts) are controlled by the Association of British Ports. Associated British Ports Holdings plc (which became a public company in 1983) is a holding company that owns and operates 21 ports throughout the United Kingdom. There are also ports registered as privately owned limited companies, which are subject to the Companies Act 1985.[11]

3 POWERS, DUTIES AND LIABILITIES OF HARBOUR AUTHORITIES

3.1 Powers of harbour authorities

A harbour authority, by s 51 of the HDPCA 1847, has the power to appoint a harbour master who has powers of direction to regulate the time and manner of ships' entry to, departure from and movement within the harbour waters (s 52 of the HDPCA 1847). The harbour master obtains his powers from by-laws. The authority's by-laws may include provisions for regulating the powers and duties of the harbour master. The harbour master is accountable to the authority for the safety of operations in the harbour.

Reference must be made to the local Acts and orders. Powers are derived either from special Acts of Parliament, the Harbour Acts, mentioned earlier, or from general Acts of Parliament relating to harbours and enabling them to make bylaws. The MSA 1995 contains several powers of the harbour authorities. If these powers are exceeded, the acts of the harbour authority will be *ultra vires*.[12] Similarly, if a company is registered by an Act of Parliament to operate public services (as, for example, for railway and market services), the company cannot abandon its objects without statutory sanction, even if the services are no longer required.[13]

The major Acts under which harbour authorities have received their powers are those referred to above, having amended or repealed previous Acts.

The DVA 1985, s 2, empowers harbour masters to give instructions to refuse entry, or to require the removal of dangerous vessels. However, it also enables the Secretary of State to countermand the directions of harbour masters, if he considers that this is necessary to secure the safety of any person or vessel.[14] A harbour master may detain a vessel if he has reason to believe that it has committed an offence by discharging oil, or a mixture containing oil, into the waters of a harbour (s 144 of the MSA 1995).

---

11 For more details, see op cit, Douglas and Geen, fn 8, Chapter 2.
12 *Dundee Harbour Trustees v Nicol* [1915] AC 550.
13 *Re Salisbury Rly & Market House* [1969] 1 Ch 349.
14 Donaldson (Lord), *Command and Control*, op cit, fn 3, DETR, Appendix 4, 'Specific intervention powers'.

In addition to the 1985 Act, harbour authorities have powers to regulate the activities of other persons at harbours and give directions to a casualty and to ships involved in salvage operations in order to ensure safety and prevention of pollution.[15] This is enhanced by the Maritime Safety Act 2003.

The Merchant Shipping (Prevention of Pollution) Regulations 1996, together with the provisions of the MSA 1995, give powers to harbour authorities to regulate the discharge of oil into the sea. Section 131 of the MSA 1995, as amended by s 7 of the MSMSA 1997, created a criminal offence if any oil or a mixture containing oil is discharged from a ship into UK national waters which are navigable by sea-going ships. Both the owner and the master of the ship shall be guilty of the offence. Section 144 of the MSA 1995 gives power to the harbour master to detain the ship. The general responsibility is in the hands of the Secretary of State. General powers of the Secretary of State derive from s 137 of the MSA 1995, as amended by the MSMSA 1997.[16]

Apart from statutes, additional powers of harbour authorities derive from EC Directives, which are implemented by regulations. Directive 93/75/EEC 'The Hazmat Directive', requiring reporting of ships carrying dangerous or polluting goods, was implemented by Merchant Shipping (Reporting Requirements for Ships Carrying Dangerous or Polluting Goods) Regulations 1995. Further developments are shown in Chapter 20, below. The Merchant Shipping (Port State Control) Regulations 1995 implemented Port State Control. The Directive 95/21/EC on Port State Control has been amended to include monitoring of traffic and inspections in ports, having as its main objective the banning of substandard ships (see Chapter 20).

3.2 Duties of harbour authorities in a risk management era

A harbour authority has duties of three kinds: some are statutory duties; but there are, in addition, general common law duties, and fiduciary duties.

These duties include an obligation to conserve, and facilitate the safe use of, the harbour; and a duty of care against loss caused by the authority's negligence.

Duties to ensure the safety of marine operations are matched with general and specific powers to enable the authority to discharge these duties.

3.2.1 The duty to assess and manage risks

Informal risk assessment has been practised for years, in one form or another, whether or not people realised that they were applying their mind to it. But, since 2001, there has been a requirement by the implementation of the Port Marine Safety Code to set in place systems for formal risk assessment and ensure that the safety management system is comprehensive and fully effective. This was the recommendation of the report made after the accident of *The Sea Empress* at Milford

---

15 See op cit, Douglas and Geen, fn 8, Chapter 6.
16 See, further, op cit, Douglas and Geen, fn 8, Chapter 9, 'Prevention of Oil Pollution'.

Haven, and it is in line with the International Safety Management Code which applies to ship operators and their ships, as seen in Chapter 8.

Harbour authorities typically have an express duty to take such action as the harbour authority consider necessary or desirable for or incidental to the maintenance, operation, improvement or conservancy of their harbour.

By the Port Marine Safety Code 2001, ports have the following duties:[17]

(1) Each harbour authority is accountable for managing operations within the port safely and efficiently and its board members should hold themselves responsible for ensuring that it does so.

(2) Each harbour authority should make a clear published commitment to the standard of marine safety required to comply with this Code.

(3) The Code represents the national standard against which the policies, procedures and performance of harbour authorities may be measured.

(4) Executive and operational responsibilities for marine safety must be clearly assigned, and those to whom they are entrusted must be held accountable for their performance.

(5) Harbour authorities must have a designated person to provide independent assurance about the operation of its marine safety management systems, who has direct access to the board.

The guide of good practice on port marine operations complements the Code for Port Marine Safety Operations, gives guidance for risk assessment in ports, and requires harbour authorities to publish policies, plans and periodic reports setting out how they comply with the standards set by the Code.

Such policies, plans and procedures should be based on a formal assessment of hazards or risks, and harbour authorities should have formal safety management systems (SMS). The aim of the SMS is to ensure that all risks are tolerable and as low as reasonably possible and the SMS depend upon competence standards applied to all parties involved.

Every harbour authority's statutory powers to regulate marine operations should be exercised in accordance with its SMS, which should include verification and audit procedures and deal with preparedness for emergencies.

Harbour authorities have a duty to take reasonable care, so long as the harbour is open for the public use, that all who may choose to navigate it may do so without danger to their lives or property. This includes an obligation to conserve, and facilitate the safe use of, the harbour; and a duty of care against loss or injury caused by the authority's negligence.

3.2.2 Duty to operate the port

Section 33 of the HDPCA 1847 provides for what is called the 'open port duty'. It is incorporated, or substantively contained, into local legislation of harbour authorities, and imposes the duty on harbour authorities to operate harbours, keep them

---

17 Department for Transport: www.dft.gov.uk.

open for anyone wishing to use them, and to offer facilities. In particular, it provides that:

> Upon payment of the rates made payable by this and the special Act (that is, the Act which incorporates s 33) and subject to the other provisions thereof, the harbour, dock and pier shall be open to all persons for the shipping and unshipping of goods and the embarking and landing of passengers.

A wide construction should be given to the interpretation of this section of the Act, said the House of Lords in the following case.

LNER v British Trawlers Federation Ltd [18]

The appellants in this case were owners of a railway, a harbour and dock. They operated a fish market on their dock quays. The respondents were fish merchants and owners of fish trawlers. The appellants sought to impose a restriction as to the manner in which or place to which the fish was to be utilised or removed, as a condition of admitting the respondents' vehicles to their harbours. The position of the markets was such that they could only be reached by the private roads and approaches which formed part of the appellants' estate. The question was how far the appellants, in exercise of their statutory powers, were entitled to impose restrictions upon the access to the fish market by those desiring to buy or remove fish. The appellants were seeking to exclude all vehicles which did not carry a licence granted by appellants. The respondents argued that the appellants were not entitled to impose any restriction and commenced an action to obtain an injunction and damages. Section 33 of the HDPCA 1847 was the issue for construction.

The House of Lords held in favour of the respondents. Lord Tomlin, referring to s 33, said:

> First, I think that upon the true construction of the Acts governing the statutory undertaking . . . the carrying on and control of the fish markets is either expressly or by necessary implication authorised as part of or incident to the harbour and docks undertaking . . . In fact, they (the harbour) have been authorised by statute to acquire lands for the extension of the markets and to exercise powers in relation to them beyond those which they could exercise as mere proprietors. The result, in my opinion, must be that as long as they do carry on the markets (and it is not necessary to determine whether they are bound to carry them on) there is necessarily implied a right of access on the part of those who bona fide desire to resort to the markets, subject only to such regulation as may be imposed by valid bylaws duly confirmed by the competent authority. [19]

For the purpose of s 33, the harbour authority must make facilities for the operation of tugs, which may be necessary for the loading, or unloading, of cargo.

In *JH Pigott & Son v Docks and Inland Waterways Executive*, [20] the defendants were the administrators of Immingham docks under delegation from the British Transport Commission. They were subject to statutory restrictions including that in s 33 of the HDPCA 1847. They also owned two tugs, which performed most of the

---

18   [1934] AC 279.
19   Ibid, pp 297, 298.
20   [1953] 1 QB 338.

towage services required at the docks. The question was whether the defendants, as the body responsible for the dock undertaking, were entitled to exclude competing tugs of the plaintiffs and others and reserve towage services to their own tugs, or such as they wished to hire to assist the services.

It was held that the defendants were not entitled to exclude other tugs. Following the decision in *LNER v British Trawlers*, Sellers J held that s 33 was not to be narrowly constructed. He stated, thus:

> In interpreting the section, I would hold that any of the persons providing any of the facilities which I have mentioned and the persons engaged in such activities are persons to whom a dock must be open if it is to be open for the shipping and unshipping of goods. I can see no real distinction between the contractor who, by his vehicles, brings in the goods for shipment or removes them after discharge, the tugowner who, by his tugs, brings in and takes out vessels engaged in the shipping and unshipping of goods, and the shipowner who brings his ship to the port aided or unaided by tugs. They are all performing services without which goods cannot be shipped or unshipped by vessels using the port; and the section makes no discrimination between persons. Provided they resort to the docks for the shipping and unshipping of goods, they are on an equality, and the shipowner does not appear to have any greater or better right than a stevedore or a haulage contractor, or, I could add, a tugowner, though the rights of all are subject to the payment of the appropriate dues which the dock authority may prescribe and subject to any regulation and control which the authority may have power, expressly or impliedly, to exercise.[21]

With regard to special rights given to users by a contract, Donaldson J (as he then was) said, in **Thoresen Car Ferries Ltd v Weymouth and Portland BC,**[22] that, under s 33, a harbour authority is obliged to keep their harbour open to any person. Subject to rights of others to use it, it was possible to grant regular use to some persons by contract, such as the right to use a specific berth, to an operator who needs access regularly. A provision can be included in the local legislation by which a harbour may set aside or appropriate part of the port or equipment for the exclusive or preferential use for a certain trade or by certain people. No other person may use the facilities of the appropriated part without the consent of the harbour master.[23] Any appropriation must be narrowly construed to derogate as little as possible from the freedom enshrined in s 33. If there is a berth available, then s 33 dictates that the authority must allow a lawful user to use it.[24]

Whether a port authority has power to restrain lawful trade in order to prevent unlawful protest came for judicial review in **R v Coventry CC ex p Phoenix Aviation and Others.**[25]

It concerned the issue whether public authorities – operating air and sea ports – were entitled to ban the flights or shipment of livestock by animal exporters; if so, whether they could properly refuse to handle that trade in response to the demands of unlawful protesters for animal rights. Two applications were made by livestock

---

21   Ibid, p 348.
22   [1977] 2 Lloyd's Rep 614.
23   Dover Harbour Revision Order 1969.
24   *R v Coventry CC ex p Phoenix Aviation and Others* [1995] 3 All ER 37, p 54.
25   Ibid.

exporters, who relied on statutory provisions relating to availability of facilities for lawful trade on equal terms to all without discrimination: Article 78(3) of the Air Navigation Order 1989 and s 33 of the HDPCA 1847, respectively. The third application was by the local authority for judicial review of the decision of a statutory body not to ban the export of livestock. It relied on the ground that the local authority had discretion, under s 40 of the HA 1964, to refuse the use of dock services to those engaged in a particular trade for the reason that a substantial police force was needed to control animal protesters. The first two applications were granted and the third was refused on the following grounds:

(a) the public authority had no general discretion under their respective statutory powers to distinguish between different lawful trades;

(b) the rule of law did not allow public authorities to respond to unlawful protest and threats from pressure groups by surrendering to their dictates, but required them, in co-operation with the police, to safeguard the right of others to go about their lawful business without disruption.

3.2.3 Statutory duty to provide navigational safety and safety procedures

3.2.3.1 Good practice on port marine operations and other statutory provisions

Each harbour authority is accountable for managing operations within the port safely and efficiently and its board members should hold themselves responsible for ensuring that it does so. The guide of good practice on port marine operations (mentioned under para 3.2.1, above) reinforces the statutory duties and represents the national standard against which the policies, procedures and performance of harbour authorities may be measured. Executive and operational responsibilities for marine safety must be clearly assigned and those to whom they are entrusted must be held accountable for their performance. Harbour authorities must have a 'designated person' to provide independent assurance about the operation of its marine management systems, who has direct access to the board.[26]

Lighthouses, beacons and buoys[27] for marking channels and providing warning of dangers to users of the port, as well as removing any obstructions, are functions of utmost importance. Now, the MSA 1995, Pt VIII has consolidated all provisions included in the previous MSAs and the HA 1964, as well as the Port Act 1991, concerning powers, functions, division of duties between general and local lighthouse authorities, rights and liabilities. Section 195 of the MSA 1995 imposes responsibility on the harbour authority for the management and superintendence of lighthouses and general maintenance of all property vested in them. Sections 197 and 198 deal more specifically with the duties of lighthouse authorities in this respect.

Chapter I of Part IX of the MSA 1995 allocates rights and duties with respect to

---

26 Op cit, DETR, fn 9, Section 2, 'Accountability of the duty holder'.

27 See definitions in s 223 of the MSA 1995; s 77 of the HDPCA 1847 is incorporated in special legislation of harbour authorities and requires the harbour authority to lay down buoys for guidance of vessels.

salvage and wrecks; Chapter II deals with vessels in distress and the duties of harbour authorities in dealing with wrecks.[28] The power to remove wrecks causing obstruction is granted by s 252 of the Act in Chapter III, which grants extensive powers to the authorities even to destroy the wreck, as well as providing for rights in claiming wreck removal expenses.[29] In addition, s 56 of the HDPCA 1847, which is incorporated in almost all special legislation of harbour authorities, empowers the authority and the harbour master to remove wrecks or other obstructions impeding navigation. Intervention is justified when the wreck causes an obstruction to navigation and, hence, a hazard to other ships, or a threat to the environment. The conservancy duties of a harbour authority have been stated in several decisions (see paras 3.2.3 and 3.2.4, below).

While maritime States may have legislation dealing with wrecks in their territorial waters, immense problems can arise when the wreck is on the high seas, posing a risk of pollution to coastal waters. There is, as yet, no power permitting States to force the owners of wrecks to incur the expenses of wreck removal.[30]

In this respect, the Legal Committee of the IMO, at its 92nd session held in Paris between 16–20 October 2006, approved the draft of the Wreck Removal Convention, which was adopted at the Diplomatic Conference, held from 14 to 18 May 2007, at the United Nations Office in Nairobi, Kenya. Thus, the Convention is called **The Nairobi Wreck Removal Convention 2007**.

Once it is ratified and comes into force, the new Convention will provide the legal basis for States to remove, or have removed, from their exclusive economic zones (EEZs) wrecks that may pose a hazard to navigation or, because of the nature of their cargo, to the marine and coastal environments, or to both. The new Convention will also require shipowners to take out insurance to cover the costs of removal, and provide States with a right of direct action against insurers.[31] The Convention covers risks to the safety of navigation and the risk of damage to the marine environment, or to the coastline. It should apply to all types of danger to navigation, especially the danger posed by drifting ships and other ships which may reasonably be expected to result in wrecks. It provides uniform international rules aiming to ensure the prompt and effective removal of wrecks located beyond the territorial sea of States into their Exclusive Economic Zone (EEZ). It enables State parties to apply certain provisions of the Convention in their territorial sea (see further Section C below).

In addition, under the Merchant Shipping (Port State Control) Regulations 1995, Pt 1, reg 15(3), if a port authority, in exercising its normal duties, learns that a ship within its port has deficiencies which may prejudice the safety of the ship or pose an unreasonable threat of harm to the marine environment, the authority must inform the Maritime Safety Agency. Failure to do so will result in the port authority being guilty of an offence.

---

28   For interests in wrecks, see Palmer, N, and McKendrick, E (eds), *Interests in Goods*, 2nd edn, 1998, LLP, Chapter 7.

29   There can be forfeiture of the right to claim expenses if the obstruction was caused by the fault of the harbour authority: *The Oxbird* (1937) 58 LlL Rep 346. Here, the authority had no defence under statute because it had contracted with the owner of the wreck to raise it but, due to its negligence in failing to light the wreck, a collision occurred.

30   Gaskell, N, 'Interests in wrecks', para 3.2, in op cit, fn 28, Palmer and McKendrick.

31   IMO; www.imo.org.

It is important to refer also to the Merchant Shipping (Carriage of Cargoes) Regulations 1999, which came into force by a statutory instrument[32] on 15 March 1999. They consolidate the previous 1997 Regulations, which implemented Chapter VI of the International Convention for Safety of Life at Sea (SOLAS) 1974, and its Protocol 1978, as amended. Basically, these regulations require the master of the ship and the terminal representative to agree a loading plan prior to the loading of bulk cargoes to ensure safe loading and unloading of ships.[33]

Furthermore, at the EU level, there are other new safety procedures for monitoring, control and information with regard to traffic in European waters and with regard to inspection of ships at European ports and prevention of oil pollution, as well as increased controls imposed upon ship inspection organisations and administrations (discussed in Chapter 20, below).[34]

3.2.3.2 Abandonment of wreck by its owner and powers of harbour authorities

Sometimes, the owner of a sunken ship may abandon his ownership rights of the wreck by showing a positive intention to relinquish his rights in the property. But, by doing so, the owner cannot relinquish accrued liabilities.[35]

A problem connected with the removal of a wreck, which has been abandoned by its owners within territorial waters, has been the recovery of the expenses incurred by the authority. The authority has statutory powers to sell the wreck and in that way recover its expenses, but very often the wreck removal expenses may exceed the value of the wreck.

The problem of port authorities recovering their surplus expenses is now dealt with by local legislation and the MSA 1995 (see later). In the past, problems of interpretation of s 56 of the HDPCA 1847 arose in old cases, such as *The Crystal*.[36] Unless there was a statutory provision expressly granting the authority a cause of action to sue the relevant owner, who was the owner of the ship at the time of the sinking and before abandonment, the expenses could not be recoverable because the right to claim them against the owner would not have accrued at the time of sinking, but after the owner had abandoned the wreck, or ceased to be its owner.

Thus, in *The Crystal*, the House of Lords decided against the claiming authority, because the expenses were incurred after the abandonment by the owners[37]

---

32 SI 1999/336.

33 See, also, Chapter 20 regarding the EU Directive to enhance procedures for safe loading and unloading of bulk carriers at European ports.

34 See, further, Chapters 8, 11 and 20.

35 See op cit, Gaskell, fn 30, Chapter 7, para 2.2, in op cit, Palmer and McKendrick, fn 28.

36 [1894] AC 508.

37 In this connection, it should be noted that a similar problem of recovery of wreck removal expenses arose under a charterparty (*The Fajal* [2000] 1 Lloyd's Rep 473), in which the parties had agreed that 'in the event of the vessel becoming a wreck or obstruction to navigation the charterer shall indemnify the owner against any sum whatsoever which the owner shall become liable to pay and shall pay in consequences of the vessel becoming a wreck or obstruction to navigation'. Upon arrest of the ship, being the ship of the bareboat charterer, by the owners to recover indemnity, Rix J decided that, when the owners became liable to pay the wreck removal expenses after the sinking of the ship, the charterers had ceased to be the charterers of the ship. In the light of this decision, the clause should contain express words that the charterers' liability to indemnify the owners shall accrue at the time of the sinking and irrespective of when the owners pay such expenses.

of the wreck, who were not the owners within the meaning of s 56 of the HDPCA 1847:

> It is clear to my mind, that, prima facie, the owner of the wreck must be the person to whom the wreck belongs during the time when the harbour master chooses to exercise his statutory powers. That appears to me to be the primary and natural meaning of the words. It may, of course, be displaced by force of the context. But I can find nothing in the context to suggest that the words were intended to have any other than their natural meaning.[38]

It was held that expenses could not be recovered from the owner, for the additional reason that the wreck had been removed by destruction and the Act only gave the harbour authority power to 'remove' and not to 'destroy'.

Much later, in 1988, the problem was rectified by an amendment to the old statutes by the MSA 1988, Sched 5, para 2.[39] The MSA 1995, which repealed and replaced the previous statutory provisions about wrecks, including Sched 5, para 2 of the MSA 1988, gives very wide powers (ss 252–55) to the harbour authority for the removal or destruction of a wreck.[40] A power of sale of the wreck, and reimbursement for the expenses incurred in respect thereof out of the proceeds of sale, is also included.[41] But the section does not give the relevant authorities a personal cause of action against the owners of the sunken ship to recover their expenses. However, local legislation provides that the owner will compensate the port authority for its wreck removal expenses. In particular, s 46(6) of the Medway Ports Authority Act 1973 supplements s 252, for the purpose of raising wrecks, and defines 'owner' as the person who was the owner of the vessel at the time of the sinking, stranding or abandonment.

3.2.3.3 The duty to mark wrecks and liability to third parties – risk management issues

When a ship sinks and becomes a wreck, questions of liability for resulting damage to third parties whose ships navigate the area of the sunken wreck will arise. Wrecks present a risk to navigation and, unless they are properly dealt with will, sooner or later, cause damage to others navigating territorial waters within which the harbour authorities can exercise their statutory powers. There are certain statutory provisions which provide that the authority should place the appropriate light and use the appropriate shape of a buoy in such a distance so as to give a sufficient warning to others that there is a sunken wreck at that position.

Issues with respect to risk management of these liabilities merit consideration in raising awareness of what must be done and by whom in order to prevent possible liability to third parties.

---

38 *The Crystal* [1894] AC 508, p 522.
39 Eg, the MSA 1894, s 531, which dealt with wrecks, was amended by the MSA 1988, Sched 5, para 2, which created a personal debt of the wreck-owner and changed the test of ownership.
40 Similar powers are given to lighthouse authorities by s 253.
41 With regard to a statutory right to detain the *res* and power of sale of the port authority to recover its expenses and priority of claims, see *The Sea Spray* [1907] P 133; *The Queen of the South* [1968] P 449, Chapter 4, above.

In old cases a very important question had arisen as to who would be liable in damages to a passing vessel which collided without its own fault with an unmarked or unlit wreck, the owner or the harbour authority. The owner of the wreck would be liable if, having control over his sunken ship, he did not place a warning light or a buoy and did not warn the harbour authority.[42] But, if the harbour authority, after notice given to it by the owner, had undertaken to buoy the wreck, the authority, and not the owner, would be liable, as was held by the Court of Appeal in *The Douglas*.[43]

The principle that, once the port authority has, under its statutory powers, undertaken control and management of the wreck, it will be accountable and liable to third parties in the event of damage caused to their ships using the port, if the wreck is the cause of the damage, was confirmed by the Privy Council in *The Utopia*,[44] in which the principles derived from previous authorities were confirmed:

> The owner of a ship sunk whether by his default or not (wilful misconduct probably giving rise to different considerations) has not, if he abandons the possession and control of her, any responsibility either to remove her or to protect other vessels from coming into collision with her. It is equally true that, so long as, and so far as, possession, management and control of the wreck be not abandoned or properly transferred, there remains on the owners an obligation in regard to the protection of other vessels from receiving injury from her. But, in order to fix the owners of a wreck with liability, two things must be shewn, first, that in regard to the particular matters in respect of which default is alleged, the control of the vessel is in them, that is to say, has not been abandoned, or legitimately transferred, and, secondly, that they have in the discharge of their legal duty been guilty of wilful misconduct or neglect.

It should be noted that a common law liability for negligence could not be wiped out by abandoning that which has caused the damage and doing nothing else to prevent accidents.[45] If the owner of the wreck employs an independent contractor to raise the wreck, he cannot be absolved from liability to third parties caused by the negligence of the contractor. In *The Snark*,[46] the Court of Appeal held that the owners of the wreck, who had not abandoned it nor transferred management or control, were bound to see that the necessary precautions were taken to prevent danger to the public, and could not escape from liability by throwing the blame on the contractor employed by them to do the work.

When a harbour authority, in the exercise of its statutory powers, assumes responsibility for marking the wreck, it owes a duty of care to all persons lawfully using the port to carry out that marking with reasonable skill and care.[47] Provided that such duty is discharged, and subject to causation issues, the authority will not

---

42 See *Harmond v Pearson* [1808] 1 Camp 515.

43 [1882] 7 PD 151.

44 [1893] AC 492, pp 498–99 (PC).

45 *Dee Conservancy Board v McConnell* [1928] 2 KB 159: a ketch sank, through the negligence of her owners, who became liable at common law for the damage caused by the obstruction to the navigation of the river and the blocking of the approach to the wharf. They could not escape liability for that damage by abandoning the wreck.

46 [1900] P 105.

47 *The Tramontana II* [1969] 2 Lloyd's Rep 94.

be liable for an accident caused due to the negligence of a third party by not keeping a good lookout or by not appreciating the message conveyed by the warning.[48]

3.2.4 *Duty to maintain the port in good condition and risk management*

Non-compliance with its statutory duty to maintain the port in good condition, as well as non-compliance with the Port Marine Safety Code and the guide of good practice, which require port authorities to commit to risk assessment and management in marine operations, will expose the port or harbour authority to liabilities towards those using the port. Marine operations mean the moving, berthing and unberthing of ships and other marine craft within the limits and approaches of a harbour authority. The guide provides advice and information on these operations and all the various activities which affect safety of life, property and the environment.

A port or harbour authority will be liable to third parties for breach of the statutory provisions to the extent to which the statute provides. The statute will also provide for the standard of care.

Apart from the statutory duty of harbour authorities to keep the port safe for navigation, public authorities are subject also to the common law duty of care in making the port safe. Failure to take reasonable care will result in liability to pay damages.

In *Mersey Docks Trustees v Gibbs*,[49] the port was unfit to be navigated, by reason of accumulated mud in the port. The principle with regard to the common law duty of the port authority was restated, referring to previous authorities:

> When such a body is constituted by statute, having the right to levy tolls for its own profits, in consideration of making and maintaining a dock or a canal, there is no doubt of the liability to make good to the persons using it any damage occasioned by neglect in not keeping the works in proper repair . . . And the common law in such a case imposes a duty upon the proprietors to take reasonable care, so long as they keep it open for the public use of all who may choose to navigate it, that they may do so without danger to their lives or property.

It did not make any difference that, in this case, the trustees did not collect tolls for their own profit, but merely as trustees for the benefit of the public.

A warranty of accessibility of the port will be implied, if the port authority, in the exercise of its statutory powers, represents to the public that the port has a certain depth or other characteristics. In *Bede SS v River Wear*,[50] the harbour commissioners were authorised and required by statute to execute works of improvement and maintenance in a harbour, and were empowered to make and maintain docks and to take harbour and dock tolls in respect of the use of the harbour and docks. They advertised that there was a certain depth of water on the sill of a dock belonging to them. Shipowners sent their ships to the dock on the faith of that

---

48 Ibid.
49 (1866) LR 1 HL 93.
50 [1907] 1 KB 310.

advertisement. Where, in such a case, the commissioners had not used reasonable care, but had allowed silt to accumulate at the entrance of their harbour, and a ship had consequently been detained for four days in the dock, the commissioners were liable to the shipowners in damages for the detention of their ship on the ground of breach of the warranty.

Failure by the trustees, in whom a harbour had been vested by statute, to examine whether a berth was safe was breach of the duty to take reasonable care. They could not shift this duty to the local pilots, who were not their servants.

In **The Bearn**,[51] the owners of the steamship sued the harbour trustees for damage to their vessel due to the defective condition of the berth. They also sued the owners of the wharf, a railway company. The trustees argued that, as they had not received any report from the local pilots, upon whom the duty was imposed by by-laws to make periodical inspections and take soundings, they had not been negligent in being unaware of the defective condition of the berth. The owners of the wharf argued that, as the responsibility of keeping the berth in proper condition rested with the trustees, they were not negligent in being unaware of a defect which was due to a breach of the harbour by-laws by persons unknown.

The Court of Appeal held, affirming the decision of the court below, that both defendants were liable: the trustees, because they had negligently omitted to perform the duty laid down in *Mersey Docks Trustees v Gibbs*, of taking reasonable care to see whether the harbour, including the berth in question, was in a fit condition, and they could not shift this duty on to the local pilots who were not their servants, and whose duty to take soundings was for the purpose of enabling them to navigate the vessels employing them. The railway company was liable under the rule in *The Moorcock*,[52] because, as wharf-owners, they had invited the plaintiffs' vessel alongside for profit to themselves, and could not rely upon the pilots performing the duty cast upon them by the trustees, for, in their capacity as wharf owners, they had the opportunity of ascertaining the condition of the berth, and should, therefore, have either satisfied themselves that it was reasonably fit, or warned those in charge of the vessel that they had not done so.

Even when no dues are charged, there is a general benefit derived from the use of the port, and the duty to use reasonable care exists.

In **The Grit**,[53] the plaintiffs' motor barge received damage by taking the ground on some large stones in a berth alongside the defendants' wharf, where she was loading a cargo of slag. The defendants, a railway company, owned the wharf, but not the bed of the river alongside the wharf, and they charged no dues in respect of the use of the wharf. The arrangements for the cargo to be loaded into the barge at the wharf were delegated to an agent. A year previously, the agent had warned the defendants that the berth might be dangerous to vessels using it, because stones had been placed to protect the river bank from falling into the bed of the river. The defendants took some soundings, but did nothing else.

---

51 [1906] P 48.
52 (1889) 14 PD 64.
53 [1924] P 246.

Although the defendants did not charge dues for the use of the wharf, they were held liable because they derived benefit by reason of the freight earned for the land carriage of the cargo and they were in the position of persons who had invited vessels to use the wharf. They owed a duty, therefore, if they had not taken steps to see that the berth alongside the wharf was safe for vessels and for failing to warn that they had not done so.

These are good examples concerning risk management and, had the port authorities been aware of formal risk assessment at that time, these cases would perhaps not have gone to court!

Vessels using ports are invitees and, today, the Occupiers' Liability Acts 1957 and 1984 will also apply.

By charging dues, a special relationship is created between the harbour authority and the users of the port which imposes duties analogous to the common law duties existing between invitor and invitee to take reasonable care.[54]

In a recent decision, *Carisbrooke Shipping CV5 v Bird Port Ltd*,[55] the port was held liable to the ship owners under the Occupiers' Liability Act 1957 and in negligence, in respect of damage caused to their ship while she was using the berth. The court pinpointed that the underpinning cause of the damage was lack of safe operations by the port, which required a system of regular inspections.

The berth at B's port was within a dock which could be closed by gates (described as 'not always afloat but safely aground'). It was expected that vessels would or might take the ground at low water. The bottom of the berth was typically covered with a layer of silt or mud that came in with the tide. When operational considerations permitted, dredging operations were carried out in the dock. Steel coils were commonly loaded and discharged at the port. Before the vessel had arrived at B's port, no ingress of water into the ballast tanks (or into the fuel tanks) had been reported and no unusual trim had been observed at sea. After leaving the port, soundings had revealed an increasing amount of water in the vessel's ballast tanks. An inspection showed that the vessel's bottom shell plating had suffered a circular indentation about 80mm in depth, causing damage over a diameter of about 1.5–1.6 metres, including fractures of the plating and buckling of the internals. At the centre of the circular indent, there was a dimple. The owners claimed the cost of repair and lost hire, on the basis that the damage had been caused when the vessel sat on a steel coil at the bottom of the berth.

Giving judgment for the ship owner, the judge held that the nature of the damage was cogent evidence that the damage was caused whilst the vessel was alongside the berth in B's port. B had not shown that the coil had been removed from the berth. The ship owner established, on the balance of probabilities, that the damage suffered by the vessel was caused by the vessel sitting down on a steel coil in the berth. It was not a proper discharge of B's duty of care to dredge only when operational requirements permitted. Safe operation of the dock required a system of

---

54   *Maclenan v Segar* [1917] 2 KB 325; *St Just Steam Ship Co Ltd v Hartlepool Port and Harbour Commissioners* (1929) 34 LlL Rep 344.

55   [2005] 2 Lloyd's Rep 626.

inspection and regular dredging. B's system was inadequate, and in breach of its duty of care to port users, and that failure was causative of the damage. The ship owner was entitled to recover (a) lost hire; (b) the costs of an employed super-intendent, on the basis that the cost of the employee time could be taken as an approximation for the loss of revenue, as if an external expert was engaged;[56] and (c) an 'agency' claim in the sum of 1 per cent of the proved claim, to reflect expend-iture or revenue loss by reason of disruption and expenditure of management time.[57]

In an old decision, *The Neptun*,[58] the court did not find the port liable, nor did it hold – contrary to the *Bede v River Wear* case (mentioned earlier) – that publishing information and charts gives rise to a warranty about the minimum depth of the water.

The Neptun became a total loss by stranding at a port in which the defendant, Humber Conservancy Board, were the buoyage and beaconage authority charging dues for their services. It was their duty to exercise reasonable care in the perform-ance of their functions to keep the channels safe for vessels to navigate in, and to place lightships in such positions as would indicate to vessels where the deep water channels were. The information supplied by the defendants indicated a minimum depth of 3 feet at low water ordinary spring tides throughout the Whitton channel. The owners of *The Neptun* argued that this amounted to a warranty. It was shown in evidence that the channels in the Upper Humber changed their course frequently and rapidly, that the lightships had constantly to be moved, and that the Upper Whitton lightship had been shifted before the accident happened. No notice had been issued this time about the shallowness of the water.

It was held that the liability of the defendants depended upon the special rela-tionship which arose through their taking dues; that this relationship, though not exactly that of invitor and invitee, imposed duties analogous to the common law duties existing between invitor and invitee to take reasonable care; that the issue of the information and charts did not give rise to a representation or warranty that a minimum depth of 3 feet would be found on any given date in a bed of a river which was constantly changing; that the defendants had not been negligent as regards the frequency or extent of their soundings, or in the placing of the lightships; and that the action failed.

The correctness of this decision is doubtful today, particularly with the extra responsibilities imposed on ports to implement risk assessment practices to prevent risks arising from misinformation and old charts. It is submitted that *Bede v River Wear* is a reliable authority on the important issue that publishing information and charts with regard to certain characteristics of the port amounts to a warranty of accessibility, breach of which will render the port liable to persons suffering loss or damage by relying on the representation.

The place and method of mooring vessels within a port are within the authority

---

56   *Admiral Management Services Ltd v Para Protect Europe Ltd* [2002] EWHC 233.
57   *Owners of the Kumanovo v Owners of the Massira* [1998] 2 Lloyd's Rep 301.
58   [1938] P 21.

of the harbour master or port captain. Where, by a harbour master's orders, two vessels were removed from moorings and negligently re-moored and retained in new positions, so that, on the occurrence of an extraordinary flood, both were carried away and lost, it was held by the Privy Council that the harbour board were liable for the acts of their officer.[59]

Limitation of liability of owners or trustees of harbours, docks and piers will be seen in Chapter 17 on limitation.

3.2.5 Contractual duty to make the port reasonably safe

In cases where a private dock owner invites shipowners to use his dock, a warranty is contained in the contract between the parties, namely, that the dockowner has taken reasonable steps to see that the berth offered to the boat is safe. If it is not safe, the dockowner will give notice of the fact to the shipowner.[60]

The dockowner may exempt himself from liability for negligence by placing a notice to this effect at a visible place in clear and unambiguous language. For example, in *The Ballyalton*[61] case, the vessel lying at berth sustained serious damage by reason of the unevenness of the berth.

Her owners brought an action alleging negligence, breach of contract and breach of warranty by the owners of the dock. However, the defendant had put a notice up of which the claimant had knowledge.

> Notice is hereby given that vessels . . . have to take the ground after high water, and it must be understood that, while the corporation take steps to keep [berths] in order, they do not ensure the berths always being level . . .
>
> . . . vessels . . . must be and are at the risk of the owners . . . AND NOT OF THE CORPORATION, who will not be responsible for and will repudiate any liability in respect of any damage . . . to vessel . . . resulting from using [a berth], or taking ground thereat . . .
>
> . . . owners must satisfy themselves that the vessels both in their construction and the disposition in them of the cargo, may safely take the ground and lie in the berths, and of the condition of the berths, as the corporation will not be responsible for and will repudiate any liability in respect of any damage . . . to vessel . . . resulting from using the quays or river diversion, or either of them, or taking the ground thereat or therein, or from the berths thereat or therein . . .

It was held that the defendants were protected by the notice, excepting them from liability for damage to vessels. Not only were the words of the exemption clause wide and unambiguous enough to cover negligence, but they would have been meaningless on any other interpretation.

Exception clauses will be subject to the test of reasonableness of the Unfair Contract Terms Act 1977 and, of course, liability cannot be excluded for death or personal injury, under s 2(1) of that Act.

---

59 *East London v Caledonian Shipping* [1908] AC 271.
60 *The Moorcock* (1889) 14 PD 64.
61 [1961] 1 WLR 929.

3.2.6 The duty to provide efficient pilotage services

Following the accident of *The Sea Empress* at Milford Haven in 1997, and the comments made by the Marine Accidents Investigation Branch (MAIB) about the role of the port authority in the handling of the accident through their pilots, it was thought necessary to review the functions conferred on harbour authorities by the PA 1987.[62]

The main points emphasised in the report of the review were that:

(a) pilotage ought to remain a harbour authority function and become fully integrated with other port safety services under the control of the authority;

(b) harbour authorities should use their powers to ensure that there is a clear practical assignment of responsibility for the safety of piloted vessels;

(c) harbour authorities should keep under formal regular review the specific powers and duties imposed by the 1987 Act, relating to use of powers and direction, as well as the recruitment, authorisation, examination, employment status and training of pilots;

(d) harbour authorities should be made more accountable for all their port safety functions, with a new reserve power for the Secretary of State to direct improvements where neglect of safety duties may cause a danger to public navigation.

The principal proposal of the report was that a Marine Operations Code for Ports should be developed, covering all port safety functions, and not just pilotage. This should serve as a national standard, among other things, for training and examination of pilots, a guide to best practice, and a framework for the preparation of published policies and plans by harbour authorities.

It also required the harbour authority to have available competent pilots and properly certified boats for their use. The Authority should ensure that the assigned pilot to every ship is fit and appropriately qualified for the task and that, under the PA 1987, pilotage services provided by a harbour authority should be based upon a continuing process of risk assessment. Authorised pilots should be accountable to their authorising authority for the use they make of their authorisation and harbours should have contracts with authorised pilots, regulating the conditions under which they work, including procedures for resolving disputes.[63]

The Code was swiftly drafted and is supplemented by the guide of good practice, incorporating the points of the report. It was published at the end of January 2001.[64]

The Code is directed at harbour authorities empowered to regulate shipping movements and the safety of navigation within their harbours; most of these are competent harbour authorities within the meaning of the PA 1987. The Code

---

62 *Review of the Pilotage Act 1987*, Consultation Paper, 27 July 1998, updated 7 March 2001.

63 Op cit, DETR, fn 9, Section 9, 'Pilotage'.

64 See para 3.2.3, above.

does not apply to duties and powers other than those relating to marine operations.[65]

The PA 1987 provides for a competent harbour authority to use an agent for pilotage services and to have formal joint arrangements with other competent harbour authorities for the discharge of pilotage functions (s 11).

A further relevant amendment to pilotage law and the PA 1987 is based on EU Directive 1999/42/EC[66] relating to the mutual recognition of qualifications and experience of pilots which should be recognised as between Member States. It enshrines a general principle that qualifications and experience awarded in one Member State should be recognised in another. In view of the lacuna existed in the PA 1987 in this respect, in that it placed no constraints on the way that a competent harbour authority might determine the qualifications of pilots, it was necessary to make it explicit in the Act that the principle of the Directive should be followed; thus, the Act was amended by Regulations in 2003.[67]

The amendment specifies the qualifications of pilots and requirements of experience, as set out in Sch A1.

In s 3(1) of the Act, a subsection (1A) has been inserted: 'In considering whether a person is suitably qualified (a) to be authorised under subsection (1) above to act as a pilot (i) in inland waters only, or (ii) in inland waters and other waters, or (b) to continue to be authorised, a competent harbour authority shall act in accordance with Sch A1 to this Act (which makes provision about persons with qualifications obtained in EEA states other than the UK)'.

After s 3(2), subsection (2A) is inserted, which prohibits the authority from acting in such a way as to contravene Sched A1 when it makes its determination about the qualifications of a pilot.

Section 2 of the PA 1987 states the duty of a competent harbour authority, which is to provide pilotage services where they are needed, and to designate areas which, in the interests of safety, would be compulsory pilotage areas. Section 4 provides for the employment of pilots by the authority, either under contracts of employment or under a contract for services. Section 22(3) provides for limitation of liability of the authority where an authorised pilot – without any personal act or omission of the authority – has caused any loss or damage. Section 22(8) provides that the harbour authority shall not be liable for any loss or damage caused by any act or omission of a pilot authorised by it, merely because of a fault simply in authorising the pilot. On the issue of liability of harbour authorities for acts of pilots, see Section B of this chapter.

It is important at this point to mention that the harbour authority may be criminally liable for permitting the pollution of waters, under s 85(1) of the WRA 1991, which provides for strict liability, namely: 'A person contravenes this section if he

---

65 Other functions are regulated by regulations made under the Health and Safety at Work Act 1974. Many other functions are regulated by the MSA 1995, administered by the Maritime and Coastguard Agency (MCA).

66 OJ L201 31.7.1999 p 77.

67 Pilotage (Recognition of Qualifications and Experience) Regulations 2003, SI 2003/1230, reg 2, in force 30 May 2003, amending the PA 1987.

causes . . . any . . . polluting matter to enter any controlled waters.' This may arise in connection with an inexperienced pilot, as it did in *The Sea Empress*.[68]

Briefly, the ship was laden with light crude oil when she struck the mid-channel rocks in the entrance to Milford Haven, North Wales, due to negligent navigation of her pilot, who had been trained and authorised by the Milford Haven Port Authority. Then she grounded in Mill Bay, causing a large-scale oil spill in the area. The port authority was prosecuted under this section, pleaded guilty without admission of fault, and the case came before the admiralty judge, David Steel, to determine the application of the section to the facts and the fine. Assisted by a House of Lords authority[69] in the interpretation of this section, the judge said that the section would apply if there was a positive act, not an omission, by the defendant, which need not be the immediate cause of the oil escape. With regard to causation, the section would apply if the defendant caused a situation in which the polluting matter could escape, but a necessary condition of the actual escape was also the act of a third party. If that act were a matter of ordinary occurrence, as opposed to an extraordinary, it would not negative the causal effect of the defendants' act, even if it were not foreseeable.

Having analysed the scope of the section, the judge had no difficulty in concluding that the port authority, being the operator of the port of compulsory inward pilotage, which trained and authorised the pilot, whose experience for this type of vessel was sketchy, did something which caused pollution, bearing also in mind that the pilot's negligence was a normal occurrence. He made no finding of fault, but on the basis of strict liability he fined the authority £4 million, reflecting the genuine and justified public concern.

The Sea Empress prompted the British Government, in addition to the review of the functions and accountability of harbour authorities, to take other measures as well. It accepted a proposal made by Lord Donaldson for an official representative of the Secretary of State (SOSREP) to have powers of intervention and agree a salvage plan with the salvage master to prevent situations arising, such as in *The Sea Empress* case, where the local pilot cannot have such powers (see Chapter 13, above).

4 LIABILITY OF SHIPOWNERS FOR DAMAGE CAUSED TO HARBOURS

In England and Wales, ports or harbours, whether privatised by an Act of Parliament, or publicly owned, are regulated by statutes and bylaws. Their obligations and their rights for damage caused to their property are to be found in statutory provisions.

Under s 74 of the HDPCA 1847, there is strict liability imposed upon shipowners whose ship causes damage to any of the property of the harbour or port

---

68 [1999] 1 Lloyd's Rep 673.
69 *Empress Car Co v National Rivers Authority* [1998] 1 All ER 481.

authority. In other words, the shipowner will be liable, whether or not the damage was caused by his or his servants' negligence. This means that the port authority does not have to prove that the damage was caused by negligence. There may be a defence that the damage was caused by the intervention of a non-human agent when, for example, the ship was a derelict, or had been abandoned by her crew because of tempestuous weather. As it will be seen in the following cases, the courts had a great deal of difficulty in construing this section (fully quoted below). It is important to quote fairly large parts of these decisions in order to show the distinction between the liability created by this section and liability at common law.

River Wear Commissioners v Adamson [70]

The defendants' ship was driven on shore by a storm in endeavouring to make the port of Sunderland. The crew were taken off with difficulty, and the ship, being a complete wreck, was afterwards driven by the winds and waves against the pier belonging to the harbour and caused damage to it, for which the commissioners brought an action against the owners under s 74 of the HDPCA 1847.

The question was whether the defendants were liable to pay the commissioners for the damage suffered. This depended on the interpretation of s 74, which reads:

> The owner of every vessel or float of timber shall be answerable to the undertakers for any damage done by such vessel or float of timber, or by any person employed about the same, to the harbour, dock, or pier, or the quays or works connected therewith, and the master or person having the charge of such vessel or float of timber, through whose wilful act or negligence any such damage is done, shall also be liable to make good the same; and the undertakers may detain any such vessel or float of timber until sufficient security has been given for the amount of damage done by the same: provided always, that nothing herein contained shall extend to impose any liability for any such damage upon the owner of any vessel where such vessel shall, at the time when such damage is caused, be in charge of a duly licensed pilot, whom such owner or master is bound by law to employ, and put his vessel in charge of.[71]

The issue was whether it was the intention of the legislature that the owner was not to be excused, even for liability caused by such tempestuous weather amounting to an act of God. Mellish LJ, in the Court of Appeal, said that:

> I think, looking at the language of the section, it clearly was the intention of the legislature to extend the liability of the owners of vessels, in favour of the owners of piers and harbours, beyond the liability which is imposed on them by common law: because, if that is not the intention, it is not easy to see the object of the section at all. Looking at the pointed language in which negligence or wilful act is brought in, looking to the fact that the section goes on to speak of the master, or the person having the charge of the vessel, it seems to shew clearly that the owner is intended to be liable even in the case where neither the master nor the crew had anything to do with it. But the question arises, because we may decide, on the language used, that

---

70 (1876) 1 QBD 546 (HL).

71 The proviso of s 74 (last sentence) has been overruled by the provisions of the PAs since 1913, which made the owner answerable to any damage caused by pilot's negligence while he is in control of navigation of the ship, whether or not pilotage is compulsory; see para 8, below.

the owner may be made liable where it is not proved that he or the master was guilty of negligence, are we bound to hold that in every case whatever, where the vessel physically damages the pier, etc, the owner is so liable? I am of opinion that the statute only contemplates the case where either directly or indirectly, through the act of man, the vessel is caused in some way or other to run against the pier. It is quite consistent with our law that in certain cases a person may be made liable as insurer against the acts of all the men whom he may have under his control.[72]

Denman J, also sitting in the Court of Appeal, said:

I am of the same opinion. No doubt, taking the words of s 74, it is possible to hold that they impose an absolute liability to the dockowner on the part of the owner of the vessel. The words are strong, intelligible, and grammatical (referring to the first part of the section). But I am of opinion, taking the rest of the section, some qualification must be put on those words, not by introducing fresh words into the Act of Parliament, or supposing a clause to exist in it which does not exist, but by qualifying those words by the principle of law which is so well known, and which must be taken to override the language of an Act of Parliament. I apprehend that there is no principle of law better established than this, that in an Act of Parliament words are not to be construed to impose upon individuals liability for an act or acts done, if those acts are not done by the individual, or not caused by his property or his servants, but are acts which are substantially caused by a superior power, such as the law calls the act of God. In this case, there can be no doubt, from the facts, that the injury occasioned by the vessel was not the result of any neglect on the part of the owner, or on the part of any person having charge of the vessel, or, indeed, of any human being, but it was really the effect of the violence of the winds and waves overcoming all control on the part of the master or owner of the vessel, and forcing the vessel against the pier. Under those circumstances I apprehend, on the general principle that every statute is to be so construed as to leave untouched a principle of common law which applies to all similar cases, we are not bound to hold – and ought not to hold – that the damage was done by the vessel within the meaning of the Act of Parliament; but that, on the contrary, it was damage occasioned by the act of God, and therefore no action lies.[73]

Therefore, the defendants (respondents) were held not liable because, as the Court of Appeal thought, the statute intended to excuse the owner, in the same way as common law excuses the common law carrier, when an act of God was the cause of the damage.

On appeal to the House of Lords,[74] although the House disagreed with the broad and liberal construction given to the words of the statute by the Court of Appeal, their Lordships affirmed its judgment for different reasons. The majority held that a strict liability was created by the statute, and there was no intention in the statute to excuse the owner for an act of God in the same way as the common law carrier is. The liability under the statute is different from that under common law. From careful reading of what the majority said and their conclusion, it would seem implicit that they were prepared to excuse the owner when the master and

---

72 (1876) 1 QBD 546, p 553.
73 Ibid, p 555.
74 (1877) 2 App Cas 743.

crew had been compelled, as on the facts of this case, to escape from the vessel, and had, consequently, no control whatever over it (no human agency factor).[75]

In particular, the Lord Chancellor (Lord Cairns) explained that:

In my opinion, these expressions (stated above by the Court of Appeal) are broader than is warranted by any authorities of which I am aware. If a duty is cast upon an individual by Common Law, the act of God will excuse him from the performance of that duty. No man is compelled to do that which is impossible. It is a duty of a carrier to deliver safely the goods entrusted to his care; but, if in carrying them with proper care, they are destroyed by lightning, or swept away by a flood, he is excused, because the safe delivery has by the act of God become impossible. If, however, a man contracts that he will be liable for the damage occasioned by a particular state of circumstances, or if an Act of Parliament declares that a man shall be liable for the damage occasioned by a particular state of circumstances, I know of no reason why a man should not be liable for the damage occasioned by that state of circumstances, whether the state of circumstances is brought about by the act of man or by the act of God. There is nothing impossible in that which, on such an hypothesis, he has contracted to do, or which he is by the statute ordered to do, namely, to be liable for the damages. If, therefore, by the section to which I have referred, it is meant that the owner of every vessel shall, independently of whether anything has happened which would, at Common Law, give a right of action against anyone, pay to the undertakers the damage done by a ship to the pier, I should be unable to see any reason why the payment should not be made in the manner required by the statute.

I cannot, however, look upon this section of the statute as intended to create a right to recover damages in cases where, before the Act, there was not a right to recover damages from some one. The section and those which follow it are in an Act which collects together the common and ordinary clauses that it was the habit of Parliament to insert in the private bills authorising the construction of piers and docks.[76]

Confusion arose in the interpretation of this judgment, because Lord Cairns elaborated further that there was no new substantive right created by the statute, but a new procedure. In other words, as a matter of procedure, a claim could be brought against the owner under s 74 and there was no need to prove negligence; but, by reason of the defence of compulsory pilotage, as provided at the end of the section, the owner could recover over what he would have to pay to the port authority, if the damage was caused by the negligence of the pilot.[77]

Lord Hatherley, concurring, delivered a more crisp judgment[78] of what the construction of s 74 should be:

When we look at the whole construction of the clause, it appears to me that it speaks,

---

75 Lord Gordon, dissenting, said: 'On the ground that the intention of the legislature in passing the Act must be decided by the ordinary meaning of the words used, and here the words used in the first portion of the section were words creating a liability without any restriction whatever.'

76 (1877) 2 App Cas 743, p 750.

77 He meant that the owner would have to prove negligence of the pilot, which if proved would have the effect of surpassing the strict liability element of his liability to the port authority. The defence of compulsory pilotage, that was applicable under s 74 of this Act, became obsolete by the PA 1913 (see under Section B, 'Pilotage', paras 6 and 8, below), so there is no longer an issue in this respect.

78 (1877) 2 App Cas 743, pp 752–54.

in the first place, of damage done by a vessel without regard to anyone being on board or not; then it speaks in the second place of damage done by any person employed about the vessel; and then it says that the master or person in charge of a vessel is to be liable if damage is done through his wilful act or negligence; and then the excepted case occurs of the pilot, because he had been compulsorily, and against any power of resistance on the part of the owner, placed on board and in charge.

Now, my Lords, we have to see whether or not damage arising from the act of God, that is to say in the particular case a tempest, should be held to be excepted. There might be other cases which would be similar to this of a tempest; the vessel might have been driven on the pier in some other way, or have been injured and become unmanageable by lightning, or the like. However it occurred, if the pier was damaged by the vessel in the way which was called, by the learned judge in the court below, the act of God, is there anything in the Act of Parliament to say (and this clause seems to contain all that is said in the Act about it) that the owner of the vessel shall not be responsible for the damage, but that there shall be an exception in respect of damage so caused?

One can easily conceive that the legislature might think it desirable that those who provide this great accommodation for the navigation of the country, those who provide harbours of refuge and the like, which are greatly wanted in many parts of the coasts of the UK, should be indemnified against the possible damage which may accrue to their docks, or to other works which they construct in discharge of the duties in question, and in the exercise of those powers which they have for making docks and other works. Those promoters might say, 'We offer protection to the public at all times, only, in consideration of the benevolent hospitality which we so afford, protect us from having our works damaged.' There is nothing, as it appears to me, utterly unreasonable in such a proposition reasonably carried out. It is quite true that many cases, put by the learned judges in the court below, are cases in which it would seem to be a very rigid enactment indeed that damage to a very large and extensive amount, exceeding the value of the vessel itself, should be compensated by the persons whose vessel has done this damage, being made answerable to make it good to the full amount of the damage done, which might even go to the destruction of the principal works, and might therefore result in the ruin of those persons whose vessel had been so forced against them. But, on the other hand, if there was any intention at all of giving a relief of this kind, which must be sought of course in the words of the Act, then I apprehend that the exception of a storm or tempest would be a very singular one, because it is a probable case to happen.

Lord Blackburn gave the substantive reasons that existed behind this legislation by saying:

My Lords, reading the words of the enactment, and bearing in mind what was the state of the law at the time when it was passed, it seems to me that the object of the legislature was to give the owners of harbours, docks, and piers more protection than they had. It seems to have occurred to those who framed the statute, that in most cases where an accident occurs, it is from the fault of those who were managing the ship – and in most cases those are the servants of the owners – but that these were matters which in every case must be proved, and consequently that there was a great deal of litigation incurred before the owner, though he really was liable, could be fixed: and with a view to meet this, the remedy proposed was that the owner, who was generally really liable (though it was difficult and expensive to prove it), should be liable without proof either that there was negligence, or that the person guilty of neglect was the owner's servant, or proving how the mischief happened, and this is expressed by saying that the owners shall be 'answerable for any damage done by the vessel or by any person employed about the same' to the harbour . . .

My Lords, on reading the words of the enactments, I am brought to the conclusion that such was the scheme of legislation adopted by Parliament; the mischief being the expense of litigation; the remedy that the owners should be liable without proof of how the accident occurred.[79]

It seems clear from the above extracts that the majority decided that the words used in the statute imposed strict liability, and did not generally give any indication of an exception to strict liability for damage caused by an act of God. The variation made to this general principle – taking into account the facts of this case – was that the only exception to liability would arise when there was no human agency on board the ship at the time of the tempest, as happened in this case. Lord Gordon,[80] who dissented from the majority as to the outcome of the decision with great hesitation, was of the view that the owners, even on the facts of this case in which the crew were forced by the tempest to abandon ship, should not be excused from liability.

Although the decision of the majority was not obscure, it was thought, nevertheless, by shipping lawyers and judges, that it created an ambiguity arising from the *dicta* of Lord Cairns that no new substantive right of action was created. As a result, there were no clear guidelines for the courts below, as is shown in *The Mostyn*. The House of Lords felt the need to interpret *Adamson* in its later decision, *Great Western Rly Co v Owners of SS Mostyn (The Mostyn)*. The question was whether s 74 extends the liability of a ship owner to the port beyond what common law provides, so as to create a new substantive right.

The Mostyn [81]

The appellants, who were the owners of the docks at Swansea, brought this action against the respondents, the owners of the steamship, *The Mostyn*, to recover an agreed sum by way of damages for negligence, or alternatively an amount for which the respondents were liable under s 74 of the HDPCA 1847, for the damage done by *The Mostyn* to the Swansea docks. In a masonry chase-way, electric cables were laid for lighting purposes and the supply of power. During the night, while *The Mostyn* was proceeding along the channel to the Prince of Wales' Dock, her port anchor fouled and damaged some of these cables, with the result that the docks were plunged in darkness. The cables were part of the dock works.

The President came to the conclusion, on the evidence, that no negligence was proved against the respondents, and held, on the authority of the House of Lords' decision in *River Wear v Adamson*, that, where negligence was disproved, liability under s 74 of the HDPCA 1847 did not lie. He, therefore, gave judgment for the respondents. Evidently, the President misapplied the *Adamson* case.

The Court of Appeal (Bankes, Atkin and Sargant LJJ) affirmed the judgment of the President.

---

79 (1877) 2 App Cas 743, pp 768–69.
80 Ibid, p 780.
81 [1928] AC 57 (HL).

The House of Lords dealt with the question in more detail and in broader terms, drawing a general principle for guidance in subsequent cases; the majority of (Viscount Haldane, Lord Shaw of Dunfermline, and Lord Blanesburgh; Viscount Dunedin and Lord Phillimore dissenting) held:

> Under s 74 of the HDPCA 1847, the owner of a vessel doing damage to a harbour, dock or pier, or works connected therewith, is responsible to the undertakers for the damage, whether occasioned by negligence or not, where the vessel is at the time of the damage under the control of the owner or his agents.

When commenting on *River Wear v Adamson*, Viscount Haldane said, in particular:

> My Lords, the massive legal intelligence even of Lord Cairns does not seem to me to have wholly disposed of the question before us. He was dealing with a case in which human agency had been superseded. Here, we are dealing with one in which there was human agency, although there was no breach of duty. I think that he meant to go further, and to suggest that, even if there was human agency, there would be no liability created provided that there was no breach of duty at common law. But that question was not before him, and what he suggests was not necessary for the decision of the *Adamson* case. It is, therefore, important to see whether his suggestion was concurred in by the other noble and learned Lords who took part in the decision.

> The very power of rhetoric which Lord Cairns commanded when stating his conclusions about matters of legal principle makes it the more desirable to see that we are following the substance rather than the form of his propositions. Even if we accept his view that the section is one creating a new procedure, that of suing the owner . . ., I am quite unable to see how this leaves the existing substantive law intact and relates to procedure alone. The owner could not be sued under that law unless he had violated some duty. If he can be sued at all, even with a right to recover over, it must be because some new substantive liability has been imposed on him by the statute. I think, therefore, that it follows that the common law has been altered and that a new right of action has been created depending on the alteration. This is much more than mere procedure. Did his colleagues who heard the appeal with him accept his view as I interpret it? I think they did not . . .

> Lord Hatherley was a very careful judge. I think that his disposition here was to hold that the words of the Act were so free from ambiguity that they covered cases in which there was no human agency, though he did not say so in terms. He was content to express his general agreement with the view of Mellish LJ that the statute only applied where human agency had intervened, and that it was because it was absent in the *Adamson* case, that he concurred in the judgment of the Court of Appeal. I doubt whether Lord Hatherley himself was ready to accept even this restriction of its scope, but he thought it at least a possible one, and if true it was enough to take the circumstances in the case before him, where there was no human agency, outside the language of the Act . . .

> Lord Gordon in *Adamson* expressly dissented. At the conclusion of an elaborate judgment, he expressed the opinion that the statute ought not to be construed as if it contained any exemption from liability where it occurred even from the act of God. The words appeared to him to be express and unambiguous, and being so, he thought that they ought to be read according to their ordinary construction.

> My Lords, there remain to be considered the opinions of Lord O'Hagan and Lord Blackburn, with a view to ascertaining whether these noble and learned Lords concurred in the view which had been expressed by Cairns LC, that no new right of action at all was created, whether or not human agency was present.

My Lords, upon scrutiny of the words used by Lord O'Hagan, I have come to the clear conclusion that he did not concur in the *dictum* of the Lord Chancellor, so far as it went beyond the facts of the case before him, that the statute created no new right of action, but was confined in its scope to procedure only. The language, Lord O'Hagan thought, was prima facie sufficient to cover all cases, including those in which no human agency came in. But he was of opinion that, reading the whole of the section, and particularly the reference to 'such' vessel in the words declaring the liability of the master or person having charge of it, an intention was expressed to confine the liability of the owner to vessels 'in charge of a master or somebody else'. On this point he expressed his concurrence with Mellish LJ. The owner is therefore placed in a worse position than he would have been at common law, but not so bad as that in which he would have been had he been made liable when no one had charge on his behalf . . .[82]

My Lords, when the expressions used by Lord Blackburn are considered. I cannot find in them concurrence with the *dictum* of Lord Cairns that no new right of action was created, even where human agency came in, and that the wide words at the beginning of the section were intended to introduce nothing more than what Lord Cairns had spoken of as a new form of procedure, which would indeed assist the dockowner to pursue a new kind of remedy, but conferred on him no fresh substantive right. On this point, the opinions delivered appear to me to leave us under the duty of deciding, unfettered by authority, whether when the vessel which caused the damage was under the control of the owner's agents, he is liable notwithstanding that there was no breach of the duty not to be negligent on their and his part.

I do not think that *River Wear Commissioners v Adamson* settles the point of non-liability where the vessel was in charge, at the time of the accident, of the owners' agents. It seems to me that the words of the statute are too clear to admit of this conclusion, and that the decision of this House in the earlier case is not in truth any authority for it . . . If there was no human agency, then what I have said does not apply in that case. I comment on the decision in the *Adamson* case on the assumption that, notwithstanding what was said by Lord Blackburn, there was no such human agency. For, if there was, that in my view brings the case within the uncontrolled words, and would render it analogous to the present case. But, on the facts set out in the report, I think that the vessel must be taken to have become out of human control.

It appears to me to be bound by the authority of the Adamson case to hold that the section in question is not to be read literally, but as applying when the damage complained of has been brought about by a vessel under the direction of the owner or his agents, whether negligent or not. The decision further exempts the owner when the vessel is not under such control but is, for instance, derelict. When there are facts to which it applies, it effects an alteration in the common law which imposes a new liability to be sued on the owner, and to that extent changes not merely procedure but also substantive law.

My Lords, if these things are true I think that, on the facts established in the present case, we must find the owners liable, reverse the judgment of the court below in their favour, and give judgment for the appellant railway company for damages, the agreed amount of which is 226l.[83]

---

82 [1928] AC 57, pp 67–69.
83 [1928] AC 57, pp 71–72.

The difference on the facts between the *Adamson* and *The Mostyn* cases was that, in the former, the ship had been abandoned because of the extreme weather while, in the latter, the ship was under the control of its master and crew when the accident happened.

The issue of strict liability was questioned again later in the context of damage suffered by the harbour authority, which was due partly to its fault. The House of Lords had another opportunity to clarify the application of s 74 in this context in *The Towerfield*[84] (which is considered fully later under shipowners' liability for pilot's negligence).

The facts were briefly these. In 1941, a ship in the charge of a compulsory pilot, approaching an English harbour through a channel, went aground on an undredged accumulation of river silt, sustaining damage. It was conceded on behalf of the shipowners that she had also caused damage to the harbour. The harbour authority was found, on the facts, partly negligent for not having maintained the approaches to the harbour clean, which contributed to the casualty. The pilot on board the ship, which stranded, was also found partly negligent for the stranding of the ship and the damage caused to the property of the harbour.

On the issue of whether the application of strict liability of the owner was excluded because of the fault of the harbour authority, it was held that contributory negligence by the harbour authority was no defence to a claim by them under s 74 of the HDPCA 1847, for damage caused by the ship to the harbour (Lord Porter, Lord Normand, Lord Morton of Henryton and Lord Radcliffe; Lord Oaksey dissenting).

Applying *The Mostyn*, Lord Potter said:

> ... the majority of their Lordships took the view that the shipowner was responsible for damage done to harbour works whether he was in fault or not, save in a case similar to that decided in the *River Wear* judgment. Accordingly, where the ship had been abandoned and was therefore out of the control of its owners, they agreed that no liability attached under the section. But save for that concession they decided in terms, as I think, that the only exception from liability was that afforded to an abandoned ship.
>
> My Lords, until *The Mostyn* decided the true effect of the wording of the section a profound difference of view as to its construction was to be found amongst those who practised in that branch of the law which is devoted to shipping matters, ... I cannot think that fine distinctions should be introduced which would limit the generality of the decision which has been reached.[85]

In short, the effect of the interpretation of the *Adamson* decision, given by the House of Lords in *The Mostyn*, is that shipowners will be liable for any damage caused by their ship to the property of public harbour, or dock authorities, whether caused by negligence of their servants or not, or even if it is caused by an act of God, unless the ship is abandoned because of tempestuous weather, by reason of which the ship is not under human direction. Since s 74 imposes strict liability in this respect, *The*

---

84 *Workington Harbour Dock Board v Towerfield (Owners)* [1951] AC 112.
85 Ibid, p 136.

Towerfield case added to this principle that the fault of the port authority contributing to the loss would not be a defence for the shipowner. Such an addition to the principle as derived from *The Mostyn* and *Adamson* on the interpretation of s 74 is, however, questionable.

The Towerfield is irreconcilable with the statutory and common law duty of port authorities to maintain the port in a safe condition, considering that the damage was caused primarily because the ship went aground on an undredged accumulation of river silt. At the time the incident in that case occurred, in 1941, there was no contributory negligence defence allowed at common law. Could one assume that the Law Reform (Contributory Negligence) Act (LR(CN)A) 1945 would make a difference if the case were to be decided today? *The Mostyn* decided that there is a new substantive right created in favour of the port authority by s 74, whether or not there is a breach of duty by the ship owner's servants, but it did not go as far as to allow such right to extend into cases in which the port authority was in breach of its duties. In any case, the wording of s 74 does not warrant such a result. Supposing a ship causes damage to the port through no fault of its own, but because the port is unsafe to navigate in: would the port then be allowed to benefit from its own fault? The owner will have a separate cause of action against the port authority to claim damages caused to his ship for breach by the port authority of the common law duty of care and statutory duties under the Occupiers' Liability Act 1957 as seen in a recent decision earlier under para 3.2.4.

As far as recoverable damages are concerned, in an action based on s 74, the damages that can be claimed by a jetty or pier owner will include physical damage to the property as well as consequential financial loss arising from the consequential delay to repair the port or jetty, which will inevitably delay the business in the port, causing the port to become liable to third parties with whom the port had entered into contracts, as was decided on the facts of an Austrian decision.[86] However, on the facts of *The Towerfield* (see later), Lord Potter did not wish to go as far as to embrace amongst damages any loss of revenue to which the harbour board had suffered.

A question as to who is the owner under s 74 was recently considered. An argument was advanced by the defendants in ***The Chevron North America***[87] that the word 'owner' in s 74 meant the person who had possession of the vessel and employed, and had the right to control, the master and crew, for example demise charterers or bareboat charterers. The House of Lords, in rejecting this interpretation, stated that there was a public policy reasoning behind s 74 to enable claims to be made quickly and efficiently. Such an interpretation would run counter to these objectives, and so the word 'owner' is to be taken to mean the registered owner of the vessel.

---

86   *Texada Mines Ltd v The Ship Afovos* [1974] 2 Lloyd's Rep 168.
87   [2001] UKHL 50, [2002] 1 Lloyd's Rep 77.

5 HARBOUR DUES

The harbour authority has a statutory power of detention and a right to arrest a ship and have it sold, if port dues are not paid.[88] The authority's claim for their expenses of removal or conservation of a wreck has priority over other claims, even those giving rise to maritime liens, such as collision damage and salvage. The reason for this is that, had the authority not preserved the *res*, there would be no property left for the satisfaction of these claims, provided the proceeds are sufficient.[89]

The Veritas [90]

The Veritas was in distress outside the Mersey Docks. Salvage services were rendered to her, bringing her into the Mersey. Thereafter, a collision occurred between *The Veritas* and another steamship. Salvage services were again rendered to her by two tugs and she was brought alongside the dock wall. However, she drifted against a landing stage, doing damage to the stage and, finally, she sank. The Mersey Docks and Harbour Board, under the statutory powers conferred upon it, removed her. An action was instituted by the salvors against *The Veritas* in respect of the salvage services rendered. The board intervened in the action and the vessel was released to the board, which sold it. After deducting its expenses, it paid the proceeds of the sale into court. The present action was to determine priorities between the judgment creditors. It was held that the claim of the board took priority over that of the salvors. This was because the lien of the board was one which arose *ex delicto* as opposed to one arising *ex contracto* or quasi *ex contracto*. Gorell Barnes J stated that:

> It is also clear that liens arising *ex delicto* take precedence over prior liens arising *ex contracto*. The principal ... [reason is] that the person having a right of lien *ex contracto* becomes, so to speak, a part-owner in interest with the owners of the vessel. He has chosen to enter into relationship with the vessel for his own interests whereas a person suffering damage by the negligent navigation of a ship has no option. Reparation for wrongs done should come first.[91]

SECTION B – PILOTAGE LAW

1 INTRODUCTION

The term 'pilot' refers to a person with specialised knowledge of local conditions and navigational hazards, who is generally taken on board a vessel at a specific place for the purpose of navigating or guiding a ship through a particular channel, river, or other enclosed waters to or from a port. His functions are: to guide vessels

---

88 *Corps & Corps v The Queen of the South* [1968] 1 Lloyd's Rep 182.
89 *The Sea Spray* [1907] P 133.
90 [1901] P 304.
91 Ibid, p 313.

from open sea into port, or vice versa; to guide a ship from anchorage to a berth, or from berth to a terminal within a port; or to help a ship to dock or undock within a port.

The history of pilotage in the UK can be found in Douglas and Geen.[92] The authors say that, in 1514, Henry VIII granted a charter to the Trinity House giving it powers to control the operations of ships, pilots and mariners throughout the country. This charter was confirmed by the succeeding Tudors. In 1604, James I gave Trinity House a more comprehensive charter, but this was dissolved by Parliament in 1647, being considered as having Royalists tendencies. Charles II restored this charter and in 1685 there was a new charter under James II, which strictly stated that no person would be permitted to act as a pilot unless he had first been appointed and authorised by the Trinity House. There have been various successive Acts of Parliament relating to London Trinity House, of a general nature, since the 18th century. It became apparent in the early 20th century that a confusion had been created by the variance between the general statute law and the special provisions of local Acts regulating the business of pilots. As a result, the PA 1913 was passed to consolidate and amend the law relating to pilotage.

This was amended by the MSA 1979, upon recommendations of an Advisory Committee on Pilotage, which established the Pilotage Commission to act as an advisory body. But, in 1983, both the 1913 Act and the pilotage provisions of the MSA 1979 were repealed and replaced by the PA 1983. The responsibility of administering a pilotage district was upon a pilotage authority, which licensed pilots for its district and, where there was a compulsory pilotage, it granted pilotage certificates to masters. Its other functions were the making and enforcement of bylaws, pilotage charges and approval of pilots' boats. It could also employ pilots, but the majority of pilots, however, were self-employed.[93]

Finally, a new statute was passed in 1987, which came into force in 1 October 1988, to simplify the law of pilotage. It made radical changes to the provision of pilotage services by transferring the functions of pilotage from a pilotage authority to the harbour authorities. Nevertheless, there had been some provisions in this Act which lacked clarity and, perhaps, contributed to the problems encountered by the Milford Haven port authority in *The Sea Empress*. This resulted in the review of pilotage and the duties of the harbour authorities by the implementation of a Code for Port Marine Operations in 2001, as mentioned under Section A of this chapter. In addition, the Act was amended by the Pilotage (Recognition of Qualifications and Experience) Regulations 2003 in order to implement the EU Directive 1999/42/EC on mutual recognition of qualifications and experience of pilots by Member States.

By s 1 of the PA 1987, the responsibility for provision of pilotage services was placed upon a class of harbour authorities, which are managing their harbours under statutory powers, designated as 'competent harbour authorities', the functions of which will be seen later.

---

92 Op cit, Douglas and Geen, fn 8, Chapters 19 and 20, for a detailed history and development of legislation in pilotage law.

93 Op cit, Douglas and Geen, fn 8, Chapter 19.

A pilot is defined in s 31(1) of the PA 1987, as amended by the MSA 1995, as 'any person not belonging to a ship who has the conduct thereof'.[94]

2 DUTIES OF A COMPETENT HARBOUR AUTHORITY IN RELATION TO PILOTAGE

2.1 Provision of pilotage service

Competent harbour authorities have specific powers under the Pilotage Act (PA) 1987 to enable them to discharge the pilotage duties imposed under that Act. They have a duty by s 2(1) of the Act to keep under consideration the following:

(a) whether any and, if so, what pilotage services need to be provided to secure the safety of ships navigating in or in the approaches to its harbour; and

(b) whether in the interests of safety, pilotage should be compulsory for ships navigating in any part of that harbour or its approaches and, if so, for which ships and in which circumstances and what pilotage services need to be provided for those ships.

Furthermore, each competent harbour authority shall, in performance of its duties, have regard, in particular, to the hazards involved in the carriage of dangerous goods or harmful substances by ships.

By s 2(3) of the Act, each competent harbour authority should provide such pilotage services as it considers necessary. Section 11 allows that the duty of providing pilotage services – as considered to be necessary by a competent harbour authority under s 2 – may, by arrangement, be provided on its behalf by another competent harbour authority or an agent.

The designation of an area as a compulsory pilotage area is left at the discretion of the competent harbour authority, by s 7 of the Act, if it considers that it would be necessary in the interests of safety. Unlike the 1983 Act, the present statute does not contain any classes of ships which would be exempt from compulsory pilotage, such as Her Majesty's ships and ferryboats. The only exempt ships are small boats of less than 20 metres long, or fishing boats registered as being less than 47.5 metres in length (s 7(3)).

The harbour authorities must ensure that any vessel which they own or operate and use in the exercise of their functions, otherwise than for pilotage, is subject to the same pilotage obligations as any other vessel (s 9).

These duties should now be read in conjunction with the Code of Good Practice

---

94 Detailed provisions relating to pilot ladders and safety issues can be found in Merchant Shipping Notice (MSN 1716) which includes the IMO Resolution on Pilot Transfer Arrangements, amplifying SOLAS 1974, Chapter V, reg 17. The Merchant Shipping (Pilot Transport Arrangements) Regulations 1999 (SI 1999/17) replaced the Merchant Shipping (Pilot Ladders and Hoists) Regulations 1987 and implemented SOLAS 1974, Chapter V, reg, 17. It came into force on 10 February 1999, and includes duties of the shipowner, master and officers of the ship in relation to safety, providing for penalties in the event of contravention of its provisions, which is made a criminal offence.

for Port Marine Operations, seen earlier.[95] The principle of accountability, which has been the main objective of the review of pilotage services, applies to the discharge of the authority's statutory duties. The harbour authority's duty relates to safety of navigation and regulation of marine operations. Safety of navigation is a public right; provision of pilotage is a specific duty to facilitate the public right. But, harbour authorities are not publicly accountable at large.

However, a harbour authority which fails to provide adequate services of pilots might incur liability to the owner of a ship which sustains damage in consequence of the absence of pilots in the port.[96] If a pilot is provided but he is incompetent, it has been uncertain whether the authority will be liable to the owner for damage sustained by his ship. Such uncertainty has arisen because of the interpretation given to s 22(8) of the PA 1987 which excludes liability of the harbour authority for damage caused by an act or omission of a pilot authorised by it (as will be seen later under paras 7 and 8). But, in the light of the review of the duties of the harbour authorities after *The Sea Empress* and the recent Code of Good Practice, harbour authorities should guard against such risks of pilots' incompetence by proper risk management and seek to obtain insurance cover. In addition, the harbour authority may be liable under other statutes.

In *The Sea Empress*,[97] the Milford Haven port authority was prosecuted by the Environment Agency under s 85(1) of the Water Resources Act 1991, it pleaded guilty to the offence which imposes strict liability, and paid a fine. The inexperience of the pilot involved, and the lack of a coherent policy by the port in pilotage services, were highly criticised by the court and raised great concerns in the industry which led to the introduction of rules of best practice for training and familiarisation of pilots.

2.2 Authorisation of pilots

There has been a major change introduced by the 1987 Act in the engagement of pilots. By contrast to the PA 1983, which gave power to a pilotage authority to license pilots, now, by s 3 of the 1987 Act, it is the harbour authority that has power to **authorise** (instead of merely licensing) persons to act as pilots in their harbour. Although, under each Act, the purpose has been to ensure that pilots have the necessary qualifications, the difference is that, in the past, a licence enabled the pilot to act in the district in which he was licensed, while, under s 3 of the present Act, the authorisation must be coupled with a contract of employment or otherwise enable him to act as an authorised pilot in a particular harbour.

By s 3, as amended by the Pilotage (Recognition of Qualifications and Experience) Regulations 2003, each competent harbour authority may authorise suitably qualified pilots in its area. Authorisations may relate to ships of a particular description and to particular parts of the harbour. The authority must follow the

---

95 See Section A of this chapter.

96 *Anchor Line (Henderson Bros) Ltd v Dundee Harbour Trustees* (1922) 38 TLR 299; the case is still good law under the present statute.

97 [1999] 1 Lloyd's Rep 673.

guidelines of Sched A1 (inserted into the Act by the above Regulations) in determining the qualifications and experience for authorisation and, once the person is authorised, he should have an adaptation period. The authority may employ the person under a contract of employment, which must be offered to him, or a contract for services (s 4).

The employment status of pilots has been a contentious issue. Whatever arrangements are made for the use of pilots, they must safeguard the authority's position of control. Employment is a default option and the easier way of integrating pilotage services. Pilots should become direct employees of the port authority and not of a subsidiary of the authority, as was the Milford Haven Pilotage Ltd.[98]

An authorisation must specify the area within which it has effect and it may limit the pilot's authority to certain parts of the harbour or types of ships. The authorisation may be suspended if the pilot is found guilty of misconduct or has ceased to have the relevant qualifications, or when the number of pilots required exceeds the needs of the area.

Section 8 allows a competent harbour authority to issue exemption certificates, upon the application of a master or mate of a ship, where a pilotage is compulsory, to enable him to navigate that ship in the area concerned without a pilot, if it is satisfied that his experience, skill and knowledge of the local area and of the English language are sufficient.

All of these duties have been reviewed by the recent consultation paper on pilotage services (see under Section A above) regarding the Code for Port Marine Operations, and an emphasis has been placed on the duty of the harbour authority properly to train pilots and keep pilotage and safety procedures under constant review by systematic application of risk assessment and management.

3 CHARGES BY THE COMPETENT HARBOUR AUTHORITY

The authority is authorised, by s 10 of the PA 1987, to make reasonable charges for the services of pilots authorised by it, and for expenses reasonably incurred in connection with the pilot's services. Such charges may include:

(a) charges for the services of an authorised pilot;

(b) charges for expenses incurred by the pilot in providing his services;

(c) penalties for failure to keep an estimated arrival or departure time;

(d) charges for providing, maintaining and operating a pilot boat;

(e) any other costs in providing and maintaining the authority's pilot organisation.

Pilotage charges must be published in such manner as to bring them to the notice of those persons likely to be interested.

There is no maritime lien for pilotage charges. The charges are recoverable as a debt, which is enforceable under s 20(2)(i) of the Supreme Court Act 1981 by an *in rem* claim form.

---

98 Op cit, Consultation Paper, fn 62.

4 DUTIES OF MASTERS AND PILOTS IN A COMPULSORY PILOTAGE AREA

Once a compulsory pilotage area is designated, a ship navigated in that area must be under the pilotage of an authorised pilot, accompanied by an assistant, if that is required, or the master must hold an exemption certificate that he is qualified and, thus, he does not need a pilot (s 15). A master who navigates in a compulsory pilotage area, without notifying the competent harbour authority that he proposes to do so, will be guilty of an offence and liable of summary conviction (s 15(3)).[99] If any ship is not under such pilotage after an authorised pilot has offered to take charge of the ship, the master will be guilty of an offence, liable on summary conviction (s 15(2)).

It is not an offence, nor is it prohibited, to be in a compulsory pilotage area without a pilot if an offer has not been made, but the master has to look out for one.[100]

What constitutes an offer by a pilot? The offer must be clearly communicated in relation to the particular movement of the ship and it is a question of fact.[101] Mere display of the pilot flag may not be sufficient to constitute an offer (s 15). An offer made on the basis that the pilot would return next morning, instead of offering his services during the evening tide, would not be a reasonable offer.[102]

However, these principles as derived from old decisions should now be questioned in the light of the pilotage review and the review of the duties of harbour authorities.

The master of the ship is also under an obligation, by s 50, to display a pilot signal in a compulsory area. When the offer is accepted, the master has an obligation to provide information about the ship (s 18) and facilitate the pilot boarding and leaving his ship (s 20).

An authorised pilot has a right to supersede an unauthorised one. It would be an offence if the master has an unauthorised pilot on board, without first notifying the harbour authority, or if he continues to employ him after an authorised pilot made an offer (s 17).

---

99 See, also, *Muller v Trinity House* (1924) 20 LlL Rep 56; *Clayton v Albertsen* [1972] 2 Lloyd's Rep 457, where the master was prosecuted because he failed to be under pilotage and failed to display a pilot signal in circumstances in which pilotage was compulsory in the Tyne Pilotage District, for the purpose of entering and making use of the Port of Tyne, if the ship was carrying passengers, contrary to the PA 1913, ss 11 and 43. The charges were dismissed because it was found, on the facts, that the drivers of the lorries carried on the ship were not passengers!

100 *Muller v Trinity House* (1924) 20 LlL Rep 56; *Rindby v Brewis* (1926) 25 LlL Rep 26.

101 *Babbs v Press* [1971] 2 Lloyd's Rep 383.

102 *The Ignition* [1983] 1 Lloyd's Rep 382.

5 PILOT'S AUTHORITY AND DIVISION OF CONTROL BETWEEN MASTER AND PILOT

The master remains in command of the vessel.[103] A pilot is a person not belonging to a ship who has the conduct of her: s 31(1) of the PA 1987. The pilot's duties are confined to navigation and he does not supersede the master. But the pilot is the person best qualified to appraise the situation in the particular area in which he has been authorised. Co-operation and assistance, in looking out for danger, in guiding the pilot how to handle the ship, and ensuring that the crew carry out the pilot's instructions is expected from the master.[104]

Under the Merchant Shipping (Reporting Requirements for Ships Carrying Dangerous or Polluting Goods) Regulations 1995, reg 12, the master of a ship before entering port in the UK, or a port of another Member State of the European Union, must complete a checklist giving details of the ship, her equipment, crew and survey certificates, and also make that list available to any pilot boarding the ship.

Under reg 13, if the pilot engaged in berthing or unberthing a ship in UK waters learns of deficiencies in the ship, which may prejudice its safe navigation, he must immediately inform the port authority. If he boards a ship, knowing or believing that she has defects which may prejudice her safe navigation, he shall notify the master. Upon the master failing to notify the port authority of the defects in question, the pilot must himself notify the port authority (reg 14). Failure to comply with these regulations, or the deliberate making of false statements, is a criminal offence (reg 15).

An authorised pilot engaged in the berthing and unberthing of a vessel in the United Kingdom, or engaged on a vessel bound for a port within an EU Member State, must immediately inform the harbour authority whenever he learns, in the course of his normal duties, that there are deficiencies in the ship which may prejudice her safe navigation, or which may pose a threat of harm to the environment.[105] The harbour authority shall immediately inform the Maritime and Coastguard Agency.

The respective duties of a pilot and master were clearly defined as long ago as 1850, in *The Christiana*,[106] by Baron Parke:

> The duties of the master and the pilot in many respects are clearly defined. Although the pilot has charge of the ship, the owners are most clearly responsible to third persons for the sufficiencies of the ship and her equipments, the competency of the master and crew, and their obedience to the orders of the pilot in everything that concerns his duty, and under ordinary circumstances we think that his commands are to be implicitly obeyed. To him belongs the whole conduct of the navigation of the ship, to the safety of which it is important that the chief direction should be vested in one only.

The master is entitled to rely on the pilot's guidance, and he cannot interfere with

---

103 MSA 1995, s 313(1).

104 *Owners of SS Alexander Shukoff v SS Gothland* [1921] 1 AC 216 (HL); *The Nord* [1916] P 53; *The Hans Hoth* [1952] 2 Lloyd's Rep 341.

105 The Merchant Shipping (Port State Control) Regulations 1995 (SI 1995/3128, as amended), reg 15.

106 (1850) 13 ER 841.

the pilot's actions except in extreme necessity, for example, when there is a danger to his ship.[107] Otherwise, he may be held liable for negligence. However, situations of conflict or misunderstanding are not uncommon and they may vary from master to master and their underlying personalities.

The Prinses Juliana [108]

The *P* and the *E* came into collision in the entrance to Harwich Harbour. Shortly before the collision, the master of the *P* took the navigation of the vessel out of the hands of the compulsory pilot and countermanded his order. Bucknill J stated that:

> If the master sees fit to take the navigation out of the hands of the pilot and counter-mand his orders, he must satisfy the court that he was justified in so doing, and that the action which he took was at all events more calculated to avoid a collision than the manoeuvre which he countermanded.[109]

It was held that, on the facts of the case, the master of the *P* wrongly and without any justification took the matter out of the pilot's hands and without the pilot's consent. He also gave a wrong order, without which the collision would not have occurred.

Before the abolition of the defence of compulsory pilotage (by s 15 of the PA 1913) – on which a shipowner could previously rely to disclaim liability for damage caused by his ship while she was under compulsory pilotage – the pilotage authority had to prove that there was negligence on the part of the shipowner's servants. It was necessary, therefore, to distinguish between the duties of the pilot and the master. Since the above Act came into force (and the subsequent Acts, which replaced it), such need does not arise as far as English law is concerned. It will be seen later how the courts have construed this section to impose liability for the negligence of the pilot upon the shipowner.

It suffices at this point to mention that, even in compulsory pilotage areas, the duties of the master and crew remain the same, namely, to give assistance to the pilot to navigate the ship, as was illustrated by the House of Lords in *Owners of SS Alexander Shukoff v SS Gothland*,[110] per Lord Birkenhead:

> ... this rule, which is intended as a measure of security, does not mean, and must not be taken to mean, that a pilot when once he is in charge of a vessel is so circum-stanced that the master and crew owe him no duty to inform him of circumstances which, whether he has noticed them himself or not, are material for him to know in directing the navigation of the vessel. The master and crew are not mere passengers when a pilot is on board by compulsion of law. The pilot is entitled to their assist-ance, and to apply the defence of compulsory pilotage to a case where the accident would have been averted if such assistance had been given, though in fact it was not, would defeat the policy which has created the defence, and so far from increasing the safety of navigation would actually increase its risks.

---

107 'If the pilot is intoxicated, or steering a course to the certain destruction of the vessel, the master, no doubt, may interfere and ought to interfere, but it is only in urgent cases.' *The Peerless* (1860) 167 ER 16, p 17, per Dr Lushington.

108 [1936] P 139.

109 Ibid, pp 149–150.

110 [1921] AC 216 (HL), p 223.

And he went on to quote Lord Alverstone (p 224):

> In *The Tactician* Lord Alverstone CJ, stated the rule in these terms: 'The cardinal principle to be borne in mind in these pilotage cases ... is that the pilot is in sole charge of the ship ...', and he expressed his agreement with the opinions of the very learned judges, from Dr Lushington downwards. ... 'as to the danger of a divided command, and the danger of interference with the conduct of the pilot; and that if anything of that kind amounts to an interference or a divided command serious risk is run of the ship losing the benefit of the compulsory pilotage ... But side by side with that principle is the other principle that the pilot is entitled to the fullest assistance of a competent master and crew, of a competent lookout, and a well found ship ... The cases in which the master has to interfere at all with the pilot very rarely occur, but ... there is, or may be, a distinction between interference and bringing to the pilot's notice anything which the pilot ought to know. The pilot has a good many things to attend to, particularly in a place like the Thames, and certainly it is not putting the case too high to say that he is entitled to full information with regard to any surrounding fact which it is important that he should know'.

The importance of efficient team work, between the pilot, the master, the engineers and the officers on watch (e.g. the cadet and chief officer) was highlighted by the court in **The Torepo**,[111] which grounded in the Patagonian Channels of South America, perhaps due to miscommunication between those in charge of navigation, and also due to an erroneous transposition of figures on the charts.

6 LIABILITY OF A PILOT

Under s 21 of the PA 1987, a pilot may be guilty of an offence and be summarily convicted to imprisonment for a term not exceeding six months, or a fine, or convicted on indictment to imprisonment for a term not exceeding two years, or to a fine, or both, if:

(a) he does any act which causes, or is likely to cause the loss or destruction of, or serious damage to, the ship or its machinery, navigational equipment or safety equipment, or the death of, or serious injury to, a person on board the ship; or

(b) he omits to do anything required to preserve the ship or its machinery, navigational equipment or safety equipment from loss, destruction or serious damage, or to preserve any person on board the ship from death or serious injury; and

(c) the act or omission is deliberate or amounts to a breach or neglect of duty, or he is under the influence of drink, or a drug, at the time of the act or omission.

The pilot must exercise reasonable skill and care in the performance of his duties and acquaint himself with the local conditions. Whether performing compulsory pilotage or not, he will be liable for his own negligence. His liability may be limited to £1000 and the amount of the pilotage charges in respect of the voyage during which the liability was incurred (s 22(2)). Obviously, there is not much point in suing him to recover that little.

---

111 [2002] 2 Lloyd's Rep 535.

The target for a claimant who sustained damage or loss by a ship due to negligence of the pilot on board is the shipowner, even if the ship was navigated by the pilot in a compulsory pilotage area. By the passing of the PA 1913, the defence of compulsory pilotage was abolished because s 15 made the owner, or the master of the ship, answerable[112] for any loss or damage caused by the vessel or by any fault of the navigation of the vessel in the same manner as he would if pilotage were not compulsory.

There is a policy reason that the statutes on pilotage law following the 1913 Act have adopted the same provision.

It will be seen shortly that the courts have consistently held the shipowner liable not only to third parties, but also for damage sustained by his ship due to the pilot's negligence whether or not the pilot is an independent contractor or a person whose general employer might be the harbour authority. They have held that a pilot is the employee of the shipowner *pro tempora* during the time of the navigation of the ship.[113]

7 LIABILITY OF HARBOUR AUTHORITIES WITH RESPECT TO PILOTAGE

The duty of the authority under the 1987 Act is to provide adequate pilotage services and qualified pilots to do the job.

Section 22(8) expressly provides that the harbour authority shall not be liable for any loss or damage caused by an act or omission of a pilot authorised by them by virtue only of that authorisation. The PA 1983 had a similar provision (s 17).

Licensing, as it was under the older statute, or authorising pilots, as it is under the present statute, does not involve the authority in any liability for negligence of pilots so authorised. The reason given in decided cases is that the authority is not the principal in the piloting of ships, nor is it involved in the conduct of management of the particular ship which sustains damage.[114]

Upon reading s 22(3), however, which entitles the authority to limit liability for the negligence of a pilot whom they employ, it would appear that this sub-section is in conflict with s 22(8). But a distinction is intended to be drawn between the power of a harbour authority merely to authorise pilots and situations in which the authority employs qualified pilots. While the authority will not be liable for the negligence of a properly qualified pilot who is authorised by the harbour authority to act, it will be liable for the negligence of a pilot whom it employs. The authority will also be liable for damage caused by the lack or inadequate pilotage services, or the negligence of a pilot who is not properly qualified and trained for breach of both its statutory and common law duties, as seen under section A and para 2 above.

---

112 'Answerable' means responsible in terms of damage sustained by the ship due to pilot's negligence, or of damage done to third parties: *Towerfield v Workington Harbour & Dock Board* (1950) 84 LlL Rep 233 (HL).

113 *The Cavendish* [1993] 2 Lloyd's Rep 292.

114 *Fowles v Eastern and Australian Steamship Co Ltd* [1916] 2 AC 556 (PC); *The Esso Bernicia* [1989] AC 643.

It is submitted that, at present times, if a pilot is not properly qualified or trained but he is, nevertheless, authorised by the harbour authority, the latter should be accountable and liable for the damage caused due to the faults of a non-properly qualified pilot. Support for such a proposition is gained from the Code for Ports Marine Operations and the guide of good practice, in that the duty of the authority will be to ensure that pilots are properly qualified and trained for the job. The review of the duties of harbour authorities under the PA 1987 by the Code will have the effect of making the authority assume responsibility for safe pilotage.[115] The Code requires each harbour authority to hold itself accountable for the discharge of its duties and powers to the standard laid down. It requires the board members of each authority to accept responsibility for ensuring that the authority discharges its duties and powers to that standard. Duties and powers relating to the safety of marine operations in any harbour have been entrusted to a statutory authority. Board members are collectively and individually responsible for the proper exercise of their authority's legal duties. It follows clearly that it, and they, are severally and collectively the 'duty holder'.[116]

The question whether a duty of care might be owed to third parties by the harbour authority for the negligence of a non-properly qualified pilot causing economic loss will be met with the same legal considerations as those in relation to classification societies, discussed in Chapter 11; namely, that it will not be fair or reasonable to impose such a duty on the port authorities.

The limitation of harbour authorities' liability is governed by s 191 of the MSA 1995.

8 LIABILITY OF THE SHIPOWNER FOR NEGLIGENCE OF THE PILOT

Under common law, owners of vessels were always held liable whenever they took on a pilot in a non-compulsory pilotage area. But where pilotage was compulsory, the owners were not liable because the pilot could not be regarded as the owners' servant or someone for whose acts and omissions the owners should be liable. This rule had been enshrined in s 633 of the MSA 1894, which provided:

> An owner or master of a ship shall not be answerable to any person whatever for any loss or damage occasioned by the fault or incapacity of any qualified pilot acting in charge of that ship within any district where the employment of a qualified pilot is compulsory by law.

By contrast, Art 5 of the Brussels Collision Convention 1910 provided that the liability imposed by the articles of the Convention attached in cases where the collision was caused by the fault of a pilot, even where the pilot was carried by compulsion of law. This provision had effect only in collision cases, but it was not

---

115 See also Section A of this chapter; Lord Jauncey in *The Esso Bernicia* [1989] AC 643 (see para 8, above) said that, theoretically, it is possible that the general employer, port authority, may be liable if it assumes responsibility for safe pilotage.

116 Department for Transport on Port Marine Safety Code: www.dft.gov.uk.

enacted in the Maritime Convention Act 1911, which brought the Collision Convention into English law.

However, the defence of compulsory pilotage (as mentioned under para 6, above) was first abolished by s 15 of the PA 1913, which provided:

> Notwithstanding anything in any public or local Act, the owner or master of a vessel navigating under circumstances in which pilotage is compulsory shall be answerable for any loss or damage caused by the vessel or by any fault of the navigation of the vessel in the same manner as he would if pilotage were not compulsory.

Section 15 was wider than Art 5 of the Collision Convention. Next came the repeal of the 1913 Act by the consolidating Pilotage Act 1983, and s 35 of this Act was identical to s 15 of the PA 1913.

Problems of construction of the wording of this section gave rise to interesting decisions, which perhaps provided the ground for the amendment of the same provision by the equivalent section of the 1987 Act, s 16. It was thought that the new Act intended to change the law, but this was not so (see later).

It will help to consider, first, how the courts construed s 15 of the 1913 Act, and then see whether s 16 of the 1987 Act brought any change.

The Towerfield[117]

The case involved a ship in charge of a compulsory pilot, which was approaching an English harbour and went aground on undredged accumulated river silt. She sustained damage and also caused damage to the harbour. It was found, on the facts, that both the harbour authority and the pilot were negligent and their negligence contributed to the casualty. The harbour authority were negligent in that they failed to discharge their duty to ascertain the condition of the channel and to communicate the relevant information either to the master or to the pilot. The duty to give warning to the master arose from the relation of invitor and invitee. The argument by the harbour board that the pilot was intimately acquainted with the port and that he knew, or at any rate they were entitled to assume that he knew, the port's exact condition was rejected.

Regarding the pilot's negligence, the House of Lords held the shipowner responsible, not only for the damage which his ship sustained, but also for the damage to the harbour on the basis of s 15 of the PA 1913.

In particular, the issue was whether 'answerable' meant more than the damage just done by the ship to the harbour, so as to include damage suffered by the ship.

The owners' submissions were that, on the language of the section, the effect of the change of the law was that they would be liable for any loss or damage to other persons, in case the negligence of the pilot was imputed to them, but, on the other hand, the section did not prevent them from claiming damage done to their ship.

Although Lord Norman criticised the clumsy drafting of this section, he said:

> The wording of s 15 is not happy. The word 'answerable' is not the cause of the difficulty, and it is merely the equivalent of 'responsible'. But the words 'answerable

---

117 [1951] AC 112.

for any loss or damage caused by the vessel', though apt when the claim is against the owner of a ship, are incapable of applying when the claim is by the owner for damage done to his ship. The words 'answerable for any loss or damage caused . . . by any fault of the navigation of the vessel' are ill chosen and clumsy, but they are capable of applying to the shipowner's claim.[118]

Despite the admission by Lord Norman that, in his view, the words used in the section were incapable of applying to the shipowners' claim, his final conclusion cannot be supported by his interpretation of the section.

The majority of the Court of Appeal in this case had accepted that, while the liability of a shipowner for the negligence of the pilot was applicable to a claim in tort, it held that it had no application in a contractual situation. In their view of this case, the harbour had offered to receive any ship on the terms that the channel was safely dredged and, by entering the port, *The Towerfield* had accepted such an offer.

The House of Lords did not accept this, and reversed the decision. Lord Potter said robustly in this respect:

My Lords, for the purpose of this decision and without staying to consider its accuracy, I am prepared to accept the suggestion that such a contract was so formed. But I do not find myself able to agree with the contention that the withdrawal of the protection given to ships employing a compulsory pilot affects only cases where a claim in tort is made.

Taking the view which I do, that upon the true construction of the Act a shipowner is, after the beginning of 1918, to be responsible for the acts of a compulsory pilot, I do not find myself influenced by a consideration of the history of the negotiations leading to a change in the law. The provisions of the Act, as I think, themselves plainly attribute to shipowners liability for the fault of a compulsory pilot in all cases and I can, therefore, see no reason for differentiating between contract and tort, more particularly as this appears to have been accepted as the correct view from the time when the Act came into force until the present day.[119]

Lord Potter gave the following answer to the owners' submissions, and also dealt with the effect of the port authority's negligence in the light of the strict liability of the owner under s 74 of the HDPCA 1847 (which was mentioned under para 4 of Section A of this chapter). Since this will be a relevant consideration in pilotage cases as well, it is worth reviewing it in this context:

My Lords . . . the section says that the owner or master shall be answerable for any loss or damage caused by the vessel, or by any fault of the navigation of the vessel. In the present case, the damage to *The Towerfield* was undoubtedly caused by faulty navigation, but when the Act says that the owner shall be answerable for that faulty navigation, it has to be determined whether 'answerable' means more than that the damage, whether done to or done by his ship, is his responsibility or is confined to damage done by the ship. Either view no doubt is theoretically possible but I do not think that read in its context the use of the word 'answerable' would naturally convey the suggestion that, though the shipowner is liable for any damage done by the pilot's fault, yet he can recover his own damage in full. 'Answerable', as I think, simply means responsible, and a shipowner who through a compulsory pilot is

---

118 Ibid, p 145.
119 [1951] AC 112, p 134.

responsible for faulty navigation is responsible for damage to his own ship as well as for injury to the property of another . . .[120]

There remains, however, to be determined the contention put forward by the harbour board that though their negligence may be one of the causes of the disaster, yet they can recover by reason of the terms of s 74 of the HDPCA 1847.

The section has, my Lords, been considered at least four times and has twice been fully discussed . . .

In *River Wear Commissioners v Adamson* . . . where the matter was fully discussed, Lord Gordon took the first view and Lord Cairns the second. The other noble Lords agreed with Lord Cairns in holding the shipowner not liable, but with considerable doubt and in the case of the majority, as I think, because that liability only attached where the ship was still in charge of and controlled by some person. This, at any rate, seems to have been the reasoning upon which the Court of Appeal acted and your Lordships' House approved their judgment.

The next case to reach your Lordships' House was *Great Western Rly Co v Mostyn (Owners)*, but before that case was considered Roche J (in *Det Forenede Dampskibs Selskab v Barry Rly Co* followed the decision in the *River Wear* case in holding a shipowner not absolutely liable, but excused in a case where the damage to the harbour works was, in part at least, caused by the fault of the harbour authority. As I read the decision in *The Mostyn*, however, the majority of their Lordships took the view that the shipowner was responsible for damage done to harbour works whether he was in fault or not, save in a case similar to that decided in the *River Wear* judgment. Accordingly, where the ship had been abandoned and was therefore out of the control of its owners, they agreed that no liability attached under the section. But, save for that concession, they decided in terms, as I think, that the only exception from liability was that afforded to an abandoned ship . . .

I would only add that, like those of your Lordships who are of the same opinion, I would limit the damages to those directly caused to the harbour, in which, as the shipowners concede, are to be included the restoration of the channel to the condition in which it was before the stranding of *The Towerfield*, but I would not embrace amongst them any loss of revenue to which the harbour board have been put thereby. Save to this extent I think the claim and counterclaim fail.[121]

It was discussed in Section A of this chapter, under s 74,[122] that when the incident occurred in this case, the LR(CN)A 1945 was not in force, albeit that the case was decided in 1951. If the case on these facts was decided today, it is submitted that although the port authority would not have to prove negligence on the part of the owner for the purpose of s 74, the shipowner would be able to plead contributory negligence on the ground of breach of statutory duty by the port authority to maintain the port in a safe condition, which contributed to the damage suffered by both the ship and the harbour. If this is not correct, the owners would have a separate claim against the harbour authority for damage to their ship on the basis of breach of the statutory duty to maintain the port in a safe condition (see para 3.2.3 of Section A). In any case, it is time that this old section is reconsidered and amended to reflect the changes of present times. It is submitted that the ship owner

---

120 Ibid, p, 133–34.
121 [1951] AC 112, pp 135–136.
122 Section A, para 4, above.

today should be able to pursue his cause of action for damage to his ship against the authority for breach of the statutory duty to maintain the port in safe condition and provide efficient pilotage services. Such duties are reinforced by the review of harbour authorities' duties in recent years and the emphasis on their obligation to implement risk assessment for safe marine operations in ports. Information documented in relation to the safety management system pursuant to the Code for port safe marine operations will be used as evidence in support of the breach of duty. There is no justification both in principle and policy (such as protectionism) why such action should not be maintained against a harbour authority.

The construction of s 15 of the PA 1913 was again examined, almost 40 years later, by the House of Lords in the following case, but the main issue in this case was concerned with s 15. The case did not involve negligence of the harbour authority to make the port safe for navigation, as the previous case did.

The Esso Bernicia[123]

In 1978, *The Esso Bernicia* with a pilot on board was being berthed at a jetty in an oil terminal (a compulsory pilot area) in Shetland Islands with three tugs in attendance. A tow-line had been secured by one of the tugs, S. At about midnight, a coupling blew out of a hydraulic pipe above the engine exhaust of the tug. The escaped hydraulic oil caught fire and the tow-line was cut off. *The Esso Bernicia* was no longer under the control of the other two tugs and came into contact with mooring dolphins, whereby she and the dolphins sustained damage. Large quantities of bunker oil escaped. The tug S had been designed and built by Hall Russell Co Ltd for the purpose of berthing tankers at the oil terminal. The owners of *The Esso Bernicia* brought an action against the ship builders, Hall Russell, on the ground of negligence in the building of the tug, for an indemnity with respect to oil pollution liabilities incurred to third parties and for damage to the jetty. The pilotage authority were joined as third parties to the action. The shipbuilders averred that the pilot on board the vessel had caused the accident, and that the pilotage authority was vicariously liable for his acts and omissions, being an employee of the authority. When the incident happened in 1983, the PA 1913 was, just, still in force.

Despite powerful previous authorities on the issue, counsel for the shipbuilders was not deterred from arguing that the pilotage authority, being the general employer of the pilot, were vicariously liable. He maintained that while the owner was responsible throughout to third parties for the acts and omissions of the pilot, he was not the master of the pilot for the purposes of any damage which the pilot caused to him. Therefore, he could sue both the pilot (*Lister v Romford Ice and Cold Storage Co Ltd* [1957] AC 555) and, if he was employed by an authority, his employer. Thus, he argued, so far as the pilot was concerned it mattered not whether he fell to be treated as the servant of the owner, or an independent contractor for the purposes of a negligent act. In either event, the owner could recover from him subject always to any statutory limitation of liability.

Lord Jauncey took the opportunity to analyse both principle and policy:

---

123 [1989] AC 643, [1988] 2 Lloyd's Rep 8.

The critical question is whether the owner can recover from a general employer of the pilot . . .

The fact that he was an independent contractor did not alter the common law rule that when he had been engaged voluntarily by a shipowner he was, so far as any acts or omissions on his part were concerned, the servant of the shipowner. The rule operated whether he was in the general employment of a pilotage authority, or whether he was an independent contractor . . . My Lords, nothing that has been said on behalf of Hall Russell persuades me that the rationale of the line of authority to which I have referred was wrong or that there is any exception to the general application of s 15 of the Act of 1913 to damage suffered by a ship under pilotage. Subject only to what I have to say in the context of Hall Russell's second submission, the pilot is to be considered for all purposes as the servant of the owner . . . If Hall Russell's argument were correct, there would follow the curious result that the doctrine of *respondeat superior* would apply to two different masters in respect of two different claims of damage arising out of a single act of negligence. It is a well recognised principle, exemplified in cases involving crane drivers, that a servant in the general employment of A may, for a particular purpose, be treated as in the *pro hac vice* employment of B. However, there is no principle which permits a servant to be in the *de jure* employment of two separate masters at one and the same time.[124]

The shipbuilders' second argument was that the pilotage authority had assumed the responsibility of piloting ships and had held themselves out as undertaking pilotage services as principals of the pilot.

Lord Jauncey rejected this argument also, and concluded by stating a general rule:

My Lords, it may be stated as a general rule that the employer of a qualified licensed pilot is not vicariously responsible to the owner of a ship damaged by his negligence while under pilotage. All the authorities support such a rule and none appear to controvert it. The basis of the rule is twofold, namely: (1) the pilot is an independent professional man who navigates the ship as a principal and not as a servant of his general employer, and (2) s 15(1) makes him the servant of the shipowner for all purposes connected with navigation.

In stating this rule, I am not going so far as to say that an employer of a licensed pilot could never be responsible for his negligent navigation. It is theoretically possible that such an employer could himself assume the obligation of safe pilotage although, at the moment, I have very great difficulty in envisaging a situation in which such an event could occur. However, it is unnecessary to speculate further since there is nothing in the present case to take it out of the general rule.[125]

Although almost 20 years ago, Lord Jauncey could not envisage a situation in which a harbour authority could assume the obligation of safe pilotage, this does not stand today, particularly after the recent review of pilotage services by the Code of Port Safe Marine Operations by which harbour authorities assume such responsibility for safe services. Such responsibility is reinforced by the Directive 1999/42/EC, regulating the employment of competent and properly authorised and experienced pilots.

The third significant case in the line of these authorities, which is particularly

---

124 [1989] AC 643, pp 685–86.
125 Ibid, pp 690–91.

important because it was decided after the 1987 Act was in force, is *The Cavendish*. The relevant sections were ss 2 and 16 of this Act. Section 2 provides:

2(1) Each competent harbour authority shall keep under consideration:

    (a) whether any and, if so, what pilotage services to be provided to secure the safety of ships navigating in the approaches to its harbour; and

    (b) whether in the interests of safety, pilotage should be compulsory for ships navigating in any part of that harbour or its approaches and, if so, for which ships and in which circumstances and what pilotage services need to be provided for those ships.

  (2) without prejudice to the generality of sub-s (1) above, each competent harbour authority shall in performing its function under that subsection have regard in particular to the hazards involved in the carriage of dangerous goods or harmful substances by ships.

  (3) Each competent harbour authority shall provide such pilotage services as it considers need to be provided as mentioned in sub-s (1)(a) and (b) above.

Section 16 provides:

The fact that a ship is being navigated in an area and in circumstances in which pilotage is compulsory for it, shall not affect any liability of the owner or master of the ship for any loss or damage caused by the ship or by the manner in which it is navigated.

The Cavendish[126]

Briefly, the defendants, Port of London Authority (PLA), provided pilotage services under the PA 1987. They had directed that pilotage be compulsory for ships navigating in the approaches to the River Thames. The plaintiffs requested the services of a pilot to pilot *The Cavendish* from the seaward limit of their pilotage jurisdiction. A pilot was duly provided and took charge of the vessel. About 40 minutes later, the vessel struck the Sunk Head Tower and/or buoy, in the approaches to the Thames, resulting in damage to her. The plaintiff sought to recover their loss and expense from PLA. For the purpose of determining a preliminary issue about the effect of ss 2 and 16 of the 1987 Act, the parties agreed that it was to be assumed, without being admitted, that the loss suffered by the plaintiffs was caused by the negligence of the pilot.

The first issue was whether s 2 of the 1987 Act imposed a positive duty upon the authority to pilot ships, therefore, becoming vicariously liable for the negligence of the pilot. The second issue was whether PLA was liable to the plaintiffs in contract, having contracted to supply pilotage services subject to a statutory or common law implied term that such services would be performed with reasonable skill and care and that the claim was not precluded by s 16 of the Act.

Clarke J (as he then was) held on the first issue that the effect of s 2 of the 1987 Act was not to impose duties upon competent authorities to pilot ships, but to require them to supply properly authorised pilots for ships.[127] If the law had intended to provide for this new duty upon an authority, it could have been done in

---

126 [1993] 2 Lloyd's Rep 292.
127 The judge applied the principle of *Fowles v Eastern and Australian Steamship Co Ltd* [1916] 2 AC 556.

clear and unequivocal terms. In essence, s 2 gave statutory definition to duties which were, in practice, assumed by pilotage authorities under the earlier legislation. Therefore, PLA were not vicariously liable in tort for the negligence of the pilot.

On the second issue, he held that there was no basis for holding that a contract existed between the parties.[128] It was no more than an arrangement between PLA and the plaintiffs for the discharge of the shipowner's statutory obligation by taking a compulsory pilot and paying a fee provided by the regulations made under the Act.

Finally, on s 16, the plaintiffs argued that this section has changed the law, in that it prevents the shipowner from relying on the negligence of a compulsory pilot in resisting claims by third parties, but it restores the common law position so far as claims by the shipowner against the general employer of the pilot is concerned. The judge held that s 16 replaced the similar provision of the 1913 Act, and it was not intended to alter the meaning of the earlier provision but to put it into more modern language. It imposed liability for negligence of a compulsory pilot on the shipowner in respect of claims by third parties. If this was so, there was no reason for holding that the pilot was the servant of the shipowner for that purpose, but not for the purpose of making them liable to bear their own loss.

A pilot could not have two masters and, once it was held that the pilot was, for some purposes, the servant of the shipowner, he could not be at the same time the servant of his general employer, the competent authority.

This case seems to have closed any further debate on these issues, although the wording of s 16 of the 1987 Act has still not made the position clearer than its predecessor. For example, the words 'any loss or damage caused by the ship', which Lord Norman in *The Towerfield* criticised as being clumsy drafting and not capable of applying when the claim is by the owner for damage done to his ship, have been copied without any additional words referring to damage done or caused to the ship.

However, these decisions are based on policy rather than on strict legal interpretation of the wording of the relevant sections of the successive Pilotage Acts.

New issues for consideration by the courts may, however, arise in the future, and the Code on port marine operations will have to be taken into account in assisting the court, not only by way of evidence but also in redefining the scope of the duty of the harbour authorities in relation to safe marine operations. Although it is correct that the harbour authority is not in the business of piloting ships, it has a duty to provide properly qualified pilots. (*The Sea Empress* was an example of the port authority's failure to meet that duty.)

The defence of compulsory pilotage may be available by the law of the country where the wrong was committed, as in the following example.

The Waziristan [129]

The S grounded in the Shatt el Arab (in Iraqi territorial waters). The grounding was caused by an obstruction to the channel by *The Waziristan* (W), which had gone aground by negligent navigation of those on board while proceeding down the

128 The judge applied the principle in *Oceanic Crest Shipping Co v Pilbara Harbour Service Ltd* (1985) 160 CLR 626.
129 [1953] 2 Lloyd's Rep 361.

channel ahead of S. The owners of the S claimed damages from W's owners. W claimed that the grounding of S was due solely to S's negligent navigation, and that, as there was a compulsory pilot in charge on board her, they were not responsible.

Willmer J found, on the evidence, that W was not at fault for taking the ground. No negligence had been shown. He, however, went on to discuss the issue of compulsory pilotage. The question was whether the presence of a compulsory pilot on board W could be relied upon as a defence by the defendants. In Iraq, there was no equivalent provision to s 15 of the UK PA 1913 making the shipowner responsible for the negligence of a compulsory pilot. It was found that the state of the law in Iraq was such that the defendants could not be liable in this case for such negligence.

In the USA, a shipowner will be liable for the negligence of a pilot who is engaged voluntarily, but not if he is engaged in a compulsory area because the pilot will be forced by operation of law and not by choice, so as to create a relationship of a master and servant. Therefore, neither the master nor the owner of the vessel is liable *in personam* for the negligence of the compulsory pilot, provided the pilot has been solely at fault and there is no negligence on the part of the ships' personnel, or the owner, in failing to make the ship seaworthy. However, the ship itself, being regarded as a legal entity under admiralty law, is chargeable with fault for the wrong of the pilot and is subject to a suit *in rem*. The harbour authority, also, being the employer of the pilot, will be liable for the negligence of a pilot under the doctrine of *respondeat superior*.[130]

This is a sensible legal approach, and it might encourage port authorities to perform their duties more efficiently.

Limitation of liability of shipowners and others is examined in Chapter 17.

SECTION C – THE WRECK REMOVAL CONVENTION (WRC) 2007

1 INTRODUCTION

At the proofs stage of this edition, the Convention was agreed at the Diplomatic Conference in Nairobi on 18 May 2007. Only a brief summary of the main provisions of the Convention and its scope will be given here.

Although the project of the WRC had been developing for a long time, it was subordinated to the more pressing demands for the revision of the Athens Convention and the SUA (Suppression of Unlawful Acts) Protocols 2005.

As the scope of application of the Convention is to enable States to take measures to remove wrecks which are located in their Exclusive Economic Zone (EEZ), if those wrecks constitute a danger to navigation or to the marine environment, there

---

130 See Parks, A, and Cattell, E, *The Law of Tug, Tow and Pilotage*, 3rd edn, 1994, Cornell Maritime Press Inc, pp 1022–29.

were divergent views as to its scope at the meeting of the IMO Legal Committee in Paris in October 2006. It was argued that Coastal States have limited rights under UNCLOS to take action on environmental grounds in the EEZ in order to remove a wreck and there was concern that there might be incompatibility with States' sovereign rights under the Convention of the law of the sea (UNCLOS). Of course, Coastal States have jurisdiction to remove wrecks located in internal waters and their territorial sea, and as most wrecks, in reality, are found in those waters, governments, in early days of the discussions, supported the extension of the provisions of the Convention to the internal waters and territorial sea.[131] Despite opposition by some governments, this led to the 'opt-in' provision which will enable a Coastal State to make a declaration that it will apply certain articles of the Convention to wrecks in its internal and territorial waters.

The main objective of the Convention is to provide the legal basis for State parties to remove, or have removed, shipwrecks which pose a hazard to the safety of navigation, or to the marine and coastal environments, or both. Such hazard may have the potential of affecting adversely the safety of lives, goods and property at sea, including the marine environment. The Convention will fill a gap in the existing international legal framework, by providing the first set of uniform international rules aimed at ensuring the prompt and effective removal of wrecks located beyond the territorial sea. It also includes an optional clause enabling State parties to apply certain provisions of the Convention to their territorial and internal waters.[132]

2 FUNDAMENTAL PROVISIONS

The objectives and general principles of the Convention are stated in Art 2, namely, that:

a. A State party may take measures in accordance with this Convention in relation to the removal of a wreck which poses a hazard in the Convention area.

b. Measures taken by the Affected State in accordance with paragraph 1 shall be proportionate to the hazard.

c. Such measures shall not go beyond what is reasonably necessary to remove the wreck posing the hazard, and shall cease as soon as the wreck has been removed; they shall not unnecessarily interfere with the rights and interests of other States including the State of the ship's registry, and of any person, physical or corporate, concerned.

d. The application of this Convention within the Convention area shall not entitle a State party to claim or exercise sovereignty or sovereign rights over any part of the high seas.

e. State parties shall endeavour to co-operate when the effects of a maritime casualty resulting in a wreck involve a State other than the Affected State.

---

131 Report to CMI by Shaw, R., CMI News Letter No 2 May–August 2006.
132 IMO briefing 22 May 2007.

'Convention area' is defined in Art 1(1) as the EEZ established in accordance with international law or, if a State party has not established such a zone, an area beyond and adjacent to the territorial sea of that State determined by that State in accordance with international law and extending not more than 200 nautical miles from the baselines from which the breadth of its territorial sea is measured.

Articles 7, 8 and 9 set out the obligations under the Convention for locating, marking and removing wrecks which pose a hazard and that the registered owner shall remove a wreck determined to constitute a hazard, which is defined in Art 1(5) as any condition or threat that:

(a) poses a danger or impediment to navigation; or

(b) may reasonably be expected to result in major harmful consequences to the marine environment, or damage to the coastline or related interests of one or more States.

Art 6 gives extensive details of the criteria as to what may constitute a hazard.

The liability of the registered owner for the costs of locating, marking and removing the wreck is stated in Art 10, which also provides for exceptions to that liability in cases in which the maritime casualty is caused by war risks etc (being identical to the same exceptions provided for in the other Conventions, see Chapters 18 and 19 below). Art 10(1)(c) also excludes liability when the registered owner proves that the casualty was wholly caused by the negligence or other wrongful act of any Government or other authority responsible for the maintenance of lights or other navigational aids in the exercise of that function. Further exceptions to liability are provided by Art 11, in that the registered owner shall not be liable for the costs under Art 10, if, and to the extent that, liability for such costs would be in conflict with the CLC 1992, HNS 1996, the Nuclear damage Conventions, and the Bunkers Convention 2001 (see chapter 19). Compulsory insurance or financial security is extensively dealt with in Art 12 following the same pattern as is found in the other Conventions mentioned above.

Limitation of liability of the registered owner for such costs is permitted under Art 10(2), which states that nothing in this Convention shall affect the right to limit as provided for under any applicable national or international regime, such as the 1976 Limitation Convention, as amended (see chapter 17).

It is hoped that the Convention will improve the position of salvors in recovering their expenses if they are engaged to remove hazardous wrecks in EEZ of Contracting States, which may reasonably be expected to result in major harmful consequences to the marine environment, or damage to the coastline or related interests of one or more States. As discussed in chapter 13, above, apart from the LOF 1980, which provides for a safety net to encourage salvors to take steps even in the high seas in order to protect the environment, neither Art 14 of the Salvage Convention 1989, nor any LOF subsequent to 1980, provide such protection.

To prevent conflict between the WRC and the Salvage Convention, or national law, Art 11(2) of the WRC provides that to the extent that measures under this Convention are considered to be salvage under applicable national law or an international convention, such law or convention shall apply to questions of the remuneration or compensation payable to salvors. Thus, the WRC will not apply to the geographical area in which the Salvage Convention, or Art 14, applies if the measures are considered to be salvage operations.

In addition, there will be an immense contribution of this Convention, broadly, to the maritime world and the protection of the environment because the existence of a certificate of insurance will serve to allay the concerns of harbour authorities and Coastal States when there is a request for a place of refuge of a ship in distress, which might become a wreck and an obstruction to navigation in their waterways.

Among the resolutions adopted by the Conference was a resolution on compulsory insurance certificates under existing maritime liability Conventions, including this Convention, urging IMO Member States to ensure the entry into force of the other liability and compensation Conventions (seen in chapter 19) and the Athens Convention 2002 (seen in chapter 18). The Conference invited IMO (and its Legal Committee) to develop a model for a single insurance certificate which may be issued by State parties in respect of each and every ship under the relevant IMO liability and compensation Conventions.

The Convention will open for signature from 19 November 2007 until 18 November 2008, and thereby will be open for ratification or accession or acceptance. It will enter into force twelve months following the date on which ten States have either signed it without reservation as to ratification, acceptance, or approval, or have deposited instruments of ratification, acceptance, approval, or accession, with the Secretary General of IMO.

PART III

INTERNATIONAL CONVENTIONS ON CIVIL LIABILITY LIMITATION AND COMPENSATION

OVERVIEW

This Part includes limitation of liability under the London Convention 1976, as amended by the 1996 Protocol (Chapter 17), and the Athens Convention 1974 and the 2002 Protocol (Chapter 18). Pollution damage and limitation of liability under the Civil Liability and Fund Conventions 1992 are covered, as well as the Hazardous and Noxious Substances Convention 1996; Nuclear Damage Conventions, and the Bunker Convention 2001; (Chapter 19 is contributed by Elizabeth Blackburn QC).

Consideration is also given to the implications of the International Safety Management Code on the issue of breaking the right to limit.

This Part does not deal with the specifics of limitation of liability under the Hague Rules, the Hague-Visby Rules or the Hamburg Rules which apply to the carriage of goods by sea contracts, although reference is made to them by way of comparison when the bar to the right to limit is discussed, and as an overview of the right to limit provided by Conventions.

The recently adopted Wreck Removal Convention 2007 is briefly considered at the end of Chapter 16 as it was thought more appropriate to include it in the chapter of the law of harbours.

CHAPTER 17

LIMITATION OF LIABILITY FOR
MARITIME CLAIMS

1 INTRODUCTION

Historically, for 250 years, limitation of shipowners' liability for maritime claims has been designed to encourage and protect trade. It encourages shipowners to stay in business and their insurers to be able to insure risks for liability to third parties, which would, otherwise, be uninsurable.[1] Limitation of liability is not a matter of justice, but of public policy which has its origin in history and its justification in convenience.[2] It is regulated by separate regimes of limitation implemented by international conventions.

The Hague Rules 1924, the Hague-Visby Rules (HVR) 1968 and the Hamburg Rules 1978[3] regulate the carrier's obligations and liabilities with respect to the carriage of goods by sea and provide for limitation of the carrier's liability for loss of or damage to cargo 'carried on board' (known as the 'package or unit' limitation). The Athens Convention 1974, as amended by the 1976, the 1990 and the 2002 Protocols, relates to the carriage of passengers and their luggage by sea and provides for limitation of liability in this respect.[4] The Limitation of Liability Convention 1976 (the London Convention), as amended by the 1996 Protocol,[5] provides for 'tonnage' limitation of liability for a variety of maritime claims which may arise during a casualty, but it excludes pollution damage claims. These are specifically dealt with by the Civil Liability Convention 1992 and the Fund Convention 1992, as amended by the Fund Protocol 2003 which came into force on 3 May 2005 (see Chapter 19).[6]

---

1   *Limitation of Shipowners' Liability: The New Law*, 1986, Southampton University.

2   *Alexander Towing Co v Millet (The Bramley Moore)* [1964] P 200, per Lord Denning; Read, also, a thoughtful address to the British Maritime Law Association in 1993, Mustill (Lord), 'Ships are different – or are they?' [1993] LMCLQ 490, and the reply by Steel, D, QC, 'Ships are different – the case for limitation of liability' [1995] LMCLQ 77.

3   The Hamburg Rules have not been adopted by the UK, nor do they have international application, although they have been ratified by 26 countries, but not by major maritime nations.

4   The 1976 Protocol stated limits in SDR, instead of Gold Francs used in the original text, and the 1990 Protocol, which did not come into force, increased the limits. There is the 2002 Protocol, which introduces a new scheme of limitation, financial security and direct action against insurers to be in line with the pollution liability regime. (See Chapter 18 para 4, below).

5   The 1996 Protocol increased the limits and entered into force on 13 May 2004. It was implemented in the UK by SI 1998/1258, and SI 2004/1273 which adopts the amendments.

6   See comprehensive examination of the subject by De La Rue, C, and Anderson, C, *Shipping and the Environment*, 1998, London: LLP. A third tier for oil pollution compensation entered into force on 3 May 2005 in the form of the Fund Protocol 2003. The effect of this is to increase further the amount that can be claimed in those States which have adopted the Protocol. In practice, it is hoped that this will avoid the need to pro rata claims, as has been the practice in the past. For an overview of how the system operates in practice and the amount of the limits, see generally www.iopcfund.org.

The rationale for shipowners' limitation of liability was put in a nutshell by Mr Justice Staughton (as he then was) in *The Garden City*:[7]

> The reasoning behind the Convention may now be that shipowners should be encouraged to insure against liability, and limitation makes it easier for them to do so; but that limitation should not be tolerated in the case of outrageous conduct, such as deliberately or recklessly causing loss.

> However, the historical reason for the introduction of limitation appears to have been to enable British ships to trade on equal terms with those of other nations.

Some argue that limitation of liability is anachronistic and overprotective to shipowners and their insurers.[8] While, however, the original reason for limitation was to increase the number of ships and to prevent any discouragement to merchants, limitation has been encouraged and maintained over the years because it has evolved into a system for the support of a whole series of infrastructures. There is an undercurrent utilitarian philosophy for its perpetuation. Politicians and legislators would not be prepared to protect the interests of a minority (the shipowners) by legislation if, by doing so, it were not for the benefit of the community at large. In other words, the fact that the system of limitation of liability is built in to a viable insurance system facilitates trade and boosts the employment of a large part of the workforce and, consequently, allows a series of infrastructures of the service industries to operate. Furthermore, the system of limitation, as opposed to unlimited liability, ensures that insurance, and in most cases compulsory insurance, is obtained, thus, victims are protected, even if their claims are not fully met.

While it is easy for the objectors to limitation to see only the benefit to the shipowners, derived from the fact that the law allows them to limit their liability, it should not be overlooked that, had it not been for limitation, freight and fuel prices would not be competitive, insurance would be scarce – hence, there would be no guarantee for payment of claims – and the movement of goods would be slower or more difficult. It takes little imagination to envisage that the dependant and related services would suffer, which would have a knock-on effect on the prosperity of a country and, generally, on employment. This is a major reason for the consensus that has been reached internationally in favour of limitation, hence, the limitation conventions have been ratified by most of the maritime nations.

In recent years, there have been further developments to increase the limits under the various conventions as will be seen in this chapter and Chapters 18 and 19. Efforts have been made to amend the Athens Convention, and the proposed 2002 Protocol has been adopted, as it provides a fairer system than the present outdated system.[9] Also the liability and limitation system with regard to pollution damage to the environment has been reformed rapidly in recent years. The problems in this area have been highlighted by the sinking of *The Erika* and *The Prestige*, which provided the impetus for change, both at the IMO and the EU levels.[10]

---

7   [1982] 2 Lloyd's Rep 382, p 398.
8   See Guici, G (Dr), 'Limitation of liability in maritime law: an anachronism' (1995) 19(1) *Marine Policy* 65, pp 65–74.
9   See Chapter 18.
10 These are discussed in Chapters 19 and 20.

2 THE SCOPE OF TONNAGE LIMITATION OF LIABILITY UNDER THE 1976 CONVENTION

In this chapter, the law relating to limitation of liability under the 1976 Convention, which concerns tonnage limitation in relation to maritime claims, is examined. It is known as 'tonnage' limitation because it is based on the size of the liable ship, as opposed to value, as was the case under the Merchant Shipping Act (MSA) 1894. This limitation is also referred to as 'global,' because it is designed to deal with disasters in which the owner faces claims from a variety of claimants and seeks to create one overall maximum limit in relation to them.

Limitation of liability under the HVR, applying to individual contracts of carriage of goods by sea, is not examined here in detail, other than for making comparisons when necessary. In this edition, limitation of liability arising from personal injury or loss of life during the transportation of passengers under the Athens Convention 1974 (s 183 of the MSA 1995) is examined in Chapter 18. The special regime of the CLC 1992 (s 157 of the MSA 1995) is examined in Chapter 19.

Since the first edition of this book, the limits of the 1976 Convention were increased when the Protocol 1996 entered into force on 13 May 2004.

2.1 Reasons of acceptance of the 1976 Convention

The predecessor to the 1976 Convention was the International Convention Relating to the Limitation of Liability of Owners of Sea-going Ships 1957, which had not wholly been adopted by the UK, but some of its provisions were used to amend the previous regime on limitation enshrined in s 503 of the MSA 1894. This was done by the Merchant Shipping (Liability of Shipowners and Others) Act (MS(LSO)A) 1958. Limitation under these provisions could not avail the shipowner if he could not show that the incident giving rise to the claims took place without his 'actual fault or privity'. This was a difficult burden for the shipowner to discharge in the frequent litigation that ensued. This issue, coupled with a demand for a higher limitation figure, led to the International Conference for Limitation of Liability held in London in 1976, under the auspices of the International Maritime Organisation (IMO), which resulted in the adoption of the 1976 Convention. This Convention was a compromise in order to strike a balance between successful claimants and shipowners. It achieved the increase of the limitation fund to a sufficiently high level, so that the claimants could reasonably be compensated, but not so high as to make the shipowners' liability uninsurable. As a *quid pro quo* for the increase of the fund, the article providing for the breaking of limitation became tighter, so that it is almost impossible for the claimants to break the right to limit (discussed later).

The new Convention was wholly adopted by the UK for reasons of international uniformity and was given domestic effect first by s 17 of the MSA 1979. The consolidating MSA 1995 contains the Convention in Sched 7, Pt I and, by s 185 of the same Act, the Convention applies to English law, subject to certain reservations contained in Pt II, Sched 7. The Convention came into force on 1 December 1986.

Countries which have not ratified the 1976 Convention may have their own national system of limitation, or may apply the 1957 Convention.

2.2 Application of the Convention and limitations

Article 15 of the Convention (Sched 7, Chapter IV of the MSA 1995) provides that the Convention shall apply whenever any person entitled to limit (per Art 1) seeks to limit his liability before a court of a State party or seeks to procure the release of a ship, or other property, or the discharge of any security given within the jurisdiction of any such State.

Article 15(2) of the Convention allows the State parties to make their own provisions of limitation to be applied to vessels which, according to the law of that State, are ships intended for navigation on inland waters, or ships of less than 300 tons. On the other hand, the Convention forbids the courts of a State party to apply the Convention to ships constructed for, or adapted to, and engaged in, drilling:

(a) when that State has established under its national legislation a higher limit of liability than that otherwise provided for in Art 6; or

(b) when that State has become party to an international convention regulating the system of liability in respect of such ships.

2.2.1 Limitation to sea-going ships

The Convention applies to sea-going ships. However, the UK has made no alteration to the previous regime applicable under English law, and the right to limit has been reserved to apply to any ship[11] whether sea-going or not (Pt II, para 2 of Sched 7 and s 185 of the MSA 1995). Reference to a ship in the Convention, in para 12 of Pt II of Sched 7, includes reference to any structure (whether completed, or in the course of completion) launched and intended for use in navigation as a ship, or part of a ship.

The provisions of limitation which have the force of law under s 185 shall also apply to Her Majesty's ships, which are defined, by s 192(2), as ships of which the beneficial interest is vested in Her Majesty in right of Her Government in the UK, or are registered as Government ships, or which are for the time being demised, or sub-demised to, or in the exclusive possession of the Crown.

2.2.2 Hovercraft not included in the Convention

Since the provisions of the MSA 1995 apply to hovercraft (Sched 13, para 42 of the MSA 1995), the Limitation Convention under English law applies to hovercraft to the extent that it shall not apply to the baggage of hovercraft passengers to which the Carriage by Air Act (CAA) 1961 applies.[12]

---

11 'Ship' is defined in the MSA 1995, s 313, as including any description of vessel used in navigation.

12 Civil Liability Order 1986 (SI 1986/1305).

2.2.3 *Minimum tonnage*

Subject to variations from State to State with respect to minimum tonnage, as is allowed by the Convention, there is a single minimum limit for all ships of no more than 500 tons, but the UK has varied this position. There is a new minimum level of limitation for ships of less than 300 tons in respect of all claims within Art 6, not just for loss of life or personal injury claims, as was the position under s 1 of the 1958 Act. With respect to passengers' claims, the number of passengers which the ship is certified of carrying is relevant and not the tonnage, according to Art 7 of the 1976 Convention.

2.2.4 *Floating and drilling platforms excluded*

By Art 15(5), the Convention does not apply to floating platforms constructed for the purpose of exploring or exploiting the natural resources of the seabed, or the subsoil thereof.

Since the UK has not incorporated this limitation to the MSA 1995, whether such platforms are to be regarded as ships for the purpose of limitation will depend on whether the Secretary of State, who has powers by virtue of s 311 of the MSA 1995 to order that a thing designed or adapted for use at sea may be treated as a ship, so orders. Equally, the provision of the Convention (Art 15(4)) excluding drilling units from limitation does not have the force of law in the UK. So, if a drilling unit satisfies the definition of a ship, as it has now been decided that it does (see Chapter 12),[13] it will qualify for limitation under the MSA 1995.

3 PERSONS ENTITLED TO LIMIT

Article 1 provides:

(1) Shipowners and salvors, as hereinafter defined, may limit their liability in accordance with the rules of this Convention for claims set out in Art 2.

(2) The term 'shipowner' shall mean the owner, charterer, manager or operator of a sea-going ship.

(3) Salvor shall mean any person rendering services in direct connection with salvage operations. Salvage operations shall also include operations referred to in Art 2, para 1(d), (e) and (f).

(4) If any claims set out in Art 2 are made against any person for whose act, neglect or default the shipowner or salvor is responsible, such person shall be entitled to avail himself of the limitation of liability provided for in this Convention.

(5) In this Convention the liability of a shipowner shall include liability in an action brought against the vessel herself.

(6) An insurer of liability for claims subject to limitation in accordance with the rules of this Convention shall be entitled to the benefits of this Convention to the same extent as the assured himself.

(7) The act of invoking limitation shall not constitute an admission of liability.

---

13 *Perks v Clark* [2001] 2 Lloyd's Rep 431 (CA).

3.1 Shipowners and others

3.1.1 Owner, manager or operator

Under the old regime of limitation, the right to limit liability was only given to actual registered or beneficial owners of a ship, by s 503 of the MSA 1894. That right was extended to persons other than shipowners by s 3 of the MS(LSO)A 1958, which amended the earlier section (pursuant to the 1957 Convention, Art 6) to include 'charterers, any person interested in or in possession of the ship,[14] a manager or operator of the ship, and the master, crew or other servants of the owner . . . acting in the course of their employment'.

Under the 1957 Convention, a person merely in possession, but not in operation of the vessel, for example, a mortgagee, or ship-repairer, was allowed to limit his liability by s 3(1) of the 1958 Act.[15] By eliminating the words 'any person interested in or in possession of the ship' in Art 1(2) of the 1976 Convention, it is clear that the right is not given to a mortgagee, unless the mortgagee upon default by the owner takes over the management and operation of the ship (see Chapter 9, above); nor is the right given to other persons who merely hold possession of the ship, such as a ship-repairer, at a given time. A salvor, who may be in possession of the ship, can limit as is mentioned specifically in Art 1(1). The right is restricted to the shipowner which, for the purpose of the Convention, means the owner, charterer, manager or operator of a sea-going ship (Art 1(2)). The word 'manager' does not include the crewing agent but a manager who is involved in the technical management of the ship, or in the ship's operation.[16] The ship repairer will be able to rely on s 191 of the MSA 1995 to limit liability as far as English law is concerned (see para 3.4, below).

3.1.2 Charterer

A charterer can limit liability for claims for which he is liable.

Until recently, it was not clear whether or not a charterer could limit liability vis-à-vis the owner of the chartered ship when he claims to be indemnified in respect of losses suffered, due to the charterer's breach of contract or due to complying with the charterer's orders. This issue arose in *The Aegean Sea*.[17]

By a charter-party in the Asbatankvoy form, the owners let their vessel *The Aegean Sea* to Repsol Oil International Ltd (ROIL), for the carriage of a cargo of crude oil to ". . . one or two safe port(s) European Mediterranean. ROIL was a

---

14 'Any person interested in . . . the ship' meant a person having a legal or equitable interest in the ship: *McDermid v Nash Dredging & Reclamation Co Ltd* [1987] AC 906 (HL).

15 *Mason v Uxbridge Boat Centre* [1980] 2 Lloyd's Rep 592; the judge followed the precedent of the House of Lords' decision in *The Ruapehu* [1927] AC 523 (HL), which decided in favour of a dockowner acting as a ship-repairer under the previous statute of limitation, the MS(LSO)A 1900, s 2.

16 For types of management of ships, see Chapter 8, above.

17 [1998] 2 Lloyd's Rep 39; see further *The Tasman Pioneer* [2003] 2 Lloyd's Rep 713: a sub-time charterer was able to limit under the equivalent legislation on limitation in New Zealand.

trading company and was wholly owned by Repsol, a company owned by the State of Spain and which operated refineries in Spain. The cargo was loaded and the ship proceeded to Spain. While *The Aegean Sea* was proceeding to berth at La Coruña to discharge her cargo she grounded onto rocks, broke in two and exploded. The vessel and most of her cargo were lost, and there was large-scale pollution of the environment and damage to private property.

The owners sought to recover the amounts for which claims by third parties were brought against them, together with the value of the vessel, the bunkers on board and the freight from ROIL and Repsol, on the ground of unsafe port or, alternatively, on the ground of complying with the charterers' orders.

The charterers denied the port was unsafe and further contended that, in the event that they were found liable to the owners, they were entitled, as charterers of *The Aegean Sea*, to limit their liability under the provisions of the Convention on Limitation of Liability for Maritime Claims 1976 (the 1976 Convention).

Thomas J (as he then was) decided against such limitation, on the basis that the 1976 Convention did not provide (and was not intended to provide) an entitlement to charterers to limit for any of the claims (damage to ship, cargo, freight, bunkers, pollution damage claims, and consequential losses) brought by the owners against the charterers, ie ROIL, as such claims could not be reasonably brought within its language.

He approached the issue from an analysis of Arts 11, 9 and 1(2) of the Convention in that, under the Convention, there is only one fund established (under Art 11) on behalf of the owner, charterer and operator, and a separate fund on behalf of the salvor. A fund constituted by one of the persons mentioned in art 9 (1)(a), (b) or (c) shall be deemed constituted by all persons mentioned. The Convention provides, by Art 9, for the aggregation of claims arising from one distinct occasion. Although a distinction can be drawn between ship owners and salvors, no such distinction is drawn between ship owners and charterers under Art 1(2). For example, when a vessel is lost carrying cargo under owner's or charterers' bills of lading, there is one limit of liability and one fund, which is for the benefit of all claimants and protects equally the owner, charterer, manager and operator in respect of those claims. There is no provision for a separate limit or separately constituted fund through which the charterer can limit his liability to the owner.

He, thus, held that it could not have been intended by the Convention that the limitation fund be reduced by direct claims by the owners against the charterers for the loss of the ship, or the freight or the bunkers; the fund was intended for claims by cargo interests and other third parties external to the operation of the ship against those responsible for the operation of the ship; to permit claims of the type advanced by the owners against the charterers, for the direct losses they suffered, to come within the scope of the limitation fund would diminish what was available to others. Even if, on the assumption that the 1976 Convention covered claims by the shipowner against the charterer, the loss of the ship was not the loss of 'property . . . occurring in direct connection with the operation of the ship' in Art 2(1)(a), because it was the operation of the very ship that must have caused the loss of property, the ship could not be the object of the wrong.

In the subsequent decision of *CMA CGM SA v Classica Shipping Co Ltd (The*

CMA Djakarta),[18] Steel J at first instance held in the same way as Thomas J, that the charterer could not limit, because the all-embracing category of 'ship owners' suggested that individual members of that class, such as charterers, operators, managers, may be exposed to claims by reason of activities usually associated with ownership. Shipment of a dangerous cargo which was the cause of the ship's loss was not an activity associated with ownership but it was done in the capacity as charterer. The property damaged could not be the very same thing as the operation of which caused the damage, and the ship could not be at the same time the other property.

The Court of Appeal in *The CMA Djakarta*[19] disapproved of the reasoning of both Thomas J and Steel J, and held that the word 'charterer' in Art 1(2) of the 1976 Convention connoted a charterer acting in his capacity as such, not a charterer acting in some other capacity. To say that a charterer had to be acting as owner was to impose a gloss on the wording of Art 1(2) of the Convention and accord it a meaning other than its ordinary meaning.

On the facts of this case, the owners' container ship was damaged by an explosion, which arbitrators found was caused by bleaching powder shipped in containers in breach of the charterers' obligations under the time charterparty on the New York Produce Exchange form, which excluded carriage of dangerous or flammable goods. The main part of the owners' claim was the cost of repair of the ship and salvage services rendered. There were other claims made by them against the charterers, to be indemnified in respect of their liability to contribute to general average and their liability to cargo owners for loss or damage to cargo. The charterers claimed to be entitled to limit their liability under Art 1(2) of the 1976 Convention, which included 'charterer' in the definition of shipowner, and had established a limitation fund in France for all claimants.

The Court of Appeal further held that the correct interpretation of Arts 2 and 9 of the Convention led to the conclusion that the claims in respect of which an owner or charterer could limit did not include claims for loss or damage to the ship relied on to calculate the limit. The judge had been right to hold that the ordinary meaning of Art 2(1)(a) did not extend the right to limit for a claim in respect of damage to the vessel by reference to the tonnage of which limitation was to be calculated. *The Aegean Sea* was approved on this point. In addition, the charterers could not limit in respect of the owners' claims to be indemnified in respect of liability to salvors or liability to contribute in general average because those claims were not within Art 2(1). On the other hand, the owners' claim for an indemnity in respect of the cargo claim against which they could limit their liability) was a claim in respect of loss of or damage to property occurring on board the ship within Art 2(1)(a), and the charterers could limit their liability in respect of that claim.

As to whether or not the word 'charterer' included all types of charterers, and not only the demise charterer as was the case under the MSA 1894,[20] the Court of

---

18   [1998] 2 Lloyd's Rep 39.
19   [2004] 1 Lloyd's Rep 460 (CA).
20   *The Hopper No 66* [1908] AC 126.

Appeal held that it would be too bold to construe the word 'charterer' in a modern international convention to mean only 'demise charterer'. As to whether the word included a part charterer, or a slot charterer, who does not hire the ship as a whole, it was argued on behalf of the owners that the framers of the Convention could not have intended that a slot charterer could limit his liability to the owner, particularly since it would be absurd that his limit would have to be calculated by reference to the whole tonnage of the vessel when he never contracted to have that tonnage available. Since this issue was not necessary to be decided in this case, the court was content to leave the answer to this question for a future case, while it observed that the court had already previously held, in the context of arrest of a ship, that a charterer under the 1952 Arrest Convention was interpreted to include a slot charterer.[21] Griggs, Williams and Farr suggest that, since the slot charterer uses only part of the ship, and there is no provision which allows a slot charterer to limit liability proportionately, the choice would seem to be between allowing him to limit according to the full tonnage of the ship, or not at all. But the authors prefer the former view, which is in line with the aim of the Convention.[22]

3.1.3 Any person for whose act, neglect or default the shipowner or salvor is responsible

The wording of Art 1(4), '. . . any person for whose act, neglect or default the shipowner or salvor is responsible, such person shall be entitled to avail himself of the limitation of liability provided for in this Convention', can potentially cause problems of interpretation as to the extent of persons for whose acts, etc, the shipowner is responsible. It should be borne in mind, however, that the provision is mainly concerned with granting an independent right of limitation to those people for whose act, neglect or default the shipowner, or charterer, or manager, or operator, or salvor will be vicariously liable. These people were, before the 1957 Convention, potentially exposed to be sued separately from the shipower, if the claimants wished to bypass the owner's right to limit.

It may be that the provision is intended to include persons other than merely the master or crew, other servants of the owner, etc, acting in the course of their employment. Such a wording was used in the 1957 Convention. Was it necessary to change it? The answer to this may be that it was done just for purpose of clarification or, in order to expand the list of people in this class. The most obvious category of those people is the stevedores who, although they are generally independent contractors, must show that, in the particular case in which they seek to limit liability, they were employed by the shipowner or the charterer as the case may be. Whether or not the Convention intended to include in this category independent contractors will not be interpreted by applying domestic principles, but by reference to broad and generally accepted principles of construction, without any

---

21   *The Tychy* [1999] 2 Lloyd's Rep 11 (CA); see Chapter 3, above.

22   Griggs, P, Williams, R, & Farr, J, *Limitation of Liability for Maritime Claims*, 4th edn, 2005, LLP, p 11; and [1997] IJSL 118–21.

English law preconceptions, as to the meaning of the word 'responsible' in Art 1(4). What are broad and acceptable principles may be difficult to know, but some such principles are enshrined in Arts 31 and 32 of the Vienna Convention 1969 on the Law of Treaties (which came into force in 1980). The duty of the court, pursuant to the guidelines of these articles, is to ascertain the ordinary meaning of the words used, not just in their context but also in the light of the evident object and purpose of the Convention. The court may have recourse to the *travaux préparatoires* and the circumstances in which the Convention was concluded.[23]

In a case of negligence of independent contractors who are appointed by the owner to repair a ship, and their negligence causes the ship to be unseaworthy, and that unseaworthiness causes loss to third parties, although the shipowner will be constructively liable to the third parties for such loss under Art III, r 1 of the HVR (*The Muncaster Castle*),[24] it does not mean that the independent contractor is a person for whose act, etc, the owner will be vicariously liable, so as to be within the meaning of Art 1(4). The owner is liable to third parties in such cases because he owes a direct personal duty to them and the duty is non-delegable.[25] The word 'responsible', in Art 1(4), ought to mean, it is submitted, that the owner or salvor is vicariously liable, for the person seeking to limit to have an independent right to limit.[26] A ship repairer will be able, under English law, to limit under s 191 of the MSA 1995 in respect of damage caused to ships, goods, or merchandise on board the ship.[27]

3.2 Salvors

The 1976 Convention introduced the right of limitation for salvors, as well as any person rendering services in direct connection with salvage operations (Art 1(3)). Article 1(1) of the Convention provides that salvors '... may limit their liability in accordance with the rules of the Convention for the claims set out in Art 2 of the

---

23   *CMA v Classica Shipping Co Ltd* [2004] 1 Lloyd's Rep 460, pp 463, 464, per Longmore LJ, referring to previous authorities.

24   [1961] 1 Lloyd's Rep 57 (HL).

25   See *Salsbury v Woodland* [1970] 1 QB 324, pp 336–37, per Widgery LJ: 'It is trite law that an employer who employs an independent contractor is not vicariously responsible for the negligence of that contractor. He is not able to control the way in which the independent contractor does the work, and the vicarious obligation of a master for the negligence of his servant does not arise under the relationship of employer and independent contractor. I think that it is entirely accepted that those cases – and there are some – in which an employer has been held liable for injury done by the negligence of an independent contractor are, in truth, cases where the employer owes a direct duty to the person injured, a duty which he cannot delegate to the contractor on his behalf'.

26   Under contracts of carriage, in which the Hague Rules apply, there is no equivalent independent right given to the carrier's servants to limit liability, unlike under the HVR; so Art 1(4) of the 1976 Convention will be useful to them for the purpose of limitation, although it is common in such contracts to include a Himalaya clause. When English law applies to such contracts, the Contracts (Rights of Third Parties) Act 1999, which applies to contracts made after 11 May 2000, enhances the protection of third parties to the contract intended by the terms of the contract to be protected in the same way as the parties to the contract (see, further, Chapter 14, para 10).

27   See under para 3.4, below.

Convention'. This new development was a direct consequence of *The Tojo Maru*. It should be noted briefly what happened in this case with regard to limitation.

The Tojo Maru[28]

A salvage agreement was signed on the Lloyd's Open Form on the 'no cure no pay' basis. After the ship had been brought to a place of safety, the salvors' diver, who was trying to repair a crack at the bottom of the ship being salved, negligently fired a bolt through the shell plating of the ship which went through a gas-filled cargo tank. This resulted in an explosion causing substantial damage to the vessel. When the salvors claimed salvage remuneration, the shipowners counterclaimed damages for the damage to be set off against any remuneration the salvors might have been entitled to. The salvors sought to limit their liability under s 503 of the MSA 1894, if they were held liable to pay damages. This section restricted limitation to acts, or omissions (which caused the damage or loss) in the navigation or management of the ship, or through the act, or omission, of any person on board the liable ship, the owners of which were seeking to limit liability. The central issue with regard to limitation was whether the negligent act of their diver which caused the explosion took place in the management of their tug or, alternatively, whether it took place on board the tug. While the owners' counterclaim for damages was upheld, it was held that the salvors were not entitled to limit their liability under s 503(1) of the MSA 1894. The salvors' contention that the negligent act of their diver was done either in the management of, or on board, the tug was rejected. Lord Reid stated, quite sympathetically:[29]

> But a court must go by the provisions which have been agreed and enacted. If the special position of salvors was unforeseen, then we must await alteration of those provisions if those concerned see fit to make some alteration.

As a result of this case the law changed. Now, the wording of Art 2(1) of the Convention specifically covers the circumstances of this case, namely that limitation applies to claims in respect of loss of life, or personal injury, or loss or damage to property occurring on board, or in direct connection with the operation of the ship, or with salvage operations, and consequential loss resulting therefrom.[30]

In addition, Art 1(4) includes the servants of the salvor in the list of people with the right to limit, if any claims under Art 2 are made against any person for whose acts, neglect or default the salvor is responsible.

3.3 The liability insurer

The Convention has innovated by including, in Art 1(6), for the liability insurer to be entitled to the benefits of this Convention to the same extent as the assured himself. This will apply in the event the insurers are sued directly by those who

---

28 [1972] AC 242 (HL) (see Chapter 13, above).

29 Ibid, p 270.

30 In Chapter 13, above, issues of offsetting damages for salvor's negligence against the salvage award, and when a salvor can limit, are discussed.

sustained damage to, or suffered loss of, property; or those who suffered personal injury, or the dependants of those whose life was lost on board, or in connection with the operation of the ship, or with salvage operations.

3.3.1 When is there a right of action against the insurer?

The right of action against insurers was first introduced by the Third Parties (Rights Against Insurers) Act 1930, which, in essence, provides for a statutory subrogation entitling the victim of the wrongdoer (the assured, insofar as the liability insurer is concerned) to bypass the privity of contract barrier and take the benefits of the contract of insurance between the liability insurer and the assured. The rights of the assured against the insurer under the contract in respect of the liability are transferred to, and vest in, the third party to whom the liability was so incurred (s 1(1) of the 1930 Act). This statutory subrogation arises in the event of insolvency or bankruptcy of the assured, in other words when he is unable to satisfy the claim.

There are two preconditions that have to be fulfilled before the third party can claim against the insurer. First, the third party must obtain a judgment, or an arbitration award, on liability against the assured and become a judgment creditor. He cannot sue the insurer unless the assured's liability to him is first established because the assured himself cannot claim his indemnity from his insurer, if such liability has not been established.[31] Second, since the assured (defendant) is insolvent and cannot satisfy the judgment debt, the judgment creditor must obtain a winding up order of the company of the assured in England.

To obtain a winding-up order when a company is foreign, as in most cases shipowning companies are, the claimant must establish jurisdiction in the UK. Although doubts existed in the past, it is now possible that such an order can be obtained if the company has assets within the jurisdiction. Insurance proceeds, payable in England under the protection and indemnity (P&I) cover, have been regarded as such an asset for this purpose.[32] The court has discretion whether or not to grant the order. The question that still arises, in the case of P&I clubs that are registered as offshore companies, is whether the insurance proceeds would be regarded as an asset within the jurisdiction for the purpose of the winding-up order, if the responsible party was paying from abroad. Would it matter, in fact, where the insurer was incorporated, or would it be sufficient that the responsibility for payment of the proceeds to the assured lay upon the managers of such P&I clubs, operating in England, or their London agents? It is submitted that the latter would be a strong reason for the court to exercise its discretion in favour of granting

---

31 *Post Office v Norwich Union Fire Insurance Co* [1967] 1 Lloyd's Rep 216: Lord Denning MR said in this case, p 219: 'I think the right to sue for these moneys does not arise until the liability is established and the amount ascertained. How is this to be done? If there is an unascertained claim for damages in tort, it cannot be proved in the bankruptcy, nor in the liquidation of the company. But, nevertheless, the injured person can bring an action against the wrongdoer. In the case of a company, he must get the leave of the court. No doubt, leave would automatically be given. The insurance company can fight that action in the name of the wrongdoer. In that way, liability can be established and the loss ascertained. Then the injured person can go against the insurance company'.

32 *The Allobrogia* [1979] 1 Lloyd's Rep 190; *The Vainqueur Jose* [1979] 1 Lloyd's Rep 557; *Re Compania Merabello San Nicholas SA* [1973] Ch 75.

the order. Once these two preconditions (a judgment on liability and a winding-up order) are satisfied, the judgment creditor 'steps into the shoes' of the assured and takes over the assured's rights against the insurer under the contract in respect of the liability incurred to the creditor (s 1(1) of the 1930 Act). However, that is not the end of the matter for the third party, in view of the 'pay to be paid' rule.

3.3.2 'Pay to be paid' rule under the rules of the liability insurer[33]

Assuming that a claimant obtained a judgment, and an English winding-up order against the debtor was granted, there is another impediment for the claimant before he can obtain payment from the insurer. First, liability insurance is subject to the terms of the contract between the assured and his P&I insurer, contained in the club rules, which require that, for an indemnity to be paid to the assured, the latter must have first paid the third party, known as the 'pay to be paid' rule.[34] This rule prohibits the third party creditor stepping into the shoes of the assured, since the reason why he needs to claim from the assured's insurer is that the assured has not paid him.

Were he, the assured, claiming indemnity from his insurer, he should first have paid the creditor, and, in this case, it would mean that the creditor should pay himself. It has been suggested that the creditor may devise ways to pay himself (pretending to be two different entities at the same time, for example, the assured, on the one hand, who hands over the money, and, on the other hand, the creditor, who receives the money due).[35] Then he may claim to be indemnified from the liability insurer, who will be entitled to limit his liability under Art 1(6). However, while cargo claimants who are supported by cargo underwriters may use this device, it is not feasible for personal injury claimants to find the money to pay themselves. The Law Commission, therefore, has made recommendations to amend the 1930 Act, so as to enable claimants of personal injury, or loss of life, to claim directly from the liability insurers. No substantial progress has been made in amending the 1930 Act. However, a significant change in the law regarding ferry and cruise ships' passengers has been made by the recent adoption of the 2002 Protocol to the Athens Convention 1974 (see Chapter 18, below). Claimants under the Athens Convention 2002, once it is in force, will have direct action against the liability insurer, with the effect that the 'pay to be paid' rule is rendered invalid.

3.3.3 Insurer's contractual and statutory defences

Since the creditor claiming against the insurer will be in the shoes of the assured, in cases other than those where there is a right of a direct action against the insurer, he will be faced with another possible difficulty in recovering from the insurer, which may arise if the assured was in breach of the contract of insurance and, in particular, of ss 39(5) and 55(2)(a) of the Marine Insurance Act (MIA) 1906.

---

33 Hazelwood, S, *The Law and Practice of P&I Clubs*, 3rd edn, 2000, LLP.
34 *The Fanti and The Pandre Island (No 2)* [1990] 2 Lloyd's Rep 191 (HL).
35 *The Vainqueur Jose* [1979] 1 Lloyd's Rep 557.

Section 39(5) provides that the insurer is not liable for any loss attributable to unseaworthiness, if the ship was sent to sea in an unseaworthy condition with the privity of the assured. Similarly, by s 55(2)(a), the insurer is not liable for any loss attributable to the wilful misconduct of the assured. On the hypothesis that the insurer could provide evidence to show that the assured was guilty of such conduct, the creditor – stepping into the assured's shoes – would be faced with the same defences that the P&I insurer would have had against the assured under the contract of insurance.

The implications of the law as it stands at present – considering the legal structures of one-ship companies – are enormous in cases of loss of life, or personal injury, where the victims may be left without any remedy other than gratuitous payments. In the first edition of this book, the implications of the inadequacies of the law were highlighted in the hope that steps would be taken, at international level, to adopt the 2002 Protocol (which proposes compulsory insurance, backed with financial security and direct action against the insurer) without delay. It is encouraging that the 2002 Protocol has been adopted and it will, hopefully, be ratified soon. The EU is also putting further pressure for reform in the law. The Athens Convention and the 2002 Protocol are examined in Chapter 18.

In short, the 2002 Protocol abolishes, in part, the presumed fault-based system which currently operates under the 1974 Convention. This is replaced by a strict liability system, up to a set amount of units of account (first tier), which can be increased to a higher maximum unless the carrier can prove the loss occurred without his fault or neglect. There is also a requirement that ship owners take out compulsory insurance or other financial security. Such insurance has to be for a minimum of 250,000 SDR per passenger. This equates to just over £200,000. In addition, the claimant can bring a direct action against the insurer, whose liability is limited to 250,000 SDR. However, the wilful misconduct defence is maintained.

3.4 Harbour authorities

Although the Convention does not include harbour authorities, or conservancy authorities, or the owners of docks or canals, in the class of persons who are entitled to limit their liability, s 191 of the MSA 1995 grants them the right of limitation in the UK in respect of claims for damage caused to ships,[36] goods, merchandise or other things whatsoever on board the ship. The basis of limitation is by reference to the tonnage of the largest UK ship, which has been within the area over which the authority discharges any functions at the time of the loss, or within the last five years before the relevant incident. According to s 191(5), the limit of liability shall be ascertained by applying the method of calculation specified in para 1(b) of Art 6, Pt II, Sched 7, read together with para 5(1)(2), Pt II. Dock includes wet docks and

---

[36] Limitation will, presumably, still apply even if the dock incurs liability by discharging its function of repairing a ship within its area The majority of the House of Lords held that the right was not confined to acts done in their capacity as dockowners but extended to acts done in their capacity as ship-repairers: *The Ruapehlu* [1927] AC 523 (HL).

basins, tidal dock and basins, locks, cuts, wharves, piers, stages, landing places and jetties (s 191(9)).

4 CLAIMS SUBJECT TO LIMITATION

Article 2 provides:

(1) Subject to Art 3 and 4 the following claims, whatever the basis of liability may be, shall be subject to limitation of liability:

    (a) claims in respect of loss of life or personal injury or loss of or damage to property (including damage to harbour works, basin and waterways and aids to navigation), occurring on board or in direct connection with the operation of the ship or with salvage operations, and consequential loss resulting therefrom;

    (b) claims in respect of loss from delay in the carriage by sea of cargo, passengers or their luggage;

    (c) claims in respect of other loss resulting from infringement of rights other than contractual rights, occurring in direct connection with the operation of the ship or salvage operations;

    (d) claims in respect of the raising, removal, destruction or the rendering harmless of a ship which sunk, wrecked, stranded or abandoned, including anything that is or has been on board such ship;

    (e) claims in respect of the removal, destruction or the rendering harmless of the cargo of the ship;

    (f) claims of a person other than the person liable in respect of measures taken in order to avert or minimise loss for which the person liable may limit his liability in accordance with this Convention, and further loss caused by such measures.

(2) Claims set out in para 1 shall be subject to limitation of liability even if brought by way of recourse or for indemnity under a contract or otherwise. However, claims set out under para 1(d), (e) and (f) shall not be subject to limitation of liability to the extent that they relate to remuneration under a contract with the person liable.

4.1 All claims whether for damages or for a debt or indemnity (Art 2(1), (2))

Article 2(1) provides that, subject to excluded claims, specified in Art 3, and when there are reasons for barring limitation, as stated in Art 4, limitation shall apply to all claims outlined in sub-paras (a)–(f), whatever the basis of liability may be for breach of contract (debt or damages) or in tort. Furthermore, it is emphasised in Art 2(2) that claims set out in para (1) shall be subject to limitation of liability, even if brought by way of recourse, or for indemnity under a contract, or otherwise.

This article has altered the position under the UK old regime of limitation when, by s 503 of the 1894 Act, as amended by the 1958 Act, limitation was applicable only to claims for which the shipowner was liable in damages and not claims for a debt or for an indemnity under contract.[37]

The result is a considerable extension of claims being subject to limitation, which is reinforced for clarification purposes by express provisions, as seen below.

4.2 Claims occurring on board or in direct connection with the operation of the ship or with salvage operations (Art 2(1)(a))

Claims under Art 2, which are subject to limitation, may arise either in contract, or in tort, or through any other cause. Article 2(1)(a) covers claims for loss of life or personal injury when, for example, the crew or passengers of one ship claim damages caused due to negligence of another ship involved in a collision. Similarly, property claims including damage to harbours are included.

As explained earlier, Art 2(1)(a) was primarily drafted this way to overcome the difficulties the salvors had with regard to their inability to limit liability in *The Tojo Maru*.

Previously, only those claims which arose due to negligent acts or omissions done by persons on board, or in the navigation or management of the ship, or in the loading, carriage or discharge of its cargo, or the embarkation, carriage or disembarkation of its passengers, were subject to limitation.

Article 2(1)(a) of the present Convention has widened the scope of limitation quite considerably.

Since the first edition of this book, there has been an opportunity for the court to consider the ambit of this article in recent cases; in *The Aegean Sea* (mentioned earlier), Thomas J analysed each heading and broadly grouped the claims with regard to property, which were relevant in this case, into two categories: (a) claims for loss of the vessel, freight and bunkers; and (b) claims for recourse or indemnity. In considering claims under Art 2(1), which states 'whatever the basis of the claim might be', one should look at the nature and not the basis of the claim, and he referred to *Caspian Basis*[38] in which Rix J (as he then was) expressed the principle in those terms.

As far as the loss of the ship is concerned, it was decided in *The Aegean Sea*, and approved later by the Court of Appeal in *CMA v Classica Shipping Co Ltd*[39] (see earlier), that the language of Art 2(1)(a), 'loss of property occurring in direct connection with the operation of the ship', does not intend to include the loss of the very thing in connection with the operation of which the damage was caused. By contrast, a claim for the loss of the ship which salvors had been trying to salve will be

---

37 *The Kirkness* [1956] 2 Lloyd's Rep 651, in which the owners of the tug, which suffered damages whilst it was towing under a contract of towage containing the usual covenant of indemnity, claimed against the owners of the tow to be indemnified. The latter could not limit their liability.

38 [1997] 2 Lloyd's Rep 507, p 522; later approved by the Court of Appeal [1998] 2 Lloyd's Rep 461, p 473.

39 [2004] 1 Lloyd's Rep 460.

within the wording, because the loss of the ship being salved (which is here the object of the damage and not the subject) occurs in direct connection with the operation of the salvor's tug (the subject of the damage).

Longmore LJ in *CMA v Classica* interpreted[40] Art 2(1)(a) to include three types of claims being subject to limitation: first, loss of life or personal injury; second, loss of or damage to property occurring on board; and, third, loss of or damage to property 'occurring . . . in direct connection with the operation of the ship'; he suggested that the most obvious reason for including this third category of claim was to cater for cases of collision with another ship. Loss of or damage to that other ship (or its cargo) would not be loss of or damage to property 'occurring on board', but it would be loss of or damage to property 'occurring in direct connection with the operation of the ship'.

Thomas J in *The Aegean Sea* further opined, although he did not have to decide the following points, that the loss of bunkers being on the ship is within the wording of Art 2(1)(a), as it happens in direct connection with the operation of the ship. As regards freight, if the freight was earned, it would be due and owing in full without limitation of liability. If it was not earned but due, then the owners of the ship should have a claim in damages. Since the loss of freight, however, was consequential to the loss of the ship (the subject of the damage), the judge thought it was not within the meaning of Art 2(1)(a).

The recourse or indemnity claims for pollution damage paid to third parties, namely for direct damage to property by pollution, clean-up claims and consequential loss of profit claims resulting from loss of cargo, were claims that occurred, in the judge's view, in direct connection with the operation of the ship and were within Art 2(1)(a). Equally, claims for loss of profit by fishermen and perhaps others will fall within this head. The philosophy of the Convention is to extend, and not to restrict, limitable claims, but Art 2(1) makes it clear that the basis of the liability is not a relevant factor.

Claims for consequential loss encompass a variety of claims. For example, the shipowner, in *The Breydon Merchant*,[41] was able to limit liability when the cargo-owners claimed compensation against him with respect to the amount their insurers had to pay to the salvors, who were engaged and successfully salved the ship and cargo in the English Channel when fire broke out on board. The claim was based in damages for breach of contract, and the cargo's contribution to the salvage award was regarded as a consequential loss resulting from the fire damage to their property for which salvage was necessary. The judge stressed that it was not a salvage claim against the shipowner, which is only allowed by salvors, so as to be excluded from limitation by Art 3.

By contrast, the charterer in *CMA v Classica* was not able to limit against the claim made by the shipowner to recover the cost incurred of salving the ship. It was held that such a claim was not within Art 2(1)(a), since a claim for loss or damage to the ship was not within that provision. Even if such a claim to recover the salvage

---

40   Ibid, p 467.
41   *The Breydon Merchant* [1992] 1 Lloyd's Rep 373.

cost was regarded as consequential loss, it was still a claim in respect of the damage to the ship and it could not be brought within Art 2(1)(a) or (f) (see below). The same principle applied to the claim by the owner to be indemnified against his liability to contribute to general average.[42]

Similarly, where a bareboat charterer claimed against the owner of the chartered ship, which suffered damage itself, needing repairs, and incurred liabilities to third parties due to a collision with another vessel, the owner of the vessel in this case, *The Darfur*,[43] was not able to limit liability as against the bareboat charterer for all claims which were consequential to the damage of the chartrered ship. It mattered not that it was the owners who were seeking to limit against claims brought by the charterer, rather than the other way round, as in the aforesaid case. The issue turned on the scope of the claims that were subject to limitation and not the class of persons entitled to limit.

On the issue of claims in respect of liability to cargo interests, the charterer in *CMA v Classica* could limit liability for claims brought (in a country in which the Convention had been ratified) by the owner to be indemnified for claims brought in tort against him by cargo interests, since the charterer was the contractual carrier under the bill of lading. It would be an anomaly if the charterer could not limit as against the owner, who passed the claim on to him, since he could limit as against the cargo interests if they brought the claim directly against him. Such a claim is a result of 'loss of or damage to property ... occurring ... on board the ship' and, thus, falls within Art 2(1)(a); in any event, it falls within Art 2(2).[44]

Another example of consequential loss would be when, after a collision incident, a wreck removal becomes necessary; the expenses incurred will be 'consequential loss' under Art 2(1)(a), save for the exception that the owner of the wreck will not be able to limit his liability to his own contractor engaged to remove the wreck, according to Article 2(2). Article 2(2), coupled with the reservation made by the UK Government in relation to no limitation against claims for wreck removal made by the port authorities (see later), gives rise to an anomaly in distributing practical justice. The anomaly is that, while the owner of the wreck, who might not even have been liable for the collision, will not be able to limit his liability with regard to the wreck removal cost, the owner of the other colliding ship will be able to limit his liability against the entire collision liability, including the wreck removal expenses paid by the owner of the wreck and claimed against him.[45]

The wording 'directly connected with the operation of the ship' is capable of encompassing claims in respect of loss of life or personal injury or loss of or damage to property etc, as enumerated in Art 2(1)(a), arising from neglect or default of a person ashore (for whose acts or omissions the shipowner is responsible, as discussed earlier under para 3.1.3). That person may be the superintendent who may be negligent while he is performing duties in connection with the operation of the ship. Such claims may also arise when the vessel is in drydock, and the damage is

---

42 Op cit, fn 39, p 469.
43 [2004] 2 Lloyd's Rep 469.
44 Op cit, fn 39, p 469.
45 See also *Marsden on Collisions at Sea*, 13th edn, 2003, Sweet & Maxwell, p 596.

caused by such a person in performance of an act ashore, being directly connected with the operation of the ship.[46]

However, the 1996 Protocol has amended the Convention, and was brought into force in the UK from 13 May 2004 by the Merchant Shipping (Convention on Limitation of Liability for Maritime Claims) (Amendment) Order 1998.[47] A new article has been inserted in para 3 *bis* of Part II of Sched 7 to the MSA 1995, which permits Member States to regulate, by specific provisions of national law, the system of liability to be applied to claims for loss of life or personal injury to passengers of ships, provided that the limit is not lower than as prescribed in para 1 of Art 7. Following this permission, the UK has excluded claims for loss of life or personal injury suffered by passengers of seagoing ships, as such claims are dealt with by the Athens Convention, apart from claims which involve non-seagoing ships to which Art 2 of the 1976 Convention applies.

A very important issue was recently decided in two cases, ***Thompson v Masterton***[48] (Royal Court of Guernsey), and ***The Robert Whitmore***[49] (New South Wales Supreme Court), which had not previously come before the courts under the 1976 Convention. The issue was whether the limitation of liability for a claim under Art 2 of the Convention is inclusive, or exclusive, of any cost order which may be made in proceedings establishing that claim. In other words, the question was this: would the defendant in the limitation proceedings be obliged to look to the limitation fund alone to satisfy both the judgment and the consequential cost order, or would he be entitled to obtain payment of the judgment out of the limitation fund and to enforce the cost order directly against the liable party? In both cases, it was held that a limitation fund under Art 11 of the 1976 Convention was exclusive of any legal costs which might be incurred in establishing a claim against the fund. Costs in establishing the claim are separate and distinct from the claim itself. The relief given to the ship owner by the limitation statutes historically has been in relation to damages and nothing else.[50] For example, if the damages to be awarded exceed the limitation fund, the practice in the UK has been that the damages will be limited to the full amount of the fund established, and there will be a separate order for costs.[51] Claims under Art 2 carry their literal meaning, which goes no further than their express words. A claim for reimbursement of the legal expenses incurred in prosecuting a disputed claim under Art 2(1)(a) is outside the scope of both this article and Art 6(1)(b) referring to 'any other claims'.[52] The Convention does not say anything about the way in which legal costs of disputed claims are to be dealt with.

---

46 See also Op cit, Griggs, William & Farr, fn 22, p 20.

47 SI 1998/1258.

48 [2004] 1 Lloyd's Rep 304.

49 [2004] 2 Lloyd's Rep 47.

50 Per Viscount Simonds in *The Stonedale (No 1)* [1955] 2 Lloyd's Rep 9, p 13; furthermore, under the Warsaw-Hague Convention, the court held in *Swiss Bank Corp v Brink-MAT Ltd* [1986] 2 All ER 188, that the limits of liability of a carrier encompasses every expense except costs to which an air carrier might be put as a result of a successful claim which equalled or exceeded the limits on liability imposed by Art 22(2) of the Convention.

51 *Wheeler v London & Rochester Trading Co Ltd* [1957] 1 Lloyd's Rep 69; *Beauchamp v Turrell* [1952] 1 Lloyd's Rep 266.

52 *The Robert Whitmore*, ibid, fn 49, pp 53, 54.

Since it is now settled that legal costs cannot be included in the limitation fund (the contrary would in fact amount to the limitation action being at the defendant's expense), it may be a blow to lawyers who may find themselves unable to recover costs in helping claimants to establish their claim in the limitation fund when the ship of a one-ship company has sunk, unless they have obtained security from the owner's P&I club. It is submitted that the decisions in both *Thompson v Masterton* and *The Robert Whitmore* are sound both in terms of principle and policy; imagine how the limitation fund would have shrunk, if claims of some claimants (defendants in the limitation action) were 'swollen' by the inclusion of their legal costs to the expense of other claimants who did not use lawyers. Domestic procedural laws, however, should provide solutions to legal costs of a successful party.

4.3 Claims for loss resulting from delay (Art 2(1)(b))

This new provision, under Art 2(1)(b), may be of particular help to the shipowner seeking to limit liability for loss suffered by the cargo-owner due to delay in delivery of the goods under the contract of carriage, as it is not certain whether Art IV, r 5(a) of the HVR includes such claims. However, this would create a conflict between the provisions of the two limitation regimes.

4.4 Claims for rights which have been infringed (Art 2(1)(c))

Claims in respect of loss resulting from infringement of rights which occur in direct connection with the operation of the ship, or salvage operations, are subject to limitation, provided they do not arise from infringement of contractual rights. This may include rights of access into a port by other ships, or the rights of the port itself, if the port is obstructed by a stranded ship which prevents a right of passage or use of the port facilities. It will also include claims for loss of profit made by fishing boat owners and others, which can properly be described as resulting from the infringement of rights other than contractual rights. But it will not include a claim by an owner against the charterer under a charterparty for loss of freight due to breach of the charter by the charterer (*The Aegean Sea*.)[53]

4.5 Cost incurred for wreck removal imposed by law (not being incurred contractually) (Art 2(1)(d), (e))

The predecessor to the 1976 Convention, the 1957 Limitation Convention, in Art 1(1)(c), had extended the right of limitation of liability imposed by law for expenses relating to removal of wreck. Despite the incorporation of this provision into UK law by the 1958 Act, a reservation was made by the same Act, as was permitted by the 1957 Convention, restricting the provision of limitation for wreck removal expenses incurred by harbour authorities, pursuant to their statutory powers, from

---

53   Op cit, fn 17, p 52.

coming into force until such a date as the Secretary of State appointed by statutory instrument. The reservation was not removed by the Secretary of State; therefore, the limitation statute remained consistent with the common law position that a shipowner could not limit his liability for the expenses of wreck removal incurred by the port authority in raising the wreck in the UK.[54]

The 1976 Convention preserves the owners' right to limit with respect to claims for expenses incurred for the raising, removal, destruction or rendering harmless of a ship which sunk, wrecked, stranded or abandoned, including anything that is or has been on board such a ship (Art 2(1)(d), provided the liability does not relate to remuneration under a contract (Art 2(2)).

The Convention, by Art 18, however, allows States to make reservations. The UK has continued to reserve the position against limitation of liability for claims of harbour authorities pursuant to their statutory powers (as provided by s 201 of the MSA 1995 and s 56 of the HDPCA 1847). Schedule 7 to the MSA 1995, Pt II, para (3) states that Art 2(1)(d) shall not apply unless provision has been made by an order of the Secretary of State for the setting up of a fund to be used for making payments to the harbour or conservancy authority, as a compensation for the reduction of their expenses by reason of Art 2(1)(d). The reason for this reservation is to protect the public authority's right to recover its expenses in relation to the raising of wrecks in full but, paradoxically, not in relation to the raising of cargo under para (1)(e).

There may have been an oversight in the drafting of the reservation, which is only made in relation to para (1)(d) of Art 2 and not in relation to para (1)(e). The latter refers to claims in respect of the removal, destruction or the rendering harmless of the cargo on board the ship. The odd result of this may be that, while a shipowner will not be able to limit, under para (1)(d), for the expenses in relation to the removal, etc, of 'anything that is or has been on board such ship', which might include the cargo on board, he may technically be able to limit under para (1)(e). Since Thomas J held in *The Aegean Sea* that claims for pollution caused by bunkers and by cargo, insofar as they relate to clean up or pollution prevention, fell within Art 2(1)(d), such claims, if made by the harbour authority, would be unlimited under (d) but limited under (e). Such issues leave academic writers perplexed and surely will be perplexing to practitioners and judges when a case comes before them.[55]

In this connection it should be noted that the Wreck Removal Convention (WRC) which was recently adopted at the Diplomatic Conference in Nairobi on 18 May 2007, provides for limitation of liability (Art 10(2)) of owners of wrecks by reference to the 1976 Convention. As under English law the owner cannot limit in respect of wreck removal expenses (as seen above), his obligation under the WRC will be to carry compulsory liability insurance only up to the amount of the limit (Art 12). The action for recovery of wreck removal expenses can be brought directly against insurers for that amount (see Ch 16, above). There is a potential conflict between the WRC and UK reservation under the (1976) Convention, unless the UK withdraws its reservation when it enacts the WRC.

---

54 See *The Stonedale (No 1)* [1956] AC 1.
55 See, further, Journal of International Maritime law, Editorial, vol 11 (Jan–Feb 2005) at 5–7, and Griggs et al, op cit, fn 22, at 23–24.

4.6 Claims in respect of measures taken in order to avert or minimise loss (Art 2(1)(f))

Sub-paragraph 1(f) should (as much as sub-para 1(d) and (e)) be read together with the second sentence of Art 2(2), which makes it clear that limitation will not apply to claims relating to remuneration under contract with the person liable, for example a claim for remuneration by a salvage contractor. It is also made clear, by the insertion of the words 'claims of the person other than the person liable' for the claim, that claims under para (f), which incur by reason of the steps taken to prevent or minimise loss, are only claims made against the shipowner (the person liable). An example of loss 'for which the person liable may limit liability' is a claim made by a cargo-owner whose cargo was in peril of loss and measures were taken by a third party to minimise such loss of the cargo on board for which the shipowner would be liable and able to limit his liability. The costs of those measures when paid in full by the cargo-owner to the salvor can be claimed against the shipowner who can limit his liability under this sub-paragraph.[56] If further damage was caused to the cargo in the course of taking such measures to avert or minimise loss, a claim for such further loss will be subject to limitation under this head.

5 CLAIMS EXCEPTED FROM LIMITATION (ART 3(a)–(e))

Article 3 provides:

1   The rules of this Convention shall not apply to:

    (a) claims for salvage including, if applicable, any claim for special compensation under Art 14 of the International Convention on Salvage 1989, as amended, or contribution in general average;

    (b) claims for oil pollution damage within the meaning of the International Convention on Civil Liability for Oil Pollution damage . . .;

    (c) claims subject to any international convention or national legislation covering or prohibiting limitation of liability for nuclear damage;

    (d) claims against the shipowner of a nuclear ship for nuclear damage;

    (e) claims by servants of the shipowner or salvors whose duties are connected with the ship or salvage operations, including claims of their heirs, dependants or other persons entitled to make such claims, if under the law governing the contract of service between the shipowner or salvor and such servants the shipowner or salvor is not entitled to limit his liability in respect of such claims, or if he is by such law only permitted to limit his liability to an amount greater than that provided for in Art 6.

5.1 Salvage and contribution in general average claims

Claims excluded from limitation under Art 3(a) are direct claims against the shipowner (as defined in Art 1(2)) by salvors, or by a party who has incurred a general

---

56   *The Breydon Merchant* [1992] 1 Lloyd's Rep 373.

average loss or sacrifice. But, as has been discussed earlier, if a cargo-owner has paid his proportion of salvage, or of general average, to the party entitled to it, he can claim that amount by way of damages or indemnity against the shipowner, in which case limitation of liability will apply to that claim under Art 2(2). Excluded claims are also now, since the 1996 Protocol came into force on 13 May 2004,[57] by which Art 3(a) was revised (as shown above), claims for special compensation under Art 14 of the Salvage Convention 1989.

5.2 Claims for oil pollution (dealt with by special legislation)

Claims for oil pollution damage, within the meaning of the Civil Liability Convention (CLC), as amended by the 1992 Protocol (see Chapter 19, below), are excluded from limitation under this Convention (Art 3(b)) because they are dealt with separately by the specialised Convention and, insofar as the UK is concerned, by s 153 of the MSA 1995. In this connection, it should be noted that, while under the 1976 Convention the owner, charterer, manager or operator of a ship may limit liability, under the CLC, only the owner can. Having excluded limitation for oil pollution from the 1976 Convention, it means that the ship-manager or operator of a ship, the charterer, or the salvor is unable to limit, unless domestic legislation addresses this gap.

Insofar as the UK is concerned, para 4(2), Pt II, Sched 7 to the MSA 1995 expressly limits the exclusion from limitation with regard to oil pollution to 'claims in respect of any liability incurred under s 153 of the MSA 1995', which refers to pollution liability of the owner of the ship. Thus, it seems that the liability for oil pollution of a ship-manager or operator, as well as of a charterer and of a salvor, may be limited under the 1976 Convention.

Similarly, since the CLC does not deal with bunker spills, nor does Art 3(b) of the 1976 Convention exclude that liability from limitation, it follows that losses from bunker spills and consequential financial losses are subject to limitation under Art 2(1)(d) and (e) respectively, as far as they relate to clean up and pollution prevention costs (*The Aegean Sea*). A new Convention on Civil Liability for Bunker Oil Pollution was agreed on 23 March 2001, which will permit limitation under the general law of limitation, whether this is applicable by national law, or by international convention. In the UK, pollution from bunkers is dealt with in s 154 of the MSA 1995 and limitation of liability by s 168, which refers to s 185 of the MSA 1995 and to Art 2(1)(a) of the 1976 Convention.

It should be noted that claims for oil pollution may include claims for pure economic loss brought by fishermen who are prevented from fishing because of the contamination of waters by oil pollution, as was indicated by the Court of Appeal in *The Sea Empress* (discussed in chapter 12). Such claims may be based on Art 2(1)(c), as it was not disputed in *The Aegean Sea* that they can properly be described

---

57 Statutory effect had been given earlier to that amendment in the UK by para 4(1) of Part II, Sched 7 to the MSA 1995.

as resulting from the infringement of rights other than contractual (see earlier and see further Chapter 19).

5.3 Nuclear damage claims

Claims subject to any international convention for nuclear damage (under Art 3(c)) are excluded from limitation, to the extent that there is an international convention dealing with these claims. However, under UK law, para 4, Pt II of Sched 7 stipulates that such claims are claims made by virtue of ss 7–11 of the Nuclear Installations Act 1965. The 1965 Act allows limitation in certain circumstances. With regard to Art 3(d), nuclear damage done by a nuclear ship is outside the scope of the 1976 Convention, but, in the UK, such damage is dealt with by a separate statute, the Liability of Operators of Nuclear Ships Act 1962 (see further about the particular Vienna and Paris Conventions and the Brussels Supplementary Conventions on nuclear damage in Chapter 19, para 9, below).

5.4 Claims by the master and crew against employers

Claims under Art 3(e) are not, strictly speaking, excluded from limitation as the title of this article indicates. Article 3(e) refers to the law governing the contract of employment of the master and crew, which may provide for limitation. If that law is the law of any part of the UK, however, s 185(4) of the MSA 1995 has re-enacted s 35 of the MSA 1979 and exercises the option of unlimited liability for claims by the master and crew against their employer. Section 185(4) provides that the provisions of the Convention shall not apply to any liability for loss of life, or personal injury caused to, or loss of or damage to any property of, a person who is on board the ship in question, or employed in connection with that ship, or with the salvage operations in question if (a) he is on board or employed under a contract of service governed by the law of any part of the UK; and (b) the liability arose from an occurrence that took place after the commencement of this Act (that is, 1 January 1996).

If the law of the contract is foreign, one has to find out whether the law governing the contract provides for unlimited liability, or for limitation which is lower than that provided by Art 6 of the 1996 Convention. If the former is provided, then the limitation of the Convention shall not apply; if the latter is provided, then the limitation of the Convention shall apply. If the limitation is greater than that of Art 6, then the greater limitation shall apply to crew claims.

6 EXCLUSION OF TOTAL LIABILITY

With regard to British ships, the old statute, s 502 of the MSA 1894, provided for exclusion of shipowners' liability for any loss or damage to property (such as cargo) caused by *fire on board, or to valuables by reason of theft, provided the nature and value of valuables had not been declared to the owner at the time of shipment.* An overriding qualification to exclusion from liability was that the loss or damage did not result from the owner's actual fault or privity. Damage by fire includes damage caused by smoke or water to put the fire out.[58] While the section requires a causal connection between the loss or damage and the fire on board, this need not be by actual contact, if it is operative in fact.[59]

This section was repealed and replaced by s 18(1)(a) of the MSA 1979, which maintained the exclusion for the same claims but adopted the test for breaking the right of exclusion from Art 4 of the 1976 Convention. The same provision is now found in s 186(1) of the MSA 1995. This section applies to property so damaged or lost on British ships (except passenger vessels[60] and claims for loss of, or damage to property of persons employed on board, or in connection with the ship, or with salvage operations).[61] Paragraph 3, s 186, adopts the same test for breaking the right to exclude liability as provided in Art 4 of the Convention (examined below). Therefore, the position with these claims for fire or theft of valuables is either total exclusion, or a bar to exclusion, if there is proof of the conduct required by Art 4 of the Convention.[62]

As far as theft of valuables on board is concerned, the exclusion of liability under s 186 of the MSA 1995 will be operative, if neither the nature nor the value of valuables carried on board were declared at the time of the shipment. The only case where the description would be sufficient without an express statement of the value would be where the shipment consists of coin, in which case it may be enough to state the number and description of the coins.[63]

The justification for this exclusion is that it would be unfair to make the shipowner liable for highly expensive cargo for which he did not have an opportunity, if its value was not declared, to charge higher freight. Again the exclusion shall not apply if the conduct required under Art 4 of the Convention is proved (s 186(3)).

Section 186 does not mention whether limitation of liability will apply when the nature and value of such valuables have been declared and loss or damage occurs,

---

58 *The Diamond* [1906] P 28: the crew on board the vessel caused an outbreak of fire by negligently overheating a stove. The plaintiffs' bags of flour and bran on board the vessel were damaged by the fire, smoke and the water used to extinguish the fire. The plaintiffs alleged that the vessel was unseaworthy because the stove was placed too near a bulkhead without any means of insulation and the defendant was privy to the position of the stove. Therefore, they alleged, the defendant was not entitled to exclude his liability on the basis of the MSA 1894, s 502(2). Also, that damage by smoke and water used to extinguish the fire were not within the scope of the statute. It was held that the stove was not placed in an improper position rendering the vessel unseaworthy. Therefore, there was no actual fault or privity on the part of the owners. The judge also held that the water and smoke were matters which occurred by reason of the fire, thus, they were covered under provisions of the statute.

59 *Louis Dreyfus v Tempus Shipping* [1930] 1 KB 699.

60 The MSA 1995, para 13, Pt II, Sched 6, which incorporates the Athens Convention 1974, expressly states that s 186 shall not relieve a person of any liability imposed on him by the Athens Convention.

61 For such claims, limitation is not allowed either by s 185(4) (and previously by s 35 of the MSA 1979).

62 With regard to contracts for the carriage of goods by sea, to which the HVR apply, there is no exclusion from liability, but s 6(4) provides that the right of the British shipowner under the MSA 1995, s 186, is to be treated as a matter of limitation of liability. HVR, Art VIII states that these rules shall not affect the rights and obligations of the carrier under any statute, for the time being in force, relating to limitation of the liability of owners of sea-going ships.

63 *Williams v The African Steam Ship Co* [1856] H&N 300, p 305.

as it is expressly stated under the Athens Convention. By comparison, Art 5 of the Athens Convention provides that the carrier shall not be liable for valuables, unless they have been deposited with the carrier for the purpose of safekeeping, in which case the carrier shall be liable up to the limit provided for by this Convention.

7 CONDUCT BARRING LIMITATION OR EXCLUSION OF LIABILITY

Limitation provisions have rules defining when the right to limit is lost, apart from the Hague Rules which do not attempt to restrict the carrier's right to limit under Art IV, r 5, where it is stated that: 'Neither the carrier nor the ship shall in any event become liable for any loss or damage to or in connection with the goods in an amount exceeding ... unless the nature and value of such goods have been declared by the shipper before shipment and inserted in the bill of lading.'

Under the 1976 Convention, it is difficult, if not impossible, to break the right to limit. The party States to the Convention agreed this stringent test in exchange for higher limits. Article 4 provides:

> A person liable shall not be entitled to limit his liability if it is proved that the loss resulted from his personal act or omission, committed with the intent to cause *such loss*, or recklessly and with knowledge that such loss would probably result.

The Athens Convention 1974, and the 2002 Protocol Art 13 provides, similarly:

> The carrier shall not be entitled to the benefit of the limits of liability prescribed in Arts 7 and 8 and para 1 of Art 10, if it is proved that the damage resulted from an act or omission of the carrier done with intent to cause such damage, or recklessly and with knowledge that *such damage* would probably result

Article IV, r 5(c) of the HVR has almost the same wording:

> Neither the carrier nor the ship shall be entitled to the benefit of the limitation of liability provided for in this paragraph if it is proved that the damage resulted from an act or omission of the carrier done with intent to cause damage, or recklessly and with knowledge that *damage* would probably result.

The Warsaw Convention 1929, as amended by Art 13 of The Hague Protocol 1955, hence, the CAA 1961, similarly provides by Art 25:

> The limits of the liability specified in Art 22 shall not apply if it is proved that the damage resulted from an act or omission of the carrier, his servants or agents, done with intent to cause damage, or recklessly and with knowledge that damage would probably result; provided that, in the case of such act or omission of a servant or agent, it is also proved that he was acting within the scope of his employment.

While, under the 1976 Convention, only 'loss' is mentioned and in the other three Conventions (the Athens Convention, the HVR and The Warsaw Convention) reference is only made to 'damage', Art 8 of the Hamburg Rules provides more certainty by referring to *loss, damage or delay*:

> The carrier is not entitled to the benefit of the limitation of liability provided for in Art 6 if it is proved that the loss, damage, or delay in delivery resulted from an act or omission of the carrier done with intent to cause such loss, damage or delay, or

recklessly and with knowledge that such loss, damage or delay would probably result.

There are slight but not insignificant differences in the wording of these provisions, which may have material effect on the test of breaking limitation to some extent, as will be discussed later.

The test for breaking limitation is, however, strict under the above provisions.

7.1 The test barring limitation under the 1957 and 1976 Conventions (comparison)

7.1.1 *Burden of proof*

Under ss 503 and 502 of the MSA 1894, as amended by the MSA 1958, following the 1957 Limitation Convention, the claimant was entitled to full compensation unless the shipowner, who claimed that he was entitled to limit, or be excluded from liability, discharged the burden of proof that the loss was caused without his 'actual fault or privity'. Many cases were litigated and it was usually difficult for the shipowner to discharge this burden.

Under the 1976 Convention the right to limit shall apply automatically, as Art 2(1) provides 'the following claims ... *shall* be subject to limitation of liability', unless it is proved by the claimant that the party seeking to limit is guilty of the misconduct barring limitation under Art 4.

The court is not obliged to investigate whether or not the person liable is guilty of conduct barring limitation when that person commences a limitation action.[64] The effect of Art 4 is that, once the person liable has established that the claim falls within the claims mentioned in Art 2, he is entitled to a decree of limitation, unless the claimant proves the facts required by Art 4[65] (for example, that the loss resulted from the personal act or omission of the shipowner, or other person liable, committed with the intent to cause such loss, or recklessly and with knowledge that such loss would probably result).

It is obvious that not only is the burden of proof difficult to discharge, but also it is now upon the claimant and not upon the shipowner, as it used to be under the old law.[66] The same applies under the other Conventions mentioned earlier but with the following differences.

(a) *Whose act or omission?* It is the carrier's act or omission under the Athens Convention, the HVR and the Hamburg Rules, while under the 1976 Convention it is emphasised that it is the ***personal*** act or omission of the person liable as referred to therein (see, further, para 7.1.2, below). Under the Warsaw Convention, it is the act or omission of the carrier his servants or agents.

(b) *Whose conduct?* Article 1 of the 1976 Convention defines the persons who are

---

64   *The Bowbelle* [1990] 3 All ER 476, per Sheen J.
65   *The Capitan San Luis* [1994] 1 All ER 1016, per Clarke J.
66   *The Norman* [1960] 1 Lloyd's Rep 1 (HL).

entitled to limit and who have a separate right from each other, that is, the 'person liable'. It is the conduct of that person (as regards a corporate body, see para 8, below). The other Conventions define who is the carrier – whose conduct is important. Under the HVR, Art 1, the 'carrier' includes the owner or the charterer who enters into a contract of carriage covered by a bill of lading, or similar document of title. Under the Athens Convention, and the 2002 Protocol Art 1, 'carrier' means the person in whose name the contract is concluded. He remains responsible, by Art 4, even if the performing carrier performs the contract. The performing carrier means a person other than the carrier, who may be the owner, or the charterer, or the operator of the passengers' ship, who actually performs the whole or a part of the carriage (Art 1(b)). Under the Hamburg Rules, the 'carrier' is the person named in the contract of carriage, and 'actual carrier' is the person entrusted by the carrier to perform the contract. The carrier remains responsible for the acts or omission of the actual carrier and of his servants and agents.

(c) *In relation to what loss or damage?* The conduct mentioned in the 1976 Convention is related to 'such loss' and in the Athens Convention is related to 'such damage' that occurred. The Hamburg Rules, more explicitly, refer to 'such loss, damage or delay'. The HVR and the Warsaw Convention refer to 'damage' (for the interpretation of these words, see para 7.1.6, below).

7.1.2 *Personal act or omission versus acts or omissions of others*

Section 503 of the 1894 Act, as amended, provided that:

(1) The owners of a ship, British or foreign, shall not, where all or any of the following occurrences take place without their actual fault or privity ... be liable beyond the following amounts.

It is important to set out para (c) of this section in order to compare it with the present Convention in relation to 'act or omission':

(c) Where any loss of life or personal injury is caused to any person not carried in the ship through the act or omission of any person (whether on board the ship or not) in the navigation or management of the ship in the loading, carriage or discharge of its cargo or in the embarkation, carriage or disembarkation of its passengers, or through any other act or omission of any person on board the ship.

Similar wording had been adopted in relation to loss of or damage to property under para (d). It is to be noted that, under the old law, it was the 'act or omission of any person', whether on board the ship or not, acting in the navigation or management of the ship etc, and not just the 'personal act or omission' of the person claiming limitation, that was taken into account for limitation purposes.

On the construction given to this wording by the courts, the owners were not able to limit their liability incurred by the fault of a person to whom a task had been delegated by them, such as the managers of the ship (see *The Marion* at para 7.1.4, below), unless they could show that the particular occurrence took place without their actual fault or privity.

By contrast, Art 4 of the 1976 Convention has restricted the 'act or omission' or the 'fault of any person' to the 'personal act or omission' of the person liable (see

The Leerort, as contrasted with *The Saint Jacques* at para 7.1.5, below). For example, even if the act or omission which causes the loss is that of the master of the ship, or any of the crew members acting in the course of their employment, the owner, or salvor, or the charterer or the manager or operator of the ship, whoever was vicariously responsible for the acts or omissions of those servants, would still be able to limit his liability, even if the employee was guilty of the misconduct described in Art 4. Also, if the act or omission is that of the owner's agent, for example, the manager of the ship, the owner will be able to limit, whilst under the old law he was not able to limit for the fault of his agents or servants, if he could not prove that the damage occurred without his actual fault or privity.[67]

The manager or operator, or the master and crew will be able to limit independently, provided their act or omission which caused the loss was not committed with intent to cause such loss, or recklessly and with knowledge that such loss would probably result.

If, however, the manager or operator is not a third party ship-management company, but is integrated within the owner's corporate structure, questions may arise with regard to who was the 'directing mind'[68] of the owning and managing companies, as, invariably, the mind and control of both companies may be the same.

A material difference exists in the wording of Art 25 of the Warsaw Convention, which states that it is also the misconduct of the carriers' servants or agents which will disqualify the carrier from limitation.

The other Conventions do not require 'a personal' act or omission of the carrier, but just 'act or omission of the carrier'. However, there is no material difference other than using the word 'personal' for emphasis in the 1976 Convention. It can be derived from the *travaux préparatoires* to these Conventions that it is only the misconduct of the carrier himself which will defeat the right to limit. This interpretation has been accepted by the English courts in relation to the HVR and the Athens Convention.[69]

7.1.3 'Actual fault or privity' under the 1957 Convention

It is important to look at the leading or accepted Court of Appeal decisions on this issue, since this Convention is still applicable by some maritime nations, and also for the purpose of comparison with the test under the 1976 Convention.

In *Lennard's Carrying Co Ltd v Asiatic Petroleum Co Ltd*,[70] the ship, loaded with cargo of benzene, stranded and then caught fire. The shipowners were a limited company and the managing owners, JM Lennard & Sons Ltd, were another limited company. The managing director of the latter, John Lennard, was the registered managing owner and took an active part in the management of the ship on

---

67 *The Marion* [1984] 2 Lloyd's Rep 1.

68 The concept of the *alter ego* is discussed in para 8, below.

69 Diamond, A (QC), 'The Hague-Visby Rules' [1978] LMCLQ 225; *The European Enterprise* [1989] 2 Lloyd's Rep 195; *The Lion* [1990] 2 Lloyd's Rep 144.

70 [1915] AC 705.

behalf of the owners. Upon a claim by the cargo interests for loss of their cargo, on the ground of unseaworthiness of the ship by reason of the defective condition of her boilers, the owners admitted liability and sought to exclude liability on the basis of s 502 of the MSA 1894. The judge found that the ship was unseaworthy, that the fire and the loss of the cargo were due to that unseaworthiness, and that the loss did not happen without the owners' actual fault or privity. The case reached the House of Lords, and the question for decision was whether the fault of the managing owner was the fault of the company itself for the purpose of s 502.

Lennard was director of both companies entrusted with the management of the vessel. He appeared to be the spirit in the joint stock company. So, Lennard knew or had the means of knowing of the defective condition of the boilers, but he gave no special instructions to the captain or the chief engineer regarding their supervision, and took no steps to prevent the ship putting to sea with her boilers in an unseaworthy condition.

Viscount Haldane said:[71]

> For, if Mr Lennard was the directing mind of the company, then his action must, unless a corporation is not to be liable at all, have been an action which was the action of the company itself, within the meaning of s 502 . . . It must be upon the true construction of that section in such a case as the present one that the fault or privity is the fault or privity of somebody who is not merely a servant or agent for whom the company is liable upon the footing *respondeat superior*, but somebody for whom the company is liable because his action is the very action of the company itself. It is not enough that the fault should be the fault of a servant in order to exonerate the owner, the fault must also be one which is not the fault of the owner, or a fault to which the owner is privy; and I take the view that when anybody sets up that section to excuse himself from the normal consequences of the maxim *respondeat superior* the burden lies upon him to do so.

In *The Lady Gwendolen*,[72] the ship collided with a vessel at anchor during fog.

It was held by the Court of Appeal, confirming the judgment below, that the causes of the collision were, briefly: inadequate use of radar and excessive speed in fog; and the master, who took command of *The Lady Gwendolen*, had had no experience in radar and was given no instructions as to its use or misuse.

The assistant managing director (Williams) was responsible for the vessels and was the *alter ego* of the owning company. The radar problem merited his personal attention. Although the owners' main business was that of brewers, in their capacity as ship owners, they were to be judged by the standard of conduct of the ordinary reasonable ship owner in the management and control of vessels in all matters of safety at sea. The installation of radar required particular vigilance of ship owners through the person (in this case, W) who was responsible, in the capacity of the owners, for the running of the ships. The owners had failed in that vigilance and had failed to consider or appreciate the problems which had arisen through the use of radar and to impress their master with the gravity of risks he was taking. Therefore, they failed to prove that the accident happened without their actual fault or privity.

---

71 Ibid, p 714.
72 [1965] 1 Lloyd's Rep 335.

The marine superintendent in *The Lady Gwendolen*, Mr Robbie, had perused the logs in the performance of his duty, but failed to detect the master's habit of navigation in such dangerous circumstances, or if he did, or suspected it, he failed to warn the master, or deter him from this practice, or take any step to see that the regulations were complied with. He also failed to inform his employers, who, throughout, seemed to have been unaware of the risks the master of this ship was taking. The superintendent did not supervise properly, though the judge was satisfied that he knew enough to enable him to do so.

On these facts, Willmer LJ explained:[73]

> I think the true view is that where shipowners delegate the performance of a duty of the kind conveniently described as 'non-delegable' they are held constructively guilty of fault of its non-performance. This means that, so far as liability is concerned, they cannot escape. But such fault falls short, in my view, of what is meant by 'actual fault' within the meaning of s 503 of the Act. Constructive fault goes only to liability, and leaves untouched the question whether there is such actual fault on the part of the shipowners themselves as will defeat their right to limitation. This seems to me to accord with the view expressed by Lord Justice Buckley in *Asiatic Petroleum Company Ltd v Lennard's Carrying Company Ltd*, p 432, as follows:
>
> > 'The words "actual fault or privity" in my judgment infer something personal to the owner, something blameworthy in him, as distinguished from constructive fault or privity such as the fault or privity of his servants or agents . . .'
>
> I think it is necessary to examine in detail the facts of each particular case in order to see what, in fact, the shipowners did, or omitted to do, which could fairly be said to constitute actual fault on their part . . . .

The word 'privity' was interpreted by Lord Denning MR in ***The Eurysthenes*,[74]** in the context of s 39(5) of the MIA 1906 and, in doing so, he examined the origin and history of the development of the concept of 'fault or privity' in old cases and statutes. His interpretation was adopted in cases in which the courts had to consider the meaning of 'actual fault or privity' under the old system of limitation of liability. Useful extracts of Lord Denning's judgment below sufficiently explain the evolution and meaning of the concept:

> According to the old common law, the master of a servant was only responsible for the acts of his servant if they were done 'by his command or with his privity'. But, if the acts were done by the servant in the course of the master's service, and for his master's benefit, they were presumed to be done by the authority of the master 'although no express command or privity of his master was proved'[75] . . . On the other hand, the owner of a ship was absolutely liable for the loss of goods, because he was a common carrier and liable by the custom of the realm, even though they were stolen without his fault or privity. That was settled in 1674 in the great case of *Morse v Slue*.[76] (It) operated so harshly on shipowners that in 1734 Parliament passed the first of the MSAs (7 Geo 11 c 65) saying that a shipowner was not to be held liable for any loss or damage occasioned by the master or mariners 'without the privity and knowledge' of the owner to an amount greater than the value of the ship. This

---

73 Ibid, pp 344, 345.
74 [1976] 2 Lloyd's Rep 171 (CA).
75 See *Turberville v Stamp* (1697) Raym 264; *Huzzey v Field* (1835) 2 CM&R 440.
76 (1674) 1 Vent 190, p 238.

was followed by a succession of MSAs, all of them directed to limiting the responsibilities of the shipowner for the acts or defaults of his servants. He was not to be liable for acts done 'without his fault or privity' beyond the value of the vessel. The object of these Acts was to limit his liability for his servants on the basis of *respondeat superior*, but to leave him fully liable for faults done by himself personally or with his privity[77] ... This distinction underlies the provision of the MSA 1894, which limits the liability of a shipowner for damage or loss of goods which takes place 'without his actual fault or privity' but leaves him fully liable for acts done by his actual fault or with his privity.

Lord Denning continued:

This historical survey shows to my mind that, when the old common lawyers spoke of a man being 'privy' to something being done, or of an act being done 'with his privity', they meant that he knew of it beforehand and concurred in it being done. If it was a wrongful act done by his servant, then he was liable for it if it was done 'by his command or privity', that is, with his express authority or with his knowledge and concurrence. 'Privity' did not mean that there was any wilful misconduct by him, but only that he knew of the act beforehand and concurred in it being done. Moreover, 'privity' did not mean that he himself personally did the act, but only that someone else did it and that he knowingly concurred in it. Hence, in the later MSAs, the owner was entitled to limit his liability if the act was done without his 'actual fault or privity'. Without his 'actual fault' meant without any actual fault by the owner personally. Without his 'privity' meant without his knowledge or concurrence.

Such is, I think, the meaning we should attach to the word 'privity' in s 39(5). If the ship is sent to sea in an unseaworthy state, with the knowledge and concurrence of the assured personally, the insurer is not liable for any loss attributable to unseaworthiness, that is, to unseaworthiness of which he knew and in which he concurred.

To disentitle the shipowner, he must, I think, have knowledge, not only of the facts constituting the unseaworthiness, but also knowledge that those facts rendered the ship unseaworthy, that is, not reasonably fit to encounter the ordinary perils of the sea. And, when I speak of knowledge, I mean not only positive knowledge but also the sort of knowledge expressed in the phrase 'turning a blind eye'. If a man, suspicious of the truth, turns a blind eye to it, and refrains from inquiry – so that he should not know it for certain – then he is to be regarded as knowing the truth. This 'turning a blind eye' is far more blameworthy than mere negligence. Negligence in not knowing the truth is not equivalent to knowledge of it.[78]

Thus, under the old limitation system, without his 'actual fault' meant without any actual fault by the owner, personally, and the fault of an inefficient manager appointed by the owner would be imputed to the owner, as a matter of law, in a sense of being his actual fault or a fault committed with his privity (*The Marion*, see below). Without his 'privity' meant without his knowledge of and concurrence in the faults of others, but not necessarily amounting to wilful misconduct.

---

77 See *Wilson v Dickson* (1818) 2 B&A 2; *The Spirit of the Ocean* (1865) B&L 336, p 339, per Dr Lushington; *Asiatic Petroleum Co v Lennard's Carrying Co* [1914] 1 KB 419, p 432, per Buckley LJ.
78 [1976] 2 Lloyd's Rep 171, pp 178–79.

7.1.4 Faults of ship-managers under both Conventions (compared)

The extent of managerial duties of owners and managers, especially in relation to the supply of navigational information and publications to their vessels, was in issue in some cases from 1960. The House of Lords, in *The Norman*,[79] shed new light on the duty of managers and, since then, it has no longer been permissible for managers to wash their hands of all questions of navigation or to leave everything to the unassisted discretion of the masters. Any company which embarks on the business of shipowning must accept the obligation to ensure efficient management of its ships, if it is to enjoy the very considerable benefits conferred by the statutory right to limitation.[80]

In 1984, there was the famous limitation of liability case, *The Marion*.[81] The vessel was owned by a Liberian company and was managed by professional managers, an English company, who were insured for third party liabilities with the same P&I club as co-assured of the owners of the ship.

It is important to note in what way the managers were at fault, which prevented limitation by the owners under the old system. What was said in this judgment sounds like the prelude to the kind of supervision needed under the ISM Code today. Such conduct will be relevant when the shipowners' and managers' safety management systems, which they are obliged to maintain under the provisions of the ISM Code, are scrutinised. Defects of the system, however, may or may not amount to the conduct required under Art 4 of the 1976 Convention for the purpose of limitation.[82]

The Marion

The vessel's anchor fouled an oil pipeline on the seabed causing damage to it due to the negligence of the master, who was relying on out-of-date charts. The owners had delegated the management of the ship to third-party managers, an English company. It was the managers' duty to oversee that there were up-to-date charts on board and that the master used them. There was evidence that the master was in the habit of being superficial in this respect and, had he used the new charts, he would have seen the position of the pipeline, so the accident would not have happened. Upon a claim made by the pipeline owners for $25 million, the shipowners admitted liability but sought to limit their liability under s 503 of the MSA 1894, as amended. The issue for the court was whether the damage occurred without the owners' actual fault or privity.

The questions to be decided by the court were: (1) what action should have been taken by the managers as reasonably prudent ship-managers to ensure that *The Marion* was supplied with up-to-date charts? (2) If the answer to this question showed that there was fault on the part of the managers, was that fault a fault for which the owners were liable upon the footing of *respondeat superior*, or was it the

---

79 [1960] 1 Lloyd's Rep 1.
80 *The Lady Gwendolen* [1965] 1 Lloyd's Rep 335, pp 345, 346, per Sir Gordon Willmer; and *The England* [1973] 1 Lloyd's Rep 373, p 383.
81 [1984] 2 Lloyd's Rep 1.
82 See Chapter 8, para 5.8, above, and later in this chapter.

fault of somebody for whom the owners were liable because his action was the very action of the company itself? The judge held that, on the evidence, there was no fault on the part of the managers, so he allowed limitation. He was overruled by the Court of Appeal, which held that the owners had not established that the casualty was caused without their actual fault or privity. The shipowners appealed to the House of Lords. The thrust of the issue was whether the managers had, in their management and operation of *The Marion*, a system by which the managing director ensured that an adequate degree of supervision of the master to keep and observe the up-to-date charts was exercised, either by himself or by his subordinates. Although, in the absence of the director from the office, his subordinate had written to the master to follow the new charts, as had been pointed out by the report on the ship by the flag State, Liberia, he omitted to follow this up and ensure that the master, in fact, did so. The director was in communication with the office but he was not informed about this report. The inference by the House of Lords was that his instructions in this respect to his subordinates were insufficiently clear, so his system of supervision was defective.

Confirming the decision of the Court of Appeal, Lord Brandon said:

> My Lords, in the result, I conclude that there were two actual faults of the appellants: first, in Mr Downard's (director of the managers) failure to have a proper system of supervision in relation to charts; and, secondly, in failing, when he departed to Greece, to give to Mr Lowry and Mr Graham (his subordinates) instructions with regard to the matters about which he required to be kept informed which were sufficiently clear, precise and comprehensive.[83]

Lord Brandon approved the approach of the Court of Appeal in *The England*,[84] in which it had been settled that it was not sufficient to appoint a competent master and delegate all matters to him for the owners or managers to discharge their responsibilities. On the facts of this case, the manager ought to have realised that the master had a propensity to navigate with obsolete charts, requested him to abandon such habit and, if he was incapable of reform, he should have been relieved of his command as captain. Lord Brandon referred to his previous decision in *The Lady Gwendolen* and repeated what he had said in that case, that ship owners must accept the obligation to ensure efficient management of their ships if they are to enjoy the very considerable benefits conferred on them by the statutory right to limitation.

Thus, the owners were not able to limit liability because the fault of the manager constituted, as a matter of law, actual fault of the owners, and such fault caused or contributed to the damage of the pipeline.

If the case were to be decided under the present system of limitation, it would be the managers, separately from the owners, who would seek limitation. Regardless of the fault of Mr Downard, the owners would be able to limit because his fault, which should qualify as a personal omission under Art 4 of the Convention, would not be the personal omission of the owners.[85] However, whether or not the

---

83 [1984] 2 Lloyd's Rep 1, p 8.
84 [1973] 1 Lloyd's Rep 373.
85 See the identification theory, para 8.2, below.

managers would be able to limit under the 1976 Convention, it would depend on proof by the claimants that such personal omission amounted to a reckless conduct and, also, that the person liable was aware that such loss would probably result from his omission (for the interpretation of the words used in Art 4, see below).

While the information in the system of management, which will now be transparent because of the ISM Code, will assist the claimants in the burden of proof under Art 4, it will be a matter of degree as to whether the conduct of the person liable in a particular case amounts to recklessness coupled with the required knowledge. On the facts of *The Marion*, it might be considered reckless under the present system not to have dismissed a master of a ship who was known to be in the habit of navigating with outdated charts and to disregard instructions, but such conduct might not in itself amount to knowledge that the loss suffered would probably result (see paras 7.1.5 and 7.1.6, below).

7.1.5 'Intent or recklessness and with knowledge' under the 1976 Convention

'Intent or wilful misconduct'

There is no difficulty in defining this term, which has been defined in the context of other statutes. In the context of air carriage, it was defined in *Horabin v British Overseas Airways Corp*:[86]

> Wilful misconduct is misconduct to which the will is a party, and it is wholly differ- ent in kind from mere negligence or carelessness, however gross that negligence or carelessness might be. The will must be a party to the misconduct, and not merely a party to the conduct of which complaint is made ... To establish wilful misconduct on the part of ... [the] pilot, it must be shown, not only that he knowingly (and in that sense wilfully) did the wrongful act, but also that, when he did it, he was aware that it was a wrongful act, ie that he was aware that he was committing misconduct ...

More recently, and in the context of safety practices as envisaged by the regulations in air carriage, it was said in *Rolls Royce plc v Heavylift-Volga Dnepr Ltd*:[87]

> For the finding of wilful misconduct the court must find on a balance of probabilities that the acts (or omissions) alleged to constitute the misconduct must not only fall below the standards to be expected of persons acting reasonably, but be sufficiently below such standards as to be capable of being regarded as 'misconduct', and not just as careless, or very, or grossly careless. Second, the person must know that he is misconducting himself when he does (or fails to do) the acts complained of and does them intentionally or recklessly as to the consequences.

'Recklessness'

The present system clearly requires either wilful misconduct ('intent') or 'reckless- ness' and, in addition to recklessness, the person liable must have had particular 'knowledge that such loss would probably result'.

---

86 [1952] 2 Lloyd's Rep 450, p 459.
87 [2000] 1 Lloyd's Rep 653.

These words have been interpreted in criminal law and, in the context of Art 25 of the Warsaw Convention, in connection with claims by air passengers. Since the first edition of this book, there have been a few cases on the meaning of these words under Art 4 of the 1976 Convention, which will be seen later.

First, it is important to look at how 'recklessness' is treated in criminal law, as there has been a recent re-examination of the test. Then, it will be demonstrated how these words have been interpreted under both the Warsaw Convention and the 1976 Convention.

Under criminal law, 'intent' means the subjective intent (*mens rea*) of the person liable. The test of 'recklessness' was defined 24 years ago by Lord Diplock in *R v Caldwell*[88] in the context of s 1 of the Criminal Damage Act 1971:

> A person charged with an offence under section 1(1) . . . is reckless . . . if (1) he does an act which in fact creates an obvious risk that property will be destroyed or damaged and (2) when he does the act he either has not given any thought to the possibility of there being any such risk or has recognised that there was some risk involved and has none the less gone on to do it . . .

> to decide whether someone has been 'reckless' as to whether harmful consequences of a particular kind will result from his act, as distinguished from his actually intending such harmful consequences to follow, does call for some consideration of how the mind of the ordinary prudent individual would have reacted to a similar situation. If there were nothing in the circumstances that ought to have drawn the attention of an ordinary prudent individual to the possibility of that kind of harmful consequence, the accused would not be described as 'reckless' in the natural meaning of that word for failing to address his mind to the possibility; nor, if the risk of the harmful consequences was so slight that the ordinary prudent individual upon due consideration of the risk would not be deterred from treating it as negligible, could the accused be described as 'reckless' in its ordinary sense if, having considered the risk, he decided to ignore it.[89]

Thus, the test as set by Lord Diplock was that there must be an obvious risk assessed by the standards of a reasonable prudent man.

Lord Hailsham in *R v Lawrence*[90] agreed with Lord Diplock's definition of recklessness by saying:

> I share the distaste for the obsessive use of the expressions 'objective' and 'subjective' (test) in crime. In all indictable crime, it is a general rule that there are objective factors of conduct which constitute the so called '*actus reus*,' and a further guilty state of mind which constitutes the so called '*mens rea*' . . . It is, of course, true that in a legal context, the state of mind described as 'reckless' is discussed in connection with conduct objectively blameworthy, as well as dangerous.[91]

The *Caldwell* test, which had, until recently, been followed, adopted (by a majority of 2:1) the wider interpretation of recklessness, namely that the term covers advertent and inadvertent wrongdoing. By bringing within the reach of s 1(1) of the CDA 1971 cases of inadvertent recklessness, the decision in *Caldwell* became a source of

---

88   [1982] AC 341 (HL).

89   Ibid, p 354.

90   [1982] AC 510 (HL).

91   Ibid, pp 520–21.

potential injustice, as Lord Steyn said in the following decision. Lord Diplock's test was criticised by academics and judges that it amounted, in effect, to not examining the state of mind of the accused.

Thus, the House of Lords in *R v G*[92] (in which two boys set fire in a shop by setting fire to some newspapers) was asked to re-examine the meaning of the word 'recklessness' in the context of s 1 of the CDA 1971, and it departed from the test in *Caldwell* by placing emphasis on a *subjective awareness of the risk.*

It was held that, in order to convict of an offence under s 1, it had to be shown that the defendant's state of mind was culpable in that he acted recklessly in respect of a circumstance if he was aware of a risk which did or would exist, or in respect of a result if he was aware of a risk that it would occur, and it was, in the circumstances known to him, unreasonable to take the risk. The accepted meaning of recklessness involved foresight of consequences. The shift is towards adopting a subjective approach by looking at the matter in the light of how it would have appeared to the defendant.

'Recklessness and with knowledge'

In the context of interpretation of words used in Conventions, however, the Court of Appeal, in *Goldman v Thai Airways International*[93] (which, at the time, had to look at the test of *Caldwell*), cautioned against construing an international Convention on the basis of English statutes, and Eveleigh LJ said:

> When conduct is stigmatised as reckless, it is because it engenders the risk of undesirable consequences. When a person acts recklessly he acts in a manner which indicates a decision to run the risk or a mental attitude of indifference to its existence. . . . One cannot, therefore, decide whether or not an act or omission is done recklessly without considering the nature of the risk involved. In the present case, the omission relied upon was the failure to order seat belts to be fastened. The risk with which we are concerned, therefore, is the risk of injury to the passenger whose belt should have been fastened. If the article had stopped at the word 'recklessly', I would have been prepared to say that, on the judge's findings, the plaintiff had proved his case. This is because, on those findings, the pilot had deliberately ignored his instructions which he knew were for the safety of the passengers, and, thus, demonstrated a willingness to accept a risk. Also, it might be said that he thought that he knew better than those responsible for the manual and, while this might mean that he in his own mind saw no risk, he was, in fact, taking the risk that his judgment was better than that of other experts. If this is so, I would be prepared to say, as did the judge, that a deliberate disregard of the rule must be considered recklessness in the circumstances of the case. I shall consider later whether or not a deliberate disregard of instructions has been proved. However, the doing of the act or omission is not only qualified by the adverb 'recklessly', but also by the adverbial phrase 'with knowledge that damage would probably result'. If the pilot did not know that damage would probably result from his omission, I cannot see that we are entitled to attribute to him knowledge which another pilot might have possessed or which he himself should have possessed. I appreciate that, when introducing an English version to coincide with a French text, there is naturally an inclination to

---

92 [2003] UKHL 50, [2003] 3 WLR 1060.
93 [1983] 1 WLR 1186.

follow the pattern of that text and where possible to avoid a free translation. Even so, I cannot believe that lawyers who intended to convey the meaning of the well known phrase 'when he knew or ought to have known' would have adopted 'with knowledge'.[94]

... An act may be reckless when it involves a risk, even though it cannot be said that the danger envisaged is a probable consequence. It is enough that it is a possible consequence, although of course there comes a point where the risk is so remote that it would not be considered reckless to take it. We look for an element of rashness which is perhaps more clearly indicated in the French text *'temerairement'*, Art 25, however, refers not to possibility, but to the probability of resulting damage. Thus, something more than a possibility is required. The word 'probable' is a common enough word. I understand it to mean that something is likely to happen. I think that is what is meant in Art 25. In other words, one anticipates damage from the act or omission.[95]

Lord Eveleigh continued:

I say at once that, reading Art 25 as a whole for the moment and not pausing to give an isolated meaning to the word 'recklessly', the article requires the plaintiff to prove the following: (1) that the damage resulted from an act or omission; (2) that it was done with intent to cause damage; or (3) that it was done when the doer was aware that damage would probably result, but he did so regardless of that probability; (4) that the damage complained of is the kind of damage known to be the probable result.[96]

The revised test of recklessness in criminal law by the House of Lords in *R v G*, putting emphasis on the subjective realisation that the risk or the result would occur, has close affinity with Lord Eveleigh's test of recklessness, save for the particular emphasis in the Convention that the person seeking to limit must also have had knowledge that the kind of damage complained of would probably result. Thus, a person acts recklessly and with knowledge that damage would probably result when he anticipates that damage would be likely to follow from his act or omission.

An interesting examination of 'knowledge' can be found in the judgment of the Court of Appeal in *Nugent v Michael Goss Aviation*,[97] concerning Art 25 of the Warsaw Convention, where the knowledge of the pilot was under scrutiny. Three types of knowledge were examined: actual knowledge, background knowledge, and imputed knowledge. It was stressed that the approach of the court is to identify actual knowledge and to reject imputed knowledge. As to the background knowledge, it was more difficult to determine its effect on actual knowledge, and it was argued that it should be regarded as the 'store' of knowledge being part of actual knowledge, albeit that it may be forgotten at the time. The majority decided that the intention of the legislation is to attribute a narrow scope to the provision of limitation, and that was voted by a majority at the 1955/56 Hague Conference which amended Art 25 of the Warsaw Convention. It was not sufficient to show that, by reason of his training and experience, the pilot ought to have known that damage

---

94 Ibid, p 1194.
95 Ibid, p 1196.
96 Ibid, p 1194.
97 [2000] 2 Lloyd's Rep 222 (CA).

would probably result from his act or omission. There was no basis for concluding that those who agreed the text of Art 25 intended to include background knowledge. But this is not to say that background knowledge is totally ignored; the greater the obviousness of the risk, the more likely the tribunal is to infer recklessness and that the defendant, in so doing, knew that he would probably cause damage. Inference is different from imputing.[98] There could not be a deeming provision of knowledge if the person did not have that knowledge present in his mind at the time. The article requires that there should be knowledge of the probable consequences.

There is a clear distinction in the legislature between what a person ought to (or should) have known and what a person must have known (or did know).[99]

The same approach is followed with regard to the interpretation of Art 4 of the 1976 Convention. Unlike in the past, there have recently been a few decisions on Art 4. In *The MSC Rosa M*,[100] the cargo interests, in their defence to a limitation decree (applied for by the demise charterers of the ship), alleged that there were various defects in the fuel and ballast systems which caused the ship to take in water and list, with the result that it had to be abandoned by the crew and eventually salved. The cargo interests became liable to a substantial amount of salvage. They contended that, as the captain and technical director had been advised of these defects, he ought to have known of them. His failure to give instructions to check the cross-connections of the valves amounted to reckless disregard for the safety of the ship and that, as a master mariner and technical director of the company, he would know that failure to take those steps would lead to the risk of a serious incident.

Steel J held that, as regards knowledge under Art 4, this meant actual and not constructive knowledge. It was insufficient to make an allegation that the relevant person ought to have known something. The judge was not persuaded, following *Nugent*, that it was open to the cargo interests to say that the kind of 'shut-eye' knowledge, as explained by Lord Denning in *The Eurysthenes* (ie refraining from asking relevant questions in the hope that, by his lack of enquiry, he will not know for certain), constitutes actual knowledge for the purpose of Art 4. Although he did not have to decide the point, he said that in this case it was not suggested that the demise charterer consciously suspected other defects and he deliberately chose not to check, so as to avoid turning suspicion into awareness (which is a different inquiry).[101] It must be shown by cargo interests that, at the time of those alleged acts or omissions, the alter ego of the demise charterers actually knew that a capsize would probably result.

By contrast, in *Saint Jacques II and Gudermes*,[102] a case which was described by the judge to be exceptional, there was a real prospect of defeating the right to limit.

---

98 Ibid, pp 227, 232: 'But as a matter of proof, the two will often stand or fall together'.

99 See *Rolls Royce v HVD* [2000] 1 Lloyd's Rep 653, p 659; also, in the context of s 39(5) of MIA 1906, such distinction was made in *The Star Sea* [1997] 1 Lloyd's Rep 360, p 378 (CA) and [2001] 1 Lloyd's Rep 389, and in the following cases concerning limitation of liability: *Nugent v Michael Goss Aviation* [2000] 2 Lloyd's Rep 222; *The MSC Rosa M* [2000] 2 Lloyd's Rep 399.

100 [2000] 2 Lloyd's Rep 399.

101 The test applied to s 39(5) of MIA 1906; see *The Star Sea* [2001] 1 Lloyd's Rep 389.

102 [2003] 1 Lloyd's Rep 203.

The *Saint Jacques* was navigating across the Traffic Separation Scheme, as a rogue vessel contravening reg 10 of the Collision Regulations. Both the skipper, who happened to be the owner of the vessel, and the deckhand were aware of the contravention, and they were doing this in order to reach the fishing grounds before other vessels. She collided with *Gudermes*. The skipper commenced the limitation action. The judge decided that the matter should go to trial but, on the issue of reckless navigation, he decided that the conduct of the claimant was a repeated practice in flagrant breach of the Collision Regulations, directed personally by the claimant for commercial reasons, and there was a real prospect for the defendant to defeat the claimant's right to limit at trial.

In *The Leerort*,[103] an anchored ship on berth was struck by another, entering the harbour, resulting in breaching one hold, which caused flooding and damage to its cargo. It was held that the limitation provisions of the 1976 Convention provide even greater protection to the person seeking to limit than those applicable in relation to carriage by air. It must be the causative personal act or omission of the person liable which could defeat the right to limit, and the test required a foresight of the very loss that actually occurred. Limitation was permitted.

Under the Warsaw Convention, it is also the act or omission of servants or agents which are taken into account; see *Nugent v Michael Goss Aviation*[104] in which, as regards 'knowledge', it was restated by the Court of Appeal that those who drafted Art 25 of this Convention did not intend that anything less than actual conscious knowledge would suffice. An interesting question was raised at first instance as to whether 'turning a blind eye' would be consistent with the knowledge required by Art 25. The judge ruled that it would not be consistent, but Pill LJ, who dissented on appeal only on the issue of whether background knowledge was relevant (see earlier), disagreed with the judge. The matter does not appear to have been dealt with by the majority, as it was not relevant to the decision, but the outcome of the reasoning of the majority points towards agreement with the judge. It is important, however, to note what Pill LJ said in this respect:

> The article does not permit in my view the actor to say that his knowledge is no longer his knowledge because he has made a conscious decision to put it out of his mind.[105]

Such statement is in accord with what the House of Lords said in *The Star Sea*[106] in the context of s 39(5) of the MIA 1906, where it was stated, by way of drawing a parallel, that:

> Privity in its ordinary meaning connotes knowledge. 'Blind-eye' knowledge approximates to knowledge. Nelson at the battle of Copenhagen made a deliberate decision to place the telescope to his blind eye in order to avoid seeing what he knew he would see if he placed it to his good eye. It is, I think, common ground – and if it is not, it should be – that an imputation of blind-eye knowledge requires an amalgam

---

103 [2001] 2 Lloyd's Rep 291.
104 [2000] 2 Lloyd's Rep 222.
105 Ibid, p 231.
106 [2001] 1 Lloyd's Rep 389, p 413.

of suspicion that certain facts may exist and a decision to refrain from taking any step to confirm their existence.

In other words, this statement should mean that actual knowledge is deliberately suppressed.

Although it has been stressed, in the decisions cited above, that actual knowledge is necessary for the purpose of Arts 25 and 4 of the respective conventions, it is submitted that actual knowledge should be inferred if the facts show that a deliberate action was taken to obscure the realisation of actual knowledge, once it was consciously realised that such knowledge should be put out of mind. In that sense, 'blind-eye' knowledge should be taken into account in the test.

7.1.6 'Loss' and 'such loss'

Under the old system of limitation, s 503 of the MSA 1894, as amended, referred to occurrences with respect to which the owner would not be liable beyond certain limits, and then referred to 'such loss, damage, or infringement' in relation to which the conduct, 'actual fault or privity', barring limitation would bite.

Under the 1976 Convention, there is only reference to 'loss' in Art 4; this should be relevant to damage also in relation to various claims outlined in Art 2, although it is curious why the word 'damage' has been omitted. By contrast, the word 'damage' is used in Art 25 of the Warsaw Convention, the HVR, Art IV, r 5(e), and in Art 13 of the Athens Convention, while in the Hamburg Rules the words 'loss, damage or delay' are used.

Although the provisions of limitation under the various Conventions are not identical, it must have been intended that the bar to limitation would be applicable to either 'loss' or 'damage'. Etymologically, 'damage' is harm from which one suffers loss; 'loss' embraces damage, and it should embrace loss resulting from delay. Another difference also exists between the Conventions with regard to loss or damage that relates to the mental element. For example, the 1976 Convention refers to 'with intent to cause *such* loss, or recklessly and with knowledge that such loss would probably result'; the Athens Convention refers to 'such damage'; while the Hamburg Rules refer to 'such loss, damage or delay'. By contrast, the HVR and the Warsaw Convention, as amended, link the misconduct generally to 'damage' without using the word '*such*'. This may, or may not, be of a material significance when reading the interpretation given to these words by Eveleigh LJ, when he said, in *Goldman*:

> It is with rather less confidence that I have said that the damage anticipated must be of the same kind of damage as that suffered. I have reached my conclusion because Art 25 is designed to cover cases of damage both to the person – in other words, injury – and to property . . . There may be occasions when an act can be said to be done recklessly in regard to one possible kind of damage, although morally wholly justified as the price of averting some other more serious hurt. Perhaps, one could resolve this matter by saying that recklessness involves an element of moral turpitude. If all that can be anticipated is the spilling of a cup of tea over someone's dress, it does seem wrong that the pilot should be blamed for unexpected personal injuries. Whether or not I am right in this, I am satisfied that the pilot must have knowledge that damage will result from his omission. With respect to the judge, I cannot see that the fact that a wine glass may slip from a tray and cut a passenger's leg should make

the carriers liable for unlimited damages in respect of an injury suffered because there was no seat belt to protect him. The damage, whether it is referred to as 'the damage' or merely 'damage,', refers to something which results from the omission. The French text, by the use of the word '*en*', clearly establishes this.[107]

Purchas LJ said that 'damage' involves probable damage contemplated by the article.[108] This is also reflected in the fourth limb of the test of Eveleigh LJ (see under para 7.1.4, above): 'that the damage complained of is the kind of damage known to be the probable result'. The examples given by Eveleigh LJ above require pause for thought. He juxtaposed anticipated minor damage with a very serious one, and suggested that the right to limit should not be barred if the serious one was not anticipated. This is similar to the remoteness rule in damages and makes sense.

Since the first edition of this book, where it was suggested that 'such loss' might mean the type of loss and not the very loss suffered, which must have been anticipated, there have been some maritime cases on this point: in *The MSC Rosa M,*[109] Steel J said that:

> ... The person challenging the right to limit must establish both reckless conduct and knowledge that the relevant loss would probably result.

In *The Leerort,*[110] Lord Phillips MR said:

> It seems to me that this requires foresight of the very loss that actually occurs, not merely of the type of loss that occurs ... the words 'such loss' clearly refers back to the loss that has actually resulted and which is the subject matter of the claim in which the right to limit is asserted.

There was emphasis that the wording of the limitation provisions in relation to merchant shipping provides even greater protection than air carriage and requires restrictive interpretation.

What if the anticipated loss was a collision damage? Should the liable person have anticipated that a collision may occur with the particular ship? or with any ship? This was dealt with in *The Leerort* but it was not necessary to decide which alternative was correct. In either event the reality was, the court said, that:

> When damage results from collision the ship owner will only lose his right to limit if it can be proved that he deliberately or recklessly acted in a way which he knew was likely to result in the loss of or damage to the property of another in circumstances where, inevitably, the same consequences would be likely to flow to his own vessel.[111]

8 CORPORATE PERSONALITY AND WHOSE MISCONDUCT SHOULD BE ATTRIBUTED TO THE COMPANY

The owners, managers or operators, or charterers of ships are corporate bodies. In law, a personality is attributed to a corporation by a fiction. Since a corporation is

---

107 [1983] 1 WLR 1186, p 1196.
108 Ibid, p 1202.
109 [2002] 2 Lloyd's Rep 399, p 401.
110 [2001] 2 Lloyd's Rep 291, p 295.
111 Ibid, p 295.

not a living person with mind and hands to carry out its intentions, certain rules of attribution of liability have developed. The first rule of attribution is commonly known as the *'alter ego'* doctrine, which has been understood to mean the directing mind of the company. Later, this was better expressed as the 'identification' doctrine, because the exercise has been to identify the persons in the company who make the decisions and are commonly described as the 'brains and nerve centre' of the company. The second rule of attribution of liability to a company is known as the 'vicarious liability' doctrine, by which liability can be attributed to a company through the acts or omissions of its servants or agents who are lower in the hierarchy than the board of directors, but carry out activities on behalf of the company during the course of their employment.

However, since in certain circumstances, neither the identification doctrine nor the vicarious liability one has given satisfactory answers to all questions of attributing liability to a company, a new more flexible approach to attributing liability has developed. This is known as 'the *Meridian* rule of attribution', derived from the name of the case in which it was developed.[112] By this approach, the court has to interpret the substantive rule of law under which liability is sought in order to determine whether the policy or the intention of the substantive rule, which is usually a statute or convention, requires the court to attribute liability to the company in question, even if the damage or loss claimed of, or the breach of duty, was caused or committed by a person lower in the hierarchy of the company's directing mind.

It is important to recapitulate, in this context, how these concepts developed over the years and which rule of attribution would seem to be appropriate in the context of limitation of liability under the 1976 Convention, while also making a comparison with the old system of limitation.

8.1 The concept of the *'alter ego'* of a corporation

The alter ego concept was first developed by English judges to ascribe a mind to a corporation. In 1915, the issue arose in relation to the 'fault or privity' of the owner, under s 502 of the MSA 1894, in **Lennard's Carrying Co Ltd v Asiatic Petroleum Co Ltd** (seen earlier).[113] Viscount Haldane stated:[114]

> A corporation is an abstraction. It has no mind of its own any more than it has a body of its own; its active and directing will must consequently be sought in the person of somebody who for some purposes may be called an agent, but who is really the directing mind and will of the corporation, the very ego and centre of the personality of the corporation. That person may be under the direction of the shareholders in general meeting; that person may be the board of directors itself, or it may be, and in some companies it is so, that that person has an authority co-ordinate with the board of directors given to him under the articles of association, and is appointed by the

---

112 See a summary of these principles in Chapter 8, para 5.5, above, and *Meridian Global Funds Management Asia Ltd v Securities Commission* [1995] 3 All ER 918, under para 8.3, below.

113 [1915] AC 705.

114 Ibid, p 713.

general meeting of the company, and can only be removed by the general meeting of the company . . .

In the well-known decision of *The Lady Gwendolen*,[115] the Court of Appeal was prepared to attribute actual fault to the company, for the purpose of no limitation of liability under s 503 of MSA 1894, through the fault of persons below the board and a person who was not a director but head of the traffic department and the registered ship's manager.[116] It did not have to reach a final conclusion, however, because, in the particular circumstances of the case, all concerned from the board of directors downwards were guilty of actual fault for failures in the management of their ship.

With the obvious sources of fault lying with the master and the marine super-intendent (as seen under para 7.1.3, above) the Court of Appeal held:

> It is on account of the introduction of radar and the learned judge's view of an owner's obligation with regard to the supervision of its use. Reliance on a competent master and an efficient marine superintendent has been held by him not to be enough to exonerate the owners.

> Mr D Williams was the assistant managing director of the plaintiff company. He had previously been the head brewer. Later, he took charge of the traffic depart-ment, whose function it was to manage and control the ships owned by the com-pany for the purpose of distributing its product. Mr DW Boucher was the traffic manager, but his training and experience had not been with ships, but with rail-ways. He was no doubt expert in arranging the dispatch of the cargo. The highest in the management who had any real knowledge of ships was Mr Robbie, the marine superintendent.

Per Willmer LJ (at 344, 345):

> It is necessary to look closely at the organisation of the company in order to see of what individual it can fairly be said that his act or omission is that of the company itself. The decision in *Lennard*'s case, of course, affords valuable guidance in the conduct of this inquiry. . . .

> But neither in the Court of Appeal nor in the House of Lords was said that a person whose actual fault would be the company's actual fault must necessarily be a dir-ector. Where, as in the present case, a company has a separate traffic department, which assumes responsibility for running the company's ships, I see no good reason why the head of that department, even though not himself a director, should not be regarded as someone whose action is the very action of the company itself, so far as concerns anything to do with the company's ships. In the present case Mr Boucher was not only the head of the traffic department, but he was also the registered ships' manager.

As seen earlier, Lord Denning MR, in *The Eurysthenes*,[117] unravelled the mean-ing of 'privity' in relation to the *alter ego*, and said:

---

115 [1965] 1 Lloyd's Rep 335.

116 However, such dicta were disapproved of by Lord Diplock in *Tesco Supermarkets v Nattrass* [1972] AC 153 (HL), p 200 (see below under para 8.2 fn 130).

117 [1976] 2 Lloyd's Rep 171, p 179.

The knowledge must . . . be the knowledge of the shipowner personally, or his *alter ego*, or, in the case of a company, its head men or whoever may be considered their *alter ego*.

In 1989, Mustill LJ (as he then was) did not wish to draw a general rule restricting *alter ego* to the board of directors, in *The Ert Stefanie*.[118] In particular, he said:

The board of directors of a corporation may not always comprise the whole of the group of people who together constitute the governing mind and will of the corporation, for the cases show clearly that the fault of a senior manager below board level may on occasion be included in the group. Nevertheless, it seems to me that any director must necessarily be a member of the group unless formally dis-seised of responsibility in the manner just described. Thus, I would prefer to steer clear of generalisations about the constituent elements of the *alter ego*. Each case must turn on its own facts.[119]

The concept of the 'alter ego', as distinguished from the 'ego' of a company, was more clearly explained by Lord Reid in the *Tesco* case (see below).

8.2 The 'identification' doctrine

In 1944, three justices of the Divisional Court, in **DPP v Kent and Sussex Contractors Ltd**,[120] overruled the court below in a criminal case, in which the court was of the opinion that the company could not, in law, be guilty of the offences charged. It was explained by Viscount Caldecote CJ that:

[In the present case] the offences created by the regulation are those of doing something with intent to deceive or of making a statement known to be false in a material particular. There was ample evidence, on the facts as stated in the special case, that the company, by the only people who could act or speak or think for it had done both these things.[121]

Furthemore, Hallett J said:

With regard to the liability of a body corporate for torts or crimes, a perusal of the cases shows, to my mind, that there has been a development in the attitude of the courts arising from the large part played in modern times by limited liability companies. At one time, the existence, and later the extent and conditions of such a body's liability in tort was a matter of doubt, due partly to the theoretical difficulty of imputing wrongful acts or omissions to a fictitious person, and it required a long series of decisions to clear up the position. Similarly, the liability of a body corporate for crimes was at one time a matter of doubt, partly owing to the theoretical difficulty of imputing a criminal intention to a fictitious person and partly to technical difficulties of procedure.[122]

In 1957, the concept of identification of the relevant persons in a company hierarchy was clearly defined, when Denning LJ approved the approach of the court in the

---

118 [1989] 1 Lloyd's Rep 349.
119 Ibid, p 352.
120 [1944] KB 146.
121 Ibid, p 156.
122 Ibid, p 157.

last case, and stated that the same principle should apply in both civil and criminal cases. He said, in *HL Bolton (Engineering) Co Ltd v TJ Graham & Sons Ltd*:[123]

> A company may in many ways be likened to a human body. It has a brain and nerve centre which controls what if does. It also has hands which hold the tools and act in accordance with directions from the centre. Some of the people in the company are mere servants and agents who are nothing more than hands to do the work and cannot be said to represent the mind or will. Others are directors and managers who represent the directing mind and will of the company and control what it does. The state of mind of these managers is the state of mind of the company and is treated by the law as such. So you will find that, in cases where the law requires personal fault as a condition of liability in tort, the fault of the manager will be the personal fault of the company. That is made clear in Lord Haldane's speech in *Lennard's Carrying Co Ltd v Asiatic Petroleum Co Ltd*. So, also, in the criminal law, in cases where the law requires a guilty mind as a condition of a criminal offence, the guilty mind of the directors or the managers will render the company itself guilty.

In 1972, the identification doctrine was adopted by the House of Lords in *Tesco Supermarkets v Nattrass*, in the context of offences under the Trade Descriptions Act (TDA) 1968, and in which the concept of the *alter ego* was, for the first time, questioned.

Tesco Supermarkets v Nattrass [124]

The defendants, a body corporate owning supermarket stores, were charged with an offence, under the TDA 1968, for failing to display the correct prices on goods at a branch. They sought to raise a defence under s 24(1) on the grounds that the commission of the offence was due to the act or default of another person, namely, the manager of the store at which the offence was committed, and that they had taken all reasonable precautions and exercised all due diligence to avoid the commission of such an offence. The shop manager was not a person within s 20, carrying out functions as a director, manager, secretary or other similar.

Lord Reid said:

> I must start by considering the nature of the personality which by a fiction the law attributes to a corporation. A living person has a mind which can have knowledge or intention or be negligent and he has hands to carry out his intentions. A corporation has none of these: it must act through living persons, though not always one or the same person. Then the person who acts is not speaking or acting for the company. He is acting as the company and his mind which directs his acts is the mind of the company. There is no question of the company being vicariously liable. He is not acting as a servant, representative, agent or delegate. He is an embodiment of the company or, one could say, he hears and speaks through the persona of the company, within his appropriate sphere, and his mind is the mind of the company. If it is a guilty mind then that guilt is the guilt of the company. It must be a question of law whether, once the facts have been ascertained, a person, in doing particular things, is to be regarded as the company, or merely as the company's servant or agent. In that case, any liability of the company can only be a statutory or vicarious liability . . .

---

123 [1957] 1 QB 159, p 172, relating to the intention of a limited company owning property and managed by its directors.

124 [1972] AC 153 (HL).

Normally the board of directors, the managing director and perhaps other superior officers of a company carry out the functions of management and speak and act as the company. Their subordinates do not. They carry out orders from above and it can make no difference that they are given some measure of discretion. But the board of directors may delegate some part of their functions of management, giving to their delegate full discretion to act independently of instructions from them. I see no difficulty in holding that they have thereby put such a delegate in their place, so that within the scope of the delegation he can act as the company.[125]

In some cases, the phrase *alter ego* has been used. I think it is misleading. When dealing with a company the word *alter* is I think misleading. The person who speaks and acts as the company is not *alter*. He is identified with the company. And when dealing with an individual, no other individual can be his *alter ego*. The other individual can be a servant, agent, delegate or representative, but I know of neither principle nor authority which warrants the confusion (in the literal or original sense) of two separate individuals . . .

I have said that a board of directors can delegate part of their functions of management so as to make their delegate an embodiment of the company within the sphere of the delegation. But here, the board never delegated any part of their functions. They set up a chain of command through regional and district supervisors, but they remained in control. The shop managers had to obey their general directions and also take orders from their superiors. The acts or omissions of shop managers were not acts of the company itself.[126]

Viscount Dilhorne and Lord Pearson suggested that one has to determine who are in actual control of a company, which may vary from one company to another.[127] Viscount Dilhorne said, in particular:

If, when Denning LJ referred to directors and managers representing the directing mind and will of the company, he meant, as I think he did, those who constitute the directing mind and will, I agree with his approach. These passages, I think, clearly indicate that one has, in relation to a company, to determine who is or who are, for it may be more than one, in actual control of the operations of the company, and the answer to be given to that question may vary from company to company depending on its organisation.[128]

Similarly, Lord Pearson said:[129]

In the case of a company, the ego is located in several persons . . . in similar position of direction or general management. A company may have an *alter ego*, if those persons who are or have its ego delegate to some other person the control and management, with full discretionary powers, of some section of the company's business. In the case of a company, it may be difficult, and in most cases for practical purposes unnecessary, to draw the distinction between its ego and its *alter ego*, but theoretically there is that distinction.

[In this case] Mr Clement, being the manager of one of the company's several hundreds of shops, could not be identified with the company's *ego*, nor was he an *alter*

---

125 Ibid, pp 170–72.
126 [1972] AC 153 (HL), pp 174–75.
127 This approach is similar to that followed by the CA in *The Star Sea* [1997] 1 Lloyd's Rep 360.
128 *Tesco v Nattrass* [1972] AC 153 (HL), p 187.
129 Ibid, p 193.

ego of the company. He was an employee in a relatively subordinate post. In the company's hierarchy, there were a branch inspector and an area controller and a regional director interposed between him and the board of directors.

It was suggested in the argument of this appeal that, in exercising supervision over the operations in the shop, Mr Clement was performing functions of management and acting as a delegate and *alter ego* of the company. But supervision of the details of operations is not normally a function of higher management: it is normally carried out by employees at the level of foremen, charge hands, overlookers, floor managers and 'shop' managers . . .

This decision has made an important clarification of the concept known as *'alter ego'*. It was stressed by their Lordships that the person acting as the company, having control of the company, is not a delegate but the embodiment of the company. Such person is not an *'alter ego'* but the *'ego'* of the company although for practical purposes it may be difficult to draw such a distinction (per Lord Pearson). If the persons in control, the directors of a company, delegate control by giving full discretionary power to the delegate to perform certain tasks, his acts will be acts of the company (the *'alter ego'*). Supervision of details of a function by a manager is not making him the *'alter ego'* in that sense.

Lord Diplock emphasised, in the following passage, that no extension of the class of people identified with a company should be made beyond those who are entrusted with the control of the company by the articles of association:

There has been in recent years a tendency to extract from Denning LJ's judgment in *HL Bolton (Engineering) Co Ltd v TJ Graham & Sons Ltd* [1957] 1 QB 159, pp 172, 173, his vivid metaphor about the 'brains and nerve centre' of a company as contrasted with its hands, and to treat this dichotomy, and not the articles of association, as laying down the test of whether or not a particular person is to be regarded in law as being the company itself when performing duties which a statute imposes on the company.

In the case in which this metaphor was first used, Denning LJ was dealing with acts and intentions of directors of the company in whom the powers of the company were vested under its articles of association. The decision in that case is not authority for extending the class of persons whose acts are to be regarded in law as the personal acts of the company itself, beyond those who by, or by action taken under, its articles of association are entitled to exercise the powers of the company. Insofar as there are *dicta* to the contrary in *The Lady Gwendolen* [1965] P 294, they were not necessary to the decision and, in my view, they were wrong.[130]

In 1994, **The Safe Carrier**[131] concerned the duty of shipowners, charterers and managers to take reasonable steps to ensure the safe operation of their ships. Breach of this duty is a criminal offence by statute, s 31 of the MSA 1988 and now s 100 of the MSA 1995.

The House of Lords held that there would be a breach of duty if there was a failure to take steps which, by an objective standard, were held to be reasonable steps to take in the interests of the safe operation of a ship; the duty which the section placed on the owners, charterers or managers was a personal one. The

---

130 *Tesco Supermarkets v Nattrass* [1972] AC 153 (HL), p 200.
131 [1994] 1 Lloyd's Rep 589 (HL).

owner, charterer or manager would be criminally liable if he failed personally in the duty, but would not be criminally liable for the acts or omissions of his subordinate employees, if he himself had taken all such reasonable steps. The identification doctrine was applied, as was clarified in the *Tesco* case.

It is clear from these decisions that, as a general rule, the embodiment of a company is its directors (the *'ego'*). Depending on the policy of a company, a person below the level of directors may be given control and full discretionary power to perform certain tasks, whereupon he will, exceptionally, be the 'alter ego' of the company for those specific tasks. In such a case, his acts or omissions will be those of the company for the purpose of attributing liability to the latter.

However, the identification doctrine could not apply to statutory offences satisfactorily in all cases. When a duty is imposed upon a company by statute, the question of law is whether or not that duty is personal to the company. Upon construction of the particular statute, it may transpire that the intention of the legislation has been that acts of the management could be attributed to the company, and it would not matter at what level in the hierarchy of employees the system of management broke down.[132]

What is important is to look at the overall scheme and purpose of the statute or the Convention, or the rule of law, which is the subject matter for interpretation. Such approach was followed by the courts in the mid-1990s, and was formulated by the Privy Council in the *Meridian* case, as explained below.

8.3 The *'Meridian* rule of attribution' by interpretation of the substantive rule of law

In 1995, the Privy Council considered, in **Meridian Global Funds Management Asia Ltd v Securities Commission**,[133] the principle of the identification theory and introduced flexibility in approach as to what acts or omissions can be attributed to a corporation. It was emphasised that it was not merely a question of identifying the relevant person in the company hierarchy, but the rule of attribution was a matter of interpretation or construction of the relevant substantive rule of law in each case. The rule of attribution was defined by Lord Hoffmann, thus:

> ... [When] the court considers that the law was intended to apply to companies, although it excludes ordinary vicarious liability, insistence on the primary rules of attribution would, in practice, defeat that intention. In such a case, the court must fashion a special rule of attribution for the particular substantive rule. This is always a matter of interpretation: given that it was intended to apply to a company, how was it intended to apply? Whose act (or knowledge or state of mind) was for this

---

132 In *Re Supply of Ready Mixed Concrete* [1995] 1 All ER 135 (HL), the company was held guilty of contempt of court for breach of an injunction due to the act of junior management, despite specific instructions having been given by senior management not to act in the manner it did; in *Regina v British Steel plc* [1995] 1 WLR 1356 (CA), the senior management was held criminally liable for the death caused at work by negligence of their employees upon construction of the relevant statute, the Health and Safety at Work Act 1974. It was said, p 1363: 'He will only be exposed to the risk if the system (if any) designed to ensure his safety has broken down and it does not matter for the purposes of s 3(1) at what level in the hierarchy of employees that breakdown has taken place.' For this reason, the *Tesco* case was distinguished.

133 [1995] 3 All ER 918 (PC).

purpose intended to count as the act, etc, of the company? One finds the answer to this question by applying the canons of interpretation, taking into account the language of the rule (if it is a statute) and its content and policy.[134]

The issue is one of choice of the appropriate attribution rule for corporate liability. In the case of a tort committed by employees of a company in the course of their employment, the choice of the attribution rule will be the general rule of vicarious liability. In cases where a particular law (or otherwise the substantive rule of law with which the court is dealing) imposes liability to a company on the basis of a personal fault and a kind of conduct which is either wilful misconduct or more than just mere negligence, requiring a mental element of intention or a personal know-ledge of the facts that would be likely to result in the harm inflicted, the choice of the attribution rule will be the identification doctrine. The articles of association, or board decisions, of the company will assist in finding the person who is the direct-ing mind of the company. If, however, the purpose behind the substantive rule of law, as derived from the language used in the statute or Convention under which liability is sought to be imposed, requires one to look at persons other than the directors of the company, the court will fashion a special rule to be applied to the particular substantive rule of law.

The *Meridian* approach suggests that the choice of the attribution rule depends on the purpose behind the rule of substantive liability.[135] The purpose will vary from one substantive rule of law to another. When statutory criminal offences are considered, the conduct of persons in managerial as opposed to directorial posi-tions might be taken into account with regard to the liability of the company for the offence committed, if that intention was derived from the policy behind the statute. When the substantive rule of law is, for example, an international convention, the court would have to look at the overall purpose of the Convention as may be found in the *travaux préparatoires*, so that there is a uniform application of the Convention.

For example, the interpretation of the provision as regards limitation of liability under the 1957 Convention will be differently construed from Art 4 of the 1976 Convention. The decisions in which the intention behind the 1957 Convention was construed show that faults of servants, agents, or managers of the ship owner were imputed to the owner because, as it was stated, it was up to him to ensure the efficient management of his ships. If he failed to do so, it has been decided that the fault of the delegated persons constituted, as a matter of law, actual fault of the owner personally. The words used in this Convention are the 'act or omission of any person, whether on board the ship or not, acting in the navigation or manage-ment of the ship' etc, and not just the 'personal act or omission' of the person claiming limitation, as is stated in Art 4 of the 1976 Convention, the test of which is further tightened by the requirement of the mental element (see paras 7.1.2–7.1.5, above).

In this connection, it is now relevant to interpret these provisions in the context of the ISM Code (see further Chapter 8 para 5.5).

---

134 *Meridian Global Funds Management Asia Ltd v Securities Commission* [1995] 3 All ER 918, p 924.
135 See, further, Armour, J, 'Corporate personality and assumption of responsibility' [1999] LMCLQ 246.

8.4 The effect of the ISM Code on limitation and risk management

Applying the principles enunciated in the relevant authorities, it is submitted that the interpretation of the substantive rule of law and policy behind the 1976 Limitation Convention will not permit the extension of the class of people who, under the articles of the company's association, or decisions of the Board pursuant to those articles, are entrusted with the control of the company or of particular functions of it. It is the philosophy and purpose behind the 1976 Convention that does not permit the rule of attribution to cross the board level. The identification doctrine, as explained in the *Tesco* case, sufficiently satisfies the purpose of this Convention in identifying the relevant persons who have the control of the company for the purpose of attributing liability.

It follows that the delegation of supervision of safety matters, in a ship or the shore management, to the designated person, appointed pursuant to the Code, will not make the designated person a person whose acts or omissions will be those of the company, unless he is a director, (the '*ego*' of the company) or he is delegated with full discretionary powers and control for the tasks (the '*alter ego*' of the company, according to the analysis of the concept in the *Tesco* case).[136]

Unlike the 1957 Limitation Convention, the misconduct of the designated person will not bar limitation of his employers under Art 4 of the 1976 Convention. This requires proof that the loss resulted from the personal act or omission of the 'controlling mind and will' of the company, committed with intent to cause such loss, or recklessly and with knowledge that such loss would probably result. In other words, the '*ego*' of the company must have consciously anticipated the kind of, or the very, loss claimed.

If the designated person is sued personally, he will have the right to limit under the 1976 Convention, provided that he passes the test under Art 4.

The direct access of the designated person to the senior management and his duties of reporting to them, as provided by the Code, will undoubtedly expose the senior management and their system of management practices to questions as to how and why the particular incident causing liability could not be prevented (see Chapter 8).

In this connection, it is important to refer to a relevant recent decision of the English court, *Rolls-Royce plc v Heavylift-Volga Dnepr Ltd*,[137] concerning limitation of liability, under Art 25 of the Warsaw Convention. The liability arose in relation to damage caused by the negligence of Servisair's employees to a Rolls-Royce engine being unloaded from Rolls-Royce's lorry with a 10-ton forklift truck at East Midlands Airport. Similar provisions of safety regulations apply to cargo handling operators in airports to those applicable to onshore management of ships. Breach of those regulations, in particular with regard to monitoring and providing a co-ordinated system of safety, as well as negligence, was found on the part of the company's safety and security manager, on the part of the designated 'competent'

---

136 See the author's earlier article: 'The International Safety Management Code in perspective' (1996) 10(6) P&I International, June, p 107, pp 109–10.
137 [2000] 1 Lloyd's Rep 653.

person and on the part of the employee involved in the unloading. The right hand was apparently unaware of what the left hand was doing, and the designated person had failed to ensure that all his staff were aware of all risks which they might encounter. It was pointed out that someone responsible in the company's safety systems should have picked up his failures. It was even commented by the court that any competent management would have foreseen the need to make sure that their staff did not operate this vehicle if it was not in proper condition. Nevertheless, the court held that:

> For the finding of wilful misconduct the court must find on a balance of probabilities that the acts (or omissions) alleged to constitute the misconduct must not only fall below the standards to be expected of persons acting reasonably, but be sufficiently below such standards as to be capable of being regarded as 'misconduct', and not just as careless, or very, or grossly careless. Second, the person must know that he is misconducting himself when he does (or fails to do) the acts complained of and does them intentionally or recklessly as to the consequences.

> Overall, Servisair were guilty of negligence. What might have avoided the accident would have been proper training on the heavier forklift truck. The company's failure to have a proper system of work which would have ensured that only properly trained and qualified people operated such vehicles was causative of the accident. However, neither separately nor in the aggregate did the failures of the various persons identified as being at fault amount to misconduct or to recklessness with knowledge under the Convention.[138] Thus, limitation was allowed.

This decision may be borne in mind in limitation cases under the 1976 Convention, when similar failures in the system of safe operation of ships may arise under the ISM Code, but, as this case indicates, it will still be difficult for the claimant to break limitation.

It is interesting to note the chain of responsibility in this case, as it may be relevant in cases where similar duties are delegated to a designated person under the ISM Code.[139] That does not mean to say, however, that the delegation will necessarily extend the class of persons (whose acts are to be regarded in law as the personal acts of the company itself) beyond those who, by the articles of association, are entitled to exercise the powers of the company.[140]

Different criteria apply to cases of criminal liability arising from breach of statutory offences, as specified by the statutory instrument making the ISM Code part of English law, because of the wording of those offences, being the substantive rule of law for interpretation according to the Meridian attribution rule.[141]

However, the person who seeks to limit ought to be warned that the factual situations of *The Lady Gwendolen*,[142] *The Marion*,[143] *The Garden City*[144] and *The*

---

138 [2000] 1 Lloyd's Rep 653, p 659.

139 See the reference to delegation by Lord Reid in *Tesco v Nattrass* [1972] AC 153 (HL), para 8.2, below.

140 As Lord Diplock said in *Tesco v Nattrass* [1972] AC 153 (HL).

141 See Chapter 8, para 5.8.1, above.

142 *The Lady Gwendolen* [1965] 1 Lloyd's Rep 335 (defective radar lookout, coupled with excessive speed in fog).

143 [1984] 2 Lloyd's Rep 1.

144 [1982] 2 Lloyd's Rep 382.

Anonity[145] are situations to be avoided at all costs. Were these cases to be decided today, questions would be raised as to how and why the directing mind of the company was not able to ensure that a proper safety system was in operation. This inquiry may lead to a train of inquiries, which may reveal that the directing mind of the company was reckless in not attending to the deficiencies. But that alone will not be sufficient for the test of Art 4 to be met. It must further be shown that the directing mind had actual knowledge that the loss of the same kind as the loss sustained would probably result (*The MSC Rosa M* and *The Leerort*, see earlier) and, despite such knowledge, did nothing to correct the deficiencies which must have caused the loss claimed. The information contained in the ISM documentation may point to the required knowledge. It has been suggested, but not decided, that the test of Art 4 may be met if the relevant person consciously suspected defects and deliberately chose not to check, so as to avoid turning suspicion into awareness.[146]

To put matters into perspective for risk management purposes, it is worth summarising the salient features of the aforesaid cases and comments made.

In *The Lady Gwendolen*, the evidence disclosed a serious failure in the management of the ships which contributed to the collision. It was noted, at first instance, on the facts that: 'If the marine superintendent is put upon inquiry for an obvious disregard of the regulations, he should take steps about it, and if his steps fail, he must go higher until something is done about it.' This may be relevant under the ISM Code, to the extent of showing how far the questioning of the practices of the directors in the management of the ships might go.

In *The Marion*, there were two types of fault noted here, which may be relevant to the questioning of directors of shipowners or managers by virtue of the ISM Code: first, failure of the managing director to have a proper system of supervision; and, second, failure to give instructions on what matters he would like to be kept informed. Although such failures alone, without more in the conduct of directors, will not break the limit under Art 4 of the 1976 Convention, as it did under the 1957 Convention, they are, however, worth keeping in mind, particularly because the DP has direct access to the senior management who should give clear instructions about what matters they would require to be informed.

In *The Garden City*, Staughton J (as he then was) said that the top management of every shipowning company ought to institute a system for the supervision of navigation and detection of faults. Although there was a system here providing for two officers to be on the bridge when the vessel was navigating in fog, the master did not keep to it. In this case, however, no fault of the director was found. Under the ISM Code, today, the director would be questioned why such a habit of the master had not been detected, but, to break the limitation under Art 4, there must be evidence of a conscious realisation (drawn from previous collision incidents that might have been caused by the master's same disregard of instructions) that the loss suffered was anticipated as very likely to happen and, nevertheless, recklessly, no preventive measures were taken. The recent example of the factual situation in *Saint Jacques* (seen earlier) is to be borne carefully in mind.

---

145 [1961] 1 Lloyd's Rep 203.
146 *The MSC Rosa M* [2000] 1 Lloyd's Rep 399, p 402, per Steel J.

In *The Anonity*, the issue on the facts was whether adequate instructions were given by the shipowners to their servants as to the extinguishing of galley fires when the ship was lying alongside an oil jetty. The sparks that escaped caused fire to the jetty, which was destroyed. On the evidence, circular instructions about galley fires had been sent by the marine superintendent to the master. The *alter ego* of the company, Mr Everard, was very strict about compliance by the crew in all matters, but the master, who had been at the employ of Mr Everard for 16 years, was disobedient and perhaps sloppy. He filed the circular instructions in his desk and forgot about it, after a brief discussion with the chief and second officers. Under the old system of limitation, the owners could not limit liability because the circular was not enough; there ought to have been instructions from the owners, exhibited by a notice next to the galley fire prohibiting its use at oil berths.

In any event, the facts of these cases should be borne in mind in case the jurisdiction for limitation of liability is in a country in which the 1957 Convention applies.

9 ESTABLISHMENT OF THE LIMITATION FUND

9.1 Procedural matters under the Convention

Article 11 of the 1976 Convention provides for the establishment of a limitation fund, which will be distributed by the court to satisfy the claims being subject to limitation:

> Any person alleged to be liable may constitute a fund with the court or other competent authority in the State Party in which legal proceedings are instituted in respect of claims subject to limitation.

The article implies that the person seeking to limit has an option to establish a limitation fund in the court of a State party in which the liability proceedings have been brought, but beyond that it states nothing with regard to other jurisdictional options.

In practice, it has been quite common for the person seeking to limit to start limitation proceedings in a jurisdiction of his choice before the liability action is brought (as has been seen in Chapters 5 and 6, above) and the English courts do not have any difficulty in permitting limitation actions to be brought in a different forum from that of the liability action.[147]

Only recently was the issue of whether or not there can be a free-standing limitation action under Art 11 brought before the court in *The Denise*[148] (Steel J) and *The Western Regent*,[149] in which the Court of Appeal approved the approach of the judges in both *The Denise* and in this case.

---

147 See, for example, *Caspian Basin v Bouygues No 4* [1997] 2 Lloyd's Rep 507, p 525; *The Happy Fellow* [1998] 1 Lloyd's Rep 13, and other examples in Chapters 5 and 6.

148 (2004) 3 December, unreported.

149 [2005] 2 Lloyd's Rep 359 CA.

The Western Regent

The vessel was operating in the North Sea, towing six steamers. Two of the steamers came into contact with a buoy, resulting in damage to the head installation of the oilfield. It was accepted that the collision and the damage were due to the negligence of the demise charterer. Both the registered owners and the demise charterer brought limitation proceedings in England. Section 20(1), (3), (7) of the SCA 1981 confers jurisdiction on the court in respect of limitation actions in relation to all claims wherever arising. The owner of the oil installation, a British company, who suffered damage to its property and loss from interruption of business, brought proceedings in Texas, a year later, where the limitation is based on the value of the ship after the collision and not on the 1976 Convention. The claimants in the limitation action applied for summary judgment and for an anti-suit injunction restraining the defendants from pursuing the proceedings in Texas.[150] The defendants applied for a declaration that the court had no jurisdiction, alleging that neither the Convention nor the MSA 1995 contemplates the possibility of a pre-emptive strike by the ship owner before any proceedings on liability had been brought.

It was held by the Court of Appeal that there was nothing in the language of the Convention, or the SCA 1981, or the CPR 1998, which required the person seeking to limit to wait until a claimant brought proceedings in England.

Clarke LJ commented that, if a case involves many claimants, they may commence proceedings in different jurisdictions, and the owner may choose to start limitation proceedings and constitute a fund under the Convention in any such jurisdiction.

Paragraph 8(3), Pt II of Sched 7 to the MSA 1995 gives the court, in which the fund has been constituted, discretion to stay any proceedings, relating to any claim arising out of that occurrence, which are pending against the person by whom the fund has been constituted.

Article 13(1) of the Convention provides that, when a limitation fund has been constituted, any person having a claim against the fund shall be barred from exercising any right in respect of that claim against other assets of the person on whose behalf the fund has been established. Paragraph (2) of Art 13 provides that after a limitation fund has been constituted in accordance with Art 11, any ship belonging to a person on behalf of whom the fund has been constituted, which has been arrested within the jurisdiction of a State party for a claim which may be raised against the fund, or any security given, may be released by order of the court of such State. Such a release is mandatory if the limitation fund has been constituted either:

(a) at the port where the occurrence took place; or

(b) at the port of disembarkation (in respect of loss of life, or personal injury claims); or

(c) at the port of discharge in respect of cargo claims; or

(d) in the State where the arrest is made;

---

150 Issues arising with regard to the anti-suit injunction are discussed in Chapter 7, above.

provided always that the rules of the above paragraphs shall apply only if the claimant may bring a claim against the limitation fund and the fund is actually available and freely transferable in respect of that claim.

Any person who has a claim arising out of the same incident may, nevertheless, pursue to break limitation. Regardless of whether a claimant contends that he can prove that the shipowner was guilty of conduct barring limitation, the combined effect of Arts 2 and 13 of the 1976 Convention is that a person liable can only be compelled to constitute one fund, in accordance with Art 11, and not be also compelled to put up bail for the release of his ship.[151]

An interesting issue on Art 13(2) and (3) arose recently in the following case:

The ICL Vikraman[152]

After a collision incident and the sinking of the vessel *The ICL Vikraman*, the cargo interests arrested a sister ship and obtained a LOU from the P&I club of the owners in lieu of the release of the ship. The cargo interests proceeded to arbitration, as provided by their contract of carriage, and obtained an award. Since the LOU did not contain any restriction with regard to tonnage limitation, the owners of the ship applied for limitation and established a limitation fund. They also sought an injunction to prevent the claimants from presenting the LOU to the club. They obtained leave to serve the limitation claim form out of the jurisdiction and were also granted the injunction. The claimants applied to set aside both, alleging that, since they had obtained security (unlimited by reference to limitation) after the arrest of the sister ship, they were not bound by the establishment of the fund.

Colman J held that the purpose of Art 13 was to protect the person who had properly constituted a limitation fund in any State party from enforcement of a claim in respect of the same occurrence against his ships, or property, or such security, as might have been given which were subject to the jurisdiction of the same or any other State party. Once the fund was established, there was jurisdiction to give leave to serve the limitation claim out of the jurisdiction. However, the LOU stood as the only security in the pending *in rem* action in Singapore, which remained alive despite the arbitration award in London, and it stood in place of the released ship, so it could be released only by order of the Singaporean court. Since Singapore was not a State party to the 1976 Convention, there was no basis for the operation of Art 13(2). The security regime provided by the Convention was confined to States that are parties to it. The Convention could not be construed so as to create a power in the country of one State party to interfere by order with the disposition of security within the jurisdiction of a non-State party. If that was wrong, then under Art 13(3) the limitation fund established in this country was available to a given claimant, notwithstanding that there was no limitation decree at the material time. Thus, the absence of a limitation decree would not be a ground for refusing the release of the LOU.

Once the release of the ship has been ordered after the constitution of the limitation fund, there is a bar to other actions but the person whose ship has been

---

151 *The Bowbelle* [1990] 3 All ER 476.
152 [2004] 1 Lloyd's Rep 21.

released shall be deemed to have submitted to the jurisdiction of the court (para 10, Pt II).

The law applicable to the constitution and distribution of the fund shall be the law of the State in which the fund is constituted (Art 14).

No lien or other right in respect of any ship or property shall affect the proportion in which, under Art 12, the fund is distributed among several claimants (para 9, Pt II).

9.2 Counterclaims

Article 5 of the Convention provides:

> Where a person entitled to limitation of liability under the rules of this Convention has a claim against the claimant out of the same occurrence, their respective claims shall be set off against each other and the provisions of this Convention shall only apply to the balance, if any.

Thus, limitation of liability applies after the respective claims of the parties have been set off. The limits provided by the Convention apply to the balance. An interesting question, which has not been authoritatively answered, is this: if a ship after an accident receives salvage services and during the salvage operations damage is caused to the ship by the negligence of the tug, for which the salved will have a counter-claim in damages against the salvor (as in *The Tojo Maru*), would a claim for salvage award and the claim for negligence be regarded as being out of the same occurrence, so that the respective claims are set off against each other and the limitation provisions then apply to the balance? It is doubtful that Art 5 is meant to apply in such a situation because a claim for salvage is excluded from limitation under the rules of the Convention. It is submitted that this article should apply to claims and counter-claims for which the Convention permits limitation and which arise, for example, out of a collision between two ships.

In *The Khedive*,[153] the House of Lords had decided on this issue as is provided in art 5.

Two ships *V* and *K* came into collision. Both ships were held to blame. The owners of the *K* brought an action to limit their liability under the then Merchant Shipping Amendment Act 1862 and paid the amount of their liability into court. The damage to the *V* was greater than that to the *K*, and the fund in court was not sufficient to satisfy all the claims for which the owners of the *K* were answerable in damages.

It was held that limitation of liability applied to the balance remaining after deducting the smaller from the larger claim. The owners of the *V* were entitled to prove against the fund their damage, less the damage sustained by the *K*, and to be paid in respect of the balance due to them (after such deduction) *pari passu* with the other claimants out of such fund.

---

153 (1882) 7 App Cas 795 (HL).

9.3 Amount of limitation

The 1996 Protocol has substantially increased the limits provided for by the Convention and it came into force on 13 May 2004 internationally.

In the UK, two statutory instruments (SI 1998/1258 and SI 2004/1273) contain the amendments made to the 1976 Convention by the 1996 Protocol and the details as to the determination of the unit of account into sterling. It has, particularly, provided for the avoidance of an overlap of limitation under the Athens Convention for claims to which the latter applies, as well as under the International Convention on Liability and Compensation for Damage in Connection with the Carriage of Hazardous and Noxious Substances by Sea 1996, which is not yet in force.

The general limits for claims other than passenger claims (Art 7) arising on any distinct occasion are calculated on the basis of a sliding scale, depending on the size of the vessel's tonnage (Art 6(1)). It is the gross tonnage of the ship that is relevant. For hovercrafts, however, limitation is calculated by reference to the maximum operational weight.

Claims for *personal injury or loss of life* are treated preferentially to other claims. Article 6(1), as amended by the Protocol, provides for 2 million units of account for a ship not exceeding 2000 tons. Then there is a sliding scale upwards, as shown below.

In the UK, for a ship up to 300 tons, the limit is 1,000,000 units of account; between 301 tons and 2,000 tons, the limit is 2,000,000 units; from 2,001 to 30,000 tons, 800 units of account per ton are added; from 30,001 to 70,000 tons, 600 units of account per ton are added; and, in excess of 70,000 tons, 400 units of account per ton are added.

The limit in respect of *any other claims* starts in the UK at 500,000 units of account for vessels below 300 tons. Under Art 6(1), as amended by the Protocol, the limit of 1,000,0000 units of account applies to a ship with a tonnage not exceeding 2,000 tons. For a ship in excess of 2,000 tons, there is again a sliding scale of tonnage to which more units of account are added per ton, in addition to that applicable to the first scale: 2,001 to 30,000 tons, 400 units of account per ton; 30,001 to 70,000 tons, 300 units of account per ton; in excess of 70,000 tons, 200 units of account per ton.

Two separate funds are provided for each category of claims, personal claims and other claims, but the fund for other claims is available to meet any unsatisfied balance of the personal claims, which then rank rateably with the other claims (Art 6(2)).

The unit of account is defined in Art 8 and is stated in Special Drawing Rights (SDR), as defined by the International Monetary Fund (IMF). It is based on the daily value of a basket of currencies and is converted into the national currency of the State (Member of the IMF) in which limitation is sought, according to the value of that currency at the time. If the State is not a Member of IMF, the value of the national currency in terms of SDR shall be calculated in a manner determined by that State (Art 8 of the 1976 Convention and Art 7 of Pt II, Sched 7 to the MSA 1995).

The 1976 Convention provides for a global limit and applies to each distinct occasion of injury. The aggregate of claims that arise from any distinct occasion is taken into account, under Art 9 of the 1976 Convention.

Article 7 of the 1976 Convention provides for a separate limitation fund for passengers in the amount of 46,666 units of account, multiplied by the number of passengers the ship is authorised to carry, but not exceeding 25 million units of account. Article 7, as amended by the Protocol, provides that the limit of liability in respect of any claims arising on any distinct occasion for loss of life or personal injury to passengers of ships shall be an amount of 175,000 units of account, multiplied by the number of passengers which the ship is authorised to carry.

However, the Carriage of Passengers and their Luggage by Sea (UK Carriers) Order 1998[154] has increased the limit for death or personal injury claims to 300,000 units of account per passenger. It came into force on 1 January 1999 and applies only to carriers whose principal place of business is in the UK.

9.4 Procedure in the Admiralty Court in relation to limitation (brief account)

There are three ways of enforcing the right to limit: the admiralty Practice Directions provide that limitation may be relied upon by way of defence to any claim;[155] a limitation claim may be brought by counterclaim with the permission of the Admiralty Court;[156] a limitation claim is begun by the issue of a claim form in admiralty.[157]

If the defendant invokes the right to limit by way of defence and counterclaim and is found liable, the limit of that liability will apply only to that claim. Therefore, to avoid separate proceedings, if it is envisaged that many claims will be brought, the best method of proceeding would be to institute a limitation action, in which the limitation fund will be valid against all claimants who claim against the fund.

As seen under para 9.1, above, there is no provision in the Convention with regard to the jurisdiction of limitation claims, nor a requirement that the limitation action must be brought in the court in which liability is determined. As seen in Chapters 5 and 6, above, a limitation claimant may choose the forum of his choice (forum shopping), and it has recently been confirmed that there can be a free-standing limitation action (*The Western Regent*).

The only restriction on jurisdiction has been brought by Art 6A of the Brussels Convention, now Art 7 of the Brussels Regulation, which provides that the court which has jurisdiction in actions relating to liability shall also have jurisdiction over claims for the limitation of such liability. This provision, however, applies when the liable party is sued in a Member State (see, further, Chapter 6). There are further restrictions now imposed by the decisions of the ECJ in *Gasser v MISAT* and *Owusu v Jackson*, as discussed in Chapter 6. If for example, the person seeking to limit issues proceedings for a declaration of no liability or for limitation in a Member State in which he has his domicile, and the claimant then brings liability

---

154 SI 1998/2917.
155 PD 61, para 10.18.
156 CPR, r 61.11(22).
157 PD 61, para 10.1; Form No ADM15.

proceedings in another Member State, the court second seised will have to stay its proceedings pursuant to Art 27 until the court first seised determines its jurisdiction. If the claimants bring proceedings in a jurisdiction outside the member States, which may be the natural forum, application of the *forum non-conveniens* doctrine will not be permitted, if the defendant is domiciled in a Member State.

When a limitation fund has been constituted, a caveat against arrest will be issued.

Once the limitation decree is granted, the Admiralty Court may order the stay of any proceedings relating to any claim arising out of the same occurrence; or order the claimant to establish the fund, if he has not already done so. But the court has no power to order a party seeking to limit to constitute a limitation fund by way of security.[158]

The court may give directions for the advertisement of the decree, if it is a general and not a restricted one.[159] Claimants against the fund are invited in the advertisement to submit their claims.

Any person other than a named defendant may apply to the admiralty registrar, within a time fixed in the decree, to set aside the decree.[160]

The limitation fund is distributed to claimants in proportion to their established claims against the fund (Art 12(1) of the 1976 Convention), and no lien or other right in respect of any ship or property shall affect the proportions in which, under Art 12, the fund is distributed among the several claimants (para 9, Pt II, Sched 7 to the MSA 1995).

---

158 *The Tasman Pioneer* [2003] 2 Lloyd's Rep 713 (NZHC).
159 CPR, r 61.10(13).
160 CPR, r 61.10(16).

CHAPTER 18

PASSENGERS' CLAIMS AND LIMITATION OF LIABILITY

1 INTRODUCTION

Carriers who perform carriage services to passengers on board ships are faced with different risks than those carriers who transport cargoes. Passenger risks, being a third party liability, are also covered by P&I insurance, but the function of insurance, as is the case with all maritime risks that are covered by insurance, is to indemnify a carrier for losses that have been incurred. Obtaining insurance cover is not a way of managing risks in a sense of preventing their occurrence by compliance with international conventions, regulations and EU Directives concerning the safe operation of passenger vessels (see Chapters 8 and 20). Managing risks involved with passenger vessels has become more complex, particularly with regard to the modern and large cruise ships which carry a large number of people.

The purpose of this chapter is to look at the international regime that deals with the civil liability of carriers to passengers for losses incurred due to loss of life or personal injury or loss of or damage to their property and the provisions concerning limitation of liability.

Such a regime is known as the Athens Convention 1974, which entered into force on 28 April 1987, and provides for a system whereby carriers may limit their liability for any incident which causes death, personal injury, or loss of or damage to passengers' luggage. The Convention is in force in 32 States, including the UK.[1] Since its entry into force, however, it has been subject to criticism for imposing too low a limit of liability for carriers. Although seen as sufficient in 1974, by the time of its entry into force in 1987, the limits were outdated. Successive Protocols to the Convention were made in 1976 and 1990; the former came into force in 1989, but has also become outdated. The 1990 Protocol was ratified by only six countries[2] and is unlikely to enter into force internationally.

In 2002, a new Protocol was agreed, which went further than merely raising the limits. This Protocol, known as the Athens Convention 2002, provides a new system of liability and is modelled largely on the modern conventions that have been agreed recently.[3] In view of industry concerns with regard to insurance capacity and terrorist risks, and in order to follow limitation of liability for claims relating to war or terrorism, a Reservation and Guidelines for implementation of the

---

1   For details of the Convention and the 2002 Protocol, see Griggs, Williams and Farr, *Limitation of Liability for Maritime Claims*, 4th edn, 2005, LLP, Chapter 4; the enabling statute for the Athens Convention can be found in s 183 of, and sched 6 to, the Merchant Shipping Act 1995.

2   Croatia, Egypt, Germany, Spain, Switzerland and Tonga.

3   See Chapter 19, below.

Convention issued by the IMO were finally adopted in Paris on 19 October 2006 so that the ratification of the Athens Convention 2002 can progress (see para 4, below).

This chapter concentrates first on outlining the system of passenger liability under the Athens Convention 1974 highlighting the problems of its inadequate protection to passengers. How it interacts with the Limitation of Liability Convention 1976 is also shown.[4] Then it provides an overview of the Athens Convention 2002, as consolidated with the 1974 Convention.

2 THE ATHENS CONVENTION 1974 OUTLINED

This Convention may have only a short life, if the 2002 Convention is ratified internationally, but it is important to outline its provisions in order to understand why the 2002 Protocol has been necessary.

2.1 Application and scope

The Athens Convention 1974 provides for a fault-based system of liability. It applies to any 'international carriage', which means any carriage in which, according to the contract of carriage, the place of departure and the place of destination are situated in two different State parties to the Convention.[5] In the UK, however, the Athens Convention 1974 has been extended in scope to apply also to all domestic carriage.[6] The Convention has been incorporated into UK law by virtue of s 183 of the MSA 1995.

Article 2 goes on to state that, in order to be covered by the Athens Convention, the ship has to be either: flying the flag of a State party to the Convention; or is registered in a State party, or else the contract of carriage to which the voyage relates has to have been made in a State party, or have the place of departure or destination in a State party.

2.2 Definition of ship

Article 1 of the Athens Convention contains the definitions that are applied throughout. 'Ship' is defined[7] as being only a seagoing vessel, excluding an air-cushion vehicle.

---

4 See Chapter 17, above.

5 Athens Convention 1974, Art 2(1). The definition of international carriage also allows the place of departure and destination to be in a single State, so long as there is an intermediate port of call in another State. This covers a range of modern-day cruises, where the place of departure and destination of the cruise itself is the same port, but calling at several others over the course of the voyage.

6 By virtue of s 184 of the MSA 1995, the Government may, by Order in Council, extend the application of the Convention to domestic carriage: Carriage of Passengers and their Luggage by Sea (Domestic Carriage) Order 1987, SI 1987/670.

7 Op cit, fn 5, Art 1(3).

2.3 Persons liable

Both the carrier and the performing carrier are made liable under the Convention, pursuant to Arts 3 and 4, and where both carriers are liable, their liability shall be joint and several (Art 4(4)). Under Art 1(1)(a), (b), 'carrier' is the person by or on behalf of whom the contract of carriage has been concluded, whether or not the carriage is actually performed by him or by a performing carrier. 'Performing carrier' means the person other than the carrier, being the owner, charterer or operator of a ship, who actually performs the whole or part of the carriage.

The Convention provides that the carrier shall be liable for his own fault or neglect, or for the fault or neglect of his servants and agents, acting within the scope of their employment.[8]

The liability of the carrier only arises upon proof by the claimant (Art 3(2)) of fault or neglect of the carrier, or his servants or agents. This amounts to the common law definition of negligence.[9] In certain circumstances such fault and neglect is presumed,[10] unless the carrier is able to prove otherwise. The specified instances, where such a presumption arises, are where the death or personal injury to a passenger or the loss of or damage to cabin luggage arose from or in connection with the shipwreck, collision, stranding, explosion or fire, or defect in the ship itself (Art 3(3)).

As far as loss of or damage to other luggage is concerned, fault or neglect is presumed in all circumstances, unless the carrier is able to prove otherwise (Art 3(3)).

Where death or personal injury or loss of or damage to cabin luggage occurs aside from the specified events above, the burden of proving such fault or neglect, so as to be covered by the Convention, rests with the claimant, as does the burden of proving that the incident which caused the loss or damage and its extent occurred in the course of the carriage.[11]

Where a death has occurred, for example through drowning when falling overboard, it may be difficult for the next of kin to establish the fault or neglect of the carrier. This is more so if the next of kin claiming was not aboard the ship when the incident took place; but the court, nowadays, will look beyond the immediate cause and examine the operational diligence of the carriers as to whether or not they applied proper risk assessment and training practices, as it did in the following case.

Davis v Stena [12]

During a very rough ferry crossing from Ireland to Wales, the claimant's husband fell overboard into the sea from the ro-ro ferry, *Koningen Beatrix*, owned and operated by Stena. The use of *Koningen Beatrix*'s lifeboats was ruled out due to the severe weather conditions. He was spotted by a crew member of a container ship, *Celtic*

---

8   Op cit, fn 5, Art 3(1).
9   *Davis v Stena Line Ltd* [2005] 2 Lloyd's Rep 13.
10 Op cit, fn 5, Art 3(3).
11 Op cit, fn 5, Art 3(2), (3).
12 *Davis v Stena Line Ltd* [2005] 2 Lloyd's Rep 13.

King, which was in the vicinity and had a lifeboat, with a full crew, on standby to launch. During the course of attempted rescue by *Koningen Beatrix*'s crew, Mr Davis died.

The widow of Mr Davis sued Stena. The issue before the court was whether or not Mr Davis had died as a result of the negligence of the defendants and their crew, in particular the captain in charge of the rescue operation. Possible reasons for the claimant's husband having gone overboard included the finding that, close to the time of the sighting of Mr Davis in the water, the ship had made a sudden change of course in order to avoid a collision. It was mooted that, maybe at this time, he had stumbled into the safety railing and gone over it into the water, or that he fell over a gap in the railing that had been left open. When the police examined the ship in Wales, there was not found to be anything untoward aboard the ship, although the point was also made that a crew member could have come across the gap in the safety railings before docking and closed the open gate without realising the significance that this had! There was no evidence that Mr Davis deliberately jumped overboard, or that he had taken a foolish and reckless action.

Since the claimant's claim did not fall within any of the presumptions listed in Art 3(3) of the Convention, the burden was upon her to prove negligence, which from the facts appeared inconclusive. However, the court held that both Stena as a company and the captain of *Koningen Beatrix* were negligent, and that this led to the death of the claimant's husband. The following reasons relied upon by the court were given:

(i) It was a known fact in the maritime industry, since the publication of the report of the *Estonia* disaster, that a ship like *Koningen Beatrix*, which was described as a high-sided vessel, made a rescue of a man overboard virtually impossible.

(ii) The crew were negligent for failing to give any consideration as to how Mr Davis was to be rescued. The defendants (Stena) were negligent in that neither the master nor the officers and crew had received advice or guidance or undergoing training with regard to rescue of a man overboard in such circumstances.

(iii) Stena had not carried out any appropriate risk assessment of such an emergency. Even if Stena's shortcomings were representative of the standards of the industry at the time, that did not excuse them.

(iv) It should have been obvious to the master that *Celtic King*'s fast rescue boat was in a position to rescue Mr Davis much more quickly and with far less danger to him than the planned retrieval to *Koningin Beatrix*.

This is a very good example for passenger carriers to bear in mind from a risk management perspective.

2.4 Limits of liability

The carrier, performing carrier and servants or agents of both (if they prove that they acted within the scope of the carrier's employment) shall be entitled to limit their liability as provided by this Convention (Arts 7–11). The carrier and the passenger may agree, expressly and in writing, to higher limits of liability than those prescribed below (Art 10(1)).

2.4.1 Limits applied for death or personal injury

The Athens Convention 1974 allows the carrier to limit his liability on the basis of 'per capita', eg per passenger claiming. The limits provided for in the Convention, as amended by the 1976 Protocol, for death or personal injury to a passenger, is 46,666 SDR,[13] which is then multiplied by the number of passenger actually on board, on each occasion. The conversion SDR rate fluctuates, but roughly the above amount could be the equivalent to £35,839.49 per passenger.[14] The total figure arrived at is the total fund available, regardless of the number of people claiming. Therefore, the same size fund would be available if only one person is claiming, or if all the passengers are claiming.

Perhaps 30 years ago, at the time of the conclusion of the Convention, this limitation figure might have been satisfactory, but certainly not today.

Article 7(2) allows States parties to the convention to impose higher limits than the 46,666 SDR provided for by the Convention. The UK has done so. For a carrier whose principal place of business is in the UK, the limit for death or personal injury under the Athens Convention 1974 is now 300,000 SDR,[15] which is the equivalent of about £230,400.

2.4.2 Limits applied for loss of or damage to luggage

Under Art 8 of the Athens Convention, as amended by the 1976 Protocol, loss of or damage to cabin luggage is limited to 833 SDR per passenger per carriage; equivalent to about £639.74.[16] Damage to vehicles, including whatever luggage is carried within the vehicle, is limited to 3,333 SDR, which is equivalent to about £2,559.74.[17] All other luggage not covered by the above is limited to 1,200 SDR, which is equivalent to about £921.60.[18]

2.4.3 Losing the right to limit

It is possible that the carrier or performing carrier will not be entitled to limit his liability under the Athens Convention. Article 13(1) states that:

> The carrier shall not be entitled to the benefit of the limits of liability prescribed in Arts 7, 8 and 10(1) if it is proved that the damage resulted from an act or omission of the carrier done with the intent to cause such damage, or recklessly and with knowledge that such damage would probably result.

---

13 Article 7(1). The wording of the original text of the Convention refers to 700,000 gold francs per carriage, which was to be converted to monetary units, each unit consisting of 65.5 milligrams of gold, by virtue of Art 9. The 1976 Protocol stated the limits in 'Special Drawing Rights' (SDR), which enables a standard currency to be used in all Conventions so that it is converted accurately into a country's national currency.

14 Eg on the basis of SDR rate 0.768 to the pound sterling, calculated on 1 March 2007, but the value of the SDR in the national currency shall be calculated at the date of judgment or the date agreed by the parties (Art 9).

15 The Carriage of Passengers and their Luggage by Sea (United Kingdom Carriers) Order 1998, SI 1998/2917, Art 3. This amended SI 1989/1880 which imposed a figure of 100,000 SDR.

16 Op cit, fn 14.

17 Op cit, fn 14.

18 Article 8(3), and fn 14.

The same test applies to servants or agents of the carrier or of the performing carrier by Art 13(2) if they seek to limit liability for damage resulting from their act or omission.

This test is identical to the test that is incorporated into the Limitation Convention 1976, save for the word 'loss' instead of 'damage' used in the 1976 Convention. The analysis of the test is provided in Chapter 17, above.

2.5 Carriage of valuables

The carrier shall not be liable for the loss of or damage to valuable items such as jewellery, gold, silver, ornaments, art-work and monies, except where such valuables have been deposited with the carrier for the agreed purpose of safe-keeping, in which case the carrier shall be liable up to the limit provided for in Art 8(3), unless a higher limit is agreed upon in accordance with Art 10(1). (See a recent decision, *Lee v Airtours Holidays*, later, interpreting this provision.)

2.6 Contributory negligence

Article 6 of the Convention provides that, if the carrier proves that the death of or personal injury to a passenger or the loss of or damage to his luggage was caused or contributed to by the fault or neglect of the passenger, then the court trying the claim may exonerate the carrier wholly or partly from his liability in accordance with the provisions of the law of that court. As far as the UK is concerned, the law of contributory negligence is dealt with by the Law Reform (Contributory Negligence) Act 1945.

2.7 Liability arising through negligence of servants or agents of the carrier

It was thought that, even though the carrier is liable for the acts of his servants or agents whilst engaged in their employment with the carrier, passengers may try to circumvent the limits of the Athens Convention by seeking to claim directly against the servant or agent. In order to prevent this from occurring, Art 11 of the Convention allows a servant or agent to bring themselves within the Convention and its limits, as long as they are able to prove that their acts which led to the damage being claimed occurred when they were acting in the scope of their employment.

2.8 Time limit

There is an overall time limit for any action under the Convention of two years, provided for by Art 16. For personal injury claims, time starts to run from the date of the passenger's disembarkation. For claims relating to the death of a passenger, time starts to run from the date when the passenger should have disembarked. If the passenger suffers a personal injury, which leads to his or her death, then the time starts from the date of death, as long as this does not exceed three years from the disembarkation date. For the loss of or damage to luggage, time starts from the date of disembarkation or from the date when disembarkation should have taken place, whichever is later. Since this article imposes numerous ways in which to calculate the time period, there is an all-encompassing time bar on any action being brought in any State after a period of three years from the date of disembarkation or from when disembarkation should have taken place, whichever is the later.

In addition, Art 15 provides that the passenger shall give written notice to the carrier or his agent in case of apparent damage to luggage, before or at the time of disembarkation, as far as cabin luggage is concerned, and before or at the time of re-delivery as far as all other luggage is concerned. If the damage is not apparent, such notice should be given within 15 days from the date of disembarkation or the redelivery date, or from the time when such re-delivery should have taken place. In the event of failure to comply with this provision, it shall be presumed, unless the contrary is proved, that the luggage was received undamaged.

2.9 Jurisdiction

When a claimant pursues a claim against a carrier under the Athens Convention, there are provisions dealing with the jurisdiction in which to bring the action. As the UK is a member of the EU, the governing regulation dealing with jurisdictional issues is Council Regulation (EC) 44/2001.[19] This states that, in claims relating to tortious actions, the place to sue is the place where the harmful event took place. Under the Regulation, a claimant would therefore have to sue the carrier in a foreign country, if that were the place where the death or injury took place. This may discourage potential claimants from pursuing their claim, as they may be unfamiliar with the governing law of that particular country and it may prove more costly. If the incident occurred on the high seas, there is also the added complication of which State would have jurisdiction: the State of the last port of call, or the State of the next port of call. This is all resolved by Art 17 of the Athens Convention, which affords the claimant a choice of jurisdiction in which to sue the carrier. As long as the court concerned is located in a State party to the Convention, the claimant may bring a claim against the carrier in: the permanent residence of the defendant, or the defendant's principal place of business; the place of departure or destination; the domicile of the claimant; or the State in which the contract of carriage was concluded, provided that the defendant has a place of business in such a country.

The parties may agree, after the occurrence of the incident, that the claim shall be submitted to any jurisdiction or to arbitration.

---

19 Council Regulation (EC) 44/2001 of 22 December 2000 on jurisdiction and the recognition and enforcement of judgments in civil and commercial matters (OJ L12, 16/12/2001, p 1); see, further, Chapter 6, above.

2.10 Contracts of travel or holiday through travel agents

Contracts made in the UK will include standard terms of the cruise operator's contract, the UK Package Travel Regulations (PTR) 1992,[20] and the Athens Convention.

Regulation 15 of the PTR 1992 provides that a cruise operator is liable to the consumer for the proper performance[21] of the obligations under the contract, whether performed by him or by other suppliers, and is liable to the consumer for any damage caused to him by the failure to perform the contract or the improper performance of the contract, unless the improper performance is due neither to any fault of the cruise operator nor to that of another supplier of services. The exception is linked to either the fault of the consumer, or to unforeseen or unavoidable circumstances, which could not have been avoided by the exercise of due care, or an event which, even with all due care, could not have been foreseen or forestalled.

The decision in *Hone v Going Places Travel Ltd*[22] clarifies whether reg 15 of the PTR 1992 imposed a strict or fault-based liability on tour operators for the 'proper performance' of a holiday contract. The case concerned a claim made for personal injury suffered during an air flight.

Hone (H) appealed against the dismissal of his claim against a travel agent, Going Places (G), brought under reg 15 of the PTR 1992, for injury to his back sustained whilst descending from an aircraft via the emergency chute following a crash landing on the return flight from a package holiday. While in the chute, he collided with a large lady passenger and he was then hit on the back by the hard-heeled shoes of his fiancée who followed him. He kindly attempted to help the large lady to stand to her feet and he hurt his back again. The judge concluded that H had failed to show that there had been improper performance of the contract agreed for the package tour, in that he had failed to establish that his injuries were attributable to the fault of the party supplying services in relation to the tour. H submitted, inter alia, that the liability imposed under reg 15 was strict or absolute, subject to defences which G could not show were available. The Court of Appeal, dismissing the appeal, held that liability under reg 15 was not strict. Regulation 15(2) imposed a liability upon G for any damage caused to H by improper performance of a contractual obligation and it was necessary to refer to the terms of the contract in order to determine what constituted improper performance. There was no express obligation to execute safe air carriage and, in the absence of such a term, the implication was that the air carriage would be performed with reasonable skill and care.

In a recent decision in the UK, *Norfolk v My Travel Group Plc*,[23] an attempt by claimants to circumvent the Athens Convention 1974 failed. Modern cruise holidays are generally booked through intermediaries, such as travel agents, rather

---

20 The Package Travel, Package Holidays and Package Tours Regulations 1992, SI 1992/3288, implementing Council Directive 90/314/EEC on package travel for the protection of consumers.

21 The test is that reasonable skill and care will be used in the rendering of services: *Hone v Going Places* [2001] EWCA Civ 947.

22 [2000] All ER (D) 1854 (confirmed in the Court of Appeal [2001] All ER (D) 102).

23 *Norfolk v My Travel Group Plc* [2004] 1 Lloyd's Rep 106.

than direct with the cruise operator. Customers who therefore suffer personal injuries aboard a cruise ship may not realise that the time-bar in which to bring claims under the Athens Convention 1974 is shorter than for regular personal injury claims in the UK.[24] In the *Norfolk* case, the claimant passenger had booked her cruise holiday through a travel agent. She suffered personal injury during the carriage. After the two-year time limit had lapsed – in order to avoid the Athens Convention 1974 framework altogether – she attempted to present the claim for personal injury as a statutory claim for damages for improper performance of the contract between the customer and the travel agent, bringing the claim within the PTR 1992. The Plymouth County Court rejected this approach, with the result that a claim for any personal injury suffered aboard a cruise ship when the Athens Convention 1974 applies will fall within the scope of the Convention and the claim was time barred. The court further held that the fact that the Regulations flowed from a Council Directive did not affect the standing of the international Convention, and the provision of the Human Rights Convention had no bearing on the interpretation of international conventions.[25]

An interesting test case, which has important implications with regard to claims by passengers carried in a cruise ship, highlights problems of possible conflict between the Athens Convention and the PTR 1992. In *Lee v Airtours Holidays Ltd*,[26] the contract for a cruise holiday on *Sun Vista* (which caught fire and sank, with passengers' valuables on board) had been made, again, through a travel agent. The claim was brought under reg 15 of the PTR 1992 against the travel agent for, inter alia, loss of valuables. Judge Hallgarten QC held that the Regulations represented an alternative regime to the Convention. Insofar as the Regulations conflicted with UK domestic law, the regime of the Regulations must prevail, pursuant to the European Communities Act.

This is a point of great significance and it should be tested by a higher court, because the UK domestic law to which the judge referred is the law that has implemented an international convention. Should this decision be correct on this point, it would seem that the claimant's claim in the *Norfolk* case (see above) should not have been time barred). But Hallgarten J further held that, if there was no express incorporation of the Athens Convention in the contract, and here the booking was done on the phone using a credit card, no terms and conditions being mentioned, the PTR 1992 prevailed over the Athens Convention 1974 to the extent that the two conflicted. Regulation 15(3) gives an opportunity to the operator to insert the Athens Convention in the contract, or particular aspects of it. The defendant tour operator relied on the Athens Convention 1974 so as to entitle them to limit their liability with regard to personal injury and exclude it with regard to the lost valuables. However, since the defendant had not expressly incorporated the limitation aspects of the Convention into the contract with the claimant, he could not rely on

---

24 Under the Limitation Act 1980, the time limit in which to bring a claim for personal injury is three years. Under the Athens Convention, however, the limit is two years from the date of disembarkation.

25 The judge gained support for his view from the judgment of Lord Hope in a previous case, relating to the Warsaw Convention, in *Sidhu v British Airways Plc* [1997] 2 Lloyd's Rep 76, [1997] AC 430.

26 [2004] 1 Lloyd's Rep 683.

the provisions therein and faced unlimited liability to the claimant. If, contrary to this conclusion, the judge further held, the Athens Convention did apply, the claimant's valuables had not been deposited with the carrier, as the Convention requires by Art 5, for the agreed purpose of safe-keeping. The alternative deposit in the cabin safe could not be said to be 'with the carrier'. However, the carrier has to provide appropriate facilities for safe carriage; either those were not available, or the claimant's tender was wrongfully rejected. In either case, the carrier was in breach, and the amount recoverable would be subject to the limit provided by the Athens Convention, if it applied, and therefore liability was not excluded.

3 RELATIONSHIP WITH THE LIMITATION CONVENTION 1976

As has been seen in Chapter 17, above, under the Limitation of Liability Convention for Maritime Claims 1976,[27] ship owners (and others) are able to limit their liability for any maritime claim, subject to exceptions in Art 3, provided they are able to bring the various claims within Art 2. The Convention provides for a 'global' limitation of liability: in other words, it caps the amount that the ship owner is liable for to various different claimants. Article 7 of the 1976 Convention repeats the 46,666 SDR limit per passenger (being the same amount used by the Athens Convention 1974), but the amount is multiplied by the number of passengers which the vessel is certified to carry (as opposed to the number of passengers actually on board, as is the case under the Athens Convention). The limit is capped to 25 million SDR. The net effect of this is that, for all passenger ships with a carrying capacity of over 500 passengers, the amount that each passenger would be able to claim would be reduced further. With the fact that most modern-day cruise ships have a carrying capacity of 1,500 and above, it is clear that the amount to be claimed, if a ship owner is able to limit his liability under the 1976 Convention, is quite inadequate.

A modern example will serve as an illustration. The Cunard-owned cruise-ship *Queen Mary 2* sailed from Southampton on her maiden voyage in January 2004. With a carrying capacity of 2,600, she represents the modern approach of cruise-ships to resemble hotels. If the ship foundered with its passengers, the amount that each representative of the deceased would be able to receive would be the equivalent to about £7,384.62.[28] For claims arising from death or serious personal injury, this amount is clearly insufficient.

3.1 The 1996 Protocol to the 1976 Limitation Convention and implementation in the UK

Just as the limits in the 1974 Athens Convention were seen as inadequate by the time of its entry into force, so too were the limits in the 1976 Convention. In 1996, there was a Protocol agreed upon which, among other things, raised the limits and

---

27 See Chapter 17, above.
28 Op cit, fn 14.

introduced a procedure which would simplify the process of raising the limits in the future. For passenger claims, Art 7 limits were raised to 175,000 SDR per passenger, and the 25 million SDR ceiling was removed. This equates to about £134,400[29] per passenger, and is the figure provided for in the 1990 Protocol to the Athens Convention, which certainly is not likely to enter into force internationally particularly now that the 2002 Protocol represents current trends.

The 1996 Protocol to the 1976 Convention entered into force on 13 May 2004 and, at the time of writing, has 27 State parties signed up to it. Whenever a ship owner seeks to limit his liability in a court of a State party to it, the 1996 Protocol limits apply. With 27 signatories to date, however, compared to the 47 State parties to the main Convention, there is still the possibility that a limitation fund will be constituted in a State party which is a Party to the 1976 Convention, but not to the Protocol, and avail himself of the lower limits there and, hence, in relation to passenger claims, the ceiling that is imposed.

The UK is a State party to the 1996 Protocol[30] and, accordingly, the 1976 Convention has to be read in accordance with the 1996 Protocol. However, the UK enabling power has made slight alterations to the regime, which directly affects the Protocol's interaction with passenger claims. Article 7(b) of the Order restricts the application of death and personal injury claims under the 1976 Convention to non-seagoing ships.[31] This means that, for all passenger ferries' and cruise-ships' claims initiated in the UK courts, the 1976 Convention, as amended by the 1996 Protocol, does not apply. For non-seagoing ships, art 4(b) of the Order amends Art 7 of the 1976 Convention, so that the limit to be applied is 175,000 SDR per passenger.

The UK approach makes sense in practice. By taking seagoing ships (of carriers whose principal place of business is in the UK) out of the 1976 Convention regime and making them subject to the Athens Convention 1974, the limits available are higher due to the UK statutory instrument (see para 2.4.1, above), increasing the limits to 300,000 SDR per passenger. Most travel agents in the UK use the UK as their principal place of business, and are therefore subject to the higher limits. However, for carriers facing action in the UK courts with a place of business outside the UK, the limits to be imposed remain the lower levels of the Athens Convention 1974, until the 2002 Protocol comes into force.

The Athens Convention also by Art 14 restricts claimants for passenger claims to bring such claims against the carrier, or performing carrier, otherwise than as provided by the Athens Convention.

---

29 Op cit, fn 14.

30 The enabling power which brought the 1996 Protocol into force nationally was the Merchant Shipping (Convention on Limitation of Liability for Maritime Claims) (Amendment) Order 1998, SI 1998/1258. (See further Chapter 17, above).

31 Article 7(b) of the Order, which amends the 1976 Convention, provides: 'before paragraph 3 there shall be inserted, 2A. Paragraph 1(a) of article 2 shall have effect as if the reference to "loss of life or personal injury" did not include a reference to loss of life or personal injury to passengers of seagoing ships.' Article 7(e) of the Order further expressly provides: "Article 7 [of the 1976 Convention] shall not apply in respect of any seagoing ship; and shall have effect in respect of any ship which is not seagoing . . ."

4 THE 2002 PROTOCOL TO THE ATHENS CONVENTION

When the previous edition of this book was published in 2001, the proposed draft Protocol had just been put before the IMO Diplomatic Conference. Since then, there have been a plethora of consultations within the industry and, following several years of work at the IMO's Legal Committee meetings, a new Protocol to the Athens Convention was concluded on 1 November 2002, after its acceptance by the Diplomatic Conference on 20 October 2002. In so doing, it was decided that it would be known as the Athens Convention 2002 and, when it enters into force, it will entirely replace the Athens Convention 1974. A precondition of the Protocol is that States ratifying it have to denounce the 1974 Convention and the subsequent Protocols of 1976 and 1990.[32] It will enter into force 12 months after at least 10 States have either signed it *without reservation as to ratification*, acceptance or approval, or have deposited instruments of ratification, acceptance, approval or accession with the Secretary General of the IMO.[33] At the time of writing, there have been nine states that have signed the Protocol[34] and only four have ratified it.

In the following paragraphs, an overview of the main consolidated changes that the 2002 Convention will make to the Athens Convention 1974 is provided, with some comparative examples at the end. Briefly, the Protocol introduces a no-fault, or strict liability, basis of liability, up to a certain limit, matched with financial security and direct action against insurers, as well as a substantial increase in the limit.

4.1 The two-tier system of liability (strict and fault-based)

Article 3 of the Athens Convention 2002 introduces a new system of liability for the carrier. It will be remembered that the 1974 Convention uses a fault-based system, with presumptions of fault in favour of the claimant in certain instances. The 2002 Convention is designed on a two-tier system, namely: for loss suffered as a result of the death of or personal injury to a passenger caused by a *shipping incident*, Article 3 provides strict liability up to a certain limit (see below), and fault-based liability if the claimed amount exceeds the first tier of limit. If such loss, as mentioned above, is caused by a *non-shipping incident*, the fault-based system is applied.

In particular, Art 3(1) of the 2002 Convention applies strict liability to death or personal injury caused by a 'shipping incident', which encompasses shipwreck, capsizing, collision or stranding of the ship, explosion or fire in the ship, or defect in the ship.[35] The provision about 'defect in the ship' will raise issues of whether or not

---

32 Athens Convention 2002, Art 17(5).

33 Ibid., Art 20.

34 Albania, Finland, Germany, Latvia, Norway, Spain, Sweden, Syria and the UK.

35 Article 3(5)(a). A defect in the ship is further defined in sub-paragraph (c) of the Article as meaning any: 'malfunction, failure or non-compliance with applicable safety regulations in respect of any part of the ship or its equipment when used for the escape, evacuation, embarkation, and disembarkation of passengers, or when used for the propulsion, steering, safe navigation, mooring, anchoring, arriving at or leaving berth or anchorage, or damage control after flooding; or when used for the launching of life-saving appliances'.

there has been a proper implementation of the safety management systems of the company under the ISM Code, and the other provisions on safety of passenger ships under the SOLAS Convention. In this respect, owners or operators of passenger ships will need to show that they have implemented a systematic approach to the management of risks (see Chapter 8, above).

Strict liability on the carrier is imposed up to a limit of 250,000 units of account, which (by Art 9) are defined to be SDR. (This equates to about £204,325 and it is the first tier.) The carrier (as defined in Art 1(1)(a)(b)(c)) will escape strict liability for a shipping incident if he can prove that the incident fell within two categories of exception as provided by Art 3(1)(a), (b).

The first category includes the results of acts of war and natural phenomena 'of an exceptional, inevitable and irresistible character'. The second category covers incidents which were 'wholly caused by an act or omission done with the intent to cause the incident by a third party'. It has been assumed that, in the second category, terrorist activities causing the incident of loss are an exception, and neither the carrier nor its insurer would be liable for damage 'wholly' caused by terrorists. Therefore, insurance for such damage would not be a requirement by the Convention. However, the said exception will apply only to incidents 'wholly' caused by terrorism. Therefore, such a wording gave cause for serious concern among the P&I Insurance Group, which is a non-war risk insurance. Consequently, the matter had to be dealt with by the Legal Committee of the IMO.

In the light of the IMO Guidelines to States for the implementation of the Protocol and the Reservation adopted by the Legal Committee at its 92nd session on 19 October 2006 and issued on 20 November 2006, insurance cover for all terrorist risks causing loss are to be dealt with by a special war insurance cover (see para 4.10, below).

If, and to the extent that, the loss resulting from a 'shipping incident' exceeds the above limit, the carrier shall be further liable up to SDR 400,000[36] (second tier), unless he proves that the incident which caused the loss occurred without his fault or neglect. 'Fault or neglect' includes the fault or neglect of the servants of the carrier, acting within the scope of their employment (Art 3(5)(b)).

If any death or personal injury loss is not caused by a 'shipping incident', liability is determined on the fault-based system but, in these cases, the claimant bears the burden of proving such fault or neglect.[37] The liability of the carrier shall in no case exceed 400,000 units of account (SDR) per passenger on each distinct occasion (Art 7), unless the right to limit is lost, as provided in Art 13 (as seen above, under para 2.4.3).

For loss suffered as a result of the loss of or damage to cabin luggage, the carrier shall be liable if the incident which caused the loss was due to the fault or neglect of the carrier; but, if the loss was caused by a 'shipping incident', the fault or neglect of the carrier shall be presumed.[38] The presumption may be rebutted by evidence. For loss of or damage to any luggage other than cabin luggage, the carrier shall be

---

36 Art. 7
37 Article 3(2).
38 Article 3(3).

liable, unless he proves that the incident which caused the loss occurred without his fault or neglect.[39]

Article 3(6) specifically states that the liability of the carrier under Art 3 relates only to loss arising from incidents that occurred in the course of the carriage. The burden of proof that the incident occurred in the course of the carriage, and the extent of the loss, shall lie with the claimant.

With any incident, if the carrier proves that the death of or personal injury to a passenger, or the loss of or damage to his luggage, was caused or contributed to by the fault of or neglect of the passenger, the court seised of the case may exonerate the carrier wholly or partly from liability in accordance with the provisions of the law of that court (Art 6, contributory fault seen under para 2.6, above).

By Art 4, the carrier shall remain liable for the entire carriage, according to the provisions of the Convention, even if the performance of the carriage has been entrusted to a performing carrier. Furthermore, the carrier shall be liable for the acts and omissions of the performing carrier's servants and agents acting within the scope of their employment. The performing carrier shall also be subject and entitled to the provisions of the Convention for the part of the carriage performed by him. Where, and to the extent that both the carrier and the performing carrier are liable their liability shall be joint and several.

4.2 Financial security (compulsory insurance and direct action)

The idea of compulsory insurance for carriers is not new. Indeed, in the field of oil pollution, the International Convention on Civil Liability for Oil Pollution Damage (CLC) 1969 now CLC 1992 included the use of compulsory insurance as a means of forcing carriers to meet any potential liability. Furthermore, both the HNS Convention 1996[40] and Bunker Convention 2001[41] have included compulsory insurance as part of their scheme (see Chapter 19, below). The Wreck Removal Convention 2007, which was approved recently on 18 May 2007 in Nairobi, provides also for compulsory insurance and direct action against insurers.

Under the Athens Convention 2002, all ships that are registered in a State party, and are licensed to carry 12 or more passengers, have to carry insurance or some other form of financial security,[42] at least up to the sum of 250,000 SDR per passenger on each distinct occasion, which is the ceiling at which the carrier is strictly liable,[43] for claims arising out of death or personal injury. A model form of the certificate required is produced as an Annex to the Athens Convention 2002.

It is recognised that many ships that are in operation may not be registered in any country that is likely to be a State party to the Athens Convention 2002. In order

---

39 Article 3(4).

40 International Convention on Liability and Compensation for Damage in Connection with the Carriage of Hazardous and Noxious Substances 1996.

41 International Convention on Civil Liability for Bunker Oil Pollution Damage 2001.

42 Article 4*bis*.

43 Article 4*bis* (1).

to encourage ships which are registered in non-Athens Convention countries, the Convention also obliges State parties to refuse access to their ports for all ships which are licensed to carry 12 or more passengers and do not carry the requisite financial security, wherever they are registered.[44]

Also in keeping with modern conventions that are in existence, the Athens Convention 2002 contains a provision allowing claimants to seek direct action against the carrier's insurers for any claim that may arise.[45] This is a move which will make it easier and faster for claimants to obtain judgment for any claim arising under the Convention. The theory behind this provision is that it may be costly and time-consuming for a claimant to find out where to sue a large company, that may have several offices and subsidiary companies in several jurisdictions. By going straight to the insurer, claims can be more efficiently settled, leaving the insurers to take action against their assured, if necessary.

By Art 4*bis*, the limit of compulsory insurance is 250,000 SDR per passenger, and applies also as a limit of liability of the insurer, or provider of financial security, even if the carrier, or performing carrier, is not entitled to limit.[46]

The insurer may invoke the defences (other than the bankruptcy of the carrier) which the carrier would have been entitled to invoke against the claimant in accordance with the Convention. A contested issue had been, at the time of consultations relating to the drafting of the Convention, as to whether the insurer should be entitled to rely on the defence of wilful misconduct of the assured; it was finally settled in Art 4*bis* (10) that this defence may be invoked,[47] but the insurer shall not invoke any other defences which he might have been entitled to invoke in proceedings brought by the assured against him.

4.3 Limits of liability

The limits prescribed below apply to the aggregate of the amounts recoverable in all claims arising out of the death or personal injury to any one passenger or the loss of or damage to his luggage. If the carriage is performed by a performing carrier, the aggregate of the amounts recoverable from the carrier and performing carrier, or their servants and agents, shall not exceed the highest amount which could be awarded against either the carrier or performing carrier under the Convention; but none of the persons mentioned shall be liable for a sum in excess of the limit applicable to him (Art 12). The test for the loss of the right to limit is the same as under the 1974 and 1976 Conventions (Art 13).

4.3.1 Limits applied for death or personal injury

The Athens Convention 2002 contains provisions limiting the carrier's liability for any incident which causes death or personal injury. The limit under Art 7 applies to claims which exceed the first-tier limit, for which there is strict liability up to

---

44   Article 4*bis* (13).
45   Article 4*bis* (10).
46   Ibid.
47   The implications of this are discussed in para 4.5, below.

250,000 SDR under Art 3. It will be remembered that, under the Athens Convention 1974, the limit was 46,666 SDR per passenger, with the UK increasing it (with regard to carriers whose principal place of business is in the UK) to 300,000 SDR under the 1998 Order.[48]

Under the Athens Convention 2002, the upper limit in Art 7 has now risen to 400,000 SDR per passenger, which equates to about £307,200.00.[49] Again, there is a provision within the Convention allowing national States to increase the limits within their own national laws.[50]

4.3.2 Limits applied for loss of or damage to luggage and vehicles

Under the Athens Convention 2002, the limit for loss of or damage to luggage is 2,250 SDR (£1,728) per passenger. For damage to vehicles, including any luggage within the vehicle, the limit is 12,700 SDR (£9,753.60) per vehicle. For all other luggage, the limit is 3,375 SDR (£2,592).[51]

The latter limit also applies to valuables, on condition that they have been deposited with the carrier for the agreed purpose of safe-keeping. If they are not so deposited, the carrier shall not be liable for their loss or damage (Art 5).

4.4 Comparison of the limits between the Athens Conventions 1974 and 2002

The table below shows the difference, under the two Conventions, of the limitation figures in practice, by using modern examples of average capacity of cruise liners or passenger vessels and the respective limits imposed under both the 1974 and the 2002 Conventions. At the end, figures are also shown of the limits under the 1976 Limitation Convention and its 1996 Protocol, and these are compared with the 2002 Convention.

With 3500 passengers, the exposure under the Athens Convention 2002 will be US$2.1 billion and, for 1000 crew, US$1 billion, making a total of US$3.1 billion. However, the P&I Group has reached an arrangement for an overall limit of US$3 billion as an excess overall reinsurance cover to be obtained from the market for large passenger ships. The restructuring of the overall market reinsurance cover of the group is serving the purpose of preserving the principle of mutuality with regard to issues that might arise in relation to modern large passenger ships.

---

48   See para 2.4.1, above.
49   Article 7(1).
50   Article 7(2).
51   See conversion rate, fn 14.

Table Comparing Total Limits available (in UK£)[52] under Athens Convention 1974 and 2002 respectively

Name of Ship	Queen Mary 2	Queen Elizabeth 2	Val de Loire (Brittany Ferries Passenger ship)	MV Estonia
Maiden Voyage	12 January 2004	2 May 1969	1993	(Foundered in 1994)
Passenger Carrying Capacity[53]	2,620	1,791	2,140	1,400
Maximum Limits under Athens Convention 1974[54]	Total Fund of £93,899,458.56	Total Fund of £64,188,523	Total Fund of £76,696,504.32	Total Fund of £50,175,283.20
Maximum Limits under Athens Convention 2002[55]	Total Fund of £804,864,000 Total of £503,040,000 available for direct action	Total Fund of £550,195,200 Total of £343,872,000 available for direct action	Total Fund of £657,408,000 Total of £410,880,000 available for direct action	Total Fund of £430,080,000 Total of £268,800,000 available for direct action

3000 passengers under old limit of 1976 Limitation Convention = SDR 25,000,000.
3000 passengers under new limit of the 1996 Protocol to 1976 Convention = SDR 525,000,000.
3000 passengers under the Athens Protocol 2002 at SDR 400,000 per passenger = SDR 1,200,000,000.

4.5 The implications of the 2002 Protocol in case of bankruptcy of the owner

The aim of the imposition of compulsory insurance is to protect passengers in the event of insolvency of the liable party. In addition, claimants – by having the right of direct action against the insurer – are greatly helped, instead of having to pursue a paper company in a remote jurisdiction. Furthermore, compulsory insurance will raise the standards of ships, because financial security will not be provided to substandard owners who should be expelled by the other mutually insured owners.

Direct action has two significant effects: first, it enables victims to overcome the hurdles imposed by the Third Parties (Rights Against Insurers) Act 1930; and, second, it renders the P&I clause in the clubs' rules, namely 'pay to be paid' (meaning that the insured owner has to pay the claimant first before it can be indemnified by

---

52   An SDR rate of 1 SDR = 0.768 GBP, as calculated on 1 March 2007, is used here to convert the SDR limits under both Conventions.
53   Assuming, for this comparison, that the number of passengers stated were on board.
54   The calculation is made by multiplying the limit of 46,666 SDR by the number of passengers on each occasion (carried on board each vessel), which is then converted into sterling.
55   The calculation is made by multiplying the limit of 400,000 SDR by the number of passengers carried on each vessel, which is then converted into sterling. The direct action limit is calculated by multiplying the limit of 250,000 SDR per passenger by the number of passengers carried on board, which is then converted to sterling.

the insurer), invalid. The issue of direct action had been contested by the clubs during the consultation process. Article 4bis (10) provides now that the insurer in a direct action has the benefit of the limits, even if the carrier or the performing carrier is not entitled to limitation of liability. The insurer may further invoke the defences (other than the bankruptcy or winding up) which the carrier would have been entitled to invoke in accordance with this Convention, and also the defence that damage resulted from the wilful misconduct of the assured under s 55(2)(a) of the Marine Insurance Act 1906. However, the insurer shall not invoke any other defence which he might have been entitled to invoke in the proceedings brought by the assured against the insurer.

Despite lengthy discussions and recommendations to the IMO's Legal Committee about dropping the 'wilful misconduct' defence, since the purpose of compulsory insurance is to protect the victims of disasters, it is unfortunate that it has been maintained. It is also unfortunate that the alternative proposal for protection of victims by the provision of accident insurance, which is not subject to the defence of wilful misconduct, was not accepted. One argument in support of retaining the defence of wilful misconduct is that it will discourage owners who may be minded to scuttle their ship for gain, or deliberately do not maintain the ship in a seaworthy condition. However, such an argument is flawed: in the first place, insurers should not insure such owners, and second, such owners will not be deterred by maintaining the defence against the victims, who will have no asset of the bankrupt owner against which to proceed. The other argument in favour of maintaining this defence is that it will be unfair to the other owners who are insured mutually in the P&I clubs to have to finance the insurance for such conduct by substandard owners. However, the P&I managers and directors of the mutual insurance are in a better position to evaluate the credentials of owners who enter with the particular club (and refuse the insurance of substandard owners), than ferry passengers who may board a substandard ferry boat.

4.6 Time limit for claims and jurisdiction

Other changes by the Athens Convention 2002, which affect the current regime, include an amendment to the time limits before the action is barred. The requirement that the time bar expires after two years is maintained. However, due to the different ways in which the beginning of the time run can be calculated, the all-encompassing limit has moved from three to five years, which begins with the date of disembarkation or when disembarkation should have occurred, whichever is the later.[56] Alternatively, three years beginning with the date when the claimant knew or should reasonably have known of the injury, loss or damage caused by the incident, if this is earlier than the previous option.[57]

Furthermore, a slight change has been introduced with regard to Art 17 of the Protocol in the light of Council Regulation (EC) 44/2001 on jurisdiction, which is based on the domicile of the defendant. One of the jurisdiction provisions in the

---

56   Article 16(3)(a).
57   Article 16(3)(b).

Protocol was originally based on the domicile of the claimant; that would not be in accord with the Regulation. Therefore, after presentations to the IMO Legal Committee by the Commission, there has been the following addition to the jurisdiction of the domicile of the claimant, that is 'provided the defendant has a place of business and is subject to the jurisdiction in that State'.

The other three heads of jurisdiction provided are the same as in the Athens Convention 1974 (seen earlier).

4.7 Invalidity of contractual provisions

It is clearly stated, in Art 18, that contractual terms concluded before the occurrence of the incident causing the death of or personal injury to a passenger, or the loss of or damage to the passenger's luggage, purporting to oust the provisions of the Convention with regard to liability, burden of proof and the limits, as specified by the Convention, shall be null and void, but the nullity of those provisions shall not render the contract of carriage void, which shall remain subject to the provisions of the Convention.

4.8 Tacit acceptance procedure

Under the 1974 Athens Convention, the procedure required in order to make any amendments to the Convention involves the ratification by a certain number of States before it enters into force. It is for this reason that the 1990 Protocol has not entered into force. By the time the requisite number is reached, the changes made are already outdated. This is also seen as the reason why the Athens Convention 1974 itself has been ratified by only a small number of States.

The Athens Convention 2002 has included a measure designed to simplify the procedure for raising the limits of liability. Amendments (which shall be submitted to the IMO's Legal Committee for prior consideration) shall be adopted by a two-thirds majority of the State parties to the Convention, as revised by the Protocol, on condition that at least one half of the State parties to the Convention shall be present at the time of voting (Art 23(5) of Final Clauses). Certain restrictions are stipulated on proposals to amend the limit, such as: no amendment may be considered within five years from the date the Protocol was offered for signature, or from the date of entry into force of a previous amendment; and no limit may be increased by more than 6% per year.

Any amendment adopted as per Art 23(5) shall be notified to the all State parties by IMO. The amendment shall be deemed to have been accepted at the end of a period of 18 months after the date of notification. An amendment deemed to have been accepted as above shall enter into force 18 months after its acceptance, and shall bind the State parties unless they denounce this Protocol at least 6 months before the amendment enters into force (Arts 23(8)–(10), 21).

Revision or amendment of the Protocol shall be requested by not less than one-third of the State parties (Art 22 of Final Clauses).

4.9 Competence of regional organisations

An unusual provision in the Convention permits a Regional Economic Integration Zone to sign the Convention on behalf of its members.[58] This is defined as being a group of sovereign States who have transferred certain competencies to the organisation which the Convention affects. An example of such an organisation is the European Union, which has competency to rule on issues concerning maritime safety. A provision such as this may prove to dissuade a body like the EU from creating its own, more stringent, laws which would only affect the area in which it is authorised to rule upon. In this way, the Convention encourages a uniform application of the law around the world.

Indeed the EU Parliament passed a Resolution on 25 April 2007 on the proposal for a Regulation of the EU Parliament and of the Council on the liability of carriers of passengers by sea and inland waterways in the event of accidents. After negotiations with industry bodies, the Regulation will include the Reservation and IMO Guidelines (see below) for the implementation of the 2002 Athens Convention by EU member States through the EU Regulation. The Regulation, as amended, will exclude the application of the Convention to inland the waterways, to be in line with the Convention.

4.10 Industry concerns and solutions

The fact that the Athens Convention 1974 is not ratified by many States is testament to the difficulties of the regime. The framework is adequate and workable in theory, but the cumbersome means of amending the limits has led to delays in improving them. By the time the 1974 Convention entered into force in 1987, the limits were widely seen as out of date, leading to a 1990 Protocol, which did not gain the requisite number of signatures and its limits, anyway, have by now become out of date. The result has led many national States to create their own system of liability for passenger claims. The UK, for instance, has retained the framework of the Athens Convention 1974, but has introduced higher limits for carriers based in the UK. Many States who are not parties to the Convention have leaned more towards a system of open-ended liability. With modern cruise liners now having a carrying capacity of over 3000 passengers, the old system of limitation embodied in the 1974 Convention is clearly unacceptable and inadequate.

The Athens Convention 2002 should, therefore, be a welcome move, since it has solved the two main problems which have dogged its predecessor. On the one hand, the limits that are imposed are much higher, and properly reflect what is seen as acceptable compensation for death and personal injury claims in the modern age. On the other hand, there is a procedure introduced which provides for an easier method of upgrading the limits when the need arises in the future.

It has taken six years to produce the Protocol, which was met with an undercurrent of opposition from ship owners and the insurance market.[59] In the meantime,

---

58 Final Clauses, Art 19.
59 Griggs, Williams and Farr, op cit, fn 1, p 132.

since no progress was being made to implement the Protocol, the EU took steps to oblige its members to implement the Protocol into their national legislation. As a first step, the Commission presented a proposal for a Council Decision in June 2003, by which the Community would become a contracting party to the Protocol. Later, since the industry and the governments were not moving towards implementation by 2005, the Commission proposed that the Protocol should be implemented at the EU level by a passenger liability Regulation.[60]

The areas of concern about the implementation had been the introduction of compulsory insurance for passenger ships coupled with direct action against the P&I insurers, who had also been concerned about the steep increase of the limits. It had been argued that there would not be sufficient insurance capacity in the market. Since P&I clubs, which insure third party liabilities, operate on the principle of mutual insurance, they were, understandably, concerned that non-passenger carriers, who are members of the clubs, would refuse to cover the high risks posed by the owners of large passenger ships.

Such concerns have now abated. It has been accepted that, like the other modern Conventions which provide for compulsory insurance and direct action against the insurer, the 2002 Protocol should be in line with those Conventions. The issue of market capacity has also been resolved. A solution has been found also for the issue of mutuality, by restructuring the overall excess insurance cover of the P&I Group through the reinsurance market (see para 4.4, above).

A further serious issue of concern for P&I clubs, which had been a stumbling block to the progress of ratification of the Protocol, was the enormous potential exposure of P&I clubs to terrorist risks, when an incident of loss was partially caused by terrorists' activities and partially by the failure of the owners to protect passengers adequately from terrorism. Such loss would not be covered by the exception of Art 3(1)(b) of the 2002 Protocol. P&I clubs do not insure liabilities arising from terrorist acts and, considering that there is aggregation of claims with regard to passengers carried on a ship, the prospect of liability for damage arising from terrorist acts was unattractive. It was necessary, therefore, to find a solution. It was recommended by the IMO Legal Committee, at its 90th session, that if terrorist risks were excluded from the Convention by a Reservation when a State ratifies the Convention, this would speed up the ratification process because it would be possible to obtain insurance for those risks from a separate entity. Then, the P&I clubs would be prepared to issue Athens insurance certificates if war and terrorist risks were kept out.

The European Commission took note of these concerns, which were addressed at global level within the IMO, and halted its action to impose a solution at a regional level.

The problems were solved in Paris, 16–19 October 2006, where the IMO Legal Committee at its 92nd session adopted the proposed Guidelines and Reservation for the implementation of the Protocol, and the IMO issued a circular No 2758 (dated 20 November 2006) containing the Guidelines and Reservation, mentioned earlier. The Guidelines, which represent a good compromise, confirm a broad

---

60 COM(2005) 592 final.

consensus that the 2002 Protocol should be ratified and enter into force; such adoption is final, not requiring another Diplomatic Conference.[61] Marsh insurance brokers have offered to arrange terrorist risk insurance cover.

Liability incurred due to war or terrorism is capped by the reservation to 250,000 SDR per passenger in each distinct occasion, or to 340 million SDR overall per ship on each distinct occasion. It is said that this will match the level of market insurance. Such insurance shall cover, under Guideline 2.2, liability for loss suffered as a result of death or personal injury to a passenger caused by:

- war, civil war, revolution, rebellion, insurrection, or civil strife arising there from, or any hostile act by or against a belligerent power;
- capture, seizure, arrest, restraint or detainment, and the consequences thereof or any attempt threat;
- derelict mines, torpedoes, bombs or other derelict weapons of war;
- act of any terrorist or any person acting maliciously or from a political motive and any action taken to prevent or counter any such risk;
- confiscation or expropriation.

This liability may be subject to the following exceptions, limitations and requirements

- War automatic termination and exclusion clause.[62]
- In the event the claims of individual passengers exceed in the aggregate the sum of 340 million SDR overall per ship on any distinct occasion, the carrier shall be entitled to invoke limitation of his liability in the amount of 340 million SDR, always provided that:
  - this amount should be distributed amongst claimants in proportion to their established claims,
  - the distribution of this amount may be made in one or more portions to claimants known at the time of the distribution, and
  - the distribution of this amount may be made by the insurer, or by the court or other competent authority seised by the insurer in any State party in which legal proceedings are instituted in respect of claims allegedly covered by the insurance.

Guideline 2.3 provides that non-war insurance should cover all perils subject to compulsory insurance, other than those risks listed in Guideline 2.2.

Regarding non-war/terrorism risks, the exposure under the Athens Protocol 2002 for ships of 3500 passengers will be US$2.1 billion and, for 1000 crew, US$1 billion, making a total of US$3.1 billion. However, the P&I Group has reached an arrangement for an overall limit of US$3 billion as an excess overall reinsurance cover to be obtained from the market for large passenger ships.

---

61 Rosaeg Erik, 'Light at the end of the tunnel for passengers', editorial in the Journal of International Maritime Law, vol 12, issue 5, October 2006; Professor Rosaeg, Director of the Scandinavian Institute of Maritime Law, University of Oslo, Norway, played an instrumental role in the process of finding solutions to the various issues involved in the Protocol.

62 The insurance cover shall terminate automatically upon the outbreak of war between the UK, USA, France, the Russian Federation, and the People's Republic of China.

There will be a 'Blue Card' issued by a war insurer as evidence of insurance cover, and another 'Blue Card' issued by a non-war insurer. The wordings of both cards, and of a model certificate of insurance, are provided in Appendix B to the Guidelines.

Both war and non-war insurance are subject to exceptions with regard to loss or damage caused by radioactivity and cyber attack.

It is hoped that, in the near future, the Athens Convention 2002 will be ratified by a large number of States.

CIVIL LIABILITY FOR MARINE POLLUTION, DAMAGE BY HAZARDOUS/NOXIOUS SUBSTANCES, NUCLEAR INCIDENTS AND COMPENSATION

This chapter, contributed by Elizabeth Blackburn QC,[1] provides an overview of the international liability system relating to pollution at sea. For the rules and regulations made at the regional level by the European Union concerning environmental protection and maritime safety, including the Criminalisation Directive and Framework Decision for ship-source pollution, see Chapter 20, below.

1 INTERNATIONAL CONVENTIONS CONCERNED WITH POLLUTION

1.1 UNCLOS: the protection and preservation of the marine environment

Article 24 of the 1958 Convention on the High Seas called on States to draw up regulations to prevent the pollution of the seas by the discharge of oil or the dumping of radioactive waste, and Part XII of the United Nations Convention on the Law of the Sea 1982 (UNCLOS) now deals with the protection and preservation of the marine environment.

1.1.1 Sovereign powers, jurisdiction and obligations of Member States to legislate

Article 192 of UNCLOS provides that States have the obligation to protect and preserve the maritime environment, and Art 211(1) and(2) provide that States, acting through the International Maritime Organisation (IMO), or general diplomatic conference, shall establish and keep under review international rules and standards to prevent, reduce and control pollution of the marine environment from vessels, and promote the adoption, in the same manner, of routing systems designed to minimise the threat of accidents which might cause pollution of the marine environment, including the coastline, and pollution damage to the related interests of Coastal States. States are to legislate for the prevention, reduction and control of pollution of the marine environment from vessels *flying their flag, or of their registry,*[2] and Art 211(4) also provides that States can adopt laws and regulations for the

---

1   Stone Chambers, Gray's Inn.
2   UNCLOS, Art 211(2).

prevention, reduction and control of pollution in their *territorial sea*, including vessels exercising the right of innocent passage, but such laws and regulations are not to hamper innocent passage of foreign vessels. Pursuant to Art 19(2)(h) of UNCLOS, the only act of pollution which can deprive a foreign ship of the right of innocent passage in the territorial sea is an 'act of wilful and serious pollution contrary to the Convention'. Hence, in the absence of a wilful and serious act of pollution, passage by a foreign ship in the territorial sea of a coastal State must be considered to be 'innocent passage'.[3]

Part V of UNCLOS deals with exclusive economic zones (EEZ), which are areas beyond and adjacent to the territorial sea, and such zones are subject to the specific legal regime established in this Part of the Convention, under which the rights and jurisdiction of the coastal State and the rights and freedoms of other States are governed. Such a zone cannot extend beyond 200 nautical miles from the baselines from which the breadth of the territorial sea is measured. Article 56 provides that the coastal State has jurisdiction as provided for in the relevant provisions of UNCLOS, inter alia, with regard to the protection and preservation of the marine environment in the economic zone. Article 221 in turn recognises the right of States to take and enforce measures beyond their territorial sea, proportionate to the actual or threatened damage, in order to protect their coastline or related interests, including fishing, from pollution or threat of pollution, following upon a maritime casualty or acts relating to such a casualty which may reasonably be expected to result in major harmful consequences.

Article 58 establishes the rights and duties of other States in the EEZ: such as the freedom of navigation of the high seas, over flight, and laying of submarine cables and pipelines. However, in exercising these rights, such States should have due regard to the rights, duties and laws of the coastal State and, in exercising its rights and performing its duties under the Convention in the EEZ, the coastal State shall have due regard to the rights and duties of other States, and shall act in a manner compatible with the provisions of this Convention.

Article 211(6) states that, where the international rules and standards referred to in Art 211(1) are inadequate to meet special circumstances, and coastal States have reasonable grounds for believing that a particularly clearly defined area of their respective EEZ is an area where the adoption of special mandatory measures for the prevention of pollution from vessels is required for recognised technical reasons in relation to its oceanographical and ecological conditions, as well as its utilisation or the protection of its resources and the particular character of its traffic, the issue can be referred to the IMO for determination, and any consequent implementation.

In addition, coastal States have jurisdiction physically to inspect, and to commence proceedings against, ships in their territorial waters and EEZ where there are clear grounds for believing that the ship concerned has violated domestic or international pollution regulations.[4] It should be further noted that a State, in whose port

---

3   Mensah, T, presentation on 'Sovereign Rights in Legislation of Member States', 8th Cadwallader Memorial Lecture, 4th October 2005, The London Shipping Law Centre, www.london-shipping-law.com.

4   UNCLOS, Art 220.

a vessel is, may take legal proceedings against that vessel not only for breaches of the pollution laws of that State, but also in respect of any discharge outside its internal and territorial waters or its EEZ, in violation of applicable international rules and standards.[5]

As set out in Art 235, States are responsible for the fulfilment of their international obligations concerning the protection and preservation of the marine environment, and are liable in accordance with international law. States must ensure that recourse is available, in accordance with their legal systems, for prompt and adequate compensation or other relief in respect of damage caused by pollution of the marine environment by persons under their jurisdiction. With the objective of assuming prompt and adequate compensation in respect of all damage caused by pollution of the marine environment, States are to co-operate not only in the implementation of existing international law but also in the further development of international law relating to responsibility and liability for the assessment of and compensation for damage and the settlement of related disputes, as well as, where appropriate, development of criteria and procedures for payment of adequate compensation, such as compulsory insurance and compensation funds.

1.2 Other key international conventions concerned with pollution[6]

MARPOL

The International Convention for the Prevention of Pollution from Ships 1973 (MARPOL) and the 1978 Protocol are concerned with all forms of pollution from ships apart from dumping. Detailed standards are laid down covering oil, noxious liquid substances in bulk, harmful substances carried by sea in packaged form, sewage and garbage. It covers ships flying the flag of, or operated under the authority of, a State party, but does not apply to warships or State-owned ships used only on governmental non-commercial service.

MARPOL empowers and obliges every State party to 'prohibit' any violation of its requirements. Each State party is required to establish sanctions under its laws for such violations, subject to the limitations and constraints as provided mainly by MARPOL which is also subject to the overarching principles of UNCLOS.[7]

Each State party undertakes to conduct an investigation of a casualty occurring to any of its ships if it has produced a major deleterious effect upon the marine environment. It imposes a duty on the master to report such incidents and if the vessel is abandoned or in the event of a report from the ship being incomplete or unobtainable, the owner, charterer, manager or operator of the ship or their agents shall to the fullest extent possible assume the obligations imposed on the master.

---

5   Art 218.
6   For a detailed analyis of marine environmental law, see De La Rue and Anderson, *Shipping and the Environment*, 2nd edn, 2005, LLP.
7   See Mensah, op cit, fn 3, for further interpretation.

SOLAS

The International Convention for the Safety of Life at Sea 1974 (SOLAS) and its 1978 Protocol contain detailed provisions covering oil tankers, and include mandatory provisions for ships carrying dangerous cargoes in bulk (the IBC Code, which is also mandatory under MARPOL) and for those carrying liquefied gases in bulk (IGC Code). Chapter IX makes mandatory the application of the International Safety Management (ISM) Code, which requires safety management systems to be run on those ships to which the ISM Code applies. This involves establishing environmental protection policies, and having instructions and procedures to ensure protection of the environment in compliance with international and flag State legislation.[8]

Intervention

The 1969 Intervention Convention (as amended by its 1973, 1991 and 1996 Protocols) confirms the coastal State's right to take measures beyond the territorial sea in cases of maritime casualties which cause or threaten to cause pollution. By Art I, the parties to the Convention may take such measures on the high seas 'as may be necessary to prevent, mitigate or eliminate grave and imminent danger to their coastline or related interests from pollution or threat of pollution of the sea by oil (defined by article II as crude oil, fuel oil, diesel oil and lubricating oil), following upon a maritime casualty or acts related to such a casualty which may reasonably be expected to result in major harmful consequences'.

Article V of the Intervention Convention provides that measures taken by the coastal State shall be proportionate to the damage (actual or threatened) to it, such measures shall not go beyond what is reasonably necessary to achieve the end mentioned in Art I, and the measures shall not unnecessarily interfere with the rights and interests of the flag State, third States and of any persons, physical or corporate, concerned.

In considering whether the measures are proportionate to the damage, account shall be taken of (a) the extent and probability of imminent damage if those measures are not taken; (b) the likelihood of those measures being effective; and (c) the extent of damage which may be caused by such measures. Article III of the Intervention Convention provides for a system of consultation and notification when a coastal State is exercising its right under Art I, including consultation with a list of experts maintained by IMO.

In English law, maritime intervention is particularly dealt with in ss 137 to 141 of the Merchant Shipping Act 1995 (MSA 1995), as amended by ss 2 and 3 of the Merchant Shipping and Maritime Security Act 1997. Intervention is now allowed not only in respect of polluting oil, but also pollution by other substances liable to create hazards to human health, to harm living resources and marine life, and to damage amenities or to interfere with other legitimate uses of the sea.

It should be particularly noted that there is a right to compensation from the Secretary of State if the action taken was not reasonably necessary to prevent or

---

8   About the ISM Code, see Chapter 8, above.

reduce the pollution; or was such that the good it did, or was likely to do, was disproportionately less than the expense incurred or damage suffered as a result of the action: see s 138 of the MSA 1995, as amended.

The powers of the Secretary of State under s 137(4) may be delegated,[9] and such delegation has been made to 'the Secretary of State's Representative' (SOSREP). SOSREP has been appointed to provide overall direction for all marine pollution incidents involving the salvage of ships or offshore installations that require a national response. As set out in the National Contingency Plan for Marine Pollution from Shipping and Offshore Installations, the normal arrangement is for him to exercise operational control. As recommended in Lord Donaldson of Lymington's report on Salvage and Intervention and their Command and Control, Ministers and senior officials should not attempt to influence SOSREP's operational decisions while operations are in progress – in Lord Donaldson's words, they should 'back him or sack him'.

OPPRC

The International Convention on Oil Pollution Preparedness, Response and Co-operation 1990 is concerned with ensuring prompt and effective action in the event of a pollution incident, and requires ships to carry detailed plans for dealing with pollution emergencies. The Convention requires incidents to be reported without delay, national and regional systems to be set up for dealing with such incidents, and the State parties agree to co-operate and provide advisory services, technical support and equipment. This is covered in English law in s 128(1)(d) of the MSA 1995, and the order and regulations made under that section. The Protocol on Preparedness, Response and Co-operation to Pollution Incidents by HNS 2000 came into force on 14 June 2007.

Dumping

The right to dump or jettison cargo, bunkers, slops etc is severely circumscribed by various Conventions, such as the London Convention on the Prevention of Marine Pollution by Dumping of Waste and Other Matter at Sea 1972; and the Convention on the Protection of the Marine Environment of the North East Atlantic 1992 (the OSPAR Convention).

Salvage

Under the London Salvage Convention 1989 (set out in Sched 11 to the MSA 1995), the salvor owes a duty to the owner of the salved vessel, or other property in danger, to carry out the salvage operations with due care and, in performing that duty, to exercise due care to prevent or minimise damage to the environment; and the Convention defines 'damage to the environment' as meaning substantial physical damage to human health or to marine life or resources in coastal or inland waters or areas adjacent thereto, caused by pollution, contamination, fire, explosion or similar major incidents (see Chapter 13, above).

---

9   See s 137(5) of the MSA 1995, and Chapter 13, para 15, above.

Information on most of these conventions can be found on the IMO website[10] and on the CMI website.[11]

1.3 The system in the United States

In the USA, there are both federal and State statutes relating to damage caused by pollution. The main federal Statutes are the Clean Water Act, the Federal Water Pollution Control Act, the Comprehensive Environmental Response Compensation and Liability Act, and the United States Oil Pollution Act (OPA) 1990.

2 THE INTERNATIONAL OIL POLLUTION COMPENSATION REGIMES

2.1 Introduction

The dramatic grounding in 1967 of the Liberian tanker *Torrey Canyon* off the Cornish coast of the UK, and the consequent spilling of 119,000 tonnes of crude oil, was the first major tanker disaster, and prompted the international community, through the IMO, to take measures to introduce compensation for victims of pollution damage. An ad hoc Legal Committee was established to deal with the various issues raised by the casualty, and the Committee soon became a permanent organ of the IMO, presently meeting twice a year to deal with any legal issues raised at IMO.

In 1969, a conference convened by IMO adopted the International Convention on Civil Liability for Oil Pollution (1969 CLC) which dealt with the civil liability of the registered shipowner for pollution damage caused by spills of persistent oil from tankers. However, it emerged during the course of the diplomatic conference that some delegates felt that the liability limits established under 1969 CLC were too low and that adequate compensation might not be available to victims; another diplomatic conference was convened in 1971 which resulted in the adoption of a sister convention, the 1971 International Convention on the Establishment of an International Fund for Compensation for Oil Pollution Damage (the 1971 Fund Convention). The two Conventions entered into force in 1975 and 1978 respectively.

The 1984 Protocol, by which an increase of the limits had been proposed, did not receive sufficient ratification. However, a second attempt at more substantial reforms in the 1990s resulted in the 1992 Protocols to the CLC and Fund Conventions, and the amended Conventions are now known as the 1992 Civil Liability Convention and the 1992 Fund Convention. The 1992 Protocols entered into force on 30 May 1996.

The 1971 Fund Convention ceased to be in force on 24 May 2002. The 1971 Fund continues to pay compensation for claims arising from incidents which occurred when the 1971 Fund was in force, but it does not apply to incidents occurring after

---

10 www.imo.org.
11 www.comitemaritime.org.

that date. However, it should be noted that a number of States have remained parties only to the 1969 CLC. The main differences between the 1969 CLC and the 1992 CLC are discussed below.

Simply put, the 1992 CLC/Fund regime provides for two 'tiers' of available compensation. The victim first looks to the registered shipowner and his CLC insurer (normally his P&I club) for the initial tier of compensation which is governed by the 1992 CLC and is subject to a tonnage type 'limitation' ceiling. The registered shipowner has to maintain insurance to cover his CLC limited liability,[12] and claims can be brought directly against the CLC insurer.[13] From 1 November 2003, the shipowner's limitation ceiling was increased,[14] and now ranges from 4.51 million SDR (approximately US$7 million) for a ship not exceeding 5,000 units of gross tonnage, up to 89.77 million SDR (approximately US$136 million) for a ship of 140,000 gross tons or over. As usual in modern limitation regimes, the shipowner is only deprived of the right to limit if it is proved by the claimant that the discharge, or escape or relevant threat of contamination, resulted from anything done or omitted to be done by the owner, either with intent to cause any such damage or cost, or recklessly and in the knowledge that any such damage or cost would probably result. However, as will be seen, the CLC guarantor/insurer is always entitled to limit his liability under CLC.

The second tier, which is governed by the 1992 Fund Convention, is provided by the International Oil Pollution Compensation Fund 1992, a world-wide intergovernmental organisation, which exists to pay compensation in certain circumstances, when those suffering oil pollution damage do not obtain full compensation under the 1992 CLC. The 1992 Fund is financed by contributions levied on any person who has received, after sea transport, in one calendar year, more than 150,000 tonnes of crude oil and/or heavy fuel oil in a State party to the 1992 Fund Convention. That person then becomes liable for costs arising from any incident in the next calendar year and for payments in respect of that incident in subsequent years. Annual contributions are levied to meet the anticipated payments of compensation and administrative expenses during the coming year, and are paid direct to the 1992 Fund.

From 1 November 2003, the compensation payable by the 1992 IOPC Fund for any one incident has been increased,[15] and is now limited to 203 million SDR (approximately US$307 million), but this maximum amount also includes any limitation sum actually paid by the shipowner or his insurer under the 1992 CLC first tier.

If the total amount of the established claims exceeds the two tiers, the compensation paid to each claimant will be reduced proportionately, and when there is a risk that this situation will arise, the 1992 Fund may have to restrict compensation payments to ensure equal treatment.

---

12 1992 CLC, Art 7(1).
13 1992 CLC, Art 7(8).
14 This followed amendments made to the 1992 Protocols to the CLC and Fund Conventions, which were adopted at the 82nd Session of the IMO's Legal Committee in October 2000.
15 Ibid.

Increasingly, the maximum compensation afforded by the 1992 Conventions is proving insufficient to meet compensation needs in some Contracting States, and this has led to the need to pro-rate payments in cases such as *The Prestige* [Spain 2002], resulting in claimants not being paid in full and delays in obtaining compensation.

In the light of the devastating consequences of the sinking of both *The Erika* and *The Prestige*, in May 2003, a diplomatic conference adopted the 2003 Protocol on the Establishment of a Supplementary Fund for Oil Pollution Damage, which entered into force on 3 March 2005,[16] ie three months after the date on which the requirements for entry into force were met. The new 2003 Protocol will provide an optional *third tier* of compensation by means of a Supplementary Compensation Fund, which will afford additional compensation over and above the compensation available under the 1992 Conventions, but only in those States to the 1992 Fund Convention who choose to 'contract in' to the new Protocol. The Supplementary Fund will only cover incidents which occur after the entry into force of the 2003 Protocol. 1992 Fund States which consider that they cannot join the Supplementary Fund (for whatever reason) need not do so, and they will still continue to enjoy the benefit of the compensation offered by the existing 1992 CLC/Fund regime.

The aggregate amount of compensation which will be available to victims if the relevant State is a party to the 1992 CLC, 1992 Fund and the 2003 Protocol will be 750 million SDR (just over US$1,000 million).

2.2 Information on Contracting States

Information on the regime, including the Contracting States to each of the Conventions, is available on the IOPC Fund's website[17] and on the IMO website.[18]

In addition, the IOPC Fund publishes a Claims Manual, and the Fund's Annual Reports are a very useful source of information relating to the worldwide casualties dealt with by the IOPC Fund, and include outlines of defences taken and points on the construction and application of the regime.

2.3 The relevant UK legislation

In the United Kingdom, the 1992 CLC/Fund Conventions are the relevant law, as enacted in ss 152 to 182 of the Merchant Shipping Act 1995. However, it should be particularly noted that the terms of the Conventions have not themselves been specifically enacted into or scheduled to the UK legislation. Nevertheless, in construing the relevant sections of the 1995 Act, the legislation should be given a liberal and broad rather than a restricted construction, and so construed, if reasonably possible, to conform to the language of the conventions.[19] The UK has become a

---

16 The 2003 Protocol came into force in the UK on 8 September 2006.
17 www.iopcfund.org.
18 www.imo.org.
19 *Algrete Shipping Co Inc (RJ Tilbury and Sons (Devon) Ltd) v IOPC Fund 1971: The Sea Empress* [2003] EWCA Civ 65; [2003] 1 Lloyd's Rep 327, P 332.

Contracting State to the 2003 Protocol, and has enacted it in the MSA (Pollution) Act 2006.

2.4 The 1992 CLC regime

2.4.1 Application to sea-going vessels carrying persistent oil in bulk

The CLC 1992 regime applies to any sea-going vessel or any seaborne craft of any type whatsoever, constructed or adapted for carrying persistent hydrocarbon mineral oil in bulk as cargo, but a ship capable of carrying oil and other cargoes *will be regarded as a ship only for these purposes when it is actually carrying the oil in bulk as cargo, or during any voyage following such carriage*, unless it is proved that it has no residues of such carriage of oil in bulk aboard.[20] The regime does not apply to warships or other ships owned or operated by a State and used, for the time being, only on government non-commercial service.[21]

The term 'persistent' is used to describe those oils which, because of their chemical composition, are usually slow to dissipate naturally when spilled into the marine environment and are likely to spread and require cleaning up, such as crude oil, fuel oil, heavy diesel oil and lubricating oil. Non-persistent oils tend to evaporate quickly when spilled and do not require cleaning up. Neither persistence nor non-persistence is defined in the Conventions. Bitumen and asphalt can come within the CLC regime, but damage caused by spills of non-persistent oil, such as gasoline, light diesel oil and kerosene, is not compensated under the Conventions.

There have been a number of cases on whether the relevant ship is a 'vessel' for the purposes of CLC 1992. For example, the 1992 Fund Assembly has indicated in Committee that offshore craft, such as floating storage units and floating production, storage and offloading units, should be regarded as 'CLC ships' only when they carry oil as cargo on a voyage to or from a port or terminal outside the oil field in which they normally operate. In *The Al Jaziah 1* [UAE, January 2000], the casualty was about 40 years old, she had a rudder and propeller, but did not carry basic navigation equipment, and her design at build had been approved by the Dutch small ship inspectorate as an inland waters motor tank ship. She had a very low forecastle but, at the time she sank, she was operating in open seas. The 1992 Fund Committee took the view that, if a vessel was actually operating at sea at the time of the loss, she came within the regime. In *The Dolly* [Caribbean, 5 November 1999], the vessel had been built in 1951 as a general cargo ship, but at some date three tanks for carrying bitumen had been installed in the hold, and the opening of the original hatch had been closed with steel plates. The Committee concluded that she was a CLC ship, because she had been adapted for the carriage of oil in bulk. (See also *The Slops*, Greece, June 2000).

In *The Maritza Sayalero* [Venezuela, June 1998], the incident fell outside the CLC Convention because the oil was non-persistent, and also because the maritime

---

20 1992 CLC, Art 1, and ss 153(3), (4), 170(1) of the MSA 1995.
21 1992 CLC, Art 11, and s 167(1) of the MSA 1995.

transport of the oil had been completed, and the spill came from a hose belonging to the oil terminal that had ruptured at a distance of 40 metres from the ship's manifold.

It should be noted, however, that the Committee's decisions are not binding, and a party can always refer the issue to the relevant national court. The Court of Appeal indicated in *Algrete Shipping Co Inc (RJ Tilbury and Sons (Devon) Ltd) v IOPC Fund 1971: The Sea Empress*[22] that decisions made by the 1992 Fund Assembly are not even particularly persuasive.[23]

2.4.2 Geographical application when there is pollution damage

Waters

The 1992 Conventions apply to 'pollution damage' caused in the territory or territorial sea of a State which is a party to the Convention in question, and to pollution damage caused in the exclusive economic zone (EEZ) of such a State or, if a contracting State has not established such a zone, in the 'quasi EEZ' – ie an area beyond and adjacent to the territorial sea of that State in accordance with international law and extending not more than 200 nautical miles from the baselines from which the breadth of its territorial sea is measured. In the UK, the relevant area beyond the territorial sea is defined in s 129(2)(b) of the MSA 1995[24] and the orders made thereunder.[25]

Provided that the relevant vessel is a sea-going vessel, the regime would appear to apply to pollution damage caused on inland waterways. For example, in October 2003 the 1992 IOPC Fund Executive Committee considered the question of whether the CLC regime applied to pollution damage in the inland, non-tidal reaches of rivers in the context of *The Victoriya* where the incident occurred in the upper reaches of the Volga River, some 1,300 kms inland from the Caspian Sea and the Sea of Azov. *The Victoriya* was registered for river and sea navigation, and traded regularly in the Mediterranean, Black Sea and Baltic. Since 2002, she had traded in Turkey, Greece and the Ukraine, and at the material time was en route to a non-Russian port in the Black Sea. The Fund Executive Committee concluded that *The Victoriya* was a 'ship' for CLC purposes; and, under general principles of public international law, the concept of territory of a State covers inland waters, including rivers. However, during the discussion, some delegations expressed reservations about the applicability of the 1992 Conventions, drawing attention to the preamble of the 1992 CLC, which referred specifically to pollution posed by the worldwide maritime carriage of oil and the exclusion of inland waters from the scope of application of UNCLOS.

---

22 Op cit, fn 19.

23 In May 2003, the Administrative Council of the IOPC Fund adopted a Resolution in which the Council expressed the view that the courts of State parties should take into account the decisions of the governing bodies of the Fund relating to the interpretation and application of the Conventions.

24 1992 CLC, Art 2; s 170(4) of the MSA 1995.

25 Merchant Shipping (Prevention of Pollution) Limits Regulations 1996, SI 1996/2128, made pursuant to Art 2 of the Merchant Shipping (Prevention of Pollution) (Law of the Sea Convention) Order 1996, SI 1996/282.

Section 153 of the MSA 1995 defines the geographical extent by using the words 'in the territory of the United Kingdom', which would appear to encompass inland waters.

Pollution damage

'Pollution damage' is defined as 'loss or damage caused outside the ship by contamination resulting from the escape or discharge of oil from the ship, wherever such escape or discharge may occur, provided that compensation for impairment of the environment other than loss of profit from such impairment shall be limited to the costs of reasonable measures of reinstatement actually undertaken or to be undertaken'.[26] If the material vessel comes within the definition of a 'CLC vessel', loss or damage caused outside the ship by contamination resulting from the escape or discharge of bunkers will be compensated.[27] The definition of pollution damage also extends to the costs of preventive measures (ie any reasonable measures taken by any person after an incident has occurred, to prevent or minimise pollution damage in the above-mentioned areas of a State party to the Convention in question, wherever these measures are taken)[28] and further loss or damage caused by such preventive measures.[29]

Incident

In turn, 'incident' is defined as meaning 'any occurrence, or series of occurrences having the same origin, which causes pollution damage or creates a grave and imminent threat of causing such damage'.[30] It follows that, if a response on the high seas or within the territorial waters of a non-Contracting State party succeeds in preventing or reducing pollution damage within the territorial sea or EEZ of a Contracting State, that response qualifies for compensation. The expense of reasonable preventive measures is recoverable, even if no spill of oil occurs, provided that there was a grave and imminent threat of causing such pollution damage.[31]

2.4.3 Application to types of claim

Anyone who has suffered pollution damage in a 1992 Contracting State party may bring a claim. Compensation is payable for not only the cost of reasonable clean-up measures and to combat the oil and defend sensitive resources, but also for reasonable costs associated with the capture, cleaning and rehabilitation of wildlife; and for the reasonable costs of cleaning, repairing or replacing property that has been contaminated by oil. Compensation is payable for loss of earnings suffered by the owners of such contaminated property, and it can also be payable in certain circumstances where property has not been polluted, for example, when a fisherman has

---

26 1992 CLC, Art 1(6).
27 See the definition of oil in 1992 CLC, Art 1(5) and s 153(7) of the MSA 1995.
28 1992 CLC, Art 1(7), and s 153(1)(b) of the MSA 1995.
29 1992 CLC, Art 1(6).
30 1992 CLC, Art 1(8).
31 See also s 153(2) of the MSA 1995.

been prevented from fishing because the fishing grounds have been polluted or where a hotelier located close to a polluted beach has lost business. Compensation for impairment of the environment is limited to loss of profit from such impairment and costs of reasonable reinstatement measures[32] directed at accelerating natural recovery of environmental damage actually undertaken or to be undertaken. Loss or damage caused by measures to prevent or minimise pollution is also compensated. For example, if clean-up measures result in damage to roads or piers, the cost of the resulting necessary repairs is an admissible claim. Examples of other types of allowable claims can be found in the IOPC's Claims Manual, which provides a very helpful analysis of how claims are evaluated and dealt with by the Fund.

The Manual emphasises that any expense or loss must actually have been incurred, and it must relate to measures which are deemed reasonable and justifiable. However, a claimant's expense/loss or damage is admissible only if, and to the extent that, it can be considered as caused by contamination resulting from the spill: there must be a reasonably close link of causation between the expense/loss or damage covered by the claim and the contamination caused by the spill. There must be a reasonable degree of proximity between the contamination and the loss or damage sustained and, when considering whether such a close link exists, account is taken of the following factors: geographic proximity between the claimant's activity and the contamination; the degree of economic dependence on the affected resource; the extent to which a claimant had alternative sources of supply or business opportunities; and the extent to which a claimant's business formed an integral part of the economic activity within the area affected by the spill. A claimant is entitled to compensation only if he has suffered a quantifiable economic loss, and he has to prove the amount of his loss or damage by producing appropriate documents or other evidence. The extent to which claimants are able to reduce their losses is taken into account.

However, the regime does not provide a right to compensation to a claimant whose loss is of an indirect relational pure economic nature: the 'but for' test (ie but for the incident, the loss would not have occurred) is not applicable, and the shipowner is not liable to compensate an indeterminate number of claimants. A claim is not accepted solely because a pollution incident occurs. In *The Sea Empress*,[33] the Court of Appeal held that a whelk-processing company located in Devon was not entitled to recover its loss of profit after a fishing ban was imposed off Milford Haven to prevent any health hazards through pollution, so that the local fishermen were stopped from supplying whelks under a contract with the processing company. The claimant's resultant loss arose from its inability to carry out processing and packing and deliveries of processed and packed whelks at points far away from the contaminated areas, and the court concluded that this was a form of secondary economic loss, which was outside the intended scope of a statute which was closely focused on physical contamination and its consequences.[34] (See further, Chapter 12, para 3.12.3.4).

---

32 1992 CLC, Art 1(6)(a), and s 156(3) of the MSA 1995.
33 Op cit, fn 19.
34 For a similar decision in Scotland, see *Landcatch v IOPC* [1999] 2 Lloyd's Rep 316.

Claims are assessed by the Fund on the basis of objective criteria, and one of the prime benefits of the regime is that, provided causation is established, and the costs can be shown to be reasonable, the Fund endeavours to settle claims out of court, applying Fund practice, and the Fund then pursues its subrogated rights. Costs, however, are not accepted when it could have been foreseen that the measures taken would be ineffective.

If matters cannot be compromised, the claimant has the right to bring his or her claim before the competent court in the State in which the damage occurred.

2.4.4 Possible claims by salvors

There is one other type of claim which might arise under the CLC regime if there have been salvage services. As discussed in Chapter 13 (above), under the London Salvage Convention 1989 the salvor owes a duty to the owner of the salved vessel or other property in danger to carry out the salvage operations with due care and, in performing that duty, to exercise due care to prevent or minimise damage to the environment. Damage to the environment in the context of the 1989 Salvage Convention means substantial physical damage to human health or to marine life or resources in coastal or inland waters or areas adjacent thereto, caused by pollution, contamination, fire, explosion or similar major incidents.

Salvage operations on a casualty may, therefore, include an element of pollution prevention, but, according to the IOPC Manual, such operations can be considered as 'preventive measures' for the purposes of CLC compensation, only if the primary purpose is to prevent pollution damage. If the operations have another purpose, such as salving hull and cargo, the costs incurred are not admissible under the Conventions. The IOPC Manual suggests that, if the activities are undertaken for the purpose of both prevention and salving the ship and cargo, but it is not possible to establish with any certainty the primary purpose of the operations, the costs are apportioned between pollution prevention and other activities. The Manual goes on to point out that the assessment for compensation for activities which are considered to be preventive measures would not be made on the basis of the criteria applied for assessing salvage award, but would be limited to costs, including a reasonable element of profit.

There is some controversy about whether the salvor could bring such a claim under the CLC/IOPC regime. For example, Brice[35] submits that, in the event that a salvor is not able to recover a salvage reward under Art 13 of the 1989 Salvage Convention, it is unlikely that the salvor could, as an alternative, recover his costs under the CLC/IOPC regime. The reasoning is developed on the basis that any measures taken by a salvor to prevent or minimise pollution damage are generally measures taken to further the salvage operation; what a salvor is doing is performing salvage services, and any apparent preventive measures are purely incidental; a salvor, unlike any other class of person, has his own remedies under Arts 13 and 14 of the 1989 Salvage Convention, and it is unlikely that it was the intention under any of the conventions to give him concurrent remedies to recover his costs.

---

35 *Brice on the Maritime Law of Salvage*, 4th edn, 2003, Sweet and Maxwell, para 6-178.

However, it could equally be argued that, as the salvor owes a duty to the owner of the salved vessel or other property in danger, not only to carry out the salvage operations with due care, but also in performing that duty to exercise due care to prevent or minimise damage to the environment, in an appropriate case, the activities are being undertaken for the purpose of both prevention and salving the ship and cargo and, as suggested in the IOPC Manual, the costs should be apportioned.

This point could perhaps become relevant if, for example, the SCOPIC Clause[36] has been incorporated into the material Lloyd's Form relating to a CLC vessel; SCOPIC has then been invoked at a later stage of the salvage services, so that the special compensation provisions of Art 14 of the Salvage Convention are replaced in effect by SCOPIC; and the casualty is suddenly lost. The salvor would be out of pocket in respect of the earlier part of his work, prior to the invocation of SCOPIC, and his only potential remedy would be under the CLC/IOPC regime.

2.4.5 Defences

The 1992 CLC provides that the registered shipowner[37] is strictly liable for pollution damage caused by his ship, unless he proves that the damage or the threat of contamination:

(a) resulted from an act of war, hostilities, civil war, insurrection or a natural phenomenon of an exceptional, inevitable and irresistible character; or

(b) was wholly caused by an act or omission done with intent to cause damage by a third party, not being a servant or agent of the owner (eg sabotage/terrorism); or

(c) was wholly caused by the negligence or other wrongful act of any Government or other authority responsible for the maintenance of lights or other navigational aids in the exercise of that function.[38]

If the pollution damage resulted, wholly or partially, either from an act or omission done with intent to cause damage by the person who suffered the damage or from the negligence of that person, the owner may also be exonerated wholly or partially from his liability to such person.[39]

It should also be borne in mind that the claimant will have to prove that the pollution damage resulted from an incident involving the shipowner's vessel.

The deletion of the word 'unforeseeable' from a proposed Russian amendment of the CLC Art 3(2)(a) 'natural phenomenon' defence at the 1969 Diplomatic Conference perhaps indicates that, although something out of the ordinary is required, the relevant natural phenomenon or phenomena does not have to be so out of the ordinary or unusual as to be unforeseeable.

Although there is a difference in wording in the Art 3(2)(a) defence, where the

---

36 The SCOPIC clause, in effect, provides for agreed tariff rates to be paid as remuneration from the time when written notice is given to the vessel's owners (see Chapter 13, para 14, above).

37 In the absence of registration, 'owner' means the person or persons owning the ship; and where a ship is owned by a State and is operated by a person registered as the ship's operator, 'owner' means the person registered as its operator: s 170 of the MSA 1995.

38 1992 CLC, Art 3(1), (2), and s 155 of the MSA 1995.

39 1992 CLC, Art 3(3), and s 153(8) of the MSA 1995.

words 'resulted from' are used, in contrast to the other defences where the words 'wholly caused by' are used, the inclusion of the words 'inevitable' and 'irresistible' in the natural phenomenon defence indicates that causative acts by the shipowner (or a third party) would usually render the defence inapplicable, unless the natural phenomenon was so overpowering that the ship would have been overwhelmed in any event.

It would appear that, in order to establish the defence, the shipowner would have to demonstrate not only that he and his employees could not have avoided the phenomenon relied upon, but also that the phenomenon relied upon could not have been withstood.

This raises another issue, namely whether the shipowner has to prove only that the exceptional natural phenomenon was (a) unavoidable by the vessel itself (or by ships of the same category), and (b) was unable to be withstood by the vessel itself (or by ships of the same category); or does he have to go further and prove these matters in respect of any ship?

This question has been the topic of some academic debate. In his article 'Civil Liability of Shipowners for Oil Pollution', Malcolm Forster[40] suggests that the word 'inevitable' cannot mean 'unavoidable by the party concerned' because, so constrained, the word would add nothing to the word 'irresistible', and he therefore argues that it should be understood as meaning 'beyond all human power to prevent'. However, this analysis appears to be somewhat flawed, because the two words 'irresistible' and 'inevitable' have different meanings: the latter fits more happily with the concept of actions being taken by persons to avoid the casualty, whereas the former appears to reflect the physical strength of the exceptional forces acting upon the casualty. As a matter of principle, it is difficult to see that the drafters of the Convention intended to discriminate against the owners of smaller ships, which have been constructed and operated according to appropriate international standards. It is at least arguable, therefore, that the exception is concerned with the vessel itself. Gotthard Gauci[41] has perhaps more persuasively submitted that:

> . . . the wording of the paragraph in question – being in the nature of an exception – would justify a strict interpretation to the effect that reference should be made to that category of ships when gauging irresistibility; going beyond that to gauge irresistibility on the basis of any ship in existence might be taking the spirit of the Convention too far and might mean imposing a quasi-impossible burden of proof on the shipowner.

However, if the shipowner is successful in his defence, the IOPC Fund becomes liable to claimants for the full admissible claims up to the Fund's overall limit, unless the pollution damage resulted from act of war, hostilities, civil war or insurrection; or the claimant cannot prove that the damage resulted from an incident involving one or more ships as defined by the CLC, or if there has been contributory negligence. However, in the context of contributory negligence, as will be seen, the Fund is not exonerated with regard to preventive measures.

In *The Nissos Amorgos* [Venezuela, February 1997], the registered shipowner and

---

40 [1973] Journal of Business Law 23.
41 *Oil Pollution at Sea: Civil Liability and Compensation for Damage*, 1997, Wiley & Sons, p 73.

his P&I club ran a defence (supported by the 1971 Fund) based on (c) above, taking the position that the incident and resulting pollution were due to the fact that the Maracaibo Channel was in a dangerous condition, due to poor maintenance, and this was known to the Venezuelan authorities, but that its full extent was concealed and that the arrangements for alerting mariners to the dangers which existed were unreliable.

In *The Nakhodka* [Sea of Japan, January 1997], the shipowners denied liability on the grounds that the combined state of the natural conditions facing the ship at the time of its loss amounted to an exceptional natural phenomenon in the particular part of the Sea of Japan, which could not have been avoided nor withstood by *Nakhodka* or ships of the same category. The case raised interesting issues on the ambit of this defence, including whether the Art 3(2)(a) defence required a court to limit the defence only to exceptional phenomena which could be categorised within a single description, such as earthquake or Tsunami; or whether a court could properly decide that combinations of phenomena fell within the defence, provided they met the individual criteria in Art 3(2)(a). In the end, the case was compromised, so these arguments were not tested in the Japanese courts.

2.4.6 Compulsory insurance or other financial security

The shipowner is obliged to maintain insurance (or other financial security) to cover his liability under the 1992 CLC, in the sum fixed by applying the limits of liability prescribed under the CLC regime,[42] unless the ship is carrying less than 2000 tonnes of oil in bulk as cargo; and claims for compensation under the 1992 CLC can be brought directly against the CLC insurer/guarantor,[43] who will normally be one of the Protection and Indemnity Associations which insure the third party liabilities of shipowners. The Third Parties (Rights against Insurers) Act 1930 is not applicable to this specific contract of insurance covering the CLC limitation fund liability,[44] and the insurer only has a defence to his CLC liability if (a) the shipowner's defences set out above are applicable; or (b) he can prove that the discharge or escape or the threat of contamination was due to the wilful misconduct of the owner himself. However, as set out below, the insurer will always be entitled to the benefit of limitation under the CLC regime.

It should also be noted that the shipowner will probably have additional cover exceeding the CLC limitation figure with his P&I club. In some 1969 CLC cases, where limitation was theoretically easier to break, being the old 'actual fault and privity' test, the IOPC Fund had hoped to break the limit as against the shipowner under the CLC, making the shipowner's CLC liability unlimited, so that the Fund could then stand in the shipowner's shoes to sue the owner's P&I club under this additional insurance cover under legislation such as the Third Parties (Rights against Insurers) Act 1930.

However, P&I clubs normally have 'pay to be paid' clauses, or other related

---

42   1992 CLC, Art 7(1) and s 163 of the MSA 1995.
43   1992 CLC, Art 7(8) and s 165 of the MSA 1995.
44   See s 165(5) of the MSA 1995.

clauses, which mean that the shipowner has had to pay the claim first before any claim can be made against the club (see further, Chapter 18, above). The P&I club will also reserve its position to investigate the casualty, in case it emerges that the shipowner has breached any of the Club Rules, so that cover could be avoided. It will be difficult to break the limit under the 1992 CLC, but some countries still apply the CLC 1969.

2.4.7 The shipowner's rights of subrogation

Normally, the 1992 Fund co-operates closely with the relevant P&I Club in the settlement of claims, and a local claims office will usually be set up when there has been an incident which has given rise to a large number of claims. Claimants can be private individuals, partnerships, companies, States, or local authorities. Article 5(5) of the 1992 CLC provides that, if, before the fund is distributed, the shipowner and his insurers have paid compensation for pollution damage, they acquire by subrogation the rights which the person so compensated would have enjoyed under the CLC. However, in certain jurisdictions there have been problems with the national court recognising these rights of subrogation.

2.4.8 The so-called 'channelling' provisions and the shipowner's rights of recourse

Claims for compensation for pollution damage can now only be made in the UK (and in other CLC States) against the registered owner of the relevant ship pursuant to CLC,[45] but this does not preclude victims from claiming compensation outside the Convention from persons other than the registered owner. However, unless the damage resulted from their personal act or omission committed with the intent to cause such damage, or recklessly and with knowledge that such damage would probably result, the so-called 'channelling provisions' of the 1992 CLC[46] expressly prohibit claims being brought against:

(a) the servants or agents of the shipowner or the members of the crew;

(b) the pilot or any other person who, without being a member of the crew, performs services for the ship;

(c) any charterer, however described and including a bareboat charterer, manager or operator of the ship;

(d) any person performing salvage operations with the consent of the owner or on the instructions of a competent public authority;

(e) any person taking preventive measures; and

(f) all servants or agents of the persons mentioned at (c), (d) and (e) above.

However, it should be particularly noted that nothing in the CLC regime prejudices any right of recourse that the shipowner has against third parties, including those persons who are covered by the 'channelling' provisions.[47] It follows, for example,

---

45 1992 CLC Art 3(4) and ss 156(1) and 166(2) of the MSA 1995.
46 1992 CLC Art 3(4) and s 156 of the MSA 1995.
47 1992 CLC Art 3(5) and s 169 of the MSA 1995.

that a salvor could be sued by the registered owner if there has been causative negligence; and likewise a bareboat charterer. Action has been taken outside the CLC regime in appropriate cases against, for example, port authorities.

Provision is also made in the 1992 CLC regime for situations where damage has resulted from an incident involving two or more 'ships', each of which is a ship within the regime. Article 4 of the CLC provides that 'when an incident involving two or more ships occurs and pollution damage results therefrom, the owners of all the ships concerned, unless exonerated under Article 3 of the Convention, shall be jointly and severally liable for all such damage which is not reasonably separable'.[48]

2.4.9 Limitation of liability under CLC

CLC pollution damage is excluded from the 1976 Limitation Convention and has its own limitation regime. The 1992 CLC allows the shipowner to limit his CLC liability to an amount determined by the size of the ship. Prior to 1 November 2003, the limits were as follows: for a ship not exceeding 5000 units of gross tonnage, 3 million Special Drawing Rights (SDR); with a tonnage between 5,000 and 140,000 units, 3 million SDR, plus 420 SDR for each additional unit of tonnage; and for a ship of 140,000 units of tonnage or over, 59.7 million SDR. These limits were increased from 1 November 2003 in respect of incidents occurring after that date, as follows: for a ship not exceeding 5000 units of gross tonnage, 4,510,000 SDR; with a tonnage between 5,000 and 140,000 units of tonnage, 4,510,000 SDR, plus 631 SDR for each additional unit of tonnage; and for a ship of 140,000 units of tonnage or over, 89,770,000 SDR.[49]

The limitation fund has to be constituted in the relevant court of the Contracting State in which the claimant's action has been brought, or could be brought, under Art 9.[50]

As usual in modern limitation regimes, the owner is only deprived of the right to limit if it is proved by the claimant that the discharge, or escape or relevant threat of contamination, resulted from anything done or omitted to be done by the owner, either with intent to cause any such damage or cost, or recklessly and in the knowledge that any such damage or cost would probably result.[51] As can be seen from the recent decisions of the English courts on the similarly worded Art 4 of the 1976 Limitation Convention,[52] it will be very difficult to break the right to limit under CLC 1992 in the UK: see, for example, The MSC Rosa M,[53] The Leerort,[54] and The Gudermes,[55] referred to in Chapter 17, above.

However, as set out above, the CLC insurer/guarantor is always entitled to

---

48 See also s 153(6) of the MSA 1995.
49 See the Merchant Shipping (Oil Pollution Compensation Limits) Order 2003, SI 2003/2559.
50 1992 CLC, Art 5(3).
51 1992 CLC, Art 5, and s 157(1) of the MSA 1995, as amended.
52 See, further Chapter 17, para 7.
53 [2000] 2 Lloyd's Rep 399.
54 [2001] 2 Lloyd's Rep 291.
55 [2002] EWHC 2452; [2003] 1 Lloyd's Rep 203.

limit his own CLC liability (if any) under the regime.[56] As set out in s 165(4) of the MSA 1995, where the shipowner and the insurer each apply to the court for the limitation of his liability, any sum paid into court in pursuance of either application shall be treated as paid also in pursuance of the other.

Claims in respect of expenses reasonably incurred, or sacrifices reasonably made, by the owner voluntarily to prevent or minimise pollution damage ranks equally with other claims against the limitation fund.[57] If the owner or any of his servants or agents or his CLC insurer has paid compensation for pollution damage, such person acquires subrogated rights, up to the amount he has paid.[58] The court, where the fund has been constituted, may also order that a sufficient sum shall be provisionally set aside where the shipowner/insurer establishes that he may be compelled to pay compensation at a later date.[59]

The limitation fund has to be constituted in the relevant court of the Contracting State in which the action has been brought or could be brought.

Under Art 6, where the shipowner has constituted a CLC limitation fund and is entitled to limit his liability, no claimant is entitled to exercise any right against any other assets of the owner in respect of such claim, and the court has to order the release of any ship or other property belonging to the owner which has been arrested in respect of the claim, and shall similarly release any bail or other security furnished to avoid such arrest. However, these provisions only apply if the claimant has access to the court administering the fund and the fund is actually available in respect of his claim.

It would appear, from the wording of Art 6 and s 159 of the MSA 1995, that the shipowner needs a finding from the court that he is entitled to limit, before this relief is triggered, and in this respect Art 6 and s 159 may differ from the position under the provisions of Art 13 of the 1976 Limitation Convention, where a limitation decree does not appear to be required before similar relief is granted[60] (see Chapter 17, above).

As set out in s 160 of the MSA 1995, where, as a result of any discharge or escape of oil from a ship or as a result of any relevant threat of contamination, the owner of the ship incurs a liability under s 153 and any other person incurs a liability,

---

56   1992 CLC, Art 7(8) and s 165(3) of the MSA 1995.
57   1992 CLC, Art 5(8) and s 158(6) of the MSA 1995.
58   1992 CLC, Art 5(5) and (6), and s 158(5) of the MSA 1995.
59   1992 CLC, Art 5(7) and s 158(7) of the MSA 1995.
60   In *The ICL Vikraman* [2003] EWHC 2320; [2004] 1 Lloyd's Rep 21, where Colman J was dealing with Art 13(2) of the 1976 Limitation Convention, he indicated that a 1976 limitation fund established in the English courts is actually available to a given claimant notwithstanding there being no limitation decree at the material time; and the availability continues unless and until a claimant discharges the burden of proving that the shipowner is not entitled to the decree. Colman J went on to find that the protection afforded by Art 13(2) works only by reference to the jurisdiction of the State party within which the ship or other property has been attached, or some other form of security has been given, and the court where the limitation fund has been established has no jurisdiction on this aspect of the 1976 Convention. Colman J also found that the 1976 Convention could not be construed so as to create a power in the courts of one State party to interfere by order with the disposition of property or other security within the jurisdiction of a State that was not a party to the 1976 Convention. The security regime provided by the Convention was clearly confined to States that were party to it.

otherwise than under that section, for any such damage or cost as is mentioned, then, if the owner has been found to be entitled to limit his liability and has paid that sum into court, and the other person is entitled to limit his liability in connection with 'the ship' by virtue of s 185 or 186 of the MSA 1995, no proceedings shall be taken against the other person in respect of his liability; and, if any such proceedings were commenced before the owner paid the sum into court, no further steps shall be taken in the proceedings except in relation to costs.

Section 161 of the MSA 1995 (entitled 'establishment of limitation fund outside UK') also provides that, where the events resulting in the liability of any person under s 153 also resulted in a corresponding liability under the law of another Liability Convention country, s 160 and s 159 (restriction on enforcement after establishment of limitation fund) shall apply as if the references to ss 153 and 158 included references to the corresponding provisions of that foreign law, and the references to sums paid into court include references to any sums secured under those provisions in respect of the foreign law liability.

2.4.10 Jurisdiction

Under Art 9, actions for compensation under the 1992 CLC against the shipowner or his insurer may only be brought before the courts of the State party in whose territory, territorial sea or EEZ the pollution damage occurred, or in respect of which the preventive measures were taken to prevent or minimise such pollution damage. However, as set out in Art 9(3), after a limitation fund has been constituted, the courts of the State in which the fund is constituted is exclusively competent to determine all matters relating to the apportionment and distribution of the fund.

Section 153 of the MSA 1995 provides for a cause of action only where damage has been caused in the territory of the United Kingdom, which, by virtue of the provisions of s 170, includes the specified areas beyond the territorial sea; or where preventive measures have been taken to prevent or minimise damage in such territory. However, where a shipowner incurs a CLC liability in two Convention countries, such as the UK and France, and a claim is brought in England under s 153(5) of the MSA 1995, the shipowner is also liable in the UK for any damage or cost for which he would be liable in France.[61]

2.4.11 Procedure

Section 20(5) of the Supreme Court Act (SCA) 1981 provides that s 20(2)(e) [the admiralty jurisdiction of the High Court in respect of any claim for damage done by a ship] extends to any claim in respect of a liability incurred under s 153 of the MSA 1995 and any claim in respect of a liability falling on the 1992 IOPC Fund.[62] It follows that, where pollution damage has been suffered or preventive measures have been taken in the specified areas, an action can be brought against both the

---

61 1992 CLC, Art 9(2), and s 153(5) of the MSA 1995.
62 The appropriate extension of the admiralty jurisdiction in Scotland is dealt with in s 166(1) of the MSA 1995.

registered shipowner and the CLC insurer. As set out in the Practice Direction to Part 61 of the Civil Procedure Rules, such an action will proceed in accordance with Part 59 of the Rules (ie the Commercial Court Practice), and where necessary, permission will be given to serve any claim form on the defendants if they are out of the jurisdiction. An *in rem* action could also be brought against the polluting ship or a sister ship in England, provided that the requirements of s 21(4) of the SCA 1981 are met (see Chapters 2 and 3, above). However, it is doubtful whether a maritime lien would be available to a claimant in the UK, because the claim for compensation for pollution damage derives from a statutory liability. The Admiralty Practice Direction (PD61) also deals with the IOPC's Fund right to intervene in claims being brought under the 1992 CLC.

2.4.12 Time bars

Under Art 8, claimants will ultimately lose their right to compensation under the 1992 CLC unless they bring a court action against the shipowner and his insurer within three years from the date when the damage occurred. In no case, however, shall an action be brought after six years from the date of the incident which caused the damage.[63] Where the incident consists of a series of occurrences, the six-year period runs from the date of the first such occurrence. In the Scottish decision of *Gray v Braer Corporation*,[64] the court held that to be timeous any action had to be raised within three years from the date on which the claim arose, and in any event, it must be raised within six years from the date of the relevant occurrence, or the first occurrence of the relevant occurrences: these requirements were cumulative, not optional.

2.4.13 Recognition and enforcement of a CLC judgment

Any judgment given by a court with jurisdiction in accordance with Art 9 which is enforceable in the State of origin where it is no longer subject to ordinary forms of review, shall be recognised in any Contracting State, except where the judgment was obtained by fraud or where the defendant was not given reasonable notice and a fair opportunity to present his case.[65] A judgment so recognised shall be enforceable in each Contracting State as soon as the formalities have been complied with, but those formalities shall not permit the merits of the case to be re-opened.[66]

2.4.14 Differences between the 1969 CLC and 1992 CLC

The main differences between the 1969 CLC and the 1992 CLC can be briefly summarised as follows.[67] The 1969 CLC applies only to escapes and discharges from laden tankers, and does not cover purely preventive measures where there is only a threat of escape or discharge; it has different geographical application, applying

---

63 See s 162 of the MSA 1995.
64 [1999] 2 Lloyd's Rep 541.
65 1992 CLC, Art 10(1).
66 1992 CLC, Art 10(2).
67 See also *Marsden on Collisions at Sea*, 13th edn, 2003, Sweet & Maxwell, paras 10-05 to 10-36.

only to pollution damage in the territory/territorial waters; it has less extensive provisions prohibiting claims being brought against persons other than the registered shipowner; and it has different limitation provisions from its 1992 Protocol, namely a smaller limitation fund, but the owner is not entitled to limit, where the incident was a result of his actual fault or privity.

2.5 The 1992 Fund Convention

The primary purposes of the Fund Convention are:

(i) to provide compensation for pollution damage to the extent that the protection afforded by the CLC is inadequate; and

(ii) to give relief to shipowners in respect of the additional financial burden imposed on them by the CLC, but such relief is subject to conditions designed to ensure compliance with safety at sea and other conventions.

2.5.1 Applicability of the 1992 Fund Convention

The 1992 Fund Convention applies only to pollution damage caused in the territory, including the territorial sea and the EEZ/quasi 'EEZ' of a Contracting State, and to preventive measures, wherever taken, to prevent or minimise such damage.[68] (Such terms have the same meaning as in Art 1 of the 1992 CLC.)[69] The Convention does not apply to damage which occurs in a State which is not a member of the 1992 Fund. The relevant English law is to be found in ss 172 to 182 of the MSA 1995.

As the 1971 Fund ceased to be in force on 24 May 2002, where pollution damage now occurs in a 1969 State, a claimant will have no rights of redress under the 1992 Fund, unless the claim is in respect of measures to prevent or minimise pollution damage in the territory, territorial sea and EEZ/quasi 'EEZ' of a 1992 Fund State.

The International Oil Pollution Compensation (IOPC) Fund 1992 is liable to pay compensation to any person suffering pollution damage only if such person has been unable to obtain full and adequate compensation for the damage under the terms of the 1992 CLC for the following reasons:

(a) because no liability for the damage arises under the 1992 CLC; or

(b) because the owner liable for the damage under the 1992 CLC is financially incapable of meeting his obligation in full, and any financial security that may be provided under Article VII of the CLC does not cover or is insufficient to satisfy the claims for compensation for the damage; an owner is treated as financially incapable if the person suffering the damage has been unable to obtain full satisfaction of the amount of compensation due under the 1992 CLC after having taken all reasonable steps to pursue the legal remedies available to him;[70] or

---

68 1992 Fund Convention, Art 3.

69 1992 Fund Convention, Art 1(2).

70 In *Landcatch v IOPC Fund* [1999] 2 Lloyd's Rep 316, the Outer House of the Court of Session made it clear that the Fund's liability was secondary, and no decree against the Fund could be granted until this condition had been satisfied.

(c) because the damage exceeds the owner's liability under the 1992 Liability Convention, as limited pursuant to Art 5(1) of that Convention.[71]

Thus, the Fund's liability is secondary.

Article 4(1) of the Fund Convention expressly provides that expenses reasonably incurred, and sacrifices reasonably made, by the shipowner voluntarily to prevent or minimise pollution damage are to be treated as pollution damage, and the shipowner can claim these expenses from the Fund as if he were a claimant.[72]

Any proceedings by or against the Fund may either be instituted by or against the Fund in its own name, or be instituted by or against the Director of the Fund as the Fund's representative.[73]

2.5.2 Fund defences

The defences available to the 1992 Fund are more limited than those available to the shipowner.

The 1992 Fund does not pay compensation if the pollution damage resulted from an act of war, hostilities, civil war or insurrection, or if the claimant cannot prove that the damage resulted from an incident involving one or more ships, as defined by CLC.[74]

As set out above, the two Conventions do not apply where pollution damage has been caused by a spill from a warship or other ship owned or operated by a State and used, at the time of occurrence, only on Government non-commercial service.

Likewise, if the Fund proves that the pollution damage resulted, wholly or partially, either from an act or omission done with the intent to cause damage by the person who suffered the damage or from the negligence of that person, the Fund may be exonerated, wholly or partially, from its obligation to pay compensation to such person, but there is no such exoneration with regard to preventive measures.[75] The Fund is in any event exonerated to the extent that the shipowner may have been exonerated under Art 3(3) of the 1992 CLC (ie if the owner proves that the pollution damage resulted wholly or partially either from an act or omission done with intent to cause damage by the person who suffered the damage or from the negligence of that person); but, likewise, there is no such exoneration of the Fund with regard to preventive measures.[76]

The 1992 Fund will pay compensation if the shipowner has established the 'natural phenomenon' defence or the defences set out in CLC Art 3(2)(b) or (c).

---

71 1992 Fund Convention, Art 4(1), and see s 175 of the MSA 1995.

72 See also s 175(6) of the MSA 1995.

73 Section 180 of the MSA 1995, and 1992 Fund Convention, Art 2(2).

74 1992 Fund Convention, Art 4(2) and s 175(7) of the MSA 1995. See also the Incident in Germany (June 1996) in the IOPC Fund's Annual Report where the German Government, as claimant, had to establish that the pollution damage was caused by oil which had escaped from a CLC ship.

75 1992 Fund Convention, Art 4(3), and s 175(8) and (10) of the MSA 1995.

76 1992 Fund Convention, Art 4(3), and s 175(9) and (10) of the MSA 1995.

2.5.3 Rights of subrogation

Although claimants have the right to take their claims to the competent national court, in practice, the 1992 Fund seeks to settle claims out of court, so that claimants receive compensation as promptly as possible, and the 1992 Fund then acquires by subrogation[77] the rights that the person so compensated may enjoy under CLC 1992 against the shipowner and his club.

The Fund also has rights of recourse or subrogation against persons other than the owner and the club.[78] For example, after the grounding of *The Sea Empress*, the Fund sued the Milford Haven Port Authority on the basis that the port authority was allegedly in negligent breach of duty in relation to safe navigation within the Haven and its approaches, and that the necessary causative link between the alleged breaches and the incident existed. In the event, the claim was compromised.[79]

It should also be noted that, under Art 9(3) of the Fund Convention, a Contracting State or agency thereof which has paid compensation for pollution damage in accordance with provisions of national law also acquires, by subrogation, rights which the person so compensated would have enjoyed under the Fund Convention. In this regard, s 179(2) of the MSA 1995 provides that, in respect of any sum paid by a public authority in the UK as compensation, that authority acquires by subrogation the rights which the recipient had against the Fund.

2.5.4 The limit of the 1992 Fund's liability

Prior to 1 November 2003, the compensation payable by the 1992 Fund for any one incident was limited to 135 million SDR, but this sum was increased in respect of incidents which occurred after that date,[80] so that the total amount available under the 1992 Conventions is 203 million SDR (approximately US\$310 million).[81]

If the total amount of the claims approved by the 1992 Fund, or established by a court, for a particular incident exceeds the total amount of compensation available under the 1992 Conventions, the compensation paid to each claimant is reduced proportionately.

2.5.5 Time bar and jurisdiction

Claimants will ultimately lose their right to compensation under the 1992 Fund Convention unless they bring court action against the 1992 Fund within three years of the date when the damage occurred, or make formal notification to the 1992 Fund of a court action against the shipowner or his insurer within that three-year period.

---

77 1992 Fund Convention, Arts 9(1) and 4(1), and s 179(1) of the MSA 1995.
78 1992 Fund Convention, Art 9(2).
79 See IOPC Annual Report 2003, pp 58–62.
80 Ibid, fn 14 and 16.
81 1992 Fund Convention, Art 4, and s 176 of the MSA 1995, as amended by the Merchant Shipping (Oil Pollution Compensation Limits) Order 2003, SI 2003/2559.

In no case shall an action be brought after six years from the date of the incident which caused the damage. [82]

Pursuant to Art 7(1), actions for compensation under the 1992 Fund Convention against the 1992 Fund may only be brought before the court which would be competent under Art 9 of the 1992 CLC. However, if an action for compensation under the 1992 CLC has been brought before a court in a State party to the 1992 CLC, but not to the Fund Convention, any action against the Fund shall, at the option of the claimant, be brought either before the court of the State where the Fund has its headquarters or before any court of a State party to the Fund Convention competent under Art 9 of the 1992 CLC.[83] The Fund has its headquarters at the present time in London.

2.5.6 Judgments

As set out in Art 7(6) of the 1992 Fund Convention and s 177 of the MSA 1995, where, in accordance with rules of court, the Fund has been given notice of liability proceedings brought against the shipowner or CLC insurer/guarantor under the 1992 CLC, any judgment shall, after it has become final and enforceable, be binding on the Fund in the sense that the facts and evidence in the judgment may not be disputed by the Fund, even if the Fund had not intervened in the proceedings.[84]

Subject to any decision concerning the pro-rating of claims, any final type judgment given against the Fund by a court having jurisdiction under Art 7(1) and (3) shall be recognised and enforceable in each Contracting State pursuant to Art 8 of the Fund Convention.[85]

2.6 The 2003 Supplementary Fund Protocol [86]

2.6.1 Introduction

As has been demonstrated by recent pollution incidents (such as *The Braer*, 1993, *The Sea Empress*, 1996, in the UK, *The Nakhodka*, 1997, in Japan, *The Erika*, 1999, in France, *The Prestige*, 2002, in Spain), it was recognised that the level of compensation available from the IOPC Fund was not sufficient to provide financial security to victims. The Protocol was adopted under the auspices of the IMO on 16 May 2003, and its purpose is to increase the amount of compensation available to victims of pollution damage arising from a serious incident involving the carriage of persistent oil as cargo by sea. It was negotiated against the background of *The Erika* casualty, following the European Union's move to promote the establishment of a

---

82 1992 Fund Convention, Art 6, and s 178 of the MSA 1995.

83 1992 Fund Convention, Art 7(3), and see s 175(2) of the MSA 1995.

84 See also PD61, para 11.

85 See also s 177 of the MSA 1995.

86 For a detailed analysis of the 2003 Protocol, see *The 2003 Protocol to the International Convention on the Establishment of an International Fund for Compensation for Oil Pollution Damage 1992: one bridge over some particularly troubled water*, JIML [2003] 9(6), 530, by Elizabeth Blackburn QC.

European Compensation Fund for Oil Pollution in European Waters, with a proposed fund of €1 billion (see further, Chapter 20, below). The subsequent *Prestige* disaster in Spain caused the acceleration of the adoption of the Protocol.

Thus, the 2003 Protocol to the 1992 Fund Convention entered into force on 3 March 2005. The text of the Protocol does not allow the EC to become a party to it but, by Council Decision 2004/246/EC, EU Member States are authorised to sign, ratify or accede to the Protocol (see Chapter 20, para 3.3). The UK – by the authority of the Houses of Lords and Commons – has passed the Merchant Shipping (Pollution) Act 2006 to enable effect to be given to the Supplementary Fund Protocol 2003, and the Protocol came into force in the UK on 8 September 2006.

2.6.2 Applicability

Only Contracting States to the 1992 Fund convention will be able to become Contracting States to the Protocol,[87] and if such a State chooses to become a contracting State to the Protocol, the Supplementary Fund, in certain circumstances, will provide a third tier of additional compensation, over and above the compensation available under the 1992 CLC and 1992 Fund regime, for pollution damage caused in the territory, including the territorial sea, and the EEZ/quasi-EEZ of such a Contracting State and to preventive measures, wherever taken, to prevent or minimise such damage.[88] The Supplementary Fund will only cover incidents which occur after the entry into force of the 2003 Protocol.

The Supplementary Fund will pay compensation to any person suffering pollution damage if that person has been unable to obtain full and adequate compensation for an 'established claim' for such damage under the terms of the 1992 Fund Convention, because the total damage exceeds, or there is a risk that it will exceed, the applicable limit of compensation laid down the 1992 Fund Convention in respect of any one incident.[89] Such compensation will be paid when the Assembly of the 1992 Fund has considered that the total amount of the established claims exceeds, or there is a risk that the total amount of established claims will exceed, the aggregate amount of compensation available under the 1992 Fund Convention, and as a consequence the Assembly of the 1992 Fund has decided provisionally or finally that payments will only be made for a proportion of any established claim. The Assembly of the Supplementary Fund will then decide whether, and to what extent, the Supplementary Fund shall pay the proportion of any established claim not paid under the 1992 CLC and the 1992 Fund Convention.[90]

'Established claim' is defined in Art 1(8) of the 2003 Protocol as meaning a:

claim which has been recognised by the 1992 Fund or been accepted as admissible by decision of a competent court binding upon the 1992 Fund not subject to ordinary forms of review and which would have been fully compensated if the limit set out in article 4 paragraph 4 of the 1992 Fund Convention had not applied to that incident.

---

87 2003 Protocol, Art 19(3).
88 2003 Protocol, Art 3. Such terms have the same meaning as in Art 1 of the 1992 CLC.
89 2003 Protocol, Art 4(1).
90 2003 Protocol, Art 5.

The aggregate amount of compensation which will be available if a Contracting State is a party to the 1992 CLC, 1992 Fund and the 2003 Protocol will be 750 million SDR (approximately £610 million).[91]

2.6.3 The 'membership' fee

As set out in Art 10 of the 2003 Protocol, this third optional tier will be financed in the States which become parties to the Protocol, primarily by those oil receivers in that State who, in a calendar year, have received, in total, quantities exceeding 150,000 tons in the ports or terminal installations of the State by sea carriage, and in any installations situated in that territory which have been carried by sea and discharged in a port or terminal installation of a non-Contracting State.[92] However, the Protocol includes a novel provision in Art 14, which ensures that there is 'a membership fee' for countries with smaller oil receipts to obtain the benefits of the Supplementary Fund. If the actual receipts of contributing oil in the State are less than 1 million tons, there is deemed to be a minimum receipt of 1 million tons of contributing oil in the State, and the Contracting State, which chooses to become a party in such circumstances to the Protocol, assumes the liability to pay the contribution based on the deemed 1 million ton receipt, or the difference between the 1 million tons deemed receipt and the actual receipts within the State which fall within the Protocol.[93] Where the aggregate quantity of contributing oil received in a Contracting State is less than 1 million tons, the Contracting State assumes the obligations that would be incumbent under the Protocol on any person who would be liable to contribute to the Supplementary Fund in respect of oil received within the territory of that State, insofar as no liable person exists for the aggregated quantity of oil received.[94]

2.6.4 Communication obligations and the denial of compensation

Contracting States will be obliged, pursuant to Art 13 of the 2003 Protocol, to communicate to the Director of the Supplementary Fund relevant information on oil receipts,[95] and, where a Contracting State does not fulfil its obligations to submit this communication and this results in a financial loss for the Supplementary Fund, that State will be obliged to compensate the Supplementary Fund for such loss.

If, as set out above, there is no such receiver or person in the Contracting State who meets the conditions of Art 10 of the 2003 Protocol, the Contracting State will also be obliged under Art 15(1) of the Protocol to inform the Director of the Supplementary Fund accordingly.

These are the two relevant communication obligations imposed on Contracting States.

---

91 2003 Protocol, Art 4(2). The maximum figures for compensation under the 2003 Protocol, proposed at the outset of the Diplomatic Conference by various States, ranged from 400 million SDR to 800 million SDR.

92 2003 Protocol, Art 10.

93 2003 Protocol, Arts 12(2) and 14.

94 2003 Protocol, Art 14(2).

95 In accordance with Art 15 of the 1992 Fund Convention.

The temporary denial of compensation

If a Contracting State fails to honour the communication obligations provided for in Arts 13(1) and 15(1) of the Protocol, serious repercussions may follow. Under Art 15(2) of the 2003 Protocol, if the Contracting State has failed to communicate to the Director of the Supplementary Fund information on oil receipts in accordance with Art 13(1) and a casualty occurs, then no compensation will be paid by the Supplementary Fund for pollution damage in the territory, territorial sea or the EEZ/quasi-EEZ of that State until the obligation to so communicate has been complied with for all years prior to the occurrence of the incident. The same applies if the Contracting State has failed to comply with the communication obligation imposed by Art 15(1) of the Protocol (ie notification that there is no person/receiver in the Contracting State who meets the conditions of Art 10 of the 2003 Protocol).[96]

The permanent denial of compensation

Where compensation has been denied temporarily in accordance with Art 15(2), compensation will be denied permanently in respect of that incident if the obligations to communicate to the Director under Arts 13(1) and 15(1) have not been complied with, within one year after the Director has notified the Contracting State of its failure to report.[97] Otherwise, as set out in Art 6 of the 2003 Protocol, rights to compensation against the Supplementary Fund are extinguished only if they are extinguished against the 1992 Fund under Art 6 of the 1992 Fund Convention, ie if the claim is time barred. A claim made against the 1992 Fund is to be regarded as a claim made by the same claimant against the Supplementary Fund.[98]

2.6.5 Rights of subrogation

The Supplementary Fund again acquires (a) the victim's rights of subrogation under the 1992 CLC against the owner or his insurer; and (b) the rights that the person compensated may enjoy under the 1992 Fund Convention against the 1992 Fund.[99] Again, nothing in the 2003 Protocol prejudices any right of recourse or subrogation of the Supplementary Fund against persons such as port authorities.[100]

A Contracting State or agency thereof, which has paid compensation for pollution damage in accordance with provisions of national law, also acquires by subrogation the rights which the person so compensated would have enjoyed under the 2003 Protocol.[101]

2.6.6 Jurisdiction, recognition and enforcement

Jurisdiction is dealt with in Art 7 of the 2003 Protocol and, for the most part, mirrors the provisions of the 1992 Fund Convention. However, where an action for com-

---

96 2003 Protocol, Art 15(2)
97 2003 Protocol, Arts 15(3) and 6(1).
98 2003 Protocol, Art 6(2).
99 2003 Protocol, Art 9(1), (2).
100 2003 Protocol, Art 9(3).
101 2003 Protocol, Art 9(4).

pensation for pollution damage has been brought before a court competent under Art 9 of the 1992 CLC against the shipowner or his insurer/guarantor, such court shall have exclusive jurisdictional competence over any action against the Supplementary Fund for compensation, unless that court is in a Contracting State which is not a party to the 2003 Protocol, in which case, the action against the Supplementary Fund shall, at the option of the claimant, be brought either before a court of the State where the Supplementary Fund has its headquarters or before any court of a Contracting State to the 2003 Protocol competent under Art 9 of the 1992 CLC.[102] Also, if an action for compensation against the 1992 Fund has been brought before a court in a Contracting State to the 1992 Fund Convention, but not to the 2003 Protocol, any related action against the Supplementary Fund shall, at the option of the claimant, be brought either before a court of the State where the Supplementary Fund has its headquarters or before any court of a Contracting State to the 2003 Protocol which is competent under Art 7(1) of the 2003 Protocol.[103]

Recognition and enforcement are dealt with in Art 8 of the 2003 Protocol, which again mirrors the provisions of the 1992 Fund Convention. Article 8(2) was inserted into the 2003 Protocol for the purposes of the European Judgments Regulation, and it provides that a Contracting State may apply other rules for the recognition and enforcement of judgments, provided that their effect is to ensure that judgments are recognised and enforced at least to the same extent as under Art 8(1) of the 2003 Protocol.

The Supplementary Fund has its headquarters in London and has a joint Secretariat with the 1992 Fund.

3 FURTHER DEVELOPMENTS: STOPIA AND TOPIA

As discussed above under the 2003 Protocol, since the new third tier of compensation will be financed primarily by the oil receivers in the States which become parties to the 2003 Protocol, and there is growing international pressure (particularly within the European Union) for further contribution from the carrying ship and its P&I insurers, the IOPC Working Group has been involved, since 2000, in an extensive review of the CLC/Fund Conventions.

The review has been considering the shipowner's liability and related issues, such as further increases in the limitation fund, the possibility of including charterers' (usually cargo owners') liability in the compensation regime, and an additional layer of liability to be used where the spill involves a deficient oil tanker.

The European Union has been very much an active supporter of reform, supporting the extension of civil liability to charterers, classification society or flag States in the event of fault, as well as the amendment of the right to limit, aiming to revert to the old test of 'actual fault or privity'. In a report to the EU Parliamentary

---

102 2003 Protocol, Art 7(2).
103 2003 Protocol, Art 7(3).

Assembly dated 30 March 2005, the Committee on the Environment suggested that, in the event of a persistent refusal of the IMO to move in this direction, a threat should be made, jointly with other EU Member States, to leave the CLC Convention.

However, a clear majority for the revision of the CLC regime would be required if substantial amendments were to be made, and a large number of governments voiced their objections to revising the international regime.

The IOPC Fund Assembly met in October 2005 and decided that, since there was insufficient support to continue the revision process, the revision was removed from the Assembly's agenda and the working group was disbanded.

For many States, the decision to stop revision of the CLC regime was made in reliance on the offer made by shipowners through their P&I clubs to share the overall cost of claims equally with oil receivers.

Since the revision was abandoned, the Boards of all International Group P&I Clubs agreed to put in place a mechanism for voluntarily increasing the minimum limit of shipowner liability under CLC 1992 in respect of small ships (up to 29,548 GT), and this has become known as the Small Tanker Oil Pollution Indemnification Agreement (STOPIA). This agreement came into effect at the same time as the entry into force of the 2003 Protocol, namely 3 March 2005. It will apply to approximately 6,000 tank vessels, representing about 75% of the world fleet of tankers falling within the CLC 'ship' definition.

STOPIA only applies in the event of a small tanker (up to 29,548 GT) causing pollution damage in a 2003 Protocol State when liability is imposed under the 1992 CLC. Under STOPIA, the owner of the relevant tanker agrees to reimburse the 1992 Fund in respect of claims paid in excess of the shipowner's relevant CLC limit of liability, up to a ceiling of 20 million SDR per incident, as opposed to the minimum limit of 4.5 million SDR applicable under CLC 1992. STOPIA has already been reviewed, in 2006, and will apply to all States which are parties to the 1992 Fund, not just parties to the Supplementary Fund.

In addition, the discussions and consultations that took place between the Fund Secretariat, OCIMF, the P&I clubs' Boards, Intertanko and ICS, resulted in an additional agreement by which shipowners will be contractually bound to indemnify the Supplementary Fund in respect of 50% of the amount of any claim falling on the Supplementary Fund, so that the burden imposed under the 2003 Protocol will be equally shared. This agreement has been entitled TOPIA (Tanker Oil Pollution Indemnification Agreement 2006) and, in contrast to STOPIA, it applies to all relevant tankers, regardless of size.

Following approval by members of P&I clubs on 1 February 2006, an amendment to the clubs' rules, with effect from 20 February 2006, enables mutual members to enter into these agreements.

The implementation of STOPIA and TOPIA is reflected in the Memorandum of Agreement (MOU) between the IOPC Funds and the International Group of P & I Clubs, in order to give effect to the clubs' undertakings to provide automatic entry in STOPIA and TOPIA and provide cover for the liabilities arising. The MOU gives the right to the 1992 and Supplementary Funds of direct action against the clubs regarding those liabilities.

4 SECTION 154 OF THE MERCHANT SHIPPING ACT 1995

The 1992 Conventions do not apply to spills of bunker oil from ships other than tankers, such as dry cargo ships. In England, s 154(1) of the MSA 1995 provides for shipowner liability for damage and the cost of preventive measures in the territory of the UK where, as a result of an occurrence, oil is discharged or escapes from a ship other than a CLC ship, including a ship which is not seagoing. Section 154(2) also provides for shipowner liability where, as a result of any occurrence, there arises a grave and imminent threat of damage being caused by the contamination which might result if there were a discharge or escape of oil from the non-CLC ship. However, it should be particularly noted that this liability under s 154 is now limitable under the 1976 Limitation Convention, as amended by the 1996 Protocol to that Convention, pursuant to s 168 of the MSA 1995.

Section 154(3) also provides for joint and several liability where the occurrence involves two or more vessels and the liability cannot reasonably be separated. The Law Reform (Contributory Negligence) Act 1945 applies in relation to any damage or cost for which a person is liable under s 154, but which is not due to his fault.

5 COMMON LAW

Marine pollution incidents which fall outside the ambit of the CLC/IOPC regime would fall to be decided in England under normal tortious principles at common law, and the following causes of action may be relevant, namely public nuisance, private nuisance, trespass, negligence, and possibly the rule in *Rylands v Fletcher*.[104] If the shipowner is dealing with common law claims, he will also be able to limit his liability under the 1976 Limitation Convention, as amended by its 1996 Protocol.

6 TOVALOP AND CRISTAL

TOVALOP was the Tanker Owners' Voluntary Agreement concerning Liability for Oil Pollution, which increased the shipowner's level of limited liability. CRISTAL (Contract Regarding an Interim Supplement to Tanker Liability for Oil Pollution) was the complementary scheme introduced by the oil industry. Both supplemented the 1969 CLC and 1971 Fund Conventions, and expired in February 1997, although there are still a few outstanding claims relating to rights and obligations which had accrued by that date.[105]

---

104 See, further, *Marsden on Collisions at Sea*, 13th Edition, 2003, Sweet & Maxwell, paras 10-74 to 10-85, and the discussion of basic tortious liability in *Esso Petroleum Co Ltd v Southport Corporation* [1956] AC 218. It should be noted that, on its facts, this case would now be decided under the CLC/Fund regime.

105 The TOVALOP and CRISTAL schemes are discussed in detail in the 12th Edition of *Marsden on Collisions at Sea*, para 10-70 and following.

7 FUTURE DEVELOPMENTS

There are two further international pollution damage conventions (not yet in force) which will be of relevance in the near future: the Bunker Oil Pollution Damage Convention 2001 (Bunker Convention), based on the CLC model, which deals with pollution damage caused by hydrocarbon mineral oil, including lubricating oil used for the operation or propulsion of the ship and any residues of such oil; and the Hazardous and Noxious Substances Convention 1996 (HNS Convention), based on the CLC and the IOPC Fund model.

All EU States were authorised to ratify both the Bunker Convention[106] and the HNS Convention.[107] It is anticipated that they will probably enter into force in the EU fairly soon.

A summary of these Conventions follows.

7.1 The Bunker Oil Pollution Damage Convention 2001

This Convention will require ratification by 18 States, including 5 States each with ships whose combined tonnage is not less than 1 million gross tons.[108] Once these entry into force criteria have been met the Convention will come into force internationally 12 months later.

The Convention covers bunker pollution from any seagoing vessel and sea-borne craft[109] and again follows the CLC precedent, with some exceptions.[110] The scope of geographical application is the same as in CLC, but the Bunker Convention includes a wider definition of the 'shipowner' than that contained in CLC, and covers not only the registered owner, but also the bareboat charterer, manager and operator of the ship.[111] Pollution damage is defined under this Convention as meaning loss or damage caused outside the ship by contamination resulting from the escape or discharge of bunker oil (hydrocarbon mineral oil, including lubricating oil, used or intended to be used for the operation of propulsion of the ship, and any residues of such oil)[112] from the ship, and the costs of preventive measures,

---

106 Council Decision of 19 September 2002 authorising the Member States, in the interest of the Community, to sign, ratify or accede to the International Convention on Civil Liability for Bunker Oil Pollution Damage 2001 (OJ L 256, 25/09/2002, p 7).

107 Council Decision of 18 November 2002 authorising the Member States, in the interest of the Community, to sign, ratify or accede to the International Convention on Liability and Compensation for Damage in Connection with the Carriage of Hazardous and Noxious Substances by Sea 1996 (OJ L 337, 13/12/2002, p 55).

108 Bunker Convention, Art 14.

109 Bunker Convention Art 1(1), but, again, warships, and other ships owned or operated by a State and used, for the time being, only on government non-commercial service, are excluded by Art 4(2).

110 For a more detailed analysis of the Bunker Convention, see Tsimplis, MN, *The Bunker Pollution Convention 2001: completing and harmonizing the liability regime for oil pollution from ships* [2005] LMCLQ 83.

111 Bunker Convention, Art 1(3).

112 Bunker Convention, Art 1(5).

including further loss or damage caused by preventive measures.[113] The Bunker Convention does not apply to pollution damage as defined in the 1992 CLC, as amended, whether or not compensation is payable in respect of it under that Convention.[114]

The limited exemptions from liability afforded to the shipowner mirror the exemptions contained in 1992 CLC,[115] but, where there is more than one person who is liable under the Convention, the liability is joint and several.[116] Where an incident involving two or more ships occurs and pollution damage results, the shipowners of all the ships involved, unless exonerated under the provisions of Art 3, shall be jointly and severally liable for all such damage which is not reasonably separable.

The Bunker Convention does not have its own limitation fund provisions of the sort seen in the 1992 CLC and the HNS Conventions. Such claims, however, may be limitable by the shipowner under the Convention on Limitation of Liability for Maritime Claims 1976, as amended, and Art 6 specifically provides that nothing in the Convention shall affect the right of the shipowner to limit liability under any applicable national or international regime, such as the 1976 Limitation Convention. However, the Limitation Convention 1976 may give the shipowner no general right of limitation for bunker pollution claims which do not involve physical damage to property, and a specific provision of the type presently found in s 168 of the MSA 1995 may be required in the future to ensure that the shipowner can limit his liability under the Bunker Convention.

Compulsory insurance up to the Limitation Convention 1976 limit (and any amendments) is dealt with in the Bunker Convention, and is an obligation which rests with the registered owner, to the exclusion of the other persons who come within the definition of 'shipowner'.[117] This obligation applies to ships having a gross tonnage greater than 1,000 gross tons.[118] However, there can be an exemption to this obligation for compulsory insurance in relation to ships operating exclusively on 'domestic voyages' within the territorial sea.[119] Again, there is a direct action provision against the insurer, who can always limit his liability to the amount equal to the 1976 Limitation Convention, and the insurer has the same defences as contained in the 1992 CLC.[120]

The time limit, jurisdictional and enforcement provisions also mirror the 1992 CLC.[121]

---

113 Bunker Convention, Art 1(9).
114 Bunker Convention, Art 4(1).
115 Bunker Convention, Art 3(3).
116 Bunker Convention, Art 3(2).
117 Bunker Convention, Art 7(1).
118 Bunker Convention, Art 7(1), (12).
119 Bunker Convention, Art 7(13).
120 Bunker Convention, Art 7(10).
121 See Bunker Convention, Arts 8, 9 and 10.

7.2 The Hazardous and Noxious Substances Convention 1996

7.2.1 Introduction

Compensation for damage caused by the carriage by sea of hazardous and noxious substances (HNS) is regulated by the International Convention on Liability and Compensation for Damage in Connection with the Carriage of Hazardous and Noxious Substances by Sea 1996 (HNS Convention), which is largely modelled on the oil pollution CLC/Fund regime.

Compensation payments to be made by the HNS Fund will be financed by contributions levied on persons who have received, in a calendar year, contributing cargoes after sea transport in a Member State in quantities above the thresholds laid down in the HNS Convention. However, in contrast to the IOPC Fund, the HNS Fund will have a general account which will be divided into sectors, and will also have separate accounts in respect of (a) oil; (b) liquefied natural gases of light hydrocarbons with methane as the main constituent (LNG); and (c) liquefied petroleum gases of light hydrocarbons with propane and butane as the main constituents (LPG).[122] The contributions to finance the compensation payments will be made post event, and levies may be spread over several years in the case of a major incident.

As set out above, the Convention is not yet in force, although the enabling legislation is in place in England pursuant to the Merchant Shipping and Maritime Security Act (MSMSA) 1997.[123] The Convention will enter into force 18 months after ratification by at least 12 States, subject to the following conditions: (a) four States must each have a registered ships' tonnage of at least 2 million GT; and (b) contributors in the States that have ratified must, between them, have received during the preceding calendar year a minimum of 40 million tonnes of cargo consisting of bulk solids and other HNS liable for contributions to the general account.

The Convention does not apply to warships or ships on government non-commercial service.[124] The Convention also allows a State to exclude its application to ships which do not exceed 200 gross tonnage and carry HNS only in packaged form and while the ships are engaged on voyages between ports or facilities of that State.[125]

7.2.2 Damage covered

The HNS Convention covers both pollution damage and damage caused by other risks, eg fire and explosion. It does not cover pollution damage caused by persistent oil, since such damage is already covered under the 1992 CLC and Fund

---

122 HNS Convention, Art 16.

123 See MSMSA 1997, s 14, Sched 3, which amends the MSA 1995 by adding new ss 182A, 182B and 182C, and a new Sched 5A which sets out the text of the Convention.

124 HNS Convention, Art 4(5).

125 HNS Convention, Art 5(1).

Conventions.[126] However, non-pollution damage caused by persistent oil, eg damage caused by fire or explosion, is covered by the HNS Convention. The HNS Convention covers a large number of substances including liquefied natural gas, and liquefied petroleum, and will apply to the residues from the previous carriage in bulk of such cargoes, except where the previous carriage has been of packaged items.[127] HNS is defined largely by reference to lists of individual substances that have been previously identified in a number of international Conventions and Codes. It does not apply to damage caused by class 7 radioactive material.

In addition to loss of or damage to property outside the carrying ship, the Convention also applies to loss of life or personal injury on board or outside the ship carrying the HNS, provided that such damage is caused by those substances.[128] 'Damage' also includes loss or damage caused by contamination of the environment, loss of income in fishing and tourism, and the cost of reasonable preventive measures (such as clean-up or removal of HNS from a wreck if the HNS presents a hazard or pollution risk) and further loss or damage caused by such measures.

The Convention applies to claims other than claims arising out of any contract for the carriage of goods and passengers, and applies to:

(a) any damage caused in the territory, including the territorial sea, of a State party;

(b) to damage by contamination of the environment caused in the EEZ Quasi-EEZ of a State party;

(c) to damage, other than damage by contamination of the environment caused outside the territory, including the territorial sea, of any State, if this damage has been caused by a substance carried on board a ship registered in a State party or, in the case of an unregistered ship, on board a ship entitled to fly the flag of a State party; and

(d) to preventive measures, wherever taken (see Art 3).

7.2.3 The registered shipowner's HNS liability

Under the Convention, assuming that he can limit his liability, the registered shipowner is liable for the loss or damage up to a certain amount which is covered by insurance.[129] The shipowner is required to take out insurance in respect of this limited sum or maintain other acceptable security and, as under the CLC regime, claims for compensation may be brought directly against the HNS insurer/guarantor.[130]

No claim for compensation may be made against the same category of people as set out in the 'channelling' provisions of 1992 CLC, unless the damage resulted from their personal act or omission, committed with the intent to cause such damage, or recklessly and with knowledge that such damage would probably result.[131]

---

126 HNS Convention, Art 4(3).
127 HNS Convention, Art 1(5)(b).
128 HNS Convention, Art 1(6).
129 HNS Convention, Arts 1(3), 7, 9(1), (2), and 12.
130 HNS Convention, Art 12.
131 HNS Convention, Art 7(5).

However, as in the CLC regime, the registered shipowner does have rights of recourse against these people where appropriate, including rights against the people referred to in the channelling provisions.[132]

The Convention only begins to apply from when the HNS enters the ship's equipment, or passes its rail on loading, and ends when the HNS ceases to be present in any part of its equipment or passes the rail on discharge.[133]

The compensation is distributed among claimants in proportion to their established claims, but loss of life/personal injury claims have priority over other claims, and up to two-thirds of the available shipowner's limitation fund is reserved for such claims.[134]

The registered owner of the ship is usually strictly liable to pay compensation, unless he can prove that:

(a) the damage resulted from an act of war, hostilites, civil war, insurrection or a natural phenomenon of an exceptional, inevitable and irresistible character; or

(b) the damage was wholly caused by an act or omission done with the intent to cause damage by a third party eg sabotage/terrorism; or

(c) the damage was wholly caused by the negligence or other wrongful act of any government or other authority responsible for the maintenance of lights or other navigational aids in the exercise of that function; or

(d) (in addition to the CLC types defences) the failure of the shipper or any other person to furnish information concerning the hazardous and noxious nature of the substances shipped either:

(i) has caused the damage, wholly or partly; or

(ii) has led the owner not to obtain insurance in accordance with Art 12;

provided that neither the shipowner, nor his servants or agents, knew or ought reasonably to have known of the hazardous and noxious nature of the substances shipped.[135]

Again, if the shipowner proves that the damage resulted wholly or partly either from an act or omission done with intent to cause damage by the person who suffered the damage or from the negligence of that person, the shipowner may be exonerated wholly or partially from its obligation to pay compensation to such person.[136]

Provision is also made in the HNS regime for where damage has resulted from an incident involving two or more 'ships', each of which is a ship within the respective regime. Article 8 of the HNS Convention provides that each owner, unless exonerated under the relevant provisions of the Convention, shall be liable for the damage. The owners shall be jointly and severally liable for all such damage which is not reasonably separable. However, the owners are entitled to the limits of

---

132 HNS Convention, Art 7(6).
133 HNS Convention, Art 1(9).
134 HNS Convention, Art 11.
135 HNS Convention, Art 7(2).
136 HNS Convention, Art 7(3).

liability applicable to each of them under the Convention. Again, nothing in this article prejudices any right of recourse of an owner against any other owner.

7.2.4. Limitation

The test for limitation is the same as under the CLC.[137] The shipowner's limitation of liability is calculated on the basis of the units of gross tonnage of the ship, as follows:

(a) 10 million SDR for a ship not exceeding 2,000 tons;

(b) for a ship in excess of 2,000 tons, 10 million SDR, plus:

(i) for each unit of tonnage from 2001 to 50,000 GT, 1,500 SDR; and

(ii) for each unit of tonnage in excess of 50,000 GT, 360 SDR.

The aggregate amount of the shipowners' liability shall not exceed 100 million SDR.[138]

7.2.5. Jurisdiction

Claimants can only take legal action in a court in the State party in whose territory, territorial waters or EEZ/quasi EEZ the damage occurred, or in respect of which the preventive measures have been taken: see, in this respect, Art 38(1). However, Art 38(2) provides that, where an incident has caused damage exclusively outside the territory, including the territorial sea, of any State parties, and either damage (other than damage by contamination of the environment) has been caused by a substance carried on board a ship registered in a State party (or, in the case of an unregistered ship, on board a ship entitled to fly the flag of a State party); or preventive measures have been taken, actions for compensation may be brought against the owner or HNS insurer/guarantor only in the courts of the State party where the ship is registered or, in the case of an unregistered ship, the State party whose flag the ship is entitled to fly; or the State party where the owner has habitual residence or where his principal place of business is established, or where the shipowner's limitation fund has been established.

7.2.6 The HNS Fund's liability

The HNS Fund (which will mirror the organisation of the IOPC Fund) will pay compensation when the total admissible claims exceed the shipowner's liability; or where the shipowner is exonerated from liability; or the shipowner is financially incapable of meeting his obligations.[139] A claimant must be able to prove that there is a reasonable probability that the damage resulted from an incident involving one or more ships, and the Fund will be liable to pay compensation even if the particular ship can not be identified.[140] The Fund is not liable if the damage was caused by

---

137 HNS Convention, Art 9(2).

138 HNS Convention, Art 9(1).

139 HNS Convention, Art 14(1).

140 HNS Convention, Art 14(3).

an act of war, hostilities, civil war or insurrection, or by HNS discharged from a warship or from a vessel on government non-commercial service. If the HNS Fund proves that the damage resulted wholly or partially either from an act or omission done with the intent to cause damage by the person who suffered the damage or from the negligence of that person, the Fund may be exonerated wholly or partially from its obligation to pay compensation to such person. But there is no such exoneration of the Fund with regard to preventive measures.[141]

The maximum amount payable by the HNS Fund in respect of any single incident is 250 million SDR, including the sum paid by the shipowner or his insurer.[142]

Actions against the HNS Fund should be brought before the same court as actions taken against the shipowner. Where an incident has occurred and the ship involved has not been identified, legal action may be brought against the Fund only in State parties where damage occurred.[143]

7.2.7 Time bars

Under Art 37(1), rights to compensation from the shipowner are extinguished unless an action is brought within three years from the date when the person suffering the damage knew, or ought reasonably to have known, of the damage and of the identity of the owner. Rights to compensation from the HNS Fund are extinguished within three years from the date when the person suffering the damage knew, or ought reasonably to have known, of the damage unless an action is brought or a notification has been made to the Fund that HNS proceedings have been brought against the shipowner or HNS insurer/guarantor.[144]

In no case shall an action be brought against the shipowner or the HNS Fund later than 10 years from the date of the incident which caused the damage. Where the incident consists of a series of occurrences, the 10-year period runs from the date of the last of such occurrences.[145]

8 OTHER PROVISIONS OF THE MERCHANT SHIPPING ACT 1995 RELEVANT TO OIL SPILLS

Sections 131[146] to 134, 136 and 143 of the MSA 1995 deal with the criminal liability for oil spills, defences thereto and the obligation on the owner or master to report spills. It should be noted that s 134 gives some protection for acts done in exercise of certain powers of harbour authorities. There is a power to detain ships for s 131 offences.[147]

---

141 HNS Convention, Art 14(3), (4).
142 HNS Convention, Art 14(5).
143 HNS Convention, Art 39.
144 HNS Convention, Arts 37(2) and 39(7).
145 HNS Convention, Art 37(3), (4).
146 As amended by s 7 of the MSMSA 1997.
147 See ss 144–146 of the MSA 1995, as amended by the MSMSA 1997.

Section 135 of the MSA 1995 deals with the restrictions on transfer of oil at night, and s 142 and 147 relate to the keeping of oil records. The relevant criminal sanctions are dealt with in s 142.

Section 139 provides for criminal penalties in respect of any failure to comply with orders given during maritime intervention by the Secretary of State under s 137.

If fines are not paid, s 146 provides for enforcement by arrest and sale of the vessel, and the court also has power to direct that the fine be paid to those who have suffered damage or incurred expenses in relation to a discharge of oil covered by s 131.

The MSA 1995 also provides powers to board and inspect vessels to investigate discharges or escapes of oil, and sanctions for the failure to produce the relevant records.[148]

Where proceedings are being brought under s 131 and the shipowning company is out of the jurisdiction, service on the master is good service under s 143(6).

Section 293 of the Act covers the functions of the Secretary of State in relation to marine pollution and, as amended by s 6 of MSMSA 1997, enables him to indemnify those who assist counter-pollution operations.

9 NUCLEAR DAMAGE CONVENTIONS

9.1 Introduction

There are two international liability regimes dealing with civil liability for nuclear damage: the International Atomic Energy Agency's (IAEA) Vienna Convention on Civil Liability for Nuclear Damage 1963,[149] and the Organisation for Economic Co-operation and Development's (OECD) Paris Convention on Third Party Liability in the Field of Nuclear Damage of 1960,[150] which was extended by the Brussels Supplementary Convention 1963, the Additional Protocol of 1964 and the 1982 Protocol. These two systems were linked by the Joint Protocol Relating to the Application of the Vienna Convention and the Paris Convention 1988, which was intended to preclude any possible conflicts of law in the case of international transport of nuclear material, and which also expanded the cover provided by the two Conventions. The Joint Protocol entered into force in 1992.

Thereafter, the 1997 Protocol to the Vienna Convention, which broadened the definition of nuclear damage to cover environmental damage and preventive measures, extended the geographical scope and increased the liability limits to a

---

148 See ss 259 and 260 of the MSA 1995.
149 In force from 1977.
150 In force from 1968.

figure not less than 300 million SDRs, entered into force in 2003, but it has few members at the present time.

In 1997, the IAEA parties adopted a Convention on Supplementary Compensation for Nuclear Damage, but this Convention is not yet in force.

In 2004, the contracting parties to the Paris and Brussels Conventions signed Amending Protocols, which broadened the definition of nuclear damage, widened the scope of application and set new limits of liability. These Protocols are not yet in force, but will be brought into force in due course.[151] However, many States with nuclear power reactors are not yet parties to any international nuclear liability convention.[152]

The Vienna and Paris Conventions share the following common aims and principles. Whatever the nationality, domicile or residence of a victim of nuclear damage, if nuclear damage occurs in a contracting State (or, in certain circumstances, in the course of transport to or from a non-contracting State), liability is channelled exclusively against the operator of the relevant nuclear installation in that State, or by reason of a nuclear incident involving nuclear substances coming from such an installation, and that liability is strict, save where the damage caused by a nuclear incident was directly due to an act of armed conflict, hostilities, civil war, insurrection, or (except insofar as the legislation of the contracting Party in whose territory the nuclear installation is situated may provide to the contrary) a grave natural disaster of an exceptional character. The operator, in relation to a nuclear installation, means the person designated or recognised by the competent public authority as the operator of that installation. Liability is limited under both regimes. Under the Paris and Brussels Conventions, the maximum liability is a total of 300 million SDR. Under the Vienna Convention, the ceiling is not fixed, but it may be limited by legislation in each contracting State. The operator must maintain insurance or other financial security for an amount equal to his limit of liability, and, beyond this level, the installation State can provide public funds but can also have recourse against the operator. Generally, rights to compensation are extinguished under both regimes, if an action is not brought within 10 years, although in the case of theft, loss, jettison or abandonment of the nuclear fuel or radioactive products, the period shall in no case exceed 20 years.

Many EU countries, including the UK, are parties to the Paris Convention and the Brussels Supplementary Convention.

9.2 The Paris Convention

Article 2 of the Paris Convention provides that the Convention does not apply to nuclear incidents occurring in the territory of non-contracting States or to damage suffered in such territory, unless otherwise provided by the legislation of the

---

151 Section 76 of the Energy Act 2004 will be used in due course for this purpose in the UK.
152 See Civil Liability for Nuclear Damage UIC Nuclear Issues Briefing Paper No 70, June 2004.

contracting party in whose territory the nuclear installation of the operator liable is situated, and except in regard to rights referred to in Art 6(e).[153]

However, Art 4 provides that, in the case of carriage of nuclear substances, including storage incidental thereto, without prejudice to Art 2, the operator of a nuclear installation shall be liable for damage, upon proof that it was caused by a nuclear incident outside that installation and involving nuclear substances in the course of carriage therefrom, only if the incident occurs (a) before express contractual liability (in writing) with regard to nuclear incidents involving the nuclear substances has been assumed by another nuclear installation; or (b) in the absence of such express terms, before the operator of another nuclear installation has taken charge of the nuclear substances; or (c) where the nuclear substances are intended to be used in a reactor comprised in a means of transport, before the person duly authorised to operate that reactor has taken charge of the nuclear substances; or (d) where nuclear substances have been sent to a person in a non-contracting State, before they have been unloaded from the means of transport by which they have arrived in that territory.

Conversely, Art 4 goes on to provide that the operator of the nuclear installation in the Contracting State shall be liable for damage if the incident occurs after express contractual liability (in writing), with regard to nuclear incidents involving the nuclear substances, has been assumed by the operator in the Contracting State; or, in the absence of such express terms, after he has taken charge of the nuclear substances; or after he has taken charge of the nuclear substances from a person operating a reactor comprised in a means of transport; but where the nuclear substances have, with the written consent of the operator been sent from a person in a non-contracting State, after they have been loaded on the means of transport by which they are to be carried from the non-contracting State.

Pursuant to Art 6(b), no person other than the operator shall be liable for damage caused by a nuclear incident, but this provision does not affect the application of any international agreement in the field of transport in force or open for signature, ratification or accession at the date of the Paris Convention. As can be seen from the relevant English legislation, s 12(4) of the Nuclear Installations Act 1965 indicates that the relevant transport agreements include the Hague Rules 1924, various Air Transport Conventions, and the Convention on the Contract for the International Carriage of Goods by Road 1956. Under Art 6(d) of the Paris Convention, any person who has paid compensation in respect of damage caused by a nuclear incident under any such international agreement or under any legislation of a non-contracting State shall, up to the amount which he has paid, acquire by subrogation the rights under this Convention of the person suffering damage whom he has so compensated.

As set out above, under Art 6(e), any person who has his principal place of

---

153 Under Art 6(e), any person who has his principal place of business in the territory of a contracting party or who is the servant of such a person and who has paid compensation in respect of damage caused by a nuclear incident occurring in the territory of a non-contracting State or in respect of damage suffered in such territory shall, up to the amount which he has paid, acquire the rights which the person so compensated would have had against the operator but for the provisions of Art 2.

business in the territory of a contracting party, or who is the servant of such a person, and has paid compensation in respect of damage caused by a nuclear incident occurring in the territory of a non-Contracting State or in respect of damage suffered in such territory shall also, up to the amount which he has paid, acquire the rights which the person so compensated would have had against the operator, but for the provisions of Art 2.

The operator has a right of recourse only if the damage caused by a nuclear incident results from an act or omission done with intent to cause damage, against the individual acting or omitting to act with such intent; or if and to the extent that it is so provided expressly by contract.[154]

Article 7 sets out the limitation provisions, and provides that the aggregate of compensation required to be paid in respect of damage caused by a nuclear incident shall not exceed the maximum liability established in accordance with this article. The maximum liability is 15 million SDR, but a contracting party may establish a greater or lesser amount, provided that in no event shall any amounts be less than 5 million SDR. Article 7(c) states that compensation for damage caused to the means of transport on which the nuclear substances involved were at the time of the nuclear incident shall not have the effect of reducing the liability of the operator in respect of other damage to an amount either less than 5 million SDR or any higher amount established by the legislation of a contracting party. These amounts shall apply to the liability of such operators wherever the nuclear incident occurs. Any interest and costs awarded shall not be considered to be compensation, and shall be payable in addition to any sum for which the operator is liable. However, art 15 then goes on to provide that any contracting party may take such measures as it deems necessary to provide for an increase in the amount of compensation specified.

To cover the liability under the Paris Convention, the operator is required to have and maintain insurance or other financial security.[155]

Article 13 covers jurisdiction, and provides that jurisdiction lies only with the courts of the contracting party in whose territory the nuclear incident occurred but, where a nuclear incident occurs outside the territory of the contracting parties, or where the place of the nuclear incident cannot be determined with certainty, jurisdiction over such actions shall lie with the courts of the contracting party in whose territory the nuclear installation of the operator liable is situated. Judgments entered by the competent court shall become enforceable in due course in the territory of any of the other contracting parties. The Convention shall be applied, according to Art 14, without any discrimination based upon nationality, domicile or residence. National law and legislation means the law and legislation of the court having jurisdiction under the Convention over claims arising out of a nuclear incident, and shall apply to all matters, both substantive and procedural, not specifically governed by this Convention.

---

154 Article 6(f).
155 Article 10(1).

9.2.1 Losses which fall outside the ambit of the Paris Convention

In the 1997 Protocol to amend the Vienna Convention, the definition of 'nuclear incident' was extended as follows: 'any occurrence or series of occurrences having the same origin which causes nuclear damage or, but only with respect to preventive measures, creates a grave and imminent threat of causing such damage' so as to include the costs of preventive measures. The Paris Convention may well cover the cost of cleaning up and preventive measures taken in mitigation of the damage by the owner of the property which has been damaged. However, it would appear that the Paris Convention in its present form does not cover matters where only a grave and imminent threat of damage has arisen and preventive measures are taken by authorities.

9.3 The 1963 Supplementary Convention

The 1963 Brussels Supplementary Convention is subject to the Paris Convention, and was intended to increase the amount of compensation for damage which might result from the use of nuclear energy for peaceful purposes. Article 2 states that the system of the 1963 Convention shall apply to damage caused by nuclear incidents (other than those occurring entirely in the territory of a State which is not a party to this Supplementary Convention), for which an operator is liable under the Paris Convention, and which is suffered in the territory of a contracting party; or on or over the high seas on board a ship registered in the territory of a contracting party, or on or over the high seas by a national of a contracting party provided that, in the case of damage to a ship, the ship is registered in the territory of a contracting party: provided in each case that the courts of a contracting party have jurisdiction pursuant to the Paris Convention.

Under the Supplementary Convention, as amended by the 1982 Protocol, the contracting parties undertake that compensation shall be provided up to the amount of 300 million SDR per incident, which shall be provided (a) up to an amount of at least 5 million SDR out of funds provided by insurance or other financial security, such amount to be established by legislation in the State in whose territory the nuclear installation of the operator is situated; (b) between this amount and 175 million SDR, out of public funds to be made available by the contracting party in whose territory the nuclear installation of the operator is situated; and between 175 and 300 million SDR, out of public funds to be made available by the contracting parties according to a formula set out in Art 12 of the Convention.

Article 3 goes on to provide that each contracting State shall either establish the maximum liability of the operator at 300 million SDR, or establish the maximum liability of the operator at an amount at least equal to 5 million SDR, and provide that, in excess of such amount, the public funds shall be made available by some other means. Interest and costs are still payable in addition, as set out in Art 3(f), so that the operator will be liable in part for the interest and costs in a very large claim, and wholly in a claim which falls within his limit.

Where the operator has a right of recourse under the Paris Convention, the contracting party in whose territory the nuclear installation is situated shall take such legislative measures as are necessary to enable both that contracting party and the other contracting parties to benefit from this recourse, to the extent that public funds have been made available.

9.4 Limitation of liability

Article 3(c) of the 1976 Limitation Convention provides that the rules of the 1976 Convention shall not apply to claims subject to any international convention or national legislation governing or prohibiting limitation of liability for nuclear damage (see Chapter 17).

9.5 The UK legislation

In the UK, the relevant legislation covering both conventions is to be found in ss 7–21 and 26 of the Nuclear Installations Act 1965, as amended by the Energy Act 1983. In the UK, the operator's only defence is if the occurrence or the causing thereby of the injury or damage is attributable to hostile action in the course of any armed conflict.[156] It should be noted that a claim under the 1965 Act does not give rise to any lien or other right in respect of any ship or aircraft, pursuant to s 14.

9.6 The 1971 Convention relating to Civil Liability in the Field of Maritime Carriage of Nuclear Material

The 1971 Convention relating to Civil Liability in the Field of Maritime Carriage of Nuclear Material (NUCLEAR 71) to which, for example, France, Spain and Germany are contracting parties, but not the UK, provides that any person who by virtue of an international convention or national law applicable in the field of maritime transport might be held liable for damage caused by a nuclear incident shall be exonerated from such liability: if the operator of a nuclear installation is liable for such damage under either the Paris or the Vienna Convention; or if the operator is liable for such damage by virtue of a national law governing the liability for such damage, provided that such law is in all respects as favourable to persons who may suffer damage as either the Paris or Vienna Convention.

The exoneration also applies in respect of damage caused by a nuclear incident to the means of transport upon which the nuclear material involved was at the time of the nuclear incident for which the operator is not liable, because his liability for such damage has been excluded by the provisions of the Paris or Vienna Convention or by equivalent provisions of national law.

The provisions of NUCLEAR 71 do not, however, affect the liability of any individual who has caused the damage by an act or omission done with intent to cause damage.

---

156 See s 13(4) of the 1965 Act.

PART IV

SAFETY AT SEA

OVERVIEW

Part IV concerns mainly developments with regard to safety at sea that have taken place since the first edition. The chapter on European legislation, as compared with the parallel steps taken by the IMO, has been overhauled. Technological developments in the running of ships, public concern for protection of the environment and criminalisation, international regulations for safety at sea, the campaign for quality shipping, and insurance concerns have all influenced the development of maritime law in recent years.

The epilogue in this Part gives an overview of the approach to risk management, and highlights its significance by bringing the Parts of this book together.

CHAPTER 20

EU LEGISLATION IN MARITIME SAFETY AND PARALLEL IMO DEVELOPMENTS

1 INTRODUCTION

Since the last edition of this book, there has been a great deal of activity in the EU, following serious marine accidents and terrorist activities, which led to new and proposed legislation in connection with maritime safety, the protection of the environment and security.

There is, of course, a series of conventions[1] with regard to ensuring safety at sea and the protection of the environment drawn up under the auspices of the IMO following several disasters, such as *Torrey Canyon* in 1967 and *Exxon Valdez* in 1989. MARPOL 1973/1978 regulates both accidental pollution (caused by unforeseen events) and operational pollution (caused by deliberate acts).

Following the sinking of the oil tanker *The Erika* in December 1999 off the coast of France, the European Commission set out on 21 March 2000[2] a communication for general strategy on the safety of 'seaborne oil trade', and made proposals for consideration by the Council and the European Parliament with a view to tightening up safety measures, so that a recurrence of this type of accident is prevented in the future.

The proposals incorporated measures for:

(i)   the elimination of manifestly sub-standard ships;

(ii) increased inspection of vessels posing risks;

(iii) increased information obligations;

(iv) monitoring traffic to EU ports and reporting;

(v)   the imposition of higher standards for inspection organisations;

(vi) phasing out single-hull vessels;

(vii) the establishment of a European Maritime Safety Agency (EMSA) for surveillance of maritime safety and prevention of pollution from ships; and

(viii) the establishment of a Committee on safe seas and the prevention of pollution from ships (COSS).[3]

In addition, the catastrophic event of the terrorist attacks of September 11 2001 on the World Trade Centre in New York necessitated the development of legislation

---

1   MARPOL 1973, as amended in 1978; SOLAS 1974, as amended in 1978; UNCLOS 1982; Salvage Convention 1989; OPPRC 1990; CLC 1969, as amended by the 1992 Protocol; Fund Convention 1971, as replaced by the 1992 Protocol, and further amended by the 2003 Protocol; HNS Convention 1996; Bunkers Convention 2001.

2   COM(2000) 142, Brussels, 21 March 2000.

3   Regulation (EC) 2099/2002.

for the implementation of security measures on ships and ports. Regulation (EC) 725/2004 of the European Parliament and the Council (31/03/04) entered into force on 19 May 2004[4] to enhance maritime security adopted by the IMO in 2002, which amended the SOLAS Convention and established the International Ship and Port Facility Security Code (ISPS Code).

The purpose of this chapter is to focus on new developments in legislation with regard to maritime safety originating from the EU in the last five years, and to pinpoint how far the EU is in line with the IMO legislation.

1.1 Safety measures with regard to non-tanker vessels

With regard to non-tanker vessels, there has been a Directive, 2001/96/EC, issued by the European Parliament and Council on 4 December 2001 and brought into force in 2002,[5] with regard to requirements for safe loading and unloading of bulk carriers when calling at terminals in Community ports. The Directive which was implemented in the UK in 2003, aims to reduce the number of bulk carrier casualties – being due to structural failures – by reducing the stresses and physical damage to the ship's structure during loading or unloading. The objective of the Directive is to provide a Community framework for harmonised implementation of the code of practices for the safe loading and unloading of bulk carriers adopted by the IMO in December 1997.

The Commission has also taken steps to tighten up the safety rules and standards for passenger ships by amending the previous Council Directive 98/18/EC by Directive 2003/24/EC of the European Parliament and the Council[6] and, further, by laying down a uniform level of specific stability requirements for ro-ro passenger ships (Directive 2003/25/EC of the European Parliament and the Council).[7]

1.2 General safety measures

To ensure compliance with the MARPOL provisions, requiring ports to provide adequate reception facilities for ship-generated waste and cargo residues, Directive 2000/59/EC aims to harmonise the procedures for co-operation between ship and terminals.

Further, there has been a Directive (2001/25/EC)[8] on reinforcing the minimum level of training for seafarers having regard to training standards agreed at international level; it determines minimum standards of training, certification and watch keeping for seafarers serving on board Community ships, and aims at ensuring that the STCW Convention 1978, as revised, is implemented simultaneously and consistently in all Member States. With regard to the recognition of mariners'

---

4 OJ L 129, 29/4/04.
5 OJ L 13, 16/1/2002 (see also MS (Safe Loading and Unloading of Bulk Carriers) Regulations 2003 (S1 2003/2002) implementing the Directive into UK).
6 OJ L 123, 17/05/2003.
7 OJ L 123, 17/5/2003.
8 In force since 7 June 2001 (OJ L 136, 18/5/01).

certificates of competency issued outside the EU, Directive 2003/103/EC[9] aims at simplifying procedures.

High priority was given to safety measures since the sinking of the oil tanker *The Prestige* in November 2002, which prompted the European Commission to present proposals to the European Council for a Directive with regard to ship-source pollution, introducing criminal sanctions for infringements. This was in addition to the Commission's actions of speeding up the phasing out of single-hull ships – a measure which can be traced back at EU level to the sinking of *The Erika*. Furthermore, the furore surrounding Spain's refusal to grant *The Prestige* safe haven prior to its sinking led to both the Commission and the IMO proposing and debating legislation obliging Member States to issue a list and grant 'places of refuge' to ships in distress.

These proposals of the European Commission are known as the Erika I, the Erika II, and the Erika III packages of measures. According to the Commission, these measures are designed to bring about a change in mentality with regard to safety at sea. With more powerful dissuasive incentives, it is believed that carriers, charterers, classification societies and other key bodies involved will be persuaded to give higher priority to quality considerations. At the same time, the Commission's intention is to tighten up the net on those who pursue short-term personal financial gains at the expense of safety and the marine environment. A brief account of these measures is set out in the following paragraphs.

2 ERIKA I MEASURES

The oil tanker, *The Erika*, broke in two in December 1999, just 40 miles off the coast in Brittany, France. More than 10,000 tonnes of heavy oil were spilt into the sea, creating one of the biggest ecological disasters in history. The public outcry prompted the European Commission to take action. It was decided that more stringent safety measures needed to be put in place in order to minimise the risk of further environmental damage occurring in the seas of Member States. The need for such action was further highlighted, in November 2002, when *The Prestige* broke in two and sank off the coast of Spain, spilling a reported 70,000 tonnes of oil which washed up on the shores of Spain, France and Portugal.

The outcome of the consultations, which took place after these disasters, resulted in the aforesaid three-tier action plan. The first tier comprised measures which were able to be implemented immediately, consisting mainly of amending existing legislation. This was known as Erika I, and entered into force on 22 January 2002, giving Member States until 22 July 2003 to implement the measures into their national laws.[10] It comprises three elements:

---

9   In force since 14 February 2003 (OJ L 326, 13/12/03).

10   To date, the following actions have been taken by the European Commission as a result of Member States' failure to implement part or all of the Erika I measures: 30 March 2004, the Commission reported Finland to the European Court of Justice (ECJ), for failing to implement Directive 2001/106/EC on Port State Control; Belgium, Greece, France, Italy, the Netherlands, Austria, Finland and the United Kingdom were reported to the ECJ on 15 December 2004 for

(i)   amendments to the Inspection of Ships Directive;

(ii) phasing out of single-hull tankers; and

(iii) amendments to the Port State Control Directive.

2.1 Directive 2001/105/EC[11] on inspections of ships (amending Directive 94/57/EC)

The adoption of the previous Council Directive 94/57/EC[12] had established a set of common rules and standards concerning the activities of ship inspection organisations and maritime administrations. The inspection organisations are the classification societies to which Member States delegate the verification of safety standards on ships, and the maritime administrations are the flag States. The Directive provides that Member States are under a duty:

> to ensure that their competent administrations can assure an appropriate enforcement of the provisions of the international conventions, in particular with regard to the inspection and survey of ships and the issue of certificates and exemption certificates.[13]

Such duties are only to be entrusted to 'recognised organisations' (normally classification societies) and are assessed against criteria listed in an Annex to the Directive. Member States are responsible for authorising such organisations.

The Directive introduced financial liability of recognised organisations in the event of non-performance, or negligence or misconduct.

Council Directive 2001/105/EC[14] made subsequent amendments to the 1994 Directive providing for closer supervision of the activities of both classification societies and flag States. The Commission, through a Committee, is now involved in the process of granting initial authorisation to the classification societies for recognition, through the carrying out of various assessments of the applying society.[15]

The Commission is also able to initiate draft decisions for the withdrawal of

---

failing to notify the Commission of measures taken to implement at national level Directive 2002/59/EC on vessel traffic monitoring and information systems. Such measures should have been reported by 5 February 2004. As a point of reference, the UK adopted the provisions of the Directive under the Merchant Shipping (Vessel Traffic Monitoring and Reporting Requirements) Regulations 2004 (SI 2004/2110), which came into force on 20 September 2004. On 22 June 2004, in Case C-439/02, the ECJ found France guilty of not carrying out sufficient inspections of ships under Directive 95/21/EC.

11 19/12/2001.

12 Council Directive 94/57/EC of 22 November 1994 on common rules and standards for ship inspection and survey organisations and for the relevant activities of maritime administrations (OJ L 319 12/12/1994, pp 20–27).

13 Ibid, Art 3(1).

14 Directive 2001/105/EC of the European Parliament and of the Council of 19 December 2001, amending Council Directive 94/57/EC, on common rules and standards for ship inspection and survey organisations and for the relevant activities of maritime administrations (OJ L 19 22/01/2002, pp 9–16).

15 Ibid, Art 4.

recognition of an organisation.[16] The revised Directive includes regular inspections of recognised organisations by the Commission in conjunction with Member States. Under the original Directive, the Committee's only role was to monitor the classification societies once they had been granted authorisation. Further, the new Directive has extended the reasons for withdrawal of recognition. Under the 1994 Directive, Member States were directed to withdraw recognition from those societies which did not fulfil the criteria set out in the Annex. This is preserved under the 2001 Directive, along with a provision which withdraws recognition of those societies which do not meet 'safety and pollution prevention performance records'.[17]

Under the new Directive, the Commission is granted the authority to carry out regular assessments directly on all recognised organisations, which occur at least every two years.[18] This is in addition to the obligation placed on the Member States to regularly assess those organisations that fall within their responsibility, which was provided for under the 1994 Directive also.

The most significant change to the 1994 Directive concerns financial responsibility. It is now provided that, if a flag administration is found liable in a court of law of an incident, with the requirement that they compensate the injured parties for any loss, damage, personal injury or death, then they will be able to claim compensation from the recognised organisation to the extent to which that organisation is held by the court to be liable.[19] If such damage is caused by a wilful act or omission, or by gross negligence on the part of the organisation, such liability is unlimited.[20] If such damage is caused by negligence or recklessness, then liability may be limited to at least €4 million for death or personal injury,[21] and at least €2 million for loss of or damage to property.[22] However, Member States may opt to set higher limits, as Italy has chosen to do. In the UK, the limits are the minimum provided for. Such a provision is experimental, and the Directive goes on to provide that 'the Commission shall, not later than 22 July 2006, submit a report to the European Parliament and to the Council evaluating the economic impact of the liability regime'.[23]

In recognition of the need to enhance the quality of inspections of ships by the flag administrations, the IMO has also implemented a plan involving self-regulation and assessment by flag States. Flag States have to participate in a voluntary audit carried out by each other.

In Chapter 8, above, reference was made to the issue of a missing link in the

---

16 Ibid, Art 9(2).
17 Ibid. This is defined further in the article as being those records taken from the Paris Memorandum of Understanding on Port State Control (see Chapter 8 above) and also reports from Member States, which they are required to make to the Commission and flag State concerned whenever they discover a ship which represents a serious threat to safety and the environment, or any evidence pointing to the negligent behaviour of the organisation concerned.
18 Ibid, Art 11.
19 Ibid, Art 6(2).
20 Ibid, Art 6(2)(b)(i).
21 Ibid, Art 6(2)(b)(ii).
22 Ibid, Art 6(2)(b)(iii).
23 Ibid, Art 6(5).

campaign for quality shipping, and it was suggested that statutory controls to ensure proper enforcement of international conventions by flag States, would be an effective way of dealing with substandard flag States. The European Union is keen to follow the auditing system applicable to the International Civil Aviation Organisation in the aviation industry. It has suggested that this should be the model in shipping, and the IMO should be given the power to audit flag States by using internationally acknowledged inspectors.

However, the difficulties for the IMO in devising a system which is akin to that applicable in the aviation industry may be insuperable – considering that the IMO membership comprises fee-paying flag States, which adopt legislation agreed upon at Diplomatic Conferences. Thus, it is submitted that it is not within the IMO remit to provide statutory controls. Another route of dealing with auditing may be for the UN to establish a neutral statutory body, to provide statutory control mechanisms governing the way in which the international rules are applied throughout the world. Such a UN body – financed by all UN members – would supervise uniform enforcement of international conventions by flag States, and would enforce sanctions in case of failure by flag States to live up to their obligations under the international conventions. Such sanctions may include the expulsion, from the list of permitted flag States, of those flag States which fall below the international regulatory standards. The UN body could be called: International Organisation for Maritime Audit (IOMA).

At present, the 'blacklisting' system imposed upon flag States by the amended PSC Directive (see para 2.3, below) partially serves this purpose, but only insofar as ships flying the flags of those States visit European ports. A current version of the list is published every six months.

2.2 Phasing out single-hull tankers

The Commission has been determined to speed up the process of banning single-hull oil tankers and phase in double-hull by a Regulation. The original proposal of 21 March 2000 was amended to take into account the amendments suggested by the European Parliament on 30 November 2000.[24] The Commission accepted the recommended amendment concerning: (i) the phase-out schedule for single-hull tankers, (ii) the exclusion of tankers between 600 and 3000 dwt from the phase-out schedule, and (iii) withdrawal of its proposal for financial incentives and disincentives. It was accepted that it was desirable to adopt a joint approach with the IMO with regard to amending the existing international MARPOL regulations and to agree the dates of implementation.

As a result, the final Regulation reflected largely the stance taken by the IMO. The 49th Plenary Session of the Marine Environment Protection Committee (MEPC) of the IMO, on 14–18 July 2003, proposed several amendments to the phase-out timetable of single-hull tankers, which had been agreed at the 46th Plenary Session in April 2001. The amendments took the form of accelerating the phase-out schedule; this was a direct reaction to the breaking up and sinking of *The*

---

24 Amended proposal COM(2000) 848 12 December 2000.

Prestige in November 2002. The proposed amendments were adopted at the 50th session of the MEPC, on 1–4 December 2003, and entered into force on 5 April 2005. The MARPOL Convention provides for three categories of oil tanker: broadly, Category 1 is for oil tankers of 20,000 or more dwt carrying crude oil, fuel oil, heavy diesel oil, or lubricating oil as cargo, or more than 30,000 dwt if carrying any other oil, without being protectively located in segregated ballast tanks; Category 2 has the same requirements as Category 1, but these tankers must have a protectively located segregated ballast tank; and Category 3 is for oil tankers of 5,000 dwt. The respective phase-out dates for single-hull tankers are as follows:

CATEGORY OF OIL TANKER	DATE OF PHASE-OUT
Category 1	5 April 2005
Categories 2 and 3	5 April 2005: ships delivered on 5 April 1977 or earlier
	2005: ships delivered after 5 April 1977, but before January 1978.
	2006: ships delivered 1978–1979
	2007: ships delivered 1980–1981
	2008: ships delivered in 1982
	2009: ships delivered in 1983
	2010: ships delivered in 1984 or later
	2015: complete ban on single-hull tankers

Regulation (EC) 417/2002[25] was subsequently amended by Regulation (EC) 1726/2003[26] and Regulation (EC) 2172/2004,[27] to reflect the above changes adopted by the IMO in 2003. They apply to all tankers of 5,000 dwt or above which are either: (a) entering or leaving a port or offshore terminal, or anchoring in an area under the jurisdiction of a Member State; or (b) flying the flag of a Member State. There is scope for single-hull tankers to enter and leave ports of Member States when they would otherwise be banned: Art 5 provides for single-hull tankers of 15 years of age or older, and which fall within categories 2 and 3, to be able to enter and leave ports of Members States, provided they comply with a condition assessment scheme. Basically, the scheme is a system of enhanced surveys, which are designed specifically to detect structural weaknesses in single-hull tankers.

In response to the sinking of *The Prestige*, Regulation (EC) 1726/2003[28] was

---

25 Regulation (EC) 417/2002 of the European Parliament and of the Council of 18 February 2002, on the accelerated phasing-in of double hull or equivalent design requirements for single-hull oil tankers, and repealing Council Regulation (EC) 2978/94 (OJ L 64, 7/03/2002, pp 1–5) came into force on 27 March 2002.

26 Regulation (EC) 1726/2003 of the European Parliament and of the Council of 22 July 2003, amending Regulation (EC) 417/2002 on the accelerated phasing-in of double hull or equivalent design requirements for single-hull oil tankers (OJ L 249, 01/10/2003, pp 1–4) came in force on 21 October 2003.

27 Commission Regulation (EC) 2172/2004 of 17 December 2004, amending Regulation (EC) 417/2002 of the European Parliament and of the Council of 18 February 2002, on the accelerated phasing-in of double hull or equivalent design requirements for single-hull oil tankers, came into force on 7 January 2005.

28 Op cit, fn 18.

enacted, not only to speed up the phasing out of single-hull oil tankers, but also to ban from European ports all single-hull tankers carrying heavy grades of oil.[29] This applies to all tankers with a deadweight tonnage of 600 and above.[30]

2.3 Directive amending Port State Control (PSC)

The objective of Directive 2001/106/EC[31] is to make compulsory, rather than discretionary, the system of inspections of certain potentially dangerous ships, and to tighten up measures relating to manifestly sub-standard ships for the more effective implementation of the original Directive (95/21/EC).[32] The Directive applies to all ships calling at a port of a Member State or at an off-shore installation, or anchored off such a port or such an installation.[33]

Under the previous law, the inspection authorities of Member States had a broad discretion as to whether to select ships for so-called 'expanded inspection'. This led to non-uniformity in Member States' implementation, and so ships falling within Annex V of the Directive now face mandatory inspection. Such ships are, broadly, oil tankers and passenger ships over 15 years of age, gas and chemical tankers over 12 years of age, and bulk carriers over 12 years of age.

Under a new Art 7b, Member States are also obliged to refuse access altogether to their port, if the ship in question[34] either flies the flag of a State appearing in the blacklist of the Paris Memorandum of Understanding (MOU), and has been detained more than twice within the last two years in a port of a signatory State of the MOU; or flies the flag of a State described as 'very high risk' or 'high risk' in the MOU's blacklist and has been detained more than once in the last three years in a port of a signatory State of the MOU.

Another way in which the Directive provides for additional safety precautions is the introduction of a mandatory programme for the installation of Voyage Data Recorders (VDRs). These systems are the equivalent to 'black boxes' found on aircraft, and assist in the investigation of accidents that occur. Under Annex XII of the Directive, passenger ships built after 1 July 2002 have to have them installed. For those built earlier, installation became mandatory from 1 July 2004. For passenger

---

29 Heavy grades of oil include, under Art 3(14) of Regulation (EC) 417/2002, as amended by Regulation (EC) 1726/2003, heavy fuel oil, heavy crude oil, waste oils, bitumen and tar. Regulation (EC) 1726/2003 amends Art 4 of Regulation (EC) 417/2002, inserting sub-para (3), which bans all single-hull tankers from carrying heavy oil in European ports.

30 Op cit, fn 18, Arti 1(2), amending Art 2(1) of Regulation (EC) 417/2002.

31 European Parliament and Council Directive 2001/106/EC (OJ L 19, 22/01/2002); final date of implementation was 22 July 2003.

32 Council Directive 95/21/EC concerning the enforcement, in respect of shipping using Community ports and sailing in the waters under the jurisdiction of the Member States, of international standards for ship safety, pollution prevention and shipboard living and working conditions (Port State Control) (OJ L 157, 07/07/1995, p 1). It was amended to take account of amendments to the MARPOL and SOLAS Conventions and resolutions of the IMO and of the Paris MOU, by Council Directive 98/25/EC (OJ L 133, 7/05/98) and by Commission Directives 98/42/EC (OJ L 184, 27/06/98) and 1999/97/EC (OJ L 331, 23/12/99).

33 Article 3(1).

34 Under Annex XI of the Directive, these are gas and chemical tankers, bulk carriers, oil tankers and passenger ships.

ships built before 1 July 2002 which also carry cargo on-board, so-called 'ro-ro' passenger ships, it is mandatory to have VDRs installed before the first survey on that ship which occurs on or after 1 July 2002. Other classes of ships with a 3,000 dwt or more, constructed after 1 July 2002, must also have a VDR installed.

The above requirements reflect exactly the amendments the IMO made to Chapter V of the International Convention for the Safety of Life at Sea 1974 (SOLAS), under regulations that were adopted in 2000 and entered into force for IMO members on 1 July 2002.

Since, at this stage, the IMO had yet to agree on phasing in requirements for existing cargo ships, Annex XII of the Directive provides for the date of installation on cargo ships to be set by the IMO but, in the absence of such a decision, no later than 2007 and 2008 respectively, depending on the tonnage of the vessel.

In December 2004, the IMO adopted further amendments to Chapter V of SOLAS as follows: for cargo ships of 20,000 dwt and above, a VDR must be fitted at the first scheduled dry-docking after 1 July 2006, but not later than 1 July 2009. For cargo ships of 3,000 dwt, but less than 20,000, at the first scheduled dry-docking after 1 July 2007, but no later than 1 July 2010. For these classes of ships, the VDRs required can be simplified VDRs. Although not storing the same level of detailed data as VDRs, it is still required to store information relating to the position, movement, command and control of a vessel in the period leading up to and after an accident.

A general related Directive 2002/84/EC[35] aims to speed up and simplify the incorporation of international rules on maritime safety, prevention of pollution from ships, and shipboard living and working conditions into Community legislation. The Directive is closely linked to Regulation (EC) 2099/2002 which established the Committee on safe seas (COSS). The implementation of legislation will be assisted by COSS.

3 ERIKA II MEASURES

This second set of measures was confirmed at the Biarritz European Council on 14 October 2000. The European Commission issued its 'Erika II Package' of measures on 6 December 2000.[36]

The package contains three sets of proposals dealing with:

(i) more effective monitoring and control of ships operating in EU waters by amending the previous Directive 93/75/EEC, by Directive 2002/59/EC;

(ii) the creation of a European Maritime Safety Agency (EMSA) to provide the Commission and Member States with support in enforcing and monitoring compliance with Community law; and

---

35 European Parliament and Council Directive 2002/84/EC (OJ L 324 29/11/2002); final date of implementation was 23 November 2003.

36 In COM(2000) 802, 6 December 2000.

(iii) improving the liability and compensation for damage to the environment regimes in force.

Although the existing international legislation regulating shipping is extensive, the Commission felt that such legislation fails to deliver the safety imperative because it is not consistently and rigorously enforced.

3.1 Directive 2002/59/EC for a Community monitoring, control and information system (CMCIS)

Reporting requirements for dangerous or polluting goods and bunker fuels on board had already been provided for by Directive 93/75/EEC, which had been in force since 1995 and was known as the Hazmat Directive. Pursuant to this Directive, the masters or operators of a ship carrying dangerous or polluting goods were required to provide information to the competent authorities designated by the Member States. However, this Directive was not so well understood and had limitations.

A major limitation was that it applied only to ships bound for, or leaving, a Community port and carrying dangerous or polluting goods. The new Directive extended the provisions to all ships, whether or not they were bound to call at or leave a Community port, and whether or not they were carrying dangerous or polluting goods.

Another major limitation of Directive 93/95/EEC was that there were no proper means of enforcement, in that the only sanction upon a ship was refusal of access for failure to provide notification after leaving the port of departure outside the Community. The Commission felt that a system of financial penalties would provide the requisite mechanisms necessary for effective enforcement.

The new Directive 2002/59/EC[37] entered into force on 5 August 2002. It gave Member States until 5 February 2004 to adopt the necessary regulations within their national laws in order to give effect to the Directive. From this date, the previous Directive 93/75/EEC was repealed.

The Directive provides for:

(a) improving the identification of ships in areas of high traffic density, requiring them to carry an automatic identification system (AIS);

(b) extending the reporting requirements provided for by the previous Directive;

(c) making systematic use of electronic data interchange to simplify and harmonise the transmission of data on dangerous or polluting goods carried on board;

(d) requiring ships calling at Community ports to carry voyage data recorders (VDRs), in order to facilitate the investigation of accidents;

(e) enhancing the powers of intervention of Member or coastal States where there is an accident risk or threat of pollution off their coasts; and

---

37 Directive 2002/59/EC of the European Parliament and of the Council of 27 June 2002, establishing a Community vessel traffic monitoring and information system and repealing Council Directive 93/75/EEC.

(f) prohibiting ships from leaving ports in weather conditions where there is a serious threat to safety or the environment.

The monitoring of ships (posing a serious threat to marine safety and environment) and circulation of information among Member States, in order to take any preventive action, is an essential measure in the new Directive.

The monitoring includes a wider obligation upon ships entering European waters to declare their entry, and will require them to carry on-board automatic identification systems (AIS).

The Directive also includes the further development of common databases and networking of centres responsible for managing the information received under the Directive, and the enhancement of powers of intervention of the Member States, as coastal States. With the information that it is hoped will be gathered by the implementation of the new Directive, Member States will be able, before accepting high-risk ships into their ports, to ask for additional information in order to check compliance by the ship with international conventions and, if necessary, to carry out on-board inspections under the Port State Control Directive.[38]

A much-debated issue involves a requirement that Member States receive ships in distress in ports of refuge. This aims to make it easier to seek a port of refuge in the event of trouble at sea, and also to prevent the risk of accident by prohibiting ships from leaving ports of call in the Community if particularly bad weather and sea conditions increase the risk of an accident. The IMO has also taken a pro-active role in this respect, particularly after the incident of the gasoline carrying vessel, *The Castor*, being in distress outside Spanish waters. This issue has been through lengthy consultations, and its present status is to be found in the Erika III proposals below.

3.2 The European Maritime Safety Agency

The creation of a European Maritime Safety Agency (EMSA) in June 2002[39] was seen as one of the key initiatives in the enhancement of maritime safety and pollution control following the *Erika* disaster. Largely based on the Aviation Safety Agency, it entered into force on 25 August 2002, and the implementing Regulation gave a one-year window in which to get EMSA fully operational.[40] From January 2004, EMSA became fully operational.

EMSA is a legal body of the Community,[41] and its functions are numerous. Its tasks include providing technical assistance, organising training activities, gathering data and exploiting databases on maritime safety, monitoring navigation, evaluating and auditing classification societies, carrying out on-the-spot inspections, and participating in enquiries following accidents.

---

38 See para 2.3, above.
39 Regulation (EC) 1406/2002 of the European Parliament and of the Council of 27 June 2002, establishing a European Maritime Safety Agency (OJ L 208, 05/08/2002, pp 1–9. EMSA's website can be accessed at http://www.emsa.eu.int.
40 Ibid, Art 23.
41 Op cit, fn 29, Art 5(1).

On one level, the body exercises a supervisory function, overseeing the implementation of Community legislation in connection with maritime safety. This is by means of monitoring the Member States' arrangements in relation to the implementation of Port State Control and the directives relating to classification societies and double-hull tankers. EMSA also plays a pro-active role in the future development of maritime safety and pollution prevention legislation, assisting the Commission in updating and producing legislation in this area, as well as assisting the Member States and the Commission in technical aspects concerning maritime safety, traffic and pollution fields.

As an addition to its powers,[42] EMSA now has specific tasks relating to the prevention of oil pollution. This includes the powers to draw up an Action Plan for the implementation of pollution response initiatives. The Regulation also provides that, in the event of a pollution incident, EMSA shall assist the Member State concerned, with the Member State retaining the authority for the clean-up operations associated with the pollution incident. EMSA's budgetary authority, the European Parliament and Council, agreed the provision of €17.5 million in 2005 in order for EMSA to contract a fleet of vessels for use as pollution response vehicles.

EMSA's Administrative Board is made up of one representative from each of the 25 EU Member States, four Commission representatives, and four professionals from the maritime sector. The latter group are appointed by the Commission and do not have the right to vote. There are also mechanisms in the Directive to allow third countries to join the board. Each elected member, including the Executive Director, serves a five-year term, which is allowed to be renewed once only. Decisions of the Administrative Board are taken by a two-thirds majority.[43]

3.3 Compensation fund for oil pollution damage

Following the *Erika* disaster, it was proposed[44] that the Commission would introduce a Regulation to set up what would have become known as the Compensation for Oil Pollution in European Waters Fund (COPE). In essence, the fund would step in and pay compensation to victims of oil spills in European waters whenever the current schemes embodied in the CLC and IOPC Fund[45] had been exhausted. However, following the adoption by the IMO (on 16 May 2003) of the 2003 Protocol to the International Convention on the Establishment of an International Fund for Compensation for Oil Pollution Damage 1992 (the 2003 Fund Protocol), the European Council changed their approach. The proposed COPE Fund was abandoned

---

42 Regulation 724/2004 of the European Parliament and of the Council of 31/03/2004, amending Regulation (EC) 1406/2002 establishing a European Maritime Safety Agency (OJ L 129, 29/04/2004, pp 1–5).

43 Op cit, fn 29, Art 14(1).

44 COM (2000) 802 final (OJ C 120 E, 24/04/2001). The proposal was amended in June 2002 before it was submitted to the European Parliament.

45 For a detailed overview of the operation of these two schemes, see Chapter 19, above.

and, in its place, the Council adopted a Decision which authorised Member States to sign, ratify or accede to the 2003 Fund Protocol.[46]

The 2003 Fund Protocol entered into force on 5 March 2005. A Private Members' Bill allowing for the provisions of the 2003 Fund Protocol was introduced and, after discussion by both the House of Lords and House of Commons in July 2005, the Merchant Shipping (Pollution) Act 2006 was passed. Further details on the pollution legislation can be found in Chapter 19, above.

4 FOLLOW-UP WORK

4.1 The establishment of a Committee on Safe Seas and the Prevention of Pollution from Ships

Regulation (EC) 2099/2002[47] established a single committee to carry out the tasks assigned to it by the various directives and regulations in the field of maritime safety, the prevention of pollution from ships and shipboard living and working conditions. Known as COSS, it came into force on 19 December 2003. Its purpose, in essence, is to streamline the tasks that had been assigned to various different committees in the field of maritime safety.

The main directives and regulations affected by this, referred to above, are the directives relating to the monitoring, control and information systems; common rules and standards for ship inspection and survey organisations; port state control, and the regulation relating to the phasing out of single-hull tankers.

As well as carrying out such tasks, another important function of COSS, in the short term, is its role in the conformity checking procedures, which are provided for in the Regulation.[48] Under this procedure, the Commission and Member States will co-operate in order to agree a common position internationally to reduce the risks of conflict between Community maritime legislation, on the one hand, and international conventions relating to maritime law on the other.

4.2 The Criminalisation Directive on ship-source pollution

Ship-source pollution, whether caused by an accident involving a ship or deliberately, is dealt with by international maritime standards provided for by the MARPOL Convention 1973/1978. However, the European Commission considered

---

46 Council Decision of 2 March 2004 authorising the Member States to sign, ratify or accede to, in the interest of the European Community, the Protocol of 2003 to the International Convention on the Establishment of an International Fund for Compensation for Oil Pollution Damage, 1992, and authorising Austria and Luxembourg, in the interest of the European Community, to accede to the underlying instruments (OJ L 78, 16/03/2004, pp 22–24).

47 Regulation (EC) 2099/2002 of the European Parliament and of the Council of 5 November 2002, establishing a Committee on Safe Seas and the Prevention of Pollution from Ships (COSS), and amending the Regulations on maritime safety and the prevention of pollution from ships (OJ L 324, 29/11/2002, pp 1–5), amended by Commission Regulation (EC) 415/ 2004 of 5 March 2004 (OJ L 68, 06/03/2004, pp 10–11).

48 Ibid, Art 5.

that these standards are not uniformly applied by MARPOL Member States or are being regularly ignored. Therefore, it was decided that dissuasive and proportionate criminal penalties were needed, and the European Commission proposed a Directive immediately after the sinking of *The Prestige* in 2002.

After considerable deliberations, and despite grave concerns raised from all sides of the industry including the European Parliament, the European Parliament and the Council of the European Union were persuaded to finalise the Directive. After certain amendments, the Directive on ship-source pollution and introduction of sanctions for infringements (2005/35/EC), together with the Council Framework Decision (2005/667/JHA), supplementing the Directive, were published on 30 September 2005.[49] The implementation date for the Directive by EU Member States was 1 March 2007, and for the Framework Decision was 12 January 2007, failing which the Commission can launch infringement proceedings, but see further developments under 4.2.3 below.

4.2.1 The essence of the Directive and Framework Decision

It is stated, at Preamble 7 of the Directive, that:

Neither the international regime for the civil liability and compensation of oil pollution not that relating to pollution by other hazardous or noxious substances provide sufficient dissuasive effects to discourage the parties involved in the transport of hazardous cargoes by sea from engaging in substandard practices; the required dissuasive effects can only be achieved through the introduction of penalties applying to any person who causes or contributes to marine pollution; penalties should be applicable not only to the ship owner or the master of the ship, but also to the owner of the cargo, the classification society or any other person involved.

It is also stated, at Preamble 8, that:

Ship-sourced discharges of polluting substances should be regarded as infringements if *committed with intent, recklessly or by serious negligence*. These infringements are regarded as criminal offences by and, in the circumstances, provided for in Framework Decision 2005/667/JHA supplementing the Directive.

Article 1 of the Directive states that its purpose is to incorporate international standards for ship-source pollution into Community law, and to ensure that persons responsible for discharges are subject to adequate penalties in order to improve maritime safety and to enhance protection of the marine environment from pollution by ships.

By Art 3, the Directive applies, in accordance with international law, to discharges of polluting substances from any ship (except warships or government-owned ships) irrespective of its flag (i) in the territorial sea of a Member State; (ii) in straits used for international navigation; (iii) in the Exclusive Economic Zone (EEZ); or (iv) on the high seas.

Articles 4 and 5 define the scope of infringements and the exceptions provided. They distinguish between penalising provisions for pollution in territorial sea, on the one hand, and on the high seas or in the EEZ on the other. With regard to

---

49   OJ L 255/11/2005 and OJ L 255/164/2005 respectively.

discharges *within the territorial sea* of a Member State, there will be an infringement for any party associated with the ship involved, without exceptions, if they are committed with intent, recklessly or by serious negligence. Therefore, reg 11(b) of Annex I, and reg 6(b) of Annex II, of MARPOL (see next sub-paragraph) are disapplied. By contrast, discharges *on the high seas, or in the EEZ of a Member State*, are an infringement for all operators, other than the owner, master or crew, if they are committed with intent, recklessly, or by serious negligence. Such discharges, therefore, will not be an infringement for owners, masters, or crew, acting under the master's responsibility, provided all reasonable precautions have been taken to prevent or minimise the discharge, and these parties have not acted either with intent to cause damage or recklessly and with knowledge that damage would probably result (the MARPOL test, under reg 11(b) of Annex I).

The Framework Decision provides the specific criminal penalties for such infringements. If the pollution damage is done with intent or recklessly, it is punishable with imprisonment of between 2–5 years. If pollution is caused by serious negligence, the penalty is imprisonment between 1–3 years, unless the offence also causes death or serious injury to persons, whereupon the punishment is 2–5 years imprisonment.

4.2.2 *International perspective*

The UNCLOS Convention 1982, Part XII, Art 211 provides briefly: by Art 211(1): Member States, through the competent international organisation or diplomatic conference, shall establish international rules and standards to prevent, reduce and control pollution of the marine environment from vessels; Art 211(2): States shall adopt laws and regulations for the prevention etc of pollution from vessels flying their flag; such laws shall at least have the same effect as that of generally accepted international rules and standards established through the competent international organization or diplomatic conference; Art 211(4): Coastal States may, in the exercise of their sovereignty within their territorial sea, adopt laws and regulations for the prevention etc of pollution from foreign vessels, including vessels exercising the right of innocent passage. Such laws or regulations shall not hamper innocent passage of foreign vessels; Art 211(5): With regard to EEZ, coastal States may adopt laws and regulations for the prevention of pollution from vessels conforming and giving effect to generally accepted international rules and standards as established by the competent international organisation, or diplomatic conference.

Article 230(1) of UNCLOS provides only for monetary penalties which may be imposed in case of infringements of pollution regulations committed by foreign vessels beyond the territorial sea. Article 230(2) provides that monetary penalties may only be imposed also with respect to violations of national laws or applicable international rules and standards for the prevention, reduction and control of pollution of the marine environment committed by foreign vessels in the territorial sea, except in the case of a wilful *and* serious act of pollution in the territorial sea.

Further, under Art 230(1), the coastal State has no sovereignty to legislate beyond the territorial sea otherwise than is provided by this article.

Unlike the EU Directive, under para 2 of Art 230, non-monetary penalties may only be imposed for a *wilful and serious* act of pollution, being a criminal offence which requires *mens rea*. Apparently, these words have been misinterpreted by the drafters of the Directive, as is apparent from the insertion of 'serious negligence' as part of the test of the EU Directive offence. In other words, the word 'serious' in Art 230(2) of UNCLOS, which is linked to 'wilful', is taken out of context by replacing the conjunctive 'and' with the disjunctive 'or', and adding after 'serious' the word 'negligence'.[50]

Although the UNCLOS Convention, by Art 2, recognises the sovereignty of coastal States over their territorial sea, such sovereignty must be exercised subject to this convention and the other rules of international law. This has not been observed by the EU Directive. Nevertheless, the Commission's position has been that the Directive is in accordance with Arts 211 and 230(2) of UNCLOS. Moreover, under UNCLOS, ships have a right of innocent passage through the territorial sea (Art 17), which means that it is innocent so long as it is not prejudicial to the peace, good order or security of the coastal State. A wilful and serious pollution by a foreign ship in the territorial sea will be prejudicial and, hence, it will be in breach of this provision (Art 19). However, pollution caused accidentally after a marine accident, provided precautions are taken after the accident to prevent or minimise the discharge of polluting substances in accordance with Annex I, reg 11(b) of MARPOL (see below), will not be prejudicial in the sense of Art 17.

The MARPOL 1973/78 Convention, being adopted under the auspices of IMO, aims to regulate pollution from ships and came into force in 1983, after its revision by the 1978 Protocol.

All EU Member States are parties to both MARPOL and UNCLOS.

MARPOL distinguishes operational discharges (Annex I, regs 9 and 10) from accidental ones. With regard to operational discharges, regs 9 and 10 involve restrictions prohibiting discharges in special areas, within a minimum distance from land or in excess of maximum stipulated rates of discharge per nautical mile. Except when a list of conditions is satisfied, discharges of oily mixtures from ships are prohibited, and contracting States are required to penalise the offenders. On the other hand, accidental spills are treated differently.

Most accidental spills would be in breach of regs 9 and 10, unless the conditions of reg 11 applied. Regulation 11(a) excludes breach of regs 9 and 10 if the discharge of oily mixture is necessary for the safety of the ship or saving life at sea. Regulation 11(b) is very relevant in this context, and provides that the discharge of oily mixture resulting from damage to a ship or its equipment is not a breach, provided:

(i) all reasonable precautions have been taken after the occurrence of the damage or discovery of the discharge for the purpose of preventing or minimising the discharge; and

(ii) except if the owner or the master acted either with intent to cause damage, or recklessly and with knowledge that damage would probably result.

Therefore, under this Convention, accidental oil spills falling within reg 11(b) are not prohibited. Annex II, regs 5 and 6 deal with noxious liquid substances.

---

50 The same observations have been made by Professor Mukherjee in his paper 'Criminalisation and Unfair treatment: The Seafarers' Perspective', presented to the CMI Conference in February 2006, held in Cape Town.

It is apparent from the brief resume of the relevant provisions of these conventions that the EU Directive (see earlier) conflicts with the provisions of those conventions and, hence, is contrary to the Convention obligations of the EU Member States. Furthermore, the Directive will have serious consequences upon seafarers who may be detained on a presumption of criminal negligence.

These issues were highlighted at the 7th and 8th Cadwallader Lectures of the London Shipping Law Centre in October 2004 and 2005 respectively. The presentations and discussions that ensued provided the catalyst to the EU Directive and the impetus required for the shipping industry to initiate an action in the English courts challenging the Directive.

4.2.3 The Validity of the Directive and Framework Decision referred to ECJ

Mr Justice Hodge, in the application of Intertanko, Intercargo, Lloyd's Register, ISU and GSCC against the UK Secretary of State for Transport, held that the arguments in support of a reference to the ECJ were well founded and handed down his judgment on 30 June 2006,[51] in favour of referring the matter to the ECJ (pursuant to Art 234 EC) to answer the following questions:

(a) In relation to straits used for international navigation, the Exclusive Economic Zone or equivalent zone of a Member State and the high seas, is article 5(2) of Directive 2005/35/EC valid insofar as it limits the exceptions in Annex I regulation 11(b) of MARPOL 73/78 and in Annex II regulation (6)(b) of MARPOL 73/78 to the owners, masters and crew?

(b) In relation to the territorial sea of a Member State:

   (i) Is article 4 of the Directive invalid insofar as it requires member states to treat serious negligence as a test of liability for discharge of polluting substances; and/or

   (ii) Is article 5(1) of the Directive invalid insofar as it excludes the application of the exceptions in Annex I regulation 11(b) of MARPOL 73/78 and in Annex II regulation (6)(b) of Marpol 73/78?

   (iii) Does article 4 of the Directive, requiring Member States to adopt national legislation which includes serious negligence as a standard of liability and which penalises discharges in territorial sea, breach the right of innocent passage recognised in the United Nations Convention on the Law of the Sea, and if so, is article 4 invalid to that extent?

   (iv) Does the use of the phrase 'serious negligence' in article 4 of the Directive infringe the principle of legal certainty, and if so, is article 4 invalid to that extent?

At the time of writing, the ECJ has not yet issued its judgment. The question of validity of the Framework Decision of the Council (mentioned above) was also put before the ECJ by an action brought by the Commission against the Council of the European Union on 8 December 2005.

---

51 [2006] EWHC 1577 (Admin), case no CO/10651/2005.

The Commission of the European Communities claims that the Court should:

(i) declare that Council Framework Decision 2005/667/JHA of 12 July 2005 to strengthen the criminal-law framework for the enforcement of the law against ship-source pollution is unlawful;

(ii) annul that framework decision.

The Commission argues that having regard to the Court's functional approach in Case C-176/03 *Commissiom v Council* [2005] ECR I-0000 and also to the fact that the measures provided for in Articles 1 to 10 of Framework Decision 2005/667/JHA constitute criminal law measures necessary to ensure the efficacy of the common transport policy, as developed by Directive 2005/35 EC, the Commission considers that the entire Framework Decision Infringes Article 47 EU, on account of its indivisibility, and is therefore unlawful.

5 ERIKA III MEASURES

On 23 November 2005, the European Commission published its third maritime safety package (Erika III package) as a line of defence against sub-standard ships, taking account of the experience acquired in implementing the Erika I and II packages.

The proposal consists of the following seven proposals:

(i)   a proposal for a directive on the conformity requirements of flag States

(ii) an amendment of the Directive on classification societies;

(iii) an amendment of the port state control Directive;

(iv) a proposal for a Directive on accident investigation;

(v)   a Regulation on liability and compensation for damage to passengers in accidents;

(vi) a Directive on the extra-contractual liability of shipowners; and

(vii) an amendment of the Traffic Monitoring Directive.

The Commission felt that, despite the reduction in the number of maritime accidents, the threat relating to failure to comply with safety standards still remained. Therefore, the seven measures intend to supplement the European rules concerning maritime safety and improve the efficiency of existing measures. At the time of writing, these proposals are undergoing discussion and consultation.

5.1 Conformity requirements of flag States

The Commission believes that improved monitoring by Member States of ships flying their flags is the main 'missing link' in EU maritime legislation. The proposed Directive will ensure that all Member States fully apply international rules on ships sailing under their flags.

5.2 Classification societies

The Commission aims to improve the quality of those responsible for inspecting and certifying ships, and introduce common quality control structures, as well as harsher penalties for those societies that fail to meet Community requirements.

5.3 Port State Control (PSC)

A further amendment to PSC is planned, aiming to reform the frequency and quality of on-board ship inspections. The proposal places emphasis on targeting suspect ships by extending the pilots' role in detecting dangerous ships and introducing sanctions, including the banishment of such ships from EU waters.

5.4 Accident investigation

The Commission believes that there are currently no rules on conducting maritime investigations following accidents, and intends to provide clear guidelines similar to those used in aviation accident investigations.

5.5 Passengers' compensation

The Commission has taken steps to incorporate the Athens Convention, as amended by the Protocol 2002,[52] into European legislation.

5.6 Civil liability and financial guarantees for damage done by ships

Further, the Commission intends to introduce mandatory implementation by all Member States of the London Limitation of Liability Convention 1996 and incorporate the Convention into Community law. In addition, it will seek a mandate for negotiations with IMO to review the Convention. Ships flying the flag of a State that is not a party to the Convention will be subject to a more severe liability regime. In such cases, the shipowner will be unable to limit liability if it is proved that the damage resulted from his personal act or omission, committed with intent to cause such damage or through gross negligence.

For the protection of accident victims, the Commission considers supplementing the legislation on liability by setting up a system for obligatory financial guarantees, to be provided by shipowners, irrespective of the flag of their ships. The financial guarantee is proposed to be a sum equivalent to double the ceiling laid down by the 1996 Convention. Financial security should also be provided for

---

52 See Chapter 18.

abandonment of seafarers. The proposal for a Directive is embodied in Communi-cation 2005/0242. Direct action for third party claims against the provider of the financial guarantee is also proposed. The defence that damage was the result of intentional fault on the part of the owner, and the defences which the owner would be entitled to invoke (with the exception of those based on the owner declaring bankruptcy), will be available to the provider of the financial guarantee.

5.7 Places of refuge

5.7.1 Background

Places of refuge are locations to be designated, into which a ship in need of assist-ance or in distress can be brought, so that its condition can be stabilised and further damage to the ship can be averted, so that damage to the marine environment is prevented.

The notion of providing places of refuge for ships in distress had been raised at IMO during the late 1980s, when the International Convention on Salvage was considered, but it was not appropriate to deal with an issue of a public law rule in a private law Convention. The issue was seriously raised after *The Erika* accident, and has been discussed since then at the IMO by the Legal Committee for Maritime Safety (MSC), particularly after *The Castor* incident, in 2001, and the issue was further highlighted by *The Prestige* sinking in 2002.

Although international law, under Art 2 of the UNCLOS Convention, recog-nises the right of a State to regulate entry into its ports, the right of a foreign ship to enter a port or internal waters of another State in situations of *force majeure* or distress is not regulated by UNCLOS. But it is not precluded to adopt rules or guidelines complementing the provisions of UNCLOS.

However, the right of coastal States to take action to protect its coastline from marine pollution is well established in international law (UNCLOS, Arts 194–199, 211, 221, 225, and Salvage Convention, Art 9). On the other hand, the duty to render assistance to vessels and persons in distress is a well-established principle in international maritime law (UNCLOS, Art 98).

Therefore, it was identified by the IMO secretariat that there was no legal barrier to the development of guidelines on the subject of places of refuge. The MSC was greatly assisted by the research carried out by the CMI, and gave serious consideration to issues of liability and compensation arising from a decision by the coastal State to grant access to a ship in distress. However, the Legal Committee did not agree with CMI's view that a new Convention on places of refuge would be needed. CMI's view has been that the present international regime on liability and compensation is unsatisfactory because it does not contain clear guidelines identifying the duties and obligations of shipowners, States and others involved when making a request for a place of refuge. Thus, in CMI's view, the present legislative regime contained in the four principal Conventions dealing with liabil-ity arising from pollution damage (namely, the 1969 CLC with its Protocols, the 1992 Fund Convention, the HNS Convention 1996 and the Bunkers Convention

2001) does not sufficiently encourage States to grant places of refuge to distressed ships.[53]

5.7.2 *The IMO Guidelines*

Given this short background, it has been possible for IMO to develop Guidelines, instead of a Convention, on places of refuge for ships in need of assistance, in a manner which retains a proper and equitable balance between the rights and interests of coastal States and the need to render assistance to ships which are damaged or disabled or in distress at sea.[54] The Guidelines give guidance to all persons and coastal States, in the legal context of the relevant international conventions,[55] for action with regard to assessment of risk, contingency planning and the decision-making process. It is made clear in the objectives of the Guidelines that they will apply when a ship is just in need of assistance but safety of life is not involved. Should safety of life be involved, or there is a need for rescue operations, the Search and Rescue (SAR) Convention will have priority over the Guidelines. The Guidelines were adopted by the IMO Assembly (Annex Resolution 949(23)) in December 2003, and IMO expects its Member States to adopt them.

Once the HNS and Bunker Conventions (which provide for financial guarantees) come into force, it is believed that the system will work better. IMO will encourage the ratification of the pollution liability conventions by its Member States. In the meantime, the IMO Legal Committee on places of refuge will keep the Guidelines under review.

5.7.3 *Status of places of refuge in the UK*

In the UK, the Marine Safety Act 2003 provides for powers of intervention and direction to the Secretary of State's Representative, known as SOSREP. The UK has established a system that works with the SOSREP, who oversees all incidents in UK waters where there is significant risk of pollution. He takes responsibility and makes decisions, assisted by the MCA, the counter-pollution and response branch, and harbour masters. They maintain and use experts in salvage and pollution response. Anywhere on the UK's coast could be a place of refuge. The SOSREP system (see Chapter 13, above) is based on the overriding decision-making power of an independent competent authority. The system is also supported by the UK Government, which gives assurance that the port accepting the ship will be compensated for any damage suffered.

---

53 Report at the 38th CMI Conference in Vancouver (June 2004), and 'Places of Refuge' Work in Progress www.cmi.org. See also the study by the Scandinavian Institute of Maritime Law, University of Oslo, 'Liability and Compensation with regard to Places of Refuge', final report, October 2004, by Professor Erik Rosaeg and Director Henrik Ringbom.

54 IMO Resolution A.949(23): 'Guidelines on places of refuge for ships in need of assistance', 5 March 2004, and Resolution A.950(23), 'Maritime Assistance Services (MAS)': www.imo.org.

55 SOLAS 1974, MARPOL 1973/78, LLMC 1976, SAR 1979, UNCLOS 1982, OPPRC Convention 1990, CLC and Fund Conventions 1992; and will be subject to the HNS and Bunker Conventions once they come into force.

5.7.4 *The proposed EC Directive on Traffic Monitoring and Places of Refuge*

The proposed amendment to the traffic monitoring Directive will include a concise legal framework on safe harbours and places of refuge, and also provides for the further development of a maritime data exchange network. There will be an amendment to provide for places of refuge for ships in distress. Member States shall have to draw up plans for responding to threats presented to ships in distress. The Directive introduces an independent competent authority which will have a final and overriding decision-making power about the place where a ship in distress shall be accommodated after an assessment of the situation. There will be an inventory of potential places. The IMO guidelines must be taken into account.

However, the protection of coastal States from serious financial consequences, in case damage is caused to them by ships in distress which are offered shelter in their waters, has been a major issue. To address this issue, it is proposed that there should be a financial guarantee, or insurance certificate, provided by the owner covering liability for damage caused by the ship.[56] Although the absence of financial security will be no valid reason to deny access, the 1996 LLMC ceiling of limit of liability will be doubled.

Unlike the CMI draft proposal on places of refuge, which envisages that access should be conditional on providing financial security to the port receiving the request, and also that indemnity should be provided to the owner of the ship for damage caused by negligence of the port authority of the coastal State, access under the proposed EC Directive is not conditional, and indemnity to the owner is not considered.

6 CONCLUSION

As it seems from the progress made by both the EU and the IMO on legislation, it is very encouraging that these bodies are now willing to co-operate and, in fact, have worked in parallel with regard to some projects for the protection of the environment. There is hope, therefore, that achieving harmonised international legislation is possible in order to meet the common objectives for maritime safety and liability in the future. It is further hoped that such harmonisation will be achieved with regard to criminalisation legislation and, in this respect, the decision of the ECJ (to which the EU Directive has been referred) will be of enormous importance.

---

56   The Commission followed recommendations made on the issue of places of refuge, by the Scandinavian Institute of Maritime Law, University of Oslo: 'Liability and Compensation with regard to Places of Refuge', final report, October 2004, by Professor Erik Rosaeg and Director Henrik Ringbom.

RISK MANAGEMENT CULTURE AND COLLECTIVE RESPONSIBILITY

1 INTRODUCTION

Since the first edition of this book, it is pleasing to witness that many shipping companies have been implementing risk management systems in relation to operational and regulatory safety. There have been pressures upon shipping companies – not only from regulators but also commercial partners and insurers – to show that there is a proper implementation of the ISM Code, and that risk analysis and evaluation is systematically practised. Further safety and quality systems and industry best standards have been implemented (see Chapter 8) in line with the risk management thinking of the 21st century. Lawyers also are now advising their clients about risk management, which, on the face of it seems hardly to be in their best interests, as the more risk management is seriously implemented by companies, the less accidents will occur and, hence, less work might be the result for lawyers. It is interesting to recall that, when the first edition of this book was reviewed by an academic, he questioned the purpose of including a risk management overview chapter in this book. However, many readers of this book, commercial and legal practitioners as well as students, have appreciated its value. One cannot divorce the law, particularly maritime law, from the broader picture of risk management. The management of risk is central to shipping.

To appreciate this, it is important to understand the infrastructures involved in the setting up, operating and trading of shipping companies. The interrelations between such infrastructures are complex, and they would require a separate study from the sociological, psychological and economic perspectives. Therefore, it is only intended that this epilogue presents a framework against which risk management can be evaluated and highlights the areas in which legal risk management can be integrated with the other systems of risk management of a shipping company. It is appropriate to deal with definitions first.

1.1 What is a risk?

In common parlance, 'risk' generally means the taking of chances in the hope that everything will turn out to be both safe and profitable, depending on the circumstances of risk taking. Many factors, such as personality traits, experience and knowledge, financial incentives and commercial considerations, determine whether or not a person is prepared to take risks, other than the ordinary risks of everyday living. Although this definition of risk is commonly understood to be applicable to all strata of life, private or business, risk also carries an additional connotation of a hazard that needs to be covered by insurance.

For our purposes, risk can be understood as the possibility of harm or loss associated with an activity, or the likelihood of an incident happening that may result in danger to life, property, the environment, or may lead to commercial disputes and litigation. That being so, risks need to be evaluated in terms of their significance to the business, the probability of occurrence and the company tolerance of their consequences. There are many different methodologies available to shipping companies for risk evaluation and assessment, ranging from basic qualitative assessment to complex formal risk assessment. The method used generally depends on the level of risk being assessed.

1.2 What is risk management?

The phrase 'risk management' is used in different contexts. To a layperson it may mean the management of risks by good housekeeping, while, to a professional, it broadly means, a systematic approach to taking safety precautions at all levels of business, including the management of financial and commercial risks, and the obtaining of insurance cover. Legal risk management is a somewhat indetermine term, which generally means the management of risks arising from the drafting and/or performance of contracts. In broader terms, it encompasses any risks which may potentially result in legal consequences including litigation, or dispute resolution, risks. The examples of cases in this book amply illustrate that lack of proper crew training or defective ship equipment can lead to accidents and liabilities in law. Managing such risks before liabilities are incurred is part of legal risks managment.

In broad terms, risk management is now understood as the analysis of exposure to risks and the evaluation of the best possible way of handling such exposure taking into account the risk profile and risk tolerance of the company. It is a discipline for dealing with identifiable risks.

1.3 What is risk exposure?

Risk exposure will result from failing to identify potential risks, evaluate their frequency, probability of recurrence and their potential consequences. The consequences may include criminal or civil liabilities resulting in financial losses, loss of reputation and possibly criminal prosecution.

It would be impossible to enumerate all the situations of risk exposure.

The broad categories of risks to which a company may be exposed concern: (a) risks inherent in particular forms of corporate structures; (b) risks with regard to the operation of ships; (c) financial risks; (d) risks of liabilities to third parties; and (e) criminal liabilities. More specifically, they all concern risks which, if they are ignored, have potential legal consequences.

If one were to break down the categories of risks into their various components, the exercise would produce a long list of risk items, which business people may take into account, either consciously or sub-consciously, every day. The difference between this exercise and one of proper and systematic risk management is that, in the latter case, a system of identification, evaluation and assessment of risks is set up for the purpose of taking prophylactic measures to ensure prevention, or minimisation and control, of identified and potential risks.

For example, a corporation may be exposed to legal proceedings either for non-compliance with statutory provisions (see Chapters 8 and 12), or for accidents occurring due to non-compliance with navigational regulations (Chapter 12), or losses incurred due to unwise corporate structures (Chapter 3), or due to badly drafted contractual terms (Chapters 9, 10, 11 and 14), or for accidents occurring due to improper implementation of safety systems, lack of, or superficial, training, non-compliance with international conventions, or EU Directives and Regulations (Chapters 8, 19 and 20).

The common element in all these types of risks is that the lack of a systematic approach to the probability of their occurrence, and the lack of a system being in place for reduction or minimisation of their recurrence, will result in undesirable legal consequences with financial repercussions.

The matter is not academic. In the experience of the writer, there are some owners who, at first, seem complacent about their systems and who rely only on their in-house quality managers. In the end, however, the ones who are really committed to safety realise that their quality assurance managers cannot possibly have all the skills and knowledge required for this purpose, and that experts from outside can conduct a more wide ranging and objective review of their systems.

1.4 What is risk profile?

A company's risk profile can be assessed by identifying and evaluating the risks that the company has experienced or it may encounter. The company can develop a programme for the monitoring and controlling of risks. This process involves the listing of identified risks, measuring their frequency, and assessing their consequences. Then, an assessment of risk acceptability can be made for the purpose of setting priorities as to which risks need to be monitored or controlled by taking appropriate action. This is part of the risk assessment process.

While diligent companies are carrying out risk analysis, particularly since the implementation of the ISM Code, others do risk assessment ad-hoc, just for the purpose of mere compliance. With the SMS being integrated with other quality systems, the company can establish its objectives and targets, evaluate results and take corrective action, communicate progress, and develop action plans for the individual responsibilities of its key people and staff.

Failure to comply with international regulations will certainly be caught at the next visit to a Port State Control, and this will inevitably affect the company's risk profile.

However, not all kinds of risks are assessable. Assessment invariably depends on the subjective perception of its assessors, or a risk may only become apparent with the benefit of hindsight. The way in which the SMS assists in this respect is that it imposes an obligation upon the management of a company: (1) to have a system of recording incidents and the situations in which they have occurred; (2) to undertake conscious observation and graphic analysis of how they occurred; (3) to take action to prevent their recurrence; and (4) to visualise unsuspected exposure. The ISM Code requirement of team work, as assisted by external advisers, should ensure that a systematic risk assessment and evaluation is made, so that it is likely that the subjective element of risk assessment will be reduced and risk awareness increased.

1.5 What is risk tolerance?

Risk tolerance is the level at which risks may be accepted depending on the nature of risks and on various other factors. The best known measure of risk tolerance is described by the mnemonic 'ALARP', meaning: 'As Low As Reasonably Practicable.' First and foremost are the commercial pressures to engage the ships in profitable markets. Freight fluctuations, overcapacity creating more supply than demand, financial commitments to the mortgagee, internal pressures from partners, staffing costs and venture capital are influential in the evaluation of risk tolerance. These considerations may cause the management of a company to be more tolerant of a certain level of risk and, as a result, it may economise on the employment of high-quality trained crew, or on the maintenance of its ships. If a risk is insurable, there may be a tendency to take risks (provided the conduct is not such as to prejudice the insurance contract) and respond to a loss or liability incurred reactively, instead of pro-actively.

On the other hand, the need to observe regulations and consider the consequences of non-compliance is a factor reducing a company's risk tolerance.

1.6 What is safety culture?

'Safety culture' means that the management of a company adopts the appropriate attitude and values towards safety, and ensures commitment to safety by all in the company. A company with a good safety culture aims for transparency of management and operational practices, and the minimisation of all possible risks that are due to the human element (see Chapter 8).[1] Regular audits, risk assessment and evaluation, as well as implementation of plans to control risk exposure, should enhance the safety culture and lead to a company almost free from risk incidents. But, in the real world, there are factors of safety that are not within the control of the ship-owning or managing companies. Part of the challenge for management is causing the interlocking infrastructures of the company to work in harmony with each other.

This leads to an examination of the importance of infrastructures.

2 UNDERSTANDING INFRASTRUCTURES OF SHIPPING COMPANIES

Without wishing to state the obvious, shipping is a very competitive service industry which operates to make profit for those who are brave enough to take on the

---

1   See also 'Alert', which is a monthly journal reporting on the significance of the human element in maritime accidents, issued under the auspices of the Nautical Institute and sponsored by Lloyd's Register.

risks involved. Risk management cannot be understood without understanding how the infrastructures of the business as a whole interrelate. As one writer,[2] on managing risks in shipping, has put it: 'Commercial pressures are ever present and, for every constructive improvement, risks are taken to innovate and exploit opportunities'.

The infrastructures are divided for simplicity into: internal, relational and external.

2.1 Internal infrastructures

A company is made up of the aggregate of personalities of people who are working in it. It is very important that, at the selection and recruitment level, those who hold managerial positions are chosen very carefully to fit in with the culture of the company and are capable of meeting the objectives set by it. In the future, they may exercise their influence to change the culture of the company's approach to safety matters and risk management. Within the internal infrastructure, one should look at how a company communicates its objectives and procedures to its staff, and what is the company's philosophy to safety or safety culture, and risk tolerance.

People employed at the top, who are the 'mind and will' of the organisation (see Chapters 8 and 17), determine the safety culture and the risk tolerance of the company. The staff employed in the technical operations, or in the shore management or in the navigation of ships, are performing the core business of the company. Proper and clear communication channels between themselves and their superiors are essential for the avoidance of accidents and losses. Without clear communication and training, which have become even more essential for compliance with the International Safety Management Code (ISMC) and the Standard of Training Certification and Watchkeeping Convention (STCW), the company is at risk. Examples of accidents caused through poor communications have been given in Chapters 8, 12 and 17.

An effective management is one that implements the following objectives: leadership, clear communication, and the benchmarking of areas in need of improvement; consistency in approach and the reward of excellence; cultivation of co-operation; and the defusing of conflict.

The staff's trust, co-operation, commitment and identification with the company, for the fulfilment of its objectives, can be gained in various ways that are beyond the scope of this book. To maintain levels of co-operation and efficiency from top management to the deck[3] is crucial for the image of the company, and the results the company aims to achieve, from both financial and risk management perspectives.[4]

---

2   Parker, CJ, *Managing Risks in Shipping: A Practical Guide*, 1999, The Nautical Institute, p 2.
3   Elementary reading: Cowling, A, Stanworth, M, Bennett, R, Curran, J, and Lyons, P, *Behavioural Science for Managers*, 2nd edn, 1988, Edward Arnold; Armstrong, M, *How to be an Even Better Manager*, 4th edn, 1994, Kogan Page; Mulling, L, *Management and Organisational Behaviour*, 2nd edn, 1989, Pitman.
4   The author has made a special study and written about organisational behaviour in complex organisations.

2.2 Relational infrastructures

2.2.1 Corporate interrelations

Ship-owning companies are complex organisations. The simplest form of a corporate structure is the one-ship company. The next stage of complexity is the owner who owns two to five ships, each registered under one-ship companies. A parent company may control these subsidiaries, and the management of all these ships may be in the hands of the same people operating as a management company. Some of these ships may be chartered to a bareboat charterer who charters them in turn to different time charterers. The control may, or may not, remain with the parent company.

The next evolution in corporate structures is a complex one and may involve a venture between multinational companies, where it may be difficult to ascertain easily whether there is congruence of opinion in policy and safety matters. Ships may be owned by various subsidiary companies, owned and controlled by one or two parent companies. The ships may be entered into pools or consortia and may be let – via bareboat charters – to various time charterers, who sub-charter down the line to other charterers.

The distance created from the real owners, through complex corporate structures, is a legitimate method of limiting liability and, thus, controlling risk exposure (see examples of legitimate corporate structures in Chapter 3). Such a distance, however, has created concerns of regulatory bodies about lack of transparency as to who is behind the ship-owning companies (the beneficial owners) particularly in case of environmental disasters, or in cases involving security issues. Some of these concerns may be valid in terms of security issues. In cases of environmental protection, international conventions, if ratified by all maritime nations, take care of liabilities through compulsory insurance and the imposition of strict liability and channeling (see Chapters 18, 19 and 20).

Nevertheless, inter-corporate relationships are a crucial factor influencing the risk profile of the ship-owning companies. Differences of opinion as regards policy objectives and orientation between the top people in each company, as well as the inevitable reduction of effective communication down the line may give rise to incidents or accidents, the cause of which may have escaped the notice of the top people, so that an inefficient system of assessment and evaluation of risk may result.[5] Pinning responsibility upon the 'directing mind' of the company for the purpose of attributing liability, or for breaking the limit under Art 4 of the 1976 Convention, is virtually impossible, particularly in complex corporate structures (see Chapters 8 and 16). On the other hand, the availability of more resources and access to financial capital markets ought to facilitate the implementation of a viable safety system in each respectable company.

---

5   See, for example, *The Herald of Free Enterprise* (Chapter 8).

2.2.2 *Owners and others*

There may be a delicate relationship between owners and their bankers which may have a significant impact upon the company's risk profile. For example, banks, in exercising due diligence, are expected to select reputable owners to whom they lend money.

There is also a delicate relationship between owners and professional managers. Experienced owners may not easily delegate full management to professional managers, as they prefer to control technical and operational matters themselves, as well as controlling the cost of maintenance of their ships for the purpose of compliance with regulations (see Chapter 8).

The nationality and experience of owners, and the nationality of the crew employed, does affect the acceptance of their ships by charterers for trading and by insurers.

The relational infrastructure includes, also, the owners' relationships with the Ship's Flag State, Port States, the classification society, shipbuilders or repairers and government representatives, all of which affect the risk profile of a particular company.

2.3 External infrastructures

While external infrastructures seem to overlap with the previous category, to a certain extent, what is outlined under this category is the effect of external pressures upon risk exposure of a ship-owning or management company, and the 'third parties' factors' to it, as can be seen below.

2.3.1 *Regulatory and fiscal*

The importance of regulations has been stressed throughout this book. A great deal depends, however, not only on whether or not the owners or managers have a system of compliance in place (safety management system (SMS)), but also on whether the people delegated with the continuous implementation and mainten-ance of the systems are carrying out their duties conscientiously and efficiently. Here, the importance of continuous training is critical for the company's continuity in business and profitability. In addition, the role of the auditing organisations which inspect ships to verify compliance with international conventions is also crucial.

An original proposal was made by a speaker at a London Shipping Law Centre seminar,[6] to the effect that a solution to this problem may lie in a new Code of Honesty, Respectfulness and Integrity of Surveyors in their Tasks (CHRIST). This is not to be treated lightly, because the role of a surveyor, whether it be that of a classification society, or of any other professional body, is central in maintaining safety at sea. Indeed, it has, in recent years been recognised that controls should be

---

6 Coutroubis, A, 'Flag States, Port States, classification societies and shipowners', lecture in the series On Corporate Structures, held at the London Shipping Law Centre, 18 October 2000.

imposed upon the activities of classification societies and also of Flag States in the inspection of ships (see Chapters 8 and 20).

Equally, Flag States that neglect the enforcement of international regulations should be more rigorously controlled. But one major reason why shipowners have chosen registration of their ships with 'flags of convenience' is that the governments of most respectable registers have encouraged 'flagging-out' to tax havens by creating themselves a disadvantageous taxation system for corporations or directors (Chapter 8). However, since the first edition of this book, measures are being taken by IMO to tackle issues arising from the failure of some Flag States to enforce the implementation of Conventions vigilantly.

2.3.2 *Third parties' factors*

Shippers, charterers, port authorities, port state control, shipbuilders, classification societies, brokers, insurers, terminal operators and government agencies, are all to be regarded as sharing responsibility for the risk exposure of owners and managers, insofar as the external infrastructures are concerned. Dangerous cargo can do more harm to a ship and to the environment than the ship can do to cargo. Charterers who disregard safety matters, either with respect to the cargo, or in their choice of substandard ships to cut costs, or their choice of unsafe ports, equally can do more harm than is usually perceived (see chapter 8, paras 1.3, 1.3.6). Terminal operators accustomed to unsafe practices would also need to exercise risk management to minimise risks to ships and to the environment (see port authorities' duties in Chapter 16). Refusal of entry into a port of refuge by port authorities can indirectly have irreparable consequences for the environment (see Chapters 13 and 20).

Port States may not always be consistent in their policies of inspecting and penalising ships for deficiencies, which inevitably leads to confusion and discrimination.

Defects in the design and construction of ships are not infrequently found to be a predominant cause of a marine disaster. Shipbuilders, who may construct defective hatch covers or weak bulkheads, or ship-repair yards, which may repair defects superficially, cannot be left out of the equation in a global culture of safety. Fortunately, since the first edition of this book, measures are being taken to harmonise the standards of ship construction (see Chapters 8, 10 and 20). Classification societies have also taken on a greater role in the management of risk in the last decade than in the past, as they have largely been entrusted with the auditing of ships and companies for regulatory compliance. If there is going to be a significant change in the culture of safety, it is important to bear in mind this question: *Quis custodiet custodes?* There has been a tendency primarily to blame the owners for accidents, and only recently has there been awareness of the problems caused by classification societies and the Flag States which delegate the performance of statutory inspections to classification societies (see Chapter 8).

Insurance brokers and the insurers of sub-standard ships should be taken into account in this equation. Since the first edition of this book, there has been a study on this aspect, as mentioned in Chapter 8, which highlights the importance of making the insurer accountable for insuring sub-standard ships.

2.3.3 Market forces

What drives the management of a company are the objectives of: enhancing the company's position through the profitable engagements of the ships; placing the company in a favourable competitive position by long-term plans of employment; ensuring the good reputation of the company externally and with its financiers. In these respects, the management's perspective is interwoven with market forces, demand and supply, market capacity and quality.

When shipowners provide 'quality services', offering ships which do not cause problems to the contracting parties or to the environment, and the owners/managers have a good reputation of dealing with third parties, there will be a positive correlation between employment and demand. Quality marketing and public relations will strengthen the company's position. Apart from quality, however, other factors, such as overcapacity of ships of the same type, demand for particular commodities, technological advancements, and the like, will affect the matrix of correlation between demand and employment.

We have, however, witnessed in recent years a thriving freight market and a boom in shipbuilding. But shipping markets have their rises followed by falls, as statistical and historical data have shown.

Survival in this competitive business may lead owners or managers to cut the budget required for maintaining quality performance in order to be able to accept lower rates of freight or hire and, at the same time, overlook the increase in risk exposure that such a policy implies. In the long run, however, it should be remembered that due diligence and a systematic approach to risk management will pay dividends. There are several examples given in this book of cases, which reached the courts, due to these underlying factors and, not infrequently, due to bad management practices, as well as a lack of knowledge as to how to implement a coherent and systematic approach to risk management.

3 COLLECTIVE RESPONSIBILITY AND COMMITMENT

The objectives of safety of people, property and the environment, as well as prevention of liabilities to third parties, are a matter of collective responsibility and commitment, not only of the company concerned, from the top of the hierarchy to the workplace, but also of all players involved in the complex infrastructures. Congruency in policy and approach to risk management of the owner or manager will enable the company to surpass most problems posed from the outside. In particular, if the framework of procedures, discussed below, becomes part of the company's practices, a reduction in accidents and an increase of risk control will result. It is recognised, however, that it is not possible to eliminate all marine casualties. In this respect, a Lloyd's underwriter,[7] speaking at a conference on risk management, said: 'Because of the nature of the business in which we operate, accidents and

---

7   Redmond, S, 'The apparent cyclical nature of marine insurance and its effect on risk assessment and management', IBC Conference on Maritime Risk Assessment Management and Control, 1997.

losses will continue to happen in the most safety conscious environments. But we all have a collective responsibility to work together in order to ensure that these losses are reduced to the lowest possible level.'

The philosophy of collective responsibility was enshrined, in fact, in the ISM Code, which, as seen in Chapter 8, briefly provides for each company to:

(i) adopt a philosophy of safety culture at all levels; in other words, to commit to a mission for safety, to cultivate the right attitude and motivate its employees;

(ii) provide for safe practices by putting procedures in place and recording incidents; ensuring competence and training of the crew and carrying out equipment maintenance within the time required, or recommended;

(iii) strive for continuous improvement by monitoring, auditing, evaluating faults and preventing their recurrence; and

(iv) prevent accidents and protect the environment, paying particular attention to the human element and man–equipment interface in accidents.

For collective responsibility to be understood there must first be standards for risk control and second a systematic approach of application at each stage, as shown below.

3.1 Risk management standards for risk control

Standards derive from policies and policy objectives for safe management systems and procedures, supported by guidelines on each individual aspect and stage of risk management. The stages at which risk management standards should be implemented for risk control, following the exercise of identification, evaluation and assessment explained earlier, are examined below, by way of illustration only. These stages have been divided into five categories: (i) risks at the incorporation of the company; (ii) risks in ship operations; (iii) risks at the contractual stage; (iv) risks at the performance of voyage stage; and (v) risks at the dispute resolution stage.

3.2 The stages of risk management

3.2.1 Risks at the incorporation stage

As discussed in Chapter 3, properly constituted corporate structures are a legitimate way of limiting liability when a legal distance is kept between companies in the same group through the careful formation of one-ship companies. The formation of this type of corporate structure is even more advisable now, particularly as the effect of The Indian Grace[8] decision is that there is a personal jurisdiction against the defendant, interested in defending the claim in the *in rem* proceedings, from the service of the proceedings. This means that a judgment obtained, even in default of appearance, will be executable against the other ships in the fleet, if they are under the ownership of the same company.

---

8 See Chapter 3.

Care must be taken to avoid transfer of a ship within the same group of companies, or by forming a new company after claims have arisen, as the court may find such a transfer to be a sham. While separate corporate structures provide a shield to the lifting or piercing of the corporate veil, it should be borne in mind that an incident of proven fraud has been held to be a valid reason for the courts to pierce the corporate veil.

While making provisions through third party liability insurance to meet legitimate claims, a ship arrest is a disruption to business. It may be thought prudent to keep separate accounts, separate stock, separate directors and officers, separate operations, separate financial statements and tax returns between a parent and subsidiary companies, to protect exposure of the assets held by the subsidiaries, in case a ship owned by them calls in jurisdictions where associated arrest of ships is favoured by the legal system.

Of course, there are the investment and financial risks involved, depending on the structure of borrowing and mortgaging for the purchase of the ships.

It should also be borne in mind that the safest way of minimising risk exposure would be to have a system in place by which care is taken to control or reduce liabilities before they arise. What follows is a guide for such a system.

3.2.2 Risks in ship operations

This is the core of the business, for which risk management is paramount. The informed choice of competent personnel and crew and their training is the beginning of risk management. Compliance with the requirements of the STCW Convention, and the management of the fatigue factor is a key focus for IMO. However, no matter how much training or instructions the crew are given, if they are not able to absorb what is taught or appreciate what is expected of them, the human element in risk exposure will not be under control. Equally, the masters of the ships, the designated person and marine superintendent must be fully committed and able to obey instructions, as well as understand the importance of recording and reporting incidents, which need the managers' or directors' attention.

Incidents of collisions at sea, discussed in Chapter 12, as well as incidents where the company was not able to limit liability under the 1957 Convention, discussed in Chapter 17, are examples of inattention to the collision regulations, or failure to follow instructions. If the circumstances of such incidents are systematically plotted and evaluated, followed by an assessment of the liability exposure of the company and by an action plan for their monitoring and control, the company should save money, not only in terms of minimising liabilities to third parties, reducing the management time spent in handling accidents or incidents, but also in terms of insurance premiums and legal costs.

Routine maintenance, fire drills, training facilities and prevention of fatigue at work are essential practices of well-functioning operational systems. Lack of these practices may result in loss of life and criminal liabilities; and perhaps expose the owners to inability to limit liability or prejudice their insurance cover (see the implications of non-compliance with the ISM Code in Chapter 8).

The importance of integration of risk management procedures in this area into the overall risk management systems cross-departmentally cannot be underestimated.

3.2.3 Risks at the contract stage

As has been discussed in this book, the clumsy drafting of contracts is frequently at the root of risk exposure. Examples of badly drafted or unfavourable clauses in contracts have been seen in various chapters. For example, in the drafting of mortgage covenants, care should be taken to limit the mortgagee's right of possession to occasions of financial default (Chapter 9); in the area of ship building, skilful negotiations are needed so that the standard terms of contract offered by shipbuilders are made more acceptable (Chapter 10). As regards sale and purchase of used ships (Chapter 11), there are many examples of cases that ended up in litigation, either because the parties, through their brokers, did not make their intentions clear, or because the standard terms of Norwegian Sale Forms are very much in favour of the seller, or contain ambiguous clauses. The buyers' attention has been drawn to when an undertaking or an indemnity is given in the contract by the seller for encumbrances or claims, which may be worth only the value of the paper that it is written on.

In contracts of towage (Chapter 14), there is a need to spell out clearly what the parties expect from each other. As regards salvage contracts (Chapter 13), the introduction of the Special Compensation of Protection and Indemnity Clause (SCOPIC) for compensation of salvors in protecting the environment from pollution damage has brought some clarity in the expectations of the parties and safeguards for the salvors. A great deal of effort has been made to produce this result through negotiations and careful drafting. Yet, there is still a need for more clarity regarding the benefits and incentives provided for salvors.

There are numerous other areas of contracts such as charter parties in which risks can be controlled at the drafting stage, but these are beyond the scope of this book. The same principles discussed in this epilogue can be applied to contracts of affreightment from which many disputes arise.

There is also the risk of a disappearing debtor, which must always be borne in mind at the stage of contracting. There will be very little that the law can do if a party, appearing to contract for another, disappears, leaving no undisclosed principal behind. Checking the solvency and credibility of a putative contracting party is more important than just succumbing to market forces.

3.2.4 Risks at the performance stage

While due diligence should have been exercised at the technical and operational stage, to make the ship seaworthy in all respects, in order to prevent risks from arising, many other risks can arise at the performance stage. Such risks may either stem from badly drafted clauses in the contract (see above), or may be linked to the inherent dangers of the sea voyage, or be due to the human element. Although some of them might be minimised, or controlled, complete elimination would be impossible.

This stage concerns the physical handling of the ship by those on board, and also the directions given from the shore during a voyage on how to handle loading or discharge, port authorities, deal with unexpected situations, shippers, charterers, stevedores, or those who have come to assist the ship in an emergency. Several judicial decisions in this book provide examples of such incidents.

While, again, the human element risk can be considerably reduced by equipping seafarers with the knowledge and skills required, 'seafarers have an innate ability to understand and assess the risks that the job places before them and undertake intuitive risk analysis'.[9] However, it is the management of the company itself that must have clear goals and policies about safety, regardless of commercial pressures, so that clear communications and expectations are established to prevent confusion.

The following (non-exhaustive) areas are of paramount importance as part of the risk management of the company:

(a) Has the company taken care of: careful voyage planning; up-to-date navigational charts[10] and notices on board; weather forecast, tidal forecasts; draught restrictions; collision regulations observance,[11] with particular reference to the voyage planning; fatigue factors in watch keeping; familiarisation of new members of crew;[12] sufficient and quality bunkers for the voyage; clear guidelines and procedures?

(b) Has the management set clear instructions on what it expects from the master and crew during loading, to have the ship ready to receive the cargo, during stowage and lashing of the cargo, as well as when signing bills of lading?[13]

(c) Stowaways are a frequent and costly risk for owners and their protection & indemnity (P&I) clubs. Although it is not always easy to detect their entry into the ship, extra watch and vigilance should be exercised to look in suspected places and, in case of container ships, to investigate non-sealed containers.

(d) Port restrictions, weather conditions and manoeuvring the ship out of or into port will depend on the knowledge of and co-operation between the pilot and crew of the ship. Their co-operation and understanding of the circumstances and of each other are crucial in avoiding accidents, for example, such as *The Sea Empress*. The management must stress the importance of it to the master and crew.

(e) Proper training of the crew at the operational stage will ensure their knowledge of how to check the cargo for lashing, temperature, ventilation, or water ingress, any leakage of cargo, or any overheating which may result in combustion or fire in the holds. Fire drills and exercises should ensure that the crew know how to deal with unexpected fire on board (such as in the case of *The Eurasian Dream*).

(f) The test of whether or not the cargo has been properly stowed and securely lashed will be when the ship encounters heavy storms, particularly a tropical cyclone. Although a well-maintained and securely loaded ship with well-trained crew and an experienced master will be able to withstand bad weather,

9 Bailey, T (Captain), 'Managing risk on board ship', in op cit, Parker, fn 1, Chapter 3.
10 *The Marion* [1984] 2 Lloyd's Rep 1, see Chapters 8 and 16.
11 See Chapter 12.
12 *The Safe Carrier* [1994] 1 Lloyd's Rep 589; *The Eurasian Dream*, see Chapter 8.
13 See Cook, J et al, *Voyage Charters*, 2004 edn, LLP.

the unpredictability of sea conditions should not be under-estimated, even if meteorological information is of the highest standard. Most reported accidents are due to severe weather conditions, which perhaps hit a less well-maintained, or well-prepared, ship. It should be noted, however, that not all these accidents are preventable, although their effect may be minimised with careful voyage planning. Only seafarers know how difficult it is to handle the ship in a severe tropical cyclone.

(g) Grounding accidents, perhaps, could be prevented if an up-to-date chart and publications of local waters are always available and are observed. Collisions should be preventable with due care and compliance with the collision regulations, observance of bridge equipment procedures, familiarisation and training, as well as prevention of fatigue. Engine failures during the voyage could equally be preventable if, at the operations and preparation stage of the voyage, sufficient care is taken. But these do occur due to other reasons, perhaps a latent defect, or a survey that has failed to detect faults. In the same vein, bulkhead failures and stresses may depend either on construction, or survey faults, or miscalculation of the stresses on the ship, with a particular cargo on board.

(h) Although a systematic risk management practice will be capable of reducing risk exposure to a significant extent, it would be naive for one to believe that everything will be 100% perfect. What is important, however, is whether the company's policy or approach to the eventuality of accidents is pro-active, or how the management reacts to such occurrences. For example, fear of losing the co-operation of insurers may lead the owner to invent a less plausible cause of the accident, while it is essential to keep to the facts as they occurred. Nevertheless, it is important that the insurers, themselves, adopt an attitude of collective responsibility, as has been stressed in this chapter. Sometimes, overzealousness of insurers, or their lawyers, make things worse, and the trust between the insurer and the insured is undermined, resulting in protracted litigation. There are numerous examples of marine insurance claims (which are not within the scope of this book) in which the approach of insurers and their lawyers has been such as to alienate the insured, instead of endeavouring to resolve or minimise the impact of the accident by co-operation.

(i) If a serious accident occurs, the company should have emergency procedures in place, which should include prior training of the senior management in media handling.

(j) The possibility of loss of life during the performance of ship operations, caused by serious management faults amounting to gross negligence may result in the company being liable for corporate manslaughter depending on where the incident causing death occurred. Although the law is still developing, the trend of criminalisation legislation, particularly in the area of environmental pollution, has greatly concerned the shipping industry (see Chapters 8 and 20).

(k) The voyage may be completed uneventfully, but there may be problems at the discharge port. The owners' P&I clubs provide extensive guidelines on how to deal with various circumstances, such as obnoxious receivers, or threats of arrest of the ship for alleged shortage of cargo, or demand for delivery without production of or without the correct bills of lading, which should be referred to and followed. Clear communications and instructions at this stage are important, as well as obtaining professional advice and resolving disputes in the best way possible. If not, then the next stage would inevitably follow.

3.2.5 Risks at the dispute resolution stage

Litigation can at times be bedevilled by procedural entanglements, either because procedural rules may have more than one interpretation, or because they are unskilfully drafted, or because the litigants' lawyers might make procedural mistakes. Examples of these have been encountered in Part I of this book.

It would be better to avoid reaching this stage, by practising a systematic process of risk management in the first place. Litigation risks are costly and prejudice long-term business relationships.

Forum shopping in disregard of an agreement on jurisdiction will not be looked upon favourably by English judges. The criteria of an appropriate forum, for the interests of all parties and for the ends of justice, and the consequences of breach of jurisdiction agreements have been examined in Chapters 5, 6 and 7. Forum shopping in limitation actions has been discouraged by the English courts. Litigants have been warned not to waste litigation costs but to follow the clear guidelines laid down by the House of Lords in *The Spiliada*. Neither England, nor another forum, will be a good place to shop in if the interests of justice and comity to other nations' jurisdiction are not observed.

The rules applicable under the Brussels Regulation on jurisdiction and enforcement of judgments have recently brought significant changes (see Chapters 6 and 7). Parties to a dispute should consider finding an amicable solution through the assistance of a mediator or conciliator. Mediation of maritime disputes still has a long way to go to convince shipping companies of its advantages particularly in relation to saving legal costs. Unpredictable results can arise from the disclosure procedures in litigation as well as the performance of witnesses. The uncertainty involved in litigation should encourage the parties to mediate.

3.3 Enhancing safety culture through collective responsibility and commitment

For business productivity and profitability, enhancing safety culture is not a matter of a mechanical compliance with regulations and of preparing the systems just for the time of external auditing. It is a continual process involving collective responsibility with the ultimate goal of long-term benefits to the company. This may be stating the obvious, but there is no doubt that a great deal still needs to be done within the industry, in terms of education, to achieve the adoption of a long-term safety culture.

3.3.1 Adopting a systematic process

It derives from the foregoing, and from what other experts in risk management have advocated, that it is imperative for every shipping company to establish a systematic approach to risk management and change the company's philosophy to one of quality and safety. A change in attitude of knowing how to do things may be necessary by adopting an open-minded approach. As part of the system of improving the company's risk profile by identifying, evaluating and assessing risks, there should be a process for monitoring and reviewing risk exposure. Such a system would be enhanced by increased dialogue, training and further education for the purpose of increasing awareness of potential risks and their management.

Reinforcement of the requirement for implementation of a systematic approach to risk management is shown, for example, by the guidelines issued by the oil majors, who require tanker owners to show commitment to safety by strictly adhering to the guidelines defined in the Tanker Management Self Assessment (TMSA) programme, discussed in Chapter 8 of this book. Under these guidelines, or key performance indicators (KPI), ship operators have to re-examine not only their operating practices but also their philosophy by taking safety issues seriously. The KPI include:

- management leadership and accountability;
- recruitment of shore and ship staff policy and training;
- reliability and maintenance of critical equipment/application of standards;
- navigational safety systems and procedures;
- systems and procedures for cargo, ballast, mooring operations;
- management of change;
- incident investigation and analysis;
- safety management and environmental management;
- emergency preparedness and contingency planning; and
- measurement analysis and improvement.

3.3.2 Funding for risk control and training

It is common sense that, if investment is made to control risks pro-actively, the cost of prevention or minimisation of risks will be less than the costs of reacting to risks after their occurrence, and meeting the liabilities or losses resulting from them. While it may seem more time consuming and cost inefficient to devote the resources necessary for a systematic audit of the risk exposure of a company, to assess, analyse and control risks, when other priorities are pressing, it is wrong to assume that the result will be less cost efficient overall.

3.3.3 Commitment to change and collective responsibility

Quality shipping is a matter of collective responsibility, as has been stressed throughout this book. It can be presented like a ring, with the owners and managers of ships in the centre, their internal infrastructure of personnel and related

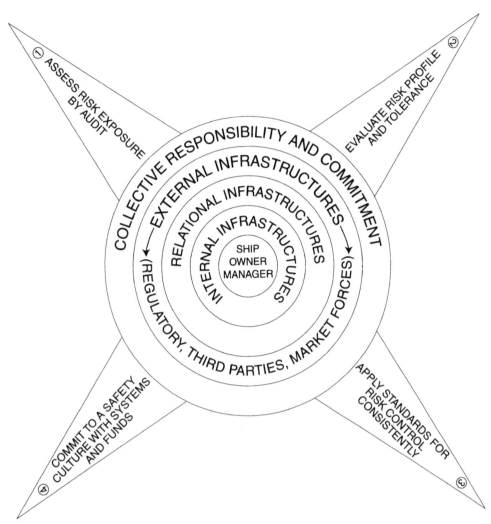

companies in the next ring, and all other players mentioned earlier in extended surrounding rings, as is shown in the following diagram.

Quality shipping is a worthwhile objective with long-term rewards and it is a must for all those wishing to stay in the business. It will make the company more competitive resulting in greater profitability; it may have the effect of lower insurance premiums, it will enhance freight returns, and it will open other opportunities for investment.

It is worth remembering the much quoted observation: 'if you think safety is expensive, try an accident'.

INDEX

A

Abandonment
  collisions 567–69
  Crown rights 62
  s 74 (HDPCA 1847) and abandoned ships
    832, 834–36
  salvage 653–54
  wrecks 567–69, 817–18, 819
Accident investigations 1008
Acts of God 828–32
Actual knowledge
  See Knowledge, actual and constructive
Actus novus interveniens 580–84
Admiralty Court
  See also In personam claims; *In rem* claims;
    In rem claims, 'non-truly'; Jurisdiction
  Company Courts and 134–35
  composition of 12
  historical overview of 5–8
Admiralty Marshal
  arrest warrants 117
  custody of property 118–19
  port authorities and 136–37, 139, 140
  priority of costs of 142
  role of 12
  sale of ships by 130–34, 136–37, 138–39,
    140, 403
Admiralty Registrar, role of 12
Agents
  disbursements 59–61
  fiduciary duties 306–08
  general principles 303–04, 323, 728–30
  heads of claim 53
  of necessity 674–83, 728, 730–31
  reasonable care and diligence 306
  receivers and mortgagees 403–04
  ship managers 299–300
    authority of 302–06
    breach of contract 308–09
    duties of 306–08
    framework 300–302
    indemnity 310
    insurance and risk management 311–12
  ship sales 472–73
  'shipbrokers and agents' 299
  tugmasters 731–33
  wages of crew 59
Agreements to sell 424
  See also Sale of ships; Shipbuilding
    contracts
Aircraft
  certification 529–31

defective products 463
heads of claim 51, 52, 63
in rem claims 114
salvage 636, 645
Warsaw Convention 1929 886, 888, 889,
  895, 897–99, 900, 901
Alcohol 554
'*Alter ego*' of company 329–31, 903–05
Alternative danger, defence of 584–86
Anti-suit injunctions
  See also Foreign jurisdiction agreements
    (outside Brussels Regulation)
  breach of contract cases 249, 271
    arbitration agreements 250–60
    English jurisdiction agreements
      (outside Brussels Regulation)
      260–62
    judicial discretion 262
  comity reasons, non-intervention for 188,
    248–49, 265–66, 269–70, 271
  generally 243, 245, 249–50
  mixed cases 267
  non-contract cases 263, 271
    new formula 265–66
    principles in early 1980s 263–65
  non-exclusive jurisdiction clauses 188
  practical considerations 258, 270
  prohibited (Brussels Regulation applies)
    243–45, 246–47
  risk management 270
  'vexatious and oppressive conduct'
    268–69
Appraisement 130
Arbitration
  anti-suit injunctions 243, 245, 250–60, 262,
    268–71
  Brussels Regulation 199
  charterparties 50
  enforcement of awards 50–51
  freezing orders 63
  maintenance of or release from arrest
    120–21, 193
  New York Convention 193, 250, 252, 253
  stay of proceedings 189–93
  time limits 155
Arrest
  arbitration agreements 120–21, 193
  caveats against 117–18, 919
  caveats against release 118, 134–35
  co-owners 297, 298–99
  Convention 1952
    jurisdiction under 196, 218–22, 225

S

Related Titles

Principles of Maritime Law
by Susan Hodges and Chris Hill
(2002)

Risk Management in Port Operations,
Logistics and Supply Chain Security
by Khalid Bichou, Michael G. H. Bell and Andrew Evans
(2007)

Shipping Law Handbook, 4th Edition
by Michael Bundock
(2007)

Southampton on Shipping Law
by the Institute of Maritime Law
(2008)

An Introduction to Admiralty Law and
Practice: A Self Study Course
from Informa Professional Academy
(2009)